W9-AZV-298

CLASSICAL AND MEDIEVAL LITERATURE CRITICISM

Guide to Gale Literary Criticism Series

When you need to review criticism of literary works, these are the Gale series to use:

If the author's death date is:	You should turn to:
After Dec. 31, 1959 (or author is still living)	*CONTEMPORARY LITERARY CRITICISM* for example: Jorge Luis Borges, Anthony Burgess, William Faulkner, Mary Gordon, Ernest Hemingway, Iris Murdoch
1900 through 1959	*TWENTIETH-CENTURY LITERARY CRITICISM* for example: Willa Cather, F. Scott Fitzgerald, Henry James, Mark Twain, Virginia Woolf
1800 through 1899	*NINETEENTH-CENTURY LITERATURE CRITICISM* for example: Fedor Dostoevski, Nathaniel Hawthorne, George Sand, William Wordsworth
1400 through 1799	*LITERATURE CRITICISM FROM 1400 TO 1800 (excluding Shakespeare)* for example: Anne Bradstreet, Daniel Defoe, Alexander Pope, François Rabelais, Jonathan Swift, Phillis Wheatley
	SHAKESPEAREAN CRITICISM Shakespeare's plays and poetry
Antiquity through 1399	*CLASSICAL AND MEDIEVAL LITERATURE CRITICISM* for example: Dante, Homer, Plato, Sophocles, Vergil, the Beowulf Poet

---

Gale also publishes related criticism series:

CHILDREN'S LITERATURE REVIEW

This ongoing series covers authors of all eras. Presents criticism on authors and author/illustrators who write for the preschool through high school audience.

SHORT STORY CRITICISM

This series covers the major short fiction writers of all nationalities and periods of literary history.

ISSN 0896-0011

Volume 1

CLASSICAL AND MEDIEVAL LITERATURE CRITICISM

Excerpts from Criticism of the Works of World Authors from Classical Antiquity through the Fourteenth Century, from the First Appraisals to Current Evaluations

Dennis Poupard
Jelena O. Krstovic
Editors

Thomas Ligotti
Associate Editor

Gale Research Company
Book Tower
Detroit, Michigan 48226

STAFF

ISBN 0-8103-2350-8
ISSN 0896-0011

Computerized photocomposition by Typographics, Incorporated
Kansas City, Missouri

Printed in the United States

Contents

Preface

The literatures of the ancient and medieval world provide the foundation of all subsequent literatures. In fact, the philosophical, stylistic, and thematic elements of these literatures echo constantly throughout literary history to the present day. For that reason, the study of the literature and philosophy of ancient and medieval authors is important to the education of any individual. Through such study we achieve a greater understanding of ourselves and of the continuity of human experience.

Literary criticism provides an essential guide to the literature of the past, and so, by extension, to the nature of the human condition. Similarly, because the criteria by which a work is judged reflect the philosophical and social attitudes of an era, the study of criticism can also provide insight into the moral and intellectual climate of a society. The range of critical response to a work of literature thus helps us to understand the work, the author, the world of the author, and our own world.

The Scope of the Series

Classical and Medieval Literature Criticism (CMLC) is designed to serve as an introduction to the authors and literary works of antiquity through the fourteenth century as well as to the most significant commentators on these authors and works. The great poets, prose writers, dramatists, and philosophers of these centuries form the basis of most literature, humanities, philosophy, and classics curriculums, so that virtually every student will encounter many of these works during the course of an advanced education. Since a vast amount of critical material confronts the student, *CMLC* presents significant passages from the most important criticism published in English to aid students in the location and selection of commentaries on the authors of this period.

The need for *CMLC* was suggested by the usefulness of the Gale series *Contemporary Literary Criticism, Twentieth-Century Literary Criticism, Nineteenth-Century Literature Criticism, Literature Criticism from 1400 to 1800,* and *Shakespearean Criticism.* With the appearance of *CMLC,* the Gale literary criticism series is now able to include criticism about every major author and literary work from the beginning of recorded history to the latest Nobel Prize winner. For further information about Gale's other criticism series, please consult the Guide to Gale Literary Criticism Series preceding the title page of this volume.

Each volume of *CMLC* is carefully compiled to include major authors and works representing a variety of nationalities and time periods. For example, in the first volume of *CMLC* Homer represents ancient Greece, Apuleius the age of Rome, *Beowulf* and *The Song of Roland* medieval Europe, and Lady Murasaki ancient Japan. In addition to these widely recognized authors and works, *CMLC* also presents surveys of lesser-known authors and works which are important to an understanding of the literature of their nation, to the development of philosophy or a literary genre, or to an appreciation of the shared and unique elements of cultures separated by time and distance. An example of such a work in the first volume of *CMLC* is *The Song of Igor's Campaign,* a major work of Russian culture that is deserving of study but is not as well known as its European counterparts *Beowulf* and *The Song of Roland.*

Each entry in *CMLC* provides an overview of major criticism on an author or literary work. For that reason, the editors include only four to six authors in each 500 page volume so that the subject of each entry may be thoroughly discussed. Although the editors have attempted to include the most important criticism from all eras, they have emphasized nineteenth- and twentieth- century appraisals, which are more accessible to the student and which often summarize or subsume the work of critics from previous centuries. Each entry attempts to provide a historical survey of *critical* response to an author or work, presenting as many varied interpretations as possible; for that reason, we have excluded philological, linguistic, and historical studies which, though of great importance, are of less immediate interest to our readers—secondary school students, undergraduates, and graduate students seeking general critical reaction. References to these studies may be found in the additional bibliography appended to each entry. The length of an entry is intended to reflect the amount of critical attention the subject has received from critics writing in English and from foreign criticism in translation. Critical articles and books that have not been translated into English are excluded. Every attempt has been made to identify and include excerpts from seminal essays on each author or work.

An author may appear more than once in the series because his or her writings have been the subject of such a vast amount of criticism that the editors have chosen to discuss specific works or groups of works in separate entries.

For example, Homer will be represented by three entries, one devoted to the *Iliad,* one to the *Odyssey,* and one to the Homeric hymns.

Organization of the Book

Each entry in the series consists of the following elements: an author or title heading, historical and critical introduction, list of principal English translations, excerpts of criticism (each preceded by an explanatory note and followed by a bibliographical citation), illustrations, and an additional bibliography for further reading.

- The *author heading* consists of the author's full name, followed by birth and death dates, or the complete title of the literary work discussed in the entry, followed by the most common form of the title in English translation and the date of original composition. In entries devoted to a single author, the unbracketed portion of the name denotes the form under which the author is most commonly known. If an author wrote consistently under a pseudonym, the pseudonym will be listed in the author heading and the real name given in parentheses on the first line of the historical and critical introduction. Also located at the beginning of the introduction to the author entry are any name variations under which an author wrote, including transliterated forms for authors whose languages use non-Roman alphabets. Uncertainty as to a birth or death date, or the date of composition of a literary work, is indicated by a question mark when the date is thought to be a specific year or by circa when more precise dating is not possible.

- The *historical and critical introduction* contains background information designed to introduce the reader to an author or literary work and to the critical debate represented in the entry. Problems in the dating of works or in assigning birth and death dates to authors will be explained in the introduction, and textual information will be provided when necessary to an understanding of the work or author in question.

- Most of the entries include *illustrations,* such as manuscript pages, historic artifacts, maps, charts, or representations of significant events or places.

- The *list of principal English translations* is chronological by date of first publication and is included as an aid to the student seeking translated versions of these works for study. The list will focus primarily upon twentieth-century translations, selecting those works most commonly considered the best by critics.

- *Criticism* is arranged chronologically in each entry to provide a useful perspective on changes in critical evaluation over the years. All titles featured in the critical entry are printed in boldface type to enable the user to ascertain without difficulty the subject of the criticism. Also for purposes of easier identification, the critic's name and the publication date of each essay are given at the beginning of each piece of criticism. Unsigned criticism is preceded by the title of the journal in which it appeared. When an anonymous essay is later attributed to a critic, the critic's name appears in brackets at the beginning of the excerpt and in the bibliographical citation. Many critical entries in *CMLC* also contain translated material to aid users. Unless otherwise noted, translations within brackets are by the editors; translations within parentheses are by the author of the excerpt. Publication information (such as publisher names and book prices) and parenthetical numerical references (such as footnotes or page and line references to specific editions of a work) have been deleted at the editor's discretion to provide smoother reading of the text.

- Critical essays are prefaced by *explanatory notes* as an additional aid to students using *CMLC.* The explanatory notes provide several types of useful information, including: the reputation of a critic, the importance of a work of criticism, the specific type of criticism (biographical, psychoanalytic, structuralist, etc.), a synopsis of the criticism, and the growth of critical controversy or changes in critical trends regarding an author's work. Dates in parentheses within the explanatory notes refer to a book publication date when they follow a book title and to an essay date when they follow a critic's name.

- A complete *bibliographical citation* designed to facilitate location of the original essay or book by the interested reader follows each piece of criticism.

- The *additional bibliography* appearing at the end of each author entry suggests further reading on the author or work. In some cases it includes essays for which the editors could not obtain reprint rights.

An appendix lists the sources from which material in each volume has been reprinted. It does not, however, list every book or periodical consulted in preparation of the volume.

Cumulative Indexes

Each volume of *CMLC* includes a cumulative index to authors listing all the authors who have appeared in *Contemporary Literary Criticism, Twentieth-Century Literary Criticism, Nineteenth-Century Literature*

Criticism, Literature Criticism from 1400 to 1800, Short Story Criticism, and *Classical and Medieval Literature Criticism* (as well as individual works when the authors of those works are unknown), along with cross- references to the Gale series *Children's Literature Review, Authors in the News, Contemporary Authors Autobiography Series, Dictionary of Literary Biography, Concise Dictionary of American Literary Biography, Something about the Author, Something about the Author Autobiography Series,* and *Yesterday's Authors of Books for Children.* Readers will welcome this cumulated author index as a useful tool for locating an author within the various series. The index, which lists birth and death dates when available, will be particularly valuable for those authors who are identified with a certain period but whose death date causes them to be placed in another, or for those authors whose careers span two periods. For example, F. Scott Fitzgerald is found in *TCLC,* yet a writer often associated with him, Ernest Hemingway, is found in *CLC.*

Each volume of *CMLC* will also contain a title index, which will cumulate with the second volume. Primary works under critical consideration are listed, followed by the corresponding volume and page numbers where criticism may be located. Foreign language titles that have been translated are followed by the titles of the translation, for example: *Slovo o polku Igoreve (The Song of Igor's Campaign).* Page numbers following these translated titles refer to all pages on which any form of the title, either foreign language or translated, appear. Titles of novels, dramas, nonfiction books, as well as poetry, short story, or essay collections are printed in italics, while all individual poems, short stories, and essays are printed in roman type within quotation marks. In cases where the same title is used by different authors, the author's surname is given in parentheses after the title, e.g., *Collected Poems* (Horace) and *Collected Poems* (Sappho).

An index to critics, which will cumulate with the second volume, is another useful feature of *CMLC.* Under each critic's name are listed the authors and/or works on whom the critic has written and the volume and page number where the criticism may be found.

Acknowledgments

No work of this scope can be accomplished without the cooperation of many people. The editors especially wish to thank the copyright holders of the excerpted criticism included in this volume, the permissions managers of many book and magazine publishing companies for assisting us in securing reprint rights, and Anthony Bogucki for assistance with copyright research. We are also grateful to the staffs of the Detroit Public Library, the Library of Congress, the University of Detroit Library, the University of Michigan Library, and the Wayne State University Library for making their resources available to us.

Suggestions Are Welcome

Readers who wish to suggest authors or works to appear in future volumes, or who have other suggestions, are cordially invited to write the editors.

Authors to Appear in Future Volumes

Abelard, Peter 1079-1142
Abu Nuwās, Hasan ibn Hānai 762-c.815
Aelfric c.955-c.1020
Aeschylus c.525-456 B.C.
Aesop 6th century B.C.
Agathon c.445-c.399 B.C.
Albertus Magnus 1206-1280
Alcuin 735-804
Amadís de Gaula c. 14th century
Ambrose 339-397
Anacreon c.570-c.485 B.C.
Ancrene Riwle c.1200?
Anglo-Saxon Chronicle 9th -12th centuries
Anna Comnena 1083-c.1153
Antiphon c.480-411 B.C.
Apollonius Rhodius c.295-? B.C.
Aquinas, St. Thomas c.1225-1274
Aristarchus c.217-c.143 B.C.
Aristides, Aelius c.117-189
Aristophanes c.450-c.385 B.C.
Aristotle 384-322 B.C.
Arnaut, Daniel fl. c.1200
Artemidorus 2nd century
Aucassin et Nicolette c.1200
Augustine, St. 354-430
Augustus 63 B.C.-A.D.14
Aurelius, Marcus 121-180
Barlaam and Josaphat 13th century
Basil, St. 329-379
Batrachomyomachia 5th century B.C.?
Bede 673-735
Bertran de Born fl. c.1140
Bhavagad gita c.200 B.C.
The Bible
Bion c.325-c.255 B.C.
Boccaccio, Giovanni 1313-1375
Boethius, Anicius Manlius Severinus c.480-524
Bogurodzica c. late 13th century
Book of Odes c.1000-c.700 B.C.
Books of Chilam Balam
Caedmon ?-c.670
Caesar, Gaius Julius 100-44 B.C.
Carmina Burana 13th century
Cassiodorus, Flavius Magnus Aurelius c.487-44 B.C.
Cato, Marcus Porcius 234-149 B.C.
Catullus, Gaius Valerius c.84-c.54 B.C.
Chrétien de Troyes 12th century
Chrysostom, John c.350-407
Ch'u Elegies 125
Cicero, Marcus Tullius 106-43 B.C.
Cinna, Gaius Helvius c.70-44 B.C.
Claudian c.370-404
Claudius 10 B.C.-A.D.54
Clement of Alexandria c.150-214
Columba, St. c.520-597
Compagni, Dino c.1255-1324
Confucius c.551-c.479 B.C.
Conon de Béthune c.1150-c.1219
Constantine Porphyrogenitus 905-959
Corinna 6th century B.C.
Cynewulf 8th-9th centuries
Cyprian, St. c.200-258
Cyril of Scythopolis c.524-c.560
Dante Alighieri 1265-1321
Democritus c.460 B.C.
Demosthenes 384-322 B.C.
Diodorus Siculus fl. 60-30 B.C.
Diogenes Laertius early 3rd century
Dionysius of Halicarnassus fl.80-30 B.C.
Eckhart, Meister c.1260-1327
Eddas c.900-1200
Egils saga Skalla-Grímsonnar 13th century
Egyptian mythology
Einhard c.770-840
Empedocles c.493-c.433 B.C.
Epic of Gilgamesh c.2700 B.C.
Epictetus c.55-135
Epicurus 341-271 B.C.
Euripides c.484-406? B.C.
Eustathius of Thessalonica ?-c.1195
Fioretti di San Francisco 14th century
Francis, St. c.1182-1226
Fredegar 7th or 8th century
Galen c.129-199?
"Gawain Poet" fl. 1370
Geoffrey of Monmouth 1100?-1154
Gesta Francorum
Gesta Romanorum c.1300
Gísla saga Súrssonar c.1225
Gottfried von Strassburg fl. 1210
Greek mythology
Gregory of Tours c.540-594
Grettis saga c.1300
Grosseteste, Robert c.1168-1253
Gui, Chatelain de Coucy d.1203
Guy of Warwick
Hadrian 76-138
Han Yü 768-824
Hartmann von Aue fl. 1190-1210
Heliodorus 3rd century
Heraclitus fl. c.500 B.C.
Herodotus c.484-c.420 B.C.
Hesiod 800-700 B.C.
Hippocrates of Cos c.460-380 B.C.
Historia Augusta c.360
Horace 65-8 B.C.
Hugo von Trimberg c.1230-c.1313
Imru'u'l-Qais ?-c.540
Isocrates 436-338 B.C.
Jacques de Vitry c.1160-1240
Jalâl al-Dîn 1207-1273
Jaufre Rudel 12th century
Jean Bodel c.1165-c.1210
Jean Renart fl. early 13th century
Jerome, St. c.348-420
John of Salisbury c.1115-1180
Josephus 37?-?
Julian 331?-363
Juvenal 60?-130?
Kakinomoto Hitomaro c.700
Kalidasa c.400
Kamasutra
Kojiki c.712
Konjaku monogatari c.1050
Koran c.632
Langland, William c.1331-1399?
Lao Tzu 6th century B.C.
Leo VI 866-912
Li Po 701-762
Livy 59 B.C.-A.D. 17
Longinus 1st century
Lucan 39-65
Lucretius c.95-c.55 B.C.
Mabinogion early medieval period
Macrobius, Ambrosius Theodosius 4th-5th centuries
Mahabharata c.400 B.C.-A.D. 200
Maimonides 1135-1204
"Mandeville, Sir John" fl. 1350
Manuel, Don Juan 1282-1345
Marie de France fl. late 12th century
Meleager c.140-70 B.C.
Menander 341-290 B.C.
Morte Arthure 14th century
Mystère d'Adam c.1150-1170
Nachmanides 1194-c.1270
Native American legends and tales
Nibelungenlied c.1200
Norse sagas
Novellino, Il late 13th century
Odyssey 8th century B.C.
Omar Khayyâm ?-1122?
Ono Komachi c.850
Origen c.185-253
Ovid 43 B.C.-A.D. 17?
The Owl and the Nightingale c.1200
Petrarch, Francisco 1304-1374
Petronius Arbiter, Gaius c. 1st century
Philemon c.361-262 B.C.
Pindar 518-438 B.C.
Plato c.429-347 B.C.
Plautus, Titus Maccius c.254-184 B.C.
Pliny the Elder 23-79
Pliny the Younger c.61-c.114
Plotinus 205-70

Plutarch c.46-c.127
Po Chü-i 772-846
Poema de mio Cid 12th century
Polo, Marco 1254?-1324
Propertius, Sextus c.54-c.16 B.C.
Pseudo-Dionysius the Areopagite c.500
Ptolemy fl. 121-51
Quintilianus c.30-c.100
Rāmāyana
Razón de amor early 13th century
Rgveda c.1500-1000 B.C.
Roman de la rose c.1225-1277
Roman de Renart c.1174-1205
Russian Primary Chronicle 12th century
Sa'dî c.1215-1292?
Sappho c.612-? B.C.
Saxo Grammaticus c.1150-c.1206
Sei Shōnagon c.1000
Seneca, Lucius Annaeus, the Younger 4 B.C.-A.D.65
Simonides c.556-c.468 B.C.
Snorri Sturulson 1179-1241
Socrates 469?-399 B.C.
Solon c.640-c.560 B.C.
Sophocles c.496-406 B.C.
Sordello fl. mid 13th century
Sumerian mythology
Su Shih 1036-1101
Tacitus, Cornelius c.55-?
Talmud
Tannhäuser fl. mid 13th century
Terence 195?-159 B.C.
Tertullianus, Quintus Septimus Florens c.160-c.225
Theocritus c.310-250 B.C.
The Thousand and One Nights
Thucydides c.455-c.399 B.C.
Tu Fu 712-770
Upanishad c.800-500 B.C.
Veda 1500-500 B.C.
Virgil 70-19 B.C.
Wace, Robert c.1100-1184
Walther von der Vogelweide c.1170-c.1230
William of Malmesbury c.1090-c.1143
Wolfram von Eschenbach fl. early 13th century
Wyclif(fe), John c.1328-1384
Xenophon c.430-c.354 B.C.
Zeno of Elea fl. c.450 B.C.
Zosimus 5th century

(Lucius) Apuleius (Madaurensis)

125?-175?

Roman novelist and orator.

Apuleius is the author of *Metamorphoses,* or *Asinus Aureus (The Golden Ass),* the earliest Latin novel to survive in its entirety and one of the most spirited prose works of the ancient world. He also wrote *Apologia sive oratorio de magia (The Apology),* the only Latin forensic speech to survive from imperial Roman times, and *De deo Socratis (On the God of Socrates),* an influential discourse on the *daimonion,* or divine element, elucidated by Socrates in Plato's *Apology.* A skilled rhetorician and original stylist noted for his polished, exuberant, and highly rhythmic Latin, Apuleius is credited with raising Latin prose to new heights, and his works, especially *Metamorphoses,* have long been admired as epitomes of classical humor, satire, and wit. The province of historians, literary critics, and general readers alike, Apuleius's writings are valued as illustrations of ancient life and thought, and *Metamorphoses* is especially enjoyed as a superb entertainment.

Bibliotheque Nationale, Paris

Details of Apuleius's life are drawn primarily from *The Apology* and *Metamorphoses,* although neither source is comprehensive and neither may be considered entirely reliable. Almost certainly the son of prosperous parents, Apuleius was born about 125 in the North African city of Madaura—near modern Mdaourouch in eastern Algeria. According to Apuleius, he was educated as a young man in Carthage and Athens, and, in the latter city, drank "the elegant draught of poetry, the clear cup of geometry, the sweet one of music, the stiff one of dialectic, and the inexhaustible nectar of universal philosophy." From Athens Apuleius went to Rome, where he became closely associated with the city's elevated literary circles, probably wrote *Metamorphoses,* and was initiated into the mysteries of the Egyptian goddess Isis. He was impoverished by the enormous expenses involved in the Isiac rites, and therefore began work as a rhetorician. He pleaded legal cases, oversaw the preparation of legal and civil documents and developed his skills as an orator. Restless by nature and insatiably curious about life in the outer reaches of the Empire, he left Rome and set out for Alexandria, probably in the year 156. While visiting Oea (now Tripoli), he fell dangerously ill and took up temporary residence at the home of Sicinius Pontianus, whom he had known as a student in Athens, thereby unwittingly ensnaring himself in a well-intentioned but ill-considered scheme to marry him to Pontianus's rich, widowed mother, Pudentilla. In time the marriage took place, but soon after Apuleius was brought to trial by members of his new family, first for murdering Pontianus, who had died suddenly following a journey, and secondly for coercing Pudentilla's affections by using black magic—both unfounded charges. The murder charge was quickly dismissed, but the black magic allegation, apparently made to prevent Apuleius from controlling his in-laws' fortune, led to a formal indictment, and Apuleius was called to defend himself at the assizes in Sabratha. His speech there, *The Apology,* was his exculpation, but it is unclear whether Apuleius was acquitted or whether the case was dismissed as unproved. In any event, he appears to have left Oea not long after the trial, for by the early 160s he had won a great reputation as an orator in Carthage: statues were erected in his honor, he was made priest of Aesculapius, and he became a major advocate of emperor-worship as a demonstration of provincial loyalty. The remainder of his life was apparently devoted to literature, philosophy, and translation. It is believed that he died at Carthage, probably at around fifty years of age.

Apuleius is best known for *Metamorphoses,* an eleven-book, first-person novel that relates the purported adventures of a restless and insouciant traveler named Lucius. The story begins in Thessaly, where Lucius hears of a murder committed by a witch in Hypata, the town to which he is journeying. Arriving there, he stays with Milo, husband of another witch, Pamphile. At a party, Lucius is again told a witch story, and on his way home he kills three bandits who, upon closer inspection, prove to be animated wineskins. Later, assisted by Fotis, Pamphile's serving maid, he watches Pamphile use a magic ointment to transform herself into an owl. His curiosity roused, Lucius attempts the same transformation on himself; a mistake, however, turns him into a jackass instead. Stolen by robbers and taken to their hideout, Lucius the ass overhears the story of the lovers Cupid and Psyche and witnesses the rescue of a kidnapped girl, Charite. Next he is present at the depraved orgies of Syrian priests, after which he hears four indecorous tales. These incidents are followed by three horror stories: the first about a nobleman's abuse of a poor family; the second about a lecherous stepmother who tries to poison her unresponsive stepson; and the third about a sadistic woman who commits five murders. The sadist of the third story is to be punished by public sexual intercourse with Lucius, but he is so appalled by the idea that he flees his captors for Cenchreae, where he falls asleep and dreams. In the final book of *Metamorphoses,* the transformed Lucius is visited in his sleep by Isis, who, with a wreath of roses, makes him human again. Out of devotion to his savior, he goes to Rome and is initiated into the mysteries of Isis and Osiris.

Metamorphoses is generally deemed a reflection of its author's religious and philosophical principles. The work treats not only the subject implied by its title, transformation, but is also concerned with divinity, individual salvation, the relationship of the real to the imaginary, human capacity for evil, and the supernatural. Based in part on earlier narratives, including, critics believe, the Greek work *Lucius; or, The Ass,* attributed to Lucian, and the lost *Metamorphoses* of Lucius of Patrae, Apuleius's *Metamorphoses* explores the foibles of humanity, promoting mystical thought and religion, especially the cult of Isis, over reliance on rational thought. Apuleius himself called *Metamorphoses* a collection of "Milesian tales"—frivolous, amusing, generally erotic stories—but modern scholars agree that the work is more than this. An episodic novel in the ancient Roman sense—that is, a long fictional prose narrative with a connected sequence of events—*Metamorphoses* presents its hero in the process of continuous development, and many commentators suggest that the work ultimately attains unity through Apuleius's allegorical treatment of *curiositas,* or curiosity, as a vehicle for Lucius's inadvertent spiritual quest. Stylistically the novel is at once archaic and innovative, combining antiquated diction and artistically mannered rhetoric with neologisms and colloquial language to create a highly individual Latin style.

Apuleius also wrote a number of forensic and philosophical works, the most important of which are outstanding examples of Roman Silver Age oratory and rhetoric. These include *The Apology, On the God of Socrates,* and *Florida. The Apology,* the speech Apuleius delivered in defense against the charge of practicing magic, is praised for its erudition and power, and, critics argue, must have held its original audience spellbound. Laced with rhetoric and sophistry and colored by digressions which are often more ornate than forceful, the work is structured by an argument that is logical, convincing, clear, and, in a few places, coldly analytical. More than just a courtroom document, *The Apology* is full of irony, gossip, and light humor, although never at the expense of the matter at hand, justice under the law. *On the God of Socrates* is an elaborate and declamatory oration noted for its expert synthesis of Greek and Roman philosophy. The subject of the work is a traditional one: the nature of demons or intermediary spirits, first discussed by Hesiod and later treated by a number of writers, including Pythagoras, Plato, and Plutarch. Along with the minor work *De Platone et eius dogmate (Plato and His Doctrine), On the God of Socrates* is the basis for calling Apuleius a Platonist. *Florida* is a collection of excerpts from Apuleius's public and private orations on moral, ethical, and occasional themes. Probably an abridgment of a collection now lost, this work is an energetic treatment of the sophist's usual subjects: science, including geography, natural history, and ethnography; the lives and deeds of great men; mythology and history; and the art of sophistry itself.

Apuleius's critical legacy is an ancient and distinguished one. Around the beginning of the fifth century, at least two persons, Saint Augustine of Hippo and Ambrosius Theodosius Macrobius, wrote on Apuleius's conception of intermediary spirits. The former commented also on *The Apology,* calling it "a most copious and eloquent oration," and stating his belief that the ass-transformation described in *The Golden Ass*—this is the title which Augustine used in referring to *Metamorphoses* and the one which has since often been applied to the work—may really have taken place. This belief continued well into the Byzantine period, and brought Apuleius a reputation for wizardry. *Metamorphoses* was not unknown during the Middle Ages, but its author was not recognized as an accomplished storyteller until the end of the fifteenth century. By 1566, the Englishman William Adlington could comment both on the moral purpose of *Metamorphoses*—"Verily under the wrap of this transformation is taxed the life of mortall men"—and on the aesthetic characteristics of the work: "[It is written in] so darke and high a stile, in so strange and absurd words, and in such new invented phrases, as hee [Apuleius] seemed rather to set it forth to show his magnificencie of prose, than to participate his doings to other." Toward the end of the next century, John Dryden applied a generic and historical perspective to the work, linking *Metamorphoses* with Varronian satire, a particularly mocking and comic form of the genre. In the second half of the eighteenth century, William Warburton saw *Metamorphoses* as a calculated, anti-Christian piece of pagan propaganda—a view that has been largely discredited. The early-nineteenth-century critic and translator Thomas Taylor focused on Apuleian Platonism, concluding from his reading of *Metamorphoses* and *On the God of Socrates* that Apuleius was "undoubtedly the greatest of the ancient Latin Platonists." The late nineteenth and early twentieth centuries saw the germination of new critical approaches, ones which proved to be the foundation of much later criticism. Walter Pater, for instance, focused on the purely literary qualities of *Metamorphoses.* He praised the work's "quaint terms and images picked from the early dramatists," and admired its "archaisms and curious felicities." Similarly, Charles Whibley called *Metamorphoses* a "brilliant medley of reality and romance" and "a beginning of modern literature"—an evaluation that foreshadowed intricate studies of the work's structure, genre, intent, and historical importance.

The twentieth century brought a new standard of rigorous academic criticism to all of Apuleius's works, although commentators continued to concentrate on *Metamorphoses.* Major *Metamorphoses* issues included the purpose of the Cupid and Psyche story, the relationship of Book 11 to the rest of the work, the unity of the novel as a whole, the value of the work as a reflection of Roman provincial life, the relation of the narrative to its antecedents, and Apuleius's overall originality. These and other issues were treated from many points of view. In an essay which exemplifies the sociohistorical approach to the work, Elizabeth Hazelton Haight called the narrative "a veritable Odyssey of the life of an extraordinary hero in the age of the Antonines." Later, employing an essentially comparative approach, F. A. Todd viewed *Metamorphoses* as "a novel which may justly be regarded as the greatest achievement of the ancients in prose fiction, with the sole possible exception of the *Satiricon.*" Perhaps the highest compliment came from Kenneth Rexroth: "Apuleius blows up rhetoric until it explodes. His is one of the most extraordinary styles in all literature, comparable to the fantastic obscurities of medieval Irish, or the invented language of the Japanese erotic novelist Saikaku, of James Joyce's *Ulysses* or even sometimes *Finnegans Wake.*"

Although Apuleius's exclusively rhetorical writings may not be widely read today, their author's reputation as a highly original novelist endures, due in large measure to the simple entertainment *Metamorphoses* offers and to the intellectual stimulation it affords. Critically lauded and extremely influential—Giovanni Boccaccio, François Rabelais, Miguel de Cervantes, William Morris, and Robert Bridges made extensive use of its techniques in their own works—*Metamorphoses* is a valuable witness to the versatility of the Latin language, a testament to the power of religious conversion, a statement about human nature, and a matchless mirror of ancient life. Moreover, it is an uncommonly engaging and diverting work, one that is, in the words of Peter Quennell, "one of the five or six volumes that an intelligent Crusoe would hope to discover on his desert island."

PRINCIPAL ENGLISH TRANSLATIONS

The XI Bookes of the Golden Asse (translated by William Adlington) 1566
The Transformations of Lucius, Otherwise Known as "The Golden Ass" (translated by Robert Graves) 1951
The Story of Cupid and Psyche as Related by Apuleius (translated by Louis C. Purser) 1982

LUCIUS APULEIUS (essay date c. 150-75)

[*In the following preface to* Metamorphoses, *which first appeared c. 150-75, Apuleius explains the purpose of his narrative.*]

That I to thee some joyous jests may show in gentle glose,
And frankly feed thy bended ears with passing pleasant prose:
So that thou deign in seemly sort this wanton book to view,
That is set out and garnished fine, with written phrases new.
I will declare how one by hap his human figure lost,
And how in brutish formed shape his loathed life he tossed.
And how he was in course of time from such estate unfold,
Who eftsoons, turned to pristine shape, his lot unlucky told.

What and who he was attend a while, and you shall understand that it was even I, the writer of mine own ***Metamorphoses*** and strange alteration of figure. Hymettus, Athens, Isthmia, Ephyrus, Taenaros, and Sparta, being fat and fertile soils (as I pray you give credit to the books of more everlasting fame) be places where mine ancient progeny and lineage did sometime flourish: there I say, in Athens, when I was young, I went first to school. Soon after (as a stranger) I arrived at Rome, whereas by great industry, and without instruction of any school master, I attained to the full perfection of the Latin tongue: behold, I first crave and beg your pardon, lest I should happen to displease or offend any of you by the rude and rustic utterance of this strange and foreign language. And verily this new alteration of speech doth correspond to the enterprised matter whereof I purpose to entreat; I will set forth unto you a pleasant Grecian jest. Whereunto, gentle reader, if thou wilt give attendant ear, it will minister unto thee such delectable matter as thou shalt be well contented withal. (pp. xxiii-xxiv)

Lucius Apuleius, in a preface to Apuleius, the Golden Ass: Being the Metamorphoses of Lucius Apuleius, *translated by W. Adlington, revised by S. Gaselee, 1915. Reprint by William Heinemann Ltd., 1965, pp. xxiii-xxiv.*

AMBROSIUS THEODOSIUS MACROBIUS (essay date c. 390-410)

[*A Latin encyclopedist who probably lived in the late fourth and early fifth centuries, Macrobius is known to be the author of at least three works:* Commentary on the Dream of Scipio, *a Neoplatonic study of the last book of Cicero's* De republica; Saturnalia, *an account of a winter symposium held by a group of savants and litterateurs; and* On the Differences and Similarities of the Greek and Latin Verb, *a lost treatise known only by its medieval abridgment. In the following excerpt from the first-named work, which appeared c. 390-410, Macrobius designates Apuleius's "narrative"—undoubtedly a reference to* Metamorphoses—*as a work that entertains rather than instructs.*]

Philosophy does not discountenance all stories nor does it accept all, and in order to distinguish between what it rejects as unfit to enter its sacred precincts and what it frequently and gladly admits, the points of division must needs be clarified. Fables—the very word acknowledges their falsity—serve two purposes: either merely to gratify the ear or to encourage the reader to good works. They delight the ear as do the comedies of Menander and his imitators, or the narratives replete with imaginary doings of lovers in which Petronius Arbiter so freely indulged and with which Apuleius, astonishingly, sometimes amused himself. This whole category of fables that promise only to gratify the ear a philosophical treatise avoids and relegates to children's nurseries. The other group, those that draw the reader's attention to certain kinds of virtue, are divided into two types. In the first both the setting and plot are fictitious, as in the fables of Aesop, famous for his exquisite imagination. The second rests on a solid foundation of truth, which is treated in a fictitious style. This is called the fabulous narrative *(narratio fabulosa)* to distinguish it from the ordinary fable; examples of it are the performances of sacred rites, the stories of Hesiod and Orpheus that treat of the ancestry and deeds of the gods, and the mystic conceptions of the Pythagoreans. Of the second main group, which we have just mentioned, the first type, with both setting and plot fictitious, is also inappropriate to philosophical treatises. The second type is subdivided, for there is more than one way of telling the truth when the argument is real but is presented in the form of a fable. Either the presentation of the plot involves matters that are base and unworthy of divinities and are monstrosities of some sort (as, for example, gods caught in adultery, Saturn cutting off the privy parts of his father Caelus and himself thrown into chains by his son and successor), a type which philosophers prefer to disregard altogether; or else a decent and dignified conception of holy truths, with respectable events and characters, is presented beneath a modest veil of allegory. This is the only type of fiction approved by the philosopher who is prudent in handling sacred matters. (pp. 84-5)

Ambrosius Theodosius Macrobius, "Commentary on Scipio's Dream," in his Commentary on the Dream of Scipio, *translated by William Harris Stahl, Columbia University Press, 1952, pp. 79-248.*

SAINT AUGUSTINE (essay date c. 413-26)

[Widely considered the greatest thinker of Christian antiquity, Augustine was Bishop of Hippo in Roman Africa from 396 to 430 and has long been revered as a doctor of the Roman Catholic Church. A devout Manichaean early in life, he later embraced Catholicism thanks largely to the influence of St. Ambrose, then bishop of Milan, whose teachings Augustine followed passionately. Markedly Neoplatonic, Augustine's Christian philosophy centers on epistemology, cosmology, and ethics, and is distinguished by its intense interest in three types of love: amor, the moral dynamic that impels us into action; agape, love in the New Testament sense of the word; and caritas, charity. A profound intellect, Augustine was also an outstanding prose stylist whose major works, including his autobiography, Confessions, *and* The City of God, *a treatise on the "beginnings, courses, and destined ends" of the elect and the damned, have been praised often and lavishly. Intimately acquainted with the works of Apuleius, Augustine is generally deemed one of the Roman author's most attentive and systematic explicators. In the following excerpt from* The City of God, *which first appeared c. 413-26, he examines Apuleius's concept of demons as presented in* On the God of Socrates *and discusses what he considers to be the apparent transformation of Apuleius recounted in the* Metamorphoses.]

[Of rational souls and of demons] many have written: among others Apuleius, the Platonist of Madaura, who composed a whole work on the subject, entitled, ***On the God of Socrates.*** He there discusses and explains of what kind that deity was who attended on Socrates, a sort of familiar, by whom it is said he was admonished to desist from any action which would not turn out to his advantage. He asserts most distinctly, and proves at great length, that it was not a god but a demon; and he discusses with great diligence the opinion of Plato concerning the lofty estate of the gods, the lowly estate of men, and the middle estate of demons. These things being so, how did Plato dare to take away, if not from the gods, whom he removed from all human contagion, certainly from the demons, all the pleasures of the theatre, by expelling the poets from the state? Evidently in this way he wished to admonish the human soul, although still confined in these moribund members, to despise the shameful commands of the demons, and to detest their impurity, and to choose rather the splendour of virtue. But if Plato showed himself virtuous in answering and prohibiting these things, then certainly it was shameful of the demons to command them. Therefore either Apuleius is wrong, and Socrates' familiar did not belong to this class of deities, or Plato held contradictory opinions, now honouring the demons, now removing from the well-regulated state the things in which they delighted, or Socrates is not to be congratulated on the friendship of the demon, of which Apuleius was so ashamed that he entitled his book ***On the God of Socrates,*** whilst according to the tenor of his discussion, wherein he so diligently and at such length distinguishes gods from demons, he ought not to have entitled it, ***On the God,*** but *Concerning the Demon of Socrates*. But he preferred to put this into the discussion itself rather than into the title of his book. For, through the sound doctrine which has illuminated human society, all, or almost all men have such a horror at the name of demons, that every one who, before reading the dissertation of Apuleius, which sets forth the dignity of demons, should have read the title of the book, *On the Demon of Socrates,* would certainly have thought that the author was not a sane man. But what did even Apuleius find to praise in the demons, except subtlety and strength of body and a higher place of habitation? For when he spoke generally concerning their manners, he said nothing that was good, but very much that was bad. Finally, no one, when he has read that book, wonders that they desired to have even the obscenity of the stage among divine things, or that, wishing to be thought gods, they should be delighted with the crimes of the gods, or that all those sacred solemnities, whose obscenity occasions laughter, and whose shameful cruelty causes horror, should be in agreement with their passions. (pp. 259-60)

The same Apuleius, when speaking concerning the manners of demons, said that they are agitated with the same perturbations of mind as men; that they are provoked by injuries, propitiated by services and by gifts, rejoice in honours, are delighted with a variety of sacred rites, and are annoyed if any of them be neglected. Among other things, he also says that on them depend the divinations of augurs, soothsayers, and prophets, and the revelations of dreams; and that from them also are the miracles of the magicians. But, when giving a brief definition of them, he says, "Demons are of an animal nature, passive in soul, rational in mind, aerial in body, eternal in time." "Of which five things, the three first are common to them and us, the fourth peculiar to themselves, and the fifth common to them with the gods." But I see that they have in common with the gods two of the first things, which they have in common with us. For he says that the gods also are animals; and when he is assigning to every order of beings its own element, he places us among the other terrestrial animals which live and feel upon the earth. Wherefore, if the demons are animals as to genus, this is common to them, not only with men, but also with the gods and with beasts; if they are rational as to their mind, this is common to them with the gods and with men; if they are eternal in time, this is common to them with the gods only; if they are passive as to their soul, this is common to them with men only; if they are aerial in body, in this they are alone. Therefore it is no great thing for them to be of an animal nature, for so also are the beasts; in being rational as to mind, they are not above ourselves, for so are we also; and as to their being eternal as to time, what is the advantage of that if they are not blessed? for better is temporal happiness than eternal misery. Again, as to their being passive in soul, how are they in this respect above us, since we also are so, but would not have been so had we not been miserable? Also, as to their being aerial in body, how much value is to be set on that, since a soul of any kind whatsoever is to be set above every body? and therefore religious worship, which ought to be rendered from the soul, is by no means due to that thing which is inferior to the soul. Moreover, if he had, among those things which he says belong to demons, enumerated virtue, wisdom, happiness, and affirmed that they have those things in common with the gods, and, like them, eternally, he would assuredly have attributed to them something greatly to be desired, and much to be prized. And even in that case it would not have been our duty to worship them like God on account of these things, but rather to worship Him from whom we know they had received them. But how much less are they really worthy of divine honour—those aerial animals who are only rational that they may be capable of misery, passive that they may be actually miserable, and eternal that it may be impossible for them to end their misery! (pp. 262-63)

In vain, therefore, have Apuleius, and they who think with him, conferred on the demons the honour of placing them in the air, between the ethereal heavens and the earth, that they may carry to the gods the prayers of men, to men the answers of the gods; for Plato held, they say, that no god has intercourse with man. They who believe these things have thought it unbecoming that men should have intercourse with the gods, and the gods with men, but a befitting thing that the demons should have intercourse with both gods and men, presenting to the gods the petitions of men, and conveying to men what the gods have granted; so that a chaste man, and one who is a stranger to the crimes of the magic arts, must use as patrons, through whom the gods may be induced to hear him, demons who love these crimes, although the very fact of his not loving them ought to have recommended him to them as one who deserved to be listened to with greater readiness and willingness on their part. They love the abominations of the stage, which chastity does not love. They love, in the sorceries of the magicians, *"a thousand arts of inflicting harm,"* which innocence does not love. Yet both chastity and innocence, if they wish to obtain anything from the gods, will not be able to do so by their own merits, except their enemies act as mediators on their behalf. Apuleius need not attempt to justify the fictions of the poets, and the mockeries of the stage. If human modesty can act so faithlessly towards itself as not only to love shameful things, but even to think that they are pleasing to the divinity, we can cite on the other side their own highest authority and teacher, Plato. (p. 264)

[Was] it before Christian judges that Apuleius himself was accused of magic arts? Had he known these arts to be divine and pious, and congruous with the works of divine power, he ought not only to have confessed, but also to have professed them, rather blaming the laws by which these things were prohibited and pronounced worthy of condemnation, while they ought to have been held worthy of admiration and respect. For by so doing, either he would have persuaded the judges to adopt his own opinion, or, if they had shown their partiality for unjust laws, and condemned him to death notwithstanding his praising and commending such things, the demons would have bestowed on his soul such rewards as he deserved, who, in order to proclaim and set forth their divine works, had not feared the loss of his human life. . . . (p. 265)

But there is extant a most copious and eloquent oration [***Apology***] of this Platonic philosopher, in which he defends himself against the charge of practising these arts, affirming that he is wholly a stranger to them, and only wishing to show his innocence by denying such things as cannot be innocently committed. But all the miracles of the magicians, who he thinks are justly deserving of condemnation, are performed according to the teaching and by the power of demons. Why, then, does he think that they ought to be honoured? For he asserts that they are necessary, in order to present our prayers to the gods, and yet their works are such as we must shun if we wish our prayers to reach the true God. Again, I ask, what kind of prayers of men does he suppose are presented to the good gods by the demons? If magical prayers, they will have none such; if lawful prayers, they will not receive them through such beings. But if a sinner who is penitent pour out prayers, especially if he has committed any crime of sorcery, does he receive pardon through the intercession of those demons by whose instigation and help he has fallen into the sin he mourns? or do the demons themselves, in order that they may merit pardon for the penitent, first become penitents because they have deceived them? This no one ever said concerning the demons; for had this been the case, they would never have dared to seek for themselves divine honours. For how should they do so who desired by penitence to obtain the grace of pardon, seeing that such detestable pride could not exist along with a humility worthy of pardon? (pp. 265-66)

[No] credence whatever is to be given to the opinion of Apuleius and the other philosophers of the same school, namely, that the demons act as messengers and interpreters between the gods and men to carry our petitions from us to the gods, and to bring back to us the help of the gods. On the contrary, we must believe them to be spirits most eager to inflict harm, utterly alien from righteousness, swollen with pride, pale with envy, subtle in deceit; who dwell indeed in this air as in a prison, in keeping with their own character, because cast down from the height of the higher heaven, they have been condemned to dwell in this element as the just reward of irretrievable transgression. But, though the air is situated above the earth and the waters, they are not on that account superior in merit to men, who, though they do not surpass them as far as their earthly bodies are concerned, do nevertheless far excel them through piety of mind—they having made choice of the true God as their helper. (p. 269)

[What] is the difference between good and evil demons? For the Platonist Apuleius, in a treatise on this whole subject [***On the God of Socrates***], while he says a great deal about their aerial bodies, has not a word to say of the spiritual virtues with which, if they were good, they must have been endowed. Not a word has he said, then, of that which could give them happiness; but proof of their misery he has given, acknowledging that their mind, by which they rank as reasonable beings, is not only not imbued and fortified with virtue so as to resist all unreasonable passions, but that it is somehow agitated with tempestuous emotions, and is thus on a level with the mind of foolish men. (p. 281)

[If] any one says that it is not of all the demons, but only of the wicked, that the poets, not without truth, say that they violently love or hate certain men—for it was of them Apuleius said that they were driven about by strong currents of emotion—how can we accept this interpretation, when Apuleius, in the very same connection, represents all the demons, and not only the wicked, as intermediate between gods and men by their aerial bodies? The fiction of the poets, according to him, consists in their making gods of demons, and giving them the names of gods, and assigning them as allies or enemies to individual men, using this poetical licence, though they profess that the gods are very different in character from the demons, and far exalted above them by their celestial abode and wealth of beatitude. This, I say, is the poets' fiction, to say that these are gods who are not gods, and that, under the names of gods, they fight among themselves about the men whom they love or hate with keen partisan feeling. Apuleius says that this is not far from the truth, since, though they are wrongfully called by the names of the gods, they are described in their own proper character as demons. To this category, he says, belongs the Minerva of Homer, "who interposed in the ranks of the Greeks to restrain Achilles." For that this was Minerva he supposes to be poetical fiction; for he thinks that Minerva is a goddess, and he places her among the gods whom he believes to be all good and blessed in the sublime ethereal region, remote from intercourse with men. But that there was a demon favourable to the Greeks and adverse to the Trojans, as another, whom the same poet mentions under the name of Venus or Mars (gods exalted above earthly affairs in their heavenly habitations), was the Trojans' ally and the foe of the Greeks, and that these demons fought for those they loved against those they hated—in all this he owned that the poets stated something very like the truth. For they made these statements about beings to whom he ascribes the same violent and tempestuous passions as disturb men, and who are therefore capable of loves and hatreds not justly formed, but formed in a party spirit, as the spectators in races or hunts take fancies and prejudices. It seems to have been the great fear of this Platonist that the poetical fictions should be believed of the gods, and not of the demons who bore their names. (pp. 286-87)

Perhaps our readers expect us to say something about [the transformations which seem to happen to men through the art of demons]; and what shall we say but that men must fly out of the midst of Babylon? For this prophetic precept is to be understood spiritually in this sense, that by going forward in the living God, by the steps of faith, which worketh by love, we must flee out of the city of this world, which is altogether a society of ungodly angels and men. Yea, the greater we see the power of the demons to be in these depths, so much the more tenaciously must we cleave to the Mediator through whom we ascend from these lowest to the highest places. For if we should say these things are not to be credited, there are not wanting even now some who would affirm that they had either heard on the best authority, or even themselves experienced, something of that kind. Indeed we ourselves, when in Italy, heard such things about a certain region there, where landladies of inns, imbued with these wicked arts, were said to be in the habit of giving to such travellers as they chose, or could manage, something in a piece of cheese by which they were changed on the spot into beasts of burden, and carried whatever was necessary, and were restored to their own form when the work was done. Yet their mind did not become bestial, but remained rational and human, just as Apuleius, in the books he wrote with the title of ***The Golden Ass,*** has told, or feigned, that it happened to his own self that, on taking poison, he became an ass, while retaining his human mind.

These things are either false, or so extraordinary as to be with good reason disbelieved. But it is to be most firmly believed that Almighty God can do whatever He pleases, whether in punishing or favouring, and that the demons can accomplish nothing by their natural power (for their created being is itself angelic, although made malign by their own fault), except what He may permit, whose judgments are often hidden, but never unrighteous. (pp. 623-24)

Saint Augustine, in his The City of God, *translated by Marcus Dods, with Rev. J. J. Smith and Rev. George Wilson, The Modern Library, 1950, 892 p.*

WILLIAM ADLINGTON (essay date 1566)

[*Adlington was an English editor and translator. He was, by his own claim, connected at some time with University College, Oxford, and it is likely that he wrote the anonymous moral poem* A Speciall Remedie against the Force of Lawless Love *(1579). In the following excerpt from an introduction to his 1566 translation of* Metamorphoses, *Adlington discusses how he came to produce the first English translation of Apuleius's novel and analyzes its style and substance.*]

When that I had (gentle Reader) slightly here and there runne over the pleasant and delectable jeasts of Lucius Apuleius (a man of antient descent, and endued with singular learning) written in such a franke and flourishing stile, as he seemed to have the Muses at his will, to feed and maintaine his pen. And when againe I perceived the matter to minister such exceeding plenty of mirth, as never in my judgment the like hath been shewed by any other, I purposed according to my slender knowledge (though it were rudely, and farre disagreeing from the fine and excellent doings now adayes) to translate the same into our vulgar tongue, to the end that amongst so many sage and serious works (as every man well nigh endeavour daily to encrease) there might bee some fresh and pleasant matter to recreate the mindes of the Readers withall. Howbeit, I was eftsoones driven from my purpose by two causes: First, perceiving that the Author had written his work in so darke and high a stile, in so strange and absurd words, and in such new invented phrases, as hee seemed rather to set it forth to shew his magnificencie of prose, than to participate his doings to other. Secondly, fearing least the translation of this present Booke (which seemeth a meere jeast and fable, and a Worke worthy to be laughed at, by reason of the vanity of the Author) might be contemned and despised of all men, and so consequently I to be had in derision, to occupie my selfe in such frivolous and trifling toyes. But on the other side, when I had thoroughly learned the intent of the Author, and the purpose why hee invented so sportfull a jest, I was verily perswaded that my small travell should not onely be accepted by many, but the matter it selfe allowed and praised of all. Wherefore I intend, God willing, as nigh as I can, to utter and open the meaning thereof, to the simple and ignorant, whereby they may not take the same, as a thing only to jest and laugh at (for the fables of Æsop and the feigning of Poets were never written for that purpose) but by the pleasantnesse thereof bee rather induced to the knowledge of their present estate, and thereby transforme themselves into the right and perfect shape of men. The argument of the book is, how Lucius Apuleius the Author himselfe travelled into Thessaly, being a region in Greece, where all the women for the most part bee such wonderfull Witches, that they can transforme men into the figure of brute beasts: Where after he had continued a few dayes, by the mighty force of a violent confection hee was changed into a miserable Asse, and nothing might reduce him to his wonted shape but the eating of a Rose, which after the indurance of infinite sorrow, at length he obtained by prayer. Verily under the wrap of this transformation is taxed the life of mortall men, when as we suffer our mindes so to bee drowned in the sensuall lusts of the flesh, and the beastly pleasure thereof (which aptly may be called the violent confection of Witches) that wee lose wholly the use of reason and vertue, which properly should be in man, and play the parts of brute and savage beasts. By like occasion we reade, how divers of the companions of Vlysses were turned by the marvellous power of Circe into swine. And finde we not in Scripture, that Nabuchadnezzar the ninth King of Babylon, by reason of his great dominions and realmes, fell into such exceeding pride, that he was suddenly transformed of Almighty God into an horrible monster, having the head of an Oxe, the feet of a Beare, and the taile of Lion, and did eat hay as a Beast. But as Lucius Apuleius was changed into his humane shape by a Rose, the companions of Vlysses by great intercession, and Nabuchadnezzar by the continual prayers of Daniel, whereby they knew themselves, and lived after a good and vertuous life: so can we never bee restored to the right figure of our selves, except we taste and eat the sweet Rose of reason and vertue, which the rather by mediation of praier we may assuredly attaine. Againe, may not the meaning of this worke be altered and turned in this sort: A man desirous to apply his minde to some excellent art, or given to the study of any of the sciences, at the first appeareth to himselfe an asse without wit, without knowledge, and not much unlike a brute beast, till such time as by much paine and travell he hath atchieved to the perfectnesse of the same, and tasting the sweet floure and fruit of his studies, doth thinke himselfe well brought to the right and very shape of a man.

Finally, the metamorphosie of Lucius Apuleius may be resembled to youth without discretion, and his reduction to age possessed with wisedome and vertue. (pp. 5-7)

[Among the works of Apuleius] now extant are the foure books named ***Floridorum,*** wherein is contained a flourishing stile, and a savory kind of learning, which delighteth, holdeth, and rejoiceth the Reader marvellously; wherein you shall finde a great variety of things, as leaping one from another: One excellent and copious Oration [***Apology***] containing all the grace and vertue of the art Oratory, whereby he cleareth himselfe of the crime of art Magick, which was slanderously objected against him by his Adversaries, wherein is contained such force of eloquence and doctrine, as he seemeth to passe and excell himselfe. There is another booke [***On the God of Socrates***], whereof S. Augustine maketh mention in his booke of the definition of spirits, and description of men [see excerpt dated c. 413-26]. Two other books of the opinion of Plato, wherein is briefly contained that which before was largely expressed. One booke of Cosmography, comprising many things of Aristotles Meteors. The ***Dialogue of Trismegistus,*** translated by him out of Greeke into Latine, so fine, that it rather seemeth with more eloquence turned into Latine, than it was before written in Greeke. But principally [the] eleven Bookes of the ***Golden Asse,*** are enriched with such pleasant matter, with such excellency and variety of flourishing tales, that nothing may be more sweet and delectable, whereby worthily they may be intituled, ***The Bookes of the Golden Asse,*** for the passing stile and matter therein. For what can be more acceptable than this Asse of Gold indeed. Howbeit there be many which would rather intitle it ***Metamorphosis,*** that is to say, A transfiguration or transformation, by reason of the argument and matter therein. (pp. 10-11)

William Adlington, in an introduction to The Golden Asse of Lucius Apuleius *by Lucius Apuleius, translated by William Adlington, Simpkin, Marshall, Hamilton, Kent & Co. Ltd., 1922, pp. 5-7, 10-11.*

JOHN DRYDEN (essay date 1693)

[*Regarded by many as the father of modern English poetry and criticism, Dryden dominated literary life in England during the last four decades of the seventeenth century. By deliberately and comprehensively refining the English language in all his works, he developed an expressive, universal diction which has had immense impact on the development of speech and writing in Great Britain and North America. Recognized as a prolific and accomplished dramatist, Dryden also wrote a number of satirical poems and critical works, some of which are acknowledged as his greatest literary achievements. In the former, notably* Absalom and Achitophel *(1681),* Religio Laici *(1682), and* The Hind and the Panther *(1687), he displayed an irrepressible wit and forceful line of argument which later satirists adopted as their model. In his critical works, particularly* Of Dramatic Poesy *(1668), Dryden effectively originated the extended form of objective, practical analysis that has come to characterize most modern criticism. In the following excerpt from his* Discourse Concerning the Original and Progress of Satire, *which first appeared in 1693, he links* Metamorphoses *with the work of the second-century Roman satirist Marcus Terentius Varro.*]

This we may believe for certain, that as [Varro's subjects] were various, so most of them were tales or stories of his own invention. Which is also manifest from antiquity, by those authors who are acknowledged to have written Varronian satires, in imitation of his; of whom the chief is Petronius Arbiter, whose satire, they say, is now printed in Holland, wholly recovered, and made complete: when 'tis made public, it will easily be seen by any one sentence, whether it be supposititious, or genuine. Many of Lucian's dialogues may also properly be called Varronian satires, particularly his *True History;* and consequently the ***Golden Ass*** of Apuleius, which is taken from him. Of the same stamp is the mock deification of Claudius, by Seneca: and the *Symposium* or *Cæsars* of Julian, the Emperor. Amongst the moderns, we may reckon the *Encomium Moriæ* of Erasmus, Barclay's *Euphormio,* and a volume of German authors, which my ingenious friend, Mr. Charles Killigrew, once lent me. In the English, I remember none which are mixed with prose, as Varro's were; but of the same kind is *Mother Hubbard's Tale,* in Spenser; and (if it be not too vain to mention anything of my own), the poems of *Absalom* and *MacFleckno.* (pp. 66-7)

John Dryden, "A Discourse Concerning the Original and Progress of Satire," in his Essays of John Dryden, Vol. II, *edited by W. P. Ker, Oxford at the Clarendon Press, 1926, pp. 15-114.*

WILLIAM WARBURTON (essay date 1738-66)

[*Warburton was an English prelate, critic, editor, and theological controversialist who edited Shakespeare's plays, prepared an amply annotated edition of Alexander Pope's works, and wrote numerous philosophical and apologetic commentaries. He is best remembered as the author of* The Divine Legation of Moses *(1738-66), a lengthy, rambling treatise designed to demonstrate the reasonableness and necessity of Christianity. In the following excerpt from that work, he argues that* Metamorphoses *was conceived primarily as a pagan diatribe against Christianity.*]

[How essential the mysteries] were esteemed to RELIGION, we may understand by the ***Metamorphosis*** of Apuleius; a book, indeed, which from its very first appearance hath passed for a trivial fable. Capitolinus, in the life of Clodius Albinus, where he speaks of that kind of tales which disconcert the gravity of philosophers, tells us that Severus could not bear with patience the honours the Senate had conferred on Albinus; especially their distinguishing him with the title of *learned,* who was grown old in the study of old-wives-fables, such as the Milesian-Punic tales of his countryman and favourite, Apuleius. . . . [Macrobius] seems to wonder that Apuleius should trifle so egregiously: and well he might [see excerpt dated c. 390-410]. For the writer of the ***Metamorphosis*** was one of the gravest and most virtuous, as well as most learned, philosophers of his age. But Albinus appears to have gone further into the true character of this work, than his rival Severus. And if we may believe Marcus Aurelius, who calls Albinus "homo exercitatus, vita tristis, gravis moribus" ["a disciplined man of melancholy mien, bearing a deathly burden"], he was not a man to be taken with such trifling amusements as Milesian fables. His fondness therefore for the ***Metamorphosis*** of Apuleius shews, that he considered it in another light. And who so likely to be let into the author's true design, as Albinus, who lived very near his time, and was of Adrumetum in the neighbourhood of Carthage, where Apuleius sojourned and studied, and was honoured with public marks of distinction! The work is indeed of a different character from what some Ancients have represented it; and even from what modern Critics have pretended to discover of it. Those Ancients, who stuck in the outside, considered it, without refinement, as an idle fable: the Moderns, who could not reconcile a work of that nature to the gravity of the author's character, have supposed it a thing of more importance, and no less than a general satire on the vices of those times. . . . But this is far short of the matter. The author's main purpose was not to satyrize the specific *vices of his age* (though, to enliven his fable, and for the better carrying on his story, he hath employed many circumstances of this kind) but to recommend PAGAN RELIGION as the only cure for *all vice whatsoever.*

To give what we have to say its proper force, we must consider the real character of the writer. Apuleius, of Madaura in Afric, was a devoted Platonist; and, like the Platonists of that age, an inveterate enemy to Christianity. . . . His superstitious attachment to the *Religion of his country,* is seen in his immoderate fondness for the MYSTERIES. He was initiated, as himself tells us, into almost all of them: and, in some, bore the most distinguished offices. . . . His great devotion to Paganism, therefore, must needs have been attended with an equal aversion to Christianity; and it is more than probable, that the oration he speaks of [in his ***Apology***] as made in honour of Æsculapius, was in the number of those INVECTIVES, at that time so well received by the enemies of our holy faith. For, not to insist on the success of his oration, which, he tells us, was in every body's hands, a thing common to discourses on subjects that engage the public attention, but rarely the fortune of such stale ware as panegyrics on a God long worn into an establishment; not, I say, to insist upon this, we may observe that Æsculapius was one of those ancient heroes, who were employed, by the defenders of Paganism, to oppose to JESUS; and the circumstances of Æsculapius's story made him the fittest of any in fabulous antiquity, for that purpose. (pp. 287-90)

[In consideration of] what there was in the common passion of his Sect, and in his own fond mode of superstition, to indispose Apuleius to *Christianity;* let us inquire what private provocation he might have to prejudice him against it; for, a private provocation, I am persuaded, he had; occasioned by a personal injury done him by one of THIS PROFESSION; which, I suppose, did not a little contribute to exasperate his bigotry. He had married a rich widow, against the good liking of her first husband's Relations; who endeavoured to set aside the marriage on pretence of his employing sorcery and enchantments to engage her affections. Of this, he wasjudicially accused by his wife's brother-in-law, Licinius Æmilianus, before the Proconsul of Africa. Now his Accuser, if I am not much mistaken, was a CHRISTIAN, though this interesting circumstance hath escaped the notice of his commentators. . . . 1. Now, irreligion and atheism, we know, were the names Christianity at that time went by, for having dared to renounce the whole family of the gentile Gods together. . . . That the Atheism of Æmilianus was of this sort, and no *courtly* or *philosophic* impiety, appears from his Character and Station. He was neither a fine Gentleman, nor a profound Inquirer into nature; characters indeed which are sometimes found to be above Religion; but a mere Rustic, in his life and manners. Now plain, unpolished men, in such a condition of life, are never without some Religion or other: When therefore, we find Æmilianus not of the *established,* we must needs conclude him to be a *Sectary* and a CHRISTIAN. 2. His neglect of his country Gods was not a mere negative affront of forgetfulness. He gloried in being their despiser; and took kindly to the name of MEZENTIUS, as a title of honour— . . . which I would consider as a further mark of a *Christian, convict.* 3. He even held it an *abomination* so much as to put his hand to his lips, (according to the mode of adoration in those times) when he passed by an Heathen Temple; . . . the most characteristic mark of a *primitive Confessor,* by which he could never be mistaken; nor, one would think, so long overlooked. 4. By the frequent and sarcastical repetition of the word *verum* [''truth''], Apuleius seems to sneer at that general title which the Faithful gave their *Religion,* of THE TRUTH. (pp. 290-92)

The aversion, therefore, which Apuleius had contracted to his Christian accuser . . . would without doubt increase his prejudice to that Religion. I am persuaded he gave the Character of the Baker's wife, in his ***Golden Ass,*** for no other reason than to outrage our holy faith. Having drawn her stained with all the vices that could deform a Woman; to finish all, he makes her a Christian. (p. 293)

Let us see now how this would influence his writings. There was nothing the PHILOSOPHERS of that time had more at heart, especially the *Platonists* and *Pythagoreans,* than the support of sinking Paganism. This service, as hath been occasionally remarked, they performed in various ways and manners: some by *allegorizing their Theology;* some by *spiritualizing their Philosophy;* and some, as Jamblichus and Philostratus, by writing the *lives of their Heroes,* to oppose to that of CHRIST; others again, as Porphyry, with this view *collected their oracles;* or as Melanthius, Menander, Hicesius, and Sotades, *wrote descriptive encomiums on their* MYSTERIES. Which last, as we shall now shew, was the province undertaken by Apuleius; his ***Metamorphosis*** being nothing else but one continued RECOMMENDATION of them.

But to give what we have to say its proper force; let us, 1. enquire into the motives our Author might have for entering at all into the defence of Paganism: 2. His reasons for choosing this topic of defence, *the recommendation of the Mysteries.*

1. As to his defence of paganism in general, we may observe, 1. That works of this kind were very much in fashion, especially amongst the Philosophers of our author's Sect. 2. He was, as we have seen, most superstitiously devoted to pagan worship: and, 3. He bore a personal spite and prejudice to the Christian profession.

2. As to his making the defence of the *Mysteries* his choice, still stronger reasons may be assigned. 1. These were the Rites to which he was so peculiarly devoted, that he had contrived to be *initiated* into all the *Mysteries* of note, in the Roman world; and in several of them had borne the most distinguished offices. 2. The *Mysteries* being at this time become extremely corrupt, and consequently, in discredit, needed an able and zealous Apologist: both of which qualities met eminently in Apuleius. The corruptions were of two kinds, DEBAUCHERIES and MAGIC. . . . 3. Our author's close attachment to *Mysterious rites* was, without question, the very thing that occasioned all those suspicions and reports, which ended in an accusation of *Magic:* And, considering . . . the corrupt state of the *Mysteries,* the reader will not wonder that it should.

Such then being the general character of the *Mysteries,* and of this their great Devotee, nothing was more natural than his projecting their defence; which, at the same time that it concurred to the support of Paganism in general, would vindicate his own credit, together with an Institution of which he was so immoderately fond. And the following considerations are sufficient to shew, that the ***Metamorphosis*** was written after his ***Apology:*** for, 1. His accusers never once mention the fable of the ***Golden Ass*** to support their charge of Magic, though they were in great want of proofs, and this lay so ready for their purpose. For, we are not to suppose that he alludes to the ***Metamorphosis*** in [the ***Apology*** when he refers to *anileis fabulas*]. . . . The *idle tales* here hinted at, are the gossiping stories which went about of him, and which he afterwards exposes in the course of this defence. 2. He positively asserts before the tribunal of Maximus Claudius, that he had never given the least occasion to suspect him of *Magic.* . . . (pp. 293-94)

Now Antiquity considered INITIATION INTO THE MYSTERIES as *a delivery from a living death of vice, brutality, and misery; and the beginning of a new life of virtue, reason, and happiness*. This, therefore, was the very circumstance which our Author chose for the subject of his recommendation.

And as in the *Mysteries,* their moral and divine truths were represented in *shews* and *allegories,* so, in order to comply with this method of instruction, and in imitation of the ancient Masters of wisdom, who borrowed their manner of teaching from thence, he hath artfully insinuated his doctrine in an agreeable Fable; and the fittest, one could conceive for his purpose, as will be seen when we come to examine it.

The foundation of this Allegory was a *Milesian Fable,* a species of polite trifling then much in vogue, and not unlike the modern *Arabian tales*. To allure his readers, therefore, with the promise of a *fashionable* work, he introduces his ***Metamorphosis*** . . . [by] plainly intimating that there was something of more consequence at bottom. But the *fashionable* people took him at his word; and, from that day to this, never troubled their heads about a further meaning. The OUTSIDE engaged all their attention, and sufficiently delighted them; as we may gather from the early title it bore of ***Asinus Aureus.*** And, from the beginning of one of Pliny's epistles, I suspect that AUREÆ was the common title given to the *Milesian,* and such like tales as Strolers used to tell for a piece of money to the rabble in a circle. (pp. 294-95)

Upon one of these popular Fables, [Apuleius] chose to ingraft his instruction; taking a celebrated Tale from the *collections* of one Lucius of Patræ; who relates his transformation into an Ass, and his adventures under that shape. Lucian has epitomised this story, as Apuleius seems to have paraphrased it: and the subject being a METAMORPHOSIS, it admirably fitted his purpose; as the METEMPSYCHOSIS, to which that superstition belongs, was one of the fundamental doctrines of the *Mysteries*. But from Photius's account of Lucius Patrensis one would be inclined to rank him amongst those who composed books of *Metamorphosis* . . . according to the popular Theology, rather than a writer of Milesian fables. . . . And after having said that Lucian borrowed his *Ass* from thence, to ridicule pagan religion, he goes on; "but Lucius giving a more serious turn to his Metamorphosis, and treating as realities these changes of Men into one another, of Men into Beasts, and so on the contrary, hath weaved together these and many other of the trifles and absurdities of the Ancient Mythology, and committed them to writing for the entertainment of the Public." This will account for the oddness of Apuleius's expressions, with which he introduces his *Fable*. . . . (p. 295)

The Fable opens with the representation of a young man, personated by himself, sensible of the advantages of *virtue* and *piety,* but immoderately fond of PLEASURE, and as curious of MAGIC. Apuleius takes care to keep up the first part of this character as he goes along, *familiaris* CURIOSITATIS *admonitus,* . . . *familiari* CURIOSITATE *attonitus*. . . . And *Curiosus* and *Magus* were used by the Antients as Synonymous. . . . Hence it is that [Apuleius himself] is represented as having been initiated in all the *corrupt Mysteries,* where Magic was professedly practised. . . . As to the second, we have his adventure with *Byrrhena* and *Pamphile,* which seems to be borrowed from Prodicus's fable of the contest between *Virtue* and *Pleasure* for the young *Hercules*. Byrrhena meets our adventurer; pretends to be his relation, and tells him that she brought him up from his infancy: by which is intimated that virtue was most natural to him. She leads him home to her house, which is described as a magnificent palace: one of its principal ornaments is the history of Diana; where the punishment of Actæon is not forgotten, as a seasonable lesson against *vicious curiosity*. And to keep him to herself, she promises to make him heir of all her fortunes. Then taking him apart, she warns him to beware of the mischievous practices of his hostess Pamphile. (p. 296)

[Lucius] had promised to observe *Byrrhena's* admonitions, and to return to her again: but a circumstance of immoderate mirth intervening, he found in himself a more than ordinary aversion to keep his word. . . . This is a fine circumstance, nothing being so great an enemy to modesty and chastity (figured in the person of Byrrhena) as immoderate mirth. He gives a loose to his vicious appetite for *Pleasure* and *Magic:* and the crimes and follies into which they lead him soon end in his transformation to a BRUTE.

This contrivance of the introductory part is artful; and finely insinuates the great moral of the piece, THAT BRUTALITY ATTENDS VICE AS IT'S PUNISHMENT: and punishment by actual transformation was keeping up to the popular opinion. His making a passion for *Magic* contribute to this dreadful change is no less ingenious, as it cleared both *himself* and the *Mysteries* from that imputation; for it appeared that *Magic* was so far from being innocent, that in his opinion, it was attended with the severest punishment; so far from being encouraged by the *Mysteries,* that they only could relieve men from the distresses which this vicious curiosity brought upon it's votaries; as is shewn by the catastrophe of the Piece.

St. Austin permitted himself to doubt whether Apuleius's account of his change into an ASS was not a true relation [see excerpt dated c. 413-26]. . . . I shall say nothing to so extravagant a doubt, but only observe, that it appears from hence, that St. Austin esteemed Apuleius a profligate in his manners, and addicted to the superstitions of *Magic*. And yet it is by no means credible, that he who took so much pains, in a very serious and public way, to free himself from these imputations, should afterwards wantonly undo all he had so successfully performed in support of a doubtful reputation, by an unnecessary narrative of his own early debaucheries. But it may be said, that all this happened in his youth; and that his subsequent *Initiations* had purified his manners: But neither will his ***Apology*** admit of this supposition; for there he expressly insists on the virtue of his youth. . . . What have we then to conclude but that the representation of himself in this *Fable,* under a debauched character, is entirely feigned? Yet still it would be as absurd to imagine that a grave and moral Philosopher should chuse to exhibit himself to the public in the odious, and false light of a *Magician* and *Debauchee;* and take a pleasure in dwelling upon the horrors of so detestable a Character, for no other purpose than to amuse and entertain a set of dissolute readers. We must needs therefore go a step further, and conclude that he assumed it only for the sake of the GENERAL MORAL, and the better to carry on his Allegory; which was, to recommend the MYSTERIES as the certain cure for all the DISORDERS OF THE WILL.

This being his end, he was but too much encouraged by the example of the most moral of the ancient Satirists, to particularize the various maladies to which he was applying a remedy. Let this, and his copying only what he found in his original Author, stand for some kind of excuse in a wretched Pagan; and it is the best we have, for all the obscenities with which his Fable abounds.

But to proceed with his plan. Having now shewn himself thoroughly brutalized by his crimes; he goes on to represent at large the miseries of that condition, in a long detail of his misadventures; in the course of which he fell, by turns, under the dominion of every vicious passion; though the incidents are chiefly confined to the mischiefs of unlawful love: And this, with much judgment, as one of the principal ends of the *Mysteries* was to curb and subdue this inordinance, which brings more general and lasting misery upon Mankind than all the other. And as it was the great moral of his piece to shew *that pure religion* (such as a platonic Philosopher esteemed pure) *was the only remedy for human corruption;* so, to prevent the abuse or mistake of this capital Principle, he takes care to inform us, *that an attachment to superstitious and corrupt Religion does but plunge the wretched victim into still greater miseries.* This he finely illustrates, in the history of his adventures with the BEGINNING PRIESTS OF CYBELE, whose enormities are related in the eighth and ninth books; and whose CORRUPT MYSTERIES are intended as a contrast to the PURE RITES OF ISIS: With which, in a very studied description and encomium, he concludes the *Fable*.

In the mean time, matters growing from bad to worse, and Lucius plunged deeper and deeper in the sink of vice, his affairs come to a crisis. For this is one great beauty in the conduct of the Fable, that every change of station, while he remains a brute, makes his condition still more wretched and deplorable. And being now (in the *ninth* book) about to perpetrate one of the most shocking enormities; NATURE, though so deeply brutalized, REVOLTS; he abhors the idea of his projected crime; he evades his keepers; he flies to the seashore; and, in this solitude, begins to reflect more seriously on his lost condition. This is finely imagined; for we often see men, even after a whole life of horrors, come suddenly to themselves on the hideous aspect of some Monster-vice too frightful even for an hardened Reprobate to bear. Nor is it with less judgment that the Author makes these beginnings of reformation confirmed by solitude; when the unhappy victim of PLEASURE hath broken loose from the companions and partakers of his follies.

And now, a more intimate acquaintance with his hopeless condition obliges him to fly to Heaven for relief. The MOON is in full splendour; and the awful silence of the night inspires him with sentiments of Religion. . . . He then purifies himself in the manner prescribed by PYTHAGORAS; the Philosopher most addicted to *Initiations* of all the early Sages, as Apuleius, of all the later; and so makes his prayer to the *Moon* or ISIS; invoking her by her several names of the *Eleusinian Ceres,* the *celestial Venus, Diana* and *Proserpine:* when betaking himself to repose, she appears to him in a dream. This was not a circumstance of the Fabulist's mere invention. Pausanias tells us "that in Phocis there was a Chapel consecrated to Isis, of all the places of worship; which the Greeks erected to this Egyptian Goddess, by far the most holy: that to this sacred place it was not lawful for any to approach, but such whom the Goddess had invited, and appeared to, in a *Dream,* for that purpose." Here she appears under the SHINING IMAGE so much spoken of by the *Mystics,* as representing the divine nature in general. . . . [Apuleius describes] several symbolic Attributes, the *lucid Round,* the *snakes,* the *ears of corn,* and the *sistrum,* represent the tutelar Deities of the *Hecatæan, Bacchic, Eleusinian* and *Isiac* MYSTERIES. That is, MYSTIC RITES IN GENERAL; for whose sake the allegory was invented. As the black Palla in which she is wrapped, embroidered with a silver-moon, and stars, denotes the TIME, in which the Mysteries were celebrated, namely the dead of NIGHT; which was so constant and inseparable a circumstance, that the author calls *initiation,* NOCTIS SOCIETAS. (pp. 296-300)

[She] then reveals to Lucius the means of his recovery. Her festival was on the following day; when there was to be a Procession of her Votaries. The Priest who led it up (she told him) would have a chaplet of ROSES in his hand, which had the virtue to restore him to his former shape. But as breaking through a habit of vice is, of all things, the most difficult; she adds encouragements to her promises. . . . Alluding to what was taught in the *Mysteries,* that the *assistance of Heaven* was always *present* to second the efforts of virtue. But in return for the favour of releasing him from his brutal shape, i.e. of reforming his manners by *Initiation,* she tells him she expected the service of his whole life; And this, the *Mysteries* required: Nor should her service (she said) go unrewarded, for he should have a place in ELYSIUM hereafter; And this, too, the *Mysteries* promised. (pp. 300-01)

Lucius is at length confirmed in his resolution of *aspiring* to a life of virtue. And on this change of his dispositions, and intire conquest of his passions, the Author finely represents all Nature as putting on a new face of chearfulness and gaiety. . . . And to enjoy Nature, in these her best conditions, was the boasted privilege of the *Initiated,* as we may see from a Chorus in the *Frogs* of Aristophanes.

And now the Procession, in honour of ISIS, begins. Where by the way, we must observe, that the *two first days* of the celebration of the *Eleusinian Mysteries* are plainly described. . . . The Priest or Hierophant of the Rites leads up the train of the Initiated with a garland of Roses in his hand. Lucius approaches, devours the Roses, and, according the promise of the Goddess, is restored to his native Form; by which, as we have said, no more was meant than a change of Manners, from vice to virtue. . . . The *garland* plainly represents that which the aspirants were crowned with at their *initiation:* just as the *virtue* of the Roses designs the *Mysteries*. At his transformation he had been told, that ROSES were to restore him to Humanity: so that, amid all his adventures, he had still this remedy in view. Particularly in a circumstance of great distress, he met with a species of them called *rosa laurea;* but on examining its properties, he found that, instead of a restorative, it was a deadly poison to all kind of cattle. . . . Who can doubt then, but by this *rose-laurel* was meant all *debauched, magical, and corrupt Mysteries,* such as those of the SYRIAN GODDESS, whose Ministers he represents in so abominable a light; in opposition to what he calls "sobriæ religionis observatio" ["the moderate observance of religion"]: and in those Rites, *initiation* was so far from promoting a life of virtue, that it plunged the deluded Votary into still greater miseries. These *emblematic Roses* were not of our author's invention. For the Rose, amongst the Ancients, was a symbol of SILENCE, the requisite quality of the *Initiated*. And therefore the statues of Isis or Diana Multimammea, (images consecrated to the use of the *Mysteries*) are crowned with chaplets of Roses; designing what we now mean, when we say, in proverbial speech, UNDER THE ROSE.

Our Author proceeds to tell us, that the people wondered at this instantaneous Metamorphosis. . . . For the *Mysteries* boasted the power of giving a sudden and entire change to the mind and affections: And the advocates of Paganism against Christianity used to oppose this boast to the real and miraculous efficacy of GRACE.

As soon as Lucius had recovered the integrity of his nature, by *initiation,* the Priest covers him, naked as he was, with a Linen garment: A habit always bestowed upon the Aspirant, on his admission to the *Mysteries;* the *rationale* of which, Apuleius himself gives us in his ***Apology.***

When all was over, the Priest accosts his Penitent. . . . (pp. 301-03)

Here the MORAL OF THE FABLE is delivered in plain terms; and, in this *moral,* all we have advanced, concerning the purpose of the work, fully confirmed. It is expressly declared, that VICE and inordinate CURIOSITY were the causes of Lucius's disasters; from which the only relief was INITIATION into the MYSTERIES. Whereby the Author would insinuate, that nothing was more abhorrent from those holy rites than DEBAUCHERY and MAGIC; the two enormities they were then commonly suspected to encourage.

It hath been observed above, that by Lucius's return to his proper Form, was meant his *initiation;* and accordingly, that return is called (as *initiation* was) *the being born again* . . . ; but this was only to the LESSER, not the GREATER *mysteries.* The first was to *purify* the mind: hence it was called by the Ancients . . . a *separation from evil:* the *second* was to *enlighten* it, when purified, and to bring it to the knowledge of divine secrets. . . . Hence they named [the mysteries] . . . PURIFICATION and PERFECTION. The *first* is here represented in the incident of Lucius's being restored to humanity by the use of *roses:* The *second,* as the matter of chief importance, the Author treats more circumstantially.

He begins with making the Priest take occasion, from the benefit already received, to press Lucius to enter into the GREATER MYSTERIES of Isis. . . . But at the same time makes him inform the Candidate, that nothing was to be precipitated: for that not only many previous Rites and Ceremonies, concerning religious diet, and abstinence from prophane food, were to be observed; but that the Aspirants to these *higher Mysteries* were to wait for a CALL. . . . Accordingly, he is initiated into the GREATER MYSTERIES. The ceremony is described at large; and we find it to agree exactly with what . . . other ancient writers more professedly deliver concerning it. (pp. 303-04)

[The] Author, in the next place, takes occasion, agreeably to his real practice and opinions, to recommend a MULTIPLICITY OF INITIATIONS. He tells us how *Isis* counselled him to enter into the *Mysteries* of *Osiris:* how, after that, she invited him to a third *initiation:* and then rewarded him for his accumulated Piety with an abundance of temporal Blessings.

All this considered, we can no longer doubt but that the true design of his work was to recommend INITIATION INTO THE MYSTERIES, IN OPPOSITION TO THE NEW RELIGION. We see the Catastrophe of the piece, the whole Eleventh Book, entirely taken up with it; and composed with the greatest seriousness and superstition.

And, surely, nothing could be better conceived, to recommend the *Mysteries,* than the idea of such a plan; or better contrived than his execution of it. In which he omits no circumstance that might be plausibly opposed to CHRISTIANITY; or that might recommend the MYSTERIES with advantage to the Magistrate's protection: as where he tells us, that in these Rites, *they prayed for the prosperity of all Orders in the* STATE. . . . (p. 305)

This interpretation will throw new light on *every part* of the ***Golden Ass.*** But I have been so long upon the subject, that I have only time to give one instance; and this, chiefly because it reflects light back again on my general interpretation of the Fable.

In the fifth and sixth books is the long episode of CUPID and PSYCHE; visibly allegorical throughout; and entirely foreign to all the rest of the work, considered as a mere Milesian fable;

Engraved title page to a 1624 edition of Apuleius's collected works.

but very applicable to the Writer's purpose, if he had that moral to inculcate which we have here assigned unto him.

There was no man, though he regarded the ***Golden Ass*** as a thing of mere amusement, but saw that the story of CUPID and PSYCHE was a *philosophic allegory of the progress of the soul to perfection, in the possession of divine love and the reward of immortality.* The Amour of Cupid and Psyche was a subject which lay in common amongst the Platonic writers. And though originally founded on some obscure tradition of the *Fall of Man,* yet every one fashioned this agreeable fiction (as our Author has done here) according to the doctrines he had to convey under it. By this means it could not but become famous. The remaining monuments of ancient sculpture convince us that it was very famous; in which, nothing is so common as the figures of CUPID and PSYCHE in the various circumstances of their adventures. Now we have shewn at large, that the professed end of the *Mysteries,* in the later ages of their celebrity, was to restore the soul to it's ORIGINAL RECTITUDE, and, in every age, to encourage good men with the promises of *happiness in another life.* The fable, therefore, of ***Cupid and Psyche,*** in the fifth and sixth books, was the finest and most artful preparative for the subject of the eleventh, which treats professedly of the *Mysteries.* (pp. 305-06)

William Warburton, "Book II," in his The Divine Legation of Moses Demonstrated, Vol. I, *edited by*

J. Nichols, tenth edition, Thomas Tegg, 1846, pp. 165-406.

THOMAS TAYLOR (essay date 1822)

[Taylor was an important and prolific English philosopher, translator, mathematician, and classical scholar. Overtly Neoplatonic in attitude and interests, he was the first of his countrymen to translate systematically the Orphic hymns, and his five-volume translation of Plato's Works *(1804), prepared along with Floyer Sydenham, markedly increased public interest in Greek philosophy. Not always admired for his scholarship—one of his contemporaries said of him: "The man is an ass, in the first place; in the second he knows nothing of the religion of which he is so great a fool as to profess himself a votary; and thirdly, he knows less than nothing of the language about which he is continually writing"—Taylor nevertheless stands out prominently as an influential advocate of Plato's works and of Neoplatonic literature. In the following excerpt from the introduction to his 1822 translation of* Metamorphoses, *he surveys Apuleius's major works, examines his Platonism, and defends* Metamorphoses *against the charge of lasciviousness.]*

[Apuleius] is undoubtedly the greatest of the ancient Latin Platonists, a portion of whose writings have been preserved to the present time; and though, in consequence of living at a period in which the depths of the Platonic philosophy had not been fathomed, and its mysteries luminously unfolded, as they afterwards were by certain Coryphæan Greeks, he is not to be classed among the chief of the disciples of Plato, yet he will always maintain a very distinguished rank among those who have delivered to us the more accessible parts of that philosophy with consummate eloquence, and an inimitable splendour of diction. (pp. v-vii)

The works of Apuleius which have escaped the ravages of time are, his ***Metamorphosis,*** or, as it is generally called, ***The Golden Ass,*** in eleven books; his treatises ***Of Natural and Moral Philosophy; On the Categoric Syllogism;*** and ***On the God of Socrates,*** . . . And besides this there are extant, his ***Apology,*** his ***Florida,*** and his treatise ***De Mundo,*** which is nothing more than a translation from the Greek of a treatise with the same title which is generally ascribed to Aristotle. The Latin translation also of the Asclepian Dialogue of Hermes Trismegistus, is attributed to Apuleius; and though it is entirely destitute of that splendour of diction which so eminently distinguishes the writings of our author, yet it is not improbable that it is one of his productions; since a translator, if he is faithful, will not only give the matter, but the manner also of his original. (pp. xiii-xiv)

[The] ***Metamorphosis*** is the most celebrated of all the works of Apuleius. A great part of this fable may be said to be a paraphrase of the Ass of Lucian, which was originally derived from a work of Lucius Patrensis, who wrote in Greek, and was of Patræ, a city of Achaia. The most important parts however of the ***Metamorphosis,*** viz. the fable of Cupid and Psyche, and the eleventh book, in which Apuleius gives an account of his being initiated in the mysteries of Isis and Osiris, are not derived from any sources with which we are at present acquainted. I call these the most important parts, because in the former, as it appears to me, the very ancient dogma of the pre-existence of the human soul, its lapse from the intelligible world to the earth, and its return from thence to its pristine state of felicity, are most accurately and beautifully adumbrated. . . . And as to the eleventh book, though the whole of the ***Metamorphosis*** is replete with elegance and erudition, yet this book excels all the rest, in consequence of containing many important historical particulars, and many which are derived from the arcana of Egyptian philosophy and religion. What he says about his initiation into the mysteries in particular, is uncommonly interesting and novel.

Dr. Warburton formed an opinion of the design of the ***Metamorphosis,*** which, in one part of it at least, appears to me to be singularly ridiculous and absurd; viz. that the author's main purpose was to commend Pagan religion as the only cure for all vice whatsoever; and to ridicule the Christian religion. There may be some truth in the former part of this assertion; but it is wholly incredible, that at a period when the Christian religion was *openly* derided and execrated by all the Heathens, Apuleius should have written a work one part of the intention of which was to ridicule *latently* that which, *without any concealment,* and with the sanction of the existing government, was generally despised. One passage indeed occurs in which he speaks *contemptuously* of the Christians; but then his meaning is so far from being latent, that it must be obvious to every one. The passage I allude to is the following in book the ninth, in which Apuleius, speaking of the nefarious wife of a baker, says of her: "Then despising and trampling on the divine powers, instead of the *true religion,* counterfeiting a nefarious opinion of God, whom she asserted to be the only deity; devising also vain observances, and deceiving all men, and likewise her miserable husband, she enslaved her body to morning draughts of pure wine, and to continual adultery." In the tenth book also, he denominates a most execrable character *cruciarius,* which according to Plautus signifies *discipulus crucis, a disciple of the cross;* and perhaps in thus denominating this murderer, he intended to signify that he was a Christian; but there are no other parts of this work in which there is a shadow of probability that Apuleius had the Christian religion in view; except it should be said that he alludes to it, when in the eleventh book he calls the heathen the *most pure, magnificent, and eternal religion.*

What then was the real design of Apuleius in composing this work? Shall we say, with Macrobius, that Apuleius sometimes diverted himself with the tales of love, and that this is a kind of fable which professes only to please the ear, and which wisdom banishes from her temple to the cradles of nurses [see excerpt dated c. 390-410]? This, however, is by no means consistent with that dignity and elevation of mind which are essential to the character of a Platonic philosopher. Is it not therefore most probable that the intention of the author in this work was to show that the man who gives himself to a voluptuous life, becomes a beast, and that it is only by becoming virtuous and religious, that he can divest himself of the brutal nature, and be again a man? For this is *the rose* by eating which Apuleius was restored to the human, and cast off the brutal form; and, like the moly of Hermes, preserved him in future from the dire enchantments of Circe, the Goddess of Sense. This, as it appears to me, is the only design by which our author can be justified in composing the pleasing tales with which this work is replete. Indeed, unless this is admitted to have been the design of Apuleius, he cannot in certain passages be defended from the charge of lewdness; but on the supposition that these tales were devised to show the folly and danger of lasciviousness, and that the man who indulges in it brutalizes his nature, the detail of those circumstances through which he became an ass, are not to be considered in the light of a lascivious description, because they were not written with a libidinous intention; for every work is characterized by its ultimate design. Hence, what Iamblichus says [in *De mysteriis*] respecting the consecration of the phalli among the ancients in the spring, and the obscene language which was then employed, may be said in defence of these passages in the*Metamorphosis:* viz. "The powers of the human passions that are in us, when they are entirely restrained, become more vehement; but when they are called forth into energy, gradually and commensurately, they rejoice in being moderately gratified, are satisfied; and from hence, becoming purified, they are rendered tractable, and are vanquished without violence. On this account, in comedy and tragedy, by surveying the passions of others, we stop our own passions, cause them to be more moderate, and are purified from them. *In sacred ceremonies, likewise, by certain spectacles and auditions of things base, we become liberated from the injury which happens from the works effected by them.* Things of this kind, therefore, are introduced for the sake of our soul, and of the diminution of the evils which adhere to it through generation, and of a solution and liberation from its bonds. On this account, also, they are very properly called by Heraclitus *remedies,* as healing things of a dreadful nature, and saving souls from the calamities with which the realms of generation are replete." Notwithstanding, however, there is no real lasciviousness in these passages. . . . (pp. xiv-xxi)

[With respect to the treatises ***Of Natural Philosophy*** and ***Of Moral Philosophy***] they may be considered as a good epitome of the physiology and ethics of Plato; certain parts of those sciences being excepted, the depths of which Apuleius had not fathomed, in consequence, as I before observed, of the more abstruse dogmas of Plato not having been developed at the time in which he lived. And his treatise ***On the Categoric Syllogism*** is a useful introduction to the logic of Aristotle. The treatise ***On the God of Socrates*** is on the whole an admirable work, and contains some things of a most interesting and remarkable nature. . . . (p. xxi)

Thomas Taylor, in an introduction to The Metamorphoses, or Golden Ass, and Philosophical Works of Apuleius *by Lucius Apuleius, translated by Thomas Taylor, Robert Triphook and Thomas Rodd, 1822, pp. v-xxiv.*

[J. GIBBS] (essay date 1851)

[In the following excerpt, Gibbs comments on the structure, purpose, and language of Metamorphoses.]

The ***Metamorphoses*** of Apuleius are not suited to modern taste, though they well deserve notice. . . . The structure of the story is like that of Gil Blas. In both the adventures of the hero form the groundwork; but in both also, more than half the book consists of stories and incidents from their own lives, told by the different personages. This resemblance is probably due to the fact, that Apuleius, like Le Sage, worked up into his book materials provided by preceding novelists. (p. 472)

[Apuleius] was a philosopher as well as a satirist, and desired, in portraying, to reform his generation. We are aware that this has been denied by many critics, both in ancient and modern times; but on any other supposition a large portion of the book is unintelligible, and inconsistent with what we know of his character. (pp. 473-74)

Critics have perplexed themselves to find a hidden meaning in the book. They have supposed it an allegory, representing the soul invited by Virtue and Vice;—like the old story of the Choice of Hercules. Thus Byrrhæna is Virtue, warning Lucius against Pamphile and Fotis, the impersonation of Vice; but led astray by curiosity and love of pleasure, he neglects the warning, and his transformation typifies his fall into sensuality. In the end, his better nature,—the human reason beneath the asinine form,—roused and strengthened by misfortune, becomes victorious, and induces him to pledge himself to Virtue by initiation among the worshippers of Isis. Warburton has lent his support to this theory. His ingenuity has tempted him to carry it a step further. He exalts Apuleius into a controversialist, and an inveterate enemy of Christianity; and he considers the true design of the story to be "to recommend Initiation into the Mysteries, in opposition to the New Religion." This interpretation is founded on the character of the baker's wife, and a passage in the ***Apology*** from which Warburton concludes that his accuser was a Christian. For the honour of the African Church, we hope the conclusion is false; and assuredly, if Apuleius had intended to single out Christianity for his attack, he would have made his meaning clearer. Nor do we think the tale an allegory. It was not new; we have it in Lucian, and both are said to have copied from an earlier writer—Lucius of Patræ.

But Apuleius introduced two remarkable additions,—the account of the Mysteries, and an allegory, closely connected with them, representing the fall, the trials, and the ultimate restoration of the soul to the love of what is divine,—the legend of Cupid and Psyche. In the Greek account Lucius regains his human form on merely tasting rose-leaves; Apuleius, by his version, obviously intended to use the old story as a vehicle for a panegyric on the "Mysteries." The advantage of initiation was an established tenet of the philosophy of the day, and in his ***Apology*** he boasts of having studied "many sacred systems, rites, and ceremonies, in the pursuit of truth and the exercise of piety." Now, by the side of the true mysteries had grown up a race of impostors, who brought discredit upon them by their debauchery, magic, and lying divinations. . . . [Against the superstitions of this race] Apuleius levelled his satire. They were gloomy and infernal; nay, more, they were caricatures of the truth. His object was to bring out the contrast. The best commentary on the book is his own confession of faith made on his trial:—"We, of the Platonic School, believe in nothing but what is joyous, cheerful, festive, from above, heavenly."

One word upon his Latinity. Grammarians place him with Tertullian and Cyprian, in the African School, the chief peculiarity of which is an affectation of old forms of speech. Punic was the common language of the north of Africa, and Apuleius learnt his Latin in the schools of the rhetoricians. The rhetoricians were indebted for the important position they then occupied to the patronage of Hadrian; and, in return, they echoed his imperial criticism, that Cato ranked above Cicero, Ennius above Virgil. Apuleius caught their spirit, and in every page we have the florid declamation of a later age studded with archaisms and expressions which, even when new, are stamped to resemble an early coinage. He is not one of those authors who live by their style. As a novelist he has had his day; but to the student of the history of literature and society during the decay of the Roman Empire, he will always be a useful and amusing companion. (pp. 488-89)

[J. Gibbs] "The Metamorphoses of Apuleius," in The Edinburgh Review, *Vol. 94, October, 1851, pp. 472-89.*

C. G. PROWETT (essay date 1873)

[Prowett was an English barrister, critic, and journalist. In the following excerpt he examines Apuleius's approach to the story

of Lucius's transformation, which had also served as the basis for works by other authors.]

[We] may very well take for granted, from what we know of Apuleius, that he would look on [the story of the "golden ass"] with the eye of a moralist and a disciple of Plato. To him the transformation of Lucius would be an obvious allegory. He is transformed in consequence of his amour with the wicked coquette Fotis; and as he thus typifies the fall of a man sunk by the indulgence of his lower passions into the most brutish of all creatures, so, after penance duly done, he is redeemed to humanity by the exalting influences of religious reverence, within which he is brought through the mysteries of Isis. There is nothing of the controversial spirit in all this, and Tertullian himself might have written the ***Golden Ass,*** substituting, as he probably would have done, for the gorgeous procession in the eleventh book, the simple *mysterium* of the Christian Eucharist, which the Church offered in exchange for the pompous pageantries of Eleusis and Samothrace. Dismissing Warburton's attempt to make out Apuleius an anti-Christian controversialist, we need not dwell on the Bishop's ingenious efforts to trace this controversial purpose through the various incidents of the story. In the main features of his narrative, Apuleius would no doubt keep his moral in view; but in carrying out its details he was quite capable of giving himself up to the enjoyment which an imaginative writer feels in his own fancies, and which he is thus best enabled to convey to his readers. It is true that we have not in the tale of Lucius the wondrous fancy with which Shakespeare conjured up the adventure of Bottom the weaver; that quaint humour, full of the grotesque faëry of the scene, revelling in that weird bewilderment, that dreaming half-consciousness of something absurd in the situation, which will make all generations delight in the "translated" Bottom. Lucius is thoroughly and painfully alive to the transmutation which has passed upon him. He knows exactly how it happened, and is not therefore dazed with Bottom's bewilderment. Nor has he that practical sagacity which leads Bottom to make the best of his position. "Good hay, sweet hay, hath no fellow," is the ready avowal of the cheery Athenian weaver; unless, indeed, there is something in these words of a humorous sarcasm at his own expense. But Lucius was too serious about the matter to take kindly to his hay. In the first place he objected to feeding with his own horse and with an ass (he does not call it *another* ass), and adds plaintively. "Besides, under any circumstances, I was not accustomed to dine upon hay." No wonder that he envied the dogs who enjoyed the remnants of the rich man's feast, while he was fain to meditate bitter curses on Fotis, because she had not at least blundered him into a dog rather than an ass. Sometimes, however, he is inclined to play a little with his own misfortune; as when, listening to the wicked confidences which his mistress exchanges with her gossip in his presence, he derives some consolation from the length of his ears which put such secrets in his power. There is an odd humour, too, in the view which he takes of the relations between his own personality and the shape which he is condemned to wear; as when he speaks of himself as *asinus meus* ["my asinine self"] looking forward to the time when he should resume his proper figure. And he is evidently half amused at his own abortive attempts at human vocalisation; as when, passing through a populous village, he would fain invoke assistance by the cry of *O Quirites,* the utterance of a Roman citizen under circumstances which would induce an Englishman to shout "Police!"—the one call being probably as effectual in most cases as the other. He rounds the *O* to a most sonorous deliverance, but his *Quirites* is a failure, and, notwithstanding all his efforts, will not be brayed. (pp. 478-79)

C. G. Prowett, "Apuleius," in Fraser's Magazine, *Vol. VIII, October, 1873, pp. 464-82.*

WALTER PATER (essay date 1885)

[*Pater was an English essayist, novelist, and critic who is recognized as one of English literature's greatest proponents of aestheticism and as the formulator of an explicitly aesthetic philosophy of life. Widely admired in his day but nevertheless extremely controversial, he advocated the "love of art for art's sake" as life's greatest offering, a belief he exemplified in his influential* Studies in the History of the Renaissance *(1873) and elucidated in his novel* Marius the Epicurean: His Sensations and Ideas *(1885), the latter work an account of the fictional character Marius as he searches for a satisfactory philosophy of life in Aurelian Rome. In the following excerpt from* Marius, *the boy Marius and his youthful companion, Flavian, discover the artistry of* Metamorphoses.]

The two lads were lounging together over a book, half-buried in a heap of dry corn, in an old granary. . . . What they were intent on was, indeed, the book of books, the "golden" book of that day, a gift to Flavian. . . . It was perfumed with oil of sandal-wood, and decorated with carved and gilt ivory bosses at the ends of the roller.

And the inside was something not less dainty and fine, full of the archaisms and curious felicities in which that generation delighted, quaint terms and images picked fresh from the early dramatists, the lifelike phrases of some lost poet preserved by an old grammarian, racy morsels of the vernacular and studied prettinesses:—all alike, mere playthings for the genuine power and natural eloquence of the erudite artist, unsuppressed by his erudition, which, however, made some people angry, chiefly less well "got-up" people, and especially those who were untidy from indolence.

No! it was certainly not that old-fashioned, unconscious ease of the early literature, which could never come again; which, after all, had had more in common with the "infinite patience" of Apuleius than with the hack-work readiness of his detractors, who might so well have been "self-conscious" of going slipshod. And at least his success was unmistakable as to the precise literary effect he had intended, including a certain tincture of "neology" in expression. . . . What words he had found for conveying, with a single touch, the sense of textures, colours, incidents! "Like jewellers' work! Like a myrrhine vase!"—admirers said of his writing. "The golden fibre in the hair, the gold threadwork in the gown marked her as the mistress"—*aurum in comis et in tunicis, ibi inflexum hic intextum, matronam profecto confitebatur*—he writes, with his "curious felicity," of one of his heroines. *Aurum intextum:* gold fibre:—well! there was something of that kind in his own work. And then, in an age when people, from the emperor Aurelius downwards, prided themselves unwisely on writing in Greek, he had written for Latin people in their own tongue; though still, in truth, with all the care of a learned language. Not less happily inventive were the incidents recorded—story within story—stories with the sudden, unlooked-for changes of dreams. He had his humorous touches also. And what went to the ordinary boyish taste, in those somewhat peculiar readers, what would have charmed boys more purely boyish, was the adventure:—the bear loose in the house at night, the wolves storming the farms in winter, the exploits of the robbers, their charming caves, the delightful thrill one had at the question—"Don't you know that these roads are infested by robbers?" (pp. 55-7)

[In] truth, all through the book, there is an unmistakably real feeling for asses, with bold touches like Swift's, and a genuine animal breadth. Lucius was the original ass, who peeping slily from the window of his hiding-place forgot all about the big shade he cast just above him, and gave occasion to the joke or proverb about "the peeping ass and his shadow."

But the marvellous, delight in which is one of the really serious elements in most boys, passed at times, those young readers still feeling its fascination, into what French writers call the *macabre*—that species of almost insane preoccupation with the materialities of our mouldering flesh, that luxury of disgust in gazing on corruption, which was connected, in this writer at least, with not a little obvious coarseness. It was a strange notion of the gross lust of the actual world, that Marius took from some of these episodes. "I am told," they read, "that when foreigners are interred, the old witches are in the habit of out-racing the funeral procession, to ravage the corpse"—in order to obtain certain cuttings and remnants from it, with which to injure the living—"especially if the witch has happened to cast her eye upon some goodly young man." And the scene of the night-watching of a dead body lest the witches should come to tear off the flesh with their teeth, is worthy of Théophile Gautier.

But set as one of the episodes in the main narrative, a true gem amid its mockeries, its coarse though genuine humanity, its burlesque horrors, came the tale of Cupid and Psyche, full of brilliant, life-like situations, *speciosa locis* ["set in a splendid place"], and abounding in lovely visible imagery (one seemed to see and handle the golden hair, the fresh flowers, the precious works of art in it!) yet full also of a gentle idealism, so that you might take it, if you chose, for an allegory. With a concentration of all his finer literary gifts, Apuleius had gathered into it the floating star-matter of many a delightful old story. (pp. 60-1)

Walter Pater, "The Golden Book," in his Marius the Epicurean: His Sensations and Ideas, Vol. I, *Macmillan and Co., Limited, 1911, pp. 55-91.*

CHARLES WHIBLEY (essay date 1893)

[*An English critic, Whibley had a special interest in the literature of the sixteenth and seventeenth centuries. He wrote the celebrated study* Book of Scoundrels *(1897), contributed essays to a variety of periodicals, and cofounded* Tudor Translations *(begun 1892), a series of reprints of Elizabethan and Jacobean versions of literary works from the classical and other languages. In the following excerpt from an essay originally published in 1893, he discusses the prose style of* Metamorphoses, *compares Apuleius's narrative with Lucian's earlier rendition of the same story, and examines the supernatural and macabre incidents which Apuleius made central to his novel.*]

The Golden Ass of Apuleius is, so to say, a beginning of modern literature. From this brilliant medley of reality and romance, of wit and pathos, of fantasy and observation, was born that new art, complex in thought, various in expression, which gives a semblance of frigidity to perfection itself. An indefatigable youthfulness is its distinction. As it was fresh when Adlington translated it "out of Latine" three centuries since, so it is familiar to-day, and is like to prove an influence to-morrow. Indeed, it is among the marvels of history that an alien of twenty-five—and Apuleius was no more when he wrote his ***Metamorphoses***—should have revolutionised a language not his own, and bequeathed us a freedom which, a thousand times abused, has never since been taken away.

A barbarian born, a Greek by education, Apuleius only acquired the Latin tongue by painful effort. Now a foreigner, not prejudiced by an inveterate habit of speech, seldom escapes a curiosity of phrase. Where the language is the same, whether written or spoken, art is wont to lapse into nature. But there was no reason why Apuleius, who could not but be conscious of his diction, should ever deviate from artifice. His style, in truth, he put on as a garment, and it fitted the matter without a crease. His exotic vocabulary was the fruit of the widest research. He ransacked the ancient plays for long-forgotten words. He cared not where he picked up his neologisms, so they were dazzling and bizarre. Greece, his own Carthage, the byways of Rome, contribute to the wealth of his diction, for he knew naught of that pedantry which would cramp expression for authority's sake. The literary use of slang was almost his own invention. He would twist the vulgar words of every day into quaint, unheard-of meanings, nor did he ever deny shelter to those loafers and footpads of speech which inspire the grammarian with horror. On every page you encounter a proverb, a catchword, a literary allusion, a flagrant redundancy. One quality only was distasteful to him: the commonplace. He is ever the literary fop, conscious of his trappings and assured of a handsome effect.

In brief, he belonged to the African School, for which elaboration was the first and last law of taste. . . . No wonder poor Adlington, whose equipment of Latin was of the lightest, hesitated for a while! No wonder that he complained that "the Author had written his work in so darke and high a stile, in so strange and absurd words, and in such new invented phrases as hee seemed rather to set it forth to shew his magnificencie of prose than to participate his doings to others!" [see excerpt dated 1566]. But the difficulty is not invincible; and the adventurous have their reward. The prose sparkles with light and colour. Not a page but is rich inlaid with jewels of fantastic speech. For Apuleius realised centuries before Baudelaire that a vocabulary is a palette, and he employed his own with incomparable daring and extravagance.

Though his style be personal, the machinery of his story is frankly borrowed. The hero who, transformed by magic to an ass, recovers human shape by eating roses was no new invention. He had already supplied two writers with a motive; and the learned have not decided whether it was from Lucian (so-called) or from Lucius of Patrae that Apuleius got his inspiration. But a comparison of the Latin version with its Greek forerunner, commonly attributed to Lucian, proves the debt a feather's weight. Whatever Apuleius conveyed, he so boldly changed and elaborated as to make the material his own. His method is a miracle of simplicity. He accepts the [work attributed to Lucian] as a framework, sometimes following it word for word, yet decorating it with so lavish an array of phrases, tricking it out with episodes so fertile and ingenious, as to force you to forget the original in the copy. Only in a single incident does his fancy lag behind. His hero's interview with the serving-maid is chastened and curtailed. The professionally elaborate detail, wherewith Lucian enhances this famous episode, is touched by Apuleius with a light and summary hand. But elsewhere he appropriates to adorn. Though again and again the transference is verbal, the added ornament is entirely characteristic, and it is as unjust to charge the author with plagiarism as it were to condemn the Greek tragedians for their treatment of familiar themes.

Indeed, the two writers approach the matter from opposite points of view. Lucian's austere concision is purely classical.

He has a certain story to present, and he reaches the climax by the shortest possible route. The progress is interrupted neither by phrase nor interlude, and at the end you chiefly admire the cold elegance wherewith the misfortunes of Lucius are expressed, as it were, in their lowest terms. Apuleius, on the other hand, is unrestrainedly romantic. He cares not how he loiters by the way; he is always ready to beguile his reader with a Milesian story. . . . (pp. 1-4)

His masterpiece, in truth, is magnificently interlaced with jests, sometimes bound to the purpose of the story by the thinnest of thin threads, more often attached merely for their own or for ornament's sake. But not only thus is he separate from his model. Though he is romantic in style and temper alike—and romanticism is an affair of treatment rather than of material—he never loses touch with actuality. He wrote with an eye upon the realities of life. Observation was a force more potent with him than tradition. If his personages and incidents are wholly imaginary, he could still give them a living semblance by a touch of intimacy or a suggestion of familiar detail. Compare his characters to Lucian's, and measure the gulf between the two! Lucian's Abroea is a warning voice—that, and no more. Byrrhena, on the other hand, is a great lady, sketched, with a quick perception of her kind, centuries before literature concerned itself with the individual. And is not Milo the miser leagues nearer the possibility of life than Hipparchus? Even Palaestra, despite the ingenuity of one episode, is not for an instant comparable in charm and humour to Fotis, most complaisant of serving-maids.

Nor is it only in the portrayal of character that Apuleius proves his observation. There are many scenes whose truthful simplicity is evidence of experience. When Lucius, arrived in Hypata, goes to the market to buy him fish, he encounters an old fellow student—Pythias by name—already invested with the authority and insignia of an ædile. Now he, being a veritable jack-in-office, is enraged that Lucius has made so ill a bargain, and overturning his fish, bids his attendants stamp it under foot, so that the traveller loses supper and money too. The incident is neither apposite nor romantic; it is no more Milesian than mystical; but it bears the very pressure of life, and you feel that it was transferred straight from a note-book. Again, where will you find a franker piece of realism than the picture of the mill, whereto the luckless Ass was bound? Very ugly and evil-favoured were the men, covered only with ragged clouts; and how horrible a spectacle the horses, with their raw necks, their hollow flanks, their broken ribs!

The Greek author, disdaining atmosphere, is content to set out his incidents in a logical sequence. Apuleius has enveloped his world of marvels in a heavy air of witchery and romance. You wander with Lucius across the hills and through the dales of Thessaly. With all the delight of a fresh curiosity you approach its far-seen towns. You journey at midnight under the stars, listening in terror for the howling of the wolves or the stealthy ambush. At other whiles, you sit in robbers' cave and hear the ancient legends of Greece retold. The spring comes on and "the little birds chirp and sing their steven melodiously." Secret raids, ravished brides, valiant rescues, the gayest of intrigues—these are the diverse matters of this many-coloured book. The play of fancy, the variety of style, the fertility of resource are inexhaustible. Mythology is lifted into life, and life itself transformed to mystery at the wizard's touch. The misery and terror of the Ass's life are intercepted by the story of Cupid and Psyche, set forth with rare beauty and distinction of style. And yet this interlude, exquisitely planned and phrased . . . , is the one conspicuous fault of the book. Admirable in itself, it is out of proportion as well as out of key; though you turn to it again for its own sake, you skip it industriously when it keeps you from robbery and witchcraft.

But the most remarkable characteristic of ***The Golden Ass*** is the ever-present element of sorcery, of the *Macabre,* as Mr. Pater calls it [see excerpt dated 1885]. Grim spectres and horrid ghosts stalk through its pages. The merriest Milesian jest turns sudden to the terror of death and corruption. The very story which Boccaccio borrowed is shifted by Apuleius to a weird conclusion. The baker, having most wittily avenged his wife's deceit, is lured into a chamber by a meagre, ragged, ill-favoured woman, her hair scattering upon her face, and when the servants burst open the door to find their master, behold! no woman, but only the baker hanging from a rafter dead! And where for pure horror will you match Meroe's mutilation of Socrates? Secretly the witch attacks him in his sleep, drives her sword deep into his neck, and dragging out his heart stops the wound with a sponge. Aristomenes, unwilling witness of the cruelty, half believes it a dream, and gladly they resume the journey, until, when Socrates goes to the river to drink, the sponge falls out and with it the last faint pulse of life. Again, when Thelyphron watches in the chamber of the dead lest witches should bite off morsels of the dead man's face, and falling asleep at sight of a weasel, loses his ears and nose, who so callous as to feel no shudder of alarm? But the most terrific apparition of all is the obscene priest of the Syrian goddess, with his filthy companions, carrying the divine image from village to village and clanging their cymbals to call the charitable. This grimy episode, with its sequent orgies, is related with an incomparably full humour which, despite its Oriental barbarity, is unmatched in literature.

So there is scarce a scene without its ghostly enchantment, its supernatural intervention. And herein you may detect the personal predilection of Apuleius. The infinite curiosity wherewith Lucius pries into witchcraft and sorcery was shared by his author. The hero transformed suffered his many and grievous buffetings because he always coveted an understanding of wizardry and spells; and Apuleius, in an age devoted to mysticism, was notorious for a magic-monger. Seriously it was debated, *teste* ["as is testified by"] St. Augustine, whether Christ or he or Apollonius wrought the greatest marvels; and though the shape wherein the romance is cast induced a confusion of author and hero, it is recorded that Apuleius was a zealous magician, and doubtless it is himself, not Lucius, he pictures in his last book among the initiate. (pp. 4-7)

Charles Whibley, "An Essay on Apuleius," in Apuleius, the Golden Ass: Being the Metamorphoses of Lucius Apuleius *by Lucius Apuleius, translated by W. Adlington, revised edition, Liveright Publishing Corp., 1927, pp. 1-18.*

***THE BOOKMAN*, LONDON (essay date 1894)**

[*In the following excerpt, the critic notes the distinctive features of the prose style and narrative of* Metamorphoses *and compares Apuleius's novel with fin-de-siècle literature.*]

[In ***The Golden Ass***], which is outside the close circle of the classics, and which certainly took few of their precautions to secure for itself immortality—full of mannerisms is it, tricks of speech and affectations—it must be some surpassing quality which has kept it alive from the second century right down to our own days. The quality is just life itself. . . .

Did Apuleius write for edification? Taylor, of course, thought so, finding the romance veined with Platonism [see excerpt dated 1822]. Adlington made of his stories moral allegories in conventional fashion. "In this feigned jest of Lucius Apuleius is comprehended a figure of man's life, ministering most sweet and delectable matter" [see excerpt dated 1566]. Or was he but a fine teller of tales? Inconsistently and capriciously he was probably what his commentators believed him to be. The perceptible allegory in his story is beautiful, from the metamorphosis of Apuleius to his initiation by the eating of the rose and by prayer to the final mysteries. But first of all is his narrative for its own sake good. It was that narrative, not as allegory, but pure narrative, full of episode, and high spirits, quick wit, ingenuity, the unexpected, the magical, everything save the commonplace, that made him the inspirer, at least the fecund suggester, of the long line of romancists since his time, Boccaccio, Cervantes, Lesage, Scarron, of all the romance of the road.

As for his style, apart from mere verbal tricks and feats, it is peculiarly modern. Anything further removed from classical austerity would be impossible to find. And it is not one modern style you find in him, but many. Our passion after exactness, fine-shading, our realism, our impressionism, are here. Can you not understand the mannerism of Bellerophon as he told his tale, "So lapping up the end of the table cloath and carpet together, hee leaned with his elbow thereon, and held out the three forefingers of his right hand in manner of an orator, and sayd, When I was a young man, etc." For gruesome realism could the watch by the dead man's body be surpassed? The description of nature is neither cold nor general, but warm and individual. He will have even an ass express himself with picturesqueness and articulately. "Then I (willing to show as much joy as I might, as present occasion served) set and pricked up my long ears, I ratled my nosethrils, and cryed stoutly, nay rather, I made the towne to ring againe with my shrilling sound."

But its special interest for to-day lies behind all that. When the fruits of our present day literature are gathered up, it will be found that our passion for observation of the life that is round us, for reporting exactly vocabulary and accent, for expressing all that we know, see, or surmise, by literal or symbolic means, is not a more marked characteristic than our reaction against content with the common facts of life. A curiosity in all that is behind the commonplace, into the weird, the magical, a search full of feverish morbid excitement, leading now and then through unwholesome dark valleys, with poison enough to kill all but the sturdy, but visited by novel lights, giving strange opportunities to the adventurous soul, and aiming at the full initiation into the final mysteries—these form the undercurrent of the most influential art and literature of today. There on that ground Apuleius meets us. Every page of his is crossed by beams of the strange light we watch for. Glamour plays in the eyes of every reader who does not throw him aside as childish. Only such an one will wonder why his old romance should be named "Golden."

A review of "The Golden Ass," in The Bookman, *London, Vol. 5, No. 30, March, 1894, p. 189.*

S[TEPHEN] GASELEE (essay date 1915)

[Gaselee was an English scholar and bibliographer with varied interests, including Latin literature, paleography, hagiography, and medieval studies. He achieved particular distinction for his anthology The Oxford Book of Medieval Latin Verse *(1928). In the following excerpt, he elucidates the sources and language of* Metamorphoses.]

In the ***Metamorphoses*** (or ***Golden Ass,*** as it is often called) the author's religious and philosophical views take a less important place than in most of his other works; and indeed the last book, which contains an elaborate account of the hero's initiation into various mysteries, is of less value than the rest of the work except to professed students of the various Oriental religions which had to contend with the rising Christianity of the second century. The references to magic, which occur throughout, are of greater interest, and the story of the transformation of the hero into an ass, which is the main thread of the plot, so deeply impressed some of his contemporaries and successors that we find St. Augustine writing: "Yet had he his humane reason still, as *Apuleius* had in his asse-ship, as himself writeth in his booke of the golden asse; bee it a lie or a truth that hee writeth (*aut indicavit aut finxit*)" [see excerpt dated c. 413-26]. The plot, however, was not his own, but taken from a still extant Greek work . . . which was formerly ascribed to Lucian, though it is almost certainly not his. It was very greatly improved by Apuleius, who cut down one or two of the scenes of the original and then greatly enlarged it with an abundance of excellent stories of love, sorcery, jests, and robbers; and, in particular, inserted in the middle of his work the long and beautiful allegory of Cupid and Psyche.

It seems probable that many of these stories belonged to the various collections of *facetiae* which were common in the later Greek and Roman literature, though now unfortunately almost completely lost. The most famous collection was known as the *Milesian Tales,* originally collected by one Aristides, and translated into Latin by the historian Sisenna in late republican times: it is likely that, besides those contained in the ***Metamorphoses,*** we have specimens of a couple in the earlier novel of Petronius. These were almost universally, it must be confessed, of more than doubtful morality; but as told by Apuleius in his rollicking fashion they give the reader little more than an impression of fun and high spirits, and the general effect may perhaps be compared with that of Boccaccio's *Decameron.* (pp. vi-vii)

Apuleius is by no means an easy author, delightful as he is, to read in the original Latin. Latin was not his native or natural language, and when he mastered it he worked out for himself a most extraordinary style, which seems to contain the genius of some quite other tongue clothed in a Latin dress. He would make use of rare and outlandish words, as well as reviving others which had dropped out of the ordinary language since pre-classical times, and combined the whole into a curious mosaic, not at all unsuitable, indeed, to the weird and jolly stories that he had to tell, but disconcerting to those accustomed to the sobriety and regularity of classical Latin. (p. viii)

Stephen Gaselee, in an introduction to Apuleius, the Golden Ass: Being the Metamorphoses of Lucius Apuleius *by Lucius Apuleius, translated by W. Adlington, revised by S. Gaselee, 1915. Reprint by William Heinemann Ltd., 1965, pp. v-x.*

BURTON RASCOE (essay date 1933)

[An American essayist and literary critic noted for his perceptive recognition of new or obscure talent, Rascoe served on the staffs of several influential periodicals and newspapers during the early and mid-twentieth century, including the Chicago Tribune, New York Herald Tribune Books, Bookman, *and* American Mercury. *In the following excerpt, he discusses the narrative structure of* Metamorphoses *and considers the moral issues raised in the work.]*

The Golden Ass is not a work of immaturity, even of the immaturity of an extremely precocious writer. The flawless story of Cupid and Psyche which is embedded in it, is proof that it is not. That is a story which has enchanted readers in all ages from Apuleius' time down to our own; it has provoked imitation, inspired poets and dramatists and novelists, challenged the ingenuity of interpreters, and caused translators to labor over it with love. (p. 182)

It is true, as Whibley points out, that the story of Cupid and Psyche in ***The Golden Ass*** is out of proportion to the rest of the novel [see excerpt dated 1893]; but as we shall see later on, it is the keystone of the structure. The novel, in the main, is made up of a series of disconnected episodes and bits of erotica, held together only by the itinerary of Lucius in search of the magical meal of roses which would restore him to human shape after he had been transformed into an ass. One character only emerges vital and distinct, Fotis, the jolly and sensual serving-maid; but there is a whole tapestry pageant of thieves, ingenious lovers, depraved old men, deceptive wives, pagan priests, witches, tradesmen, soldiers, magistrates, and sorcerers, woven against a somber, twilit background. Murder, mutilation, flagellation, nocturnal horror, bats and specters contribute to the sustained macabre effect of the first three and a half and the last five books. Bawdy anecdotes which Lucian would have presented in a witty and amusing fashion are related by Apuleius in a manner at once precious and gross, provoking neither a chuckle nor a smile.

Apuleius is interesting, indeed, but not funny, however much he tries to mingle comedy with pathos, romance, mystery and thrills. The reason is that Apuleius is essentially a moralist and, strangely enough for his time and place, a moralist of a peculiarly Pauline character. His distrust of women amounted almost to a monomania. His married women are uniformly lascivious and full of wiles, often resorting to magic to gain their carnal ends and cruelly resourceful in their vengeance when their wills do not prevail. Matrons murder their husbands to gain easy access to their lovers and to their husbands' fortunes; others bewitch young men and, failing this, take magical potions which transform them into fowl that they may fly to the men they desire; others make mock of their husbands' stupidity and give them horns in the most indecent and abandoned manner.

By converting his hero, Lucius, into an ass for having drunk, by mistake, one of the magical potions used by an adulterous wife in her escapades, Apuleius hit upon an excellent device for visiting the moral opprobrium upon ordinary human conduct that he had gained as an ascetic and tonsured priest of Isis. As an ass Lucius is witness to a great deal of behavior of which he seriously disapproves. Often he wants to cry out, but all he can achieve is the first word of the sentence he wants to utter; and this word is taken as a bray: no attention is paid to it. So Lucius in his avatar as an ass kicks the top of a hogshead off to disclose to a husband his wife's paramour and shows his distaste for breaches of monogamy by all the overt actions performable by a morally censorious donkey.

Apuleius, indeed, is, like Baudelaire, fascinated and repelled by evil, and in his spirit we see working some of that ferment which produced among early Christian adherents that mortification of the flesh and that apprehension of supernal forces, both malign and angelic, which resulted in the Manichean doctrine of the invisible war between Good and Evil, set St. Augustine in his middle years to retaste and repudiate his past, and made St. Simeon Stylites sit for years upon a pillar in mortification of his flesh to show a gaping crowd below what an awful heller he would be if he gave in to the devil that was tempting him.

Yet there was this in Apuleius—that he had a notion that love might be physical, pleasurable and innocent like the love of Lucius and Fotis, or spiritual, pleasurable and innocent like the love of Cupid and Psyche. He confused matters, I think, as Dante and many others after him confused them, by allowing that there was any necessarily conflicting difference between the two. (pp. 182-85)

Burton Rascoe, "Apuleius," in his Prometheans: Ancient and Modern, *G. P. Putnam's Sons, 1933, pp. 173-92.*

ELIZABETH HAZELTON HAIGHT (essay date 1936)

[Haight was an American classicist and critic. Her works, which include Apuleius and His Influence *(1927),* Essays on Ancient Fiction *(1936), and* Essays on the Greek Romances *(1943), trace the development of story-telling in the ancient world, thereby introducing unfamiliar aspects of the classics to the scholar and general reader alike. In the following excerpt, she examines the unique narrative style of* Metamorphoses.]

The novel of Apuleius called the ***Metamorphoses*** is unique in Latin literature. It is the one complete Latin novel extant. It is entirely different from the fragmentary *Satyricon* in style, theme and scope. It is linked to the Greek novels that were being written in the same period only by general plot and by the tales of adventure which it shares with them. It deserves special study as a novel because of its own brilliancy and because of its position in the history of fiction. Apuleius' preface to the Reader presents its greatest claim for consideration, its entertaining character: *lector intende; laetaberis*. ["Reader, give heed; you will enjoy yourself"]:

In the same preface Apuleius himself states the sources of his novel. It is a Greek story. In it various Milesian tales are woven together. Paper and pen are Egyptian. Its theme is the transformation of human beings into different shapes and their retransformations to themselves. The language is an exotic and rhetorical Latin learned by a foreigner who had acquired Greek first. (p. 151)

[Part of the narrative art of Apuleius] consists in the personality of the narrator and his relation to his audience. The ***Metamorphoses*** is an *ich-roman*, a story told by Lucius in the first person to the reader who is often directly addressed. This personal character of the narration is diversified by having several of the major stories told by some special character to a special audience. The story of Socrates and the witch is told to two fellow-travelers on the road, one of whom is Lucius, so here the chief narrator of the novel becomes the audience. This is true in the story of Thelyphron and the witches, which is told by Thelyphron at a dinner-party for the benefit of the guest of honor, Lucius. The three stories of robber chiefs are told by one robber to the rest of the band at dinner in their cave while Lucius the ass listens. Lucius himself narrates the long tale of Charite but the inset, Cupid and Psyche, is told by the old crone who keeps the robbers' cave to the kidnaped bride, and the third part of Charite's story by a servant from her family. In the four Milesian tales that follow Lucius the ass recounts the stories of the Lover under the Tub and the Baker's Wife, but in the two stories included in that of the Baker's Wife an old procuress tells the story of the Sandals under the Bed to the Baker's Wife, and the Baker relates the story of the Fuller's

Wife to his own spouse. Lucius the ass is the narrator of the next story about the Rich Man and the Poor Man but in it a messenger appears as in Greek tragedy to relate the awful deaths of the three sons of the poor man's neighbor. Lucius the Ass tells the tragic romance of the Amorous Stepmother and the tale of the Murderess of Five. Lucius too recounts the crucial events which motivate the entire plot, his transformation and his retransformation.

A certain subtle development in the relation of Lucius to the reader may be traced in the progress of the novel. The first chapter brings him *en rapport* with his audience. Lucius identifies himself as a Greek with progenitors of Athens, Corinth and Sparta. He states his theme, the transformations and retransformations of men and their fortunes. He states the sources of his novel: a Greek story, Milesian tales. He declares that his style is exotic and forensic, due to the fact that Latin was an acquired language. But he assures the reader that if he listens to the story, he will be entertained.

After Lucius is transformed into an ass, he often reminds the reader that though now a perfect ass he has retained human intelligence and curiosity. He makes moral comments on the characters in the novel, on the venality of women, on the blindness of Fortune. He reflects that his ass form has given him the opportunity of Odysseus to visit many cities and people and to attain knowledge and wisdom. He is aware, as he utters diatribes against the corruption of lawyers and judges, that someone will exclaim: "Really! Shall we now permit an ass to philosophize for us?" Finally in the last book, before the description of his own initiation, he addresses the reader as *studiose* ["studious"], declares that perhaps now the reader is excited by a religious longing and expects him to hear and believe the truth as Lucius reveals his ecstatic experience in initiation. Through these various appeals to the reader there is suggested a subtle change in his assumed attitude. First the reader is to be entertained. Then the story is to be made plausible to him. Next his curiosity about life and men is to be gratified. And though he may resent the ass's philosophizing, he is finally carried along with Lucius in an intense desire to know the truth about a religious experience which will set him free. (pp. 185-87)

[The stories] divide into simple, progressive narratives, groups of stories in sequence, and convoluted story within story within story for contrast or emphasis. Within these rather simple plans, multiplex and varied devices are used for gaining effects.

There is no monotony in the settings of the stories. The reader is transported to bedroom in inn, dinner party in palace, courtroom, house of miser, hut of poor old baggage, elegant palace, robbers' mountain fastness, a baker's mill, a rich tyrant's farm. In the story of Charite the scene shifts from her home to the forest where the boar hunt takes place, from her bedroom where she puts out the eyes of Thrasyllus to the sepulchre of her husband where she kills herself. In the story of Cupid and Psyche with almost cinematic shifting we behold the house of her parents, the lonely mountain top, the palace of Cupid, Venus' golden bedroom, the temples of Ceres and of Juno, the royal palace of Jupiter, the lower world, Olympus with all its glorious assemblage of gods. Part of the brilliancy of the narrative consists in many a *purpureus pannus* ["purple patch"] of vivid description of some special scene: the robbers' cave, Byrrhaena's house, Cupid's palace, the baker's mill, and in these pictures realistic details develop the atmosphere desired of horror, of beauty, or of pathos.

Even more varied than the settings of the stories are the characters who pass swiftly before our eyes in this pageant of adventure. With Lucius, man or ass, always leading the procession, advance witches, miser, pompous aedile, wanton maid, elegant matron, Chaldean charlatan, thaumaturgic Egyptian, bandits with brave chieftains, terrified old cook, kidnaped bride, gallant husband, false lover, phantom ghosts, poor shepherds with their flocks and dogs, cruel masters, rich tyrants, wanton wives, deceived husbands, cunning lovers, murderesses and corrupt slaves, venal physician and upright physician, lewd Syrian priests, rapt Egyptian priests, bright Olympian deities made in the image of man, and last of all the mystic figure of Isis, goddess of many-names, goddess of salvation. No chance for boredom is afforded the reader in this great cinema of innumerable scenes and characters.

And the cinema is a talking movie, rich in conversations and speeches. A character that has been given no name and has seemed a mere type speaks and is revealed no automaton but a human being whom we understand from his words. Turn the pages of the ***Metamorphoses*** rapidly as though it were a novel of today and you will see how much conversation and direct speech enlivens the narrative. (pp. 187-89)

Throughout the novel one of Apuleius' most effective methods is this varied use of conversation and speeches. Sometimes a simple short question reveals the point of the whole story. "In this place are dead men wont to run away?" Again a long speech with cumulative effect sets the atmosphere of the tale as when Socrates describes at length the powers of the witch, Meroe. Characters are effectively painted by their own words: for example, the wicked sisters of Psyche reveal in conversation their jealousy, venality and cruelty. Certain speeches highly colored by emotion advance plot or form climax. When the outraged Venus angrily upbraids Cupid, we see that Psyche has made a dangerous enemy who will torture her with long suffering. The impassioned denunciation by Charite of the sleeping Thrasyllus prepares us for her act of vengeance and her suicide. The short speech of the amorous stepmother to the grave young hero lays the corner-stone of this tragedy. In the eleventh book, the inner meaning of the worship of Isis is developed by the ardent prayers of Lucius, by the mystic revelation in long speech of the goddess herself, and by the consolation of her priest's great benediction for the hero, her new follower.

These few illustrations serve to suggest Apuleius' skillful art. In stories short and long on rather simple general outlines he shows the practiced technique of the great story-teller by his skillful use of different narrators and audiences, of various settings and detailed descriptions, of a multitude of vital persons whose own natural words portray their characters and tell their stories. And that exotic Latin for which he apologized with its prodigious vocabulary, its compelling melodies, its peculiar contrasts, its sudden simplicities, clothes the novel in very rococo garments that suit its picaresque corporality. (pp. 189-90)

[To] the thoughtful reader it must be evident that through all the adventures of this novel the hero is in quest of a permanent satisfaction. He is ever eager to penetrate beyond the visible and the tangible to phenomena less evident but more vital. So first he pursues magic art, gathers information, experiments disastrously. Yet in the long period of his transformation he becomes intuitively aware of strange identities in nature of man and beast and enters vicariously into the lives of both. This identification of himself with a four-footed creature serves to open a world of folk-lore to him and brings him through old *mârchen* into a fairy realm of chanting waters, serving winds, gossiping gull, friendly ants, musical reed. And in that world echoes of a far-off dimly remembered Platonism come to him so that he thinks of Amor and Psyche as bright youths in love, one god, one mortal, surrounded by deities. And through these strange glasses of folk-lore and Platonic philosophy the Olympian hierarchy is seen in a new Lucianic light as part of a brilliant story, wherein the great gods are very near man in form and character.

But the old story fails to satisfy, and the hero must struggle on, viewing every corruption of religion, of family life, of social life, until at last he is forced to be a part of these horrors and must submit in ass's shape to obscene degradation in public spectacle. Then his own horrified revolt effects his escape and through prayer, vision, ecstasy and benediction he is saved and restored to human shape by Isis, and her mystic cult. If Lucius is not meant to be Everyman or Everyass at least he conveys to every reader the sense of universal experience, the homo facing fundamental concepts of mind and matter, of body and soul, of sex and religion, of subconscious and superconscious forces in conflict for or in his life. The significant conclusion of the novel in the startling eleventh book is the experience of mystic ecstasy, by revelation, conversion and adoration. Lucius descends to hell and ascends into heaven, wanders through all the elements, meets the gods face to face, finally becomes the worshiper and lover of the goddess Isis forever. The central story of the novel, the love-story of Cupid and Psyche, in which Psyche is made immortal seems to forecast this story of conversion in which man is transformed into votary worthy of his divine Lady and worshiped by the people as a god himself.

Perhaps I may seem to have overemphasized a theme of spiritual quest and growth in Apuleius' novel but for me it is there, now vaguely hinted, now clearly developed. May it not be significant that when Apuleius is converted he no longer goes four-footed but again rides his white horse, Candidus, strangely restored to him? Certainly the central position in the novel of the Cupid and Psyche story with its suggestions of hidden meaning makes it more than a fairy-story or a love-story. And the solemn nature of the long final book with its impressive pageantry, visions, prayers, conversion, exaltation, benedictions, must convince any reader that at the end Lucius the votary of Isis is a far different person from the Lucius of the first book, the curious traveler in Thessaly, land of magic.

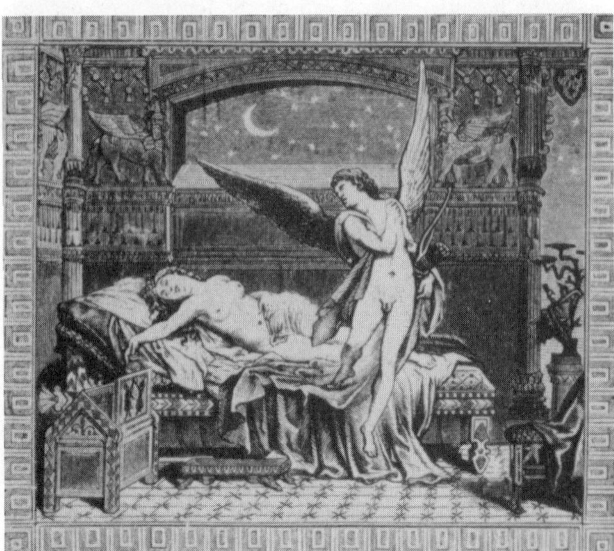

1872 illustration for the tale of Cupid and Psyche.

The very art of Apuleius conceals in the rich overlay of stories this change in his hero's point of view and nature. Anyone who reads the ***Apologia,*** the speech of self-defense which Apuleius made in his trial for the use of magic, must be convinced that the writer was a sophisticated artist who calculated and understood his effects on hearers or readers. And his ***Florida*** confirms this belief. In his novel I think that Apuleius was working out the besetting problems of his age and his relation to them, not by deep thinking or systematic philosophy but pragmatically through adventure, experience and reflection. The ***Metamorphoses*** seems to me indeed, as Lucius himself hinted, a veritable Odyssey of the life of an extraordinary hero in the age of the Antonines. (pp. 192-94)

Elizabeth Hazelton Haight, "Apuleius' Art of Story-Telling," in her Essays on Ancient Fiction, *Longmans, Green and Co., 1936, pp. 151-94.*

ROBERT GRAVES (essay date 1947)

[Graves is a prolific English man of letters who is considered one of the most accomplished minor poets of the twentieth century. Strongly influenced by both World Wars and by his literary and emotional attachment to American writer Laura Riding, Graves displayed in his work a mixture of disquietude and cheerful romanticism. Although his subject matter is often characterized as traditional, he is credited with ingenious structural and linguistic experimentation. Also considered an accomplished prose stylist, he is well known for his historical novel I, Claudius *(1934) and for his retellings of the Greek myths, both of which demonstrate his scholarly but eccentric interest in classical history and literature. In the following excerpt, he evaluates the prose style of* Metamorphoses, *enumerates the religious principles of its author, posits the sources and import of Lucius's transformation in the story, and compares Apuleius as a man and author with St. Augustine.]*

William Adlington, in whose vigorous early-Elizabethan translation [***The Transformation of Lucius Apuleius of Madaura*** or ***The Golden Ass***] is still best known, remarks in his introduction that Apuleius wrote "in so dark and high a style, in so strange and absurd words and in such new invented phrases, as he seemed rather to set it forth to show his magnificent prose than to participate his doings to others" [see excerpt dated 1566]. Adlington has missed the point: Apuleius, who could write a good plain prose when he chose, as his ***Discourse on Magic*** and his ***God of Socrates*** prove, was parodying the extravagant language which the "Milesian" story-tellers used, like barkers at country fairs today, as a means of impressing simple-minded audiences. The professional story-teller, or *sgéalai,* is still found in the West of Ireland. I have heard one complimented as "speaking such fine hard Irish that Devil two words together in it would any man understand"; but this hard Irish, like Apuleius's hard Latin, is always genuinely archaic, not humorously coined for the occasion.

Why did Apuleius choose to write in this eccentric style? For the same reason that Rabelais did. The parallel is close. Both were priests—pious, lively, exceptionally learned, provincial priests—who found that the popular tale gave them a wider field for their descriptions of contemporary morals and manners, punctuated by philosophical asides, than any more respectable literary form. (pp. ix-x)

The main religious principles that Apuleius was inculcating were wholly opposed to those of the Christianity of his day. The first was that men are far from equal in the sight of Heaven, its favour being reserved for the well-born and well-educated, in so far as they are conscious of the moral responsibilities of their station: that only such can be admitted into the divine mysteries and so mitigate their fear of death by a hope of preferential treatment in the after-world. Slaves and freedmen cannot possibly acquire the virtue, intelligence or discretion needed to qualify them for initiation into these mysteries, even if they could afford to pay the high fees demanded. Slavery carries a stigma of moral baseness; and Apuleius's slaves are always cowardly, wicked, deceitful or treacherous.

To be abjectly poor, though free, he regarded as a sign not necessarily of moral baseness but of ill-luck, and his second main religious principle was that ill-luck is catching. The virtuous nobleman does not set his dogs on the poor man, and there is nothing to prevent him from sending a slave round to relieve his immediate distresses; but, like the priest and the Levite in Jesus's parable of the Samaritan, he should carefully avoid all personal contact with ill-luck. Thus when Aristomenes the provision merchant, in Apuleius's opening story, found his old friend Socrates in such a shocking plight at Hypata, he should have been content to toss him a coin or two, spit in his own bosom for luck, and leave him to his fate; instead of officiously trying to rescue and reform him—actually dragging the reluctant wretch into the baths and scrubbing his filthy body with his own hands! Socrates was in any case fated to die miserably, and his bad luck fastened securely on Aristomenes, who soon found himself in Socrates's position—forced to change his name, abandon his wife and family, and become a hunted exile in daily terror of death.

The fault which involved Lucius in all his miseries was that, though a nobleman, he decided on a frivolous love-affair with a slave-girl. A slave-girl is necessarily base; baseness is unlucky; ill-luck is catching. He also transgressed the third main religious principle: he meddled with the supernatural. His ulterior motive in making love to the girl was to persuade her to betray the magical secrets of her mistress, who was a witch. Yet he had been plainly warned against this fault in Byrrhaena's house at Hypata by being shown a wonderful statue of Actaeon's transformation into a stag, his punishment for prying into the mysteries of Diana. A nobleman should not play with black magic: he should satisfy his spiritual needs by being initiated into a respectable mystery cult along with men of his own station; even then he should not thrust himself on the gods but patiently await their summons. Lucius's punishment was to be temporarily transformed not into an owl, as he had hoped, but into an ass.

The owl was a bird of wisdom. The ass, as the Goddess Isis herself reminded Lucius at Cenchreae, was the most hateful to her of all beasts in existence; but she did not account for her aversion. Adlington's explanation, that the ass is a notoriously stupid brute, does not go far enough. The ass was in fact sacred to the God Set, whom the Greeks knew as Typhon, her ancient persecutor and the murderer of her husband Osiris. In Apuleius's day the ass typified lust, cruelty and wickedness, and Plutarch—from whom he claimed descent—had recorded an Egyptian festival in which asses and men with Typhonic colouring (*i.e.*, sandy-red like a wild ass's coat) were triumphantly pushed over cliffs in vengeance for Osiris's murder. When Charitë, in Apuleius's story of the bandit's cave, escapes and rides home on ass-back, he remarks that this is an extraordinary sight—a virgin riding in triumph on an ass. He means: "dominating the lusts of the flesh without whip or bridle." (pp. xii-xiv)

Until nearly the end of his life as an ass, in the course of which he gets involved in the hysterical and fraudulent popular rites of the Syrian Goddess, Lucius is a beast of ill-luck. And ill-luck is catching: each of his masters in turn either dies violently, is locked up in gaol or suffers some lesser misfortune. The spell begins to lift only when he enters the household of Thyasus, the Corinthian judge, and is there encouraged slowly to reassert his humanity.

The seasonal transformations of the variously-named god of the mystery-cults, the Spirit of the Year, were epitomized in the Athenian *Lenaea* festival and corresponding performances throughout the ancient world, including north-western Europe. The initiate identified himself with the god, and seems to have undergone twelve emblematic transformations—represented by Lucius's "twelve stoles"—as he passed through the successive Houses of the Zodiac before undergoing his ritual death and rebirth. "Transformations" therefore conveys the secondary sense of "spiritual autobiography"; and Lucius had spent twelve months in his ass's skin, from one rose-season to the next, constantly changing his House, until his death as an ass and rebirth as a devotee of Isis. (p. xv)

Evidently St. Augustine and his credulous contemporaries had not read Lucius of Patra's popular novel *The Ass,* now lost, or Lucian of Samosata's *Lucius, or the Ass,* still extant, which is based on it; otherwise, they would have realized that Apuleius had borrowed the plot of ***The Transformations*** from one or other of these two sources. (Lucius's date is unknown; but Lucian and Apuleius were close contemporaries). Lucian's novel is shorter and balder than ***The Transformations.*** His slave-girl Palaestra has none of the charm that excuses Apuleius's intimate account of the love-affair with her counterpart Fotis; she merely plays the female drill-sergeant, initiating her recruit into the discipline of sex as one teaches arms-drill by numbers. Lucian includes none of Apuleius's incidental stories, such as the stories of Aristomenes, Thelyphron, Cupid and Psyche; nor the Festival of Laughter episode—there really was such a festival at Hypata—nor the hoodooing of the baker; and his hero returns to human shape at Thessalonica, not Corinth, during his exhibition in the amphitheatre, when without divine assistance he manages to grab some roses from one of the attendants. The comic climax of Lucian's story comes when the ex-ass returns hopefully to the rich woman who has recently played Pasiphaë with him and proposes to renew their intimacy: she throws him out of her house, greatly aggrieved that he is now a mere man, quite incapable of satisfying her needs. Lucian's stories all leave a bad taste in the mouth; Apuleius's do not, even when he is handling the same bawdy situation. His rich Pasiphaë, for example, is no mere bestialist, but shows her genuine love for the ass by planting pure, sincere, wholly unmeretricious kisses on his scented nose.

Apuleius constantly uses a device now known on the variety stage as the "double take." The audience applauds, but finds that it has applauded too soon; the real point, either funnier or more macabre than anyone expected, was yet to come. The brilliance of his showmanship suggests that he turned professional story-teller during his wanderings in Greece, using Lucius of Patra's *Ass* as his stock piece—he felt its relevance to his case and Lucius happened to be his own name—and stringing a number of popular stories to it. (pp. xvii-xviii)

[Apuleius] probably invented none of his stories, though it is clear that he improved them. The story of Cupid and Psyche is still widely current as a primitive folk-tale in countries as far apart as Scotland and Hindustan; but taking hints from passages in Plato's *Phaedo* and *Republic* he turned it into a neat philosophical allegory of the progress of the rational soul towards intellectual love. This feat won him the approval even of the better sort of Christians, including Synnesius, the early fifth-century Bishop of Ptolemais; and ***Cupid and Psyche*** is still Apuleius's best known, though by no means his most golden, story. His devotion to Platonic philosophy is shown in the ***God of Socrates,*** which St. Augustine attacked violently [see excerpt dated c. 413-26].

St. Augustine's dislike of his fellow-countryman Apuleius seems to have sprung from an uncomfortable recognition that they would one day come up together for the judgement of posterity. He was born near Madaura, Apuleius's birthplace, whose inhabitants he addresses in his 232nd Epistle as "my fathers," and went to school there; then, like Apuleius, he went on to Carthage University. Book II of his *Confessions* begins: "I will now call to mind my past foulness and the carnal corruption of my soul. . . . In that sixteenth year of the age of my flesh, when the madness of unlicensed lust took rule over me and I resigned myself wholly to it . . . I walked the streets of Babylon and wallowed in the mire thereof as if in a bed of spices and precious ointments." He goes on to describe how he took up with a gang of young Mohocks (like the ones that terrorized Hypata) and so fell into the mortal sin of theft. Still following the footsteps of Apuleius, he studied oratory at Rome. It is not until Book VIII that after a severe struggle with himself he hears a voice from Heaven directing him to read a text from St. Paul, becomes suddenly converted, once more like Apuleius, and determines to devote his life to God.

His father Patricius, a nominal Christian, was a violent, vulgar fellow from whom he inherited neither rank, money nor a predisposition to virtue; so that even had he wished to become a priest of Isis he could not have qualified for the honour. But the Christian mysteries were open to everyone, slave or noble, of good or evil life, and the greater the sinner the warmer his welcome to the fold. Though his conversion was as genuine as that of Apuleius, it does not seem to have made his life nearly so happy. Tormented by the memory of his sins, he flaunts his dirty linen for our detestation: "Alas, terrible Judge, I began by robbing a pear-tree, I ended in adultery and the hateful Manichaean heresy!" Apuleius does nothing of the sort. His ***Transformations*** is as moral a work as the *Confessions;* but he presents his errors in humorous allegory, not as a literal record, and admits that he learned a great deal from them which has since stood him in good stead: granted, his love affair with Fotis was a mistake, and he paid dearly for it, but it would be hypocritical to pretend that it was not a charming and instructive experience while it lasted.

St. Augustine described with horror the fascination that the amphitheatre and the study of oratory had held for him in his unregenerate days. Apuleius, though a priest of Osiris, continued to practise as a barrister and in later life organized the gladiatorial and wild-beast shows for the whole province of Africa. St. Augustine rejected Platonic philosophy as insufficient for salvation; Apuleius was true to it and showed his scorn of contemporary Christianity by making the most wicked of his characters, the baker's wife, "reject all true religion in favour of the fantastic and blasphemous cult of an Only God" and use the Christian Love-feast as "an excuse for getting drunk quite early in the day and playing the whore at all hours." One of St. Augustine's biographers, E. de Pressensé, has written approvingly: "He kept dragging along the chain of guilt . . . and unlike his fellow-countryman Apuleius whose greatest pleasure was to arrange words in harmonious order and who had no desire beyond that of calling forth applause . . . still felt sick at heart." This is unfair to Apuleius. His greatest desire was not applause: it was to show his gratitude to the Goddess whom he adored, by living a life worthy of her favour—a serene, honourable and useful life, with no secret worm of guilt gnawing at his heart as though he had withheld some confession from her or mistrusted her compassion. (pp. xix-xxi)

Robert Graves, in his introduction to The Transformations of Lucius, Otherwise Known as The Golden Ass, *by Lucius Apuleius, translated by Robert Graves, Farrar, Straus & Young, 1951, pp. ix-xxii.*

PETER QUENNELL (essay date 1950)

[Quennell is a prolific and distinguished English biographer and literary critic. In the following excerpt, he considers the literary merits of Metamorphoses *and notes the value of the novel as a mirror of the social life of its time.]*

[Walter Pater's appreciation of ***The Golden Ass*** (see excerpt dated 1885)] has not lost its value. Evidently there was much to be said about ***The Golden Ass*** that he refrained from saying; but the imaginative charm he stresses is still its greatest quality. Apuleius was an incomparable story-teller; and, while human beings love to be told stories and to wander in the mysterious borderland dividing fact and fantasy, the book will continue to gather admirers and will remain one of the five or six volumes that an intelligent Crusoe would hope to discover on his desert island. It was part of the small library, we are informed, that T. E. Lawrence carried everywhere with him during his Arabian campaigns. Nor is the selection difficult to understand; for, although Lawrence was an ascetic and, at least towards the end of his career, a self-torturing misogynist, and Apuleius a reformed rake, a polished advocate and a man of the world, the texture of the novel is extremely various—as various as the extraordinary scenes through which Lucius, condemned to an asinine garb, strays seeking the mouthful of fresh roses that will restore him to his human shape. It is both highly romantic and brutally realistic, a fantasy derived from the immemorial realm of fairy tales and a satirical panorama of everyday life in a backward Roman province, the whole narrative coloured by strong religious feelings. . . .

[***The Golden Ass***] is essentially a pattern of contrasts, a picaresque novel with a poetic and philosophic background. Lucius's affair with Fotis introduces the theme of sensual satisfaction. The passage has a lyrical glow. But soon afterwards Lucius loses his human shape and is immediately plunged into the outer darkness reserved for slaves and animals, harried from pillar to post, beaten and humiliated by his brutal masters, among the ugliest of mankind and the wretchedest of beasts of burden. Then, in midst of his worst sufferings, penned in the robbers' cave, he hears the exquisite fable of the marriage of Cupid and Psyche; and on the heels of his most demoralising experience—his seduction, while he is still an ass, by a rich and vicious matron—he escapes from public shame in the amphitheatre and enjoys the resplendent vision of Isis that brings his wanderings to a happy close.

Was it not an important part of the novelist's design to clothe the harshness and nastiness of many of the scenes he described—scenes drawn, no doubt, from his own knowledge of the second-century provincial world—in a style as literary and learnedly allusive as anything attempted by the author of *Ulysses* and *Anna Livia Plurabelle?* . . . ***The Golden Ass*** is a miraculously absorbing tale, which makes fantasy credible and reality fantastic, a symbolic representation of life that never degenerates into vulgar allegory. (p. 126)

Besides its imaginative charm, as a picture of his social period, Apuleius's novel is permanently interesting. The sun of the *pax romana* [''Roman peace''] had seldom shone more brightly; but, at any rate in the north of Greece, the roads are infested with huge bands of well-armed brigands, and landowners, surrounded by their armies of slaves, seem to have begun to retire into an almost feudal isolation. Sorcery is rife, and the influence of the eastern mystery religions is everywhere increasing; the chaste and dignified cult of Isis is paralleled by the crude and orgiastic cult of Cybele, whose mendicant eunuch priests go prancing in paint and rags through the Thessalian towns and villages. Apuleius despised the followers of Cybele and did not love the Christians; and the only Christian to emerge in his tale is the cruel and licentious baker's wife who ''professed perfect scorn for the Immortals and rejected all true religion in favour of a fantastic and blasphemous cult of an 'Only God','' practising in his honour ''various absurd ceremonies which gave her the excuse of getting drunk quite early in the day and playing the whore at all hours.'' Nor had he attention and sympathy to spare for the depressed and servile classes: ''Apuleius's slaves [Robert Graves points out (see excerpt dated 1947)] are always cowardly, wicked, deceitful or treacherous.'' At heart he was still the provincial aristocrat, a priest, a rhetorician and an advocate who shone in the courts, proud of his erudition and literary accomplishments, devoted to the tenets of the enlightened religion he had adopted, very much a man of the ancient world, yet endowed with an imaginative sensibility that hints now and then at the art and literature of modern Europe. It is as though, behind the solid and stately facade of organised Roman peace and plenty, he divined the ''picturesque'' Mediterranean landscape of a later epoch—the fascinating ruins that Piranesi drew, the wild torch-lit figures of a Magnasco or a Salvator Rosa. (p. 127)

Peter Quennell, in a review of ''The Golden Ass,'' in The New Statesman & Nation, *Vol. 40, No. 1012, July 29, 1950, pp. 126-27.*

MOSES HADAS (essay date 1952)

[*Hadas was a distinguished American academic and scholar whose many works, including* A History of Greek Literature *(1950), A* History of Latin Literature *(1952), and* Hellenistic Culture: Fusion and Diffusion *(1959), range over the whole of classical literature. In the following excerpt, he surveys Apuleius's major writings and comments on their prose style.*]

[The ***Metamorphoses*** of Apuleius], and especially the story of Cupid and Psyche embedded in it like a jewel, assure Apuleius' position as one of the handful of Latin authors with a legitimate and perennial claim on the attention of lovers of literature. (pp. 339-40)

[The] ***Apology*** (it is called ***Pro se de magia liber*** in the manuscripts) is our best introduction to second-century Latinity as well as very valuable for the abundant light it throws on the private life and intellectual atmosphere of the time. The speech as we have it is too long to have been delivered, but it was probably enlarged for publication, like Cicero's *Pro Milone* or the Younger Pliny's *Panegyric to Trajan*. But the main part of the speech was surely delivered; it is not a wholly fictive speech like Cicero's *Against Verres* or *Second Philippic*. The first portion of the speech disposes of the charge of wizardry. With a flamboyant display of learning Apuleius overwhelms his puny adversaries and makes them ludicrous. The second portion defends his marriage with Pudentilla and justifies his dealings with his stepsons. The only parallel to the detailed and merciless portraiture of the villainous turpitude of his accusers and the base ingratitude of his stepsons and their unlovely domestic life is Cicero's *Pro Cluentio*. Nor, despite its extravagant Asianism, is the style of the ***Apology*** as different as we should expect, on the basis of the ***Metamorphoses*** and the ***Florida,*** from the classic norm. Here is genuine indignation and the practical necessity of securing acquittal from a serious charge. In prose employed as an instrument for practical ends, then, divagations from the classical norm were only such as might be expected from the natural course of development, remembering the dominant influence of rhetorical education. The display pieces would then fall into a distinct and separate category, where virtuosity in language was an end in itself.

Renascence scholars regarded the peculiarities of Apuleius' style as being due to his African origin and spoke of his *tumor Africus* [the turgidity and bombast of his African style]. Modern scholarship has shown that there is nothing distinctly African either in Apuleius or in other African writers, though each province may have retained words which had fallen into disuse in the capital. Apuleius' style is the style of the second century. Unlike Fronto, who was a conscious archaizer, Apuleius used all available resources, ancient and contemporary, to make his style effective. The noticeable characteristics of that style are balance and symmetry, attained by devices of structure and sound; diffuseness and redundancy, by the use of synonyms, periphrases, and rhetorical repetitions; variety, by conscious syntactical alternations; alliteration and assonance, in many forms; diminutives, Grecisms, neologisms. Walter Pater (*Marius the Epicurean,* Chapter 5) aptly describes Apuleius' style as ''full of archaisms and curious felicities in which that generation delighted, quaint terms and images picked from the early dramatists, the life-like phrases of some lost poet preserved by an old grammarian, racy morsels of the vernacular and studied prettinesses'' [see excerpt dated 1885].

But it is rather to the ***Florida*** that ''his rococo, very African, and, as it were, perfumed personality'' (Pater, Chapter 20) applies. These are excerpts from his epideictic declamations, which Apuleius himself had probably published in four books under some such title as *Orationes*. At a later period some admirer selected an anthology (which is the meaning of *florida*) of choice bits, retaining the book division of the original, which is very unsystematic, for the selected pieces. The excerpts are elaborately polished and have an ornate kind of stateliness, though all are essentially trivial and some grotesque. Some are from speeches on public occasions, some contain moralizations, legends, or picturesque stories. There are, for example, a detailed description of the flight of an eagle; the contest of Apollo and Marsyas; a note on the flautist Antigenidas; remarks on India and the gymnosophists; the artistic taste of Alexander the Great; a comparison of his own versatility with that of the sophist Hippias; on the parrot; on the Cynic Crates; on Samos, Polycrates, and Pythagoras; on the comic poet Philemon; on the familiar dispute of the sophist Protagoras and his disciple Euathlos concerning tuition charges. . . . (pp. 342-43)

Of the same class as the declamations of which we have excerpts in the ***Florida*** is ***On the God of Socrates.*** The *daimonion* of which Socrates speaks as directing his conduct in Plato's *Apology,* Apuleius says, was one of the spirits intermediary between God and man who are "in nature animal, in intellect rational, in mind subject to emotion, in material airy, in duration eternal. The first three characteristics they have in common with men; the fourth is peculiar to themselves; the fifth they share with the immortal gods; but they differ from them in being subject to emotion." They are intermediaries in both directions: they execute divine behests for mankind, and they convey to the gods the prayers and offerings of men. The doctrine is ancient; it is found in Hesiod, and in the account of the birth of Eros in Plato's *Symposium*. Plutarch found it extremely useful in reconciling a perfect deity with an imperfectly administered universe, and his writings on the subject, especially *On the Obsolescence of Oracles* and *On the Face in the Moon,* were very influential. Apuleius' treatise certainly follows, if it does not translate, a Greek original. Because it was the first work in Latin on a subject important equally to pagans and Christians, Apuleius' treatise enjoyed a vogue out of all proportion to its merit.

Apuleius has been praised as a *Platonicus* (St. Augustine, *City of God* 8.12) [see excerpt dated c. 413-26], but his ***De Platone et eius dogmate*** is such a summary as an undergraduate might write. The book begins with a brief biography of Plato and continues with an account of the Platonic theories of the world and the soul, based mostly on the *Timaeus*. The second book, addressed to *Faustine fili* ["his son Faustinus], summarizes Plato's views on ethics and politics, drawing largely on *Gorgias, Republic,* and *Laws*. These books show no real knowledge of Plato, but are the heaped-up learning of the rhetorician, with no judgment or critical faculty. It has been suggested that Apuleius' immediate authority for his Platonic writings was his contemporary Albinus. The ***Peri hermeneias*** on formal logic which used to be regarded as the third book of ***De Platone*** is Aristotelian and Stoic rather than Platonic, and is a separate work, if indeed it is Apuleius'. If the *fili* in the dedication of the second book is literal, the work must derive from Apuleius' last years; if it is metaphorical, the book may have been written at any period in Apuleius' career. ***De mundo (On the Universe)*** is a free and often inaccurate translation of an extant Greek treatise entitled *Peri kosmou,* falsely ascribed to Aristotle and dedicated to one Alexander, probably the apostate nephew of Philo Judaeus. This dedication Apuleius alters to *Faustine fili,* leaving the impression that the work was his own. Efforts to save Apuleius' honor by making him author of both the Greek and Latin are misguided. The treatise strikes a note of lofty monotheism almost Christian in character. (pp. 345-46)

We come now to the ***Metamorphoses,*** upon which Apuleius' reputation in literature rests, for without the ***Metamorphoses*** he would have been forgotten by all but professional scholars. Apuleius himself does not speak of the book, and it is difficult to know at what point in his career he wrote it. . . . [Some] considerations point to a date late in Apuleius' life. On the other hand, it is held that the ebullience of the writing implies youth and that the accounts of the initiations and other biographical details in the eleventh book reflect recent experience, and hence that the ***Metamorphoses*** must have been written in Apuleius' Roman period. . . . On neither side are the arguments completely cogent. The genius of the work is timeless, and perhaps it is not essential that we date it to a definite year in its author's life. (pp. 346-47)

Apuleius is a more characteristic phenomenon in Latin literature than might at first glance seem likely. Latin literature was from its beginnings consciously "literary," and Apuleius succeeds in making his very "literary" Latin to the highest degree effective. Latin literature from the beginning set itself the task of harvesting, broadcasting, and perpetuating the artistic achievements of its predecessors; Apuleius' harvest was rich and varied, and he did broadcast and perpetuate it, with his special cachet. And from the beginning Latin literature at its best endowed its borrowings with a gravity and seriousness of purpose. Such gravity and seriousness are not wanting in Apuleius. (p. 350)

Moses Hadas, "The Age of Hadrian," in his A History of Latin Literature, *Columbia University Press, 1952, pp. 334-52.*

ANDRÉ-JEAN FESTUGIÈRE (essay date 1954)

[In the following excerpt, Festugière studies the relationship of Book XI of Metamorphoses *to the rest of the work.]*

There are two ways of looking at [the ***Metamorphoses*** of Apuleius]. One may see in it simply an amusing story—the model for which was furnished by a Greek novel (the *Ass* of Lucian offers a parallel)—to which Apuleius would then have added an edifying conclusion having no direct connection with what precedes. Or one may suppose that, from the beginning, Apuleius had in mind the events at the end of the work, and may consequently consider the whole novel as a story of a sin and a redemption, a conversion in the proper sense of the word—the passage from a sinner's miserable condition to a pure and sanctified life. For my part I should incline to this second interpretation, for the following reasons. (1) There are in the text itself very clear indications that the role of Isis in the XIth book is conceived in opposition to the role of Fortune or Destiny in the rest of the novel, and that there is therefore a relationship of contrast intended between these two divine powers, with Isis triumphing in the end. (2) It is evident that the misfortunes of Lucius and his moral degradation are actually the consequences of a sin from which he is cleansed and saved by Isis, through whom he comes to lead a new life.

It is a *Leitmotiv* of the novel, especially marked from book VII on, that Lucius is a plaything in the hands of Fortune. Whenever it seems that Lucius' condition is bound to improve, and that he is on the point of reaching a safe harbor, Fortune submerges him once more. Let us choose an example from the VIIth book. In the beginning of this book, after the ass has been rescued from the bandits, his fellow captive Charite, in whose deliverance he was instrumental, in order to show her gratitude, entrusts him to the head groom so that he may graze in leisurely fashion in the fields. However, instead of letting him graze, the groom's wife makes him turn a millstone all day long, striking him whenever he stops. One day he is sent to the fields, but it turns out that the proximity of horses is a martyrdom for the ass. Thus "I was already crushed by these miseries, when relentless Fortune gave me over to new torments." . . . Next the ass is separated from the horses, and he thinks he is saved. Alas, it is only to fall into the hands of a little slave who does not cease to persecute him; thus "Fortune, that could not have enough of my torments, had devised a new pain for me." . . . This little slave leads Lucius, the ass, to the mountainside, where he cuts wood and loads it on the animal. One day, however, the ass, frightened by the sight of a bear, takes flight and is caught and mounted by a passer-by. Lucius believes that his trials are over. But he falls into the hands of wicked shepherds, who, to punish him for having abandoned the child, prepare to kill him; "Fortune, ever bent on my distress, put an end with hideous swiftness to my happy escape, and set new snares for me." . . . Later, put up for sale in a populous and famous city, perhaps Berea in Macedonia, Lucius the ass, wanted by no one, falls into the hands of the lowest of the low—pervert priests of the Syrian Goddess. "But that savage Fortune of mine, from whom I fled through so many lands but could not escape, and whom all the miseries I had undergone did not appease, once more turned her blind eyes upon me." . . . While he is in the service of these priests, upon the occasion of their being invited to a banquet in a village by a devotee of Atargatis, Lucius finds himself in deadly peril. At the last moment, a haunch of venison having been eaten by a dog, the cook gets ready to roast and serve the ass Lucius. He flees, and runs headlong into the banquet hall, where he breaks everything. Once more he believes that his misfortunes are at an end: "But assuredly if Fortune is against it, nothing good can come to mortal man; and there is no plan so carefully worked out and no device so clever that it can undo or change in any way the fate previously ordained by the gods." . . . (pp. 72-4)

Why this cruelty, this relentlessness on the part of Fortune? It is because she is a blind goddess, who is partial only to the wicked and the unworthy, who accords reputation in such contrary wise that the evildoer passes for a good man, and the most innocent for guilty." . . . (p. 74)

Over against malicious Fortune is set, in a striking contrast, the good and merciful Isis. No one can prosper if Fortune is against him, we read . . . , nor can he cancel or amend the fate previously ordained by the gods. No one, that is, except Isis, who by her providence saves men: "Give over thy weeping and leave off thy lamentations; for, by my providence, the day of deliverance already dawns for thee." . . . "And here at last came the good things which the divinity most present to aid had promised me. The priest came along bearing in his right hand my destiny and deliverance itself in the form of the wreath of roses commanded by the goddess. . . . And fitting it was that it was a crown, . . . for at last I was to be victor over the Fortune that had so cruelly fought against me." . . . This contrast between the two goddesses is strikingly brought out by the priest after the miracle of Isis.

> Having undergone hardships many and varied, having been driven by the violent storms of Fortune and buffeted about by her highest winds, thou hast come at last, Lucius, to the haven of Rest and the altar of Mercy. Neither thy high birth, nor thy standing, nor again the learning in which thou dost shine, was anywhere of the slightest help to thee. Thou didst fall on the slippery surface of vigorous youth into servile pleasures and didst reap the bitter fruit of an ill-starred curiosity. But nonetheless Fortune in her blindness, by the very enormity of the ordeals to which she subjected thee, succeeded only in bringing thee to thy present religious felicity—so improvident was she in her malice. Let her go now, let her give free rein to her utter fury, let her find another victim on which to exercise her cruelty. Ill luck has no foothold against the lives of those whom the majesty of our goddess has saved to be her servants. The robbers, the wild beasts, thy slavery, thy wanderings back and forth over the roughest roads, thy daily fear of death—of what avail were these to spiteful Fortune? Now thou art safe under the protection of a Fortune, but of one that is not blind; by the splendor with which she shines she gives light even to the other gods. Put on now a more joyful countenance to match the shining raiment thou wearest, join with exultant steps the procession of the goddess who is thy deliverer. Let the godless see, let them see and recognize the error of their ways; behold how Lucius, delivered from his former troubles, now by the providence of mighty Isis doth joyfully triumph over his Fortune. . . .

We have here a living commentary on the last verse of Isis' aretalogy: "I am victorious over Destiny; Destiny obeyeth me."

Another connection, as we said above, between book XI and the other books is that XI concerns a conversion, the passage from a state of impurity to a pure life. This too is stressed by the priest after the miracle: "Thou didst fall . . . into servile pleasures and didst reap the bitter fruit of an ill-starred curiosity." . . . Two reasons are given for the downfall and degradation of Lucius: first, curiosity about magic, which led him to make his unfortunate experiment at Hypata . . . ; and secondly, his voluptuous relations with Photis, the young slave of the magician Pamphile. This last is quite unusual in an author of antiquity, for the ancients considered love as a sickness at the worst, never as a real sin. Moreover, the case of Hippolytus shows that, by refusing love, one actually offends a goddess, Aphrodite. We may ask ourselves whether, in the expression "servile pleasures," the accent be not upon "servile"; but the ancients had no prejudices in that respect. Besides, the blunders of Lucius are presented as imprudent rather than sinful. It is by a chain of imprudent actions—his affair with Photis, and the dabblings in magic to which his curiosity impels him, with Photis as accomplice—that Lucius falls into the hands of Fortune, who proves herself relentless. Again, even in the shape of an ass, Lucius preserves the instincts of a sound and honest lad. Nevertheless, it must be admitted that the frivolous tone of books I to X is in contrast with the steadfast self-discipline imposed upon Lucius in book XI.

One may therefore speak, in a sense, of *conversion*. It follows that, as a conversion may not be understood except in relation to the way of life which preceded, there is obviously a connection between book XI and the rest of the novel.

Now all the interpreters of book XI have noted that the tale here takes on an autobiographical character, especially from the time of Lucius' arrival at the temple at Cenchreae. There are at this point accents of warmth and sincerity which are unmistakable; he who speaks thus has been himself initiated, and is recalling his own experience. What is at first only a very strong impression registered on the reader is later confirmed by a slip—perhaps a voluntary slip—in the text itself. . . . Lucius is at Rome, a year passes, when he is notified in a dream that he must be initiated into the mysteries of Osiris at the hands of a certain pastophorus named Asinius Marcellus. The latter, for his part, has been advised by the god that he must initiate "a citizen of Madaura, truly a very poor man. . . . This citizen of Madaura is obviously Apuleius himself, who has taken the place of his hero.

It is, then, certainly Apuleius who speaks. Now we know that Apuleius was pious; he speaks in the ***Apology*** of a statuette of Hermes, to which he addressed his prayers. We know that he was initiated into various mysteries. We also know that he practiced magic; at least he was accused of it, put on trial with that indictment, and it is in vain that he repudiates the accusation, for his defense, which we read in the ***Apology,*** is scarcely convincing. If we bear all that in mind, the account of book XI of the ***Metamorphoses*** and the relation of book XI to the rest of the novel take on a much more interesting aspect. It is no longer merely a matter of the artificial joining of a Greek tale—which, as everything leads us to believe, was nothing but a succession of amusing adventures—to an edifying conclusion. The substance of such a tale remains, but Apuleius has changed the spirit. The work, in its entirety, becomes a human document. Lucius was punished for having tried to practice magic. For the same reason Apuleius underwent a very serious prosecution, which might have cost him his life. Like Lucius, he was at that time a young man. Is it absurd to think that the memory of this experience still obsessed him when he wrote the ***Metamorphoses,*** and that he has there traced for us the story of a soul which fell, which suffered by reason of that fall, and which the merciful hand of Isis raised up and saved? (pp. 74-7)

André-Jean Festugière, ''Popular Piety: Lucius and Isis,'' in his Personal Religion Among the Greeks, *University of California Press, 1954, pp. 68-84.*

MICHAEL GRANT (essay date 1954)

[*Grant is a prolific English classicist known both for his scholarly works and for his popular studies of ancient cultures, especially the Roman Empire. In the following excerpt from* Roman Literature, *he discusses* Metamorphoses *in the context of life and literature in second-century Rome.*]

[***Metamorphoses***] is the only Roman novel which has survived complete. It is a fantastic story about a certain Lucius who is accidentally turned into a donkey and has many strange adventures. To this central theme the work owes its usual modern title, ***The Golden Ass.*** Theme and title recall a shorter Greek story called *Lucius or the Ass,* and it is possible that both versions may go back to an unknown Greek *Metamorphoses*. . . . But the title ***Metamorphoses*** recalls to memory, as it was intended to, that Ovid had constructed his greatest poem, of the same name, out of a whole collection of such transformation scenes.

The language of Apuleius is startlingly brilliant, florid and extravagant. Its exuberance has been attributed to his African origin. But it is hard to say how far this is true, since comparison with other writers is difficult: for a large proportion of the greatest writers of this and subsequent generations were North Africans. This is perhaps the Latin of an epoch, rather than of a country. It is in part the daily speech of the educated people of the time. But it contains also a rich added decoration, part of which is due to the influence of travelling ''sophists.'' Ciceronian grammar is rapidly breaking down, and modern ''Latin'' languages are almost in sight. Another feature of this period, and of Apuleius, is a return to archaisms—to the language of Plautus, eclipsed in the intervening centuries by the literary language of Ciceronians, and then Augustans, and then Silver Latin writers.

This second-century movement of colloquialism combined with archaism was known by one of its originators (Marcus Aurelius' tutor, Fronto) as the New Speech: its greatest exponent was Apuleius. ''In him, style celebrates its orgies with the impetuous dizziness of bacchants, launching into the furies of the whirlwind, evaporating into a sea of floating clouds, into a fantastic disorder.'' We have come far from the pure classical spirit; but Apuleius justifies his unorthodoxy by his success. One feature of his writing and of his epoch—not found in Petronius—is the ecstatic belief in mystery religions which marked, in some sense, the transition between state-paganism and Christianity. Apuleius seems to record a deeply felt experience of his own when he describes his hero's initiation to the mysteries of the Egyptian Isis: and to her he devotes the riches of his imagination. It is not nearly enough to see such passages from the viewpoint of orthodox classicism. This was not just a bad version of an old age; it was a new age.

It was an age of interest in natural and supernatural phenomena—an age of what St. Augustine was to call, in words that do not require translation, *damnabilis curiositas.* The second century A.D. recalls the epoch between our two Great Wars, in its love of sensation and of rapid movement from place to place. Apuleius was a versatile representative of his time. He was novelist and ''sophist,'' lawyer and lecturer, poet and initiate. It is not surprising that he was accused of magic—a charge from which he defends himself in a dazzling and outrageous speech, the ***Apologia,*** one of our few surviving Latin speeches apart from those of Cicero.

Just as the novel of Petronius [*The Satyricon*] contains its ''inset'' *Dinner of Trimalchio,* so Apuleius, too, introduces the even more famous story of ***Cupid and Psyche.*** This elaborate story of the ''Fairy Bridegroom'' contains many features of folk-lore which reappear, as is the mysterious habit of folklore, in the tales of widely separated lands. It is a masterpiece of narrative and descriptive art. (pp. 125-27)

Michael Grant, ''Fact and Fiction,'' in his Roman Literature, *Cambridge at the University Press, 1954, pp. 84-132.*

FRANCES NORWOOD (essay date 1956)

[*In the following excerpt, Norwood argues that Apuleius intended* Metamorphoses *to be entertaining rather than didactic and comments on the characters and narrative pace of the work.*]

The last book—or chapter—of ***Metamorphoses*** fails to hang together with the first ten. After their secularity its sudden exalted mysticism comes to most readers as a brutal shock. Such a violent and unprepared change of key must strike any modern critic as bad art. Imagine the climax of *The Pilgrim's Progress* tacked on to the end of *Tom Jones* and try to justify the result!

Of course attempts have been made. [In his *Il significato e il valore del romanzo di Apuleio,* B. Lavagnani] observed that Apuleius' hero passes through ten books of adventures before he reaches the haven of Isis, and undergoes ten days of preparation before he becomes her initiate. Surely, he concludes, such correspondence of numbers argues a design. [H. Riefstahl asserts in *Der Roman des Apuleius*] that the gaiety, licentiousness, and suffering of the first ten books represent a complete, realistic picture of The World: the hero, having learned by bitter experience that magic gives him no refuge from this world and no control over his fortunes, finds his real refuge from it in the worship of Isis. This does, to be sure, make unity out of diversity and lessens our surprise at the change of tone in the last book. But it is hard to believe that a writer with any such plan in mind would have failed to give some clue to it in the earlier books. It is still harder to believe that any religious devotee could write with such obvious relish of the world which he had learned to regard as Dead Sea fruit.

There is another explanation of the changed mood in the last book. This I advance diffidently because it amounts to no explanation at all. Have we any right to expect Apuleius to satisfy our modern ideas about artistic unity? Some Greek tragedies fulfil present canons of drama: others do not. Ought we to castigate the writers of these latter for getting the rules wrong when *they* had no rules to go by? Were there, in Apuleius' day, any rules for an extensive work in prose fiction? Merely, I imagine, the general precept to keep one's readers entertained. And this, to a professional rhetor, would mean that very variety of mood and tone which we now condemn because it offends our modern standards. Apuleius probably regarded his last chapter as a *tour de force* where he might display his skill with sacerdotal language and mystic ideas, as a juggler keeps his best trick for the climax of the performance. I am encouraged in such a view by the fact that the early novel was not a place where one expected profundity. The Greek romances, for example, were simply entertainment—escape literature as we call it now. The unassailable virtue of their leading characters is not moral philosophy but part of the haze of unreality which shimmers over the plot. Apuleius was far too accomplished a student of literature to place the gem of philosophy in the wrong setting: he would have considered it bad taste to endow a novel with a serious moral lesson. "But is not the last chapter about religion?" you may ask. Of course: mystery religions were popular, the cult of Isis particularly so. To include in his novel a long purple patch about religious ecstasy was in keeping with the taste of the times and with his own avowed interests. But to write the entire novel as a piece of religious propaganda advertising the wrong and the right paths to salvation was an altogether different matter. If such was his intention Apuleius was, so far as we know, a pioneer. If such was his intention, moreover, he failed to make it clear to ancient literary critics. Macrobius dismisses his fiction as designed solely for pleasuring the ear, and therefore much less valuable than the myths of Plato or Cicero's *Dream of Scipio* [see excerpt dated c. 390-410]. Critics do at times fail to understand authors, but surely never so wantonly as this! (pp. 4-6)

[A consideration of the plot of ***Metamorphoses*** reveals that although] it is Lucius' quest for knowledge which brings about his unlucky transformation, few of the donkey's experiences are brought about by his quest for roses. In fact he forgets the roses for pages at a time and actually fails to mention them when he is bought by a gardener, surely an appropriate moment for a reference to flowers. Let us then call the novel picaresque or episodic, and be content with what little unity Apuleius has seen fit to give us. (p. 7)

[Apuleius] expands his work by introducing tales along the way. The great number of these is startling, and nothing better illustrates the capricious inventiveness of the author than the manner of their insertion and the variety of their subject-matter, both seeming to defy analysis. The jewelled fairy-story of Cupid and Psyche, which forms a great centrepiece of the romance almost two books in length, is typical of the surprises Apuleius has in store for his reader. It is told in a robbers' den by a filthy old woman: one would expect a narrative about common folk uttered in colloquial language. Instead, the author, with a lordly disregard for verisimilitude, has lavished on the lines all the richness of his thought, all the splendour of his Latin. He has taken a folk-tale of the Beauty-and-the-Beast order, with wicked sisters, talking insects, and the like. To it he has added the divinities of Olympus, glorious in their majesty but revealing clay feet in most diverting fashion—as when Venus objects to her son's marriage because it would make her, the goddess of beauty, a grandmother. . . . Over these two elements Apuleius has shed a curious glamour by the opulent embroideries of language which describe fairy palaces or dark, dragon-guarded crags with words as romantic as the scenes they invoke.

It is characteristic of a great work of art that it not only communicates a spiritual experience of its creator but by that communication inspires in others a spiritual experience of their own. Hence down the centuries this enchanting tale has wakened many echoes, from translations which are themselves works of art to elaborate allegorical exegeses which see in it the soul of Man raised to divinity by Love. But if Apuleius intended any moral by the tale it seems to me only this: it was curiosity that brought Psyche to grief just as it was curiosity that ruined Lucius. Psyche is Lucius in Fairyland.

In contrast to the gorgeous detail of the Cupid and Psyche narrative ***Metamorphoses*** contains stories of half a dozen lines. The tragedy of the foolish slave . . . is stripped bare of all ornament, its horrors follow one upon the other, unrelieved, until the dreadful climax when the slave is tied to a tree, smeared with honey, and left to be devoured by ants. Only then does Apuleius permit one touch of beauty to soothe our harrowed feelings: it is not the torments of the slave with which the tale ends, but with a picture of his white bones gleaming against the darkness of the fatal tree. (p. 8)

A professional orator must be skilled in description as well as narration. The Greek romances provide accounts of pictures, statuary, and the like, usually ascribed to the interest in visual arts that characterized the period of their composition: such accounts were more probably inserted because the author was a rhetorician. But contrast the clumsy hand of an Achilles Tatius with the subtlety of Apuleius. The former opens his novel [*Leucippe and Clitophon*] by describing a picture. What links it with the narrative which follows? There is a Cupid in the picture and the novel is about love, a connection solemnly explained by the hero with a *naïveté* which reduces criticism to awed silence. Apuleius is both more reticent and more refined. The pause to display a work of art he uses only once—possibly he regarded it as too much like a school-boy's exercise for one of his powers. Moreover, the work described is perfectly in tune with the main plot. Lucius tells of a sculptured group of Diana and Actaeon which he observed in his relative's house . . . ; readers of that day would be familiar with the tale of Actaeon, whose unseemly curiosity caused his transformation and subsequent suffering, perhaps also familiar with the story of Lucius himself, who was so soon to encounter a similar experience. Apuleius could have chosen no more appropriate subject for his art-description. But he does not kill our pleasure in the appropriateness by telling us to observe it: few authors can so resist nudging their readers in case they miss a point.

Apuleius uses another type of description which is of more interest to modern critics—a great tableau of a crowd at a festival. There are three of these, each introduced to halt us at a crisis in the hero's fortunes. All are in a sense religious festivals yet each is elaborated in an entirely different way to illustrate the author's inventive genius. The Festival of Laughter, immediately before Lucius is transformed, presents a great trial scene. . . . Here it is the mass of people which engages the author's attention, overflowing the seats, twined round columns, perched on statues, peeping through windows—the scene is like a Giles' cartoon, with heads bobbing up in the most unlikely places. The Festival of Triumph, just before the ass runs away for the last time, describes a theatrical presentation of the Judgment of Paris . . . with emphasis now on stage *décor,* music, and dancing. No expense had been spared with the production and no detail is spared in its description: Paris is ''discovered'' on a mountainside where real grass and a real spring give refreshment to real goats; Minerva dances to Dorian music but Venus very properly to the Lydian mode—Apuleius was a Platonist and knew about the effect of music on the emotions. In the Festival of Isis . . . , when Lucius is about to be restored to human shape, it is the diversity of the celebrants upon which the writer has chosen to dwell: happy masqueraders, shaven initiates, surpliced priests pass before us in procession as bright with colour as Lucius' roses. The late Professor E. K. Brown has drawn attention [in his *Rhythm in the Novel*] to the modern novelist's employment of repetition with variations. It is fascinating to reflect that a device found, for instance, in the several *soirées* of Proust was used in much the same way by one of the earliest authors of the European novel.

No novelist may be dismissed without a word about his characterization. It is here perhaps that we are most conscious of Apuleius as an explorer in his *genre,* feeling his way towards our current notion of presenting a personality in the round. For instance, he aids our imagination by giving us full details of his hero's colouring and height . . .—an elementary trick, to be sure, but one seldom found in classical Latin. We can moreover discern in Lucius, both as man and donkey, qualities other than the curiosity which chiefly distinguishes him: he appears in situations that illustrate his good nature and good manners, his self-consciousness and simplicity, and his rather endearing lack of heroism. Lucius is, in short, nearer to a character in modern fiction than he is to an Aeneas. It is true that the character does not develop: a later author would have delighted in showing psychological changes in Lucius under his sufferings. But at least there is consistency, and to maintain this in such unusual circumstances is no mean achievement. Present-day writers may plume themselves on their experiments with new types: few have gone so far as Apuleius. His hero for a great part of the book is a donkey. But that is not all—he is a donkey with human thoughts and impulses which must always be restrained by the donkey's capacity for action. So we find him able to describe the theatrical spectacle only because the gates were left open . . . : Apuleius is saying in effect ''I am not such a fool as to leave you thinking that my donkey occupied a seat in the theatre!'' Again, when the ass gallops away from the robbers' den with the maiden on his back, his emotion makes him turn his head to kiss her feet—but he carefully pretends to be seeking an itchy spot on his own skin. (pp. 8-11)

Why, after all, does one author succeed in depicting character while another fails? The most interesting feature of Apuleius' characterization is the clue he provides to this riddle. Reading through his book we cannot fail to observe that no sooner is Lucius transformed than the tempo of the action alters markedly: the pace of the last seven books is, in general, much more rapid. It is precisely where the tempo is slow that characters are alive, which suggests that the best way to create a character is to insert seemingly unnecessary details. Those who on the strength of this statement feel encouraged to begin a character-novel must be warned that the choice of these unnecessary details requires skill: such phrases as, ''He tamped out a cigarette,'' or, ''Miss Silver coughed,'' do less to make

Woodcuts from a 1516 edition of Metamorphoses. *Top to bottom: the transformed Lucius becomes the lover of a wealthy noblewoman; he receives Isis's promise that he will be returned to human form; he begins the final transformation while eating the wreath of roses.*

a character than their fond authors imagine. Apuleius had the requisite skill. We can all imagine dining with Lucius' host Milo, that irritating blend of meanness and good manners, whose conversation is interrogation. We have all encountered a Pythias, the petty official performing his humble duties with a pomposity worthy of a proconsul. But these excellent characters appear early in the novel. Later, when the ass is being hurried from one adventure to another, it is significant that only twice is there any attempt at real characterization: first, in the Cupid and Psyche story, which is notably elaborate; second, when Apuleius delays the progress of the narrative to dwell on a fiendish donkey-boy, one of the most ingenious imps who has ever romped across the pages of literature. For the rest, we meet with rich men, poor men, beggar-men, and thieves, in luxuriant variety, but they flit past too rapidly to do more than give an impression of teeming life and provide historians with material for studying social conditions under the Antonines.

The little flash of seemingly irrelevant detail is not, it must be added, encountered solely in the sphere of characterization. Few Latin authors give us details of an action not significant to their main theme; Apuleius practises no such economy. What housewife does not recognise with delight the action of the market-clerk of Hypata when he shakes up the basket of fish to see those at the bottom . . .? Who has not sat like Lucius on a bed, with feet up and arms twined about his knees . . .? Such trivialities are not important to the plot but—and herein lies their importance—they give us a part in it: we are not merely reading about the experiences of a certain Lucius: we share them.

Unfortunately these touches of everyday life help to account for Apuleius' reputation as a difficult author. A study of Gibbon and Burke would be of small service to a Pole bent on reading Dickens: Cicero and Livy are no more useful in preparing us for Apuleius. But his obscure Latinity cannot be explained only by the fact that he is a novelist: the *Elocutio Novella* [''New Speech''] which flourished during his period sought its models in early authors like Cato and compensated for simplicity of structure by virtuosity in the use of language. To this fashion Apuleius added his own fondness for rhetorical affectation and contrast, so that his style ranges incredibly. . . . (pp. 11-12)

Had Apuleius been discovered last month, too recently to have influenced anyone, it would not make his book one degree the worse—or the better. The traces of his style which may be found in Tertullian, the echoes of his stories in Boccaccio, Cervantes, Lafontaine, and Morris may tell us how widely ***Metamorphoses*** was read but not that it deserved reading. Many a book which comes to us trailing clouds of imitators occupies its honoured place on our curricula because of *their* greatness, not because of its own. Away then with the lists of writers influenced by Apuleius! What of the influences exerted *on* him? . . . Such things, I admit, should be known if the novel is to be appreciated fully. But what of the sources—were there not ancient tales and other writings from which Apuleius gathered themes for his various narratives? Knowledge of them adds nothing to our pleasure in the book. Apuleius did not write for scholars but for the reading public, and the reading public may approach his work with all confidence . . . remembering his own promise in the first chapter: ''*laetaberis*—you will enjoy yourself!'' (p. 12)

Frances Norwood, ''The Magic Pilgrimage of Apuleius,'' in The Phoenix, *Vol. X, No. 1, 1956, pp. 1-12.*

WILLIAM E. STEPHENSON (essay date 1964)

[In the following excerpt, Stephenson explores the function of evil in Metamorphoses.*]*

The comic stories of Apuleius, in ***Metamorphoses,*** are easy to appreciate simply for their brilliant bawdiness and use of ancient comic types—the ardent young man, the clever slave, the old crone, the miser, and so on. But a fuller appreciation is possible if one can see how these stories also reflect the change and development in Lucius, Apuleius' narrator and central character, from his first appearance to his last. . . . The tales he hears and retells, as well as his accounts of his experiences while turned into an ass, are Apuleius' device to reveal the deepening, darkening perception of the world's evil that leads Lucius from one state to the other.

Certainly the stories a man deems worth retelling at various times will reflect his state of mind at those times. As Lucius grows more aware of worldly evil, and as he becomes more and more sure that evil can be averted only by supernatural means, his stories fall into a pattern of ever-greater underlying sombreness. After the first story (of the bewitching of Aristomenes and Socrates), which is intended to set a mood for the enchanted city of Hypata, he begins with tales where the chief emphasis is on supernatural adventure and heroic deeds in the face of death (the stories of Thelyphron and of the bandits). He further tells stories which dwell on human love (Charite, Cupid and Psyche), but with a consideration of love's relationship to death and the enduring life of the soul. Then he goes on to stories which stress the laughable baseness of purely physical attraction (the lover under the tub, the sandals under the bed) and further to stories of the perversion and misery of sex without a spiritual sanction (the fuller's wife, the baker's wife). After his account of the murder of the baker, he begins to tell stories which emphasize the unrelieved misery of *all* life unless there is supernatural guidance and intervention to save man (the feudal despot, the stepmother, the sadistic poisoner). The first desires of young Lucius for adventure and the thrill of sexual love, apparent in the earlier stories, are completely removed by the time Apuleius is through with him. In the end he is truly ready to give up his life to the protecting Isis, when she at last appears to him; he is ready to believe that because Isis has directed him to do so, an act of as little earthly meaning as eating roses can be his salvation, more than a garland, ''my crown to deliver me from cruel fortune . . .'' (Book XI).

If the developing darkness of the stories is due to a growing assumption of overwhelming worldly evil, the prevailing tone of comedy depends no less on an assumption that evil can be averted. A basis of evil for the comedy of Apuleius may not be immediately apparent. The clearest way to indicate such a quality, it seems, is to compare Apuleius with Terence—another, equally notable, writer of comedy in Latin. Apuleius and Terence are similar in that both try in their works to show the education of young men for a better state of being; both consider the struggles of that education to have a ''happy ending.'' Their great difference, outside of purely formal considerations, comes in the way they portray the earthly state of man: the essential capacity for evil of the world surrounding man, and man's relative strength in comparison to ''cruel fortune'' or the blind forces of the world. A second difference is in the nature of their happy endings: Terence gives his young heroes an education for life; Apuleius gives Lucius an education for death.

One might say, drawing on a common division between kinds of tragedy, that Terence writes a comedy of character and Apuleius writes a comedy of fate. For Terence, the moment of comic resolution comes when two discordant forces, two men equally well-intentioned and equally susceptible to folly, meet and through prevailing human goodness move toward a happy concord of social well-being. It is for him a moment of *direction*. For Apuleius, in the comedy of fate, any and all men are single elements hurled against a force of crushing evil absolutely unknown in Terence. Apuleius' moment of comic resolution comes when a man in some miraculous fashion is able to avoid, more or less briefly, mankind's fated misery and destruction. His moment is, in the fullest sense of the word, one of *diversion*.

Perhaps this point can be illustrated best by comparing the details with which the two writers develop comic deceptions. Terence's deceptions are instigated by youths and their familiar slaves, in rebellion against parental authority. They learn to be better men and citizens by trying their tricks—which are played out in front of the family home, as innocent as sidewalk games. The deceptions only comically turn against the perpetrators, as in *Heautontimorumenos,* where the trick is perceived by the father supposed to be deceived. In the end both old and young are reconciled and a better ensuing state of life is promised.

But in the tale of the sandals under the bed from ***Metamorphoses,*** which has the standard Terentian characters of lover and mistress and slave-accomplice, the lover is an audacious, unrepentant adulterer and both slave and erring wife bend to his will entirely for money: "according to the light nature of women, when she heard him speak of so great a sum, (she) put her chastity in pawn to the vile money. Myrmex, seeing the intent of his mistress, was very glad, and hastened to the ruin and breaking of his faith . . ." (Book IX). There is nothing jocund about the conduct of the cuckolded husband: "Barbarus went through the street towards the justice with a countenance of fury and rage, and Myrmex fast bound followed him weeping . . . he cried bitterly and called upon the mercy which availed him nothing . . ." (Book IX). Myrmex, having done real evil, is in real danger of death. Only the comic chance of a successful lie diverts the danger from him. There is no improvement of the situation, and no feeling that the same situation will not arise again with a dire outcome for one or all of the characters.

The barely-submerged threat of real cruelty and evil, together with a first suggestion that only the divine can subdue them, is to be found in the important early scene of deception in ***Metamorphoses,*** when Lucius is hauled from the bed of Fotis to be tried before the tribunal of a strange town for a drunken triple murder. He panics, and with good cause: he remembers stabbing at three men in the dark. He is appalled to see instruments of death by torture prepared before the trial is over. Faced with the rack and red-hot iron, he grovels in terror while the townsmen laugh merrily. Then, forced to uncover with shrinking hand what he thinks are the corpses, he finds that he has abased himself to the dust before three inflated wineskins. It has all been a practical joke. While the assembled town roars with laughter, he bursts into tears of relief and shame.

He is told: "put away then all sorrow out of your heart and banish this anguish of mind: for this day (is the one) we celebrate once a year in honour of the god Laughter . . . he will not suffer that you should be sorrowful, but he will diligently make glad your countenance with serene beauty." (Book III) Young Lucius has come too near death by popular demand, too near the fate of many a convenient scapegoat far from home, to treat the deception as a jolly joke. He can only withdraw, and brood. It is true, however, that the gift of laughter and a detached point of view (as one might say, the presence of the divine Risus) *does* protect Lucius until he humbly and seriously becomes the ward of Isis in the last book.

To be sure, Apuleius' Risus is a cruel god and demands frequent sacrifice. In the Apuleian world, even at the moment of highest comedy, someone is being hurt. Furthermore, the danger of being hurt is greater in Apuleius than in Terence because his world is so much larger and of such different contour. In Terentian geography one has a street, leading one way to a harbor and the other way to a public square; in its furthest extension the street leads out to the country residence of the *paterfamilias*. But Apuleius leads one down a road through a wilderness, past the uncanny toward the unforeseeable. After Lucius is transformed into an ass, he goes forth into a world unimaginable within Terence's city limits: among other things, he sees a despot intent on seizing another man's goods and land in open contempt of Roman law (a far cry from Demea's humorous badgering of Micio, in *Adelphoi,* to part with his wealth) and a centurion of uncomplicated brute ruthlessness (utterly unlike the bumbling soldier Thraso in *Eunuchos*). In Terence the city street has been familiar since childhood; but the city of Hypata is never home to Lucius in ***Metamorphoses***—instead, it has a fearful attraction because it is known as the weirdest nest of witches in Thessaly. In Terence a young man goes to the country to avoid his captious mistress; in Apuleius the girl Charite is found in the country because she has been ravished away from her home by marauding brigands.

The idea that the road leads forever *onward* comes as the saving grace in Apuleius. Only the feeling that all things are momentary, an incident in passing, makes each moment one of comedy rather than of tragedy. The story of Charite is probably the fullest illustration of this point. Where the young men of Terence's plays seemed to emit a glow of good spirits which protected them against any mishap, the innocence of youth is nakedly vulnerable to the evil at large in ***Metamorphoses.*** Only a further moment of life brings hope: Charite is abducted, but hopes to escape; her escape is a failure, but she hopes for rescue; she is rescued, but a rival to her bridegroom Tlepolemus kills him like an animal. If death ended hope, it would be a grim tale indeed. But death in Apuleius is the beginning, not the end, of real hope. Lucius has already told of the corpse reanimated in the tale of Thelyphron, to bring justice to his murderer; Apuleius shows, also, in the tale of Cupid and Psyche that lovers may be united in the afterworld. Now when Charite's husband is murdered, he comes back to her as a spirit, his love unchanged and the essence of his being. She joins him in death, which becomes a "happy ending" of spiritual fulfillment.

It is hardly too strong to say that the whole idea of intervening gods and a waiting afterworld is Apuleius' chief comic device, for it is the highest "diversion" he knows from the evil surrounding man on earth. Death for him never has tragic finality. He may thrust his lovers into an earthly chamber of horrors—pretty, gentle Charite raves and screams in anguish at her husband's death, guilefully deludes the murderer with a mask of turpitude, drugs and mutilates him, then kills herself—but instead of a black ending at that moment, Apuleius points down a road of escape to "blessed release."

The idea of being reunited in a life after death, which ends the story of Charite, is generally considered basic to the "Oriental" religions of the Mediterranean area, whether the Isis cult of Apuleius or that religion Yeats says in "Two Songs from a Play" grew out of the "fabulous, formless darkness" around a virgin and her Star; for much of the world since the time of Christ, the catastrophe of death has been the only finally happy ending. Viewing death as a gateway to a better world allows Apuleius a sojourner's humorous tolerance of conditions, and the witty, detached tone recurrently found in his observations. One may see emerging in ***Metamorphoses,*** indeed, the world view which was to be expressed again more than a thousand years later in Chaucer's ending to *Troilus and Criseyde* when Troilus has gone up to "the eighthe sphere":

> And down from thennes faste he gan avyse
> This litel spot of erthe, that with the se
> Embraced is, and fully gan despise
> This wrecched world, and held al vanite . . .
> And in hymself he lough right at the wo
> Of them that wepten for his deth so faste . . .

Lucius never ceases to need such a road of escape. Only the promise of a new life buoys him up in his later days, not any contentment to settle down to worldly society in the Terentian fashion. In the incidents he relates about himself, as much as in his stories of others, he shows a never-lightened assumption of helplessness before the world's evil. Several times he exercises his increasingly penetrating sense of right and wrong, and tries to speak out against the evil he sees. But what happens after his transformation to an ass, when he is stolen by thieves? "And on a time when it was high day, as I passed through a village . . . where was a great fair, I came amongst a multitude, and I thought to call upon the renowned name of the Emperor in that same Greek tongue, and I cried out cleverly and aloud, "O," but "Caesar" I could in no wise pronounce: but the thieves, little regarding my unmusical crying, did lay on and beat my wretched skin in such sort, that after it was neither apt nor meet for leather nor sieves." (Book III) In other episodes, such as his denunciation of the perverted eunuch priests in Syria, he has no better success.

The attempts of the transformed Lucius to act in the name of right and justice fail as completely as his attempts to speak words of condemnation. After he carries off Charite in an attempt to escape the bandits, he is foiled because the girl tries to pull him by force onto the road the bandits use. Charite is recaptured, Lucius is beaten and led back to camp with a sore hoof, and there an old woman has hanged herself because she let the girl escape.

Again, when the ass steps on the fingers of the young lover in order to expose the infidelity of the baker's wife, the result is a forcible act of perversion upon the adulterous young man, then a beating for him, then the murder of the baker by his wife through witchcraft, and finally the dissolution of the household by the grieving daughter.

Even when Lucius finally impresses his latest owner with his "human" qualities, the man only values him as a performing animal, an amusing sport thrown out by nature. The human spirit of Lucius overcomes the abyss between species of animals. He achieves union with a woman. Their night of love at least comes close to being believably tender because of Lucius' new perception of the emotions on both sides. One might say the ludicrous physical coupling is exalted by the union of the spirits involved, that truly the entire scene is of a higher order than the youthful sexual battle between Lucius and the maidservant Fotis in the first book, which he described as an exciting though tiring sport.

But the result, as always, is pain and disappointment and need to escape—because the owner's slave, who was a witness to the episode, reveals it to his master. The master, in turn, can think only of revealing the animal's trick (as he considers it) to the world in the public theater. Since Lucius' partner is too noble a lady to "perform" publicly, the new sweetheart chosen for him is a depraved murderess who is to go from his embrace to the jaws of a lion, to make a public amusement. Lucius' final moment of "diversion" from earthly misery comes when he escapes one more time, and is allowed to swear devotion to Isis by the edge of the sea.

Much of Apuleius' view of the evil world, developed gradually in Lucius and the stories he tells, is also presented briefly and intensely in the central tale of Cupid and Psyche. In Psyche exists all the weakness of character, together with its endearing sweetness, which one perceived little by little in the young Lucius. Like Lucius she is fond of human beings, however dubious in character, to the point of peril. Like Lucius, she is curious about the supernatural forces which surround her, and suffers more than once from meddling with them. Like Lucius, she finally learns to give up the earth entirely.

Both Cupid and Psyche must find their "happy ending" in the rarefied retreats of Mount Olympus, not in any city of men. Nowhere in the world, though at different moments he can summon up a palace of surpassing beauty from the earth and can harness the West Wind, can even Cupid be safe from the evil the world does. The power of evil rages beneath all beauty: before Psyche's sisters ruin themselves and die like beasts on the rocks of the cliff, they first invade and destroy the happiness of the lovers in their magical solitude, and scar Love himself by inciting Psyche to spy on him with a lamp.

In the abode of the gods, to be sure, Psyche is first met by the rage of Venus—affronted as goddess and mother. But the difference is clear: now it is Psyche's misfortune which is momentary, not her felicity. No earthly ants have been known to sort out spilled grain to help a maiden; on earth they would bear it away for themselves. No earthly green reeds would warn Psyche of the dangerous golden flock; on earth, they would bend silently. In the afterworld, for the first time, man's surroundings work for him rather than against him.

The romance of Cupid and Psyche, like Terence's comedies, ends in marriage and birth. The story of Lucius, unlike anything in Terence, ends in withdrawal from the world into holy mysteries. But both rely alike on a belief in divinity able to place men outside the power of earth's evil; this is always Apuleius' final escape, whether for Psyche or Lucius or Charite, and is the basis of his comic view of the world. Where Terence says that if man will do right then right shall be returned to him, Apuleius says that man's only hope is to substitute, for rights and duties, rites and devotions. Only as the priest of Isis, secure in the goddess' promise of a better life to come, can Lucius finally say to his audience what the celebrants at the festival of Risus first said to him: laugh at the moment's anguish, and "put away then all sorrow out of your heart." (pp. 87-93)

William E. Stephenson, "The Comedy of Evil in Apuleius," in Arion, *Vol. 3, No. 3, Autumn, 1964, pp. 87-93.*

C. S. LEWIS (essay date 1964)

[Lewis is considered one of the foremost Christian and mythopoeic authors of the twentieth century. Indebted principally to George MacDonald, G. K. Chesterton, Charles Williams, and the writers of ancient Norse myths, he is regarded as a formidable logician and Christian polemicist, a perceptive literary critic, and—most highly—as a writer of fantasy literature. Lewis also held academic appointments at Oxford and Cambridge, where he was an acknowledged authority on medieval and Renaissance literature. A traditionalist in his approach to life and art, he opposed the movement in modern criticism toward biographical and psychological interpretation, preferring instead to practice and propound a theory of criticism that stresses the author's intent, not the reader's presuppositions and prejudices. In the following excerpt, he discusses On the God of Socrates, *focusing on Apuleius's exposition and interpretation of Plato's concept of demons and noting as well Apuleius's importance as a conduit of Platonic thought.]*

[Apuleius] is now usually (and deservedly) remembered for his curious romance, the ***Metamorphoses*** or ***Golden Ass.*** For a medievalist, however, his essay ***On the God of Socrates*** is more important.

Two passages from Plato underlie it. One is in the *Apology* . . . , where Socrates explains why he abstained from political life. "The reason," he says, "is one you have often heard me mention. Something divine and daemoniac . . . happens to me. . . . It has been so ever since I was a boy. There comes a voice which, whenever I hear it, always forbids something I am about to do, but never commands."

"God" and "daemon," as present here in their adjectives "divine" and "daemoniac," may be synonyms, as, I take it, they often are for other Greek writers both in prose and verse. But in the second passage [from the *Symposium*] . . . , Plato draws a clear distinction between them which was to be influential for centuries. Daemons are there creatures of a middle nature between gods and men—like Milton's "Middle spirits—Betwixt the angelical and human kind." Through these intermediaries, and through them alone, we mortals have any intercourse with the gods. . . . [As] Apuleius translates it . . . , no god converses with men. The voice that spoke to Socrates was that of a daemon, not a god.

About these "middle spirits" or daemons Apuleius has much to tell us. They naturally inhabit the middle region between Earth and aether; that is, the air—which extends upwards as far as the orbit of the Moon. All is, in fact, so arranged "that every part of nature may have its appropriate animals." At first sight, he admits, we might suppose that birds provide the "appropriate animals" for the air. But they are quite inadequate: they do not ascend above the higher mountain-tops. *Ratio* demands that there should be a species genuinely native to the air, as gods are to the aether and men to the Earth. I should be hard put to it to choose any single English word as the right translation of *ratio* in this context. "Reason," "method," "fitness," and "proportion" might all put in a claim.

The daemons have bodies of a finer consistency than clouds, which are not normally visible to us. It is because they have bodies that he calls them animals: obviously, he does not mean that they are beasts. They are rational (aerial) animals, as we are rational (terrestrial) animals, and the gods proper are rational (aetherial) animals. The idea that even the highest created spirits—the gods, as distinct from God—were, after their own fashion, incarnate, had some sort of material "vehicle," goes back to Plato. He had called the true gods, the deified stars . . . , animals. Scholasticism, in regarding the angels—which is what the gods or aetherial creatures are called in Christian language—as pure or naked spirits, was revolutionary. The Florentine Platonists reverted to the older view.

The daemons are "between" us and the gods not only locally and materially but qualitatively as well. Like the impassible gods, they are immortal: like mortal men, they are passible. . . . Some of them, before they became daemons, lived in terrestrial bodies; were in fact men. That is why Pompey saw *semidei Manes,* demigod-ghosts, in the airy region. But this is not true of all daemons. Some, such as Sleep and Love, were never human. From this class an individual daemon (or *genius,* the standard Latin translation of *daemon*) is allotted to each human being as his "witness and guardian" through life. . . . (pp. 40-2)

[***On the God of Socrates***] illustrates the sort of channel through which scraps of Plato—often scraps which were very marginal and unimportant in Plato's own work—trickled down to the Middle Ages. Of Plato himself they had little more than an incomplete Latin version of a single dialogue, the *Timaeus.* That by itself, perhaps, would hardly have sufficed to produce a "Platonic period." But they also received a diffused Platonism, inextricably mixed with neo-Platonic elements, indirectly, through such authors as Apuleius. . . .

In the second place, Apuleius introduces us to two principles—unless, indeed, they are really the same principle. . . . (p. 43)

One is what I call the Principle of the Triad. The clearest statement of it in Plato himself comes from the *Timaeus:* "it is impossible that two things only should be joined together without a third. There must be some bond in between both to bring them together." The principle is not stated but assumed in the assertion of the *Symposium* that god does not meet man. They can encounter one another only indirectly; there must be some wire, some medium, some introducer, some bridge—a third thing of some sort—in between them. (pp. 43-4)

The other is the Principle of Plentitude. If, between aether and Earth, there is a belt of air, then, it seems to Apuleius, *ratio* herself demands that it should be inhabited. The universe must be fully exploited. Nothing must go to waste. (p. 44)

C. S. Lewis, "Selected Materials: The Classical Period," in his The Discarded Image: An Introduction to Medieval and Renaissance Literature, *Cambridge at the University Press, 1964, pp. 22-44.*

L. A. MacKAY (essay date 1965)

[In the following excerpt, MacKay considers the moral and spiritual intent of Metamorphoses.*]*

[At] what was Apuleius aiming [in his ***Metamorphoses***], Apuleius, rhetorician and Platonist? Not primarily at satire, though the narrative is enlivened by numerous satirical touches. Certainly not satire against priests and quacks; only one group of priests, in one episode, is attacked, and only one quack, in a minor story, not really involving Lucius. One might be tempted to imagine a suggestion that becoming a priest of Isis and Osiris is only another way of becoming an ass; but if Apuleius had meant this, he is not so inexpert a writer as to have failed to make it clear. No considerations of prudence could operate to make him veil his meaning; the religion of Isis was tolerated, but even Julius Ceasar did not attempt to make it official. It is closer to the mark to suggest that the book is a satire on a whole state of society, on the idea expressed by Apuleius' contemporary, Aelius Aristides, that the age of the Antonines was a second Golden Age. But the Psyche story, and the Eleventh Book, go beyond this.

We must also reject the idea that the central theme is a conflict between magic and religion, as avenues of understanding, that this is the symbolism involved when Lucius becomes an ass in the attempt to become an owl. Athena's bird is the *noctua* [''night owl'']; Lucius' bird is the *bubo* [''horned owl''], an ill-omened fowl, always connected with the deities of the underworld. They have nothing in common, not even a generic name; Latin has no generic name corresponding to ''owl.'' Magic is not presented as in any sense a true competitor of religion; magic does not attempt to understand the universe, but merely to manipulate available portions of it for an immediate and selfish purpose. The true alternative to Divine Providence is Fortune, blind Chance. As [Piero] Scazzoso has pointed out [in *Le Metamorfosi di Apuleio*], magic is prominent in the stories that precede the tale of Cupid and Psyche; the stories that follow it turn rather on Fortune, with little or no emphasis on magic. Scazzoso has stressed particularly the themes of curiosity and eroticism, both of them obviously and unmistakably important. More must be said, however, of a theme on which he touched, without fully developing its significance.

Curiosity has more than once been cited as the binding theme, the common and capital fault of both Lucius and Psyche. It is certainly a prominent motif in both stories; but it has always been hard to reconcile a distrust of curiosity with the lively and varied interests of the author of the ***Apology***. Nor is any contrast exploited between the improper curiosity of the magician, and the scientific curiosity of the philosopher.

It is true that magic, the attempt to command the powers of the universe for selfish ends, is rejected for religion, a willing submission to these powers. This is quite in keeping with Apuleius' Platonism; and here, surely, lies the heart of the matter. The myth of Psyche, told at such length, and given central position in the book, does provide its central and unifying theme. For the real fault of Psyche, from beginning to end of the story, is disobedience, self-will. Her curiosity is a manifestation of disobedience. From beginning to end, disobedience gets her into trouble, and obedience brings happiness. The human soul, in its arrogant self-will, rebels against, offends, and wounds the divine Love, but by a long and painful return to obedience, it is redeemed and reunited. Over and over again, from the beginning of the book, it is Lucius' stubborn self-will, in the face of repeated warnings, that gets him and others into trouble. A clear and obvious hint has been curiously overlooked; for the dominant and distinguishing characteristic of the ass in literature, from Homer on, and probably long before Homer, has been precisely stubbornness. Lucius as an ass is by no means stupid, but always stubborn and wilful. This is what is punished, and this is what is abandoned on conversion; this is his final metamorphosis, his regeneration. The moral of the story, a moral not at all surprising in a Second Century Platonist, is that power and wealth and all self-seeking are fatal to the soul—prosperity in itself brings danger, as we see particularly clearly in the end of the wanderings, where the resumption of a life of self-indulgence brings Lucius to the brink of a particularly distasteful and disgraceful death. His sufferings as an ass had taught him nothing. Only in a life of voluntary poverty, chastity, and submission to the divine will, can genuine happiness be found. This is something neither earned nor learned, but the free gift of divine grace, in answer to the suppliant's appeal. Apuleius' philosophical studies had led him to the conviction that the only logical alternative to a world ruled by divine providence is a world ruled by blind chance, and the stories of Books Seven to Ten show what kind of world that is, a world where, as often as not, the evil prosper and the good suffer, quite haphazardly. The whole book is an extended myth for the edification of the world ''whose culture from ancient times had taught that the end of man on earth was physical enjoyment and material success, and that the human body was a delightful instrument of pleasure'' [G. Downy, *Antioch*].

It would be absurd to claim that the theme of undue self-confidence monotonously dominates all the incidents. Some of them, like the scene in the fish-market, are told only for their comic value. This scene does build up the idea of Lucius as a man dogged by misfortune; but in this case he shows too little rather than too much self-assertion. At most, it shows the vulnerability of a man who has not yet accepted, or been granted, divine guidance. The same may be said of his experience in the Festival of Laughter; though certainly he had displayed a considerable degree of drunken self-confidence in attacking, as he thought, three robbers single-handed, his action was intended as a generous and decent defence of his host's house. He was more fortunate than the brothers who attempted to defend the poor man against his rich neighbor . . . ; but their story is part of the demonstration of the impotence of virtue in a world ruled by Chance.

Yet the transformation to an ass results from Lucius' obstinacy in disregarding the warnings of Byrrhaena, as he had earlier disregarded the warnings implicit in Aristomenes' tale, and from his headstrong insistence on personally experiencing the effect of magic rites. His is not an arrogant, heroic, tragic self-confidence, but an innocently gullible comic self-assurance which exposes him defenceless to the malice of Fortune, and requires the protection of divine guidance. The art of Apuleius lies in turning the comic motif into something of serious importance, in making Lucius, precisely because he is not heroic and exceptional, into a figure of Everyman, faced with the choice between, on the one hand, ruinous self-assertion in a world governed by Fortune, which delights in striking down the self-assertive, and even the good (consider the fate of the vigorous and active leaders in the robber-stories and the generous initiative of the young men in [Books VIII and IX. . .], and on the other hand, pious submission to the guidance of a benevolent Providence, a guidance which cannot be merited, but can be accepted. All Lucius' attempts to pluck the redeeming roses by his own initiative were frustrated; release was rapidly and promptly given in answer to humble prayer. There is no question of merit, of ''salvation by works''; all that Lucius has learned, and all that he needed to learn, is humility. He is justified by faith. This is Apuleius' version of the doctrine of ''election,'' which he had not the intellectual vigor, nor the background, to develop into a full theory of predestination.

It is a curious accident that two hundred years later another North African rhetorician and philosopher—a better philosopher, though a less brilliant rhetorician—reworked the basic idea more tellingly. In spite of the deliberate reference in Book Eleven to the ''man from Madaura,'' in spite of the genuine piety of that book, we cannot regard the ***Metamorphoses*** as a *Confessions*. Apuleius appears to have ended his life not in pious and abstemious retirement at a convent of Isis in Rome, but in full enjoyment of the world at Carthage. The ***Metamor-***

phoses then is not a spiritual autobiography; it is not really a picaresque, satirical, or moralizing novel; it is an extended myth, with a rambling but real unity, though Apuleius was no more able than Herodotus to resist a good story, whether of his own invention or of another's, and was keenly aware of the importance of variety and contrast in narration.

The book remains an important document in the spiritual history of the latter half of the Second Century, an age seeking direction. The old civic religion was bankrupt, the Olympians figures of fun, the immigrant Asiatic deities often figures of fear. Bankrupt too was the confident—or rampant—humanism that the age following the Great Age of Greece had bequeathed to the Great Age of Rome. The superficial security and prosperity of the Second Century of the Empire overlay a deep insecurity and destitution, both material and moral. Apuleius was no reformer, but he was a sensitive observer. His artist's intuition presages the breakdown and recovery of the succeeding century, though neither intuition nor calculation availed him to identify the predominant auspices under which that recovery was to be effected.

The ultimate significance, the serious burden, of his story finds an unexpected echo more than a millennium and a half later, in a time of security equally deceptive, of prosperity equally ill-distributed, of spiritual malaise equally distressing and perplexing, in the words of Cardinal Newman:

> I loved to choose and see my path; but now
> Lead Thou me on.
> I loved the garish day, and, spite of fears,
> Pride ruled my will.

Lucius, like Psyche, finds true happiness and that peace which the world cannot give, in the surrender of self-will to divine love. Psyche, too, we should remember, was required to forsake the world, including her own family, to enter into salvation.

Yet no one, I think, can read the ***Metamorphoses*** without feeling that the prayer of Apuleius is still, "Give me chastity and continency, only not yet." The book, for all its religious message, is not a precursor of *Pilgrim's Progress*. It is a precursor of *Candide*. (pp. 476-80)

L. A. MacKay, "The Sin of the Golden Ass," in Arion, *Vol. 4, No. 3, Autumn, 1965, pp. 474-80.*

BEN EDWIN PERRY (essay date 1967)

[*An American academic and critic, Perry was one of the most provocative and original classical scholars of the twentieth century. In the following excerpt, he notes innovations in the narrative structure of* Metamorphoses *and examines Apuleius's contribution to the development of prose narrative.*]

[The] modern reader of the ***Metamorphoses*** can scarcely help feeling that there is something magical about [Apuleius], in the sense that his book is deeply permeated with a spirit of belief in the hidden and marvellous potentialities of nature and human life, and that a kind of alchemy is wrought, as it were, by the very charm of his style, whereby whatever he touches upon, leaden though it may be by nature, is transmuted forthwith into literary gold, illumined with the glamour of poetry or of strange but graphic reality, and spellbinding in its effect upon the reader. Indeed, it is in the realm of style that Apuleius has made his most original contribution to literature; for that style—so highly colored, fanciful, and rococo, so studiously piquant and recherché, and so picturesque, varied, and opulent—is shaped in large measure by his own romantic outlook on the world; whereas the subject-matter of his books is derived in the main from Greek sources, and his knowledge of science and philosophy tends to be as superficial as his interests are wide and scattered. He likes to think of himself as a Platonic philosopher, yet he has no comprehensive grasp of Plato's thought, which he seeks to dish out in packages, and he lacks the temperament necessary for organizing a philosophical system of ideas. He cannot linger long enough on any one thing. He is ever the *desultor litterarum* ["literary leaper"], to use one of his own figures, leaping from one literary horse to another and admiring his own dexterity in so doing. He is less a thinker than a showman; not a painstaking scholar, but a dilettante and a dandy, who likes to hear himself speak on any subject because he does it so gracefully, so copiously and, to all appearances, so learnedly. For him philosophy is composed of secrets relating to the hidden powers of nature and the spiritual world, and he loves to pose before the public as the high priest and interpreter of things which it is bound to admire but does not understand.

The romantic temperament of Apuleius, and that restless spirit which seems to be in endless quest for a revelation of one kind or another, or for communion with the *anima mundi,* the mystic soul of the world which he found adumbrated in Plato, and impersonated in Isis, may be seen in his religious experience. In the ***Apology*** . . . he tells us that he had been initiated into many religious mysteries, which in his day were relatively new and popular cults, evangelistic and ecumenical in character as compared to the older cults of the city state, and for the most part oriental in origin; and in the eleventh book of the ***Metamorphoses,*** where he identifies himself almost completely with the protagonist Lucius, he describes his initiation into the mysteries of Isis with an eloquence deeply inspired and made beautiful by the force of a living religion. Here the pantheistic spirit of the second century and of Apuleius himself is brought vividly before us. (pp. 239-40)

The eleventh book of the ***Metamorphoses*** . . . tells how the protagonist Lucius becomes a devotee of Isis, regains human form miraculously through her favor, and is initiated, first into the mysteries of that goddess near Corinth, and later into those of Osiris at Rome, where, finally, he enters upon a career as orator and advocate in the Roman forum, with the necessary encouragement of Osiris, and becomes a priest with shaven head in the service of that deity. From beginning to end this last book of the ***Metamorphoses*** celebrates, in a tone of gravity and high moral seriousness nowhere relaxed, the triumph of revealed religion in a man's life over all other human concerns. It is a personal gospel in which the author intentionally makes it clear to his public that he is testifying on the basis of his own religious experience and conviction; and that "Lucius," hitherto of Corinth but now of Madaura . . . , and an advocate in the Roman forum . . . , is none other than Apuleius of Madaura, who tells us in the ***Apologia*** . . . that he had participated in many religious mysteries in Greece, and in the ***Florida*** . . . that he had carried on his studies (in oratory) at Rome.

Structurally considered in relation to the ***Metamorphoses*** as a whole, Book XI is an artistic unit standing apart by itself in strong contrast to the preceding ten books, with which it is only loosely and outwardly connected, and in which, by contrast, the real nature and *raison d'être* of the ***Metamorphoses***—primarily a series of mundane stories exploited on their own account as such for the reader's entertainment—is to be seen. The contrast in mood and nature of subject matter between the last book of the ***Metamorphoses*** and the ten that precede it is no sharper than that which marks the transition from one story or group of stories to another in the first ten books. Love of variety and the tendency to pass in rapid succession from the contemplation of one wonderful thing to another, with a minimum of logical connection, is profoundly characteristic of Apuleius in all his literary activity. (pp. 242-43)

[The] last book of the ***Metamorphoses*** was added for a very special purpose, quite apart from its interest as an eloquent description of religious experience, and independently of any specific statement or hint concerning the moral of the ***Metamorphoses*** as a whole that an imaginative interpreter may succeed in finding in it. The real purpose, as we have already explained in the preceding chapter (p. 234), was to redeem his book from the appearance of complete frivolity. To publish for sheer entertainment a lengthy work of fiction in the form of dramatically spun-out witch stories, fairy tales, and tales of sensational or scandalous adventure, all of which types of prose narrative were looked upon with disdain by his contemporaries as trivial old wives' tales (*aniles fabulae*), or tales fit only to be told on the street-corner (*aureae fabulae*), was something that Apuleius really *wanted* to do, but did not *dare* to do, without qualifying his work in such a way as would leave the impression that he had, after all, something of serious importance to convey by it, which was instructive, and high-minded, and thereby worthy of an educated writer. Book XI served that necessary purpose, but only in a very perfunctory and superficial fashion. Instead of building into the framework of his story-book as a whole an ostensible meaning in terms of satire, philosophical critique, or allegory which would be evident from start to finish, as is the case in Lucian's novels, Apuleius is content merely to tack on at the end a piece of solemn pageantry as ballast to offset the prevailing levity of the preceding ten books. With his showman's instinct for the value of immediate dramatic effects (which often leads him into self-contradiction elsewhere), he feels that all he needs to do in order to prevent the publication of his old wives' tales from becoming a scandal in the literary world, comparable to that of Aristides' *Milesiaca,* is to make a personal appearance on the stage in the last act, bow deeply and reverently before his audience, and overwhelm them with the magic of his eloquence on a subject of grave and universal import, a subject about which he speaks with earnest conviction and sincerity, but which does not belong with the story of Lucius. (pp. 244-45)

[Stated] abstractly, the changes that Apuleius has introduced in retelling the objectively comic story of Lucius, and other similar stories inserted into its framework, are somewhat as follows. The tone in which the story is told is often much more serious, more moral, and more sympathetic with the thoughts and emotions of the actors, however superstitious or credulous these may be, than in the Greek original [by Lucian]. Indeed the author frequently ascribes what are obviously his own feelings and judgments—moral, philosophical, artistic, and religious—to Lucius and at times, as notably in Book XI, actually identifies himself with the protagonist Lucius. Magic and supernatural phenomena, moreover, are described by the Latin author sympathetically from the viewpoint of the credulous believer in a spirit of awe and wonder, instead of being exhibited objectively and ironically in a spirit of burlesque, as in Lucian's satires. Here the method of Apuleius in dealing with stories of the supernatural differs from that of the Greek author in much the same way, incidentally, as the method of Pliny . . . differs from that of Lucian . . . in telling the story of the haunted house at Athens: the action in outline of the story is the same with both authors, but the Roman Pliny tells it seriously as a miracle that he thinks may be true, while Lucian treats it as farce in a spirit of ridicule. Another innovation which Apuleius makes in his exploitation of the comic novella consists in the lifelike portrayal of character and emotion for its own interest as a principal exhibit in many kinds of persons. Not content with describing outward actions in the objective manner of the Greek original, he makes many changes and additions of his own which serve to illustrate and to bring vividly before us the inner thoughts and feelings of his characters, some of whom have no necessary function in the plot of the main story but are introduced for the sake of their picturesque value. Like Euripides and the modern novelists, but unlike his predecessors in the telling of comic stories, Apuleius is studiously interested in human nature as such, in what Balzac calls the *comédie humaine* and much of his artistic effort is directed to presenting it in various aspects as vividly and dramatically as possible. Viewed broadly against the background of ancient literary history, what Apuleius has done in effect is to transfer to the comic novella the artistic aims and values of fiction which had long been confined to the essentially serious or ideal literary genres, such as epic and tragedy and poetry of various kinds. (pp. 250-51)

We have considered the qualitative changes that Apuleius made in retelling the fundamentally comic stories that he took from Greek sources; but we must not overlook the many serious or ideal stories which he has introduced into the ***Metamorphoses*** and which, as a class broadly conceived, have a very different background in ancient literary convention. These stories in the serious or ideal mood differ from one another: they include the beautiful fairy tale of Cupid and Psyche . . . , which is called a "Milesian" tale because it is an *anilis fabula;* although not in the comic tradition, the tragic story of Charite and Tlepolemus . . . , that of the three poor man's sons . . . , and such sensational stories of crime and atrocity as that of the vengeful stepmother . . . , and that about the multiple crimes of the condemned woman. . . . Before Apuleius such stories as these would have appeared in prose literature (other than the romances) only in an historiographical or a scientific context, and in summary outline. Their length and the limited extent to which they were dramatized in the telling, if at all, would be normally what it is in the paradoxographers, or the mythographers, or Plutarch, or in the collection of thirty-six stories of tragic love excerpted from local histories or summed up from the poets, which was compiled by Parthenius of Nicaea, one of Vergil's teachers, as raw material for the use of his friend, the Roman elegiac poet Cornelius Gallus. On the basis of those documentary outlines of the careers of historical or mythical lovers, Gallus would compose narratives dramatically prolonged with much character analysis and a lively portrayal of the thoughts and emotions of the characters. Ovid does this, for example, with the story of Scylla in his *Metamorphoses* . . . , and so Parthenius himself had done; but all this would be *poetry* in the form and tradition of epic or elegy, not prose. Where Apuleius found the outlines of his tragic or ideal stories, whether in poetic versions, in collections like that of Parthenius, in historiography, or in folklore, we do not know; but the artistic aims and methods that he follows in filling in the outlines so as to produce a dramatic story in the modern conception of that term—as opposed to an abstract summmation of events—are essentially the same as those followed by the poets, except for musical and verbal effects; and the fact that this is done by Apuleius for the first time, so far as we know, *in prose,* marks a new stage in the history of prose fiction in Graeco-Roman antiquity. (pp. 252-53)

In the hands of a writer whose primary purpose is to entertain the reader with a story dramatically told for its own sake, as with Apuleius and many medieval writers, a narration that was originally only a skeleton outline of events in an historiographical, philosophic, or scientific context, is padded and prolonged with the addition of many dramatic details and often with new episodes added either within or beyond the original framework of events. . . . The process by which Apuleius expands and dramatizes stories previously written only in summary outlines and abstractly often involves the addition of one or more originally independent stories as further episodes in the story with which he begins. This multiplies the amount of sheer action in the story, but tends to minimize the logical inner connection between one episode and another, so that each stands out by itself, more or less, in paratactic relation to what precedes. (pp. 253-54)

Preoccupation with the scene immediately before him often leads Apuleius as narrator into self-contradiction or logical absurdity, at times even within the limits of a short space of text. He thinks of one thing at a time in its close-up aspect, ever intent on his showmanship, passing rapidly from one exhibit to another. In so doing he often forgets or ignores as inconsequential something that he had said before about a character or situation, which contradicts what he is now saying, or he disregards the logical requirements of the situation within which a witticism or a sensational act is suddenly projected. (p. 254)

[In Book II of the ***Metamorphoses***], when a group of angry servants make a sudden attack on the character Thelyphron, the latter, speaking in the first person, tells us that the servants "picked up weapons of every kind and went after me; one punched my cheeks with his fist, another dug his elbows into my shoulder blades, another battered my ribs with the palms of his hands, they kicked me, they pulled my hair, and tore my clothes." Now a reader may not notice the incongruity involved in picking up weapons for the purpose of making an attack, then attacking in every possible way except by the use of those weapons; but for an author to narrate an action with such complete disregard of logical sequence is very unusual. And yet it is characteristic of Apuleius. He will say whatever occurs to him at the moment as being dramatic or picturesque, and in the next moment he will forget it in his preoccupation with some other fancy. (pp. 254-55)

[When in Book III of the ***Metamorphoses***] a male servant brings Lucius an invitation to dinner from his elderly kinswoman Byrrhena, verbally delivered, Lucius is made to reply as if he were speaking to Byrrhena herself, instead of to her servant: "How happy I should be to comply with your request, mother, if only honour would permit me to do so. But my host Milo . . ." Here the probability is that Apuleius has simply forgotten the person to whom Lucius is represented as speaking directly; but if one assumes, as some editors do, that these words of Lucius are dictated to the servant as a reply which he intends the servant to report literally to Byrrhena, in that case the failure of the author to tell us so explicitly is no less the result of an absent-minded disregard of plausibility in the circumstances in which Lucius speaks. (p. 255)

[These and other passages] show how negligent Apuleius can be of the context within which he introduces an action, and how completely oblivious he sometimes is of the most elementary considerations of logic, sequence, and probability, even within the limits of a very short space of text. Since that is so, it is all the more to be expected that he will neglect to harmonize discordant and contradictory elements when those elements are more widely separated, and especially when they come from originally independent stories where they had a different function and a different orientation of their own. . . . The strange conflicts in motivation, and the absence of natural sequence, which we find in [the composite narrative of Aristomenes in Book I, of Telyphron in Book II, and in the Risus festival story in Book III, each] made up of two or more originally independent stories, go far to explain the dreamland atmosphere of mystery and unreality which pervades much of the ***Metamorphoses*** in the first four books, and is not inherent in the romantic or miraculous nature of the subject matter itself, nor in the writer's artistic aim. No folktales that I have ever read or heard relating supernatural events, however paratactic or agglutinative their structure may be, have this puzzling contradictory quality which, in Apuleius, results accidentally from the artificial combination of one originally independent story with another and the author's failure to trim and shape his building blocks in such a way that they fit harmoniously into the new structure. (p. 258)

[The three composite stories mentioned above illustrate] certain features of the Apuleian narrative which are profoundly characteristic of the author, and which explain, incidentally and among other things, the unique atmosphere of mystery and surrealism that pervades the first three books of the ***Metamorphoses.*** That mysterious, unworldly effect, in a degree which is elsewhere unparalleled in narrative literature of the West, as far as I know, results from artificially joining together two or more originally independent stories in such a way that elements appropriate to only one or another of the original stories are left standing in the new composite structure, where they are either meaningless or contradictory and lead into blind alleys of motivation. Like other Roman authors who work with Greek originals, Apuleius strives constantly to add something new to a subject matter which he has borrowed and which had already been shaped organically by some other writer. In so doing, and in combining source materials, he retains carelessly, under the dramatic impulse of the moment, instead of eliminating carefully, some of the building blocks used by the original architects which at best are non-functional in his own new and larger structure, and often interfere with it and make it look queer. The reader is consequently puzzled at times to understand just what is going on and what the meaning may be of this or that incident or speech in relation to the larger context of the story as a whole. He looks instinctively but in vain for organic connections between things which the author has not given him, or, if so, falsely and unconvincingly, and which he can find for himself only by the exercise of a very free and hazy imagination. Nevertheless, in spite of its contradictions, the composite Apuleian narrative as a whole is much richer in suspense and dramatic surprise than was any one of its component parts, and that is what the author intended.

The principal aims of Apuleius in retelling a Greek story, and in adding to it, or in making one story out of two or more shorter ones, are to prolong the suspense, add to the amount of action, and to the number of surprises for the reader, and fill out with picturesque and dramatic details that which the Greek author had told in more summary and abstract terms for the sake only of its total meaning, with little or no effort having been made to dramatize the story or to entertain the reader in the process of telling it. The general effect of these Apuleian innovations, the illustration of which, if complete, would require an entire book on the subject, is to create a new kind of story which is more in accord with the modern conception of

From the 1637 French edition of Metamorphoses, *an illustration of the scene in which Pamphile transforms herself into an owl as Lucius secretly looks on.*

what a short story artistically told for its own sake as entertainment should be.

So much for the structural features of the Apuleian story and the aesthetic effects that they produce. More important, for the realization of where Apuleius with his ***Metamorphoses*** stands in the history of prose fiction, is the fact that he has superimposed upon a basically comic, picaresque or satirical narrative, which was something cold and impersonal, the warm ideal values of sympathetic character portrayal which had previously been exploited only in poetry—except insofar as they had spilled over occasionally into historiography and other prose forms wherein they were contraband elements. . . . Consider that what Apuleius did in the second century was precisely the same kind of thing, fundamentally, that Cervantes did later in *Don Quixote,* that Fielding did in *Joseph Andrews* and the Abbé Prévost in *Manon Lescaut*. It is the fusion in those books of two originally separate traditions each with its own proprieties and conventions, the one essentially comic, picaresque or satirical, the other ideal and poetic, that made the potentialities of the novel what they are today, and what they were likewise in Greek literature at the end of the second century. (pp. 280-82)

Ben Edwin Perry, "Apuleius and His 'Metamorphoses'," in his The Ancient Romances: A Literary-Historical Account of Their Origins, *University of California Press, 1967, pp. 236-82.*

KENNETH REXROTH (essay date 1968)

[Rexroth helped pioneer the revival of jazz and poetry in the San Francisco area during the 1940s and 1950s. Largely self-educated, he became involved early in his career with such left-wing organizations as the John Reed Club, the Communist party, and the International Workers of the World. During World War II he was a conscientious objector, but later became antipolitical in his work and writing. While Rexroth's early poetry was greatly influenced by Surrealism, his later verse became more traditional in style and content, though by no means less complex. It was as a critic and translator, however, that Rexroth gained prominence in American letters. As a critic, his acute intelligence and wide sympathy allowed him to examine such varied subjects as jazz, Greek mythology, D. H. Lawrence's works, and the cabala. As a translator, Rexroth was largely responsible for introducing the West to both Chinese and Japanese literary classics. In the following excerpt, he describes the structure, prose style, and allegory of Metamorphoses.]

The accidents of the centuries have left us only two great prose fictions from classical antiquity. They are both in Latin. The much larger body of Greek Romance is definitely inferior, prolix and formularized. We have only fragments of *The Satyricon* of Petronius, but we have all of ***The Golden Ass*** of Apuleius. The complete Satyricon must have been one of the greatest novels ever written. ***The Golden Ass*** is a lesser production, but still a major work.

Apuleius has been called serene and genial, and rightly so. Pythagorean, Platonist, initiate mystic of Isis—he has none of Petronius' secret agony, his melancholy of the rich and corrupt, and none of the Greek Lucian's astringent and atribilious cynicism. It was from Lucian that he took the story of a well-bred but too curious and randy scholar turned into an ass while meddling with witchcraft.

Lucius, the hero of Apuleius' novel, certainly has an abundance of comic and bawdy adventures before he regains his human shape. Ridiculous, horrible, lewd, gruesome—the episodes succeed one another at a dizzying pace; but they are all told with the most innocent humor, the most apparent desire to please. ***The Golden Ass*** is a remarkably good-tempered book, far removed from the solemn or bitter comedy of most great comic writers. Neither *Tristram Shandy* nor *Pickwick* is so easily, so unself-consciously narrated. If Apuleius is a typical representative, the paganism of the period following the collapse of belief in the official religion turns out not to suffer from the "failure of nerve" and "schism in the soul" attributed to it by modern philosophers of history. Quite the contrary. Apuleius is a confident inhabitant of a homogeneous world. There is even less sense of spiritual disunity in his view of life than in a Chinese adventure-romance like the *Water Margin* or *All Men Are Brothers*. It is the Christian Saint Augustine, his fellow North African and contemporary, who is torn and distracted and frightened by the crisis of classical civilization. He writes of Apuleius with admiration and even something close to poorly concealed envy [see excerpt dated c. 413-26].

The plotting of the many adventures of Lucius the Ass may be simple. The prose is not. Petronius, like Ernest Hemingway in our time, made a rhetoric out of anti-rhetoric. Apuleius blows up rhetoric until it explodes. His is one of the most extraordinary styles in all literature, comparable to the fantastic obscurities of medieval Irish, or the invented language of the

Japanese erotic novelist Saikaku, or James Joyce's *Ulysses* or even sometimes *Finnegans Wake*.

The Classicist taste of even the recent past found the prose of ***The Golden Ass*** barbarous, "full of affectation and meretricious ornament and that effort to say everything which prevents anything from being said well." Only Walter Pater knew better, and the fifth and sixth chapters of *Marius the Epicurean,* which include a superlative if somewhat dreamy translation of the Cupid and Psyche episode, is the best appreciation of Apuleius' style until recent times [see excerpt dated 1885]. Today, we who read Latin return far more often to the exuberance of Apuleius than to the carefully molded platitudes of Cicero. Apuleius ends his preface to the reader with the words "Read on, and enjoy yourself." His book was written both to amuse the author in writing and to delight the reader.

Although the Greek romances which he imitated are devoid of characterization, and the plots are strings of the stock situations of serial melodrama, Apuleius, like Petronius, is a psychologist, a quick and accurate portrait painter gifted with that Roman sense of the uniqueness of the individual person which gives Roman portrait sculpture its unforgettable impact. There is actually very little description in ***The Golden Ass;*** yet in the straight narration of events, nights under the stars, robbers roistering in caves, slaves toiling at the millwheel, any number of witches and warlocks and monstrous mysteries all come to life and carry a conviction of reality. Apuleius gives the impression of a photographic fantasy. When we go back and read him over, we discover that this impression is due to the incisiveness of the narrative and not to a descriptive imagism.

The Golden Ass is not just literature of entertainment. Lucius lives in the body of a donkey from June to June, from roses to roses. Inserted early in his story, apparently gratuitously, as a tale told by an old woman to a captive beauty in a robbers' cave, is the story of Cupid and Psyche, an ideal allegory of the soul redeemed by love. Many critics have been unable to account for its presence in the novel. It is not a gracious idyll intruded into a series of coarse and bawdy adventures. It is the distilled concentration of the meaning of the trials and redemption of Lucius, the man who spent a year as an ass. It is the idyllic microcosm of a comic macrocosm, like a pearl in an oyster, a crystalline lattice from which the roughhewn real world of Lucius' metamorphosis is constructed.

The Magic Flute and *The Tempest* are stories of similar import and have been called thinly disguised occult rituals. Critics have denied that ***The Golden Ass*** is an allegory. What story of this kind is not? To the anagogic eye, any tale of man in the grip of vicissitude is a re-enactment of the Great Mystery. Certainly Lucius the Ass goes through the Zodiacal houses of the Perils of the Soul and is about to play the role of the sacrificed king in an obscene and comic *hierosgamos,* a parody mystic marriage, when he is saved from all his trials in animal form, transformed into a better man, and devoted to Isis, the queen of heaven.

Even though his hero is saved, Apuleius cannot quite stop his good-humored mockery. There is the subtlest irony in his description of the way the priests mulct Lucius of all his money in one expensive initiation after another: with the result that after he has become an impoverished devotee of Isis of the third degree, he then forms such profitable connections that he ends up richer than before—not at all unlike a modern businessman or lawyer member of a fraternal organization. Irony or no, the final chapters of the book are the purest expression of Late Classical ritual mysticism—more moving, more illuminated than Plutarch's essay on the cult of Isis. Over the page of Apuleius lies the radiance of his own deep, unbreakable happiness, and his metamorphosed donkey on his comic pilgrimage shares with Christian of *The Pilgrim's Progress* the abiding sense of joy of the saved. (pp. 116-20)

Kenneth Rexroth, "Apuleius, 'The Golden Ass'," in his Classics Revisited, *Quadrangle Books, 1968, pp. 116-20.*

WILLIAM R. NETHERCUT (essay date 1969)

[Nethercut is an American academic and classical scholar. In the following excerpt, he analyzes themes and motifs that organize the diverse episodes of Metamorphoses *into a unified narrative, one which follows the spiritual progress of Lucius from his early encounter with Fotis to his ultimate reception into the cult of Isis.]*

Lucius' affair with Fotis, the maidservant of Milo's house, deserves the most careful attention. Although his interest in her is largely ancillary to his desire to gain first-hand experience in magic, and even if it is the witch herself whom Lucius intends to observe, Fotis, too, emerges as a supernatural female figure who proves of greater importance for the hero's future. Some adumbration of Fotis' lamian characteristics can be discerned in the way in which Lucius states his decision to approach the girl: "Although I may not fare well" (*licet salutare non erit . . .*), "let's see where we can get with Fotis." Additional levels of meaning for *salutaris* ["salutary"] become manifest in later books. If Lucius is thinking here only of a possible *échec* ["repulse"] amidst his amorous pursuits, yet eventually he will consider what ultimate meaning such a life holds in store and what *salvation* there can be from the existence he had followed. (pp. 98-9)

Circe-like, Fotis is of major assistance in preparing Lucius spiritually for passage into another world. . . . Few incidents in Latin literature tempt the imagination more [than the *Risus* episode, the "Festival of Laughter"]. Returning home to Fotis late at night, Lucius finds three bandits trying to break down the gate to his quarters. He attacks and kills them all. The next morning he is put on trial before everyone for murder, and, confronted with the draped bodies, is about to be sentenced. Forced to unveil them, he finds, however, nothing but three goat-skin bags. Suddenly his ears ring with laughter—the whole city bursts out in an uproar. The incredible change here from death to farce is chilling and almost mocks the comprehension.

It would be a mistake to try to clarify how this set of circumstances unfolds naturally and logically from what has taken place thus far in Lucius' story: first of all, the author has set us in an enchanted city, thus absolving himself of any responsibility for the events of his tale to "make sense." More important is the distinction between narrative that is purely discursive and that which functions dramatically for the whole. It is his skillful manipulation of the latter which allows Cervantes, in the second installment of *Don Quixote,* far to surpass the effect of his earlier effort. Such incidents as the hidalgo's descent into the Cave of Montesinos, or his encounter with the touring players who perform a wake, are thrust without warning before the reader. It is not really the relation they bear to the material immediately preceding or coming after which is of importance, but the manner in which they go together and join with other episodes (the Don's defeat by the Knight of the White Moon, for instance) to color the mood of that section of the work and to prepare the emotions for what finally develops.

In just such a way does the *Risus* festival ready us and Lucius for his transmutation into a different form and entrance into an "underworld." Aside from the fact that Lucius feels his existence to be threatened and almost at an end, when put on trial, it will be noticed that, shocked by what he has uncovered, he speaks of himself as having died: "But I, as soon as I had lifted the wrap, stood like stone, ice-cold, like nothing so much as one of the other columns or statues in the theatre. Nor did I come up from out of the underworld" (*nec . . . ab inferis emersi . . .*) "before my host, Milo, came to me." It is significant that it is here for the first time that Lucius talks of an actual descent into the nether regions; moreover, although it may be presumed fairly common to refer to the land of the dead in the midst of crisis (cf. the liberal sprinkling of *perii's* [the element denoting "peril," "ordeal," "danger," etc.; translated as "I died" or "I perished"] throughout Latin comedy), yet is seems possible to preserve a distinction between what Lucius says in this instance and the words of Aristomenes in Book 1 . . . , who, contemplating suicide, says only that "the earth parted, and I looked upon the depths of Tartarus" (*me terra dihiscente ima Tartara . . . prospexisse*) and alludes to the fact that he is heading towards the world below (*mihi ad inferos festinanti*). The point is that in this initial scene, which alone is comparable to the present one thus far, the man over whom death hangs does not really find himself within another realm in spirit.

The festival serves to prepare Lucius in another manner. Cast into the depths of horror and disbelief, he finds that misery can be viewed objectively. Man can circumvent evil by refusing to accept its existence or to acknowledge the world's cruelty. This lesson is reenforced in Book 9: an old gardener buys the ass and gives him light work, sharing with him whatever he obtains for his own plate. . . . Our sympathy is attracted. But then a soldier stops Lucius and his master on the road and requires them to serve him. Knocking down the arrogant man, the gardener takes refuge with a friend in the village. They hide Lucius in a room upstairs. When the soldier comes to search the town, he finds nothing. All is about to go well. But again Lucius' thoughtless urge to learn results in harm . . . : he sticks his head out the window to see what is taking place, and is recognized. The soldier confiscates the old man's belongings, and the innocent gardener is carted off to die. . . . Lucius remains detached. He expresses almost no sorrow for his erstwhile friend and keeper, and calmly goes where he is taken without a backward glance. He has learned.

Not only, then, is it appropriate to liken man, credulous and eager to make trial of the unknown, to an animal with long ears, but the very comparison of him to a beast which must be led around, however much it may desire to go off on its own, is fitting. In an unpredictable world in which one has no hope of setting his own direction, there is no choice but to submit and follow the currents of Fortune. It is this necessity of submission which Lucius must come to appreciate before he can approach salvation; it is this appreciation which his days as an ass serve to inculcate. The ass suggests at once the fault and the truth to be acknowledged. And it is during the festivities honoring *Risus* that he is initially confronted with a situation where he is powerless to think ahead and go where he intends. For the first time he is literally dragged and pulled, as lictors, by order of the magistrates, take him before the people. . . . It is worthy of comment that it is at this moment that Apuleius chooses to allude to Lucius as if he were a beast of burden, and pictures his head in a posture which will become all too familiar: "And although I was plodding sadly along with my head cast down to the earth—to the dead below, would be more accurate—" (*capite in terram, immo ad ipsos inferos iam deiecto*) "nevertheless, I looked up out of the corner of my eye.". . .

Having paused thus to reflect on the critical significance of Hypata's celebration of Laughter for the story, we perceive all the more clearly the essential nature of Fotis' role. This is brought to the attention by a striking discrepancy. On the first reading, one easily receives the impression that the whole festival has been carefully planned as a community project. After all, does not Lucius' hostess speak of the citizen body of Hypata as participating together? . . . Besides, the day is one which is observed every year and has been since the city was founded. . . . Yet in fact the peculiar mixture of jollity and terror we have discussed is made possible *by Fotis alone*. When Lucius returns home after the celebration, he discovers that Pamphile had sent out Fotis to a barber shop to gather the cut hair of a young man of whom she was desperately enamored. The barber, however, long since annoyed by women lurking around his premises to pick up human trimmings, told her to be off. Not wishing to disappoint her mistress, Fotis had taken some hairs from goat skins. And so when, thereafter, Pamphile had performed incantation over the hairs, binding their owners to come to her, the goat skins came to knock on the door. It was these which Lucius took for robbers and which he deflated with his sword. In all of this, there was no plan on Hypata's part which could possibly have aimed at implicating Lucius.

Lucius' reply to the apology of Fotis allows us to postulate a symmetrical arrangement of motifs in this part of the ***Metamorphoses:*** "Well then, I can register this triumph of strength as a first on my own account, after the example of Hercules' twelve, likening the skin bags I cut up to the triple body of Geryon, if you will, or, as it may be, to the threefold shape of Cerberus. Their number was equal.". . . By causing Lucius to refer to the occasion on which Hercules went down to the underworld and then returned, Apuleius places allusion to movement from this life to the next near the beginning (. . . Lucius with his head sunk *ad ipsos inferos* ["toward the very depths"]), at the very center (. . . the festival, where he stands still, his spirit in the underworld), and at the conclusion of the events of this day. . . . Secondly, just as Lucius presented himself in the posture of an animal as he was dragged off, head down, to be judged, and just as this suggestion of his bestiality was closely joined with a second suggestion—that of transition into the land of death (*capite in terram, immo ad ipsos inferos iam deiecto*)—even so, to reverse the order chiastically, at the end of the day do we encounter reference to the underworld (just discussed), quickly followed by another reminder that Lucius will pass into his new existence as an animal. (pp. 100-04)

[In Book 3], he finds himself sated and exhausted from that kind of intercourse in which humans normally indulge. His appetites revive at the prospect of sodomy. "Then indeed, although I was already tired from that indulgence which is characteristically appreciated by a man with a woman, Fotis set before me that special source of pleasure which boys learn to master" (*Tum quidem mihi iam fatigato de propria liberalitate, Fotis puerile obtulit corollarium*).

I argue that here Lucius approaches Fotis from behind, like an animal. The Latin is not so clear, saying only that Fotis now leads her lover into a new path, one along which boys lead men. If we consider the possibilities of what *puerile corollarium* might mean, they seem to be three: Fotis provides him additional gratification manually, orally, or anally. If the last is correct, further symmetry exists in the work as a whole:

when Lucius escapes from the stud farm and meets the eunuch priests, the subject of sodomy is raised once more. That is, in Books 3 and 8, approximately the same distance from beginning and end, respectively, we will find allusion to it. What will be more important, as it concerns Lucius' changing role in the work, is the contrast between Lucius, in human shape, loving Fotis in the position of an animal, and, later in Book 10, Lucius the ass, making love to the *matrona* [''married woman''] in *human* position—from the front. . . . [The] facts that Fotis and the *matrona* are the two women with whom Lucius enjoys sex during his travels, and that certain verbal echoes from scenes with the first can be identified in the scene with the second, encourage us in believing that the significant contrast the foregoing similarities prepare us to notice may well be that between a human Lucius loving like a beast, and a bestial Lucius in human posture.

Aside from contributing to the coherence of the whole, the interpretation I suggest appears to be the most logical. Apuleius stresses that what Fotis now does is characteristic of a boy. Manual and oral caresses do not suggest a practitioner of a given sex to the same extent that anal intercourse does.

What Lucius undergoes during the celebration of Laughter, what he now comes to understand of love in the fashion of an animal, he owes to Fotis. When she leads him up the stairs to the attic, it is only one more step, almost less important, following naturally from what has happened up to that time. Long before she hands Lucius the fateful ointment, Fotis has readied him for a different life.

After Lucius has daubed himself with the salve and finds that he can no longer be human in appearance, he is kidnaped by robbers who take him to carry their plunder and lead him upwards, over rough paths, toward their cave. There, enclosed within the earth, the ass will listen to the story of Cupid and Psyche.

In the ***Metamorphoses,*** high places are associated with death. For instance, it will be remembered that Psyche is taken, in accordance with the oracle, to a rock on the summit of a mountain where a deadly wedding will be hers. . . . It is from this same cliff that her envious sisters, after they goad her to look upon the face of her husband, fall to their deaths. And when Venus charges Psyche to draw water from the spring which feeds the Styx, we are told the source cascades darkly from the top of a mountain, while terrible dragons wait below to prevent anyone from coming near. . . . Here we should note that the robbers' cave in [Book 4] is described in just the same manner—water pours from the top of a mountain. . . . When Psyche learns she must go to Hades to obtain beauty for Venus, she becomes so despondent she goes to a high tower intending to throw herself off it. . . . Later on, Lucius, fearing castration, considers leaping over the side of a cliff. . . . (pp. 104-05)

Once more, to turn to the ascent at hand, the journey up to the cave is punctuated by death. Just as Odysseus loses Elpenor, and just as, in a later version, Palinurus or, again, Misenus, are lost to Aeneas—as the sacrifice of a life, in short, is a necessary step in the *rites de passage*—so Lucius witnesses the loss of one of his own kind before he climbs the final hill to the cave. Thinking to free himself of the heavy bags the highwaymen have forced him to carry, he has just decided to sink to the ground and refuse to budge or move one step more; suddenly, a second ass in the train attempts this very thing. The bandits hamstring him and throw him over the side to be crushed on the rocks below. . . . (pp. 105-06)

It has become clear that our tale embodies the sequence, familiar over the world in literature, of the individual's isolation from society and his search for knowledge on the other side of life. In the present instance, the stage has been set with care. But exactly how does the story of Cupid and Psyche relate to Lucius? How may it be said to educate him?

Lucius is exposed to a new definition of love. Central to this experience is the development which takes place in Apuleius' portrayal of Venus and Cupid. Earlier, entranced by the sight of Fotis' luxurious hair, Lucius thinks of Venus closely attended by her son and all the Graces, and then goes on to say that even the goddess of loveliness, were she to promenade bald, would not win a glance from Vulcan. . . . Fotis is compared to Venus at a second moment in the affair, when, with hair tossed into happy disarray, she yields her body to her lover's eyes and drowns his senses with knowledge of her. . . . Then, at the most important juncture of his life, when he will smear himself with the magic ointment, he entreats Fotis to change him ''so that, winged, I may stand at your side, Cupid by my Venus.'' . . .

Two points can be made. Previously, before we hear about Cupid and Psyche, Venus has appeared as tradition presents her—the desirable queen of love who brings ecstasy to her servants. Moreover, in the foregoing part of the book, Cupid and Venus are physically near one another—a harmonious team. Lucius guides his life by this premise; together, Cupid and Venus articulate and mirror his mental and spiritual commitment.

Against this background, it is suggestive to discover that the presuppositions regarding Venus which underlie the account of Cupid and Psyche are very different. At the beginning, Venus is presented with a rival. Word has spread that a second Venus has arisen—not from the sea, but from the earth. No longer is love merely love; no longer do we find reference to an established deity mythologically generalized. Directly at the start a contrast is sharply drawn between the Venus whose orgiastic worship and temple harlots were a reality on islands like Paphus and Cnidus, and a new kind of love and worship which is pure. . . . It is therefore instructive that Cupid disobeys the original Venus and deserts the post he has held beside her up to this point in the story to pursue the newcomer. Lucius has likened himself to Cupid, as we have seen, and it will be interesting to determine whether his conception of love will undergo a similar re-creation in the remainder of the work. In his marriage to Psyche, finally, Cupid becomes something more and higher than himself. Speaking of her feeling for him, Psyche says: ''For I love you and cherish you desperately, whatever your identity, like my own breath; nor would I equate you with Cupid himself''. . . . Desire, for those sympathetic to allegory, is redefined. (pp. 106-07)

[It is fair to set the story of Tlepolemus and Charite] beside the tale of Cupid and Psyche. That they are unequal in length is beside the point: such a reservation seems to stem from an assumption we are dealing with an Augustan author, in which milieu recent criticism has been almost excessively preoccupied to underline numerical balances; and it completely avoids the really significant issue of content and placement in the work. One might object that they are different in nature: ***Cupid and Psyche*** tells of a quest; **''Charite and Tlepolemus,''** of revenge. But their subjects are more importantly alike: they are the two narratives in the ***Metamorphoses*** which have as their concern a love that is pure and abiding. In both, the lovers are separated and suffer on this account; in both, jealousy is the disruptive element, and in both they are reunited, at the end, forever. A third distinction, that whereas the first story lies outside the plot, the second involves characters in it, is valuable; but it is one which actually provides all the better reason for comparing the tales, given the similarities we have just urged. For . . . tales told outside the plot in the ***Metamorphoses*** bear a close relation to events which come to pass soon after. Sometimes the relation is general—more one of mood than of specific detail—e.g., the horror of Thelyphron's adventure paves the way for that terror Lucius experiences during the *Risus* festival; but often the precise order of events is repeated, as we . . . see throughout Book 9 in the case of the baker's wife. And we . . . [witness] an intriguing reversal of the kind, whereby Tlepolemus tells of his escape as a man dressed like a woman (this is "in" the action to the extent that it directly precedes his appearance in the cave) from raids spurred by a woman disguised as a man (an account lying farther from what is taking place before our eyes). (pp. 112-13)

Let us pause briefly to appreciate the degree to which Apuleius' arrangement of subject matter, from the approach to the cave in Book 4 to the trial of the wolves and the night passage to a new land in Book 8, is a model of structural symmetry, with form underlining meaning and serving content in the best Latin tradition. The balance is perfect. The two love stories frame the two spheres in which Lucius moves: he is greeted within the gates of "hell" by the tale of Cupid and Psyche; the last thing that occurs before he departs from the farm is the messenger's account of Charite and Tlepolemus. It would be a mistake, of course, solely to focus on the architectural framework which lends form to this part of the book. Like the brick reenforcement one can see in the Roman *opus incertum* ["unproved work"], which imparts sturdiness to a wall but does not hinder contraction or expansion of the tufa from which the wall is basically made, so chiastic organization (Story—Lucius in the cave—Lucius on the farm—Story) grants definition, but does not limit movement or inhibit the plastic nature of Apuleius' narrative. If there is any constant in either Ovid or Apuleius, it is change and movement, variation. And so the two stories are importantly different. The union of Cupid and Psyche represents an ideal realized, and as such is removed from us, static and immutable; but, as Charite and Tlepolemus accompany Lucius along the road out of the cave, so does their final union, made possible by Charite's renunciation of life, imply motion and points for Lucius along a path which will carry him beyond the bounds of the world. (pp. 114-15)

[It is in the appearance of the goddess Isis in Book 11] that one is impressed by how very truly the story of Cupid and Psyche marks the way for what has now come to pass. In the first place, the promise which warmed the ass' heart in the underworld has come true: a happy ending lies just ahead. As in the story, such an ending would be impossible but for divine intercession. More specifically, not only does Lucius "leave" Venus, in a sense, judging her character adversely; he also (again, like Cupid in the tale) chooses a chaste Venus to attend. To compare Isis with Venus may appear to some extravagant. After all, the first demands abstinence from sexual participation—the great delight of the latter. Yet, just as the early paragraphs of ***Cupid and Psyche*** made the point that the goddess of Paphos and her new rival were both called by the same name among mortals . . . , so it happens, at the conclusion of the book, that Lucius' Isis is, in a very real way, Venus transformed.

This emerges when we think back over the two passionate scenes with Fotis—in the kitchen, and, later, in the bedroom. If the psycho-sexual configuration of the author of the *Satirica* can be termed that of the voyeur or exhibitionist, surely that of Apuleius belongs to the category of souls contemporary analysts denominate "bestial"—one of whose outstanding traits is fascination with hair of all kinds, particularly when it is long and luxurious. One recalls the lengthy digression on the beauties of a woman's coiffure in which Lucius indulges when he first meets Fotis. At this time . . . it occurs to him to speak of Venus, although Fotis is not compared to her directly. The equation of the two is made complete, when . . . Fotis comes to Lucius to spend the night. The passage is worth reproducing:

> I lifted my tunic, and, showing Fotis my inability to withstand Venus' torment, (*impatientiam ueneris Fotidi meae monstrans*) I said: "Have mercy upon me. Come to my aid quickly! (*miserere . . . subueni maturius*) For, as you can see, now that the battle which you took it on yourself to declare between us draws near, I stand ready at my post, drawn up at arms ever since I took Cupid's first arrow as it made its way deep inside me. And he himself now tries my bow and stretches it vigorously, so that I am very much afraid lest the string snap from being drawn so tight. But, that you may satisfy me the more completely, loosen your hair so that it can fall down, and come press me with your embrace, rippling and flowing with what I love."
>
> She obliged readily. Ridding the room of the remains of the meal, and, at the same time, herself of clothes, she shook her hair loose for festive sport. She looked like Venus, who arises from the waves of the sea (*in speciem Veneris, quae marinos fluctus subit*).

All this is closely related to the scene with Isis in Book 11. In both, Lucius prays to a female figure, asking for mercy and aid. These are the only two times he implores a woman's help in the ***Metamorphoses.*** In both, we find a goddess coming up from beneath the ocean. This in itself would be a powerful argument for asking if Fotis-Venus and Isis may not be related. But even more convincing is the fact that, when Lucius starts to tell how the vision of the goddess looked, the very first thing he mentions is her long *hair!*

> *Iam primum crines uberrimi prolixique et sensim intorti per diuina colla passiue dispersi molliter defluebant.*
>
> *("Now, first of all, her tresses were exceedingly thick and abundant. Freed on all sides, they flowed softly down, caught in ringlets, along her perfect neck.") . . .*

(pp. 127-28)

Such a correspondence between the deity of sex and a goddess whose worship requires continence is provocative and may be read in two ways. Within the limits of the story, Lucius' praise of Isis' hair can be taken to show his change of heart. Earlier, he fought in Venus' camp and served her generously tressed priestess, Fotis. That the attractions hair holds for Lucius now belong to Isis underlines the transference of his affections and may be thought to point up his conversion from one manner of living to another, drastically opposed. The appearance of this motif in different parts of the book ties together the ***Metamorphoses*** and is, in addition to (1) the fact that Lucius' journey is continuous, with clearly demarcated stages, in which no incident is without pertinence, (2) the chiastic structure of the major part of the work (not surprising in a story which tells of movement to a point and a return along a similar path), and (3) the relation of Cupid to Venus, to which allusion is made at important moments throughout the whole, one more indication of the highly unified organization it owns.

On another level, hair is a sexual symbol which is permanent in suggestion and exists above the time and days of any story. Thus we can also say that its presence at the revelation Lucius experiences speaks eloquently about the nature of illumination and conversion in the oriental faith cults—namely, that such is made possible by a redirection of the vital urge basic to existence. Whether she is called the queen of Cyprus or "Psyche," whether she be born of the sea or of the land, whether defiled or pure, the goddess, as we are told in ***Cupid and Psyche,*** bears the same name among men. Venus rules both the reborn and the non-believer equally. (pp. 128-29)

William R. Nethercut, "Apuleius' 'Metamorphoses': The Journey," in Agōn, *Vol. 1, No. 3, 1969, pp. 97-134.*

J. L. PENWILL (essay date 1975)

[In the following excerpt, Penwill examines the story of Cupid and Psyche rendered in Metamorphoses, *focusing on its relationship to the main narrative.]*

All have admired the tale of Cupid and Psyche, that long narrative which occupies the central sections of the novel. Its qualities as a fairy story and folk tale have been expatiated upon, its romanticism forms a pleasing contrast to the harsh surroundings of the robbers' cave in which it is told. For a while we feel we can escape from the depressing realities of life in an uncertain world.

Recent work on the tale has concentrated on thematic parallels between it and the main narrative. As with Lucius, Psyche's experience is seen to constitute a fall and subsequent redemption. According to this interpretation Psyche's separation from Cupid, which can be viewed as resulting from her curiosity, is the counterpart of Lucius' transformation; the persecution of Psyche by Venus parallels that of Lucius by Fortune in Books 7-10; and the intervention of Jupiter to resolve the situation foreshadows the intervention of Isis in Book 11. Psyche's trip to the underworld, the fourth of the tasks imposed on her by Venus, is seen as a precursor of Lucius' initiation. And the marriage of Cupid and Psyche at the end of the tale is seen as a resolution of Psyche's troubles, a redemption from the punishment she incurred upon herself as a result of breaking the divine prohibition, the ensuing spiritual joy being represented by the birth of Voluptas (Pleasure); this may be said to parallel the deliverance of Lucius from the toils of Fortune and the spiritual joy which follows upon his commitment to Isis.

There is no denying the obvious and definite thematic links between the Cupid and Psyche episode and the story of Lucius; it is questionable, however, whether these links are to serve the function of turning the episode into a restatement of the novel's main theme. It is hard to imagine what artistic purpose could be fulfilled by such a restatement; and if such were its nature, it would be unique among all the tales contained in Books 1-10. The thematic links are not there to create a *parallel* but to point up a *contrast*—a technique which we . . . see Apuleius employing time and time again, especially with respect to the relation between Book 11 and the rest of the work. The reader is invited to compare the stories of Psyche and Lucius, above all in the light of what happens to Lucius in Book 11; and it is in the comparison that the real significance of "Cupid and Psyche" becomes apparent.

Apuleius seems to go out of his way to emphasize the happy ending of this tale. The old woman who tells it calls it a *narratio lepida* ("pleasant story" . . .), but perhaps the most telling way in which this atmosphere is created is in the obviously intentional similarity between its plot and that of the standard Greek romance. The outstanding beauty of the heroine which leads to her being mistaken for a goddess is one typical romance motif; so is the separation of the lovers involving a series of trials and tribulations. In the end the lovers are always reunited and live happily ever after—and in Psyche's case this final cliché becomes literally true, for by Jupiter's decree she is made immortal. . . . But in this novel where appearances are so often deceptive one must always be on one's guard against being carried away by first impressions. The very emphasis on creating an expectation of a happy outcome should constitute a warning in an author who loves to indulge in surprise and sudden change.

Let us begin by looking at the final sentence . . . :

> Sic rite Psyche convenit in manum Cupidinis et nascitur illis maturo partu filia, quam Voluptatem nominamus.
>
> ("So Psyche was ceremoniously married to Cupid; and when the due time came there was born to them a daughter, whom we call Voluptas.")

All very nice—until we remind ourselves that the names of the protagonists in the tale actually mean something. Psyche of course is the Greek word for "soul," and not unnaturally leads to the conclusion that a story in which she is the heroine must in some way be an allegory involving the soul. Cupido is the Latin word for "desire"; specifically, in the case of the son of Venus, "sexual desire." Finally there is the name of the child, Voluptas, which means "pleasure." Now this last is generally interpreted in the light of the remark by Cicero (*de Finibus* . . .) made in the course of a discussion about the Epicurean doctrine of pleasure:

> Huic verbo omnes qui Latine sciunt duas res subiciunt, laetitiam in animo, commotionem suavem iucunditatis in corpore.
>
> (Everybody who knows Latin attaches to this word two ideas—that of gladness of mind, and that of a delightful excitation of feeling in the body.)

Laetitia in animo, "gladness of mind" or "spiritual joy" is the meaning normally attached to Voluptas here. So Tatum: "The birth of a child with this name, as the happy resolution to the tale of Psyche, represents the soul's discovery of spiritual joy at its deliverance from the power of blind fortune." But there is only one other example of such a use of *voluptas* in the ***Metamorphoses.*** This occurs in Book 11 where Lucius describes his feelings as he contemplates the statue of Isis . . . :

> Paucis dehinc ibidem commoratus diebus inexplicabili voluptate simulacri divini perfruebar.
>
> ("I remained there for a few days afterwards, experiencing the ineffable pleasure of the divine image.")

The extreme nature of the qualification *inexplicabilis,* "ineffable," indicates the novelty of the feeling; it defies verbal expression, renders the *voluptas* Lucius experienced with Fotis quite meaningless. But in all other cases in the novel *voluptas* denotes physical pleasure, especially sexual. Unqualified and coming at the end of a story dominated by Venus and Cupid, it is surely more likely to represent this sort of pleasure than the spiritual. (pp. 50-2)

The terms in which the marriage is described are also interesting. *Convenit in manum* is a legal term signifying that the wife comes into the power and possession of her husband. Now if Psyche is to represent soul and Cupid sexual desire, which is what the words mean, then we have the situation that the soul comes under the domination of sexual appetite. That "redemption" should take this form is a most peculiar notion for a Platonist such as Apuleius to adopt. In Lucius' case, salvation involves a *liberation* from the demands of such desires—so Isis in her epiphany instructs him . . . :

> Quodsi sedulis obsequiis et religiosis ministeriis et tenacibus castimoniis numen nostrum promerueris. . . .
>
> ("So if you deserve well of my godhead through diligent obedience, religious observances and persevering chastity. . . .")

Liberation from the bodily desires which impede the soul from apprehension of the truth is the Platonist's goal: not the binding together of soul and bodily appetite such as the marriage of Cupid and Psyche seems to signify.

At this point we may pause to consider the way in which the tale is usually interpreted in Platonist terms. According to this, Cupid represents Eros, that divine Eros in the *Phaedrus* which motivates the soul towards true imperishable Beauty. The marriage of Cupid and Psyche thus would signify the taking over of the soul by this Eros, and the *voluptas* that ensues is the pleasure of the soul which derives from its contemplation of Beauty in the intelligible world. But there is a significant indication in the tale itself that this is the wrong way to interpret it. When Cupid informs Psyche (in the course of yet another warning against the danger she faces from her sisters) that she is pregnant, he says . . . :

> Nam et familiam nostram iam propagabimus et hic adhoc infantilis uterus gestat nobis infantum alium, si texeris nostra secreta silentio, divinum, si profanaveris, mortalem.
>
> ("For we are now on the way to producing our family and this hitherto childish womb is itself carrying a child for us. If you keep our secret in silence it will be divine, but if you divulge it, mortal.")

This condition is never countermanded. Psyche contravenes it by telling her sisters the truth . . . and by disobeying Cupid's prohibition against trying to see his face. The *voluptas* that is born to them must therefore be the mortal kind, that which results from appetite gratification, rather than the divine which accompanies the contemplation of reality; it denotes the pleasure of the perishable body rather than the pleasure of the immortal soul. The distinction is brought out in Plato's *Republic* Book 9 . . . :

> Those who have no experience of wisdom and virtue, who are always at their feastings and so forth . . . have never been filled with what really is or had a taste of pure and abiding pleasure. Like brute beasts they look ever downwards, and feed stooping over the ground and poking their noses into their tables, cropping and coupling. . . . They fail either to satisfy with real things the real part of themselves, or to fill up that vessel, their body [Translation by W.H.D. Rouse]. . . .

The Voluptas begotten by Cupid is of this animal kind; and Cupid himself represents not the Eros of Socrates' second set speech in the *Phaedrus* but that of the first . . . :

> the irrational desire which overcomes the tendency of opinion towards right, and is led away to the enjoyment of physical beauty [Translation by Benjamin Jowett]. . . .

Support for such an assessment of Cupid's function in the allegory is provided by the way in which the other gods in the story are characterized. It has been observed that the Olympians are being satirized or caricatured in a manner reminiscent of Ovid in his ***Metamorphoses;*** but there is more to it than this. Again a contrast with Book 11 is being invited by means of verbal echo and thematic link. The main comparison of course is between Venus and Isis. Venus commences her jealous tirade against Psyche as follows . . . :

> En rerum naturae prisca parens, en elementorum origo initialis, en orbis totius alma Venus. . . .
>
> ("Here am I, the primeval mother of the universe, the first beginning of the elements, the whole world's 'dear Venus'." . . .)

The educated reader would no doubt smile at the humorous reminiscence of Lucretius' prologue. But the words are almost exactly repeated by Isis in her epiphany to Lucius . . . :

> En adsum . . . rerum naturae parens, elementorum omnium domina, saeculorum progenies initialis.
>
> ("See, I am here . . . the mother of the universe, the mistress of all the elements, first offspring of the ages.")

No longer comic, the repetition serves to point up the utter contrast between Venus and Isis; the portrait of Venus in this tale is such as to destroy any credibility in her as a cosmic force. The jealousy and lust for revenge she displays are as ferocious and destructive as those of Psyche's sisters. Set against this the compassion of Isis. Where Venus displays nothing but hostility and cruelty towards Psyche, Isis offers Lucius salvation and a welcome to the fold; where Venus sees the very existence of Psyche as an affront—indeed a threat—to her position and reacts with hatred and rage, Isis speaks to Lucius with the dignity and calm serenity of one who knows no jealousy because no rival is conceivable. The reaction of Venus to Psyche is to see her as a sexual rival—a natural reaction in one whose confidence in herself is derived not from her status as *rerum naturae prisca parens* ("primeval mother of the universe") but from the fact that Paris awarded her the prize . . . :

> Frustra me pastor ille, cuius iustitiam fidemque magnus comprobavit Iuppiter, ob eximiam speciem tantis praetulit deabus.

> ("In vain did that shepherd—whose impartiality and good faith were verified by great Jupiter—place me ahead of such eminent goddesses because of my exceptional beauty.")

One can discern a definite thematic parallel between Venus and the jealous lovers of Books 1-10 (e.g. Meroe, Thrasyllus and the mass murderess with whom Lucius is to copulate) who wreak fearful destruction on the innocent.

As Venus is to Isis, so Jupiter is to Osiris—though Jupiter's failings do not lie in the region of jealous rage. Indeed he appears as a genial figure at the conclusion of the story to engineer the happy ending. But this "father of gods and men" is himself a slave to passion; he speaks of the erotic desires implanted in him by Cupid as interfering with his cosmic functions . . . :

> Istud pectus meum, quo leges elementorum et vices siderum disponuntur, convulneraris assiduis ictibus.

> ("With continual blows you wound that breast of mine wherein the laws of the elements and the movements of the stars are worked out.")

Like the Lucretian allusion in the case of Venus, this literary commonplace of the king of the gods himself being overcome by love may raise a smile in the educated reader; so may the fact that the condition upon which he agrees to help Cupid is that Cupid must find him another exceedingly beautiful mortal girl—otherwise he may have difficulty keeping his hands off Psyche. But the smile may fade a little when in Book 11 the undignified antics of this playboy figure are contrasted with the serene majesty of Osiris at the close of Lucius' story . . . :

> Deus deum magnorum potior et maiorum summus et summorum maximus et maximorum regnator Osiris. . . .

> ("God more powerful than the great gods and highest of the greater and greatest of the highest and ruler of the greatest, Osiris. . . .")

It is quite plain that the Olympians are being portrayed in a manner which invites comparison with the Isiac deities. Two things may be noted. One is that the tale of Cupid and Psyche constitutes exactly that sort of story about the gods that Plato proscribes in *Republic* 2 and 3, in that it propounds a false notion of divinity. Secondly, that the gods themselves in this story are endowed with the same characteristics and failings as the human beings of Books 1-10.

In the light of these considerations we may go back to consider Psyche's progress in the tale, especially in those respects in which it is said to parallel that of Lucius. First, the so-called "fall," which in each case is attributed to excessive curiosity. Psyche's case is somewhat different from Lucius', however—indeed, quite opposite. For whereas after his disastrous experience with black magic Lucius shows no further interest in the subject, Psyche desires more and more that which she broke the divine prohibition to see. For her curiosity leads her to examine Cupid's arrows, and she accidentally pricks herself with one . . . :

> Sic ignara Psyche sponte in Amoris incidit amorem. Tunc magis magisque cupidine fraglans Cupidinis, prona in eum efflictim inhians, patulis ac petulantibus saviis festinanter ingestis de somni mensura metuebat.

> ("So without knowing it Psyche spontaneously fell in love with Love. Then, burning more and more with desire for Desire, she threw herself on him with desperate longing and kissed him with open-mouthed lascivious kisses—but hurriedly, fearing he would soon wake up.")

The conceit of falling in love with Love is not mere word play. Psyche, the soul, becomes infatuated with Cupid, sexual appetite—an infatuation which expresses itself in a very physical way—to the extent that Lucius after his metamorphosis had become even more obsessed with the subsequent separation is exceedingly painful. Indeed, after the separation Psyche wanders the world looking for Cupid. It is as though magic. Secondly, one may consider what happens when Psyche tries prayer as a solution to her troubles. In the course of her wanderings Psyche comes upon temples of Ceres and Juno, and in each case she addresses a prayer to the goddess. The rhetoric of these, especially of the prayer to Juno . . . , is very similar to that of Lucius' prayer in [Book 11]. But what is the reply? "Very sorry—we'd like to help but we can't offend Venus!" It is not the goddesses who come to assist Psyche in her troubles, but the ants, the reed, the eagle and the talking tower. Such is the aid the soul may expect from the Olympians; her approach to Ceres and Juno produces nothing but guarded sympathy; her approach to Venus results in cruel punishment and the imposition of impossible tasks: what a contrast to the result of Lucius' prayer to the Queen of Heaven! Thirdly, there is Psyche's trip to the underworld which supposedly parallels Lucius's initiation. Again, the two situations could hardly be more dissimilar. The visit does nothing for Psyche's spiritual development; indeed, it comes close to destroying her completely. She is still afflicted with curiosity—a curiosity moreover concerned with making herself more acceptable to Cupid. Forgetting the express instructions of the tower *not* to look into the box containing Proserpina's beauty,

> mentem capitur temeraria curiositate et: "ecce," inquit, "inepta ego divinae formonsitatis gerula, quae nec tantillum quidem indidem mihi delibo vel sic illi amatori meo formonso placitura," et cum dicto reserat pyxidem. Nec quicquam ibi rerum nec formonsitas ulla, sed infernus somnus ac vere Stygius. . . .

> ("Her mind seized with rash curiosity she said to herself, 'I should be a pretty stupid carrier of divine beauty if I didn't take a little bit for myself to please that beautiful lover of mine,' and so saying she opened the box. In it was no tangible thing nor any beauty, but an infernal and truly Stygian sleep.")

From the consequences of this Epimethean piece of thoughtlessness she has to be rescued by Cupid. The fact that she is motivated towards it by her desire to please Cupid clearly shows the continuing operation in her of "that irrational desire which overcomes the tendency of opinion towards right." She has learnt nothing from her experiences; indeed she is less in touch with reality here than she was at the beginning. Lucius on the other hand *does* learn from his experience, and correctly refuses to "lift the lid" on matters which are required to be kept secret. His tantalisingly summary account of his initiation is prefaced by an address to the reader:

> Quaeras forsitan satis anxie, studiose lector, quid deinde dictum, quid factum; dicerem, si

> dicere liceret, cognosceres, si liceret audire. Sed parem noxam contraherent et aures et linguae illae temerariae curiositatis.
>
> ("I imagine you would very much like to know, attentive reader, what was then said and done; I would tell you if it were permitted to speak, and you would find out if it were permitted to hear. But both your ears and my tongue would suffer an equal punishment for such rash curiosity.")

Temeraria curiositas ("rash curiosity"): once again the verbal echo points up the contrast.

Finally we return to the point at which we began: the "redemption" of Psyche and Lucius, the "happy issue out of all their afflictions" which is supposedly the climax of each tale. We have seen that Psyche's development has been one of more and more involvement with Cupid, from the time when the oracle declares that her husband will be a *saevum atque ferum vipereumque malum* ("savage, bestial and viperous evil") feared by Jupiter himself. . . . Thus the eventual marriage is on the surface a happy ending to a love-story, and no doubt, according to the values of the old lady in whose mouth the story is put, the ending *is* a happy one. But there are as we have seen strong reasons for questioning this superficial interpretation. When we place the tale in the context of the novel as a whole and note the contrasts that the author suggests between it and the story of Lucius, and view these contrasts in a Platonist light, the "lived happily ever after" with which Psyche exits from the ***Metamorphoses*** becomes highly suspect. The rescuing *deus ex machina* in her case is not occasioned by any act of contrition on her part; indeed, it follows upon the "rash curiosity" of her opening the box. There is no sense of spiritual or mental development in Psyche: rather she goes downhill in both areas as she becomes more and more infatuated with Cupid. And it is this infatuation that Jupiter perpetuates by his intervention . . . :

> Porrecto ambrosiae poculo: "Sume," inquit, "Psyche, et immortalis esto nec umquam digredietur a tuo nexu Cupido, sed istae vobis erunt perpetuae nuptiae."
>
> ("He proffered her a cup of ambrosia and said, 'Drink this, Psyche, and become immortal. Cupid will now never be parted from your embrace; this marriage of yours will last for ever'.")

Immortality for Psyche in a world controlled by Jupiter is thus contingent upon her being bound to Cupido. And when we compare the way in which Lucius' soul will achieve immortality *tenacibus castimoniis* ("with persevering chastity"), we realise that we are not dealing with a *redemption* but a *fall*. The fate of Psyche is the fate of the soul under the control of false religion: the true thematic parallels to Olympianism lie not in the cult of Isis but in black magic and the cult of the Syrian goddess both of which bind the souls of their devotees to appetite gratification of a predominantly sexual nature. Jupiter and the Olympians are in no way like the gods of the *Phaedrus* who lead the soul upwards to the ultimate reality; themselves slaves to passion they drag the soul down to their own level from a state of pristine innocence. "Cupid and Psyche" in fact is the myth which tells how *voluptas* came into the world through the enslavement of the soul to sexual appetite, and thus accounts for the present state of unregenerate man. He who would seek salvation must, like Lucius in Book

An 1872 illustration of the scene in Metamorphoses *in which Lucius seduces the servant girl of Pamphile the witch.*

11, *break* the tie between Psyche and Cupid: only then can he come to an understanding of the truth. (pp. 50-9)

J. L. Penwill, "Slavish Pleasures and Profitless Curiosity: Fall and Redemption in Apuleius' 'Metamorphoses'," in Ramus, *Vol. 4, No. 1, 1975, pp. 49-82.*

ARTHUR HEISERMAN (essay date 1977)

[*Heiserman was a distinguished twentieth-century American authority on classical prose fiction. In the following excerpt, he discusses* Metamorphoses *as an essentially comic work.*]

For over a thousand years the story of the ass-man has been honored as an allegory of man's salvation, as a masterpiece of conversion literature, as an eloquent piece of propaganda for Isis. I think it is better than any of these things. I honor it as a comedy of the marvelous. I do so because all of its parts—its characters, episodes, ancillary tales, fervid style—make a whole designed, as Apuleius himself says, to "charm" us, to make us "marvel," not to move us to adopt an opinion, attitude, or action. Ideas play in it the subsidiary role they play in the comedy of *Clitophon* (though Apuleius needs fewer of them), not the determinate role they play in the comedy of *Daphnis*. ***The Golden Ass*** is of course very different from these works in other important ways. It is in Latin. It is a "picaresque" novel. It is "realistic"—though it contains episodes more fantastic than any in Greek romance. It uses none of the vital conventions of romance except in the romantic tales it incorporates. And the story in its main outlines is not original with the author. Still, if I must answer the question of genre which ***The Golden Ass*** has always demanded of its critics, I must say it is primarily a comedy.

Apuleius adapted, and probably augmented several fold, a comical satire by the witty skeptic, Lucian of Samosata, whose life overlapped Apuleius'. Since only an epitome of this Greek work survives, it is impossible to say exactly what Apuleius added to the original (if he knew it); but the adventures of Lucian's hapless young hero, named Lucius, are essentially those of Apuleius' hapless Lucius. Curious about magic, both Luciuses seduce a servant girl in order to spy on an obscene witch, and both are by mistake transformed into donkeys. Both are taken by robbers to caves, attempt to escape with a captive maiden, are recaptured, and finally are rescued, along with the fair captive, by a posse. Both suffer grievously at the hands of the maiden's slaves and are then sold, first to a band of lascivious eunuch-priests of the Syrian mother goddess, then to a gardener, and finally to a cook, who, observing poor Lucius' unnatural cleverness, panders him to a lady whose erotic ambitions he satisifies. The ass's ability to apply himself like a man wins him a role in the theater (of mounting a condemned woman); but at the crucial moment he escapes, eats some roses, and is transformed back into human shape. Lucian's Lucius now returns to the lady for more fun, but she, eyeing his now merely human equipment, scornfully dismisses him; whereupon he goes home to Patras. Apuleius' Lucius, turning his life toward Isis, the mother goddess whose power has restored his manhood, unhappily struggles toward the top rank of her priesthood in Rome and ends as a shaven celibate whose curiosity about magic is apparently satisfied. By means of his delightful story (one-eighth the size of Apuleius' tale in the epitome), Lucian manages to satirize curiosity, magic, vicious rustics, hypocritical priests, and women. Apuleius retains all these villains and fools but transmutes satire into comedy by developing an action that includes about two hundred characters (of whom thirty-two die) and covers about seven months (in which seventy-three days are mentioned). In addition, his Lucius as man and ass overhears or participates in twenty-seven stories of desperate lovers, witches, feuds, and murders, including the celebrated tale of Cupid and Psyche; and few if any of these marvelous stories were in his source. So described, none of this added material seems particularly comic. Furthermore, the "ancillary" tales often seem even more digressive than those in the works of Apuleius' imitators, Cervantes and Fielding. They trouble any formalist who assumes that extended narratives must follow the rules of plays or lyric poems, and they invite the exegete to find in them a key moral or meaning that would unify an apparently disjointed plot. Still, it is doubtful that Apuleius and his contemporaries could have called any fiction of ordinary life, told in the first person by its protagonist, who is a likable fool, anything but a comedy, unless they adopted the phrase used by Apuleius in his prologue—"a stringing-together of various tales in the Milesian style." (pp. 145-46)

Milesian tales were short stories about conjugal betrayal, comic contretemps, and sardonic or cruel trickery resolved in surprising but not supernatural ways. . . . Whether comic or bitterly cynical, Milesian tales were "realistic" in our sense of the term; they and their characters were much inferior in status to the *erōtika pathēmata* ["classical romantic comedy"], and they were hardly worthy of a literary man's notice. And these are scratched in another sort of matter, apparently even more to be scorned: Egyptian papyrus. A great many Egyptian stories survive, but no one seems to have observed that Apuleius, in the ***Metamorphoses,*** is telling one. In Egypt such tales seem to have enjoyed among the scribes a much higher literary status than the Milesian tales did among Hellenic literary men, and there is no reason why Apuleius could not have heard some of them or perceived that Lucian wrote one in the Greek *Ass*. Like the Milesian tales, they were brief; but they were of more diverse character, for they include mythological tales, historical anecdotes, philosophical apologues, and a few elegant autobiographical tales that seem to derive from the lives of real men (these Gustave Lefebvre terms *"romans"*). But one characteristic they have in common: they all involve the marvelous—the deeds of sorcerers, speaking animals, witches. As Lefebvre says [in his *Romans et contes égyptiens de l'époque pharaonique*], "the marvelous is nearly inseparable from the Egyptian *conte*." The basic stuff of the ***Metamorphoses*** is indeed marvelous—not only all the witch stories Apuleius adds to Lucian but the fundamental story of a man's transformation into a donkey and back again with the aid of the Egyptian mother goddess. And in this Egyptian material are embedded comic and bitter Milesian tales of "realistic" tone. This seems to be a paradoxical mix of opposites, in itself a marvel. But the Milesian and the Egyptian are similar on one vital score—they both deal in the pleasures of surprise, wonder, astonishing reversals, and recognitions. In this sense, both involve the marvelous, and Apuleius correctly tells us that he welds them together so that we may marvel.

I suggest also that Apuleius may have borrowed his narrative method from some Egyptian literary habits. Egyptian tales were sometimes strung together by being assigned to a single teller who is in some sort of predicament, like Scheherazade in *The Thousand and One Nights*. Poor Lucius does tell all the various fables of ***The Golden Ass,*** but after his escape. His own story, however, is like those Egyptian autobiographies intended

> to sum up the characteristic features of the individual person in terms of his positive worth and in the face of eternity. His person should live forever, in the transfigured form of the resurrected dead, and his name should last forever in the memory of the people [Miriam Lichtheim, *Ancient Egyptian Literature*].

In fact, Lucius predicts that his story will have such an effect. In book 2 he boasts that a sorcerer once predicted that he (Lucius) would win great fame and that his life would be a marvelous tale that would provide material for books. The sorcerer was right. But in Apuleius' book, Lucius is not a paragon but a likable fool, and his autobiography is a comedy of marvels. (pp. 151-52)

Apuleius has in fact written one of the bitterest of comedies. The sadistic cruelties of men and circumstances, the masochistic enslavement of a hero who suffers more blows than Don Quixote and Sancho Panza combined, the hypocrisy of venal and perverted clergies, the monstrous passions of women—all have charmed our kindly ears because they have been conveyed through the author's incantatory murmur. This murmur is partly a verbal style that is at once idiosyncratic and characteristic of the second century; it is arch, frenetic, extravagant. But when used by a narrator whose perceptions and experiences are themselves extravagant, it also becomes a style appropriate to comedy and in itself a source of comedy. Its unremitting cleverness can absorb the horror of the most hideous events and thereby permit us to enjoy saying, with a kind of cynical confidence, "Yes, this is the world as it is." Furthermore, we can be charmed by horrors when they themselves are as extravagant—as incredible and marvelous—as the ridiculous hero's style. Style, action, and character combine, therefore, to make us marvel; and when the extravagant twists of Milesian fables are entwined with the extravagant wonders of Egyptian ones, our marveling becomes unexpectedly complex: the "realistic" betrayals, blows, dismemberments, and murders of the Milesian materials become as incredible as the marvels of witchcraft, metamorphoses, and salvation of the Egyptian materials; while, contrariwise, the marvels of the Egyptian stories become as credible as the grimly mundane deeds of the Milesian ones. This melding of the credible, this writing of Milesian stories on Egyptian papyrus, fulfills Apuleius' promise to make us marvel. He makes us marvel at extremes—the worst of life, the most fearsome; and the best, the most desirable. And they are so extreme, they are experienced by such a frantic fool of an ass-man, that the worst and the best both become ludicrous, and this makes the ***Metamorphoses*** one of the most bitter and profound of comedies. (pp. 165-66)

Arthur Heiserman, "Antonine Comedy," in his The Novel before the Novel: Essays and Discussions about the Beginnings of Prose Fiction in the West, *The University of Chicago Press, 1977, pp. 117-66.*

JOHN J. WINKLER (essay date 1985)

[*In the following excerpt from his study* Auctor & Actor: A Narratological Reading of Aupuleius's "Golden Ass," *Winkler analyzes the complex relationship in* Metamorphoses *between narrator (auctor) and character (actor).*]

Let us begin with a simple, common-sense notion of ***The Golden Ass*** as an utterance by a narrator named Lucius about his past life and see just where that notion becomes inadequate.

The I who tells us he was heading for Thessaly [in Book 1] is not conventionally identified by personal name or city of origin but, following a technique familiar from the dialogues of Plato and Lucian, the reader is gradually and indirectly given a great deal of information about him. The conveyance of this information is made to seem merely an unavoidable consequence of reporting what was actually said and done by others. Thus, the narrator of the [***Golden Ass***] never says in so many words to the reader, "My name is Lucius," but we learn that name late in Book 1 when his friend Pythias addresses him as Lucius. From similar situations we learn that Lucius has been in Athens, has studied there along with Pythias under a teacher named Adytius, that he is upper-class, handsome, modest in manner, and still young. His parents' names are Theseus and Salvia, and his mother's illustrious marriage, judged by the comparatively humble one of her wealthy relative Byrrhena, implies that Lucius's family, in wealth and eminence, must be *la crème de la crème*. The magistrates of Hypata are evidently not exaggerating when they say, "The nobility of your famous family does honor to our entire province." . . .

Lucius the narrator also informs us about the significant psychological characteristics he then displayed, chief among them curiosity and a certain impetuousness. Lucius, then, as an agent and role player in events had a specific social identity and personal character that Lucius as narrator gradually reveals to his readers. Whether Lucius as narrator still has those same traits of character is an open question, but obviously he still has the same social identity. In that sense he is the same fictional character, though he may have a different moral character. *Qua* narrator he has a different perspective on himself then than he did then, a perspective that entitles him to stand outside himself (that is, his then self) and present the self he was as a character along with others. His access to the knowledge and feelings of that character in the story is of course privileged, but though he can know that character better than all the others (Milo, Photis, Charite), Lucius is nonetheless presented as a character acting in a story.

But at the very beginning (for first-readers, whose experiences at this point are very hard for us second-readers to pin down), ***The Golden Ass*** is not at all a story *about* Lucius. Most critical second-readers seem to forget that the *ego* of this narrative is only gradually *discovered* to be the central character in a plot. The erasure of this experience of discovery is the result of exclusively synchronic analysis that ignores the actual process of reading as a mental act that occupies a space of time. Thus what is arguably the most important reidentification of a character in Books 1-10 (narrator becoming the central actor) is overlooked. Parallel to the naturalistic method of introducing information about the *ego* as having a well-characterized identity is the much more important discovery that the *ego* is not only a storyteller but a teller of stories about *himself.* Let us examine this initial period of getting the focus right—from blurry to sharp—as the reader's sense of who is speaking and from what perspective gradually becomes clear.

The I of the prologue says, "I will thread together for you various tales," a phrase that ought to mean that he is an anthologist, selecting separate short narratives. This is also the obvious implication of his reference to "figures and fortunes of persons converted to other images." If he is introducing not a novel but a story *collection,* the tentative sense of the phrase, "We begin a Greeklike tale" is not "I am starting a novel (or even a frame tale) set in Greece," but rather "the *first* story of my anthology is set in Greece." Perhaps the subsequent stories will have different locales—Egyptian, Milesian, whatever. As far as the first-reader knows, the storyteller may, after completing the Greeklike tale with which he begins, jump around from country to country and perhaps from time to time, the only connecting thread being the storyteller himself.

The next few paragraphs of the [***Golden Ass***] set the scene for the narrator's meeting with a storyteller, Aristomenes. The content of those paragraphs is essentially an elaboration of "Once on the road to Thessaly I heard the following story." This extended introduction does not demand to be read as the beginning of a story about Lucius. As far as the first-reader is given to know, the narrator will skip, after Aristomenes' tale is finished, to another point in his life when he heard another good story. This would be fully in accord with the expectations set up in the prologue. When we learn at the close of Aristomenes' tale that the narrator means to continue an account of his journey to Hypata, we make a small adjustment to our earlier expectations: the narrator is either going to hear more tales in Hypata or he is going to confirm there the tale of Aristomenes, which was clearly said to be set in that city and verifiable by all its inhibitants. When he subsequently . . . refers to Hypata as the city where Aristomenes encountered the witch Meroë, either of these possibilities may seem to be confirmed. The introduction of further tales in Book 2, however, gradually changes the reader's sense of the storyteller's anthological method. Apparently he (whose name we now know to be Lucius) will give an account day by day of the various taletellers he met. The string stitching the tales together will be not just himself as a storyteller but a continuous account of his life as a witness of tales.

It is a further modification of this to learn, at the beginning of Book 3, that Lucius himself is the subject of tales. By this time the two series reinforce each other: (i) the gradual characterization of Lucius as an agent, and (ii) the gradual specification of the narrative as not a serial anthology but a life, and then not a life as witness but a life as hero. Most efforts to interpret the [***Golden Ass***] forget the original experience of the first-reader groping to understand the form of the narrative as it slowly reveals itself. It is important to remember that the original storyteller *became* a characterized agent and that the various tales *became* an autobiographical narrative. The prologue speaker does not say that he will tell a long, continuous story about himself; if anything he creates the opposite impression. The slow approach to the correct awareness of the form in which he is writing allows the author to play with the reader's undefined sense of what might be appropriate in this text. If we were told in the first sentence that "This is the story of my life and the experiences I underwent," we would pay a different attention to what the narrator says about himself from the beginning. As it is, we are given first a strong sense of disconnected, discrete *fictions* and then an autobiographic account that continually and playfully asserts that it is true.

Consider Lucius as a characterized actor in the plot. We are given the elements of his specific identity (name, city of origin, class, etc.) and we are told something of his personal traits (curiosity, impetuosity). These characteristics belong to Lucius no matter who tells the story of his journey to Thessaly and his transformation. It would be incorrect therefore to use the term "characterized narrator," meaning that the narrator *qua* narrator is wealthy or curious or impetuous. But the narrator *qua* narrator does have characteristics: he has, for instance a tendency to postpone information for the sake of surprise or suspense, a marvelous narrative skill, and a mastery of many literary qualities pertaining to style, description, dialogue, and innuendo. These characteristics have nothing to do with Lucius the agent or actor. They are the qualities of the *ego* who offered in the prologue to whisper delightful stories and whose presence is established by the performance of the text long before the separate characterization of Lucius as central actor in the narrative. There is a kind of deception induced here: the reader might well come to think that Lucius is simply telling what happened to him and that it was very interesting indeed. This is what I referred to above as "a simple, common-sense notion of the [***Golden Ass***] as an utterance by a narrator named Lucius about his past life." This notion *forgets* that the character of the narrator as a gifted, clever teller of tales had been earlier established and is not replaced but only overlaid by another form of discourse, the connected autobiography.

As the reader progresses through the text two sets of characteristics are gradually perceived and assembled—those of Lucius then and those of the narrator now (*actor* and *auctor*). Though the narrator now claims to be the same person as Lucius then, the [***Golden Ass***] contains many obvious tokens for the innocent first-reader that the narrator is a teller of fictional stories rather than true stories. First, the prologue speaker had announced "various tales" "to amaze you" and "to enjoy." Then there is the sustained incredibility of the events, not only their magical content but their obvious dramatic quality. Everyone's life may contain a few good scenes and a few startling events worth telling just as they happened, but the unremittingly dramatic and storied quality of Lucius's life is itself a strong indicator that it is a thing not only reshaped by an autobiographical narrator who has learned to make the most of what really happened to him but that it is fundamentally a fiction made up from amazement and enjoyment. To say this is, in a sense, to beg the question of the entire text, which repeatedly plays with the issue of the truth of tales and converts that play into a serious issue in Book 11. But it should be obvious at least that the "simple, common-sense notion" with which we began—that of Lucius telling us what happend to him—is not adequate to account for what happens in the text.

We have to speak instead of two duplicities and a playful slippage between them. The first duplicity is that of the writer pretending to be a certain Lucius who tells us his story. This relation of *auctor* (whom we may call Apuleius, though his name is irrelevant to the analysis) to *actor* (Lucius) accounts for the high level of narrative delight, the incredible coincidences, exciting characters, and in general the storied quality of the book. Insofar as such a narrative is a game of Let's Pretend, this duplicity carries a connotation of confessed deceit. The second duplicity is the relation of *auctor* (Lucius as narrator) to *actor* (Lucius as actor). This duplicity is a mere doubleness between past and present selves, with no implication of deceit. Nothing in the [***Golden Ass***] leads us to think that Lucius, considered as a concrete person, is altering his real past or deceiving his audience in any fashion. (pp. 135-40)

Consider first the relation of *auctor* Lucius to *actor* Lucius (present narrator to his past self). The remarkable feature about this pair is the constant and steady suppression of the *auctor* Lucius's present reality. The speaker of the [***Golden Ass***] conceals the conversion to which the narrative (evidently) leads; he makes not even the broadest guessable allusion to some special event that will cap the narrative (such as "Little did I know that my misery as an ass was a path to special glory," *vel sim.*). Each event of the past is told for immediate effect, with virtually no intrusion of the present speaker judging, condemning, commenting on the action. The few comments he does make are not intrusions in the character of an Isiac deacon on his misguided past but those of a mere survivor who lived to tell the tale. . . . [All] intrusions of the present speaker's judgment are strictly designed to heighten the vividness of the story and the reader's control of the units of action. They provide the first-reader with no sense that the story will reach a serious *telos* when it catches up with the narrator's present.

From at least one angle Augustine's *Confessions,* if held up to Apuleius's ***Asinus Aureus,*** presents an interesting reversal or mirror image. Both narratives might be described (with serious foreshortening, of course) as sequences of spicy and dramatic episodes. (An *ad hoc* case for their relatedness might include the fact that Augustine began his lessons in literature in Apuleius's city of Madauros. . . .) But in writing his autobiographical conversion story, Augustine refuses to relive those events except in the burning spotlight of his present conciousness of his god. Each past episode is drawn into the present relationship of Augustine to his god and examined for what it now means, with some regretful comments on what it used to mean to the past Augustine. The present narrator invades his past as an enemy territory, using his god as a powerful ally to destroy the lingering vestiges of the pleasure he originally felt. Apuleius's narrator, though he is a deacon of Isis, describes in luscious detail his seduction dialogue, his foreplay, and each sexual position he assumed with Photis; Augustine, the priest of Iesus, gives virtually no details of his love life, withholding even the name of his devoted mistress and quite obscuring his strong attraction to men. . . . Not what nowadays we would call a confession. The title *Confessions* names the present speaker's act, as the *Ass* in Apuleius's title names the past self of the speaker. The difference in titles aptly sums up the opposite weights given to the I now telling and the I then acting in the two works.

What are we to make of the suppression in the [*Golden Ass*] of the I now narrating in relation to the I then acting, a suppression that becomes problematic not merely in comparison with a differently structured text such as Augustine's but in the light of its own conclusion—Book 11? (pp. 140-42)

[What] Apuleius tells us about the narrating I in the [***Golden Ass***] is exactly gauged to maximize the immediate, dramatic effectiveness of each episode for the first-reader *and* to be an uncanny torment about the end for the second-reader. . . . [In the relationship between the two *actors*] Lucius now/Lucius then and [the two *auctores*] Apuleius author/Lucius fictional narrator, the search for a single perspective on the dual structure is endless: a reader may decide to stop at some point in the cycle of shifting points of view, but the authoritative voice of the text makes no declaration about what the reader should choose. Apuleius neither affirms nor denies any of the perspectives—he merely signifies that they are there. (p. 142)

The complexity of self in the [***Golden Ass***] cannot be accounted for simply in terms of two fixed locations for Lucius as present narrator and past actor. It also requires that the *auctor* be thought of sometimes as Apuleius the novelist and sometimes as Lucius the narrator. The slippage between one *auctor* (Apuleius the novelist) and the other *auctor* (Lucius the narrator) takes place along what I will call three axes where the text shifts its meaning in such a way that the reader must sense a fiction writer behind the character of Lucius narrating. Now this is of course a quite ordinary feat of impersonation, analyzable into author (scriptwriter) behind actor (person who reads the lines) behind character (role played), as in any stage comedy. But what is extraordinary about Apuleius's script is that the three axes, or types of oscillation in reference frame of the narrative, set up two different effects simultaneously: they determine for the first-reader an intelligible *system* of interplay, characterizing the book itself as a sophomoric text, while for the second-reader the same facetious, boundary-violating play becomes an ongoing allusion to the problem of Book 11. . . . Along what I call the three axes, the [***Golden Ass***] plays almost every imaginable game of self-conscious and self-referential duplicity.

The first axis is that of class—the [***Golden Ass***] slides back and forth between the opposite extremes of high seriousness and low comedy. The second axis is that of unity—the [***Golden Ass***] fluctuates between seeming to be a whole whose parts have an integral relation to each other and seeming to be a disjointed, episodic work. The third axis is that of authority—the [***Golden Ass***] variously indicates either that it contains a message or story that the author endorses and takes responsibility for or that it has no center of authority. Since a sudden change along one axis does not entail a change along the other two, I tend to visualize this image of three axes not as a set of intersecting coordinates but as three parallel lines that cover the same territory. On them may be diagramed three acts of the mind performed by the reader of the [***Golden Ass***] as he or she asks the ordinary questions we bring to anything we read or watch in performance: What is the decorum of this text—high or low or varying? What is the progressive buildup or coherence of its parts—tightly or loosely organized, or fluctuating? And what is the character of the author who has put out this text—one hidden behind the inherited authority of other texts, masked in a *persona,* or seriously present in his own person? Insofar as these three axes represent the typical coordinates along which we locate works of literature (not by genre but by rhythm, style, and I.Q.), the complex and quite particular performance of ***The Golden Ass*** sketches a comprehensive model of narrating identity.

One may observe that these three oscillations have affinities, but they do not entail each other. On one side of the cognitive field they depict a text that is (a) ideally noble, (b) unified, and (c) makes a responsible utterance; on the other side, a text that is (a) vulgar, (b) disorganized, and (c) inconsistent for no reason. Some types of text vary on one axis but not on the others: parodic and seriocomic texts may shift class by introducing unexpected patches of vulgarity or sublimity while maintaining a unity of plot or argument and a coherence of purpose. Anthological or episodic texts may have parts that are quite unrelated to each other, omissible at will, but without varying in tone or overall intention. It is harder to illustrate the third axis with any other ancient work than the [***Golden Ass***] (or possibly the *Satyrika* of Petronius), for the degree of responsibility or fixity of purpose is the most fundamental unity in any work that has a single author. The degree of responsibility for different texts may be high or low—low for the author who collects without endorsing, high for the author who assembles and actively integrates and argues for the value of his or her perspective—but that degree of authority is almost always invariable within the bounds of a single text. (pp. 153-55)

High literature, low trash; a single tale, a heterogeneous collection; a responsible narrator, a man who can't help himself: the [***Golden Ass***] is characterized by its obsessive shifts along the axes of class, unity, and authority. For the first-reader ***The Golden Ass*** entertains by shifting its frames of reference. That makes the novel inconsistent, but inconsistent in a funny way

Illustration from a 1637 French edition of Metamorphoses *depicting a scene from the story of Socrates and Aristomenes.*

and within a system. For the second-reader the system itself is a problem. Because of the leap to Book 11, the existence of the three dimensions of volatility seems now to be somehow or other significant. Significant of what? I should say: of the impossibility of authorizing an answer to the question of the meaning of the whole, any whole. The text can raise the question, play with a variety of answers, but cannot successfully endorse and hand over a solution to *such* a question.

Obviously this is a distinct thesis in and about the field of religious knowledge, a skeptical or aporetic position. There are alternatives that assert, for instance, that all claims to higher knowledge are phony . . . or that a single deity is the correct one because it is alone true . . . or more true than others. . . . In this sense the [***Golden Ass***] takes up a particular, endorsed position in opposition to those alternatives, or rather it causes the reader tentatively to adopt those other positions, *fabulae gratia,* one after another, but gives no grounds to conclude that one is correct. Instead it presents a value-free description of what a conversion with cosmic, life-reorienting consequences would be like. . . . [Here] I would endorse the remark of Ninian Smart: "This should not blind us to the fact that such [value-free] descriptions also must be in a certain way value-rich, for they need to be evocative rather than flat, though the evocations themselves are of course bracketed" [Ninian Smart, *The Science of Religion and the Sociology of Knowledge*]. ***The Golden Ass*** is an evocation of a religious experience bracketed in such a way that the reader must, but cannot, decide the question of its truth. (pp. 178-79)

John J. Winkler, in his Auctor & Actor: A Narratological Reading of Apuleius's "Golden Ass," *University of California Press, 1985, 340 p.*

ADDITIONAL BIBLIOGRAPHY

Birley, Anthony. "Apuleius: Roman Provincial Life." *History Today* 18, No. 9 (September 1968): 629-36.

Approaches *The Apology* as an account of Roman provincial life "with the lid off."

Boberg, Inger Margrethe. "The Tale of Cupid and Psyche." *Classica et Mediaevalia* I (1938): 177-216.

Places Apuleius's Cupid and Psyche tale among its chief antecedents and descendants.

Browning, Elizabeth Barrett. Letter to John Kenyon. In her *The Letters of Elizabeth Barrett Browning,* edited by Frederic G. Kenyon, Vol. I, pp. 249-50. New York: The Macmillan Co., 1897.

1845 letter in which the author comments: "Apuleius is *florid,* which favored the poetical design on his sentences. Indeed he is more florid than I have always liked to make my verses."

D'Amico, John F. "The Progress of Renaissance Latin Prose: The Case of Apuleianism." *Renaissance Quarterly* 37 (Autumn 1984): 351-92.

Explores the imitation of Apuleius's language and prose style by Renaissance Latinists.

Dowden, Ken. "Apuleius and the Art of Narration." *Classical Quarterly* 32, No. 2 (1982): 419-35.

Probes the various modes of narration in *Metamorphoses.*

Drake, Gertrude C. "Candidus: A Unifying Theme in Apuleius's *Metamorphoses.*" *The Classical Journal* 64, No. 3 (December 1968): 102-09.

Studies equine themes and references in *Metamorphoses,* centering on the ancestors in Greek and Roman mythology of the horse Candidus.

———. "The Ghost Story in *The Golden Ass* by Apuleius." *Papers on Language & Literature* 13, No. 1 (Winter 1977): 3-15.

Elucidates Hellenic, Roman, Mithraic, and Isiac components in *Metamorphoses,* chiefly as they appear in Thelyphron's tale in Book II.

Duff, J. Wight. "An Epilogue—The Second Century and After." In his *A Literary History of Rome in the Silver Age: From Tiberius to Hadrian,* pp. 650-58. New York: Charles Scribner's Sons, 1927.

Analyzes the prose style of *Metamorphoses,* concluding: "The phrasing is unusual, often bizarre: it is a fantastic blend of elaborate archaism and bold innovation—now poetic, now colloquial."

Ebel, Henry. "Apuleius and the Present Time." *Arethusa* 3, No. 2 (Fall 1970): 155-76.

Discusses the construction and function of *Metamorphoses*'s major motifs, focusing on such issues as Fortuna and vicissitude, metamorphosis, restless curiosity, death and resurrection, magic, and true and false religion.

Griffiths, J. Gwyn. *The Isis-Book* (Metamorphoses, *Book XI*), by Apuleius of Madauros. Edited and translated by J. Gwyn Griffiths. Leiden, Netherlands: E. J. Brill, 1975, 439 p.

Lengthy introduction and commentary elucidate the historical, biographical, religious, and linguistic aspects of the last book of *Metamorphoses.*

Haight, Elizabeth Hazelton. *Apuleius and His Influence.* New York: Longmans, Green and Co., 1927, 190 p.

Surveys Apuleius's major works and traces their influence from the early Middle Ages to the end of the nineteenth century.

———. "A Comparison of the Greek Romance and Apuleius' *Metamorphoses*." In her *Essays on the Greek Romances*, pp. 186-201. 1943. Reprint. Port Washington, N.Y.: Kennikat Press, 1965.
Compares *Metamorphoses* with its principal Greek source, Lucian's *Lucius; or, The Ass*, noting especially the two works' generic features.

———. "Apuleius and Boccaccio." In her *More Essays on Greek Romances*, pp. 113-41. New York: Longmans, Green and Co., 1945.
Considers Apuleius's influence on Boccaccio, particularly as seen in the latter author's *Decameron* and *De genealogiis deorum*.

———. "A Coronation and Two Ancient Pageants." *The Classical Journal* 49, No. 2 (November 1953): 57-63.
Compares the coronation of Elizabeth II of England with the pageant of Isis in Book XI of *Metamorphoses*.

Hijmans, B. L., Jr., and van der Paardt, R. Th., eds. *Aspects of Apuleius' Golden Ass*. Groningen, The Netherlands: Bouma's Boekhuis, 1978, 275 p.
Excellent collection of fifteen original papers treating a variety of Apuleian issues.

Hooker, Ward. "Apuleius's 'Cupid and Psyche' As a Platonic Myth." *The Bucknell Review* 5, No. 3 (May 1955): 24-38.
A source study of the Cupid and Psyche tale in *Metamorphoses*, centering on the myth's allegory and plot.

Kenny, Brendan. "The Reader's Role in *The Golden Ass*." *Arethusa* 7, No. 2 (Fall 1974): 187-209.
Maintains that the satirical elements in *Metamorphoses* subserve the recognition that the world of experience is "inexplicable, random, fortune-ruled."

Lactantius. *The Divine Institutes: Books I-VII*, translated by Sister Mary Francis McDonald, O.P., pp. 334ff. The Fathers of the Church: A New Translation, edited by Roy Joseph Deferrari, Vol. 49. Washington, D.C.: The Catholic University of America Press, 1964.
An early-fourth-century apologetic treatise containing scattered comments on Apuleius's supernatural powers.

Lang, Andrew. "Cupid, Psyche, and the 'Sun-Frog'." In his *Custom and Myth*, pp. 64-86. New York: Harper & Brothers, 1885.
Sketches the early history of the Cupid and Psyche myth, linking the version in *Metamorphoses* with its apparent antecedents.

Lewis, C. S. Letter to Arthur Greeves. In his *They Stand Together: The Letters of C. S. Lewis to Arthur Greeves (1914-1963)*, edited by Walter Hooper, pp. 182-84. New York: Macmillan Publishing Co., 1979.
1917 letter in which Lewis admires, in passing, the "brooding magic," "occasional voluptuousness," and "ridiculous passages" of Apuleius's works.

Mallock, W. H. "The Golden Ass of Apuleius." *Fraser's Magazine* n.s. XIV, No. LXXXI (September 1876): 363-74.
Explores *Metamorphoses* as "a literary Pompeii" mirroring the provincial life of its day.

Mayrhofer, C. M. "On Two Stories in Apuleius." *Antichthon* 9 (1975): 68-80.
Challenges the view advanced by Ben Edwin Perry (see excerpt dated 1967) that the stories of Aristomenes and Thelyphron in *Metamorphoses* are essentially incoherent.

Millar, Fergus. "The World of the *Golden Ass*." *The Journal of Roman Studies* LXXI (1981): 63-75.
Approaches *Metamorphoses* as a source document especially useful for the historian of communal life in a Roman province.

Nethercut, William R. "Apuleius' Literary Art: Resonance and Depth in the *Metamorphoses*." *The Classical Journal* 64, No. 3 (December 1968): 110-19.
Examines Apuleius's technique of reintroducing a single story element at different places in *Metamorphoses*.

Neumann, Erich. *Amor and Psyche: The Psychic Development of the Feminine—A Commentary on the Tale by Apuleius*. Translated by Ralph Manheim. Bollingen Series, No. LIV. New York: Pantheon Books, 1956, 181 p.
A close mythological reading of the Cupid and Psyche tale in *Metamorphoses*.

Perry, B. E. "The Significance of the Title in Apuleius' *Metamorphoses*." *Classical Philology* XVIII, No. 3 (July 1923): 229-38.
Concludes that *Metamorphoses* "seems to be a humorous and ironical, though good-natured, commentary on metamorphoses and the students of magic."

———. "On Apuleius' *Metamorphoses* II, 31-III, 20." *The American Journal of Philology* 46, No. 183 (1924): 253-62.
Maintains that, although the Risus festival in *Metamorphoses* Books II and III is "an excellent jest and well told," it is not original to Apuleius's story and delays its progress.

———. "The Story of Thelyphron in Apuleius." *Classical Philology* XXIV, No. 3 (July 1929): 231-38.
Suggests that the story of Thelyphron in *Metamorphoses* is a somewhat awkward compound of three different stories, one of which contradicts the other two.

Rouse, W. H. D. Preface to *Cupid and Psyche and Other Tales from The Golden Ass of Apuleius*, by Lucius Apuleius, edited by W. H. D. Rouse, pp. ix-xxvii. London: The De La More Press for Alexander Moring, 1904.
Traces the evolution of the legend of Cupid and Psyche, noting Apuleius's achievement in writing the "most beautiful and charming" tale in the world.

Rubino, Carl A., S. J. "Literary Intelligibility in Apuleius's *Metamorphoses*." *The Classical Bulletin* 42, No. 5 (March 1966): 65-9.
Sees *Metamorphoses* as an illustration of "all the insecurity and complexity of its time."

Schlam, C. C. "The Scholarship on Apuleius since 1938." *The Classical World* 64, No. 9 (May 1971): 285-309.
A useful annotated bibliography of Apuleius criticism from 1938 to 1970.

Scobie, Alexander. "The *Golden Ass:* Its Generic Connections and Nature" and "The Portrayal of Character in the *Golden Ass*." In his *Aspects of the Ancient Romance and Its Heritage: Essays on Apuleius, Petronius, and the Greek Romances*, pp. 30-54, 55-82. Beiträge zur klassischen Philologie, edited by Reinhold Merkelbach, No. 30. Meisenheim am Glan, Germany: Verlag Anton Hain, 1969.
A careful study of both the genre of *Metamorphoses* and the work's characterization, focusing on the narrative's stylistic roots and examining Lucius and Fotis as evidence of Apuleius's creative skills.

Skulsky, Harold. "*The Golden Ass:* Metamorphosis as Satire and Mystery." In his *Metamorphosis: The Mind in Exile*, pp. 62-106. Cambridge, Mass.: Harvard University Press, 1981.
Explores changes between shape and fortune in *Metamorphoses*, maintaining that in the narrative "a radical change in one's . . . circumstances will inevitably force a change in shape."

Smith, Warren, S., Jr. "The Narrative Voice in Apuleius' *Metamorphoses*." *Transactions and Proceedings of the American Philological Association* 103 (1972): 512-34.
Explores the narrator's perspective in *Metamorphoses* as a key to Apuleius's narrative method as a whole.

Swahn, Jan-Öjvind. "Apuleius' 'Cupid and Psyche'." In his *The Tale of Cupid and Psyche (Aarne-Thompson 425 & 428)*, pp. 373-80. Lund, Sweden: C. W. K. Gleerup, 1955.
Compares the Cupid and Psyche tale in *Metamorphoses* with modern folk tradition and antique religion.

Tatum, James. "Apuleius and Metamorphosis." *American Journal of Philology* 93, No. 2 (April 1972): 306-13.
Considers why Apuleius titled his best-known work *Metamorphoses*.

———. *Apuleius and "The Golden Ass."* Ithaca: Cornell University Press, 1979, 199 p.

A full-length study focusing on how *Metamorphoses* can be related to Apuleius's other literary activities.

———. "Apuleius (*b. ca.* A. D. 120)." In *Ancient Writers: Greece and Rome,* Vol. II: *Lucretius to Ammianus Marcellinus,* edited by T. James Luce, pp. 1099-1116. New York: Charles Scribner's Sons, 1982.

A useful introduction to Apuleius's life and major works, including comments on Apuleius as philosopher and novelist.

Thompson, Stith. "The Folktale in Ancient Literature: Latin." In his *The Folktale,* pp. 281-82. 1946. Reprint. Berkeley and Los Angeles: University of California Press, 1977.

Describes folktale elements in the tale of Cupid and Psyche.

Ward, Philip. *Apuleius on Trial at Sabratha.* Stoughton, Wis.: The Oleander Press, n. d., 27 p.

A brief chronicle of Apuleius's trial for practicing magic.

Winter, Thomas Nelson. "The Publication of Apuleius' *Apology.*" *Transactions and Proceedings of the American Philological Association* 100 (1969): 607-12.

Considers the question, "How did the text of Apuleius's *Apology* originate?"

Wright, Constance S. "'No Art at All': A Note on the Proemium of Apuleius' *Metamorphoses.*" *Classical Philology* LXVIII, No. 3 (July 1973): 217-19.

Suggests that in the proemium to *Metamorphoses,* Apuleius is at pains to dissociate himself from the narrator Lucius.

Beowulf

Circa Eighth Century

English poem.

Beowulf is the first major poem in English literature and an outstanding depiction of the life and thought of its age. The story of the virtues and exploits of the Scandinavian hero Beowulf, this anonymous work is many things at once: artifact, history, epic, elegy, folklore, and linguistic document, to name a few. The poem is remarkable both as a historical milestone and as a work of literature, and, critics note, is as compelling for what it conceals as for what it reveals. For although theories abound, it is not known when the poem was written, or how, or for what purpose. Moreover, the textual history of the work—*Beowulf* was written long after the events it describes and exists in a manuscript that may have been compiled centuries after the poem was composed—is complicated by the strong possibility that the poem was altered repeatedly before being set down in its present form. Notwithstanding these mysteries, *Beowulf* is an essential object of study for linguists, historians, and literary critics alike, for whom the poem is a window on medieval culture, an Old English document of the first order, and a deeply felt study of man's fate in an uncertain world.

Although a mere objective narration was not the *Beowulf* poet's chief aim, the story of the poem may be briefly stated. Beowulf, nephew of Hygelac, king of the Geats, learns of the nightly ravages of a monster called Grendel in the hall of Heorot, seat of Hrothgar, king of the Danes. With a band of men, Beowulf travels by sea to Denmark, where he is welcomed by Hrothgar, who had known Beowulf's father. Beowulf kills Grendel, but the monster's vengeful mother carries on her son's murderous attacks. Beowulf therefore slays Grendel's mother in her dwelling at the bottom of a haunted mere. Richly rewarded with treasure, he returns to Hygelac's court, where he is acclaimed. He then participates honorably in the Geats' wars, eventually being made king of that people. After a fifty-year reign, Beowulf is called on to defend the Geats from the attacks of a firedrake. Despite abandonment by his men and his own certainty that battle with the creature will lead to his death, Beowulf attacks the firedrake singlehandedly, ultimately killing it with the help of his only loyal retainer, Wiglaf. After discovering treasure in the dragon's barrow, Beowulf dies of his wounds. A funeral pyre is raised, and the poem ends with lines in praise of its hero.

Beowulf survives in only one known manuscript, an Old English miscellany copied out probably around the year 1000 and later joined with another Old English manuscript. It is not known by or for whom the *Beowulf* manuscript was prepared. Its earliest identified owner, the sixteenth-century English antiquary Laurence Nowell, left no record of where he obtained it, thereby contributing to a paucity of evidence concerning the early history of the work. In 1731, after it had become part of the manuscript collection formed by the English collector Sir Robert Cotton, the *Beowulf* manuscript was badly scorched in a fire. As a result, the book became brittle and crumbled in places, initiating a gradual loss of letters and words, primarily at the corners and edges of pages, which was arrested only in the nineteenth century. Because of this progressive deterioration, the first two transcriptions of *Beowulf,* made in 1787 by the Icelander Grímur Jónsson Thorkelin, are considered indispensable records of many portions of the text that are now lost. In fact, Thorkelin's transcriptions, known as "Thorkelin A" and "Thorkelin B," were the basis of the first printed edition of *Beowulf* and are incorporated in all modern editions of the poem.

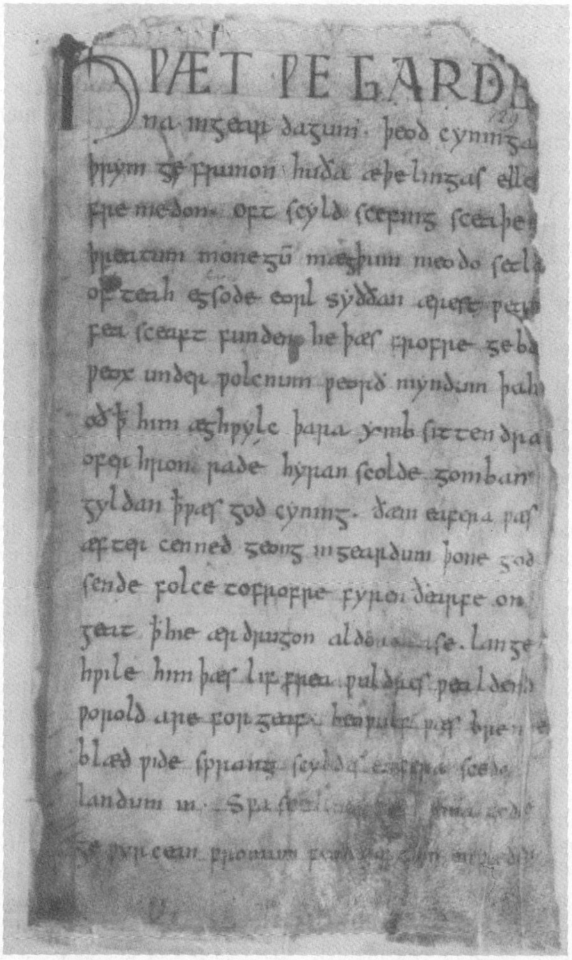

Evidence for the composition date and place of origin of *Beowulf* is highly speculative, mainly because it is not known whether the work contains deliberately archaic, atmospheric elements, or whether parts of the narrative were altered over time. The earliest date proposed by modern scholars is the first half of the seventh century. This date, which is occasionally assigned to a hypothetical antecedent of *Beowulf* but only rarely to the poem as we know it, is based on the poem's language, Germanic character, and blend of paganism and Christianity. The language of *Beowulf,* especially the level of culture and literacy it suggests and its apparent indebtedness to classical literature, has been used to assign the poem to the first half of the eighth century, the so-called "Age of Bede," to pinpoint its origin to Northumbria, and, according to some commentators, to locate its author among the monks of that region. Some scholars prefer a slightly later date. Citing the assimilation of ecclesiastical culture in the poem, Dorothy Whitelock, for example, posited an origin at the late-eighth-century court of King Offa of Mercia, while other commentators, perceiving a tension in the poem between paganism and Christianity, have also proposed this date, if not always this place of origin. A few students of *Beowulf* have assigned the poem to the ninth, tenth, or eleventh centuries, but such late dates are usually discounted by critics, who see positive portrayal of the Danes as impossible after 793, when Danish raids began in northern England. Although there is no consensus concerning the composition date of *Beowulf,* nearly all critics agree that the events recounted in the poem and the composition date of the poem itself are separated by at least a century, possibly much more. This gap in time, the critics point out, is confirmed by the poet's call to think back to earlier times and by external, historical evidence concerning some incidents in the poem.

Students of *Beowulf* agree that an understanding of the formal elements and cultural background of the poem enhances an understanding of the meaning of the work. *Beowulf* is composed in the unrhymed four-beat alliterative meter common to Old English poetry. Each verse line is in two parts—half lines commonly known as "a" and "b"—each of which is an independent metrical unit tied to the other by the repetition of initial sounds. The language of the poem is acknowledged to be mainly traditional, strictly poetic, often stereotyped, and frequently formulaic, employing numerous synonyms, picturesque expressions, and, as fully one third of its four-thousand-word vocabulary, circumlocutory, metaphorical words and phrases known as kennings. Some examples of kennings in the poem are "hilde-leoma" ("battle-flame"), "helm-berend" ("the helmet-bearing one"), and "swan-rade" ("swan-road"), the latter compound meaning "sea." Also common with much Old English poetry, the trope of litotes—understatement in which an affirmative is expressed by the negative of the contrary—occurs throughout *Beowulf,* as in the narrator's interjected comment in the description of Beowulf clutched in the claws of Grendel's mother: "he was not at all happy about that." The poet also makes occasional use of the typically Germanic practices of variation and parenthetic exclamation, the former involving the double or multiple statement of a single idea in order to suggest new aspects or shades of meaning, the latter consisting of direct address to the audience by the narrator. Yet, while the rhetorical elements of *Beowulf* are for the most part derivative, critics stress that the poet's use of them is often extremely original.

The generic and narrative sources of *Beowulf* have been described by C. L. Wrenn in the following manner: "The poet of *Beowulf* drew on two traditions: Germanic for his verse-form, history, geography, social and physical culture, folklore, and myth; Romano-Christian for some of his diction, symbolism, Biblical and patristic learning, classical parallels, and hagiographical models; and both for many of the genres subsumed in his overall structure, such as elegy, flyting, gnome, encomium, allegory, set speeches, and his conceptions of epic and tragedy." In connection with the generic elements of the poem, commentators often note that the culture portrayed in *Beowulf*—that is, the culture of the Danes and the Geats, not necessarily that of the author or first audience of the poem—was an oral rather than a literate one: distinctions between hearsay and fact or history and legend were either vague or nonexistent, with the collective memory of the society keeping alive stories of past deeds and heroes. Because the composition date of *Beowulf* is several generations removed from the action of the poem, few critics describe the work as the direct product of an oral culture, but most agree that the poem shares certain characteristics with the literature of such a culture, including formulaic diction, fixed verse forms, and conservative narrative patterns; folktale-like battle scenes; a recollective way of knowing and describing past events; the use of numerous traditional stories, most evident in the poet's stated awareness of his audience's foreknowledge of certain events; a marked interest in blood feuds and kinship; and a politically unstable setting. These links with oral culture have, like speculation concerning the composition date and place of origin of the poem, led to disputes concerning the authorship of *Beowulf.* Although few critics believe the poem was composed orally, opinion is strongly divided over whether *Beowulf* is the work of one man, or several, or many. Commentators agree, however, that the stories in *Beowulf* were not invented out of thin air: whoever gave the poem its final form was just one link in a long chain of poetic storytellers, a late-arriving "scop," or maker of tales, who adapted, fashioned, and passed on an inherited, evolving canon of traditional stories.

The society portrayed in *Beowulf* is based on the Germanic *comitatus* relationship, a code of social conduct which stresses the reciprocal obligations of lord and thanes: generosity and protection from the overlord, service and loyalty from his retainers. In their discussions of the society portrayed in *Beowulf,* commentators note an emphasis on the overlord's obligation to provide his retainers with land and treasure and to supply opportunities for martial ambition. Critics also recognize the Germanic commonplace that, because an individual warrior's first duty is personal fealty and no disgrace is deeper than disloyalty, a retainer's greatest misfortune is to be deprived of a protecting lord. The pivotal interests of *comitatus* society are battle, death, strength, duty, valor, and blood revenge, with heroism leading to a desire for fame and glory, both in life and posthumously, and a man's "wyrd," or fate, properly accepted with resignation.

It is not known how much of *Beowulf* is historical truth. Only one of the events in the poem, Hygelac's disastrous Frankish raid, has been positively confirmed: according to Gregory of Tours's sixth-century *Historia Francorum,* this excursion took place in about 521. The existence of Beowulf himself is considered unlikely, but few critics rule it out absolutely, and most agree that the hero of the poem, if nonexistent, was at least prominent in contemporary folk mythology. Among the Danes, Hrothgar and Hrothulf are mentioned by the late-twelfth-century chronicler Saxo Grammaticus, and Hrothgar's hall, which is also mentioned in the Old English poem *Widsith,* has been connected with a village now called Lejre. The fourth-century Ostrogothic king Eormenric is known from several medieval sources, and the historicity of the royal Swedes in the poem has been confirmed by twentieth-century archaeological work. Regarding the English, Offa, the fourth-century king of the Angles on the Continent, is mentioned in the poem, and Hengest, who figures in the Finn episode, has been cited as the closest link with English history. Recent work on the seventh-century ship burial at Sutton Hoo, Suffolk, has confirmed the richness of the type of treasure described in *Beowulf,* and weapons found at Sutton Hoo have been shown to correspond well with some historical matters implied in the poem. It is therefore generally conceded that, while much of *Beowulf* is mythological or fantastic, the poem is cast in a historical mold full of historical allusions, some of which are unquestionably genuine, others of which may be genuine but which cannot be proven at this time.

Critical responses to *Beowulf* have been extremely varied. When not focusing exclusively on the linguistic or historical import of the work, the first known commentators often judged *Beowulf* by standards derived from other forms of literature. Thus the early-nineteenth-century critic John Josias Conybeare saw the poem as "entitled in some degree to the name of Epic," but added that, by lacking "unity of plan," the poem offended against "the received canons of the heroic muse." Other nineteenth-century students of *Beowulf* were primarily concerned with establishing two things about the poem: that it was written by a Christian author, and that it deserved to be read as literature. Turn-of-the-century commentators demonstrated a desire to refrain from the extra-literary concerns of their predecessors by concentrating on purely aesthetic matters, but their judgments were not always favorable. W. P. Ker, for instance, while valuing *Beowulf* as "the specimen by which the Teutonic epic poetry must be judged," also described the poem as "defective from the first in respect of plot," and Arthur Quiller-Couch labeled *Beowulf* "a shapeless monstrosity." There was, however, no dearth of praise at this time; Edmund Gosse, for example, extolled the poem as "one of the strongest and most stimulating products of the medieval mind," and William Witherle Lawrence considered the Finn episode "finer matter than the tale of Oedipus, in that pursuing Fate lies in men's own passions, not in external influences determining their destinies." Still, early-twentieth-century critics were reluctant to assess *Beowulf* solely on its aesthetic characteristics, valuing it instead as an artifact only incidentally able to stand alongside more esteemed works of literature.

J. R. R. Tolkien's 1936 lecture "*Beowulf:* The Monsters and the Critics," in which the author approached the poem as pure art, completely altered the course of *Beowulf* studies. Tolkien called *Beowulf* "a composition not a tune" and saw in the poem "a method and structure that within the limits of the verse-kind approaches rather to sculpture or painting." In contrast to most earlier critics, he concluded that the poem "is not an 'epic,' not even a magnified 'lay'," describing the work as "the most successful Old English poem because in it the elements, language, metre, theme, structure, are all most nearly in harmony." In the wake of this highly favorable assessment, critics probed the poem for evidence of marked artistry. Joan Blomfield, for example, called the author of the poem "in fact a true poet," admired the "tragic unity" of the poem, and found evidenced in the work "the poet's eye which splits and recombines the elements of everyday perceptions." C. S. Lewis also approached *Beowulf* as a work of art, noting that "one of Homer's great passages is like a cavalry charge; one of *Beowulf*'s, like blows from a hammer or the repeated thunder of breakers on the beach." From such observations gradually emerged a critical concentration on three broad aesthetic issues: the structural unity of the poem, including the purpose of the episodes usually labeled "digressions"; the impact of the poet's Christianity on the artistry of the work; and the major thematic concerns of the poem, including the nature and identity of the monsters Beowulf fights, the narrator's function in the work, the nature of heroism and social responsibility, and the analogues and purpose of the quest motif. Throughout their discussions of these issues, most post-Tolkien critics acknowledge the artistic achievement of the *Beowulf* poet, echoing Stanley Greenfield's 1965 evaluation of the poem as "one of the triumphs of English poetry."

By any standard *Beowulf* is a difficult and puzzling work that hides its deepest character from the casual reader. Nearly lost to happenstance and fire, the poem is a treasured artifact of European culture, a mirror of medieval life, and the foundation of English literature. Essentially the story of one man's fate, it reveals the philosophical foundations of a medieval society and provides extraordinary insight into an ancient world.

PRINCIPAL MODERN TRANSLATIONS

Beowulf, the Oldest English Epic (translated by Charles W. Kennedy) 1940
Beowulf: A Verse Translation into Modern English (translated by Edwin Morgan) 1952
Beowulf (translated by David Wright) 1957
Beowulf (translated by Burton Raffel) 1963
Beowulf: A New Translation (translated by E. Talbot Donaldson) 1966
Beowulf (translated by Michael Alexander) 1973
Beowulf: A Dual-Language Edition (translated by Howell D. Chickering, Jr.) 1977
Beowulf (translated by Albert W. Haley) 1978
Beowulf: A Verse Translation with Treasures of the Ancient North (translated by Marijane Osborn) 1983
Beowulf (translated by Kevin Crossley-Holland) 1984

JOHN JOSIAS CONYBEARE (essay date 1826)

[Conybeare was a nineteenth-century English geologist and language scholar whose antiquarian interests led him to the study of, among other things, mineral tallow, the Cornish subsoil, Latin verse, and Old English poetry. To the latter subject he contributed the important Illustrations of Anglo-Saxon Poetry *(1826), an edition of several Old English texts augmented by an examination of their meter. In the following excerpt from that work, he discusses the narrative and structural elements of* Beowulf, *contending that the poem is as worthy of study as the epics of classical civilization.]*

[Independently] of its value as ranking among the most perfect specimens of the language and versification of our ancestors, [***Beowulf***] offers an interest exclusively its own. It is unquestionably the earliest composition of the heroic kind extant in any language of modern, or rather of barbarous, Europe. (p. 30)

[The writer of ***Beowulf***] speaks of his story as one of ancient days, and more than once appeals for his authority either to popular tradition or to some previously existing document. Whatever was his age, it is evident that he was a Christian, a circumstance which has perhaps rendered his work less frequent in allusions to the customs and superstitions of his pagan ancestors, and consequently somewhat less interesting to the poetical antiquary than if it had been the production of a mind acquainted only with that wild and picturesque mythology which forms so peculiar and attractive a feature of the earlier productions of the Scandinavian muse. (pp. 33-4)

The internal evidence of [***Beowulf***'s] language, and the structure of its sentences, in which it much resembles the poems attributed to Cædmon, would appear to justify our attributing it, in its present form, to the same æra which produced those singular compositions.

That its phraseology and allusions are frequently less intelligible may be readily accounted for by the greater obscurity of the subject. . . . (p. 34)

The narrative . . . of Beowulf's successful expedition against the Grendel, occupies nearly two-thirds of the manuscript; and, had the poet terminated his labours at this point, his composition would have added to the other qualifications which entitle it in some degree to the name of Epic, that of unity of plan; a praise seldom perhaps to be conceded to the earlier and more barbarous efforts of the heroic muse. He proceeds however, without interruption or apology, to the details of an adventure in which the same hero, fifty years after his elevation to the throne, was destined to engage, as might naturally be anticipated, with far other success. (p. 65)

[As] a specimen of language and composition, as a picture of manners and opinions, and in some measure even as an historical document, [***Beowulf***] possesses claims upon the notice of the scholar and the antiquary far beyond those which can be advanced by any other relique, hitherto discovered, of the same age and description. (p. 79)

It can hardly have escaped notice that the Scandinavian bard, in the general style and complexion of his poetry, approaches much more nearly to the father of the Grecian epic, than to the romancers of the middle ages. If I mistake not, this similarity will readily be traced in the simplicity of his plan, in the air of probability given to all its details, even where the subject may be termed supernatural; in the length and tone of the speeches introduced, and in their frequent digression to matters of contemporary or previous history. (pp. 79-80)

It may perhaps be thought scarcely worth while to offer any opinion on the poetical merits of our author. In some it may even excite a smile to hear a production so little resembling the purer models of classical antiquity dignified by the name of poetry, or considered as an object of criticism. We are all, I am fully conscious, liable not unfrequently to be misled by a natural prepossession in favour of that upon which we have employed any considerable portion of our time and labour. From this prepossession I do not pretend to be exempt; but I still apprehend that he who makes due allowance for the barbarisms and obscurity of the language (an obscurity much increased by our still imperfect knowledge of its poetical construction and vocabulary) and for the shackles of a metrical system at once of extreme difficulty, and, to our ears at least, totally destitute of harmony and expression, will find that ***Beowulf*** presents many of those which have in all ages been admitted as the genuine elements of poetic composition.

The plan (as it has been already stated) is sufficiently simple. The characters, as far as they are developed, are well sustained, and their speeches usually natural and well appropriated. The narrative is by no means so encumbered with repetitions as that of the reputed Cædmon; nor is the style so ambitious and inflated. Over the almost unintelligible rhapsodies of the Edda (for these are the fairest points of comparison) it possesses a decided superiority; nor are there many among the metrical romances of the more polished Normans, with which it may not fairly abide a competition.

If we except perhaps the frequency and length of the digressions, the only considerable offence against the received canons of the heroic muse is to be found in the extraordinary interval of time which elapses between the first and last exploits of the hero. . . . (pp. 80-1)

John Josias Conybeare, "Anglo-Saxon Poem Concerning the Exploits of Beowulf the Dane," in his Illustrations of Anglo-Saxon Poetry, *edited by William Daniel Conybeare, Harding and Lepard, 1826, pp. 30-167.*

ISAAC DISRAELI (essay date 1841)

[Although probably most famous as the father of novelist and British prime minister Benjamin Disraeli, Isaac Disraeli was a noted essayist and critic who wrote several popular and important studies of English literature. In the following excerpt from a book originally published in 1841, he compares the social customs portrayed in Beowulf *with those depicted in the Homeric epics.]*

The Anglo-Saxon poetical narrative of [***Beowulf***] forms a striking contrast with the chronological paraphrase of Cædmon. Its genuine antiquity unquestionably renders it a singular curiosity; but it derives an additional interest from its representation of the primitive simplicity of a Homeric period—the infancy of customs and manners and emotions of that Hero-life, which the Homeric poems first painted for mankind:—that Hero-life of which Macpherson in his Ossian caught but imperfect conceptions from the fragments he may have collected, while he metamorphosed his ideal Celtic heroes into those of the sentimental romance of another age and another race. (p. 51)

The war-ship and the mead-hall bring us back to that early era of society, when great men knew only to be heroes, flattered by their bards, whose songs are ever the echoes of their age and their patrons.

We discover these heroes, Danes or Angles, as we find them in the Homeric period, audacious with the self-confidence of their bodily prowess; vaunting, and talkative of their sires and of themselves; the son ever known by denoting the father, and the father by his marriage alliance—that primitive mode of recognition, at a period when, amid the perpetual conflicts of rival chieftains, scarcely any but relations could be friends; the family bond was a sure claim to protection. Like the Homeric heroes, they were as unrelenting in their hatreds as indissoluble in their partisanship; suspicious of the stranger, but welcoming the guest; we find them rapacious, for plunder was their treasure, and prodigal in their distributions of their golden armlets and weighed silver, for their egotism was as boundless as their violence. Yet pride and glory fermented the coarse leaven of these mighty marauders, who were even chivalric ere chivalry rose into an order. The religion of these ages was wild as their morality; few heroes but bore some relationship to Woden; and even in their rude paganised Christianity, some mythological name cast its lustre in their genealogies. In the uncritical chronicles of the middle ages it is not always evident whether the mortal was not a divinity. Their mythic legends have thrown confusion into their national annals, often accepted by historians as authentic records. But if antiquaries still wander among shadows, the poet cannot err. Beowulf may be a god or a nonentity, but the poem which records his exploits must at least be true, true in the manners it paints and the emotions which the poet reveals—the emotions of his contemporaries. (pp. 51-2)

Isaac Disraeli, "Beowulf: The Hero-Life," in his Amenities of Literature, Consisting of Sketches and

Characters of English Literature, *edited by the Earl of Beaconsfield, revised edition, Frederick Warne and Co., 1881, pp. 51-8.*

HIPPOLYTE A. TAINE (essay date 1863)

[Taine is often considered the founder of the sociological school of literary criticism. In his Histoire de la littérature anglaise *(1863-69;* History of English Literature, *1871) and other works, he argued that a work of literature is best understood as a product of three influences: race, moment, and milieu. By "race" Taine meant the combined physical traits and specific mental habits of a nation. Today, especially after the abuse of the term by the Nazis and by others, race is usually considered a weak and constricting criterion for judging literary works. Critics do not agree on what Taine meant by "moment," but it is often thought that the term implies either the sum of race and milieu, or simply the milieu of a particular time. "Milieu" is the only term that is still useful to critics. It includes, according to Taine's definition, not only the physical environment in which a work is produced but also the political and social conditions surrounding it. In the following excerpt from* History of English Literature, *Taine utilizes his tripartite theory of determinism in an examination of the character of Beowulf and the poetic merits of the work.]*

[***Beowulf*** contains the stories] which the thanes, seated on their stools, by the light of their torches, listened to as they drank the ale of their king; we can glean thence their manners and sentiments, as in the *Iliad* and the *Odyssey* those of the Greeks. Beowulf is a hero, a knight-errant before the days of chivalry, as the leaders of the German bands were feudal chiefs before the institution of feudalism. (p. 43)

[Beowulf's service to his people] is thorough and real generosity not exaggerated and pretended as it will be later on in the romantic imaginations of babbling clerics, mere composers of adventure. Fiction as yet is not far removed from fact: the man breathes manifest beneath the hero. Rude as the poetry is, its hero is grand; he is so, simply by his deeds. Faithful, first to his prince, then to his people, he went alone, in a strange land, to venture himself for the delivery of his fellowmen; he forgets himself in death, while thinking only that it profits others, "Each one of us," he says in one place, "must abide the end of his present life." Let, therefore, each do justice, if he can, before his death. Compare with him the monsters whom he destroys, the last traditions of the ancient wars against inferior races, and of the primitive religion; think of his life of danger, nights upon the waves, man grappling with the brute creation, man's indomitable will crushing the breasts of beasts; man's powerful muscles which, when exerted, tear the flesh of the monsters: you will see reappear through the mist of legends, and under the light of poetry, the valiant men who, amid the madness of war and the raging of their own mood, began to settle a people and to found a state. (p. 45)

Hippolyte A. Taine, "The Saxons," in his History of English Literature, Vol. I, *translated by H. Van Laun, Hurst & Company Publishers, n.d., pp. 33-56.*

HENRY WADSWORTH LONGFELLOW (essay date 1871)

[A nineteenth-century American poet, novelist, essayist, critic, and translator, Longfellow was one of the most popular American writers of his day. His reputation, however, suffered a serious decline after his death, when the very characteristics which made his poetry popular in his own day—gentle simplicity and a melancholy reminiscent of the German Romantics—fell out of favor, leading to critical reaction against his work. Notwithstanding the continuing debate over his literary stature, Longfellow is credited with having helped introduce European culture to American readers and with popularizing American folk themes abroad. In the following excerpt from the 1871 revision of his celebrated survey of European literature, The Poets and Poetry of Europe *(1845), he praises the epic and poetic qualities of* Beowulf.]

One of the oldest and most important remains of Anglo-Saxon literature is the epic poem of ***Beowulf.*** Its age is unknown; but it comes from a very distant and hoary antiquity; somewhere between the seventh and tenth centuries. It is like a piece of ancient armor; rusty and battered, and yet strong. From within comes a voice sepulchral, as if the ancient armor spoke, telling a simple, straight-forward narrative; with here and there the boastful speech of a rough old Dane, reminding one of those made by the heroes of Homer. The style, likewise, is simple,—perhaps one should say, austere. The bold metaphors, which characterize nearly all the Anglo-Saxon poems we have read, are for the most part wanting in this. The author seems mainly bent upon telling us, how his Sea-Goth slew the Grendel and the Fire-drake. He is too much in earnest to multiply epithets and gorgeous figures. At times he is tedious; at times obscure; and he who undertakes to read the original will find it no easy task. (p. 4)

[***Beowulf***] is filled up with abundant episodes and warlike details. We have ale-revels, and giving of bracelets, and presents of mares, and songs of bards. The battles with the Grendel and the Fire-drake are minutely described; as likewise are the dwellings and rich treasure-houses of these monsters. The fire-stream flows with lurid light; the dragon breathes out flame and pestilential breath; the gigantic sword, forged by the Jutes of old, dissolves and thaws like an icicle in the hero's grasp; and the swart raven tells the eagle how he fared with the fell wolf at the death-feast. Such is, in brief, the machinery of the poem. It possesses great epic merit, and in parts is strikingly graphic in its descriptions. As we read, we can almost smell the brine, and hear the sea-breeze blow, and see the main-land stretch out its jutting promontories, those sea-noses (*sæ-næssas*), as the poet calls them, into the blue waters of the solemn main. (pp. 4-5)

Henry Wadsworth Longfellow, "Anglo-Saxon Language and Poetry," in his The Poets and Poetry of Europe with Introductions and Biographical Notices, *revised edition, Houghton, Mifflin and Company, 1882, pp. 1-7.*

JOHN EARLE (essay date 1892)

[Earle was a nineteenth-century English linguist, editor, and palaeographer who wrote extensively on Anglo-Saxon life and literature. In the following excerpt, he discusses the comitatus relationship in Beowulf.]

There is one great thought which animates [***Beowulf***], and it is a thought proper to the time. It is the germinant thought of social organism, and it provides a theme adequate for an Epic, because it is coextensive with moral and political life so far as it had then been developed, and accordingly it embraces human interests of the highest order.

The thought is this:—*Mutual dependence is the law of human society*. No one is independent; not the strongest or noblest or most exalted; for he depends upon the support of those who are under him. Consideration and generosity from him to them; honour and fidelity and devotion from them to him; these are the rudimentary foundations upon which alone it is possible to erect and edify a stable fabric of government, to build up a State.

This thought pervades the allegorical narrative as a whole, and this thought is the text of that well-abused discourse which is the centrepiece of the poem. The unity of the poem is manifested by the readiness of every part, whether action or discourse, to be interpreted by reference to this thought. In the discourse of the aged king it is expanded; in the occasional maxims interspersed it is condensed; in the narrative as a whole it is dramatically represented and illustrated.

Hrothgar's discourse is a warning of the dangers which attend high success. Nothing is worse for men, nothing more hurtful to their understanding, than the consciousness of possessing a power which none can control. This is the cause of Hrothgar's solicitude for Beowulf, towards whom he has conceived a paternal affection. It is as if he said: "Do not fall into the snare of fancying yourself out of the reach of danger, and exempt from the common liabilities of humanity. When Heremod knew he had no match, he degenerated into a hectoring bully, he became intolerable, and he was driven forth by his own subjects."

The general sense of the poem is this. There is work for the age of Blood and Iron, but such an age must yield to a better. Force is not the supreme and final arbiter of human destiny; above and behind Might is enthroned the diviner genius of Right. In this idea we recognize the essential thought of Civilization, the clue to emergence out of barbarism. And even further back, as if in barbarism itself, we see a germ of culture and the gentler forms of life. The honoured position of woman, which here rests upon ancestral custom, is full of promise for the development of the nobler instincts of Society. (pp. lxxxvii-lxxxviii)

John Earle, in an introduction to The Deeds of Beowulf: An English Epic of the Eighth Century Done into Modern Prose, *translated by John Earle, Oxford at the Clarendon Press, Oxford, 1892, pp. ix-c.*

SARAH F. McNARY (essay date 1894)

[*In the following excerpt, McNary explores* Beowulf *as a reflection of Teutonic character and ideals.*]

Whether the ***Beowulf*** had its origin in nature, myth, or hero-worship, or sober history, or whether it is a combination of all three, is the province of the scholar to determine. The adoption of any one of these theories will not change the aesthetic or ethical aspect of the poem in its present form, nor will it in any degree modify the impress of Teutonism which it bears, the stamp of the Teutonic character and ideals. (p. 530)

Over the whole poem broods the thought of Wyrd ["Fate"]. The atmosphere is gray and misty, like the marsh home of Grendel, and through the grayness go stalking the huge dim forms of the giants and *nickers* of the northern cult. The gray gloom is a reflection of the conception these folk had of life, as well as a picture of the natural scenery which they daily looked upon. The conditions of life point always in the direction of tragedy. There is, however, no disposition to sit down and weep over the melancholy of it. Beowulf stands up bravely and looks the issue in the face,—Fate must be fought against, whatever the odds. Brave before all else is this Beowulf, with the bravery of a young, strong, unsoftened people, the physical courage which not only meets an enemy unshrinkingly, but seeks him out to fight with him alone and weaponless. This is the very rapture and madness of bravery, the apotheosis of daring. It is almost imaginative—rather, it so strips off and defies imagination as to capture that quality by the abnegation of it.

The love of praise and the desire for glory breathing through every utterance in the poem, are not the evidence of a vaulting ambition which seeks its goal through crooked ways, but rather the unrestrained outbreak of the longing for appreciated activity and power. Its root is in the instinct for the ruder kind of self-expression, the impulse to fight, to overcome obstacles by muscular force. Beowulf does not seek to conceal his desire for praise. He boasts of his exploits with a child's simplicity of enjoyment. His age is too far from civilization to have attained the virtue of modesty and the vice of hypocrisy. In spite of this large boastfulness, there is a temperance in his judgment of men and things, which predicates balance of temperament and strong wisdom in the race which produced him.

The spirit of loyalty that has already grown, in Beowulf's time, into a racial institution, is strongly impressed upon the poem. The duty of the *thegn* ["thane"] to his lord, a service resting upon sentiment as well as upon necessity, is performed heartily. The germ of feudalism and the prophecy of chivalry are here discovered, but it is only a germ as yet. Scarcely a hint of the love sentiment is to be found anywhere. Woman is seen in various relations, occupying always a position of dignity, and inspiring those feelings of respect, that sense of her inviolability, which is the great honor of the Teutonic race; but the tenderer feeling that nourished feudalism into chivalry is quite beyond the pale of Beowulf's experience. (pp. 531-32)

[***Beowulf***] is pagan and of the essence of paganism. The old fragment touching the Passing of Scyld hints of the mystery of birth and death; but aside from this there is no looking beyond that after-mystery, no dwelling upon the possibilities of the hereafter. The whole work is an embodiment of the idea of practicality. Beowulf died, not to establish a principle, but to secure the golden hoard of the fire-drake, and therefore the funeral dirge of this hero knells him out of the memory of men. The history of Beowulf is the pathos of paganism and of the material. It has been said that this is a half-finished epos, benumbed in the midst of its growth. It lies frozen because it is the imperfect ideal of a single, unmixed race; because it is wanting in elements that lay hold upon the higher imagination; because it was never touched by that "natural magic," that divine spark which is of the essence of immortality. But though Beowulf, as a single concrete character, passed so early out of English thought, the elements of his being passed into the English people, and he lives to-day in enduring qualities. He appears in history and in literature in varied forms. He lives the free life of law-abiding lawlessness with Robin Hood in Sherwood Forest. His loyalty breathes again in Shakespeare's Faulconbridge,—a loyalty deepened into reverence for the kingly office, and into love of race and country. He reaches England's heart through the kindly and kingly heartiness of Henry the Fifth. He stirs the English blood to go over seas on adventure in the great days of Elizabeth. He fights again with Nelson and the Iron Duke. Was his struggle with the dragons all in vain, when a dragon-slayer is patron saint of England? If Beowulf is no longer an ideal in the higher sense, it is because he has been lived into a type. (p. 532)

Sarah F. McNary, "Beowulf and Arthur as English Ideals," in Poet Lore, *Vol. VI, No. 11, November, 1894, pp. 529-36.*

W. J. COURTHOPE (essay date 1895)

[*Courthope was an English educator, poet, literary critic, and biographer whose most notable work is his six-volume* History of English Poetry *(1895-1910). Described as a confirmed classicist in poetic theory, Courthope reacted against Romanticism, advocating a return to the heroic couplet and satiric poetry characteristic of the English Augustan Age. Markedly nationalistic in intent, Courthope's criticism often focuses upon the extent to which authors reflect the English character and traditions that had enabled the British empire to arise from the institutions of the Middle Ages. In the following excerpt, Courthope argues that* Beowulf *is a work of oral literature by a Christian minstrel-poet that provides a valuable reflection of Teutonic life.*]

[It is evident] that the style of ***Beowulf*** is not that of a literary poet, but of a minstrel. Had it been a deliberate literary composition, it would have exhibited some traces of central design, and its joints and articulations would have been carefully marked; but the poem as it stands is a medley of heterogeneous materials, singularly wanting in plan and consistency. A literary "Demiurgus" of Anglo-Saxon descent, and separated by a long period from the events which he professed to be recording, would undoubtedly have tried to produce an appearance of order in his creation, by furnishing a clue to his historical allusions. But nothing can be more careless and casual than the references to the heroic exploits, the family relationships, and the tribal feuds of the persons and nations mentioned in the course of the story. This is just what might be expected in the style of oral minstrelsy; it is indeed an exact reproduction of the style of Homer. Exceedingly Homeric, too, are the stereotyped forms employed by the narrator to indicate stages in the action: the words prefatory to speeches, *e.g.* . . . Beowulf spake, the son of Ecgtheow; . . . formularies of description, such as, "The time flew on; the ship floated on the waves; the bark lay under the hill and the seamen with alacrity climbed on to her stern; the streams rolled; the water dashed against the sands"—the descriptions of objects by means of metaphors, as ["The shepherd of the people"; "the fallow flood"; "bone-locker," meaning flesh, just as Homer speaks of the "fence of teeth,"] . . . and the use of conventional epithets like ["confident in his might"]. . . . From these and similar characteristics I am inclined to infer that the poem, in its existing form, was composed for the purpose of chanting or recitation, on lines long familiar to the Teutonic race, and by the aid of materials derived perhaps from a remote antiquity. But it is not, therefore, necessary to assent to . . . [the view] that it is a *mere* assemblage of unconnected lays, each of which may be regarded as having once formed a separate whole. The unity of the work lies in the deeds and character of Beowulf, and this central conception shows every sign of having proceeded from the mind of a single poet, though it was doubtless built by him out of materials previously existing. That he was a Christian and sang before a Christian audience is evident, but I do not think we need conclude . . . that he was an ecclesiastic. It seems to me more reasonable to suppose him a scop of the roving kind described in *The Traveller,* who was accustomed to wander from court to court, entertaining the lords who supported him with the legends of ancestors common to the race. On this hypothesis there would be no difficulty in understanding why the exploits of Danes and Swedes should have been recited in the court of an Anglo-Saxon king. Whether the poem was altered or added to after it was reduced to writing is a question of comparatively trifling importance.

Thus much it has been necessary to say in support of the proposition that ***Beowulf*** is to be regarded as a sample of the minstrelsy prevailing among the Anglo-Saxons before their conversion to Christianity. For whatever may be the date of the composition, it is clear that in the essence of its mythology, in its treatment of history, and in its representation of manners, the poem affords a vivid reflection of primitive Teutonic life. As regards mythology, it is of course impossible for us to form a clear conception of the manner in which our ancestors reasoned about nature; but the demons and monsters mentioned in ***Beowulf*** must in some way have represented to them the wasting forces of evil by which mankind are beset. Moreover, it is to be observed that the chief of these malignant beings—Grendel, Grendel's mother, and the fire-drake—are each associated with different elements. The Christian poet is indeed at much pains to point out that Grendel was a descendant of Cain; but he has preserved the ancestral belief about this fiend, which makes him "a great stepper over the mark, who held the moors, the fens, and the wilderness"—an interesting relic of the primeval religion by which all the land belonging to the mark or boundary of the tribe was left uncultivated and regarded as accursed. Grendel may, therefore, have been a personification of plague and pestilence, by which Hrothgar's bright hall of Heorot was ravaged. In Grendel's mother, the old sea-wolf, who takes vengeance on the Danes for the death of her son, we find a trace of the curious Teutonic belief that the prime power of evil was born of woman, an idea long preserved in the common English expression, "devil's dam." The description of the places haunted by this ancient fiend, when on shore, is a remarkable piece of painting, showing the terror with which the waste scenery of the mark-land filled the imagination of the people. (pp. 88-91)

W. J. Courthope, "The Poetry of the Anglo-Saxons," in his A History of English Poetry: The Middle Ages, Vol. I, *Macmillan and Co., Limited, 1919, pp. 79-111.*

W. P. KER (essay date 1897)

[*Ker was a noted English medievalist and an authority on comparative European literature and the history of literary forms. In the following excerpt, he favorably compares* Beowulf *with classical epics, focusing upon the structure, unity, characterizations, and fantastic elements of the English work.*]

The poem of ***Beowulf*** has been sorely tried; critics have long been at work on the body of it, to discover how it is made. It gives many openings for theories of agglutination and adulteration. Many things in it are plainly incongruous. The pedigree of Grendel is not authentic; the Christian sentiments and morals are not in keeping with the heroic or the mythical substance of the poem; the conduct of the narrative is not always clear or easy to follow. These difficulties and contradictions have to be explained; the composition of the poem has to be analysed; what is old has to be separated from what is new and adventitious; and the various senses and degrees of "old" and "new" have to be determined, in the criticism of the poem. With all this, however, the poem continues to possess at least an apparent and external unity. It is an extant book, whatever the history of its composition may have been; the book of the adventures of Beowulf, written out fair by two scribes in the tenth century; an epic poem, with a prologue at the beginning, and a judgment pronounced on the life of the hero at the end; a single book, considered as such by its transcribers, and making a claim to be so considered.

Before any process of disintegration is begun, this claim should be taken into account; the poem deserves to be appreciated as it stands. Whatever may be the secrets of its authorship, it exists as a single continuous narrative poem; and whatever its faults may be, it holds a position by itself, and a place of some honour, as the one extant poem of considerable length in the group to which it belongs. It has a meaning and value apart from the questions of its origin and its mode of production. Its present value as a poem is not affected by proofs or arguments regarding the way in which it may have been patched or edited. The patchwork theory has no power to make new faults in the poem; it can only point out what faults exist, and draw inferences from them. It does not take away from any dignity the book may possess in its present form, that it has been subjected to the same kind of examination as the *Iliad*. The poem may be reviewed as it stands, in order to find out what sort of thing passed for heroic poetry with the English at the time the present copy of the poem was written. However the result was obtained, ***Beowulf*** is, at any rate, the specimen by which the Teutonic epic poetry must be judged. It is the largest monument extant. There is nothing beyond it, in that kind, in respect of size and completeness. If the old Teutonic epic is judged to have failed, it must be because ***Beowulf*** is a failure.

Taking the most cursory view of the story of ***Beowulf,*** it is easy to recognise that the unity of the plot is not like the unity of the *Iliad* or the *Odyssey*. One is inclined at first to reckon *Beowulf* along with those epics of which Aristotle speaks, the *Heracleids* and *Theseids,* the authors of which "imagined that because Heracles was one person the story of his life could not fail to have unity."

It is impossible to reduce the poem of ***Beowulf*** to the scale of Aristotle's [summary of the] *Odyssey* without revealing the faults of structure in the English poem. . . . (pp. 158-60)

Aristotle made a summary of the Homeric poem, because he wished to show how simple its construction really was, apart from the episodes. It is impossible, by any process of reduction and simplification, to get rid of the duality in ***Beowulf.*** It has many episodes, quite consistent with a general unity of action, but there is something more than episodes, there is a sequel. It is as if to the *Odyssey* there had been added some later books telling in full of the old age of Odysseus, far from the sea, and his death at the hands of his son Telemachus. The adventure with the dragon is separate from the earlier adventures. It is only connected with them because the same person is involved in both. (p. 160)

Homer had not to wait for ***Beowulf*** to serve as a foil to his excellence. That was provided in the other epic poems of Greece, in the cycle of Troy, in the epic stories of Theseus and Heracles. It seems probable that the poem of ***Beowulf*** may be at least as well knit as the *Little Iliad,* the Greek cyclic poem of which Aristotle names the principal incidents, contrasting its variety with the simplicity of the *Iliad* and *Odyssey*.

Indeed it is clear that the plan of ***Beowulf*** might easily have been much worse, that is, more lax and diffuse, than it is. This meagre amount of praise will be allowed by the most grudging critics, if they will only think of the masses of French epic, and imagine the extent to which a French company of poets might have prolonged the narrative of the hero's life—the *Enfances,* the *Chevalerie*—before reaching the *Death of Beowulf*.

At line 2200 in ***Beowulf*** comes the long interval of time, the fifty years between the adventure at Heorot and the fight between Beowulf and the dragon. Two thousand lines are given to the first story, a thousand to the *Death of Beowulf*. Two thousand lines are occupied with the narrative of Beowulf's expedition, his voyage to Denmark, his fight with Grendel and Grendel's mother, his return to the land of the Gauts and his report of the whole matter to King Hygelac. In this part of the poem, taken by itself, there is no defect of unity. The action is one, with different parts all easily and naturally included between the first voyage and the return. It is amplified and complicated with details, but none of these introduce any new main interests. ***Beowulf*** is not like the *Heracleids* and *Theseids*. It transgresses the limits of the Homeric unity, by adding a sequel; but for all that it is not a mere string of adventures, like the bad epic in Horace's *Art of Poetry,* or the innocent plays described by Sir Philip Sidney and Cervantes. A third of the whole poem is detached, a separate adventure. The first two-thirds taken by themselves form a complete poem, with a single action; while, in the orthodox epic manner, various allusions and explanations are introduced regarding the past history of the personages involved, and the history of other people famous in tradition. The adventure at Heorot, taken by itself, would pass the scrutiny of Aristotle or Horace, as far as concerns the lines of its composition.

There is variety in it, but the variety is kept in order and not allowed to interfere or compete with the main story. The past history is disclosed, and the subordinate novels are interpolated, as in the *Odyssey,* in the course of an evening's conversation in hall, or in some other interval in the action. In the introduction of accessory matter, standing in different degrees of relevance to the main plot, the practice of ***Beowulf*** is not essentially different from that of classical epic.

In the *Iliad* we are allowed to catch something of the story of the old time before Agamemnon,—the war of Thebes, Lycurgus, Jason, Heracles,—and even of things less widely notable, less of a concern to the world than the voyage of Argo, such as, for instance, the business of Nestor in his youth. In ***Beowulf,*** in a similar way, the inexhaustible world outside the story is partly represented by means of allusions and digressions. The tragedy of Finnesburh is sung by the harper, and his song is reported at some length, not merely referred to in passing. The stories of Thrytho, of Heremod, of Sigemund the Waelsing and Fitela his son (Sigmund and Sinfiotli), are introduced like the stories of Lycurgus or of Jason in Homer. They are illustrations of the action, taken from other cycles. The fortunes of the Danish and Gautish kings, the fall of Hygelac, the feuds with Sweden, these matters come into closer relation with the story. They are not so much illustrations taken in from without, as points of attachment between the history of ***Beowulf*** and the untold history all round it, the history of the persons concerned, along with Beowulf himself, in the vicissitudes of the Danish and Gautish kingdoms. (pp. 160-63)

In the episodic passages of ***Beowulf*** there are, curiously, the same degrees of relevance as in the *Iliad* and *Odyssey*.

Some of them are necessary to the proper fulness of the story, though not essential parts of the plot. Such are the references to Beowulf's swimming-match; and such, in the *Odyssey,* is the tale told to Alcinous.

The allusions to the wars of Hygelac have the same value as the references in the *Iliad* and the *Odyssey* to such portions of the tale of Troy, and of the return of the Greek lords, as are not immediately connected with the anger of Achilles, or the return of Odysseus. The tale of Finnesburh in ***Beowulf*** is purely an interlude, as much as the ballad of Ares and Aphrodite in the *Odyssey*.

Many of the references to other legends in the *Iliad* are illustrative and comparative, like the passages about Heremod or Thrytho in ***Beowulf.*** "Ares suffered when Otus and Ephialtes kept him in a brazen vat, Hera suffered and Hades suffered, and were shot with the arrows of the son of Amphitryon." . . . The long parenthetical story of Heracles in a speech of Agamemnon . . . has the same irrelevance of association, and has incurred the same critical suspicions, as the contrast of Hygd and Thrytho, a fairly long passage out of a wholly different story, introduced in ***Beowulf*** on the very slightest of suggestions.

Thus in ***Beowulf*** and in the Homeric poems there are episodes that are strictly relevant and consistent, filling up the epic plan, opening out the perspective of the story; also episodes that without being strictly relevant are rightly proportioned and subordinated, like the interlude of Finnesburh, decoration added to the structure, but not overloading it, nor interfering with the design; and, thirdly, episodes that seem to be irrelevant, and may possibly be interpolations. All these kinds have the effect of increasing the mass as well as the variety of the work, and they give to ***Beowulf*** the character of a poem which, in dealing with one action out of an heroic cycle, is able, by the way, to hint at and partially represent a great number of other stories.

It is not in the episodes alone that ***Beowulf*** has an advantage over the shorter and more summary poems. The frequent episodes are only part of the general liberality of the narrative.

The narrative is far more cramped than in Homer; but when compared with the short method of the Northern poems, not to speak of the ballads, it comes out as itself Homeric by contrast. It succeeds in representing pretty fully and continuously, not by mere allusions and implications, certain portions of heroic life and action.

The principal actions in ***Beowulf*** are curiously trivial, taken by themselves. All around them are the rumours of great heroic and tragic events, and the scene and the personages are heroic and magnificent. But the plot in itself has no very great poetical value; as compared with the tragic themes of the Niblung legend, with the tale of Finnesburh, or even with the historical seriousness of the *Maldon* poem, it lacks weight. The largest of the extant poems of this school has the least important subject-matter; while things essentially and in the abstract more important, like the tragedy of Froda and Ingeld, are thrust away into the corners of the poem.

In the killing of a monster like Grendel, or in the killing of a dragon, there is nothing particularly interesting; no complication to make a fit subject for epic. ***Beowulf*** is defective from the first in respect of plot.

The story of Grendel and his mother is one that has been told in myriads of ways; there is nothing commoner, except dragons. The killing of dragons and other monsters is the regular occupation of the heroes of old wives' tales; and it is difficult to give individuality or epic dignity to commonplaces of this sort. This, however, is accomplished in the poem of ***Beowulf.*** Nothing can make the story of Grendel dramatic like the story of Waldere or of Finnesburh. But the poet has, at any rate, in connexion with this simple theme, given a rendering, consistent, adequate, and well-proportioned, of certain aspects of life and certain representative characters in an heroic age.

The characters in ***Beowulf*** are not much more than types; not much more clearly individual than the persons of a comedy of Terence. In the shorter Northern poems there are the characters of Brynhild and Gudrun; there is nothing in ***Beowulf*** to compare with them, although in ***Beowulf*** the personages are consistent with themselves, and intelligible.

Hrothgar is the generous king whose qualities were in Northern history transferred to his nephew Hrothulf (Hrolf Kraki), the type of peaceful strength, a man of war living quietly in the intervals of war.

Beowulf is like him in magnanimity, but his character is less uniform. He is not one of the more cruel adventurers, like Starkad in the myth, or some of the men of the Icelandic Sagas. But he is an adventurer with something strange and not altogether safe in his disposition. His youth was like that of the lubberly younger sons in the fairy stories. "They said that he was slack." Though he does not swagger like a Berserk, nor "gab" like the Paladins of Charlemagne, he is ready on provocation to boast of what he has done. The pathetic sentiment of his farewell to Hrothgar is possibly to be ascribed, in the details of its rhetoric, to the common affection of Anglo-Saxon poetry for the elegiac mood; but the softer passages are not out of keeping with the wilder moments of ***Beowulf,*** and they add greatly to the interest of his character. He is more variable, more dramatic, than the king and queen of the Danes, or any of the secondary personages.

Wealhtheo, the queen, represents the poetical idea of a noble lady. There is nothing complex or strongly dramatic in her character. Hunferth, the envious man, brought in as a foil to Beowulf, is not caricatured or exaggerated. His sourness is that of a critic and a politician, disinclined to accept newcomers on their own valuation. He is not a figure of envy in a moral allegory.

In the latter part of the poem it is impossible to find in the character of Wiglaf more than the general and abstract qualities of the "loyal servitor."

Yet all those abstract and typical characters are introduced in such a way as to complete and fill up the picture. The general impression is one of variety and complexity, though the elements of it are simple enough.

With a plot like that of ***Beowulf*** it might seem that there was danger of a lapse from the more serious kind of heroic composition into a more trivial kind. Certainly there is nothing in the plain story to give much help to the author; nothing in Grendel to fascinate or tempt a poet with a story made to his hand.

The plot of ***Beowulf*** is not more serious than that of a thousand easy-going romances of chivalry, and of fairy tales beyond all number.

The strength of what may be called an epic tradition is shown in the superiority of ***Beowulf*** to the temptations of cheap romantic commonplace. Beowulf, the hero, is, after all, something different from the giant-killer of popular stories, the dragon-slayer of the romantic schools. It is the virtue and the triumph of the poet of ***Beowulf*** that when all is done the characters of the poem remain distinct in the memory, that the thoughts and sentiments of the poem are remembered as significant, in a way that is not the way of the common romance. Although the incidents that take up the principal part of the scene of ***Beowulf*** are among the commonest in popular stories, it is impossible to mistake the poem for one of the ordinary tales of terror and wonder. The essential part of the poem is the drama of characters; though the plot happens to be such that the characters are never made to undergo a tragic ordeal like that of so many of the other Teutonic stories. It is not incorrect to say of the poem of ***Beowulf*** that the main story is really less important to the imagination than the accessories by which the characters are defined and distinguished. It is the defect of the poem this should be so. There is a constitutional weakness in it.

Although the two stories of ***Beowulf*** are both commonplace, there is a difference between the story of Grendel and the story of the dragon.

The story of the dragon is more of a commonplace than the other. Almost every one of any distinction, and many quite ordinary people in certain periods of history have killed dragons; from Hercules and Bellerophon to Gawain, who, on different occasions, narrowly escaped the fate of Beowulf; from Harald Hardrada (who killed two at least) to More of More Hall who killed the dragon of Wantley.

The latter part of ***Beowulf*** is a tissue of commonplaces of every kind: the dragon and its treasure; the devastation of the land; the hero against the dragon; the defection of his companions; the loyalty of one of them; the fight with the dragon; the dragon killed, and the hero dying from the flame and the venom of it; these are commonplaces of the story, and in addition to these there are commonplaces of sentiment, the old theme of this transitory life that "fareth as a fantasy," the lament for the glory passed away; and the equally common theme of loyalty and treason in contrast. Everything is commonplace, while everything is also magnificent in its way, and set forth in the right epic style, with elegiac passages here and there. Everything is commonplace except the allusions to matters of historical tradition, such as the death of Ongentheow, the death of Hygelac. With these exceptions, there is nothing in the latter part of ***Beowulf*** that might not have been taken at almost any time from the common stock of fables and appropriate sentiments, familiar to every maker or hearer of poetry from the days of the English conquest of Britain, and long before that. It is not to be denied that the commonplaces here are handled with some discretion; though commonplace, they are not mean or dull.

The story of Grendel and his mother is also common, but not as common as the dragon. The function of this story is considerably different from the other, and the class to which it belongs is differently distributed in literature. Both are stories of the killing of monsters, both belong naturally to legends of heroes like Theseus or Hercules. But for literature there is this difference between them, that dragons belong more appropriately to the more fantastic kinds of narrative, while stories of the deliverance of a house from a pestilent goblin are much more capable of sober treatment and verisimilitude. Dragons are more easily distinguished and set aside as fabulous monsters than is the family of Grendel. Thus the story of Grendel is much better fitted than the dragon story for a composition like ***Beowulf,*** which includes a considerable amount of the detail of common experience and ordinary life. Dragons are easily scared from the neighbourhood of sober experience; they have to be looked for in the mountains and caverns of romance or fable. Whereas Grendel remains a possibility in the middle of common life, long after the last dragon has been disposed of.

The people who tell fairy stories like the *Well of the World's End,* the *Knight of the Red Shield,* the *Castle East o' the Sun and West o' the Moon,* have no belief, have neither belief nor disbelief, in the adventures of them. But the same people have other stories of which they take a different view, stories of wonderful things more near to their own experience. Many a man to whom the *Well of the World's End* is an idea, a fancy, has in his mind a story like that of Grendel which he believes, which makes him afraid. The bogle that comes to a house at night and throttles the goodman is a creature more hardy than the dragon, and more persevering. Stories like that of Beowulf and Grendel are to be found along with other popular stories in collections; but they are to be distinguished from them. There are popular heroes of tradition to this day who are called to do for lonely houses the service done by Beowulf for the house of Hrothgar. (pp. 163-70)

There are people, no doubt, for whom Peer Gynt and the trolls, Uistean Mor and the warlock, even Selkolla that Bishop Gudmund killed, are as impossible as the dragon in the end of the poem of ***Beowulf.*** But it is certain that stories like those of Grendel are commonly believed in many places where dragons are extinct. The story of Beowulf and Grendel is not wildly fantastic or improbable; it agrees with the conditions of real life, as they have been commonly understood at all times except those of peculiar enlightenment and rationalism. . . . Grendel in the poem of ***Beowulf*** is in the same order of existence as [the portents of the Sirens or of Calypso in the *Odyssey*]. If they are superstitions, they are among the most persistent; and they are superstitions, rather than creatures of romance. The fight with Grendel is not of the same kind of adventure as Sigurd at the hedge of flame, or Svipdag at the enchanted castle. And the episode of Grendel's mother is further from matter of fact than the story of Grendel himself. The description of the desolate water is justly recognised as one of the masterpieces of the old English poetry; it deserves all that has been said of it as a passage of romance in the middle of epic. Beowulf's descent under the water, his fight with the warlock's mother, the darkness of that "sea dingle," the light of the mysterious sword, all this, if less admirably worked out than the first description of the dolorous mere, is quite as far from Heorot and the report of the table-talk of Hrothgar, Beowulf, and Hunferth. It is also a different sort of thing from the fight with Grendel. There is more of supernatural incident, more romantic ornament, less of that concentration in the struggle which makes the fight with Grendel almost as good in its way as its Icelandic counterpart, the wrestling of Grettir and Glam.

The story of ***Beowulf,*** which in the fight with Grendel has analogies with the plainer kind of goblin story, rather alters its tone in the fight with Grendel's mother. There are parallels in *Grettis Saga,* and elsewhere, to encounters like this, with a hag or ogress under water; stories of this sort have been found no less credible than stories of haunting warlocks like Grendel. But this second story is not told in the same way as the first. It has more of the fashion and temper of mythical fable or romance, and less of matter of fact. More particularly, the old sword, the sword of light, in the possession of Grendel's dam in her house under the water, makes one think of other legends of mysterious swords, like that of Helgi, and the "glaives of light" that are in the keeping of divers "gyre carlines" in the *West Highland Tales.* Further, the whole scheme is a common one in popular stories, especially in Celtic stories of giants; after the giant is killed his mother comes to avenge him.

Nevertheless, the controlling power in the story of ***Beowulf*** is not that of any kind of romance or fantastic invention; neither the original fantasy of popular stories nor the literary embellishments of romantic schools of poetry. There are things in ***Beowulf*** that may be compared to things in the fairy tales; and, again, there are passages of high value for their use of the motive of pure awe and mystery. But the poem is made what it is by the power with which the characters are kept in right relation to their circumstances. The hero is not lost or carried away in his adventures. The introduction, the arrival in Heorot, and the conclusion, the return of Beowulf to his own country, are quite unlike the manner of pure romance; and these are the parts of the work by which it is most accurately to be judged.

The adventure of Grendel is put in its right proportion when it is related by Beowulf to Hygelac. The repetition of the story, in a shorter form, and in the mouth of the hero himself, gives strength and body to a theme that was in danger of appearing trivial and fantastic. The popular story-teller has done his work when he has told the adventures of the giant-killer; the epic poet has failed, if he has done no more than this.

The character and personage of Beowulf must be brought out and impressed on the audience; it is the poet's hero that they are bound to admire. He appeals to them, not directly, but with unmistakable force and emphasis, to say that they have beheld ("as may unworthiness define") the nature of the hero, and to give him their praises.

The beauty and the strength of the poem of ***Beowulf,*** as of all true epic, depend mainly upon its comprehensive power, its inclusion of various aspects, its faculty of changing the mood of the story. The fight with Grendel is an adventure of one sort, grim, unrelieved, touching close upon the springs of mortal terror, the recollection or the apprehension of real adversaries possibly to be met with in the darkness. The fight with Grendel's mother touches on other motives; the terror is further away from human habitations, and it is accompanied with a charm and a beauty, the beauty of the Gorgon, such as is absent from the first adventure. It would have loosened the tension and broken the unity of the scene, if any such irrelevances had been admitted into the story of the fight with Grendel. The fight with Grendel's mother is fought under other conditions; the stress is not the same; the hero goes out to conquer, he is beset by no such apprehension as in the case of the night attack. The poet is at this point free to make use of a new set of motives, and here it is rather the scene than the action that is made vivid to the mind. But after this excursion the story comes back to its heroic beginning; and the conversation of Beowulf with his hosts in Denmark, and the report that he gives to his kin in Gautland, are enough to reduce to its right episodic dimensions the fantasy of the adventure under the sea. In the latter part of the poem there is still another distribution of interest. The conversation of the personages is still to be found occasionally carried on in the steady tones of people who have lives of their own, and belong to a world where the tunes are not all in one key. At the same time, it cannot be denied that the story of the *Death of Beowulf* is inclined to monotony. The epic variety and independence are obliterated by the too obviously pathetic intention. The character of this part of the poem is that of a late school of heroic poetry attempting, and with some success, to extract the spirit of an older kind of poetry, and to represent in one scene an heroic ideal or example, with emphasis and with concentration of all the available matter. But while the end of the poem may lose in some things by comparison with the stronger earlier parts, it is not so wholly lost in the charms of pathetic meditation as to forget the martial tone and the more resolute air altogether. There was a danger that Beowulf should be transformed into a sort of Amadis, a mirror of the earlier chivalry; with a loyal servitor attending upon his death, and uttering the rhetorical panegyric of an abstract ideal. But this danger is avoided, at least in part. Beowulf is still, in his death, a sharer in the fortunes of the Northern houses; he keeps his history. The fight with the dragon is shot through with reminiscences of the Gautish wars: Wiglaf speaks his sorrow for the champion of the Gauts; the virtues of Beowulf are not those of a fictitious paragon king, but of a man who would be missed in the day when the enemies of the Gauts should come upon them.

A badly damaged page of the Beowulf *manuscript, showing the effects of the Cottonian fire.*

The epic keeps its hold upon what went before, and on what is to come. Its construction is solid, not flat. It is exposed to the attractions of all kinds of subordinate and partial literature,—the fairy story, the conventional romance, the pathetic legend,—and it escapes them all by taking them all up as moments, as episodes and points of view, governed by the conception, or the comprehension, of some of the possibilities of human character in a certain form of society. It does not impose any one view on the reader; it gives what it is the proper task of the higher kind of fiction to give—the play of life in different moods and under different aspects. (pp. 171-75)

W. P. Ker, "'Beowulf'," in his Epic and Romance: Essays on Medieval Literature, *1897. Reprint by Dover Publications, Inc., 1957, pp. 158-75.*

STOPFORD A. BROOKE (essay date 1898)

[Brooke was an Anglo-Irish clergyman, poet, critic, and educator whose Primer of English Literature *(1876) was popular with generations of students and whose other works on literature, including*

Theology in the English Poets *(1874),* English Literature from the Beginning to the Norman Conquest *(1898), and* Naturalism in English Poetry *(1920), were widely read and admired. In the following excerpt, he discusses the subject and poetic craft of* Beowulf, *noting several differences between the poem and traditional epic poetry and contending that the work is more properly viewed as a personal narrative.*]

[***Beowulf***] has been called an epic, but it is narrative rather than epic poetry. The subject has not the weight or dignity of an epic poem, nor the mighty fates round which an epic should revolve. Its story is rather personal than national. The one epic quality it has, the purification of the hero, the evolution of his character through trial into perfection—and Beowulf passes from the isolated hero into the image of an heroic king who dies for his people—may belong to a narrative poem. Moreover the poem is made up of two narratives with an interval of some sixty years, an interval which alone removes it from the epic method, which is bound to perfect the subject in an ordered, allotted, and continuous space of time. But as a narrative, even broken as it is, it attains unity from the unity of the myth it represents under two forms, and from the unity of the hero's character. He is the same in soul, after fifty years, that he was when young. There is also a force, vitality, clearness and distinctiveness of portraiture, not only in Beowulf's personality, but in that of all the other personages, which raise the poem into a high place, and predict that special excellence of personal portraiture which has made the English drama so famous in the world. Great imagination is not one of the excellences of ***Beowulf,*** but it has pictorial power of a fine kind, and the myth of summer and winter on which it rests is out of the imagination of the natural and early world. It has a clear vision of places and things and persons; it has preserved for us two monstrous types out of the very early world. When we leave out the repetitions which oral poetry created and excuses, it is rapid and direct; and the dialogue is brief, simple and human. Finally, we must not judge it in the study. If we wish to feel whether ***Beowulf*** is good poetry, we should place ourselves, as evening draws on, in the hall of the folk, when the benches are filled with warriors, merchants and seamen, and the Chief sits in the high seat, and the fires flame down the midst, and the cup goes round—and hear the Shaper strike the harp to sing this heroic lay. Then, as he sings of the great fight with Grendel or the dragon, of the treasure-giving of the king, and of the well-known swords, of the sea-rovings and the sea-hunts and the brave death of men, to sailors who knew the storms, to the fierce rovers who fought and died with glee, to great chiefs who led their warriors, and to warriors who never left a shield, we feel how heroic the verse is, how passionate with national feeling, how full of noble pleasure. The poem is great in its own way, and the way is an English way. The men, the women, at home and in war, are one in character with us. It is our Genesis, the book of our origins. (pp. 81-3)

Stopford A. Brooke, "Beowulf" and "Beowulf—The Poem," in his English Literature: From the Beginning to the Norman Conquest, *1898. Reprint by Macmillan and Co., Limited, 1921, pp. 58-67, 68-83.*

W. P. KER (essay date 1904)

[*In the following excerpt, Ker comments on the stylistic strengths and weaknesses of* Beowulf.]

A reasonable view of the merit of ***Beowulf*** is not impossible, though rash enthusiasm may have made too much of it, while a correct and sober taste may have too contemptuously refused to attend to Grendel or the Firedrake. The fault of ***Beowulf*** is that there is nothing much in the story. The hero is occupied in killing monsters, like Hercules or Theseus. But there are other things in the lives of Hercules and Theseus besides the killing of the Hydra or of Procrustes. Beowulf has nothing else to do, when he has killed Grendel and Grendel's mother in Denmark: he goes home to his own Gautland, until at last the rolling years bring the Firedrake and his last adventure. It is too simple. Yet the three chief episodes are well wrought and well diversified; they are not repetitions, exactly; there is a change of temper between the wrestling with Grendel in the night at Heorot and the descent under water to encounter Grendel's mother; while the sentiment of the Dragon is different again. But the great beauty, the real value, of ***Beowulf*** is in its dignity of style. In construction it is curiously weak, in a sense preposterous; for while the main story is simplicity itself, the merest commonplace of heroic legend, all about it, in the historic allusions, there are revelations of a whole world of tragedy, plots different in import from that of ***Beowulf,*** more like the tragic themes of Iceland. Yet with this radical defect, a disproportion that puts the irrelevances in the centre and the serious things on the outer edges, the poem of ***Bęowulf*** is unmistakably heroic and weighty. The thing itself is cheap; the moral and the spirit of it can only be matched among the noblest authors. It is not in the operations against Grendel, but in the humanities of the more leisurely interludes, the conversation of Beowulf and Hrothgar, and such things, that the poet truly asserts his power. It has often been pointed out how like the circumstances are in the welcome of Beowulf at Heorot and the reception of Ulysses in Phæacia. Hrothgar and his queen are not less gentle than Alcinous and Arete. There is nothing to compare with them in the Norse poems: it is not till the prose histories of Iceland appear that one meets with the like temper there. It is not common in any age; it is notably wanting in Middle English literature, because it is an aristocratic temper, secure of itself, and not imitable by the poets of an uncourtly language composing for a simple-minded audience. (pp. 252-54)

W. P. Ker, "The Teutonic Language," in his The Dark Ages, *1904. Reprint by Thomas Nelson and Sons Ltd., 1955, pp. 228-318.*

JAMES ROUTH (essay date 1911)

[*Routh was an American academic, poet, and journalist who, in addition to his several studies of the history of English criticism, wrote widely on philological and other technical issues of English language and literature. In the following excerpt, he describes the value of* Beowulf *as a work of literature and discusses the strengths and shortcomings of the poem.*]

[Regardless] of popularity, what is the real value of . . . the ***Beowulf***? The unlearned and the learned are alike vague in their answers. "The ***Beowulf,***" says one, "oh yes, great literature for that people in that age, but crude." It is the opinion of the average critic, who in all probability has never read a line of it, except in a translation,—which is like looking at a red rose through blue glasses. At the other extreme are the philologists. When a philologist approaches this subject, too often he leaves behind all sense of comparative values, and focuses his microscope solely upon the ***Beowulf*** and its contemporaries. The result is characteristic. As the contemporaries are mostly worthless, the ***Beowulf*** looms by contrast to prodigious and Homeric proportions. To the reader whose interest is primarily in literary, not in philological, values, these extreme decisions are equally unsatisfactory. That the ***Beowulf*** is not the yawp of a savage, but literature worth reading, is a commonplace. On the other hand, it is certainly not one of the first among the great epics of the world. Where then is its place in literature?

Again, what is the character of this enigmatic poem? To many critics anything old is the source of an archaeologically aesthetic thrill. There is about it something unreal, and stagey, and alluring. . . . All life, to [these critics] is a stage, on which literary types play their parts according to preconceived ideas. From this school we can evidently get nothing of the spirit of the ***Beowulf.***

If we turn to the philologists we are not much better off. We ask, for example, if the ***Beowulf*** is a part of the great epic tradition of mankind: does it show us the mystery of blind mankind wandering in darkness, or the tragedy of death and its night-dark hereafter? Is there about it the sublimity of a human character rising above the gloom of world-wide ignorance and helplessness? There is no answer from philology; though we are told that the poem has repeated phrases, recurring allusions, and such like, and that these are signs of an epic style. Analysis there is, among the philologists, of the majesty and music of the verse form. But except for this, there is little explanation of the spirit of the poem.

The question, then, for the literary reader is not the position of the ***Beowulf*** in literary history, not the manners and customs of the people for whom it was composed, not even the question of whether it be all by the same hand or by different hands. Still less it is a question of archaic thrills. The question is: first, What is the absolute value of the poem as literature when compared with the *Faerie Queen* and *Paradise Lost,* the *Canterbury Tales* and the *Idylls of the King;* second, What is the meaning of the poem to us, not as historians of the twentieth century, but merely as men? (pp. 29-30)

That the poem as a whole is incoherent, digressive, and totally lacking in plot-organization, must be admitted. To say that the poet had no means, in his day, of knowing how to compose a plot, is not to the purpose. Regardless of what information he had, the fact that he could not build a plot marks his production as primitive to that extent; therefore, from the standpoint of absolute values, to that extent weak. Were the architectonic qualities of the ***Beowulf*** the only ones to be considered, the poem would be a matter merely of antiquarian interest. But, fortunately for our great epic, there is something more to a verse story than plot-construction.

We cannot go into the subject of the rhythm of the poem, as it would involve us in too many technicalities. Suffice it to say that the rhythm is as perfect of its sort, as polished, as artificial even, as Milton's. There is not the slightest trace of that crudity which ignorance has attributed to it. That the language is harsh, and the system of metrics intrinsically inferior to the Latin and to the modern English, may be conceded, without its being granted that they are any the less beautiful enough to be intrinsically and in themselves worth while. The strength and swing, and even variety, of the Anglo-Saxon metre, are things for which we may look in vain in classic or in later tongues, and things without which universal literature would be distinctly the poorer. That this peculiar metre has not survived is due less to any real weakness or defect in it than to the fact that no modern language of civilization retains the strongly accentual and explosive form of utterance which was essential to its use. In the matter of rhythm, then, though the ***Beowulf,*** judged by absolute standards, is distinctly inferior to the verse of classic or later languages, yet the inferiority is far less than is ordinarily supposed, and is in some measure compensated for by the fact than no other metre is capable of expressing exactly the strength and swing of this. To take an hypothetical, but just, test, suppose that modern literature were to produce a counterpart of the ***Beowulf,*** in a similar metre. In the matter of rhythm, we should adjudge it inferior to *Paradise Lost* and to most of Tennyson, Shelley, or Keats. But we would not spurn it as merely primitive, any more than we spurn the *vers libre* or Whitman's lines; and we would rate it considerably above either. Such metre, then, has a distinct value, and a value not far below the best.

But there is a third quality of verse as important as either organization or rhythm. It is the aptness, force, and beauty of the scene when considered in detail, and the quality of the language in which they are sketched. And here we come to the noblest traits of the ***Beowulf.***

To take a single quality, the picturesque, that is the vividness and freshness of the scenes. Other poems have longer or more fully developed pictures, carefully and often painfully elaborated. But the ***Beowulf*** scenes are oftentimes equally strong, and yet require no such careful elaboration. They have the brevity and force of epigrams. There is something essentially Shakespearean in the ability, the knack, the trick if you will, of producing effects of tremendous vividness in a few flashing words. For example, take any one of the descriptive passages from Shakespeare, as this from *Midsummer Night's Dream:*

The starry welkin cover thou anon
With drooping fog, as black as Acheron,

Compare with this the similar swift effectiveness of the ***Beowulf.*** The warriors were prepared for battle with Grendel, when

Over all darkening night
Came striding, the dim shadow-shapes,
Black under the clouds.

Or again, compare these two passages. The Shakespearean—from *Macbeth*—is richer in allusion and figure, but scarcely in the sort of vividness that belongs to a picture:

Now o'er the one half-world
Nature seems dead, and wicked dreams abuse
The curtain'd sleep; witchcraft celebrates
Pale Hecate's offerings; and wither'd murder,
Alarum'd by his sentinel, the wolf,
Whose howl's his watch, thus with his stealthy pace,
With Tarquin's ravishing strides, towards his design
Moves like a ghost.

The situation in the other passage is similar. Grendel, the monster, is going to the Danes' hall for his nightly slaughter:

In dark night came
Striding the shadow-goer. The warriors slept
That were to hold the hornèd hall,
All but one

. . . . . .

Then from the moor under the misty slopes
Came Grendel going—God's anger he bore upon him—
He thought to himself that he would seize unawares
One of the men in the high hall.
So fared he forth 'neath the clouds to where he well knew
Was the wine-hall, the gold-hall of men.
Shining with plates of gold.

At other places the poem reminds us more of Homer. For example, on the first approach of Beowulf to Heorot, the hall of the Danish King, the watch by the sea, who has challenged the Geats on their landing, says:

Let your battle-shields here await you,
And your wooden spears.

Beowulf then goes to the hall:

The great chieftain then arose,—around him stood his warriors,
The brave band of thanes: some abode there,
And kept the armor, as the chieftain bade.
The others hurried forward together; the guide directed them
Under Heorot's roof: boldly went Beowulf
Stern under his helmet, till he stood in the hall;
Then he spoke—the chain-mail shone upon him,
The linked net-work, forged by the smith,—
'Be thou, Hrothgar, hail.'

Again we have the same effect, when Beowulf has returned from killing Grendel's mother, and has brought the head of the monster with him. . . . In other places we get touches which remind us of the mystic, horror-loving spirit of the Middle Ages. . . . More often, though, the spirit seems one that recalls no other literature very strongly. Take, for example, the queen's courtesies to Beowulf and the other warriors, when he is first entertained in the Danish hall. . . . Again, in the same connection we may be permitted one more [example]. . . . It is of the sort that is used by pseudo-antiquarians to produce archaic thrills. Needless to say, the [account of Beowulf's funeral procession and final rituals], despite the element of strangeness and sombreness, had all the reality to the Anglo-Saxon that, say, a military funeral has to us. Only you must substitute for the dim colors of the cathedral aisle the melancholy of the misty northern glow on the sea-cape. . . . The spirit is plainly not Shakespearean, not Homeric, not in the customary sense mediæval. It is a native Anglo-Saxon spirit, tremendously impassioned, but withal calm, restrained, and melancholy. It is a spirit that lies too near the heart for words, and so, feeling the cheapness of language, expresses itself in comonplaces that ring from the very depths of life and are resonant with its mystery and its melancholy.

In the same spirit are many of the allusions to fate. The religion of the poem is fatalism tinctured with Christianity. The fatalistic conception comes out in many places; for example, in a remark with which Beowulf ends a speech addressed to Hrothgar. It is just before the fight with Grendel, and Beowulf requests that if he be slain, his burnie, or coat of chain armor, be sent to Hygelac, his sovereign and uncle. Then he adds, ''Goes aye fate as it will.''. . . In another place the poet says:

It is not easy
To elude death (try it who will),
But every one of soul-gifted men, of the earth-dwellers,
Shall come to the fated spot.
There his body fast in his death-bed
Shall sleep after this feast.

Sometimes the poet is at pains to explain that though fate *(wyrd* or *wierd)* is ordinarily supreme, God may overrule it. Some critics hold this to prove that the poem is a pagan writing interpolated,—and so rendered theologically innocuous,—by a later Christian redactor.

Finally, among the more important strong qualities to be found in the ***Beowulf,*** is the spontaneous reality of the character-drawing. There are no fine distinctions, but elemental traits are handled with naïve vigor, and put into the right places. Sometimes the character element is entirely obvious, as in the exclamation:

So it is sorrowful to an agèd churl
To live to see his bairn hang
Young on the gallows.

But more frequently the obvious trait is one of the sort that make us wonder why we never thought of it ourselves. For example, when Beowulf first offers to champion the Danes against Grendel, Hunferth, a local hero, is moved with jealousy, and addresses Beowulf in very much the tone of the jeering small-boy, who explains to the other that he has an exaggerated conception of himself (''Aw, you aint so fine''). He recalls to mind a swimming match in which Beowulf was defeated. Here we should expect the hero of divine lineage to keep contemptuous silence. But not so. Beowulf is human,—and explains at great length that he was not defeated, after which he ends with a malicious dig at Hunferth by recalling the fact that that redoubtable warrior had stained his career by the murder of his brothers, an incident that has nothing to do with the question of valor, and which shows an almost feminine irrelevancy of repartee.

Another humanizing touch appears, naively and without apparent guile on the part of the bard, in the frequent allusions to braggadocio and love of praise among the warriors. There is something childlike about the simple emotions of most of them. It is probably this note that rings in the closing words of the poem, when the companions of Beowulf, in praising the dead hero, end by declaring him—in terms of high laudation,—

To his folk most kind and fondest of praise.

Oftentimes the character-effect appears, in this way, in the turn of a phrase merely. At the banquet of the Danes, given for Beowulf,

The ring-adorned queen,
Noble in mind, the mead-cup bore.

How much more significant that terse phrase ''Noble in mind'' than any possible description of her ''majestic bearing,'' her ''courtly grace,'' or other similar descriptive qualities. Another effective, but more sombre, bit of character realization occurs in the picture of the aged warrior, who, many years before the time of the story, buried the dragon's hoard of treasure. The old man, lonely, bereft of friends, discouraged rather than disillusioned, but none the less weary of life, sadly puts away his treasure:

There's no joy of harp,
No joy of glee-wood, nor does the good hawk
Fly through the hall, nor the swift horse
The castle court paw.

We have, then, in the ***Beowulf*** at least five distinct strong points of spirit or temper: a sort of Shakespearean vividness of scene, Homeric simplicity of narrative, mediæval mysticism, native force, and an elementary but very much alive element of character-drawing. Against these, though, must be set—besides the lack of organization—a further defect of detail, a defect of excessive digression and parenthesis. This is a trait of Anglo-Saxon poetry in general rather than of the ***Beowulf.*** Yet it cannot but be considered a national weakness of the period. This trait shows itself most noticeably in the little moralizing asides which the poet irritatingly thrusts between exciting passages of action or adventure, when he should go straight ahead, oblivious alike of himself and of his sentiments. The last part of the poem sins more in this respect than the first, which may, perhaps, though doubtfully, lend color to the supposition that it is a later addition. But even if this supposition be true, the fault is not wholly with the redactor, for many of the digressions are woven into the poem in such manner as almost to preclude the idea of interpolation. Perhaps, though, we should not quarrel too much with a minstrel—who was probably an old man with all the characteristics of age,—if he fall into the bad habit of digressing to give good advice. It was dramatically in keeping with his character, though the result may be defective literature.

In a few cases the digressions of this sort are not bad, as when the bard, after describing Beowulf's preparation to fight with the fire-dragon single-handed, pauses to exclaim, "Such is no coward's work." In fact, we have clear evidence that this digressiveness is part of a distinct and consistent style, which characterizes the whole poem. Though a defect, it is a defect peculiar to that style, a fact which can scarcely be omitted from consideration. The style itself is the story-teller's style, the sort of thing that survives to-day, in modified form, in children's stories. It is a style similar to that of the fairy-tale—about the dragon and the prince—told to the children some howling winter night about the blazing fireside. The surest evidence of this is the presence of those very asides. Also exclamatory asides, such as "That was a good king!" "That was no coward's work!" Another significant phrase, which the poem shares with most Anglo-Saxon poems, is the introductory "I have heard it told that;" as we say to-day in our stories, "I have heard that once upon a time."

Again the bard is colloquial in his anticipations of what is to come. Before Grendel is slain, he says,

It no longer was fated
That he more of the race of man
Might devour by night.

Before the fight with the dragon, the anticipatory remarks become so numerous as to suggest conscious art rather than a merely instinctive colloquial style. Before the dragon fight is recounted, the bard intimates that Beowulf is about to die: and that intimation is given, not once, but at five different points of the narrative. The concluding scene of the whole epic is too tremendous in import for the reader to be allowed merely to blunder into it as into an accidental adventure. He is carefully prepared for it, and his mind by anticipatory sorrow is brought into just that state in which the foreseen tragedy shall come, not as an adventure, but as a mighty, melancholy, and passionate climax.

Often he uses the device common to the recounter of a long story—of reminding his hearers of the preceding events. In three places he reminds his hearers of the fate of Grendel, though he has himself already narrated the whole event in detail. The strange legend that Grendel is descended from Cain is also repeated when the poet comes to Grendel's mother. Near the end of the poem, when Beowulf's companion in the dragon-fight sees him dying, the poet—though he has already killed off the dragon—pauses to repeat [the account of the dragon's death]. . . . These repetitions and anticipations of the story have been taken to indicate the work of a bungling redactor. When, however, the *recitative* character of the poem and of its style is once recognized, and the literary effect is fully appreciated, these qualities of the poem appear entirely in keeping with the spirit of the whole, which is that of the spoken or chanted story.

Such are, in a few dashes of the brush, the best and the worst features of the poem. That, despite its unquestioned defects, it is a great poem, is a conviction that is taking ever firmer hold upon competent critics. . . . [As] the poet himself says, "Goes aye fate as it will;" and there are signs that the fate which makes or unmakes the popularity of poems, is slowly relenting towards this the most ancient, the most native poem of the English language. (pp. 32-42)

James Routh, "Our Earliest English Masterpiece," in The Sewanee Review, *Vol. XIX, No. 1, January, 1911, pp. 29-42.*

SIR ARTHUR QUILLER-COUCH (essay date 1916)

[Most commonly known by his early pseudonym "Q," Quiller-Couch was a versatile and prolific turn-of-the-century English man of letters whose learned but popular works, including the best-selling Oxford Book of English Verse *(1900) and several collections of lectures, earned their author a wide readership that admired the clarity and conciseness of his judgments. In the following excerpt, Quiller-Couch disparagingly compares the poetics of* Beowulf *with those of Homer's* Iliad.]

I, who construe Anglo-Saxon with difficulty, must admit [***Beowulf***] to contain many fine, even noble, passages. Take for example Hrothgar's lament for Æschere [in lines 1321-29]. . . . (p. 194)

This is simple, manly, dignified. It avoids the besetting sin of the Anglo-Saxon gleeman—the pretentious trick of calling things "out of their right names" for the sake of literary effect (as if *e.g.* the sea could be improved by being phrased into "the seals' domain"). Its Anglo-Saxon *staccato,* so tiresome in sustained narrative, here happens to suit the broken utterance of mourning. In short, it exhibits the Anglo-Saxon Muse at her best, not at her customary. But set beside it [any] passage in which Homer tells of a fallen warrior—at haphazard, as it were, a single corpse chosen from the press of battle. . . . (p. 195)

[Could anyone] compare the two passages and miss to see that they belong to two different kingdoms of poetry? I lay no stress here on "architectonics." I waive that the *Iliad* is a well-knit epic and the story of ***Beowulf*** a shapeless monstrosity. I ask you but to note the difference of note, of accent, of mere music. . . . To assure yourselves that [Homer can] . . . express the extreme of majesty and of human anguish in poetry which betrays no false note, no strain upon the store of emotion man may own with self-respect and exhibit without derogation of dignity, turn to the last book of the *Iliad* and read of Priam raising to his lips the hand that has murdered his son. I say confidently that no one unable to distinguish this, as poetry, from the very best of ***Beowulf*** is fit to engage upon business as a literary critic.

In ***Beowulf*** then, as an imported poem, let us allow much barbarian merit. It came of dubious ancestry, and it had no progeny. The pretence that our glorious literature derives its lineage from ***Beowulf*** is in vulgar phrase "a put up job"; a falsehood grafted upon our text-books by Teutonic and Teutonising professors who can bring less evidence for it than will cover a threepenny-piece. Its run for something like that money, in small educational manuals, has been in its way a triumph of pedagogic *réclame* [''puffing'']. (pp. 196-97)

Sir Arthur Quiller-Couch, ''On the Lineage of English Literature (I),'' in his On the Art of Writing, *G. P. Putnam's Sons, 1916, pp. 176-200.*

OLIVER FARRAR EMERSON (essay date 1921)

[*Emerson was a late-nineteenth- and early-twentieth-century American philologist whose pioneering works on Old, Middle, and contemporary English phonology earned him a wide reputation in his day. In the following excerpt from one of his few non-philological works, he discusses the Christian emphasis of* Beowulf, *which he finds embodied in the reasons for Grendel's attacks upon the Danes.*]

In the only detailed account of his raids (***Beow.*** 739-45) Grendel appears as a man-eating monster who seeks food, ''a full meal'' (wyst-fylle 734), and who devours the body ravenously (743), as if hunger were his only thought. Nothing in the earlier account of his attack [89 f.] is at variance with this savage satisfaction of hunger, although it is there merely said that the first time he ''seized in their sleep thirty thanes'' (122-3), and with the booty went to his home. In the third account of the event (1580-84), we are more exactly told that Grendel ate on the spot fifteen of the thirty victims, carrying the other fifteen away. During his attack of the following night, as we are informed in more general terms, Grendel ''accomplished more of murderous evil'' (135-6). When the monster's mother comes to avenge her son (1278), she is discovered too quickly to make clear what she might have done. She has time only to seize ''one of the nobles'' (1294) and the bloody hand of Grendel, when she hastens away to save her life. Escaping to the entrance of her watery cave, however, she too takes time to devour Æschere's body, but for some reason—a fortunate circumstance for her pursuers and perhaps intended as such by the poet—she leaves his bloody head upon the cliff (1420-21).

In curious contrast with all this fondness for a cannibalistic feast—Grendel has the form of a man (1352)—we are told of the monster's making the attack because he ''bore hardly that he heard each day loud mirth in the hall'' (88-9). This mirth is then described as ''sound of the harp'' and ''song of the scop (minstrel),'' while as an example of the latter there is repeated to us a hymn in praise of the Creator. Again, in lines 99-100, we are informed that when the attack was made ''men were living in happiness blessedly.''

This inconsistency between motive and accomplishment has not been commented upon before. (p. 113)

That we should be told this man-eating monster was inspired to assail the Danes by envy of their happiness, rather than by hunger for human flesh, seems ridiculously insufficient. But the poet . . . intends to make all clear by immediately following the passage with his characterization of Grendel as a ''hellish fiend'' (feond on helle, 101), and reciting at length his origin in the devilish progeny of Cain (lines 104-14), an origin which he again asserts in a later passage (1258-68). In other words, this is the reason for introducing a passage which has always been a stumbling block to those who saw only a heathen story in the poem, and which occasioned what now seems the extraordinary interpolation theory. As of devilish origin, Grendel merely exhibits a devilish characteristic in being carried away by envy of the happy Hrothgar and his court, a community accepting God as Creator and benefactor—in other words, essentially Christian.

It would seem scarcely necessary to argue at length for envy as a characteristic of the devil according to medieval conception. Envy of the Creator was joined with pride in his own powers to cause the fall of Lucifer. Indeed, St Augustine gave envy as the prime motive. . . . Envy stands next to pride in the list of the seven ''deadly sins.''. . . (pp. 116-17)

Envy of man's happiness was also fully recognized in medieval times as a devilish characteristic. Jewish legend, on which so much of Christian demonology was based, placed the envy of Adam and its accompanying jealousy before the fall of Lucifer. . . . (p. 117)

That Grendel's envy of the Danes did not show itself in tempting them to their spiritual fall, as commonly with the devils, was due to his belonging to the race of Cain's descendants, corporeal monsters with physical characteristics. According to medieval conception these corporeal demons . . . were bloodthirsty in the most literal sense. (p. 118)

So far I have not considered the Hymn of Creation (***Beow.*** 90-98) sung by the Danish minstrel as a reason for Grendel's attack. It is not a reason, I take it, because it praises the Creator, toward whom envy would have been natural on the part of any demon. The song is primarily an example of the peaceful pleasures of the Danish people, and probably not intended as an indication of how they ''lived blessedly'' (99-100) in any Christian sense. On the other hand, the words ''lived blessedly'' might have such meaning, especially as the hymn is in quite extraordinary contrast with the other songs of the scop introduced into the poem. The latter, as the Praise of Beowulf (872 f.) and the Song of Finn (1086 f.), are strictly in keeping with the natural characteristics of a warlike race. The only approach to the ideas of the Hymn of Creation are the words of the devout Hrothgar, as in lines 928 f. and 1700 f.

It may be contended that Grendel's dislike of the Danish revelry belonged to the original story. That is not impossible, and perhaps even probable. Even in that case, however, we must consider how a Christian poet of medieval England would have looked at such a matter, and how far he would have retained it if he had regarded it as essentially heathen. It is clearly not heathen to have the revelry of the Danes include a Hymn of Creation similar to that of the Christian Caedmon, whose follower the ***Beowulf*** poet must have been. Besides, the fact that the poet at once accounts for Grendel in exactly the manner in which the medieval Christian was wont to explain such monsters, leaves implications which cannot be accounted for on any heathen basis. The explanation of Grendel's motive as envy of man's happiness seems to account for the introduction of the Cain descent as it has not been accounted for before. With this explanation, that descent seems less than ever dragged in unnecessarily.

It was then, as our poet conceives, because Grendel was of devilish origin that he was prompted, by envy of the Danes in their happiness and innocent pleasures, to make his earliest attack, and to become their persistent enemy until the hero Beowulf comes to the rescue. Thus, at the foundation of this part of the ***Beowulf*** story, is a conception which can be fully accounted for only on a Christian basis. Let us add it to the Christian elements, as one of the significant evidences that only a Christian poet could have written the old English epic. (pp. 118-19)

Oliver Farrar Emerson, ''Grendel's Motive in Attacking Heorot,'' in The Modern Language Review, *Vol. XVI, No. 2, April, 1921, pp. 113-19.*

J. MIDDLETON MURRY (essay date 1921)

[*Murry is known as one of the most significant English critics and editors of the twentieth century. Anticipating later scholarly opinion, he championed the writings of Marcel Proust, James Joyce, Paul Valéry, D. H. Lawrence, and Thomas Hardy through his positions as the editor of the* Athenaeum *and as a longtime contributor to the* Times Literary Supplement *and other periodicals. As with his magazine essays, Murry's book-length critical works are noted for their impassioned tone and startling discoveries; such biographically centered critical studies as* Keats and Shakespeare: A Study of Keats' Poetic Life from 1816-1820 *(1925) and* Son of Woman: The Story of D. H. Lawrence *(1931) contain esoteric, controversial conclusions that have angered scholars who favor more traditional approaches. Notwithstanding this criticism, Murry is often cited for his perspicuity, clarity, and supportive argumentation. His early exposition on literary appreciation,* The Problem of Style *(1922), is recognized as an informed guidebook for both critics and general readers to employ when considering not only the style of a literary work but also its theme and viewpoint. In it Murry espouses the theoretical premise underlying all of his criticism: that in order to evaluate fully a writer's achievement, the critic must search for the crucial passages that effectively "crystallize" the writer's innermost impressions and convictions. In the following excerpt, Murry applies this premise to his evaluation of the claim that* Beowulf *is "the English epic."*]

[The] principal grievance against ***Beowulf*** is not that it is harsh, but that it is dull. It has its moments, no doubt; but the effect of the whole is a dim confusion, lit by brief, fragmentary lights. Whoever the writer was, he was incapable of resisting a digression, and it was beyond his power to seize the dramatic moments of what is in outline a very exciting fairy-tale. Further, ***Beowulf*** has nothing whatever to do with England except that it happens to have been written in an Anglian dialect at the end of the seventh century. Why it should be called by Mr. Moncrieff [in his 1921 edition of the poem] and others "the English epic" is not at all clear. The *Iliad* is the Greek Epic, the *Æneid* the Roman epic, the *Chanson de Roland* the French epic. We decline to have ***Beowulf*** foisted on to us. For one thing, it is a Danish or Swedish or Norwegian epic; for another, it is not good enough. . . .

The handling is more primitive than the story. The poet has but a small gift of putting what he describes before our eyes, and still less of conveying feeling to us. He is at his best in the short passages in which he evokes the sea and the swift ships that dare it; and there is one brief passage [lines 32-52] in the induction to the poem, describing the obsequies of Shield of the Sheaf, the first king of the Danes, in which the feeling for the sea and the feeling for death are remarkably combined. . . . Very little of ***Beowulf*** is on that level. There is, however, a real visual beauty in the description (which may without undue exaggeration be called Homeric) of Beowulf's setting out to cross the sea to Hrothgar [lines 208-24]. . . . These are the purple patches, and they are, in their way, right Tyrian. There is one other which Mr. Moncrieff singles out as the most imaginative passage in the poem. It occurs at the opening of the final movement. The writer imagines the sorrow and the loneliness of the ancient hero who bade bury the treasure which the Worm guards. The lines are too many to quote, and to our thinking they are not quite the best in ***Beowulf,*** but they are admirable in their simplicity.

A handful of such passages, is, however, not enough to redeem ***Beowulf*** from dullness. The world is dim in which these Viking heroes have their being. We can discern the glitter of the sea, but when we pass inland from the shore a thick mist descends. Within the mist lurk terrors by night and day. We are conscious of death by sea and land, but of what life may be we have no idea. It seems to hold no joys; there is no light to reveal it. Beowulf himself is only a great shadow in the surrounding gloom. He might be a Patagonian for all we know about him, or indeed for all we care. (p. 147)

A great deal of unnecessary fuss has been made about [Beowulf]. In the main he is treasure-trove only for the historian and the philologist; as literature, he is a relic of the times before English literature had begun, an antediluvian curiosity. As such he has his interest. . . . If we must have an English epic, let it be Malory. (p. 148)

J. Middleton Murry, in a review of "Beowulf," in The Nation & The Athenaeum, *Vol. XXX, No. 4, October 22, 1921, pp. 147-48.*

FRIEDERICH KLAEBER (essay date 1922)

[*Klaeber was a late-nineteenth- and early-twentieth-century Prussian-born American philologist and textual critic whose outstanding contributions to Old English studies remain essential reading for students of the period. A rigorous and meticulous editor, he is best known for his copiously illustrated edition of* Beowulf *(1922, with later supplements), for his service to the Simplified Spelling Board, and for his role in stimulating the study of early English among Americans. In the following excerpt from the introduction to his critical edition of* Beowulf, *he discusses the Christian elements of the poem and examines the structure and narrative methods used by the poet. For a criticism of Klaeber's view that the poem is not structurally unified, see the excerpt by Joan Blomfield dated 1938.*]

The presentation of the story-material in ***Beowulf*** has been influenced, to a considerable extent, by ideas derived from Christianity.

The poem abounds, to be sure, in supernatural elements of pre-Christian associations. Heathen practices are mentioned in several places, such as the vowing of sacrifices at idol fanes (175 ff.), the observing of omens (204), the burning of the dead (3137 ff., 1107 ff., 2124 ff.), which was frowned upon by the Church. The frequent allusions to the power of fate (*wyrd* . . .), the motive of blood revenge (1384 f., cp. 1669 f., 1256, 1278, 1546 f.), the praise of worldly glory (1387 ff., cp. 2804 ff., 884 f., 954 f.) bear testimony to an ancient background of pagan conceptions and ideals. On the other hand, we hear nothing of angels, saints, relics, of Christ and the cross, of divine worship, church observances, or any particular dogmatic points. Still, the general impression we obtain from the reading of the poem is certainly the opposite of pagan barbarism. We almost seem to move in normal Christian surroundings. God's governance of the world and of every human being, the evil of sin, the doings of the devil, the last judgment, heaven and hell are ever and anon referred to as familiar topics. . . . Though mostly short, these allusions show by their remarkable frequency how thoroughly the whole life was felt to be dominated by Christian ideas. The author is clearly familiar with the traditional Christian terminology in question and evinces some knowledge of the Bible, liturgy, and ecclesiastical literature. Of specific motives derived from the Old Testament (and occurring in *Genesis A* also) we note the story of Cain, the giants, and the deluge (107 ff., 1261 ff., 1689 ff.), and the song of Creation (92 ff.).

Furthermore, the transformation of old heathen elements in accordance with Christian thought may be readily observed.

The pagan and heroic cremation finds a counterpart in the peaceful burial of the dead, which the Church enforced (1007 f., 2457 f., cp. 445 f., 3107 ff.). The curse placed on the fateful treasure is clothed in a Christian formula (3071 ff.) and is declared to be void before the higher will of God (3054 ff.). By the side of the heathen fate is seen the almighty God. *Gæð ā wyrd swā hīo scel* [''Fate will go as it must''], exclaims Beowulf in expectation of the Grendel fight, 455, but again, in the same speech, he avows: *ðær gelyfan sceal / Dryhtnes dōme sē þe hine dēað nimeð* [''Whoever death takes will have to trust in the judgment of God] 440. The functions of fate and God seem quite parallel: *wyrd oft nereð / unfægne eorl . . .* [''So fate often saves an undoomed man''] 572; *swā mæg unfæge ēaðe gedīgan / weān ond wræcsīð sē ðe Waldendes / hyldo gehealdeþ* [''Thus, when the Ruler's favor holds good, an undoomed man may easily survive dangers in exile''] 2291. . . . Yet God is said to control fate: *nefne him wītig God wyrd forstōde / ond ðæs mannes mōd* [''had not wise God and Bēowulf's courage changed that fate''] 1056. Moreover, the fundamental contrast between the good God and the blind and hostile fate is shown by the fact that God invariably grants victory (even in the tragic dragon fight, 2874), whereas it is a mysterious, hidden spell that brings about Bēowulf's death, 3067 ff.

Predominantly Christian are the general tone of the poem and its ethical viewpoint. We are no longer in a genuine pagan atmosphere. The sentiment has been softened and purified. The virtues of moderation, unselfishness, consideration for others are practised and appreciated. The manifest readiness to express gratitude to God on all imaginable occasions . . . , and the poet's sympathy with weak and unfortunate beings like Scyld the foundling . . . and even Grendel . . . and his mother . . . , are typical of the new note. Particularly striking is the moral refinement of the two principal characters, Bēowulf and Hrōđgar. Those readers who, impressed by Bēowulf's martial appearance at the beginning of the action, expect to find an aggressive warrior hero of the Achilles or Sigfrit type, will be disposed at times to think him somewhat tame, sentimental, and fond of talking. Indeed, the final estimate of the hero's character by his own faithful thanes lamenting his death is chiefly a praise of Beowulf's gentleness and kindness. . . .

The Christian elements are almost without exception so deeply ingrained in the very fabric of the poem that they cannot be explained away as the work of a reviser or later interpolator. In addition, it is instructive to note that whilst the episodes are all but free from those modern influences, the main story has been thoroughly imbued with the spirit of Christianity. It is true, the action itself is not modified or visibly influenced by Christianization. But the quality of the plot is changed. The author has fairly exalted the fights with fabled monsters into a conflict between the powers of good and of evil. The figure of Grendel, at any rate, while originally an ordinary Scandinavian troll, and passing in the poem as a sort of man-monster, is at the same time conceived of as an impersonation of evil and darkness, even an incarnation of the Christian devil. Many of his appellations are unquestionable epithets of Satan . . . , he belongs to the wicked progeny of Cain, the first murderer, his actions are represented in a manner suggesting the conduct of the evil one . . . , and he dwells with his demon mother in a place which calls up visions of hell. . . . Even the antagonist of the third adventure, though less personally conceived than the Grendel pair, is not free from the suspicion of similar influences, especially as the dragon was in ecclesiastical tradition the recognized symbol of the archfiend. (pp. xlviii-li)

[The poet has raised the champion] to the rank of a singularly spotless hero, a ''defending, protecting, redeeming being,'' a truly ideal character. In fact, we need not hesitate to recognize features of the Christian Savior in the destroyer of hellish fiends, the warrior brave and gentle, blameless in thought and deed, the king that dies for his people. Nor is the possibility of discovering direct allusions to the person of the Savior to be ignored. While there are not lacking certain hints of this kind in the first part of the poem (942 ff., 1707 ff.), it is especially in the last adventure that we are strongly tempted to look for a deeper, spiritual interpretation. The duality of the motives which apparently prompt Bēowulf to the dragon fight may not be as unnatural as it has sometimes been considered. Still, it is somewhat strange that the same gold which Bēowulf rejoices in having obtained for his people before the hour of his death . . . , is placed by his mourning thanes into the burial mound; they give it back to the earth. . . . Nay, Wīglāf, in the depth of his sorrow which makes him oblivious of all else, expresses the wish that Bēowulf had left the dragon alone to hold his den until the end of the world. . . . The indubitably significant result of the adventure is the hero's death, and, in the structural plan of the poem, the aim and object of the dragon fight is to lead up to this event,—a death, that is, which involves the destruction of the adversary, but is no less noteworthy in that it partakes of the nature of a self-sacrifice. . . . [Some] incidents in the encounter with the dragon lend themselves to comparison with happenings in the garden of Gethsemane. . . . (p. li)

Though delicately kept in the background, this Christian interpretation of the main story on the part of the Anglo-Saxon author gives added strength and tone to the entire poem. It explains one of the great puzzles of our epic. It would indeed be hard to understand why the poet contented himself with a plot of mere fabulous adventures so much inferior to the splendid heroic setting, unless the narrative derived a superior dignity from suggesting the most exalted hero-life known to Christians.

The poem of ***Beowulf*** consists of two distinct parts joined in a very loose manner and held together only by the person of the hero. The first of these does not in the least require or presuppose a continuation. Nor is the second dependent for its interpretation on the events of the first plot, the two references to the ''Grendel part'' being quite cursory and irrelevant (2351 ff., 2521). The first part, again, contains two well-developed main incidents (which are closely enough bound together to constitute technically one story), while its third division, ''Bēowulf's Home-Coming,'' only serves as a supplement to the preceding major plot. . . . [There] is a decided structural parallelism in the unfolding of the three great adventures, the fights with the fabulous monsters, namely in setting forth the ''exciting cause,'' the preliminaries of the main action, the fight itself, and the relaxation or pause following the climax.

At the same time we note a remarkable gradation in the three great crises of the poem. The fight against Grendel is rather monotonous and seems altogether too short and easy to give much opportunity for excitement—in spite of the horrors of the darkness in which the scene is enacted. The second contest is vastly more interesting by reason of its elaborate, romantic scenery, the variety and definiteness of incidents, the dramatic quality of the battle. The hero is fully armed, uses weapons in addition to his ''hand-grip,'' and yet is so hard pressed that only a kind of miracle saves him. There is, moreover, an element of justice in representing the combat with Grendel's mother as more formidable and pregnant with danger. Grendel, who has ravaged the hall because of the innate wickedness of his heart, deserves to be overcome without difficulty. His mother, on the contrary, is actuated by the laudable desire for revenge (1256 ff., 1278, 1305 f., 1546 f., . . .) and, besides, is sought out in her own home; hence a certain amount of sympathy is manifestly due her. Finally, the dragon (who likewise has a kind of excuse for his depredations) is entirely too much for his assailant. We tremble for the venerable king. He takes a special measure for protection (2337 ff.), and is strengthened by the help of a youthful comrade, but the final victory is won only at the cost of the hero's own life. The account of this fight, which, like that against Grendel's mother, falls into three clearly marked divisions, receives a new interest by the introduction of the companions, the glorification of one man's loyalty, and the added element of speech-making.

The plot of each part is surprisingly simple. In the use of genuine heroic motives the main story of ***Beowulf*** is indeed inferior to the Finnsburg legend. But the author has contrived to expand the narrative considerably in the leisurely epic fashion, which differentiates it completely from the type of the short lays. Subsidiary as well as important incidents are related in our epic. Extended speeches are freely introduced. There is not wanting picturesque description and elaborate setting. In the first part of the poem, the splendid life at the Danish court with its feastings and ceremonies is graphically portrayed in true epic style. The feelings of the persons are described, and general reflections on characters, events, and situations are thrown in. Last not least, matter more or less detached from the chief narrative is given a place in the poem by way of digressions and episodes.

About 450 verses in the first part and almost 250 in the second part are concerned with episodic matter. . . . (pp. li-liii)

[Several] of these digressions contain welcome information about the hero's life; others tell of events relating to the Scylding dynasty and may be regarded as a legitimate sort of setting. The allusions to Cain and the giants are called forth by the references to Grendel's pedigree. The story of Creation is a concrete illustration of the entertainments in Heorot. Earlier Danish history is represented by Heremōd, and the relation between Danish and Frisian tribes is shown in the Finn story. Germanic are the legends of Sigemund and of Eormenrīc and Hāma. To the old continental home of the Angles belongs the alllusion to Offa and his queen. The digressions of the second part are devoted chiefly to Geatish history, the exceptions being the "Elegy of the Last Survivor" and the "Lament of the Father," which (like the central portion of Hrōðgār's harangue in the first part) are of a more general character. The frequent mention of Hygelāc's Frankish raid is accounted for by the fact that it is closely bound up both with Geatish history in general and with Bēowulf's life in particular. Accordingly, sometimes the aggression and defeat of Hygelāc are dwelt upon (1202 ff., 2913 ff.), in other passages Bēowulf's bravery is made the salient point of the allusion (2354 ff., 2501 ff.).

Most of the episodes are introduced in a skilful manner and are properly subordinated to the main narrative. For example, the Breca story comes in naturally in a dispute occurring at the evening's entertainment. The legends of Sigemund and of Finnsburg are recited by the scop. The glory of Scyld's life and departure forms a fitting prelude to the history of the Scyldings, who, next to the hero, claim our chief interest in the first part. In several instances the introduction is effected by means of comparison or contrast. . . . Occasionally the episodic character is clearly pointed out. . . . The facts of Geatish history, it cannot be denied, are a little too much in evidence and retard the narrative of the second part rather seriously. Quite far-fetched may seem the digression on Þrȳð ["might" or "strength"], which is brought in very abruptly and which, like the Heremōd tale, shows the poet's disposition to point a moral.

In extent the episodic topics range from cursory allusions of a few lines . . . to complete and complicated narratives (the adventure with Breca, the Finnsburg legend, the Heaðo-Bard feud, the battle at Ravenswood).

A few passages, like the old spearman's speech (2047-56) and the recital of the Ravenswood battle (2924 ff.), give the impression of being taken without much change (in substance) from older lays. The Elegy of the Last Survivor reminds us of similar elegiac passages in Old English poetry (see *Wanderer* . . . and *Ruin*). The fine picture of Scyld's sea-burial, and the elaboration of detail in the Bēowulf-Breca adventure seem to be very largely, if not exclusively, the poet's own work. Most of the episodes, however, are merely summaries of events told in general terms and are far removed both from the style of independent lays (like the *Finnsburg* Fragment) and from the broad, expansive epic manner. The distinctly allusive character of a number of them shows that the poet assumed a familiarity with the full story on the part of his audience.

On the whole, we have every reason to be thankful for these episodes, which not only add fulness and variety to the central plot, but disclose a wealth of authentic heroic song and legend, a magnificent historic background. Still we may well regret that those subjects of intensely absorbing interest play only a minor part in our epic, having to serve as a foil to a story which in itself is of decidedly inferior weight.

Upwards of 1300 lines are taken up with speeches. The major part of these contain digressions, episodes, descriptions, and reflections, and thus tend to delay the progress of the narrative. But even those which may be said to advance the action, are lacking in dramatic quality; they are characterized by eloquence and ceremonial dignity. (pp. liv-lv)

By far the most felicitous use of the element of discourse is made in the first part, especially in the earlier division of it, from the opening of the action proper to the Grendel fight (189-709). The speeches occurring in it belong largely to the "advancing" type, consist mainly of dialogue (including two instances of the type "question: reply: reply," 237-300, 333-335), and are an essential factor in creating the impression of true epic movement. As the poem continues, the speeches increase in length and deliberation. The natural form of dialogue is in the last part completely superseded by addresses without answer, some of them being virtually speeches in form only.

The "Grendel part" also shows the greatest variety, as regards the occasions for speech-making and the number of speakers participating (Bēowulf, the coast-guard, Wulfgār, Hrōðgār, Unferð, the scop, Wealhþēow). . . .

In spite of a certain sameness of treatment the poet has managed to introduce a respectable degree of variation in adapting the speeches to their particular occasions. Great indeed is the contrast between Bēowulf's straightforward, determined vow of bravery (632-638) and Hrōðgār's moralizing oration, which would do credit to any preacher (1700-1784). Admirable illustrations of varying moods and kinds of utterance are Bēowulf's salutation to Hrōðgār (407-455) and his brilliant reply to the envious trouble-maker Unferð (530-606). A masterpiece is the queen's exhibition of diplomatic language by means of veiled allusion (1169 ff.). A finely appropriate emotional quality characterizes Bēowulf's dying speeches (2729 ff., 2794 ff., 2813 ff.).

That some of the speeches follow conventional lines of heroic tradition need not be doubted. This applies to the type of the *gylpcwide* [''boasting speech''] before the combat (675 ff., 1392 ff., 2510 ff.), the ''comitatus'' speech or exhortation of the retainers (2633 ff. . . .), the inquiry after a stranger's name and home (237 ff. . . .). The absence of battle challenge and defiance . . . is an obvious, inherent defect of our poem.

The reader of the poem very soon perceives that the progress of the narrative is frequently impeded. Looseness is, in fact, one of its marked peculiarities. Digressions and episodes, general reflections in the form of speeches, an abundance of moralizing passages . . . interrupt the story. The author does not hesitate to wander from the subject. When he is reminded of a feature in some way related to the matter in hand, he thinks it perfectly proper to speak of it. Hence references to the past are intruded in unexpected places. The manner of Scyld's wonderful arrival as a child is brought out incidentally by way of comparison with the splendor of his obsequies (43 ff.). Bēowulf's renown at the height of his career calls to mind the days of his youth when he was held in disrespect (2183 ff.). No less fond is the poet of looking forward to something that will happen in the near or distant future. The mention of the harmony apparently reigning at the court of Hrōðgār gives an opportunity to hint at subsequent treachery (1018 f., 1164 f., 1180 ff.). The building of the hall Heorot calls up the picture of its destruction by fire (82 ff.). It is not a little remarkable that in the account of the three great fights of the hero, care has been taken to state the outcome of the struggle in advance. . . . Evidently disregard of the element of suspense was not considered a defect in story telling.

Sometimes the result of a certain action is stated first, and the action itself mentioned afterwards (or entirely passed over). . . . In this way a fine abruptness is attained. . . . Thus it also happens that a fact of first importance is strangely subordinated (as in 1556).

There occur obvious gaps in the narrative. That Wealhþēow left the hall in the course of the first day's festival, or that Bēowulf brought the sword Hrunting back with him from the Grendel cave, is nowhere mentioned, but both facts are taken for granted at a later point of the story (664 f., 1807 ff.).

Furthermore, different parts of a story are sometimes told in different places, or substantially the same incident is related several times from different points of view. A complete, connected account of the history of the dragon's hoard is obtained only by a comparison of the passages, 3049 ff., 3069 ff., 2233 ff. The brief notice of Grendel's first visit in Heorot (122 f.) is supplemented by a later allusion containing additional detail (1580 ff.). The repeated references to the various Swedish wars, the frequent allusions to Hygelāc's Frankish foray, the two versions of the Heremōd legend, the review of Bēowulf's great fights by means of his report to Hygelāc (and to Hrōđgār) and through Wīglāf's announcement to his companions (2874 ff.; cp. also 2904 ff.) are well-known cases in point.

Typical examples of the rambling, dilatory method—the forward, backward, and sideward movements—are afforded by the introduction of Grendel . . . , by the Grendel fight . . . , Grendel's going to Heorot (702 ff.), and the odd sequel of the fight with Grendel's mother (1570-90). The remarkable insertion of a long speech by Wīglāf, together with comment on his family, right at a critical moment of the dragon fight . . . , can hardly be called felicitous. But still more trying is the circuitous route by which the events leading up to that combat are brought before the reader. . . . (pp. lvi-lix)

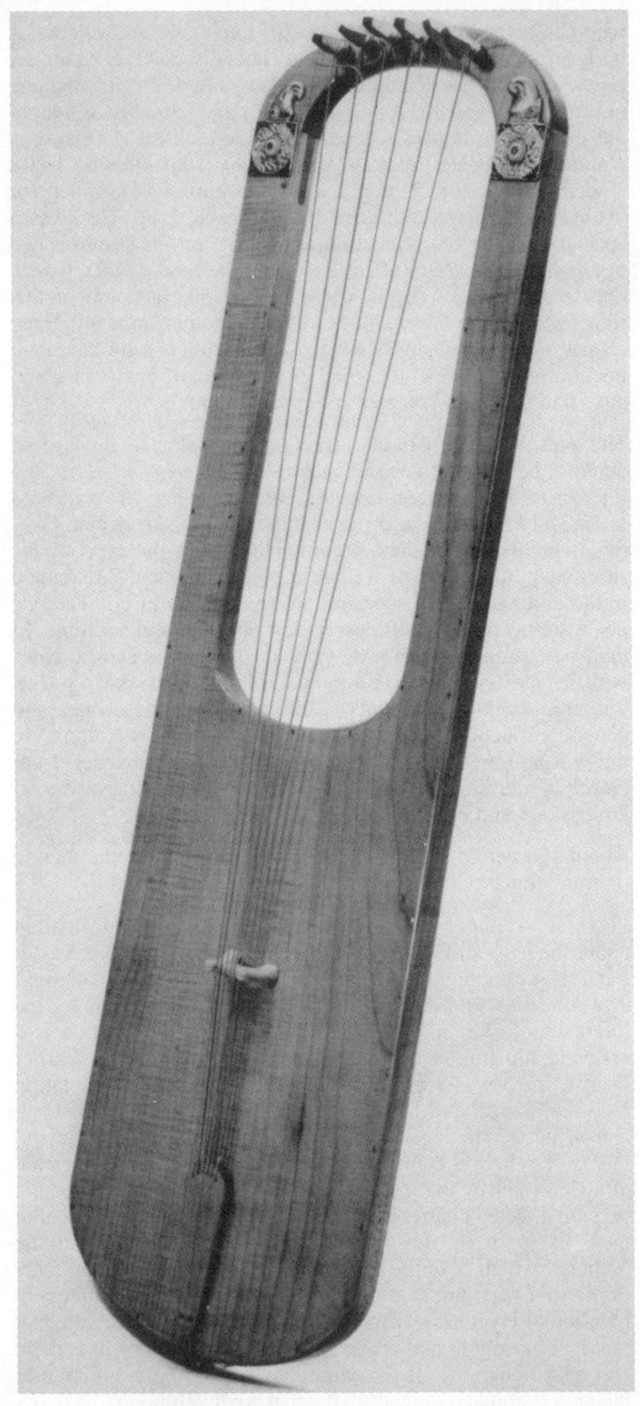

A reconstruction of an Anglo-Saxon round lyre found in the Sutton Hoo, England, ship burial. The British Museum.

Friederich Klaeber, in an introduction to Beowulf and The Fight at Finnsburg, *edited by Friederich*

Klaeber, D. C. Heath and Company, 1922, pp. ix-cxxii.

EDMUND GOSSE (essay date 1923)

[*Gosse's importance as a critic is due primarily to his introduction of Henrik Ibsen's "new drama" to an English audience. He was among the foremost English translators and critics of Scandinavian literature and was decorated by the Norwegian, Swedish, and Danish governments for his efforts. Among his other works are studies of John Donne, Thomas Gray, Sir Thomas Browne, and important early articles on French authors of the late nineteenth century. Although Gosse's works are varied and voluminous, he was largely a popularizer, with the consequence that his commentary lacks depth and is not considered in the first rank of modern critical thought. However, his broad interests and knowledge of foreign literatures lend his works much more than a documentary value. In the following excerpt, Gosse argues that* Beowulf *is neither English in subject or character nor Christian in perspective.*]

[***Beowulf*** is] one of the strongest and most stimulating products of the mediæval mind. (p. 162)

[How] does this outermost planet, this mysterious Neptune of our poetic system, strike an unbiased reader . . .? In the first place, I am struck with its luminous darkness. It is a picture, not like Chaucer's or Spenser's, in the camera lucida, but in the camera obscura. It is almost submarine in its effect; we seem to be looking down into a translucent pool of ocean, fringed and shaded by seaweeds, in whose depths monstrous fishes are slowly swimming, and fierce crustaceans are energising, and noiselessly engaging in combat. The Icelandic poems, of the *Elder Edda* and what not, are mysterious, too, but they are suffused with the upper sunlight. The atmosphere of ***Beowulf*** is almost lunar, or rather it is permeated by an inexplicable radiance of which we cannot trace the source. To pass to particulars, it is steeped in aristocratic romance, of a kind which seems new, that is to say, which leaps over the civilisation of Latin and Greek fancy, and returns to a primeval, even to a savage ancestry. It is partly historical, and to this it owes its peculiar fascination, because here is something definite, based on the long progress of the race. Here are persons, who, remote as they are, share in some measure our own passions and capacities, but it is embroidered, as it were, with ornament of sheer fabulous invention, which transcends our experience, and is indeed incredible and preposterous. Here are real kings and fighting men, actual ships and familiar landscape, and here are also giants and genii, impossible monsters and feats of physical endurance to which the wildest credulity, it would seem, could never give credence. This mingled stuff, melted in a sombre colouring of romance, is the central feature of ***Beowulf.***

It seems to me that the commentators have in some respects misread the poem. In the first place, I am quite unable to see that it deserves the sentimental prominence which has been awarded to it as the earliest expression of the English attitude to life and action. People have talked as though the author of ***Beowulf*** was a far-away precursor of Mr. Rudyard Kipling.

This is surely a patriotic illusion. There is nothing English about ***Beowulf,*** so far as I can see, except the curious and agreeable fact that it comes to us composed in the language employed in Mercia, that is to say, Leicestershire, about the year 700. Not an English place or person is mentioned in it, except one king who may or may not be English, for I have my doubts about Offa. Whether it is likely that a poem mainly describing the seacoast and maritime adventure should have been conceived in the neighbourhood of Ashby-de-la-Zouch I leave to more learned pens than mine. But all the scenes and all the personages are clearly Scandinavian. The good King Hrothgar obviously built his hall of Heorst or Hart on the eastern shore of Denmark—Mr. Chambers thinks it was at Leire, in Zealand; the Geats who avenged his wrong must have come over the Cattegat from Sweden.

The landscape is consistently Danish; Beowulf and Breca had their swimming match under what closely resembles the Klint of Moen; the Whale's Headland where Beowulf's barrow stood, and where the dead dragon was flung over into the sea, is evidently a ness in the Baltic. There is nothing English in all this, and I ask myself in vain how the bard in Mercia, who, unless he had travelled, can never have smelt salt water, imagined such scenes. I feel that we have not the material for even a conjecture as to how, by an accident most fortunate for us, a purely Scandinavian poem came to be composed in an English dialect.

Another amiable fallacy seems to be that ***Beowulf*** is suffused with the spirit of Christian piety. I fail to find a trace of Christianity in it. The writer was so far not a heathen that he believed in one God and rejected, or neglected, the mythology of a still earlier race. He was apparently acquainted with some parts of the Old Testament. Grendel and his mother are described as of the seed of Cain, and the poet seems to have heard of Noah's Flood. There is not unfrequent reference to a "Wielder of Victories," a power that gives wisdom to earls and kings, and "wieldeth times and climes." Especially is a tribute paid to this "Wisest Lord, the Justice of Heaven," when the hero overcomes the powers of evil.

But the allusions are all deistical; there is not a trace of acquaintance with Christ or the Christian plan of salvation. The poet is removed from the Icelanders, who worshipped Odin and Thor, solely by his belief in one God instead of many. It has been said that the author of ***Beowulf*** was "a pious Christian." I am sure he was "pious," for his reflections are inspired by a lofty morality, but the signs of his Christianity escape me. The methods of the poet are so contradictory that it is dangerous to take his intention for granted, but it seems to me that it was not the adventures of Beowulf so much as his character which attracted the poet, and if this is true it sharply distinguishes him from the Scandinavians, for whom the story was everything and the psychology accidental.

Judged by any modern standard, the method of ***Beowulf*** is bewildering in the extreme. The poet seems to have drawn no distinction between the real and the unreal. Sometimes he is delightfully exact in his descriptions, and we move amongst actual persons. It strikes me that he must have been a sailor by profession, perhaps a pirate, because the moment he begins to write about ships and their movements a veil seems to fall, and a vivid scene unrolls itself. The critics have generally praised, as the most brilliant passage in the poem, the swimming match between Beowulf and Breca, which is elaborately told and extremely engaging. But when Unforth, who relates this particular episode, assures us that the heroes swam for seven days and nights without resting, holding drawn swords in their hands to protect them against *nicors,* or sharks . . . , that "a mighty mer-deer" dragged Beowulf to the bottom of the sea, where he fought and rose again, and continued his swim, we feel we are in the realm of fable. Whereas the description of how the ships started to the help of Hrothgar is truth itself. . . . This is experience; and so is the still more vivid account of the return of "the crowd of haughty bachelor-men," laden with honour and treasure, to their Geatish haven.

The same inconsistency marks the conduct of the story itself. Hrothgar, the melancholy chieftain, throned with his gentle queen in the gold-decked wine hall he had built, sitting in serenity encircled by his thanes, is an actual human figure. But Grendel, the giant who comes marching down on them over the misty moors, and slits open the sleeping warriors and sucks their blood, is a mere shadow thrown by ghastly fear. There is a grandeur in the solemn horror of his approach, but he is not an individual, he is a theory of destructive wickedness. As for his mother, who follows him, with like cannibal intent, and steals a thane and eats him, and dives to the bottom of a pool where she has a cave,—unless we suppose her story to be an echo of a raid actually made upon a human coast colony by some hungry sea-beast, she is insufferably absurd.

But the reader must turn to the mysterious little epic . . . and judge for himself. . . . There is something uplifted, something morally magnificent, about this sombre story which gives it a unique significance. (pp. 163-67)

Edmund Gosse, "Beowulf," in his More Books on the Table, *Charles Scribner's Sons, 1923, pp. 159-67.*

R. W. CHAMBERS (essay date 1925)

[*Chambers was an English scholar and writer on English language and literature whose interests ranged from early German legends to English authors of the seventeenth century. In the following excerpt, he argues that the spirit of* Beowulf *is Christian and compares the poem's method of composition with that of classical epics. This essay first appeared in 1925 as a foreword to Archibald Strong's translation of* Beowulf.]

[It] seems clear that ***Beowulf*** was written under the influence of . . . vernacular Christian poetry. It may have been inspired by lost works of Cædmon and of Aldhelm. At any rate, there are striking points of verbal resemblance between ***Beowulf*** and the Christian poems of the school of Cædmon. And the whole spirit of ***Beowulf*** is Christian. It looks as if some man, by no means convinced that there is nothing "in common between Ingeld and Christ," had set to work to write a poem which should bring in the great heroes of Germanic minstrelsy, Ingeld and Froda, Hrothgar and Hrothulf, Sigemund and Heremod, Offa and Scyld. But the poet is careful to avoid anything incompatible with the Christian faith and morals. He goes further, and, after the manner of Aldhelm, "works in words of Scripture among the more amusing matter." It is an event of the greatest importance when book-learned men, like Aldhelm, or those Northumbrian clerics who interested themselves in Cædmon, begin to pay attention to the composition of verse in the vernacular. (pp. 61-2)

In ***Beowulf*** the combination of Christian and heathen elements, though sometimes incongruous, is certainly better harmonized than in the passage from the *Andreas* [in which St. Andrew's disciples refuse to desert their master]. The scholars of a generation ago were chiefly interested in trying to strip off the Christian element in ***Beowulf***—the work, as they believed, of monkish interpolators and revisers. Thus they hoped to be able to disentangle the original heathen lays from which they believed that ***Beowulf*** had been pieced together. Here and there a stalwart scholar can still be discovered engaged on this labour. But most students have long ago abandoned the attempt, and have come to agree [with Friederich Klaeber] that "the Christian elements are, almost without exception, so deeply ingrained in the very fabric of the poem that they cannot be explained away as the work of a reviser or later interpolator. Whilst the episodes are all but free from these modern influences, the main story has been thoroughly imbued with the spirit of Christianity" [see excerpt dated 1922].

Nobody of course doubts that, before ***Beowulf***, as we know it, was composed, there existed a number of short lays and traditions handed down by word of mouth, dealing with the stories told in ***Beowulf***. For many of these stories are historic, and the short lay is the most likely medium through which a knowledge of these tales can have come down from the Fifth and early Sixth Centuries, when the events happened, to the Seventh and Eighth. But the assumption that ***Beowulf*** was composed simply by fitting together a number of these short lays, which had come down from heathen times, and adding various Christian interpolations, rests, in its turn, upon another assumption which has only to be stated to be seen to be very perilous. It is assumed that each of these heathen lays dealt with a limited portion of the story, but treated it in an elaborate way, and with the full "epic breadth" which characterizes the elaborate long poem. It is assumed, in fact, that nothing was needed but a man with a talent for arrangement and interpolation, who could "assemble the parts," fit one lay on to another, and so produce a complete epic. But an examination of existing short lays shows us that they are not of the kind which can be pieced together, so as forthwith to make an epic. Very often a short lay will hurry through a story as complicated as that of a long epic. Take, for example, the *Lay of Weyland* in the *Elder Edda*. In bulk, this is much shorter than the shortest of the twenty-four books of the *Iliad*, or of the *Odyssey*. But the story it tells is more complicated than the main story of the *Iliad* or of the *Odyssey*, and the length of time occupied by it is longer. It would be easier to summarize in one sentence the story of the Wrath of Achilles or the Return of Odysseus than the tale of Weyland.

The men who made the short lays made them for their own pleasure: they were not thinking of providing material convenient for the purpose of some epic poet who was to come after them. Therefore it should not be assumed, without evidence, that these lost lays of heathen times were of such a character that an epic could easily be made by fitting them together. Half a dozen motor-bikes cannot be combined to make a Rolls-Royce car.

How the long epic, as opposed to the short lay, came to be written in England, is a question difficult to answer. It is likely enough that but for the example of the classical epic this would never have happened. (pp. 62-4)

Not all are in agreement with the view so cautiously expressed by Professor W. P. Ker [see excerpt dated 1904]. Yet it is difficult not to suspect the influence of the classical epic in ***Beowulf***, when we notice how carefully the rules of the game are observed. The story begins *in medias res*, but the hero recounts his earlier adventures at a banquet: the poet is not satisfied with telling us that there was minstrelsy at the banquet: he must give us a summary of the lay sung. And such classical influence is not, on *a priori* grounds, at all unlikely. Enthusiasm for Virgil was a possible thing enough in Northumbria at this date: Alcuin, when a boy of eleven in the school of York, was "a lover of Virgil more than of the Psalter."

However that may be, there is a likeness sufficiently strong to challenge comparison, not merely between ***Beowulf*** and the *Aeneid*, but between ***Beowulf*** and the *Iliad* or the *Odyssey*.

The inferiority of ***Beowulf*** is manifest first of all in the plot. The main story of ***Beowulf*** is a wild folk-tale. There are things equally wild in Homer: Odysseus blinds the Cyclops, and Achilles struggles with a river-god: but in Homer these things are kept in their right places and proportions. The folk-tale is a good servant, but a bad master: it has been allowed in ***Beowulf*** to usurp the place of honour, and to drive into episodes and digressions the things which should be the main stuff of a well-conducted epic. (pp. 64-5)

[In] both [***Beowulf*** and in Homer's works] we have a picture of society in its Heroic Age. The society of ***Beowulf*** is in many respects cruder and less developed, just as the hall of Hrothgar is a less elaborate thing than the hall of Odysseus. But there is a fundamental likeness in the life depicted.

Now in Anglo-Saxon England this Heroic Age was brought into contact with Christianity, and with all the civilization of the Mediterranean which came to England with Christianity. It is just this which makes the Seventh Century in England so exciting an epoch. Christian gentleness, working upon the passions of the Heroic Age, produces at once a type which is the rough outline of what later becomes the medieval ideal of the knight, or the modern ideal of the gentleman. (p. 65)

In the epoch of ***Beowulf,*** an Heroic Age more wild and primitive than that of Greece is brought into touch with Christendom, with the Sermon on the Mount, with Catholic theology and ideas of Heaven and Hell. We see the difference if we compare the wilder things—the folk-tale element—in ***Beowulf*** with the wilder things in Homer. Take for example the tale of Odysseus and the Cyclops—the No-Man trick. Odysseus is struggling with a monstrous and wicked foe, but he is not exactly thought of as struggling with the powers of darkness. Polyphemus, by devouring his guests, acts in a way which is hateful to Zeus and the other gods: yet the Cyclops is himself god-begotten and under divine protection, and the fact that Odysseus has maimed him is a wrong which Poseidon is slow to forgive.

But the gigantic foes whom Beowulf has to meet are identified with the foes of God. Grendel is constantly referred to in language which is meant to recall the powers of darkness with which Christian men felt themselves to be encompassed: "inmate of Hell," "adversary of God," "offspring of Cain," "enemy of mankind." Consequently, the matter of the main story of ***Beowulf,*** monstrous as it is, is not so far removed from common medieval experience as it seems to us to be from our own. It was believed that Alcuin as a boy had been beset by devils because he neglected divine service in order to read Virgil. Grendel resembles the fiends of the pit who were always in ambush to waylay a righteous man. And so Beowulf, for all that he moves in the world of the primitive heathen Heroic Age of the Germans, nevertheless is almost a Christian knight. If Spenser had known ***Beowulf,*** he would have found a hero much nearer to his Red Cross Knight than Achilles or Odysseus. The long sermon on humility which Hrothgar preaches to Beowulf after his victory, is as appropriate as the penance in the House of Holiness which the Red Cross Knight has to undergo (and, the scoffer will here interject, hardly less painful).

Beowulf, then, has yet a third claim on our attention. Here we find the character of the Christian hero, the medieval knight, emerging from the turmoil of the Germanic Heroic Age. Not but what many of Beowulf's virtues can be traced back to that Heroic Age. For example, Beowulf's loyalty, when he refuses to take the throne at the expense of his young cousin Heardred, is a part of the Teutonic code of honour, though a part often not put into practice. But the emphasis placed upon gentleness, humility, and judgment to come is a thing in which we can trace the influence of the new faith. In his dying speeches, Beowulf rejoices that he has sought no cunning hatreds, nor sworn oaths unrighteously: "For all this may I have joy, though sick with deadly wounds, that the Ruler of men may not charge me with the slaughter of kinsfolk." And he thanks the Lord of all, the King of glory, that he has been able to win such treasure for his people. (pp. 66-7)

Many different standards and ideals were brought into contact in England in the Seventh Century and the generations following: the civilization of Rome, the loyalties and the violence of the Germanic Heroic Age, the teaching of Christianity. We see these things combining, in different ways, [in ***Beowulf***]. . . . The elements are, as yet, not perfectly fused: from their combination the civilization and ethics of modern Europe were to grow in the fullness of time. (p. 68)

R. W. Chambers, "'Beowulf', and the 'Heroic Age' in England," in his Man's Unconquerable Mind: Studies of English Writers, from Bede to A. E. Housman and W. P. Ker, *Jonathan Cape, 1964, pp. 53-69.*

WILLIAM WITHERLE LAWRENCE (essay date 1928)

[An American scholar, Lawrence wrote critical studies of William Shakespeare's works, Geoffrey Chaucer's Canterbury Tales, *and* Beowulf. *In the following excerpt, he discusses the form, content, and thematic purpose of the Finn episode in* Beowulf *while relating it to the independent* Finnsburg Fragment.]

Quite unconnected with the main business of [***Beowulf***] is the tragic story of the feud between Danes and Frisians, the paraphrase of the lay sung by Hrothgar's minstrel at the ceremonial banquet after the slaying of the demon Grendel. . . . It far transcends in dramatic interest the historical legends [associated with the poem], and it is purely realistic, with no intrusion of the supernatural, and with little epic exaggeration. Actual events may well be mirrored in it, although there is unfortunately little to aid in determining this. No historical documents or poetic narratives, except the *Finnsburg Fragment,* give other versions of the story. But its general character is plain. Even if it is not a record of fact, imaginatively treated, it is a record of what might have been fact, true to the spirit and customs of the times. The chief emphasis lies upon human passions, upon the tragic crises which confronted men and women in the unsettled yet highly conventional life of the Heroic Age. Certain typical situations, frequently utilized for poetic effect elsewhere in ***Beowulf*** and in Germanic story-telling in general, stand forth with great vividness. The shadows are as strong as the high lights; much is left in obscurity. The minstrel's own words are not quoted, as many editions suggest, but summarized, just as in the song sung in Beowulf's honor during the return from the Haunted Mere. . . . The way in which this paraphrase is arranged shows that the Finnsburg story as a whole was perfectly familiar, and that a knowledge of its outlines was taken for granted by the ***Beowulf*** poet. He was thus free to get special effects by stressing tragic and pathetic situations. This allusive method is tantalizing for us to-day; the course of events has to be reconstructed by conjecture and by study of analogous material. Patient labor has yielded a reasonably satisfying and connected narrative, but with many obscurities of detail. A completely different interpretation of the main outlines is by no means beyond the bounds of possibility.

We are singularly fortunate in being able to supplement the ninety lines of the minstrel's lay by a detailed treatment of one scene, in a little less than fifty lines, which is not elaborated in the epic. (pp. 107-08)

By common consent, [this detailed treatment] has long been known as the *Finnsburg Fragment,* in contradistinction to the *Finnsburg Episode* (1063-1159) in ***Beowulf.*** It is defective both at the beginning and at the end. How many lines have been lost, no one can tell. It seems probable, from internal stylistic evidence, that not a great deal is missing, and that, if it were preserved in its entirety, it would form a good illustration of the Anglo-Saxon short epic lay. It contrasts sharply with the *Episode* in treatment. The latter is retrospective, stressing, in the outlines of a complicated story, special scenes of pathos, tragedy, and revenge. The *Fragment* gives a vivid and detailed account of a single scene, a night attack upon a hall, and its successful defence. The reader must bear in mind that, though telling a scene in the same story, the *Fragment* is absolutely independent of the *Episode*.

The circumstances under which the minstrel sang his lay in Hrothgar's hall are important for an interpretation of the story. The subject was selected with a view to giving pleasure to the feasting Danish warriors, celebrating the triumph of a foreign hero, who had performed a feat that they had themselves striven in vain to accomplish. This might well be a little galling to them. That it actually was so is shown by the speech of Unferth at the banquet before the fight with Grendel. So the court poet adroitly selected a tale of Danish heroism and Danish vengeance, a tale of the complete and satisfying victory of the Danes over their ancient enemies, the Frisians. And this would have been equally pleasing for Beowulf to hear. His own people were no friends to the Frisians; Hygelac later selected their coast as the objective point of the great raiding expedition in which he lost his life, and in the later part of the epic Frisian enmity against the Geatas is much emphasized. The whole *Episode* must be read, then, with the grand climax at the end in mind: the absolute and complete vengeance of the Danes for the injury inflicted upon them by the Frisians. (pp. 109-10)

In a nutshell, the action is as follows. A band of Danes under their prince, Hnæf, are attacked at night, while quartered in a hall as guests of Finn, king of the Frisians. Many warriors on both sides are slain, among them Hnæf. Since they have fought indecisively, and to utter exhaustion on both sides, a truce is arranged, whereby the Danes are to remain for the winter under the overlordship of the Frisian king, and be treated with all honor. In the spring, Hengest, the leader of the Danes, is driven by the restlessness of his men to take vengeance on the Frisians. In the ensuing attack, Finn is killed, and his queen and treasure are taken back to Denmark in triumph. The whole tale falls naturally into two parts: the events preceding and following the long winter during which the Danes brood darkly on schemes of revenge. In the first part, the poet is most interested in the scene after the hall-fight, with the terms of the truce, which are set forth in detail, the funeral of the slain warriors, and the despair of Hildeburg, the queen of Finn, a sister of Hnæf, who has lost both a brother and a son, fighting on opposite sides. In the second part, the slow oncoming of spring is pictured, and the mental struggle of Hengest, torn between fidelity to his oath to Finn and the duty of vengeance for his dead prince. (pp. 112-13)

[The] opening lines (1063 ff.) [of the *Episode*], which give the setting of the whole, and introduce the paraphrase of the minstrel's lay, are important. . . . The poet . . . alludes at the outset to the end of the tale, the moment for which the listening warriors in the hall waited, "the swift attack falling on warriors of Finn," the final vengeance of the Danes. There was no objection to anticipating the outcome, since this was already known. Interest in heroic story lay, not in suspense, but in opportunities for emotional effect afforded by tragic complications and for alluring details of narrative.

After the brief introduction, the story proper begins, with the attack on the Danes and the death of Hnæf. Since this was a temporary triumph for the Frisians, and would be no very agreeable subject for the feasting Danish warriors to linger over, it is quickly dismissed, in two lines, and the poet concentrates attention on the woes of Queen Hildeburg. The *Finnsburg Fragment,* which describes this attack fully, can do so with no loss of dramatic effect, since it is in no way connected with the setting of the lay in Hrothgar's hall. Queen Hildeburg, we are told, "could in no wise praise the good faith of the Eotens"—the typical Anglo-Saxon method of saying that she could well accuse them of treachery. Did Finn invite the Danes to his court with the design of murdering them? Or did some unlucky word or deed set the ancient quarrel new abroach, and lead to a tragic violation of hospitality? Were the Danes themselves in some degree responsible for the quarrel? We cannot tell. It is easy, however, to recognize typical situations of Germanic poetry,—the princess married as a "peace-weaver" to a foreign king, who has earlier been hostile to her people; the treacherous hospitality with murder looming up darkly in the background; the bloody hall-fight after a night-attack; and the sufferings of the unhappy lady. The details and treatment of these situations vary from tale to tale, but there are striking parallels in the story of Ingeld and Freawaru, in the scene at the court of Attila in the Nibelung legends, in the crime of King Siggeir and the dreadful revenge of Signy in the Volsung story. It is noteworthy that the first point which the ***Beowulf*** poet selects for emphasis is the tragic conflict in the heart of Hildeburg. Her pathetic desolation as she stands in the gray morning, looking at the bodies of her son and her brother, loathing the treachery that has caused it all, sorrowing for the hard-pressed kinsmen from her homeland, yet bound by years of marriage to their hated foemen—all this is the very bone and sinew of Germanic lyric and epic poetry.

Not less significant is the fact that the poet devotes twenty lines to the truce concluded after the hall-fight. This, indeed, does require explanation. The strict ethics of the *comitatus* made it a disgrace to survive the death of a leader, unless he could be fully avenged; and in this instance, not only is the Frisian king not killed in reprisal, but the Danish warriors agree to accept his overlordship. For the satisfaction of the listening Danish warriors in Hrothgar's hall, the extraordinary circumstances that led to this arrangement had to be fully explained. It is clear that the Frisian party suffered great losses in the hall-fight; "battle snatched away all the thanes of Finn, save a few survivors." . . . But, on the other hand, the Danes, a relatively small body at the start, could not conquer the Frisians, especially after the loss of their leader, Hnæf. Both sides had fought to a standstill, and to utter exhaustion. At this point, Finn made a proposition to the Danes: they were to have another hall, all their own, with a high-seat for the chief; they would have equal rights with his own men, and receive from him as much as the Frisians in the usual distributions of treasure,—provided they would accept him as their lord. It was a dreadful situation for the Danes; Finn was the *bana* ["slayer"] of Hnæf . . . , the man who bore the technical responsibility for his death, even though the actual slaying had been done by somebody else.

To accept him as their over-lord was a terrible breach of tribal custom. But what were they to do? Winter was upon them; they could not take ship and return home; they had to have food and shelter, and they had fought so long (five days, says the *Fragment*) that they could fight no more. It was an *impasse;* an irreconcilable conflict between human endurance and the ethics of a rigid code. So the Danes finally accepted Finn's terms. All the emphasis, as would be expected in a telling of the tale to Danes, is upon the promises made by the Frisians and their allies. Finn expressly agreed that his enemies should have every consideration. If any Frisian should taunt the Danes with having taken service with the *bana* of their lord, the sword should be the end of him. The situation was a dreadful and impossible one, but "it was forced upon them." . . . They had no choice. Just here lay the fascination of the tale for a Germanic audience. . . . [Poets] loved to draw themes for drama from conflicts between different aspects of tribal duty, or between such obligations and the facts of human life. The situation was not comfortable for the Frisians; it was big with tragic possibilities for them. They must have recognized that the truce could be only a temporary expedient for getting through the winter, until the sea should be navigable in the spring, and the Danes could leave for their own country. Later on, there would inevitably be fresh trouble; the duty of revenge would assert itself once more.

The funeral of the dead warriors of both parties is etched in a few vivid lines. A huge pyre was erected, adorned with armor and gold. Upon it were placed, among the rest, Hnæf the Dane and his nephew, the son of the Frisian king. Beside the fire stood the heartbroken Frisian queen. The flames sprang up, crackling and roaring, the bodies burst with the heat, blood poured down the pyre beneath the curling smoke. When all was over, the Frisian warriors returned to their own homes, and all settled down for the winter. The Danes, with heavy hearts and grievous wounds, occupied their hall, while the winter storms raged outside.

Here the first part of the tale ends. Before tracing the tragic sequel, we must look with some care at the account of the hall-fight in which Hnæf lost his life, as told in the *Fragment*. This is a remarkable piece of rapid and vivid narrative. The Danes are quartered in a hall by themselves. Apparently they are the honored guests of Finn; if there have been presentiments or foreshadowings of trouble, we are not informed of them. The "battle-young" Hnæf keeps watch while his followers sleep. Suddenly a gleam in the moonlight attracts his attention. Is it a dragon flying through the air? is it the first beams of dawn? is it a fire in the gable of the hall? No, an attack! Their shining armor has betrayed the stealthy traitors. Hnæf rouses his men, and they rush to arms; Sigeferth and Eaha defend one door, and Ordlaf and Guthlaf the other. Outside the hall Garulf, son of Guthlaf, calls out in a clear voice, asking the name of the defender at the door within. The proud answer comes back: "Sigeferth is my name; I am prince of the Secgan, a wandering champion known far and wide. Many woes and hard fights have I survived; as for you, it remains to be seen what fate you will suffer at my hands." Guthlaf, not heeding the counsel of a more prudent companion, Guthere,—the definiteness of the names gives great realism to the scene,—rushes to the attack, and is the first of the besiegers to fall. The fight is on, the raven hovers above, swords gleam as if all Finnsburg were in flames! Well do the thanes of Hnæf repay the generosity of their leader. Five days they fight, and no one of them falls; they defend the hall successfully. Then one of the besiegers retires, the king (Finn) asks after the wounded,—and the *Fragment* is at an end.

On the whole, all this agrees very well with the narrative in the *Episode*. We should indeed expect the divergences to be greater, in view of the characteristic shiftings of epic narrative. There are one or two minor inconsistencies. The Ordlaf of the *Fragment* is no doubt the Oslaf of the *Episode*. Garulf, the impetuous young hero who first attacks, is called "son of Guthlaf," and Guthlaf was one of the defenders of the doors. If they are father and son, why are they fighting on opposite sides? Possibly circumstances have allied the two with different parties—a common device to arouse interest in Germanic poetry; possibly the father of Garulf is another Guthlaf than the Dane inside the hall; possibly the phrase "Guthlaf's son" . . . is a scribal error for "Guthere's son." . . . Again, the *Episode* apparently states that not only Hnæf but others . . . fell; the *Fragment* states certainly that no one of the defenders fell. This looks like epic exaggeration, a desire to exalt the supreme valor of the Danes. The *Episode* would have no point without the death of Hnæf and the obligation of vengeance, which motivate the entire tragic situation. In the *Fragment,* a detached lay, apparently, no such event was required. However, in discussion of the narrative as a whole, the discrepancies between the two accounts may be dismissed as of little importance.

The second part of the story has been aptly termed "the tragedy of Hengest." He was apparently not of royal blood, but the chief retainer of the dead Hnæf, the ablest man in the party, on whom the command of the Danes devolved. His position was one of extreme difficulty and delicacy. He and his men were in a foreign land, in the dead of winter, among bitter enemies. They were bound by oath to keep the peace, and he, as leader, was additionally responsible. They all longed to return home, but this was impossible until spring. Desire for revenge and a burning sense of wrong filled their hearts. Decision as to future action depended upon Hengest. They could, of course, mature a plan for revenge to be executed after they had left Finn's domains. But could they leave without striking a blow at the *bana* of their lord Hnæf? Nothing but the oath to Finn stood in their way, but this oath was of the most solemn and binding character, allegiance to an over-lord. In this dilemma, Hengest temporized. Finally spring came, the bosom of the earth grew fair, the stormy sea subsided—and the restless Danes could contain themselves no longer. One day the son of Hunlaf came to him, bearing a sword, the edges of which "were well known among the Eotens,"—which probably means that it had done service earlier in the hall-fight,—and formally presented it to him. Hunlaf was apparently (on the evidence of the *Skjoldungasaga*) a brother of the princes Guthlaf and Oslaf (Ordlaf). Perhaps he had been killed in the hall-fight, and his son was especially desirous of vengeance for his slain father. At all events, the presentation of the sword was a call to action, and Hengest wavered no longer. He recognized the superior claim of immediate vengeance. And "horrid bale fell upon Finn in his own home." Just what happened is not told; probably the Danes surprised the Frisians in an unguarded moment, after the long months of inaction. But one thing is clear: that the final attack upon Finn and his men forms the great climax of the story, the whole point of the telling of the tale at Hrothgar's feast. Danish revenge was accomplished with dreadful thoroughness. Grim exultation and bitter reproach accompanied it; Guthlaf and Oslaf cast in Finn's teeth all the woes that had befallen them since that first fateful journey across the sea to Finnsburg. Finn was slain in his own hall, which ran red with the blood of his men. Hengest and his followers, taking with them all Finn's treasures and his unhappy queen, sailed back to their own country in triumph.

Is not this final victory clouded by dishonor? Does not the fact that Hengest proved false to his oath to Finn place him and his warriors in a bad light? No offence had been given by the Frisian party, so far as we know, since the conclusion of the truce; they had played the game fairly. Would it not have been a more satisfying tale, from the Danish point of view, if Hengest had waited until, after a stay in his own land, he could return and wipe out the old score? The submission to Finn had obviously been only an expedient for getting through the winter; it cannot have been thought of by either party as a permanent arrangement. Finn could not have expected that the Danes would remain with him after a return to their own land became possible, but he had every reason to think that they might observe the terms of the oath until after their stay in his domains was over. Does not the whole tale, then, involve the moral shame of the Danes, despite the satisfaction of the great duty of blood-revenge?

No. If this had been the case, the lay could hardly have been sung to gladden the feasting warriors in the hall of Hrothgar. In the first place, Hengest had to choose between conflicting moral obligations. He finally chose the one which seemed to him the more imperative, and which seemed so to his men. It is hard for us at the present day to realize the shame felt by a Germanic warrior if he failed in his full duty to his leader, or the disgrace of having to give allegiance to the slayer of his prince. Nothing could obliterate such humiliation, even though sealed by a forced oath, excepting thorough and bloody revenge. . . . Hengest, when confronted with the supreme duty of taking vengeance for his lord, finds in oaths sworn to an enemy under compulsion no permanent and binding sanctity. (pp. 113-23)

Had the poet of ***Beowulf*** striven to make his narrative [of the Finn story] baffling and obscure, while preserving his general artistic aim, he could not have succeeded better. He has left us unsatisfied, but the has nevertheless allowed us to catch the blurred outlines of a great and moving tragedy. Its wild passion strikes, like a vivid cross-light, athwart the placid epic atmosphere of its setting. It would lend itself readily to dramatic form, with its sharply contrasted scenes—the treacherous attack on the hall in the moonlight, the breaking of dawn on the slain warriors and the weeping queen, the blazing pyre lighting up the grim and bloodstained faces of deadly enemies, the long, gloomy winter vigil of the desperate and humiliated Danes, the secret presentation of the sword, the fierce attack on Finn's hall amid curses and reproaches, and the final voyage of the treasure-laden ship with the triumphant Danes taking a last look at the bloodstained Frisian land. It is finer matter than the tale of Œdipus, in that pursuing Fate lies in men's own passions, not in external influences determining their destinies. Somewhere in the lost poetry of the Heroic Age there lies, perhaps, an epic narrative not unworthy of the greatness of the theme. (p. 128)

William Witherle Lawrence, in his Beowulf and Epic Tradition, *Cambridge, Mass.: Harvard University Press, 1928, 349 p.*

LEVIN L. SCHÜCKING (essay date 1929)

[In the following excerpt from an essay originally published in the MHRA Bulletin *in 1929, Schücking discusses Germanic and Christian definitions of the responsibilities of kings and compares them with the role of the leader in* Beowulf.]

[No] moment of human existence characterizes Christian and non-Christian attitudes so unequivocally as that of death. How does the dying Beowulf conduct himself? He throws a backward glance over his life, expresses satisfaction for having administered his kingdom so well that no enemy dared to attack it. Nor has he committed malicious deeds, broken an oath, or perpetrated wrong against his relatives. Great emphasis is placed, therefore, on the idea of performing that duty which also has first place in the code of morals of the Germanic people, namely *Treue* [''loyalty'']. . . . The Anglo-Saxon word ''treow'' itself has, by the way, just the three meanings with which we here are concerned:

1. Truthful behavior (Cf. ''no malicious deeds'')

2. Faithfulness, in the sense of loyalty (Cf. ''relation to relatives'')

3. Keeping of word or promise (Cf. ''no oaths broken'')

The concept that no enemy dared to attack him is, however, clearly also a traditional formula—not specifically Christian—for a glorious reign, as for example, the description of Edgar's reign contained in the *Peterborough Chronicle:* no enemy was so daring as to threaten his possessions, no army so strong as to devastate his country as long as he ruled over it. Thus, what one would expect of the dying Christian is lacking here. Even in the Byrhtnoth Poem—entirely filled with warlike spirit—at least there is put in the mouth of the leader at the moment of departing, the request to be admitted into Heaven. In contrast thereto, Beowulf's thought that the sight of the earthly goods which he acquired makes death easier for him is even decidedly un-Christian. There is little harmony between the Christian penitential axiom that we are all sinners, and the beautiful pride of duty-performed that emerges from his parting words with which he goes confidently before his Judge. The spirit which these words breathe is then much more what Heusler, relying primarily on Nordic materials, designates as the essence of the Germanic-heathen religiosity: ''No terrified awareness of Deity, no humble submissiveness, but tones of comradely trust as between men and lords.'' Such a mental attitude occurs more than once in the poem. True pride, esteem for one's own achievement, dignity do not disappear in the religious relations. Byrthnoth, a shade more Christian, knows, for example, a prayer of entreaty for use before the battle (262), Beowulf by contrast only prayers of thanksgiving. Many other characteristic Germanic features are to be found in the poem; for example, the fatalistic belief in fate (Gæð a wyrd swa hio scel [''Fate goes ever as it must'']), which occurs throughout Germanic literature. . . . An additional Germanic feature, not infrequent, is the emphasis on the duty of revenge which Heusler calls the greatest highlight of the old Germanic code, equal to loyalty of the vassal and heroic death. (pp. 36-7)

However, if it had been the glorification of these features which mattered to the author, he could have written an Ermanarich epic. If he did not do so, he had obviously quite particular reasons for it. Here, too Heusler has already indicated the right way by showing that Beowulf, the fighter of monsters, must have been a much better hero for a Christian mirror of princes, than a representative of the old heroic world of sagas. Looking at things in this manner it becomes especially clear that the specifically Germanic features enumerated disclose to a large extent a certain selection by which they are granted their place

Zoomorphic ship's figurehead, probably dating from the ninth century, discovered in the River Scheldt at Appels, Belgium. The British Museum.

in a world view which in the last analysis is differently constituted. For there are in the poem very clearly un-Germanic features as, for example, the following. Neckel says: "It does not glorify champions and benefactors of the people as such." That, however, is precisely what it does. King Beowulf dies for his people, and his comfort in dying is to have acquired for his loyal people such precious possessions. Klaeber, who has the merit of having proved more exactly how Christian ***Beowulf*** is in fundamental conception, in spite of all its heathen Germanic elements, thinks he can even see in this motif an allegory of the Savior. He supports this parallel further by certain correspondences of the final action, namely the events at the sacrifice of the king's life, where the companions desert him in cowardice—and this is said to be a reminiscence of Gethsemane. The question is, however, whether the final action, like the whole concept, does not bring into being rather an ideal of kingship. Such an ideal has by degrees acquired an almost dominating character from the contemporary church literature, namely that of *imperator felix* ["successful emperor"] or *rex justus* ["just king"] of Augustine.

The teaching of Augustine, which continues to live with only little change in Gregory the Great, Pseudo-Cyprian, Sedulius Scotus, Hincmar of Reims, etc., spiritualizes the authoritative office by asking from its bearer above all wisdom, piety, and kindness. The prince must be master of his desires and passions, and especially, not yield power over himself to the greatest and for him the most dangerous sin—pride (superbia), but remain modest and humble. His rule should be a service in love, benevolence, sympathetic care. . . . He is indulgent and pardons easily. If he is forced to act harshly, he tries to compensate by mercy and ample charity. His purpose is to bring and keep for himself and his people the true peace of God on earth. For the highest purpose of life is harmony (ordinata concordia ["harmonious order"]) between states, within the state and within the family. In contrast to such a "rex justus" ["just king"] who always appears as a *good shepherd* and with the *qualities of a father,* is the "tyrannus" or "rex iniustus," who is ruled by the "radix vitiorum" ["root of vices"], "superbia" ["pride"] or "amor sui" ["love of self"]. . . . Out of *amor sui* spring all other vices, such as "invidia, ira, tristitia, avaritia and ventris ingluvies" ["envy, wrath, sadness, avarice and gluttony"]. (pp. 38-9)

[How far] does the Augustinian interpretation of kingship shine forth in the ***Beowulf*** epic in spite of . . . [its] Germanic elements? First and foremost, it is evident in the conception of the theme, which shows a hero and king not only by great deeds but by the "prodesse" ["help"], which is according to Augustine the essence of the royal office. Beowulf, who kills the dragon, is the good shepherd, who perishes in protecting his flock. But the old King Hrothgar, too, in the first part of the poem embodies this ideal of "rex justus" ["just king"]. He is a prince of peace, full of fatherly benevolence, caring for the welfare of his people. The "ordinata concordia" ["harmonious order"] is for him a high ideal. He rejoices in the treaty of peace between the Danes and the Gauts . . . as well as the happy accord within the Danish community ("Her is æghwylc oþrum getrywe") ["Here is each loyal to the other"]. Further, like Beowulf, he accepts decisions from God's hands on most important matters without grumbling, and with Gregorian "obedientia" ["obedience"]. Especially remarkable, however, is his conduct towards his people. When his loyal Aeschere is torn away from him by death, he mourns for him in terms of highest praise just as he would for one of his peers. He even uses the designation "sincgifa" ("treasure-giver," line 1342) for the deceased as if speaking of a king, just as if he intended to bear out Gregory's demand: "Sit rector bene agentibus per humilitatem socius" ["Let the ruler be through humility a companion to those who conduct themselves well."]. . . . The final words of the epic celebrating the deceased as the kindest and friendliest of all men characterize most strongly this striving to show benevolence and warmth of heart in his relation with those around him.

Such strong emphasis on a prince's popularity and on good relations between a king and his people runs through the entire ***Beowulf,*** and perhaps contrary to what one might think, is in no way like the ideal of a king to be found in Vergil. King Latinus of the *Aeneid* is "pious, prudent, generous, just, tender of heart . . . but with the Latin poet, great popularity and the striving for popularity play no role. Evidently, Germanic conceptions are blended in the ***Beowulf*** to a high degree. That the king is, for example, always designated briefly as "wine" (Cf. "wine Scyldinga") means that the word for "friend" and "lord" is the same, evidently derived from the atmosphere of the life of the comitatus. Just this democracy within the governing class is typically Germanic. Still, the basis for the democracy is again Christian. The speech of Hrothgar against Pride ("superbia"), for example, breathes a typical Augustinian-Gregorian spirit. . . . Also the counter example of "tyrannus," who is more obedient to the devil than to God,—here, it is the gloomy Heremod—is in itself completely borrowed from the way of thinking of the Church Fathers, who, for example, liked to contrast Moses and Solomon or turn to account the picture of Saul (Hincmar, Pseudo-Cyprian); the details, it is true, are fitted out with the appropriate Germanic features. The basic vice of the evil ones is designated as "lufu" . . . , a word the use of which in this place has remained unexplained but which perhaps only renders Augustine's *amor sui*.

Finally, striking in the ***Beowulf*** is the strong emphasis on the king's inellectual powers. Likewise, in the picture of the ideal figure of the martyr king, Edmund, in Ælfric's Homily . . . , prudence is cited in first place (*snotor* and wurðfull ["wise and worthy"]). This prudence, it is true, is of a very different kind. . . . But the king is still in the first place the "wise one"—and to this, moreover, according to the proposition that wisdom presupposes age . . . , is tied the notion of being well advanced in years, which is also customarily connected with other expressions for "prudent," namely "frod" and "snotor." Again and again, Beowulf is thus designated as "se wisa." . . . His intellectual achievement in the epic is shown not the least by the fact that he is wise in a special way, namely, "wis wordcwida," that is, he is a good orator. But this, too, is neither foreign nor un-Germanic. "To be gifted as an orator," says [Gustav Neckel in *Altgermanische Kultur* (1934)], "is always well-becoming to a Germanic king." In the Christian ideal of a king, however, this feature is particularly prominent. The "persuabilitas (in verbis)" ["power of persuasion" ("by means of words")] belongs to the "eight pillars" of royalty. Such an ability for speaking is at the same time an ability for teaching, just as the deserted vassal in the *Wanderer* . . . yearns to return to the "*larcwidum*" ("teaching") of the king; indeed, sometimes, it passes over directly into the sermon. But to see so distinctly the teacher in the king is, I suppose—one should think of Gregory's *Cura Pastoralis*—a clerical ideal. (pp. 40-3)

Levin L. Schücking, "The Ideal of Kingship in 'Beowulf,'" in An Anthology of Beowulf Criticism, *edited by Lewis E. Nicholson, University of Notre Dame Press, 1963, pp. 35-49.*

J.R.R. TOLKIEN (lecture date 1936)

[*Tolkien is famous as the author of the mythopoeic* Lord of the Rings *trilogy (1954-56) and of its simpler prequel,* The Hobbit *(1938). With C. S. Lewis, Charles Williams, and others, Tolkien was a central member of the Oxford Christians, or "Inklings," a group of like-minded writers and friends who met weekly to discuss literature and read works-in-progress. A longtime professor of medieval English literature and philology at the University of Oxford, Tolkien had conservative literary tastes; for years he campaigned to keep "modern" (nineteenth- and twentieth-century) English literature off the curriculum at Oxford. Like Lewis, he disliked nearly all of the formal developments in twentieth-century writing, his reading tending instead toward the traditional epic, with his favorite literature being the ancient Norse sagas. In the following excerpt from a 1936 British Academy lecture, Tolkien presents his view that, in addition to having a historical and linguistic interest,* Beowulf *is primarily a work of art whose aesthetic qualities make it the most successful Old English poem. Throughout, Tolkien refutes those critics who question the ethical and aesthetic qualities of the poem, paying particular attention to structure, plot, and portrayal of characters in the work. Translations in this excerpt are taken from* Beowulf: A Dual-Language Edition *by Howell D. Chickering, Jr.*]

I have read enough, I think, to venture the opinion that *Beowulfiana* is, while rich in many departments, specially poor in one. It is poor in criticism, criticism that is directed to the understanding of a poem as a poem. It has been said of ***Beowulf*** itself that its weakness lies in placing the unimportant things at the centre and the important on the outer edges. This is one of the opinions that I wish specially to consider. I think it profoundly untrue of the poem, but strikingly true of the literature about it. ***Beowulf*** has been used as a quarry of fact and fancy far more assiduously than it has been studied as a work of art. (pp. 245-46)

So far from being a poem so poor that only its accidental historical interest can still recommend it, ***Beowulf*** is in fact so interesting as poetry, in places poetry so powerful, that this quite overshadows the historical content, and is largely independent even of the most important facts (such as the date and identity of Hygelac) that research has discovered. It is indeed a curious fact that it is one of the peculiar poetic virtues of ***Beowulf*** that has contributed to its own critical misfortunes. The illusion of historical truth and perspective, that has made ***Beowulf*** seem such an attractive quarry, is largely a product of art. The author has used an instinctive historical sense—a part indeed of the ancient English temper (and not unconnected with its reputed melancholy), of which ***Beowulf*** is a supreme expression; but he has used it with a poetical and not an historical object. The lovers of poetry can safety study the art, but the seekers after history must beware lest the glamour of Poesis overcome them.

Nearly all the censure, and most of the praise, that has been bestowed on ***The Beowulf*** has been due either to the belief that it was something that it was *not*—for example, primitive, pagan, Teutonic, an allegory (political or mythical), or most often, an epic; or to disappointment at the discovery that it was itself and not something that the scholar would have liked better—for example, a heathen heroic lay, a history of Sweden, a manual of Germanic antiquities, or a Nordic *Summa Theologica*. (pp. 247-48)

It is not surprising that it should now be felt that a view, a decision, a conviction are imperatively needed. But it is plainly only in the consideration of ***Beowulf*** as a poem, with an inherent poetic significance, that any view or conviction can be reached or steadily held. (pp. 249-50)

Although there is plainly considerable difference between the later Norse and the ancient English form of the story alluded to in ***Beowulf,*** already there it had these two primary features: the dragon, and the slaying of him as the chief deed of the greatest of heroes—*he wæs wreccena wide mærost* [''he was the most famous hero-adventurer'']. A dragon is no idle fancy. Whatever may be his origins, in fact or invention, the dragon in legend is a potent creation of men's imagination, richer in significance than his barrow is in gold. (pp. 257-58)

Beowulf's dragon, if one wishes really to criticize, is not to be blamed for being a dragon, but rather for not being dragon enough, plain pure fairy-story dragon. There are in the poem some vivid touches of the right kind—as *þa se wyrm onwoc, wroht wæs geniwad; stonc æfter stane* [''By then, also, the dragon had wakened and with it new strife. It slithered and sniffed along the stone walls''], 2285—in which this dragon is real worm, with a bestial life and thought of his own, but the conception, none the less, approaches *draconitas* [''dragonishness''] rather than *draco* [''dragon'']: a personification of malice, greed, destruction (the evil side of heroic life), and of the undiscriminating cruelty of fortune that distinguishes not good or bad (the evil aspect of all life). But for ***Beowulf,*** the poem, that is as it should be. In this poem the balance is nice, but it is preserved. The large symbolism is near the surface, but it does not break through, nor become allegory. Something more significant than a standard hero, a man faced with a foe more evil than any human enemy of house or realm, is before us, and yet incarnate in time, walking in heroic history, and treading the named lands of the North. And this, we are told, is the radical defect of ***Beowulf,*** that its author, coming in a time rich in the legends of heroic men, has used them afresh in an original fashion, giving us not just one more, but something akin yet different: a measure and interpretation of them all.

We do not deny the worth of the hero by accepting Grendel and the dragon. Let us by all means esteem the old heroes: men caught in the chains of circumstance or of their own character, torn between duties equally sacred, dying with their backs to the wall. But ***Beowulf,*** I fancy, plays a larger part than is recognized in helping us to esteem them. Heroic lays may have dealt in their own way—we have little enough to judge by—a way more brief and vigorous, perhaps, though perhaps also more harsh and noisy (and less thoughtful), with the actions of heroes caught in circumstances that conformed more or less to the varied but fundamentally simple recipe for an heroic situation. In these (if we had them) we could see the exaltation of undefeated will, which receives doctrinal expression in the words of Byrhtwold at the battle of Maldon. But though with sympathy and patience we might gather, from a line here or a tone there, the background of imagination which gives to this indomitability, this paradox of defeat inevitable yet unacknowledged, its full significance, it is in ***Beowulf*** that a poet has devoted a whole poem to the theme, and has drawn the struggle in different proportions, so that we may see man at war with the hostile world, and his inevitable overthrow in Time. The particular is on the outer edge, the essential in the centre. (pp. 258-60)

Beowulf is not . . . the hero of an heroic lay, precisely. He has no enmeshed loyalties, nor hapless love. *He is a man, and that for him and many is sufficient tragedy.* It is not an irritating accident that the tone of the poem is so high and its theme so low. It is the theme in its deadly seriousness that begets the dignity of tone: *lif is læne: eal scæceð leoht and lif somod* [''life is transitory: all men leave this world and life together'']. So deadly and ineluctable is the underlying thought, that those who in the circle of light, within the besieged hall, are absorbed in work or talk and do not look to the battlements, either do not regard it or recoil. Death comes to the feast, and they say He gibbers: He has no sense of proportion.

I would suggest, then, that the monsters are not an inexplicable blunder of taste; they are essential, fundamentally allied to the underlying ideas of the poem, which give it its lofty tone and high seriousness. The key to the fusion-point of imagination that produced this poem lies, therefore, in those very references to Cain which have often been used as a stick to beat an ass—taken as an evident sign (were any needed) of the muddled heads of early Anglo-Saxons. (pp. 260-61)

It is through [a blending of Christian and Norse materials and traditions] that there was available to a poet who set out to *write* a poem—and in the case of ***Beowulf*** we may probably use this very word—on a scale and plan unlike a minstrel's lay, both new faith and new learning (or education), and also a body of native tradition (itself requiring to be learned) for the changed mind to contemplate together. The native ''learning'' cannot be denied in the case of ***Beowulf.*** Its display has grievously perturbed the critics, for the author draws upon tradition at will for his own purposes, as a poet of later times might draw upon history or the classics and expect his allusions to be understood (within a certain class of hearers). He was in fact, like Virgil, learned enough in the vernacular department to have an historical perspective, even an antiquarian curiosity. He cast his time into the long-ago, because already the long-ago had a special poetical attraction. He knew much about old days, and though his knowledge—of such things as sea-burial and the funeral pyre, for instance—was rich and poetical rather than accurate with the accuracy of modern archaeology (such as that is), one thing he knew clearly: those days were heathen—heathen, noble, and hopeless. (pp. 263-64)

[***Beowulf***'s author] is concerned primarily with *man on earth,* rehandling in a new perspective an ancient theme: that man, each man and all men, and all their works shall die. A theme no Christian need despise. Yet this theme plainly would not be so treated, but for the nearness of a pagan time. The shadow of its despair, if only as a mood, as an intense emotion of regret, is still there. The worth of defeated valour in this world is deeply felt. As the poet looks back into the past, surveying the history of kings and warriors in the old traditions, he sees that all glory (or as we might say ''culture'' or ''civilization'') ends in night. The solution of that tragedy is not treated—it does not arise out of the material. We get in fact a poem from a pregnant moment of poise, looking back into the pit, by a man learned in old tales who was struggling, as it were, to get a general view of them all, perceiving their common tragedy of inevitable ruin, and yet feeling this more *poetically* because he was himself removed from the direct pressure of its despair. He could view from without, but still feel immediately and from within, the old dogma: despair of the event, combined with faith in the value of doomed resistance. He was still dealing with the great temporal tragedy, and not yet writing an allegorical homily in verse. Grendel inhabits the visible world and eats the flesh and blood of men; he enters their houses by the doors. The dragon wields a physical fire, and covets gold not souls; he is slain with iron in his belly. Beowulf's *byrne* was made by Weland, and the iron shield he bore against the serpent by his own smiths: it was not yet the breastplate of righteousness, nor the shield of faith for the quenching of all the fiery darts of the wicked.

Almost we might say that this poem was (in one direction) inspired by the debate that had long been held and continued after, and that it was one of the chief contributions to the controversy: shall we or shall we not consign the heathen ancestors to perdition? What good will it do posterity to read the battles of Hector? *Quid Hinieldus cum Christo?* [''What has Ingeld to do with Christ?''] The author of ***Beowulf*** showed forth the permanent value of that pietas [''piety''] which treasures the memory of man's struggles in the dark past, man fallen and not yet saved, disgraced but not dethroned. It would seem to have been part of the English temper in its strong sense of tradition, dependent doubtless on dynasties, noble houses, and their code of honour, and strengthened, it may be, by the more inquisitive and less severe Celtic learning, that it should, at least in some quarters and despite grave and Gallic voices, preserve much from the northern past to blend with southern learning, and new faith.

It has been thought that the influence of Latin epic, especially of the *Aeneid,* is perceptible in ***Beowulf,*** and a necessary explanation, if only in the exciting of emulation, of the development of the long and studied poem in early England. There is, of course, a likeness in places between these greater and lesser things, the *Aeneid* and ***Beowulf,*** if they are read in conjunction. But the smaller points in which imitation or reminiscence might be perceived are inconclusive, while the real likeness is deeper and due to certain qualities in the authors independent of the question whether the Anglo-Saxon had read Virgil or not. It is this deeper likeness which makes things, that are either the inevitabilities of human poetry or the accidental congruences of all tales, ring alike. We have the great pagan on the threshold of the change of the world; and the great (if lesser) Christian just over the threshold of the great change in his time and place: the backward view. . . . (pp. 265-67)

But we will now return once more to the monsters, and consider especially the difference of their status in the northern and southern mythologies. Of Grendel it is said: *Godes yrre bær* [''he bore God's wrath'']. But the Cyclops is god-begotten and his maiming is an offence against his begetter, the god Poseidon. This radical difference in mythological status is only brought out more sharply by the very closeness of the similarity in conception (in all save mere size) that is seen, if we compare ***Beowulf,*** 740 ff., with the description of the Cyclops devouring men in *Odyssey,* ix—or still more in *Aeneid,* iii. 622 ff. In Virgil, whatever may be true of the fairy-tale world of the Odyssey, the Cyclops walks veritably in the historic world. He is seen by Aeneas in Sicily, *monstrum horrendum, informe, ingens* [''a fearful, hideous, prodigious monstrosity''], as much a perilous fact as Grendel was in Denmark, *earmsceapen on weres wæstmum . . . næfne he wæs mara þonne ænig man oðer* [''misshapen, stalked marshy wastes in the track of an exile, except that he was larger than any other man'']; as real as Acestes or Hrothgar. (p. 267)

[Southern mythology does not have] the monsters in the centre—as they are in ***Beowulf*** to the astonishment of the critics. But such horrors cannot be left permanently unexplained, lurking on the outer edges and under suspicion of being connected with the Government. It is the strength of the northern mythological imagination that it faced this problem, put the monsters in the centre, gave them victory but no honour, and found a potent but terrible solution in naked will and courage. ''As a working theory absolutely impregnable.'' So potent is it, that while the older southern imagination has faded for ever into literary ornament, the northern has power, as it were, to revive its spirit even in our own times. It can work, even as it did work with the *goðlauss* viking, without gods: martial heroism as its own end. But we may remember that the poet of ***Beowulf*** saw clearly: the wages of heroism is death. . . .

I think that the passages in ***Beowulf*** concerning the giants and their war with God, together with the two mentions of Cain (as the ancestor of the giants in general and Grendel in particular) are specially important.

They are directly connected with Scripture, yet they cannot be dissociated from the creatures of northern myth, the ever-watchful foes of the gods (and men). The undoubtedly scriptural Cain is connected with *eotenas* and *ylfe* [''giants'' and ''elves''], which are the *jötnar* and álfar of Norse. But this is not due to mere confusion—it is rather an indication of the precise point at which an imagination, pondering old and new, was kindled. At this point new Scripture and old tradition touched and ignited. It is for this reason that these elements of Scripture alone appear in a poem dealing of design with the noble pagan of old days. For they are precisely the elements which bear upon this theme. Man alien in a hostile world, engaged in a struggle which he cannot win while the world lasts, is assured that his foes are the foes also of Dryhten, that his courage noble in itself is also the highest loyalty: so said thyle and clerk.

In ***Beowulf*** we have . . . an historical poem about the pagan past, or an attempt at one—literal historical fidelity founded on modern research was, of course, not attempted. It is a poem by a learned man writing of old times, who looking back on the heroism and sorrow feels in them something permanent and something symbolical. So far from being a confused semi-pagan—historically unlikely for a man of this sort in the period—he brought probably *first* to his task a knowledge of Christian poetry, especially that of the Cædmon school, and especially *Genesis.* He makes his minstrel sing in Heorot of the Creation of the earth and the lights of Heaven. So excellent is this choice as the theme of the harp that maddened Grendel lurking joyless in the dark without that it matters little whether this is anachronistic or not. *Secondly,* to his task the poet brought a considerable learning in native lays and traditions: only by learning and training could such things be acquired, they were no more born naturally into an Englishman of the seventh or eighth centuries, by simple virtue of being an ''Anglo-Saxon,'' than ready-made knowledge of poetry and history is inherited at birth by modern children.

It would seem that, in his attempt to depict ancient pre-Christian days, intending to emphasize their nobility, and the desire of the good for truth, he turned naturally when delineating the great King of Heorot to the Old Testament. In the *folces hyrde* [''guardian of the people''] of the Danes we have much of the shepherd patriarchs and kings of Israel, servants of the one God, who attribute to His mercy all the good things that come to them in this life. We have in fact a Christian English conception of the noble chief before Christianity, who could lapse (as could Israel) in times of temptation into idolatry. On the other hand, the traditional matter in English, not to mention the living survival of the heroic code and temper among the noble households of ancient England, enabled him to draw differently, and in some respects much closer to the actual heathen *hæleð* [''hero'' or ''warrior''], the character of Beowulf, especially as a young knight, who used his great gift of *mægen* [''strength''] to earn *dom* [''glory''] and *lof* [''praise''] among men and posterity.

Beowulf is not an actual picture of historic Denmark or Geatland or Sweden about A.D. 500. But it is (if with certain minor defects) on a general view a self-consistent picture, a construction bearing clearly the marks of design and thought. The whole must have succeeded admirably in creating in the minds of the poet's contemporaries the illusion of surveying a past, pagan but noble and fraught with a deep significance—a past that itself had depth and reached backward into a dark antiquity of sorrow. This impression of depth is an effect and a justification of the use of episodes and allusions to old tales, mostly darker, more pagan, and desperate than the foreground. (pp. 268-71)

The criticism that the important matters are put on the outer edges misses this point of artistry, and indeed fails to see why the old things have in ***Beowulf*** such an appeal: it is the poet himself who made antiquity so appealing. His poem has more value in consequence, and is a greater contribution to early mediaeval thought than the harsh and intolerant view that consigned all the heroes to the devil. We may be thankful that the product of so noble a temper has been preserved by chance (if such it be) from the dragon of destruction.

The general structure of the poem, so viewed, is not really difficult to perceive, if we look to the main points, the strategy, and neglect the many points of minor tactics. We must dismiss, of course, from mind the notion that ***Beowulf*** is a ''narrative poem,'' that it tells a tale or intends to tell a tale sequentially. The poem ''lacks steady advance'': so Klaeber heads a critical section in his edition [see excerpt dated 1922]. But the poet was not meant to advance, steadily or unsteadily. It is essentially a balance, an opposition of ends and beginnings. In its simplest terms it is a contrasted description of two moments in a great life, rising and setting; an elaboration of the ancient and intensely moving contrast between youth and age, first achievement and final death. It is divided in consequence into two opposed portions, different in matter, manner, and length: A from 1 to 2199 (including an exordium of 52 lines); B from 2200 to 3182 (the end). There is no reason to cavil at this proportion; in any case, for the purpose and the production of the required effect, it proves in practice to be right.

This simple and *static* structure, solid and strong, is in each part much diversified, and capable of enduring this treatment. In the conduct of the presentation of Beowulf's rise to fame on the one hand, and of his kingship and death on the other, criticism can find things to question, especially if it is captious, but also much to praise, if it is attentive. But the only serious weakness, or apparent weakness, is the long recapitulation: the report of Beowulf to Hygelac. This recapitulation is well done. Without serious discrepancy it retells rapidly the events in Heorot, and retouches the account; and it serves to illustrate, since he himself describes his own deeds, yet more vividly the character of a young man, singled out by destiny, as he steps suddenly forth in his full powers. Yet this is perhaps not quite sufficient to justify the repetition. The explanation, if not complete justification, is probably to be sought in different directions.

For one thing, the old tale was not first told or invented by this poet. So much is clear from investigation of the folk-tale analogues. Even the legendary association of the Scylding court with a marauding monster, and with the arrival from abroad of a champion and deliverer was probably already old. The plot was not the poet's; and though he has infused feeling and significance into its crude material, that plot was not a perfect vehicle of the theme or themes that came to hidden life in the poet's mind as he worked upon it. Not an unusual event in literature. For the contrast—youth and death—it would probably have been better, if we had no journeying. If the single nation of the *Geatas* had been the scene, we should have felt the stage not narrower, but symbolically wider. More plainly should we have perceived in one people and their hero all mankind and its heroes. This at any rate I have always myself felt in reading ***Beowulf***; but I have also felt that this defect is rectified by the bringing of the tale of Grendel to Geatland. As Beowulf stands in Hygelac's hall and tells his story, he sets his feet firm again in the land of his own people, and is no longer in danger of appearing a mere *wrecca,* an errant adventurer and slayer of bogies that do not concern him.

There is in fact a double division in the poem: the fundamental one already referred to, and a secondary but important division at line 1887. After that the essentials of the previous part are taken up and compacted, so that all the tragedy of Beowulf is contained between 1888 and the end. But, of course, without the first half we should miss much incidental illustration; we should miss also the dark background of the court of Heorot that loomed as large in glory and doom in ancient northern imagination as the court of Arthur: no vision of the past was complete without it. And (most important) we should lose the direct contrast of youth and age in the persons of Beowulf and Hrothgar which is one of the chief purposes of this section: it ends with the pregnant words *oþ þæt hine yldo benam mægenes wynnum, se þe oft manegum scod* [''till age took from him the joy of his strength—a thing that harms many''].

In any case we must not view this poem as in intention an exciting narrative or a romantic tale. The very nature of Old English metre is often misjudged. In it there is no single rhythmic pattern progressing from the beginning of a line to the end, and repeated with variation in other lines. The lines do not go according to a tune. They are founded on a balance; an opposition between two halves of roughly equivalent phonetic weight, and significant content, which are more often rhythmically contrasted than similar. They are more like masonry than music. In this fundamental fact of poetic expression I think there is a parallel to the total structure of ***Beowulf. Beowulf*** is indeed the most successful Old English poem because in it the elements, language, metre, theme, structure, are all most nearly in harmony. Judgement of the verse has often gone astray through listening for an accentual rhythm and pattern: and it seems to halt and stumble. Judgement of the theme goes astray through considering it as the narrative handling of a plot: and it seems to halt and stumble. Language and verse, of course, differ from stone or wood or paint, and can be only heard or read in a time-sequence; so that in any poem that deals at all with characters and events some narrative element must be present. We have none the less in ***Beowulf*** a method and structure that within the limits of the verse-kind approaches rather to sculpture or painting. It is a composition not a tune.

This is clear in the second half. In the struggle with Grendel one can as a reader dismiss the certainty of literary experience that the hero will not in fact perish, and allow oneself to share the hopes and fears of the Geats upon the shore. In the second part the author has no desire whatever that the issue should remain open, even according to literary convention. There is no need to hasten like the messenger, who rode to bear the lamentable news to the waiting people (2892 ff.). They may have hoped, but we are not supposed to. By now we are supposed to have grasped the plan. Disaster is foreboded. Defeat is the theme. Triumph over the foes of man's precarious fortress is over, and we approach slowly and reluctantly the inevitable victory of death.

"In structure," it was said of ***Beowulf***, "it is curiously weak, in a sense preposterous," though great merits of detail were allowed. In structure actually it is curiously strong, in a sense inevitable, though there are defects of detail. The general design of the poet is not only defensible, it is, I think, admirable. There may have previously existed stirring verse dealing in straightforward manner and even in natural sequence with the Beowulf's deeds, or with the fall of Hygelac; or again with the fluctuations of the feud between the houses of Hrethel the Great and Ongentheow the Swede; or with the tragedy of the Heathobards, and the treason that destroyed the Scylding dynasty. Indeed this must be admitted to be practically certain: it was the existence of such connected legends—connected in the mind, not necessarily dealt with in chronicle fashion or in long semi-historical poems—that permitted the peculiar use of them in ***Beowulf***. This poem cannot be criticized or comprehended, if its original audience is imagined in like case to ourselves, possessing only ***Beowulf*** in splendid isolation. For ***Beowulf*** was not designed to tell the tale of Hygelac's fall, or for that matter to give the whole biography of Beowulf, still less to write the history of the Geatish kingdom and its downfall. But it used knowledge of these things for its own purpose—to give that sense of perspective, of antiquity with a greater and yet darker antiquity behind. These things are mainly on the outer edges or in the background because they belong there, if they are to function in this way. But in the center we have an heroic figure of enlarged proportions.

Beowulf is not an "epic," not even a magnified "lay." No terms borrowed from Greek or other literatures exactly fit: there is no reason why they should. Though if we must have a term, we should choose rather "elegy." It is an heroic-elegiac poem; and in a sense all its first 3,136 lines are the prelude to a dirge: *him þa gegiredan Geata leode ad ofer eorðan unwaclicne* ["the Geatish people then built a pyre on that high ground, no mean thing"]: one of the most moving ever written. But for the universal significance which is given to the fortunes of its hero it is an enhancement and not a detraction, in fact it is necessary, that his final foe should be not some Swedish prince, or treacherous friend, but a dragon: a thing made by imagination for just such a purpose. Nowhere does a dragon come in so precisely where he should. But if the hero falls before a dragon, then certainly he should achieve his early glory by vanquishing a foe of similar order.

There is, I think, no criticism more beside the mark than that which some have made, complaining that it is monsters in both halves that is so disgusting; one they could have stomached more easily. That is nonsense. I can see the point of asking for *no* monsters. I can also see the point of the situation in ***Beowulf***. But no point at all in mere reduction of numbers. It would really have been preposterous, if the poet had recounted Beowulf's rise to fame in a "typical" or "commonplace" war in Frisia, and then ended him with a dragon. Or if he had told of his cleansing of Heorot, and then brought him to defeat and death in a "wild" or "trivial" Swedish invasion! If the dragon is the right end for Beowulf, and I agree with the author that it is, then Grendel is an eminently suitable beginning. They are creatures, *feond mancynnes* ["solitary sinners against mankind"], of a similar order and kindred significance. Triumph over the lesser and more nearly human is cancelled by defeat before the older and more elemental. And the conquest of the ogres comes at the right moment: not in earliest youth, though the nicors are referred to in Beowulf's *geogoðfeore* ["period of youth"] as a presage of the kind of hero we have to deal with; and not during the later period of recognized ability and prowess, but in that first moment, which often comes in great lives, when men look up in surprise and see that a hero has unawares leaped forth. The placing of the dragon is inevitable: a man can but die upon his death-day.

I will conclude by drawing an imaginary contrast. Let us suppose that our poet had chosen a theme more consonant with "our modern judgement"; the life and death of St. Oswald. He might then have made a poem, and told first of Heavenfield, when Oswald as a young prince against all hope won a great victory with a remnant of brave men; and then have passed at once to the lamentable defeat of Oswestry, which seemed to destroy the hope of Christian Northumbria; while all the rest of Oswald's life, and the traditions of the royal house and its feud with that of Deira might be introduced allusively or omitted. To any one but an historian in search of facts and chronology this would have been a fine thing, an heroic-elegiac poem greater than history. It would be much better than a plain narrative, in verse or prose, however steadily advancing. This mere arrangement would at once give it more significance than a straightforward account of one king's life: the contrast of rising and setting, achievement and death. But even so it would fall far short of ***Beowulf***. Poetically it would be greatly enhanced if the poet had taken violent liberties with history and much enlarged the reign of Oswald, making him old and full of years of care and glory when he went forth heavy with foreboding to face the heathen Penda: the contrast of youth and age would add enormously to the original theme, and give it a more universal meaning. But even so it would still fall short of ***Beowulf***. To match his theme with the rise and fall of poor "folk-tale" Beowulf the poet would have been obliged to turn Cadwallon and Penda into giants and demons. It is just because the main foes in ***Beowulf*** are inhuman that the story is larger and more significant than this imaginary poem of a great king's fall. It glimpses the cosmic and moves with the thought of all men concerning the fate of human life and efforts; it stands amid but above the petty wars of princes, and surpasses the dates and limits of historical periods, however important. At the beginning, and during its process, and most of all at the end, we look down as if from a visionary height upon the house of man in the valley of the world. A light starts—*lixte se leoma ofer landa fela* ["its gold-hammered roofs shone over the land"]—and there is a sound of music; but the outer darkness and its hostile offspring lie ever in wait for the torches to fail and the voices to cease. Grendel is maddened by the sound of harps.

And one last point, which those will feel who to-day preserve the ancient *pietas* towards the past: ***Beowulf*** is not a "primitive" poem; it is a late one, using the materials (then still plentiful) preserved from a day already changing and passing, a time that has now for ever vanished, swallowed in oblivion; using them for a new purpose, with a wider sweep of imagination, if with a less bitter and concentrated force. When new ***Beowulf*** was already antiquarian, in a good sense, and it now produces a singular effect. For it is now to us itself ancient; and yet its maker was telling of things already old and weighted with regret, and he expended his art in making keen that touch upon the heart which sorrows have that are both poignant and remote. If the funeral of Beowulf moved once like the echo of an ancient dirge, far-off and hopeless, it is to us as a memory brought over the hills, an echo of an echo. There is not much poetry in the world like this; and though ***Beowulf*** may not be among the very greatest poems of our western world and its tradition, it has its own individual character, and peculiar solemnity; it would still have power had it been written in some time or place unknown and without posterity, if it contained no name that could now be recognized or identified by research. Yet it is in fact written in a language that after many centuries has still essential kinship with our own, it was made in this land, and moves in our northern world beneath our northern sky, and for those who are native to that tongue and land, it must ever call with a profound appeal—until the dragon comes. (pp. 271-78)

J.R.R. Tolkien, "Beowulf: The Monsters and the Critics," in Proceedings of the British Academy, *Vol. XXII, 1936, pp. 245-95.*

JOAN BLOMFIELD (essay date 1938)

[*In the following excerpt, Blomfield outlines the structural unity of* Beowulf, *in direct contradiction of the opinion of Friederich Klaeber (see excerpt dated 1922). Translations in this excerpt are taken from* Beowulf: A Dual-Language Edition *by Howell D. Chickering, Jr.*]

The unity of ***Beowulf*** has long been taken for granted, but the sure construction of the poem has only of late been wholeheartedly affirmed. Discrepancies and weaknesses which have puzzled earlier critics now begin to fall into their rightful places in a scheme of poetic conception with its own values. I do not attempt to probe these underlying values, but rather to indicate how they emerge in the plan and method of the poem. It is unfortunate that ***Beowulf*** is in many ways unique. Since no other poem of sufficient scope on the full heroic plan has survived, only in ***Beowulf*** can we follow the crystallization of structural processes in style and observe the features that certain modes of thought produce in each.

The setting out of the material is not in ***Beowulf*** an evolution, following one main line or connecting thread. Instead, the subject is disposed as a circumscribed field in which the themes are drawn out by a center of attraction—in this case, the character of the good warrior. Far-flung tales and allusions, apparently scattered material and disconnected events are grouped in a wide sweep around the hero's character. In fact, these *are* his character, and their significance in the poem consists in this particular relation; by comparisons we are shown Beowulf's nature, by searchlights into the past and future we are to sense the magnitude and true import of his achievements. From this periphery he draws his substance and reality. By these means he lives and his destiny impregnates the whole poem. The good warrior is displayed as a being consummated through all phases of his life and in all aspects of his character. The whole progress from adventurous youth to wisdom-weighted old age, many discrete elements—the bear-warrior strength, the knightly courtesy, vanity beside humility, and so on—are comprehended in this static unity. It has often been observed that there is no development of plot or character. The concluding state of affairs must be implicit in the beginning. With such a plan, a pre-ordained course of events, familiar topics, and stock situations are essential for the achievement of depth and scope. Not by transitions and transformations but by suggestion of the ever-present identity of seed in fruit and fruit in seed does the poet adjust the emotional tension. The reference to the burning of Heorot woven into the description of its first glories, and the forecast of family strife while yet all is well in Hroðgar's court are straightforward instances. More complex is the messenger's announcement of Beowulf's death: at great length he recounts the rising to power of the Geats—now to fall a prey to peoples they had overcome; their downfall will be the direct consequence of Beowulf's death—who died in defending them; he *þe us beagas geaf* ["who gave us rings"] has gained with his last breath yet more *beagas* ["rings"], treasure which is thus his personal perquisite, which in perishing with him on the pyre, shall symbolize the joys now to pass for ever from the Geats. This tendency to antithesis, frequently verging on paradox, and the constant play of irony are but stylistic manifestations of those movements of the poet's thought which shape the very stuff of the poem.

Stylistic detail might be expected to give reliable indications of the lines on which the theme is constructed; and it is fortunate that the style of ***Beowulf*** has attracted a large share of the most discerning criticism. Analysis of style is in this case a justifiable approach to analysis of structure. The general impression that ***Beowulf,*** lacking clarity and speed, is remarkable rather for depth and vibrancy needs explanation in terms both of style and of structure. These effects are partly due to a method of evocation and cross-reference in which contrast is an important element. Notable examples of description by contrast are the allusions to Sigemund, Heremod, and Offa; and there are constant lesser instances of this method and its corollary, parallelism. As a structural principle, it may be traced in the antiphonal exordium. We hear first of the mighty destiny and wide fame of the Scyldings. The crescendo of Scylding power rouses opposing forces of cunning evil ever lurking to reverse the prosperity of mankind; by Grendel's raids the fame of the Scyldings is blasted, the utmost human effort frustrated, the mightiest of rulers made impotent. Beowulf is then introduced in the all-powerful enterprise of untried youth. Here the concentration of the double flow increases: for Beowulf is connected with Hroðgar both by grateful allegiance, because of the favour shown to his father, and by his undertaking the trial of valour where others have failed. Complementing the knowledge of that Hroðgar his *hold wine* ["trusty friend"] is in need is Beowulf's desire to crown his exploits by the supreme enterprise of *ðing wið þyrse* ["this giant demon"]. The duty of allegiance emerges in Hroðgar's recapitulation of Beowulf's *æþelu* ["nobility"] (457-72), the demands of Beowulf's career in his own account of his setting forth (405-41). Both are presaged in the greeting of Wulfgar (338-9), who recognizes in the bearing of Beowulf the *wlenco* ["daring"] and *hige þrymm* ["greatness of heart"] which have brought him to Heorot, as contrasted with *wræcsið* ["exile" or "misery"] (which brought his father). The allusion is oblique—Wulfgar is challenging Beowulf as a stranger—and its application by so much the more pointed. This same alternation is at work throughout the poem. The suspension of the theme—the "balance" of which Professor Tolkien speaks [see excerpt dated 1936]—demands a constant confrontation of similar and dissimilar.

A fundamental element in this balance is the poet's distribution of his material within the orbit of a central idea. The descriptive method of recurrence-with-elaboration distributes epithets and qualifying phrases in this way. The simplest form is piling of varied repetition, of the type: *eorlscipe efnde, ealdre geneðde, mærðo fremede* ["to show my courage in the press of waters, put life in danger, that I might work fame"] (2, 132-3). More complicated is the type: *þonne heoru bunden, hamere geþruen, sweord swate fah swin ofer helme ecgum dyhtig andweard scireð* ["when wrought sword, forged under hammer, the iridescent blade, blood-wet, cuts through enemy's boar-guard, an edge ever firm''] (1285-7), or *forðon he ær fela nearo neðende niða gedigde, hildehlemma, syððan he Hroðgares, sigoreadig secg, sele fælsode; ond æt guðe forgrap Grendeles mægum laðan cynnes* [''since he had endured much violence before, taken great risks in the smash of battles, after he had cleansed Hrothgar's hall, rich in his victories, crushed out Grendel and his kin in battle, a hateful race''] (2, 349-53). Here the amplification of several interdependent ideas is carried through by turns, so that the parts of the sentence are interlocked by a spaced and cumulative reinforcement—a method which reaches its ultimate development in the poetry of the Norse skalds. And in the last analysis, the ''synonyms'' so characteristic of Old English poetic diction express in little the multiplicity, the resolution into separate aspects, shown in the presentation of the theme itself.

For the structure of the poem is not sequential, but complemental; at the outset certain parts of a situation are displayed, and these are given coherence and significance by progressive addition of its other parts. Already Klaeber [see excerpt dated 1922] has noticed a circumscribing movement, and in the most penetrating passages of his criticism he constantly recurs to this idea. He recognizes ''an organic relation between the rhetorical characteristics and certain narrower linguistic facts as well as the broader stylistic features and peculiarities of the narrative'' . . . , citing in particular ''retardation by means of variations and parenthetical utterances'' and further elaborating the idea in his statement: ''The preponderance of the nominal over the verbal element, one of the outstanding features of the ancient diction, runs parallel to the favourite practice of stating merely the result of an action and of dwelling on a state or situation.'' Yet having worked out this organic relation and as good as stated the pervading conception imposing form on the whole material out to its fringes of verbal detail, he can suggest no structural unity, but speaks instead of ''looseness'' and ''matter more or less detached from the chief narrative.'' . . . (pp. 396-99)

Klaeber has noted the outstanding instances of a circumambient structure, although the heading under which he groups them—Lack of Steady Advance—again shows that he does not allow the principle its fundamental importance. Most clearly in the fight with Grendel, but also to some extent in the slaying of Grendel's mother and the account of the dragon's hoard, we see the unfolding of an event into its separate aspects. Apparently, the sum of them all—synchronism and the momentary visual impression—is the one aspect not considered poetically significant. The course of the fight in the hall is several times reviewed, each time in different terms and with varying emphasis. Grendel's movements and motives and his final sense of defeat are first described (745-57). The poet next reverts to Beowulf's grapple, considered as a fulfilment of his *æfenspræc* [''evening-speech'']. In 764-5 the climax, the tearing off of Grendel's arm, is obscurely stated in a metaphor. The fight is then represented from the point of view of the Danes (765-90) who hear the din raging within their hall; the climax is here marked by the shriek of defeat, which is elaborated at some length (782-88). Lastly, the sensations of the Geats when they see their lord at grips with the monster provide an opportunity for contrasting Grendel's magic immunity from bite of iron with his impotence against the decrees of providence (801-15); these reflections are concluded with an explicit account of the severing of the claw, darkly alluded to before. The outcome for each of the three parties—Beowulf, Grendel, and the Danes—is then summed up, and the severed claw again mentioned, this time as the proof and symbol of Grendel's final defeat. A similar disregard for the synchronizing of the separate aspects of an action is seen in the defeat of Grendel's mother. Throughout the struggle the poet draws out the implications of each stage; he describes the virtues of the magic sword which Beowulf seizes in his desperation (1,557 ff.), occupies seven lines with the brandishing and victorious thrust, and next proceeds to display in one of his rare similes the flash of light which marks the defeat of the sorceress (1,570-2). The beheading of Grendel's corpse is also worthy of note. Much space is given to the retribution implied in this act, and the appearance of the huge headless body is touched upon: only in the final phrase is it stated *ond hine þa heafde becearf* [''and I cut off the head''].

We learn of the dragon and his hoard by the same method of distributing essential parts of a situation into distinct groups. The first mention of the dragon . . . is followed by the incursion of the thief, which leads on to a description of the hoard as the heritage of a vanished line. By means of the last survivor's speech as he consigned them to the earth, the treasures are shown as emblems of mortal joys stilled by death in the dim past. We hear no more of the history of the hoard until the fight is over, and the Geats have only to look upon the ruin and perform the exequies of their lord. Then another feature is brought into play: the hoard is the direct cause of the deaths of the dragon and Beowulf by reason of the heavy curse laid upon it. Thus the functions of the hoard, as provoker of strife and as bringer of the inevitable *worulde gedal* [''world-parting''], are elaborated in the appropriate contexts: not to mention its subsidiary contributions by way of contrast and symbolism.

To illustrate yet wider distribution of elements cohering in one theme, we may take the knitting together of Danish and Geatish history and the relation between Beowulf's account of the fights at Heorot and the earlier description. In the central portion of the poem, which is dominated by domestic and dynastic affairs and courtly observances, one of the three essential elements in the warrior's character is displayed. He must have violence and strength as of a beast, most fully exemplified in youth when he must win his spurs by marvellous deeds. Wisdom and submission to the decrees of providence again are essential. But equally he must take his place as an aristocrat fit to move among kings. When communal court life first comes into the scene (491-661) it is little more than a scaffolding for Beowulf's adventure with the sea-monsters and his *beot* [''boast'']. Its next appearance (1,008-1,237) is much more substantiated. The affairs of both Danish and Geatish courts are included: allusions to the *facenstafas* [''treachery''] between Hroðgar and Hroþulf (1018, 1164), the tale of Hnæf Scyldinga who fell in Freswæle, and also the downfall of Hygelac (1202). Beowulf is very honourably taken into this milieu, and his sphere extending over both courts is delineated. The next episode . . . is entirely occupied with the glorification of Beowulf; the part he is to play as king of the Geats (1,707-9, 1,845-53) and the function of kingship is defined, by contrast with Heremod and by comparison of the tried wisdom of the elder ruler with the sagacity already apparent in the younger (1,842-3).

Beowulf returns to the Geatish court (1,928). In accordance with the filling and deepening of the courtly scene in this part, a disquisition on the ideal type of high-born lady, shown by contrast with Þryðo just as the ideal king is contrasted with Heremod, is attached to the person of Hygd. In Beowulf's subsequent relation of his adventure, the stress on the affairs of the Danish court is accentuated by a full account of the Heaðobard attack merely hinted at in connection with the building of the hall (82 ff.). All this helps to fill out the picture of court life. This strain is concluded in 2,199, where we hear that Beowulf is accorded a position among the Geatish nobility differing only in degree from that of Hygelac himself. The account of the fights at Heorot depicts the value of these episodes as an approach to an assured position in the knightly hierarchy. The struggles are much toned down. Savage and fantastic elements are attributes of the earlier, more primitive Beowulf: here is no mention of the *leoht unfæger* [''ugly light''] streaming from Grendel's eyes, nor of the fearful din and the cry, nor of the fens beyond; of the severed claw it is said merely *him sio swiðre swaðe weardade* [''his right hand stayed behind'']. . . . Room is found for prosaic and curious detail, such as the name of the warrior Grendel devours and the description of the *glof* [''glove''], neither given elsewhere. Emphasis is laid on the advancement of Beowulf's career: the princely rewards given (2,101-3, 2,134, 2,142-7), his rôle as emissary of the Geats (2,095-6), and his reliance on his *heafodmaga* [''near relative''] Hygelac (2,148-51). The theme is brought out still further by innuendos defining knightly conduct by contrast (2,166-9, 2,177-83), and is finally closed on the dominant of Beowulf by a description of his boorish beginnings (2,183-8)—a fact we learn only when it is introduced to heighten Beowulf's eminence and substantiate the comment that a *tireadig mann* [''famous man''] will always make good.

The poetry of this time (like the visual art) reaches a high degree of abstraction and formalism. As far as his medium, a sequence of words, will allow, the poet has detached his theme from the processes of time and space and disregarded the appearances which for practical purposes constitute reality. He is able to evaluate his ''action'' directly, by exhibiting the parts in their æsthetic and moral relations. Hence the ''moralizing'' passages should be regarded as an integral part of the subject and are in no sense digressions—indeed, they are inextricably blended with some of the finest poetry in ***Beowulf.*** Emphasis on the causal relation is not required. The structure is not a progression, and follows no direct line. The writer of ***Beowulf*** is in fact a true poet; he has created a tragic unity, he sees with the poet's eye which splits and recombines the elements of everyday perceptions. The signs and symbols that he uses are now unfamiliar, representations which need to be interpreted; we should not be misled into thinking them accidents. The ritual of language and exploitation of its metaphysical aspects which are the most outstanding features of this style have repeatedly won the attention of critics, and provide the best clues to the underlying structural unity. (pp. 399-403)

Joan Blomfield, ''The Style and Structure of 'Beowulf','' in The Review of English Studies, *Vol. XIV, No. 56, October, 1938, pp. 396-403.*

C. S. LEWIS (lecture date 1941)

[Lewis is considered one of the foremost Christian and mythopoeic authors of the twentieth century. Indebted principally to George MacDonald, G. K. Chesterton, Charles Williams, and the writers of ancient Norse myths, he is regarded as a formidable logician and Christian polemicist, a perceptive literary critic, and—most highly—as a writer of fantasy literature. Lewis also held instructional posts at Oxford and Cambridge, where he was an acknowledged authority on medieval and Renaissance literature. A traditionalist in his approach to life and art, he opposed the movement in modern literary criticism toward biographical and psychological interpretation. In place of this, Lewis practiced and promoted a theory of criticism that stresses the importance of the author's intent, rather than the reader's presuppositions and prejudices.

In the following excerpt from one of his celebrated applications of this theory, A Preface to ''Paradise Lost'' *(originally presented in 1941 as a lecture at the University College of North Wales), Lewis compares the epic qualities of* Beowulf *with those of the Homeric poems.*]

The older critics divided Epic into Primitive and Artificial, which is unsatisfactory, because no surviving ancient poetry is really primitive and all poetry is in some sense artificial. I prefer to divide it into Primary Epic and Secondary Epic—the adjectives being purely chronological and implying no judgements of value. The *secondary* here means not ''the second rate,'' but what comes after, and grows out of, the *primary.*

The Primary Epic [may be] illustrated from the Homeric poems and from the English ***Beowulf.*** . . . Both ***Beowulf*** and the Homeric poems, besides being poetry themselves, describe poetical performances, at feasts and the like, proceeding in the world which they show us. From these descriptions we can gather what the epic was in a heroic age; but it does not follow that ***Beowulf*** and the Homeric poems are themselves the same kind of thing. They may or may not *be* what they *describe.* (p. 13)

[In ***Beowulf*** we hear nothing at all] about poetry outside the court. But we can supplement ***Beowulf*** from other sources. In Bede's account of Caedmon . . . we get the glimpse of a feast among men apparently of peasant's rank, where each sang in turn as the harp came to him. It is just conceivable that what each sang was a very short heroic lay, but there is no reason to suppose this. Certainly the Anglo-Saxons had songs of a very different type. Alcuin's letter to Hygebald in 797 is always quoted because, in deploring the use of heathen poetry in religious houses, he mentions *Hinieldus* who is probably Hrothgar's son-in-law Ingeld. But it should also be remembered that he asks for ''the voice of the reader in the house rather than the laughter of the mob in the streets'' (*voces legentium in domibus tuis non ridentium turvam in plateis*). This ''laughter'' would not be connected with heroic lays. No doubt, Alcuin may be referring to ribald conversation and not to poetry at all. But it seems to me very likely that he means comic poetry, and that comic, or at least light, poems were sung at the feast which Caedmon attended. This is admittedly conjecture; but it would be very odd if the ancestors of Chaucer, Shakespeare, Dickens, and Mr. Jacobs produced no funny stories.

When we turn to ***Beowulf's*** picture of the court we are on surer ground. In lines 2105 and following we have a performance given by Hrothgar himself. We learn that he sometimes (*hwilum*) produced a *gidd* or lay which was *soþ* and *sarlic* (true and tragic), sometimes a tale of wonders (*sellic spell*), and sometimes, with the fetters of age heavy upon him, he began to recall his youth, the strength that once was his in battle; his heart swelled within him as he remembered the vanished winters. Professor Tolkien has suggested to me that this is an account of the complete range of court poetry, in which three kinds of poem can be distinguished—the lament for mutability (*hu seo þrag gewat*) now represented by the *Wanderer* and the *Seafarer,* the tale of strange adventures, and the ''true and tragic'' lay such as the *Finnsburg* poem, which alone is true epic. ***Beowulf*** itself contains elements of the *sellic spell,* but it is certainly *sarlic* and probably much of it was regarded as *soþ.* Without pressing these distinctions too far, we can certainly conclude from this passage that the author of ***Beowulf*** is aware of different kinds of court poetry. Here, as in Homer, Epic does not mean simply whatever was sung in hall. It is one of the possible entertainments, marked off from the others, in Homer by the spontaneity and quasi-oracular character of the poet's performance, and in both Homer and ***Beowulf*** by tragic quality, by supposed historical truth, and by the gravity that goes with "true tragedy." (pp. 15-16)

About ***Beowulf*** there is no external evidence [that it either was or was not composed for recitation]. It is easily recitable, and would take perhaps three hours; this, with a break in the middle, would not be too long. But about ***Beowulf,*** and about the Homeric poems, there is internal evidence. They both have the oral *technique,* the repetitions, and stylized diction of oral poetry. If not oral themselves, they are at least closely modelled on work that was. (pp. 18-19)

It remains to ask if they are court poetry. ***Beowulf*** clearly is. Its preoccupation with honour, its exclusive attention to the life of courts, its interest in etiquette (*duguþe þeaw*) and in genealogy, put the matter beyond doubt. Homer is more doubtful. We have seen that in historical times it was recited not in courts, but at great national festivals, and it is possible that it was also composed for these. In other words, it is either court-poetry or festival poetry. If it is the latter, then epic, since the time of the earliest lays, has moved up, not down. The original *solemnity* of the hall has been replaced by the greater *solemnity* of the temple or the forum. Our first picture of the epic poet needs to be modified by the associations of incense, sacrifice, civic pride, and public holiday; and since this change certainly occurred sooner or later we may as well make the adjustment now. We move a stage *further away* from the solitary, private, and armchair associations which the word "poetry" has for a modern.

Homer and ***Beowulf,*** then, however or whenever they were actually produced, are in the tradition of Primary epic, and inherit both its oral technique and its festal, aristocratic, public, ceremonial tone. (p. 19)

The most obvious characteristic of an oral technique is its continual use of stock words, phrases, or even whole lines. It is important to realize . . . that these are not a second-best on which the poets fall back when inspiration fails them: they are as frequent in the great passages as in the low ones. In 103 lines of the parting between Hector and Andromache (justly regarded as one of the peaks of European poetry) phrases, or whole lines, which occur again and again in Homer are twenty-eight times employed. . . . Roughly speaking, a *quarter* of the whole passage is "stock." In Beowulf's last speech to Wiglaf (***Beow.*** 2794-820) "stock" expressions occur six times in twenty-eight lines—again, they are about a quarter of the whole. (p. 20)

To a limited extent the technique of ***Beowulf*** is the same as that of Homer. It, too, has its reiterated expressions, *under wolcnum, in geardum,* and the life, and its "poetical" names for most of the things the author wants to mention. One of its differences from Homer, indeed, is the number of synonymous words which the poet can use for the same thing: Homer has no list of alternatives to compare to the Beowulfian words for man—*beorn, freca, guma, hæleþ, secg, wer*. In the same way, Beowulf is fonder than Homer of partial repetition, of using slightly varied forms of a poetic phrase or compound. Thus, [*Wuldorcyninge* occurs only once in the poem], but *wuldres wealdend* and *wuldres hyrde* do. *Wordum secge* is similarly a partial repetition of *wordum bædon, wordum wrixlan,* and *wordum nægde; wyrd forsweop,* of *wyrd fornam, deaþ fornam,* and *guþdeaþ fornam*. In part, this difference of technique goes with a shorter line, a language more full of consonants, and doubtless a slower and more emphatic delivery. It goes with

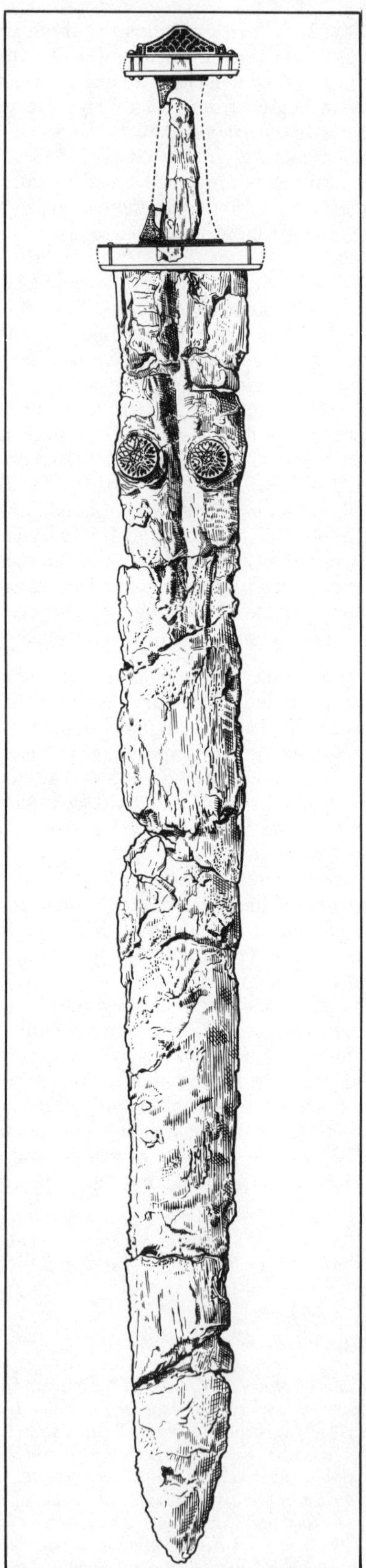

Sword found in the Sutton Hoo ship burial. The British Museum.

the difference between a quantitative metre and one which uses both quantity and stress accent, demanding their union for that characteristic of alliterative verse which is called weight. One of Homer's great passages is like a cavalry charge; one of ***Beowulf***'s, like blows from a hammer or the repeated thunder of breakers on the beach. The words flow in Homer; in ***Beowulf*** they fall apart into massive lumps. The audience has more time to chew on them. Less help is needed from pure reiteration.

All this is not unconnected with a deeper difference of temper. The objectivity of the unchanging background which is the glory of Homer's poetry, is not equally a characteristic of ***Beowulf.*** Compared with the *Iliad,* ***Beowulf*** is already, in one sense, "romantic." Its landscapes have a spiritual quality. The country which Grendel haunts expresses the same things as Grendel himself: the "visionary dreariness" of Wordsworth is foreshadowed. Poetry has lost by the change, but it has gained, too. The Homeric Cyclops is a mere puppet beside the sad, excluded *ellorgast,* or the jealous and joyless dragon, of the English poem. There is certainly not more suffering behind ***Beowulf*** than there is behind the *Iliad;* but there is a consciousness of good and evil which Homer lacks.

The "proper" oral technique of the later poem, that which distinguishes it most sharply from Homer, is the variation or parallelism which most of us have first met in the Psalms. "He that dwelleth in heaven shall laugh them to scorn; the Lord shall have them in derision." The rule is that nearly everything must be said more than once. The cold prose about the ship in which Scyld's dead body was sent away (***Beow.*** 50) is that nobody knew what became of it. The poetical rendering is that "Men knew not to say for a truth, the talkers in the hall knew not, warriors under the sky knew not, who received that cargo." (pp. 25-6)

C. S. Lewis, "Primary Epic" and "The Technique of Primary Epic," in his A Preface to Paradise Lost, *1942. Reprint by Oxford University Press, 1961, pp. 13-19, 20-6.*

CHARLES W. KENNEDY (essay date 1943)

[*Kennedy was a distinguished American academic, critic, and scholar who concentrated his studies on Old English poetry and theories of sportsmanship. In the following excerpt, he contends that, despite its Scandinavian setting,* Beowulf *demonstrates the heroic ideals of English society.*]

To what extent is the ***Beowulf*** an old tale retrold merely for the joy of the telling? To what extent is it developed as an exemplification of noble kinghood and the Christian ideal? An epic tale lends itself gracefully to purposes of doctrine, as the tradition of the epic so richly shows. A well-known letter of Edmund Spenser, outlining the design and structure of the *Faerie Queene,* sets forth in clear terms the underlying purpose with which the author had shaped the allegory of his immortal poem: "The generall end therefore of all the booke, is to fashion a gentleman or noble person in vertuous and gentle discipline."

It is never a simple matter to separate in a work of art didactic purpose from the aesthetic aims of creation. And in the case of the ***Beowulf*** we have no such statement of purpose as Spenser's to throw light upon the poem, and no knowledge of the poet's identity, or way of life, by which to guide interpretation of his underlying intent. Many would define his purpose quite simply, as the desire to tell an old tale of heroism in verse, and to tell it well.

Yet many passages in the poem suggest that the author had more in mind than the mere retelling, however well, of a heroic tale. There is a difference between tales of heroism and a narrative of a heroic life, and in the story of ***Beowulf*** the reader is made to feel that the author is conscious of this difference. The Old English Christian poet . . . had his moralizing strain and, like his Renaissance successor, may have felt that a narrative of a heroic king, elevated to epic dignity and illumined by the Christian ideal, could well serve for the fashioning of men to magnanimous and noble living.

Certain it is that under the pen of the ***Beowulf*** poet the stubborn stuff of Scandinavian legend is tempered and refined, and there emerges the figure of a noble and Christian king. The poem reflects the spirit, not of Scandinavia, but of English life of the seventh and eighth centuries, presenting a blending of old folkways with new, a welding of pagan heroism with Christian virtue. The miracle of the ***Beowulf*** is the artistry of its refashioning. However widely the poem may range through the tribal lands of Scandinavia, the mood and spirit are the mood and spirit of England; the poetic ideal is the Christian ideal. The pagan backgrounds of the poem sink into shadow. The old dark tales of men and lands beyond the sea echo as from a vast distance. The story of Beowulf becomes an English poem. It becomes a poem suited to a Christian court, and fitted for the shaping of men in "vertuous and gentle discipline." Even an ancient tale of pagan heroism, transformed by Christian spirit, could become an element in the stream of influence that flowed from the Christian Church. Lives of saints and martyrs formed a literature for the stirring of men's souls to faith and virtue and, side by side with such spiritual heroisms, the ancient tale of Beowulf's struggle with monster and dragon may well have lent itself to the uses of Christian allegory.

The unmistakable English strain in the ***Beowulf*** is perhaps clearest in the elegiac tone and moral temper of the poem. The elegiac element, which twice wells up with a poignancy suggestive of the lyric sadness of the *Wanderer* and the *Ruin,* is the poetic symbol of early English life amid the scattered and ruined reminders of the Roman settlement. And in the moral temper of the poem there is clear reflection of the birth and shaping, largely through the dawning influence of the Christian faith, of nobler concepts of human relations and political duty. Feud and treachery, murder of kindred and usurpation, have illustration in the poem, it is true, as they had illustration in contemporary English annals. But a new order of life is symbolized in the condemnation and repudiation which, in the poem, are unfailingly directed against such manifestations of violence and crime.

The youthful Beowulf of the beginning and the aged king of the final scenes alike illustrate the chivalry of spirit that ennobles heroism. The Beowulf of the Grendel adventure was in essentials a knight-errant of his age. It was no call of duty which urged him across the sea to stake his life against monsters. Indeed, though his personal followers urged him on, Hygelac had endeavored to dissuade him from the undertaking. So we learn from his uncle's words at the banquet after Beowulf's return:

I had no faith   in this far sea-venture
For one so beloved.   Long I implored
That you go not against   the murderous monster,
But let the South-Danes   settle the feud
Themselves with Grendel.

Such were the words of expediency! It can be granted that the poet portrays a youthful hero fired with love of adventure. But there is more than love of adventure that urges Beowulf on; there are demons to kill, and a curse to be lifted. More than once his words to Hrothgar reflect the sober spirit of one who strives with the powers of evil: "I will fight to the death, foe against foe; then let the one whom death takes put his trust in the Judgment of God." In all the young lad does and says, there is courage. But, more important, there is also magnanimity.

The tradition of doom in the dragon fight is a survival from the pagan world. But it has taken on new depth of implication. The tragic glory of the conflict is its illustration of man's heroic war with powers of darkness and evil beyond his strength. The tragic glory of Beowulf's death is its illustration of that fated courage which fights to the utmost, knowing the utmost will not avail, and fighting on.

It is in the exercise of the powers and responsibilities of kingship that the poet stresses most Beowulf's magnanimity, and the Christian ideal. In his early manhood, refusing power for himself, Beowulf served as Protector of the young king Heardred. Becoming king at Heardred's death he had for fifty years ruled wisely and well. At the end, as he lay dying, his thoughts were of the needs of his people. For himself, as he looked back upon his life, he rejoiced that after death the Lord of mankind could not charge against him the killing of kinsmen. His reign had been a reign of peace and justice. Abiding by his appointed lot he had sworn no unrighteous oaths, had kept his own well, had courted no quarrels. As the smoke of his funeral pyre rose to the sky, his people lamented the passing of the kindest of earthly kings, the mildest and most gentle.

The ***Beowulf*** is a priceless heritage from the earliest age of English poetry. Forgotten for centuries, and rediscovered, it has at last by the devotion of many scholars come into its own, unfolding before us its ancient excellence. Across the centuries from the Age of Bede it proclaims the ideal of gentleness united to strength, and valor ennobled by virtue. It speaks to the modern world in moving accents of honor, of courage, and of faith. It is a tale of a vanishing age retold in the dawn of a new day. The pagan gods were fading into the darkness; new light was upon the world. The flash and thunder of Thor were not wholly forgotten; but the bolt was spent and the echoes dying. The old legends of violence and blood formed shadowy background for a tale of Christian courage and virtue. Twice in a heroic lifetime mortal valor was pitted in crucial conflict with the ravening forces of evil. Twice a hero turned back the invading dark. In his youth he conquered and lived; in age he conquered and died. To live or to die was as fate might ordain. To conquer was all. (pp. 97-100)

Charles W. Kennedy, "Beowulf," in his The Earliest English Poetry: A Critical Survey of the Poetry Written before the Norman Conquest with Illustrative Translations, *Oxford University Press, 1943, pp. 53-100.*

HERBERT J. C. GRIERSON AND J. C. SMITH (essay date 1944)

[Grierson was a Scottish academic and scholar who wrote authoritative studies of the lives and works of John Milton, John Donne, and Sir Walter Scott. Smith was a Scottish academic, editor, and critic. In the following excerpt, they assess the merits and failings of Beowulf.*]*

[***Beowulf***] is swollen out with three episodes to something like epic dimensions. It was composed in Britain by a Christian scribe, probably about A.D. 700; but the material from which it was composed belongs to an earlier date and to a distant and a pagan land. . . . ***Beowulf*** is no *Iliad*. The story is mere folklore: Beowulf—the bees' foe, the bear—is one of those folktale heroes who have been suckled by a wild beast and imbibed its strength, and his three exploits are too like one another. The story, then, is a poor one, and there is not enough of it: it has to be padded out to 3000 lines with digressions and long speeches. Yet there are noble things in ***Beowulf***—not only loyalty and dauntless courage but courtesy in hall and respect for ladies; the style too has a grave dignity throughout; and the figure of the old king going out to fight and, as he knows, to die for his people, is truly heroic. How much of what is noblest in the poem is due to the Christian scribe we cannot tell; but loyalty and courage at least are pagan virtues. ***Beowulf,*** we have said, is no *Iliad;* yet the hero's funeral—

> Men of the Weders . made thereafter
> A barrow on the sea-cliff . broad and high,
> That wave-farers . might see from far—

is not unworthy to be compared with the funeral which the Trojans held for Hector, the tamer of horses. (pp. 2-3)

Herbert J. C. Grierson and J. C. Smith, "Anglo-Saxon Poetry," in his A Critical History of English Poetry, *1944. Reprint by Chatto & Windus, 1965, pp. 1-7.*

JAMES R. HULBERT (essay date 1946)

[An American medievalist, Hulbert concentrated his studies on Old and Middle English literature, English verse forms, and the early history of the English language. In the following excerpt, he favorably compares the narrative structure of Beowulf *with the structure of classical epics, noting dissimilarities and explaining the effectiveness of the techniques used by the* Beowulf *poet.]*

Comparison with the classical epics and general concepts of what constitutes effective story-telling have led to the judgment that ***Beowulf*** is at fault because it does not always proceed directly, in chronological order; because it contains digressions or episodes by which material from other legends is incorporated into the poem; because it uses a dramatic, rather than a simple, narrative method; and because its central action is of fairy-tale character. . . .

The objection made most generally is to the use in ***Beowulf*** of digressions and episodes, by which is meant the incorporation of two types of material: (1) epitomes of heroic stories (or references to some elements in them) introduced as illustrations or as reports of minstrels' recitations; (2) retrospective and anticipatory accounts of events in the main narrative, or achievements of principal characters in it. (p. 65)

[In weighing this objection] it will be well to bear in mind three considerations: (*a*) the artistic value for the poem of the episodes and digressions; (*b*) the use of such devices elsewhere; and (*c*) the proportion of digressions to direct narrative in ***Beowulf.*** (p. 66)

[It] is clear that the objection to the ***Beowulf*** poet's practice is really not to his use of digressions but to some such fault as his failure to make clear transitions from the main narrative to episodes and back again and the amount of the digressions in proportion to the whole. . . . In these respects, certainly, the author's practice is not that of classical epic writers. In the spaciousness of the epics, the poets allow themselves as many lines as seem desirable to a clear and leisurely introduction of episodes and a return to the main narrative. In ***Beowulf*** this is not so. Episodes are introduced with the slightest of transitions or with no transition at all. (pp. 67-8)

Further, the classical epics develop their episodes with much the same leisureliness and completeness as they do their basic narrative. The ***Beowulf*** poet compresses and omits; sometimes, as in the case of Heremod, he refers so allusively and briefly as to tantalize the modern reader who does not know the whole story of that bad example. Finally, the proportion of episodes to the main narrative is unusually high in ***Beowulf.*** The poem is packed with allusions to other stories and summaries of them, with bits of anticipatory and retrospective narrative and with details in nonchronological order (e.g., the account of the Swedish-Geatish wars). Indeed, of the total number of lines in the poem—3,182—Klaeber's figures show that approximately 700 are devoted to episodic matter of all sorts [see excerpt dated 1922]. I have no comparable figures for any classical epic. But the proportion is certainly much smaller. For long stretches the narration is direct, unimpeded, chronological; digressions are so rare as to be unusual and perhaps refreshing.

Clearly, therefore, there is a difference in the use of those devices between ***Beowulf*** and the classical epics. Whether this difference justifies those who object to the ***Beowulf*** writer's involved methods is not so sure, since it might be that the writer made an effective extension of the use of digressions and episodes. Their objections demonstrate, however, that to some learned and able readers the author's ways in this respect seem unsuccessful. One will encounter such "reactions" to later writers also: e.g., Conrad, whose devices are quite similar to those we have been considering, and Meredith (in his novels) and Browning, whose methods are at least as involved as are those of the ***Beowulf*** poet. To some readers such development of narrative stuff has an immense attraction; to others it is annoying and destructive to any interest or willingness to continue. To some it may be effective when not overused. (p. 68)

Beyond this point, we cannot go. If a reader does not like an allusive, indirect method of narration, he will certainly feel that ***Beowulf*** is as badly developed as [some other scholars have done]. . . . But devotees of Browning and Conrad should find delight in such indirectness. The narrative irregularities of ***Beowulf*** have never troubled me since I first encountered them forty years ago. . . . But, then, my only complaint concerning Conrad is that he did not write more novels like *Nostromo.*

A problem remains which I cannot solve: Did the author of ***Beowulf*** consciously choose to use this allusive, backward, forward, and sideward movement, or did he follow this method because he was not completely master of his craft? Is what we have a clumsy production of one who "bit off more than he could chew," or is it the work of a sophisticated artist who disdained mere clarity and consciously composed for a highly cultivated and subtle "intelligentsia"? No doubt many readers will not hesitate to suppose that he was simply unskilful. . . . Yet, because of the poet's success in maintaining with ease and naturalness a consistently dignified style and because of his remarkable ability to secure just the effect he desires in particular scenes, I think he consciously intended to do what he did, as Browning and Meredith certainly chose their allusive, indirect development. . . .

[It has been argued elsewhere that if the author of ***Beowulf***] really had been greatly interested in his main story, he would have limited himself chiefly to that and would not have made such extensive digressions as appear in the poem. Of course, that argument has no validity. If it did, it would convict the authors of classical tragedy of the same lack of interest because of their use of retrospective narrative and the elaboration of the messengers' speeches which interrupt the greatest suspense near the end of their plays; Tudor dramatists because of their use of subplots; and modern novelists because of the episodes and secondary actions in their novels. It should not be necessary to argue the point further.

Nor should it be necessary to argue that the author of ***Beowulf*** does full justice to his main action. The narratives of Beowulf's combats are as exciting as such stories can be made. (p. 69)

[The] author of ***Beowulf*** had ample authority in the classics for revealing the outcome before narrating a sequence of events. It is astonishingly naïve in the critics, however, to imply that such precognition destroys suspense. It might do so if the writer had not sufficient skill. But in the work of a skilful artist its use results in building suspense as to how the end will be reached, as to the motives of an action or the effect of it upon the characters, or as to some other element in the events. The device is not limited to the epic, of course, but is found frequently enough in modern fiction. It has been used even in detective stories, which, if they lacked suspense, would be nothing. The murderer may be known from the beginning of such a story, and suspense may be built on the difficulty of proving his guilt, the hazards encountered by the detective in accomplishing that result, and so on. The authors of epics and other narratives have intentionally used this device, for obvious reasons, and have not forfeited suspense in doing so. In the epics and ***Beowulf*** the usual purpose of foreshadowing the end of an action is to get a tragic effect and thus increase the impression of nobility in heroes and dignity and impressiveness in the narrative. In securing that effect, the authors do not lose suspense; if they did, no one, not compelled by a college assignment, would read their poems. It is unthinkable that any intelligent reader of the epics or of ***Beowulf*** is not quite as eager to find out what will happen next as he would be if the results of the episodes had been kept from him until the end of the episodes. . . .

[W. P. Ker] finds one great defect in ***Beowulf,*** the *Märchen* ["fable-like"] quality of the hero's adventures [see excerpt dated 1896]. (p. 71)

If one judges literature absolutely, one must acknowledge the truth of this criticism. But usually one considers the time and audience for which a book is composed. To the people of this author's time, trolls and dragons were as real as people and much more awful. The author doubtless was right in selecting such material in preference to a story like that of Walter of Acquitaine for the hearers of his own time. And, as Ker seems to imply, his poem does grip modern readers. It certainly did Ker himself; for, however he expresses himself here, he had a taste for such stories as ***Beowulf*** and *Gawain and the Green Knight.*

It is significant that, to enforce his point, Ker compared ***Beowulf*** not with the classical epic but with Germanic legends, for in the classical epic also the *fabelhaft* ["fabulous"] element is large. It is found not only in the narratives about the gods but in long episodes like the stories of Circe and Polyphemus. In fact, it may be a question whether anything like the epic impressiveness of ***Beowulf*** or the Homeric poems can be secured without a supernatural element. Certainly, it is not in Ekkehard's *Waltarius;* and *Hildebrand* and *Waldere* are too short to serve as specimens of epic without the supernatural. On the other hand, long narratives of early date which retain no mythological or supernatural features—e.g., the Icelandic sagas such as *Njal* or *Laxdaela*—though immensely impressive, have a different type of effect from that of the epics. Perhaps for epic effect a mixture of legendary and mythological or fairy-tale elements is necessary.

In making comparisons with classical epic, no scholar, as far as I am aware, has dared to assert that ***Beowulf*** is in any respect superior. Impressed by the admirable planning of the *Iliad* and the *Odyssey;* by their combination of many parts, properly proportioned to each other, to fill out perfectly a large design; and by the unity of tone and style which they maintain, critics perhaps have thought that such virtues as they could perceive in ***Beowulf*** were too minor to be worth mention. Yet it is only fair to state these virtues; to some types of mind they may even outweigh the best qualities of the classical epics. (p. 72)

[One] respect in which, for many readers, ***Beowulf*** is superior is its conciseness. This has disadvantages . . . [in] the episodes and digressions; perhaps it is carried to an extreme, and the development would have been easier to follow and more pleasing if the author had allowed himself more space. But at least, in reading ***Beowulf,*** we are spared the many genealogies even of minor characters, the long narratives of battles which are always the same in details, and the unnecessary repetitions without the addition of any new features (e.g., Achilles' recital of his wrongs to his mother in Book i of the *Iliad*). Even Aristotle considered the Homeric epics rather too long.

The emotional effect of ***Beowulf*** is intensified not only by its compression but by its style. This has not the plainness which Arnold emphasized as a characteristic of Homer but is formal, elaborate, dignified. Though it lacks the Homeric simile, it is, in many respects, more ornate than the style of Homer. It should be said, however, that in reading ***Beowulf*** one feels no self-consciousness or striving for effect. The elevated style used seems to be the natural mode of expression for this author. (p. 73)

There is another respect in which ***Beowulf*** seems to me better than the Homeric poems. Perhaps it should not be presented here because it is a matter not of literary artistry but of a difference in ideals and conceptions between the classical Greeks and the Anglo-Saxons. As it can hardly fail to make an impression on readers, however, and affect their enjoyment of the poems concerned, it seems to me proper to mention it here. The author of ***Beowulf*** maintains a much higher ideal of nobility of speech and action than Homer does. His figures always have a dignity which the classical heroes frequently lack. Agamemnon and Achilles, for example, talk and act like boasting, spoiled boys. The very cause of Achilles' wrath may seem to modern readers ignoble, and the uniform refusal of mercy to vanquished enemies is repugnant to us. Hardly less acceptable to a modern reader is the omnipresent action of the gods. There is such incredible inanity in their speech and deeds that a modern cannot comprehend how such beings could seem to be gods at all to Homer's contemporary readers. By contrast, the consistent nobility of speech and action in all the characters of ***Beowulf*** (except Unferth, of course) is refreshing to the readers of our time.

To some minds at least, the next difference to be mentioned must be a cause of dissatisfaction. The heroes in Homer have essentially no freedom of action: what they do is ordained and controlled by the gods. Perhaps the ancient Greeks could hear of this divine meddling with human affairs reverently and with equanimity, though it looks to me like a convention very slightly believed. But at least it detracts seriously from a reader's feeling of the initiative and heroism of the classical warriors. By contrast, Beowulf acts "on his own," supplies his own determination to meet dangers, expects and receives no aid from protecting gods.

Though clumsy in some details of development and too compressed and allusive, ***Beowulf*** is, in the main, well conceived and planned. There is logical sequence in the main narrative of Beowulf's journey to Denmark, his reception at Hrothgar's court, the contests with Grendel and Grendel's mother, his return to Geatland, his becoming king, and, finally, his slaying of the dragon and loss of his own life. Into this main narrative the author incorporates summaries and references to a mass of old Germanic legend. By this combination he made . . . from a narrative which might have been suitable only for children or peasants, a poem fit for kings and courtiers and full of deepest interest to readers of today.

In developing the parts of this large work, the poet's means are always adequate for the effects that he desires to secure. For instance, the story rather requires that, on his return from Denmark, Beowulf report to Hygelac on his experiences. Readers expect such a passage to be incorporated in the poem because an adventurer in Beowulf's position really would have made such a report and because they like to see the adventure concluded with recognition by the "home folk" of the hero's achievement. Yet they would be bored if the report were a verbatim repetition of parts of the preceding text. The author solves the difficulty easily by omitting some details previously presented and adding others not mentioned before. Indeed, he always "rises to the occasion," for example, in the description of the "haunted mere," which affords so good a setting for the combat with Grendel's mother. The origin of the dragon's hoard need not have been told, but the author rightly feels that some account of it will add to his effect. So he inserts the elegiac passage about the last survivor of an ancient family with its charmlike address to the earth. Finally, the ease with which he makes a perfect end of his poem should be mentioned—the narrative of the funeral races and the summary of his hero's qualities expressed as the words of the mourners.

Altogether, ***Beowulf*** stands comparison with the classical epic better than is commonly admitted. The author did not attempt the form of classical epic with its twenty-four books (or the Vergilian twelve), its great length, and slow, stately pace. If he was, as some have thought, familiar with the *Aeneid,* he either did not realize its form and structure (as Chaucer did not realize the form of the Petrarchan sonnet and perhaps did not perceive the epic structure of Boccaccio's *Teseide*), or he did not choose to imitate that form. His aim was merely to tell his story as vividly and impressively as possible, to exhibit noble actions and a noble hero. And he accomplished his purpose so well that he had no need to feel disturbed at the effect of a comparison, which he doubtless never anticipated, of his work with the classical epics. (pp. 74-5)

James R. Hulbert, "'Beowulf' and the Classical Epic," in Modern Philology, *Vol. XLIV, No. 2, November, 1946, pp. 65-75.*

KEMP MALONE (essay date 1948)

[Malone was an American essayist, editor, academic, and philologist who is best known today for his studies of the works of Shakespeare and Chaucer. In the following excerpt, he discusses the marriage of Germanic traditions and Christian morality in

Beowulf, *noting that the poem concentrates upon exploits that demonstrate broad moral import as well as physical valor arising from pagan codes of heroism. Malone also analyzes the dual focus of the two parts of the poem: Beowulf in the flush of youth and power, and the aged warrior confronting death with equanimity.*]

[***Beowulf***] holds a unique place in the literature of Europe. Its fundamentally Christian orientation is now widely recognized, and needs no discussion in this paper. Nevertheless, one cannot properly classify it as a religious poem in any strict or narrow sense. The action of the poem takes place in a part of ancient Germania and at a time thought of by the poet as ancient and therefore pagan. The characters are not Christians and know nothing of Christianity. The hero is a virtuous pagan. He is made as Christ-like as the setting permits, but all his virtues can be explained quite naturally as growing out of the heroic ideals of conduct traditional among the English as among the other Germanic peoples.

The monkish author, devout Christian though he is, finds much to admire in the pagan cultural tradition which, as an Englishman, he inherited from ancient Germania. It is his purpose to glorify this heroic heritage, this spiritual heirloom, this precious birthright of his nation. He accomplishes his purpose by laying stress upon those things in Germanic tradition which agree with Christianity or at any rate do not clash seriously with the Christian faith. In particular, his hero in all he says and does shows himself high-minded, gentle, and virtuous, a man dedicated to the heroic life, and the poet presents this life in terms of service: Beowulf serves his lord, his people, and all mankind, and in so doing he does not shrink from hardship, danger, and death itself. In many passages the poet's own Christianity comes to the surface; most notably, perhaps, in the so-called sermon of the aged King Hrothgar, who out of the fulness of his wisdom warns the youthful hero against the sin of pride. But even here the king's words, though obviously based on Christian teaching, are not put in specifically Christian terms, and most of the time the author keeps his Christianity below the surface. Nor does he falsify Germanic paganism by leaving out those features of it inconsistent with the Christian faith. Thus he puts in the mouth of Beowulf himself the following piece of pagan wisdom:

it is better for every man
to avenge his friend than to mourn much.

The poet's picture of the Germanic past is idealized but not distorted. The devil-worship of the Danes (as the medieval Christians conceived it to be) is mentioned with perfect frankness in a famous passage (lines 175 ff.). Anachronisms are fewer and less serious than one would expect in a poem of the eighth century. Indeed, perhaps the most remarkable though not the most important feature of the poem is the relatively high standard of historical accuracy which it maintains. The author was clearly a man learned in the traditional lore of his people, and concerned to tell the truth as he saw it. (pp. 162-63)

It would hardly do to think of [the ***Beowulf*** poet] as an eighth-century humanist, born 600 years before his time, since his interest lay, not in the philosophy of life of classical antiquity but in that of Germanic antiquity. Nevertheless his case is not unlike Petrarch's, in that both authors, Christians though they were, sought and found spiritual as well as stylistic values in a pagan literary culture: each in the particular culture which was his own by inheritance. In this matter the ***Beowulf*** poet did not stand alone. The author of *Deor* taught the virtue of patience under affliction by exempla drawn from pagan Germanic story, and the author of *Maldon* sang a Christian lord and dright who fought and died for the faith, inspired and sustained by the same heroic ideals that their heathen forefathers had cherished. These ideals held their own to the very end of Old English times, and made many a man a hero in life and death not merely by force of ordinary tradition but also, and in large measure, by force of poetic tradition. (p. 164)

[The ***Beowulf***] poet deals in detail with two chapters only of the hero's life, and . . . these two chapters stand in sharp contrast. In the first, the hero is young; he is represented as an ideal retainer; he undertakes a task which he is not in duty bound to perform; full of the generous spirit of youth, he goes out of his way to do good; he fights single-handed against two foes (taken one at a time); he wins, and goes home in triumph. In the contrasting chapter, the hero is old; he is represented as an ideal king; the task which he undertakes is one which he cannot avoid without failing in his duty to his own people; sad at heart, he meets the issue without flinching; he fights, with a helper beside him, against a single foe; he wins, but at the cost of his own life.

The two chapters, however, have one feature in common: in both, Beowulf fights as the champion of mankind, against monstrous embodiments of the forces of evil, adversaries so formidable that only the greatest of heroes could possibly cope with them. Our Christian poet makes much of the hero as monster-queller, not only because a fight with a monster in the nature of the case is more dangerous and therefore more heroic than a fight with another man, but also, and chiefly, because the struggle between hero and monster symbolizes the struggle between good and evil in our earthly life. Mere man-to-man fighting lends itself far less readily to treatment in terms of right and wrong, and the poet accordingly makes little of his hero's military career. Here our author goes his own way, the way of a Christian moralist, departing deliberately and radically from the practice usual in heroic story, where the hero's exploits in battle get plenty of attention.

The poet's neglect of Beowulf's deeds of valor in ordinary warfare must have been deliberate. Certainly he was well informed about them. He tells us himself, though with the utmost brevity, about one of the many battles which his hero had survived with honor. In this particular battle, fought in the Low Countries, Beowulf had covered himself with glory: he had killed no less than thirty of the enemy in hand-to-hand conflict; one of them, the Frankish champion Dæghrefn, he slew with his bare hands. The poet informs us further that Beowulf was the only man on his side to survive the battle. His own triumph over the enemy was so complete that, though his fellows all lay dead, he held the field alone and stripped from the bodies of the thirty men he had slain the armor to which his victory over them gave him honorable title, the surviving Franks not daring to interfere and allowing him to fall back to the sea unmolested. The story of King Hygelac's ill-fated expedition to the Netherlands, and in particular the story of the last stand of the doomed army, the fall of Hygelac, and the death of man after man of the king's devoted dright, until at the end Beowulf stood alone—this was surely a fight worthy of celebration in song. The ***Beowulf*** poet, in four scattered passages, has something to say about the expedition and its outcome. But he fails to make even an episode of it, much less a major part of the poem. Some poets would have thought it enough for a whole epic.

But I do not wish to blame the poet for what he left undone. He knew what he was about. Hygelac's expedition had no high moral purpose. The king and his men were out for booty, and our pious poet, though he loved a good fight as well as anybody, chose for extended treatment tasks undertaken and carried through by the hero for the benefit of mankind.

One exploit of Beowulf's remains to be considered: his swimming match with Breca. This match makes a clean-cut episode, to which more than 100 lines are devoted. The story of the match is not told as such, however. It is set in a frame: the fliting between Unferth and Beowulf. The integration of frame and story is beautifully complete: the swimming match is the subject of the fliting, each contender in the war of words giving us his own version of the story of the match. In consequence, this story is told twice. The repetition is characteristic of the ***Beowulf*** poet, who loves to tell a story more than once. We have already seen that Hygelac's expedition up the Rhine is spoken of no less than four times. The most elaborate piece of repetition in the poem, of course, is Beowulf's report to Hygelac when he comes back from Denmark; this report amounts to a retelling of the story of the fight with Grendel and Grendel's mother. Many other cases of repetition occur in the course of the narrative. The poet repeats himself in a masterly fashion; the device as he employs it not only emphasizes and clarifies but also gives esthetic pleasure. When we come to a given repetition we know what to expect in a general way, but we always find novelty enough in word and thought. The two versions of the swimming match differ markedly, of course, in point of view, and therefore are highly differentiated, much more so than is the case with the other repetitions in the poem.

But why does the poet make so much of the swimming match? It comes under the head of the hero's *enfances,* or exploits of boyhood, a familiar feature of heroic story, but one fundamentally trivial in character. Beowulf mentions some other boyish feats of his when he first addresses King Hrothgar. His speech begins,

> Be thou hale, Hrothgar! I am Hygelac's kinsman and retainer. I did many glorious deeds when I was a boy.

This is pretty vague, of course, but later on in the speech he tells Hrothgar, more specifically, that he had been a giant-killer, that he had taken five giants captive, that he had slain sea-monsters by night, and that he had fought with success against certain unnamed foes of his own people. Obviously if Beowulf fought monsters as well as that in his boyhood he ought to be able to cope with Grendel now that he has become a full-grown man. In other words, Beowulf's catalogue of his early exploits is meant to convince the king that here at last is the man he needs. The catalogue serves also to instruct the reader or hearers of the poem; they learn out of Beowulf's own mouth—that is, from the most authoritative source possible—that he is a redoubtable champion; in particular, that he is a monster-queller. This device of self-characterization is familiar in literary art. One finds it in Shakespeare, for example. The ***Beowulf*** poet's use of it is, in all likelihood, highly traditional and conventional.

Beowulf's mention of sea-monsters which he had slain by night takes us back to the swimming match with Breca, one detail of which is precisely this monster-quelling on the part of the hero. The quelling, as Beowulf himself points out, is of benefit to mankind, and may be taken for a kind of prelude to the more important quelling which is to follow at the Danish court. But after all, the two boys, when they agreed and vowed to swim to sea, had no thought of rendering a service to their fellow men. They risked their lives in this swimming match on the high seas in a spirit of recklessness. They were showing off. In Beowulf's story of the swim we catch the apologetic note: "we were both still in our boyhood," he says. The implication is clear that the Beowulf who had reached young manhood would not have undertaken such a match. One should not risk one's life in vain.

It now becomes clearer why the poet makes a good deal of the swimming match. The story of the match gives us a short but vivid view of the adolescent hero in action. We get other glimpses of him as a boy, but nowhere else is any event of his boyhood told in detail. The poet reserves the main fable for his hero as a young man and as an old man, but in one episode he presents him in his immaturity. Here the future champion of mankind against the world of monsters is already a monster-queller, though not yet informed with a high moral purpose. He plays with the heroic life to which, later on, he will dedicate himself in earnest.

Most of the episodic matter in the poem, however, is concerned, not with the hero himself but with his setting. The author, as we have seen, was not only a Christian moralist. He was also an Englishman; that is, a man of Germanic stock and traditions. He chose a hero of his own race, and gave him for setting the golden age of ancient Germania, that glorious period of migration when the Germanic tribes overran the Roman Empire and made its provinces into Germanic kingdoms. . . . [In the eighth century] the English, so far as their culture was concerned, still belonged, in part, to a commonwealth of nations, the Germania of their Continental forefathers. Within that commonwealth they were at home, and felt the Goth, the Swede, the Langobard alike to be cultural fellow-countrymen. The ***Beowulf*** poet was intensely patriotic; his poem shows at every turn the warmth of his love for his native culture and his native race. But his patriotism embraced Germania as a whole; it was no narrowly English affair. It is particularly significant, I think, that his hero lived and died in southern Scandinavia, the heart of the old Germanic homeland, the cradle of the race, the region least affected by foreign influences. Moreover, it was from the Jutland peninsula, a part of this very region, that the English themselves had come, in their great migration to Britain. We must not forget that England in its earliest centuries was still colonial territory. The stream of settlers from the Germanic motherland had probably stopped flowing by the time of the ***Beowulf*** poet, but the English had not forgotten their origin nor yet the source of their cultural traditions. Above all, ***Beowulf*** is a poem of the past, of a past thought of by the poet as remote. The action of such a poem obviously must take place in the homeland, not in a colony of recent foundation.

It may be worth our while, however, to speculate about the poet's reasons for not making King Offa the hero of his poem. Offa is the only English king of the Continental period about whom we have much information. We learn of him both in ***Beowulf*** and in *Widsith.* The ***Beowulf*** poet calls him the best of all mankind, and adds that he was held in high esteem far and wide because of his generosity and his success in warfare. The poet also tells us that Offa ruled his country with wisdom. In *Widsith* we get more specific information about Offa's achievements: while still a boy he overthrew "with single sword" (that is, by his own efforts, without help from others) the kingdom of the Myrgings, and dictated a boundary between his own kingdom and theirs, a boundary which his successors were able to keep. Moreover, we have reason to think that Offa was the first English king whose realm included western as well as eastern Sleswick. . . . It seems clear that Offa was a man eminently suitable for celebration in song. An English poet in particular might be expected to make Offa the hero of a poem set in the Germania of the migration period, the heroic age of the Germanic peoples. Why did our poet choose Beowulf instead? The answer, I think, is simple. Beowulf was famous chiefly as a queller of monsters, whereas Offa won his fame as a queller of men. The poet, pious Christian that he was, found spiritual values in Beowulf's monster-quelling which he could not find in Offa's man-quelling. Nevertheless he did not like to leave Offa out of his poem altogether. The great hero of his own tribe must be brought in somehow. The episode in which Offa figures I describe elsewhere as having been introduced by a *tour de force*, and this may well be a correct statement of the case. But the poet's technic of linkage here has a parallel in at least one other episode. I will take up Offa first.

King Offa is introduced, not directly but by way of his wife, Queen Thrytho, and most of the episode is devoted to the lady, whose unorthodox behavior makes her more interesting than her pattern of a husband. The introduction of a husband through his wife, however, is certainly no *tour de force*. It is the introduction of Thrytho herself which makes trouble for modern readers. The poet gets her in by contrasting her with Hygd, wife of King Hygelac. Beowulf has come back home after his Grendel adventure and is approaching Hygelac's hall to make his report of the journey. The author stops at this point to comment on the hall, the king, and the king's wife. But he disposes of hall and king in a line and a half; Queen Hygd is the one he gives most of his attention to. She is characterized in accordance with the etymology of her name. *Hygd* means "thought" and the queen is represented as thoughtful indeed: wise, well behaved, and mindful of other people's wishes and feelings. The poet explains Hygd's exemplary conduct as the fruit of deliberation, study, mental activity. He says,

> The good queen of the people [i.e., Hygd] bore in mind (wæg) the haughtiness, the terrible violence of Thrytho.

In other words, Hygd took warning by the example of Thrytho. She took care to behave differently. This brings the poet to Thrytho's own behavior, which was certainly not very encouraging to would-be suitors, for she objected so strongly to the attentions of men that if one of them so much as looked at her she had him put to death. The poet goes on to say, "that is no way for a lady to do." We learn, however, that Thrytho turned over a new leaf after her marriage to Offa, whom she loved dearly. King Offa, it would seem, proved master of the situation at home as well as on the field of battle.

Linkage by contrast also serves to bring in the second Heremod passage (lines 1709-1722), a part of the so-called sermon of Hrothgar. The aged king after praising Beowulf speaks of Heremod as Beowulf's antithesis. He brings the passage to an end by exhorting Beowulf to profit by the evil example that Heremod has set. The sad fate of Heremod should be a lesson to the young hero. The same device of contrast is used in the first Heremod passage (lines 901-915), but here this type of linkage comes at the end of the passage; the poet, by contrasting Heremod with Beowulf, brings the narrative back to his hero. This passage about Heremod is introduced by the use of a different device: sequence in time. The poet has been speaking of the famous hero Sigemund, the dragon-slayer. He shifts to Heremod very simply, saying that Sigemund flourished after Heremod had had his day. We get no hint that the two men are connected in any other way, and the device which serves to link them in the poem strikes us as artificial enough. In this case, however, the Scandinavian evidence makes it clear that Sigemund and Heremod were traditionally associated, though just what the association was we are unable to make out. This information, gained from a study of Icelandic poetry, forces us to revise our opinion of the artistic technic of the ***Beowulf*** poet. We now see that the true linkage between Sigemund and Heremod was left unexpressed and needed no expression, since it was already firmly fixed by tradition in the minds of the poet's audience, to be evoked at will be a mere mention of the names. It is our misfortune, but not the poet's fault, that we in our ignorance miss the true link and have to depend altogether on that sequence in time which the poet uses, as an external device only, in proceeding from the one member of the heroic pair to the other.

The device of contrast, too, now begins to have a different look. One may well suspect, though one certainly cannot prove, that the coupling of Beowulf and Heremod, and of Hygd and Thrytho, belong to tradition and have their roots deep in Germanic story. If so, the English poet took up these characters together, not as a mere device for changing the subject, but because they went together in the songs that had come down to him, the sources he drew upon for the tale he had to tell.

What functions do the episodes have in the economy of the poem? . . . [Most] of them bring out the setting in which the hero lived and died. This setting was ancient Germania; more particularly, the Scandinavia of the fifth and sixth centuries of our era. The story of Scyld, mythical founder of the Danish royal house, gives us a taste of an old legend, and the description of his funeral takes us back to pagan rites dim with antiquity. The tale of Ecgtheow's feud with the avengers of Heatholaf makes the father of the hero more than a name to us and links him with the Wulfing tribe, famous in heroic story from Iceland to the Mediterranean. When Hrothgar's scop, after singing Beowulf's praises, goes on to the exploits of Sigemund, he puts our hero side by side with a hero of Frankish legend, one of the chief figures of Germanic story. That night the scop sang once more; this time he told the tale of Finn, an ancient story very welcome at the Danish court, since it ends with a Danish victory. The tale of Ingeld the English poet puts in the mouth of Beowulf himself, as part of his report to Hygelac on the state of Denmark. All these passages serve to make our hero part and parcel of the heroic age of Germanic antiquity.

It is possible, however, to make a distinction here between those episodes which have been drawn into the narrative and those that remain external to it. Examples of the former are the passages about Scyld, Ecgtheow, and the swimming match; examples of the latter are the passages about Sigemund, Finn, and Ingeld. In part two of the poem the integration of the historical passages into the story of the dragon fight has been done in such a way as to disturb many modern readers. Thus, Klaeber says . . . ,

> The facts of Geatish history, it cannot be denied, are a little too much in evidence and retard the narrative . . . rather seriously [see excerpt dated 1922].

This verdict does less than justice to the narrative art of the poet, who in part two tells the story of his hero's tribe: past, present and future. The attack of the dragon on that tribe, and Beowulf's counter-attack, ending in the death both of the hero and of his monstrous antagonist, make part of the tribal story, a part which we may call the present crisis (present, that is, from the point of view of the hero). The poet gives us his account of this crisis, not continuously but in sections, sections which alternate with accounts of earlier crises in the tribe's history. The death of the dragon ends the present crisis, but the messenger of Wiglaf foresees disaster for the tribe in the future, now that they have lost their great king. He justifies his forebodings by reminding his hearers of certain events of the past, events which in due course will lead to ruin, want, and exile. The poet himself adds that the messenger's fears are fully justified. The poem ends in the present, with the funeral of the hero.

It will be seen that the author of ***Beowulf*** in part two of his poem uses a technic of alternation between events of the present and events of the past. He restricts himself throughout to his hero's own tribe, in marked contrast to his procedure in part one, where he ranges widely over Germania. The unity of part two, in theme and form alike, is noteworthy. As for the technic of alternation which the poet uses to drive home this unity, it is a technic very familiar today, especially in the narrative art of screen and novel. Many recent screen plays follow this method of shifting repeatedly from present to past. In Hollywood they have a name for the shift backwards in time: they call it a flashback. . . . In the novel, just as in part two of ***Beowulf,*** the action is restricted to one day, but the flashbacks take us deep into the past. It is not likely that the novelists and scenario writers of today learned this technic by studying ***Beowulf,*** but theirs is the technic of the ***Beowulf*** poet none the less.

The shift from present to past occurs three times in the narrative of part two. The poet makes the transition in a different way each time. In all three cases he manages the shift with great skill. The second transition is of special interest, as an example of the poet's craftsmanship. Beowulf and his little band of men had reached the immediate neighborhood of the dragon's lair. Beowulf was to go forward alone from that point. He sat down on the headland, and bade his followers goodbye. The aged king fell to thinking about his childhood and youth, and began to talk. His reminiscences take up nearly 100 lines of verse. The technic seems almost realistic here. What could be more natural than for an old man to talk about old times?

One may now ask whether the three long passages on the history of the Geatas incorporated in part two should really be looked upon as episodic. Without them the story of the dragon fight would remain, but would lose greatly in spiritual quality, since we should not know as we do the people for whom Beowulf was giving his life. As the poem stands, the fate of the hero and the fate of the tribe are bound together in such a way that each lends weight and worth to the other. We mourn for the Geatas as well as for their king, and this double mourning deepens as well as widens the sweep of the tragic march of events. One cannot doubt that the poet meant it so. For him, Beowulf would not have been a hero if he had not had a people to die for. The ***Beowulf*** poet was above all a patriotic poet.

We end as we began, with a look at the poem taken in the large. As we have seen, ***Beowulf*** falls into two parts, devoted respectively to the hero in young manhood and the hero in old age. Part one is predominantly cheerful in tone, as befits a period of youth. When one reads the Sigemund episode, for instance, one feels that it is good to be alive in a world made for heroic adventure. Even the Finn episode has a happy ending if one sides with the Danes, as our poet does. Now and then the shadows of feuds that are to come darken the picture of

The jewelled lid of a purse discovered in the Sutton Hoo ship burial. The British Museum.

the Danish court, and the aged Hrothgar is fond of talking about his own troubles and those of others, but the hero takes all this in his stride and goes home in triumph, leaving a cleansed and happy Herorot behind him.

Utterly different is the tone of part two. Old age has come, and death is near at hand from the start. No longer does the hero leave home, to fight the good fight in other lands. He stands strictly on the defensive. He is sad at heart; his breast surges with dark thoughts. But there is one thought which he does not have. It does not occur to him to give up. Great though the odds against him, he take the field and fights to the last. In this world defeat and death are sure to come in the end. The hero is he who, like Beowulf, faces the worst without flinching and dies that others may live. (pp. 165-72)

Kemp Malone, "'Beowulf'," in English Studies, *Vol. XXIX, No. 4, December, 1948, pp. 161-72.*

GILBERT HIGHET (essay date 1949)

[*A Scottish-born writer and critic, Highet was a classical scholar and distinguished educator. As a literary personality on a weekly radio program in New York, he used a witty, urbane manner to present diverse works of literature—from Greek and Latin classics to contemporary novels—in an interesting and understandable form. Although Highet was sometimes harshly criticized for his popularizing techniques, his scholarly studies* The Classical Tradition: Greek and Roman Influences on Western Literature *(1949) and* The Anatomy of Satire *(1962) received wide recognition in the literary community. In the following excerpt from* The Classical Tradition, *Highet finds the artistry of* Beowulf *lacking when compared to the epics of Homer and Vergil. Highet also discusses the "half-barbarous" audience addressed by the* Beowulf *poet.*]

The most important poem in old English literature is an epic called ***Beowulf.*** It deals with two heroic exploits in the life of a warrior chief, but also covers his youth, his accession to the throne, his kingship, and his death. Beowulf is his name, and he is called prince of the Geatas. This tribe is believed to have lived in Götaland, which is still the name of southern Sweden; and one of the battles in which the poem says he fought is known to have occurred about the year A.D. 520. The chief tribes mentioned are the Angles, the Swedes, the Franks, the Danes, and the Geatas themselves. The material of the poem was therefore brought over from the Baltic area by some of the fierce war-bands who invaded Britain after the Romans left it.

Its chief interest is that it shows us an earlier stage of development in European civilization than any other comparable document, Greek and Roman books included. Compare it with Homer. The type of life described, a disorganized world of tribal states, raiding-parties, and gallant chiefs, is pretty much the same. Beowulf himself would have been welcomed in the camp of the Achaeans outside Troy, and would have won the swimming prize at Patroclus' funeral games. But there are important differences:

(*a*) In ***Beowulf,*** the conflict is between man and the sub-human. Beowulf's chief enemy Grendel is a giant cannibal living in a cave. (Apart from Grendel's terrific size, he is not necessarily a mere fable. As late as the seventeenth century there are reports from outlying parts of Europe of cannibal families inhabiting caves not unlike Grendel's. The most famous case is Sawney Bean, in southern Scotland.) The other opponent of Beowulf is a firedrake, a flame-spitting dragon guarding a treasure. So the story represents the long fight between brave tribal warriors on the one side and, on the other, the fierce animals of the wilderness and the bestial cave-beings who live outside the world of men and hate it. But in the *Iliad* the war is between raiding tribesmen from a Greece which, though primitive, is not empty of towns and commerce, and the rich civilized Asiatic city of Troy, with rich and civilized allies like Memnon. There is no prolonged conflict between men and animal monsters in Homer. (Bellerophon was forced to fight against a lion-goat-snake monster, the Chimera, which breathed fire; but that incident takes only five lines to narrate. The chief Homeric parallels to this aspect of ***Beowulf*** are to be found in the *Odyssey,* where they are located in wild regions far outside the Greek world: Grendel's nearest kinsmen are the Cyclopes of the Sicilian mountains, or the man-eating Laestrygones in the land of the midnight sun.) Compared with Homer, Beowulf's adventures take place, not in the morning light of civilization, but in the twilight gloom of that huge, lonely, anti-human world, the forest primeval, the world so beautifully and horribly evoked by Wagner in *The Ring of the Nibelungs;* or that of the weird Finnish *Kalevala,* which is ennobled in the music of Sibelius.

(*b*) The world of ***Beowulf*** is narrower and simpler than that of Homer. Men's memories are very short. Their geographical range is small: north central Europe, bounded by pathless forest and serpent-haunted sea, with no trace of Slavs or Romans beyond. Within this frontier their settlements are lonely, scattered, and ill organized. When new champions face each other in the *Iliad,* or when Odysseus makes a new landfall in the *Odyssey,* there is usually a polite but clear exchange of information which shoots rays of light into the surrounding darkness. We hear of great cities in the distance and great heroes in the past. The result is that the epics gradually build up a rich collection of historical and geographical knowledge, rather like the books of Judges and Samuel in the Bible. But ***Beowulf*** contains far less such information, because its characters and composers knew far less of the past and of the world around. Any three thousand lines of *Iliad* or *Odyssey* take us into a wider, more populous, more highly explored and interdependent world than all the 3,183 lines of ***Beowulf;*** and the customs, weapons, stratagems, arts, and personalities of Homer are vastly more complex than those of the Saxon epic.

(*c*) Artistically, ***Beowulf*** is a rude and comparatively unskilled poem. Epic poetry is, like tragedy, a highly developed literary growth. Its wild ancestors still exist in many countries. They are short poems describing single deeds of heroic energy or suffering: the ballads of the Scottish borders, the songs about Marko Kraljević and other Serbian chiefs, the fine Anglo-Saxon fragment, *Maldon,* about a battle against the invading Danes. Sometimes these are roughly linked together, to make a cycle or a chronicle telling of many great exploits performed in one war, or under one dynasty, or by one group of strong men. But still these do not make an epic. All the adventures of Hercules, or King David, or King Arthur and his knights, will form an interesting story, but they will not have the artistic impact of a real epic. An epic is made by a single poet (or perhaps a closely linked succession, a family of poets) who relates one great heroic adventure in detail, connecting it with as much historical, geographical, and spiritual background as will make it something much more deeply significant than any isolated incident, however remarkable, and causing it to embody a profound moral truth.

Now, most of the heroic poetry in the world belongs to the first stage of this development. It tells the story of Sir Patrick

Spens, or the battle of Otterburn, and then stops. There is an Anglo-Saxon poem like this, called *Finnsburh,* which we can also find built into ***Beowulf*** in a different shape, like the little chapel which later architects have worked into a large and complex church. The Icelandic sagas correspond to the second stage, the long chronicle—although a few, like *Njála,* have the nobility of true epic. ***Beowulf*** is a dogged, though unskilled, attempt to reach the third stage, and to make a poem combining unity and variety, heroic action and spiritual meaning. Here is its skeleton:

100-1,062 Beowulf fights the giant Grendel;
1,233-1,921 Beowulf fights Grendel's mother;
2,211-3,183 Beowulf fights the fiery dragon, and dies.

So the poem is mostly occupied by relating two (or at most three) heroic adventures, which are essentially similar, not to say repetitious. Two happen in a distant country and the third at the end of Beowulf's long life; while his accession to the throne and his fifty years' reign are passed over in less than 150 lines. The other episodes, evoking the past, comparing Beowulf with earlier heroes, and foretelling the gloomy future, were designed to coordinate these adventures into a single multidimensional structure; but the builder could scarcely plan well enough. It would have been astonishing if the age which made only the most primitive churches and castles and codes of law could have produced poets with the power to conceive a large and subtle plan and to impose it on the rough recalcitrant material and half-barbarous audiences with which they had to deal. The style and language of the poem, in comparison with the greater epics of Greece and Rome, are limited in range, sometimes painfully harsh and difficult; yet, even if awkward, they are tremendously bold and powerful, like the hero of whom they tell.

There is apparently no direct classical influence on ***Beowulf*** and the other Anglo-Saxon secular poems. They belong to a different world from that of Greco-Roman civilization. Attempts have been made to prove that ***Beowulf*** imitates the *Aeneid,* but they consist mainly in showing that both poems describe distantly similar heroic incidents in heroic language; and on these lines we could prove that the Indian epic poets copied Homer. The differences in language, structure, and technique are so striking as to make any material resemblance merely coincidental, even if it were probable that a poet working in one difficult tradition at such a period would borrow from another even more difficult. When early craftsmen like the creator of ***Beowulf*** know any classical literature, they are forced by its superior power and elaboration to adapt it very carefully and obviously.

There is, however, a certain amount of Christian influence—although it is evidently peripheral, and later than the main conception of the poem. ***Beowulf,*** like the world in which it grew, shows Christian ideals superimposed upon a barbarous pagan substructure, and just beginning to transform it. We see the same thing in some of the Icelandic sagas and in the Gaelic legends. Lady Gregory tells how Oisin argued with St. Patrick from the old heroic standpoint, and said to him:

> "Many a battle and many a victory was gained by the Fianna of Ireland; I never heard any great deed was done by the King of Saints (i.e. Jesus), or that he ever reddened his hand."

So ***Beowulf*** both begins and ends with a thoroughly pagan funeral. It is significant also that, when Heorot the haunted palace was first opened, a minstrel sang a song about the first five days of Creation (evidently based on Genesis, like Cædmon's hymn); but later, when the ogre began to attack the palace, the chiefs who debated about preventive measures vowed sacrifices to "the slayer of souls" (= the devil = a pagan divinity). Such inconsistency can be a sign either of interpolation or of the confusion of cultures. What Christian influence does appear is strictly Old Testament tradition. The audience of ***Beowulf,*** the "half-barbarous folk" to whom Aldhelm sang vernacular songs, was scarcely at an intellectual and spiritual level which would permit it to appreciate the gospels and the Pauline epistles. God is simply a monotheistic king, ruler, and judge, venerable because of His power. There is no mention of Jesus Christ, of the cross, of the church, of saints, or of angels. One or two early Old Testament stories appear, as it were grafted upon paganism: the giant Grendel, together with "ogres and elves and sea-monsters," is said to come of the race of the fratricide Cain; and there is a mention of the Flood. But all this, although it comes through the Latin Bible, is classical influence at its very thinnest. Greece and Rome had no immediate influence on ***Beowulf*** and its kindred poems, any more than on the Welsh *Mabinogion,* the stories of Fingal and his warriors, the great legends of Arthur, and other heroic tales which grew up along the frontiers of the dissolving civilization of Rome. Classical influence, if it reached them and their makers at all, reached them through the church. After the Greek world had been cut off and the Roman world barbarized, the church civilized the barbarians. ***Beowulf*** allows us to see how it began: gradually and wisely, by converting them. After many dark centuries, Europe regained civilization, urged forward largely by feeling, once again, the stimulus of the spirit of Greece and Rome; but it was the church which, by transmitting a higher vision through that influence, began the reconquest of the victorious barbarians upon the ruins of the defeated empire. (pp. 22-7)

Gilbert Highet, "The Dark Ages: English Literature," in his The Classical Tradition: Greek and Roman Influences on Western Literature, *Oxford University Press, 1949, pp. 22-47.*

GEORGE K. ANDERSON (essay date 1949)

[*Anderson was a prolific American scholar of Old and Middle English literature, the works of Chaucer, and twentieth-century English and American fiction and poetry. In the following excerpt, he discusses several important aspects of* Beowulf: *the poem as demonstration of the Germanic code of the hero, the intricate and complex structure of the work, and the question of authorship and date of composition.*]

Unquestionably the most important monument of Old English epic literature . . . is the poem ***Beowulf.*** Its importance lies not alone in the fact that it embodies in characteristic fashion the ideals of the Germanic warrior; it is also the only example in Old English poetry of a heroic epic in what seems to be a complete state. It is in addition a happy hunting-ground for the linguist, the scholar, and the critic. In ***Beowulf,*** we are beyond the first stage of the heroic folk-epic, the individual lay concerning an epic feat by an individual hero—no good illustration of which can be found in Old English literature—and have come to the second stage, the concatenation of more than one feat by a single hero, covering in fact the essential achievements of the hero's entire career. In these manifold deeds of the hero are portrayed the ideals of the Geatish people—ideals which may properly be considered the ideals of the Germanic hero no matter what his tribal origins. . . . And on the other side of the coin ***Beowulf*** depicts the loyalty of warrior to chieftain; of freeman, earl, and churl to their king—a whole-souled devotion to which the Anglo-Saxon was ready to dedicate his life. "Death is better for every earl than a life of shame!" cried young Wiglaf at his lord Beowulf's passing.

Beowulf, to the reader who first meets it, is a rather confusing succession of incidents, although a closer acquaintance with the work will reveal that the confusion is more apparent than real and that the author knew well where he was going. In spite of the admitted multiplicity of these incidents, however, the poem falls into two general parts: that having to do with the adventures of Beowulf the Geat at the Danish court of King Hrothgar, and that dealing with the mighty struggle between Beowulf and the fire-dragon at home in Geatland. Into the first part stalk two great mortal enemies of Beowulf, Grendel and Grendel's mother. There is also detailed reference in this section to a previous feat by Beowulf, the swimming-race with Breca. In the second part, during the narrative of Beowulf and the fire-dragon, there come many shreds of other stories—allusions, often of some length, to incidents in the wars between the Geats and the Swedes or between the Danes and the Heathobards, and to isolated figures of Germanic legendry who stride majestically through a few lines.

Beowulf the hero stands forth as a man of dignity and polish, in the sense that he knows to perfection the complicated etiquette expected of a champion. There is a suggestion that as a youth he was considered slow and lazy; but it is further apparent that as a child of seven winters he was, according to the custom of Germanic princes, taken from the keeping of his father and brought up by some one else—in this case, by his grandfather Hrethel, then King of the Geats. His training must, in the long run, have been successful; but in the "slowness" of Beowulf as a youth we see illustrated that common theme of folklore: the unpromising stripling who makes good, the "male Cinderella." As a young man in his twenties, however, Beowulf has physical attributes which are nothing short of overpowering; he is a fabulous swimmer and diver, for one thing. Nothing could be more appropriate than to find a maritime colossus as the hero of the only complete surviving epic in Old English literature. For even if Beowulf is not himself Anglo-Saxon, he has the attributes of a seafaring man, for which the English have always been famous. As examples, there is first of all his swimming-contest with Breca, a feat of epic proportions; there is next his even more remarkable accomplishment of covering the sea-stretches from the mouth of the Rhine to his home in Geatland (presumably in the Baltic), with thirty coats-of-mail on his back. The whole Breca episode should be read with one eye upon the muscularity and grim vigor of the text. . . . Combined with the sinewy indefatigability of Beowulf in the water is his superb lung-capacity. He can dive into the mere after Grendel's mother and follow down into the inky depths for a day before he can perceive the bottom of the sea. . . . Finally, Beowulf possesses at least by reputation the strength of thirty men in his hand-grip; it is sufficient, at any rate, to tear out the arm of the monster Grendel. Indeed, Beowulf relies upon this grip to the exclusion of the sword in fighting Grendel; and that unfortunate monster, "the shepherd of crimes,"

> Knew that he never had met in this world,
> In the four quarters of the whole wide earth
> In any other man a mightier hand-grip.

These physical attributes, then, are Beowulf's peculiar contribution to the epic tradition of great strength and prowess. They are comparable to Roland's mighty blasts on the horn, to the weight-throwing gift of Ajax, to Cuchulain's marvelous dexterity and eyesight. But these are, after all, physical attributes only. In addition to qualities of bodily strength there are in Beowulf moral virtues of more than passing worth: there is nobility and gravity and an unshaken courage. Yet this courage is translatable chiefly into terms of action. It is more physical than moral. It is sober and sure but never brilliant; there is little in it of hot impetuosity. Even if one discounts the usual amount of conventional boasting in which Beowulf, as any good epic hero, indulges before a combat, there still remains an aura of confidence about him which is extraordinary. Neither the grim ferocity of the "mighty merewife," Grendel's mother, nor the flames pouring from the head of the fire-dragon dissuade Beowulf from his advance into danger. If there is any appreciable flaw in his character—any tragic defect of body or spirit which brings about his downfall, such as Achilles or Siegfried or Roland suffered—it is a superabundance of this valor and a resulting overconfidence which prompts him to sally forth against the fire-drake with inadequate protection at a too advanced age.

There is more than enough of platitude and of Christian admonition in the poem. The bloodiest and crudest of primitive battle-narratives will jostle against the most approved rules of conduct, either practical or spiritual. There are some, incidentally, who believe that the poem was intended, in its present form, as a book of conduct for kings and princes to follow; but this point of view, while attractive, need not be accepted. In many passages Fate (*Wyrd*) and her warriors, both the doomed and the undoomed, wrestle with the Christian God for supremacy. Such inconsistencies, however, are easily enough understood when we remember that ***Beowulf*** as we have it today has a story many features of which belong to the pagan Germanic world of the sixth century or earlier and a form which belongs to Christian England of the eighth century as regards language and of the early eleventh century as regards manuscript. (pp. 63-8)

The more one reads and studies ***Beowulf,*** the more one is impressed by the design of the Beowulf Poet, in spite of the fact that his gift for digressive incidents is remarkable. There are forward pointings and backward glances sufficient to demonstrate that the poet was not indulging in an amateurish crazy-quilt of incident. Besides, the admittedly episodic structure illustrates in the main the individual epic lay, the narrative unit which serves as the individual tile in the mosaic which is the full narrative poem. For that reason it would be well to enumerate the major lays which present themselves in ***Beowulf.*** It will be noted that the subject-matter of these lays is often very remote from the Beowulf story. But, to stick at first to the lays in ***Beowulf*** having reference to the Geats and the Danes, there is, for example, the brief account of Beowulf's conduct in the battle fatal to his king Hygelac (2354-2379). This incident is alluded to more than once in the poem. It is at least one event mentioned in ***Beowulf*** which seems to be historically authentic. Again, there is the lay of the death of Ongentheow, king of the Swedes, in the first of the Geatish-Swedish wars (2472-2509). This is an elemental passage with a singularly romantic turn. The Swedes, under Ongentheow, had been at first victorious over the Geats; but when the tide of battle turned, the old Swedish king is brought to bay and killed by a rather obscure young Geatish warrior, Eofor. As a reward for this decisive blow the Geatish king, Hygelac, gives Eofor his only daughter in marriage. There are still other allusions to the Geatish-Swedish wars and to the feud between the Danes and Heathobards, as well as to the famous Finnsburg conflict (1060-1159).

But some of these lays, on the other hand, are extraneous and didactic in purpose. There is the rather chance allusion to the "unapproachable queen" Thryth, or Modthryth, a figure reminiscent of Atalanta, Brunhild, and others (1931-1962). This originally evil person is described as a contrast and foil to a sympathetic character, Queen Hygd of the Geats. Similarly, there are two references to a tyrannical King Heremod, a more or less legendary ruler in Danish tradition, who is everything that a king should not be; he is thrown into sharp contrast with Beowulf and with the great North Germanic hero Siegmund (901-915). All these allusions are, in effect, individual epic lays, which, if expanded and linked to other lays about the same character, would produce an heroic epic of full dimensions. The appearance of these lays, digressive and instrusive as they are, indicates that the Beowulf Poet was well versed in Germanic legendry and could use his material for whatever purpose he saw fit. It is impossible to say whether he is following closely some current epic material on the subject of these miscellaneous lays or whether he is improvising. We can be sure, however, that there was plenty of actual copying of manuscripts either in whole or in part; in other words, the material was there to be used by other poets. (pp. 73-4)

[A] striking . . . passage in ***Beowulf*** . . . [describes] the lair of Grendel and his dam (1357-1377). In these twenty lines lives one of the earliest pieces of landscape poetry in English literature. . . . The resemblance of the landscape in these lines to that of the approach to the underworld found in the classical epics, notably to the scene in Book VI of Virgil's *Aeneid,* has been frequently discussed. There is no reason whatsoever why the Beowulf Poet should not have known Virgil's epic and used it as an inspiration for secondary details; but the actual scene is described elsewhere in Germanic legends where there is no need to assume Virgilian influence. It is not inconceivable that the mountain-vistas of Norway might be even more influential than Virgil, if the author of these lines was familiar with them; or he may have had in mind the Lake Country of northwestern England. The reader can decide for himself.

Two other sections of ***Beowulf*** . . . [illustrate another type of Old English literature]—elegiac verse. The first of these is the implied lament of a father for a son who has been hanged (2444-2462). . . . The second is the excellent piece of lyric poetry uttered by the last survivor of the race of men guarding the gold-hoard—that sinister gold-hoard of which the fire-dragon eventually becomes a jealous custodian (2247-2266). . . . (pp. 76-8)

These two passages should be considered along with the rather magnificent harangue [in lines 1724-68] of the garrulous, somewhat Polonius-like Hrothgar, as he makes his banquet-speech celebrating Beowulf's victory over Grendel but warning him of the inevitable end of man. . . . It should be observed . . . that the Beowulf Poet, on the evidence of these passages alone, must have been a man of considerable literary background for his time. As I have remarked before, the description of Grendel's cave contains some Virgilian echoes; the elegiac passages demonstrate that the Beowulf Poet was steeped in the poetic traditions of his own people. Moreover, there emanates from Hrothgar's homily a strong Biblical and scriptural atmosphere; it can be shown that many phrases in ***Beowulf*** exhibit the influence of the Vulgate Bible. We are probably justified in assuming this threefold literary material—classical, Biblical, and native—to have been the stock-in-trade of the English writers of the period before the Norman Conquest. (pp. 78, 80)

[The] name of the Beowulf Poet, the *scop*—or the priest—who shaped so worthily the 3,182 lines of the poem ***Beowulf,*** and the names of the two scribes who have given us our existing manuscript-version are alike unknown. In pondering this mystery of the Beowulf Poet, we should bear one fact in mind—the civilization portrayed in ***Beowulf*** is not necessarily the civilization in which the Beowulf Poet actually lived. In fact, it could not be, for Beowulf the Geat moves in a setting fundamentally heathen, epic, and heroically exaggerated, whereas the Beowulf Poet breathed a Christian atmosphere. The question of the authorship of ***Beowulf,*** whether single or multiple, has raged since Thorkelin's first edition of the poem in 1815. Much has been made of the historicity of the characters and of the possibility that some of the events of the poem have a basis in fact. None of the questions of authorship, however, seems to depend upon whether or not this event or that one is actually true. It might be one individual, "laden with stories of glorious deeds," who composed the poem which we have before us; it could just conceivably be more than one, the first being the *scop* who celebrated some single event mentioned in the poem. The same question, of course, can be raised concerning any heroic epic unless, as with the *Aeneid* or *Paradise Lost,* we recognize the unmistakable fact of single authorship of a "literary" epic. But all epics are in that sense "literary," and the inevitability of a single author for any completed poem is clear whenever the matter has been carefully considered.

Gregory of Tours, a contemporary chronicler, has given authority to that last, fatal battle in which Hygelac engaged; according to him, it took place about 520. Obviously this makes that event stand out apart from other events in the work; it affords a convenient *terminus a quo* for certain parts of the story. At the same time, there is no longer any reason to accept this particular battle as the only historical happening in ***Beowulf.*** It is simply that it is an event which held great authority for the earlier editors of the poem. Since the mid-nineteenth century . . . , other chronicles have received attention, so that it is now possible to infer a reasonably satisfactory account of the Danish tribes during the time covered by the action of the poem.

One man, however, could put into place the individual lays into which the structure of ***Beowulf*** can be broken down, and he could do it better than several. As in *Widsith,* there are portions of ***Beowulf*** which belong to pagan legendry and are dateless. There are also parts of the poem which have relation of a vague sort to history. Now it is unlikely that any poem so Scandinavian in sympathy would be written in England before the Danish invasions had at least begun. Hrothgar and his people are Danes and so need no further discussion as Norsemen. The identity of the Geats, however, is still obscure; they are scarcely the Jutes of Jutland, but more likely the Old Norse Gautar, a tribe inhabiting the southern tip of what is now Sweden. At any rate they were Scandinavian. A poem so thoroughly Norse in subject-matter as ***Beowulf*** would probably not be well received in Anglo-Saxon territory during the actual progress of the Danish invasions, which began in the eighth century and reached peaks in the late ninth and late tenth centuries. It will be remembered that the Danes overran Northumbria and Mercia; their influence both in language and in literature showed itself first in the northern sections of England. Yet the manuscript of ***Beowulf*** is written in a dialect generally West Saxon, with a considerable degree of Anglian admixture.

It is likely, then, that the *manuscript* of the poem is the work of West Saxon Christians writing at a time when Danish influence was strong even in the south of England—in other words, about the time of the Danish Conquest (1014). This date checks well with the scribal evidence. But the date of *original composition* is another matter. The poetic forms and devices, to say nothing of the language, indicate that ***Beowulf*** was written in the heyday of bardic poetry in England—the eighth century. Most scholars assign the poem a date near 725, though some are willing to venture a date either half a century earlier or more than a century later. This, therefore, would be the time of the flourishing of the Beowulf Poet, who might be of Danish ancestry, living in Anglia and writing his poem in an Anglian dialect—probably Mercian, possibly Northumbrian. These details, however, can be only speculation. We are agreed that he was a cleric, a scholar beyond the average for his time, and a poet of high order.

The period from the *terminus a quo* in 520 to 725—a span of two centuries—is not at all excessive for the slow growth of an heroic epic; in that time the patchwork structure, while still too obvious, will nevertheless have taken on more settled lines, perhaps a rude pattern. It will only remain then for a gifted synthesizer to come along, as the Beowulf Poet came. The very early dates of the authentic historical events in ***Beowulf*** are of little importance in reference to the completed literary form; they only go to show the manifest fact that the saga has all its vital roots in the Germanic Heroic Age, at a time when the tribes which gave it birth were still on the Continent. If one takes the period from about 725 to about 1000, both the Beowulf Poet and the final scribes belong to the era of Christianity in England, and the blend of paganism and Christianity in ***Beowulf*** has been consummated.

And so, to summarize, one may grant the pagan qualities of the original story; one may further assume that one or more bards contributed descriptive details, didactic passages, elegiac lays, some historical or legendary digressions, until eventually a more gifted individual, known as the Beowulf Poet, put the accumulated epic and lyric material down into his individualized concept, much as we have it now. This Beowulf Poet may have composed the major part of the poem as it now exists—perhaps all of it—or he may only have transcribed the poem as he knew it from a predecessor or predecessors. But he is responsible for ***Beowulf*** as we understand it, and he composed it some time in the eighth or ninth century. The poem came to be incorporated in the Beowulf Manuscript—Cotton Vitellius A XV—near the year 1000. Whether or not the scribes who compiled Cotton Vitellius A XV made important alterations in the poem composed by the Beowulf Poet cannot be shown; but it is not likely that much was changed. Beyond this one cannot go in a survey of this kind; but it can be insisted that a theory of single authorship of a piece is much more practical than a theory of multiple authorship.

Needless to say, parallels to certain features of the Beowulf story appear in other Germanic literature. The conception of the fire-drake guarding a treasure is established in Germanic folklore; and in ***Beowulf*** itself there is reference to a combat between the hero Siegmund and just such a dragon. This may or may not be the same story as the one later attributed to Siegfried, son of Siegmund. It is sufficient to note that it affords a parallel. Then again, the deeds which Beowulf performed at the court of Hrothgar, when he rescued the Danish ruler and his people from the desolation wrought by Grendel and his dam, were evidently referred to other Germanic heroes, especially in the Norse sagas of the thirteenth century. The *Grettissaga* tells of a male and female monster, of men disappearing at night from a particular house; and the hero Grettir grapples with this gigantic female troll, cutting off her arm. There is even a cave underneath a waterfall, which the hero must reach by diving, and a magic sword hanging on the wall of the cave. The episodes are strikingly similar to those in ***Beowulf.*** The same reminiscences of these particular happenings appear in the *Thorsteinsaga* (*Vikinssonar*), the *Hrolfssaga,* and the *Ormssaga* (*Orms thattr Storolfssonar*).

A comparison of ***Beowulf*** with the superb Homeric poems is naturally highly disadvantageous to the Old English epic; but as a head-piece to English literature, ***Beowulf*** deserves a most honored position. The weakness of the poem lies in its architectonics, but too much has been made of its alleged laxity of structure. Perhaps the episodes are not always too well proportioned; yet when it is recalled that the entire work is a typical stringing together of separate epic materials, such a state of affairs is not surprising. On the other hand, Beowulf the hero, who is endowed with an undeniably strong personality, serves excellently as an integrating influence. Besides, it is impossible to deny that the poem has power, a massive strength, and a more than adequate amount of poetic atmosphere. In spite of its digressions, it tells its story well. Best of all, it touches the universal situation of danger to be faced and odds to be overcome, both outward terrors and inward fears, life for a people opposed to death for an individual. In these respects alone ***Beowulf*** has elements of true greatness. Yet it is a mistake to insist, as many scholars in the Old English period have done, that this poem is the only significant achievement of Old English literature. There are, as it happens, too many other pieces which can vie with it. But ***Beowulf*** admittedly has one point of preeminence.

> So the people of the Geats lamented
> The death of their lord, did his hearth-companions;
> They said that he was among the kings of this world
> The mildest of men and the most gentle,
> Kindest to the people and most eager for praise.

With this touching and simple little tribute the poem ends. Indeed, the hero himself has passed from the world more than two hundred lines before, to reappear only as a corpse on the funeral-pyre. The somber pomp of his obsequies has subsided. There is no reason to suppose that any more lines followed. Beowulf has departed to seek "the judgment of the righteous." He leaves no heir behind, probably not even a widow. If we are right in these suppositions, then ***Beowulf*** stands apart as the only complete heroic epic surviving from Old English literature—complete in its narrative and complete in its portrayal of a mighty man of deeds. (pp. 81-5)

George K. Anderson, "The Old English Heroic Epic Poems," in his The Literature of the Anglo-Saxons, *Princeton University Press, 1949, pp. 56-104.*

DOROTHY WHITELOCK (lecture date 1950)

[*Whitelock was a distinguished English scholar known for her contributions to Anglo-Saxon studies, including* The Beginnings of English Society *(1952) and* English Historical Documents c. 500-1042 *(1955; 2nd ed., 1979). In the following excerpt from a series of lectures delivered in 1950 and later published as* The Audience of "Beowulf," *she discusses the nature and interests of the Old English audience of* Beowulf *and posits a date of composition for the poem.*]

[The ***Beowulf*** poet] was composing for Christians, whose conversion was neither partial nor superficial. He expects them to understand his allusions to biblical events without his troubling to be explicit about them. He does not think it necessary to tell them anything of the circumstances in which Cain slew Abel, or when, and why, "the flood, the pouring ocean, slew the race of giants." He assumes their familiarity not merely with the biblical story, but with the interpretation in the commentaries—not, of course, necessarily at first hand, but through the teaching of the Church. His hearers would not have understood why it was "the race of giants" that were destroyed by the flood, unless they were aware of the identification of the giants of Genesis vi. 4 ("There were giants in the earth in those days"), with the progeny of the union of the descendants of Seth with those of Cain, a union thought to be implied in Genesis vi. 2 ("The sons of God saw the daughters of men, that they were fair"). The passing reference earlier in the poem to "giants, that fought against God for a long time; He paid them out for it" would have been altogether cryptic and obscure to a newly converted audience. In fact, it is unlikely that a recently converted people would have known the word the poet uses for giants, for it is a Latin loan-word coming most probably from the Latin Bible, and the poet gives no explanatory gloss. It is not the only ecclesiastical Latin loan-word which he uses; *candel* ["light"], used only in a metaphorical sense, applied to the sun, *forscrifan* ["to proscribe or condemn"], a formation from the Latin *proscribere* ["to proscribe"], are other instances; and, most significant of all, as Professor Girvan has pointed out [see Additional Bibliography], the word *non* has had time to be generalized from its original application to a church service at the ninth hour till it indicates merely a certain time of day. It is interesting to contrast the practice of the poet of the *Heliand* with that of the ***Beowulf*** poet in this respect, for while the latter says casually in a secular context "Then came noon of the day" the former normally glosses the term; for example, he says: "the noon of the day at the ninth hour" and "at noon, when it was the ninth hour of the summer-long day." It is only when he uses the term for the third time that he allows it to stand unsupported. The poet of ***Beowulf*** expects the word to be understood; more than that, the context in which he uses it suggests that it no longer even had an ecclesiastical flavour. (pp. 5-6)

An audience which understands biblical references will also be familiar with the stock metaphors of the homiletic tradition, themselves often of biblical origin. The poet is not afraid of being misunderstood when he speaks of "the slayer . . . who shoots wickedly from his bow" or of the man who, when the "guardian of the soul" sleeps, "is struck under his helmet with a sharp arrow." The metaphors of the spiritual armour against the arrows of the devil are too much the common property of sermon literature for it to be worth while to look for a specific source for their use in ***Beowulf.*** They occur, for example, in Vercelli homily No. IV. The poet need not have been conscious of passages like Ephesians vi. 16. What is important is that he regards such metaphors as instantly intelligible to his hearers, and this could not have been the position in the earliest days after the conversion of the English.

It is in keeping with all this that the poet assumes that the conception of a last judgement, of retribution after death for sins, of eternal life for the righteous, will be accepted without question. He does not labour these matters; he does not need to; he is not asserting them against a different point of view. His audience accept the Christian dogmas and the poem is free from religious polemic.

I would go further than claiming that the audience of ***Beowulf*** was thoroughly acquainted with the Christian religion. I believe that it was also accustomed to listen to Christian poetry. There is no general difficulty in the way of such an assumption, unless one wishes to date the poem very early indeed. (pp. 7-8)

[The] poet did not himself invent all his poetic expressions for Christian conceptions, but drew them from a common store that had gradually grown up among poets dealing with religious subjects. I will elaborate a little on this opinion. The poet uses a great number of Christian expressions that are also to be found in surviving religious verse. This verse shares with ***Beowulf*** not only many of the poetic periphrases for the divinity, such as *wuldres wealdend, lif-frea, wuldorcyning, sigora waldend, heofena helm, dæda demend,* but many other expressions also: e.g. *miclan domes* "of the great judgement," *werhðoo dreogan* "suffer damnation," *ece rædas* "eternal benefits," *lænan lifes* "of this transitory life"—all of them complete half-lines—, *God eaðe mæg* "God can easily," always used as a second half-line with its object in the following line. Much of the verse in which these expressions occur is probably later than ***Beowulf,*** none can be proved to be earlier, for I consider the expression *ece Dryhten* "eternal Lord," shared by ***Beowulf*** and Caedmon's Hymn, to be too obvious an epithet for the divinity for it to carry any weight in this argument. It would therefore be possible to claim that the other poets who use these expressions were borrowing them from ***Beowulf.*** But is it likely? It would indeed be odd if it first occurred to a poet whose theme is not primarily religious to invent so much new phraseology for Christian conceptions, sometimes apparently by translating expressions in the Vulgate or the early Christian hymns, and if subsequent poets, composing on religious themes, used this predominantly secular work as a store-house of Christian phrases. It is easier to imagine the ***Beowulf*** poet and these religious poets deriving the diction they have in common from the same source, earlier religious verse which has not survived. (pp. 9-10)

It is not necessarily a sign of very early date that the poet should expect his audience to be interested in the vivid and impressive funeral rites of the heathen period, and should therefore describe at length the ship-burial of Scyld and the cremation of Beowulf. It would be a different matter if it could be proved that these descriptions were based on eye-witness accounts. . . . [As] long as it is open to us to believe that these descriptions were drawn from earlier accounts, in poetry or otherwise, we need not date the poem within living memory of these ceremonies. The poet may have found similar scenes described in the sources from which not only he, but his hearers also, had gained their knowledge of the heroic stories alluded to in the poem. . . . [Before] so Christian a poet—and here I would add so Christian an audience—can take pleasure in detailed accounts of heathen burial rites, those rites must be so far in the past as to have lost much of their association with other, more obnoxious, heathen ceremonies. As long as the fate of Christianity in England was in any way insecure, its more pious adherents could hardly enjoy hearing of the practices of a heathenism from which they had only recently been released, even if purely heathen poems were still being listened to by their less religiously minded contemporaries.

Neither is it a sign of early date that the audience is assumed to be interested in the blood-feud, to judge by the frequent references to stories which turn on this motive. If this implies a people not fully weaned from heathen ethics, the same could be said with equal justice of the Anglo-Saxons throughout their history. For the duty of protecting one's kindred, or one's lord, or one's man, and of exacting retribution from the slayer and his kindred if any of these were killed, was not superseded by Christianity. (pp. 12-13)

It think it is important, if we wish to estimate the effect of our poem on its contemporaries, to realize that there is no period in Anglo-Saxon history when the interest taken in the carrying out of vengeance would be merely antiquarian. The tales referred to in the poem would not be regarded simply as violent, dramatic tales of the bad old days, or, in nostalgic mood, the good old days. . . . [Any] man of the audience might find himself suddenly forced to become an avenger by necessity, perhaps in circumstances that involved his acting counter to his inclination and affections. The dilemma of an Ingeld or a Hengest might one day be his own. The poet's allusions to characters such as these give his poem more than an ''historical'' background; they hint at a problem that was real to the poet's contemporaries. (p. 17)

One may reach the conclusion that the audience of ***Beowulf*** was a Christian company, and one which admitted that vengeance, in unavoidable circumstances and carried out in accordance with the law, was a binding duty. This second consideration is of no help at all in our dating of the poem; but the first, its Christianity, is. The depth of its Christian knowledge is for this purpose far more important than that of the poet himself, for his Christian education might be exceptional; it would be unsafe to argue from it to the general conditions of his day. Nor would the extent of the audience's Christianity be of much assistance in dating the poem if there were any reason to suppose that the poet was addressing himself to ecclesiastics alone. My choice of the term ''audience'' has already indicated that I do not believe that ***Beowulf*** was composed merely for people who could read, which is almost equivalent to saying, for the clergy. Nothing that is recorded of the ecclesiastics of Anglo-Saxon England lends countenance to a view that they were in the habit of composing long poems on secular themes solely for circulation among themselves. It is difficult to imagine any bishop or abbot approving the use of so much expensive parchment for a work which he would not regard as directly edifying to men of religion. Some of these were interested in the tales of the Germanic heroes, and scandalized Alcuin in 797, but nothing in the letter in which he reproved the monks of Lindisfarne for their interest in songs about Ingeld suggests that this taste was pandered to in monastic scriptoria. ***Beowulf,*** though it may contain elements intended for edification, is surely first and foremost literature of entertainment, and as such, intended mainly for laymen. . . . It would be hazardous to postulate a considerable reading public of laymen, and I do not consider the length of ***Beowulf*** an insuperable obstacle to the view that it was intended for oral recital. It could easily have been delivered in three sittings. It is perhaps not by accident that the second episode, the fight with Grendel's mother, begins with a neat synopsis of what has gone before; this may be intended to inform newcomers and remind the previous audience of what has happened in the first part. The third episode, the dragon fight, is intelligible by itself. The ease with which the work divides in this way does not force us to suppose that it was intended for oral performance, but it supports such a view if this is probable on other grounds.

For a lay company to be so steeped in Christian doctrines, a considerable time must have elapsed since the acceptance of Christianity. This is still more certain if the terminology of Christian vernacular poetry has become so familiar that it can be used in a generalized and weakened sense; for, if we are to believe Bede, it was not until late in the seventh century that the native poetic technique was first applied to religious subjects. One must allow no short time for the spread of this habit till the point is reached when a poet could take for granted his audience's familiarity with the conventions of Christian poetry. But even apart from this consideration, it is doubtful whether the attitude to Christianity and the knowledge of it, which are implied by the poem, could be as early as the seventh century, and perhaps not even early in the eighth. The spread of the new faith was not so rapid as all that. . . . Bede, writing in 734, is of the opinion that the Church in Northumbria is far too understaffed for effective instruction in the Christian faith to be given to the laity throughout the kingdom. If, then, it is desired to date ***Beowulf*** in Bede's lifetime, it must be assumed that it was intended for a section of the community with a degree of religious education far above that of the average layman; or, alternatively, that it was composed outside Northumbria, and that this kingdom was worse off than other parts of England in this matter of religious education. (pp. 19-22)

In view of these difficulties, it might be as well to consider if we really are forced to date ***Beowulf*** in the age of Bede (*c.* 672-735). Of late years, it seems to have become widely accepted as a dogma that that is where the poem must be placed. (p. 22)

The poem is surely pre-Viking Age. It may be true that we should not attach an exaggerated importance to the high terms of praise and respect with which the poet speaks of the Danes and their rulers. Heroic poetry shows respect to kings and chieftains as such; the poet would probably have used similar terms of the Goths, the Lombards, or the Burgundians, or any other nation, if the story he was telling had happened to be located in their courts. It is not in order to pay honour to the Danes, but to heighten the dignity of his subject, that the poet lays such stress on the might and splendour of the court where his monsters' ravages take place. All this I would readily yield. Yet, I doubt whether he would have spoken in these terms during the Viking Age, or whether his audience would have given him a patient hearing if he had. It is not how men like to hear the people described who are burning their homes, pillaging their churches, ravaging their cattle and crops, killing their countrymen or carrying them off into slavery. So, if the poem is later than the time when Viking invasions began in earnest, about 835, it can hardly be placed before the tenth century, and even then it would have to be put . . . in the court of an Anglo-Danish king in the Danelaw. It could hardly be located in English England until the reign of Cnut, and that is later than our surviving manuscript. (pp. 24-5)

Though I cannot concur in [a Viking Age] date for our poem, I think it desirable to reconsider the evidence on which so many scholars put their final limit about 750. Why do they so firmly exclude the second half of the eighth century? The evidence they depend on is partly linguistic, partly historical. Metre shows that the poem contained some early linguistic features which do not occur in the poetry of Cynewulf and his school. But there is very little contemporary evidence to help us to put an absolute date to the sound changes involved, and even the arranging of the various poems in a relative chronology is completely valid only if there is reason to suppose that they come from approximately the same part of the country. The rate of development need not have been uniform in the various dialects. . . . I suspect that the belief that linguistic evidence forbids a later date than 750 for ***Beowulf*** is to a great extent based on too early a dating of the work of Cynewulf. . . . (pp. 26-8)

As for historical reasons for fixing the date of the poem . . . , it is not enough to show, however convincingly, that the poem fits into a certain historical context, unless one can also show that no other historical context exists into which it could equally well be fitted; and, as our evidence is fragmentary and unequally distributed, there may well have been contexts about which we know little or nothing which would have suited our requirements very well. The fullness of the records for the age of Bede has made it possible for a case to be made out for the court of Aldfrith of Northumbria (685-705) as the place where ***Beowulf*** was first produced; but enough is known about Eadberht Eating, king of Northumbria from 737 to 758, to show that he could have sponsored such a poem, while quite a number of rulers about whom, by accident, less is known may be eligible for the position of patron to our poet. On historic grounds alone, one could not reject the great Mercian kings, Æthelbald and Offa, or Ælfwald of East Anglia, to whom Felix dedicated his *Life of St. Guthlac,* or Alhred and Ælfwald of Northumbria, or Ine and Cynewulf of Wessex, or various Kentish kings. One can sympathize with a desire to assign ***Beowulf*** to the age of Bede, and thus make it contemporary with the masterpieces of Northumbrian art, such as the best Anglian crosses and the Lindisfarne Gospels; and I should like to make it clear that I do not wish to argue that the poem *could* not have been composed them, but merely that it *need* not have been. It is not that I wish to substitute a different date from that so commonly held, but rather to extend the later limit to include the later eighth century within the range of possibility, because I believe that the interests of Beowulfian scholarship will be best served by a refusal to settle securely into too definite a dating at present. . . . (pp. 28-9)

[Perhaps] I may be allowed to indulge in speculation on how the poet wished to affect [his audience], and to consider why he chose for his central subject a story of monster-slaying, using heroic stories merely as illustration or as background. It is no longer usual for scholars to spend time regretting that he did so, or accusing him of a perverted sense of proportion. He was composing for men of his own day, and he doubtless had good reason for his choice of theme. Nor is it likely that it was forced on him because all the good "historical" themes had been used up. His main story would be as real to his audience as would have been an account of the strife for the Danish throne among the members of the Scylding dynasty; and in the course of it, the poet has placed the race of monsters in relationship to a Christian universe, and has shown that they can be overcome by human beings of courage and fortitude who fight them with faith in God. He has shown that humanity is not left helpless in the hands of the evil powers. That was no trivial theme to the men of that day.

Yet one may wonder why he was so concerned that his hearers should at the same time have present in their minds certain stories about human conflicts. It was not, however, unusual for allusions to such stories to be introduced to enrich a theme. Even the small fragments which are all that is left of the *Waldere* poem—a work which, if it told the full story as known from other sources at the leisurely pace of these fragments, must have been little shorter than ***Beowulf***—include references in passing to the tales of Weland and Theodric; while in the short poem *Deor* allusions to heroic legends are used to point a general moral. In ***Beowulf*** such references add dignity and solidity to the central theme: it was not just any hall that was haunted, it was a splendid royal hall, famous in story; it was no vague and nebulous region which the dragon ravaged, but one inhabited by a mighty people, who had played their part in stirring events. Nevertheless, the so constant reminder of these things makes one doubt if this is an adequate explanation of their presence. Perhaps there is more to it than that.

I do not, however, believe that the poet's intention was to pander to his audience's taste, in that he expected it to be more interested in human histories of the clash of personalities, of the conflict between ambition and duty, between affection and duty, between conflicting duties; nor that he was himself irresistibly drawn to such subjects and thus inserted references to them on the slightest provocation. If this were so, why should he have failed to emphasize similar situations in his hero's career? What was Beowulf's dilemma when his lord and kinsman Heardred was killed by the Swedish king, Onela? He could, presumably, have raised the forces of his own province and brought them, to inevitable defeat, against the whole Swedish host; or he could come to terms and bide his time, though it meant accepting a kingdom from the slayer of his lord, and surely that would involve an oath of allegiance. He accepted the kingdom, but later he supported a rival of King Onela and helped to kill him, thus avenging his lord Heardred. The poet was eager to present a similar dilemma in the case of Hengest, but he skates over it hastily in his hero's life, so hastily that one hardly notices it. He simply says that Onela "let Beowulf hold the throne and rule the Geats."

The poet must deliberately have refrained from enlarging on this incident. To have done so would have been to spoil a contrast which, I think, he is making: not a contrast between unreal adventures and realistic stories, but one between noble, disinterested deeds for the good of the human race and actions of violence and passion, arising from divided loyalties, or, worse still, from ambition and treachery. The tales he recalls are well known to his audience, but perhaps he is putting an unusual type of emphasis on them, stressing the suffering caused to innocent persons rather than the triumph of successful warfare and vengeance. Maybe he is asking: "What would Hildeburh have said of the way in which the retainers of Hnæf repaid the shining mead?" Their loyalty cost her a son, a husband, and a home. And did not Hygelac bring disaster on his people when he made his celebrated Rhineland raid, attacking "out of pride" a people with whom he was not at war? There must, however, be no uncertainty about the beneficent effect of Beowulf's deeds; hence the poet does not care to emphasize a situation in his career that puts him on a level with the characters of heroic legend.

Besides providing a foil of this kind to the main events, the sub-themes have another result. The poet seems determined not to let us forget how temporary are the effects even of good actions in this world. Heorot is freed from Grendel, only to witness the destruction of the Scylding dynasty through the evil passions of its members; Beowulf ruled his people well and saved them from the dragon, but foreign enemies lie in wait to pounce on them and destroy them once their king is dead. It is this which has caused the poem to be called pessimistic. It is full of the sense of the temporal nature of all earthly success. But the hero lived his life so that the final words of the poem can claim: "Of the kings of the world, he was the mildest of men and the gentlest, the kindest to the people, and the most eager for fame"—words which remind us of what King Alfred said in his *Boethius:* "I desired to live worthily as long as I lived, and to leave after my life to the men who should come after me my memory in good works." Beowulf had taken Hrothgar's advice and chosen the *ece rædas* ["eternal gains"]. Seen in relation to the things which last for ever the poem is not pessimistic. (pp. 95-8)

Reconstruction drawings of the stag on the scepter found in the Sutton Hoo ship burial. The British Museum.

Dorothy Whitelock, in her The Audience of Beowulf, *Oxford at the Clarendon Press, Oxford, 1951, 111 p.*

ADRIEN BONJOUR (essay date 1950)

[*Bonjour is a Swiss academic and scholar whose professional interests span ancient and modern literature. In the following excerpt, he describes the artistic and thematic value of the episodes and digressions in* Beowulf.]

It is perhaps no exaggeration to say that few other features are more characteristic of the ***Beowulf*** than the use of numerous digressions and episodes. Though they represent less than a quarter of the poem, the investigations and comments to which they have given rise are probably as numerous as those which have been devoted to the rest of the poem. (p. xi)

What does this episodic material actually consist in? As regards the form and presentation of the digressional units, two types may be distinguished: the episodes and the digressions. Strictly speaking, an episode may be considered as a moment which forms a real whole and yet is merged in the main narrative, whereas a digression is more of an adjunction and generally entails a sudden break in the narrative. As a genuine type of episode we have, of course, the Finnsburg Tale. Though its style is somewhat allusive, that part of the legend recited by the scop at the royal court is complete in itself; as a specimen of what the king's gleeman used to sing on such occasions, it is part of the description of the festivities in Heorot. As a type of digression we may cite the allusion to Modthrytho and Offa (introduced with reference to the young Geatish queen), which rather abruptly interrupts the narration of Beowulf's return.

Needless to say such a distinction is not absolute. Some critics give the word "episode" a very restricted sense whereas others use the terms "episode" and "digression" as synonyms.

As regards their subject matter and length, on the other hand, the digressional units are of the greatest diversity. Events relating to early Danish history, to Geatish and Swedish history or to Germanic legends, as well as allusions to the hero's youthful adventures and references to Biblical passages, not to speak of moralizing or elegiac topics of a general character, all these form the substance from which the episodic matter has been drawn. In extent the digressional units "range from cursory allusions of a few lines," such as the anticipation of the burning of Heorot, "to complete and complicated narratives," such as the Finnsburg Tale or the Heathobard feud.

Now if each individual digression has its own problems—and some of them are of great interest and variety—the one great question which is raised by the presence of so many and various digressions in the poem is that of their relation to the main story. (pp. xi-xii)

Generally speaking . . . , the main advantages which the poem owes to the introduction of so many various episodes are the following. First, the very number and variety of the episodes renders the background of the poem extraordinarily alive; they maintain a constant interest and curiosity in the setting and, by keeping continuously in touch with "historical" events, represent the realistic note serving as a highly appropriate foil to the transcendental interest of the main theme with its highly significant symbolic value. The way in which many digressions are presented, the allusive manner that so often suggests rather than describes, the light and subtle undercurrent of implications and connotations that runs beneath the vivid pageantry of many scenes, all contribute to create that "impression of depth" which, as pointed out by Professor Tolkien, justifies the use of episodes and makes them so appealing [see excerpt dated 1936].

Now by what means did the poet manage, or at least attempt, to avoid the dangers and drawbacks that the use of so many various digressions was almost inevitably bound to carry with it? The most obvious of these drawbacks and the most difficult to overcome was that such an extensive use might have endangered the organic unity of the poem and created an impression of confusion highly detrimental to its artistic value. That many critics have been tempted to think that such was actually the effect of the episodes on the poem, or that some of them were not relevant, perhaps even interpolations, is proof enough of the reality of such a danger. We suggest . . . that the poet actually succeeded to a very large extent in overcoming that danger; and this precisely owing to his artistic sense.

In the first place he was careful to create a number of various links between the different episodes and some aspect of the main story, or between two or more convergent episodes so grouped as to achieve an artistic effect which has a bearing on the main theme; in the latter case each particular episode of the group often happens to have also its own links with its immediate context. These links are extremely varied, some of them very obvious and direct, others much more subtle and implicit—but, however differing in degree, they are all so many links of relevance that weave the main theme and its highly dramatic and diversified background into an elaborate and impressive tapestry.

Most of these links are made tangible by the constant use of parallelism and contrast. Such a repeated use of the element of contrast (to take but the favourite device of the poet) almost systematically applied, might easily have resulted in an appearance of artificiality and rigid symmetry. Yet, precisely because the very number and diversity of the episodes allowed so many variations in the use of the device, that danger was avoided too. Thus the use of the contrast, which is at the basis of so many of the connecting links, thereby contributes to avoid the confusion such a number and variety of digressions might have created; and reciprocally the very number and diversity of digressions, by permitting frequent variations in the use of contrast prevented its appearing as an automatic device suggesting an impression of sheer artificiality. There we have, indeed, a hint of the poet's artistic sense.

Even in episodes where no such links of relevance seem to be visible we have a particular atmosphere that merges at a given point in the general mood and contributes to its intended effect. Consequently we shall draw the important conclusion that behind all the episodes is found a definite artistic design, clear enough to allow us to say that each one plays a useful part—however minute or important—in the composition of the poem.

If we want to classify the digressions according to their respective rôles . . . we meet a difficulty owing to the fact that most of the digressions have actually more than one part to play. Yet, without aiming at completeness or, to put it in Professor Tolkien's expressive way, looking rather to the strategy and neglecting the minor tactics, we shall attempt a brief and schematical summary which, though imperfect, may be useful at least.

It will be convenient to distinguish two great divisions: in the one we shall class those episodes that concern, above all, the background of the poem: to the other belong the episodes directly connected with the main theme.

I. Here we have the group of four successive episodes dealing with the *Swedish-Geatish Wars*. Each one has its own immediate object, and yet the ultimate purpose of those digressions can only be fully understood if they are considered as a group. Following one upon another (in a succession unparalleled in the poem), they bring home to the audience the theme of the Swedish-Geatish enmity in an impressive gradation. The recurrence of the theme subtly conveys the impression of an impending doom, and leads to the epic prophecy of the downfall of the Geats after Beowulf's death. The dramatic effect of that prophecy is thus considerably heightened.

Indirectly linked with these are—in the first part of the poem—the *Finn* and *Heathobards Episodes*. By illustrating the inexorability of "wyrd" and the powerful urge for revenge in two rival tribes, both episodes, which have in common the theme of the precarious peace, serve as foreshadowing parallels to the Swedish-Geatish enmity and help to give it its full force. Thereby they prepare the way for that dramatic aspect which gives the background of the poem its portentous significance and finds its climax in the great epic prophecy.

The two *Elegies* finally, by their striking atmosphere of gloom and sadness, help to prepare, and effectively contribute to, the predominantly sombre and oppressive mood in which this climax, and more generally the end of the poem, is steeped. The Elegy of the Last Survivor, moreover, gives us an ominous and subtle premonition of the catastrophe in store for the Geats, so vividly suggested and almost materialized by the great picture of desolation closing the messenger's speech.

Carried to such a degree of dramatic force, this background is certainly the fittest and most effective for the main story; it echoes the great motive of which that story is likewise—though on a universal plane—the fine illustration: "līf is lǣne."

II. We may put the following digressions in a first group: the *Youthful Adventures of Beowulf,* the *Unferth Intermezzo* and *Beowulf in Friesland*. Their principal purpose is to contribute to the presentation and to our better knowledge of the hero by stressing some of his characteristic traits. Some are physical traits such as his fabulous strength and endurance which are to give us confidence in the success of his great undertaking. Others are psychological, such as his courtesy towards the King of Denmark, his keen wit in the dispute with Unferth and his sense of humour, all of which cannot but heighten our esteem of the hero. Besides, the story of the youthful adventures, Unferth's attack and Beowulf's version of the Breca contest are three movements which form a kind of dramatic prologue to the main action. Finally, the psychological situation which motivates the *Ecgtheow digression* incidentally sheds some light on one aspect of the Unferth incident.

A second group consists of the episodes known as *Sigemund and Heremod, Heremod's Tragedy,* together with the last Heremod allusion in conjunction with *Beowulf's Inglorious Youth*. Their object is a glorification of the hero by means of parallels and significant contrasts. The Sigemund and Heremod episode may indeed be considered as a hymn in praise of Beowulf, to which both the scop and the ***Beowulf*** poet contribute. As to Hrothgar's admonition, which again implies a contrast between Heremod and Beowulf, it is, at the same time—by its subtle anticipation of a new turn in Beowulf's life—a preparation and prologue to the hero's future career. Even the allusion to Beowulf's sluggish youth which emphasizes his prodigious ascent, and the way this ascent is implicitly contrasted to Heremod's disastrous downfall after a few years of great promise, again contribute to the glorification of the hero. One aspect of the *Modthrytho-Offa* digression may, perhaps, allow us to include it in the group.

The short digression on the *Fate of Heorot* and the allusion to the *Brosinga mene* give slight but significant touches representing first minor (and premonitory) variations on a fundamental theme in the poem: the transience of all earthly things, even the most beautiful. A "vanitas vanitatum" theme illustrated on a larger scale in the course of the poem.

The digressions of the *Biblical Group* show us, and represent, the point of fusion between Northern myth, which gave the poet the frame (or "accident") of his story, and Christianity, out of which he made the substance.

There only remains the *Scyld Prologue*. Together with the Finnsburg and Heathobards episodes which—though already grouped elsewhere—may, at the same time, be put under this new heading, it forms an artistically important group of episodes contributing to the unity of the poem. . . . [They] provide significant links between the two main divisions of the poem. In the case of the Scyld Prologue those links consist, on the one hand, in the parallelism between the "lordless" time from which the Danes suffered before Scyld's advent, and that which is announced at the end of the poem, and, on the other hand, in the symbolic value of both funeral scenes: one that opens the poem and suggests a brilliant future, the other that closes it and represents a glorious past . . . while imminent disaster is looming in the background. The transition between those two main divisions of the poem is furthermore prepared by the Heremod parallel in Hrothgar's sermon, the trend of which shows that the old King addresses and advises Beowulf as a future ruler. Consequently those two closely connected episodes can also be classed within the same group. (pp. 70-5)

[Each] digression brings its distinct contribution to the organic structure and the artistic value of the poem. In other words . . . , all of them, though in different degrees, are artistically justified. (p. 75)

The result obtained by the use of the artistic criterion, though it does not amount to an actual proof, thus decidedly points to, and eloquently speaks in favour of, the unity of authorship. Even if it does not exclude other possibilities concerning the genesis of the poem, the subtle and consummate art that underlies the use of digressions in ***Beowulf*** can best be explained by its unity of authorship. With the poetic power which reached such heights in the treatment of the main story, as interpreted by Professor Tolkien, an interpretation which we hold to be most attractive, can be paralleled the high artistic sense shown in the use of episodes.

Those aspects of the art of ***Beowulf*** that are revealed in the treatment of its episodes were indeed well worth pointing out. It is for that artistic achievement . . . quite as much as for its documentary value that the ***Beowulf*** poem deserves to survive, and with it the memory of its unknown author: "Hwæt!"—to use one of his own expressions—"þæt wæs gōd scop!" (pp. 75-6)

Adrien Bonjour, in his The Digressions in Beowulf, *Basil Blackwell, 1950, 80 p.*

C. L. WRENN (essay date 1953)

[*Wrenn was a leading English medievalist and the editor of an important edition of* Beowulf, *entitled* Beowulf and the Finnesburg Fragment *(1953; 2d ed., 1958). In the following excerpt, which is from the introduction to a 1973 revised edition of that work, he outlines the historical context of* Beowulf.]

The historicity of Beowulf himself must be, at best, but very shadowy. It is true that the mere attribution to him of supernatural feats of strength need not in itself imply that he had in fact no existence. For, as Ritchie Girvan has well argued in the third lecture of his *Beowulf and the Seventh Century* [see Additional Bibliography], such a view would also make King Richard I a mere figment of the mediæval romantic imagination because of the miraculous deeds attributed in romance to Richard Cœur-de-Lion. But from the beginning the poet seems to assume that Beowulf is capable of more than human actions while at the same time remaining a very human hero; and the fact that no clear allusions to this hero have so far been found outside the poem, and that the name Beowulf is only once found in O.E. [Old English] in ordinary use (in the *Book of Life* of the Lindisfarne monks of the early ninth century) and in two not very secure early place-names, tells against historical reality. True, we should expect the audience to look for a hero from the known or traditional Germanic past: but Beowulf may well have been known to them as a great hero from a kind of "historicized folk-mythology" much as was Weland (*cf.* l. 455), the Germanic hero, artificer in metals, and magician. True again, the one fully authenticated historical fact repeatedly mentioned in ***Beowulf*** is the closing event of the life of the Geat king Hygelac, Beowulf's uncle—and there are reasons for believing that the accounts of Geatish happenings in the poem are more accurate than those concerned with Hrothgar the Dane. Yet there is no mention of this greatest of poetic heroes known to England before the Normans in *Widsith,* which contains so much of remembered names from Germanic history. On the other hand, *Widsith* does not know of the undoubtedly historical Hygelac the Geat, though it knows both Hrothgar the Danish king and his nephew and successor Hrothulf.

In addition to the negative evidence, there is the positive: Beowulf's name does not alliterate with those of his family (including his father) or of his tribe. The feats attributed to him are not only more than human: they are paralleled in a number of well-nigh ubiquitous (but especially Scandinavian) folk motifs. In a poem where many of even the minor names can be documented, that of the hero is anomalous and almost anonymous. Much can be said for the view that the poet either deliberately chose a highly obscure figure for his hero, or indeed invented him out of whole cloth, in order to provide himself with a protagonist more adaptable to his purpose, one whose associations would not be so clear-cut as those of, say, Ingeld or Sigemund already were.

Hrothgar and Hrothulf are known to the Danish Latin chronicler of the late twelfth century, Saxo Grammaticus, to Old Norse saga-tradition, and to the Anglo-Saxon *Widsith*. Indeed, the tragic civil war between Hrothulf, who had benefited so much from the generosity of his uncle Hrothgar, and Hrothgar's son whom he slew, is used by the ***Beowulf***-poet as one of those ironic anticipatory allusions to events to come which are well known to the audience that are one of his devices for producing a tragic atmosphere. These lines (1014-19) are closely paralleled in *Widsith* 45-49. *Widsith* here mentions together (the second only by implication) the overcoming by the Danish royal pair of an attack on Heorot by the Heathobards under Ingeld, and the civil war between Hrothulf and Hrothgar's loyal retainers. Hrothgar is the Roe of Saxo Grammaticus's *Gesta Danorum,* and Hrothulf (*Hrothwulf* in *Widsith*) is Rolfo: in Old Norse the two Royal kinsmen appear respectively as Hróarr and Hrólfr. But very little is to be had from such sources about Hrothgar, who seems to have been a traditional figure whom our poet could freely adorn with patriarchal qualities not uninfluenced by the Old Testament. Much, on the other hand, is written of Hrothulf; but the saga devoted to his prowess, *The Saga of Hrolf Kraki (Hrólfssaga Kraka)* is a relatively late example of a type which the Icelanders distinguished from historical sagas proper by the name of *Sagas of the Men of Old (Fornmanna Sǫgur);* and the events it narrates are often remote from reality and include the account of a monster-slaying somewhat like those in ***Beowulf.***

Hrothgar's hall Heorot, which is also mentioned in the passage noted above from *Widsith,* has been placed very plausibly at a village now called Lejre near the ancient Cathedral town of Roskilde. That is to say, it has been assumed that this Lejre is the descendant of the *Lethra* of Saxo Grammaticus and the *Hleiðargarð* of the saga, which was the royal seat of King Hrólfr or Hrothulf; and there are certainly ancient grave-mounds near the site. That the Danes were already a powerful tribe by the close of the fifth century (when Hrothgar should have reigned) is attested by the Greek Procopius, who wrote in the middle of the sixth century, and by others.

Of Hrothgar's predecessors on the Danish throne, Scyld is the most significant, but scarcely historical except in a quite general sense as bearing a name meaning "shield" or "protector" which suggests that he embodies the legend of the founding of the Danish kingdom. He is called *Scioldus* by Saxo, which is a latinizing of the expected Norse form of the name. His "terrifying of the Heruli" (l.6) may, if the attractive conjecture which so explains the passage is right, indicate that he was remembered in tradition as a strong king who overcame the most terrible and warlike tribe then living in Denmark, and first consolidated the Danish state. But his legend has been confused with a folk-tale of a child who arrived in a ship with his head pillowed on a sheaf of corn as a sign that he would bring prosperity.

The Danish royal family were called *Scyldingas,* and in O.N. *Skjǫldungar (Scioldungi* in Saxo Grammaticus): and it is likely that the name *Scyld* was made for their legendary founder from this, corresponding to O.N. *Skjǫdr (Scioldus* in Saxo). Such warlike names as *Scyldingas* = "men of the shield" were frequent in the Germanic world, and we may compare *Wylfingas* of 471 with *Wulfingas* of *Widsith* 29—"men of the she-wolf" and "men of the wolf" respectively. Probably *Scēfing,* meaning "with a sheaf" (W.S. *Scēafing*), came to be regarded by folk-etymology as = "son of Scef or Sceaf" owing to confusion with the patronymic *-ing* at a time when the original had been forgotten. Hence the *Scēaf* of the genealogies. (pp. 34-6)

The Beowulf of l. 18, Scyld Scefing's son, seems to be an error for *Bēow* or *Bēowa* of the Anglo-Saxon genealogies through confusion with the more famous hero of the poem; but he must be considered quite without known historical support. Heremod, who is the subject of two historical references at ll. 901 ff. and 1709 ff. was a Danish king; but he seems to have been brought in by the poet to emphasize by contrast the heroic virtues of Beowulf. There are no details known from the other documents about Heremod; and it may be that he was a traditional figure about whom there were few things known to the audience, so that the author was free to portray him artistically as a foil to his hero. Unferth, whose name "unpeace" (or perhaps "nonsense") suggests that he was a literary creation rather than a historical person, serves the poet again as a foil to Beowulf, but also to bring out certain points in the hero's character. The other Danish persons in ***Beowulf,*** though some of them are recorded as names in Scandinavian material, cannot be said to have historical significance beyond the fact that they were known to tradition.

Turning now to the Geat characters in ***Beowulf***—apart from the hero, who has already been dealt with—we come to the one central and fundamental historical fact of the poem, upon which all chronological or similar examination must depend. Hygelac, Beowulf's lord, is recorded on unimpeachable evidence as having made the raid upon the Frisian territory of the Franks wherein he met his death (*cf.*ll. 1202 ff., 2354 ff., 2501 ff., and 2910 ff.) about A.D. 521. The Frisians concerned were part of the Frankish Merovingian empire at the time of Hygelac's campaigns; and it is from Frankish sources that the incident is first verified, in the *Historia Francorum* of Bishop Gregory of Tours, who wrote towards the close of the sixth century and lived only a generation after the event he describes. Gregory does not mention the name of the tribe attacked, but only that it was at a village in the kingdom of Theudoric (the Merovingian king) that Hygelac made his raid. (pp. 37-8)

[Hygelac's] nephew Beowulf, who is said to have shared in Hygelac's last fight, has been shown to be possibly, but not probably, historical; and his deeds in Heorot would have occurred near the beginning of the sixth century. But it may seem strange that so relatively little is known historically of these Geats despite the one outstanding fact of Hygelac's raid. The Geats . . . seem to have lived in southern Sweden in Götland. . . . The wars between Geats and Swedes which figure in the latter part of ***Beowulf*** give the impression of authenticity; and the fact that the Geats are not heard of in history after about the middle of the sixth century corroborates the implication in ll. 2999 ff. and 3015 ff. of the complete overthrow of the Geats by the Swedes after the death of Beowulf. While the O.E. heroic tradition in poetry knows something of the Danish royal family and its doings, as witness *Widsith* in its allusive reference to Hrothgar and Hrothwulf, we know of the Geatish kings and their deeds only through prose histories and the account of Hygelac's last raid given in the [eighth-century collection of stories about monsters and strange beasts known as the] *Liber Monstrorum* because this gigantic king's bones were preserved to be shown to visitors on an island at the mouth of the Rhine. Miss Whitelock pertinently asks whether the poet of ***Beowulf*** may not be giving the Geatish happenings in relatively fuller detail than Danish events just because he must assume less knowledge in his audience of matters of Geatish than of Danish history. . . . Yet, though *Widsith* knows nothing of the Geatish royal family, the fact that the Geats are among the peoples visited by the Traveller may imply that the poetic tradition of the heroic age did indeed include them. It may be that it is merely the very fragmentary state of the surviving O.E. poetry which is responsible for this odd-seeming gap concerning the Geats. Nothing is known to history for certain of any of the Geatish kings save only Hygelac, the evidence for whose historical existence is the basic fact in ***Beowulf*** for the historian.

The Goths, whose traditions so often appear in Germanic heroic poetry, supply one definitely historical name in ***Beowulf***—that of the far-famed Ostrogothic king Eormanric, who reigned over a vast empire in central Europe and died about the close of the third quarter of the fourth century when his empire fell to the Huns. This king, called in Latin *Ermanaricus,* is described by an almost contemporary historian, Ammianus Marcellinus, and more fully by the Gothic historian Jordanes in his *Getica* of the mid-sixth century. Eormanric, the ruthless hero-king, receives four mentions in *Widsith* (8, 18, 88, and 111), and is the subject of a longer passage in *Deor* (21-26); and it is evident from these that the story of his might, wealth, and ruthlessness was one which an Anglo-Saxon audience could be assumed to know well and to recognize by the smallest allusions. The ***Beowulf*** reference (1200-1) merely implies this legend in alluding to Hama's stealing the magic necklace *(Brōsinga mene)* from Eormanric; so that nothing but the name can definitely be said to be historical in the strict sense.

Of the Swedish kings in ***Beowulf,*** Ongentheow is mentioned at *Widsith* 31, and is known in Scandinavian tradition as *Angantýr*. Like his father and son and nephew (who are not in *Widsith*), he has been thought to have been buried in a mound at Old Uppsala, though he is not treated in the Old Icelandic saga of Swedish kings, the *Ynglingasaga,* nor by Snorri Sturluson in his historical work *Heimskringla* of the thirteenth century. He must have been killed early in the sixth century, as the fight in which he lost his life (***Beowulf*** 2484 ff.) took place early in Hygelac's reign. Along with his sons Onela (O.N. *Áli*) and Ohthere (O.N. *Óttarr*) and his nephew Eadgils (O.N. *Aðils*) he has been authenticated by archæologists as well as in Scandinavian tradition—though these others are touched upon definitely in the *Ynglingasaga* and by Snorri, as he is not. The historicity of the royal Swedes of ***Beowulf*** has been confirmed by work done in the last thirty years on the famous burial-mound of *Óttarr Vendilkråka* (Vendel-crow) at Vendel in Sweden, where Ohthere or Óttarr (cf. ***Beowulf*** 2932 and elsewhere) was buried about the year 525 A.D. . . . . If the evidence of the Óttarr burial-mound and those at Old Uppsala which are to be dated in the first part of the sixth century—just about the time when the burials must have occurred—agrees clearly with the accounts of Ongentheow, Onela, Ohthere, and Eadgils in ***Beowulf,*** and if the Scandinavian traditions in literature generally also are consistent with our poet's statements and allusions, then we may fairly conclude that the Swedish events in ***Beowulf*** are mainly historical.

Of the less clearly mentioned peoples in ***Beowulf,*** there is no doubt about the Franks, nor of the Frisians and Hetware who lived within the Frankish Merovingian empire. Though the MS. spelling *merewioingas* (gen. sing.) at l. 2921 looks corrupt, this reference to enmity from the Merovingian king, caused by Hygelac's part in fighting the Hetware, seems to fit in excellently with its context. But the Heathobards of the so impressively poignant and puzzling Ingeld episode (2024 ff.) have not been identified, though the alluding passage in *Widsith* ll. 45-49 to the destruction of Ingeld and his *Heaþobeardan* in their attack on Heorot pointedly seems to parallel ***Beowulf*** ll. 81-85 and ll. 1013-19, where the burning of Heorot through war between Ingeld and his father-in-law Hrothgar, and the feud between Hrothgar and his nephew Hrothulf after much friendship, are alluded to as devices of tragic anticipation. Ingeld, indeed, receives the support of apparently widespread popularity as a poetic hero among the early Anglo-Saxons, as implied in the oft-cited letter of *797* from Alcuin to the Lindisfarne monks, reminding them that the harp should not be listened to, but the Scriptures, the discourses of the Christian Fathers, not songs of the pagans, and posing the famous rhetorical question: "Quid enim Hinieldus [*Ingeld*] cum Christo?" ["What has Ingeld to do with Christ?"] There were clearly lays about the tragic feud of Danes and Heathobards and the tormented struggles in Ingeld the Heathobard prince between his love for his bride Freawaru (Hrothgar's daughter) and the duty of avenging the slaying in battle by the Danes of his father Froda. Ingeld receives more confused mention in Scandinavian tradition; but history, as distinct from heroic legend, has nothing definite to say of Ingeld and the Heathobards. (pp. 39-41)

[Offa, the] fourth-century king of the Angles on the Continent, is the centre of the episode beginning at l. 1931 dealing with his arrogant queen (Thryth) and his own noble deeds, and . . . this same Offa is especially praised in *Widsith* (35 ff.) and in a way which might be an indirect reference to Offa's Dyke. As this earlier Offa is well attested by other historical evidence . . . and was the direct ancestor of the historical Mercian king Offa II who reigned over a wide Mercian empire in the latter half of the eighth century, we may regard him as connected with a genuinely English part of the background to ***Beowulf.*** Finn, son of Folcwalda, who appears in ***Beowulf*** (the Finn episode beginning at 1068) and in the *Finnesburg Fragment,* is also attested by *Widsith* (27). This Finn, who rules a branch of the Frisians both in ***Beowulf*** and *Widsith,* like Offa the Angle, is named in the *Mercian Genealogy* of the ninth century . . . , as are also Offa's father Garmund (*Wermund* in the *Genealogy*) and his son Eomer (written *Eamer* in the *Genealogy* and by scribal confusion *Geomor* in *Beowulf* 1960). Now Finn, who rules the East Frisians, seems in the episode about him in ***Beowulf*** to be also a Jute (Jutes and Frisians being very closely related ethnically and linguistically) who could rule Frisians from somewhere just outside of Frisian territory proper, and to have had his own Jutish *comitatus*. But beyond this kind of hypothetical connexion with perhaps the Jutes of Kent, Finn's connexion with England cannot be pressed. (pp. 43-4)

With Hengest, who figures in both the Finn episode of ***Beowulf*** and in the *Finnesburg Fragment* as well as in the *Mercian Genealogy,* we are on far more important ground: for if Hengest is to be connected with England, he must be the Hengest of history and therefore the one authentic character in the poem who played a direct part in English history. If the *Healf-Dene* of ***Beowulf*** 1069 may be taken as a band of Jutes who had taken service with the Danish king under their leader Hnæf—and because they are among tribes serving the Danes are called "Half-Danes" as well as Danes (1090)—then Hnæf's successor in the leadership of these Half-Dane Jutes is Hengest, who could fit into the framework of history in the poem as the Hengest who conquered Kent in the middle of the fifth century according to tradition as preserved in the *Anglo-Saxon Chronicle*. The archetype of the *Finnesburg Fragment,* a poem preserved only in Hickes's version from a lost eleventh-century copy, seems clearly to have been in an older heroic style than ***Beowulf,*** and the Finn episode, based on the original of the *Fragment,* one may suppose, was thought of as being recited by Hrothgar's scop (1068 ff.) at the beginning of the sixth century. Now, allowing for the usual space of about a hundred years (which it seems to require for an historical event to become an heroic legend), we might take the story of Finn and Hengest as dealing with events which occurred in history early in the fifth century; so that a young Hengest the Jute could have performed the deeds alluded to in the Finn episode and *Fragment* before coming to conquer Kent in the middle of that century. The "historical" Hengest appears pretty consistently in Old and early Middle English tradition (*cf.* Lazamon's *Brut*) as both an exile and a mercenary—exiled from his Continental home and taking mercenary service under the British king Vortigern. In the Finn episode too he seems to have both these rôles. As a "Half-Dane" (1069) he seems to be a mercenary—and since Hnæf is *hæleđ Healf-Dena,* Hengest must be also a Half-Dane as his successor, and therefore a Jute; and at l. 1137 it is Hengest who is the "exile" (*wrecca*). (pp. 44-5)

It is inevitably difficult or impossible certainly to distinguish heroic legend from heroic history, or again heroic legend from folklore proper; but one can recognize several heroic legends which cannot be properly historical in ***Beowulf*** but which we know from Germanic literature to have been part of the Anglo-Saxon poetic tradition. Mention has already been made of the magician smith Weland, who is said at l. 455 to have been the maker of Beowulf's corslet, which was an heirloom from his grandfather the Geat king Hrethel. (p. 46)

Another famous Germanic legend is that of the necklace *Brísinga men* in the Edda, made originally by the *Brīsingas* or "fire-dwarfs," originally belonging to the goddess Freyja, which possessed magical properties. By a scribal error this magic necklace appears in ***Beowulf*** (1199) as *Brōsinga mene,* where it seems to have been stolen from the fabulous treasury of Eormenric the Gothic emperor, by Hama. (pp. 46-7)

More significant is the legend of Sigurðr and his slaying of a treasure-guarding dragon in the Sigemund episode beginning at l. 874. This tragic tale is told in the Old Icelandic Eddic poems and in the later saga of the Volsungs. . . . In ***Beowulf,*** it would seem, the deeds of the son Sigurðr have been transferred to his father Sigmund (Sigemund); but it is quite as likely that the Old English, being set down several centuries before the Norse accounts, has the older tradition, and that it is right in that sense in attributing the dragon-slaying to Sigemund rather than to his son Sigurðr as do all the Norse sources. His other son and nephew is called *Sinfjǫtli* in Old Norse, and *Fitela* (879) in ***Beowulf***—Fitela being a shortened form of his nickname. This is not found in the Old English. But Fitela plays only a secondary part in ***Beowulf***: it is his father Sigemund who slays the dragon, though Fitela had shared many of his strenuous heroic adventures. This cycle of tales of Sigmund and Sigurðr is one of the greatest and most moving Germanic heroic tragedies, which caught the sombre imagination of the whole Germanic people, and has left us the great poetry of the *Nibelungenlied* and is nowadays familiar to its widest audiences in the operas of Wagner (in which Sigurðr has become the German Siegfried). It is right that the poet of ***Beowulf*** should have chosen the most poignant of ancient Germanic tragic tales to foreshadow at long distance the end of his own hero. (p. 47)

The ancient Germanic world endowed weapons with something like a personality, and hence swords with proper names, like Beowulf's sword *Nægling* and Unferth's *Hrunting*. The golden-hilted sword "made of old by supernatural beings" with which Grendel's mother had been slain (1677) is described (1688 ff.) as having pictured on its blade the *Genesis* story of the flood and of the overthrow of the giants, with runes engraved on the golden plates of its hilt, in a manner blending Christian and pre-Christian styles which reminds one of the Franks Casket: and it is worth noticing how the Biblical story has been used in exactly the same way as the Germanic legends proper. (pp. 47-8)

The heroic legendary material . . . in ***Beowulf*** plays a very considerable part in framing the proper setting for the tale of the poem. But, unlike the historical elements, it cannot be explored with any precision, nor the results of such exploration effectively checked. But that it is like the historical material proper in being taken from a shared inherited culture by the poet for his audience cannot be doubted. The problem of the Ingwine is one in which heroic legend touches folklore and mythology. . . .

It is obvious that the simple tale which is the primary plot of ***Beowulf*** is a blend of heroic traditions with folklore and mythology. Demons and such supernatural beings of evil were part of human life in Anglo-Saxon times, as can be seen from the many place-names which commemorate haunted cliffs and even dragons. . . . There is a well-known passage in the so-called *Gnomic Verses* saying that a dragon is in the habit of dwelling in a barrow: and it is not difficult to see how the notion of some supernatural power guarding the treasure-filled barrow in which a great chieftain had been laid to rest grew up. For a stupendous expression of the powers of evil which a hero must fight, the dragon would come quite naturally to the Anglo-Saxon poet and his audience; and both would have been already familiar with tales of similar beings. Similarly, both Grendel and his mother must have come at some point from folklore, and the same type of conflict as those of Beowulf with them is found in Old Norse saga. The saga of the historical and well-authenticated Icelandic hero Grettir (who was killed in about the year 1031) attributes to him two fights against supernatural beings—the one closely resembling Beowulf's fight with Grendel, and the other that which he had with Grendel's mother in the demon-haunted mere. The resemblances are too close to be fortuitous; and one must suppose common folkloristic elements lying behind both—since the late thirteenth-century *Grettissaga* cannot be supposed to have "borrowed" these ideas from *Beowulf,* which was not then known in Iceland. (p. 49)

The hero who was thought to be sluggish and of little worth as a boy is typical of folklore of the widest distribution. Of Beowulf is said (2183 ff.):

> For a long time he was contemned, as the children of the Geats knew him not to be brave, nor would the lord of the Geats do him much honour at the mead-bench. They very much suspected [that] he was slothful, a feeble princeling.

The Latin *Lives of the Two Offas (Vitæ Duorum Offarum),* written *circa* A.D. 1200 at St Albans Abbey, attributes miraculously cured dumbness to the early years of both Offa the Angle (the hero of the episode in ***Beowulf*** in ll. 1931 ff.) and to the great King Offa II of Mercia of the late eighth century: and Grettir, in chapter 21 of the *Saga,* shows the same feature of youthful slackness. To this day there is remembered in Denmark the famous Holger the Dane, pictured as a boy of twelve asleep through the ages, leaning over a table with a vast beard, too slothful to use his great strength till a time shall come when Denmark shall be in its utmost need: then he will arise and save his country. (p. 50)

The poet of ***Beowulf*** drew on two traditions: Germanic for his verse-form, history, geography, social and physical culture, folklore, and myth; Romano-Christian for some of his diction, symbolism, Biblical and patristic learning, classical parallels, and hagiographical models; and both for many of the genres subsumed in his overall structure, such as elegy, flyting, gnome, encomium, allegory, set speeches, and his conceptions of epic and tragedy. The more overt of these two traditions is the less well documented outside the poem itself: we have a fragmentary O.E. poem on Finnesburg, literary analogues for the Sigemund episode, evidence that there was an Ingeld lay, and a hint at least from lines 499 ff. that there may have been a Breca lay as well; but otherwise little can be said about the form in which the poet encountered the Germanic material or the way in which he learned the verse-form through which he mediated it. Much more remains to us of the Latin tradition, both classical and Romano-Christian, that characterized Anglo-Saxon culture of the eighth century, but its impact on the poem is at most covert, and hence a matter of interpretation in which no clear consensus has developed. . . . What, then, can truly be said of "sources"?

First, it will now be clear that the central notion of Beowulf's fights with the monsters may have been suggested by legend and folklore and the beliefs of later Germanic paganism—since doubtless the beliefs of the pagan Norsemen would be shared by the immediately pre-Christian Anglo-Saxons, at least in fundamentals. Secondly, the historical setting, which adds dignity and the feeling of greater reality to the main subject, would be derived from already existing poetry and other oral traditions; this too would apply to the quasi-historical heroic legends. The primary sources, then, are the inherited traditions of the poet's own people.

But the implicit symbolism in the accounts of Grendel and his mother, for instance, suggests that the newer Christian inheritance, which an early eighth-century poet and his audience would share, is also a source: and . . . the use of expressions which link the monsters with devils in early Christian style, such as *man-cynnes fēond* and *helle hæfta,* or the use of the pre-Christian Germanic word *hell* with some of the newer Christian implications. Such expressions are mostly in the poet's own moralizing comments or asides, and neither Beowulf nor the other characters (except Hrothgar) use specifically Christian—as distinct from merely monotheistic—expressions. The Bible itself is, however, assumed to some extent to be known to the audience, though Cain and Abel (*cf.* ll. 107-8 and 1261) are the only Scriptural characters in fact named. There is clearly assumption of remembrance of the passage in Genesis vi. 4 ff. in the description of the account of the giants and their destruction by the Flood engraved on the blade of the ancient sword of ll. 1688 ff. (pp. 51-2)

[The poet] of ***Beowulf*** must have known the new Christian heroic poetry introduced by Cædmon, and . . . at least the older parts of the *Genesis A* poem in the Junius MS. were almost certainly in his mind. Even though it be true that lays of the creation of the world by God are by no means confined to Christian sources (as can be seen from the early part of the *Vǫluspá*), the scop's song at ll. 90 ff. is clearly derived from the story in Genesis, and the expression *se Ælmihtiga* (92) points to Christian setting. . . . But the Scriptural influence is generally rather implicit than explicit: and naturally, as the poet is carrying his audience back in imagination to a pre-Christian antiquity, specific Christian references are not normally appropriate and are avoided. Hrothgar, like Beowulf, acknowledges God, who receives his thanks for favours: but neither—except in the famous homily of Hrothgar at ll. 1724 ff.—shows specific Christian beliefs. (p. 53)

Another possible "source" is Virgil's *Æneid,* in which it is not very difficult to find parallel passages to ***Beowulf.*** The phrase *under sceadu bregdan* of l. 707 makes one think of the *ire sub umbras* ["ire beneath the shadows"] of Dido's last words in *Æneid* IV on her death: but such a metaphorical expression has naturally and quite independently arisen in many languages. . . .

We may conclude . . . in quite general terms—since there can be no more specific details—that the sources of ***Beowulf*** are the inherited culture and traditions, both Germanic and Christian, of the poet's own people, including history, heroic pagan story, and the Cædmonian heroic style; and secondarily, the Bible and familiar expressions from the Fathers. It is possible, too, that there may be some general influence from Virgil, though ***Beowulf*** is not in any way an epic in the Classical sense, nor a patriotic poem, nor even a narrative of its hero's life; further, that the poet knew heroic lays such as those of Ingeld and Finn, and possibly also an elegiac poetic treatment of Beowulf himself. (p. 54)

C. L. Wrenn, in his Beowulf, with the Finnesburg Fragment, *edited by C. L. Wrenn, revised edition, St. Martin's Press, 1973, 301 p.*

E.M.W. TILLYARD (essay date 1954)

[Tillyard was an English scholar of Renaissance literature and the author of widely respected studies of John Milton, William Shakespeare, and the epic genre. In the following excerpt from his influential study The English Epic and Its Background *(1954), he evaluates the claim that* Beowulf *is an epic.]*

From what remains of Old English narrative poetry it seems that a principal part of its strength lay from beginning to end in what can be called the heroic episode. ***Beowulf, Waldhere,*** the *Fight at Finnesburh, Judith, Andreas,* and the *Battle of Maldon* ranging from the early eighth to the eleventh centuries, can all be put in that category. Whether ***Beowulf*** breaks out of it into that of the epic is not likely to cease to be a matter of dispute. The answer does not depend ultimately on the facts of quality or cultural affinities. It seems agreed that ***Beowulf*** is very good in its way. And it does not make a fundamental difference how much Christianity and sophistication you see in it. Even if the author was a monk who had read Virgil and had modelled Beowulf's reminiscences on Aeneas's (as an extreme view would make him), it remains true that what gives the poem its character is its picture of early Teutonic life and morality. Even if Hrothgar and Beowulf have some share in the Christian virtue of patience, we should not dream of going to ***Beowulf*** rather than elsewhere to find a classic expression of that virtue. In emphasis the Christian patience pictured in ***Beowulf*** counts for little compared with a tradition of daring and of endurance that long antedated the arrival of Christianity among the Anglo-Saxons. It may be that eighth-century England showed an astonishing mixture of English and Mediterranean and that we should not forget that ***Beowulf*** and Bede's *Ecclesiastical History* are near each other in date. But once again it is not to ***Beowulf*** that we go to become greatly aware of that mixture. Primarily ***Beowulf*** depicts the old Teutonic world, and the present question is whether it does so broadly enough and at the same time dramatically enough to reach to epic height.

Intensity of a sort no one can deny to ***Beowulf.*** The descriptions of Beowulf's journey to Heorot, the watchman's challenge to him and his company when they land, and of the journeys to and from the mere are brief and clear and exciting. Beowulf's own courage is cool and powerful to a degree, as when he tells Hrothgar before the fight with Grendel that he will need no burial if he loses, for Grendel will gnaw his bleeding body as he carries it to his lair. But one has only to think of the *Odyssey* on the one hand and of the Icelandic Sagas on the other to see that the world of ***Beowulf*** is comparatively narrow, that the poem does not truly fulfil the epic function of conveying the sense of what it was like to be alive at the time the author wrote. There are no touches of ordinary feeling or of homely quotidian life to supplement the grim exercises of heroic will-power or princely bounty: nothing like the sudden picture of the labourer returning home with the mist rising behind him which Milton inserted in the last lines of *Paradise Lost*. The true epic amplitude is not here. The characters are powerful and adequate to the comparative narrowness of the world they inhabit. But there is no inner conflict, and they do nothing to widen by their own richness the setting in which they are placed. However evolved and sophisticated the art of ***Beowulf*** may be, that sophistication does not include the motivation of the actors. (pp. 121-22)

E.M.W. Tillyard, "The Outskirts," in his The English Epic and Its Background, *Oxford University Press, 1954, pp. 113-33.*

KINGSLEY AMIS (essay date 1957)

[An English novelist, poet, essayist, and editor, Amis was one of the Angry Young Men, a group of British writers of the 1950s whose works expressed bitterness and disillusionment with society. Common to the fiction of the Angry Young Men is an anti-hero who rebels against a corrupt social order in a quest for personal integrity. Amis's first and most widely praised novel, Lucky Jim *(1954), is characteristic of the school and demonstrates its author's skill as a satirist. Amis has since rejected alliance with any literary group, maintaining instead that he is only interested in following his artistic instincts. Throughout his career, Amis has also had an interest in science fiction, coediting the* Spectrum *science fiction anthologies and writing one of the first major critical surveys of the genre,* New Maps in Hell *(1960). In the following excerpt from his review of David Wright's 1957 prose translation of* Beowulf, *Amis questions the literary merits of the poem.]*

Deciding which is the most boring long poem in English is, even given the existence of *Piers Plowman,* by no means an easy task. If the matter is probed, a correlation emerges between a proneness to the more spacious or inflatable poetic forms and an indifference to what has often been considered the prime literary subject, relations between human beings. Thus *The Faerie Queene* and *Paradise Lost,* in their different ways the two most ambitious poems in our language, are also among the most remote and frigid. . . .

The Old English poem ***Beowulf,*** though not on the same scale as the works I have mentioned, has the property of seeming to be. It occupies a unique position in both English literature and English studies. Its 3,200-odd lines account for something like one-tenth of the whole corpus of surviving Old English verse, an accident which has had some remarkable results. The poem, after more than a century of peaceful ransacking and discussion by antiquarians and philologists, has comparatively recently attracted some attention as a literary work. This development can be traced back to the foundation of the Oxford English School and the inclusion within it of Old and Middle English studies in the evident hope of causing the syllabus to be, or look, as hard as that of other Schools. . . .

The result was a stealthy upgrading of Old and Middle English texts into a position of alleged aesthetic importance. . . . But it was the Old English stocks, helped on perhaps in spite of much talk about "sophisticated culture" by sentimentality about primitiveness, which really soared. ***Beowulf*** . . . [naturally] soared highest. After all, the thing was an epic, at least it has some narrative about it, and a hero, and one great single action—well, three actually, the last taking place fifty years after the other two, but that could be got over by discovering an "essential unity." ***Beowulf*** became a great poem—*nem. con.,* for the experts were all in the movement, and what inexpert dissenter could endure to gather ammunition by studying the text? . . .

With this established, there was now a theoretical extrinsic reason for going into all that stuff about the scribes and the transcripts and the relative frequency of the weak form of the adjective used without the article: it was like, or fairly like, getting up the references in *Paradise Lost*. The new situation, however, aggravated instead of lightening the burden of the student, who was henceforth required to think up reasons for admiring the poem as well as remembering why the impossible MS reading *hrærgtrafum* in line 175 is significant. But let this flash of science deceive nobody; I am not, thank heaven, an expert, and the merit I think I can glimpse in two or three Old English poems, and even here and there in ***Beowulf*** itself, is to that extent faint and far off. If I were an expert, no doubt I should be throwing imputations of greatness around with the best of them. Most scholars are men of foggy æsthetic sense, the ideal audience for their own propaganda; even so, the confidence with which these claims are made is astounding and discreditable. The body of Old English poetry is so meagre, one might have thought, as to defeat inquiry on many points prerequisite to the forming of a literary judgement. A good poem is not just good, but good of its kind: when, as with ***Beowulf,*** there is only one of the kind in existence, the critic would do well to move cautiously.

Mr. David Wright, introducing his prose version of the poem, is ready to affirm that ***Beowulf*** is great—a point, he adds quaintly, "until recently often overlooked." And why, or how, or in what is it great? The answer, for Mr. Wright, lies in its theme: "it is about how the human being ought to behave when he is without hope." Is this true of any but the closing stages? Alternatively, the theme is "the conflict of good and evil." Is it? Granted that it is, this conflict remains one between a man and three assorted monsters, and whatever weight of symbolism we may attach to these it is hard to see the core of the poem as existing in any but non-human terms. ***Beowulf,*** in fact, exhibits to the full that endemic weakness of [*Paradise Lost*]: poverty of human interest. This is perhaps debatable, but Mr. Wright's emphasis on theme has other aspects which connect with his emphasis on matters of construction and narrative—odd focuses of interest, incidentally, in a work so episodic, so slow-footed and so sparing of incident.

Kingsley Amis, "Anglo-Saxon Platitudes," in The Spectator, *Vol. 198, No. 6719, April 5, 1957, p. 445.*

ARTHUR GILCHRIST BRODEUR (essay date 1959)

[In the following excerpt, Brodeur discusses the most significant elements of Beowulf's battles with Grendel, Grendel's mother, and the dragon.]

A gold buckle found in the Sutton Hoo ship burial. The British Museum.

It is a far cry from any extant heroic lay to the complex and well-ordered poem of ***Beowulf.*** If that poem rests upon a number of lays, each of which presented a portion of the hero's career, then its author faced and accomplished a task much more involved than the mere joining of their narratives into a single work. He has so managed the substantially distinct parts of his hero's career that, though they constitute a deliberate balance, both exhibit the same heroic ideal; and in both parts, in triumphant death as in glorious victory, all the hero's words and deeds arise out of, and express, the same noble qualities of character.

The three great events of the main plot—the killing of Grendel, the victory over Grendel's dam, and the fight with the dragon—display striking structural similarities, and equally striking variety of narrative treatment. In each case, the inciting cause is very much the same: the destruction wrought by a monster; in each, the hero, after a hard and dangerous struggle, slays his foe—though the hero himself is fatally hurt in his last fight. In each, the fight is preceded by an exposition of the hero's state of mind; the fights with Grendel and his dam are each followed by his report of the combat to Hrothgar, and by an account of the gratitude and praise heaped upon him by the Danish king. Each of Beowulf's monster-killings is undertaken to deliver a people sorely afflicted; and in each case the people involved, though saved from present affliction, is nevertheless doomed to suffer ultimate catastrophe.

Yet, within these similar frames there is wide diversity: diversity in setting, in attendant circumstance, and in manner of treatment. . . . In his narrative of the fight with Grendel, the poet several times assures us of a happy outcome; yet he overbalances each assurance with effects of horror so calculated and climactic, and imparts so vividly the impact of the terror of battle upon his dramatic audience, that the listeners' sense of fear and peril is maintained almost to the end. In the story of the fight with Grendel's dam he deliberately withholds any assurance that the hero will prevail; and through impressively fearful setting and vivid alternation of the fortunes of fight he keeps us anxiously uncertain of the hero's victory, or even of his survival, until the instant before the means of victory is discovered and used. It is . . . quite otherwise with the dragon-fight: here we are told repeatedly that both Beowulf and the dragon will perish; and these direct forecasts are reinforced by expositions of the hero's states of mind, from just before battle is joined through each phase in the movement of the fight to the very end.

Quite evidently these differences in mood and treatment represent the author's deliberate choice: we are dealing with the work of a poet "who subdued existing narrative material to a controlling artistic purpose of his own." If what he told derives from popular and heroic tradition, the whole manner of the telling, the motivations, the characterization, the whole plan and direction of the story into a single heroic and ethical channel are the work of a fine craftsman and a great poet. Attempts to prove plural authorship, or to show that individual passages are interpolations, have shipwrecked on the tough cohesiveness of the work. The style of ***Beowulf*** is as nearly uniform as the style of so long a poem can be expected to be, and as varied as the effects at which the poet aims demanded: it is unique in power and beauty in the whole course of Old English poetry. . . . [So] large a proportion of the vocabulary of the poem is elsewhere unmatched that it presents every appearance of striking originality within a highly developed conventional usage. The well-designed, balanced structure which Tolkien discerned [see excerpt dated 1936], and the pervasive irony, no less than the magnificence of language, show the hand of an artist in complete command of his material and his medium. We have, then, no reason for surprise at the fine congruity between the major stages of the action and their settings.

If we compare the narrative of Beowulf's monster-slayings in Denmark with the corresponding action in any of the analogues, we discover two sharp differences: first, the settings of the combats in ***Beowulf*** are infinitely richer and more elaborate than the settings in any other version; and secondly, the settings in the epic are not only beautifully calculated to enhance the effect of the main action, but are also so contrived as to suggest something beyond it, something at once magnificent and tragic. The settings in the first part of the poem are at once dramatic and symbolic: they reveal a present splendor and intimate its imminent ruin.

These differences reflect, of course, dissimilar levels of tradition. Even in *Grettissaga* the underlying folk-tale of the purging of a hall still bears the stamp of its popular origin, although the story has been somewhat rationalized and elevated in consequence of its circulation among a logical-minded people and its attachment to the historical figure of Grettir. In ***Beowulf*** it has found its way into the poetry of art, and has been transformed through association with a royal court and princely personages—and finally through the genius of a great poet—into the stuff of heroic poetry.

The story of the purging of a hall of an invading monster or pair of monsters came to the author of ***Beowulf***—as it later reached the compiler of *Grettissaga*—in a form which required two distinct though not widely separated settings: the haunted hall, and the lair of the trolls that ravaged it. The more formidable of the two trolls made a practice of raiding the hall for his victims; the hero's first fight therefore took place (or, as in *Grettissaga,* began) in the hall. The second troll had to be sought out and destroyed in its lair. For us it is a minor matter that, in *Grettissaga,* it is the female monster which raids the hall and is killed first; it is of greater importance that both in the saga and in ***Beowulf*** the she-troll is the more dangerous adversary.

The differences in the action of these two versions concern us less than the differences in setting. In *Grettissaga* the hall is the house of a farmer; in ***Beowulf*** it is a royal residence. In *Grettissaga* the abode of the monsters is a cave behind a waterfall in a river-gorge near the house: the terrain is rough and mountainous, but it has none of the trappings of terror which envelop the Haunted Mere. Hrothgar's description of the region, and the poet's account of the march to it, seem to imply that a considerable distance separates it from Heorot.

These differences, to a degree, accurately reflect the differences between the cultural level, and the milieu, of the two versions: farmers' dwellings are common in Iceland, royal halls non-existent; and, . . . the Sandhauger episode in *Grettissaga* is relatively close to the folk-tale. But the poet of ***Beowulf*** was not content to use Heorot simply as the scene of the fight with Grendel; it is also the splendid and luxurious home of Hrothgar, and the setting of nearly all of Part I. We see the personages—Beowulf and his followers as well as the Danes—inhabiting this royal residence, enjoying all its pleasures and amenities: it is, indeed, the most comprehensive and detailed picture of Germanic aristocratic life that has come down to us from any source. The scene as a royal court was supplied by the poet's source; its lavish embellishment, its luxury and splendor, the courtesy and charm of the life within it so vividly pictured, are the gift of the poet. So, too, many of the features of the Haunted Mere may have been present in the poet's source; but it was certainly our poet who first perceived how admirably they could be used to envelop the fight with Grendel's dam in an atmosphere of terror.

Neither in *Grettissaga* nor in any of the folk-tale analogues is there any clear and logical link between the two monster-slayings: the second, where it exists, is motivated weakly or not at all. In *Grettissaga* the hero visits the gorge and finds the second troll merely out of curiosity: he does not expect to find another monster. The connection between the settings is the simplest possible: the house at Sandhaugar lies near the river. The two stages of the action are almost wholly unconnected. (pp. 108-12)

The very nature of the theme—the purging of a hall—requires the fight with Grendel to be staged in Heorot; the fury of the struggle is dramatically conveyed through the poet's report of its terrific din, the breaking of benches, and the almost shattering effect of the struggle upon the building itself. It is in the hall, too, that Æschere is killed; there, too, that Beowulf and his men receive rich rewards at the feast in celebration of the victory over Grendel; there that Beowulf brings his trophies, after the second combat, to astonish the Danes who had thought him slain. The unity of the action is provided by the hall Heorot itself. . . . (p. 113)

It might seem somewhat surprising that this combat with Grendel, fought to purge Heorot, should prove so much less dangerous to the hero than the fight with Grendel's dam. Yet it is so as well in all those analogues which preserve the twofold fight: the female monster is a much more desperate adversary than the male. Grettir, like Beowulf, is in grave danger of death in his fight with the she-troll, and has little difficulty disposing of her male companion. It is characteristic of stories of trolls that the female is the more aggressive and the more terrible opponent: few male monsters compare for sheer horror with the man-eating, hall-raiding she-troll killed by Arnljot Gellini; she is very like to her counterpart at Sandhaugar, and to Grendel's dam. The poet of ***Beowulf,*** in representing the male Grendel as the persistent and terrible raider of the hall, and permitting the female to invade Heorot only as her son's avenger, departed from an ancient and common pattern. We cannot tell whether this departure was of his own devising, or whether he found it in his source; at least, in the poet's hands the departure proved most fortunate, for it permitted him to order his hero's exploits climactically. It also involved him in a grave difficulty, which he resolved brilliantly.

The difficulty has left its marks on the story of the fight with Grendel: in spite of the long and horrific record of Grendel's ravages in Heorot, in spite of the carefully built effects of terror in Grendel's last march upon the hall, his horrible appearance within the door, and the devouring of Hondscio, Grendel does not give Beowulf a really good fight. Though capable of killing thirty Danish thanes in one night, there is no aggression left in him once he feels the power of Beowulf's grip; he struggles not to destroy, but to escape. Since there is little glory in an easy victory, the poet was compelled to find effective means of making Grendel *seem* a more dangerous enemy than he was. He achieved this precisely by making the most of Grendel's ruthless ravages among the Danes, by constructing for his last invasion of Heorot a tremendous machinery of terror, culminating in the ghastly devouring of Hondscio, and by imparting the sense of panic produced among the Danes by the din of the fight and Grendel's shrieks of pain. After the fight is over, the awesome power of Grendel is further communicated by the description of his monstrous hand and arm. Very skillfully the poet has made the fight seem worthy of the prize; actually it is not.

The poet was sufficiently remote from popular tradition to feel compelled to represent Grendel's dam as inferior in strength to her son; but the compulsions of his story could not be wholly escaped. His hero *must* come closer to death in the second struggle than in the first. His artistic sense pushed him in that same direction; therefore, having committed himself to the untraditional but logical admission that the she-troll was not so strong as Grendel, he was obliged so to manage Beowulf's combat with her as to place him in mortal danger. This he accomplished . . . through his skillful management of the conditions of the fight: Beowulf is seized unaware in the water, taken by surprise, and dragged down into a milieu unfamiliar to him and favorable to his antagonist. The poet's representation of the Haunted Mere is not the consequence of failure to apprehend the nature of the setting in the folk-tale; it results from the necessity resting upon him to fashion the setting so that it will both oppress the hero's spirit and place in his way obstacles calculated to prevent him from using his strength to best advantage. This he has done, and done triumphantly: for his description of the region of the mere not only accounts for the terror of the combat, but also constitutes one of the glories of the poem. (pp. 113-15)

[The poet] brings before us a twofold dramatic contrast. Against the magnificence of Heorot, the very building of which was so glorious an act, the ruthless incursions of Grendel and his dam stand out with greater horror; and after Grendel's death, the future treachery and murder of kinsmen afford a still more tragic contrast with present pride and glory. The first of these contrasts gives vividness and shocking force to the main action; the second lends tragic pathos to the matter of the subplot. After the slaying of Grendel, the darker side of the first contrast is represented by the killing of Æschere; the second contrast is subtly suggested in the narrative of the feast in Heorot.

Six hundred and sixty lines separate the conclusion of the fight with Grendel from Beowulf's encounter with Grendel's dam. This lull in the main action is occupied by an account of the celebrations of Grendel's death by the jubilant Danish warriors, and by a much longer account of the feast. (pp. 115-16)

The scene, stately and splendid, is suffused with tragic irony, displayed in two contexts. First, against the joy, the seemliness, and the splendor of the feast and the gift-giving, the poet reminds us that these Danes, still united in fellowship and loyalty, and imagining neither treason nor rebellion, will one day be divided by civil war; secondly, even as Hrothgar and his men leave the banquet and go to bed with full confidence that their afflictions are ended, the poet warns us that they are to be tragically disillusioned. The warning in lines 1233b-37a and 1240b-41 points in both directions; the lines following it reinforce the irony with a ringing affirmation of the vigilant valor with which the Danish warriors, full-armed, guard the hall—in vain.

The feast is treated at great length and *con amore*; on the surface, it exhibits every outward aspect of noble and generous conduct; underneath, it is omnious and threatening. Whatever basis there may have been in the poet's sources for a scene of jubilation, these tragic undercurrents, and the dramatic irony which edges the poet's treatment of his minor theme, are certainly his own; for them there could have been no model. Much of the external splendor of the scene must also have been of his creation; and there can hardly have been any source other than the poet's perceptive imagination for the balancing, against that magnificent background, of the hidden clash of loyalty with ambition, the rising conflict of opposed interests, and the subtly dramatic use of the queen's attempt to forestall fate. It is not the pageantry of the feast, but the manner in which the author places his personages within its setting and invests them with tragic meaning, which gives the scene its greatness. As, in the *Odyssey*, Homer used the visit of Telemachus to the court of Menelaus to exhibit the unhappy fortunes of the great Achæan lords after the fall of Troy, so the poet of *Beowulf* employs the feast in Heorot to foreshadow the ruin of the noble house of the Shieldings.

The poet's love of contrast has been frequently remarked; but it neither springs from a propensity to didacticism nor reflects undue preoccupation with "the unwar wo or harm that comth behynde." Contrast is the essence of all tragedy; and ***Beowulf*** is a tragedy. (pp. 116-17)

The most obvious contrast within Part I is that between the settings of the two combats: one, the stately and luxurious hall of Hrothgar and the gallant life of heroes for which it was designed; and the other, the terrible landscape of the Haunted Mere. The first envelops darker and deeper contrasts: first and most immediately important, that between the joys for which the hall was built and the bloody persecution of its inmates by Grendel; secondly, the contrast between the present solidarity and good-will among the Danes, and the treason and bloodshed to be enkindled by Hrothulf's ambition. The first warning of the troublous times in store for Hrothgar's realm occurs immediately after the announcement of his greatest peaceful triumph, the completion of Heorot and his munificence within it: "The hall towered, lofty and wide-gabled; it awaited the surges of battle, hostile fire; nor was it long until that edged hate between father-in-law and son-in-law was destined to awaken in furtherance of murderous hostility." Although Hrothgar and Hrothulf were to beat back the invasion of the Heaðobards, the stately hall was to be destroyed.

The setting for the second combat contains no such contrasts; but . . . the perfect congruence between it and the action within it is followed by a swift succession of striking dramatic contrasts. (pp. 117-18)

The contrast between present joy and future catastrophe in the narrative of Part I is afforded by the balance between the glorious events of the main action and the tragic subplot; by the underlying antithesis between the hero as God's instrument against the kin of Cain and the hero as prince and statesman vainly intervening in purely human affairs and frustrated by Fate. In Part II, Fate has tipped the balance against the hero, and this contrast vanishes; instead, the poet constantly confronts us with the contrast between past and present; between the heroic youth that has been and the heroic old age that has lost nothing of youth's courage and little of its strength, but well-nigh everything of its good fortune. Indeed, Part II is one long, mournful contrast to the splendor and glory of Part I. The mighty nation of the Geats has become weak; the hero is doomed to die, and his people to suffer conquest. This contrast is so swiftly introduced that it strikes us with sudden shock. . . . (p. 122)

The beautifully conceived interchange between Beowulf and Hygelac with which Part I concludes leaves the listener in precisely the state of mind which the poet must have intended. At this moment Beowulf is in the flower of youth and strength, and at the height of his renown; the Geatish kingdom is at the peak of its power. The great king has a matchless champion as his right-hand man, and they are united in a deep and abiding love. Hard upon this triumphant note comes, at once, the crashing dissonance of the opening of Part II. In a few breathless lines the poet announces the sequent fatalities which have weakened the Geats and left them ringed round with powerful enemies. Hygelac has fallen; his son Heardred has been slain in battle with the Svear. Beowulf has come to the throne, and has held it well for fifty winters—*until* a dragon ravages his land. The eleventh line, with its fateful *until,* forecasts the hero's own fall, which is to entail the ruin of his people. Of all the many contrasts in the poem, this is the most dramatic. Here, at the outset of the last action, the tragic close in anticipated.

It is a first principle of storytelling that setting must be appropriate to the action which unfolds within it. The major action of the second part of ***Beowulf*** is the dragon-fight; its causes are the theft of a precious vessel from the dragon's hoard, and the dragon's savage retaliation upon the Geats. Its vengeance is swift and terrible. . . . The hero must now meet the dragon, and both must die. (pp. 125-26)

The main action calls for one major setting: the barrow in which the dragon guards its treasure, with its immediate environs; and one minor setting, which is so barely sketched that one can hardly visualize it at all: that of Beowulf's cremation and entombment.

The major setting lacks the fullness, the complexity, and the vividness of detail which give brilliance to the settings of Part I (the hall Heorot, and the landscape of the mere). This is as it should be, in view of the singleness and the simple directness of the action of Part II. The second part of the poem concentrates upon the dragon-fight and its consequences for the hero and his people; there are no complicating factors. (p. 126)

The setting . . . is in its general outlines fixed by tradition; the poet elaborates the conventional aspects of a dragon's lair only by a somewhat detailed description of the barrow, and of the treasure contained in it as that treasure is examined by Wiglaf after the dragon's death. Those elements which impress one as of the poet's invention are the burning brook, the rocky approaches to the barrow, the stone "seat" on which Wiglaf sits to gaze on the stone "arches" of the barrow; and the account of the treasure (lines 2757-70). (p. 128)

The narrative of the dragon-fight is swift and furious; except for the lines which set forth the flight of Beowulf's thanes and explain the role of Wiglaf and the origin of his sword, it is uninterrupted. This single break is essential: the desertion of the thanes is required, to give full plausibility to the representation of Beowulf's mortal peril. The hero's men had not deserted him in his fight with Grendel, nor even at the Haunted Mere, when they thought him slain. It is the panic of all but one of his bravest men which convinces us that, in the dragon, he faces a foe far more terrible than Grendel or Grendel's dam. The intervention of Wiglaf is equally necessary, both to demonstrate the extremity of the hero's peril and to supply him, in his darkest hour, with a companion as loyal as he himself had been to Hygelac. Moreover, it is the devoted gallantry of Wiglaf which justifies Beowulf's sacrifice: if none of the Geats had stood by him, we should feel that their impending conquest by the Svear was fully justified, and that Beowulf's death for them was a futile gesture. Moreover the poet wished to assure us that, fatal as it was to prove to his people, Beowulf's fall did not leave the Geats utterly leaderless.

The main action, then, vigorous and fierce, and in the main uninterrupted, is enclosed in a setting the major elements of which are traditional, but which the poet has elaborated in his description of the barrow and the treasure. It remains, however, a setting appropriately lean and stark. This is to the good: in a more elaborate setting the action would have lost something of its fury and its force.

The minor setting, in the two scenes of Beowulf's burning and interment, is very lightly suggested. Poetic names adorn these scenes: the place of cremation is called *Hrones-næs;* the site of Beowulf's burial mound is *Earna-næs;* both are close to the sea. The mound is "high and broad, widely visible to seafarers"; a seemly wall is wrought about the hero's ashes, and the treasure is buried with him. The fashion of his pyre, and the account of his burning, resemble rather closely the details of the burning of the warriors slain at Finnsburg (lines 1107-24); in both instances the pyre is hung with armor, and the dead placed amidst the helms and corselets; flame roars, and smoke ascends to heaven. In both, moreover, the principal mourner is a woman: Hildeburg in the one case, and apparently Beowulf's widow in the other. (pp. 129-30)

Nevertheless the accounts of the burning of the dead Danish and Frisian warriors after Finnsburg and the cremation of Beowulf differ in two significant respects. First, although the ritual details are very similar, they are expressed in different terms: if the elements of the two descriptions are essentially conventional, the conventionality is not evident in the diction. Secondly, the lamentation of Hildeburg expresses simply her grief for those slain at Finnsburg; the grief of the woman who mourns for Beowulf is not only for his death, but for its consequences to herself and to the Geatish people. . . . The mourning of "Beowulf's widow" reinforces the forecasts of Wiglaf and the Messenger with respect to the downfall of the Geatish nation; it is symbolic rather than personal. Klaeber is wrong, then, in believing that "she was introduced, awkwardly enough, merely in the interest of a conventional motive"; the fears expressed in her lamentation afford the last and strongest intimation of the ruin to fall upon Beowulf's people through his death. Justly enough, Beowulf's warriors chant around his ashes the praises of their dead lord; the woman clearly sees, and grieves for, the destruction of his people. (pp. 130-31)

Arthur Gilchrist Brodeur, in his The Art of Beowulf, *University of California Press, 1959, 283 p.*

MAURICE B. McNAMEE, S.J. (essay date 1960)

[*McNamee is an American academic, scholar, and Jesuit priest who is best known for his studies of medieval and Renaissance visual art and literature. In the following excerpt, he portrays Beowulf as the embodiment of the Christian virtue of magnanimity, which demands the recognition of God as the bestower of all honors and abilities and the use of those abilities in the service of others.*]

There is nothing new . . . in seeing Beowulf as a Christian hero; but it seems to me that the extent of his Christian spirit is seen with new clarity when his character and actions are examined in the light shed upon them by the Christian notion of magnanimity. Such a scrutiny reveals how completely Beowulf exemplifies the virtue of magnanimity as Christian writers in all ages conceived it. These writers are willing to admit, with Saint Paul, that in itself there is nothing wrong in the great man's seeking honor as long as that pursuit is limited by two things: the clear recognition and admission (1) that whatever he has that merits honor he has from God, that whatever he achieves he achieves with the providential help of God, and that, therefore, to God should go the greater honor and glory; and (2) that all the talents and powers that have made him great were given him not for himself alone but in order that he might employ them in the service of his neighbor as well as of himself. In other words, the true Christian can never make the pursuit of honor an unqualified end in life; it must always be limited by humility, or the recognition of his dependence upon God for all that he is and all that he does, and by charity, or the recognition that he is his brother's keeper and that he cannot, therefore, ignore his brother's rights and needs in the pursuit of his own personal honor and glory. The Christian notion of honor so circumscribed by the Christian virtues of humility and charity loses the excessive selfishness and egotism of the Greek ideal and becomes one of the clearest norms for distinguishing the Christian from pagan values in both literature and life. When that norm is employed to interpret Beowulf, the extent to which his character and actions were created under the new influence of the "gentler qualities of Christian virtue" becomes very much more apparent.

The first prerequisite for the magnanimous man . . . is that he be a man of genuine heroic stature, pre-eminent in all the virtues. Even a cursory reading of ***Beowulf*** makes it clear that the ***Beowulf*** poet has striven to give his hero pre-eminence in both physical and spiritual qualities. Over and over again he is described as "the strongest of men," towering over all his followers in physical stature, and with a handgrip of thirty men. All his own brag speeches and the various flashbacks upon his past exploits reveal him as a man of almost giant strength and matchless courage. But besides his physical prowess, Beowulf is consistently represented as possessed of an innate nobility of character that wins him the instinctive respect of followers, friends, and strangers alike. When he comes to the land of the Danes, the herald declares that he has never seen a nobler man than Beowulf. "Never have I seen a mightier noble upon earth, a warrior in armour, than is one of you; that is no retainer dignified by weapons, unless his countenance, his peerless form belies him." And later, when he announces the newcomers to King Hrothgar, the herald says of Beowulf: "Assuredly the chief is doughty who has led these battle-heroes hither." As he appears at the beginning of the poem—mighty, brave, and virtuous—so he is described at the end when he goes forth fearlessly to meet the firedrake. . . . And in this last deadly conflict, Beowulf acquits himself as the mighty, brave, and noble hero he has been pictured to be throughout the poem.

A superficial reading of the poem might suggest that Beowulf in all his exploits was dominated by the very same motives that prompted Achilles. The very last words of the poem sung in praise of their hero by his loyal followers describe him as a man "most eager for fame." And several times in the course of the poem fame as a motive of Beowulf's actions comes to the fore, either in the speeches of the hero himself or in the remarks of those who surround him. The greeting of Hrothgar's herald, Wulfstan, is somewhat ambiguous, but, taken by itself, it might seem to have the old heroic ring: "I believe you have sought out Hrothgar, not from exile, but from prowess and from loftiness of spirit." Again in Beowulf's first brag speech to Hrothgar, we seem to be hearing nothing different from the boastful self-confidence of Achilles:

> I have in my youth undertaken many deeds of daring. . . . My people, the noble and wise men, advised me thus, Lord Hrothgar,—that I should visit thee, because they knew the strength of my might. They had themselves looked on, when, blood-stained from battles, I returned from the fight, where I bound five, laid low a brood of giants, and slew by night sea-monsters on the waves . . . And now I will decide the matter alone against the monster, the giant, Grendel! . . . Moreover, I have learnt that in his rashness the monster recks not of weapons. Hence,—so that Hygelac, my prince, may be glad at heart on my account, I renounce that I should bear a sword, or ample shield, or yellow buckler to the battle; but with the fiend I will close with grip of hand, and contend for our lives, foe against foe.

On the face of it, this seems to be as arrogant a boast as any that Achilles ever made. And in a like tone Beowulf later tells the gracious Queen Wealtheow that he will display his courage against the monster Grendel or die in the attempt. . . . It would seem . . . from all this that in Beowulf we have another example of the self-centered pursuit of glory that puts him in the company of Achilles. The character of Beowulf has sometimes been so interpreted.

But so to interpret him is to ignore the consistent qualifications that the ***Beowulf*** poet puts on his hero's pursuit of glory all through the poem. Those qualifications . . . are the identical ones enumerated by Saint Paul in his Second Epistle to the Corinthians and by Pope Saint Gregory in his letter to Saint Augustine—the recognition of one's dependence upon God for all one's talents and the employment of those talents not merely or primarily for oneself but for one's neighbor.

Reference to one providential God Who created and governs all, and Who will eventually judge all men is persistent throughout the poem. It is to this one providential God and Lord of all that Beowulf gives all the credit for his achievements, great and small. When he and his men land in Denmark, their first act, after they have drawn their ships up on the shore, is an act of thanksgiving to God for their safe arrival. When Beowulf makes his first speech at the court of Hrothgar and assures the old king that he is ready to challenge the monster Grendel, he resigns himself to the will of God in the outcome: "He whom death carries off shall resign himself to God's judgment." As he prepares himself for the advent of the monster, he is described by the poet as trusting firmly "in his proud might, the favor of the Creator." Here the poet seems definitely to be introducing the Christian notion that whatever one has he has as a gift from the Creator. (pp. 89-94)

But striking as is Beowulf's recognition of his dependence upon God for all that he is and does, the degree in which this Christian idea pervades the poem becomes even more apparent when we consider Hrothgar's attitude toward this matter in the first two episodes. Hrothgar is an old man who has learned much from the experience of years, and there are two things that he has learned in particular: that whatever happens to man happens under the guidance of a providential God, and that a man can achieve nothing without the help of God. When he hears of Beowulf's arrival, he is confident that "the holy God has of his mercy sent him to us West-Danes . . . to meet the terror of Grendel." When he recounts to Beowulf the ravages that Grendel has made upon his followers, he also declares his confidence in God's providential help: "God can easily restrain the wild ravager from his deeds." The old king, in fact, looks upon Beowulf as the instrument of God's providence in saving the Danes from the ravager. And when Grendel has finally been done to death by the mighty grip of Beowulf, Hrothgar speaks with a true Christian instinct when he gives glory to

God rather than to Beowulf himself—to the God who had given such might to man. (pp. 96-7)

As we have seen, Beowulf was certainly not unaffected by the motive of personal honor, but it was to be won through the generous service of others. The chief motive for his actions in all three of the major episodes of the poem is the succor and welfare of others—of those who were not even his own countrymen in the first two episodes, and of his own subjects in the third episode. He knowingly risks his life in the first two episodes to save the Danes from the ravages of Grendel and his troll-mother; and in the last episode he sacrifices his very life to save his own people from the ravages of the dragon.

The poet leaves us with no possible room for doubt that charity is a prominent motive in the poem. The point is made explicit repeatedly by both Beowulf himself and by Hrothgar. When Beowulf heard about the terrible inroads of Grendel upon the subjects of Hrothgar, he "bade make ready for himself a good ship for the crossing of the waves,—said he would seek the warrior-king, the noted prince, over the swan's-road, since he was in need of men." And he was seconded in his generous impulse by all his fellow wise Geats. They "did not blame him at all for the expedition, though he was dear to them; they urged on the stout-hearted one." (pp. 100-01)

The motive of "kindly aid" comes to the fore again when Hrothgar is helpless in the face of the avengeful depradations of Grendel's mother. He admits that Beowulf alone can help his people in their distress. "Now once more is help to be had from thee alone." And Beowulf again assures the troubled king that he is ready to succor him: "Sorrow not, wiseman. Better is it for each one of us that he should avenge his friend." And with that Beowulf is off to avenge his friend Hrothgar for the loss of his counselor Aeschere—at the risk of his own life. When he plunges into the dreadful mere his thoughts are not of himself but of his followers, whom he entrusts to the care of the king should he see the end of his days in the struggle with the monster below. And when triumphant and loaded with gifts from the grateful Hrothgar, he is making his farewell speech before departing for his home country, he makes another generous offer of help, should the king be again beset by his enemies. (pp. 101-02)

If any further evidence for the fact of Beowulf's spirit of Christian humility and charity is needed, it is provided by a comparison of his character with that of the noble Hrothgar and by a contrast with that of the less noble Unferth. (p. 103)

Part of the unity of the whole poem is achieved by [the] resemblance of the mature Beowulf of episode three to the Hrothgar of episodes one and two. It is a relationship of type to prototype, and it appears that the ***Beowulf*** poet wishes us so to conceive it. The virtues which Hrothgar exemplifies so well in the first two episodes are exemplified to perfection by Beowulf in very similar circumstances in episode three. And the transition between the second and third episodes is achieved through the farewell speech of Hrothgar in which he urges Beowulf to learn by his experience and matured wisdom that the way to personal happiness and to peace and security for his future subjects is the way of humility, gentleness, and kindly service. Arrogance, violence, and selfishness, he warns Beowulf, can lead only to chaos and unhappiness for himself and his people. (p. 104)

If Hrothgar . . . acts as a positive foil for the virtues of both the young and the mature Beowulf, Unferth certainly serves as a negative foil for them. He is in every respect inferior to Beowulf. He lacks his physical strength, his courage, and especially his moral integrity. In contrast to Hrothgar, he reacts with the typical jealousy of a small man to the obvious superiority of the Geatish hero. He tries to deflate Beowulf's reputation by reference to the Breca episode in the hero's past in which he was bested (so Unferth asserts) in a swimming contest. In contrast to the scathing wrath with which Achilles might be expected to meet such an envious thrust, Beowulf quite calmly recounts the true story which, without boastfulness, enhances his own reputation and quietly deflates Unferth's. And he also lays bare the truth of the present situation when he reminds Unferth of his own shady past as a murderer of his kin and of his present inability to cope with the destructive monster Grendel. The whole function of Unferth in the first two episodes, in fact, is to enhance the moral stature of Beowulf. Beowulf's very restraint in dealing with the unjust taunt of this jealous man disarms him and ultimately redeems him. Unferth gives him his own sword for the encounter with Grendel's dam; and, although it proves useless against the water troll, Beowulf returns it to its owner after the struggle with thanks and with no reference to its uselessness in the fight. The significance of this situation is vastly strengthened by imagining the rejoinder that Achilles might have made in a like situation. The degree of Beowulf's unselfish magnanimity on this occasion is perhaps measured by the fact that, so far from carrying any grudge against Unferth for his jealousy and discourteous taunt on his arrival, he pays him an unsolicited compliment when he departs. Here Beowulf again shows himself to be the truly Christian magnanimous man who can overlook a slight to himself because he is interested in something bigger and more ennobling than his mere personal reputation. Beowulf is here totally unlike Achilles, who was willing to sacrifice the whole Greek army to reinstate his own personal honor in the eyes of the host.

One of the chief ways in which the barbaric pagan spirit showed itself among the Nordic races in general was in the family feuds which were constantly breaking out and resulting in murderous intrigues of all kinds. The new Christian doctrine of brotherly love, therefore, had a special significance for these Nordic peoples. The ***Beowulf*** poet seems to be weaving this part of the Christian message into the movement of his whole poem. In this connection, added significance is given to the fact that the monster Grendel is the offspring of the fratricidal Cain and that the ravages of the firedrake are occasioned by the theft of a fugitive from justice. Unferth is accused by Beowulf of having murdered his kin, and there is a veiled reference to a future family feud in the household of Hrothgar that will wreck the peace which he has established. One of the great sources of comfort to Beowulf at the end of his life is that he has not been guilty of murdering his own kin. The many references to the instinct for such fratricidal feuds throughout the poem put us in touch with a very barbaric aspect of these Nordic races, indeed; but their presence gives greater point to the refining and civilizing influence of the new Christian ideal of gentleness and charity that is so admirably exemplified in both Hrothgar and Beowulf. (pp. 106-08)

Maurice B. McNamee, S.J., "Beowulf, Christian Hero," in his Honor and the Epic Hero: A Study of the Shifting Concept of Magnanimity in Philosophy and Epic Poetry, *Holt, Rinehart and Winston, Inc., 1960, pp. 86-117.*

KENNETH REXROTH (essay date 1965)

[Rexroth was one of the leading pioneers in the revival of jazz and poetry in the San Francisco area during the 1940s and 1950s.

Largely self-educated, he became involved early in his career with such left-wing organizations as the John Reed Club, the Communist party, and the International Workers of the World. During World War II he was a conscientious objector, but later became anti-political in his work and writing. Rexroth's early poetry was greatly influenced by the surrealism of André Breton, but his later verse became more traditional in style and content, though by no means less complex. However, it was as a critic and translator that Rexroth gained prominence in American letters. As a critic, his acute intelligence and wide sympathy allowed him to examine such varied subjects as jazz, Greek mythology, the works of D. H. Lawrence, and the cabal. As a translator, Rexroth was largely responsible for introducing Western readers to many Chinese and Japanese classics. In the following excerpt, he discusses the differences between Northern European epics and those of Southern European realms.]

Like the more hardy and noble fish, the kinds of men that we heirs of the Anglo-Saxon tradition think most heroic thrive best amidst the colder seas. The figures of the Norse, Welsh, and Irish Heroic Ages possess a magnanimity, courage, and contempt for triviality that we do not find in the heroes of Homer. Nor do our heroes come to their doom because they have pushed their normal endowment of great pride to the point of existential conceit; nor are they haunted by irresponsible fate or plagued by the frivolities of the gods.

For these reasons ***Beowulf*** seems essentially heroic in a way that the epics of the Mediterranean do not; its hero fulfils our insistence upon a moral heroism. His legend is one with those of Gordon, Florence Nightingale, Wellesley, or of Jesse W. Lazear and other martyrs of public health. Modern criticism has devalued our nineteenth-century heroes, but Beowulf is far away; all we know of him is a single document, so he stands as a mythic paradigm of the brave, generous, self-sacrificing aristocrat. . . .

The most unexpected quality in ***Beowulf*** is its abiding communication of joy. In contrast with the Mediterranean glitter of the *Odyssey,* plagued by fatigue and melancholy, ***Beowulf*** takes place in an atmosphere of semi-darkness, the gloom of fire-lit halls, stormy wastelands, and underwater caverns. It is full of blood and fierceness. Its rhythms have the tone of peremptory challenge and the clang of iron. Men exult in their conflict with each other and the elements. The sea is not a jealous, cantankerous, senile deity. It is a cold, thrilling antagonist. Even Grendel and his mother are serious in the way Greek demons never are. They may be horrors survived from the pagan Norse world of frost giants, wolf men, and dragons of the waters, but nobody would ever dream of calling them frivolous. They share Beowulf's dogged earnestness; what they lack is his joy, which suffuses the book in spite of a countersuffusion—a doom that haunts the far background of the narrative, like a few drops of ink and milk spreading into water from opposite directions.

Though they glory in themselves as successful animals, always we feel that ***Beowulf*** is a tale of men at the end of their tether. Not only do life and splendor fall to ruin but a hand is writing, ''Mene, mene tekel upharsin'' in the firelight on the walls of Hrothgar's banqueting hall. This civilization is almost over. The onrushing twilight of the gods is ominous in the distance. The refrain of another great Anglo-Saxon poem: *''Thaes ofereode, thisses swa maeg!''* (That passed away, this will too.) might as well have occurred every twenty lines or so in ***Beowulf*** or again, ''Mood be the more as our might lessens.'' . . . [***Beowulf***] takes place against the imminent end of the Heroic Age of the Teutonic peoples, but in addition a specific tragedy is unfolding in the background. The immediate personal future of Hrothgar's family was filled with treachery and disaster. The author knew this and so did his audience. Foreboding echoes as a counterpattern of rhythm and symbolism against all the poem's exultation.

This is a specifically northern epic theme. Arnold Toynbee, quoting John Knox, calls it ''the monstrous regimen of women.'' Both Helen and Penelope determine the Homeric epics only by the passive exercise of their femininity. The queens and enchantresses of the North interfere actively. It is their machination that brings disaster.

Grendel and his mother, devourers of men, inhabitants of subterranean depths, embody the demonic past whose claims can be destroyed with the facility only of courage and strength—but the future cannot be destroyed. Its doom depends on the deliberate evils of its participants, not on karma, not on myth, not on the unconscious. It will be played out in treachery, the murder of kinsmen, and civil war. All through the poem the poet inserts carefully muted ambiguous references to the dynastic ruin that is about to overwhelm all the participants except Beowulf himself. It is this tension between the easily subjugated occult and the inchoate and ungovernable overt fact of human destiny that gives the poem its irony, its pathos, and its structure. Once this tension is understood, ***Beowulf*** ceases to seem a folkloristic collection of Scandinavian legends and emerges as a strictly organized but muted tragedy—an elegiac drama.

Beowulf dies and is buried ''above the battle,'' overlooking the pale, cold sea, the perfect example of heroic transcendence. His grave must have been much like the ship burial discovered in our own generation at Sutton Hoo in England on the western shore of the same sea of adventure. Among the surviving treasures of that anonymous hero are the enameled clasps of his sporran, ornamented with a figure of a man strangling two beasts—the Gilgamesh motif come to the far North across 4,000 years.

Kenneth Rexroth, ''Beowulf,'' in Saturday Review, *Vol. XLVIII, No. 15, April 10, 1965, p. 27.*

STANLEY B. GREENFIELD (essay date 1965)

[*Greenfield is a recognized authority on Old English literature. In the following excerpt, he contends that the complexity and richness of* Beowulf *are due to the poet's intricate use of structural and thematic contrasts.*]

Though Beowulf has his analogues in such Scandinavian heroes as Boðvarr Bjarki and Grettir the Strong, he seems to be unique to the Old English epic to which, in modern editions, he gives his name. His origins, that is, along with those of the monsters he fights, are more to be found in folktale than in heroic story. But in the hands of the ***Beowulf*** poet he has become epically proportioned like the Homeric and Vergilian heroes of an earlier Heroic Age, and he has been given, along with other epic accoutrements, an historical setting involving him with the fates of two dynasties, the Danish Scyldings and the Geatish Hrethlings. As an additional layer in ***Beowulf,*** there is the Christian ethos, undoubtedly the contribution of the monastery which probably produced the written poem, though certain Christian elements may already have ''lain in solution,'' as it were, in oral songs about ***Beowulf*** utilized by the religious poet. The fusion of these three levels by the more-than-capable anonymous author leads to the richness and complexity of this sole complete surviving Germanic epic. (pp. 81-2)

Whatever the disagreements about details and about the interpretation of small passages and large sections, and whatever the disagreements about the ultimate unity of the poem and about its *significatio* [''import and meaning''], the narrative movement of ***Beowulf*** is clear enough. It revolves around the three great monster fights in the hero's career: against Grendel, Grendel's mother, and finally against the dragon. (p. 83)

[The] anonymous poet's sense of structure [is evident] in the ''movements'' of the three contests: in the differing natures and motivations of the antagonists; in the progressive difficulties Beowulf has in conquering his foes; in the shift of locales from the friendly confines of Heorot to the submerged cavern to the windy headland. Also involved in the structural movement is the progressive isolation of the hero: in the Grendel fight his band of retainers draw their swords in an attempt, however vain, to help their leader; in the second contest this band can only sit on the shore of the mere—the Danes already having departed in despair—suffering and yet hoping for the reappearance of their beloved chieftain; and in the dragon fight, Beowulf's *comitatus,* with the exception of Wiglaf, deserts him, abandoning him to the ultimate isolation of death. This last structural variation clearly impinges upon theme, the concept of loyalty vs. disloyalty that pervades the poem and that was integral to the Germanic secular ethos. As the ethical norm we are given Beowulf's almost unparalleled loyalty to his uncle and lord, Hygelac, in his refusal to accept the crown in lieu of Heardred, Hygelac's son, after the king has been killed in Frisian fields; and as one of several contrasts we find suggested the latent treachery in Heorot, in the character of Unferth, who has killed his kinsmen in battle, and in Hrothulf, Hrothgar's nephew and co-ruler, who will one day usurp the Danish throne.

The complexity and richness of the poem may perhaps be best summarized in the concept of *contrast*. For contrasts (and parallels) are what bind the poem into a unity, operating in the larger structural elements, character presentations, theme, and even in the most detailed stylistic matters. It is this unifying technique that allows the poet to bring into his poem the many apparent digressions, whether they be legendary—as they largely are in the first part of the poem—or historical—as in the second part. And it permits the Christian and pagan elements to coexist meaningfully within the framework of the poem.

The two major structural divisions provide the over-all contrast of youth *vs.* age: with youth in Part I is connected the ideal of the perfect retainer, in Beowulf's strengths of mind, body, and character, and in his conception of service to both Hrothgar and to his proper lord, Hygelac; with old age in Part II, in the ideal of the Germanic king, in Beowulf's attempt not only to protect his people but to provide them with treasure as part of the *comitatus* bond. One of the critical problems in this respect is whether the aged Beowulf is indeed ''perfect,'' either as a secular hero or as an exemplar of the Christian hero, receiving the ''doom'' of the righteous as his eternal reward; or whether he is ''flawed'' in his eagerness for treasure, thus tragically exemplifying the degeneration and sinful pride which Hrothgar in his homily (11. 1735ff.) had warned him of; or whether Beowulf, though admirable by the ''inner'' secular standards of the poem, falls short from the ''outer'' Christian perspective of the poet, being subject to the curse and damnation laid upon the dragon's hoard, with only the ''hope of heathens'' for an afterlife reward—the hope which is hell.

The youth-age structural contrast is also related to success and failure and, in a widening sense, to the rise and fall of nations. In Part I, the rise of the Scylding dynasty in Denmark is outlined as a prelude to the story proper, and the glory of the hall and court of Hrothgar at the peak of its opulence, with its Germanic aura of singing, feasting, and drinking, gift-giving and magnanimity of spirit is set scenically and directly before our eyes. Indeed the panorama of heroic life is suggested by the allusions to and digressions on heroic stories from the whole realm of Germania. In Part II the focus is on the end of the Geatish nation. The setting, in contrast to that of Part I, is the desolate headland and barrow where Beowulf fights the dragon, his own hall having already been destroyed by the dragon's breath. The panorama is now historical rather than legendary, unfolding in flashbacks by the poet himself, then by Beowulf, and finally by Wiglaf's messenger: it reveals the progressive elimination of the members of the Hrethling dynasty—the eldest son of King Hrethel accidentally slain by bowshot at his brother Hæthcyn's hands, Hæthcyn killed by the Swedes, and the last brother, Hygelac, humbled in Frisia and his son Heardred later killed by the Swedes; and Beowulf, the last survivor, is childless. The messenger prophesies the final defeat and dispersal of the Geats in a memorable passage [lines 3015-27] incorporating the ''useless treasure'' theme. . . . (pp. 85-7)

The rise and fall of nations that is the extension of the youth and age of the hero is emphasized further in the contrast between the *tones* of the two halves of the poem. The heroic dominates in the first part, with the evocation of such a concept as that of the good king, or in the heroic resolution Beowulf exhibits in confrontation with Wyrd or Fate, or in Beowulf's advice to Hrothgar upon Æschere's death that

> It is better for us all
> To avenge our friends, not mourn them forever.
> Each of us will come to the end of this life
> On earth; he who can earn it should fight
> For the glory of his name; fame after death
> Is the noblest of goals.

The elegiac dominates the second part, from the elegy of the last survivor (11. 2247ff.) who buries the hoard the dragon takes possession of, to the lament of Hrethel for his son Herebeald and the elegy of the old man whose son hangs on the gallows, to the final lament around Beowulf's funeral mound.

On the one hand, the larger contrasts just mentioned are modified by such matters as the arrival and ship burial of Scyld, which serves as a prolegomenon to the whole poem and which enhances both the heroic and elegiac within itself as well as affording a larger parallelism to the burial of Beowulf at the poem's conclusion; the seeds of downfall in the Danish dynasty sown in the significant allusions to future treachery and to the burning of Heorot; age in the figure of King Hrothgar himself; and the central helplessness of the Danes under the ravages of the Grendel clan. Further, there is the *historical* allusion in Part I to the death of Hygelac, an allusion made at the moment Wealhtheow bestows the necklace upon Beowulf; and Hygelac's fall serves to unify the impending doom of both Danish and Geatish nations. In Part II the elegiac is qualified somewhat by the heroic actions recounted, and especially by Wiglaf's behavior in coming to Beowulf's rescue in the face of the flight of the other retainers; but though his aid is not too little it is too late, serving only to heighten the *lif is laene* 'life is transitory' theme that is so central to the epic.

On the other hand, the larger structural contrasts are reinforced by lesser antitheses throughout the poem, as the qualifications in the preceding paragraph have already suggested. To these might be added the use of character contrasts, as in Hrothgar's scop's allusions to Sigemund (good) and Heremod (bad) in connection with his "improvised lay" about Beowulf on the way back from the mere, or in the Thryth (niggardly, wicked)-Hygd (liberal, gentle) contrast. There are, furthermore, symbolic contrasts, good and evil finding their correspondences in light and darkness, joy and sorrow. And, on the most detailed stylistic level, within the semantic and syntactic collocations of the poetic line, we find such moments as the one in which Beowulf comes, the morning after the celebration of Grendel's death, to ask whether Hrothgar has spent the night pleasantly. "Ne frin þu æfter sælum! Sorh is geniwod/Denigum leodum. Dead is Æschere," replies the king. ("Ask not after joys! Sorrow is renewed to the people of the Danes. Dead is Æschere.") The opposition of joy and sorrow is suggested in one way by the syntactic break in the line, yet the alliterative connection of *sælum* and *sorh* underlies the confluence of the emotions. Similarly, in the passage in which Grendel stalks Heorot: "Com on wanre niht / scriðan sceadugenga. Sceotend swæfon," (In the dark night the walker in shadows came striding. The shooters slept), the moving Grendel and the sleeping warriors are effectively contrasted through the syntactic severance and the chiastic use of the verbs, yet brought into their soon-to-be-realized association by the alliteration and metrical pattern.

These are but samples of the range of the ***Beowulf*** poet's accomplishments in drawing the many disparate elements of his poem into one of the triumphs of English poetry. One further example, at a little greater length, will have to suffice. . . . The Finn Episode (11. 1068-1159), a sample of the entertainment provided by the scop in Heorot after the defeat of Grendel, is an excellent tragedy in itself, focusing as it does on the conflicting claims imposed upon Hengest: to revenge his dead leader Hnæf on the one hand, and to keep the peace pact he has been forced to make with Hnæf's slayer, King Finn of Frisia, on the other. The final resolution with Hengest and the Danes slaughtering Finn and his retainers in their hall, and thus exacting revenge, is presented by Hrothgar's scop as a Danish victory, and on this level alone would find its *raison d'être* in the context of ***Beowulf.*** But the Episode operates on more subtle lines in the over-all unity of the poem. For though the scop has concentrated on Hengest, the ***Beowulf*** poet himself gives another perspective through Hildeburh's wretchedness: her loss of brother (Hnæf), son, and finally of husband (Finn), so that the heroic-elegiac pattern of the whole poem is reflected in miniature in this story. On another level, the theme of treachery is emphasized at the beginning, in the litotical comment that Hildeburh, Finn's wife, had "little reason to speak well of the loyalty of the Jutes," and the theme of treachery runs throughout the piece, to be picked up after the scop finishes his song when the ***Beowulf*** poet alludes to the future treachery in Heorot itself. In another way, the Episode reveals the failure of human attempts to achieve peaceful compromise, a theme echoing throughout the ***Beowulf;*** and the unenviable position of Queen Hildeburh has its immediate parallel in Wealhtheow, who will be the loser when nephew Hrothulf usurps, and a more distant parallel in Wealhtheow's daughter Freawaru, whose future suffering will be adumbrated by Beowulf in his report to Hygelac. Finally, the Finn Episode is balanced in Beowulf's report by the Ingeld Episode, for the former treats of a past triumph within the perspective of disaster, while the latter foretells future disaster within the perspective of triumph (at least we know from *Widsith* that Ingeld, though he burned Heorot, was defeated by Hrothgar and Hrothulf). In this balanced presentation of past and future, we can see one more way in which the poet has gained epic scope for the folktale contests that are the narrative basis upon which he so expertly and admirably built. (pp. 87-91)

Stanley B. Greenfield, "Secular Heroic Poetry," in his A Critical History of Old English Literature, *New York University Press, 1965, pp. 80-101.*

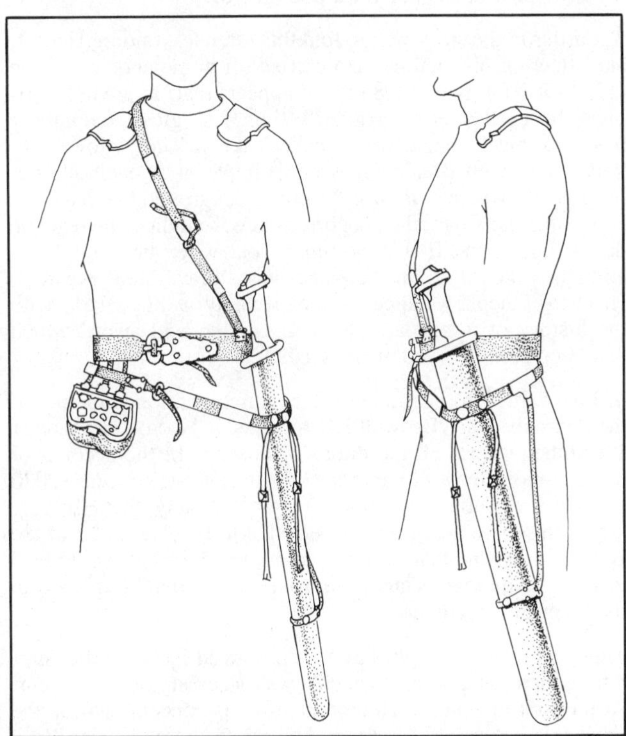

Gold regalia as it may have been worn in Anglo-Saxon times. The British Museum.

KENNETH SISAM (essay date 1965)

[*Sisam was a distinguished New Zealand-born English editor, philologist, and critic who is remembered both for his editorial work at Oxford's Clarendon Press and for his many contributions to Old and Middle English studies. In the following excerpt, he discusses seeming irrelevancies in two sections of* Beowulf *considered extraneous by many critics: Beowulf's expedition to the mere and return to Hygelac's hall.*]

The possibility that the expedition [in lines 837-927 in which Beowulf and his men travel to and from the mere] is a later addition cannot be excluded, but there are considerations on the other side. To follow Grendel's tracks was a natural thing to do; it had probably been done before (132), and after the attack by Grendel's Mother her tracks were followed (1390 f., 1402 ff.). He might be found dead on the way, or lurking somewhere, still alive and dangerous. If he had reached a refuge, it was important to know exactly where. At sight of the bloodstained mere, an immediate release of high spirits—horse-racing and acclamations of Beowulf—was also natural, and there is no place for it once the ceremonial thanksgiving begins with Hrothgar's appearance.

But an improbability arises from the accepted interpretation. Though the mere was not many miles from Heorot (1361 f.), an expedition which followed Grendel's tracks on the way there, and heard all the adventures of Sigemund, with more besides, on the way back, must take a considerable time. . . . Is it credible that on this great day Hrothgar would stay so late in his bedchamber, instead of coming as early as possible to see the evidence of his deliverance? It will not do to say that he was old and infirm, for after the unexpected attack by Grendel's Mother, he had heard the news and summoned Beowulf at first light (1311).

The explanation is better found in a well-known characteristic of primitive narrative: two things happening at the same time are described one after the other with no technical device to show that they were contemporaneous. Here the setting out of the party who follow Grendel's tracks and Hrothgar's appearance to join the crowd outside the door of Heorot are nearly simultaneous. A poet who knew Virgil could have used *pars . . . pars . . .* , taking care to keep the first member short. Instead, the poet of ***Beowulf*** describes the expedition to the mere elaborately, and when he comes to the scene at the hall, is unable to make a smooth connexion. He simply repeats the note of time; for I take *Đa wæs morgenleoht / scofen ond scynded* to be practically a variation of *on morgen* (837), meaning "it was full daylight" or perhaps "the sun rushed up."

Whatever explanation of the extant text is preferred, the impressions of the way to the mere given on this occasion and on the following day (1357 ff., 1408 ff.) are strikingly different. If interpolation is excluded, it must be allowed that the poet used to the limits an artist's privilege of varying or selecting material in order to express a mood. (pp. 30-2)

[Beowulf's return in lines 1888-2199] has had few admirers. . . .

As a bridge between the first two adventures and the last it is unsuccessful, since lines 2200 ff. would come little less abruptly if they followed line 1887 or line 1904. But no clear break defines the beginning of the passage. The pause before line 1888, which is the starting-point preferred by later scholars such as [Levin L. Schücking in his *Beowulfs Rückkehr* (1905)] and Tolkien [see excerpt dated 1936], is due to the appreciation of Hrothgar (1885-7) which marks his passing out of the narrative. Beowulf remains and this is his story.

The poet seems unable to contrive an effective stopping-point once Beowulf's work at Heorot is done; and in the narrative, as distinct from the episodes, he follows a course which requires no power of inventive construction. (p. 44)

Every step in the sequence of the narrative is obvious. Nor is the framework "loaded with ore." The Geatish court is lifeless: Hygelac and Hygd are little more than names of a good king and his good queen. Yet the dignified expression remains and there is no demonstrable falling-off in the technical quality of the metre. The "Return" reads like the work of a well-equipped poet who has temporarily lost his inspiration, and drifts when he has not another adventure to tell of.

Beowulf's recapitulation (2000-2162), the longest speech in the poem, has been criticized for its length, for its repetition of what has been told already, and for its variations from the earlier narrative. On the first two counts some defence can be made. He had a great deal to report, and to shorten this speech appreciably would make still more noticeable the thinness of the whole passage under discussion. There is also a question of verisimilitude. In early times, when the sources of news were few, a traveller's story on his return was a rare opportunity. A man so famous as Beowulf, who had gone on a great adventure, would be expected to report what had happened. In the circumstances, repetition was inevitable.

The variations from the early narrative have been taken as evidence of interpolation, or of the use of two parallel versions. Others have explained them as intended to relieve the monotony of repetition, though this purpose would not account for all of them. Consideration should also be given to the conditions of pre-literary composition and oral delivery, for ***Beowulf*** shows many characteristics of verse that was not composed in writing or intended to be read, among them kinds of variation that seem strange to a careful modern reader.

1. Beowulf told Hrothgar that the wise leaders of his people encouraged him to undertake the fight with Grendel (415 ff., cf. 202 f.). Yet, on his return, Hygelac, whose advice mattered most, says he had urged him again and again not to meddle with the murderous ogre, but to let the Danes fight their own battle (1992 ff.). This illustrates a way of presentation which I have noted [in the discussion of the return from the mere]: the poet exaggerates a mood or argument in order to make a strong impression, and at another place, for the same immediate purpose, says something inconsistent. When Beowulf reached Heorot, he had to convince Hrothgar that he was a match for Grendel, and the unanimous advice of the wiser Geats who knew his powers would confirm his claims. To mention Hygelac's fears would have spoiled the effect. When Beowulf comes home safe, Hygelac expresses the joy and relief of the Geats—feelings which are effectively conveyed by emphasizing previous anxiety about the outcome of his adventure.

2. Verisimilitude helps to account for the naming of Hondscio at line 2076. When the poet described the struggle in Heorot, it was enough that Grendel began by seizing and devouring one of Beowulf's men. But for Beowulf, back in Hygelac's hall where his small company were all well known, "one of my men" would not do. The name must be given, with the explanation that he was sleeping nearest to the hall-door, perhaps the post of honour for a bodyguard.

3. Earlier in the story we are told that Grendel, raiding Heorot, ate fifteen of his victims, and carried off home another fifteen (123, 1582 f.). Now (2085 ff.) it appears that, as a bag for his prey, he used a *glof*—a giant's fingerless glove, cunningly made by black magic from snakes' skins. The "glove" involves no inconsistency. It is an example of a technique noticeable elsewhere in ***Beowulf***: from a background that has been kept completely dark the poet brings into the light some realistic detail, not at the first opportunity, but when he wants it to embellish the story. In the same way "brave Heoroweard," Hrothgar's nephew, appears unexpectedly at line 2161, with the history of a standard, helmet, corslet, and sword which had been simply listed at lines 1020-3.

4. Freawaru, Hrothgar's daughter, is not mentioned on any of the occasions when Beowulf is entertained in Heorot. Her mother Wealhtheow does all the duties of hostess. In the account of his reception Beowulf mentions the queen first, but adds (2020 ff.) that Freawaru was also serving the company; that Hrothgar hoped to secure peace by her betrothal to Ingeld, leader of the Heathobards; and that, in his opinion, the marriage would lead to a tragic quarrel. Thus he introduces the Ingeld episode in the form of a prediction.

Though Freawaru might have been noticed in the earlier narrative, there is no point at which it was necessary or convenient. At the first meeting in Heorot attention is concentrated on the principals—Beowulf, Hrothgar, Unferth (to introduce the Breca story), and Wealhtheow. There is plenty of subject-matter; and even if there were room, Beowulf could not express his misgivings while he was the guest of the Danish court. It was different when he reported to Hygelac, for whom the alliances and quarrels of his neighbours the Danes had a special interest. A first-hand opinion from his right-hand man that there would be war with the Heathobards was great news; and Beowulf's prediction, which the audience knew to be accurate, was intended to show his wisdom and foresight. Any long break in the narrative has formal disadvantages; but this episode seems to me to be skilfully introduced at the best place.

5. No such aptness can be claimed for the so-called "Thryth" episode. In the transmitted text, with editorial patching, it falls so ineptly that Sir William Craigie thought it was a scrap from the manuscript of another poem which had got into the scribe's pattern copy by some mischance. It is the story of an arrogant princess who had been criminally merciless to suitors until the Continental Offa (Offa I) married her, when she became an excellent queen. [I maintain] that *modþryðo,* with which it begins, is the accusative of an abstract noun, as in so many phrases with *wæg,* e.g. *Genesis* 2238 *higeþryðe wæg;* and that the episode is mutilated at the beginning, where one would expect to find the names of the princess, her father and her people.

Even so it is a crude excrescence. With Hygelac's hall in view and great news for his king, Beowulf is held back on the beach where he landed while the poet tells this story. To say that it is relevant because, before she was married, the cruel princess was unlike Hygd, does not justify the construction: almost anything could be dragged in on the ground of more or less likeness or unlikeness. The old suggestion that this passage points to contact with the court of the Mercian Offa (d. 796) is attractive because it ends with the names of three members of the Mercian royal house. But perhaps it is a sufficient explanation that the poet aimed at entertainment. If the extraneous stories he wanted to use fitted neatly into the narrative, so much the better; if not, they were still good entertainment. "Beowulf's Return" would be thinner and more monotonous without the two episodes. As a whole, the "Return" appears to be an extension of the two older stories of Grendel and Grendel's Mother made by the poet who gave ***Beowulf*** substantially the form in which it has survived. (pp. 45-50)

Kenneth Sisam, in his The Structure of Beowulf, *Oxford at the Clarendon Press, Oxford, 1965, 88 p.*

EDWARD B. IRVING, JR. (essay date 1968)

[Irving is an American academic who has written extensively on Old English literature. In the following excerpt, he examines selected negative rhetorical constructions in Beowulf, *noting the way the poet uses such constructions to define both the ideal hero and the nature of a monster and to comment on the meaning of human fate.]*

[Negative constructions] have always been recognized as a striking feature of Germanic rhetoric. They surely play a major role in creating the impression of a persistent tone of irony and understatement that modern readers receive from this poetry, and they also have much to do with the usual representation of behavior in extreme terms. . . . [One form of rhetorical heightening] is provided by the frequent combination of a negative clause or phrase with the adversative conjunction *ac* ["but"] or with other words such as *hwæðre* or *swa þeah* ["nevertheless"] with the general meaning usually something like: "It is by no means A; on the contrary it is B."

The poet may use negative terms to state or amplify his conception of what a true hero should be in two different ways. He may mention what a true hero is not or does not do (namely, bad things), or he may mention what a nonhero is not or does not do (namely, good things).

Let us begin by looking at some examples [in ***Beowulf***] of the second kind of statement, in which characters or behavior more or less sharply defined as being the opposite of heroic are typically described. Two such examples occur in the passage in Hrothgar's sermon where the wicked king Heremod is described. Heremod is, to be sure, an antitype of the ideal king rather than of the ideal hero, but the passage illustrates the principle of the construction especially well.

Ne wearð Heremod swa
eaforum Ecgwelan, Arscyldingum;
ne geweox he him to willan, ac to wælfealle
ond to deaðcwalum Deniga leodum.
(1709b-12)

Heremod was not so [helpful] to the descendants of Ecgwela, to the honorable Scyldings; he did not grow up to be what they wished—far from it, he grew into the slaughter and violent death of the Danish people.

In such a passage we can sense the full rhetorical effect of this adversative form of statement. Here we have the energetic clash of powerful opposites: growth, potentiality for good, and the people's will on one hand; murder and destructiveness on the other. On one side of the *ac* fulcrum is stated (in negative terms) one ideal of true kingship: that the king grow into what his people wish him to be, or that he grow to become loved by his people. On the other side of the *ac* the two tautological compounds *wælfealle* and *deaðcwalum* put particularly heavy stress on the anarchic violence we actually find in this king. Heremod's brutality leads to alienation from humanity, as we see in the following lines:

breat bolgenmod beodgeneatas,
eaxlgesteallan, oþþaet he ana hwearf,
mære þeoden, mondreamum from.
(1713-15)

In furious anger he cut down his table-companions and comrades in arms, until at last he went off alone, that famous prince, away from men's joys.

Keeping two opposites alive simultaneously in the hearer's mind (in this instance, attributes of good and bad kings) may be the most important function of this form of rhetoric.

What we find here, and in many similar passages, is a form of statement in terms of extremes, where poetic energy may originate in the violent oscillation of sense from one extreme to another. Our second example, from the passage immediately following the lines we have quoted, shows just such an effect.

Ðeah þe hine mihtig god mægenes wynnum,
eafeþum stepte, ofer ealle men
forð gefremede, hwæþere him on ferhþe greow
breosthord blodreow. Nallas beagas geaf
Denum æfter dome; dreamleas gebad
þæt he þæs gewinnes weorc þrowade,
leodbealo longsum.
(1716-22a)

> Even though mighty God had favored him and exalted him beyond all men in joys of might and strength—still a bloodlust grew in his secret heart. He gave no rings to any Danes to gain glory; no, he lived to be joyless and to suffer pain for his violence, and longlasting affliction.

Here *hwæþere* serves as the rhetorical fulcrum. We are told that, on the one hand, God, by giving Heremod the same gift of heroic strength he has given Beowulf, has encouraged him and raised him above other men. But Heremod suddenly turns to evil, and to a particular form of evil (stinginess, not giving rings) that is peculiarly ironic in view of God's generosity toward him. The very willfulness of his behavior is signaled by the abrupt adversative transitions *hwæþere* and *nallas*. The expression "not giving rings" is in fact here a notable understatement, since Heremod apparently murders his subjects. We see the same expression later in Hrothgar's sermon, in the exemplum of the man corrupted by pride and the devil's arrows, a man much resembling Heremod:

Þinceð him to lytel   þæt he lange heold,
gytsað gromhydig,   nallas on gylp seleð
fædde beagas,   ond he þa forðgesceaft
forgyteð ond forgymeð,   þæs þe him ær god sealde,
wuldres waldend,   weorðmynda dæl.

(1748-52)

> What he has held for so long now seems to him too little; he covets fiercely—never any longer does he proudly bestow ornamented rings; and he then ignores and scorns the created world, the great share of honors which God, Ruler of glory, had given him.

Even if we leave murder out of the picture, avarice itself is always something more serious than mere stinginess in Germanic heroic poetry; it represents the immoral violation of a personal relationship that happens to be symbolized by the exchange of material wealth. In this light we may with some justice regard avarice as a form of extreme behavior.

Unferth, the Dane who insultingly challenges Beowulf when he arrives at the great Danish hall of Heorot, is in some respects another antitype of the hero. One negative phrase of the type we are examining is applied to him:

Gehwylc hiora his ferhþe treowde,
þæt he hæfde mod micel,   þeah þe he his magum nære
arfæst æt ecga gelacum.

(1166b-68a)

> Each of them trusted his spirit, that he had a great heart, even though he had not been honorable to his kinsmen in the play of sword-edges.

The past history of Unferth and his position at Hrothgar's court are by no means clear and may never be, but this remark by the poet, couched as it is in the habitual ironic mode of understatement, can hardly mean anything other than that Unferth has murdered his kinsmen.

Again, the cowardly retainers who retreat from the dragon's attack and hide in the forest are certainly pictured as nonheroes:

Næs ða lang to ðon
þæt ða hildlatan   holt ofgefan,
tydre treowlogan   tyne ætsomne.
Ða ne dorston ær   dareðum lacan
on hyra mandryhtnes   miclan þearfe,
ac hy scamiende   scyldas bæran,
guðgewædu,   þær se gomela læg,
wlitan on Wilaf.

(2845b-52a)

> It was not long before those slow in battle came out of the forest, ten cowardly faith-breakers together; they had not dared to make play with their spears in their lord's moment of great need; on the contrary, in shame they bore shields and armor to where the old man lay, and they looked at Wiglaf.

Now that the dragon is dead and the danger over, they come forward quickly, although when they were needed they did not come at all. But the negative clause here (2848-49) serves to define very plainly their primary obligation as retainers: to come to their lord's help when he has need of them. The clause with *ac* that follows presents a minor problem in interpretation, however. Precisely what is being opposed to what? If the emphasis in the preceding clause is on *scamiende,* is the chief contrast then between the retainers' previous shamelessness in flight and their present feelings of mortification? More interesting is the possibility of an ironic contrast between the help they did not bring when it was so urgently needed and the useless shields and corselets they now officiously carry to the place where Beowulf lies dead.

Another passage in which the retainers' duty is stated flatly and unequivocally by means of a negative phrase is the following:

Nealles him on heape h*a*ndgesteallan,
æðelinga bearn,   ymbe gestodon
hildecystum,   ac hy on holt bugon,
ealdre burgan.

(2596-99a)

> In no way did those war-comrades, those sons of noblemen, take their stand around him in formation as fighting-men should; no, they fell back into the forest and took care of their own lives.

This is again rhetorical statement in terms of the polarizing of possible behavior into two extreme kinds. The alliteration here of *hildecystum* and *holt* draws our attention to the alternatives: to stand in military formation or to go hide in a forest. As so often in Old English poetry, and in Germanic literature generally, this kind of statement vividly dramatizes a character's free choice of action, at the same time that a phrase like *aeðelinga bearn* reminds us of his hereditary aristocratic obligations. Heroic life is consistently presented as a series of such radical choices.

Another possible violation of heroic decorum, though in this instance certainly a venial one, may be the storm of emotion that overwhelms King Hrothgar when he says farewell to Beowulf, as the hero takes leave of Denmark and returns home.

Wæs him se man to þon leof
þæt he þone breostwylm   forberan ne mehte,
ac him on hreþre   hygebendum fæst
æfter deorum men   dyrne langað
beorn wið blode.

(1876b-80a)

> That man was so dear to him that he could not hold back the surge in his breast; on the con-

> trary, a secret longing in his bosom for the dear
> man strained against rational restraints, burned
> in his blood.

Beowulf's feelings on this occasion are not described. Assuming that he too feels some measure of grief, one may perhaps see a contrast between his stoical behavior and Hrothgar's yielding to the expression of emotion (a moment before we were told of Hrothgar's tears). But the more important contrast here is between youth and age (often referred to in this part of the poem) rather than between heroic self-restraint and emotionalism. Hrothgar's long experience in disappointment has taught him that they will probably never see each other again; Beowulf is still too young to see the world this way. The rhetorical structure of this sentence differs somewhat from the structure of the previous examples, in that here we have a parallel rather than the usual contrast, for the ideas of the dearness of the man, the fight for self-control, and the hot wave of emotion are really to be found here on both sides of the *ac* fulcrum. Possibly the *ac* construction in this instance may serve simply to emphasize in a general way the strength of Hrothgar's feelings, since such a construction ordinarily suggests some form of emotional tension.

Let us turn now to some examples of the more common way of defining the heroic ideal by negations, this time by negating or denying the nonheroic. It goes without saying that courage is the most important heroic attribute; consequently there are a number of negative expressions that allude to the hero's courage in terms of his "not fearing" or not showing other signs of cowardice. Not only phrases but *un* compounds like *unforht* or (in *The Battle of Maldon) unearg* (uncowardly) fall into the same category.

In *Maldon,* as I have suggested [in my 1961 study "The Heroic Style in *The Battle of Maldon*"], constant reminders of the possibility of flight from battle do much to increase the dramatic tension of the poem. There, of course, such verbal reminders operate in the context of a narrative that in fact describes mass flights. While the flight of the cowardly retainers does of course take place in ***Beowulf,*** it does not have as much relative importance in the poem; it is merely one dark background stroke in the tremendous heightening and brightening of the figure of Beowulf. Even though they are used less intensively than in *Maldon,* such formulas probably serve to keep alive at the edge of the audience's consciousness the thought that it is after all normal behavior to be frightened under such conditions.

From an assortment of negative phrases describing other nonheroic attributes, we might construct an interesting model of the Anglo-Saxon nonhero: a man who kills his companions over drinks and secretly weaves an ensnaring net of malice for others; who has a ferocious temper and the bad manners to find fault with gift swords. Behavior like this may well have been common in England in the seventh or eighth century, perhaps even common enough to be called a realistic norm. But, since such speculation takes us beyond the bounds of our poem, it would be more profitable to examine these expressions in context. Three of them happen to occur in the same scene.

The final lines (2101-62) of Beowulf's report to Hygelac after he has returned to Geatland project an image of Hrothgar as ideal king, stressing as they do the grief Hrothgar had to suffer under the oppression of Grendel, the warmth of his affection for Beowulf, and, above all, his great generosity. The speech comes to its climax when Beowulf orders Hrothgar's splendid gifts to be brought into the hall and presents them formally to his uncle Hygelac. Hrothgar's magnanimity is used here (as nearly everything in the poem is used sooner or later) to reveal to us Beowulf's own virtues: in this instance, his love, generosity, and loyalty.

The occurrence of three of our negative expressions in this triumphant scene is of interest partly because it reveals what comes into the poet's mind as he contemplates uncle and nephew. A central theme all through this passage is fidelity, symbolized as usual by the exchange of gifts, and, again as usual, we are urged to think both of the affection that inspires the gifts and the obligations they entail. It is entirely characteristic of Old English poetic style that fidelity must be defined or set off or deepened in meaning by strong hints of its opposite.

In his presentation speech to Hygelac, Beowulf mentions that the arms Hrothgar has given him once belonged to Heorogar, Hrothgar's older brother, and that Hrothgar had not wished to give them to Heorogar's son Heoroweard. We are not told what Hrothgar's reason for this last decision may have been, but later versions of the story in Saxo Grammaticus and in the saga of Rolf Kraki make it seem at least possible that Heoroweard, like his cousin Hrothulf, may also have been eying his uncle's throne. In any event the reference to the Scylding royal family must at least have reminded the poet of some plotting nephew, whether Heoroweard or Hrothulf, for otherwise the ensuing description of Beowulf as a nephew loyal to Hygelac would have had little point.

> Swa sceal mæg don,
> nealles inwitnet oðrum bregdon
> dyrnum cræfte, deað ren[ian]
> hondgesteallan. Hygelace wæs,
> niða heardum, nefa swyðe hold,
> ond gehwæðer oðrum hroþra gemyndig.
> (2166b-71)

> This is how a kinsman should behave—and not
> be secretly weaving a treacherous net for others
> or laying a deathtrap for a comrade. His nephew
> [Beowulf] was indeed very loyal to war-tough-
> ened Hygelac, and each of them was attentive
> to the happiness of the other.

This passage is a good example of the rhetorical effect we have been discussing. The semantic rhythm here is positive *(swa sceal mæg don)*—negative (the *nealles* clause)—positive (Beowulf's own loyalty). From a different point of view one could see it as constructed in another way: the first two parts are statements of ethical alternatives, while the third is a specific instance of choice. Beowulf has chosen one of the two possible modes of behavior.

What is done in miniature in this brief passage is done on a larger scale in the scene as a whole. Into this scene of absolute and dedicated fidelity in Hygelac's hall the poet introduces a flood of dark reminders of treachery in Heorot, chiefly through references to Hrothgar (2155), to Hrothgar's queen Wealhtheow and the marvelous necklace she gave Beowulf at the great banquet, and to an unnamed hypothetical nonhero who bears some resemblance both to Unferth and to the evil Danish king Heremod, as we can see in the following passage:

> Swa bealdode bearn Ecgðeowes,
> guma guðum cuð, godum dædum,
> dreah æfter dome, nealles druncne slog

heorðgeneatas; næs him hreoh sefa,
ac he mancynnes mæste cræfte
ginfæstan gife, þe him god sealde,
heold hildedeor.

(2177-83a)

Thus Ecgtheow's son [Beowulf], a man known in battles, showed his bravery in heroic deeds, lived to gain glory; never was he the one to strike comrades over drinks by the hearth; his temper was never savage. No, with the greatest strength of mankind this valorous man kept safe the abundant gifts which God had given him.

Strength and courage are essential to the hero but they are not enough. Heremod and Unferth, both fatally undisciplined, showed their aggressiveness in the violent disruption of social order; Beowulf, while assuredly a veteran warrior, a *guma guðum cuð,* saved his fighting for the battlefield. The negative image of the nonhero is needed here for clearer definition of the moral requirements of true heroism, as they are embodied in Beowulf.

Elsewhere and in somewhat different ways, negative phrases are used to differentiate Beowulf from other men. The Danish coastguard's awed reactions to his first sight of Beowulf, for example, are largely conveyed in a rapid series of expressions that define the nature of the hero by excluding the expected, the normal, the usual, by saying what he is not:

No her cuðlicor cuman ongunnon
lindhæbbende; ne ge leafnesword
guðfremmendra gearwe ne wisson,
maga gemedu. Næfre ic maran geseah
eorla ofer eorþan ðonne is eower sum,
secg on searwum; nis þæt seldguma,
wæpnum geweorðad, næf*ne* him his wlite leoge,
ænlic ansyn.

(244-51a)

Never have shield-bearers arrived here in a more open way, yet you were not sure of the permission of our fighting-men or the consent of our kinsmen. I never saw a bigger man on earth than one of you, that fighter in armor. He is certainly no hall-lounger, unless his looks belie him, his noble face.

How can the puzzled coastguard establish the identity of these strange visitors? He can do it only by excluding them from successive categories. Their behavior is entirely different from that of previous visitors to Denmark, who apparently have come either as deferential guests or as furtive spies. But these men come openly and confidently; they walk as if they already had the password. Indeed all the password they need walks among them in the person of Beowulf. And so at the end of this passage the coastguard singles out Beowulf from the rest of the band: he is bigger, braver, of a more resolute and heroic appearance. Yet it is interesting to see how such a luminous and compelling image is constructed out of negative expressions.

Later Wulfgar, who keeps the door of Hrothgar's hall, further distinguishes Beowulf and his men from other visitors. After a moment's inspection, he concludes that these men are not only brave men but that they are responsible and honorable volunteers rather than *wreccan,* that type so common in Germanic literature, roving professional adventurers or refugees from foreign vendettas.

Wen ic þæt ge for wlenco, nalles for wræcsiðum,
ac for higeþrymmum Hroðgar sohton.

(338-39)

I believe that you have come to see Hrothgar out of sheer pride and greatness of spirit, certainly not as adventurers in exile.

Another negative construction (if we may take *forhicge* as expressing an essentially negative idea) sets Beowulf apart from ordinary warriors in respect to his method of fighting:

Ic þæt þonne forhicge . . .
þæt ic sweord bere oþðe sidne scyld,
geolorand to guþe, ac ic mid grape sceal
fon wið feonde ond ymb feorh sacan,
lað wið laþum.

(435-40a)

I have no intention on that occasion . . . of carrying any sword or wide yellow-bordered shield to battle; on the contrary, I will be obliged to grapple with the fiend with my hands and fight for life, one enemy against another.

Other warriors in heroic poetry make much of the process of assembling their weapons for battle, but Beowulf is different. The difference is most clearly dramatized in the half-ironic "disarming of the hero" scene just before the fight with Grendel, in the course of which Beowulf methodically divests himself of all the traditional accouterments of the epic fighter in order to meet the monster with his bare hands.

Finally, as king, Beowulf differs from others in his response to Queen Hygd's offer to him of the throne of the Geats:

No ðy ær feasceafte findan meahton
æt ðam æðelinge ænige ðinga,
þæt he Heardrede hlaford wære
oððe þone cynedom ciosan wolde;
hwæðre he hi*ne* on folce freondlarum heold,
estum mid are, oððæt he yldra wearð,
Wedergeatum weold.

(2372-79a)

None the sooner could the destitute Geats prevail on the prince in any way to become Heardred's lord or willingly to accept the kingdom; no, he [Beowulf] went on to maintain Heardred in his proper place in the nation by his friendly advice and respectful affection, until he [Heardred] grew up to rule over the Storm-Geats.

Placed in a situation of this kind, where the king is only a child, most men would yield readily to the reasonable pleas of their people to assume power. Many men would be only too glad to seize the royal authority. But Beowulf goes to the other extreme: far from plotting to seize power for himself, he devotes himself to keeping young Heardred in power by his friendly counsels. He will not accept a position that he thinks he does not deserve, even when it is freely (and probably legally) offered to him by a majority of the Geats and by their queen.

Just as the hero can be effectively defined by the use of negatives, so negatives can serve to describe the hero's chief antagonist Grendel, especially in his relation to some familiar human norm. In fact it may well be that the essential reality of Grendel is best understood in terms like these, for in many ways Grendel could be called an instance of Negative Man. As a fighter and as a "visitor" to the Danish hall that he devastates, he is often treated ironically as a peculiar kind of human warrior. But he is set off from ordinary warriors in one respect, for example, because, as Beowulf points out [in lines 681-849], for all his courage and ferocity he does not even know how to fight with a sword. . . . (pp. 2-16)

Not only is Grendel cut off from the normal concerns of a Germanic warrior by his ignorance of the use of weapons, but he is further excluded from the ranks of noblemen because he has no father, or at least his father's name is not known by men. . . . Since, in all epic poetry, a patronymic is at least as necessary to a hero as a sword, Grendel's title to heroic identity is wholly obscured.

Unlike normal men, Grendel does not pay the Danish people the honor they surely deserve, but instead he obeys his own fierce impulses in disposing of them:

Nymeð nydbade, nænegum arað
leode Deniga, ac he lust wigeð,
swefeð ond sendeþ, secce ne weneþ
to Gardenum. Ac ic him Geata sceal
eafoð ond ellen ungeara nu,
guþe gebeodan.

(598-603a)

He extorts toll, and honors no man of the Danish nation; quite the contrary, he does just as he pleases, butchers and sends to death (?), expecting no resistance from the Spear-Danes. But I am the one who will show him very soon now the strength and courage and fighting-power of Geatish men.

In this passage we see Grendel beyond the control of any of the Danes and equally beyond the control of any code of conduct that would be binding on noblemen.

Grendel and his mother of course live somewhat beyond the pale, in a lake-bottom home which no human being has ever seen:

No þæs frod leofað
gumena bearna, þæt þone grund wite.

(1366b-67)

No one of the sons of men lives so old and wise that he knows the bottom [of that lake].

The range of human experience and wisdom cannot even reach the place where Grendel lives.

As was already suggested, several negative expressions of this kind are closely related to the poet's consistent and ironic presentation of Grendel as a mock thane, and serve to provide particularly compact and vivid statements of the irony. Grendel is first shown to us as a wretched exile from the human race, living in the darkness of social disgrace and spiritual isolation, perpetually bearing God's anger. Infuriated by the harmonious sounds of human joy in Heorot, he comes first as a "guest" to visit the hall; perhaps he is even viewed ironically as the good neighbor paying a social call on the new arrival (Heorot has just been completed and occupied). When the Danes abandon Heorot, Grendel "rules" there; it is in the context of a passage describing the wholesale evacuation of the hall by the terrified Danes that Grendel is called a "hall-thane" (142). But Grendel's authority in Heorot has limits.

Heorot eardode,
sincfage sel sweartum nihtum;
no he þone gifstol gretan moste,
maþðum for metode, ne his myne wisse.

(166b-69)

He lived in Heorot, that treasure-bright hall, in the black nights; but he was never permitted to draw near the gift-throne or the treasure because of the Lord, and did not know pleasure in it.

Even though Grendel seems to be living in the hall, he cannot (perhaps has no wish to) approach the gift-throne—that is to say, make proper use like an ordinary retainer of the treasure for which Heorot is so famous. While the much-discussed phrase *for metode* might possible mean "in the presence of a secular lord (who is distributing treasure to his men)," more likely it refers to God and hence suggests that a supernatural order in the world must finally set limits to the outrages of such creatures as Grendel.

In another well-known passage, the same kind of irony is used to bring out Grendel's distance from mankind. It is almost as if the Danes in the poem (or at least the audience listening to the poem) were being invited to try to bring Grendel into some meaningful and familiar pattern of reference, some relationship to the structure of human society. In this case the frame of reference is the Germanic wergild system of monetary compensation for wrongs done.

Sibbe ne wolde
wið manna hwone mægenes Deniga,
feorhbealo feorran, fea þingian,
ne þær nænig witena wenan þorfte
beorhtre bote to ban*an* folmum,
[ac se] æglæca ehtende wæs,
deorc deaþscua, duguþe ond geogoþe,
seomade ond syrede, sinnihte heold
mistige moras; men ne cunnon
hwyder helrunan hwyrftum scriþað.

(154b-63)

He wished no peace-settlement with any man of the Danish force, and he refused to remove the deadly evil or to compound by making payment. No wise man had any cause to hope for the bright remedy from that butcher's hands! Far from it—that terrifying creature, the dark death-shadow, kept on plaguing them, young and old, tirelessly lying in wait and ambushing them, ruling the misty moors in endless night. Men do not know where such mysterious hellions go in their roamings.

The lines just preceding this passage have strongly emphasized the violence of Grendel's feud with Hrothgar *(heteniðas, fyrene, fæhðe, sæce)*. But, as we see later in the poem in the story of Beowulf's own father Ecgtheow, human feuds can be resolved and peace can be restored, if the participants in feuds want peace. But *sibbe ne wolde*—Grendel does not want peace, nor indeed relationship of any sort with any human being, no matter how such relationship is (ironically) extended to him. Denied here emphatically is the (ironic) hope that he will abide by human laws and pay the fine for his murders, even though the idea is toyed with almost humorously for a few lines.

The verses that follow (here I assume that the *ac se* supplied by most recent editors in line 159 to replace letters lost from the manuscript is almost certain) move us abruptly, in the usual way of an *ac* construction, away from this temporary accommodation with mankind, this way of seeing Grendel as somehow human. A man as well as a monster could be called an *æglæca,* an inspirer of fear—Beowulf himself is called one in line 2592—but no man is a *deorc deaþscua,* a dark shadow of death. And then we move out quickly even further from the human center into perpetual night, the misty moors, all those areas beyond any ordering powers of the human imagination. As we cannot know his motives, so we cannot know Grendel's dwelling-places: *men ne cunnon.*

An ironic transaction of a somewhat similar kind is described by Beowulf in his report to Hrothgar on the fight with Grendel. In order to save his life, Grendel had left his arm behind when he fled. The act of leaving his arm seems to be represented as some kind of involuntary offering (and, if we take *feasceaft* literally, all he could pay) but this down payment nets him nothing.

No þær ænige swa þeah
feasceaft guma frofre gebohte;
no þy leng leofað laðgeteona,
synnum geswenced, ac hyne sar hafað
mid *ny*dgripe nearwe befongen,
balwon bendum. Ðær abidan sceal
maga mane fah miclan domes,
hu him scir metod scrifan wille.

(972b-79)

> But the destitute man did not purchase any comfort by this action; the horrible plunderer, crippled by sin, lived none the longer for it; on the contrary, pain had seized him tight in an inescapable grip, in the bonds of death. And in that place he must wait, that man branded with crimes, to see how bright God will wish to judge him at the Great Judgment.

Perhaps it is significant that the words *guma* and *maga,* common words for man, are applied to Grendel in this passage, for what is stressed here is Grendel's sinfulness *(synnum geswenced, mane fah)* and his ultimate responsibility for his actions in the face of the Last Judgment. However badly Grendel may seem to fit the usual patterns of human society and behavior, he is not an animal; in some higher scheme of order he is seen as human and therefore responsible. Yet, just as the sacrifice of his arm gains him no respite, his suffering and death gain him no pity. A total failure as hero, he wins no glory or reputation in the eyes of others; he does not even win their momentary sympathy:

No his lifgedal
sarlic þuhte secga ænegum
þara þe tirleases trode sceawode.

(841b-43)

> His parting from life did not seem pitiable in any way to any of the men who looked at the trail of one devoid of glory.

These curious ironic expressions, constantly bringing as they do the possibility of Grendel's humanity into the periphery of our consciousness even in the act of emphatically denying it, have considerable importance in the meaning of the poem. . . . For, despite all his inhuman and monstrous attributes, it is ultimately Grendel's human ancestry that makes him the kind of monster he is—the renegade who has deserted humanity to live in the wilds of exile, the frantic destroyer of the society he was once symbolically driven from in his ancestor Cain, the bearer always of the mark of murderer, and the bearer too of the mark of man. (pp. 16-22)

That Tolkien's famous essay on ***Beowulf*** ends with the phrase "—until the dragon comes" [see excerpt dated 1936] is appropriate, for the phrase reminds us of many such expressions with "until" that constitute a major theme pattern in the poem. . . . [The construction of these expressions places] one kind or quality of human experience (usually success or the hope of success) in sharp and dramatic contrast with another kind of experience (usually failure or disaster). Here only those sentences that actually contain the words *oð* or *oððæt* (until) will be studied.

There are thirty-six instances of these words in ***Beowulf.*** For purposes of this study we can discard some thirteen as being "neutral," that is, carrying no specific emotional charge, serving merely to describe journeys or movements in space or the passage of time. It should be added immediately, however, that some of these are much less neutral than others; the term is quite relative. In a sentence like this, which describes the Geats' arrival at Heorot, the construction seems straightforward:

Guman onetton,
sigon ætsomne, oþþæt hy [s]æl timbred,
geatolic ond goldfah, ongyton mihton.

(306b-08)

> The men hastened on, marching together, until they could see the well-constructed hall, stately and gold-bright.

But the following sentence, on the other hand, contains a perceptible suggestion of suspended terror:

Hordweard onbad
earfoðlice oððæt æfen cwom.

(2302b-03)

> The guardian of the hoard [the dragon] waited in impatient misery until evening came.

The more interesting rhetorical uses of the construction, however, can be broken down into simple descriptive categories. For our purposes we may use the naïve terms "good" and "bad" to describe events or situations that, in their context, are either desirable or undesirable from the point of view of the poet or his human characters. The pairs of events described in an "until" phrase may then be roughly classified as follows in these terms:

good follows good —4
good follows bad —3
bad follows bad —6
bad follows good —10

In the first category, good follows good, three of the four passages are concerned with some form of hereditary succession. The Danish king Beow rules well in Denmark until Healfdene is born to succeed him (53-57a); Hrothgar prospers in war until a new generation of warriors grows to maturity (64-67a); Weohstan keeps the arms given him by Onela until his son Wiglaf is old enough to use them (2620-22). The fourth passage is similar in that it describes Beowulf's friendly protection of young Heardred until he is old enough to rule the Geats (2377-79b). The theme here is obvious: in the heroic world, strong rulers are the sole source of order. Social stability and continuity consists in the orderly succession of strong rulers.

In two of the three instances of ''good follows bad,'' we can see that the change is the result of heroic character and initiative. Scyld is at first a destitute child in Denmark, but he lives to see consolation for that suffering and to exact obedience from all his neighbors (6b-11). Grendel rules Heorot until at last death comes to him at Beowulf's hands (1253-55a). In the third passage spring follows winter, melting the fetters of ice, as Henges sits unhappily in Finn's hall (1131b-36a); Hengest and the Danes are then free to carry out their delayed vengeance against Finn.

Few generalizations can be ventured about the category of ''bad follows bad.'' Persistence in a course of violence is sometimes stressed. In the Ingeld episode, this passage occurs:

> Manað swa ond myndgað mæla gehwylce
> sarum wordum, oððæt sæl cymeð
> þæt se fæmnan þegn fore fæder dædum
> æfter billes bite blodfag swefeð,
> ealdres scyldig.
>
> (2057-61a)

> In this way he will remind and admonish him
> on every occasion with words of pain, until the
> time comes that the woman's retainer will sleep
> bloodstained from the sword's bite, forfeiting
> his life for the deeds of his father.

The old retainer's rekindling of hatred in the young man is seen almost as the normal fulfillment of natural process. So, in Germanic literature generally, feuds once set in motion tend to grind on to their conclusion. Other events in a career of violence are connected with *oððæt* constructions: Grendel kills some of the Danes and rules until Heorot stands unusable for Hrothgar and his men (144-46a); Heremod slaughters his subordinates in fury until at last he goes away into ''exile'' (1713-15); Ongentheow attacks the Geats and then pursues them into a trap at Ravenswood (2928-35).

We come now to the largest of these categories. That most of these ''until'' constructions should be ''bad follows good'' is in perfect keeping with the grim tone of the poem as a whole, its emphasis on tragic unawareness and unpreparedness, and its long perspective over several generations of men.

The passage in this category that happens to occur first in the poem may be taken as representative of this pattern; it deserves attention besides because it is one of the most elaborate rhetorical structures of the poem. The *oððæt* construction is at its very center, but the context should be quoted at some length.

> Ða se ell*or*gæst earfoðlice
> þrage geþolode, se þe in þystrum bad,
> þæt he dogora gehwam dream gehyrde
> hludne in healle; þær wæs hearpan sweg,
> swutol sang scopes.
>
> (86-90a)

> Then that alien spirit suffered longlasting misery, the one who lurked in darkness, because every day he heard joy loud in the hall, there where the harp's song was, and the clear voice of the minstrel.

Then, after the scop's song of the creation of the world, which offers its own brief and memorable impressions of light and vitality, the poet continues:

> Swa ða drihtguman dreamum lifdon
> eadiglice, oððæt an ongan
> fyrene fre[m]man feond on helle.
> Wæs se grimma gæst Grendel haten,
> mære mearcstapa, se þe moras heold,
> fen ond fæsten.
>
> (99-104a)

> That was how those noble men lived in luck
> and joy—until one fiend from hell began to
> commit crime. That fearful creature's name was
> Grendel, a well-known prowler of the borders,
> ruling over moor, fen, and wild country.

Then there follows the account of Grendel's descent from Cain and the origin of the race of monsters. Finally Grendel comes to Heorot:

> Gewat ða neosian, syþðan niht becom,
> hean huses, hu hit Hringdene
> æfter beorþege gebun hæfdon.
>
> (115-17)

> He came then, after night fell, to visit that lofty
> house, to see how the Ring-Danes had settled
> into it after the pouring of beer.

Note first the paralleling, for purposes of strictest contrast, of *earfoðlice* 86 with *eadiglice* 100, and of *þrage geþolode* 87 with *dreamum lifdon* 99. The formal antithesis suggested on a small scale by such verbal patterns extends of course to much larger contrasts. The explanation in the scop's song of how the universe was created, following as it does upon the description of the building of Heorot and the establishment of the great Danish civilization it represents (its light gleams over many lands), has its complement in the explanation of Grendel's origin—how dark evil came into being in the midst of a universe of sunlight and green leaves. On one side of this great opposition we have human society in harmony with the divine plan, dazzling in images of light, song, and joy; on the other side we have Grendel-Cain, the individual who has freely chosen to rebel against human society and who is now outcast in a world of darkness, misery, and violence. (pp. 31-6)

At the very center of this opposition is the *oððæt* phrase, which, by introducing the element of time into the static opposition, sets the active conflict of the poem in motion. They lived in joy until. . . . The construction here (perhaps partly because of its semi-formulaic use in similar contexts) points both to human capacities for happy unawareness of the darkness outside and to the nature of a world that sooner or later always brings in on us its merciless ''until,'' where time, change, and disaster operate outside man's powers of control.

The particular ''good'' broken in on by such ominous untils is, as this Heorot-Grendel contrast implies, most often a social good. Social order is to be succeeded by social chaos. At one extreme, the social good may take the form of a friendly, if rivalrous, community of two: Breca and Beowulf stay together in their swim (partly for mutual protection) until a storm drives them apart. At the other end of the range, it may take the form of the peace and order of an entire nation over a long period of time: Beowulf ruled the Geats well for fifty years, until a dragon began to gain power on dark nights.

The reference to dark nights suggests that most primitive, durable, and effective of all poetic dichotomies, the opposition of light and dark, and images of light and dark are often associated with these constructions. We see this contrast used to good effect, for example, in this sentence from Beowulf's report to Hygelac:

> Swa we þær inne   ondlangne dæg
> niode naman,   oððæt niht becwom
> oðer to yldum.
>
> (2115-17a)

> In this way we enjoyed ourselves indoors the whole long day, until another night arrived for men.

The poet combines the idea of being *inne*—inside, warm, and secure—with what seems to be suggested by *ondlangne dæg*, namely, the possession of a long space of time for relaxed enjoyment free from interruption, and thrusts against this combination the contrasting image of night (both darkness and time itself) arriving among men as an assailant or intruder.

Attention to such patterns of imagery may even provide some help in reaching satisfactory interpretations of such passages as . . . the poet's account [in lines 642-51] of the first night in Heorot, when Hrothgar decides to retire to sleep. . . . Like many others, this passage reveals the heavy emphasis that the poem places on the cyclic rhythms of joy and sorrow in human experience. The feast here is really a great outburst of joy and hope, which follows twelve long years of anxiety and despair for the Danes. But the sound of merriment is no sooner heard than a change is signaled, within the very space of a single alliterative line: *sigefolca sweg, oþþæt semninga*. . . . Hrothgar's sudden decision to retire is not in itself occasion for alarm except insofar as it marks the end of communal joy, but the poet seems to touch here, as often, on such simple but profound primitive fears as the child's reluctance at bedtime to leave the warm safe circle. The next few lines are not clear beyond dispute, but we seem to be told that Hrothgar knew that Grendel had been waiting all day (or possibly all evening, from the beginning of sunset until total darkness) to make his assault on Heorot. Perhaps this knowledge on Hrothgar's part is offered as a kind of reason for his retirement from the scene; at night it is now Grendel's hall, as it has been for twelve years—or else it may now be Beowulf's hall, for Hrothgar's last act before leaving Heorot is to deed over the hall to Beowulf: *hafa nu ond geheald husa selest* (658).

In a more strictly poetic way, several effective contrasts are made here. In the final lines of the passage, through the channel of Hrothgar's imagination, the outside world of darkness is permitted to come into our consciousness; it comes rushing in—*scriðan cwoman*—on the heels of the *oþ* phrase, after having been staved off and held at a distance for those brief moments of light. The similarity in the language here to that used to describe Grendel when he actually comes (*com on wanre niht / scriðan sceadugenga* 702b-03a) points to the close identification of Grendel, who indeed is later described as *æfengrom* (2074) (evening-ferocious), with darkness itself. Yet he is no more than a conspicuously energetic pseudopod of that darkness. Here and throughout the poem we are to think of the ultimate darkness of chaos and nonbeing which hangs first over this proud and splendid civilization of Denmark (if only because we are so often reminded of the destructive feuds in prospect) and which, beyond that, hangs over all human institutions and all men. Against a background of this immensity the hall becomes a crucial symbol, and the defender of the hall the embodiment of a profound kind of courage even beyond ordinary heroism.

Old age and death figure in two instances of the "until" construction. Beowulf survives many battles until that one day when he is obliged to face the dragon. And great Hrothgar was always blameless, especially in his generosity, until age took the joy of his strength from him, as it has often injured many a man. These are the universal untils that come to all.

Weapons that outlast their owners are used as symbols of the pathos of human existence more than once in the poem. . . . One "until" phrase gives expression to this idea. The weapons and armor worn by the Danes in the Ingeld episode were once the property of the Heathobards, who (it is implied) had rejoiced in the excellent qualities of these arms until they lost their comrades in battle, and afterwards lost their own lives.

Finally, in the partially Christianized sermon that Hrothgar preaches to Beowulf, there is a passage containing both [a negative-plus adversative] . . . and an *oððæt* construction. Hrothgar is speaking of the fortunate man who can see no end to his prosperity.

> Wunað he on wiste;   no hine wiht dweleð
> adl ne yldo,   he him inwitsorh
> on sef*an* sweorceð,   ne gesacu ohwær
> ecghete eoweð,   ac him eal worold
> wendeð on willan   (he þæt wyrse ne con),
> oðþæt him on innan   oferhygda dæl
> weaxeð ond wridað.
>
> (1735-41a)

A reconstruction of the mask helmet found in the ship burial at Sutton Hoo. The British Museum.

> Life for him is a feast. Disease and old age never block his path; evil sorrow never darkens his mind; no quarrels bring the savage attack of swords. No, for him the whole world goes as he wishes—he has no knowledge of something worse—until within him an enormous pride grows and puts forth shoots.

In its allusions to the common lot of human suffering from which this man thinks himself exempt, the rhetorical series of negative phrases leads us toward the "until" climax of unrealistic pride. But it is worth observing that the "until" construction here suggests something different from what is suggested by other examples in the poem. There such external forces as death, old age, or attack by evil creatures, all aspects of what we call fate and all beyond human control, are seen as arriving from outside to disrupt or destroy human happiness. That the "until" here is clearly internalized and placed in a pattern of moral cause and effect significantly reflects the Christian thinking of this sermon. It is important to recognize, however, that such a pattern is exceptional in ***Beowulf.*** (pp. 36-42)

Edward B. Irving Jr., in his A Reading of "Beowulf," *Yale University Press, 1968, 256 p.*

JOHN HALVERSON (essay date 1969)

[Halverson is an American scholar of medieval literature. In the following excerpt, he surveys the responsibility of the hero and king for maintaining social order in the world of Beowulf. *Translations in this excerpt are taken from* Beowulf: A Dual-Language Edition *by Howell D. Chickering, Jr.]*

In the first part of ***Beowulf,*** Heorot is the center of the world. Almost all movement is focused on it. Grendel seeks it out for destructive purposes; Beowulf comes to cleanse it. All the nobles assemble there; there the King presides and distributes treasure. It shines out over many lands (311), a beacon of civilization; it is the people's place ("folcstede"—76). For the dwellers on earth it is the foremost building under the heavens (309-310). It towers "healærna mæst" (78), spacious and gold-adorned (1799 f.), on a high place (285). Lavishly adorned, it is a splendid, shining structure. It is the work of many hands (992); many a people is called upon to decorate the people's place (74-6): it is the product of social enterprise. It is a place of protection (1037), a place of safety (2075), above all, a place of communal joy, of light, warmth, song, and companionship. The festivities of the hall are suffused with the social pleasures of food and drink and the music of the harp. The queen, adorned with gold, moves among the people, greets them, proffers a cup (612 ff.). There is always the pleasant sound of human voices. . . .

The hall is where treasure is distributed, a function uppermost in Hrothgar's mind when he builds Heorot (71-2). "Nor did he belie that promise; he distributed bracelets, treasure at the feast" (80-1). Common *heiti* for Hrothgar (as for kings generally in Old English) denote a giver of treasure; *sincgifa, goldgyfa, sinces brytta, beaga brytta,* etc. Heorot is not only a monumental artifact, an achievement of *homo faber* ["man the maker"]; it is also the center for *homo politicus* ["man among civil men"], the place of social joy, music, drinking and feasting, the source of pleasure, where friends and kinsmen are together in peace. The hall embodies all the good things of this world; it represents the principle of harmony: everything is in order.

At the center of the center is the King, Hrothgar. It is his hall. . . . His presence dominates the assemblies. Petitions are addressed to him, and it is he who makes all decisions. He is the source of food, drink, and treasure. And he is the protector of his people: the most frequent *heiti* for him are combinations with *helm, hleo, hyrde, eodor,* and *weard,* and Hrothgar himself speaks of this role of the king (1769-71). He gives extended advice to Beowulf about the role and duty of the king (1700 ff.), and cites the negative example of Heremod. . . . The ruler who abandons his primary duties of protection and liberality becomes a monster, solitary and joyless. He will die and another succeed him who shares treasure, the ancient wealth of earls, without regret, without fear. . . . Hrothgar, self-evidently, and by Beowulf's later confirmation, is such a *god cyning*. . . . Expressions such as *æfter dome* and *Þeawum lyfde* reveal the basis of the king's prestige in his steadfast adherence to the old customs; he is the guardian of time. The good king maintains his country, his retainers and people, and their traditions; he is the protector, the champion of his people, not their bane. Such a ruler is Hrothgar; so was Offa (1957 ff.); so will Beowulf be.

As the center of the community, the King receives the deference that is his due. Hrothgar's pre-eminence in the court is obvious. The centrality of his position is implied in Beowulf's first approach to him, from sentinel to Heorot to the King's intermediary ("ar ond ombiht"—336) to the King himself: Beowulf moves in definite stages from the periphery to the center. Heorot and Hrothgar seem to be identified by Grendel; not only does the demon hate the joyful sounds and appearance of the great hall, but he also carries on a feud with its king. . . . That Grendel's feud is not personal may be surmised from the fact that Grendel makes no attempt to find the King and kill him.

Even the digression of the swimming contest is directed toward Hrothgar insofar as the conclusion of the episode is his reassurance in Beowulf (608-10). Narrative divisions are often marked by the entrance or exit of Hrothgar or by Beowulf's going to him. Beowulf's journey is completed the moment he is in the King's presence. Their first long interview is closed by Hrothgar's departure (662) and the stage left for Beowulf's encounter with Grendel. The next scene, an interlude before the fight with Grendel's mother, opens with Hrothgar's arrival in state to look at Grendel's arm (920-2) and closes with the King's departure, exactly as before (1236-7). The depredations of the monster follow. Then Beowulf goes to the King (1316-9) and learns the news; the two go off to the mere together (1400-1); when the pool becomes bloody, the King returns home (1601-2); when Beowulf emerges, he goes directly to greet Hrothgar (1644-6). The presence of the King defines the movement of the narrative.

The poet also shows more interest in the state of Hrothgar's emotions—his sorrow and joy, his feelings of confidence, hope and doubt—than in anyone else's. His opinions, judgments, and feelings are central. His movements and speech are formal, nearly ritual. A courtly protocol is maintained, as we learn at the time of Beowulf's first audience when Wulfgar is implicitly commended because "cuþe he duguðe Þeaw" ["he knew the noble custom"] (359). Hrothgar is nearly always surrounded by a retinue: "Hroðgar sæt / eald ond anhar mid his eorla gedriht" ["Hrothgar sat, old, gray-bearded, surrounded by nobles"] (356-7). There is a slight suggestion in these passages of hierarchy, of an incipient differentiation of court and nobility. There is a distinct suggestion of the ceremonial, or ritual, magnification of the king. His movements frequently have such a tone: he goes "tirfæst" or "geatolic" and is accompanied by a splendid retinue. When he speaks, everyone becomes silent (1699).

Hrothgar has some of the numen that in many cultural traditions surrounds the royal person. A particularly striking sequence at the beginning of the poem draws an implicit parallel between Hrothgar as maker and God as creator. The King's first significant act is the construction of the great hall, for which he "shapes" the name Heorot ("scop him Heort naman"—78). Following almost immediately is the song of the scop about the creation of the world. The Almighty constructed the earth, set out the sun and moon, luminaries as light for dwellers of the land . . . , and adorned the regions of the earth with branches and leaves, and also shaped life. . . . Heorot is such a luminary . . . for the dwellers in the land . . . and much adorned. . . . Indeed, the king as builder and lord of the hall is exactly the extended metaphor for Christ that begins the poem of that name. A similar parallel is implicit when we are told of the giants who fought against God a long time (. . . 113-4) and shortly after, that Grendel fought against Hrothgar a long time (. . . 151-2).

So there are a number of suggestions in the representation of Heorot and Hrothgar of God and his creation. The importance of the assimilation is in the idea of creating or making, which is seen as a God-like act. As God brought form out of chaos, light out of darkness, so the king brings order to his world and maintains it. If the construction of Heorot is conceived as a repetition of the original cosmogonic act, then its destruction by fire would correspond closely to the end of the world as envisioned by the Old Norse *Voluspa,* and the death of Hrothgar to that of Othin. The meaningfulness of the center is obvious in ***Beowulf,*** as it is in all the Old English elegiac literature, particularly in the theme of exile. The lord's hall defines meaningful reality.

At the political-social level, the struggle for order is very clear, and the achievement as clearly tenuous. The role of kinship groups in the development of medieval forms of social organization was fundamental; in ***Beowulf*** the *winemæg* ["friend and kinsman"] relationship is the most important of social ties. The solidarity of the kinship group is evident in the obligation of vengeance that fell on the kinsmen of a slain person and the corresponding responsibility for sharing the punishment of a malefactor. This obligation and mutual responsibility were still virtually unquestioned even at the end of the middle ages. The psychological foundation of the *winemæg* relationship is the nature of the family: its interdependence, its proximity, its "natural" solidarity. If anything was secure and reliable, it was first of all the immediate family. At least one's kinsmen could be trusted. The primary bond of society became *treow,* "good faith, trust," as epitomized by the family tie; the hoped-for result is indicated by the fact that the word *sib* means both "kinship" and "peace." The most edifying personal associations in ***Beowulf,*** those the hero has with Hrothgar, Hygelac, and Wiglaf, find expression in the family relationship. Wiglaf and Hygelac are both blood relatives to Beowulf, and Hrothgar's highest tribute to the hero is to adopt him as his son (946-9). Besides these admirable examples of the loyalty and love of kinsmen are those illustating the despised opposite. The prototype is Cain, who slew his own brother (108, 1261-3). Unferth is guilty of the same crime according to both Beowulf (587) and the poet (1166-8). Hints are given of treachery to come from Hrothgar's nephew, Hrothulf:

Þa godan twegen
sæton suhtergefæderan; Þa gyt wæs hiera sib
ætgædere,
æghwylc oðrum trywe.

(1163-5; cf. 1015 ff.)

["Wealhtheow came forth, glistening in gold,
to greet the good pair, uncle and nephew; their
peace was still firm, each true to the other."]

The disruption of that *sib* by Hrothulf's rebellion was to begin the tragic downfall of the Danes.

The war of kinsman against kinsman is a terrible thing. It is one of Beowulf's chief virtues that he never injured kinsmen—or companions. The extension of the social organization of the family and its ethical principles to a larger group, the companions of the hall, is obviously not difficult, especially as relatives proliferate and the distinction between *wine* and *magas* becomes blurred. In any event, the organization of the *duguþ* ["body of retainers"] relies on the same trust as that of the family. The extension is discernible in such terms as *sibbegedryht* ["band of kinsmen"], used twice for Beowulf's followers in the first part of the poem, where there is no indication that they are his kinsmen. Loyalty to the lord is the primary virtue of retainers, but it is conditional on the lord's liberality. His obligation to distribute treasure is cited again and again in ***Beowulf*** and in Old English literature generally; just as consistently, the regular form of battlefield exhortation is to remember the gifts of the lord. We hear it not only from Wiglaf, but from Brytnoth's retainers in *The Battle of Maldon* and even from Satan in *Genesis B* (409 ff.). Thus the tie between lord and retainers is more formally contractual than that obtaining in the kinship group. The contract eventually develops into the ritual of fealty with its attendant complications, but at this earlier period, duties and responsibilities are relatively simple and immediate. The most striking carry-over from kinship ethics is the duty to revenge a slain lord. A mere contract would terminate with the death of the lord; obligations would cease at that moment. But the ideal of vengeance for the slain earl is everywhere in evidence and a principal source of the drama of *The Battle of Maldon* and of the Finn episode of ***Beowulf.***

In that passage and in two or three other places in the poem, the final extension of the trust-ethic can be seen, that is, in the relationships between different peoples. At this level formal oaths are required, supported by the giving or exchanging of gifts, including women in political marriages. After the fall of his lord, Hengest swears a truce with Finn, but the duty of vengeance rankles until it can be fulfilled. Hrothgar settles with the Wylfings by sending ancient treasures and receiving oaths (470-2); he looks forward to amity with the Geats, brought about by Beowulf and to be confirmed by the gifts and tokens of love that his ship will take over the sea: the two nations will be strongly allied "after the old fashion" (1855-65). Wealhtheow, it is implied by her designation as "friðusibb folca," was married to Hrothgar as a peace-pledge of peoples, and her daughter, Freawaru, is similarly allied to Ingeld of the Heathobards in the hope of settling that feud. The purpose of the king's giving of treasure is quite clear in Hrothgar's actions and statements: it is the cement of the political structure.

But it is tragically ineffective. An atmosphere of anxiety broods over all the social relationships of ***Beowulf,*** familial and political. Justly, for kinsman rises against kinsman, retainer against lord, the lord against his companions; political feud breaks out again after tentative settlement; the Danes will destroy themselves in internecine war, the Geats will be overthrown by their enemies; oaths are broken, the peace-pledges forgotten. Nothing is secure, nothing stable. And Heorot will go up in flames. (pp. 593-99)

The contrast and conflict of two worlds—inside and outside, the world of man and the world of monsters, the world of order and the world of chaos—constitute the basic philosophical and psychological structure of ***Beowulf.*** On one side is the world enclosed by the walls of Heorot and presided over by Hrothgar. It is a man-made world, its construction requiring cooperative labor, art and technology; in it men speak and act rationally and according to custom; there is about it a sense of material and social form. It is a world that represents the imposition of order and organization on chaotic surroundings. The results of this ordering are (temporarily) security, light and warmth. It is a socially collective world, where the pleasures of human companionship can be enjoyed in the feasting and drinking, in the sharing of treasure, in talking, in the playing of the harp and the reciting of old tales.

The world out there—cold, dark, and cheerless—is dominated by the image of fens and moors haunted by the two monsters, solitary creatures who cannot participate in the joy of the community and who savagely hate its existence. As Hrothgar is a maker, they are destroyers. Because their world is without form, it is without security and without pleasure. It is silent, frightening, monstrous. This is the world represented by the mere when the heralding blast of the trumpet disturbs its watery silence, maddening the monster serpents, who can bear the sound of the horn no more than Grendel the sound of harps.

This polar opposition of worlds is so fundamental that it gives an inevitable, fatal quality to the critical conflict of ***Beowulf,*** the struggle between the civilized world and the world out there, which begins with the invasion of Heorot by Grendel. No reason is given for Grendel's rage against Heorot; it is sudden, gratuitous, and irrational. It would seem (though it is not an obligatory inference) that Grendel has been around for some time; it is the building of Heorot that enrages him and goads him to his depredations. Precisely directed and motivated, his attack is not against the Danes as such but against the great hall, or rather what the hall stands for and makes possible: the establishment of human order with its consequent pleasures. Though he rejoices in slaughter as he goes to seek his dwelling (124-5), still his motive is not simply dietary, for apparently everyone stays out of Heorot after dark, which seems all that is required to avoid being eaten (138-42). Presumably Grendel could find his victims someplace besides Heorot, but he doesn't. His essential purpose, then, must be what in fact he accomplishes: he empties the hall. He breaks down the doors to this little enclosed world, puts out the light, lets in the cold, and, himself the embodiment of chaos, presides in darkness over Heorot, the construct of order.

So too Hrothgar's constant affliction and woe over twelve years seem to be due as much to this fact as to actual loss of life. His great achievements are being negated by the monster, and not only the Danes suffer but the precarious status of civilization as well. The resolution of this impasse, the "bright remedy" of which the Danes despair, comes from across the sea.

When Beowulf hears of Hrothgar's peril, he takes no thought of his action, but responds instantly (194-201). It is his natural function, as it were, to restore order where it has been upset. The Danes are otherwise nothing to him. Heorot is polluted, the once bright center plunged into darkness, the enclosure of civilization broken down. The atmosphere of the land of the Danes is one of gloom, hopelessness, and stasis; Danish society has been rendered immobile and desperate. In sharpest contrast to this murky atmosphere, the introduction of Beowulf into the poem is accompanied by the flash and rattle of armor, the fresh sea air, the bustle of activity; all that Beowulf and his men do is alive with purpose, direction and hope. As Herbert G. Wright says [in his 1957 article "Good and Evil; Light and Darkness; Joy and Sorrow in *Beowulf*"], "the landing of Beowulf and his followers is the signal for the irradiation of the scene with a flood of brilliant light." The ship is readied, the men chosen and armed. They set sail, quickly cross the sea, and land. Action is all, and directed unswervingly to a single end. It is urgent and purposive. The speed of the voyage, the sea wind, begin immediately to clear the atmosphere (217 ff.). Beowulf's first announced goal is to seek out the war-king over the sea (199 f.), and his progress is single-mindedly in that direction, straight to the king, and when he is at last in the king's presence, he comes instantly to the point. He has heard of the Grendel affair; he would cleanse Heorot, "Heorot fælsian" (432). Again the hall is the center of the narrative structure. Beowulf's role is that of civilization's champion, the hero who restores order when it has been weakened or destroyed. What is wrong in Denmark is not so much that Grendel terrifies the people but that the great hall stands "idel ond unnyt." When Beowulf finally succeeds in destroying the monsters, Heorot once more becomes the center of warmth, light and companionship, and the hero's mission is accomplished.

In the last part of the poem, Beowulf's role is much the same, and the situations and incidents are also parallel to those of the first part. The crisis which the hero is called upon to deal with is the depredation of a solitary monster of the night, now a dragon. Like Grendel's lair, the dragon's barrow is an "uncuð" place. Like Grendel, the dragon hates and humiliates men. Like Grendel, the dragon directs his wrath at the dwellings of men, and his terrors are known far and wide. To Beowulf, again, the crisis is made known (2324; cf. 194-5). His own hall, "bolda selest," is consumed by fire. And like Hrothgar, he is filled with sorrow. But as he had done in the past, he acts instantly and purposefully (2337 ff.; cf. 198 f.).

The pattern of significant events is quite like that of the first part. A monster of the night who embodies all that is hostile and terrifying about the world out there threatens to annihilate the constructed human world of "bright houses." The hero, responding to this crisis with speed and purpose, assumes the role of defender and restorer of civilization. The significant difference is in the outcome of the hero's battle, for in his final struggle against the destructive forces of the world outside, Beowulf is himself destroyed.

The result of the conflict between the constructed, rationalized human world and the chaotic, frightening world out there is not reassuring. The victories of Beowulf are great ones, but they are temporary; the threat remains, and the entire poem is haunted by the vision of ultimate destruction. The life of man and the works of man are fleeting and doomed. The Christian consolation of salvation has no significant part in ***Beowulf,*** nor even the Boethian consolation of the larger view; it is something rather closer to the northern Ragnarök that is implied. (pp. 601-04)

The ending of ***Beowulf*** is dominated not only by the death and funeral of the hero but also by the gloomy expectations of Wiglaf and his messenger: there will be no more receiving of treasure, no more land rights when the far-away princes learn of the death of Beowulf and the "domleasan dæd" of his men (2884 ff.). The elegiac vision of the poem has been eloquently stated by Tolkien: "we look down as if from a visionary height upon the house of man in the valley of the world. A light starts—*lixte se leoma ofer land fela*—and there is a sound of music; but the outer darkness and its hostile offspring lie ever in wait for the torches to fail and the voices to cease. Grendel is maddened by the sound of harps" [see excerpt dated 1936]. Beowulf, Hrothgar, Heorot, the achievements of civilization constitute a brave and defiant intrusion of human order into the formlessness of the outside world. But it is a doomed enterprise, for more than a temporary establishment is as yet beyond the capacity of the struggling society represented by the poem. (pp. 604-05)

The pathos of much Old English poetry, especially ***Beowulf,*** is based on themes of isolation, exile, and the dissolution of social order. The prophecies at the end of ***Beowulf*** concern the break-up of Geatish society. There is a recurring sense of yearning for social stability and material durability: a dynasty that will not be destroyed by feud and war, a hall that will not be consumed by fire or ravaged by monsters. The way to stability, the poem seems ultimately to suggest, is through closer social ties and great common effort. This is implicit in the *treow*-ethic [ethic of truth and fidelity], but conflicts with heroic individualism.

The old social ideals are all reaffirmed in the end, though the responsibilities of Beowulf as a king are not altogether the same as his duties as a warrior. When he learns of the dragon's visitation, Beowulf at first guiltily fears having gone "ofer ealde riht." What this "ancient law" comprises becomes clear in his dying *apologia* [in lines 2736-43]. . . . He has not transgressed the old law . . . ; he has lived up to the code, protecting his people, true to his oaths, faithful to his kinsmen. His fame secure, he can die content. That the traditional contractual obligations take precedence even over the lord's commands is a direct implication of the contrasting actions of Wiglaf and the other retainers. They had all been expressly forbidden by Beowulf to take part in the struggle (2529-35). Nevertheless, when in spite of this order Wiglaf comes to Beowulf's aid, the poet commends him: "swylc sceolde secg wesan" (2708). Likewise, Wiglaf's denunciation of the deserters (2684-91) is presented as just, though they "only obeyed orders." It is the poet who calls them "treowlogan," beliers of their trust. Wiglaf recalls the obligation imposed by Beowulf's liberality; in return for his gifts it was their duty to support him at need. But he threw away his gifts on them. Once more the importance—and weakness—of *treow* ["faithfulness"] as the foundation of social order is demonstrated.

Wiglaf also makes a bold, but just, criticism of Beowulf himself [in lines 3077-81]. . . . We recall that Hygelac had long before tried to dissuade Beowulf from the Grendel adventure, but then Beowulf was not a king. His death would have been an enormous personal loss, but it would not have meant the disintegration of the Geatish nation, as it does now. The king has greater responsibility than the warrior. Wiglaf, by his implicit modification of the heroic ideal of purely individual action, hints at the idea of the precedence of the group and the office over the individual, and thus looks forward to a redefined relationship between hero and community that emerges later in the middle ages. (pp. 605-07)

Old English poetry is infused with a sense of mortality and mutability. There was no lack of awareness that life is short and hard. But there is also, as a kind of compensation, a naive cherishing of artifacts: the old treasures that survive through time and can be handed down across the generations. The supreme artifact is the house of man, Heorot, where the world's vicissitudes are transcended in a moment of human collectivity. But it is a dream. The monsters of the night invade the hall, the dragon seizes the treasure. If the hero restores the hall and treasure, it is only for the moment, for his time. (pp. 607-08)

The code of loyalty, personal or impersonal, is implicitly and potentially a means toward social unity; it expresses the intent of cooperation. Why does it fail? Because of individualism. The "cowardice" of the retainers is simply an expression of the priority of the individual over the group. Wiglaf seems dimly to see the dilemma, the glory and the curse of individualism. The retainers were not legally culpable for not coming to Beowulf's aid; they did only what they were told to do. Yet Wiglaf's denunciation and his evocation of the loyalty code are right, for the saving of their society requires the cooperative effort that the code contemplates. He also sees the limitations of individual heroism. Beowulf, the greatest of heroes, is loved and revered by his nephew, but the heroic solution is not always the best solution. It is not Beowulf's pride that brings about the ultimate catastrophe, but precisely his heroism. He is not a victim of ego inflation; he simply cannot see other alternatives to his own way. He is a victim of the heroic milieu; he is molded gloriously and inflexibly by his world. (p. 608)

John Halverson, "The World of 'Beowulf'," in ELH, *Vol. 36, No. 4, December, 1969, pp. 593-608.*

MARGARET E. GOLDSMITH (essay date 1970)

[*In the following excerpt, Goldsmith examines in detail manifestations of the various forms of religious faith held by the characters in* Beowulf. *Translations in this excerpt are taken from* Beowulf: A Dual-Language Edition *by Howell D. Chickering, Jr.*]

There are some very singular features in the religion imputed to the characters [in ***Beowulf***] and some apparent inconsistencies in the poet's own attitude towards them. (p. 146)

The first curious feature is that there are no priests and no specific religious rites, either Christian or heathen, at the courts of Hrothgar, Hygelac, or Beowulf. This can hardly reflect the real-life situation either of the historical Danes and Geats or of the Anglo-Saxon courts known to the poet. It is in marked contrast with classical epic practice, in which prayers and libations to the gods accompany every great undertaking. When Beowulf set off for Denmark his friends *hæl sceawedon* ["observed the omens"] (204), but what they actually did, and whether some rite was involved, the poet does not reveal. The disposal of the dead involves no religious ceremonial, though certain ancient customs—such as riding round the grave—are mentioned. Even when the Danes pray to idols in their fear of Grendel, no pagan god is named and the nature of their sacrifices remains mysterious (175-8).

The second strange feature is a combination of circumstances: both Danes and Geats speak of God and acknowledge his governance of the world, yet they offer no prayers to God in direct address, and the poem also says in a notoriously confusing fashion, that they did not know God:

Metod hie ne cuþon,
dæda demend, ne wiston hie drihten god,
ne hie huru heofena helm herian he cuþon
wuldres waldend.

(180-3)

> [''They knew not the Lord, the Judge of our deeds, were ignorant of God, knew not how to worship our Protector above, the King of Glory.'']

In spite of this passage, Hrothgar speaks at length to Beowulf about God's gifts to man and the need to shun the evil of pride, showing a good understanding of the doctrine and language of temptation (1700-81). This long speech, rightly regarded as a homily, has more specific relevance to the action than is usually conceded. . . . Hrothgar is credited with sound knowledge of God's law and the Devil's attempts to alienate man from God. Beowulf, too, expressly speaks of God's part in mortal affairs, and at one point fears that he has angered the eternal Lord (2329-31).

On another level of theological improbability are Beowulf's direct mention of hell and judgment in two of his speeches, one concerning Unferth's guilt as a fratricide (587-9), the other in his account to Hrothgar of Grendel's death and present wait for God's judgment upon him (974-9).

In his own voice, the poet several times speaks of God's rule over the world in all ages. He makes no reference to the Trinity: his own phrases about divine subjects are not markedly different from those put in the mouths of the characters. He imputes sin, in an allusive form of words, to Grendel (137) and to Heremod (915); he also describes Grendel as *hæþen* [''heathen''] (852, 986). This word is otherwise employed only twice, in reference to the buried gold and in the context just mentioned of the Danes' idol-worship (179). He says very little concerning the after-life; apart from the plain statement that hell received Grendel (852), the expressions he uses are notably vague and sometimes ambiguous. Nowhere does he speak of heaven outright, or of its joy.

It will be seen that the matters I have put first present no great problem; granted that a Christian poet wished to create an impression of a pre-Christian world, he would understandably not wish to revive memories of the displaced deities, or forms of worship now decently forgotten, or, worse, still lurking in the half-light of memory among the Anglo-Saxon people. . . . [If the conflict of fundamental conceptions about the Danish religion] is for the moment put aside, the other religious references can, I think, be reasonably accommodated in a theory that the poet has used his patristic learning (or that of his teachers) about the nature of man to create an imagined world upon which the revelation of God in Christ has not impinged. For information about the beliefs of good men ignorant of the scriptural law of God he would naturally turn to the Book of Job, in which a just man who was neither Jew nor Christian showed unmistakable faith in his Creator and defeated the Devil's attacks upon that faith. He would, of course, be influenced by Gregory's view of Job's life and interpretation of Job's words. Gregory frequently uses other Old Testament texts to elucidate Job's speeches, often quoting the Psalms for this purpose. Here, I suggest, lies the explanation of Beowulf's anachronistic knowledge of hell and judgment and Hrothgar's knowledge of temptation: they are modelled upon Job in this respect, and we . . . also find illumination of the attitudes imputed to them in the network of patristic thinking which formed a web round the Psalms. (pp. 146-49)

Two kinds of religious passage are to be distinguished [in ***Beowulf***]: the first kind comprising the thoughts and utterances imputed to the characters in the poem, the second, observations in the poet's own voice which state or imply his attitude towards the matter he is recounting. I begin with the former group.

Hrothgar is the first of the characters to be developed as a person. His scheme for the building of a great hall includes the thought of himself as royal provider of bounty, liberally sharing all his possessions *swylc him God sealde* [''all God had given him''] (72). This indication that Hrothgar believes in God's control over all that happens to him is borne out in several speeches. When he hears of Beowulf's coming, he says

> hine halig God
> for arstafum us onsende.
>
> (381 f.)

> [''Holy God in the fullness of mercy has sent him to us.'']

The epithet ''holy'' with its Old Testament associations no doubt seemed fully appropriate in the mouth of a pre-Christian king; *for arstafum* is one of a number of phrases in the poem which may have secular or religious overtones. (p. 157)

Hrothgar shows continuing faith in God's benevolent power, and ascribes Beowulf's victory over Grendel to *Drihtnes miht* [''the might of the Lord''] (940). In praising Beowulf he says that the hero's mother was blessed by *Ealdmetod* [''Eternal God''] (945) a unique and curious word which may have been suggested by Daniel's vision of the Judge who is called *antiquus dierum* [''the ancient of days''] (Dan 7: 9 and 7: 22); it has an appropriately antique sound in Hrothgar's mouth. This speech ends with a blessing on Beowulf which again recognizes that the hero's success has been due to divine favour (955 f.). When sorrow comes again, Hrothgar's thoughts turn to God as the Almighty Ruler who directs his life (1313 ff.), and he thanks God that his champion proves ready for the new challenge (1397 f.). Beowulf's second victory draws from the king a long speech about God's gifts to men and the deterioration that comes with age. Once more he thanks God for the death of his enemy (1778 ff.). He makes a final speech to Beowulf before they part, in which he praises the hero's wise words as sent by the Lord (1841 f.). In sum, Hrothgar's thoughts and speeches show faith in God as an almighty and benevolent Lord who is the source of men's strength and wisdom.

Queen Wealhtheow, like Hrothgar, gives thanks to God for Beowulf's aid to them (625). Of the other Danes, only one man speaks of God: the captain who guards the shore takes leave of Beowulf with a blessing on his enterprise, in the words,

> Mæl is me to feran; fæder alwalda
> mid arstafum eowic gehealde
> siða gesunde.
>
> (316-18)

> [''It is time I returned; the Father all-powerful in His mercy keep you safe through all your ventures.'']

. . . [It] is hardly necessary to look beyond the Bible for this usage; the tone of the poem is very much in accord with the fighting spirit of Psalm 88, in which the psalmist puts into the mouth of God these words concerning the warrior David:

> ipse inuocabit me, pater meus es tu,
> Deus meus et susceptor salutis meae.
>
> (Ps. 88: 27)

> ''he shall cry out to me: Thou art my father, my God, and the support of my salvation.''

It seems very probable that the ***Beowulf*** poet imagined the pre-Christian world of his heroes as being rather like the world of David; the verse I have quoted with its *pater* and *susceptor salutis* might very well have been in the poet's mind as he composed lines 316 ff. In all respects, therefore, the God of the Danes is like the God of ancient Israel. It is natural enough that the poet should use the Old Testament to supply him with suitable religious language for his pre-Christian wise men, since any authentic pagan phrases known to him would smack of error or blasphemy. Hrothgar is presented as a man to whom adversity has taught something of the true nature of human life; any purely pagan expressions put in his mouth would blur this picture in the interests of historical likelihood, a much less important aspect of story-telling in those days.

The religion of the Geats is even more lightly sketched in. Beowulf's little band thank God for their safe journey (227 f.), and on their return Hygelac gives thanks that his nephew has come back unscathed (1997 f.). Wiglaf speaks as a man with faith in God, first when he calls God as witness of his desire to die beside his lord (2650 f.), and after Beowulf's death, when he tells the deserters that God allowed Beowulf to avenge himself upon the dragon without their aid. His statement does not accord with the narrative of the dragon-slaying:

hwæðre him god uðe
sigora waldend, þæt he hine sylfne gewræc
ana mid ecge, þa him wæs elnes þearf.
(2874-6)

["However, God granted, Ruler of victories,
that he avenge himself, alone, with his sword,
when courage was needed."]

Here occurs one of those inconsistencies which arise through the habit of composing individual scenes each with their appropriate emotions and moral attitudes. It is fitting that Wiglaf should give the credit of the dragon-slaying to his king, emphasizing Beowulf's greatness beside the cowards' corporate panic, and this leads to the exaggeration of *ana mid ecge* ["alone, with his sword"] (2876), in contradiction with

Feond gefyldan (ferh ellen wræc),
ond hi hyne þa begen abroten hæfdon,
sibæðelingas
(2706-8)

["They killed their foe—courage took his life—
both of the nobles, kinsmen together, had destroyed the dragon."]

In the latter passage the narrator's mind is on the loyalty of Wiglaf in the moment of crisis (cp. 2708 f.), and the event takes on a different aspect. It would therefore be unsafe to use Wiglaf's words to the deserters as proof that the poet regarded Beowulf's dragon-slaying as an unqualified God-given victory for the hero; on the contrary, before Wiglaf enters the fray, the poet hints at defeat for Beowulf (2573-5 and 2583 f.), and it is evident from the course of the fight that Beowulf was mortally wounded before the dragon was weakened by Wiglaf's sword-stroke, and could not have finished off the monster alone (cp. 2688-705). On this occasion, Beowulf does not ascribe the death of the foe to God's aid, so Wiglaf's words of lines 2874 f. stand unsupported. The expression *sigora Waldend* ["Ruler of victories"] is probably a commonplace; many variants of the phrase are found in Old English poetry, and already in *Genesis* (1036) the synonymous *sigora Drihten* is mechanically used, without reference to a particular victory. The implication of Wiglaf's words, *him God uðe . . . þæt he hine sylfne gewræc* ["God granted . . . that he avenge himself"], that God approves blood-revenge, was no doubt in keeping with many Anglo-Saxons' views on the matter, and could certainly be regarded as part of primitive moral law, since it even has scriptural support in the Old Testament: "Propinquus occisi homicidam interficiet; statim ut apprehenderit eum interficiet" (*Num*. 35: 19). "The kinsman of him that was slain shall kill the murderer: as soon as he apprehendeth him, he shall kill him." (pp. 158-61)

[Turning now to other of Beowulf's religious utterances], I note particularly his dependence upon God in his second contest. He says himself that the issue was in the balance until God intervened (1657 f.) and that God granted him sight of the ancient sword with which he triumphed (1661 f.). Since the hero placed the issue of the first combat in God's hand, it is remarkable that no similar speeches are made about the last contest. There is, if one compares the preparations for combat, a progression away from the simple confidence that God would judge the outcome, expressed before the Grendel fight, through a concern for his men, his possessions, and his fame (1490 f.) before the second contest, to a tone of fatalism (2525 ff.) and a boast that he will win the gold (2532 ff.) in the speech which precedes the dragon-fight. . . . [The relevant point] is the apparent equation of *wyrd* and *metod* in line 2526 f. In place of *witig God, halig Dryhten* as arbiter, Beowulf here assigns the issue to the decree of *wyrd, metod manna gehwæs* ["as fate decides, the Lord, for each man"]. . . . [It appears that] no inference about Beowulf's heathenism can be drawn from his speaking of *wyrd* and *metod* in the same breath. But it would probably be reasonable to infer that Beowulf is thinking of the darker and inscrutable workings of Providence when he makes the speech under discussion. There is certainly a change from the splendid confidence in God's watch over him when he waited for Grendel's coming.

Beowulf makes three speeches near to the time of his death. He does not commend his soul to God, but his mind turns to the coming judgment of his deeds (2471 ff.), which he contemplates calmly, as one who has obeyed his Lord's laws. He does not speak of his soul; the word is never used by him, though it occurs in Hrothgar's sermon and several times in the narrative. In his dying speech, he gives thanks to God for the treasure which he is bequeathing to his people. He makes no other spiritual preparation for his journey.

One incidental reference to God comes in Beowulf's account of his perilous test of endurance in the sea as a youth. When he had shaken off the grip of the sea-monsters and killed all the hostile creatures that assailed him:

Leoht eastan com
beorht beacen godes; brimu swaþredon,
þæt ic sænæssas geseon mihte
windige weallas. Wyrd oft nereð
unfægne eorl, þonne his ellen deah.
(569-73)

["Light came from the east, God's bright beacon, and the seas calmed, till I saw at last the sea-cliffs, headlands, the windy shore. So fate often saves an undoomed man when his courage holds."]

. . . [This] triumph is an earnest of Beowulf's capability in the great underwater struggle still before him, and as in the more significant combat the victory over the evil creatures is signalled by light and calming of the waters, so in the preliminary trial the boy is aware of the Creator's presence as the sun rises and brings the hope of landfall. (pp. 165-67)

I come now to those religious passages in the poem which are spoken by the poet himself as narrator or commentator. The majority of these may be shortly summed up as affirmations of faith that God governs the lives of men in all ages: these have the subsidiary effect of reminding the audience that the events described took place in remote time. . . .

The most unexpected and violent of all the Christian comments upon the action is the denunciation of the Danes' idol-worship (175-88). Their idolatry is not in itself difficult to accept within the scheme of the poem, since the Israelites in similar fashion turned from the One God to the worship of a golden image, and the religious beliefs of the characters in ***Beowulf*** are . . . conceived as similar to the religion of ancient Israel. The inconsistency which presents the real problem is the explicit statement:

metod hie ne cuþon,
dæda demend, ne wiston hie drihten god.
(180 f.)

[''They knew not the Lord, the Judge of our deeds, were ignorant of God.'']

It is true that Hrothgar himself is not explicitly included in this statement, since he is not named among the idolaters; nevertheless, the *scop*'s song of Creation (90 ff.) and the words of the coast warden to Beowulf (316 ff.) combine to give an impression that the Danes generally reverenced their Creator; the flat denial that they knew God therefore comes as a much greater shock than the statement that they turned to idols. (p. 170)

[If] *ne wiston hie drihten God* were taken as a veiled reference to Christ, and *hie . . . herian ne cuþon* as an allusion to the worship of the Church, the curiously repetitive appearance of the lines would be explained and a way opened to fit them into the general situation of the Danes. The verb *cunnan* can mean ''to know'' in the sense ''to be familiar with the nature of (a person)'' as in the lines,

ic minne can
glædne Hroþulf, þæt he þa geogoðe wile
arum healdan . . .
(1180-2)

[''Full well I know of my gracious Hrothulf that he would rule the young men in honor . . .'']

It has already been observed above that none of the men in the poem addresses God as a person in the normal manner of Christians praying. It seems to me that they ''know of'' Metod, but they do not ''know'' him as revealed in Christ, who is completely unknown to them. The oblique mode of their thanksgiving bears out that *herian ne cuþon;* they had not been taught to worship. It is not easy to find examples of *drihten God* pointing exclusively to God the Son, largely because the doctrine of the Trinity was so important to Anglo-Saxon religious poets that separation of the Persons is not common. . . . I find some support for my supposition in verses from the First Epistle of St John (3: 2-6). . . . [Bede's] strong statement about the universality of natural law was made in comment upon this chapter, so obviously he saw no contradiction between the belief in a natural recognition of God and St John's statement that sinners have not seen or known him. Here perhaps is the answer to the strange inconsistency in the poem: the idolaters among the Danes, having no hope in God, are among the sinners, of whom it is said *et omnis qui peccat, non vidit eum, nec cognovit eum* [''and whosoever sins has not seen him nor known him'']—or, in other words, *Metod hie ne cuþon*. It seems not unlikely that this chapter from St John was in the ***Beowulf*** poet's mind, because of the verses about Cain and homicide (3: 12-15). It provides one more link between the evildoers in Heorot and the kin of Cain who haunt the hall if we can suppose that in writing of *hæþenra hyht* the poet was thinking of the verses quoted above and the *filii diaboli* [''sons of the devil''].

I suggest, therefore, that the disputed lines (180-3) mean ''They did not know God, the Judge of deeds (as a Person, because they had no hope in him, being sinners), they did not know of the Lord (Christ); indeed, they did not know how to worship the Lord of heaven, the Ruler of glory.'' It may well be objected that the biblical knowledge required to understand the passage as I have interpreted it would be outside the range of laymen. This is probably true. But untutored laymen would not be disturbed by the inconsistency. . . . The point is really of no importance to the narrative. However, it probably did not seem a particularly abstruse matter to a clerical poet . . . [who] uses a number of veiled expressions which could only have been appreciated by an intelligent and informed Christian audience. My particular concern is to vindicate the poet from the charge of ignorance or ineptitude in his handling of Christian doctrine, and this I believe the suggested interpretation will do. If it should be asked why the poet did not name Christ in line 181, supposing my surmise to be right, I can only point to the extraordinary absence of the name of Christ from the whole poem; the omission must be deliberate, and the only reason I can suggest . . . [is] that the poet wished to avoid open discussion of the salvation of the righteous heathen. He obviously feels no reticence about the damnation of the unrighteous heathen. . . . (pp. 173-75)

The phrase *herian ne cuþon* may seem to be denied by the reported performance in Heorot of a song which is somewhat similar in content to Cædmon's famous Hymn of Creation. If the two are compared, however, it is noticeable that the repeated praise of God by name which is an important feature of the Hymn is absent from the ***Beowulf*** passage; Cædmon sings of the Creator, the Dane primarily of the Creation. The distinction is very slight, but perhaps significant when one considers with it the absence from the poem of corporate or private prayer to God. Even Beowulf, whose thanksgiving and praise in his dying speech (2794-8) come very close to a Christian prayer, does not use the vocative form of address or the second person pronoun for God. The whole assemblage of near-Christian attitudes is explicable if the poet's theory was that Hrothgar and Beowulf honoured their Creator in their natural wisdom, but because of their ignorance of Christ could not progress to a personal relationship in prayer. In the case of the Danes, the custom (*þeaw*) of making vows to idols might have grown out of the panic caused by Grendel's repeated attacks and been continued during the twelve years of his oppression. Hrothgar is neither involved nor exculpated. . . . The mistake many modern readers make is to try to create a logical real-life situation out of a poem which only treats limited aspects of an imagined world. There is an ambivalence in the poet's attitude to Heorot which will inevitably produce contradictions if each distinct point is pushed further in the direction to which it tends. The liberal king and the happy community are also the impotent king and the divided, sinful, and scared *heorðwerod* [''hearth company'']; the men subjected to the *gastbona* [''devil''] are ruled by a man who has learnt in a long trial of grief and humiliation to fear the Lord and to mistrust the seeming security offered by abundance, stout walls and a strong bodyguard. Hrothgar's patient endurance and hope that one day God will change his lot present one kind of response to adversity, the idolaters' vows and prayers to their images present another kind of response to the trial. Some men emerge from adversity spiritually strong, others take the road to despair and damnation. This thought lies behind the seemingly gratuitous lines 183-8. (pp.175-76)

This brings me to the often misunderstood matter of God's role in the ravaging of Heorot. Augustine's authoritative view of persecution, punishment and humiliation as part of the workings of Providence provides the doctrinal background needed to interpret the monster-attacks in ***Beowulf.*** Though the creatures' malicious desire to harm men is their own, the power to work their evil designs is given them by Providence. Augustine, while recognizing the *occulta dispensatio prouidentiae Dei* [''Providence's secret charge''], distinguishes three reasons why Providence should permit the evildoer to have his way—to punish, to test or to martyr. I do not think the categories are exclusive: the martyr is tested before he comes to his martyrdom, and even the just man who is tested is also a sinner who may merit punishment. Certainly it is difficult to fit Hrothgar, Beowulf and their peoples simply into one category. The peoples appear to be punished like the people of Israel, the Danes perhaps for their idolatry, the Geats for no specified reason. Hrothgar is undoubtedly like Job in many respects, but in view of the idolatry of his people it is perhaps better to think of him as a leader like Aaron, who must be censured for permitting the idol-worship, who must suffer with his people, but who is, like Aaron, forgiven his weakness, when the time of tribulation is over. In the case of Beowulf, the reason for the dragon's devastations must be inferred from the hint of God's anger, but the element of *probatio* ''testing'' is also important in the combat itself. . . . (pp. 176-77)

Margaret E. Goldsmith, in her The Mode and Meaning of 'Beowulf', *The Athlone Press of the University of London, 1970, 282 p.*

PAMELA GRADON (essay date 1971)

[*An English academic, scholar, and textual critic, Gradon is perhaps best known for her highly original* Form and Style in Early English Literature *(1971), an ''exploratory and experimental'' study of the relationship between medieval language and literature. In the following excerpt from that work, she posits a threefold structure to* Beowulf—*appearance of the hero, rise to fame, death of the hero—and compares it with the structure of a later medieval poem,* Sir Gawain and the Green Knight.]

The structure of [***Beowulf***] has been a battle-ground for critics for so long that it would seem that little remains to be said. . . . Tolkien justified the [poem's] two parts by assuming a binary structure ''rising and setting'' and this view contains much truth [see excerpt dated 1936]. But, while essentially true, it seems to be an over-simplification. It does not explain why the poet chose to make the ''rising'' consist of two separate, but similar, episodes, the slaying of Grendel and the slaying of Grendel's mother, nor why the poet prefaced the ''setting'' by the elaborate section of retrospect generally termed ''Beowulf's return.'' For a poet who so ingeniously introduced a whole world of historical references (even though he misguidedly placed them on the perimeter of his tale), this is perhaps surprising. For it seems to me clear that the structure of the poem, if puzzling, is not naïve. And, indeed, if we look at the poem as a pattern of exemplary action, much becomes comprehensible. The fundamental pattern of the poem can be seen in the Scyld prologue. It is one of those elegiac themes which . . . occupied the mind of Guthlac at the point of conversion: ''antiquorum regum stirpis suae per transacta retro saecula miserabiles exitus flagitioso vitae termino'' [''the wretched deaths and the shameful ends of the ancient kings of his race in the course of the past ages'']. The *dramatis persona* is an heroic king. There are brought together into a pattern of exemplary action, the arrival, the rise to fame, and the death of the hero. All the rest of the poem is a development of, and a comment on, this schema. But the development and the comment essentially (in spite of a loose narrative frame) take the form of a paratactic arrangement of similar episodes. It has been rightly observed [by John Leyerle] that ''the narrative method involves juxtaposition of events whose logical connection, at first sight, seems vague'' [see Additional Bibliography]. The first act after the prologue shows the arrival of the hero, his slaying of Grendel and his triumph. But here the pattern of the prologue alters. The theme of the hero's success is further developed and a new theme, that of ''sorrow after joy'' introduced. Just so, the different aspects of kingship are explored in the figure of Hrothgar, in the theme of precarious peace in the Finn episode, and in the theme of succession in the Wealhtheow episode. In short, the second adventure, the slaying of Grendel's mother, is necessary, not in order to tell us any more about the hero, who simply goes on being heroic, but to introduce a new theme, the theme of the reversal of fortune. Moreover, it is significant that the elaborate account of the rejoicing after the death of Grendel is not repeated after the death of Grendel's mother even though there might seem to be more cause for rejoicing here. Grendel's head is borne back to the Danes and the whole of the fiendish race is destroyed. Yet, instead of a long ritual of panegyric and banquet, we have instead [in lines 1785-92] a remarkable example of rhetorical abbreviation. . . . In the scene of which this passage is the conclusion, the contrast is not as formerly, between the sorrow of King Hrothgar, his triumph after the death of Grendel, and renewed sorrow at the death of Aeschere, but a contrast between Beowulf's triumph and the old king's sorrow at Beowulf's departure. The scene is indeed symbolic. The old king, looking at the sword from the cave, with its reminder of the punishment which falls upon the enemies of God, is moved to warn the triumphant warrior of the dangers of greatness and of its inevitable end. It must be emphasised that the scene is a human scene, its dynamic is human emotion. This is not allegory. Nevertheless, the interest is centred, not in the actors as individuals, but as representative types. It might be entitled ''any king, in his old age, bids farewell to the warrior who has been as a son to him and warns him of the deceitfulness of power and of life's mutability.'' We see, as it were, Hrothgar in three significant postures; the grief-stricken king, the generous rewarder of heroism, and the old man, warning his beloved son of future sorrow. The initial scheme, as set forth in the prologue, arrival, fame, death, is here set forth again but, to use a musical analogy, in a developed form. In the last section, the pattern is repeated for the third and last time. Beowulf arrives home, becomes king and slays, and is slain by, the dragon. The pace is slower, the picture dilated, the king's action projected against a wide historical canvas of feud and death. We have now three pictures of the life of a hero, firstly Scyld, the triumphant hero-king whose departure is more splendid than his arrival. Even in death he seems to triumph as he departs into the mysterious unknown. Then King Hrothgar and Beowulf are seen in success and reversal of fortune; and finally we have the picture of Beowulf himself, whose rise and fall straddles and links the last two parts of the poem, and whose life presents us with a mirror image of the life of Scyld. For Scyld's death presaged the rise to glory of his people, whereas that of Beowulf presaged the downfall of his nation. If this sounds fanciful and over-sophisticated, it must be remembered that both themes and actions are conventional. No Anglo-Saxon poet would have to sit down to work out their significance to combine them into a meaningful pattern. They would surely come to him as naturally as the leaves on the tree. All the poet has told is three traditional types of story three times over, varying them at each stage of the telling. This is the technique of fairy tales the world over. I have said nothing of the "episodes and digressions." They introduce new themes and elaborate old ones but I have not discussed them in detail because the technique they imply is essentially the same as that which I have suggested for the main plot. They too come within the field of exemplary action. This is all I have to add to the immense and ingenious discussion; any interpretation of the structure of ***Beowulf*** must be in terms of the typical, the general, the conventional. The poem is not an allegory nor is it a novel, but it belongs to that large class of exemplary tales which is so characteristic of the Middle Ages and whose nature is only now coming to be understood. The exemplary character has a natural corollary in the exemplary action, and the exemplary action has a natural corollary in the thematic structure. All three I believe to be present in ***Beowulf.***

It is instructive to compare the structure of ***Beowulf*** with some medieval symmetrical structures such as *Sir Gawain and the Green Knight,* or Chaucer's *Knight's Tale*. The view I have put forward, that ***Beowulf*** is a neat threefold structure, with the last two episodes linked by a kind of thematic bracket, might suggest that I am trying to claim that its structure is as mannered as that of the two late medieval poems. This is clearly not the case. The apparent difference in the poems is perfectly real. It is true that *Gawain,* like ***Beowulf,*** has a repetitive structure. Just as similar episodes continually recur in ***Beowulf,*** two ship burials, three monster slayings, two dragon slayings, three hall defences, and so on, so the *Gawain* poet repeats themes and episodes. Thus the poem is placed in a frame of Arthurian legend. The scene at Arthur's court at the beginning is balanced by a scene at Arthur's court at the end. The challenge is made on New Year's Day; the requital is given on New Year's Day. Life at the Green Knight's court is equally symmetrical. We have three evening parties, three temptation scenes, three hunting scenes. Moreover, each hunting scene is used as a kind of frame for the equivalent temptation scene. Thus we find the episode of the first kiss inserted into the first hunt, dividing it into two parts and so with the other two. The rendering of the kiss in each case is accompanied by festivities. We have parallel journeys through a winter landscape, parallel arming scenes and so on. Why then is the structure of ***Beowulf*** obscure to a modern reader, while that of *Gawain* is lucidly clear? I think there are two reasons. In the first place, and most obviously, the Gawain poet has created suspense by a kind of encapsulating technique. The two beheadings not only match each other but the sceond was predicted at the same time as the first. The careful interweaving of the temptation and the hunting scenes is necessitated by the exchange of winnings just as the second beheading is causally connected with the first, while the ***Beowulf*** poet's plot elements are complete narratives in themselves, and the pattern is in a sense self-sufficient at each stage, with its own rise and fall. There are thus no necessary narrative links between the parts. Whereas the death of Scyld does not cause the ravages of Grendel and all that follow therefrom, nor the slaying of Grendel and Grendel's mother necessitate Beowulf's return and his death, the *Gawain* poet has given us a plot in which the events are necessitated by the actions of the characters within the story. In ***Beowulf,*** all we appear to have is a loose chronological sequence and the connections are all thematic. In *Gawain* on the other hand, the events all spring from the initial challenge; and, if the visit to Hautdesert appears at first sight yet another chivalric adventure of the kind familiar to readers of medieval romances, this is only part of the poet's practical joke upon the reader. The identity of Bertilak and the Green Knight locks the episode firmly into the structure of the whole. It is as though Beowulf's dragon should turn out to be Grendel in disguise, and Hrothgar a reincarnation of Scyld. The fact that these are only parallel types and not identical persons (if I may be allowed to term the dragon a person) makes it difficult for the modern reader to identify them. The first difference between the structure of ***Beowulf*** and *Sir Gawain and the Green Knight* is thus in the way the episodes are arranged, those of the ***Beowulf*** poet being, as it were, stood in a row, and those of the *Gawain* poet being interlaced. The structure of ***Beowulf*** is that of a folk-tale, of *Gawain* that of a *virelai* or *ballade*. It thus appears that the links which, in ***Beowulf,*** are purely thematic, are, in Gawain, part of a space-time continuum, and the episodes are linked by a pattern of causation as well as by a simple symmetry of arrangement. Something of the difference between the two poems can be seen in miniature, if we compare the *hund missera* that Grendel ravaged Heorot, with the year within which the action of *Sir Gawain and the Green Knight* takes place. In the Old English poem we are looking into the "dark backward and abysm of time," in the other at a brightly lit peep-show.

The second difference is perhaps more interesting. In ***Beowulf*** we compare a number of different people from different eras of Danish and Geatish history. To equate Beowulf with Scyld, we have to perform a process of abstraction. Only then can we understand the thematic relationship of the different parts of the poem. In Gawain it is different. We have the parts linked together in a plot-like structure. Yet the marked symmetry of structure has a function which is comparable to the technique of juxtaposition in ***Beowulf.*** (pp. 127-33)

[The Gawain poet's] intention to contrast large blocks of narrative seems to be demonstrated by the treatment of the hunting and temptation scenes where the three hunts and the three temptations are described at equal length, like contrasting and complementary triptychs. This is not the interweaving of a plot and sub-plot but a deliberate juxtaposition of amplifications. Like the ***Beowulf*** poet, he brings the camera nearer as the poem draws to its conclusion, but he is not contrasting complex narrative sequences, as the ***Beowulf*** poet does, but rather single shots, carefully laid side by side, in what is a single carefully constructed plot. One might summarise by quoting the observations of Ferdinand Lot [in *Etude sur le Lancelot en Prose* (Paris, 1918)] on the topic of *entrelacement* ["interlacing"]: ". . .Le *Lancelot* n'est pas une mosaïque d'òu l'on pourrait avec adresse enlever des cubes pour les remplacer par d'autres, c'est une sparterie ou une tapisserie; si l'on tente d'y pratiquer une coupure, tout part en morceaux" ["*Lancelot* is not a mosaic whose cubes could have been cleverly lifted in order to replace them with others, it is a sparterie or tapestry; if one attempts to tamper there with an incision, everything falls to pieces."]. (p. 139)

Pamela Gradon, "Literary Structures," in her Form and Style in Early English Literature, *Methuen & Co. Ltd., 1971, pp. 93-151.*

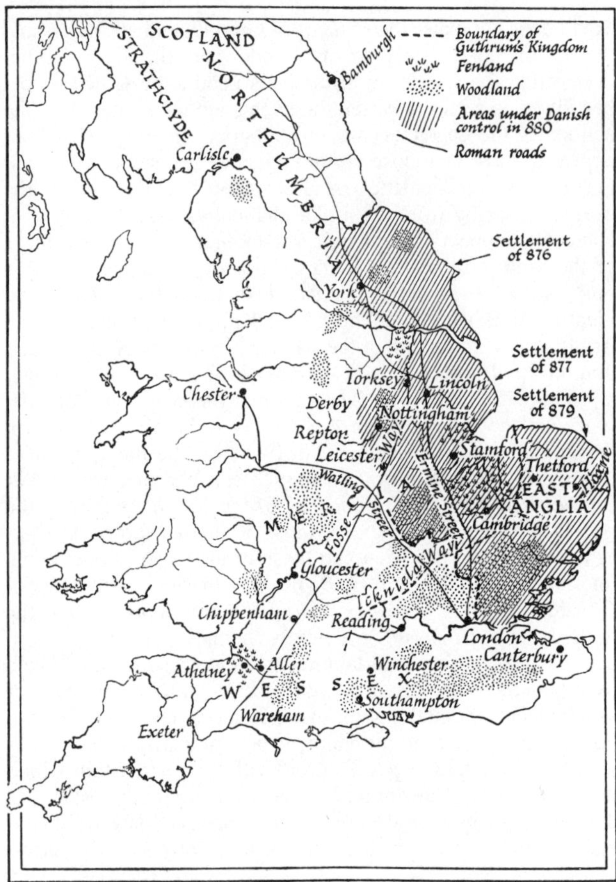

Danish settlements in England in the ninth century. From An Introduction to Anglo-Saxon England, *by Peter Hunter Blair. Cambridge University Press, 1977. Copyright © 1959, 1977 Cambridge University Press. Reproduced with permission of the publisher.*

ALVIN A. LEE (essay date 1972)

[*Lee is a Canadian scholar who specializes in Old English poetry. In the following excerpt, he explains the thematic importance of the mythic elements in four major symbolic episodes in* Beowulf.]

Beowulf is a poem about hell's possession of middle-earth. Within its overall tragic structure, the joys of the golden dryht [''noble lord''] and the actions of good kings and heroes are presented as capable of a splendid but precarious realization; the dominant vision, however, is of the defeat of man in the kingdoms of this world by the powers of darkness. (p. 171)

The ***Beowulf*** poet takes a tale of heroic action . . . and subjects it to the kind of brooding, deliberative treatment illustrated in [Old English] elegiac lyrics. The result is a romance set inside a tragedy—perhaps we could call it a ''tragic romance'' or even an ''elegiac tragedy''—serving the same Christian view of the fleeting nature of all man's earthly joys that we see throughout [Old English poetry]. But ***Beowulf,*** because of its sustained fusion of the elements of romance and tragedy, is different. Where the other poems either leave these two narrative structures, romance and tragedy, separate or with their interconnections only briefly traced (the emphasis normally being on the transcendental reality of heaven), ***Beowulf*** submits the world of the golden dryht of middle-earth to the prolonged reflections of a mind and sensibility apparently deeply attracted to that world but acutely aware of its doomed nature. (p. 172)

Beowulf is not about an individual as such but about a man of archetypal proportions, whose significance, in the broadest and deepest sense, is social. The poem is an imaginative vision of two kinds of human society, one symbolized by the gold-hall and banqueting and characterized by generosity, loyalty, and love, the other by monsters of darkness and bloodshed who prey on the ordered, light-filled world man desires and clings to. Despite the lyric overtones to the poet's presentation of his theme (that brooding, melancholy reflectiveness that every reader recognizes), ***Beowulf*** is not about a complex, individual character whose interior mental processes lead plausibly to certain actions and relations with other people. Beowulf does not have an ego, despite his boasting, and certainly has no discernible id; he is publicly conceived, all superego and controlled by the divine favor he bears. We do not know why, psychologically, Unferth behaves so oddly or what Hrothulf is thinking at any point. We learn a little more about what goes on in the mind of Hrothgar or Wealhtheow or the aged Beowulf (late in the poem) but only in terms of their functions in relation to God and to the kindred and dryht in whose social fabric their lives have meaning. They are all functionaries playing out their roles as long as wyrd [''destiny''] permits, not images of real people but exemplars of human types. (p.173)

It is generally recognized, by Klaeber, for instance [see excerpt dated 1922], that ***Beowulf*** is not, in any very consistent way, lineal in its organization. What is more, it gives little evidence of a concern on the part of the poet for plausible or realistic ordering of events according to a causal sequence. Rather, one event is associated with another—past, present, or future—because of symbolic or thematic appropriateness. The narrative is discontinuous; it does not in any representational way point out for each phenomenon mentioned its determining agents or antecedents. In fact many things happen in ***Beowulf,*** and in other Old English poems, that do not have causes in any phenomenal sense. Heaven and hell . . . are too much involved. In more purely critical terms, to use Tolkien's expression, ***Beowulf*** is a product of ''the mythical mode of imagination'' [see excerpt dated 1936]. This means that it works in implicitness of connections, in simultaneity of association, in narrative discontinuity. The images all point to the main ideas and the ideas are not time bound, not determined by orderly chronology. This kind of imagining makes unavoidable the use of metaphor, which means that the modern interpreter of ***Beowulf*** must be sensitive to poetic identities cunningly suggested in the associative imagery but not spelled out for the logical, skeptical mind. It means also, however, that he must not force identifications in ways uncongenial to the connections built up by the language of ***Beowulf*** itself or in a manner unsupported by the conventional metaphors observable in other Old English poems. (p. 174)

[One] can recognize four major myths or symbolic episodes [in ***Beowulf***], each of which is concentrated at appropriate points in the narrative but also extends its effect, with varying emphases, throughout the whole poem. In the emergence of the Scylding dynasty, climaxed by the construction of Heorot, we have a *cosmogonic myth* explicitly connected by the poet with the Christian biblical account of the origins of the created world. This in turn is followed by *the myth of the Fall and the beginnings of fratricide and crime,* as the Grendel kin of the race of Cain begin to lay waste Hrothgar's hall. Next comes the account of the advent of the hero and *the myth of the heroic* *redeemer,* and finally as the poem moves into its decisively tragic phase, we have *the myth of the hero's death and the return to chaos.*

Beowulf begins with a description of a lordless people and ends with another lordless people; the overall tonality is elegiac, and one of the major symbols of the poem's beginning, as of its conclusion, is the funeral of a great king. It is as if the poet had composed his work in the manner of a symbolist poem: starting with the effect he wanted, he then backtracked to the point from which we must begin to get that effect. From the dirgelike lament and ritualistic movements of Scyld's followers in the midst of the dynastic vision that introduces the poem, the Anglo-Saxon artist fills out and intensifies his pattern. At the same time, however, the aesthetic and thematic balance between the funerals of Scyld and Beowulf provides a very important contrast: Scyld's funeral is followed by an augmenting of the powers of his dynasty, but Beowulf's, so we are led to believe, is to be succeeded by social and political disintegration for the Geats. (pp. 177-78)

The motifs involved in [the description of the Scyldings in the beginning of the poem] are those of the golden dryht, the continual interchange of treasures, services, and protection being the very lifeblood of . . . society. This interchange takes place vertically in the imaginative space of the poem, as well as horizontally, since it is God, the "Prince of life" (16) and "Ruler of glory" (17), who sends splendid lords one by one to show generosity and protection to the Scyldings.

Hrothgar, one of the three sons of the patriarchal Healfdane, is given success and honor in war, so that his retainers follow him eagerly and his troop prospers. At the zenith of his glory (64 ff.), Hrothgar decides to have built a might mead-hall, such as the sons of men have never heard of before, as a place for feasting and the giving of gifts. With the help of many peoples throughout middle-earth, "the greatest of halls" (78) towers up "high and horn-gabled" (82). Hrothgar does not forget his promises but puts the marvelous building into use as a place of communal joy where heroes drink mead while listening to the sound of the harp and to the voice of a scop singing about God's great original gift to men, the whole created world.

The imagery of the primordial Creation [is present here]: the *wlitebeorhtne wang* (93, plain radiantly beautiful) surrounded by water, the sun and the moon as lights for land dwellers, the branches and leaves ornamenting the regions of the earth, and all living creatures. In this account of the building and initiation of Heorot, the sense of ritual repetition by man of the work of heaven is, to me, unmistakable. The implication seems to be that the construction of the gold-hall, whose light is to shine over many lands, is a hierophantic act, a manifestation of the sacred in the world of men, metaphorically identifiable with the Creation of the world itself. For the Old English thane the gift-throne is the center of the world; apart from it, he "wanders" in a life devoid of focus and meaning. The hall, the throne, and the good king can all be seen as images of the divine power that gives protection and significance to human life. Heorot is a sacred enclosure, thought of as towering upward, to ensure communication with the heavenly gift-throne and the Prince of life. It is one of several examples in Old English poems of halls built by God's champions, like those of the patriarchal princes in *Genesis,* for example, whose archetype is the celestial dryht that endures *in æternum* ["eternally"]. Heorot, like the others, is paradisal in symbolic import. Hrothgar, whose name appears to mean "glory spear" or "spear of triumph" or possibly "spear of joy," is, like the heavenly Dryhten, a lord of victories. As with God's Creation in *Genesis* so here, Hrothgar's mighty creation comes after triumph over the chaos of internecine war. Again as in heaven in numerous Old English poems (for example, *The Dream of the Rood,* 139-141), the condition of *dream* (joy) is symbolized by banqueting in the hall. Like Adam and Eve in the guest-hall of Eden, the Danes, so the poet tells us, immediately after the Song of Creation, "lived in joy, blessed" ("Swa ða driht-guman dreamum lifdon / eadiglice . . . , 99-100a). Still innocent of the *feond on helle* (fiend, or enemy in hell) who lurks without, they slept after the banquet given by their lord, not knowing "sorrow, the misery of men" ("Fand þa ðær inne æþelinga gedriht / swefan æfter symble: sorge ne cyðon, / wonsceaft wera").

The name Heorot can be explained not only in terms of naturalistic imagery to do with stag antlers on the gables of the hall, or even as a symbol of royalty like that on the Sutton Hoo standard, but also in terms of scriptural association. If we recall the psalmist's use (Ps. 42) of the analogy of the hart or stag thirsting for healing streams and the human soul in its desire for God, and if we remember that we are told later in ***Beowulf*** by the king of Heorot that the "hart strong in his antlers" will give up his life rather than enter the hellish mere (1368-1372), the possibility emerges that Hrothgar's mighty hall is imagined primarily as the earthly dwelling place of the human soul, both communal and individual. Where the mere, the poem's antithetical image for Heorot, is loathsome and terrible and infested with monsters, Heorot is described as "the most famous of buildings under heaven" (309-310a), "the bright dwelling of brave men." As a communal symbol of an ideal earthly dryht, the newly created hall is in paradisal harmony with heaven. The question of whether Hrothgar's hall in the midst of the conventional "plain" (225) has an individual reference as well as a communal one may be partially answered by [comparing the] use of the ideal-hall motif in *Guthlac A* (742). There, when the saint has triumphed in war over his enemies, his barrow, the dwelling of his newly perfected soul, is a *sele niwe* (new hall, dwelling) standing in the protection of God in the midst of a "victory plain," a very succinct correlation of the two major metaphors for Paradise in the Old English poetic mythology.

But Heorot is a fated image, existing in a double aspect. Even at the moment of its first towering upward, the poet speaks of the "fierce heat and hostile flame" that wait for it and of the "sword-hate" between son-in-law and father-in-law that will spring up because of bitter enmity (82b-85). So also, the description of the Danes living in a state of blessedness is interrupted by the first mention of Grendel and the race of Cain (99 ff.). Heorot and the world of the golden dryht exist as a splendid ideal, as *wlitige* (beautiful, fair), throughout the poem, but as earthly images they are also doomed, in the mind of a Christian poet, to become *unclæne* or polluted and thus to fall into the necessity of being "cleansed."

In the poet's use of *the myth of the Fall and the origin of fratricide,* he often specifically connects the Grendel kin with hell, which should make it easy to recognize the metaphorical structure barely concealed beneath the relatively slight surface realism of the poem. On one level of meaning, ***Beowulf*** can best be understood as a reworking of the same war between heaven and hell that emerges in its undisplaced mythical form in *Christ and Satan* and other poems. As in the Christian mythology, where demonic powers are assumed to have taken possession of the world shortly after the Creation, so in ***Beowulf*** a monster comes out of the mere and possesses the poem's *imago mundi* [''world picture''], Heorot. This necessitates a war between a heaven-sent champion and the monster, a war in which the champion's victory is a ''cleansing'' and a preliminary defeat of the feond [''fiend''] on the earthly level, as in Christ's victory on the rood. But, again as in the Christian story, the deliverer's victory in the world must be extended and consolidated by a further triumphant battle in the very depths from which the demonic attacks have come. Whether the hell referred to in ***Beowulf*** is from Teutonic myth or from Christian myth or, more plausibly, from a mixture of both does not alter the fact that the images of bondage, darkness, endless pain, joyless exile, fire, ice, wind, storm, and enmity against mankind, images associated with the monsters and their haunts, are the same ones found over and over again in the Old English poetic accounts of man apart from God. Nor does the fact that Grendel and his mother seem in some ways to be trolls from a different legendary background diminish the connotations they draw from Christian symbolism; it means only that they have this additional extension, as compared with a less poetically complex demon like the one tormenting Cynewulf's Juliana. (pp. 178-82)

Perhaps most important of all Grendel's demonic connotations is his association with Cain. Early in the poem when Grendel is first named and connected with the archetypal fratricide, the reader is confronted with a pattern highly suggestive in its possibilities for adaptation to tales of bloodthirsty feuding in Germanic society. The poet of *Maxims I* tells how, after the earth swallowed Abel's blood, Cain's criminal hatred did not die out in the world but spread, with ever-increasing malice, until it was known to all peoples. Men throughout the earth became busy with the ''strife of weapons'' and devised the hostile sword, so that shields, spears, swords, and helmets have ever since had to be ready for conflict. By his murderous action, the gnomic poet seems to be saying, Cain set the pattern in which all men are caught. This traditional view of Cain and Abel, elaborated at length in Book 15 of Augustine's *De civitate Dei*—in terms of the unending conflict throughout history of the society of carnal man, or Cain, and the society of the elect, or Abel—is also given a poetic use in *Genesis A,* apparently in an attempt to show the special significance for the poet's own period in history of fratricide and conflict among mankind. All strife and human misery are depicted metaphorically as the branches of the demonic tree which sprang up from Abel's spilled blood. The crime of Cain is linked with the guilt of Eve, and both are associated with wyrd, indicating that it is only in the fallen world that ''cruelly destructive fate'' holds sway. Cain's exile, depicted in the same formula as Adam's exile earlier, leads inevitably to an intensified enmity between Cain's descendants and God, this warfare culminating finally in the Deluge. (pp. 184-85)

There can be no tragedy in literature without a sense of glory or happiness or fulfilled ambition potentially within human grasp, a glory shown finally not to be obtainable, or, if it is obtained temporarily, not capable of being preserved. As the ***Beowulf*** poet brings his hero to work on behalf of Heorot in its ideal aspect, he demonstrates his realization of this fact of tragedy. His particular poetic version of *the myth of the heroic redeemer* has an overall tragic shape, as it combines with the myth of Fall and fratricide, but the tragic effect is possible only because Heorot in its ideal form remains as an image of what once was and what still might be, however precariously, if pride, envy, avarice, and murder could be controlled. It is to the restoration and realization of this potential Paradise—what I have been calling the golden dryht of middle-earth—that Beowulf bends his efforts in Part 1 of the poem. (pp. 196-97)

Beowulf's advent into the ruined dryhtsele [''retainer's hall''], as Hrothgar immediately perceives, is through the grace of God (381 ff.). As Hrothgar also knows, it is only God who ''can easily restrain the mad destroyer from his deeds'' (478b-479). It is as if the divine favor forfeited when Heorot fell, twelve years before, is now about to be restored. Hrothgar is an aged Adam waiting for grace and deliverance, and Wealhtheow, trying to provide for her sons a life free of crime and bloodshed, is a latter-day Germanic Eve trying to repair the ravages begun at the fateful banquet long ago in the archetypal guest-hall of Eden. In line with his elegiac rather than homiletic theme, however, the poet is careful not to censure Hrothgar and Wealhtheow but to emphasize the fateful nature of the conflict in which they are caught and to show them ready and eager to receive God's new and necessary gift to them, in the form of the hero's deeds. The underplaying of a theme of guilt in the handling of Hrothgar and Wealhtheow is analogous to the treatment of the Fall of man in *Genesis B*. . . . Beowulf, as the deliverer of the ruined dryht of the Scylding Adam is, by symbolic association, the second Adam who now comes to do battle on behalf of those who have fallen into the clutches of the fiend.

In the account of the hero's journey from Geatland, his arrival in Denmark, and his subsequent actions in restoring Hrothgar's kingdom, we see once again how in Old English poetry the myth of heroic deliverance or redemption exploits the myth of Creation for much of its imaginative significance. (p. 198)

Not since the poet has described the Song of Creation a hundred lines earlier has there been this sense of exuberant and purposive action. It is as if the heavy sense of time as duration—*fela missera, singale sæce* (many half-years, continual conflict)—into which Heorot has been plunged, is now in the process of being abolished in favor of an earlier sacred time when divine favor for Denmark was directly evident. It is also as if the experience of time only as duration brings the peril of forgetting what is fundamental, that existence itself is given by God, with the result that the Danes who now do not know the true God have fallen into devil worship. One is reminded, too, by the account of this sea voyage, of the importance in Old English poetry of the boat as a symbol of the way heroic man takes part in reenacting the divine acts of Creation and redemption. (p. 199)

Marked by God's wrath (711) and ''deprived of joys'' (721), Grendel is defeated by heaven's champion in a ferocious wrestling match, after which, mortally wounded and singing a song of defeat, he goes, the ''prisoner of hell'' (788), to seek the company of devils (808). Rejoicing in his night's work (827), the hero places the hand, arm, and shoulder of this rebel against God beneath the vaulted roof of the ''cleansed'' (825) hall. The next day the ''mar-peace'' Unferth lapses into silence, the battered Heorot is redecorated by many willing hands, gold tapestries are hung, banqueting is resumed, and again a cup is passed, giving a markedly sacramental sense of unity in one socially cohesive body. (p. 201)

With the defeat of Grendel, the Cain spirit is only temporarily quelled. Grendel's mother (1251 ff.), in strict adherence to the destructive principles of blood-feuding, rises out of the mere to wreak grisly vengeance on Heorot, taking back to the underwater hall with her the head of Æschere and the hand of

Grendel. Plunged again into profound gloom, Hrothgar describes (1345 ff.) to Beowulf what is known of the mere, that source of apparently unending hostility to his world of Heorot. At this point in the poem the myth of heroic deliverance, so far confined to the cleansing of middle-earth, is expanded to include the hellish source of evil itself, and the hero realizes that he must go "beneath the headlands" (1360) to eradicate the still-active demonic powers. Grendel's mere, although only a few miles from Heorot (1361-1362), is the opposite pole from Heorot in the poem's imaginative space. Like the splendid hall, it is primarily an image of this world, a complex symbol of all those things in nature and in human society that human desire most rejects set against the ideal aspirations embodied in the gold-hall. But also like Heorot, indeed like most images of Old English poetry, the wider significance or supernatural reference of the mere exists on the level of myth or symbolic metaphor. Unlike Heorot, however, which at certain points is the paradisal guest-hall and at others the ruined hall of the fallen world, the mere as a poetic image has no doubleness or ambivalence in its meaning. In its entirety it is demonic.

The overall tragic vision in ***Beowulf***—of a "fleeting" world caught in time as duration, in which human longings to return to the paradisal guest-hall are constantly frustrated—is clear. Similarly, the connections of the monster-infested world in ***Beowulf*** with the conventional Old English poetic vision of the ruined or fallen world are numerous. The mere is the poem's most complete concentration of fallen-world motifs as they merge, ostensibly on the level of middle-earth, with the imagery of hell. In several ways the underwater *reced* (building) or *niðsele* (hostile hall), inhabited by the *healðegn* (hall-thane) Grendel and his mother, is a grotesque parody of Heorot in its ideal aspect. Its location beneath the headlands and turbid waters, rather than in the midst of the "plain," its demonic light antithetical to the radiance of the gold-hall, its hoarded treasure (1557, 1613), its cannibalistic banqueting, its weird kinship loyalties, its total absence of *dream,* and its inveterate hostility to the harp music and loyalties of the fraternal dryht—in all these things it is a perversion of Heorot. The precise extent to which its character as a demonic dryht envelops Heorot—the making dark of the hall, the prevention of gift dispensing, banqueting, and music, and the symbolically implicit undermining of Hrothgar's *sibbegedriht* (387, 729, peaceful troop, band of kinsmen) by the spirit of Cain through the persons of Unferth and Hrothulf—is the measure of the fall or ruin of Hrothgar's world. The climactic detail of the mere's conquest of Heorot is the devil worship, the honoring by the Danes of those same demonic powers that are destroying them (175 ff.).

In terms of nature imagery, the mere, in a detailed way, is a perversion of the ideal order of Creation. Located out in the fens or moors beyond the plain surrounding the hall, it is a mist-shrouded wilderness (103-104, 162, 450, 710, 764, 820, 1265, 1348, 1405). We are told in *Christ and Satan* and in *Guthlac A* and *B* that some demons live in remote places of middle-earth and from there launch their attacks on men; this is precisely what the Grendel kin do. Encircling rocks, frost-covered trees, and the twisted roots of a "joyless wood" show the mere's wasteland setting to be the direct antithesis of the sunny, blossoming groves of the earthly Paradise described in detail in *The Phoenix* and more briefly in other poems. The motif of chaotic, treacherous water, beside which the "hart strong in its horns" (1369) will die rather than plunge in, connects with the Physiologus idea of the *deaðsele* (death-hall) of damnation being located at the bottom of the treacherous whale's domain, that hall of the dryht of hell to which Eleusius' dryht is plunged in *Juliana*. (pp. 202-05)

The ***Beowulf*** poet's sense of the fleeting or mutable character of everything in middle-earth inevitably extends in Part 2 to the person of the hero. In Part 1, as a figure of vitality and superabundance, as the heroic vehicle of divine grace, Beowulf was enabled to abolish that destructive time as duration into which Heorot—this poem's main *imago mundi*—had fallen and to restore the hall to its original freshness and radiance: "the hall rose high above him, vaulted and shining with gold; inside, the guest slept . . ." (1799b-1800). The twelve years of bondage to Grendel were in a sense canceled in favor of that sacred time contemporary with Creation, and Hrothgar appropriately gave twelve symbolic treasures to his deliverer at the end of the twelve years of misery. Now in Part 2, as the central organization of images takes on the shape of *the myth of the hero's death and the return to chaos,* we find that time and *yldo* (age) have worn the hero and his kingdom. Hrothgar was described by Beowulf as "a peerless king, altogether blameless" (1885b-1886a), defeated only because of that age which toward the end of his fifty-year reign took from him the joys of power. Now Beowulf, also an exemplary king, is first threatened and then destroyed by a fifty-foot serpent, also at the end of a fifty-year reign. The tragedy of Hrothgar's life, only temporarily relieved by Beowulf's deeds, has now become the hero's own, but no heaven-sent champion appears who can act effectively on his behalf.

There is no escape from the ruins of time in this elegiac tragedy, for the basis of the tragic vision is being in time. Even as we move through the poem's romance, through its myths of creation and heroic deliverance, we are constantly made aware that death and human defeat in middle-earth are what give tragic shape and form to the lives of the Scyldings. It is death that defines the life of Scyld, of Beow, of Heorogar, and, finally, of Hrothgar. Now, in the account of the end of Beowulf's *lændagas* (loan-days, fleeting days), again it is death that defines the shape of the heroic life. Throughout Part 2 the poet carefully establishes a sense of imminent and nearly total disaster, a disaster partly realized by the end of the action. But the catastrophe described is not apocalyptic, as in the Old English Doomsday poems. In these latter, time as duration is brought to an end, history is abolished, and what is pure and faithful within God's Creation is taken back into eternity. But ***Beowulf*** does not show an end of the world, a Ragnarok or Doomsday. It shows the defeat of heroic effort in the world of time. At the very end of the narrative the Geats are still struggling against time; they build a great barrow on the headland called *Hronesnæs* (the Headland of the Whale) that will keep alive for other seafarers the memory of their king. Within the barrow lie an ancient, useless treasure and the ashes of the hero. Outside, twelve horsemen, warriors bold in battle, sons of chieftains, circle around, uttering an ancient lament. Beowulf has died, haunted by the memory of those marvelous times when he displayed in almost godlike manner his greatest powers; Hrothgar earlier was forced to admit defeat at the hands of Grendel but also looked back nostalgically, *in geardagum* (in former days), to a time when he subdued all enemies of the Danes and doled out treasures in almost godlike manner. It is fundamental to the elegiac nature of the poem that the acts of strength, of superabundance, and of creativity are constantly pushed back into that legendary earlier and better time indicated by the hoary phrase *in geardagum.* (pp. 211-12)

The point of time in Geatish history at which Beowulf dies signals an imminent end for the Geats as a unified dryht society.

It is true that Beowulf leaves behind him Wiglaf as the *endelaf* (last remnant) of his people, placing the young hero in somewhat the same position as that of the lone survivor in the elegy, but the social disintegration is now so far advanced that there is, so far as we are told in the poem, little hope for Geatland in the fact that Wiglaf remains. (p. 213)

[Beowulf], like Heorot, becomes simply a memory. The close alignment of aged hero and dragon in Part 2 is the poem's decisive reminder that in the tragic vision even the most heroic form, perhaps most especially the heroic form, is defeated by the elemental facts of existence in time. The world that remains after Beowulf has died contains two sorts of people, cowards and outlaws, on the one hand, and those faithful to dryht loyalties (Wiglaf, the weeping woman, and the circling horsemen), on the other. By this point we have been shown the impact of heroic energy on the world of the fallen dryht and have been shown also that in such a world it is heroic energy that is destroyed while the fallen creation continues in time. The golden dryht of middle-earth and the youthful Beowulf are poetic images of the kind of joy and reality the *hæleð* [''warriors''] want, but the irony of the tragic vision decrees that life is not shaped according to human desires. The poet, with the quiet assurance of great artistry, follows his account of the roaring flames and raging winds of Beowulf's cremation with a description of the disposal of physical things: the hero's ashes are sealed in a great barrow; the rings, necklaces, and armor of the ancient treasure are returned to the earth, hidden again and useless to men. Twelve riders circle the mound, ritually containing the grief of the Geats: they eulogize the greatness and glory of their dead king, and they mourn his passing. The closing scene expresses a pronounced tragic sense of confinement, of the putting into dark places of all that is splendid in this world. It shows the stilling of heroic energy. (p. 223)

Alvin A. Lee, ''Heorot and the Guest-Hall of Eden: Symbolic Metaphor and the Design of 'Beowulf','' in his The Guest-Hall of Eden: Four Essays on the Design of Old English Poetry, *Yale University Press, 1972, pp. 171-223.*

GWYN JONES (essay date 1972)

[Jones is a prolific Welsh fiction writer, essayist, critic, translator, and anthologist who, in addition to writing a number of novels and short stories, has translated widely from the Icelandic sagas and, in two nonfiction works, A History of the Vikings *(1968) and* Kings, Beasts, and Heroes *(1972), contributed to Old English, Welsh, and Norse studies. In the following excerpt, he summarizes prevailing opinions regarding the heroic values and Christian elements of* Beowulf.]

[***Beowulf***] is most easily described as a poem of an epical and heroic nature, and in respect of its incident and action provides a notable synthesis of Germanic heroic legend and international wondertale as this latter was viewed in a Germanic context. Some have read it as pagan myth, others as Christian allegory, while some consider that its story remembers myth though its poet did not. Though not a true history, it touches closely on the matter of history, the triumphs and tribulations of kings, the winning of wars and loss of a kingdom, and has been pressed into service as a ''Gesta Danorum, Sveorum, Gothorumque,'' for the first half of the sixth century. Structurally, to a modern eye, it is less than perfect; even so its story of a young hero is compelling, of an old hero moving. It offers a noble picture of an age, its assumptions and behavior, its hierarchical bases, and the gold-decked splendour of its warrior class. It conducts its protagonist through diverse settings and episodes, by land and sea, at court and in battle, in contests with monsters and courtesies with his peers. And our poet has time for much more than adventures and monster-riddings. He was conscious, like other Anglo-Saxon poets, of the world's lack of duration. Life, he knows, is fleeting; all things are hastening to their end. Warrior and corslet crumble side by side, fair maiden moulders in her fair array; the steed that paws the stronghold yard, the falcon winging through the hall, must falter and fall; rust frets and earth devours the toil of giants and works of wondrous smiths. Also, he was deeply concerned with values: the bonds that prevented society flying apart, heroic conventions, the claims of piety, a warrior's worth and woman's excellence, the qualities of good kingship, the means to fame. In the aged Hrothgar's words to Beowulf, we like the poem's hero are bidden: ''Know what manly virtue is.'' In short, ***Beowulf*** is a poem of multiple source and episode, which combines the attractions of a brave tale with high moral seriousness, and offers a reading of life and experience. And finally, it is by any standards a good, even a fine poem; and there have been many to think it a great one—less for its movement and action, or fable, than because they find it a statement about human life and values by an artist who—by virtue of his technical ability, his command of words and metre, his power to present narrative, argument, reflection, mood, and feeling in verse—has given lasting significance to the thing he wrote, which is now the thing we read. Which means that ***Beowulf*** is worthy of our esteem for the reasons, no more, no less, for which we esteem all fine poetry. (pp. 3-5)

Beowulf is the fully valorous man. He is brave physically, just as fearless in combat when arrows shock over the shieldwall and the foot-fighters clash as when Grendel's steel-tipped claw thrusts at the halldoor or the twisted firedrake comes on a third time carrying blast and venom in his jaws. In all his life he has never drawn back for threat or peril. ''Wyrd (Fate) often spares an undoomed man when his courage holds good.'' It is a hero's duty to preserve his life by valour; and valour, Beowulf tells us, has brought him safe through many perils, times of war. He is brave in another way. In his role of hero he is schooled to accept his destiny, whatever this may be. Fate, say the pagan poets, is immeasurably strong, all-powerful, and implacable. Man is at its mercy. ''Wyrd goes ever as it must.'' Yet this in no way makes him weak and small. For if he accepts what is destined, without bowing to it, he triumphs over it. An unbreakable will makes him the equal of all-powerful Fate, and though Fate can destroy him, it can neither conquer nor humiliate him. If there are monsters to fight, fight them. If there is hardship to bear, bear it. If grief, endure. Evade nothing; complain of nothing. In all circumstances, at all times, a man must give of his best.

Without loyalty the social structure cannot hold. A leader owed it to his men, retainers owed it to their lord. Beowulf is a shining exemplar at either level. During Hygelac's lifetime he was his staunchest support. It was as Hygelac's man that he fought against Grendel in Denmark. It was by Hygelac's life that Hrothgar conjured him to fight with Grendel's Mother. It was of his followers and his lord that he spoke to ''the famous son of Healfdene'' before setting off for the mere. ''If battle carries me off, be a protector to my young retainers, my close comrades. Likewise, beloved Hrothgar, send those treasures you have given me to Hygelac. Hrethel's son, the Geats' lord, may see then by that gold, as he gazes on the treasure, that I found a good and noble ring-giver, enjoyed his bounty while I might'' (1480-86). In the event he conveys them to Hygelac himself, renders them up in love and duty, and in return is given the gold-decked sword of Hygelac's dead father, seven thousand in land, a hall and princely throne. Wherefore, "There was no need for him to seek among the Gifthas or the Spear-Danes or the people of the Swedes for a champion less good than I, buy him for money. At all times I would be before him in the host, alone in the forefront, and ever will wage battle so, so long as this sword shall last, which early and late so oft has done me service, since I killed Daeghrefn champion of the Franks with my own hands in the presence of the army" (2494-502). As with Hygelac, so with Hygelac's young son. While he lived Beowulf upheld him among his people, would not take the proffered throne himself, and when he was killed took vengeance for him. . . . The gloomy tyrant and faithless retainer, these are the rogues and deviants on whom the poet's judgement falls, in sorrow as in anger. Better die, perish in the dragon's fire, says Wiglaf, than bear shield back home in shame when one's dear lord has suffered and sunk in the fray." Death is better for any man than a life of reproach." (pp. 43-4)

In words like young Wiglaf's [in lines 2633-56], young Ælfwine called on the hard core of the English at Maldon, when all that remained was to fight on and die with their lord: "Remember those times when often we held forth at the mead-drinking, spoke vows aloud on the benches, heroes in hall, concerning hard battle. Now he who is brave can prove it." And of the retainers of Hnaef the Half-Dane beleaguered in a hall down in Frisia their poet says: "I have never heard tell of sixty victorious fighters bearing themselves better in heroic strife, and never of young men better repaying the sweet (*or* white, i.e. shining) mead than his warlike brood repaid Hnaef." Gold, weapons, mead are the recurring symbols of gift and payment, hospitality unstinted and service unto death, the full committal of lord to man and man to lord.

Beowulf records many bounteous givings: arm-rings, torques, weapons and armour, horses and harness, a tall standard with a boar-image, publicly and honourably bestowed. And true it is, no man can be mean and lordly both. It was Hrothgar's hope that he might live in Heorot and share out among his retainers everything which God had granted him, save the royal estates and the lives of men. King Onela, the Scylfings' helm, was the best of sea-kings who gave out rings in Sweden. Of Hygelac's power of giving we have just spoken. The greater the king the more lavish his dispersals. The generous gave for reward, in pay, to cement ties, from ostentation, and out of a generous heart. No Germanic, and for that matter no Celtic, poet seems to have demurred.

Wisdom, in the formal statements of the heroic age, was an embracing quality in which were subsumed education and training in the young and a wealth of digested experience in the old, observation of events and the power to draw general conclusions from them, insight into character and the ponderables of human nature, and an unfailing awareness of the personal, social, and national (or one might more safely say tribal) rights and duties, ties and acceptances, which alone made life meaningful and alone could make it good. In ***Beowulf*** wisdom is the propriety of princes, their awareness of justice, truth, and power, their distillation of the past, their insight into the future. That Hrothgar, an aged guardian of his people, should be wise is inevitable—the adjective *frōd* means both old and wise, as befits a patriarch—but wisdom is for the young too. Hrothgar has never heard a man so young as Beowulf discourse more wisely—surely the wise Lord himself had sent into his mind the words he uttered; and Hygd, the wife of Hygelac, though young, was wise and well accomplished. And if Hrothgar can make a shrewd cast into the future of the Geats, so can Beowulf into that of the Danes and Heathobards.

These virtues stand in ***Beowulf*** like four pillars in a royal hall. Kings are their surest possessors: Hrothgar, Hygelac, Beowulf himself, whose titles are not only *dryhten, frēa, cyning,* but *brytta,* breaker or dispenser (of gold), *helm,* helm or protector, *hyrde,* shepherd, keeper, guardian, *wine,* friend, and *wīsa,* leader, and many a compound, loving lord, gold-friend, gold-giver, army-leader, battle-leader, people's protector, war-king, and their like. But goodness is open to all, and without witness to the contrary is freely attributed. The presence of these unambiguous qualities, the unhedging praise they receive, and their working out in deed and ceremony, so warms and enriches the poem that the morality of ***Beowulf*** is as potent for the reader today as its wondertale narrative and heroic-historical trappings. (pp. 45-6)

[Just as] the ***Beowulf*** poet thought fit to dress a tale of monsters in rich heroic raiment, so he rounded out the lean primary virtues with a Christian addendum, and on the whole did so with tact and sensitivity. The snarl of a zealot is completely absent, and rarely does he raise a castigatory finger. He approved of the men of old, and of antique virtue no less, and his indications of the superiority of his own Christian faith are by Christian standards almost ameliorative. The heathen, he recognized [in lines 170-88], had their problems. (p. 46)

[Christianity] serves a decisive function in refining and humanizing the poem's declared values. The groundwork of story is hard and violent; the legendary and historical additions are filled with war and feud; but Hrothgar and Beowulf are strongly attractive characters, the Dane benign and gracious, temperate and affectionate, the Geat all these things, modest and forbearing too. Both men are blessed with natural piety, practise truth and right among the people, and ponder the wisdom and mystery of Almighty God in his dealings with mankind. They are wholly free of that implacable heroic imbecility beloved of Saxo and the more strenuous Fornaldar Sögur. The tribute to Beowulf with which the poem ends is a Christian amelioration of the heroic ideal. "Of all the kings of the world," said the Geats, "he was the mildest and gentlest of men, the kindest to his people, and the most eager for good report (*lofgeornost*)." The concluding adjective has begun to trouble subtle moralists, but that a hero should pursue *lof* and *dōm,* the good word of men in life and their earned commemoration after death, seems straightforward and laudable enough. For if this were vanity, as some mistakenly urge, it would be that precious refinement of it which all good men must possess if they are to strive not only for their own good name, a requisite of heroes both ancient and modern, but make a contribution to the general well-being. "Cattle die, kinsmen die, the man himself must die. One thing I know that never dies: the good name of a man who dies." These words belong to the cult of Odinn; the sentiment would be unexceptionable in any religion.

This is by no means the full spectrum of Christian colouring in ***Beowulf.*** But unless we accept quite unacceptable notions of the poem as a sustained, not to say unbroken and reinforced "Allegory of Salvation," in which Beowulf's three wondertale exploits against Grendel, Grendel's Mother, and the Dragon are to be interpreted as aspects of the Redemption or reflections of New Testament narrative and theology . . . , we find it remarkably free of specifically Christian dogma, as of formal Christian observance and ceremonial. There is a fair amount of Christian descriptive nomenclature, Father, Lord, Almighty,

Creator, God, and an appreciable quantity of Old Testament reference (the Creation, Cain and Abel, Hell, the Deluge); God's will and governance are implicit throughout, but this is no more than the minimal and inevitable apparatus of an author raised in the Christian faith, versed in its primary documents, and given to improving discourse. Much more surprising is the circumstance that Christ is never mentioned, either as Son of Man or Son of God, and that no "digression" (the brief and enigmatic reference to Hama seeking "long-lasting gain," 1197-1201, carries little or no weight) has anything to say of Christian heroes, saints, disciples, or handmaidens of the Lord. Admittedly, if we see the Dragon (to press one analogy) as Satan, the faithless warband as the twelve apostles who betrayed the Son of Man into the hands of sinners, the unhappy fugitive who stole the Dragon's treasure-cup as Judas, and Wiglaf as a kind of John, the case is altered. If we go on to reject such other interpretations of the poem's narrative and substance as myth, wondertale, heroic legend, legendary history, and historical tradition severally and jointly provide—and likewise discard the rival Christian interpretation of Beowulf as embodying the imperfect virtue of even virtuous heathendom or the flawed state of the best of good men at all times and places—it is altered still more. And if we can swallow not only the gnats of allegory but the camels too—for example, the curious circumstance that Christ's death saved mankind while Beowulf's ruined the Geats—it is altered to the point of conviction. But these are vast triadic ifs. (pp. 47-9)

Our author's most apparent poetic gift is his unflurried professional competence. We may begin by accepting that he knew what he was doing. Even in the so-called digressions he had a purpose, though at times we are less convinced than he of its validity, and once he is over his transition we find he always has good words, command of metre, an assured manner, and a mastery of mood. It is a primary virtue in an extended poem to keep it moving, which he does. And at its proper pace, which he does. Its leisureliness rests on strength, its ruminations, such as Hrothgar's homily, the passage devoted to the lone survivor's burial of a people's treasure, and the misery of the father bereft of his hanged son, are the unforced expression of matters dear to the poet's heart. It would be special pleading to call ***Beowulf*** wisdom literature, but its action is weighted with sentiments concerning virtue, life, and destiny, couched in words that convince and verse that sustains. Its author had a good eye and ear, a well-stored mind, and high expertise in verse-making. He had at command the full professional vocabulary of the Old English poet, both that abundance of synonyms and near-synonyms without which alliterative verse cannot prosper (and without which he would have been denied a sometimes conventional but frequently telling choice of names for, let us say, man, sea, ship, sword, and ruler) and that apparatus of metaphor and kenning which at its freshest gives tang and savour in almost any context: swan-road, whale-road, sail-road (sea), battle-light (sword), bone-house (body), heaven's jewel, world-candle (sun). He was a skilful manipulator of the meaningful variation of phrase, clause, or expression which is a major feature of the Old English poetic repertoire; the whole craft of alliterative verse was familiar to him, its devices and techniques, and he used it with a manly but unforced authority. (pp. 56-7)

[***Beowulf*** can be approached in many ways and admired for many reasons. Because it is unique, and because of its great assurance, and not least because of its story-telling, we may not improperly be tempted to prize it too highly, and grow recondite in its justification. There may . . . have been better poems written by better poets in the eighth and early ninth centuries even as there were brave men before Agamemnon. But this is a large assumption, and if there were they are perished, as though they had never been. But ***Beowulf*** we have, with its admirable two parts of story, its embellishments from Germanic tradition and its glimpses of early history, its patterns of excellence to imitate, its models of evil to be declined. It is concerned to teach, and acquaints us with virtue, would make us better men. And why not? No one in his right mind thinks that poetry, or any art, should make us worse. For all its monsters it portrays a warm and human world, and does it with a hundred happy touches: feasting in hall, voyaging by sea and riding afield; courteous greetings and sad farewells; the bestowing of gifts and pledging of friendship. A king sits on his throne, wise, valiant and generous; a ring-adorned queen moves through the hall, and from her jewelled hand warriors accept the brimming mead-cup; on the cliff-edge a sentinel stares out to sea, watchful for friend and foe alike; an embittered veteran broods on ancient wrongs and present revenge; a bride, young and necklaced, walks into hall on the arm of her belted escort. In no poem are we more aware of convention, and in few do we so readily accept it. Joy and sorrow are the common lot, and, under heaven, men must make of their lives what they can. For they enjoy the light and warmth and company in hall but for a while, and outside is the encompassing dark. "Presently it must happen that death will overcome you, warrior." On earth there will remain the good name of a good man; beyond earth a refuge in the Father's arms. It is satisfactory to be assured that this fierce and gentle warrior, Beowulf of the Geats, found both. (pp. 59-61)

Gwyn Jones, "'Beowulf'," in his Kings, Beasts and Heroes, *Oxford University Press, London, 1972, pp. 3-61.*

T. A. SHIPPEY (essay date 1978)

[*Shippey is an English medievalist. In the following excerpt, he examines the poetic elements of* Beowulf, *including the use of poetic compounds, variations, formulas, and the application of various poetic techniques.*]

It is . . . not disrespectful to remark on one of the sorest and least-probed points of Beowulfian style—its casual way with compound words. Consider the powerful and successful section at the end of the Grendel-fight, lines 809-36. As the monster disappears into death and darkness, the poet remarks of Beowulf:

Nihtweorce gefeh,
ellenmærþum. Hæfde East-Denum
Geatmecga leod gilp gelæsted . . .
(827-9)

[He rejoiced in his night's work, the fame his
courage won. The man of the Geats had fulfilled his boast to the East-Danes.]

Why "*East*-Danes?" The same people were "North-Danes" forty lines before (783), "South-Danes" before that (463), and "West-Danes" on Beowulf's arrival (383). They have been "Spear-Danes" and "Ring-Danes" and "Bright-Danes" too, but at least you can be all those things together, while to most people "east" definitely precludes "west," as "north" does "south." Of course *East* has been put into line 828 *only* to make the necessary alliteration with *ellen*. That is the only reason for many of the poem's other compound forms, and for many more it is the strongest reason. A few lines above *East-*

Denum the poet says that Grendel knew his end had come, *dogera dægrim*. This phrase is entirely tautologous, meaning literally "the day-number of his days." A more sensible word would be *dogorgerim* (used at line 2728) but in line 823 that would not scan. *Dæg* is thrown in, then, to make up the weight. One could balk at line 820 as well, when Grendel has to escape, *feorhseoc fleon under fenhleoðu* [flee life-sick under fen-slopes]. This is a good line, in grim contrast with the futile purpose of the next phrase, "to seek a joyless dwelling." But "*fen*-slopes?" A *hlið* is something steep, cliff or hillside or even wall. Fens, however, are flat. It is hard to resist the thought that the poet wanted a compound word which would scan, imply inaccessibility, and above all alliterate on *f;* he created *fenhleoðu,* then, by a kind of double analogy with the *misthleoðu* [misty slopes] of line 710 and the *fenfreoðu* [fenfastnesses] of 851. The word sounds all right, but it is not meant to stand close examination.

This is not to say that the ***Beowulf*** poet *never* used words imaginatively. But he did accept an element of redundance and tautology as part of his style (just as he saw no sin in heroes drinking). Compounds like *heal-reced* and *heal-ærn* (they both mean "hall-building" or even "hall-hall") are then neither tributes to the vividness of his imagination . . . nor signs of intellectual barrenness. They are, like the poet's many indistinguishable synonyms, simply functional; and their function is to create metric or alliterative pattern.

It can hardly be a coincidence that the poem's next most evident feature of style also has clear utility. This is "variation," and examples of it are everywhere. The lines just quoted about Beowulf fulfilling his boast continue:

swylce oncyþðe ealle gebette,
inwidsorge, þe hie ær drugon
ond for þreanydum þolian scoldon,
torn unlytel.

(830-33)

[Also cured all their distress, the sorrow and the malice they had endured and in painful necessity had had to endure, no little grief.]

Anyone can see that *inwidsorge* and *torn* are both "variations" of the idea first expressed in *oncyþðe,* while the whole of line 832 is an expansion of *þe hie ær drugon* just before; anyone can see, too, that the poet is enjoying the cumulative roll of vanished miseries, with the sharp litotes of *unlytel* at the end. Just the same, the "variations" in ***Beowulf*** keep on arriving even when their necessity is less than evident (for example in lines 350-55). What they do is help the poet "change step," that is, move from one essential idea to the next without losing alliteration. In this section, for instance, the poet's final and clearly deliberate stroke is to end with the image of Beowulf showing his grisly trophy, Grendel's arm, to the watching men. *Þæt wæs tacen sweotol,* he says with enthusiastic under-understatement, "it was a clear indication, once, bold in battle, he laid down the hand, the arm and the shoulder—there was Grendel's grip all together—laid it down beneath the vaulted roof" (833-6). The *tacen,* we can see, is a vital part of the section's narrative structure; but its entry has been much eased by the semantically redundant use of *torn*.

Having got so far, one can hardly avoid the concept of "orality." Does the poet's functionalism not suggest a man who will have to recite his poem to listeners who cannot be expected to ponder over every single word he says? Could it not even imply a man himself illiterate who never so much as imagined the scrupulous concepts of literary criticism? These questions (and several others) have in recent years been almost literally bedevilled by the discovery of a third stylistic feature of ***Beowulf***—the formula, sometimes called the oral-formula. The facts behind this phrase can be briefly stated. Through the whole of ***Beowulf*** about one half line in six will be repeated more or less exactly elsewhere in the poem: examples include *hine fyrwyt bræc,* already discussed, or in the lines just quoted *ellenmærþum* and *þe hie ær drugon*. Very many more will be repeated with slight (or great) changes: thus *nihtweorce gefeh* (827) is at least rather like *secg weorce gefeh* (1569), while *ond for þreanydum* (832) is virtually identical with *ac for preanedlan* (2223). Any search for repetitions in ***Beowulf*** uncovers vast but not easily organized sets of resemblances; and these once more offer radical challenge to concepts of originality, precision, the poetic mind. Thus to many the epithet *nacod niðdraca* in line 2273 seems beautifully calculated to evoke the monster's obscenely and unnaturally leathery hide, the famous armour-plating of the longworm. On the other hand the poet alliterates *nið* and *nacod* elsewhere, in line 2585, where he is talking about swords, and he has a whole range of similar phrases for the dragon, some of them ("dangerous fire-dragon," "terrible earth-dragon") no more tightly appropriate than Grendel's *fenhleoðu*. You can, in short, regard the brilliant stroke as one more accidental overlap of two repetitive systems; the formulas turn out as functional as the compounds and the variations, and as artistically neutral. Some critics welcome these implications as a gain in precision. To others the whole line of thought acts as intolerable provocation to their most cherished notions of individual art.

The problem is ours, not the poet's. Once again the overwhelming temptation for modern readers is to bring to the poem preconceived ideas of beauty and worth, to insist on praising it for what we have already decided is praiseworthy. ***Beowulf*** lends itself to these arguments, as it does to symbolic interpretations, ironic interpretations, even the neoclassic interpretations of days gone by. That does not make any of them right. Furthermore we must fear that while we pursue sterile controversies of art versus accident and oral versus literate, we are shirking the real problem, which is to see what the poet would himself have found stylistically admirable. In pursuing this objective, probably the most useful thing we can do with compounds, variations and formulas is jettison them; and with them our quasi-autobiographical curiosity about mode of composition. The latter cannot be satisfied. As for the features of style . . . , they *are* prominent and they *do* tell us something, but the most useful thing they tell us is that for the underlying charm and power of the poem—as distinct from minor local lapses or neatnesses—we shall have to look elsewhere. The style of ***Beowulf*** is clearly functional. But we want to know what aim these functions serve.

One can make a start here by considering once more the end of the Grendel fight. Here if anywhere the poet is deliberately manipulating his audience. From the start of the struggle he has been insisting that Beowulf's will is unbreakable, and so is his grip. Grendel "could not get away" (754), he "knew his fingers held in the fierce one's grip" (764-5); as for Beowulf, he "held him firmly" (788), "not for anything would he let the evil visitor escape alive" (791-2). So how does Grendel manage to flee to the fens? At the crucial moment the poet evades us, slipping from the physical bursting of bones in line 818 to the abstraction of *guðhreð,* success and glory in 819. The answer is held in suspense for fifteen lines. *Then* the poem says it was "a clear sign" [*tacen sweotol*] when Beowulf laid down the hand and arm and shoulder "beneath the vaulted roof." The hero's grip has not weakened, we see; instead it was the monster's fear which proved stronger than his flesh. (pp. 45-8)

[The] immediate point here is the strongly *visual* quality of the poet's rhetoric. One can hardly avoid saying that he "cuts" from the mighty wound to Grendel fleeing dimly into the night, that at the end he "narrows focus" to the arm "framed" by the vaulted roof. Of course all these words are cinematic, and so anachronisms. Still, they can remind us that the poet obviously did not mean his words to stay on the page, but to stimulate mental images. Sometimes he directs his audience to visualize, using words like *yþgesene:* "On the bench there over each prince you could easily have seen. . . ." More often he gives them something to look at, and characters inside the poem looking at it. The Danes pursuing Grendel's mother come upon Æschere's head with exactly the same shock as those in Heorot staring at Grendel's arm, and the poet stops to let them (and us) drink it in: *Folc to sægon,* he prompts (1422), "the people looked at it." Two hundred lines later it is Grendel's head which appears on the floor of Heorot within a frame of spectators:

Þa wæs be feaxe on flet boren
Grendles heafod, þær guman druncon,
egeslic for eorlum ond þære idese mid,
wliteseon wrætlic; weras on sawon.

(1647-50)

[Then Grendel's head was carried by its hair
on to the floor where the men were drinking,
a terrible thing for the warriors and the woman
with them, a splendid and beautiful sight; the
men looked at it.]

In between Beowulf has (quite redundantly) asked the Danes to visualize Hygelac receiving the news of his death: "Then the lord of the Geats can realize, the son of Hrethel see, when he stares at the treasure [*þonne he on þæt sinc starað*] that I found a good divider of rings . . ." (1484-7). And when the slave makes off with the dragon's cup, he shows it to his master:

frea sceawode
fira fyrngeweorc forman siðe.

(2285-6)

[For the first time the lord looked at the ancient
work of men.]

Silent vision is an important part of the poet's craft; he manufactures occasions for it. That is why we have the rapid and much-admired interchange of external and internal views as Grendel bears down on Heorot (702-27). That is equally why, after Beowulf has killed Grendel's mother in the submarine hall, the poet cannot resist switching to Hrothgar and the others fathoms above, standing and watching the blood spread in the water. Silently the Danes ride home. As silently the Geats sit and stare at the mere, wishing hopelessly that they could "see their lord himself." But the sight to which the poet redirects us is the giant sword melting like an icicle in Grendel's blood. The emotional contrasts are presented entirely visually.

Of course this makes excellent sense as a mode of narration for audiences not yet surfeited by television. What is less commonly realized, however, is how far down the stylistic scale this quality of manipulated vision goes. It is something which (unlike compound words and formulas) resists quantification. Nevertheless, the most powerful consistent feature of Beowulfian style is what may be called its 'epic brokenness'—the poet's determination not to let successive sentences resemble each other syntactically or describe events from the same point of view.

Some examples of this have already been cited. We are switched in lines 818-19 from physical "joints" to abstract "glory"; in line 825 we turn from simple past to pluperfect, as the poet invites us to consider all the courage and misery that preceded this turn of events; and in lines 827-8 we get a neat "double perspective" in time as Beowulf rejoices simultaneously over what he has done (*nihtweorce*) and what he will get (*ellenmærþum*). More generally we can see that the whole of this fight has been described in a way peripherally, with attention being repeatedly directed away from the centre to the effects that that centre produces—the echoing hall, the smashed benches, the gallant but ineffective crowd of Geats, outside them the Danes listening in horror to the screams of Grendel, "God's adversary singing a terror-song . . . the captive of hell lamenting his pain." Perhaps most remarkable, though, is the poet's occasional approach to "stream of consciousness," as for instance in his account of Ongentheow, the grim old Swedish king, falling back in sullen anger before the unexpected Geatish *revanche*. In lines 2949-57 the poet, unusually, allows this character to remain the syntactic subject of five main verbs in succession: he "went away . . . turned back; he had heard of the warfare of Hygelac, the proud man's battle-skill; he had no faith in resistance, in beating off the seamen, defending from the invaders his treasure, wife and children; again he turned away, old man beneath the earth-wall." One sees how discontinuous even this "stream" is, as the strongly implied conjunctions like "because" and "so" are omitted, as new facts like the rampart and Ongentheow's children emerge from each new clause. There are few passages in ***Beowulf*** of more direct narrative than this, and yet even here one sees the love of proceeding by a series of minor shocks—of keeping reader or listener from reaching any easy sense of predictability, while letting him see, feel, remember, conclude only those exact things which the narrator intends.

This too could be explained, incidentally, as one more accident of alliterative convention. In line 815 we have a typically sudden leap from emotion to fact, one of the poem's innumerable "changes of angle":

wæs gehwæþer oðrum
lifigende lað. Licsar gebad
atol aglæca.

(814-16)

[Each was to the other hateful while he lived.
The dreadful monster received a body wound.]

Is it coincidence, though, that in the poem *lif* and *lic* alliterate together five more times? There is an obvious reason why they should, since they mean something similar, are easily related: in line 2571 Beowulf's shield fails to protect "life and body" [*life ond lice*], in line 2743 he says he must die, "life go from body" [*lif of lice*]. But in 815 this semantic connection has become a discontinuity, separating different sentences. Is this (like *fenhleoðu* or *nacod niðdraca*) another compulsive prompting from the traditional vocabulary? Maybe so. However, the observation hardly matters. If one studies compounds and formulas in ***Beowulf,*** one can often feel that the poet's attention has wandered. When it comes to modes of revelation and concealment, however, his delight and involvement are unmistakable. Certainly he snaps up the opportunities created by traditional pairs like *lif* and *lic* or *fyr* and *flod,* and readers used to the explanatory smoothness of modern prose may feel that, for him, any excuse to change his viewpoint will do. Still, on this level his attention never wavers; there is nothing in the poem as banal visually as "East-Danes" is verbally. The poet's style is fragmented, but his voice projects control.

It is indeed typical of the poem to develop strength from what would by orthodox literary canons be weakness. Its characters do not develop or change. Admittedly Beowulf himself is presented first as young and then as old, and it has been shown how vital to the poem this final sense of age is. However, it is also true to say that the *way* this complex feeling is produced verbally is by simple combination of epithets once reserved for Hrothgar, the old and passive king (*se wisa, frod cyning, þone gomelan*), with others which remind us that the hero is still in heart what he was (*se goda, oretta, heard under helme*). What is moving is not awareness of change, but juxtaposition of fixed purpose with changed circumstance. "When I was young I did many battles," says Beowulf, as if to himself:

"gyt ic wylle,
frod folces weard fæhðe secan,
mærðu fremman. . . ."

(2512-14)

[Once more I will, old guardian of the people,
seek out violence, do famous deeds.]

Never before has he been *frod folces weard;* but *fæhðe* and *mærðu* have been his goals a dozen times already. Even this case, then, supports the assertion that Beowulfian characters do not change their true nature, though indeed this may be progressively revealed.

Sometimes the result is a peculiar inappositeness. Beowulf says of Hrothgar (2107) *"hwilum hildedeor hearpan grette"* [sometimes, bold in battle, he touched the harp]. But Hrothgar is no longer *hildedeor,* and even if he were, it would have nothing to do with his harping. Similarly, as Unferth lends Beowulf his sword, the poet remarks contemptuously that "the son of Ecglaf surely forgot, mighty in strength [*eafopes cræftig*] what he had said before, drunk with wine, now he lent his weapon to a better swordsman" (1465-8). *Eafoþes cræftig?* We feel the phrase ought to continue the criticism, and so translators tend to render it by some such word as "strapping" (which implies disapproval). Alternatively the phrase can be explained as "ironic." But the fact is that both the style and the ideology of the poem continue to use honorifics up to the moment (as with the ten cowards after line 2846) when they are formally removed. There are occasions when this inflexibility becomes a definite asset.

As Beowulf and Hrothgar part, for instance, the old king breaks down, weeping at the thought that they will never meet again. "Locked in the bonds of his heart," observes the poet, "a gloomy longing for the man he loved burnt in his blood" (1878-80). But Beowulf simply walks away:

Him Beowulf þanan,
guðrinc goldwlanc græsmoldan træd
since hremig; sægenga bad
agendfrean, se þe on ancre rad.

(1880-83)

[Away from him the gold-proud war-man trod
the grassy turf, exulting in treasure; the sea-
crosser which rode at anchor was waiting for
its lord.]

Insensitivity? The vicious pride of youth? Without the expectations of the epic style we might think so. But as it is, the shining figure trampling the grass conveys something exhilarating, the more so for the grief and foreboding which surround him. We know Beowulf is going to die; he is separated from any possible audience of the poem by a great gap of time; and yet for a moment he exists in sharp focus down the tunnel of years, real and happy and triumphant. Poetry has made him immortal. And an element in that process is the way that despair sloughs off him, leaving his character unmarked. We see the same movement at the start of the poem's last section, as the Geats turn from grief to action: "For him then the people of the Geats prepared a pyre on earth, no mean one" (3137-8). They are as correct in their silence as was Beowulf himself, confronted with the beast his men tugged from the monsters' mere: "The men gazed at the terrible stranger. Beowulf prepared himself in warriors' equipment, nothing did he care for life . . ." (1440-42). In a hard world, we might reflect, emotional stasis could be as much of a positive as sensitivity.

Line 3138, however, displays a further potential weakness of epic style in its pleonasm: the phrase *on eorðan* is redundant, for where else would you build a pyre if not on the ground? Throwing in the odd "on earth" or "under heaven" is a common device of the Anglo-Saxon poet under stress, and the author of ***Beowulf*** does not scorn it. In his poem, though, pleonasm can work; it is indeed the first stylistic device we should become aware of. As early as line 13 a child is born to Scyld, *geong in geardum* [young in the yards]. Once Scyld is dead this son rules: *Ða wæs on burgum Beowulf Scyldinga* [then in the towns was Beowulf the Scylding]. *His* son was "the high Healfdene," and to him in turn four children *in woruld wocun* [woke into the world]. Before long it is the other Beowulf, the poem's hero, who is using the same locution, for he says his father is dead and gone, *'gamol of geardum'* [old man from the yards], counterbalancing the Danish Beowulf who was born *geong in geardum* at the start, paralleling Scyld himself who "went elsewhere" in death, *aldor of earde* [as a chief from the earth]. This cluster of similar phrases works insidiously and powerfully, along with the repeated images of coming, waking up, travelling out, to create a picture of the common habitations, the homelands, the *geardas,* set in space against the universe that surrounds them and in time against the mystery of death. To these forces men oppose their fleeting happiness, their children, their social rituals of memory and inheritance. The composite image becomes deeply embedded in the poem as a whole, ready to be restimulated positively by the mention of home or inheritance (see lines 693, 912, 1127; 1960 ff., 2470 ff., 2623 ff.), or negatively by the rumour of great and ominous forces just outside the light—those for instance who sent out Scyld on his journey, *ænne ofer yðe, umborwesende* [alone over seas, being a child], and who take back his treasure-piled body in the end:

Men ne cunnon
secgan to soðe, selerædende,
hæleð under heofenum, hwa þæm hlæste onfeng.

(50-52)

[Men cannot say for sure, hall-councillors, heroes under heavens, who received that cargo.]

The heroes are heroes, one might say, because they are "under heavens" and know so little; the phrase is resonantly appropriate. It is not destroyed if one remarks that it is also an evident cliché which can (as in line 505) be used entirely mechanically.

The images of pleonasm work in fact as spatial counterparts to the rhythms of temporal opposition which the poet again extracts from formula and elevates to principle—the circle of sadness after joy and joy after sadness once more. Hrothgar explains this most openly in his long "disguised narrator" speech of lines 1700-1784, whose climax is direct appeal to Beowulf (and through him to us). Look at me, says Hrothgar, I was confident once, I ruled the Ring-Danes "beneath the clouds."

> "Hwæt, me þæs on eþle edwenden cwom,
> gyrn æfter gomene, seoþðan Grendel wearð,
> ealdgewinna, ingenga min."
>
> (1774-6)

> [To me in my home came a change from this,
> grief after pleasure, once Grendel, old enemy,
> became my invader.]

We see the use of *on eþle* in 1774, the syntactic delay of *scoþðan* in 1775, both devices already mentioned. Between them, though, lies the fierce reversal of *gyrn æfter gomene*. To this pattern the poet has drawn our attention before—*swylt æfter synnum* in 1255, *æfter wea . . . wyrp* in 909, *æfter þam wælræse willa* in 824 [death after sins, recovery after woe, desire after deadly battle]. He makes the rhythm emblematic in line 1008 as Grendel "sleeps after banquet," and as the Danish warriors are found "sleeping after banquet" in line 119, only to be betrayed by sleep to Grendel. The pattern leads readily to the repetitions of "they knew not sorrow, the fortune of men" in 119-20, and "they knew not fate, grim destiny" a thousand lines later. It finds its way from moralizing to description when the Danes wake and find their dead in line 128: "Then was after banquet lamentation raised" [*wop æfter wiste*]; and into direct speech when Hrothgar tells Beowulf: "Don't ask after joy; sorrow is renewed" [*sorh æfter sælum*]. As often, indeed, the poet and his characters turn out indistinguishable. Their shared image of human precariousness finds multiple but consistent expression.

There is little point, finally, in arguing whether the poet was or was not conscious of these repeated structures. What matters is that even if he employed them consciously, he did so un*self*consciously. His tricks of rhetoric often have learned names—pleonasm, paronomasia, essential hypotaxis. They remain, however, familiar parts of English speech; anyone who says "brain versus brawn" or "I'll love you and leave you" is using paronomasia as surely as the ***Beowulf*** poet opposing *lof* to *lif* or *wæl* to *willa*. Of course clichés do not spontaneously generate poetry. Nevertheless, the point remains: the stylistic power of ***Beowulf*** depends not on close fit of words to scenes but on bold use of familiar phrasing. The poet's art, like his philosophy, is rooted in commonplace. (pp. 48-55)

T. A. Shippey, in his Beowulf, *Edward Arnold, 1978, 64 p.*

A map of England in the tenth century. From An Introduction to Anglo-Saxon England, *by Peter Hunter Blair. Cambridge University Press, 1977. Copyright © 1959, 1977 Cambridge University Press. Reproduced with permission of the publisher.*

JOHN D. NILES (essay date 1983)

[*Niles is an American scholar who concentrates on medieval French and English literature. In the following excerpt, he discusses the function of the narrator in* Beowulf.]

The interpretation of a poem usually presupposes a "poet" and a "reader." The poet is often known by name; the reader is usually a convenient fiction, whether the author's or the critic's. The reader is assumed to be a private audience. In addressing him or her, the poet is often able to adopt a personal voice that may be ironic or confessional in tone, for both irony and confession depend on a certain private bond being established between the speaker and listener. In ironic discourse, the private bond is assumed, while in confessional discourse it is established.

To some extent the interpretation of ***Beowulf*** can be based on these conventional notions of poet and reader, but the terms do not entirely fit the text. Even the notion of "the text" as the basis of our understanding is not entirely applicable, for the poem was not primarily a text but a sequence of words spoken or sung by a performer. Like any dramatic or semi-dramatic performance, it was a dynamic event shared for a few hours by a performer and a listening audience. It did not exist in isolation, especially not in isolation on the page, but was part of an interchange among people who, in other ways as well, probably made up a group. (p. 197)

[In much of the following discussion I shall] put aside the notions of *poet* and *reader* to concentrate on the more essential terms *narrator* and *audience*. Normally these terms suggest a quiescent role for both. An audience passively hears, while a narrator passively transmits a text. I should like to use the terms in the more active sense that is appropriate to the oral poetry of societies in which skilled performers are chiefly responsible for creating and preserving a body of traditional song.

They cannot do so without audiences who bring their own special knowledge to the performance and enter actively into the process, whether by encouraging the singer or by perfecting the song in their own minds. Literature of this kind is public property. The narrator speaks with an impersonal voice that assumes some important experience shared within the group. His tone is rarely ironic or confessional, for he utters his words as spokesman for all rather than as a person sharing private perceptions.

An active narrator of this kind is sure to have provided the poem's link to a live audience. This narrator presumably had a name and character of his own and impressed his character on the work at least to the extent that a skilled musician or conductor impresses his character on a piece of music today. Although this dimension of the performance is lost, the role of the narrator in ***Beowulf*** is still not completely impossible to reconstruct, because the poet includes a part for him. From early on, one is aware of the presence of an *I*, a speaker who is not the poet himself but is the voice of the poet's alter ego in oral performance.

It is this voice that recalls the action, orchestrates it in its imposing detail, and mediates it by setting it within a value system that the listening audience would have recognized as its own. This voice is not exactly a persona, in the sense that critics use the term to speak of Chaucer's self-portrait in the *Canterbury Tales* or as Ezra Pound used the term to refer to the different masks or personalities he adopted in his shorter poems. Such a persona is always individualized and is often playful or ironic: there is an important difference between Ezra Pound and Pound's Propertius. In ***Beowulf*** one can make no such clear distinctions, for the poet's mask is nearly featureless. The chief function of the narrator's voice is to validate the story and comment on it—to "authenticate" it for the listeners. The habitual stance of the narrator has been aptly described as one of "authority based on exceptional knowledge about a common tradition.

From the poem's first lines, the narrator suppresses his individuality to present himself as one of the group, the other members of which constitute the listening audience. "Lo, we have heard," he begins, shunning the personal voice of the Anglo-Saxon elegies. The narrator claims to speak only what is common knowledge.

Eventually this first-person plural voice merges almost unnoticeably into the first-person singular. After the first line, as the story becomes more specific, the narrator never again uses the pronoun *we* in relation to his knowledge of his sources. A bare dozen times (in lines 38, 62, 74, 1011, 1027, 1196, 1197, 1842, 2163, 2172, 2694, and 2773) he uses the pronoun *I* in phrases of the sort *hyrde ic þæt,* "I have heard that"; or þa ic . . . gefrægn, "I have heard, then . . ."; or, in comparative constructions, *ne hyrde ic,* "I have not heard of" (a more comely ship, or more generous king, and so forth). Another five times (in lines 776, 837, 1955, 2685, and 2837) he uses the fixed formula *mine gefræge* "by my account" or, perhaps, "according to my version of the story." None of these phrases is meant to call up the idea of a human being with an individual sensibility or with an original story to relate. At the most, they suggest that the narrator speaks from his deep familiarity with the stories of Germanic antiquity, a familiarity that he has gained from oral tradition. Many stories of old times are told, the narrator suggests. Of these he has chosen one for retelling.

Apart from these few instances of first-person asides, ***Beowulf*** may seem to be a story that tells itself. Its immediate impression on a reader is likely to be that of direct, unmediated narrative, much like that of *Genesis A* or *Exodus*. The falsity of this impression becomes evident as soon as one considers how frequently the narrator uses gnomic statements, superlatives, and explicit ethical judgments to build up a grid of belief against which the action he recounts can be plotted. The narrator is not with us only intermittently, at moments when he speaks of his having heard the story; he is a constant presence throughout. His one great function is to put his listeners into the position of his ideal audience, an audience that nods assent to all his judgments. Because these judgments are not the property of any one person but have been handed down as collective wisdom, the narrator does not really manipulate his audience, as an author of propaganda might. One could think of the poem as a process whereby a society's traditional system of values or beliefs is articulated so that it can be appreciated more deeply by all those present.

The narrator in ***Beowulf*** is not omniscient, though he has been called that. He speaks what he knows of the actors in the story, much as Hrothgar's thane recounts "just about all that he had heard said concerning Sigemund's courageous deeds" (874b-876a). Usually he observes a respectful silence concerning things that no mortal could be expected to know. "People know not how to say truly" who received Scyld's funeral boat (50b-51a), just as "no one knows" the movements of the secret creatures of hell (162b-163). These matters he accepts as mysteries. On the other hand, his knowledge of Beowulf's adventures seems to have no limits, for he is able to describe, for example, hero's fortunes even at the bottom of Grendel's mere. At one point he moves back in time to recount the words of a speaker who died hundreds of years before this story begins (2247-66). He knows of Grendel's descent from Cain, even though there is no indication that the people in the narrative do, and he knows that Beowulf's soul is saved, even though the Geats do not. To call him "near-omniscient" hits close to the mark. Although like many a storyteller he sometimes claims knowledge that no one could really possess, he more often plays the role of an informal historian who repeats what he has heard from common report.

For the most part, his aphoristic asides are truisms: God rules over the human race (700b-702a), 1057b-58); everyone has to die (2590b-91a); death is not easy to flee (1002b-08a); misery awaits the souls of the damned, bliss the souls of the saved (183b-188); life holds good and bad in store for everyone (1060b-62); a person who has the Lord's favor can survive any difficulty (2291-93a); a good leader prospers through his generosity (20-25); kinsmen should be true to one another (2166b-69a, 2600b-01); gold does dragons little good (2275b-77); winning treasure from a dragon is no easy task (2415b-16); a good retainer will praise his lord after his death (3174b-77). These are the sorts of commonplaces that the narrator lets fall whenever the situation asks for them, as if one of his duties as spokesman for the tribe was to generalize from the particular to the universal.

The narrator feels free to appeal to customary Christian or secular wisdom even when this leads him to apparent contradictions, just as two proverbs can sometimes be cited to support opposite sides of a question. After references to Grendel's crimes and the Lord's eternal rule, for example, the narrator puts much emphasis on the virtues of discernment and forethought (1059-60a). After reporting how Beowulf trusted in his naked strength in the monsters' underwater hall, he remarks that a man who hopes to gain lasting fame should act without pausing to reflect on his safety (1534b-36). There is no real contradiction here, for the situations are different and call for a different wisdom: evil impulses are to be restrained, but a hero must sometimes act impetuously.

The narrator's gnomic voice is thus a flexible one that remains impersonal. It cannot be pinned to a single point of view, the way that the gnomic utterances set into the mouths of the characters sometimes can. Whereas Beowulf, Hrothgar, Wiglaf, and the minor personages are sometimes given aphorisms to speak, these utterances accord with their character (or help establish their character) in a way that the narrator's asides do not. The credo of action is set into the active Beowulf's mouth (1384-89), while the credo of caution is set into Wiglaf's (3077-78). The aged, gracious, somewhat humbled Hrothgar is made to speak the great fatherly warning against pride and greed (1700-84). The guardian of the Danish coast, appropriately, is given a sententious remark on the need to distinguish fair words from fair deeds (287b-89). These persons are individualized in the poem, briefly or at length, but the narrator never assumes a separate identity. If he did so he would lose his mediating role as one who speaks for all his audience, not only those with certain roles or views.

Perhaps the narrator's most disarming trait is his enthusiasm in making simple judgments. "That was a good king!" (11b), he says of Scyld. "That was a brave man!" (1812b), he later remarks of Beowulf. "That's what a man should be!" (2708b), he says of Wiglaf. There is nothing ironic or naive about these designations, as there is when the Chaucer-persona of the *Canterbury Tales* praises the Shipman with the words "and certeinly he was a good felawe!" To be a "good felawe," in the context of Chaucer's pilgrimage, is of course to be a rascal and a rogue. To be a *god cyning* in ***Beowulf*** is to rule well. Whereas Chaucer's praise can rarely be taken innocently, the ***Beowulf*** narrator seems incapable of speaking with the ironist's wink. The many superlatives of ***Beowulf*** might likewise call to mind the frequent superlatives that Chaucer applies to his gallery of pilgrims, each of whom seems to be the best or the worthiest or the most notable of his kind, but the strategies of the two poets are utterly opposed. Although Chaucer often damns with praise, as when he calls the Friar "the beste beggere in his hous," the words of the Old English poem can be taken at face value, with only a normal allowance for narrative hyperbole.

In ***Beowulf,*** everything seems larger or better or more terrible than life. Heorot is "the most illustrious building under the sky" (309-310). If Beowulf's hall is likewise "the best of buildings" (2326a), there is no contradiction here but only a plethora of praise. The lord who rules from Heorot is appropriately "the best of worldly kings between the two seas" (1684b-85), and again there is no contradiction with either Beowulf or King Offa, "the best of all mankind between the two seas" (1955-56), for these men ruled at different times, between different seas. The Danes are said to flock about their king in a bigger, more decorous retinue than any other of which the narrator has heard (1011-12). They enjoy "the choicest of feasts" (1232b), and their merriment as they flock about their king and queen is greater than any other the narrator has seen (2014b-16a). Hrothgar's gifts to Beowulf are unparalleled for their generosity (1027-29). The necklace that Wealhtheow gives the hero is the best treasure of which the narrator has heard, barring only the *Brosinga mene* (1197-99). Scyld's funeral ship is decked out more beautifully with weapons, clothes, and other treasures than any other known to the speaker (38-40a). Unferth's sword is "the best of blades" (1144a). The sword that Hygelac presents to Beowulf as a reward for his victories is better than any other among the Geats (2192b-93). The hero's corselet, another heirloom, is "the best of battle-shirts" (453a). Even the minor characters are painted in the strongest colors. Æschere is the "best," the "most beloved" of all Hrothgar's retainers (1406a, 1296b). Wiglaf is "an immeasurably good thane" (2721b). The seven Geats who rifle the barrow are "the finest" of them all (3122b).

The referent of many different superlatives in the poem is, of course, Beowulf, model hero and king. His physical attributes are described first. The narrator introduces him as "the strongest of all mankind in that day of this life" (196-197). The guard of the Danish coast notes his singular appearance and confesses that he has never seen a bigger man on earth (247b-251). After the hero's reception in Heorot, Hrothgar remarks that he has never heard a young man speak so wisely (1842b-43). Beowulf's actions in Denmark evoke further superlatives. The Danes call him the finest warrior on earth and the one most worthy of kingship (857b-61), while Wealhtheow says that people will praise him as far as the sea encircles the earth (1221-24a). At the end of his life, not his strength or ferocious deeds, but the excellence of his character is praised. To Wiglaf, he is the "most beloved" of men (2823), the "most worthy warrior over the whole earth" (3099). To the Geats who circle the barrow he is the "mildest" and "gentlest" of men and the "kindest to his people" (3181-82). The barrow the tribe builds for him is constructed with such care that knowledgeable people will find it "most worthy" (3161b-62), and the flames that consume his corpse make up "the greatest of pyres" (3143b).

If the narrator is not stingy in bestowing praise, neither does he withhold blame. Many of his judgments concern patterns of conduct that deviate from the ideal values represented by such people as Scyld, Hrothgar, Wealhtheow, and Beowulf. He is emphatic in denouncing the pagan rites of the Danes; he makes no secret of his feelings toward Grendel and the antediluvian giants as enemies of the true Lord; and he holds up the conduct of Heremod and Modthryth as examples of all that a king or queen should avoid. He explicitly points out that Unferth "lost his good name" (1470b) by declining the chance to fight Grendel's mother, and he specifies that Hygelac "asked for trouble" when he attacked the Franks and Frisians "in his arrogance" (1206). In these and other ways the narrator does not refrain from adopting a partisan voice. He lets the listening audience know exactly what he thinks of the conduct of the characters he describes, and he expresses his judgments in such a confident tone that they need no further comment or defense. Instead of trying to persuade or influence his listeners, he speaks with the absolute authority of their spokesman.

Perhaps the narrator's voice stands out most clearly by comparison with what it is not.

His judgments do not extend freely to all human affairs, unlike the judgments in a gnomic poem such as "Hávamál," but tend to be restricted to matters pertaining to the proper behavior of a lord or thane. He is not chauvinistic, unlike the author of such a piece of propaganda as "The Battle of Brunanburh," and seems to owe special allegiance to no tribe. Nowhere does he speak ill of material treasure, only of hoarding it; and unlike the author of "The Soul's Address to the Body," he makes no issue of the horrors of the grave and the corruption of all flesh. Although he implicitly warns against Hygelac's type of arrogance, he does not praise humility or advocate loving one's enemies, as does the author of "Vainglory." Most clearly, he never adopts a Cynewulfian voice, telling just who he is so that others will pray for him and, possibly, praise him by name. He does not thank God for having helped him tell the story, as the author of a saint's life might have done, nor does he urge us all to thank the Lord for His mercies, as does the author of "The Fortunes of Men." In general, he refrains from exhorting his audience as if from a pulpit, as do the authors of the Old English homilies with their direct address to the listener (*Hæleþ min se leofa,* "My dear man") or as does the speaker of "The Seafarer" with his final attempts at persuasion (*Uton we hycgan,* "Let us consider," 117). He does not have to exhort his listeners, for he and they already see eye to eye—or, at any rate, that is the effect his voice is designed to create.

Thus the narrator is a significant presence in ***Beowulf,*** even though he entirely avoids calling attention to himself except to claim the authority of oral tradition for details of his song. Although his mask is almost featureless, as befits the voice of a collective tradition, he has the important function of channeling audience response by articulating certain timeless truths and by authenticating what constitutes praiseworthy behavior. Of the many attitudes that were current in Anglo-Saxon England among different people—kings, thanes, priests, monks, nuns, farmers, craftsmen, and so on—he "activates" those basic Christian and secular values that have relevance for his story. In this way he helps create an audience that will judge the work most fittingly, without reference to inappropriate standards. As his song proceeded, one can imagine that the thoughts of his listeners merged with his until little distance between them remained. (pp. 197-204)

John D. Niles, in his Beowulf: The Poem and Its Tradition, *Cambridge, Mass.: Harvard University Press, 1983, 310 p.*

FRED C. ROBINSON (essay date 1983)

[*An American linguist and medievalist, Robinson has published several works devoted to Old English literature. In the following excerpt, he discusses the conceptions of nature, morality, and Christianity held by the* Beowulf *poet as exemplums of the world-view of their age.*]

Beowulf is one of the relatively few major poems from the distant past which, upon first reading, still capture the attention of the modern reader and leave him changed when he puts the book down. Even those who have felt the narrative method to be flawed have usually responded to the poem's bracing severity, its awesome conflation of dignity and horror, and its strange, autumnal close. To an extent the poem transcends the slow revolutions in literary taste which have taken place since the eighth century: any modern reader can feel its moving power. (p. xi)

Beowulf is about many things, and the intellectual concerns that the poet shared with his milieu were no doubt numerous, complex, and beyond total recall. . . .

[Many points] of agreement between the poem and its cultural setting will be obvious. That a Christian poet writing only a century after his nation was converted from paganism should express pious views such as those in lines 180-88 will be a surprise to no one. That a poem describing the warrior class in the Heroic Age preceding that conversion should have little to say about the farmers and craftsmen upon whom any society depends will also seem normal to anyone who has ever read an epic or romance. But other attitudes in the poem can be understood only if we pause to consider the difference between our modern thought-world and that of the ***Beowulf*** poet. Consider the respective roles of nature on the one hand and man's artifice on the other. Anyone living after Rousseau and the English Romantic poets will be familiar with the view that man is born with a natural inclination toward wholesome conduct but that he is often corrupted by the artificial forms with which society surrounds him, such as inhibitions, social customs, and city life. To restore the soul we must return to Nature, for

One impulse from a vernal wood
Can teach you more of man,
Of moral evil and of good,
Than all the sages can.

No attitude could have been more alien to the pagan Germanic society depicted in ***Beowulf*** or to the early Christian society in which the ***Beowulf*** poet lived. Men in that day found no more comfort in nature per se than a thoughtful modern man finds in typhoons, black holes, or atomic fission today. Nature seemed anarchic, inimical, and life was endurable only in so far as man had imposed rational order upon it. The vernal woods were menacing, beset with fens and wolf-slopes, fires and storms, and uncontrolled, monstrous life. Against this aimless, teeming world man poses his rational craft. He strikes roads through the wilderness and dispells the natural darkness with lighted mead-halls. His ships conquer the turbulent wave and his ringmail and weapons keep sea-monsters at bay. Readers of ***Beowulf*** must be conscious of this attitude when they see throughout the poem the many references to cunningly made armor, artfully curved ships, damascened swords, and well-wrought buildings. Each artifact is a celebration of man's triumph over the hostile wilderness that surrounds the islands of order such as Heorot. The many artifacts pictured at intervals throughout [***Beowulf***] were not merely utilitarian objects: they were reassuring signs that man's rational order can be made to prevail over a formless and malignant nature. (p. xvi)

Nor is the ***Beowulf*** poet's delight in rationalizing nature limited to external nature. Human nature, when it escapes man's control, is perhaps the most dangerous force of all. . . . We find much in ***Beowulf,*** therefore, about the forms and customs by which men ordered their lives. Greetings, speeches, preparations for battle are performed almost ritualistically. The herald who takes Beowulf's message to King Hrothgar does so standing "before his shoulder, according to the noble custom." All this is not mere *mise en scène;* it expresses a major theme in the poem, reminding us that men must ever strive for control, not yield to impulse. The same is true of the mead-serving ceremony and the formalities of seating guests and taking food. We never hear of feasts without ceremony—except when Grendel falls to his gruesome repast, or when the evil Heremod explodes with anger and slays his table companions. To the ***Beowulf*** poet such conduct as this is not human. It is natural.

The characters in ***Beowulf*** and the poet himself do not shrink from moral judgments. A man who slays his own kin is treacherous, not (as such a man might be judged today) in need of psychological counseling. A man who deserts his comrades in battle is a coward, not a respectable dissenter marching to a different drummer. A ruler who usurps the wealth that is owed to his followers is condemned and expelled; he is not, like some modern embezzlers, excused on the grounds that he was working under an emotional strain. A king whom old age has crippled may be excused as blameless even though he can no longer protect his people; but otherwise one is held responsible for his actions. Some modern critics have resisted this stern strain in the Anglo-Saxon outlook. They believe Beowulf's heroic stature is qualified by the poet, and the monsters, though evil, have something to be said in their defense. Such views smack of the modern world, not of the world of ***Beowulf.***

And yet, moral judgments in the poem are not merely simplistic. In a sense, the entire narrative is a subtle questioning of the prevailing (eighth-century) moral judgment of the Heroic Age. But to understand this we must examine one further aspect of the thought-world of ***Beowulf,*** the confrontation of Christian and pagan beliefs in Dark Age England.

The standard Christian authorities in the time of the ***Beowulf*** poet left no room for uncertainty in assessing the confrontation of Christian and pagan: Christianity was the Truth and paganism was a treacherous network of lies and deceptions fabricated by the Devil. Any devout Christian, including the ***Beowulf*** poet, would presumably have accepted this view without question. A logical corollary to this view which Christians would also have been expected to accept, is the dictum expressed most clearly by St. Cyprian: "There is no salvation outside the Church." Most Anglo-Saxons who wrote on this subject espoused Cyprian's view without difficulty, but for some the implications were troubling. For to accept this view meant that one was willing to see one's ancestors consigned to eternal damnation. To kings who traced their lineage back to Woden and aristocrats who took pride in the works and wisdom of their Continental forebears, the consequences of accepting the Christian view could involve some pain. Many, no doubt, tried not to dwell on the past, turning their minds instead toward the Christian present and future.

And yet it is precisely this condemned ancestry of the English to which the ***Beowulf*** poet has devoted his poem. Though himself a Christian, and probably the son and grandson of Christians, he does not write of the Christian heroes celebrated by many of his fellow poets but turns his gaze back to the Continent in the fifth and sixth centuries, back to his ancestors in the dark and hopeless past. He knows of their desperate situation in the Christian scheme of things, for he refers to the heathen practices of his characters (lines 175ff.):

> At times they vowed in idol-tents
> to sacrifice, &c.

and to the consequences of their heathenism:

> Woe be to him
> who because of strife must shove his soul
> to the heart of the fire! He cannot hope
> for help or change, ever.

But having acknowledged that his heroes lived in the days of heathen ignorance and having recognized the consequences of their benighted condition, he proceeds to tell their story with the deepest respect, admiring their generosity, praising their dignity, and exalting their prowess, right up to the moment that Beowulf departs this life. (pp. xvi-xvii)

[Along with] pagan details in Beowulf's characterization, the poet has in other respects portrayed his hero as a man of such virtue as to suggest, at times, the example of Christ Himself. Beowulf's entire career is one of self-sacrifice, as he repeatedly risks (and ultimately gives) his life for the salvation and protection of his people. While not a Christian, Beowulf is nonetheless deeply religious, for although he never refers to Christ or to anything pertaining to the Church, he does refer often to an all-powerful Higher Being which rules the world and men's actions. He thanks this Being for his triumphs, he ascribes his strength to Him, and near the end of the poem he worries over the possibility of his having offended this Higher Being in some way of which he is unaware. He attains to virtue by adhering to the tenets of the old Germanic code, but he does so with such piety that he seems to approach the Christian ideal. His kindness is revealed when he refuses to accept the throne which Hygd offers him, preferring out of Germanic loyalty and love to help a young, weaker man to rule. At his death, Beowulf never condemns the cowardly retainers who deserted him in his hour of need; his thoughts are always and exclusively on the survival of his people. In their conception of nature . . . and in many other things the pagan and the Christian views converged, and the poet emphasizes these points of convergence.

The poet's most imaginative device for portraying the pagan Beowulf as deserving of an honorable place in the Christian thought-world is in his conception of evil in the poem. It is in the monsters, as J. R. R. Tolkien has pointed out [see excerpt dated 1936], that we find an objective realization of all that is evil in heroic life and, at the same time, the center of evil in the Christian view. The accommodation of the two is clearest in the poet's tracing of the genealogy of Grendel in lines 105-14 (and again in lines 1261ff.). He tells us that Grendel is the descendant of Cain, thus giving him Judaeo-Christian ancestry. But the line of descent includes giants and elves and walking dead—creatures that have no place in Biblical lore but rather are from the demonology of the pagan Germanic peoples. These creatures, according to Northern mythology, were the enemies of gods and men, the forces of chaos and brute violence seeking always to undo the order that good men and good gods have brought to the world. Grendel and his mother (and later the dragon) are embodiments of the evil force as it was conceived by Christians and, simultaneously, of the evil side of the Germanic heroic life.

By pitting the hero Beowulf against the monsters thus defined, the poet has his hero join forces, unwittingly, with the Christian Anglo-Saxons of later years. This enables Christian Anglo-Saxons to identify positively with their pagan forefathers and thus retain pride of ancestry despite the theological gulf that divides them: Beowulf, though ignorant of Christian revelation, is nonetheless fighting against the same enemy that Christians of the poet's own day are fighting. While we can understand the Good only through Revelation and conversion, Evil is always the same. Cruelty and violence, whether manifested in Heremod or Cain, in the dragon of the Apocalypse or the dragon of Germanic mythology, are peculiar to no creed or culture. With this sad truth the poet of ***Beowulf*** was able to establish a place for the noble pagan in the collective memory of Christian Anglo-Saxons. (p. xviii)

Fred C. Robinson, in an introduction to Beowulf: A Verse Translation with Treasures of the Ancient North, *translated by Marijane Osborn, University of California Press, 1983, pp. xi-xix.*

J. D. A. OGILVY AND DONALD C. BAKER (essay date 1983)

[Ogilvy and Baker are American medievalists, the former specializing in early Anglo-Latin and Old English literature and culture, the latter in Old and Middle English language and literature and Renaissance writers. In the following excerpt, they discuss the sources for Beowulf, *concentrating primarily on mythic and legendary influences.]*

The sources of ***Beowulf,*** if we may call them that, are to be found in the very large body of Continental tradition that the English brought with them or acquired through continued contact with their European cousins (evidence of this continued contact includes the Old English *Genesis B,* which is an English translation of a Continental poem, and the appearance of a text of another such poem, the *Heliand,* in an English library). For its content, aside from a few minor Christian touches, ***Beowulf*** relies completely on this inherited body of folklore and legendary-historical materials. Except for the lay of creation—a passage reminiscent of Caedmon's hymn—sung by the scop in Heorot early in the poem and the linking of Grendel with the race of Cain, all the digressions and allusions in ***Beowulf,*** as well as the main story, are Continental. When and by whom this diverse material was assembled in a single tale cannot be demonstrated, but it seems most likely that it was put together by a single man—the author of ***Beowulf.***

The materials from which ***Beowulf*** was assembled were from very different strata. The oldest stratum, which the poet probably did not recognize clearly for what it was, was pagan belief. The Danish genealogy (more likely, in fact, a list of what Bede called *bretwaldas*—that is, kings paramount—of Denmark and the Scandinavian peninsula) with which ***Beowulf*** opens is a compressed form of the genealogy more or less standard for English as well as Continental monarchs. The earlier members of these lists are pagan deities: Woden (Odin), Balder, Geat, and others. Curiously enough, Woden, the nexus in whom the various lines converge as we go back in time, does not begin most of these lists. He is preceded by Scyld, Beau(w), and others, and a count of generations places him quite late, probably in the fifth century. Whether the author of ***Beowulf*** omitted Woden merely to compress the list or to expunge the name of a heathen divinity is not certain.

In Scyld Scefing (Shield Son of the Sheaf), we may have traces of a culture hero who brought grain to man, and Beowulf himself may originally have been a Germanic Hercules, a slayer of monsters (particularly marine monsters) who, as he says of himself in one passage, made the sea safe for sailors. If the Beowulf in the Danish genealogy is anything more than a slip of the pen for Beaw (the common form in the king lists), he may have been such a hero, and the author or his sources may have transferred the qualities of one Beowulf to another.

Dragons, though they appear rather infrequently in literature, were a recognized part of early Germanic natural history (their habit of guarding hoards is noted in Old English gnomic verse). We might say that they were the equivalent of the modern coelacanth and okapi—rare beasts that were seldom seen but that everyone knew existed. [One] of the digressions in ***Beowulf*** deals with the killing of a dragon by Sigemund.

Trolls, on the other hand, though well known in Scandinavia, do not seem to have become naturalized in English folklore, and it is doubtful whether the author of ***Beowulf*** recognized Grendel and his mother as of the troll kin. Yet they have two distinct troll characteristics: invulnerability to weapons and the inability to endure the light of day. If one wished to overcome a troll, he must either beat him with his bare hands by main strength or trick him into exposing himself to daylight, which would turn him to stone. Grendel's invulnerability is explained not as an innate characteristic but as the result of some special charm or spell (lines 800-805), and Beowulf's decision to fight him bare-handed is presented as a sporting gesture (lines 677-87), not as a necessary tactic. It appears that the author did not understand the original reason for this choice and put forward another explanation, which would further his purpose by emphasizing Beowulf's magnanimity.

Rather belatedly, during the dragon episode, the author brings in another explanation for Beowulf's unwillingness to use weapons: he had no luck with them because he was so strong that he always broke them (lines 2682-87). This looks like something out of a myth or a folktale—a special condition under which the hero must operate, like Antaeus's need to touch the earth or the vulnerability of Achilles' heel. Why the author does not bring up this point before the fight with Grendel is not clear. Still another folktale characteristic, brought in in isolation and, it seems, rather pointlessly, is Beowulf's sluggishness as a youth—a sort of ugly-duckling theme (lines 2183-84). . . . (pp. 88-90)

For the inability of Grendel and his dam to harry the hall by daylight or to attack the Danes outside the hall the author wisely offers no explanation. One can offer only proximate, not ultimate, explanations for natural phenomena, and magic, if one accepts it, is a natural phenomenon. Inability to endure daylight is the mark of a troll. Limitation to a certain area is the mark of a tutelary spirit. Originally Grendel's attack on Heorot may have been considered a defense of his territorial rights, but in ***Beowulf*** it is said to result from his dislike of the sounds of rejoicing. If that were the only reason, it is hard to see why the Danes should have been safe if they stayed outside the hall. Once again, the author seems to be providing an explanation for a tradition he does not completely understand.

Another element from pagan myth is probably Beowulf's preternatural underwater feats. Rationalistic explanation of some of them simply blinks the fact that the poem operates in a world where human limitations as we know them do not exist. We may point out analogues to the fight with Grendel's dam in which the hero is merely on a ledge behind a waterfall, not in the water. We may explain that, although Beowulf dives down into the mere, the sea cave into which he is dragged has trapped air in it. We can even try to explain the wrestling hold by which Beowulf was able to rip off Grendel's arm. But this is simply to strain at the gnat and swallow the camel. A hero who has the might of thirty men in his handgrip, who can swim for a week in full armor, who can fight underwater with water monsters for a day or so without coming up for air, and who can swim home from Frisia with thirty byrnies would be perfectly capable of staying underwater throughout the fight with Grendel's dam or of ripping off Grendel's arm by sheer brute strength.

Analogues such as that of the troll under the waterfall are later than ***Beowulf*** and look like attempts at rationalization of older tales. ***Beowulf*** explains them, not they ***Beowulf.*** We might as well face the fact that the author of ***Beowulf*** did not boggle at the marvelous.

A good many early scholars thought that Breca of the swimming match with Beowulf was a sea deity and attempted to equate his name with the modern "breaker," as that of Grendel was thought to mean "grinder." This idea seems to have gone somewhat out of fashion, partly because of the appearance of Breca in *Widsith* as ruler of the Brondings, along with monarchs known to have actually existed. Whatever we think of the etymology, we must, if we reflect, admit that no mere mortal could have played even the losing part in this remarkable contest. The genealogies mix gods and men, and there is no reason to think that *Widsith* is more discriminating than they. On the

Warship from the eleventh-century Bayeux Tapestry.

whole, the assumption of a pagan myth adapted to the author's purpose seems the best explanation of this passage.

It would be interesting to know exactly how the author and his audience accepted these events. Perhaps they would look upon them as they did upon dragons. None of them, probably, would assert that he had seen a dragon himself, just as few modern individuals have seen a sperm whale, but they believed that dragons existed. If they were asked whether they had ever known a man capable of Beowulf's feats, they would probably have admitted that they had not. "But," they might have added, "that was in the good old days when heroes were really heroes."

The Dark Ages do not seem to have drawn the line between the physically possible and the physically impossible, as we attempt to do today. Nor did Christianity do much to reduce credulity. Apocrypha and saints' lives contain marvels beside which those in ***Beowulf*** seem rather conservative. We should be mistaken if we thought that hearers or readers of ***Beowulf*** considered it merely a good yarn or accorded it only Coleridge's "willing suspension of disbelief for the moment that constitutes poetic faith." The characters and events of the story, they would doubtless have felt, were not what one would expect in everyday life; neither are earthquakes, tidal waves, or volcanic eruptions. But they do occur.

A very primitive element which appears both in the main plot and in some of the episodes is the uncle-nephew relationship—more specifically, in its origin at least, the relationship of the nephew and his *eam* (maternal uncle). Among some primitive peoples, such as the Polynesians, his mother's brother was a boy's closest male relative. The tragedy of the fight at Finnsburg is heightened by the fact that uncle and nephew, who fell fighting on opposite sides, are placed on the same pyre. In the digression on Sigemund, Fitela, Sigemund's companion in many of his adventures, is his nephew. Beowulf is not only Hygelac's retainer but his nephew as well, and Wiglaf is Beowulf's nephew. The author does not stress these relationships, and may not have been aware of their significance. On the other hand, he may have assumed that the audience would recognize their importance without his emphasizing it.

Above the stratum of myth we find the legendary-historic. The more recent names in the king lists represent real men, but real men as transmuted by the demands of heroic theme and epic lay, which tend to make them considerably larger than life and a good deal better or worse than they actually were—a tendency that some historians believe they observe even in Plutarch. Heremod, about whom we know very little beyond the allusion in ***Beowulf,*** appears to have been shaped into a sort of Macbeth—a good man gone very wrong indeed. Other figures, such as Sigurd, who appear elsewhere in Germanic legend have been so thoroughly wrapped in myth that the reality, if it ever existed, has disappeared. However, Finn Folcwalding (also known in the genealogies and in the Finnsburg fragment) appears to be an actual monarch whose fate lent itself to poetic treatment.

Except for Beowulf himself, the chief human characters in the central story can be found elsewhere. Hrothgar and Hrothulf appear in Scandinavian king lists as Hroar and Hrolf (or Ralph) Kraka and stand at the shadowy border of legend and history. The Swedish kings of the second half of ***Beowulf,*** though even more shadowy, doubtless lived and ruled in the fifth and sixth centuries. Ingeld appears with Hrothgar and Hrothulf in *Widsith,* and Alcuin, writing about 800, alludes to a lay or lays about him. Hygelac is vouched for by the Frankish annals and alluded to in the *Liber monstrorum,* in which his skeleton, preserved in Frisia, is said to be that of a man of gigantic stature (this statement has led to speculation that legend has confused Hygelac and Beowulf, but we might also assume that great size was a family characteristic). In other words, we can find all the important characters in ***Beowulf*** elsewhere in legend or history—except Beowulf himself.

One reason that Hygelac and the Geats do not figure in later Germanic legend may be that after the disaster predicted in the latter part of ***Beowulf*** the Geats ceased to exist as a tribe and were gradually lost to memory. In his studies of the story of Ingeld, Kemp Malone points out that, although analogues to Heathobardic tales appear in later legend, they are no longer attached to the Bards [see Additional Bibliography]. He explains this shift by pointing out that the Bards had moved away from the Baltic area and had been forgotten, so that their deeds were attributed to other tribes. Some Beowulf analogues may have a similar history.

A fair number of analogues have been pointed out, though none is very close to the poem. The favorite is Bjarki, the Bear's Son. But when we examine Bjarki, we find that, although he resembles Beowulf in certain respects, he certainly is not Beowulf. A prototype of Bjarki may have contributed something to the idea of Beowulf; just as some lost Germanic demigod may have, but that is all. In fact, when we consider the character of Beowulf, we need to distinguish the folk figure or folk figures (deity, demigod, bear's son, and what you will) who underlie the character from Beowulf the mortal man presented—and perhaps created—by the poet.

As a man, despite his incredible strength, Beowulf knows that he must die and that in each of his adventures he risks defeat. He does not even enjoy the special magical advantages of many characters in later romances. So long as Arthur had Excalibur, he could not be defeated in battle; so long as he wore the scabbard, he could not shed a drop of blood. Beowulf had no such magical guarantees. For victory, he must trust to his good byrnie, his strength, his valor, and the favor that the god of battles sometimes shows to him who fights unflinchingly for the right. Although one cannot say that his strength was as the strength of thirty because his heart was pure, one does get the impression that his high purpose was an important element in the valor without which mere strength would not have prevailed. These are qualities of human hero, not of a humanized deity or nonhuman folk figure.

The author's imperfect grasp of the nature of trolls may lead us to suspect that before it reached him the harrying of Heorot had been put together in some pagan source closer to the native land of the trolls (however the tale originated, it is an interesting example of the insertion of a supernatural tale into the life of a historical character). The blending of elements in the character of Beowulf was probably an even slower and more complicated process, but it is possible that the character of Beowulf is largely a creation of the author—original in the sense that he has shaped his diverse materials into something that is essentially new. However the poem was created, we have a very complex collection of materials frozen into a final form at a fixed point in time, no matter what their later permutations and combinations were to be. Themes, types, and characters in ***Beowulf*** turn up later in many places. The proto-Beowulf may turn up in Bjarki and other figures, a ballad on the ***Beowulf*** theme has been collected in America, analogues have been noted in French medieval literature, and so on. But ***Beowulf*** remains unique—a reflection of the English spirit in the heroic age. (pp. 90-6)

J.D.A. Ogilvy and Donald C. Baker, in their Reading Beowulf: An Introduction to the Poem, Its Background, and Its Style, *University of Oklahoma Press, 1983, 221 p.*

ADDITIONAL BIBLIOGRAPHY

Arnold, Thomas. *Notes on Beowulf.* New York and Bombay: Longmans, Green, and Co., 1898, 140 p.
An early study of *Beowulf,* touching on the geography, Scandinavian sources, and analogues of the poem.

Baum, Paull F. "The *Beowulf* Poet." *Philological Quarterly* XXXIX, No. 4 (October 1960): 389-99.
Describes the difficulties faced by the modern reader of *Beowulf.*

Berger, Harry, Jr., and Leicester, H. Marshall, Jr. "Social Structure as Doom: The Limits of Heroism in *Beowulf.*" In *Old English Studies in Honour of John C. Pope,* edited by Robert B. Burlin and Edward B. Irving, Jr., pp. 37-79. Toronto: University of Toronto Press, 1974.
A sociological examination of the portrayal of heroic consciousness in *Beowulf.*

Blackburn, F. A. "The Christian Coloring in the *Beowulf.*" *PMLA* XII, No. 2 (1897): 205-25.
Argues that *Beowulf* was originally a pagan poem to which Christian elements were later added.

Blair, Peter Hunter. *An Introduction to Anglo-Saxon England,* 2d ed., pp. 14ff. Cambridge: Cambridge University Press, 1977.
Places *Beowulf* in its social and historical context and within the canon of Anglo-Saxon vernacular poetry.

Bliss, A. J. *The Metre of Beowulf.* Rev. ed. Oxford: Basil Blackwell, 1962, 170 p.
An elaborate analysis of meter, including a line-by-line scansion of the poem.

Bonjour, Adrien. *Twelve "Beowulf" Papers, 1940-1960, with Additional Comments.* Université de Neuchâtel, Recueil de Travaux Publiés par la Faculté des Lettres, No. 30. Neuchâtel: Faculté des Lettres; Geneva: E. Droz, 1962, 194 p.
Collects and supplements twelve of Bonjour's essays on *Beowulf,* including studies of the monsters, imagery, characterization, and stylistic devices.

Bowra, C. M. *Heroic Poetry,* pp. 3ff. London: Macmillan & Co., 1952.
A rigorous study of European heroic poetry, placing *Beowulf* within the tradition.

Carlson, Signe M. "The Monsters of *Beowulf:* Creations of Literary Scholars." *Journal of American Folklore* 80, No. 318 (July-September 1967): 357-64.
Contends that Grendel and his mother are not as monstrous as is commonly supposed.

Chadwick, Nora K. "The Monsters and Beowulf." In *The Anglo-Saxons: Studies in Some Aspects of Their History and Culture Presented to Bruce Dickins,* edited by Peter Clemoes, pp. 171-203. London: Bowes & Bowes, 1959.
Outlines the Scandinavian sources of the monster narratives in *Beowulf.*

Chambers, R. W. *Beowulf: An Introduction to the Study of the Poem with a Discussion of the Stories of Offa and Finn,* 3d ed., with a supplement by C. L. Wrenn. Cambridge: Cambridge University Press, 1959, 628 p.
An in-depth survey of historical and non-historical elements in *Beowulf,* focusing on the poem's origin, date, structure, and major analogues, and containing an extensive discussion of the Finn story.

Chase, Colin, ed. *The Dating of Beowulf.* Toronto Old English Series, No. 6. Toronto: University of Toronto Press, 1981, 220 p.
Specially commissioned collection of fourteen independent essays that discuss the date of *Beowulf.*

Chickering, Howell, D., Jr. *Beowulf: A Dual-Language Edition.* Garden City: Anchor Books, 1977, 390 p.

Excellent, comprehensive introduction to the meaning and background of *Beowulf,* followed by a predominantly four-stress verse translation of the poem.

Cramp, Rosemary J. "*Beowulf* and Archaeology." *Medieval Archaeology* 1 (1957): 57-77.
Detailed study of helmet and sword references and the description of Heorot in the light of archaeological evidence.

Creed, Robert P. "On the Possibility of Criticizing Old English Poetry." *Texas Studies in Literature and Language* III, No. 1 (Spring 1961): 97-106.
Argues that, as an orally composed poem, *Beowulf* incorporates earlier, established themes containing submerged, associative metaphors.

Du Bois, Arthur E. "The Unity of *Beowulf.*" *PMLA* XLIX, No. 2 (June 1934): 374-405.
Views *Beowulf* as an artistic, organically unified, highly cultured Anglo-Saxon equivalent for drama.

Earl, James W. "The Necessity of Evil in *Beowulf.*" *South Atlantic Bulletin* XLIV, No. 1 (January 1979): 81-98.
Discusses the moral significance of *Beowulf* and comments on the complex structure of the poem.

Farrell, Eleanor. "The Epic Hero and Society: Cuchulainn, Beowulf, and Roland." *Mythlore* 13, No. 1 (Autumn 1986): 25-8.
Contains a brief overview of *Beowulf* as a reflection of Anglo-Saxon pessimism.

Fry, Donald K. *"Beowulf" and "The Fight at Finnsburh": A Bibliography*. Charlottesville: University Press of Virginia, 1969, 222 p.
Lists all located items of *Beowulf* scholarship from the earliest notices to 1969.

Gardner, John. "Beowulf." In his *The Construction of Christian Poetry in Old English,* pp. 54-84. Carbondale: Southern Illinois University Press, 1975.
Maintains that *Beowulf* is a tripartite allegory of the unattainability of *felicitas* ("happiness") in this world.

Garmonsway, G. N., and Simpson, Jacqueline, translators. *Beowulf and Its Analogues*. Including "Archaeology and *Beowulf*" by Hilda Ellis Davidson. London: J. M. Dent, 1968, 368 p.
Collects the principal literary and historical analogues of *Beowulf.*

Girvan, Ritchie. *Beowulf and the Seventh Century: Language and Content*. London: Methuen & Co., 1935, 86 p.
A linguistic, historical, and archaeological survey of *Beowulf,* suggesting that the poem dates perhaps from the second half of the seventh century.

Grant, Raymond J. S. "*Beowulf* and the World of Heroic Elegy." *Leeds Studies in English* VIII (1975): 45-75.
Considers the elegiac character of *Beowulf,* focusing on the poet's preoccupation with the transitory nature of earthly glory.

Greenfield, Stanley B. "Beowulf and the Judgment of the Righteous." In *Learning and Literature in Anglo-Saxon England: Studies Presented to Peter Clemoes on the Occasion of His Sixty-Fifth Birthday,* edited by Michael Lapidge and Helmut Gneuss, pp. 393-407. Cambridge: Cambridge University Press, 1985.
A thorough reading of Beowulf's death scene, finding Beowulf to be a peerless but vulnerable hero who seeks the judgment of the righteous.

Gulley, Ervene F. "The Concept of Nature in *Beowulf.*" *Thoth* 11, No. 1 (Fall 1970): 16-30.
Considers *Beowulf* an essentially pagan work set against a cosmic, animistic background.

Haarder, Andreas. *Beowulf: The Appeal of a Poem.* Copenhagen: Akademisk Forlag, 1975, 341 p.
Reviews the critical history of the poem from the earliest notices to the present.

Haber, Tom Burns. *A Comparative Study of the "Beowulf" and the "Aeneid."* Princeton: Princeton University Press, 1931, 145 p.
Argues that Vergil's *Aeneid* helped shape the plot, stylistic devices, and phrasing of *Beowulf.*

Hanning, Robert W. "*Beowulf* as Heroic History." *Medievalia et Humanistica* n.s. 5 (1974): 77-102.
Describes the place of *Beowulf* among medieval heroic narratives.

Howlett, David R. "Form and Genre in *Beowulf.*" *Studia Neophilologica* 46, No. 2 (1974): 309-25.
Investigates works that influenced the form of *Beowulf.*

Hume, Kathryn. "The Theme and Structure of *Beowulf.*" *Studies in Philology* LXXII, No. 1 (January 1975): 1-27.
Rejects hero-oriented readings of *Beowulf* in favor of a thematic approach that finds "threats to social order" to be the primary emphasis of the poem.

Kaske, R. E. "*Sapientia et Fortitudo* as the Controlling Theme of *Beowulf.*" *Studies in Philology* LV, No. 3 (July 1958): 423-56.
Maintains that *Beowulf* is based on an established, widely recognized ideal of heroism, wisdom, and strength.

Klaeber, Frederick. "Attila's and Beowulf's Funeral." *PMLA* XLII, No. 2 (June 1927): 255-67.
Compares Beowulf's funeral rites with those of earlier cultures.

Lanier, Sidney. "Nature in Early English and in Shakspeare: *Beowulf* and *Midsummer Night's Dream.*" In his *Shakspere and His Forerunners: Studies in Elizabethan Poetry and Its Development from Early English,* pp. 42-73. New York: Doubleday, Page & Co., 1908.
Compares the treatment of nature in *Beowulf* with the portrayal of nature in William Shakespeare's *Midsummer Night's Dream.*

Leyerle, John. "Beowulf the Hero and the King." *Medium Ævum* XXXIV, No. 2 (1965): 89-102.
Argues that *Beowulf* is structurally and thematically unified around Beowulf's three monster battles.

———. "The Interlace Structure of *Beowulf.*" *University of Toronto Quarterly* XXXVII, No. 1 (October 1967): 1-17.
Examines *Beowulf* as a typically eighth-century English "lacertine interlace."

Liggins, Elizabeth M. "Revenge and Reward as Recurrent Motives in *Beowulf.*" *Neuphilologische Mitteilungen* LXXIV, No. 2 (1973): 193-213.
Studies the *Beowulf* poet's interest in revenge, punishment, and reward.

Malone, Kemp, and Ruud, Martin B., eds. *Studies in English Philology: A Miscellany in Honor of Frederick Klaeber*. Minneapolis: University of Minnesota Press, 1929, 486 p.
Presents ten essays on such issues as the language, characters, manuscripts, and analogues of *Beowulf.*

McNamee, M[aurice] B., S. J. "*Beowulf*—An Allegory of Salvation?" *JEGP* LIX, No. 2 (April 1960): 190-207.
Interprets *Beowulf* as a salvation allegory based on Christian liturgy and New Testament theology.

Mitchell, Bruce. "'Until the Dragon Comes . . .' Some Thoughts on *Beowulf.*" *Neophilologus* XLVII, No. 2 (April 1963): 126-38.
A four-part survey of *Beowulf,* reinforcing Tolkien's view (see excerpt in entry dated 1936) of the poem as a literary masterpiece but calling attention to several minor structural shortcomings.

Moorman, Charles. "*Beowulf.*" In his *Kings & Captains: Variations on a Heroic Theme,* pp. 57-86. Lexington: University Press of Kentucky, 1971.
Studies the importance of the *comitatus* code in *Beowulf.*

Nicholson, Lewis E. "The Literal Meaning and Symbolic Structure of *Beowulf.*" *Classica et Mediaevalia* XXV (1964): 151-201.
Maintains that the setting of *Beowulf* is deliberately antediluvian and based, in part, on Old Testament typology.

———, ed. *An Anthology of Beowulf Criticism.* Notre Dame, Ind.: University of Notre Dame Press, 1963, 386 p.

Reprints and introduces eighteen late-nineteenth- through mid-twentieth-century articles on *Beowulf.*

Nist, John A. *The Structure and Text of Beowulf.* 1959. Reprint. Folcroft, Pa.: Folcroft Press, 1970, 131 p.

Reprints earlier essays on the structure, phonemics, alliterative patterns, metrics, and textual elements of *Beowulf.*

Oetgen, Jerome. "Order and Chaos in the World of *Beowulf.*" The *American Benedictine Review* 29, No. 2 (June 1978): 134-52.

Examines Beowulf's three fights as studies of the problem of order in human society.

O'Loughlin, J. L. N. "*Beowulf*—Its Unity and Purpose." *Medium Ævum* XXI (1952): 1-13.

Contends that *Beowulf* is a homogeneous unity whose oneness is implicit in the poem's purpose.

Pope, John Collins. *The Rhythm of "Beowulf": An Interpretation of the Normal and Hypermetric Verse-Forms in Old English Poetry.* Rev. ed. New Haven: Yale University Press, 1966, 409 p.

A technical, theoretical study of the meter of *Beowulf,* focusing on oral characteristics of the poem.

Raffel, Burton. "On Translating *Beowulf.*" *The Yale Review* LIV, No. 4 (June 1965): 532-46.

Surveys the ways in which *Beowulf* may be rendered in contemporary English.

Rogers, H. L. "Beowulf's Three Great Fights." *The Review of English Studies* n.s. VI, No. 24 (1955): 339-55.

Examines the *Beowulf* poet's attitude toward the inherited and invented material he used.

Shippey, T. A. "The Argument of Courage: *Beowulf* and Other Heroic Poetry." In his *Old English Verse,* pp. 17-52. London: Hutchinson University Library, 1972.

Explores the concepts of courage, honor, and heroism in *Beowulf,* focusing on the poem's theme of respect for enemies as well as friends.

Short, Douglas D. *"Beowulf" Scholarship: An Annotated Bibliography.* Garland Reference Library of the Humanities, vol. 193. New York: Garland Publishing, 1980, 353 p.

An annotated bibliography of 1,105 items of *Beowulf* scholarship dating from the first notices to 1978, focusing on the years since 1950.

Smithers, G. V. *The Making of "Beowulf."* Durham: University of Durham, 1961, 26 p.

Studies the central fable utilized by the Beowulf poet and examines the poet's shaping of his sources.

Stanley, E[ric] G[erard]. "*Beowulf.*" In *Continuations and Beginnings: Studies in Old English Literature,* edited by Eric Gerard Stanley, pp. 104-41. London: Nelson, 1966.

A valuable overview of *Beowulf,* focusing on its date, major themes, analogues, historical context, and poetic merits.

Storms, G. "The Figure of Beowulf in the O. E. Epic." *English Studies* XL, No. 1 (February 1959): 3-13.

Reviews historic and folktale elements in *Beowulf,* concentrating on the themes of loyalty and friendship in the poem.

Tietjen, Mary C. Wilson. "God, Fate, and the Hero of *Beowulf.*" *JEGP* LXXIV, No. 2 (April 1975): 159-71.

Rejects the view that *Beowulf* is an exercise in narrow Christian didacticism.

Williams, David. "The Exile as Uncreator." *Mosaic* VIII, No. 3 (Spring 1975): 1-14.

Elucidates the image of the exile in *Beowulf.*

———. *Cain and Beowulf: A Study in Secular Allegory.* Toronto: University of Toronto Press, 1982, 119 p.

Traces the influence of Latin Christianity on *Beowulf,* focusing on the impact the Cain tradition exerted on the theme and allegory of the poem.

Williams, R. A. *The Finn Episode in "Beowulf": An Essay in Interpretation.* Cambridge: Cambridge University Press, 1924, 171 p.

Interprets the Finn episode as an analogue of the medieval German saga the *Nibelungenlied.*

Wright, Herbert G. "Good and Evil; Light and Darkness; Joy and Sorrow in *Beowulf.*" *The Review of English Studies* n.s. VIII, No. 29 (February 1957): 1-11.

Analyzes contrasting opposites in the poem, noting their function as complements and illuminators of the theme and structure of the poem.

La chanson de Roland (*The Song of Roland*)

Circa Twelfth Century

French poem.

A monument of medieval literature, *La chanson de Roland* *(The Song of Roland)* is the most highly regarded and the earliest extant example of the chanson de geste, typifying yet transcending the genre. The chanson de geste—literally, a "song of deeds"—is a form of French epic celebrating heroic exploits and such feudal chivalric ideals as honor, staunch loyalty to one's liege lord and to one's peers, and unfaltering courage in battle. In addition to its literary merit, *The Song,* through its depiction of betrayal, proud resistance against all odds, and the heroic struggle of a Christian army against pagan foes, is valued for the insights it provides into the society of its time. Although many unanswered questions remain concerning the poem's origin and composition, scholars esteem *The Song* for both its artistic and historic worth.

"Once in a while a man comes along who seems to have been born more for literature than for the world he inhabits, whose very being seems overshadowed by the archetype it embodies. Such a man was Count Roland." So wrote Robert Harrison of the legendary title character of *The Song*. Of the historical Roland, and of the factual basis of the tale related in *The Song,* very little is known. Returning to France from a military venture in Spain in 778, Charlemagne, king of the Franks and Holy Roman Emperor, and his troops traveled through the Roncevaux pass in the Pyrenees. Here the baggage train and rear guard of his army were attacked and utterly decimated by Christian Basques in search of plunder. According to Einhard, a ninth-century biographer of Charlemagne, one of those who perished in the ambush was "Hruodlandus the prefect." From this passing reference arose the legend of Roland narrated in *The Song*. In the poem, Charlemagne and his men, weary after seven years of battle against pagan forces, have captured every heathen stronghold but Saragossa, whose king, Marsile, offers a false peace treaty to persuade the Frankish king to leave Spain. Charlemagne accepts the overture despite the strenuous objections of Roland, his beloved nephew and bravest knight. When the Frankish barons seek an ambassador to Marsile, Roland (whose offer of himself is rejected on the grounds that he is both too valuable and too impetuous) nominates his stepfather, Ganelon. Between Roland and Ganelon there already exists some ill-will; the latter accepts his commission not only reluctantly but furiously, publicly vowing to wreak vengeance on his stepson, who laughs derisively at the threat. In collusion with Marsile, Ganelon plans his revenge: he will see to it that Roland is given command of the rear guard, which the Saracens will ambush and destroy. The scheme proceeds as planned; as Charlemagne's army travels homeward, Roland and the rear guard, which includes the best knights of France, are attacked by Marsile's numerically superior army. Oliver, Roland's closest friend and a brave warrior in his own right, thrice begs his friend to sound his *oliphant,* or horn, to summon the aid of Charlemagne's main troop. Despite the impossible odds they face, Roland thrice refuses, citing his desire to preserve his family honor and his personal determination to win alone. When ultimate defeat is imminent, Roland at last sounds his *oliphant,* though it is patently too late to save the rear guard and though Oliver bitterly mocks him for it. Roland blows his horn so forcefully that his temples burst, but Charlemagne hears and turns around. Even with the rear guard destroyed, the Saracens are unable to vanquish Roland; after he slays Marsile's son and cuts off the king's right hand, the pagan army deserts the field, leaving Roland the sole survivor. Amid vain attempts to break his powerful sword Durendal, so that it will not be taken by a lesser knight, Roland painfully makes his way to the front of the battlefield, wishing Charlemagne and the Franks to know that he died bravely. As Roland dies from the wound he sustained sounding the *oliphant,* angels descend to accompany his soul to God.

After Roland's demise, Charlemagne and the main army wrathfully pursue and destroy Marsile's army. Charlemagne then unexpectedly finds himself facing an even more imposing foe than Marsile: the pagan Baligant. The so-called Baligant episode of *The Song* pits the Christian and pagan emperors against each other, with Charlemagne the ultimate victor. Following the Franks' return to France, the trial of Ganelon begins. Although he does not deny his role in Roland's death, Ganelon argues that his action was not treason against his liege lord, Charlemagne, but merely honorable personal revenge taken against Roland. To Chalemagne's chagrin, the Frankish barons are disposed to exonerate Ganelon, but one knight, Thierry, proposes to prove Ganelon's guilt by trial of arms against Ganelon's champion, Pinabel. Thierry, maintaining that Ganelon's action did indeed constitute treason against Charlemagne because his revenge was undertaken while Roland was acting in the king's service, vanquishes his opponent and Ganelon is brutally executed. As *The Song* ends, the weary and mourning Charlemagne is summoned by God to undertake yet another campaign against the heathen.

This is the story told in the Oxford "Digby 23" manuscript, better known as *La chanson de Roland.* Donated by Sir Kenelm Digby in the seventeenth century, the manuscript received scant attention until its first publication in 1837 by Francisque Michel. Since then, scholarship of *The Song* has been largely dominated by unresolved questions concerning the poem's origin, authorship, and date of composition. Critics generally subscribe to one of two opposing critical theories regarding the composition of *The Song:* the traditionalist and the individualist. The traditionalist viewpoint was first articulated by the French scholar Gaston Paris in his *Histoire poétique de Charlemagne* (1865), and championed most authoritatively in the twentieth century in Ramón Menéndez Pidal's *La chanson de Roland et la tradition épique des Francs* (1960). The basis of the traditionalist contention is that *The Song* can be attributed to no single author, but is rather the product of an evolving poetic tradition. Scholars postulate that soon after the actual eighth-century battle at Roncevaux, the Roland tale began to circulate, its gradual growth to legendary stature aided by the composition of *cantilènes,* or short lyrical songs, sung by traveling jongleurs. These *cantilènes,* amended and embellished through the years by succeeding generations of jongleurs, eventually became the epic poem we know today. In the traditionalist view, therefore, Digby 23 is not a definitive text of *The Song* but an arbitrary one; it is simply the version current at the time the poem was committed to parchment. The counter movement of the individualists, in turn, was spearheaded by Joseph Bédier in his *Les legendes épiques* (1908-13). According to Bédier's theory, before *The Song* was written, the Roland story existed only in local legends preserved by monks along principal pilgrimage routes. At some point in the late eleventh or early twelfth century, the local Roland legend was heard by one who then created *The Song* as a conscious act of individual genius. Although the vehemence of the traditionalist-individualist debate has lessened somewhat in recent criticism, recognition of the schism remains vital, as literary interpretations of *The Song* are frequently predicated on one or the other theory of its origin.

Regardless of whether one takes a traditionalist or an individualist approach to *The Song,* the question remains: who actually wrote the Oxford manuscript? Speculation about this issue centers around the last line of the poem: "Ci falt la gest, que Turoldus declinet." The final verb of this line has inspired much controversy among linguists and critics, resulting in such different translations as "So ends the tale which Turold hath conceived" (Charles Scott-Moncrieff); "Here ends the geste Turoldus would recite" (Dorothy L. Sayers); "The story that Turoldus tells ends here" (Robert Harrison); "Here ends the story Turoldus completes" (D.D.R. Owen); and even "Here ends the poem, for Turoldus declines" (Patricia Terry). Was Turoldus the author of *The Song,* or was he merely the scribe who copied it? Or was he, as many scholars believe, the "last redactor," acting as a freehanded editor of an already existing poem? Who was Turoldus? Attempts to assign an historical identity to him—an endeavor Harrison has wryly called "the Turoldus sweepstakes"—have been many, but thus far futile. Attempts to date *The Song* have met with better success: though their conclusions are by no means definite, most scholars have tentatively assigned circa 1100 as the poem's composition date.

Considered stylistically, *The Song* yields both additional interest and additional mystery. It is divided into about 300 strophes, called *laisses,* of varying lengths—from five to approximately thirty decasyllabic lines. The lines in each *laisse* are unified by assonance, which changes in pattern from *laisse* to *laisse*. Owen has written that "every laisse is like an individual miniature in an illuminated manuscript: memorably simple and expressive in its stylized manner, where attitude and gesture convey abstract ideas in visual terms." Scholars have demonstrated special interest in the occasional *laisses similaires,* or series of *laisses* in which the action seems to stand still, with description or narration of an event repeated, accompanied by slight changes, in each succeeding *laisse*. Among the more puzzling stylistic aspects of the poem is the apparently arbitrary use of verb tenses, and the still unexplained insertion of the letters AOI following many *laisses*. Because of the archaic language of *The Song,* linguists do not always agree on the precise meaning of words in the poem; even when the words are recognizable forerunners of modern French counterparts, their medieval connotations and nuances cannot always be adequately determined.

Evaluation of *The Song* in aesthetic terms has of necessity become entangled with historical and cultural concerns, as literary appreciation of the poem is dependent to a great extent upon an understanding of the values and ethos of the Middle Ages. The inevitable difficulties inherent in understanding a literary work at a distance of eight or nine centuries are particularly acute in the case of *The Song,* which eludes a definitive answer to even the most basic of critical questions: what is the principal theme of the poem? While scholars agree that the Christian/pagan battle motif clearly upholds the poem's flat statement that "Christians are right and pagans are wrong," further thematic interpretation is much disputed. Critical contention arises mainly from disagreement over how Roland's character and actions are to be viewed, and how they would have been viewed by *The Song*'s original audience. Some commentators have posited a fundamentally Chistian ethos for *The Song,* suggesting that Roland plays a martyr role: he is a Christ-like sacrifice to the cause of Christendom. In the same vein, others have discerned a redemption motif in Roland's story. Cursed with the sin of pride and *desmesure* (impetuosity, or a lack of due moderation and thoughtful prudence), Roland must be humbled at Roncevaux before he recognizes his folly, confesses it, and is forgiven it. As a supporter of this reading of *The Song,* Alain Renoir has called the poem "the story of the making of a saint." Dissenting critics, however, have maintained that the poem reflects and upholds not Christian but heroic virtues. George Fenwick Jones has argued that, while a medieval knight (and a medieval poet) might well pay tribute to Christianity with his words, his actions—and the basis on which those actions were judged by others—would, in fact, be predicated on a very different set of values. Thus Roland's refusal to sound the *oliphant* is not necessarily an indication of the fatal flaw of pride, but rather of a heroic and noble concern for honor and courage.

Questions of theme and characterization merge not only with regard to Roland but also in critical examination of Roland in comparison with the poem's other characters. Though Jones has written that, "foolhardy Roland is the hero of his song, not prudent Oliver," not all critics grant Roland a primary role in *The Song*. The cogency of Oliver's arguments that Roland should sound the *oliphant* before it is too late and his suggestion that Roland bears responsibility for the unnecessary deaths of Charlemagne's best knights indicate to some scholars that the narrator of *The Song* upholds Oliver's position, not Roland's. According to the text, "Rollant est proz e Oliver est sage"—Roland is valiant and Oliver is wise. Which quality has authorial sanction? Furthermore, the very fact that Roland's death removes him from the poem at its halfway point leads some commentators to believe that he does not merit heroic status. Such scholars accord that status to Charlemagne instead, for it is with him that the poem begins and ends, and to him that the task of subduing the pagans ultimately falls. Some critics have also noted ambiguity in Ganelon's character. Although *The Song* refers to his *traïsun* ("treachery"), they note that Roland does deliberately taunt and attempt to humiliate him. Historians add that Ganelon's defense at his trial—that he was justified in settling a merely personal feud—would have been accepted as a valid argument in the Middle Ages. One resolution to these conflicts is implied in Joseph Duggan's theory of "historical layering." According to Duggan, *The Song* contains and can accomodate differing and even conflicting values since it is the product of many generations of poets. Thus Roland and Charlemagne can both be heroes; Roland can be simultaneously a doughty hero and a misguided victim of his own *desmesure;* Roland and Oliver can be equally admirable. Some commentators have also contended that seeming inconsistencies of characterization or of authorial viewpoint can be explained as the conflicting attitudes of a single poet: as Owen has expressed it, "Behind the epic splendour of his poetry we hear the voice of a man who knows reality for what it is and inclines to question what he most exalts. He feels with Roland, but he thinks with Oliver."

The critical history of *The Song,* though short, has revealed much change and growth. Such early critics as Matthew Arnold in the late nineteenth and Ezra Pound in the twentieth century granted that *The Song* was "interesting," but found little else to admire. In the later twentieth century, there has been a proliferation of scholarship, as critics have focused on specific aspects of the poem in an effort to solve its many thematic riddles. For example, Renoir, Jones, and Owen, among others, have debated the issue of the poem's dominant ethos; Joseph I. Donohoe, Jr. has examined the relationship between Roland and Oliver; and Harrison has extensively studied the social and historical background of the poem.

Enigmatic though *The Song* remains, scholars rank it among the masterpieces of medieval European literature. As an historical document, the work is invaluable for its portrait of medieval society; as an artistic creation, the poem exerts a timeless appeal. Whether viewed in a Christian or heroic context, the tragedy of Roland evokes an emotional response in the twentieth-century reader just as it did in the twelfth-century listener. As Harold March has written, "We are made to feel that good and evil are absolute, not relative, that valor and loyalty and honor are realities, not mere words, and that the unseen world is very close."

PRINCIPAL ENGLISH TRANSLATIONS

The Song of Roland (translated by Charles Scott-Moncrieff) 1919

The Song of Roland (translated by Dorothy L. Sayers) 1957

The Song of Roland (translated by Robert Harrison) 1970

The Song of Roland (translated by D.D.R. Owen) 1972

The Song of Roland (translated by Gerald J. Brault) 1978

H. A. TAINE (essay date 1863-64)

[Taine was a French philosopher, critic, and historian who studied the influence of environment and heredity on the development of human character. In his well-known work, Histoire de la littérature anglaise *(1863-64;* History of English Literature, *1871), he analyzed literature through a study of race and milieu. In the following excerpt from that book, Taine cites* The Song *as an example of the lack of emotionalism in the French epic.]*

Let us look at [French] epics; none are more prosaic. They are not wanting in number: ***The Song of Roland,*** *Garin le Loherain, Ogier le Danois, Berthe aux grands Pieds*. There is a library of them. Though their manners are heroic and their spirit fresh, though they have originality, and deal with grand events, yet, spite of this, the narrative is as dull as that of the babbling Norman chroniclers. Doubtless Homer is precisely like them; but his magnificent titles of rosy-fingered Morn, the wide-bosomed Air, the divine and nourishing Earth, the earth-shaking Ocean, come in every instant and expand their purple tint over the speeches and battles, and the grand abounding similes which intersperse the narrative tell of a people more inclined to rejoice in beauty than to proceed straight to fact. But here we have facts, always facts, nothing but facts: the Frenchman wants to know if the hero will kill the traitor, the lover wed the maiden; he must not be delayed by poetry or painting. He advances nimbly to the end of the story, not lingering for dreams of the heart or wealth of landscape. There is no splendour, no colour, in his narrative; his style is quite bare, and without figures; you may read ten thousand verses in these old poems without meeting one. Shall we open the most ancient, the most original, the most eloquent, at the most moving point, the ***Song of Roland,*** when Roland is dying? The narrator is moved, and yet his language remains the same, smooth, accentless, so penetrated by the prosaic spirit, and so void of the poetic! He gives an abstract of motives, a summary of events, a series of causes for grief, a series of causes for consolation. Nothing more. These men regard the circumstance or the action by itself, and adhere to this view. Their idea remains exact, clear, and simple, and does not raise up a similar image to be confused with itself, to colour or transform itself. It remains dry; they conceive the divisions of the object one by one, without ever collecting them, as the Saxons would, in a rude, impassioned, glowing fantasy. (pp. 65-6)

H. A. Taine, "The Normans," in his History of English Literature, Vol. I, *translated by H. Van Laun, Holt & Williams, 1871, pp. 58-104.*

MATTHEW ARNOLD (essay date 1880)

[Arnold is considered one of the most influential authors of the later Victorian period in England. While he is well known today as a poet, in his own time he asserted his greatest influence through his prose writings. Arnold's forceful literary criticism, which is based on his humanistic belief in the value of balance and clarity in literature, significantly shaped modern critical the-

ory. In the following excerpt from an essay originally published in 1880, Arnold deems The Song *unworthy of comparison with Greek and Latin classical poetry.*]

It may be said that the more we know about a classic the better we shall enjoy him; and, if we lived as long as Methuselah and had all of us heads of perfect clearness and wills of perfect steadfastness, this might be true in fact as it is plausible in theory. But the case here is much the same as the case with the Greek and Latin studies of our schoolboys. The elaborate philological groundwork which we require them to lay is in theory an admirable preparation for appreciating the Greek and Latin authors worthily. The more thoroughly we lay the groundwork, the better we shall be able, it may be said, to enjoy the authors. True, if time were not so short, and schoolboys' wits not so soon tired and their power of attention exhausted; only, as it is, the elaborate philological preparation goes on, but the authors are little known and less enjoyed. So with the investigator of "historic origins" in poetry. He ought to enjoy the true classic all the better for his investigations; he often is distracted from the enjoyment of the best, and with the less good he overbusies himself, and is prone to over-rate it in proportion to the trouble which it has cost him. (pp. 11-12)

The historic estimate is likely in especial to affect our judgment and our language when we are dealing with ancient poets; the personal estimate when we are dealing with poets our contemporaries, or at any rate modern. The exaggerations due to the historic estimate are not in themselves, perhaps, of very much gravity. Their report hardly enters the general ear; probably they do not always impose even on the literary men who adopt them. But they lead to a dangerous abuse of language. So we hear Cædmon, amongst our own poets, compared to Milton . . . . [An] eminent French critic, M. Vitet, comments upon that famous document of the early poetry of his nation, the ***Chanson de Roland.*** It is indeed a most interesting document. The *joculator* or *jongleur* Taillefer, who was with William the Conqueror's army at Hastings, marched before the Norman troops, so said the tradition, singing "of Charlemagne and of Roland and of Oliver, and of the vassals who died at Roncevaux"; and it is suggested that in the ***Chanson de Roland*** by one Turoldus or Théroulde, a poem preserved in a manuscript of the twelfth century in the Bodleian Library at Oxford, we have certainly the matter, perhaps even some of the words, of the chant which Taillefer sang. The poem has vigour and freshness; it is not without pathos. But M. Vitet is not satisfied with seeing in it a document of some poetic value, and of very high historic and linguistic value; he sees in it a grand and beautiful work, a monument of epic genius. In its general design he finds the grandiose conception, in its details he finds the constant union of simplicity with greatness, which are the marks, he truly says, of the genuine epic, and distinguish it from the artificial epic of literary ages. One thinks of Homer; this is the sort of praise which is given to Homer, and justly given. Higher praise there cannot well be, and it is the praise due to epic poetry of the highest order only, and to no other. Let us try, then, the ***Chanson de Roland*** at its best. Roland, mortally wounded, lays himself down under a pine-tree, with his face turned towards Spain and the enemy—

> De plusurs choses à remembrer li prist,
> De tantes teres cume li bers cunquist,
> De dulce France, des humes de sun lign,
> De Carlemagne sun seignor ki l'nurrit.

[Then began he to call many things to remembrance,—all the lands which his valour conquered, and pleasant France, and the men of his lineage, and Charlemagne his liege lord who nourished him.]

That is primitive work, I repeat, with an undeniable poetic quality of its own. It deserves such praise, and such praise is sufficient for it . . . . [But with Homer, we] are here in another world, another order of poetry altogether; here is rightly due such supreme praise as that which M. Vitet gives to the ***Chanson de Roland.*** If our words are to have any meaning, if our judgments are to have any solidity, we must not heap that supreme praise upon poetry of an order immeasurably inferior. (pp. 13-16)

Matthew Arnold, "The Study of Poetry," in his Essays in Criticism, second series, *The Macmillan Company, 1888, pp. 1-55.*

AUBREY DE VERE (essay date 1881)

[*De Vere was an Irish poet and essayist whose works include* The Waldenses; or, The Fall of Rora: A Lyrical Sketch, with Other Poems *(1842) and* English Misrule and Irish Misdeeds *(1848). In the following excerpt, he applauds the characterizations and the spirit of loyalty and sympathy in* The Song.]

Few can read the [***Chanson de Roland***] without perceiving that it is [a poem] that deserves the fame and the wide circulation it possessed for centuries before the invention of printing, when the jongleur recited it at the village festival, in the market place of the great city, and in the castle of the noble, crowded round by priests and by ladies, as well as by rude artisans in leathern jerkins. In these days, when so much has been said about poetry as an art, it is refreshing to read a poem which, while it is simplicity itself, the work evidently of one who thought of his subject, not of himself, yet reminds us, through its grace, its pathos, and its completeness, no less than through its varied power, of Shakespeare's doctrine, "There is no art, but nature makes that art." The poet had carefully planned what he afterwards wrote with such a gladsome spontaneity. He does not scruple to depart from the details of history where the interests of his poem require it. He represents Charlemagne as of great age when he was still in his prime, doubtless in order that he might thus stand in contrast with his heroic nephew, not in competition with him. He sustains our reverence for the great Emperor by representing him as having triumphed for seven years in Spain, and left that land only when he had completed his work, though Eginhard has left us in prose a less flattering account of that expedition. He gives a greater dignity to the catastrophe by ascribing to the whole concentrated Moslem power of Spain an overthrow which was actually effected by the Basques and Gascons of the mountains. He saves the military honour of the Franks by attributing their disaster, like that of the Greeks before Troy, largely to internal dissension; while at the same time he does not, like the Italian poets, make Ganelon a mercenary traitor, but a man who revenges what he deems a deadly wrong. He vindicates poetic justice by making the fall of Roland in part a penance inflicted on wrong-doing. (pp. 386-87)

Nor is this all: many and various incidents are in this poem combined within the limits of a brief narrative. There is a corresponding variety of character; for, though all the warriors are brave, they preserve their individuality, and nothing can be less alike than the valour of Roland, which is reckless and impulsive; that of Olivier, which is equable, severe, and tempered by prudence; and that of the Archbishop, which is chiefly the crusader's zeal. Not less picturesque is the contrast between the wily and fitful audacity of the Moslem chiefs, alternating with their fears, as they bound upon their prey like a wild beast which, in the act of springing, looks another way, and the religious heroism of the Christians. The conclusion is also, as a matter of art, more elevated, though less sensational, than it would have been if the poem had ended wih the disaster of Roncesvalles. Life has its agonies; but, in the Christian estimate, a kindly Providence, not the merciless fate of the old pagan drama, rules all things, leading man out of darkness into light. The poem does not end in tragedy. Those who have died nobly are honoured in their graves; the wicked are punished; and the last image left behind on our imagination is that of the white-haired Emperor faring forth once more in search of new triumphs for the Cross. Victory, we feel, must run, like a perpetual sunrise, before his self-sacrificing spirit. It is not wonderful if to this large and far-famed monument of mediaeval literature the same specially artistic merit belongs which Coleridge attributes to the shorter poems of the Middle Ages.

But the chief merit of this poem is one which cannot be wholly supplied even by the union of nature and art. The "form" of a poem is doubtless an important matter, and many a work of high genius has missed the prize because it sinned fatally against proportion; but there are two things of yet higher importance, viz. its substance and its spirit. As regards the former, the ***Chanson*** is fortunate indeed. It has little concern either with the lower appetites of man, or with the mere conventionalities of life: it does not make its boast of speculations or of mystifications, and it does not vindicate its originality by affecting the eccentric or the quaint. It draws mainly from the springs of our moral and spiritual being. It takes for its subject the noblest relations of our universal humanity. Heroic courage and religious faith, patriotism, and honour, and friendship,—the dangers that tax our energies to the utmost, and the magnanimity that can look with equal eye on victory or defeat,—these are the subject of this poem. These things constitute its substance. Its spirit is worthy of the theme. That spirit is the spirit of self-sacrificing loyalty—loyalty not directed to a sovereign alone—or rather recognising a sovereign claim in whatever is the object of our dutiful reverence and love. It is not their own approaching death that the Paladins lament; their recurrent thought is still, how much their beloved Karl will grieve when he looks upon them dead. They think little of the loss to their proper fame; but they cannot forget how their "gentle France" will be humbled by such a defeat. It is for Roland that Olivier grieves, and Roland for Olivier: while the warlike Archbishop will not consent to death till the Paladins are brought once more to his feet, and he can extend his arms over them, if not in a last absolution, at least in a latest prayer. It is with the love of woman as with the friendship of man. Alda is but twice named in the poem, and but once appears in it. It is to ask for her betrothed husband, and to die. She is as loyal to Roland as he is to his King and his country. To her he was both of these.

Next to the spirit of loyalty the spirit of sympathy pervades this poem. As Dante sinks to the ground at the sufferings he witnesses in his *Purgatorio,* so warriors who have no pity for their own wounds swoon with grief when some loved companion in arms falls beside them;—but they do not forget to avenge him. The age described is one of vehement passions and fierce impulses: it has little benevolence outside the sphere of its sympathies; but that sphere is a wide one. It is free from that self-love which makes the love of another an unreal or a sophisticated thing; even in its enmity there is little of malice: and war, so long as it is honourable war against an honourable foe, is but a wild sport, and presupposes little of mutual hatred. In that age men seemed to dwell at once in two worlds, of which the earthlier was betrothed to the heavenlier; and while the lower one, that of human life, wore all the shifting lights and fair illusions of a poem, the world of faith, and its promises, shone out with all the vividness of reality. This, no doubt, is the fair side of a picture which had also a darker aspect—one strangely disfigured by prejudice, intolerance, and sometimes by a deplorable indifference both as to injustice and to human suffering. The ***Chanson*** gives occasional witness to these defects; but, on the whole, it is the fairer side of the age which it presents, and from which it derives its greatness and its beauty. (pp. 387-89)

Aubrey De Vere, in a review of "The Song of Roland," in The Edinburgh Review, *Vol. CLIII, No. CCCXIV, April, 1881, pp. 370-89.*

W. P. KER (essay date 1897)

[Ker was a noted English scholar of medieval literature and an authority on comparative European literature and the history of literary forms. In the following excerpt from his 1897 study of medieval epic and romance, Ker prefaces his consideration of The Song *with a general discussion of the chanson de geste in relation to other medieval literary genres.]*

The *chansons de geste* stand in a real, positive, ancestral relation to all modern literature; there is something of them in all the poetry of Europe. The Icelandic histories can make no such claim. Their relation to modern life is slighter, in one sense; more spiritual, in another. They are not widely known, they have had no share in establishing the forms or giving vogue to the commonplaces of modern literature. (pp. 288-89)

The historical influence and importance of the *chansons de geste,* on the other hand, is . . . plain and evident. Partly by their opposition to the new modes of fiction, and partly by compliance with their adversaries, they belong to the history of those great schools of literature in the twelfth and thirteenth centuries from which all modern imaginations in prose and rhyme are descended. The "dolorous rout" of Roncesvalles, and not the tragedy of the Niblungs, still less the history of Gunnar or of Njal, is the heroic origin of modern poetry; it is remembered and renowned . . . among the poets who have given shape to modern imaginative literature, while the older heroics of the Teutonic migration are forgotten, and the things of Iceland are utterly unknown.

French epic has some great advantages in comparison with the epic experiments of Teutonic verse. For one thing, it exists in great quantity; there is no want of specimens, though they are not all of the best sort or the best period. Further, it has no difficulty, only too much ease, in keeping a long regular course of narrative. Even *Beowulf* appears to have attained to its epic proportions by a succession of efforts, and with difficulty; it labours rather heavily over the longer epic course. *Maldon* is a poem that runs freely, but here the course is shorter, and it carries much less weight. The Northern poems of the "Elder Edda" never attain the right epic scale at all; their abrupt and lyrical manner is the opposite of the epic mode of narration. It is true that the *chansons de geste* are far from the perfect continuity of the Homeric narrative. (pp. 289-90)

Roland is a succession of separate scenes, with no gradation or transition between them. It still bears traces of the lyrical origins of epic. But the narrative, though broken, is neither stinted nor laboured; it does not, like *Beowulf,* give the impression that it has been expanded beyond the convenient limits, and that the author is scant of breath. And none of the later *chansons de geste* are so restricted and reserved in their design as ***Roland;*** most of them are diffuse and long. The French and the Teutonic epics are at opposite extremes of style.

The French epics are addressed to the largest conceivable audience. They are plain and simple, as different as possible from the allusive brevity of thc Northern poems. Even the plainest of the old English poems, even *Maldon,* has to employ the poetical diction, the unprosaic terms and figures of the Teutonic School. The alliterative poetry down to its last days has a vocabulary different from that of prose, and much richer. The French epic language is not distinguished and made difficult in this way; it is "not prismatic but diaphanous." Those who could understand anything could understand it, and the *chansons de geste* easily found currency in the market-place, when they were driven by the new romances from their old place of honour in "bower and hall." The Teutonic poetry, even at its simplest, must have required more attention in its hearers than the French, through the strangeness and the greater variety of its vocabulary. It is less familiar, less popular. Whatever dignity may be acquired by the French epic is not due to any special or elaborate convention of phrase. Where it is weak, its poverty is not disguised, as in the weaker portions of Teutonic poetry, by the ornaments and synonyms of the *Gradus*. The commonplaces of French epic are not imposing. With this difference between the French and the Teutonic conventions, there is all the more interest in a comparison of the two kinds, where they come into comparison through any resemblance of their subjects or their thought, as in *Byrhtnoth* and ***Roland.***

The French epics have generally a larger political field, more numerous armies, and more magnificent kings, than the Teutonic. In the same degree, their heroism is different from that of the earlier heroic age. The general motives of patriotism and religion, France and Christendom, prevent the free use of the simpler and older motives of individual heroism. The hero of the older sort is still there, but his game is hindered by the larger and more complex political conditions of France; or if these are evaded, still the mere size of the country and numbers of the fighting-men tell against his importance; he is dwarfed by his surroundings. The limitation of the scenes in the poems of *Beowulf, Ermanaric,* and *Attila* throws out the figures in strong relief. The mere extent of the stage and the number of the supernumeraries required for the action of most of the French stories appear to have told against the definiteness of their characters; as, on the other hand, the personages in *Beowulf,* without much individual character of their own, seem to gain in precision and strength from the smallness of the scene in which they act. There is less strict economy in the *chansons de geste*.

Apart from this, there is real and essential vagueness in their characters; their drama is rudimentary. The simplicity of the French epic style, which is addressed to a large audience and easily intelligible, is not capable of much dramatic subtlety. It can be made to express a variety of actions and a variety of moods, but these are generally rendered by means of common formulas, without much dramatic insight or intention. While the fragments of Teutonic epic seem to give evidence of a growing dramatic imagination, and the Northern poems, especially, of a series of experiments in character, the French epic imagination appears to have remained content with its established and abstract formulas for different modes of sentiment and passion. It would not be easy to find anything in French epic that gives the same impression of discovery and innovation, of the search for dramatic form, of the absorption of the poet's mind in the pursuit of an imaginary character, as is given, again and again, by the Northern poems of the Volsung cycle. Yet the *chansons de geste* are often true and effective in their outlines of character, and include a quantity of "humours and observation," though their authors seem to have been unable to give solidity to their sketches.

The weakness of the drama in the French epics, even more than their compliance with foreign romance in the choice of incidents or machinery, is against their claim to be reckoned in the higher order of heroic narrative. They are romantic by the comparative levity of their imagination; the story, with them, is too much for the personages. But it is still the problem of heroic character that engages them, however feebly or conventionally they may deal with it. They rely, like the Teutonic epic and the Sagas, on situations that test the force of character, and they find those situations in the common conditions of an heroic age, subject of course to the modifications of the comparatively late period and late form of society to which they belong. ***Roland*** is a variation on the one perpetual heroic theme; it has a grander setting, a grander accompaniment, than *Byrhtnoth* or *Waldere,* but it is essentially the old story of the heroic age,—no knight-errantry, but the last resistance of a man driven into a corner.

The greatness of the poem of ***Roland*** is that of an author who knows his own mind, who has a certain mood of the heroic imagination to express, and is at no loss for his instrument or for the lines of his work.

The poem . . . has a general likeness in its plan to the story of Finnesburh as told in *Beowulf,* and to the poems of the death of Attila. The plot falls into two parts, the second part being the vengeance and expiation.

Although the story is thus not absolutely simple, like the adventures of Beowulf, no epic has a more magnificent simplicity of effect. The other personages, Charlemagne, Ganelon, Oliver, King Marsile, have to Roland nothing like the importance of Agamemnon, Ajax, Diomede, or Hector, as compared with Achilles in the *Iliad.* The poem is almost wholly devoted to the praise and glorification of a single hero; it retains very much of the old manners of the earlier stages of epic poetry, before it ceased to be lyric. It is a poem in honour of a chieftain.

At the same time, this lyrical tone in ***Roland*** and this pathetic concentration of the interest on one personage do not interfere with the epic plan of the narrative, or disturb the lines of the composition. The central part of the poem is on the Homeric scale; the fighting, the separate combats, are rendered in an Homeric way. *Byrhtnoth* and ***Roland*** are the works that have given the best medieval counterpart to the battles of Homer. There is more of a crisis and a climax in ***Roland*** than in the several battles of the *Iliad,* and a different sort of climax from that of *Byrhtnoth*. Everything leads to the agony and heroic death of Roland, and to his glory as the unyielding champion of France and Christendom. It is not as in the *Iliad,* where different heroes have their day, or as at Maldon, where the fall of the captain leads to the more desperate defence and the more exalted heroism of his companions. Roland is the absolute master of the ***Song of Roland.*** No other heroic poetry conveys the same effect of pre-eminent simplicity and grandeur. There is hardly anything in the poem except the single mood; its simplicity is overpowering, a type of heroic resistance for all the later poets of Europe. This impressive effect is aided, it is true, by an infusion of the lyrical tone and by playing on the pathetic emotions. Roland is ideal and universal, and the story of his defeat, of the blast of his horn, and the last stroke of Durendal, is a kind of funeral march or "heroic symphony" into which a meaning may be read for every new hero, to the end of the world; for any one in any age whose *Mood is the more as the Might lessens*. Yet although Roland has this universal or symbolical or musical meaning—unlike the more individual personages in the Sagas, who would resent being made into allegories—the total effect is mainly due to legitimate epic means. There is no stinting of the epic proportions or suppression of the epic devices. The ***Song of Roland*** is narrative poetry, a model of narrative design, with the proper epic spaces well proportioned, well considered, and filled with action. It may be contrasted with the *Death-Song of Ragnar Lodbrok,* which is an attempt to get the same sort of moral effect by a process of lyrical distillation from heroic poetry; putting all the strongest heroic motives into the most intense and emphatic form. There is something lyrical in ***Roland,*** but the poem is not governed by lyrical principles; it requires the deliberation and the freedom of epic; it must have room to move in before it can come up to the height of its argument. The abruptness of its periods is not really an interruption of its even flight; it is an abruptness of detail, like a broken sea with a larger wave moving under it; it does not impair or disguise the grandeur of the movement as a whole. (pp. 290-95)

W. P. Ker, "The Old French Epic: ('Chansons de Geste')," in his Epic and Romance: Essays on Medieval Literature, *second edition, Macmillan and Co. Ltd., 1908, pp. 287-317.*

HENRY ADAMS (essay date 1904)

[*Adams was an American autobiographer, historian, essayist, and novelist. His work, considered less pertinent to the history of literature than to the history of ideas, embodies a particularly modern viewpoint: Adams saw the world becoming less stable and coherent and predicted that this trend would continue unabated. He developed this doctrine most thoroughly in his best-known work,* The Education of Henry Adams *(1907). As a historian, Adams is chiefly remembered for his* History of the United States of America during the Administrations of Thomas Jefferson and James Madison *(1889-91). The following excerpt is taken from his 1904 study of the cathedrals of Mont-Saint-Michel and Chartres. Adams imagines an eleventh-century performance of* The Song *before Duke William of Normandy and Earl Harold of England and discusses the spirit and style of the poem.*]

The passion for pilgrimages was universal among our ancestors as far back as we can trace them. For at least a thousand years it was their chief delight, and is not yet extinct. To feel the art of Mont-Saint-Michel and Chartres we have got to become pilgrims again: but, just now, the point of most interest is not the pilgrim so much as the minstrel who sang to amuse him—the *jugleor* or *jongleur*—who was at home in every abbey, castle or cottage, as well as at every shrine. . . . The immense mass of poetry known as the "Chansons de Geste" seems to have been composed as well as sung by the unnamed Homers of France, and of all spots in the many provinces where the French language in its many dialects prevailed, Mont-Saint-Michel should have been the favourite with the jongleur, not only because the swarms of pilgrims assured him food and an occasional small piece of silver, but also because Saint Michael was the saint militant of all the warriors whose exploits in war were the subject of the "Chansons de Geste." (pp. 29-30)

Of all our two hundred and fifty million . . . ancestors who were going on pilgrimages in the middle of the eleventh century, the two who would probably most interest every one, after eight hundred years have passed, would be William the Norman and Harold the Saxon. . . .

According to Wace's *Roman de Rou,* when Harold's father, Earl Godwin, died, April 15, 1053, Harold wished to obtain the release of certain hostages, a brother and a cousin, whom Godwin had given to Edward the Confessor as security for his good behaviour, and whom Edward had sent to Duke William for safe-keeping. Wace took the story from other and older sources, and its accuracy is much disputed, but the fact that Harold went to Normandy seems to be certain. . . . (p. 30)

[Certainly] Harold did go with William on at least one raid into Brittany, and the charming tapestry of Bayeux, which tradition calls by the name of Queen Matilda, shows William's men-at-arms crossing the sands beneath Mont-Saint-Michel, with the Latin legend: "Et venerunt ad Montem Michaelis. Hic Harold dux trahebat eos de arena. Venerunt ad flumen Coronis." They came to Mont-Saint-Michel, and Harold dragged them out of the quicksands. They came to the river Couesnon. Harold must have got great fame by saving life on the sands, to be remembered and recorded by the Normans themselves after they had killed him; but this is the affair of historians. Tourists note only that Harold and William came to the Mount: "Venerunt ad Montem." They would never have dared to pass it, on such an errand, without stopping to ask the help of Saint Michael.

If William and Harold came to the Mount, they certainly dined or supped in the old refectory, which is where we have lain in wait for them. Where Duke William was, his jongleur—jugleor—was not far, and Wace knew, as every one in Normandy seemed to know, who this favourite was—his name, his character, and his song. To him Wace owed one of the most famous passages in his story of the assault at Hastings, where Duke William and his battle began their advance against the English lines:

Taillefer qui mult bien chantout	Taillefer who was famed for song,
Sor un cheval qui tost alout	Mounted on a charger strong,
Devant le duc alout chantant	Rode on before the Duke, and sang
De Karlemaigne e de Rollant	Of Roland and of Charlemagne,
E d'Oliver e des vassals	Oliver and the vassals all
Qui morurent en Rencevals.	Who fell in fight at Roncesvals.
Quant il orent chevalchie tant	When they had ridden till they saw
Qu'as Engleis vindrent apreismant:	The English battle close before:
'Sire,' dist Taillefer, 'merci!	'Sire,' said Taillefer, 'a grace!
Io vos ai longuement servi.	I have served you long and well;
Tot mon servise me devez.	All reward you owe me still;
Hui se vos plaist le me rendez.	Today repay me if you please.
Por tot guerredon vos requier	For all guerdon I require,

E si vos voil forment preier	And ask of you in formal prayer,
Otreiez mei que io ni faille	Grant to me as mine of right
Le premier colp de la bataille.'	The first blow struck in the fight.'
Li dus respondi: 'Io l'otrei.'	The Duke answered: 'I grant.'

Of course, critics doubt the story, as they very properly doubt everything. They maintain that the ***Chanson de Roland*** was not as old as the battle of Hastings, and certainly Wace gave no sufficient proof of it. Poetry was not usually written to prove facts. Wace wrote a hundred years after the battle of Hastings. One is not morally required to be pedantic to the point of knowing more than Wace knew, but the feeling of scepticism, before so serious a monument as Mont-Saint-Michel, is annoying. The ***Chanson de Roland*** ought not to be trifled with, at least by tourists in search of art. One is shocked at the possibility of being deceived about the starting-point of American genealogy. Taillefer and the song rest on the same evidence that Duke William and Harold and the battle itself rest upon, and to doubt the ***Chanson*** is to call the very roll of Battle Abbey in question. The whole fabric of society totters; the British peerage turns pale.

Wace did not invent all his facts. William of Malmesbury is supposed to have written his prose chronicle about 1120 when many of the men who fought at Hastings must have been alive, and William expressly said: "Tunc cantilena Rollandi inchoata ut martium viri exemplum pugnaturos accenderet, inclamatoque dei auxilio, praelium consertum." Starting the ***Chanson de Roland*** to inflame the fighting temper of the men, battle was joined. This seems enough proof to satisfy any sceptic, yet critics still suggest that the "cantilena Rollandi" must have been a Norman *Chanson de Rou,* or *Rollo,* or at best an earlier version of the ***Chanson de Roland;*** but no Norman chanson would have inflamed the martial spirit of William's army, which was largely French; and as for the age of the version, it is quite immaterial for Mont-Saint-Michel; the actual version is old enough. (pp. 31-3)

All this preamble leads only to unite the ***Chanson*** with the architecture of the Mount, by means of Duke William and his Breton campaign of 1058. The poem and the church are akin; they go together, and explain each other. Their common trait is their military character, peculiar to the eleventh century. The round arch is masculine. The ***Chanson*** is so masculine that, in all its four thousand lines, the only Christian woman so much as mentioned was Alda, the sister of Oliver and the betrothed of Roland, to whom one stanza, exceedlingly like a later insertion, was given, toward the end. Never after the first crusade did any great poem rise to such heroism as to sustain itself without a heroine. Even Dante attempted no such feat.

Duke William's party, then, is to be considered as assembled at supper in the old refectory, in the year 1058, while the triumphal piers of the church above are rising. The Abbot, Ralph of Beaumont, is host; Duke William sits with him on a daïs; Harold is by his side . . . ; the Duke's brother, Odo, Bishop of Bayeux, with the other chief vassals, are present; and the Duke's jongleur Taillefer is at his elbow. The room is crowded with soldiers and monks, but all are equally anxious to hear Taillefer sing. As soon as dinner is over, at a nod from the Duke, Taillefer begins:

Carles li reis nostre empere magnes	Charles the king, our emperor, the great,
Set anz tuz pleins ad estet en Espaigne	Seven years complete has been in Spain,
Cunquist la tere tresque en la mer altaigne	Conquered the land as far as the high seas,
Ni ad castel ki devant lui remaigne	Nor is there castle that holds against him,
Murs ne citez ni est remes a fraindre.	Nor wall or city left to capture.

The ***Chanson*** opened with these lines, which had such a direct and personal bearing on every one who heard them as to sound like prophecy. Within ten years William was to stand in England where Charlemagne stood in Spain. His mind was full of it, and of the means to attain it; and Harold was even more absorbed than he by the anxiety of the position. Harold had been obliged to take oath that he would support William's claim to the English throne, but he was still undecided, and William knew men too well to feel much confidence in an oath. As Taillefer sang on, he reached the part of Ganelon, the typical traitor, the invariable figure of mediaeval society. No feudal lord was without a Ganelon. Duke William saw them all about him. He might have felt that Harold would play the part, but if Harold should choose rather to be Roland, Duke William could have foretold that his own brother, Bishop Odo, after gorging himself on the plunder of half England, would turn into a Ganelon so dangerous as to require a prison for life. When Taillefer reached the battle-scenes, there was no further need of imagination to realize them. They were scenes of yesterday and tomorrow. For that matter, Charlemagne or his successor was still at Aix, and the Moors were still in Spain. Archbishop Turpin of Rheims had fought with sword and mace in Spain, while Bishop Odo of Bayeux was to marshal his men at Hastings, like a modern general, with a staff, but both were equally at home on the field of battle. Verse by verse, the song was a literal mirror of the Mount. The battle of Hastings was to be fought on the Archangel's Day. What happened to Roland at Roncesvalles was to happen to Harold at Hastings, and Harold, as he was dying like Roland, was to see his brother Gyrth die like Oliver. Even Taillefer was to be a part, and a distinguished part, of his chanson. Sooner or later, all were to die in the large and simple way of the eleventh century. Duke William himself, twenty years later, was to meet a violent death at Mantes in the same spirit, and if Bishop Odo did not die in battle, he died, at least, like an eleventh-century hero, on the first crusade. First or last, the whole company died in fight, or in prison, or on crusade, while the monks shrived them and prayed.

Then Taillefer certainly sang the great death-scenes. Even to this day every French school-boy, if he knows no other poetry, knows these verses by heart. In the eleventh century they wrung the heart of every man-at-arms in Europe, whose school was the field of battle and the hand-to-hand fight. No modern singer ever enjoys such power over an audience as Taillefer exercised over these men who were actors as well as listeners. In the mêlée at Roncesvalles, overborne by innumerable Saracens, Oliver at last calls for help:

Munjoie escriet e haltement e cler.	'Montjoie!' he cries, loud and clear.
Rollant apelet sun ami e sun per;	Roland he calls, his friend and peer:
'Sire compainz a mei kar vus justez.	'Sir Friend! ride now to help me here!

A grant dulur ermes hoi de-serveret.' Aoi.	Parted today, great pity were.'

Of course the full value of the verse cannot be regained. One knows neither how it was sung nor even how it was pronounced. The assonances are beyond recovering; the "laisse" or leash of verses or assonances with the concluding cry, "Aoi," has long ago vanished from verse or song. The sense is as simple as the *Ballad of Chevy Chase,* but one must imagine the voice and acting. Doubtless Taillefer acted each motive; when Oliver called loud and clear, Taillefer's voice rose; when Roland spoke "doulcement et suef" ["gently and softly"], the singer must have sung gently and soft; and when the two friends, with the singular courtesy of knighthood and dignity of soldiers, bowed to each other in parting and turned to face their deaths. Taillefer may have indicated the movement as he sang. The verses gave room for great acting. (pp. 34-7)

Taillefer had, in such a libretto, the means of producing dramatic effects that the French comedy or the grand opera never approached, and such as made Bayreuth seem thin and feeble. Duke William's barons must have clung to his voice and action as though they were in the very mêlée, striking at the helmets of gemmed gold. They had all been there, and were to be there again. As the climax approached, they saw the scene itself; probably they had seen it every year, more or less, since they could swing a sword. Taillefer chanted the death of Oliver and of Archbishop Turpin and all the other barons of the rear guard, except Roland, who was left for dead by the Saracens when they fled on hearing the horns of Charlemagne's returning host. Roland came back to consciousness on feeling a Saracen marauder tugging at his sword Durendal. With a blow of his ivory horn—*oliphant*—he killed the pagan; then feeling death near, he prepared for it. His first thought was for Durendal, his sword, which he could not leave to infidels. In the singular triple repetition which gives more of the same solidity and architectural weight to the verse, he made three attempts to break the sword, with a lament—a *plaint*—for each. Three times he struck with all his force against the rock; each time the sword rebounded without breaking. The third time—

Rollanz ferit en une pierre bise	Roland strikes on a grey stone,
Plus en abat que jo ne vus sai dire.	More of it cuts off than I can tell you.
L'espee cruit ne fruisset ne ne briset	The sword grinds, but shatters not nor breaks,
Cuntre le ciel amunt est resortie.	Upward against the sky it rebounds.
Quant veit li quens que ne la fraindrat mie	When the Count sees that he can never break it,
Mult dulcement la plainst a sei meisme.	Very gently he mourns it to himself:
'E! Durendal cum ies bele e saintisme!	'Ah, Durendal, how fair you are and sacred!
En l'oret punt asez i ad reliques.	In your golden guard are many relics,
Le dent saint Pierre e del sanc seint Basilie	The tooth of Saint Peter and blood of Saint Basil,
E des chevels mun seignur seint Denisie	And hair of my seigneur Saint-Denis,
Del vestment i ad seinte Marie.	Of the garment too of Saint Mary.
Il nen est dreiz que paien te baillisent.	It is not right that pagans should own you.
De chrestiens devez estre servie.	By Christians you should be served,
Ne vus ait hum ki vacet cuardie!	Nor should man have you who does cowardice.
Mult larges terres de vus averai cunquises	Many wide lands by you I have conquered
Que Carles tient ki la barbe ad flurie.	That Charles holds, who has the white beard,
E li emperere en est e ber e riches.'	And emperor of them is noble and rich.'

This "laisse" is even more eleventh-century than the other, but it appealed no longer to the warriors; it spoke rather to the monks. To the warriors, the sword itself was the religion, and the relics were details of ornament or strength. To the priest, the list of relics was more eloquent than the Regent diamond on the hilt and the Kohinoor on the scabbard. Even to us it is interesting if it is understood. Roland had gone on pilgrimage to the Holy Land. He had stopped at Rome and won the friendship of Saint Peter, as the tooth proved; he had passed through Constantinople and secured the help of Saint Basil; he had reached Jerusalem and gained the affection of the Virgin; he had come home to France and secured the support of his "Seigneur" Saint Denis; for Roland, like Hugh Capet, was a liegeman of Saint Denis and French to the heart. France, to him, was Saint Denis, and at most the Île de France, but not Anjou or even Maine. These were countries he had conquered with Durendal. . . . He had conquered these for his emperor Charlemagne with the help of his immediate spiritual lord or seigneur Saint Denis, but the monks knew that he could never have done these feats without the help of Saint Peter, Saint Basil, and Saint Mary the Blessed Virgin, whose relics, in the hilt of his sword, were worth more than any king's ransom. To this day a tunic of the Virgin is the most precious property of the cathedral at Chartres. Either one of Roland's relics would have made the glory of any shrine in Europe, and every monk knew their enormous value and power better than he knew the value of Roland's conquests.

Yet even the religion is martial, as though it were meant for the fighting Archangel and Odo of Bayeux. The relics serve the sword; the sword is not in service of the relics. As the death-scene approaches, the song becomes even more military. . . . (pp. 38-40)

Our age has lost much of its ear for poetry, as it has its eye for colour and line, and its taste for war and worship, wine and women. Not one man in a hundred thousand could now feel what the eleventh century felt in these verses of the ***Chanson,*** and there is no reason for trying to do so, but there is a certain use in trying for once to understand not so much the feeling as the meaning. The naïveté of the poetry is that of the society. God the Father was the feudal seigneur, who raised Lazarus—his baron or vassal—from the grave, and freed Daniel, as an evidence of his power and loyalty; a seigneur who never lied, or was false to his word. God the Father, as feudal seigneur, absorbs the Trinity, and, what is more significant, absorbs or excludes also the Virgin. . . . To this seigneur, Roland in dying, proffered (puroffrit) his right-hand gauntlet. Death was an act of homage. God sent down his Archangel Gabriel as his representative to accept the homage and receive the glove. To Duke William and his barons nothing could seem more natural and correct. God was not farther away than Charlemagne.

Correct as the law may have been, the religion even at that time must have seemed to the monks to need professional advice. Roland's life was not exemplary. The ***Chanson*** had taken pains to show that the disaster at Roncesvalles was due to Roland's headstrong folly and temper. In dying, Roland had not once thought of these faults, or repented of his worldly ambitions, or mentioned the name of Alda, his betrothed. He had clung to the memory of his wars and conquests, his lineage, his earthly seigneur Charlemagne, and of "douce France" ["sweet France"]. He had forgotten to give so much as an allusion to Christ. The poet regarded all these matters as the affair of the Church; all the warrior cared for was courage, loyalty, and prowess.

The interest of these details lies not in the scholarship or the historical truth or even the local colour, so much as in the art. The naïveté of the thought is repeated by the simplicity of the verse. Word and thought are equally monosyllabic. Nothing ever matched it. The words bubble like a stream in the woods:

Ço sent Rollanz de sun tens ni ad plus.

Try and put them into modern French, and see what will happen:

Que jo ai fait des l'ure que nez fui.

The words may remain exactly the same, but the poetry will have gone out of them. Five hundred years later, even the English critics had so far lost their sense for military poetry that they professed to be shocked by Milton's monosyllables:

Whereat he inly raged, and, as they talked,
Smote him into the midriff with a stone
That beat out life.

Milton's language was indeed more or less archaic and Biblical; it was a Puritan affectation; but the ***Chanson,*** in the refectory actually reflected, repeated, echoed, the piers and arches of the Abbey Church just rising above. The verse is built up. The qualities of the architecture reproduce themselves in the song: the same directness, simplicity, absence of self-consciousness; the same intensity of purpose. . . . The action of dying is felt, like the dropping of a keystone into the vault, and if the Romanesque arches in the church, which are within hearing, could speak, they would describe what they are doing in the precise words of the poem:

Desure sun braz teneit le chief enclin	Upon their shoulders have their heads inclined,
Juintes ses mains est alez a sa fin.	Folded their hands, and sunken to their rest.

Many thousands of times these verses must have been sung at the Mount and echoed in every castle and on every battlefield from the Welsh Marches to the shores of the Dead Sea. No modern opera or play ever approached the popularity of the ***Chanson.*** None has ever expressed with anything like the same completeness the society that produced it. Chanted by every minstrel—known by heart, from beginning to end, by every man and woman and child, lay or clerical—translated into every tongue—more intensely felt, if possible, in Italy and Spain than in Normandy and England—perhaps most effective, as a work of art, when sung by the Templars in their great castles in the Holy Land—it is now best felt at Mont-Saint-Michel, and from the first must have been there at home. The proof is the line, evidently inserted for the sake of its local effect, which invoked Saint Michael in Peril of the Sea at the climax of Roland's death, and one needs no original documents or contemporary authorities to prove that, when Taillefer came to this invocation, not only Duke William and his barons, but still more Abbot Ranulf and his monks, broke into a frenzy of sympathy which expressed the masculine and military passions of the Archangel better than it accorded with the rules of Saint Benedict. (pp. 42-4)

Henry Adams, "La Chanson de Roland," in his Mont-Saint-Michel and Chartres, *1904. Reprint by The New American Library, 1961, pp. 25-44.*

J. GEDDES, JR. (essay date 1906)

[Geddes was an American educator and the author of Study of an Acadian French Dialect *(1908) and* Memoirs of a College Professor *(1945). In the following excerpt from the introduction to his modern French translation of* The Song, *Geddes deems the work "the first grand poetic monument of Latin Europe since the time of Christ" and comments generally on the poem's style and milieu.]*

[The ***Chanson de Roland***] was written a long time after the triumph of feudalism was assured, and three centuries after the events it describes, yet it preserves marked traces of the days when kingly power was well nigh absolute, and when Charlemagne was beloved and revered by all. Considering the manner in which the parts were, in all probability, at different times knit together, the unity of the epic is remarkable. It divides itself naturally into three prts that are as well balanced as the three acts of a well constructed drama. The treason of Ganelon forms the subject of the first act, which has as its result the battle and the death of Roland in the second act, leading up fittingly to the retaliation and punishment which form the third act of the drama. There are not lacking critics who claim that the poem should close with the death of Roland, and regard the last part as incongruous. . . . Nevertheless it is only natural to suppose with good judges, that it was the author's intention Roland should die conquering, and Charlemagne should avenge his death by chastising the united enemies of Christendom, the Saracens, thus heightening the author's own fame and shedding glory upon France as the defender of the faith. Indeed, it may be said that from the time of Clovis (496) down to Charlemagne's day, it was the special mission of the Franks to combat the oppressors of the Church—the Burgundians, Lombards, Saxons, and Slavs—and, above all, to check the Saracen invasions, an event which was accomplished with signal success in 732 at Poitiers, by Charles Martel. Hence the fitness, in the last part of the ***Chanson,*** of the champion of the Christian world meeting in mortal combat the head of Islam, and thus deciding the right by the defeat of the Saracen. (pp. xxiii-xxiv)

The society described in the poem belongs to the feudal aristocracy, for it was particularly in the XIth century that the nobility was strong and the king feeble. There were at least eighty immense tracts of territory, each governed by a lord absolutely independent of the king, Philip I., a weakling, who possessed in reality but a half dozen counties. It was during this century that the Normans made the conquest of England, and that they established the kingdom of the two Sicilies; that a Burgundian nobleman received as a fief the county of Portugal and that the first crusade, made up largely of Frenchmen, started for the Holy Land. The spirit of the crusades was in the air and the din of arms resounded throughout the Christian world. Besides the warrior class, there was another class that had to be reckoned with as a powerful factor in the society of the time, the clergy. The warriors who fight and the clergy who pray, taking, however, occasionally, a hand in the conflict, composed the recognized society of the eleventh century. The people appear merely as a confused indistinct mass, having no status other than that of toilers. Such, too, is their character in the ***Chanson de Roland.*** (pp. xxiv-xxv)

That the poem is warlike and religious at the same time is only what might be expected; that it remains so true to the traditions of royalty and of Charlemagne at a time when these traditions had well-nigh gone by, is surprising. But it must be remembered that the conflict described is a struggle between faith and faith, rather than between country and country; that the *Terre Majeure* [''fatherland''] is France fighting for the Christian world, and that *la douce France* is that sweet land which Charlemagne not only rules but represents. The French are right, and the pagans are wrong. In that oft repeated phrase lies the central idea of the poem of the age. Charlemagne stands for the right. He cannot well do wrong, for besides his faithful peers, do not angels counsel him? This protection from heaven serves to increase the prestige of Charlemagne and to make him more venerated and beloved.

The superstitious idea that the victory is a judgment of God, and that the Franks must win because right is on their side is as inherent a part of the belief of these old warriors as is their profound faith in God, about which there can be no controversy. Just as the *Iliad* recalls the struggle of the Greeks against the cities of Asia Minor, so here the national tradition is to defend Christianity against the Saracens. This is the great motive of the poem; the triumph of the banner, the oriflamme, symbolizing God's victory and giving the poem the character of a national epic. (pp. xxv-xxvi)

The tone, throughout the ***Chanson,*** is serious, almost severely so, as befits so noble a theme. The range of ideas is somewhat limited, as generally in all very early productions; but this is in a great measure made up for by the directness and energy with which the ideas are presented. The remarks the heroes address to each other, the epithets used, and especially the frequent repetitions recall the *Iliad* and leave much the same vivid impression upon the mind. It has been noted, too, so usual is the form of dialogue in the development of the incidents of the ***Chanson,*** that out of four thousand verses which the poem contains, sixteen hundred are pronounced in the form of address or response by one character. In both the ***Chanson*** and the *Iliad,* the general effect is enhanced by the primitive setting which carries with it a quaintness that is in itself a charm.

The few leading personages of the poem, Charlemagne, Roland, Olivier, Ganelon, are drawn somewhat roughly but vigorously, each is a well defined personality. That finer or more clearly cut distinctions might be made, no one will care to dispute, yet rough hewn as they are, they have a particular charm of primitive poetry.

The manners and customs are those of a rude civilization, in which might makes right, and where killing, hanging, and burning of all Moslems, that are not immediately converted to Christianity, is justifiable and commendable. The more sanguinary the feats of arms of the Christians, the more is the right vindicated, the nearer they themselves approach salvation. So that these tremendous blows, which shatter the helmet, buckler, and breastplate of the knight, passing on down through his body, piercing the saddle, cleaving in twain the steed, are each and all masterstrokes for Christianity, for the right, and for God. It must be admitted that they occur somewhat frequently for the literary taste and ideas of the present day, but if it be remembered that these episodes were sung by the minstrels to hearers, some of whom departed as others arrived, these repetitions would then not prove so monotonous to the audience as to the modern reader. (pp. xxvi-xxvii)

In regard to these early epics, forerunners of the national literary life of the future, it has often been remarked that, apparently, it never occurs to the poet or to his hearers that the manners and customs of other nations that he describes, can be different from those of his own . . . . The armor in which the knights on either side are encased, their arms, method of attack, way of looking at things, all appear to be essentially the same. The Saracens, to be sure, are swarthy and black; and the blacker they are, the more ungodly and dangerous do they appear. This physical trait together with religious belief is really all that constitutes the difference between the two armies. (pp. xxvii-xxviii)

As regards religion, all who do not profess the Christian faith are indiscriminately classed as Saracens. The poet describes the vows made by the Moslems to their divinities, among whom he places Apollo and Tervagant, regardless of the fact that the former ranks among Roman divinities, while the latter is merely a Gallic idol. Such distinctions, if at all appreciated, are subtleties that do not count in the momentous question of the right. It is enough that all other creeds and divinities that are not Christian, and that consequently are in the wrong, be classed and treated as Saracen. So ingrained and so far reaching is this faith, that it is invoked for the purpose of keeping a felonious agreement, as when Ganelon plights his faith to the Saracens. The idea of a Providence not only appears here and there on the surface, but also underlies the entire poem. . . . It is the old story of the conflict between light and darkness, between ignorance and vice, between good and evil. Despite the barbarity and sanguinary deeds of these old armor clad warriors, they are essentially human in all their ways; they suffer from cold and heat, from hunger and thirst, from physical and moral pain, just as we all do. They are moved by feelings of pleasure, affected by thoughts of home and the fatherland, *la douce France* [sweet France], and are moved to tears by the losses that cannot be repaired. And it is because of these human traits common to us all that we cannot help sympathizing with them, admiring their singleness of purpose, and revering the ideals they represent. Such, in general, are some of the main characteristics of the poem itself. (pp. xxviii-xxix)

Apart from its age which produces what is peculiar to it, the poem would not be understood. It awakens interest because it is the first grand poetic monument of Latin Europe since the time of Christ, what precedes it being of more interest for the study of the language than of the literature. From the Christian spirit of this popular production can be judged in a measure what a factor Christianity was in the development of early civilization. Both the ***Chanson*** and the *Iliad* represent primitive stages of two different civilizations which made possible the development of the two epics. They are not primitive, however, in the same degree, for the literature of Greece in the time of Homer was more advanced than that of France in the eleventh century. The French language was in a rude state, ill adapted to give adequate expression to much that Greek could express beautifully. One has only to think of the rich images in Homer to realize the poverty of art in the ***Chanson*** as compared with the *Iliad*. Yet, at the same time, this very poverty of expression, this simplicity in portraying, heightens the effect produced. The parting of Roland and Oliver, the death of Turpin, of Roland, of Aude, are told with childlike simplicity which adds impressiveness and imparts grandeur. And in a work of this kind, just as in the old frescoes and paintings of the middle ages, it is not facility of expression any more than correctness of line that claims human interest, but rather the idea behind it all, the spirit, the inspiration. (p. lvi)

At the very beginning, there is no invocation as in the Greek epics, and the old French poem, as has been truly said of it, begins without beginning and ends without ending; that is the action is hardly ever described, but a series of tableaux is shown to the audience listening to the minstrel's song. Thus Ganelon's treachery, upon which depends the entire action of the ***Chanson,*** is revealed in three lines, while he and Blancandrin are on their journey to Saragossa. The subject, which is anything but pleasant to dwell upon, is in this way most effectively handled, such treatment displaying literary skill of a high order.

Although it is true that the parts of the poem do not show that cohesion that may characterize particularly the product of one author, writing at one time, on one subject, nevertheless . . . the unity of the work as a whole, owing its inspiration to religious and patriotic enthusiasm, is apparent. For the disaster of Roncesvalles is the burden of the song. This disaster is the central feature, and the nucleus of what precedes and follows—Ganelon's treason and his punishment. The battle itself, a subject by no means easy to describe in a way to keep up continual interest, is splendidly introduced by the vision of Charlemagne, the preparations of the Christians and Saracens for the battle, and the first part of the episode of the horn, one of the most stirring and unique scenes in all literature, and which, too, is unlike anything else. The battle, which is represented by hand to hand conflicts between the opposing leaders, is begun by Marsile's nephew, who has the honor of being the first Saracen knight to attack Roland. The series of single handed combats between the peers on either side occupies what may be called the first act. This consists of a preliminary engagement between the rear-guard composed of twenty thousand Christian soldiers and the hundred thousand pagans forming the advance guard of the Saracen army. All of the peers of this latter host, with one exception, are slain, and of the army itself there are not two that survive, while the Christian peers remain intact. This first engagement is separated from the central one, which forms the second act of the sanguinary struggle, by Charlemagne's lament over those faithful young soldiers who have lost their lives in the battle, and are never more to see their mothers and wives; and also by the sinister forebodings to which the Franks are a prey. These are increased by the darkness which overhangs all France, and by the thunderstorms and earthquakes, all of which announce the impending doom of the rear-guard. Then follows the second act: Marsile himself comes on with the main army, and such carnage as has never before been witnessed, takes place. The Saracens fall by thousands, Roland and Oliver themselves alone killing four thousand. But when for a moment the slaughter abates, and a count is taken, alas! six of Charlemagne's peers have been slain, and but sixty knights of the faithful rear-guard survive, but sixty who shall sell their lives dearly. Then comes the second part of the episode of the horn, Roland offering to sound a blast and Oliver expostulating, the scene forming so unique a pendant to the first part. Charlemagne, thirty leagues away hears the horn, the third blast of which, faltering and feeble, strikes his followers with apprehension. Their only thought now is to hasten to the relief of the rear-guard. This forms a fitting introduction to the last act of the tragedy in which Marsile, losing his right hand by Roland's good sword Durendal, is put to flight with one hunred thousand Saracens. But all to no purpose, for the caliph, Marsile's uncle, arrives on the scene with more than fifty thousand Ethiopians. Encouraged at the sight of only a handful of Franks left, he renews with ardor the battle, the result of which is a foregone conclusion. It gives rise, however, to some of the most pathetic scenes in the poem and, indeed, in all epic poetry. Such are the parting of Roland and Oliver, the death of the latter, followed by that of the only three survivors of Charlemagne's rear-guard, Walter, the archbishop, and Roland, whose soul is borne on high by angels. While all these events are taking place, and the final struggle between the rear-guard and the Ethiopians under the caliph is drawing to a close, the vision of Charlemagne, the darkness and storm in France, the sound of Roland's horn that reaches the emperor, inform us of what is taking place in the main army of the Franks. Without any apparent artful construction, the three parts, as shown, are related to each other in as artistic a manner as are the parts of any well executed classical French drama. (pp. lvii-lix)

Whatever description may occur is very brief, details being sacrificed to the main idea, which, not infrequently, is depicted in the present tense. But one fact at a time is made prominent, and thus the tale goes on uninterrupted and with few figures of speech. The pictures of Charlemagne's camp in the orchard, of the return of the main army to France, of Roland proudly riding on Veillantif just before the battle, form tableaux complete in themselves, of great artistic merit, each contained within the limits of a *laisse*. In striking contrast in respect to the continuity of action, and simplicity of fact as well as of description, are the later *chansons de geste,* where many actions, confused adventures, and an infinity of persons are brought together. In the whole poem, there is but one genuine comparison: "Just as the stag flies before the hounds, so the pagans flee before Roland." Of weak comparisons or similes there are quite a number, but they show no originality whatever, and are evidently used naïvely either to complete the thought or the verse. Such for instance, as: "He runs swifter than a horse;" (The pagans begin) "to bark like dogs;" "Less swift of wing is the bird that flies;" "He becomes more terrible than lion or leopard."

Just as . . . the types represented in the poem are, in general, somewhat roughly outlined, so too the scenes from nature are crudely drawn. One heavy stroke renders the poet's idea. In speaking of a beautifuly day, almost the same expression occurs repeatedly: "The day was fine, the sun bright;" "The day was bright and the sun beautiful;" "The day is fine, the sun radiant;" and speaking of the moon: "The moon is bright, the stars shine." There is a certain quaintness about this kind of repetition; it suggests primitiveness and is by no means without charm. In certain places it is very effective, as where the main army is on its return to the *Terre Majeure:* "The mountains are high and the valleys are deep;" farther on: "The mountains are high and dark and vast." Describing the death of Oliver, three strophes begin with the verse: "Oliver feels that he is wounded unto death." Often a strophe begins with a verse that recapitulates the sentiment that precedes. Simple as these phrases are, there is a grandeur about them that impresses the scenes upon the mind almost indelibly. (pp. lix-lx)

There are besides these verse repetitions, strophe repetitions, or as they have been termed, *couplets similaires,* which repeat, in the same or almost the same language, some passage, or scene, or dialogue. The reason or origin of these repetitions has been much discussed. Not occurring in all the different manuscripts, it has been thought by some that they were taken from different versions and unskilfully interpolated, or were due to oversight on the part of the editor, copyist, or minstrel who sang parts of the ***Chanson*** now in one place now in another. While this is possible in some passages, it seems in many others hardly probable, because the most notable repetitions occur in the finest passages in the entire poem, the episode of the horn, thrice in the first part, twice in the second; and thrice in the Durendal sword scene. Of course such supremely beautiful passages appealed to the minstrel's audience in those days even more than to the modern reader. Nothing, therefore, is more natural than that they should be repeated. The effectiveness of such repetition was appreciated in epic poetry of a much earlier date, where instances of its happy use are of not infrequent occurrence. (pp. lx-lxi)

The contradictions in the poem have proven as fruitful a subject of discussion as have the repetitions. It is hardly possible to know absolutely the reason of some of these inconsistencies. In certain cases, nevertheless, explanations have been ingeniously suggested. Suffice it here to point out some of these passages in order to illustrate the nature of the want of agreement. When Ganelon proposes Roland as leader of the rear-guard, the latter "begins to speak like a true knight." In the next strophe, in answer to the same proposition, "he replies to his father-in-law furiously." The two strophes contradict each other in spirit and tone. It would appear that the two strophes were originally parts of different versions. Again Ganelon, upon his return from the embassy to Marsile's court, relates to Charlemagne that he has seen the caliph with 300,000 men put to sea and perish by shipwreck before they had sailed four leagues away. Later on, during the third engagement at the battle of Roncesvalles, we are suprised to see the caliph come marching on to the field at the head of 50,000 Ethiopians. When Charlemagne, lamenting the death of Roland, declares what his grief must be upon his return to France, the scene of the sorrow in the first strophe is placed at Laon and in the next at Aix-la-Chapelle, both of which towns at different epochs were capitals of the Carolingian dynasty, although Aix was founded after the battle of Roncesvalles, and Laon about the time of Charles the Simple, more than one hundred years after the battle. The discrepancy suggests versions of a different date. At the beginning of the poem, Marsile says that he has no army, and later brings on one most formidable. Ganelon, after having agreed with Blancandrin to betray the Franks, addresses Marsile in the haughtiest manner possible, thereby incurring the wrath of the king and his army. Although ambassadors when giving their messages are usually represented in old epics as using insolent language, such insolence is here hardly in keeping with the circumstances. We read that Marsile, after his defeat, offers the keys of Saragossa to the emir Baligant, but earlier in the poem we have seen Marsile in the act of handing them to Ganelon, who later delivers them to Charlemagne. Finally, Mont Saint-Michel, which is so often spoken of in the early part of the poem, and whither Marsile promised to betake himself, is not even mentioned after the death of Roland. These examples are cited not to weaken what has been said in regard to the unity of the poem as a whole, but merely as indicating the probable development of the epic, passing at different epochs through the hands of composers, or arrangers, or reciters, traces of whose influence still appear, in spite of the degree of homogeneity given to the poem in the last author's version, represented inadequately by the Oxford manuscript. (pp. lxi-lxiii)

There are not lacking throughout the poem strong passages giving vent to deep feelings of humanity which, in a measure, we all share. Ganelon, before parting on his perilous mission, thinks tenderly of *la douce France* and desires to be remembered to his wife, to his son Baudouin, and to his friend and peer Pinabel. When Charlemagne's army, after leaving the rear-guard in Spain, is on the march back to France, the thoughts of all turn toward the loved ones at home from whom they have been so long separated and there is no one who does not weep for very tenderness. When the emperor with his army returns and discovers that the rear-guard has been annihilated, weeping will not suffice, and twenty thousand Franks fall to the ground in a swoon. Such exaggerations characterize epic poetry and have there a fitness impossible elsewhere.

So serious throughout is the tone of the poem that with the exception of the short episode of Aude, which . . . is regarded as an interpolation, the sentiment of love for woman, a characteristic of the later *gestes,* is unknown. It would seem, according to the ideas of the old poet, that in the stern narrative of the struggle between Christianity and paganism, such love had no place. The only passing allusion to anything like gallantry is the remark made in speaking of Margaris de Séville, one of the Saracen peers, that "the ladies are friends of his on account of his beauty; not one of them that does not brighten on seeing him; not one of them, whether she will or not, that can keep from laughing when she sees him."

Both love, with its narrowing of interest, and humor with its episodic effect, seem to have been considered out of keeping with the times and purpose of the poem. The passage relating to the treatment of Ganelon, whom Charlemagne hands over to the cooks, who insult him by plucking out his hair, drubbing him, chaining him up like a bear, and mounting him on a beast of burden, was intended to appeal to a coarse and brutal humor common enough in those early days when refinement was uncommon. Somewhat like this passage in spirit is that in which the pagans, after the defeat of Marsile, maltreat their gods, Apollo, Tervagant, and Mohammed on account of the shame of defeat. Excepting these passages, indicative more of the coarseness of the feelings of the people than of humor, the poem preserves a uniform tone of dignity. (pp. lxiii-lxv)

Another element, too, that is conspicuously lacking in the poem when compared with many other *chansons de geste,* particularly those relating the Arthurian legends, is the miraculous, in the sense in which it appears in these other poems. In a poem like the ***Roland,*** the nature of which is sober, stately, and impressive, the insertion of fairies, enchanters, magicians,

Fifteenth-century portrayal of Roland slaying Marsile (above) and the death of Roland (below).

and all such supernatural agencies, could only weaken the effectiveness of the work as a whole. The introduction of the marvelous in the later poems is a device for attracting attention and heightening interest for the moment. But in a poem that deals with a subject so lofty and grand as the theme of the ***Roland,*** there is no need of resorting to any such trick to command attention. True it is that an angel is wont to give advice to Charlemagne, that God causes the sun to stand still in order that the emperor may have time to overtake the Saracens, that only divine interference prevents Charlemagne's death at the hands of Baligant, and that angels bear on high Roland's soul. Such miracles are not, however, pure inventions of the imagination, but have a far deeper source in that firm abiding faith that accepts without question like incidents of sacred story. The miraculous in the ***Chanson*** is simple, just, worthy of the faith, and profoundly Christian. With these old defenders of the cross, there could be no question of philosophy or theology, no discussion of any kind; in a word, they believed. (p. lxv)

In the days when the ***Chanson*** was sung to the accompaniment of a lyre by a minstrel whose arrival in the market-place was a longed-for event, its popularity was very great. Not only did it satisfy the people, but it furnished entertainment to those of the nobles who could afford to entertain the troubadour, and who delighted in hearing related the deeds of prowess of the nobility. The strong hand of Charlemagne, the national unity of France, its leadership over other Christian nations in the struggle to defend the faith, were peculiarly gratifying topics to the people of the eleventh century. And to-day the poem remains one of the principal monuments commemorative of the society of the epoch. For it is through the ***Chanson*** that we have a better idea than could otherwise have been obtained of the influence of Germanic manners, customs, and institutions. We see their traces in the power of the king limited by the nobles, by councils called together, by judicial procedure, by the spirit of brotherhood in arms, and by the strong feeling of the sanctity of the family. The noble sentiments inspired by the ***Chanson,*** of honor, of sacrifice, and of courage, exercised later on a powerful influence not only on the later French *chansons de geste,* but on the literature of the other nations of Europe. (pp. lxv-lxvi)

J. Geddes, Jr., in an introduction to La chanson de Roland: A Modern French Translation of Theodor Müller's Text of the Oxford Manuscript, *edited by J. Geddes, Jr., The Macmillan Company, 1906, pp. xvii-lxxxvii.*

EZRA POUND (essay date 1910)

[An American poet, translator, essayist, and critic, Pound was "the principal inventor of modern poetry," according to Archibald MacLeish. He is chiefly renowned for his ambitious poetry cycle, the Cantos, *which he revised and enlarged throughout much of his life. These poems are noted for their lyrical intensity, metrical experimentation, literary allusions, varied subject matter and verse forms, and incorporation of phrases from foreign languages, including Chinese ideographs and Egyptian hieroglyphs. History and politics greatly interested Pound, and many of his poems and critical writings reflect his attempt to synthesize his aesthetic vision with his political, economic, and cultural ideals. Pound considered the United States a cultural wasteland; his series of satirical poems,* Hugh Selwyn Mauberly *(1920), has often been ranked with T. S. Eliot's* The Waste Land *(1922) as a significant attack upon the decadence of modern culture. Pound is also noted for his instrumental role in the encouragement of other authors, obtaining editorial and financial assistance for Eliot, William Butler Yeats, James Joyce, and Wyndham Lewis, among others. Pound's pro-Fascist activities during World War II led to his indictment for treason and for a time diminished his reputation as one of the most innovative and creative artists of the twentieth century. In the following excerpt, Pound records his largely unfavorable impression of* The Song.]

Numerous authorities disagree with my preference of the [*Poema del Cid*], and consider the ***Chançon de Roland*** the finer poem: but in its swift narration, its vigor, the humanness of its characters, for its inability to grow old, the Spanish "geste" seems to me to surpass its French predecessor. . . . (p. 66)

The ***Chançon de Roland,*** dating in its present form from the second half of the Eleventh Century, is based upon the historic fact, which an earlier Latin chronicler dismisses thus: "In this battle Edghardus, master of the royal table, Anselmus, count palatine, and Rollandus, præfect of the borders of Brittany, with very many others, were killed." That is, Hrodland, Count of the March of Brittany, commanding the rearguard of Charlemagne's army, was defeated by the Basques in the Valley of Roncevaux, August 15, 778 (A.D.), Charles the Great being at this time thirty-six years of age.

Three centuries later this has solidified into 4002 verses, in what [Gaston] Paris terms the "national style," which style is likely to seem a rather wooden convention to an outlander. The personality of the author is said to be "suppressed," although it might be more exact to say that it has been worn away by continuous oral transmission. Summarizing further, from Paris' lecture on the "***Chançon de Roland*** et la Nationalité française": "You will remember that from their conversion the French proclaimed themselves the people beloved of Christ, chosen by him to defend his church."

This ideal pertains in the ***Chançon;*** the enemies are no longer idolaters. They are Mahometans, but the French Christians are little concerned with trifling distinctions, so far as the dramatic proportion is concerned they are "pagans." These pagans held Spain; the duty of France is to take it away from them, because they have a false religion. The poet's idea is that "The pagans are wrong, the French are right."

When Charlemagne has taken Saragossa, he converts the population *en bloc.*

En la citet n'est remis paiens
Ne seit ocis, on devien crestiens.

In the city remained no pagan
Who was not killed, or turned Christian.

Paris notes this feeling of national destiny, the love of la douce Frances, and the love of the national honor, as the three qualities which give the poem its "grandiose character." But we, who have not had our literary interest in the poem stimulated of late by the Franco-Prussian war and the feelings of outraged patriotism attendant thereupon, notice a certain tedious redundance before being charmed by this "caractère grandiose."

The poem is nevertheless quite interesting as a monument to "la nationalité française." Its championship of Christianity against Paganism makes it almost as much of Christendom as of France; it is most certainly heroic in outline, far more so than the *Cid.* (pp. 74-5)

A victim, not to the treachery of Ganelon, but to that pride which forbade him to sound the horn for aid, [Roland] dies. Perfect chivalric pose, perfect piety! The hero goes out of this chançon of gesture, and one feels that perhaps he and the rest of the characters are not wooden figures, that they are simply "latin." Heroic, his hands joined, in death he forgets not etiquette. He is the perfect hero of pre-realist literature.

But as one is grateful for Cervantes after Montemayor, one is grateful for the refreshment of the Spanish *Poema,* and for the bandit Ruy Diaz. I perhaps profane the ***Roland:*** the death scene is poignant; parts of it are natural; all of it might seem natural to minds differently poised. Poetry it has in plenty; its stiffness may often become, or seem to become, dignity; but the quality of eternal youth is not in it in such a degree as in the Spanish *Poema,* or in the old captive's song fable, *Aucassin and Nicolette.* (p. 78)

Ezra Pound, "Geste and Romance," in his The Spirit of Romance, *1910. Reprint by New Directions, 1952, pp. 64-86.*

G. K. CHESTERTON (essay date 1919)

[Regarded as one of England's premier men of letters during the first half of the twentieth century, Chesterton is best known today as a colorful bon vivant, a witty essayist, and as the creator of the Father Brown mysteries and the fantasy The Man Who Was Thursday *(1908). Much of Chesterton's work reveals his childlike enjoyment of life and reflects his pronounced Anglican and, later, Roman Catholic beliefs. His essays are characterized by their humor, frequent use of paradox, and chatty, rambling style. In the following excerpt from his introduction to Charles Scott Moncrieff's 1919 translation of* The Song, *Chesterton praises "the noble and rugged epic," claiming that to read it is to penetrate to the "human heart" of medieval history.]*

Most of us remember reading, in the school histories of our childhood, that at the Battle of Hastings, Taillefer the Jongleur went in front of the Norman Army throwing his sword in the air and singing the ***Song of Roland.*** They were naturally histories of a very Victorian sort, which passed lightly over the Roman Empire and the Crusades on the way to serious things, such as the genealogy of George I or the administration of Addington. But that one image emerged in the imagination as something alive in its dead surroundings; like finding a familiar face in a faded tapestry. The song he sang, it is needless to say, was presumably not the noble and rugged epic which Captain Scott Moncrieff has done so solid and even historic a service to letters in rendering in its entirety. The jongleur must at least have selected extracts or favourite passages, or the battle would have been unduly delayed. But the tale has the same moral as the translation; since both have the same inspiration. The value of the tale was that it did suggest to the childish mind, through all the deadening effects of distance and indifference, that a man does not make such a gesture with a sword unless he feels something, and that a man does not sing unless he has something to sing about. Dull avarice and an appetite for feudal lands do not inspire such jugglery. In short, the value of the tale was that it hinted that there is a heart in history, even remote history. And the value of the translation is that if we are really to learn history we must, in a double sense of the word, learn it by heart. We must learn it at length and as it were at large; lingering over chance spaces of contemporary work, for love of its detail and one might almost say for love of its dulness. Even a random reader like myself, only dipping here and there into such things, so long as they are really things of the period, can often learn more from them than from the most careful constitutional digests or political summaries, by modern men more learned than himself. . . . Most of the stock histories tell the young student something of what Feudalism was in legal form and custom; that the subordinates were called vassals, that they did homage and so on. But they do it somehow in such a way as to suggest a savage and sullen obedience; as if a vassal were no more than a serf. What is left out is the fact that the homage really was homage; a thing worthy of a man. The first feudal feeling had something ideal and even impersonal like patriotism. The nations were not yet born: and these smaller groups had almost the souls of nations. Now in this translation, merely because it is an honest translation, the reader will find the word "vassalage" used again and again, on a note which is not only heroic but even haughty. The vassal is obviously as proud of being a vassal as anybody could be of being a lord. Indeed the feudal poet uses the word "vassalage" where a modern poet would use the word "chivalry." The Paladins charging the Paynims are spurred on by vassalage. Turpin the Archbishop hacks the Moslem chieftain rib from rib; and the Christians, beholding his triumph, cry aloud in their pride that he has shown great vassalage; and that with such an Archbishop the Cross is safe. There were no Conscientious Objections in their Christianity.

This is a type of the truths that historical literature ought to make us feel; but which mere histories very seldom do. The one example I have already given, of the Jongleur at Hastings, is a complexity of curious truths that might be conveyed and which very seldom are. We might have learned, for instance, what a Jongleur was; and realised that this one may have had feelings as deep or fantastic as the Jogleur celebrated in the twelth century poem, who died gloriously of dancing and turning somersaults before the image of Our Lady; that he was of the trade taken as a type by the mystical mirth of St. Francis, who called his monks the Jugglers of God. A man must read at least a little of the contemporary work itself, before he thus finds the human heart inside the armour and the monastic gown; the men who write the philosophy of history seldom give us the philosophy, still less the religion, of the historical characters. And the final example of this is something which is also illustrated by the obscure minstrel who threw up his sword as he sang the ***Song of Roland,*** as well as by the ***Song of Roland*** itself. Modern history, mainly ethnological or economic, always talks of a thing like the Norman adventure in the somewhat vulgar language of success. For these it is well to note, in the real Norman story, that the very bard in front of their battle line was shouting the glorification of failure. It testifies to a truth in the very heart of Christendom, that even the court poet of William the Conqueror was celebrating Roland the conquered.

That high note of the forlorn hope, of a host at bay and a battle against odds without end, is the note on which the great French epic ends. I know nothing more moving in poetry than that strange and unexpected ending; that splendidly inconclusive conclusion. Charlemagne the Christian emperor has at last established his empire in quiet; has done justice almost in the manner of a day of judgement, and sleeps as it were upon his throne with a peace almost like that of Paradise. And there appears to him the angel of God crying aloud that his arms are needed in a new and distant land, and that he must take up again the endless march of his days. And the great king tears his long white beard and cries out against his restless life. The poem ends, as it were with a vision and vista of wars against the barbarians; and the vision is true. For that war is never ended, which defends the sanity of the world against all the stark anarchies and rending negations which rage against it for ever. That war is never finished in this world; and the grass has hardly grown on the graves of our own friends who fell in it. (pp. ix-xii)

G. K. Chesterton, in an introduction to The Song of Roland, *translated by Charles Scott Moncrieff, Chapman & Hall, Ltd., 1919, pp. ix-xii.*

T. ATKINSON JENKINS (essay date 1924)

[*Jenkins was an American educator. In the following excerpt from the introduction to his edition of* The Song, *he discusses the characters, style, and themes of the poem.*]

The ***Song of Roland,*** the oldest, the most interesting, and the most famous of the French epics, or *chansons de geste,* might also, and perhaps with greater reason, be called a *Song of Charlemagne and Roland:* when we omit from the title the name of Charles, King and Emperor of the Franks, we are laying more weight upon the subsequent interpretations and developments of the poem than upon the evident intentions of its author. (p. ix)

Thus it is Charles the King, early surnamed "the Great," who opens and closes the poem. His striking and venerable figure dominates the action from beginning to end; it is his expedition into Spain which meets with such lamentable disaster, but is avenged so thoroughly. He is the leader of "the Christian people" against heathendom; he is the right arm of the Church, the personification of civil order and personal piety; he is the favorite of Heaven, whence he receives significant dreams and visions. He rules rightfully, for, like Æneas, he is master of men because he has learned to serve the common weal. When he wages war it is not for the joy of fighting nor the lure of plunder, but to enlarge the confines of Christendom and to baptize the pagan peoples. (p. xxiii)

Charlemagne is noble, heroic, brave, powerful, wise—the poet lavishes praises upon him; at the same time he is old, and his white beard is conspicuous. He rides with his troopers, however, in amazing vigor of body, and when the Emir of Cairo offers him single battle in one gigantic duel of infidel versus true believer, he comes off victorious; not, however, without some supernatural aid. So great is the fame of his vigor and achievements that in Saragossa the King of all Spain has heard that he has attained the miraculous age of two hundred years or even more. We are invited to sympathize with, if not to pity, this great and sorely tried ruler, who, while facing rebellion on many borders and treachery within his own household, is bereft of his best soldiers, his ablest leaders, and his beloved nephew. The future for him seems dark, and his life is one of ceaseless labor and agitation.

Roland is Charlemagne's nephew, the son of his sister. This lady, whose situation could hardly be more tragic, is not named in the poem; after the death of Roland's father, she has married Count Ganelon, who becomes a traitor to France. Her son ranks next to Charlemagne himself, he is Charles' "right arm," and in council he speaks first after the Emperor. He is Count of a March, that is, Warden of a Border; he was "Britannici limitis præfectus," according to Einhard's *Life of Charles,* and we may note that the historian Adhemar of Chabannes, in the eleventh-century, spoke of "that Normandy which used to be called the March of France and Brittany." Roland is therefore properly a Marquess. His duty, when Charles' march lies in enemy countries, is to protect the main army: this he does with a force of twenty thousand, and with the aid of the Twelve Peers. It is not surprising, therefore, that he is assigned to command the rear-guard when Charles retires from Spain.

Personally, Roland is a prince among knights; riding to the hunt with the Olifant, laying waste towns or countrysides, fighting with his sword Durendal, these are his delights; at times, among his peers, he will utter his boast, his *gab,* in due form. His passion is conquest, and his idea of amusement is to present Charlemagne with all the crowns in the world, typified by a bright red apple. Roland is keenly sensitive as to his military fame, and much afraid of the satirical songs such as all soldiers sing. But he is passionately loyal to his family, to his lord Charles, and to the country of "sweet France" which Charles represents; like his master, Roland is devoted to the Christian faith, and would make it prevail everywhere by force of arms.

If Roland have enemies, they will accuse him of haughtiness, of pride, of insubordination; Ganelon hated Roland because, as the traitor explains at the Trial, Roland was overweening in his gold and wealth. When, on the tragic field of Roncesvaux, in the heat of battle and the exasperation of defeat, Oliver quarrels with his brother-in-arms, he threatens to break off the betrothal of Roland to his sister Alda, and reproaches Roland with recklessness, with heedlessness *(estoltie, legerie)*; he wishes his valiant friend might display more common sense and common prudence *(mesure).* Count Ganelon had previously declared that Roland was too indifferent to the risks run by others than himself. To these censures, which no doubt are well-founded, Roland can answer only by his silence and by his suffering; a little later, when Oliver, blinded, smites him cruelly by mistake, Roland with pathetic readiness pardons the blow. Sincerely grieving to have been the chief cause of the death of so many good knights, and of so bitter a loss to Charlemagne, Roland can only offer up his life, surrendering it, as though it were a fief, into the hands of God. After his death, Charles' soldiers hear the booming of the Olifant held by other hands than Roland's, and are moved to tears. . . . [Roland's legend] was destined to grow to phenomenal proportions, and his figure is prominent and secure in what Masefield calls "the old, proud pageant of mankind." The earliest poet (or poets) of ***Roland*** used him to embody a chivalric ideal which still makes a strong appeal. In later days, the nephew of Charlemagne was granted the aureole of the martyr; we may fittingly couple his name with that of Achilles, for the fine lines by Ernest Myers are strikingly appropriate to both:

> What gifts hath Fate for all his chivalry?
> Even such as hearts heroic oftenest win:
> Honor, a friend, anguish, untimely death.

Oliver, son of Duke Renier of Gennes (on the Loire, in Anjou?) is Roland's companion-in-arms: they watch over each other's safety, and their gain is in common. Oliver is equal to his companion in prowess. . . . For valor and courage there is little choice between them, but Oliver, perhaps by virtue of a livelier imagination, is more prudent: with him foresight and caution have their place as well as furious courage and mighty blows. As Felix Dahn said, Oliver is more of a Hellene and Roman; Roland is of the North. When ambushed by superior forces in the mountains, quicker-witted than Roland, Oliver would send for help before there has been any trial of strength; a prey to mortal anxiety, he does his utmost to make Roland listen to the voice of reason, but without success. But once overwhelmingly defeated, Oliver is just as clear that it would be shameful then to summon aid; he too will go down with all colors flying.

The poet has drawn his Roland and his Oliver with keen and evident enjoyment: there is even gaiety and humor in their relations as well as a loyal friendship tragically ended. In the early hopeful stage of the great battle, Roland watches Oliver riding through the field and despatching his Saracen opponents; Oliver's lance has lost its point, and Roland has the warrior's grim jest: "Companion, what are you about? For a fight like this, I have no use for a club. Where is your sword?" "I could not draw it," answers Oliver gaily, "I was too busy." Then "Halteclere" is drawn, and Oliver cleaves an enemy even to the backbone of the horse beneath. Roland, who is an excellent judge, enjoys the skillful swordwork with the satisfaction of a fellow-professional: "I do assure you, brother, that Charlemagne loves us for just such bits of work as that." (pp. xxiv-xxvii)

But it is necessary, granted the "dolorous rout," that loss and sorrow should predominate in the fortunes of this pair. (p. xxvii)

The poet imagined the affection between these two Peers as sincere and constant; their separation arouses deep feeling in both, and Roland, who must survive his heroic friend, grieves for him from the bottom of his heart.

Ganelon also ranks as a Count; he is "of France" but his fief is not named. He has married Charlemagne's sister, only to bring upon her a grief like Hecuba's. Their son, Baldwin, is handsome of person like Ganelon, and is near to his father's heart. An uncle, Guinemer, and a retinue of loyal knights accompany Ganelon to the war; his horse and his sword, like Roland's, are dignified by names. His spurs are of gold, his furs are of costly marten: the latter detail does not escape the cunning eye of King Marsile who, noting his preference, seeks to please him with a gift of sables.

Ganelon had been long at court, as befitted his high lineage; there, as it seems, he was known for his cupidity, for when the suspicion of his treason first enters the minds of the French chiefs they at once ascribe it only to bribery. "Accursed thirst for wealth, to what do you not drive the minds of men!" Greed for riches and display, and envy of the wealth of others, is the cause of the proud Count's downfall: at his trial, he confesses that he hated Roland because his stepson "overdid" in gold and in possessions; this irritation had led to an open quarrel in which the older man, ashamed to confess the real cause of his jealousy, raged publicly at Roland for having nominated him to a dangerous mission. One would suppose, if we did not look deeper, that Ganelon was really afraid of the danger, but events soon prove the contrary; he is certainly no coward. Count Roland has the great defects of his heroic virtues: unknown to himself he has stirred up in Ganelon, an able, proud and jealous man, the primal passions of envy, anger and malice, and out of these are born treachery and unspeakable disaster.

Count Ganelon, however, claims private venegeance as a right. He gives Roland, with Oliver and the Twelve Peers, fair notice of their danger; having lived long at court, he knows that it is not permissible to attack another knight without the *défi* ["defiance";"challenge"] in due form. One definition of "treason," in those times, was "to seek the life of one's liege lord, or that of his son"; but Ganelon, in the midst of his plans for the ambush at Roncesvaux, speaks admiringly of Charles, even affectionately. Another form of treason was to slay a fellow knight, while pretending friendship. It is his fierce grudge against Roland that Ganelon will feed fat: it is not "treason" if a *défi* is given. So let the Saracen king cut off this haughty and heedless Roland, and there will be no more Christian invasions of Spain!

In the presence of King Marsile and his pagan court Ganelon, therefore, speaks with great astuteness: he must provoke the Saracen into continuing the war, weary of the struggle as he knows him to be; but he must also dissuade the Spanish King from attacking Charlemagne. He promises that all will be well once Roland and the Peers with their small army are put out of the way. The infamous pact is sworn to on both sides, Ganelon is overwhelmed with costly gifts—"these," he says, "I am very far from refusing"—and the traitor returns to Charles' headquarters to face certain suspicion and almost certain punishment. If the treason succeed and Roland perish, his plea will be that it is permissible for one knight to avenge a personal affront, providing always due warning has been given. Charlemagne, however, in his function as king and ruler, takes the view that such private liberty must end where public injury begins, and, in the sequel, the Emperor views his sister's husband torn into pieces by fiery horses. Upon this, the poet's reflection is sober enough: "If one man betray another, he must not be allowed to glory in the deed."

Turpin, Archbishop of Reims, is the most important ecclesiastic taking part in the Spanish expedition; below him there are bishops, abbots, monks, canons and priests. History indeed knows of a Tilpin, or Tylpin, Archbishop of Reims, 753-794, who died before Charlemagne but after the disaster of Roncesvaux; Hincmar in the ninth century, and Flodoard, in the tenth, both commemorate him. The latter states that Charlemagne obtained the pallium for him, from Pope Adrian; but neither mentions his having accompanied the Emperor into Spain. When, however, in the poem, the famous rear-guard is forming, the warlike prelate comes forward with the words: *Jo irai, par mon chief!* ["I'll go, by my head!"] We know that Bishop Odo of Bayeux, at the battle of Hastings, rode armed with a club, churchmen being forbidden to shed the blood of fellow Christians; but no such scruple existed, at least in crusading days, when enemies were followers of Mohammed: Turpin is armed like the rest, and his single combats are catalogued like those of others. There fall before him Corsablis, the enchanter Siglorel, Abisme, and Malquidant; just before he himself is pierced with four spears, his marvelous steed having first been killed, he makes a prodigious clearing around him, slaying four hundred paynims. He outlives Oliver, but not Roland.

Turpin sermonizes the army before and during the battle; in him the Church speaks officially, but he is remembered particularly for his prominent part in two striking scenes: he comes forward to compose the painful quarrel between Roland and Oliver and he encourages Roland to bring in the dead bodies of the Twelve Peers, that they may be duly absolved and blessed. Seeing Roland faint, Turpin in a last supreme effort would bring him water in the Olifant. But the effort is too great, Turpin expires, and Roland must bear as best he can the terrible thirst of those who have lost much blood.

Bishop Odo of Bayeux, brother of the Conqueror, was a brutal soldier, greedy of gain, hair-brained and quarrelsome; Turpin recalls rather the venerable bishop-leader of the First Crusade, Adhemar of Le Puy, he who rode at the head of a division at Dorylæum, in whose tent the councils of war were held, and whose rôle was often that of pacifier of the turbulent leaders.

There are other personages, most of them quite definitely outlined by the poet. There is Duke Naimon, later said to be of Bavaria, the close friend and prudent counsellor of Charles: no better vassal than he in the court. There are Alda, the fair lady, betrothed to Roland, and Thierry of Anjou, victorious over Pinabel almost like David over Goliath. On the pagan side are Marsile and his Queen, their nephew Aëlroth, Baligant and his son Malprimes: these are paler figures, but there is life in them, as well as in the portrait of the handsome and irresistible Margarit of Seville. All these act and speak in their place, but in general there is scant time and space for characterization: the poet, as though oppressed by the tragic fate of his heroes and by the urgent need for more valorous Christian chevaliers to force back the menacing hosts of Turks, Arabs and Moors, is in haste to tell his moving tale: he must arouse his hearers to the great perils which threaten "the Christian people." (p. xxxii)

It is remarkable that French literature, like Greek literature, begins with a masterpiece. The conscious art of the ***Roland*** is undeniable, and recent investigation tends to strengthen rather than to weaken this statement. Gaston Paris compared the ***Roland*** to an arch at the entrance of the long highway of masterpieces of French literature, but added that the arch was perhaps "rather narrow;" it may be claimed that as our knowledge of the poem increases, this arch gains in breadth and in fairness of proportion.

Aristotle conceived of the epic as possessing a dignified theme, as having unity; within this unity the action should move with an ordered progression. In the ***Roland,*** a detachment of Charles' Christian army is waylaid in the Pyrenees by Spanish Saracens and slain to the last man: the theme is the behavior of these Christian feudal barons when confronted with successful treachery and overwhelming odds. In the action, there are three stable working factors: the perfect loyalty and amazing valor of Roland; Ganelon's personal hatred of Roland; and Charles' able leadership and his ability to achieve ultimate and signal vengeance. To avoid the defeat was still possible had there not been at work a fatal weakness of character; in this case it was recklessness, an overdoing, a *demesure* in fighting valor. The poet means to contrast the Northman's unrestrained bravery (Roland) with the cooler reason of the Roman-Hellene (Oliver). The poet also confronts devotion to public duty (Charles and Roland) with Ganelon's determination to have personal revenge at any cost.

A fair degree of epic breadth is secured by making the crisis one of religious Truth versus religious Error, as in the eighth book of the *Æneid,* and by making large the number of chevaliers engaged: twenty thousand are slaughtered on the French side, while the pagan army, which is practically destroyed, contains twenty times that number. (p. xxxiii)

The poet's power in depicting scenes is noteworthy. He has the gift of suggestion, which he uses at times in place of direct statement. Thus, at v. 119, Charlemagne is seated in an ample grove; around him are the Peers and thousands of other chevaliers, but so handsome of form and so proud of bearing is he, that—

> S'est qui'l demandet, ne'l estoet enseignier.
>
> Should any seek, no need to point him out!

In the battle, the valiant Grandónie of Cappadocia, flushed with victory, chances to meet Count Roland, whom he has not seen before; the look and bearing of the angered Roland are enough, the effect on the pagan prince is instant and electrifying—

> Ne poet muër qu'il ne s'en espavent:
> Foïr s'en voelt mais ne li valt niënt.
>
> He cannot help but he is faint with fear,
> He starts to flee, but that avails him naught.

Of the traditional epic devices, the poet makes use of visions or dreams, of which there are four in the poem. Another inheritance from the epic technique of the ancients is the enumeration of the divisions *(eschieles)* of the opposing forces.

Baist finds some traces of an attempt to give an air of archaism: the forms of Charles' army organization and the conduct of a trial by combat, he thinks, must have been obsolete by the first decade of the twelth century. It is certain that the poet did his best to be true to history but the tendency to archaize is not prominent: only three centuries separate the poet from the events he describes, and the times of Charlemagne were no more remote to him than are to us those of Cromwell.

A sober use is made of the supernatural; most of the marvelous happenings, such as the visits of Gabriel to earth and the staying of the sun, had good warrant in the Scriptures. There is some epic exaggeration, most noteworthy, perhaps, in the statement that at the sight of the slaughter at Roncesvaux twenty thousand of Charles' men fainted away upon the ground. On the other hand, it is not altogether just to say, as did G. Brandes (in a public lecture, Copenhagen, 1922): "The hero of the ***Song of Roland*** may kill 100,000 men with his sword, but Homer knows no such fantastic feats." No such statement is made in the Oxford version; at v. 2058, in an outburst of fury, Roland slays twenty of his foes, Walter six, and Turpin five. This is moderate enough. . . . (pp. xxxiv-xxxvi)

The poet's style is simple and straightforward; it is the language of action rather than that of reflection. Severer critics have called it bald or naked: it certainly lacks much of the charm and variety of the classic epics. Some of its emotional energy and rapidity has been lost by rejuvenation: many sentences, originally juxtaposed without conjunction or relative pronoun, have already in the Oxford version been weakened by the insertion of *que, qui,* etc.

Of the conventional ornaments of diction there are almost none: a single simile, a few sententious lines, and the rest is language in action with a high percentage of dialogue. There is none of that deplorable diffuseness of expression and fatal facility in ideas which are so prevalent in later epics and of which Taine so justly complained [see 1863-64 excerpt by Taine]. The ***Roland*** was written by men of action; it was written *for* men of action. (p. xxxvi)

We find in the ***Roland*** the direct and straightforward style of a poet anxious only to deliver his message: we find also an exceptional refinement and elevation of tone. "There is not a base thought in the whole poem," remarks J. Clark [in his *A History of Epic Poetry (Post-Virgilian)* (1900)]. Plebeian psychology, so prominent in many of the later epics, is absent here, or nearly so. We are far indeed from the triviality and coarseness which disfigure even so interesting a poem as the *Chanson de Guillelme*. This is the more remarkable because the poet gives scant attention to the feminine half of society; but he gives none at all to the audiences for which the *fabliaux* and the *Proverbes au Vilain* were written. His audience was an élite of princes of Church and State, army leaders, political officers, and secular-minded clergy. The poem is distinctly aristocratic in its appeal. . . . (p. xxxvii)

In contrast with Vergil's epic and with *Beowulf,* the ***Roland*** is composed in strophes: these average 14 lines in length. In Old

French, an epic strophe is called a *vers,* less commonly a *laisse;* the latter term has been preferred, as *vers* is ambiguous.

In his adaptation of the *laisse* to epic narrative the poet has shown great care and skill. The *laisse* achieves unity through the assonance, which is never the same in two successive *laisses.* Usually there is a *laisse* for each incident; change of assonance thus marks a step forward in the action. The *laisses* are often linked together by repetition of words or phrases, or by a short descriptive passage. The *laisse* and the incident often terminate with a speech or a remark (some 135 cases); often this is sententious in content, or is foreboding in tone. The last line of the *laisse* is nearly always climactic. . . . (pp. xxxvii-xxxviii)

Another rhetorical device which has attracted much attention is the *laisses similaires,* strophes in which the incident is repeated for greater effect a second, third, and even a fourth time, with change of assonance. These triads, says Tavernier [in a 1910 essay in *Zeitschrift Fuer Franzoesische Sprache und Literature*], are Turoldus' specialty; they are a form of repetition which eases the tension in an emotional crisis and imparts a sense of power and achievement, as of one who lingers a while upon an eminence. As in Homer, whole lines are not seldom repeated *verbatim,* or with slight variation. (p. xxxviii)

The assonance is exact, and not "rough" or "approximate," as is not infrequently stated. A single vowel may assonate with a diphthong, provided it is the stressed element of the diphthong which agrees. The meter is the ten-syllable, with a well marked cesura after the fourth tonic (stressed) syllable; the cesura as well as the assonance may be feminine (paroxytone). (pp. xxxviii-xxxix)

This meter is handled with notable ease and power. Not infrequently occur single lines which are memorable for content and form, and for the fusion of these two elements into an organic whole. . . . There are many such verses: they sing themselves into the memory; their vigor and simplicity, their easy flow, make them unforgettable.

The recent study of A. H. Krappe [*Alliteration in the "Chanson de Roland" and in the "Carmen de Prodicione Guenonis"* (1921)] shows an extensive use of alliteration in the poem; some eighteen lines in every hundred contain alliterative combinations. In 488 cases the alliteration is confined to a single line; in 243 cases it is a means of linking successive verses. . . . Very interesting are the six pairs of alliterating proper names which occur, three of pagan personages, three of Christian chevaliers: Gerin and Gerier, Ivoire and Ivon, Gefreit and Jozeran. It seems natural to suppose that this pairing of names is an inheritance from Germanic antiquity, being probably of specific Norse or Danish origin.

The almost total loss of the music to which the OF epics were sung has caused them and the ***Roland*** to be read, like the epic of Tasso or that of Milton; but the poet intended these verses to be sung, or chanted. (pp. xxxix-xl)

The alliance of the Frankish monarchy with Rome was one which, as Lord Bryce has said, made the fortune of both parties. But Charlemagne accepted to the full his responsibility for the welfare of the "populus christianus," and the enlightened minds of his time dreamed of a Christian Europe united and militant against the surrounding paganism. At the end of the eleventh century there is a great revival of this ideal in France; the idea is widespread of a mission to destroy the false religion of Islam, both in Spain (where it was nearest) and in the Orient. The ***Roland*** is deeply imbued with this idea of a Holy War. The chevaliers taking part in this particular expedition into the land of Spain are performing an act of piety, it is a religious duty. . . . (pp. xl-xli)

Count Roland is faithful unto death. His fidelity ennobles his character and admits him to paradise. He is faithful first of all to his friends and companions, also to his family (*parents*), also to his tribe (*les homes de son lign*), also to his chieftain-king, for whom he cherishes an unbounded admiration and affection; finally, to his country, whose welfare and honor he has deeply at heart. . . . His constant prayer is that France should not be disgraced by defeat. . . . To give effect to this admirable loyalty, the poet has endowed Roland with signal virtues. If he have a touch of the *miles gloriosus* and be frankly afraid lest the soldiers sing a song at his expense; if he wants to be first in glory, yet he is also quite willing to be first in danger, and his supreme regret is:

> Barons franceis, por mei vos vei morir:
> Jo ne vos tenser ne guarantir!
>
> Barons of France, blame *me* that you are dying:
> I cannot fend for you nor yet protect you.

Roland's courage, his bravery (*vasselage*) is superlative; he hates cowardice and dreads lest Durendal fall into unworthy hands. The poet gives the hero the fault of this virtue, makes Roland's rashness (*desmesure*) the cause of the great disaster; but, to our great satisfaction, he makes Roland's dogged obstinacy in the end melt away and yield to compassion, when the paladin views the results of his refusal to listen to the counsels of prudence. The fault is atoned for by suffering and by death. Here is the poet's greatest achievement: he has made a drama of human character and conduct, of human strength and weakness. Roland is not at the end the same person he was at the beginning: he has greatly developed, and we find here the orderly progression within unity which Aristotle demanded of the epic. (pp. xli-xlii)

T. Atkinson Jenkins, in an introduction to La chanson de Roland, *edited by T. Atkinson Jenkins, revised edition, D. C. Heath and Company, 1924, pp. ix-cxliv.*

MARIO A. PEI (essay date 1948)

[An Italian-born American educator, Pei was the author of numerous linguistic studies praised for their careful scholarship and their accessibility to the non-specialist; among these works are The World's Chief Languages *(1948) and* The Story of Language *(1949). In the following excerpt from his full-length study of the connection between* The Song *and earlier French religious literature, Pei stresses the poem's role in establishing "a line of literary continuity . . . from the ninth to the thirteenth centuries."]*

If we accept, as the bulk of learned opinion does, the ***Chanson de Roland*** as the earliest and most original sample of French epic poetry, and consider the remainder of French epic production as directly or indirectly inspired by it, we must conclude that the establishment of a comparison necessarily lies between the so-called monuments of early religious literature (*Eulalie, Passion, Léger, Alexis*) and the ***Roland.*** The connection between the latter and the balance of the epic output will not be seriously disputed by anyone. (p. v)

Is the ***Chanson de Roland*** an epic pure and simple? Above all, is it merely a feudal epic? Or may it not better be described as a religious-feudal epic, the cusp between two separate and yet related genres, the connecting link between the devotional spirit of the earlier and the feudal-military spirit of the later Middle Ages? (p. vii)

Similarities in metrical form point to the continuation and development of a native French literary tradition rather than to a borrowing by the epic from other sources, Classical or Germanic. This form is already fully set by the time Turoldus appears. (p. 100)

The use of stylistic devices is progressive. Practically no device is used in the ***Roland*** which does not appear in the earlier poetry. Literary devices are common throughout, with artistry gradually unfolding from the rough *Eulalie,* through the Biblical *Passion* (which must be in part discounted by reason of its model), on to the *Léger* and the *Alexis,* which approximates the ***Roland,*** to the ***Roland*** itself.

Religious-supernatural themes show absolutely no abatement in the epic, though the miracle is occasionally (not always) turned to a material end (but this also happens in the *Alexis*). Symbolism and the confusion of pagan gods and devils are the epic's main new contributions to this field.

The religious features are common throughout. Prayer, baptism, conversion, confession, penance, the honoring of Saints and relics, resignation to death, martyrdom, temptation, all continue from the religious poetry into the early epic. The chief new contribution of the latter is the element of violence on the part of Christ's followers, which gives a new twist to conversion, penance, and martyrdom. More earthly points of view are indicated in connection with virginity, chastity, and the desire for death, though the germs of these are to be found in the *Alexis*.

Themes which may be described as religious-feudal are perhaps the most interesting. We find appeasement, both human and divine, religious intolerance, Christian and feudal pride, religious and feudal service commingled throughout, with steady progression from the purely religious to the religious-feudal ideal, untrammeled by any clash of authority, such as appears in the purely feudal ideal of later epics. *Passion* and *Léger* supply the precedents for the ***Roland***'s olive branch, the ***Roland***'s betrayal theme, the ***Roland***'s heaping of insults upon religious and political opponents, Christian-feudal pride, Christian-feudal service. The epic's innovations consist mainly of feudal betrayal, largely divorced from religious features, and active religious persecution on the Christian side, for which the propaganda motif appears, however, in the *Passion*.

The epic's purely feudal themes all make their first bow in the religious poetry. Feudal customs, the feudal council, warfare, sieges, the striking of stout blows, and even the *enfance,* which is characteristic of later epics, first appear in the religious poems. With respect to wealth and honors we are faced with a steady progression of thought, from something to be shunned to something to be tolerated, especially in the service of God, then to something desirable *per se,* but to be relinquished at a moment's notice if God demands it.

Human themes are common to early poetry and epic, with greater stress on the human side as we advance. Learning seems to fall into decadence as time goes on. The body, as first discussed somewhat disparagingly in connection with the soul, acquires separate importance and appreciation in the *Alexis* and ***Roland,*** while its honoring after death appears throughout. Human affections became more pronounced as we advance, but human sentiments and their manifestations remain substantially the same. The epic's main innovations are a seeming indifference to learning, a keener sensitiveness to human opinion, and a greater relish in descriptions of human suffering.

Among miscellaneous themes and incidents which the religious poetry (usually the *Alexis*) and the epic hold in common are the entrusting of objects and persons, addresses to lifeless objects, unsuccessful attempts to make them conform to a human will, references to previous historical periods, the search, the arrival on the scene of death, and the sea voyage. Most of these are such that they can easily be described as coincidental, but considerable similarity appears in the case of the first three.

The question of direct influence . . . is often idle. For each item of similarity that may be advanced between the Germanic and the French epic, another may be advanced between the Classical and the French epic. It may safely be asserted that the sum total of the similarities between the religious poetry and the epic is at least equal to the others combined. Is this proof that Turoldus had read the earlier religious poems and was influenced by them? It is possible.

Of more fundamental importance is the establishing of a native French literary tradition, capable of turning into fully epic channels at the proper moment. Such a tradition is proved by the general continuance and progression of metrical forms, style, syntax, vocabulary, devices, themes and ideas. Of this literary tradition Turoldus was conscious, and he used it to the full, combining the old religious ideal with the new feudal aspects, and creating an epic which is properly styled religious-feudal. If the *Alexis* may be taken as the connecting link between the earlier works and the ***Roland,*** then the ***Roland*** itself may be taken as the connecting link between the religious poetry as a whole and all subsequent epic poetry. A line of literary continuity is thus established from the ninth to the thirteenth centuries.

In addition to all this, there is something which the religious poems and the ***Roland*** have in common that cannot be labeled as a matter of style or vocabulary, a literary feature, or even a theme. It transcends all these classifications and gives tone and life to what would otherwise be mere collections of verses. The central idea that underlies each of the five poems under consideration is the idea of death—death for a purpose, death for an ideal. Purposeful death is the least common denominator of both religious poems and ***Roland,*** the kernel about which each poem grows and develops, the hub around which each plot revolves. *Eulalie, Passion, Léger, Alexis* would not merely be incomplete without the death of their respective central characters; they would be inconceivable. Equally inconceivable would be the ***Roland*** without the inevitable loss of its main personage. It is no accident that some critics place the end of the ***Chanson de Roland*** at the lines that describe the Count's soul as being borne to Paradise, and discount all that follows as a later interpolation. . . . Whether we accept this point of view or not is immaterial for our specific problem. What matters is that our first and greatest epic differentiates itself from all the rest of the epic output by revolving completely about the death of its central character.

Let us try for an instant to think of the ***Chanson de Roland*** as a poem in which the hero escapes death. Charlemagne arrives in time to save his nephew, and the two go on side by side to do battle with the Saracens and return to France in ultimate triumph. What would we have? Undoubtedly a work of mediocre merit, something similar to the numerous (perhaps too numerous) *Chansons de Geste* that the example of Turoldus inspired in less gifted imitators. The true genius of Turoldus lies in knowing when and how to let his hero die.

Yet this death, occurring at the culmination of the hero's career, a death that has little counterpart in the subsequent epic output, is drawn bodily from the earlier religious literature. It is the crowning point of Roland's career, just as the death of Eulalie, of Christ, of Léger, of Alexis is the climax of the career of each character. Roland's death is not drawn from the Classical epic, or from Germanic sources. It is drawn from the hagiography and martyrology of the medieval Church.

Turoldus never hesitates or wavers in his determination to let Roland die. His hero's death is announced long in advance of its occurrence, by a knell of doom that rings repeatedly throughout the early part of the poem. The sacrifice of Roland is essential, inevitable, like the sacrifice of Christ on the cross, of Eulalie before the pagan emperor, of Léger in defense of his faith, of Alexis in his final renunciation of all that he was entitled to in life. There is divine intervention for all else, but not for that predestined, inevitable fate, willed by God Himself. In this respect the ***Chanson de Roland*** departs sharply from the epic model and joins the religious literature.

But it is not death alone that counts, for death appears frequently in epic poetry. It is death for an ideal. What ideal? The ideal of personal pride and glory, of wealth and earthly goods, of feudal loyalty and devotion? To some extent, but only in part. Roland's true, basic ideal, for which he sacrifices his life and that of his men, is primarily a religious one. Charlemagne's campaign is only incidentally one of plunder or conquest; fundamentally it is a religious mission, a crusade of faith. Charlemagne, his peers, Roland himself are fully willing to withdraw from Spain, to give up all that they have gained, if only Spain's ruler will embrace the Christian faith. It is the religious, not the feudal motive that is predominant in their thoughts and impels their actions. Everything else, however important it may seem at any given point, is incidental. Roland is as much a martyr for Christianity in his own way as are the Saints in theirs. The method of martyrdom has changed, but the cenral purpose is the same.

For the change in method we may bring into play the change in historical conditions, the new consciousness of Christendom as an embattled unit struggling for survival in the midst of new hostile movements. The continuity of purpose and ideals, on the other hand, definitely connects the ***Roland*** with the foregoing religious literature of France. It is a continuity destined to be broken in short order, when the remnants of the old Christian spirit, after a brief and uncertain pause in the Guillaume d'Orange poems, vanish almost completely in the Eastern and Loherian Cycles. But its clear existence in the ***Chanson de Roland*** is definite proof of a rich French literary stream flowing across the ninth, tenth, and eleventh centuries, a stream the direction of which changes in accordance with historical and social circumstances, but the existence of which can no longer be denied by those who have claimed that "before the eleventh century universal silence reigns" or that "the centuries that precede the eleventh seem incapable of producing anything." (pp. 100-05)

Mario A. Pei, in his French Precursors of the "Chanson de Roland," *Columbia University Press, 1948, 105 p.*

E. M. W. TILLYARD (essay date 1954)

[*Tillyard was an English scholar of Renaissance literature whose studies of John Milton, William Shakespeare, and the epic form are widely respected. In the following excerpt, he comments on the style, themes, and characterizations of* The Song, *noting that perhaps its best feature is "its successful tragic drama."*]

Like most English readers I first became acquainted with the text of ***Roland*** through Arnold's quotation in the *Study of Poetry*, the first essay in the second volume of *Essays in Criticism* [see 1880 excerpt by Arnold]. Arnold complains that certain poems receive excessive praise through being judged not only on their poetic merit but on their historical importance. And he cites ***Roland*** as an example. . . . I was more grateful to Arnold for introducing me to the French lines than convinced that he had said the right things about them. They seemed to be good enough poetry to make any question of primitiveness irrelevant; and to stand up pretty well to the Homeric touchstone. Here was terseness, resonance, and controlled feeling. And further acquaintance with the poem confirmed the impression.

We now know that ***Roland***, whether it dates from the eleventh or twelfth century, whether or not the song of Roland sung by Taillefer at Hastings was the same as that preserved in the Bodleian manuscript, is not primitive in its art but comes towards the end of a literary movement. If it is inferior to Homer it is so for other reasons than callowness. It is, for instance, on a much smaller scale—about 4000 lines—and if it succeeds, its success is a smaller affair. But though the movement of its lines is more abrupt than that of the roll of the Homeric hexameter, it is suited to the smaller scale of the poem. And what these facts mean is that ***Roland*** is a poem which exists in its own right as achieved poetry and can be judged on its own merits, unhampered by any Homeric comparison. What, then, are the claims of ***Roland*** to be an epic?

It is, first of all, well and coherently plotted: simple in its lines yet complex enough to allow the characters to develop. As in Shakespeare, there are doings on whose motivation one must not dwell. For instance, it is quite taken for granted that Roland's position as commander of the rear-guard when the French army cross the Pyrenees northward is one of extreme and certain peril. This is difficult to account for, because Charles was crossing the Pyrenees only because Ganelon had persuaded him that Marsilie, the king of the Saracens, had genuinely come to terms. But there is never any vague plotting where the motives of the principal persons are concerned. The source of Roland's tragedy is his recommending to Charles that Ganelon should undertake the perilous task of envoy to the Saracens (who had murdered the two envoys sent before). And the poet hints at earlier hostility between Roland and Ganelon when he tells us that Ganelon was Roland's step-father. From Ganelon's resentment at Roland's act springs his treachery, and from his treachery the various doings of Christian and Saracen that lead to Roland's death. The poem is fully rounded off by the account of Ganelon's punishment when Charles finally returns to Aix. The proportions, too, are just. The poet never dwells on an incident too long; and if he dwells longest on Roland's dying it is because that is the culmination of the poem. As far as he goes, he shows a strong controlling will; but the poem is not long enough to put the poet's will to the supreme test a full-scale epic provides.

Within the four thousand lines there is considerable variety. Like Homer and any other poets who belong to an age of artistic sophistication growing out of a more primitive one, the author of ***Roland*** had to come to terms with a legacy of crude barbarism and fantasy. He does so in a manner that is intermediate between those of *Beowulf* and the Sagas. There is no killing of monsters on the one hand nor the consistently cool realism of the Sagas on the other. There is a good deal of fantastic exaggeration; but the poet keeps it from interfering with the crucial development of the characters. Charlemagne, with his two hundred years of age and yet with the bodily vigour sufficient to kill in duel the paynim admiral, is a fabulous figure, but he serves to heighten by contrast, rather than to confound, the credible characters of Roland, Oliver, Archbishop Turpin, and Ganelon. The numbers of paynims that the first three of these kill at Roncesvalles are fabulous, but we are not worried, nor diverted from the prime human business, since they are answered by other fabulous items in the setting. When the battle reached its height there was wind and earthquake through the length and breadth of France. Then there was darkness at noon. . . . What takes the sting out of the fantasy, what reduces it to its proper proportion and makes it do its proper work as picturesque contrast is the evidence that the poet is after all close to his central human subject. Charles may be a fabulous figure, but Roland's lovely words describing what a warrior must be prepared to suffer for his lord come right out of the real France of the first crusading epoch:

The Song of Roland

Pur sun seignur deit hum suffrir granz mals
E endurer e forz freiz e granz calz;
Si'n deit hum perdre de l'sanc e de la carn.

[For his lord a man should suffer great harms and bear both hard frost and great heat. A man should lose both blood and flesh.]

Further, though there is nothing so intimately realistic as the children playing at being Mord and Hrut in *Njalsaga,* there are a few touches which have enormous value in reassuring us that the author of ***Roland*** was close to his own world. When Charles suspects Ganelon of treachery he arrests him and puts him in the custody of the cooks, who hate and insult him. This mention of the "Q" department of the army, slipped in so coolly and suddenly, recalls Homer's mention of the storekeepers in the *Iliad*.The Archbishop, who had seemed nothing but a fighter, at the height of the battle reminds us that there are other kinds of clerics. Speaking of the true knight, he says:

En bataille deit estre forz e fiers,
O altrement ne valt quatre deniers;
Monies deit estre en un de cez mustiers,
Si preierat tuz jurz noz peechiez.

[In battle he should be stout and proud; otherwise he is not worth fourpence. He should be a monk in one of those monasteries where he will pray all six days for our sins.]

There is a wonderful description of the sad and exhausted French army asleep after the rout of the Saracens who have killed Roland. Victory was so complete and exhaustion and grief so great that they do not trouble to post sentinels.

Par tuz les prez or se dorment li Franc:
N'i ad cheval ki poisset estre en estant;
Ki herbe voelt il la prent en gisant.
Mult ad apris ki bien conoist ahan.

[Over all the fields now sleep the French. There is no horse that can keep on its legs; any one that wants to graze does so lying. A man who really knows sorrow has learnt much.]

The realistic touch of the horses too tired to crop the grass standing again reminds of Homer. Sometimes realism and symbolism and the fantastic are blended. One of the great moments of the poem is when the first army of ordinary Saracens, whom Roland and his men have routed, are replaced by blackamoors. Nothing could be less realistic than this replacement. Where could they have found room to advance with an army of dead heaped up round the few surviving Frenchmen? But their colour serves superbly to shadow the coming death of Roland and to suggest that they are a worse type of paynim than that already dealt with. And they are described realistically. . . . In sum the blackamoors create, in a small space, a wonderful sense of diversity.

Another way in which ***Roland*** does much in a small place is through the sudden turn of thought or action in a single line. The passage just quoted about the weary French ended abruptly with the single gnomic line about the discipline of sorrow. Near the beginning of the poem there is the longish episode of Ganelon, on his perilous embassy to the Saracen king, Marsilie, finally agreeing to betray Roland. Marsilie praises him and promises him ten mules loaded with the finest gold of Arabia: "only be certain Roland is in command of the rearguard. If I can catch him in the narrow defiles, he will fight a mortal battle." At which

Guenes respunt: "Mei est vis que trop targe."
Pois est muntez, entret en sun veiage.

[Ganelon answered: "I think I tarry too long."
So he mounted and began his journey.]

That is the right kind of abruptness: it administers a shock and leaves us guessing. Are we to think that Ganelon left in a hurry through self-digust, or fear? Or are his motives irrelevant, the poet merely wanting to close the episode? There is no answer; yet the point is that we should be stirred to ask the questions. Most sublime of all is Roland's sudden call to re-enter into battle after his tragic self-reproaches at having caused the death of so many French lords:

Baruns Franceis, pur mei vus vei murir.
Jo ne vus pois tenser ne guarantir;
Aït vus Deus, ki unkes ne mentit!
Olivier frere, vus ne dei jo faillir;
De doel murrai s'altre ne m'i ocit.
Sire cumpainz, alum i referir.

[It is my fault, barons, that I see you die. I cannot defend or safeguard you. Help you God, who is never false! Brother Oliver, my duty is never to fail you. I shall die of grief, if no one kills me here. Sir comrade, come: let us return to smite the paynims again.]

It is the switch from self-reproach to action coming *within* the speech that is so gloriously surprising. Consider the difference if the poet had put it outside the speech, saying, "And then Roland and Oliver returned together to the battle."

Roland's speech points to what is perhaps the main virtue of the poem: its successful tragic drama. The speech itself is highly dramatic and reminds me of a culminating place in Shakespeare's *King John,* where Falconbridge, deeply perplexed at the death of Arthur and half suspicious of the king, abruptly decides on action and leaves to deal with the king's "thousand businesses." But it is only a part of a larger process of motivation which makes Roland satisfy (in a way that may be unique in medieval narrative verse) Aristotle's requirements for the tragic hero. Roland is the pattern of brave knighthood, but his fault is that his ardour is excessive. His friend Oliver says so when Roland volunteers for the dangerous mission of envoy to the Saracen: he would not make a good envoy because too impetuous. When Charles refuses to send Roland or Oliver or the Archbishop and asks for the nomination of a man from his own district, Roland unguardedly nominates his step-father, Ganelon. When later the French retire from Spain and Charles asks who is to command the rear-guard through the Pyrenees, Ganelon retaliates by nominating Roland. There is much propriety, if nothing conspicuously tragic, in Roland's incurring the price of his own impetuosity. It is when his pride involves others that the real tragedy comes in. The rear-guard Roland commands consists of twenty thousand men and includes all the first knights of France. As they hold the narrows they see a much greater force of Saracens approaching. Oliver implores Roland to sound his horn to recall Charles and the main army. Roland refuses because he will lose glory by so doing. Oliver accepts Roland's decision, though he knows it wrong, with complete loyalty. Later, Roland repents and, all too late, proposes to blow his horn; but now Oliver, as befits the slower and more reflective man, wants to abide by the earlier decision. Nevertheless, Roland has his way. He blows so fiercely that he bursts his brain. When he sees the dead French lords laid out he bitterly repents his rashness. Later, Oliver, near death and not knowing what he does, strikes Roland with his sword; and Roland forgives him. Roland dies last of all the French. The lines of the friends' characters are simple but perfectly true to basic human nature. And there is the entirely adequate irony that if Roland had blown his horn earlier he would not only have saved his fellows but spared bursting his own brain. Here is the true spirit of tragedy.

Lastly, ***Roland*** does indeed speak for a large body of people. . . . [The] essential subject of medieval epic was the Christian one of the earthly pilgrimage leading to salvation and a higher life. Such a conception accorded ill with the vigorous self-assertiveness of a heroic age. In the main the Christian world suppressed this self-assertiveness before evolving a humanism of its own. But before the great intellectual and humanist movements of the thirteenth century there did exist, and in northern France especially, compromise between the violent worldliness of the heroic age and the Christian awareness of another life. The excessive individualism of heroic society was mitigated by high notions of feudal loyalty, while the spiritual integrity on which Christian notions of salvation had at their best been founded was coarsened and simplified into crude visions of a Paradise to be attained by a technical and quite unspiritual fidelity. Thus modified, the primitive and the Christian were able temporarily to coalesce. This coalition was a genuine affair that satisfied men's hearts and enabled them to look round and to arrange some of the things that pressed upon their minds. They could take some stock of the great events that had filled recent centuries. Some of the results were the earliest crusading impulse, the strong, plain, yet neat vigour of Norman architecture, and the ***Song of Roland.***

The facts of history are in ***Roland*** excessively distorted, and yet the poem does in its queer exaggerated way faithfully express the sort of feeling that lingered in men's minds after the tremendous conflicts of Châlons and Tours. The two hundred years of Charlemagne and the immense horde of negroes who are needed for the deaths of the three last French champions are faithful correlatives of a historical epoch that, probably in its day self-blind to its own crucial importance, took on for later ages an overmastering air of the fabulous.

Roland leads the rearguard as the Saracens prepare for ambush in the lower right corner of this fourteenth-century illustration.

I quoted above three lines of one of Roland's speeches about a vassal's duty to his lord. There is another which repeats the sentiment and adds something else; in so doing it represents a whole way of thinking:

> Bien devum ci ester pur nostre rei.
> Pur sun seignur deit hum suffrir destreiz,
> E endurer e granz calz e granz freiz;
> Si'n deit hum perdre e de l'quir e de l'peil.
> Or guart cascuns que granz colps i empleit,
> Male cançun ja cantée n'en seit.
> Paien unt tort e chrestien unt dreit.
> Malvaise essample n'en sera ja de mei.

> [It is indeed our duty to stand here for our king. For his lord a man should suffer pain and bear great heat and great cold. A man should lose both skin and hair. Let each man see to it that he deals great blows that an ill song be never sung about him. Paynims are wrong and Christians are right. A bad example shall never come from *me*.]

There you have the traces of the old unmitigated heroic self-assertion, but softened by the belief that courage should be put to the public service, and given a new turn by a simple uncompromising piety. Nor can I find (with Arnold) that the expression of these great general sentiments is unworthy of them. In their sublime emphasis the last two lines are fit to be compared with Milton's Satan when, reviewing the possibility of submitting to God, he says,

> That Glory never shall his wrath or might
> Extort from me.

(pp. 126-32)

E. M. W. Tillyard, "The Song of Roland," in his The English Epic and Its Background. *Oxford University Press, 1954, pp. 126-33.*

DOROTHY L. SAYERS (essay date 1957)

[An English writer, Sayers is known as an accomplished Dante scholar, a respected writer on Christian themes, and as the creator of Lord Peter Wimsey, the sophisticated detective-hero of such acclaimed mystery novels as Murder Must Advertise *(1933),* The Nine Taylors *(1934), and* Gaudy Night *(1935). In these last-named works, Sayers attempted to fuse the detective story with the novel of manners. In so doing, she not only lent literary respectability to the genre of detective fiction, but also helped pioneer new directions for writers in that field. As a scholar, Sayers is most noted for her translation of Dante's* Divina Commedia *(1949-63; the third volume of this work, unfinished at the time of Sayers's death, was completed by Barbara Reynolds). In the following excerpt from the introduction to her translation of* The Song, *Sayers discusses several important aspects of the poem and provides a comprehensive overview of medieval society.]*

[The] extant ***Chanson de Roland*** is not a chance assembly of popular tales: it is a deliberate and masterly work of art, with a single shaping and constructive brain behind it, marshalling its episodes and its characterisation into an orderly and beautifully balanced whole.

Happily, we may leave scholars to argue about origins: our business is with the poem itself—the ***Song of Roland;*** just one, the earliest, the most famous, and the greatest, of those Old French epics which are called "Songs of Deeds"—*Chansons de Geste*. It is short, as epics go: only just over four thousand lines; and, though it is undoubtedly great literature, it is not in the least "literary." Its very strength and simplicity, its apparent artlessness, may deceive us into thinking it not only "primitive" (which it is) but also "rude" or "naïve," which it is not. Its design has a noble balance of proportion, and side by side with the straightforward thrust-and-hammer of the battle scenes we find a remarkable psychological sublety in the delineation of character and motive. But all this is left for us to find; the poet is chanting to a large mixed audience which demands a quick-moving story with plenty of action, and he cannot afford the time for long analytical digressions in the manner of a Henry James or a Marcel Proust.

The style of epic is, in fact, rather like the style of drama: the characters enter, speak, and act, with the minimum of stage-setting and of comment by the narrator. From time to time a brief "stage-direction" informs us that this person is "rash" and the other "prudent," that so-and-so is "angry" or "grieved," or has "cunningly considered what he has to say." But for the most part we have to watch and listen and work out for ourselves the motives which prompt the characters and the relationship between them. We are seldom shown their thoughts or told anything about them which is not strictly relevant to the action. Some points are never cleared up. Thus we are never told what is the original cause of the friction between Roland and his stepfather; not until the very end of the poem does Ganelon hint that "Roland had wronged [him] in wealth and in estate," and we are left to guess at the precise nature of the alleged injury. Very likely it was all part of the original legend and already well-known to the audience; or the traditional jealousy between stepparent and stepchild, so familiar in folklore, could be taken for granted. But we do not really need to know these details. The general situation is made sufficiently clear to us in the first words Roland and Ganelon speak. The opening scenes of the poem are indeed a model of what an exposition should be. The first stanza tells us briefly what the military situation is; the scene of Marsilion's council gets the action going and shows us that the Saracens are ready for any treacherous business; the great scene of Charlemagne's council introduces all the chief actors on the Christian side and sketches swiftly and surely the main lines of their characters and the position in which they stand to one another: Charlemagne—at the same time cautious and peremptory; Roland, brave to the point of rashness, provocative, arrogant with the naïve egotism of the epic hero, loyal, self-confident, and open as the day; Oliver, equally brave, but prudent and blunt, and well aware of his friend's weaknesses; Duke Naimon, old and wise in council; Turpin, the fighting archbishop, with his consideration for others and his touch of ironic humour; Ganelon, whose irritable jealousy unchains the whole catastrophe. Ganelon is not a coward, as he proves later on in the poem, and his advice to conclude a peace is backed up by all his colleagues. But it is unfortunate that, after Roland has pointed out that the proposed mission is dangerous and that Marsilion is not to be trusted, he does not at once volunteer to bell the cat himself. He lets others get in first. Charlemagne vetoes their going, and so shows that he too is aware of the danger and doubtful about Marsilion. Then Roland names Ganelon—and coming when it does, and from him, the thing has the air of a challenge. And Charlemagne does not veto Ganelon—infuriating proof that he values him less than Naimon or Turpin, less than Roland or any of the Twelve Peers. Ganelon's uneasy vanity reacts instantly: "This is a plot to get rid of me"—and Roland (who has quite certainly never had any such idea in his simple mind) bursts out laughing. That finishes it. Rage and spite and jealousy, and the indignity of being publicly put to shame, overthrow a character which is already emotionally unstable. Self-pity devours him; he sees himself mortally injured and persecuted. He is obsessed by a passion to get even with Roland at the price of every consideration of honour and duty, and in total disregard of the consequences. The twentieth century has found a word for Ganelon: he is a paranoiac. The eleventh-century poet did not know the word, but he has faithfully depicted the type.

What is interesting and dramatic in the poet's method is the way in which the full truth about Ganelon only emerges gradually as the story proceeds. We are kept in suspense about him. We cannot at first be certain whether he is a brave man or a coward. When he refuses, with a magnificent gesture, to let the men of his household accompany him to Saragossa—"Best go alone, not slay good men with me"—are we to take the words at their face-value? Is it not rather that he does not want witnesses to the treachery that he is plotting? It is, indeed. Only when, after deliberately working up the fury of the Saracens to explosion-point, he draws his sword and "sets his back to the trunk of the pine," do we realise that, so far from being a coward, he is a cool and hardy gambler, ready to stake his life in the highly dangerous game he is playing. Even when at last brought to judgement, he remains defiant, brazenly admitting the treachery, claiming justification, and spitting out accusations against Roland. If his nerve fails him, it is not till the last moment when his own head and hands can no longer serve him, and he cries to his kinsman Pinabel: "I look to you to get me out of this!" There is a hint of it, but no more.

Ganelon, like all his sort, is a fluent and plausible liar, but this, too, we only realise by degrees. His first accusations of Roland are obviously founded on fact: Roland *is* rash, quarrelsome, arrogant, and his manner to his stepfather suggests that the dislike is not all on one side. The tale Ganelon tells Blancandrin about Roland's boastful behaviour with the apple is entirely in character—invention or fact, it has nothing improbable about it. Ganelon's offensive report of Charlemagne's message certainly goes far beyond the truth, but it may, for all we know, truly express what Ganelon believes to be Charlemagne's intentions; even the further invented details *may* only be "intelligent anticipation." So far we may give Ganelon the benefit of the doubt. But when he returns to the Emperor's camp and explains his failure to bring back the Caliph as hostage by a long, picturesque, and circumstantial story which we know to be a flat lie from first to last, then we know where we are. And after that, we are not inclined to believe in the apple-story, or in Ganelon's alleged wrongs, or in anything else he says.

Similarly, we may accept, and even admire, throughout the council-scene and the scenes with Blancandrin and Marsilion, Ganelon's scrupulous deference and fervent loyalty to the Emperor. If nothing is too bad for Roland, nothing is too good for Charlemagne; this is the voice of the faithful vassal uplifted in praise of his liege-lord. But when the plot has been laid and is going well, then, as he rides homeward with Charlemagne, they hear the sound he never thought to hear again—the blast of Roland's horn. "Listen!" says Charlemagne, "our men are fighting." Ganelon answers with scarcely veiled insolence: "If any man but yourself said this, it would be a lie." And when the Emperor insists, the insolence breaks out undisguised:

> "You're growing old, your hair is sere and white;
> When you speak thus you're talking like a child."

There is in him neither faith nor truth nor courtesy; for all his wit and courage, he is rotten through and through. Yet perhaps he was not always so; he had won the love of his men, and the French held him for a noble baron; there must have been some good in the man before the worm of envy gnawed it all away.

> Before the King stood forth Count Ganelon;
> Comely his body and fresh his colour was;
> A right good lord he'd seem, were he not false.

So the poet sums him up and leaves him.

The portrait of Charlemagne is partly stylised by a number of legendary and numinous attributes belonging to his status as the sacred Emperor. The holiness of the Imperial function, handed down from Constantine through Justinian to the emperors of the West, hovers about him still. He is of unfathomable age—or rather, he is ageless and timeless, for his son and nephew are both young men: his flowing white beard, his strength unimpaired by "two hundred years and more," are hieratic and patriarchal in their symbolism; he is God's vicegerent, the Father of all Christendom, the earthly image of the Ancient of Days. Angels converse with Charlemagne, and the power from on high over-shadows him.

Beneath this larger-than-life-size figure, we discern another: the portrait of the ideal earthly sovereign—just, prudent, magnanimous, and devout. In Charlemagne, the poet has done his best to depict for us the early-mediaeval notion of what we should now call a "constitutional" monarch. He "is not hasty to reply"; he does nothing except by the advice of his Council; he has (it seems) the right to veto any proposition before it has been put to the vote, but once it has received the unanimous assent of the Council, he is bound by that decision, whether he personally approves of it or not. In this, he is carefully contrasted with the Saracen king Marsilion, who conducts most of his negotiations himself, and is at one point restrained with difficulty from throwing his javelin at an ambassador; and also with the Emir Baligant, who, when he calls a Council, merely announces his own intentions, whereupon the councillors advise him to do what he has already said he is going to do. By some writers, Charlemagne's constitutional behaviour has been reckoned as a sign of weakness; but I do not think that is at all what the poet meant. He appears to consider it very proper conduct in a monarch, though we may be doubtful about the extent to which it reflects the behaviour of any actual monarch in the feudal era. It comes much nearer to that of an English sovereign today, giving his assent to a bill duly passed by both Houses; he may doubt its wisdom, but he will not for that reason withhold his signature.

Beneath all this again is the personal character of Charlemagne—his stately bearing, his courtesy, his valour and strength, his deep religious feeling, his friendship for Naimon, his warm affection for his nephew and the Peers, and all the "young bachelors" whom he calls "his sons." He rides and fights among his barons as the greatest baron of them all.

Here too, I think we must not reckon it weakness in him that he is overcome by grief for Roland's death, that he faints upon the body and has to be raised up by the barons and supported by them while he utters his lament. There are fashions in sensibility as in everything else. The idea that a strong man should react to great personal and national calamities by a slight compression of the lips and by silently throwing his cigarette into the fireplace is of very recent origin. By the standards of feudal epic, Charlemagne's behaviour is perfectly correct. Fainting, weeping, and lamenting is what the situation calls for. The assembled knights and barons all decorously follow his example. . . . We may take this response as being ritual and poetic; grief, like everything else in the Epic, is displayed on the heroic scale. Though men of the eleventh century did, in fact, display their emotions much more openly than we do, there is no reason to suppose that they made a practice of fainting away in chorus. But the gesture had their approval; that was how they liked to think of people behaving. In every age, art holds up to us the standard pattern of exemplary conduct, and real life does it best to conform. From Charlemagne's weeping and fainting we can draw no conclusions about his character except that the poet has represented him as a perfect model of the "man of feeling" in the taste of the period.

Compared with the subtleties of Ganelon, Roland's character is simplicity itself. Rash, arrogant, generous, outspoken to a fault, loyal, affectionate, and single-minded, he has all the qualities that endear a captain to his men and a romantic hero to his audience. He has no subtlety at all; other men's minds are a closed book to him. He refuses at first to believe in Ganelon's treachery, and when the truth is forced upon him he can only suppose that the crime was committed "for gold." He never really understands why Oliver is angry with him, nor how much his own pride and folly have contributed to the disaster of Roncevaux. He has the naïve egotism of an Achilles, which will wreck a campaign for a piece of personal pride; but he is a much pleasanter person than Achilles. He never sulks or bears a grudge; he endures Oliver's reproaches with a singular sweetness of temper. Beneath all his "over-weening" there is a real modesty of heart, and a childlike simplicity of love and loyalty—to God, to the Emperor, to his friend, to his men, to his horse, his horn, his good sword Durendal. His death-scene is curiously moving.

But the picture that remains most vividly with us is that of gay and unconquerable youth. No other epic hero strikes this note so ringingly. . . . (pp. 10-16)

So he rides out, into that new-washed world of clear sun and glittering colour which we call the Middle Age (as though it were middle-aged), but which has perhaps a better right than the blown summer of the Renaissance to be called the Age of Re-birth. It is a world full of blood and grief and death and naked brutality, but also of frank emotions, innocent simplicities, and abounding self-confidence—a world with which we have so utterly lost touch that we have fallen into using the words "feudal" and "mediaeval" as mere epithets for outer darkness. Anyone who sees gleams of brightness in that world is accused of romantic nostalgia for a Golden Age which never existed. But the figure of Roland stands there to give us the lie: he is the Young Age as that age saw itself. Compared with him, the space-adventures and glamour-boys of our times, no less than the hardened toughs of Renaissance epic, seem to have been born middle-aged.

"Roland is fierce, and Oliver is wise." Oliver is Roland's "companion"—brought up with him, according to the practice of the time, sharing his pursuits and training—and he displays something of that blunt, hard-headed common-sense which is the traditional characteristic of the "hero's friend." Wisdom, in the sense of practical prudence, is a valuable, but not a showy or perhaps a very endearing quality. It is the disastrous Mary Stuarts of history, not the cautious and thrifty Elizabeth Tudors, who flame their way through the pages of ballad and romance. Oliver is a sounder soldier than Roland—more concerned with military necessities than with his own prestige. He mounts a hill before the battle to find out how many enemies they have to reckon with—an action which, by *chanson de geste* standards, scarcely becomes a gentleman; finding the odds unreasonable, he urges Roland to summon assistance—a thing which that hero considers to be beneath his dignity. He goes grimly and gallantly to a task which he knows to be impossible, but he cherishes no illusions, and is unromantic enough to feel no pleasure in the knowledge that "someone had blundered." He has not Roland's sunny disposition; he is capable of cherishing resentment, and when his forebodings have proved all too true, he has a regrettable tendency to say, "I told you so." . . . (p. 17)

He has his own pride. It flashes out, sullen and embittered, when Roland, seeing the rear-guard reduced from twenty thousand men to sixty, proposes at long last to summon Charlemagne. "When I told you to do it, you would not; if you had, you would have saved the day and saved our men. To do it now (i.e. when there is nobody to save but ourselves) would be shameful." The Archbishop intervenes, saying that although nobody can now be saved, Charlemagne can avenge them and give them all Christian burial. To this excellent argument Oliver submits in silence. He is a very reasonable young man.

The figure of Archbishop Turpin is "historical" in the same sense that those of Charlemagne and Roland are historical; that is to say, there actually was an Archbishop Tilpinus of Rheims at the end of the eighth century, but his portrait in the poem probably owes more to imagination than to fact. Not that it is an altogether impossible portrait—the warrior-priest is not unknown to Christian history; but Turpin is surely *hors concours* ["with no possible rivals"], both for prowess and for personal charm. The poet treats him with very special honour: in the first assault of the Saracens he is given a distinguished place, immediately after Roland and Oliver; in the second assault he has the honour of "opening the battle"; and he is the last left to stand beside Roland when all the rest are slain. Turpin belongs to an age, which, when the ***Song of Roland*** was made, was already passing—an age when the secular priest lived very close to the laity. At a later period, Turpin's slighting reference to the life of the cloister would have come very oddly from an Archbishop's lips; "evidently," as Marc Bloch remarks, "the Gregorian reform had not yet got round" to our poet. Yet, when the French cry: "Well doth our Bishop defend us with his crook!" (or, more literally, "In our Archbishop the crozier is strong to save"), the words are meant in a double sense. With all his fighting qualities, Turpin is a good churchman and a good pastor. He is wise in council; with strong good sense and mild but firm authority he composes the quarrel between Roland and Oliver; his address to the troops is a model of brevity and simple piety, and he takes his priestly duties seriously; his last dying action is a heroic attempt to aid another. (pp. 18-19)

This is perhaps the right place at which to speak of the essential Christianity of the poem. It is not merely Christian in subject; it is Christian to its very bones. Nowhere does the substratum of an older faith break through the Christian surface, as it does, for example, in *Beowulf*. There is no supernatural except the Christian supernatural, and that works (as being fully Christian it must) only to influence men's minds and actions, and not to provide a machinery for the story. And it is a Christianity as naïve and uncomplicated as might be found at any time in the simplest village church. These violent men of action are called on to do their valiant duty to the Faith and to the Emperor; and when they die, they will be taken to lie on beds of flowers among—strangely but somehow appropriately—the Holy Innocents, in a Paradise inhabited by God and His angels. They make their prayers directly to God Himself—no saints are invoked, not even, I think, the Mother of God; it is as simple as that.

Simplicity does not mean ignorance. The poet is not likely to have been a monk or an ecclesiastic in major orders, but he was "clerkly" enough to be acquainted with the lections and liturgy of the Church, and his theology, so far as it goes, is correct. But like most of his Christian contemporaries he has only the vaguest ideas about the Moslem religion. For him, Saracens are just "Paynims" (i.e. Pagans) and therefore (most inappropriately) idolaters. They worship an "infernal trinity," very oddly made up of Mahound (Mohammed), Termagant (a diabolic personage of obscure origin) and—rather unexpectedly—Apollo, who is in process of degenerating into the "foul fiend Apollyon" familiar to us from *The Pilgrim's Progress*. The images of these "false gods" are carried before the Saracen armies, and worshipped on bended knees; when disaster overtakes the Paynim cause they are abused, and maltreated after the manner of savage fetishes. The "law" (i.e. doctrine) of "Mahound and Termagant" is contained in a book, though it is not clear whether the poet is aware of the existence of the Koran, or is merely supposing, on the analogy of the Bible, that every religion must have a sacred book of some kind.

(That the ignorance was mutual may be seen by anybody who cares to examine the account of Christian worship and customs given in parts of the *Thousand Nights and a Night*.)

Some slight attempt is made to differentiate Oriental manners from those of the Occident. The Paynim King, Marsilion, holds his council lying down on a dais or divan, whereas Charlemagne sits upright on a faldstool (chair, or throne); the use of darts and other throwing-weapons is confined to the Saracen armies; and the description of the taking of Saragossa suggests that the poet had in mind the great walled cities of Moslem Spain, where the art of fortification was much more advanced with in Northern Europe. It is also perhaps significant that the Emir Baligant is made to promise his warriors not only booty but "fair women" as the reward of valour. Generally speaking, however, Moslem society is deemed to conform more or less closely to that of the West, and is credited with much the same kind of feudal structure. Nor is the Christian poet ungenerous to the enemy. Marsilion is, of course, treacherous, and the autocracy of the Emir is contrasted with the "constitutional" monarchy of Charlemagne; but prowess and personal courage are plentiful on both sides, and though many of the Saracen champions hail from the sinister and mysterious territories abounding in devils and sorcerers, they make no unfair military use of magical aids; it is all good, clean fighting. The great and chivalrous figure of Saladin had not yet risen up to compel the admiration of the Franks, but the reputation of the Moslem fighter stood high, and is ungrudgingly admitted. . . . Roland and his Peers are not merely overwhelmed by numbers; they are given foemen worthy of their steel. This is as it should be; you cannot make an epic out of a conflict where all the heroic qualities are on one side.

The battle-scenes are described with immense relish and, from our point of view, at rather tedious length. We must remember that for mediaeval people warfare was not only a calling but the greatest of all sports. They enjoyed the details of fights and the enumeration of the various warriors engaged as we today enjoy a running commentary upon a Test Match or a Cup-Tie Final, with biographical notes upon the players.

The fighting is all done upon horseback, and only the "noble" weapons of spear and sword are employed. There is no mention of foot-soldiers, or of the archers who played so large a part in the Battle of Hastings. This is partly due to the epic convention, but it is also historically true that at this period the most important part in a battle was played by the cavalry charge. Neither was it in fact very desirable to encumber an army with great numbers of infantry, especially in a foreign country; speed of movement was essential when long distances had to be traversed over few and bad roads, with poor facilities for transport and victualling.

Of the activities of the rank-and-file we are not told much, beyond that, in a general way, "the French" or "the Paynims" exchange good blows in the mellay; the emphasis is all placed on personal encounters between the leaders on either side. We shall notice the same thing is sober historical accounts of mediaeval battles. This, again, is not merely a convention, still less is it (as some writers would have us believe) the manifestations of an "undemocratic" spirit or a contempt for the common man. There was a very practical reason for it. Under the feudal system, it was the duty of every great lord to serve the King in battle, bringing with him so many armed vassals, each of whom in turn brought so many lesser vassals of his own, and so on down the whole scale of hierarchy. Each vassal was bound by oath of allegiance to his own lord and to his own lord only, "while their lives should last"; consequently, if a great lord was killed in battle, his followers were automatically released from their allegiance; they could—and some did—retire from the conflict and take no more part in it. Similarly, if he was taken prisoner or fled from the field, they were left without leader and tended to disintegrate. Hence it was of enormous importance that a lord should lead his men boldly, fight with conspicuous bravery and (if possible) not get killed, or even unhorsed, lest his followers should lose sight of him and become discouraged. This is why Ganelon is so insistent that, if only Roland can be got rid of, the flower of the French army, most of whom are Roland's vassals, will melt away; and this is why, when Marsilion is wounded and flees, the whole Saracen army turns tail. Similarly, when, in the final great battle, the Emperor Charlemagne and the Emir Baligant, lord of all Islam, meet face to face, the whole issue of the war hangs upon their encounter. Baligant falls; and the entire Paynim army at once flees the field.

The poem is called ***The Song of Roland,*** but only the first half of it deals with the exploits of Roland himself. He dies at the end of his great stand with the rear-guard against the treacherous assault of King Marsilion. The remainder of the story is concerned with the vengeance which Charlemagne takes for his death, and for the slaughter of the other eleven Peers and the twenty thousand French who are slain with them. By the standards of the time, the tale would be left incomplete without the vengeance, and the name of Charlemagne would be left under a cloud, for to allow the slaying of one's vassal or kinsman to go unavenged was held to be a very shameful thing. But there is more to it than that; there is a question which concerns the whole scope and function of epic, and of the ***Roland***'s right to bear that majestic title.

When, as an undergraduate, I first "did" ***The Song of Roland,*** I accepted easily enough the then-fashionable verdict upon the second part of the poem. "I cannot," said Gustave Lanson [in *Histoire de la littérature française* (1894)], "but range himself on the side of those who think that the revenge of Charlemagne upon the Emir Baligant and his Marsilion is a shabby (*mesquin*) addition, designed to flatter national vanity at the expense of the poetry." Re-reading the poem, after an interval of forty years, for the purpose of translating it, I have found it quite impossible so to range myself. (pp. 19-23)

[If] we examine Lanson's statement in the light of the ***Roland*** itself, we shall notice that he has actually got the facts the wrong way round. It is not the second part of the poem but the first that appeals to national vanity. The famous rear-guard is composed entirely of "Frenchmen of France"; when Marsilion asks on whom Charlemagne relies for his military victories, Ganelon answers: "Upon the French"; the Emperor in council "does nothing but by advice of the French." The war itself is at first presented to us as a struggle for power between (admittedly) Saracen Spain and Christian France, but, for all that, chiefly between Spain and France. It is only when the flower of the French chivalry lies dead in Roncevaux, and Marsilion has fled, mortally wounded, to Saragossa, that there loom up behind the figures of the French champions and the Spanish King the more august images of Emperor and Emir, West and East, Christ and Islam. The world expands before our eyes: we look beyond Saragossa to Alexandria and fabled Babylon; "from forty kingdoms" Baligant summons his powers. And now, embattled alongside the French, for the first time we see "the Franks," and hear the voice of all Christendom. (p. 24)

So the grand outline of the poem defines itself; a private war is set within a national war, and the national war again within the world-war of Cross and Crescent. The small struggle at the centre shakes the whole web. The evil that is done can never be undone. God is vindicated, Marsilion and Baligant slain, Saragossa taken, its inhabitants set to choose between death and baptism, Queen Bramimonda peaceably converted; but Roland is dead, and the Peers are dead, and to the war between Belief and Unbelief there is no ending. Marsilion had asked concerning Charlemagne: "He is old; when will he weary of going to the wars?" And Ganelon had replied: "Never, while Roland lives. If Roland were dead we should have peace." It was a lie. Old as he is, and bereft of his best help, Charlemagne is Christ's vassal still. "Never to Paynims may I show love or peace." The Angel summons him, and go he must.

> Small heart had Carlon to journey and to fight;
> "God!" says the King, "how weary is my life!"
> He weeps, he plucks his flowing beard and white.
>
> Here ends the geste—

It ends, like the *Iliad* and *Aeneid,* in a minor key, and on a falling cadence. I do not think it has anything to fear from the comparison. (pp. 25-6)

• • • • •

The word "mediaeval" is often loosely used to cover the whole period from the end of the Dark Ages (about the ninth century) to the beginning of the Renaissance (about the sixteenth century), and it is easy to get the impression that throughout that period European society remained much of a muchness, and was all more or less organized upon the "feudal system." That is not the case, although, of course, relics of feudalism have remained embedded in our social and legal machinery to the present day. But the genuinely feudal organization is already beginning to break up almost everywhere by about the eleventh century (the time when the ***Song of Roland*** was first written down), to yield to a more centralized type of government under the greatly increased power of the crown. By the middle of the twelfth century the whole face of society has been transformed—there is a new learning, a new literature, a new convention of behaviour as between men and women, new manners, new costumes, new armour, new interests, new developments in church and castle, camp and court. It is of these that we usually think when we hear the phrase "the Middle Ages," because story and picture have made them familiar to us. But the ***Song of Roland*** belongs to a very much more unsophisticated period, when the extreme insecurity of life made martial prowess the most necessary of all manly virtues, and it was every baron's business to be a tower of strength to the dwellers on his own land. Thus the feudal structure, as it emerged, rather than was deliberately organized, from the prevailing conditions, was that of a society permanently geared to warfare; and its songs and stories are almost all about brave warriors and heroic deeds in battle—not about ladies or enchanters or other-world adventures, like the romances of chivalry which were to take their place. The world of the French *chanson de geste* is pre-eminently a man's world—more so than the world of Homer, or that of Celtic folktale or even of the Scandinavian epic. Occasionally, indeed, a woman makes her appearance—sometimes a strong-minded lady like Guiborc, the wife of Guillaume d'Orange, as capable of keeping her husband's castle in his absence as of cooking him gargantuan meals when he returns from the battlefield; sometimes an unhappy victim of the chances of war, like fair Aude in the ***Song of Roland;*** sometimes, like the Saracen queen Bramimonda, a spirited woman with but little scope for her energies. But no powerful emotions are focused upon these female characters. The relationships which touch the heart are those which bind the vassal to his lord and the fighting man to his friend and companion in arms. The tie between fellow-soldiers has always been a strong one, and never more so than when war involves absence from home for years at a time, without letters or leave. The relationship between a Roland and an Oliver has the glamour, as well as the depth and devotion, of a love bond. But there is nothing morbid or sentimental about it. The present century has contrived so to cheapen all human relationships that it is difficult to find an unambiguous word for this strong blend of affection, admiration, and loyalty between two men. "Friendship" is a little too cool; "mutual hero-worship" a little too adolescent in its over-tones. To us, the most striking thing about it is perhaps the note of grave and formal courtesy which dignifies it from first to last; in grief or joy, in anger or in fondness, in fighting or in dying the mode of address is always: "Fair sir, companion." (pp. 29-31)

• • • • •

The social structure of the feudal age was founded upon vassalage. This was, at any rate in its origins, a *personal* bond of mutual service and protection between a lord (*seigneur*) and his dependant, and was affirmed by an oath and the rite of "homage." The vassal placed his hands, joined, as in prayer, between the hands of the lord, and swore to be "his man" (*homme*) so long as they both should live; after which the two parties kissed each other upon the mouth. Both parts of the rite clearly symbolize the reciprocity of the relationship—the submissive and the enfolding hands, and the mutual kiss. The vassal undertook to be faithful to his lord, and to serve him in a variety of ways, including (what is chiefly to our purpose here) the duty of following him to war with as many armed men chosen from his own dependents, as his wealth and rank made obligatory. The duty of the lord was to protect his vassal in life and avenge him in death, to do justice between him and his fellow-vassals, and to maintain and reward him for his services. *Maintenance* was of two kinds. In the one (*provende*), the vassal was taken into the lord's household, where he was lodged, fed, clothed, and generally "provided for" at the lord's expense. Such vassals constituted the lord's "household" or "meinie" (*maisnée*) and stood in a peculiarly personal relationship to him. The other way was called "*chasement,*" literally "housing (*casa*)"; the vassal was given a dwelling, that is to say a piece of land, from the revenues of which he was expected to maintain himself. Remuneration for services, particularly remuneration in the shape of a grant of land, was called a "fief" or "feu"—a word which has given its name to the "feudal" system. In process of time, such fiefs became hereditary, but at the beginning of the feudal period they were held only by a life tenure. The granting of a fief was symbolized by the handing-over, before witnesses, of a token—sometimes a written deed, more often a sod of turf, a straw, or (in the case of an important military appointment) a staff or standard: in a German manuscript of the *Rolandslied,* Charlemagne is shown handing Roland a standard in token of his investiture of the Marches of Spain. In the ***Chanson de Roland*** the token most commonly used for the grant or surrender of a fief is a glove.

The handing-over of a visible token as the sign of an appointment or agreement is, of course, of very great antiquity, and seems to have had two main purposes. It could be shown as evidence of the authority intrusted to one: "I come from the King; here is his king, (staff, banner, glove, or what-not) to prove it." This was particularly useful in a society where few people knew how to read. But it was also employed as a means of impressing the occasion upon the memory of participants and bystanders alike. In the same spirit, the wits of youthful witnesses to a transaction were stimulated by a smart box on the ear—as being something that they were not likely to forget in a hurry—and the glove itself may possibly represent a "token buffet" of this kind. The tokens used in the ***Roland*** include the glove (for a fief, as above), the glove and wand (for the appointment of an envoy, or messenger), and the bow which Charlemagne hands to Roland when appointing him the command of the rear-guard.

. . . . .

As used in the poem, the words "knight," "chivalry" (*chevalier, chevalerie*) do not necessarily mean men who have been admitted, by dubbing with the sword, into a formal "order" of knighthood. Neither, in spite of the derivation from *cheval,* do they simply correspond to our "horseman, cavalry." A *chevalier* is always a mounted warrior, but not every mounted warrior is a *chevalier,* for squires, sergeants, and the greater part of the army marched, and many of them also fought, on horseback. The distinguishing mark of the *chevalier* is the combination of the war-horse, or destrier, with the full equipment of arms and armour appropriate to a man of wealth and standing: the steel helmet, the metal body-armour (mail hauberk, or byrny reinforced with steel plates), the shield, the spear, and the sword. . . . A steel mare was sometimes added, though there is no mention of this in the ***Roland.*** The lower ranks were more lightly equipped, with leathern or quilted body-armour, and their horses were of correspondingly lighter build. Thus a great lord would ride to battle, followed by the knights of his household and the chief vassals belonging to his fief, who would themselves be followed by their own vassals, many of whom might also be of knightly status, and all would be attended by followers of lesser ranks, down to the serfs and peasant-proprietors who owed military service to the lords whose "men" they were. The military service demanded from the tillers of the soil was as a rule confined to a comparatively small number of days in the year, and the defence of home territory. When it came to prolonged campaigns abroad, further inducements had to be offered. The lord was always responsible for his men's food and upkeep when in the field; he might also distribute gifts in cash or kind; but the recompense that everyone, from the highest to the lowest, chiefly looked forward to was the division of the spoils of war. The arms of the vanquished, the ransom of prisoners, the tribute of the conquered, and the wealth of sacked cities, were the rewards of victory—hence the stress laid on booty ("silver and gold, and goodly battle-gear"), upon the valuable gifts (lions and bears, horses and hounds, mules laden with gold) offered by Marsilion as the price of a peace-treaty, and on the richness of all the armour described (helmets gemmed with gold, gold-plated saddles with silver saddle-bows, swords with jewelled hilts, and so forth). We may, however, note that, apart from such references as these, the general tone of the poem, and the behaviour of all the characters, is chivalrous, disinterested, and governed by a strict sense of military propriety; nobody wastes time, as Homeric warriors so often do, by stopping in the middle of a battle to strip the corpse of his adversary. Behind the savage simplicity of the battle-scenes, one feels a strict sense of decorum at work.

. . . . .

"You will observe the Rules of Battle, of course," said the White Knight to the Red Knight; and Alice, you may remember, said to herself as she watched the fight: "One Rule seems to be that, if one Knight hits the other he knocks him off his horse, and if he misses, he tumbles off himself." The Knights would have stood a very poor chance in an eleventh-century battle, where, if you were to survive at all, it was of paramount importance to keep your horse on its legs and yourself on its back. If you were knocked off, or fell off, you ran an imminent risk of either being trampled to death, or having your throat cut by any man-at-arms who happened to be handy. The mediaeval saddle, with its long stirrups, padded seat, and high bows before and behind, was designed to keep you firmly in your place—not like the modern racing saddle, to enable you to slip easily from a falling horse. The poet expressly mentions that when Roland faints in the saddle from pain and loss of blood, "he would have fallen, but was held upright by the stirrups." If the thrust of a spear bore you backwards, you were supported by the saddle-bow behind; if a heavy blow from a sword laid you flat on the horse's neck, you clung to the saddle-bow in front. The bursting of the saddle-girth was a major disaster, bringing you infallibly to the ground. This accident occurs twice in ***Roland,*** but on each occasion in a single combat and (by a happy symmetry) to both combatants simultaneously, so that they have time and room to extricate themselves and carry on.

We may, however, distinguish certain rules—or it might be better to say, a certain pattern—of battle characteristic of these epic encounters. Something must be allowed for poetic stylisation, but the general outline is probably founded upon actual practice. A fight which goes to its full length, is, ideally, a formal composition in six movements:

1. *The Defiance:* When two combatants meet face to face, the challenger opens the proceedings with a threat or insult.

2. *The Encounter with the Spear:* In the ***Roland,*** all the combatants use the spear in the modern fashion (*escrime nouvelle*): the spear is held firmly under the right arm, with the point directed at the adversary's breast or helmet, the aim being either to pierce him through, or to hurl him from the saddle by weight and speed as the horses rush together. In the Bayeux Tapestry, which is roughly of the same date as the ***Roland,*** both the old (*escrime ancienne*) and the modern fashion are shown together, some knights being depicted with the right arms raised above head-level, using the spear as a throwing-weapon. It will be noticed that the spears thus thrown have plain shafts, whereas most of those used in the modern *escrime* are adorned with a pennon of gonfalon just below the point exactly as described in the ***Roland***.

3. *The Encounter with the Sword (a) on Horseback.* If the spears are shattered without decisive result, and no squire is at hand to supply fresh ones, the combatants draw their swords to continue the fight. The sword of the period was a single-handed weapon, but it was not unusual to take both hands to it in order to deliver a particularly heavy blow, letting loose the bridle, and leaving the trained destrier to do his own work. The edge, not the point, of the blade was used, the weapon being brought down, if possible, on the opponent's head. If the blow was parried, or glanced off the steel helm, it might light upon the shoulder, inflicting a mortal wound or disabling the right arm. It is by a glancing blow of this kind that Roland

severs Marsilion's right hand at the wrist and puts him out of action.

The Encounter with the Sword (b) on Foot: If the combatants are unhorsed and are able to scramble to their feet, the sword-fight is continued on foot by the same method of hacking and hewing. [Sayers adds in a footnote: "If you unhorsed your opponent without falling yourself, it was sometimes prudent as well as chivalrous to dismount also, lest he should kill or disable your mount. This situation does not occur in the ***Roland,*** but in the *Geste* of the *Couronnement de Louis,* the hero, Guillaume Court-nez, is particularly praised for his valour in that, when contending on foot against a mounted adversary, he refrains from attacking the horse. To do so would be the obvious way of lessening the odds against him, but he would consider it unknightly behaviour—and besides, he wants the horse himself, having lost his own!"]

4. *The Mutual Summons to Surrender:* In a prolonged single combat, such as that between Charlemagne and Baligant, or in the formal Trial by Ordeal of Battle between Thierry and Pinabel, there is often a pause to recover breath. This is the moment at which it is proper for each combatant to summon the other to surrender upon terms. If both refuse, the fight is continued till one or other is vanquished.

5. *The Death-Blow:* When one adversary is disarmed or otherwise put out of action, the victor either summons him to surrender at discretion, or delivers the death-blow. In the ***Roland,*** every fight is to the death (*à outrance*), it having been announced that no prisoners will be taken.

6. *The Victor's Boast:* Having killed your enemy, you encourage yourself and your men by hurling insults at his dead body. This custom is not altogether in accordance with English notions of sportsmanship, but is part of the correct procedure in all early epic. In Homer, the Boast, like the Defiance, is often elaborated into a lengthy speech; in the ***Roland,*** it consists as a rule only of a line or so, hardly amounting to more than the "Take that, you b—!" which even modern standards may allow to be excusable in the heat of conflict.

Needless to say, it was held treacherous and unknightly to attack a man from behind. Oliver, Roland's companion, and too peerless a champion to be allowed by the poet to perish in a straight fight, is killed by a foul blow of this kind.

. . . . .

Over and above the general bond of vassalage, there are also the special ties which bind a man to the lord who has "nurtured" him, and to the man who is his "companion." It was the ancient custom to send a boy of good family to be brought up ("nurtured," or "fostered") in the household of one's overlord, where he received such education as was to be had, learned good manners, and was trained in arms, sports, and horsemanship. Two boys thus bred up side by side from early youth, and competing together in their work and play, would become special friends, or "companions"; and this intimacy and friendly rivalry would be continued in after life. The affection between companions, and that between the lord and the lads nurtured in his house was a very strong one, frequently overshadowing those of blood-relationship. Thus we hear of the "young bachelors" of Charlemagne's household, "whom he calls his 'sons'"; and we see how Roland's thoughts in his death-hour go, not only to "the men of his line," but also to "his Lord, Charlemayn, who'd bred him from a child," and in especial to his "companion," Oliver. It will be noticed also that each of the Twelve Peers has a special "companion," so that the names nearly always go together in pairs: Gerin and Gerier, Ives and Ivor, Othon and Berenger, Anseis and Sanson; (the remaining pair, Gerard of Roussillon and Engelier of Bordeaux presumably pair off together, though their "companionage" is not specially mentioned—perhaps because Gerard is represented as being an old man). (pp. 31-7)

Dorothy L. Sayers, in an introduction to The Song of Roland, *translated by Dorothy L. Sayers, Penguin Books Inc., 1957, pp. 7-44.*

STEPHEN G. NICHOLS, JR. (essay date 1961)

[An American educator and author, Nichols has written extensively on medieval literature. In the following excerpt, he explores Roland's characterization through an analysis of his behavior at Roncevaux.]

[In] the Roncevaux episode, the *jongleur* had posed a conflict which he did not really have the means to express fully. For the conflict—whether to fight or summon aid—is really a psychological one which only Roland as captain of the rearguard, can decide. As presented in *laisses* LXXXIII-LXXXVIII, it seems to be a dialogue between Roland and Oliver in which each represents an opposing view. . . . [There] is no third party intervention to resolve the issue, and it is Roland himself in *laisses* CXXVII-CXXIX who proposes the plan which he had previously opposed. He has obviously changed his mind, which implies a psychological process, although the external events have some bearing on his decision. But nowhere does the poet mention Roland as "thinking" about this problem. Furthermore, Roland, on the second occasion, uses combinations of the same formulas Oliver had used when he first urged Roland to sound his horn. The implications of the conflict within Roland underlie the whole Roncevaux episode and influence the action to the next part. It is clear, then, that the problem has a dramatic importance much greater than its explicit presentation would indicate. (p. 36)

The suggestion to call for reinforcements is made by Oliver after he has been the first to comprehend the vastness of the approaching Saracen forces. The suggestion seems reasonably well-founded on the realistic proposition: they are many and we are few, *ergo* let us call on Charlemagne's force. Roland replies with the quite natural concern that he will lose his heroic reputation in France if he seeks help. Reassuringly, he reminds Oliver of the effectiveness of his sword and avows that they can match the Saracens. These are the basic positions of Oliver and Roland, the one founded evidently on a realistic appraisal of the relative size of the two opposing forces, and the other based on the heroic over-estimation that the "twelve peers" are a match for the overwhelming pagan force. Neither position is a complicated one in appearance, and yet each represents a way of thinking which reaches deep into their personalities. One certainly would not feel this depth, however, if the *jongleur* let the question pass after the first *laisse*. But he does not. In the next *laisse* Oliver restates his proposal, this time using the verb *sucurre* which indicates his feeling that they are not just in need of light reinforcement, but real aid, as though they were helpless. As Oliver's request becomes more urgent, Roland gives more social reasons for his refusal to sound the horn. In the first *laisse,* he cited his heroic reputation (*los*); here he speaks of his obligation to his family and to *France dulce* for whose sakes he should show no cowardice. It becomes apparent that this problem has wide implications, and that the rearguard is not just a part of Charlemagne's army, but now represents France against the Saracens. They are heroes and should conduct themselves accordingly, as Roland's reference each time to his sword and the damage it will wreak reminds us. When Oliver, in *laisse* LXXXV, urges for the third time that Roland recall Charles, the importance of the conflict is emphasized beyond any single aspect of the poem to this point, since this is the first time that three consecutive *laisses* have been devoted to the same subject. Their similar wording, thrice repeated in the same order, forces our attention to focus on this problem. But again in this third *laisse* there is only the basic statement of difference: Oliver is worried about the fate of the rearguard, while Roland is concerned with their honor. Although the order of events in the fourth *laisse* of the sequence, is the same as the preceding three, i.e. Oliver speaks first, then Roland responds, the speeches are not parallel, since each of the men expresses another aspect of the situation. Oliver does not mention the horn nor Charlemagne, but rather elaborates his statement in the first *laisse* of the series: the multitude of the approaching Saracens and the inadequacy of their own numbers. The ratio of lines devoted to each of these two forces in the *laisse* is three to one, so that the larger pagan force has a greater number of lines concerned with it than does the smaller French force. So Oliver's viewpoint throughout these four *laisses* has remained static, always centered on the realistic comparison of numbers. Roland, on the other hand, has cited three reasons—personal honor, family honor, national honor—why they should not summon aid. The variety of his answers, as compared with the sameness of Oliver's urging, indicates that Roland is engaged in some mental process, even if it is only to defend his natural impulse to fight. That discretion is the better part of valor has never been an heroic attribute, at least in heroic poetry. In this fourth *laisse,* as in the other three, Roland cites two more reasons for fighting. The first is that it would not be pleasing to God if Roland sullied the *valur* of France by yielding before the pagans. Here . . . we find a *reprise* of one of the main themes: that the French are the people of God, and as such, the defenders of the faith. To Roland such a retreat from the heroic ideal (based on faith as well as tradition as we see from Charlemagne's combat with Baligant) would be a manifest lack of faith displeasing to God. Second, they are called the "twelve peers," for which they are esteemed beyond all the fighting men of France: they are above ordinary men as we understand by the word "heroic" in the Homeric sense, or rather in the Old Testament sense since Christianity precludes their being related to the gods. Charlemagne esteems them because of their fighting prowess, so they must live up to that ideal or die. . . . Oliver may have a more realistic view of the situation, but Roland understands far better their *raison d'être,* although the limits of formulaic diction make it difficult for this almost metaphysical idea to be expressed. (pp. 36-8)

At this point (*laisse* LXXXVII), before the fifth and final attempt by Oliver to have Charles recalled, the *jongleur* intervenes with descriptive epithets which . . . touch upon the general qualities of the heroes, but not upon the individual personalities that cause their heroic actions. He indicates that both Oliver and Roland are right, and that each is moved by high ideals, but in the end we see that Roland's view is the more profound in the perspective of their purpose and time. To Oliver's fifth restatement of the necessity to recall the main army, Roland firmly replies that they will stand and fight to show that they are not cowards. His final word on the subject fills the next *laisse,* where he places their obligation to fight in a fuedal context, saying in effect that the king has given him his sword, and that to acquit oneself as a *nobilie vasal* it is sometimes necessary to suffer greatly. The *laisse,* and thus the whole series end wth the words *nobilie vassal* which seem to contain the crux of the medieval hero's existence since he was not only the vassal of the emperor, but also, through the emperor, of God. This position is verified in the following *laisse* where Archbishop Turpin, next to Roland and Oliver the most effective fighter of the French heroes, blesses the French force and assures them that they are fighting for God, who will not deny his warriors Paradise (which still seems suspiciously close to Valhalla).

After this dramatic prelude which certainly increases the importance of the impending battle, the advance guard of the Saracens attacks. The order of the battle is very important to the second "horn" episode because of its relation to the interpretation of Roland's final decision to summon Charlemagne. Does his later decision to sound the Olifant indicate a basic change in his position, a conversion to Oliver's original point of view? Roland was at first confident that they would be able to defeat the Saracens. Actually, the French do defeat the advance guard of the pagans which contains the "twelve peers" of the Saracen army, including Marsile's son. With the arrival of the main body of the Saracens, however, the French are clearly doomed to succumb to the sheer weight of numbers of the enemy. Nevertheless, the French wreak great havoc among the enemy, which is forced to appeal for more aid (*laisse* CXXVI). With only sixty of the French remaining, Roland is forcibly reminded that the finest of the French chevaliers are lying dead on the field. At this point, the very ends which he felt he was serving when he refused to summon Charles seem to be defeated:

> "Bel sire, chers cumpainz, pur Deu, que vos enhaitet?
> Tanz bons vassals veez gesir par tere!
> Pleindre poums France dulce, la bele:
> De tels baróns cum or remeint deserte!
> E! reis, amis, que vos ici nen estes?"
>
> ["Dear sir, dear comrade, in God's name, what do you make of this?
> You see so many good knights lying on the ground!
> Sweet France, the fair, is to be pitied,
> How impoverished she is now of such knights!
> O dear King, what a shame you're not here!"] . . .

If Roland's reasons for not recalling Charles were based on the social concern for the honor of France, family, liege lord, and God, it is clear that this reconsideration of his former position has equally a social (as opposed to personal) basis. His lament is directed toward the loss to France of the dead barons. In other words, the tangible evidence of so many dead barons seems a contradiction to the heroic ideals which he expressed before the fight. That they died honorably, and therefore did realize those heroic ideals is the type of leisurely abstract reasoning which ill fits the battle-field. For although the heroic ideals which he first expressed were abstract, they were based on the real fact that the French rearguard was composed of superior warriors who lived by and even for fighting. Now that they are dead, it seems that they have been defeated. Here, then, is the basic conflict within Roland: the result of the battle appears to contradict the reasons for which it was undertaken. These ideals permitted Roland to predict three times before the battle:

> Jo vos plevis, tuz sont jugez a mort.
>
> [I swear to you, all are condemned to death.] . . .

Roland was referring to the Saracens, but ironically his prediction is proving true for his own force. It is impossible to tell exactly what is Roland's mental reaction to this apparent contradiction, for we can see only his actions, but evidently the shock of the reversal has caused him to realize that he may have been wrong in not recalling Charles. Personally he remains the heroic figure to the end: fighting and dying well. But as leader of the rearguard, it is evident that he becomes uncertain of his duty. Line 1697 seems almost a plea for Charles' guidance as well as his material assistance, and this feeling is reinforced in the line following when he turns to Oliver for advice. Notice also that in the next two *laisses* the order of the first series (*laisses* LXXXIII-LXXXVII) is reversed with Roland here proposing to sound the horn, while Oliver argues against the proposition. It is not the deadlock which here interests us (that is resolved as in the councils by the intervention of a third party, Turpin), but the reorientation of Roland's viewpoint. The only way we can really recognize the significant conflict within Roland is by considering the importance of the first episode, by following the progress of the battle, and then by analyzing, as we have done, his words in *laisse* CXXVIII in relation to the difference in the reality of the scene around him and that which he predicted. Then the simple statement, *Cornerai L'olifant* ["I shall sound the oliphant"] (devoid in itself of emotion), coming as it does after all that has gone before, reflects an emotional perspective in which Roland is the central figure (since the struggle is central to him), but which is also shared by the listener who has seen the growing disparity between the heroic prediction and the actual event.

Such an experience is neither traditional nor formulaic since the poet has inadequate means to give it full expression. It is clearly the work of an individual creativity which could, by deliberate repetition of important parts and by careful arrangement of the order of events, transcend the limitations of speech to hint at a complex reaction, a subtle character development taking place within the protagonist, Roland. (pp. 39-41)

Stephen G. Nichols, Jr., in his Formulaic Diction and Thematic Composition in the "Chanson de Roland," *North Carolina Studies in the Romance Languages and Literatures, 1961, 56 p.*

D.D.R. OWEN (essay date 1962)

[*Owen is an English educator whose works include* The Evolution of the Grail Legend *(1968) and* The Vision of Hell: Informal Journeys in Medieval French Literature *(1970). He is also well known as a translator of* The Song. *In the following excerpt, he posits a secular ethos for the poem, disagreeing with the conclusions reached by Alain Renoir (see Additional Bibliography) and Pierre Le Gentil (see the excerpt dated 1967).*]

In a recent number of *Speculum* Alain Renoir studied the structure and moral theme of the first part of the ***Chanson de Roland,*** with particular reference to *Laisse* CXL [see Additional Bibliography]. Interesting as the discussion was, I find it difficult to accept the main conclusions. . . . (p. 390)

Considering first the ***Chanson*** up to Roland's death, we find that the religious conflict of Christian versus pagan provides a rich backcloth throughout. But against this, the principal events of the story hold no particular religious significance: it is a tale of personal grudge and feud leading to treachery and national disaster; and such grim morals as may be drawn essentially concern warriors in their relationships to one another and to their overlord. The religious setting may charge the emotional atmosphere, but it is otherwise irrelevant to the actual plot. The key to the poet's ideological intentions is surely the character of Roland himself. Is he the devout and single-minded Christian fighter brought by events to martyrdom in the holy cause? Where, then, are his Christian virtues? Our first impression, as Renoir so clearly shows, is of a man motivated by reckless and outrageous pride. He totally lacks the Christian grace of *mesure;* on the contrary, he invites divine retribution for his display of *desmesure,* which conventional mediaeval morality regarded as a social and spiritual sin. It is nevertheless possible that the poet might yet endow Roland's role with positive Christian significance if he showed the hero undergoing some profound spiritual conversion. This, in the view of Le Gentil [see 1967 excerpt by Le Gentil] and Renoir, he has done. At the height of the battle, they claim, Roland becomes aware of his sin and, devoutly repenting his previous attitude, becomes at last worthy of his final salvation. Let us re-examine the text to see if this view of the hero's spiritual development is justifiable.

Initially the emphasis is on Roland's vanity and apparently self-centered arrogance, but already we glimpse a tenacious and more laudable regard for the maintenance of feudal honor. In Charlemagne's first council he boasts gratuitously of his own previous deeds of arms, but argues that the war should be continued to final victory in order that the Christian emissaries whom Marsile had earlier put treacherously to death mght be avenged. He does not, we notice, consider the religious aspect of the struggle. Then, when Ganelon's counter-proposal is adopted, Roland's nomination of his stepfather for the perilous embassy would seem an act of pique, or perhaps of petty vengeance in the context of some earlier quarrel. There can be no more favorable explanation, in view of Ganelon's violent reaction. At the pagan court and on his way there, Ganelon gives what seems an accurate description of Roland's character. While admitting his qualities as a warrior, he stresses his insufferable arrogance; and it is not difficult for us to be in sympathy with Ganelon.

The treachery is accomplished, and with Roland in command of the rearguard the battle will soon be joined. What now is uppermost in his mind as he prepares to grapple with the infidel? Again it is not the religious aspect of the fight, if we can judge from his own statements:

"Ben devuns ci estre pur nostre rei.
Pur sun seignor deit hom susfrir destreiz
E endurer e granz chalz e granz freiz,
Sin deit hom perdre e del quir e del peil.
Or guart chascuns que granz colps i empleit,
Que malvaise cançun de nus chantet ne seit!"

["We must make a stand here for our king
One must suffer hardships for one's lord
And endure great heat and great cold,
One must also lose hide and hair.
Now let each see to it that he employs great blows,
So that bad songs not be sung about us!"] . . .

To be sure, he adds: "'Paien unt tort e chrestiens unt dreit'" ["'Pagans are in the wrong and Christians are in the right'"], but this much-quoted line bears no particular ideological emphasis. Indeed, in the later echo line the distinction has become that between Frank and non-Frank rather than that between Christian and pagan. . . . If Roland's only thought were the triumph of the Christian cause, he might well have reconsidered his foolhardy refusal to take adequate forces when they were offered by Charles, an offer which he had brushed aside. . . . For it is this reckless self-assurance which will come near to wrecking the cause of the true religion.

If we [consider] the words spoken by Roland before and during the battle, we must conclude that he is less conscious of his duty towards his faith than of that towards his king and country, towards his family, and (most insistently of all) towards himself. . . . As the poem progresses we see more clearly the source and function of Roland's pride. It is bred of his almost fanatical regard for the feudal ideals of personal and public honor; and although it renders him incapable of prudent and rational calculation, when he is committed with his men to perilous action it sustains his own valor and has an exemplary effect on his followers and companions. (pp. 390-92)

[In *Laisse* CXXVIII], Roland sees the extent of the losses to the rearguard and expresses his sorrow at the death of so many gallant knights. This brings him to reflect for the first time on the damage done not explicitly to the Christian cause but to "France dulce, la bele" ["sweet France, the fair"]. The shock of realization makes him think of summoning Charles. This dramatic reversal of his previous attitude gives to Oliver, who apparently despairs of any mitigation of the disaster, the opportunity to taunt Roland with his own previous objections, namely that by such an act he will forfeit his own personal honor and that of his family. Although Oliver's retorts are touched with irony, we may wonder if he would have been shown opposing the sounding of the horn in this way if the poet conceived Roland's decision as the most spiritually significant of his career. Be that as it may, Roland's part in the ensuing dialogue does not convey even a flicker of contrition; indeed his reply to Oliver's taunts suggests that his pride is still with him: "Respont li quens: 'Colps i ai fait mult genz!'" ["The count replies: 'I have struck mighty fine blows!'"]. He has struck the blows he would not forgo, his sword runs with pagan blood as he had promised, and at last he believes his own and his family's honor to be secure. So foremost in his mind now is the renown of France, which is still in the balance and which can only be rescued, he sees, by the Emperor himself. With his duty towards himself and his family truly done, he will perform that towards his country—not at all in a spirit of repentance or faltering courage, but with such determination that the act of blowing the horn will burst his temples and cost him his life. There is here no recantation of an earlier purpose, but a logical pursuance by Roland of his constant ideal, the means simply being adapted to the changed circumstances. There has been no change of heart, no sudden contrition, but a steadfast adherence to a triple sense of duty. And though Roland will not live to see Charles triumph, that victory will come, and we shall know the third of his obligations, like the other two, to have been well and faithfully performed.

We can understand and sympathize with the attitude of the prudent and practical Oliver. Unrestrained idealism is indeed *desmesure,* and when, as here, it refuses to compromise with reality, common sense may well label it *estultie* ["recklessness"]. Oliver sees France's defeat as irredeemable, so why now call for help which must come too late? But while every bit as brave a warrior as his companion, Oliver by his reproof shows his own heroism to be on a lower epic plane than that of Roland. His is a practical as oposed to an idealistic heroism. Of course, he is quite right when he claims that "'. . . vasselage par sens nen est folie; / Mielz valt mesure que ne fait estultie'" [. . . "'heroism tempered wth common sense is a far cry from madness; Reasonableness is to be preferred to recklessness'"], and "'Vostre proecce, Rollant, mar la veïmes'" ["'I have come to rue your prowess, Roland'"]; but this is the truth of the world, whereas in Roland's pursuit of his ideal there lies poetic truth. "Rollant est proz e Oliver est sage" ["Roland is valiant and Oliver is wise"]: the poet has made his distinction, and here it is poignantly illustrated.

This, as I see it, is the context in which *Laisse* CXL should be studied. For a dozen *laisses* the poet has paused in his description of the fighting in order to focus attention on the mental and emotional reactions and stresses of the Christian leaders. First he reveals Roland's unexpected but logically motivated decision to summon help from Charlemagne. The ensuing tension caused by Oliver's outburst is broken by Turpin's advice and the actual blowing of the horn. Immediately we are shown the reaction of the emperor and his army and their anguished ride to the relief of Roland, who is continually at the center of our attention just as the thought of his plight dominates the minds of Charles and his barons. Now the poet wishes to lead us back into the events of the battle, and this he does in *Laisse* CXL with typical regard for balance and symmetry: by way of transition he recapitulates Roland's expression of grief at the death of his men and at the consequent loss to France; and the hero passes from reflection to action just as he had earlier paused from action to reflect on the situation.

Renoir analyses the *laisse* thus: "In the first section, Roland perceives the extent of the tragedy before him; in the second, he realizes his own responsibility and his utter helplessness; in the third, he turns to desperate action." But surely it was his perception of the extent of the tragedy which had already prompted him to blow the horn. His "utter helplessness" is confined to his inability to give further protection to those of his men who are already dead and are now in God's keeping. As for realizing his own responsibility for the disaster, this interpretation turns on the meaning of *pur mei.* Renoir rejects Bédier's reading, *pour moi* 'for my sake' in favor of Jenkins' "thru my fault," and it is on this meaning that he bases his case for Roland's repentance of his *desmesure.* He might perhaps have made more of Oliver's accusation: "'Franceis sunt morz par vostre legerie'" ["'Frenchmen have died because of your senselessness'"] of which, given his interpretation of *pur mei,* Roland's words here would be an acknowledgment. However, I think the reading "for my sake" is preferable. . . . The dead men were directly in the service of Roland as Charlemagne's representative: he was their *garant* ["guarantor"], and they fought and, as it turned out, died on his behalf. Roland himself had already stated this feudal conception of the man's duty to his lord. . . . Renoir further maintains that, in directly addressing not the sixty surviving Frenchmen but his companion: "'Oliver, frere, vos ne dei jo faillir'" ["'Oliver, my friend, I must not fail you'"], he is acknowledging that "he has relinquished his formal position as commander of the rearguard, and his only remaining duty is now toward comradeship." But this cannot be the intention of the poet, who has just exclaimed: "Deus! quels seisante humes i ad en sa cumpaigne!" ["God! What men, the sixty who are in his company!"]. Furthermore, Roland's statement: "'Jo ne vos pois tenser ne guarantir'" ["'I cannot protect or save you'"], which Renoir likens to "a compulsory and humiliating relinquishing of his command", is addressed not to the survivors but to the slain. His words to Oliver, then, do not represent the abandonment of the remnant of the rearguard, but serve to express his devotion to yet another aspect of his feudal duty, namely his duty towards his *compagnon* ["companion"]. They serve also to show that the bond between the two warriors has survived the temporary strain caused by Oliver's harsh words; and the whole situation is repeated symbolically nine *laisses* later when the blinded Oliver physically attacks Roland and is once more forgiven by him.

Throughout the battle Roland never wavers from the pursuit of his feudal ideals; and from the time when he blows the horn his eyes are set on the great task which remains for him to accomplish: the salvation of France. Though he continues to express pride in his personal valor and achievements (and this again runs counter to the idea of contrition), we glimpse no more pettiness in his character, and the stress is on his own services to his emperor and country, his grief at France's present plight, and his determination that she shall not be put to shame.

Eventually, bereft of companions and his strength ebbing away, he prepares for death. The famous scene has been called by Le Gentil "la béatification de Roland," and in it we witness "la plus belle et la plus sainte des morts" ["the most beautiful and saintly of deaths"]. . . . The scene is one of tragic force and great beauty, and to this the Christian coloring certainly contributes. But once again we must ask ourselves whether it is in fact the religious ideal which is basic to the episode.

When he has slain the last enemy remaining on the field, Roland turns his thoughts first to his sword, Durendal, which must on no account fall into pagan hands. In his apostrophe the main theme is the great deeds performed and the many lands conquered by him in the service of Charles and of France, and it is perhaps worth noting that most of the conquered lands were in fact Christian both in Carolingian times and in the eleventh century. Then it has often been pointed out that the attitude adopted by the dying hero is consonant with Christian symbolism. This may be so, but in the narraitve there is no hint that the poet had this in mind, rather:

Pur ço l'at fait que il voelt veirement
Que Carles diet e trestute sa gent,
Li gentilz quens, qu'il fut mort cunquerant.

[He did this because he earnestly desires
That Charles and all his men say
That the noble Count died as a conqueror.] . . .

Thus the text suggests that this was, on Roland's part, a final act of self-justification, prompted by thoughts of his posthumous reputation.

The climax of the scene, and the passage which most justifies Le Gentil's descriptions, is Roland's dying prayer and his reception into Paradise. The prayer takes the form of a double request for forgiveness of all past sins, couched in general and quite conventional terms; and there is even now no suggestion of specific repentance for *desmesure,* or anything which carries us beyond the orthodox end to a Christian life. Less commonplace are the lines preceding Roland's final words:

De plusurs choses a remembrer li prist,
De tantes teres cum li bers conquist,
De dulce France, des humes de sun lign,
De Carlemagne, sun seignor, kil nurrit;
Ne poet muer n'en plurt e ne suspirt.
Mais lui meïsme ne volt mettre en ubli,
Cleimet sa culpe, si priet Deu mercit.

[He began to remember many things,
The many lands he conquered as a brave knight,
Fair France, the men from whom he is descended,
Charlemagne, his lord, who raised him;
He cannot help weeping and sighing.
But he does not wish to forget prayers for his own soul,
He says his confession in a loud voice and prays for
God's mercy.] . . .

There is no mention here among his last thoughts of the holy cause in which he has been fighting, but instead we find them directed once more towards his king and country, his family, and himself. To the moment of death he has retained his sense of this triple obligation.

So Roland is received into Paradise, but not, as we now see, in token of divine approval of an act of repentance; for there has been no such act but merely the conventional *mea culpa* of the dying Christian. He is received into Paradise just as were all those slain in battle against the pagans; and Roland's destiny is different only in the emphasis placed upon it in our text. (pp. 393-97)

In view of all this, it is impossible for me to see Roland as the embodiment of a Christian ideal. On the contrary, my analysis has shown that his conduct is primarily governed by motives which, while not lacking in nobility, are strictly non-religious. These I have described as a triple sense of duty: to king and country, to family, and to self. The harm which befalls France through his apparent recklessness is in no way intended or envisaged by Roland, and in fact occurs despite his conscientious pursuit of the first ideal. In a sense, his course of action is justified by the later events, since total victory is finally achieved. There is a link, of course, between his first duty and his obligations towards the family group, for he is the nephew of the Emperor himself. And above all, these first two duties are linked to the third, in so far as the achievement of the personal ideal redounds to the credit of both country and family, a consideration which Roland always has in mind. This duty of the knight to himself involves the maintenance of his personal honor through deeds of valor eagerly accomplished. Moreover, the ideal of personal valor implies that the more difficult and dangerous the tasks performed, the greater the honor thereby achieved. In Roland's case we see this ideal pursued to the limit, with the hero deliberately increasing the danger of his situation to the point at which that situation allows the maximum exercise of his valor, i.e., to the point where the ideal claims the ultimate sacrifice of his life. And we see the hero's prowess and the difficulty of the situation he has created so perfectly matched that he dies not in defeat but in victory. He is slain by no pagan, but by his own effort in blowing the horn. Nor do the enemy triumph: they are all killed or put to flight. Roland's valor in the service of his ideal has triumphed over circumstances, although that ideal is finally attained only in death.

This, as I understand it, is the real theme of the ***Chanson de Roland:*** the illustration in concrete terms of a triple sense of duty which is not in any way dependent on a particular religious attitude. In theory a Saracen might equally well have accomplished it, although of course the poet's sympathies lie with the Christians. As it is, we actually see the pagans failing in these duties—fleeing in battle, indulging in dishonorable subterfuge, and quite prepared to sacrifice their own kith and kin in the process. So, though it is a Christian who achieves the ideal, the ideal itself is not a Christian one. It represents the needs and aspirations of a warrior feudal society encouraging, as it does, the bravery of the individual knight, the strengthening of the family unit and the unwavering loyalty of the vassal to his overlord. Roland is the embodiment and the first

Fifteenth-century representation of the battle of Roncevaux.

half of the epic is essentially the illustration of the feudal ideal, and all else is of subsidiary importance. (pp. 397-98)

I submit that the greater part of the poem as we have it, while strongly colored by the Christian outlook and practices of its age, was nevertheless composed to the glory of the secular, feudal ideal. I believe that the unknown poet was too fine and sensitive a craftsman to compromise the unity of the whole by gratuitously diverting attention to a second ideal which at times comes near to conflicting with the first. The prominence given to the militant Christian ideal in the Oxford version is therefore likely to be due to the work of some skilful redactor building on to a more compact but already admirably developed original. One may suspect that the redactor's name was Turoldus, and that he was working from a secular poem where already the opposing forces were Christian and Saracen, but where the dominant spirit was that of the lay aristocracy, seeking self-expression in the face of the cultural monopoly claimed by the clerical world. Turoldus may have appropriated secular property and camouflaged it with uncommon skill, but the old shapes continue to show through. (p. 400)

D.D.R. Owen, "The Secular Inspiration of the 'Chanson De Roland'," in Speculum, *Vol. XXXVII, No. 3, July, 1962, pp. 390-400.*

GEORGE FENWICK JONES (essay date 1963)

[*Jones is an American educator and critic who has written extensively on medieval German and French literature. In the following excerpt, he interprets* The Song *in heroic rather than Christian terms, disputing the argument of Alain Renoir (see Additional Bibliography).*]

An unbiased evaluation of ***The Song of Roland***'s ethos may . . . discredit certain literary interpretations based on the commonly accepted idea that the song is essentially Christian. As an example of such interpretations one could cite a recent study of Roland's lament in *Laisse CXL,* in which Alain Renoir stresses Roland's guilt, humility, and penitence [see Additional Bibliography]. This penetrating literary analysis proves convincingly that *Laisse CXL* "is not only a powerful piece of work; it is the focal point for the tone and structure of the first half of the poem," yet it does not prove that Roland's inner tragedy stems from guilt and remorse. By failing to investigate the song's ethical vocabulary, Renoir has fallen into the common error of attributing alien attitudes to its hero. Thus, like most of his predecessors, Renoir interprets Roland's quandry in terms of sin, remorse, and forgiveness, rather than in terms of humiliation, chagrin, and vindication. In other words, he interprets an heroic epic as if it were a hagiographical legend. (pp. 171-72)

Christian values should not be assumed for the ***Chanson de Roland*** except where the text clearly warrants. Humility, remorse, and penitence on Roland's part in this episode would clash with his character elsewhere in the song; and this is to be avoided because, as Jessie Crosland insists [see Additional Bibliography], "Roland's character . . . is all of one piece" and "the poet's psychological instinct never fails him. There is nothing incongruous or inconsistent in any of his characters."

In discussing Roland's "profound humility," Renoir says that, "like a true aristocrat, he knows how to admit the tragic extent of his failure with all the humility—and the concomitant dignity—required for such an admission." But does Turold really attribute humility to Roland? This is unlikely, since he nowhere recognizes humility as a virtue in his haughty fighting men. . . . [He] lacked a word for "humility" and used the word *humilitet* only in the sense of homage, which suggests humiliation rather than humility. . . . [In] letting Roland look *humeles* at his friends, Turold was following the classical literary tradition of praising rulers who are grim to their enemies but kind to their friends. For Turold, Renoir's expression "triumphant in humility" would have been a paradox.

In considering dignity to be concomitant with admission of failure, Renoir reflects attitudes held by Greek Stoics and by some modern men, but not by Turold and his public. . . . [Turold] branded all failure as shameful, regardless of the circumstances; and it is significant that he used the word *honte* ["shame"] to mean defeat even if the vanquished went down valiantly. Admission of failure would have been especially shameful for "a true aristocrat," for, as connoisseurs of honor from Aristotle to Ashley have agreed, nobles make the best warriers because of their great concern for their good names. Renoir's use of the word "dignity" is also questionable, since Turold did not understand such a concept. Europeans needed many more centuries to discover the innate dignity of man, as independent of rank and condition. When Shakespeare made his Montagues and Capulets "alike in dignity," he was referring to rank or social status rather than to excellence of character or innate worth. . . . [Turold] used the word *deintet* only in its sense of "sovereignty".

Renoir believes that Roland proves his penitence by acknowledging his responsibility for his men's death; and as evidence of this he cites Roland's words *Barons franceis, pur mei vos vei murir* ["French knights, for me I see you dying"]. . . . He agrees with T. A. Jenkins that Roland means "through my fault" rather than "for me," as Bédier and many others believed, because Bédier's solution presupposes "a concept nowhere intimated in this poem: that the French barons have been fighting for Roland personally rather than for their emperor or the honor of France." Here he contradicts what he has said on the previous page, namely that Roland "acknowledged their faithful service to himself and to Charles." Roland's actual words (*Si lungement tuz tens m'avez servit* ["You have served me constantly and for so long"] . . .) prove that he accepted the barons' service as a service to himself as commanding officer. Direct loyalty was then, is now, and ever shall be the essence of military chain-of-command. The subordinate owes personal loyalty to his immediate superior, and only through him to the higher commander. Although twelve of the barons at Roncevaux are Roland's "peers," they too are under his direct command during the rearguard engagement and must fight for him to their death. Although *pur mei* sometimes means "because of me," it more likely means "for my sake" in this passage, which contrasts the barons' loyal service with Roland's failure to protect them.

Believing that Roland's ordeal at Roncevaux transforms his character, Renoir considers his behavior to be "the logical outcome of his redemption from the sin of pride." But Renoir fails to prove that Roland, or even Turold, really considered pride a sin. (pp. 173-76)

Assuming that vainglory was judged blameworthy, Renoir censures Roland's braggadocio before Charlemagne early in the song and says that "not only is the outburst utterly uncouth, but Roland's uncalled-for recital of his own accomplishments constitutes an embarrassing display of the most outrageous pride." But nowhere does Turold share this aversion. Like his contemporaries, he admired the warrior who could vaunt eloquently of both his past and his future deeds; and he let Charlemagne fondly remember Roland's boast that he would advance further into the enemy territory than any of his men and that he would die as a conqueror. . . . [Roland] lists even more accomplishments in his final and longest self-adulation, which occurs after his putative remorse for having let his pride destroy his men.

If Roland's "redemption from the sin of pride" has caused a transformation in his character, then his redemption is not very permanent and Turold has failed to create a consistent character. Renoir states that "Roland's humility in the *laisse* reveals its full import only when considered in contrast to his behavior in earlier scenes, where he appears as a rash, proud, and inconsiderate warrior"; and this indicates that Renoir has failed to note that Roland is vainglorious not only in earlier but also in later scenes. . . . After Oliver's death, Roland boasts that he will never desert Turpin because of any living man, and then he brags that the best blows of all are those struck by his own sword Durendal. Immediately after praying to Gabriel, he tries to destroy his sword to escape reproach, rather than to keep his sword from being used against his fellow Christians. When the Arab approaches to take his sword and says: "Charles' nephew has been vanquished," Roland is offended and indignantly strikes him dead with his horn and then taunts him and boastfully declares that anyone who heard of this incident would consider the Arab a fool for having dared to touch him. He next tells his sword that it has won many victories and conquered many lands and that it has belonged to a brave warrior. Thereupon he again enumerates the many lands he has conquered, in which case he recalls even more than he did earlier in the song. Roland then faces the enemy so that Charlemagne and his men will *say* that he has died as a conqueror, and only then does he confess his sins, of which pride is certainly not one. His dying thoughts are of the lands he has conquered, of France, of his kinsmen, of Charlemagne who has nourished him, and then, almost as an afterthought, of his soul. He makes no mention whatever of any remorse or sense of guilt, nor does he think of the men who died because of his pride.

In view of Roland's acts and thoughts, he can hardly be called an exemplary Christian. And it is hard to agree with Renoir and others that Oliver's tongue-lashing had any salutary effect on him. He may have been chastised, but not chastened. It is even debatable whether Turold really understood remorse as distinct from regret; for he does not seem to have had any words with which to distinguish the two sentiments. He uses the word *repentir* ["repentance"] only in a secular sense, as when Charlemagne says that the Arabs will pay dearly if they do not renounce their plan of attacking, and when Baligant offers peace provided Charlemagne will give up his present policy toward him. Turold uses no word meaning "penitence." . . . [Turpin's] reference to *penitence* refers to the penance of killing pagans.

When Roland uses the word *doel* to express the emotion evoked by the sight of his dead and dying men, Renoir assumes that his emotion is grief, and this is no doubt partially true, since Roland surely regrets the death of his men. Turold sometimes uses the word *doel* to express the sorrow felt at the death of a loved one; but . . . he also uses it to express a desire to avenge rather than a desire to mourn. The latter generally seems to be the case when the word *doel* is used by or of Roland. When Aelroth slanders Charlemagne, Roland feels *doel* and immediately wreaks vengeance, and he likewise feels *doel* when he sees his friend Sansun slain by Valdabrun, whom he straightway kills. When Grandonie kills six of his friends and discourages the Franks, Roland feels such *doel* that he almost bursts and immediately curses and kills his offender.

Upon learning that his vassal Gualter has been defeated and has lost all his men, Roland has *doel* and is very angry; and just before his death he strikes ten blows with *doel* and rancor. In all these cases *doel* seems to refer to an acute vexation caused by insult or injury or by a sense of failure or frustration. This is no doubt what the word *doel* means in *Laisse CXL;* for the very next strophe tells how Roland kills Faldrun de Pui and twenty-four other Saracens and says that no other man was ever so anxious to avenge himself. . . . [Turold's] use of the words *doel, dolent, dolur, ire, irur,* and *rancune* shows that he did not distinguish clearly between anger and sorrow, and this suggests that he and his public did not categorize their emotional spectrum into the same primary colors as we do. In fact he did not have to "convert grief to anger," since the two were one.

If the word *doel* in *Laisse CXL* is translated as "chagrin," then there is no inconsistency in Roland's character or in the motivation of the song. Turold never presents Roland as crushed by feelings of guilt, whereas he constantly refers to his dependence upon other people's opinions. As Le Gentil so aptly expresses his condition, he is "a prisoner of the admiration of which he is the object." Instead of an excusable weakness, as the Stoic philosophers had maintained, solicitude for other people's opinions was a laudable virtue for twelfth-century knights, a virtue more admirable than fear of hell and damnation.

[Turold] repeatedly states that Roland fears public censure more than death. In assigning Roland to lead the rear guard, Charlemagne gives him a staff as symbol of command, and Roland boasts that people will never reprove him for letting it drop, as Ganelon had previously done. When Charlemagne offers his army for the mission, Roland declines lest he bring reproach upon his family. He extols loyalty to one's leader, but then he reveals that such virtue is performed not for its own sake but to avoid being lampooned in scurrilous songs; and this same fear later impels him to fight to the finish. He refuses to summon aid because he desires to protect his reputation in France, to save his kinsmen from reproach, and to keep people from *saying* that he did so through fear of the pagans. In every case in which Roland's motivation is clarified, his deeds are sanctioned by fear of shame and blame.

Roland has previously expressed the hope that France will not be disgraced through him because he would rather die than be reproached, and he echoes this sentiment in *Laisse CXL* in saying that he will die of *doel* if nothing else kills him first. This *doel* is chiefly the chagrin he feels upon realizing that he will lose the fame he has struggled so long to win. This explanation will seem blasphemous to those critics who see Roland as a penitent sinner, but it will accord with Ruth Benedict's observation . . . that "in a culture where shame is a major sanction, people are chagrined about acts which we expect people to feel guilty about." . . . [Shame] was Roland's chief, and almost sole, sanction. It is to escape such chagrin that Roland wishes to resume the battle and strike the enemy: death in battle will not save him from the ignominy of defeat, but at least it will save him from a life of shame. Renoir himself comments on the bitter humiliation Roland endures at being unable to defend his men, yet he seems to attribute his distress to sense of guilt rather than to loss of honor.

When Roland's *doel* is understood as chagrin, not only does all inconsistency disappear in plot and character, but Roland's tragedy becomes even more intense. For the Christian, a tragedy based on guilt and sin is always mitigated by the possibility of forgiveness. As Cardinal Newman states . . . , a sinful man can free himself of sin by one act of contrition; and this fact probably explains why there has never been a great Christian tragedy, even though hagiographies offer an abundance of potentially tragic situations. On the other hand, there is no surcease of the chagrin caused by loss of honor; for, as Cardinal Newman continues, it is impossible to restore the honor of a man once it has been sullied. Ruth Benedict continues her previous statement with the conclusion that "chagrin can be very intense and it cannot be relieved, as guilt can be, by confession and atonement."

Renoir denies that Roland "sinks into vulgar despair"; yet, vulgar or not, despair is just what Roland experiences at realizing that he will lose his honor because of his defeat and his inability to protect his men. Naimes, Charlemagne's wisest counselor, knows that Roland is despairing as soon as he hears his horn. To comprehend Roland's despondency, we should recall the mental anguish of Japanese prisoners of war in World War II, for whom defeat meant dishonor, and for whom dishonor meant severance of all social ties and consequent collapse of personal integrity. Stoic philosophers, Christian martyrs, and modern "inner-directed" men have inner resources which enable them to disregard social reprobation, provided their conscience is clear and their inner honor is still intact; but "other-directed" men lose the very source of their moral fiber when they lose the approbation of their peers. As we have seen, the major motivating force of all Roland's actions is his desire to win fame and avoid shame. Like Norfolk in Shakespeare's *Richard II,* his honor is his life, both grow in one. Take honor from him, and his life is done.

But how can we deny an obsession with sin and repentance in this scene so redolent of Christian martyrdom? How can we belittle the importance of humility and forgiveness when Roland's soul is taken up to heaven? This is easy, if we only remember how superficial Christianity was in northwestern Europe in the twelfth century. . . . [It] is tempting to think that Turold faintly recollected some holy legend, of which he borrowed the trappings, even if not the ethos.

All literary matter was grist for Turold's mill, be it holy or profane. Being the inspired genius that he was, he stamped his personality on his work and was in no way hampered by the moral intent of his sources. . . . Turold has used a clerical theme, but he has imbued it with a heroic ethos. In letting Marsilie turn to the wall to die, Turold is probably making use of some faint subconscious recollection about King Hezekiah, who did likewise. But the Hebrew king turned to the wall to pray to God, whereas the maimed and defeated king of Saragossa turned to the wall to hide his shame and sorrow. Here again the form is old, but the moral content is new.

Roland's courage, pride, and loyalty to friend and liege were qualities just as dear to the pagan Franks and Northmen as to their Christian descendants. Nowhere does he concern himself with Christian dogma or Christian ethics until a few minutes before his death, and only after it is too late to count on self-help. Even then he does not ask divine aid for his safety but only for his salvation. Unlike Charlemagne's, his campaign is in no way a holy war; and he appeals to his men's greed for glory and wealth but not to their religious duty. There is no evidence that he looks upon his men's massacre as a martyrdom. It is ironic that he first uses the word martyrdom to describe the death of the pagans; and, when he finally uses the word in connection with his own men, he is concerned with their immortal fame rather than with their eternal salvation, since he calls shame upon any who do not sell their lives dearly so that they will not bring disgrace upon France.

Roland's pride and death suggest the proverb that "pride goeth before destruction, and an haughty spirit before a fall." But, even though Roland has "an haughty spirit" even *after* his fall, this does not prevent him from rising again, at least it does not keep his soul from rising to heaven. (pp. 176-83)

Believing Roland to be truly Christian, Renoir states that Turold "specifically tells us that Roland recalls Charlemagne so that the dead French may receive Christian burial." He does not document this statement, perhaps because he could not find a single verse with which to do so. To the contrary, Roland clearly states that he is calling Charlemagne to avenge his fallen men, and he never mentions Christian burial in connection with blowing his horn. Even Archbishop Turpin stresses vengeance and only casually mentions burial. When Roland gathers the bodies of his peers, he is following Germanic rather than Christian tradition. Christ might even have let the dead bury their dead: it was Germanic custom that required a leader to recover the bodies of his men or else suffer shame. Charlemagne's efforts to preserve his men's mortal remains is primarily pagan in origin.

Having freed ourselves from all a priori assumptions, let us judge Roland's humiliation as Turold actually depicts it. To appreciate his humiliation, we must first comprehend the magnitude of the pride that preceded it. We first hear Roland boast of his past victories, and we next see him volunteer for the mission to Saragossa, only to be disqualified by Oliver because of his violent temper. When Ganelon threatens him for having nominated him for the mission, Roland laughs and says that everyone knows that he is not afraid of threats. Arriving in Saragossa, Ganelon tells Marsilie how Roland has promised to deliver all kingdoms to Charlemagne, and he predicts that Roland's pride will bring him to shame. He also warns the Saracen king that Roland will be a haughty partner when Charlemagne divides Spain between them; and he declares that Charlemagne will be safe only as long as Roland lives. When Ganelon nominates Roland for the rear guard, Roland thanks him for the opportunity and boasts that he will not let Charlemagne lose a single beast of burden; and he further boasts that he will not drop the staff that Charlemagne gives him.

Roland's reputation, i.e., his image in other people's eyes, is enhanced when each of the twelve Saracen leaders promises to defeat him; and Roland reveals his overweening self-assurance by swearing that all the pagans will die. As long as the battle goes well for the Franks, Roland remains in high spirits; but his spirit begins to falter when he sees the battle turning out badly. As he has often attested, he is not afraid of dying, but only of being dishonored by defeat, especially after he has staked his honor upon victory. At last he decides that help from Charlemagne will be less shameful than defeat, but then Oliver spitefully reverses himself and deters him from summoning help by repeating all the arguments Roland previously used when Oliver urged him to do so. Reminded of the shame he and his kinsmen will suffer, Roland refrains from blowing until Turpin convinces him that he can do so without jeopardizing his good name. Once it is too late for help, it is no longer shameful to blow the horn. On the other hand, by blowing his horn Roland assures himself that Charlemagne will avenge his death and thus partially diminish the disgrace of defeat, or at least deprive the victors of the pleasure of their victory. It will also guarantee honorable burial for the dead.

After his famous lament for his men, Roland fights with a courage born of desperation; and Turold frankly says that he and his sixty remaining followers defend themselves like men who expect no quarter. Seeing Marsilie kill several of his men, Roland curses him and boasts that he will pay for his deed and will learn the name of Roland's sword; and he fulfills his threat by cutting off Marsilie's right hand and killing his son. Thereupon most of the surviving pagans flee with their injured king, but Marsilie's uncle Marganice attacks with vastly superior numbers and gives Oliver a fatal blow from behind. Blinded by blood, Oliver strikes Roland by mistake; yet, although he is unhurt and despite their long friendship, punctilious Roland does not forgive him until he is sure that Oliver did not strike him on purpose. By asking Oliver if he has struck him on purpose, Roland clearly shows that he is still more concerned about his personal reputation than about his guilt at having caused the debacle and the death of his friends.

After Oliver's death, Roland, Gualter, and Turpin fight so fiercely that the Saracens stand back and throw their spears from a distance, thereby killing Gualter and mortally wounding Turpin. Roland continues to fight until the pagans realize that, because of his great ferocity, he can never be defeated by any mortal man; and thereupon they flee and leave him in control of the field. Thus Roland is able to vindicate his honor by conquering, as he swore he would, and by recovering the bodies of his fallen comrades. No doubt Roland deeply mourns his dead friends, as he attests in his laments, yet this neither lessens his concern for his own posthumous fame nor suggests any remorse. As we have seen, Roland tries to destroy his sword to avoid reproach, he tells his sword of his great victories, and he advances toward the enemy to prove he died victorious. As long as his comrades live, he can play to a living audience, but after they are dead and he has no witnesses to report his exploits, he must carefully set his stage so that Charlemagne will know how well and successfully he has fought. Carrying his horn and sword as proof of his victory, he seeks out a hill on which stand four large blocks of marble, as if these were a fitting monument to commemorate his heroic death.

Turold makes it amply clear that Roland has vindicated himself and has repaired his injured honor. Upon returning to Roncevaux after pursuing and destroying Roland's enemies, Charlemagne knows right where to find his body, since he remembers Roland's boast that he would lie in front of his men; and thus Roland succeeds in proclaiming to posterity that he has died as a conqueror. The whole tragedy of Roland's death can be explained in heroic terms, without reference to Christianity and without any loss of tragic intensity. An overconfident leader risks defeat and jeopardizes his followers in a foolhardy attempt to enhance his worldly fame. Realizing that his temerity has cost him his honor, he is overwhelmed by chagrin at the thought of disgrace. But, despite despair, he challenges fate and fights against superhuman odds with a strength born of desperation, until he finally vindicates his good name. Like Byrhtnoth at Maldon and like the Burgundians at Etzel's court, Roland struggles manfully against fate and relies entirely on his own efforts rather than call on human or divine aid. And, unlike Byrhtnoth and the Burgundians, he succeeds in his task even though he dies in the effort.

Nor does Roland have any more need of penitence, in its sense of contrition, than the rest of his men. His soul is taken to heaven largely because he excels in *penitence,* in Turpin's sense of the word, in which it means penance done by killing pagans. Let us try to imagine Roland's reaction if Turpin had set him some less glorious penance. Let us suppose that, to cleanse him of his sin of pride, Turpin had demanded some voluntary humiliation, such as playing the coward before his men. What would Roland have done if his penance had been to drop his sword and shield and flee to the rear, with every expectation of being chained and loaded on a pack horse for transport to Aachen and some undignified punishment? Surely his Christian faith was not strong enough to accept a penance in conflict with his martial ethos. It is a poor proof of Christianity to do in God's name what you would gladly do without ever having heard of God.

Like Germanic heroes taken to Valhalla and like Mohammedan warriors taken to paradise, the Franks achieve salvation more on their own merits and through good works than through faith. There is little evidence that Turpin's, or Turold's, idea of martyrdom differed materially from the Mohemmedan's belief in Shahid. David Wright [in an introduction to his 1957 edition of *Beowulf*] has written that "the consolation of Beowulf is not a Christian consolation but an heroic one. . . ." This is also true to a large extent of Roland, who is consoled by knowing that Charlemagne and his men will say that he has won the field and recovered the bodies of his companions and that he has advanced further than any of his men and has died as a conqueror. Roland frequently expresses deep longing for a spotless reputation, but he never expresses any deep longing for eternal life. Such a preference was by no means rare in medieval heroic literature. (pp. 184-88)

In conclusion we see that ***The Song of Roland*** portrays the inward thoughts of twelfth-century France, at least of the ruling classes of twelfth-century France, and that its ethos was acceptable to the ruling classes of the neighboring Christian countries as well. Regardless of any earlier literary tradition, ***The Song of Roland*** preserved in the Oxford manuscript depicts the moral physiognomy of the age in which it was composed, rather than that of the historical period it treats. (p. 191)

The most important terms for a study of an ethos are those which deal with right and wrong, good and bad, and honor and shame. Turold's treatment of these concepts shows that the society he depicts is a "shame culture," notwithstanding a strong admixture, or superimposition, of Christian "guilt culture." Good is what society admires, bad is what it censures. A purpose of ***The Song of Roland*** was to inspire courage and loyalty by showing that they win honor and to deter cowardice and perfidy by showing that they incur shame. In addition, courage and loyalty in the Lord's service earn eternal life in heaven.

Although its style and means of expression were strongly influenced by classical Latin literature and Christian liturgy, ***The Song of Roland*** presents and preaches an ethos basically similar to that of the heathen Germanic tribesmen. This similarity can be explained by the social predominance of the Frankish invaders and their descendants, who furnished most of the medieval aristocracy and set a social pattern scarcely affected by their acceptance of the outward forms of Christianity. The Franks' warlike ethos was later reinforced by struggle against the Scandinavian invaders and still later by assimilation with the Northmen who settled in Normandy. Friction with Mohammedans in Spain may have helped strengthen their warlike attitudes, which were theologically justified by passages in the Old Testament.

Despite much reference to Christianity, ***The Song of Roland*** shows little understanding of Christian clarity and forgiveness; and good works, mostly in the form of military service and pious endowments, are bartered in return for salvation. The Christian faith can demand great physical sacrifice from its adherents, provided it does not try to modify their traditional values, which remain martial and heroic. It can ask them to risk their lives, but not their honor; and therefore it cannot demand love in place of hate or forgiveness in place of vengeance. A man of honor must avenge all injuries to himself, his reputation, his friends, his kinsmen, and especially his sister's son. Despite many confessions, the warriors of ***The Song of Roland*** show little understanding of sin or guilt. They never question the existence of pagan deities, but merely believe their own God more powerful and more helpful. For them, love seldom means Christian charity. Sometimes it means personal affection, but at other times it merely means truce or alliance.

The chief well-spring of morality lies less in the tenets or teachings of Christ than in solicitude for public opinion, in concern for the admiration of men living and still unborn. Hope of salvation is also a strong incentive, but this incentive is usually subordinated to considerations of public repute. Religious duty is primarily a loyalty to the Church as a political entity and to Christendom as the broadest expression of the in-group, as the totality of all men fighting against a common enemy. Such a loyalty would be inculcated less by Christian ethics than by outward forms and ceremonies, splendor of buildings, elegance of costumes, wealth of church treasures, power of relics, and emotional appeal of music, to say nothing of the belief that the hierarchy held the keys to heaven.

However great their loyalty to Christendom, that is to say, to Charlemagne's universal empire, the Franks in ***The Song of Roland*** are more devoted to France proper; and it is safe to assume that their patriotism derived from Latin literature and from the Gallo-Roman occupants of Gaul.

The ethos of ***The Song of Roland*** is consistent throughout and does not indicate that any one episode was written by a different poet. However, because the Baligant episode changes the battle of Roncevaux into an apocalyptic struggle between Cross and Crescent, it could have been a later and tendentious addition, perhaps by the same author.

Even more conspicuous than the lack of Christian ethics in ***The Song of Roland*** is its lack of Stoic values, with which all Western codes of honor and decency are now imbued. The song shows little appreciation of tolerance, modesty, self-control, introspection, virtue for its own sake, or independence of other people's opinions. Oliver preaches moderation, but foolhardy Roland is the hero of the song. There is little comprehension of fair play, sportsmanship, defeat with honor, or chivalry toward the underdog, even though public fancy has subsequently ascribed these virtues to an ill-defined "age of chivalry."

This study does not mean to pass judgment on the heroes of ***The Song of Roland***—rather it argues that they must be judged by a set of standards markedly unlike those we profess today. To understand their actions and motives, and thereby to appreciate the great literary value of the song, we must free ourselves of all the ideas that values so slowly and painfully acquired by our more recent ancestors. By refusing to attribute our highest ideals and aspirations to the warriors of ***The Song of Roland,*** this study may offend certain critics who consider the song typically and essentially French. But to attribute modern French ideals to the rowdy Frankish barons of the twelfth century is to disparage the contributions of later men like Montaigne, Pascal, and Voltaire, who made French civilization what it later became. (pp. 191-94)

Even if the noble Christian knights of ***The Song of Roland*** would rate as brutal and bigoted barbarians if judged by modern standards, this in no way diminishes the literary excellence of the song. A work of art should be judged by its aesthetic rather than by its moral standards. Although built for human sacrifice, an Aztec temple may be aesthetically more pleasing than many Christian churches; and a poem by Baudelaire may be more enjoyable than one by Edgar Guest. By remembering that the basic values of ***The Song of Roland*** were more heroic than Christian, a reader will avoid being misled by the Christian and Stoic values subsequently acquired by so many of its terms. If we read Turold's words with the meanings he intended, we find the action of his epic well-motivated and his characters well-drawn. Even Ganelon acts logically, given the values and standards of his day. Being surpassed, slighted, and ridiculed by his stepson, he has lost his honor and impugned that of his kindred and has nothing more to lose but his life.

Goethe once wrote of a little boy who caught a dragon-fly and dissected it to see why it was so pretty. But, once dismembered, it was no longer pretty. Fortunately, ***The Song of Roland*** is not like a dragon-fly. It is more like a skilfully fitted timepiece. By observing the precision-made watch being disassembled, we can enhance the pleasure we get in seeing it after it is reassembled. And this has been the case during the research for this study. An analysis of ***The Song of Roland*** and a scrutiny of its parts has revealed Turold's masterful workmanship and literary genius, and a score of readings have uncovered beauties formerly missed. Charles A. Knudson advocates that all studies of the ***Roland*** "should lead us toward the poem and not away from it," and it is hoped that this study has led in the right direction. (pp. 194-95)

George Fenwick Jones, in his The Ethos of "The Song of Roland," *Johns Hopkins Press, 1963, 216 p.*

ALAIN RENOIR (essay date 1963)

[In the following excerpt, Renoir compares the heroic oath motif in The Song, *the Anglo-Saxon* Beowulf, *and the Middle High German* Nibelungenlied. *He concludes that in these works, "the initial intentions of the oath* [blur] *a little more every time it is used."]*

Ever since the beginning of recorded history, the inhabitants of the Western world seem to have entertained a decided fondness for requiring oaths from each other. . . . (p. 237)

[As] late as the end of the tenth century, Anglo-Saxon warriors swore in the hall heroic oaths which they were expected to keep on the battlefield. . . . But the heroic oath was by no means one-sided. On the contrary, just as the warriors were expected to sacrifice themselves to avenge their leader, he in turn was expected to afford them all the protection in his power; he was their formal protector. . . . (pp. 237-38)

Although the development of the feudal system changed the nature of the relationship between the leader and his retainers, it preserved the fundamental principles of the heroic oath in the form of the feudal contract. The vassal was expected to swear allegiance to his overlord and to serve in his wars for a specific period of time. (p. 238)

We should not be surprised that the heroic oath is the principal source of action in the three greatest secular epics of the Middle Ages: the Anglo-Saxon *Beowulf,* the Old French ***Chanson de Roland,*** and the Middle High German *Nibelungenlied.* We should likewise not be surprised that it brings about the destruction of the most virtuous character in each of the three poems. (p. 239)

[Roland is] the most virtuous protagonist of the ***Chanson de Roland.*** Even though we shall have occasion to see that his actions are often blatantly sinful by Christian standards, his total behavior is virtuous enough to earn him the rare reward of being taken directly to Heaven the instant he dies. . . . In the French epic, as in *Beowulf,* the action of the first half of the poem is largely due to the hero's insistence upon carrying out every detail of the heroic oath against utterly unreasonable odds. We may assume the formal feudal relationship between Roland and Charlemagne to be the same as that between Aymon and Charlemagne [in the *Chanson des Quatre Fils Aymon*]; and, just as Aymon considers himself bound to attack his own sons to keep his oath to his overlord, so Roland considers himself bound to hold his ground against an overwhelmingly superior enemy rather than surrender even one of the emperor's beasts of burden. . . . This conviction is so firmly entrenched in his mind that it leads him to sacrifice his own life and allow the massacre of the 20,000 men in his command rather than budge from the post assigned him by Charlemagne, or even call for help. (pp. 240-41)

The concept of the heroic oath is of equal importance in *Beowulf,* the ***Chanson de Roland,*** and the *Nibelungenlied,* and it fulfills similar functions in all three works. The circumstances under which the oath is carried out, however, differ greatly from one poem to the other, and this difference suggests something fundamental about each author's attitude toward the same basic theme.

The nature of the heroic oath in *Beowulf,* confusing as it may be to the modern scholarly reader, posed no serious problem for the protagonists of the poem. Even the jealous Unferth, who insultingly questions Beowulf's adequacy to deal with the monster Grendel, never openly doubts the intrinsic value of the latter's oath to rid the world of the evil doer. The only problem is the fulfillment; if Beowulf either kills Grendel, and later his mother, or bravely dies in the attempt, he will have fulfilled his oath to the letter and won eternal renown among both the Danes and the Geats. The same observation may be made about the fight with the dragon. As "Wedra helm," the hero is duty bound to fight the dragon or die in the attempt, and his only concern is to do it well. (p. 242)

Faced with the necessity of making his hero enter his last fight without even questioning the value of his action, the poet nevertheless succeeds in making us go through the soul searching which he must deny Beowulf, and he does so by presenting the episode from three different points of view—the points of view of Beowulf, his retainers, and the audience.

Although Beowulf approaches the dragon's lair with eleven armed retainers, there is no question that he must fight the monster alone. Even if age has robbed him of the nearly superhuman strength with which he overcame Grendel long ago, he still remains the "frod folces weard," and he is keenly aware that he alone has had previous experience in fighting monsters. . . . (p. 243)

The point of view of Beowulf's eleven companions, however, is not quite so simple. Common sense makes it plain that their leader is in the greatest danger, and the most fundamental rule of the comitatus demands that they stand at his side and either triumph or die with him. On the other hand, the rules of the comitatus also require obedience to the leader, and Beowulf has not only stated that the forthcoming combat is no concern of his retainers, but has specifically ordered them to keep out of the fight. . . . Torn between these two mutually exclusive, yet equally binding, duties, Beowulf's companions cannot be expected to look at the ensuing action from the same unambiguous point of view as their leader does. In fact, ten of them choose to obey his specific command, while the eleventh, Wiglaf, eventually chooses the more honorable alternative and enters the fight with the dragon. His companions are obviously misbehaving within the law, but it is significant that Wiglaf is Beowulf's only blood relative in the group, so that he has a greater incentive to disobey his orders and to succor him. (p. 244)

[We] may say that Beowulf's point of view during his last fight is devoid of any ambiguity and that both his behavior and that of his retainers are thoroughly conventional; each of them seems to think and act precisely as the audience would expect him to think and act under the circumstances. Yet we must not conclude that the passage is devoid of emotional tension, for it is perhaps one of the tensest episodes in English literature. The tension, however, is not exclusively intrinsic to the action, but is primarily due to a divergence in points of view between the audience and the participants in the action. From our position outside the poem, we know far more about the participants than they do about each other, and we have access to information necessarily unavailable to them. The result is that, while we understand their respective points of view, our own allows us to foresee the catastrophic outcome which they do not even suspect. We are, therefore, submitted to a tragic experience which is partially spared them by the limitations of their points of view, and the tension is increased by our inevitable realization that they might act differently if they only knew. (p. 245)

[We] may say that the fight with the dragon is completely devoid of suspense. The audience knows exactly what is going to happen, and everything happens according to the most conventional and time-hallowed rules of early Germanic society. Beowulf marches to his death apparently with some misgivings about his own ability to subdue his antagonist, but without the least doubt concerning the nature of his duty or the validity of the way in which he attempts to perform it. The text of the poem does not suggest even a hint of conflict on this point in his mind; it is as if the very concept of an alternative course of action were beyond his intellectual and emotional grasp. (pp. 248-49)

While the nature of the heroic oath poses no intrinsic problem in *Beowulf,* it poses a very serious one in the ***Chanson de Roland.*** One might even say that the whole poem is in one respect a long question concerning the obligations which this oath entails on the part of those who have sworn it. Perhaps the most immediately perceptible difference between the English and the French poem is one of numbers; Beowulf goes to his last battle in company with eleven warriors, Roland goes to his in company with 20,000; Beowulf never faces more than one enemy at a time within the course of the poem, Roland faces 100,000. The proportions, of course, remain the same; for a lone warrior is as easily overpowered by a single dragon or a troll as 20,000 are by 100,000 Saracens; and Roland's 20,000 men are probably not a larger percentage of Charlemagne's immense army than Beowulf's eleven in respect to the small Germanic comitatus. The larger numbers, however, entail an increased complexity which is necessarily reflected in human relationships. King Beowulf faces in person the challenge of the dragon and simply asks some trusted retainers to accompany him; Emperor Charlemagne faces the Saracen challenge by asking his peers to nominate a leader for his rearguard, and this leader in turn selects the officers who will assist him. The emperor has no direct voice in selecting the men who will die for him, he will not be on the battlefield to lead them, and the mass of them are very likely unknown to him even by sight. In comparison with the warriors in *Beowulf,* each of whom has some sort of personal relationship with his king, those in the ***Chanson*** may never have exchanged a single word with their emperor. Furthermore, although each warrior in the army owes allegiance to his own overlord, who in turn owes allegiance to Charlemagne, not every one of them has necessarily pledged allegiance to Charlemagne himself. The obvious results of this situation are two: in the first place, many a warrior may be asked to undergo all kinds of hardships in the indirect service of a rather distant potentate toward whom he has no personal obligation; in the second place, the lord who is required by oath to serve the emperor is also required to be a protector to his warriors. He is Charlemagne's *homme* [''man''; ''feudal vassal''] but he is also his men's *guarant* [''protector''; ''guarantor'']; and these two sworn duties may accidentally contradict each other. Thus, the implications of the heroic oath, not to say its very validity, are by no means so clear as they are in *Beowulf.*

The extent to which this ambiguity affects the action in the ***Chanson de Roland*** is clearly illustrated by Ganelon's betrayal of the French and his subsequent trial by his peers. When, near the beginning of the poem, Roland asks to be sent on an embassy to the Saracen King Marsilie, he is rejected as unqualified for diplomatic mission, and he then nominates Ganelon for the dangerous mission. Ganelon construes the nomination as an attempt against his life, and his furor knows no bounds. . . . Because neither man has taken an oath of allegiance toward the other, Ganelon feels free to announce publicly his intention of making his own embassy to Sarragoce an occasion for bringing about Roland's undoing. His words can be construed only as meaning that he intends to find some means of delivering Roland to the enemy, and this is precisely how they are construed by the French. (pp. 249-51)

Ganelon is indisputably correct in his assumption that he and Roland owe nothing to each other; but he never seems to realize that, in delivering him and his 20,000 men to the enemy, he is actually betraying Charlemagne himself, to whom he may be assumed to have sworn an oath of allegiance. When, at the end of the poem, he must stand trial before his peers, his justification is that he has merely avenged himself upon Roland and that [his announced intention of doing so] . . . constituted a formal challenge. . . . The interesting thing, for us, is that the barons before whom he is presenting this defense accept his argument and ask Charlemagne to set him free. . . . Ganelon, it is true, gets his well-earned punishment. . ., but the fact remains that the obligations entailed by the heroic oath in the ***Chanson de Roland*** are confused enough to allow a vassal to cause the massacre of 20,000 of his overlord's warriors and still be exculpated by a court of peers. One cannot readily imagine a similar situation in *Beowulf.* Ganelon's case, incidentally, is not the only one in Old French epic. One recalls, for instance, a similar occasion in the *Roman de Thebes,* where another court of peers fails to declare guilty a vassal of Eteocles who has traitorously turned an outer battlement of Thebes to the enemy.

Thus Roland, unlike Beowulf, is bound by a heroic oath whose precise requirements are far from unequivocal with the society in which he lives, and his tragedy is largely the result of his own failure to realize that his obligations may change according to the situation. In his own mind his bound duty is as clearly defined as was Beowulf's, and he does not hesitate to inform his men about it as soon as he learns that the Saracen hordes are about to descend upon the ill-fated rear-guard in hopelessly overwhelming number:

> Pur sun seignur deit hom susfrir granz mals
> E endurer e forz freiz e granz chalz,
> Sin deit hom perdre del sanc e de la char.
>
> [One must suffer great hardships for one's lord
> and endure severe cold and great heat, and one
> must also lose blood and flesh.]. . .

Like Beowulf, Roland is here stating his intention to conform in every detail to the strictest conventions of the oath which a vassal must swear to his overlord. Unlike Beowulf, however, he is out of tune with his society. The reader needs no great perspicuity to realize that allowing the massacre of 20,000 men rather than retreat or call for help will do little service to the emperor. Nor is this a strictly modern point of view; for it is precisely the argument with which Oliver vainly attempts to persuade Roland to blow his horn and recall Charlemagne and his army. . . . (pp. 251-52)

Roland's willingness to die rather than depart in the slightest respect from the terms of his oath is admirable, but it argues his inability to cope with the complexities of his own society. Even if we don not agree with those critics [such as George Fenwick Jones] who would make him an early Germanic warrior [see the excerpt dated 1963], we may say that his thinking, unlike that of Oliver, fits the age of *Beowulf* rather than that of the ***Chanson de Roland.*** The poet has made this situation clear with one single line: "Rollant est proz e Oliver est sage."

If we accept the definition given by the *Oxford English Dictionary* for the noun *saint*—"one of the blessed dead in Heaven"—then the ***Chanson de Roland***is in one important respect the story of the making of a saint; for, as already mentioned, we witness Roland's translation to Heaven within the course of the narrative. We know that the saints of mediaeval literature were often made rather than born, and that they not seldom followed with disturbing energy the path of evil until some revelation taught them the right way. One recalls, for instance, the legend of Gregory, who slept with his mother and later became Pope, and that of Beatrice, who was a whore before dying in holiness. Just as Beowulf's actions conform to the conventional pattern for a Germanic king, so Roland's conform to at least one conventional pattern for a saint. From the mediaeval Christian point of view, his blindness to the necessity of departing from the words of his oath in order to remain true to its spirit is in part due to pride, the most fundamental of the seven deadly sins. Roland unreasonably insists upon carrying out his oath to the letter largely because he fears that calling for help might lower his renown with the world. . . . Thus, if Roland is to prove true to type, he must learn the right way before he may die a saint.

This process of moral regeneration is carried out masterfully. The French have held their ground all day against the Saracen onslaught, and only sixty are now left alive of the 20,000 in Roland's command. . . . Roland, still convinced that he has performed his duty, would now blow his horn to recall Charlemagne. Oliver, however, argues that it is too late, now that the rearguard has been massacred, and reproachfully lays the blame for the disaster, not on Roland's misjudgment, but on his *desmesure,* the chivalric form of the sin of pride. . . . The argument is settled by Archbishop Turpin, who insists that Charlemagne be recalled so that the dead my receive Christian burial. . . . Thus, within the space of a few lines, Roland is made to realize his state of mortal sin and is faced with the necessity of performing a Christian duty. It is significant that he immediately accepts Turpin's suggestion: "Sire, mult dites bien" ["Well said, sir"]. With the very next line, we find him blowing his horn to recall Charlemagne. . . . (pp. 253-54)

At this point, one may not unreasonably argue that Roland has undergone a change. He is no longer concerned with increasing his own renown by fulfilling every detail of his oath at whatever cost; he is concerned with a purely Christian matter that will add nothing to his renown in the world, for Oliver has made only too clear the shame of recalling Charlemagne now that it is too late. . . . Roland's decision to blow his horn is thus symbolic of his moral regeneration; for in deciding to recall Charlemagne he willingly gives up the worldly fame in the pursuit of which he has just sacrificed the lives of nearly 20,000 men.

The dramatic climax of his regeneration comes a few lines later, when, with all thoughts of personal glory forgotten, he surveys the bloody battlefield. As the Saracens regroup their battalions for the final assault, the bright afternoon light bathes the battlefield in radiance. . . . Roland, inactive for the first time in the poem, may now contemplate the slaughter which his pride has caused and humbly come to a full realization of his awful responsibility:

> Rollant reguardet es munz e es lariz;
> De cels de France i veit tanz morz gesir!
> E il les pluret cum chevaler gentill:
> "Seignors barons, de vos ait Deus mercit!
> Tutes voz anmes otreit il pareïs!
> En seintes flurs il les facet gesir!
> Meillors vassals de vos unkes ne vi.
> Si lungement tuz tens m'avez servit,
> A oes Carlin si granz païs cunquis!
> Li empereres tant mare vos nurrit!
> Tere de France, mult estes dulz païs,
> Oi desertet a tant rubostl exill.
> Barons Franceis, pur mei vos vei murir;
> Jo ne vos pois tenser ne guarantir.
> Aït vos Deus, ki unkes ne mentit!
> Oliver, frere, vos ne dei jo failir.
> De doel murra, se altre ne m'i ocit.
> Sire cumpaniz, alum i referir!"
>
> [Roland gazes at the mountains and hills.
> He sees so many men from France lying dead,
> He weeps over them like a noble knight:
> "My lord barons, God have mercy on you!
> May He grant Paradise to all your souls,
> May He cause them to lie among the holy flowers!
> I have never seen worthier knights than you,
> You have served me constantly and for so long!
> You have conquered such great nations for Charles!

The Emperor raised you, but how unfortunate the outcome!
Land of France, you are a very sweet realm,
Today made desolate by such a cruel disaster!
French knights, I see you dying for my sake:
I cannot protect or save you.
May God, who never did lie, help you!
Oliver, my friend, I must not fail you,
I shall die of sorrow if nothing else kills me.
Comrade, sir, let's go strike again!'']. . . .

I have argued elsewhere that in this magnificent passage Roland is in effect surrendering his secular command to God [see Additional Bibliography]. He who was previously their proud *guarant* must now humbly acknowledge his inability to *guarantir* them in their most need. If we recall the ambiguous aspects of the feudal heroic oath noted above, we may say that Roland is here confessing his twofold failure in the world of men: in allowing the massacre of the rearguard he has failed as Charlemagne's *homme,* and in proving impotent to succor them he has failed as their *guarant*. In other words, he, who sold his life and those of his men in proud adherence to his own rigid interpretation of the heroic oath, must die with full knowledge that he has unquestionably fallen short of its two principal requirements. On the other hand, the men whom we have heard him proudly harangue on the duties of the vassal toward his lord have kept their part of the bargain, and the mangled bodies that cover the mountain slopes amply testify to the price they have paid for it.

Such is the price of the lesson which Roland learns. From the mediaeval point of view, however, the lesson is worth the cost. As the humbled commander of the rearguard relinquishes both the dead and the living to the care of God, ''ki unkes ne mentit'' [''who never did lie''], he is in effect stating what Geoffrey Chaucer will repeat some three-hundred years later at the end of *Troilus and Criseyde:*

> Repeyreth hom fro worldly vanyte,
> And of youre herte up casteth the visage
> To thilke God that after his ymage
> Yow made, and thynketh al nys but a faire
> This world, that passeth soone as floures faire.

From this point on, Roland's behavior is that of a saint. When he again addresses the remnants of his army, it is no longer to lecture on their feudal duty, but rather to assure them that they are about to suffer holy martyrdom. . . . A few lines later we hear him address his mortally wounded friend, Oliver, ''dulcement e suef'' [''softly and gently'']; and when Oliver dies Roland's humility and tenderness strike a sharp contrast against his previous pride and arrogance: ''Mult dulcement a regretter le prist'' [''He began to lament over him very softly'']. The poet further emphasizes the completeness of his hero's regeneration with an instance of supreme Christian irony. We have already seen Roland, who thrice refused to call for help when only lives were at stake, blow his horn to insure the Christian burial of his men. He immediately gives a second tremendous blast, and his effort is so great that his temples burst. . . . Now, exhausted by the self-inflicted penitential wound that will cost him his life, he gathers his rapidly failing strength in a desperate attempt to send Charlemagne a last weak call. . . . Thus, the same horn which was earlier the symbol of his worldly pride and later that of his regeneration, now becomes the symbol of his sainthood as he endures self-inflicted martyrdom in response to the bishop's Christian concern for the burial of the dead. His very death is likewise symbolic of his now complete submission to the will of God. Like the defeated knight who surrenders unconditionally to the mercy of a superior opponent whom he has fought in vain, Roland ''sun destre guant en ad vers Deu tendut'' [''offered his right gauntlet to God''].

That the poet intends God to accept Roland's surrender is evident from the fact that the hero is taken to Heaven as soon as he is dead; the conclusion of the poem affords us further evidence. The second half of the ***Chanson de Roland*** tells how the sight of the fallen rearguard sends Charlemagne back into Spain. The sinful Pagans are crushed in battle and the unrepentant survivors are treated with appropriate harshness, so that Roland's 20,000 are avenged by human intervention. Roland himself, however, is not avenged by human intervention, for we have seen that the man who engineered his death is set free by a court of peers. If we accept my earlier proposition that Roland has failed in the world of men, then it is only fair that his death should remain unavenged by men. If we further consider that he actually dies in the service of Heaven, then we must agree that the burden of avenging his death lies with God himself; and we may be sure that God will discharge His duty as well as the best feudal overlord, for we have heard Roland describe Him as one ''ki unkes ne mentit.'' When a court of peers fails to condemn Ganelon, Charlemagne requests trial by combat. Roland's friends greatly fear the outcome, but God knows better. . . . When Ganelon's champion strikes a formidable blow to his opponent, divine intervention saves him. . . . Likewise, when he is finally struck dead, the French exclaim in unison, ''Deus i ad fait vertut!'' [''God performed a miracle!'']. Thus the poet, not content with merely sending Roland to Heaven, feels the need to emphasize the point in the concluding episode. Whether or not we agree with Joseph Bédier that the author of the ***Chanson*** was an ecclesiastic, we may be sure that he would not have risked such theological audacity unless he had first intended to have his hero rid himself of the sin of pride.

Just as Beowulf dies triumphant over evil outward forces, so Roland dies triumphant over the evil forces within himself. The lesson is costly, but it is magnificent. In a way, it is the same lesson which Shakespeare has King Lear learn before he may die. Just as the *Beowulf* poet has treated the problem of the heroic oath within the conventions of early Germanic society, so the ***Roland*** poet has treated it within the conventions of feudal Christianity. In one respect, Roland's behavior is more readily understandable to the twentieth century than is Beowulf's; for our age is always ready to sympathize with the man who suffers for the sake of a change. Yet, within their respective contexts, both *Beowulf* and the ***Chanson de Roland*** present the tragedy of the heroic oath with equal mastery.

Although both Beowulf and Roland die a tragic death, their tragedies are vastly different. . . . Beowulf's death is tragic from the point of view of the audience. From his own point of view, it is rather the crowning achievement in his career as a perfect Germanic king; and it teaches him nothing that he does not already know, for he has been treading the right path ever since he became king some fifty years before. Roland's tragedy, on the contrary, is his own; he must, before his death, experience within himself the disintegration of the ideal to which he has been stubbornly sacrificing his own life as well as those of his men, and he must learn to follow a new path in the brief instants that still stand between him and death. Turning now to the *Nibelungenlied,* we find that Rüedeger also suffers a tragic death and that, like Roland's, his tragedy is his own.

Unlike Beowulf or Roland, however, Rüedeger has no control over his own tragedy and is offered no opportunity for sainthood. Beowulf goes to his death because he *wants* to discharge his heroic oath; Rüedeger goes to his because Kriemhilt *requires* him to do so. Before dying, Roland is shown the sinfulness of his interpretation of the heroic oath and is allowed to mend his ways; Rüedeger is placed into a situation where discharging his oath is almost as great a sin as failing to do so. Nor is he given the respite of believing even for a moment that he is taking the right course, for he plainly realizes his tragic plight even before complying with Kriemhilt's request. Between the time he swore to avenge any wrong done her and the time she requires him to do so, he has sworn his friendship to her brothers, the Burgundian kings whom she now wants him to fight. (pp. 254-59)

In requiring him to fight his friends, she is asking him to damn his soul. . . . His only hope of salvation is to make the queen change her mind, and even this is denied him when Etzel . . . reminds him of his duty as a vassal.

Just as the society represented in the ***Chanson de Roland*** is more complex than that in *Beowulf,* so the society in the *Nibelungenlied* is more complex than that in the ***Chanson.*** The numbers of men who move about in the two poems are approximately the same, but the German poem adds a level of complexity to that of the French. Ganelon's revenge involves only the French and the Saracens. Kriemhilt's revenge involves three different groups: the Germanic Burgundians, whose allegiance and sympathies are clearly with their kings; the Huns, whose allegiance and sympathies are clearly with Etzel and Kriemhilt; and a group of Germans in the service of the Huns, whose allegiance is to Etzel through his vassal Rüedeger, but whose sympathies are with the Burgundians. This increased complexity necessarily yields increased confusion concerning the obligations imposed by the heroic oath.

The conflicting oaths which Rüedeger swore to Kriemhilt and to her brothers are personal and voluntary, so that he may attempt to solve his dilemma by persuading the queen to change her mind. When Etzel joins his request to hers, however, he changes the nature of the dilemma by forcing his vassal to choose between friendship and feudal allegiance. As Gustav Ehrismann has convincingly argued, this is no choice, for feudal allegiance must unquestionably win out. Unable to avoid the shame of betraying his friends, Rüedeger can only restate his tragic dilemma and conclude that death in battle is the only solution. . . . (pp. 260-61)

Rüedeger's noble sacrifice can be of no avail, and, as with Beowulf, the only thing that now counts is the beauty of the act.

It is in the beauty of the act that we find what is perhaps the fundamental difference between *Beowulf,* the ***Chanson de Roland,*** and the *Nibelungenlied.* . . . [The] aesthetic accomplishment in *Beowulf* lies in the hero's unselfish devotion to the early Germanic ideals of kingship, while in the ***Chanson de Roland*** it lies in his awakening to the ideals of Christian chivalry. In the *Nibelungenlied* it lies in his adherence to the ideals of courtly chivalry. Rüedeger deplores not only the prospective damnation of his soul, but also the fact that the action he must undertake is in fact a betrayal of most cherished virtues of courtly chivalry. . . .

Just as Beowulf and Roland die in a manner that suits their ideals, so Rüedeger attempts to die like an honorable, loyal, and well-bred knight. (p. 262)

In *Beowulf* the hero himself triumphs over external evil when he kills the dragon with Wiglaf's help. In the ***Chanson de Roland*** he triumphs over internal evil when he becomes aware of his own *desmesure,* but only divine justice can vanquish external evil when Ganelon's champion loses his trial by combat. In the *Nibelungenlied* Rüedeger, like Beowulf, has no internal evil to vanquish, for . . . he is the embodiment of virtue; and external evil is crushed through the purely human intervention of Dietrich and Hildebrant. The progression is not unexpected, for *Beowulf* was surely composed during the so-called heroic age, the ***Chanson de Roland*** at the beginning of the age of Christian chivalry, and the *Nibelungenlied* during the most courtly period of German literature—during the seventy years that produced such masters of courtly poetry as Der von Kürenberc, Reimar der Alte, Hartmann von Aue, Walter von der Vogelweide, Gottfried von Strassburg, and Wolfram von Eschenbach. As western Europe changed its ideals, the poets followed suit by modifying their treatment of a common theme accordingly; and, as society grew larger and more complex, so the nature of the heroic oath grew more obscure and confusing. In *Beowulf* the hero need never think twice about what he must do to fulfill his oath honorably; in the ***Chanson de Roland*** he belatedly learns what to do; and in the *Nibelungenlied* he knows even before acting that the task is humanly impossible. Likewise, just as the nature of the oath grows more confusing with each poem, so punishment and reward become more confused. Evil in *Beowulf* is vanquished when the dragon is killed, and Beowulf himself is immediately rewarded by being granted the kind of death most coveted by early Germanic heroes. Roland, on the other hand, does not receive his reward until he is actually dead; and evil has to wait until the end of the poem to receive a punishment which it nearly escapes. In the *Nibelungenlied,* Rüedeger dies convinced that he has damned himself, and we have only our personal sense of justice to suggest that his unfailing adherence to the practices of courtly chivalry will receive its posthumous reward. (pp. 264-65)

If we accept Johan Huizinga's view [expressed in his *The Waning of the Middle Ages*] that the very concept of the heroic oath is a pagan ideal later adopted and Christianized by the feudal system, we have further evidence to argue that the transformation it undergoes in the three poems discussed here do not merely constitute an interesting coincidence, but represent three points in the development of a single phenomenon. . . . In addition to the added cultural complexities, the greater remoteness from the origin blurs the initial intentions of the oath a little more every time it issued. With the passage of time the disintegration of the original significance appears to have progressed apace. . . . In *Beowulf,* the ***Chanson de Roland,*** and the *Nibelungenlied,* however, the power of the heroic oath was still formidable enough to make it the central element in three of the greatest tragedies since classical antiquity. (p. 266)

Alain Renoir, "The Heroic Oath in 'Beowulf', the 'Chanson de Roland', and the 'Nibelungenlied'," in Studies in Old English Literature in Honor of Arthur G. Brodeur, *edited by Stanley B. Greenfield, University of Oregon Books, 1963, pp. 237-66.*

PIERRE LE GENTIL (essay date 1967)

[In the following excerpt from a book originally published in 1955 and revised in 1967, Le Gentil discusses aspects of The Song's *literary art, stating that "the author of* Roland *is clearly one of the first to have used the French language artistically."]*

Roland sounds the oliphant.

If art consists primarily of constructing and ordering a subject, of examining man and his fate, and of using realism to transcend reality, then the ***Roland*** poet clearly possesses all the elements that distinguish a great artist. (p. 125)

[To] understand the various decisions of our author is not an easy task. We are dealing with a difficult, elliptical, unintellectual style. . . . There is no explanation or commentary, not even a confidence to share, and this can be confusing. But this abrupt, intuitive compactness can be understood by those who are willing to make the effort.

Certain of these problems are not difficult to unravel. . . . [The] author likes to establish parallels and contrasts between the various events of the story, and does it with great success. A good example is to be found in the two introductory scenes. Everything in Charlemagne's camp indicates victory, breathes of strength, youth, and loyalty. But in the midst of the luxury and ostentation that surround Marsile, anxiety and treachery prevail. That this is a simple contrast does not prevent this sequence from being the best of introductions. Without an extraneous word, it puts us *in media res,* defines the subject, establishes the characters, creates the atmosphere. The poet explains by example, wants the reader to understand by observation. There is no need to accumulate a list of instances, though many immediately come to mind. To speak of sparseness of monotony in the ***Roland*** would be fallacious. The poet never uses a formula mechanically. His contrasts and repetitions are never artificial because he scorns pat devices. Ganelon's selection as ambassador parallels Roland's assignment to the rear guard but, as one initiates the drama, the other effects the treason. Although they are both carried out in the same terms, Roland, in his maliciousness, is quick and spontaneous. Ganelon's act is premeditated, the result of treacherous calculation. This distinction is a master stroke in a carefully conceived and brilliantly applied plan.

The very development of the drama demands parallels and contrasts to reveal minds and emotions, to explain both the origin and the progress of the action. The painful argument that twice opposes Roland and Oliver during the battle provides a good example. Roland finally accepts what he first rejected because something has changed in his soul, and his vision is greater. But Oliver does not change. He contradicts his previous counsel because he now sees no hope of averting the disaster. Human logic and wisdom are insufficient to explain the deed that saves Roland. There is no point in treating it as an ordinary event. (pp. 126-27)

Just as he knows how to use parallels and contrasts, the author of the ***Roland*** understands the importance of thematic groundwork. We are familiar with the role played by the theme of French weariness throughout the ***Chanson.*** It accounts for Blancandrin's offers and the debate they provoke. It explains the conflict that erupts between Roland and Ganelon, and enhances the significance of both Roland's rashness and Ganelon's weakness, clarifying the argument of one and the protestations of the other. This same theme reappears when, because of Roland's death, Charlemagne is left alone to face Baligant. And the last lines of the poem echo it, when the angel Gabriel comes to impose new trials on the old emperor, who longs for repose. The cautionary dreams and omens that suddenly threaten danger or imminent catastrophe could hardly be more skillful or striking. Is the poet's use of this groundwork so heavy-handed as to prevent any element of the unexpected? We know that he does not deserve this reproach. He is interested not in surprise but in pathos; he wants his listeners and characters to live the drama of Roncevaux. The characters can do so only if they have forebodings, and the listeners only if they know or suspect the outcome. Emotion is possible only when curiosity gives way to fear of the inevitable. It takes more than talent to meet such demands successfully.

The absence of surprise in the narrative is easily offset by the fact of its progressive intensity, which gives an unexpected perspective and meaning to events, even if they are formally announced or seem inevitable. This is nowhere better illustrated than in the last episodes of the battle, when Oliver, Turpin, and then Roland fall. These deaths, so close yet so different, form a hierarchy based on the degree and scope of each sacrifice. (pp. 128-29)

A poet has to be judged by his use of the available means of expression. The author of the ***Roland*** does not strictly depend on the most used forms of traditional rhetoric, but no one knows better than he how to make them effective by intelligent artistic handling.

A narrative is valuable not only for its organization and execution, but also for the way in which it is illustrated. Our poet describes in order to explain, but he does so with surprising restraint and admirable economy. The two contrasting scenes that serve as introduction to the poem . . . come to mind, particularly the second, rich in color and movement:

> The emperor is in a broad orchard, and with him are Roland and Oliver, the Duke Sansun, and the proud Anseis, and Gefrey of Anjou, the King's standard-bearer. Gerin and Gerer are with him also, and many others. There are fifteen thousand from sweet France. The knights are seated on white silk carpets. The clever and the elderly are amusing themselves at backgammon and chess; the quick-blooded young men are fencing. Under a pine tree near an eglantine they have set a throne of pure gold, and there sits the King who rules sweet France. His beard is white and his hair is in full flower. His body is noble and his bearing is princely. If a man were to come looking for him, there would be no need to point him out.

This is not description for its own sake; its aim is specifically to place the narrative and make it immediate. The unforgettable lines that precede the arrival of the rear guard at the pass of Roncevaux provide another example:

> The peaks are high and the valleys are dark,
> the gorges awesome under dun rocks.

The same scene is described when Charles' army sets out to aid Roland:

> The peaks are high and dark and huge, the
> valleys deep, and the torrents dash through them.
> They sound their trumpets at the head of the
> column and at the rear, and all together blare
> in answer to Roland's ivory horn.

And again, as the death throes of the hero begin:

> The mountains are high, and the trees are tall,
> and there are four great stones of marble there,
> shining. Count Roland faints on the green grass.

These repetitions are clearly not accidental; they answer and echo one another from afar. The poet closely links the setting to the action as he sustains and intensifies the emotion. The relation is schematic; but through repetition it becomes effective and, in its simplicity, takes on a vital significance. One long description would surely have been less effective. (pp. 130-32)

The author of the ***Roland*** knows how to describe a crowd. He can arrange battles and set down the elements of which they are composed. But he reveals a marked preference for single combat. The incidence of individual confrontations in his narrative is high; through repetition he probably intends to give the impression of furious animosities. More important, he wants to pay homage to personal worth and to show the courageous rivalry that impels the best to distinguish themselves from the crowd in battle. Although his use of the few available details is ingenious, they unfortunately reappear too often to remain interesting. Eventually the lances that shatter or piece the flesh up to the pennon are boring; one tires of seeing the steel, gold, and gems of the helmets that shoot sparks under the impact of swords, of watching split skulls spill out their brains and entrails being exposed in waves of blood. A hierarchy of prowess ought to correspond to the hierarchy of the heroes. But, if the least of the Christian knights can be a superman, it becomes very difficult to illustrate the superiority of Roland, let alone Charlemagne. It is hardly surprising that some fantastic blows are amusing rather than impressive, but we should be cautious in speaking of clumsiness or naiveté. The medieval public was more aware than we of what a man with a sword could do, and our poet is much too interested in pleasing his audience to have gratuitously offended them. Because of his deep conviction of the nobility of his subject, he is committed to audacity and feels free to invent the most improbable exploits. We should believe only what he asks us to believe, however. If he offers an ecstatic description of muscular force, it is obvious that he admires it. But he admires it principally because it can reveal the unconquerable heroism of a soul, the militant fervor of faith, the victorious sanctity of a cause. Whoever embodies these moral forces and finds his very motive and end in God is, must be, capable of anything. This is the logic of the ***Roland*** poet: he no more feared contradiction than he doubted his talent.

Thus he does not hesitate to describe at length the duel between Charlemagne and Baligant, though he is certainly running a risk. This duel must sum up the others without repeating or diminishing them. In particular, it must not detract from Roland's exploits. . . . Everything about this encounter recalls the previous battles. The blows dealt by these two adversaries have already been exchanged by others, in the same way and with the same effect. Others, like them, have stopped for a moment to affirm their cause or to offer a final appeal. Yet there is no doubt of the exceptional value of this passage. The poet has allowed himself repetitions, but there is no good reason to condemn in him what we admire in Homer.

The details or expressions that he has already used are skillfully altered or reordered. His effort at composition, or synthesis if you will, is rewarded and is all the more remarkable in that he has not admitted unrealistic devices. What then explains the gigantic proportions of the scene? We should first recall its context, its place in the drama, and the opponents involved. Most important is the element of supernatural intervention that is introduced to establish the scope; though subtle, it is the only occurrence of its kind in the entire poem. At the most critical moment of the battle, it is to Charlemagne alone that God reveals himself. He makes it clear that Charles is his champion, serving a cause that is sacred among all others. To unite such grandeur and such simplicity is hardly an easy task. (pp. 133-37)

[A] word now on characterization. Because of its unusual intensity, the portrait of Baligant immediately attracts attention. The poet has devoted a long strophe to him. Charlemagne's adversary is well worth such a tribute. . . . Baligant may seem to be receiving preferential treatment, but in fact the poet has not neglected his favorite heroes. Since he is always near them, and assumes us also to be at their side, he does not feel the need to set down single, complete portraits. Their images become increasingly clear in our minds as we participate in the drama of which they are the protagonists. The concise sketches that bring them to life are surprisingly evocative and, in the course of the action, reveal more of their souls than their faces. The poet relates everything that he sees or hears to these souls: conversation, attitudes, acts of heroism or ignominy. Going beyond the poet as portrayer of character, let us examine the artistry that so successfully complements the psychology he uses. A good place to start is with the portrait of Roland riding through the pass, proud, smiling, and uncorrupted, as befits the martyr that he will be in a few hours:

> Where the pass leads up out of Spain Roland has mounted Veillantif, his good swift horse. He has taken up his arms; his armor becomes him. Now with a flourish Roland the bold raises the point of his lance to heaven. Laced to the shaft is a white pennon whose fringes sweep down to his hands. He bears himself nobly; his countenance is candid and smiling. Behind him comes his companion, and the French, who regard him as their salvation. He turns and looks fiercely at the Saracens, and then humbly and sweetly at the French.
>
> (pp. 137-39)

The more important the character is, the more fragmented his portrait. This fragmentation is the result of an attempt to sustain a presence and to match the rhythms of life, and is even more true of Charlemagne's portrait than of Roland's. The emperor's attitudes are noted with care and consistency, and provide the most impressive and significant examples of the poet's style. Three magnificent lines serve to introduce the old sovereign:

> His beard is white and his hair is in full flower.
> His body is noble and his bearing is princely.
> If a man were to come looking for him, there
> would be no need to point him out.

While the barons argue, Charles is thinking, his head bowed; or, remote, he distractedly strokes his beard; suddenly he starts out of his reverie with a harsh look or an indisputable order which puts an end to the uproar and quarreling. In one scene he blesses his ambassador with the gesture of both king and priest; in another, he falls to the ground in prayer. At Roncevaux he wanders alone among the dead in search of Roland and then, leaning against a pine and supported by his barons, delivers his nephew's funeral eulogy. Confronted by Baligant, he regains his strength and rides proudly at the head of his troops, his white beard spread over his coat of mail. As Pauphilet has remarked, each of these attitudes reflects an instant in his interior life and reveals either his humanity or his grandeur. It is difficult to decide which of these many passages is the most moving or admirable.

The descriptions and portraits in the ***Roland*** are full of movement, color, and vitality, but they are valuable for other qualities as well. . . . [The exotic] occurs, for example, in regions where the olive tree is found. More important, it appears in the description of Baligant's squadrons. The poet piles up strange names and picturesque details with lavish enthusiasm. But the profusion and extravagance are neither gratuitous nor naive. Any picture of Islam and the East at the time of the First Crusade was bound to be approximate and tendentious. The author can hardly be blamed for sharing the ignorance and prejudices of his contemporaries. Quite the contrary, he should be praised for his artistic interpretation of the material provided by the oral and clerical traditions. In his descriptions he has included imaginary as well as actual characters and has given them names. Reality is not the only source of poetic inspiration; fantasy is also important, and giants and monsters are not out of place in the epic. The author of the ***Roland*** confronts his task and takes full advantage of the available possibilities. Since the drama of Roncevaux is far from ordinary, he must lead the reader beyond his usual perspective. From recollection, imagination, and a crusader's enthusiasm, he has constructed these extraordinary beings who are incarnations of the spirit of evil. His descriptions are bold and sure and sometimes achieve a verbal power that in itself justifies their creation, even though his persistence risks offending our taste. (pp. 140-41)

Neither the marvelous nor the fantastic can unsettle such a vigorous and flexible talent. Although the ***Roland*** poet is working in a tradition that goes back to biblical and pagan antiquity, he is capable of great originality. Since the marvels that announce Roland's death are so well known, I shall quote instead Charlemagne's dream on the eve of the second battle of Roncevaux:

> Charles looks up toward heaven and sees thunderbolts, hail, rushing winds, storms and awesome tempests, and fires and flames appear to him, falling suddenly upon his whole army. The lances of ash wood and of apple wood catch fire and burn, and the shields, even to the gold bosses on them. And the shafts of their sharp spears are splintered, and their hauberks and their steel helmets are broken; and he sees his knights in great distress. Then bears and leopards come to devour them, serpents and vipers, dragons and devils, and more than thirty thousand griffons, and all of them fling themselves on the French.

We can expect no less from an intelligence and an imagination that we already know to be capable of so much. The question is only whether the poet exhibits a lack of moderation or control. The truth is that he uses the fantastic; he does not abuse it. The description of Baligant's troops is the only one of its kind in the poem. Dreams, miracles, and marvels are the exception, as they should be. We . . . [note] the subtlety with which supernatural intervention is described. A few shortcomings, of which we are perhaps bad judges, count for little next to so many successes.

Edmond Faral has remarked that the ***Roland*** poet's concept of literary effect leads him to dwell on the most important and moving situations, instead of following events as they occur. The ***Chanson*** is less a narrative than a sequence of scenes. It is essentially dramatic, which no doubt explains its sustained excitement.

Let us go back to the first act of the poem. The two initial scenes that contrast the courts of Marsile and Charlemagne are clearly the work of a dramatist. The dialogue is central, the style direct. A few descriptive remarks appear here and there, but only where they are needed to establish the scene, describe the surroundings, and introduce the characters. First is Marsile's council: of a total of eighty lines, nine serve as introduction, five establish the setting, and the rest are speeches or replies. A short transitional strophe takes us to Chalemagne's camp. The famous eighth strophe . . . then names and places thc characters. In the center, on his golden throne, is the emperor; near him are Roland, Oliver, Anseis, Geoffroy, Gerin, and Gerier. On rugs of white silk the oldest knights play backgammon and chess; to one side, the youngest fence. The light is directed toward the throne, which is sheltered by a pine, and is focused on its occupant. This description is dramatic and is thus a highly appropriate introduction to a debate—the debate that will lay the way for the catastrophe. The protagonists have only to come forward and speak. As in the theater, they reveal their characters and the causes of the action through their replies and tirades. Dramatic devices, such as stage directions for an action or attitude, accompany only the decisive speeches: Roland himself springs up to be the first to speak his mind and to utter a burst of scornful laughter; Ganelon throws off his sable cloak and lets fall the glove that is entrusted to him; Charlemagne lowers his head and strokes his white beard when he is anxious, roughly separates the peers, and solemnly blesses his messenger. The anonymous crowd of barons approves or comments as would an ancient chorus. Very well, one might say—and what is true of the first council of the French is true of the second, and also of Ganelon's mission to Marsile. But is not the ***Chanson*** primarily the story of a two-stage battle?

In fact, the style of the poem does not change radically when the action shifts to Roncevaux. The poet does not recount Charles' march across the mountains. Rather, he shows him in the sinister setting of the pass. He is explaining his anxiety to Duke Naimes, who has questioned him. Dialogue recurs during Marsile's preparations for battle, and it is hardly necessary to point out . . . the two quarrels between Roland and Oliver. The unforgettable battle is broken up into several stages, and most often each stage consists of a series of single engagements. We are not offered a continuous narrative, but a collection of little scenes that focus attention on specific areas of the battlefield or on a particular pair of adversaries. And in the ***Roland*** men speak almost as much as they fight; before the battle or even in the midst of the struggle, there is time for challenge, reprimand, exhortation, monologue, and debate. Such a succession of animated, striking dramatic images inevitably recalls the technique of modern cinema: the fragmented action and shifting perspective are similar, as is the convergence of means and effects in an attempt to create a total illusion of life. Certainly this technique was well suited to the mimed declamation of the jongleurs who were entrusted with the oral transmission of the chansons.

If dialogue is so important, it must be pointed and sparing in its effect. As the more famous scenes of the poem show, the speeches follow a deliberate pattern; each person says only what he has to say, at the right time, and in terms which can best reveal his character or explain his actions. The remark that sets the drama in motion is extremely theatrical. Before Roland utters the remark, "Let it be Ganelon, my stepfather," we are at the most critical point in a heated discussion, a moment of extreme tension. These elements combine to give an incalculable weight to the words about to be spoken. Roland is either unaware or uninterested, but the poet has weighed each of the words the hero uses. Ganelon's hasty reply, "I am your stepfather, as everyone knows," foreshadows the parallel scene that results in Roland's designation: "Let it be Roland, my stepson." These interdependent replies, set off by verbal parallels, explain and control the action and make the ***Roland*** a true drama. There is no need to add that in this drama the tirades and speeches are as remarkable as the best dialogue. (pp. 142-45)

The poet's feeling for his subject is intense, and he wants us to experience it with the same fervor. As we have just seen, he first achieves this total participation by dramatic means. But it would be a mistake to overlook his other qualities, for they are no less valuable. His narrative and descriptive passages are as effective as his dialogue. Equally moving is his subtle but powerful lyricism, often expressed through *laisses similaires*. This form, which also appears in other chansons, consists of using the same group of themes and motifs, with some variation, in two or more successive verses. Practicality is not the only reason for these repetitions. The chansons were recited before a public that was boisterous and easily distracted; if the texts could not sustain or revive attention, they had at least to counteract their shortcomings with clever and timely repetitions. But what might have been mere expedience has been turned to marvelous account by our author, as can be seen in the three verses that describe Roland's last moments. . . . It could be said that these repetitions include slight changes which, though they slow down the narrative, do not impede its progress. Perhaps they detract from its clarity and strength. But on the other hand they cast a powerful spell over the emotions, for time is suspended. The crucial moment, which should be more intensely experienced than the others, is prolonged, and this suspension creates an unexpected depth. Attitudes, gestures, words, and thoughts all take on a fuller and more personal meaning. Our spirit joins that of the great hero and goes with him to the threshold of eternity.

The poet would not have achieved the same effect if he had disregarded the problem of form. But we must avoid anachronisms in our appraisal of the ***Roland***'s style, and should think both of other chansons and of the austere grandeur of Romanesque churches. We must not demand of our author's language or meter a variety and flexibility that did not yet exist. The vocabulary of Old French was extensive but quite different from the modern language. The syntactical logic was not as subtle; juxtaposition was more common than continuity. At such a distance it is difficult to appreciate fully the quality and meaning of the words or to understand all of their connotations. Of course we are familiar with the structure of the epic decasyllabic line. The strong caesura that breaks the line at the fourth syllable has not lost its effect, nor has the assonance that marks its ends; but the frequency of the epic caesura, with its overcounted unstressed syllable, is unusual. Moreover, though we know that these lines were sung or chanted, it would be difficult to say exactly what the rhythms or melodies were.

Still, to think that we were dealing with primitive poetry would be a mistake. The style of the ***Chanson*** reveals clerical influences; specifically it is not without similarities to contemporary epics in Latin. No single direct imitation of these highly artificial works—or of the *Aeneid* or the *Pharsalia,* for that matter—can be found in the ***Roland.*** Nevertheless, our author uses devices that are common in the technical jargon of the time: *oppositio* (it is true, it is not a lie), *amplificatio, interjecto ex persona poetae* (direct intervention of the poet), *addubitatio* (what should I do?), and *praemonitio* (preparation). He is familiar with apostrophe, hyperbole, the rhetorical question, alliteration, and understatement. He knew the Bible and has borrowed certain phrases from theological language. Such words as *meie culpe, paterne, Lazaron,* and *resurrexis* are taken from the Latin text of the Mass. But, having rejected one extreme, we should not go to the other: though the style of the ***Roland*** is not primitive, it is not erudite.

The ***Roland*** avoids labored affectation and unnecessary weight. Its style is marked by conciseness, precision, sparseness, and strength. This degree of austerity and steadiness presupposes a certain rigidity and monotony. The author was not familiar with such devices as the periodic sentences or enjambement, and prefers asyndeton to subordination; he tends to make an independent and self-sufficient unit of each line. This apparent fragmentation is offset by the fact that parallels, contrasts, and logical or intuitive implications link these units into considerably larger groups. Lines that are admirable in themselves are even better in context. The poet's vocabulary has the advantage of being simple and precise: he respects words. He does not waste them or weaken them by excessive or inexact use. He has no need for esoteric terms; the right word, with all its possible connotations, is enough for him. A good example is the famous line, "Roland is bold and Oliver is wise" (*Rollant est proz e Oliver est sage*). These ordinary epithets could hardly be applied with more force. When they appear, we are already familiar enough with the characters to know that the words describe them fully, without simplifying. As the action proceeds, we realize that this antithesis not only reveals the cause of the drama but also explains its evolution and determines the tragic results. And when the poet completes his description of the heroes by adding, "Both of them are renowned for their bravery" (*Ambedui unt merveillus vasselage*), he is not praising them in general terms. He evokes and embodies an ideal, creates a total epic atmosphere through these unique characters. The author of the ***Roland*** is clearly one of the first to have used the French language artistically. He has at his disposal an instrument that has not been dulled by the quest for literary effect, and he has had to learn how to handle the instrument himself. This advantage has not made his task any easier, but his success fully justifies any effort.

Since the vitality of the poet's style comes from the careful selection and location of words, he is able to avoid the use of imagery and simile. Both are very rare in the ***Chanson;*** at most he says that a horse is as swift as a swallow or a falcon, or that Charles' beard is flowing, whiter than an April flower or snow on ice. Only once is he more insistent: "As stags before the dogs, the pagans run before Roland." A writer who so carefully avoids description for its own sake must sacrifice unnecessary ornamentation to what he deems essential. Yet this same writer, so sober, so austere, and so careful in his use of words, is free in his use of repetitions and synonyms. It would be paradoxical to assume that this can be explained as carelessness. Certain epithets, descriptions, and formulas reappear throughout the ***Roland***. . . . But we must remember that repetition is a very important aspect of the poet's technique, as in the *laisses similaires*. The recurrence of a characteristic adjective can show the permanence of those very moral or physical qualities that define an individual. As an example, let us look at Charlemagne's beard, at the old monarch's pensive attitudes when he is frightened or uncertain. The majesty of his face is immutable, his spiritual anguish always deeply moving: there is no need to search for new words. Synonyms and recurring expressions can stress the depth and intensity of an emotion. The poet does not use excess phrases or padding; he strives for strength and clarity of expression. But he knows that the complexity of emotions and ideas requires the association of a number of terms that complement or qualify one another. And he knows that certain words are charged with emotional overtones. By the rhythmic incantation of repetition, which modifies the meaning as it augments it, he both intensifies and prolongs these innuendos. Some of his lines are the most evocative and suggestive in the French language. It has been said that many chansons, in which the flaws of a formulary style abound, are the product of a kind of perpetual oral improvisation, but that observation has no application here.

This brief analysis will best be concluded by focusing attention once again on the text itself, for we find the most perfect expression of the poet's artistry in the third of the three strophes that describe Roland's death. . . . The scene described in these twenty-two lines comes at the conclusion of a skillful development: from now on, the meaning of Roland's death and the reward it deserves are clear. Twice the poet has shown the hero stretched out on a hill, in the shade of a pine tree, his face turned toward Spain. By saying it a third time at the beginning of the strophe, the poet shows that he is not interested in merely describing a pose. He wants to remind us that Roland dies justified and unconquered, fulfilling the vow that he made before he fell in this strange land, far in front of his men, facing the fleeing enemy. The magnificent epic and religious theme, illustrated by the hero's sacrifice and intensified by rhythmic repetition, must resound at this supreme moment. But the glorious, triumphant note is muted by melancholy. Roland's nobility is the result of his pain. As he nears his death, the martyr of Roncevaux thinks of all that binds him to earth and life, and he glories in his conquests one last time. Without this gentle regret, his sacrifice would be worthless. He also thinks of "dulce France." Throughout the poem this expression is wrapped in a cloud of nostalgia and proud tenderness: nowhere is it more moving than when it is so simply repeated in this last farewell. The slightest elaboration would destroy the meaning of the words that follow: "des humes de son lign, / De Carlemagne, sun seignor, kil nurrit" ["the men from whom he is descended, / Charlemagne, his lord, who raised him"]. In their laconic eloquence they sum up all of Roland's emotions, all the reasons for his sorrow. They are spoken slowly. The dying man lingers over his memories and tries to prolong each precious moment as his sadness slowly gives way to serene resignation.

But melancholy leads to forgetfulness. Roland's life has involved not only precious and beautiful memories, but also faults that must be pardoned. The man must give way to the Christian, to repentance and faith. Roland realizes that he barely has enough time in which to pray. His prayer is short but intensely poignant, the essence of an old prayer for the dead.

With as much solemnity as audacity, it translates the Latin formulas into the vernacular and yet, because there is less need for eloquence than for sincerity and contrition, it remains remarkably simple. When the prayer is over, Roland acts out his speech, repeating his act of penance and homage: once more he holds out his glove and beats his breast. His humility is that of a good vassal who has delivered himself to his lord, and the fact that it takes this form is quite appropriate. As a loyal vassal and a crusader faithful to the point of martyrdom, there is no better way for Roland to express his reverence and faith. God, who wishes Roland's death to be more noble than all the others', accepts the symbolic offering of feudal Christianity that has served his cause so well. He sends his angels and saints to welcome the soul that is ready to depart from the earth. A mediocre writer would have found it difficult to resist the temptation of describing the celestial vision. Our poet confines himself to two concrete details, both of which men have the right and faculty to perceive. Roland's head falls back, and his hands are clasped together—that is all the poet presumes to describe. He barely suggests the presence of the ranks that descend from heaven. This unforgettable scene must not become a spectacle. It must be as perfectly sacred and spiritually pure as the lofty sentiment that inspires it. The actual words that describe it have become immaterial, speaking not to the eyes or to the imagination, but to the spirit.

The author of the ***Roland*** was a great poet, both vital and sensitive, who knew his craft. (pp. 147-54)

Pierre Le Gentil, in his The "Chanson de Roland," *translated by Frances F. Beer, Cambridge, Mass.: Harvard University Press, 1969, pp. 125-55.*

CONSTANCE HIEATT (essay date 1968)

[Hieatt is an American educator, translator, and medieval scholar. Among her works are adaptations for young readers of medieval literature, medieval cookbooks, and The Realism of Dream Visions: The Poetic Exploitation of the Dream-Experience in Chaucer and His Contemporaries (1967). *In the following excerpt, Hieatt suggests "ways to reconcile the extremes, and to see Roland as both a Germanic hero and a Christian."]*

It is an anomaly that most readers of the ***Chanson de Roland*** seem to side with the villain, not the hero. Improbable as it is that the poet would have sympathized with this condemnation of his hero, the usual verdict seems to be that of Ganelon—that Roland is guilty of overweening pride. For example, [Harold March's 1965] introduction to a new translation speaks of Roland's "presumptuous folly," and regards him as a "tragic" hero who sins through pride and "impetuosity," barely redeeming himself by admitting his error ("three mighty blasts of Roland's oliphant . . . proclaim his admission of error") and dying in sanctity because he is penitent. The translator [Patricia Terry] seems to agree, noting in her preface that "Roland's words of repentance [are] so convincing that he, who might well have sinned the same way again, can be carried off to heaven with angelic and human rejoicing." But an odd note creeps into the same sentence, for, she says, his "words of repentance are imprecise enough to leave his heroic stature untouched." Is heroism, then, incompatible with repentance? Perhaps this depends on what the hero repents. If Roland must repent because he has wickedly caused the slaughter of his own men, then he would seem to be more villain than hero.

A very large question remains, however, as to whether Roland is indeed repentant as described, and whether the poet intended us to see him as tragically flawed. On this question there are various opinions. Eugène Vinaver states [in a 1964 essay in *Cahiers de civilization médievale*] that the poet's view is irresolubly dual and that we cannot expect him to take sides as to who is right, be it Roland or Oliver. Others have argued, recently and not-so-recently, that questions of guilt and repentance are out of place here because Roland is basically a pagan hero of the older "Germanic" type, rather than an embodiment of Christian notions of sin and repentance. G. F. Jones, for example, considers Roland downright pagan because he does *not* specifically repent having caused the destruction of his army [see 1963 excerpt by Jones]. Comparing him to undeniably "Germanic" heroes, he says, "Like Byrhtnoth at Malden and like the Burgundians at Etzel's court, Roland struggles manfully against fate and relies entirely on his own efforts rather than call on human or divine aid." Yet the picture Jones' book projects is still not very sympathetic: Roland is termed "foolhardly," the Franks are "rowdy" and "brutal." Similarly, D. D. R. Owen, who accepts the pride but not the repentance, argues that Roland is motivated by sinful self-seeking and secular feudal concerns, and thus is not a Christian hero at all [see 1962 excerpt by Owen]. Christian references, such as Roland's dying "mea culpa," he considers merely conventional.

That such references are conventional is undoubtedly true; but they are not therefore irrelevant to the central concerns of the poem. Conventions are not by definition meaningless. If they were, little would be left in literature that we could validly discuss. Moreover, if ***Roland*** is not really a Christian poem at all, it has certainly grievously misled the many readers who have felt it was "Christian to its very bones," as Dorothy Sayers put it [see 1957 excerpt by Sayers]. Comparing it with works generally thought of as belonging to the older, originally pagan, Germanic tradition, such as *Beowulf* and the *Nibelungenlied,* makes its Christian orientation more obvious; the Christianity of the latter works seems relatively superficial (if not in actual conflict with the true nature of the material, as some have felt). But must we assume that all Germanic heroes are pagans, and thus that "Christian" and "Germanic" are mutually incompatible categories? There appear to be ways to reconcile the extremes, and to see Roland as both a Germanic hero and a Christian. (pp. 420-22)

The familiar themes and devices of Germanic heroic literature abound in the ***Chanson de Roland.*** The prominence of the themes of loyalty, treachery, and revenge, for example, so familiar to students of Old English, Old Norse, and older German works, has been noted by others. Also typically Germanic is the poet's technique of foreshadowing, both directly and indirectly, events to come. Asides that let us know right from the beginning what is going to happen are frequent, as, e.g., line 9: "Nes poet guarder que mals ne l'i ateignet!" ["He cannot prevent misfortune from befalling him there!"] The poet of the *Nibelungenlied* makes just such ominous remarks at the beginning of his work . . . , as does the *Beowulf*-poet . . . , though not in the opening lines, which are undisturbed by warnings. Indirect foreshadowing is present in dreams and portents of various sorts. Charlemagne's dreams have sometimes been cited as examples of the specifically Christian milieu here, but, as T. A. Jenkins pointed out, allegorical animal dreams are common in the Old Norse sagas. . . . The "Germanic" atmosphere of ***Roland*** is, then, evident in technique as well as in themes, and perhaps even in style, since the verse form bears some resemblance to traditional Germanic style. Most scholars who have commented on the form have noted only that it does not have systematic alliteration, and have concluded that it therefore is not in the same verse tradition. However, it does make use of the caesura to a significant extent, which is one of the characteristics of the older Germanic verse forms, and it does use rather more alliteration than most non-Germanic verse; furthermore, the use of assonance as a structural feature seems closer to traditional Germanic alliteration than the use of rhyme. If this is granted, then ***Roland*** is closer to older Germanic verse forms than is the *Nibelungenlied,* which resembles it in the use of units of verses (strophes) and in the regular caesura, but which makes use of rhyme rather than alliteration or assonance.

A number of other connections with Germanic tradition have been noted in the ***Chanson de Roland,*** but of course the most important question is the extent to which the hero himself exemplifies the traditional Germanic hero—that is, a brave warrior who proves his valor in the ultimate way, facing, with undaunted courage and resolution, certain or almost certain death and destruction. That would seem to be what a Germanic hero, by definition, is. Consider any of the heroes who deserve the name at all: Beowulf, facing first Grendel and then the fire-breathing dragon, and Hagen, decimating the vast armies of Etzel before he is finally brought down, are just the beginning of the list. In their class are Gunnar of Hlidarend, who would not have thought of forcibly taking those essential strands of hair from an unwilling Hallgerd, dying magnificently (after killing two of his assassins and wounding many others, not to mention the large number he had already overcome at previous ambushes); Skarphedin, singing as he finally dies in the burning house; Njal himself, choosing death at the hand of the Burners; another Gunnar, in the *Atlakviða,* playing a harp with his toes in a pit full of deadly serpents; Kjartan of *Laxdœla saga,* who prefers to be killed rather than to fight his sworn brother and kinsman Bolli; and, skipping innumerable others from the sagas, Byrthnoth and Byrhtwold at the Battle of Maldon. The list could go on and on.

Nor would it have occured to any of the heroes cited above to think of the safety of their followers as the primary consideration, any more than this occured to Roland. Hagen, to be sure, knew from the mermaids' prophecy that all the Burgundians were doomed anyway; but that is not evidence that he would otherwise have meekly let Kriemhild have her revenge, in order to spare the lives of his companions: such an action would clearly be out of character. Beowulf allowed Grendel to seize (and eat) one of his own men before he attacked the monster. Theoretically, Beowulf could have prevented this by lying in wait and tackling Grendel at the door before he could do any harm. But he did not, and there does not seem to be any suggestion that he was therefore morally lacking. Njal allowed his wife and grandchild to accompany him in his chosen death. If Roland was responsible for the death of his men, so was Byrhtnoth—but the Old English poet still regards him as a hero, not a villain, whatever the implications may be of the remark that he let the enemy pass "for his ofermóde" ["because of his pride"]. Contempt for those who chose to save their own skins by refusing to fight against hopeless odds is one of the most notable features of *The Battle of Maldon*. . . . To all this, the point may be raised that Roland is not really a Germanic hero, however much his actions may resemble one, but a Christian French hero. True: but the Franks were a Germanic tribe, and so were the Normans. A Norman poet writing about a Frankish hero was likely to have inherited, one way or another, Germanic notions of heroism, just as he quite evidently inherited other aspects of the Germanic heroic literary tradition. Of course Roland is a Christian (whatever we may think of his standards, or those of the poet), but so are many other Germanic heroes: a Christian Germanic hero is not quite the contradiction in terms some commentators seem to assume.

Christian ethics do not, indeed, have much to do with anyone's thinking in the *Nibelungenlied.* (pp. 422-25)

It is also true that Beowulf is never specifically Christian in his references. Gunnar of Hlidarend dies a pagan. Njal is a Christian, but in his last moments this does not seem to be a consideration. He deliberately chooses death, thus in effect committing the sin of suicide, and for an un-Christian reason: the dishonor of being unable to avenge his sons. But there are other Germanic works in the heroic tradition that are at the same time characteristically Christian in tone or outlook. *Deor* is one. It refers to the familiar names of Weland and Theodoric and Eormanric, and deals with the alternations of joy and sorrow so familiar in Germanic heroic literature, but whereas in *Beowulf* the message is generally that joy always turns to sorrow . . . , and such is the final conclusion of the *Nibelungenlied*-poet . . . , in *Deor* the speaker hopes things will turn out the other way around. After detailing various unpleasant situations, he says ["That passed away; this may too!"]. This seems to be Christian optimism, a different way of looking at the world's mutability. In precisely this respect the ***Chanson de Roland*** differs from *Beowulf* and the *Nibelungenlied:* Roland dies, but he is avenged, and the French are more victorious than ever. Sorrow for the dead hero remains, but something not inconsiderable is gained for his side. Such was not the case for Beowulf's Geats (who bury the treasure with their lord, and have little to look forward to, now that he is no longer there to defend them, but eventual defeat at the hands of the Swedes), or Hagen's Burgundians—who are, in fact, all already dead.

This Christian optimism may have some significance in relation to the structure of the ***Chanson de Roland.*** One of the most bitterly disputed points has been the role of Charlemagne and the function of the half of the poem which occurs after the death of the hero; just this sort of dichotomy splits *Beowulf,* the *Nibelungenlied,* and *Njals saga*. In each case, the first part of the work focuses our attention on the deeds of a young hero, who is either dead or grown old in the latter part. Also in each case the pattern of doom—death and destruction—is greatly expanded in the second part. In *Beowulf,* the latter part concentrates somberly on the downfall which is inevitably overtaking the Geats; in *Njals saga,* half of Iceland seems to be involved in the general pattern of lawlessness and carnage which erupts after the death of Gunnar; in the *Nibelungenlied* the Burgundian dynasty is wiped out (along with their friends as well as their opponents) in revenge for the death of one man. In all three cases, though the degree of hopelessness varies, little is salvageable from the general wreckage, while in ***Roland*** the opposite is true: the French defeat is only a temporary setback. In the end, Charlemagne defeats the heathens resoundingly. To be sure, he will have to keep on defeating others, but the reader is confident that he will continue to succeed. Heathens may attack again and again, but Christians will win in the end. . . . ["That passed away, this may too!"].

Thus the structure of ***Roland*** parallels that of certain other Germanic works, just as the themes and poetic technique do in other ways, though with a difference—and that difference would seem to be the product of a more specifically Christian outlook. Similarly, the character of the hero may be more affected by Christianity than are those of Beowulf, Hagen, or most of the others discussed above. The Germanic hero whose situation most strikingly parallels Roland's is Byrhtnoth in *The Battle of Maldon*. Like Roland, he is a Christian, leading his men in a battle in which they are hopelessly outnumbered by the enemy. As already suggested, Byrhtnoth can be held responsible for getting himself and his men into this situation, just as Roland can, through courage of the kind that later men might call "presumptuous folly." Like Roland, Byrhtnoth defends with his last strength the symbols of his position and dignity (sword and other valuables, parallels to Roland's Durendal and Oliphant) from the marauder who wishes to take them as booty. And, like Roland Byrhtnoth prays when he finds he is facing death:

> . . . [I thank you, Lord of hosts, for all the joys that I have experienced in this world. Now, merciful Lord, I have great need that you grant grace to my spirit, so that my soul may journey into your power, Lord of angels, and pass peacefully. I pray to you that hell-fiends shall not harm it.]

Both in content and organization, this prayer strikingly resembles Roland's. Both heroes first express thanks for the favors God has granted them on earth. Byrhtnoth expresses this very generally . . . , and Roland more specifically, thinking first of Durendal—the symbol of God's favor to him as well as his own responsibility to the cause he serves—then of the battles in which he has been vouchsafed victory, and the lands he has won for his king. Then, properly, both heroes ask that the mercy of God be shown to their souls. Byrhtnoth does not specifically make any confession of sin in his brief prayer, but that is to be taken for granted: if he were not a sinful man (like all other men) he would not have to fear the possibility of the torments of hell and there would be no need for him to speak at length asking God to have mercy on his soul. Roland's prayers say exactly the same thing, but in more elaborated form, as we would expect in the context of this longer and more leisurely poem. He, too, asks to be preserved from the dangers at hell . . . , but at greater length, including specific prayers for the remission of sins. There is no essential difference in the nature of these prayers unless we understand Roland to be particularizing, confessing the one specific sin of which so many readers find him guilty. But where is this particularizing? He does not say what sins he is confessing any more than Byrhtnoth says why he is in need of mercy; he simply asks forgiveness for all the sins he may have committed at any time . . . , which seems a suitable, as well as conventional, act for any Christian facing death.

The point is that Roland is *not* confessing that his own "pride" or folly has led to his death (and that of his companions). Like Byrhtnoth, he is simply dying as a Christian, with the proper prayer. Nor is there any convincing evidence that either poet regards his hero as dying the death in defeat of a man who has made one mistake too many: in death as in life they are both heroes. (pp. 425-28)

As Roland and Byrhtnoth resemble each other in being Christians, they resemble each other in the type of heroism they display. Honor, to the original audience of Germanic heroic literature, was an essential quality of manhood, not a sin; Byrhtnoth was remembered as a defender of the Church, as well as of his country, not as an example of how sinful pride leads to death and destruction. In this literary context to impute Byrhtnoth's catastrophe to the "sin of pride" or to interpret his dying words as expressing regret for what he has just done would seem obviously anachronistic, in spite of his Christianity. The similarity of Roland's character, situation, and literary context is evident. Only by applying standards other than those implicit in the poem can we either pronounce him guilty or decide that he has redeemed himself.

To see a redeeming penance in Roland's last words may be somewhat anachronistic in another way. Although the Council of Clermont in 1095 cautioned crusaders not to act in a spirit of un-Christian pride, warning about pride were certainly not the keynote of the Church's advice to prospective crusaders. Sermons of the period abounded in exhortations to fearlessness, taking the general line that one Christian is worth a hundred pagans, since God is on his side. The emphasis on penance is medieval sermons is really a later development, starting in the twelfth century and gaining impetus after the Fourth Lateran Council in 1215. Even in a later period, preachers bewailed the cowardice of knights who were afraid to go on crusades for such reasons as "the insignificance of forces on the Christian side, comparing such latter-day cowards unfavorably to Charlemagne, Roland, and Oliver, as examples of those who fought fearlessly for Church and country. (pp. 428-29)

We must, in any case, remember that the Christian sensibilities of an eleventh-century audience were not necesarily ours, nor even those of a fourteenth-century audience, any more than were their literary tastes. The audience that approved of Sir Gawain would have found Roland uncouth and discourteous, as well as lacking in Christian humility. But Beowulf and Hagen did not hesitate to proclaim their own virtues. Neither did Byrhtnoth, who threatened his enemies with death and termed himself . . . ["a noble or dauntless warrior"]. Why must we assume that Roland's defiance of the odds and confidence in himself is that pride which comes before a fall? Byrhtnoth would have appreciated it as proper behavior. That the brand of heroism Byrhtnoth, Beowulf, Hagen, and Roland show is apt to strike twentieth-century readers as foolhardiness may show only that no one would have thought very much of *us* a thousand years ago. We tend all too readily to agree with Falstaff that "the better part of valor is discretioin." Yet we still admire Hotspur, even if we think we should not. (p. 429)

Constance Hieatt, "Roland's Christian Heroism," in Traditio, *Vol. 24, 1968, pp. 420-29.*

JANET W. BOATNER (essay date 1969)

[In the following excerpt, Boatner discusses Roland's characterization, arguing "that in the name of feudal loyalty he betrays every aspect of the feudal code and that his total misunderstanding of his feudal obligations is due to the blindness of pride."]

Before embarking on yet another interpretation of the ***Chanson de Roland,*** I would like to ask two brief questions which may suggest the difficulties which hinder an acceptance of the . . . point of view [of critics who question an interpretation of Roland as Christian]: 1. If Roland is the hero of the poem and if his character and opinions remain unchanged throughout, why does the author permit Oliver, his closest friend and full equal in courage and nobility, to attack his position so unreservedly without receiving an answer and without being himself in the least disgraced? 2. If Roland undergoes no change of heart, why does an entirely different side of his nature appear after the blowing of the horn. Why, for the first time, is he shown as tender and courteous?

Actually, literature is not a scientific theory to be "proved" or "disproved" and I can hope to answer these critics only in a positive way; by explaining the pattern of the drama at Roncesvaux as it appears to me. It is notable that those who challenge the religious interpretation of the poem, and even some of its supporters, have assumed that there is a basic conflict between the feudal and the Christian ethic and that repentance and humility on Roland's part would necessarily involve inconsistency. The reason for this, in my opinion, is that they define the feudal ethic as being based on materialistic considerations plus a concern for one's reputation in the world. It is true that vassalage, in its lowest sense, was part of a primitive social system. In its highest sense, however, it implied a philosophy of personal commitment. Service was combined with devotion and loyalty with love. Actually, most men, then as in our day, were motivated by a complex of noble and ignoble motives.

The idealistic man served his lord with the same selfless devotion with which the idealist today serves a cause, since, in that more personal and concrete period "cause" and "lord" were mutually identified. There were opportunists then as now, men who served good lords for profit or for personal glory. Likewise there were mistaken idealists who served bad lords selflessly. But the desire to give oneself to something or someone greater was present in the feudal age as in our own. It is not surprising therefore, that feudal ideals influenced Christian practice and were influenced by it. The attitude of kneeling with joined hands was used both in vassal homage and in Christian prayer. The greatest sin in Dante's hell is the betrayal of a lord: the sin of Brutus and Judas.

Any ideal, however, can be more easily betrayed by its misguided supporters than by its enemies. Roland, in this poem, perceives himself as the perfect vassal who will sacrifice himself completely to serve his lord. I would like to show, however, that in the name of feudal loyalty he betrays every aspect of the feudal code and that his total misunderstanding of his feudal obligations is due to the blindness of pride. I believe this to be the basic motif of the first section of the ***Chanson.*** I would like, in short, to study Roland not as *either* a Christian *or* a vassal, but as a Christian vassal. I should add that I do not believe Roland's pride can be characterized as *desmesure,* "the carrying out of a justifiable, often noble, purpose, beyond the point of *mesure*." His fault does not lie in a lack of restraint but in a spiritual distortion that makes black appear white. Finally, I do not believe that Roland becomes a saint after his conversion, since he re-interprets the human values by which he has previously lived rather than rejecting them.

Since, in the words of Bloch, "it was the act of homage that really established the relation of vassalage under its dual aspects of dependence and protection," I should like to begin my discussion by exploring this ceremony on its symbolic level. The vassal appears before his lord bareheaded and unarmed, symbolizing vulnerability and trust. He kneels before him, in token of humility, and places his hand in his lord's hands as he speaks the words of homage. The gesture of giving his hands is an act of self-surrender. . . . Only after homage and fealty does the lord invest his vassal with the land or office he is to hold. Symbolically, then, it is only possible to enter into possession and honor by means of humility and self-surrender. We note too that as the lord must accept the service of the vassal, the vassal must accept the protection offered him, since one is necessary to the other. In the formula of homage the vassal says: "Sir, I become your vassal." It is as if he were actually transformed by entering into the relationship, and in a sense this is so. We are all defined by what we serve: our appetite, our jobs, our ideals. Note too that we expect and demand protection from what we serve. If we have chosen a bad lord we are betrayed. Let us now see how Roland "serves" his lord.

Roland knows very well that the battle of Roncesvaux is a test of his qualities as a vassal. He glories in the challenge, since he is certain of emerging with honor. . . . Yet at every crucial point in the story Roland fails to live up to his contract; indeed, he perverts it. Let us look, first, at the council scene in which Charlemagne, surrounded by his vassals, is selecting an envoy of King Marsiliun. He has refused to send Roland, Oliver, or any of the twelve peers on the grounds that their lives are too valuable to be risked on such a dangerous mission. Roland immediately says, "C'iert Guenles, mis parastre" ["I propose my stepfather, Ganelon"], thus implying that Ganelon is expendable. Not content with nominating a man for whom he has obvious contempt he then ensures disaster by reducing Ganelon to a state of blind fury with his taunts and laughter. Thus he fails one of the major duties of a vassal, to give council and advice to his lord. His behavior is the preciptating factor in the quarrel between Ganelon and himself and hence of the ultimate treachery to Charlemagne. Why does he behave in this way? The reason, obviously, is that his attention is not on the successful performance of a dangerous mission but on proving that he is the only man capable of any important job. We begin to suspect at this point what will become increasingly and tragically clear in the course of the poem. The lord that Roland really serves is not Charlemagne, but his own pride.

Later, when Roland has been nominated to the rear guard, Charlemagne offers him adequate forces to defend the pass. Roland refuses them, boasting that with only a small force he can still do better than anyone else. . . . His failure here is twofold. Charlemagne's duty, as Roland's lord, is to protect him. Roland refuses this protection, saying in effect that the contract is *not* mutual, that he can give service without accepting protection. Yet to refuse to accept is in effect to refuse to serve. Roland is actually rejecting the whole relationship which he claims to be the mainspring of his action. What he is actually saying, though unconscious of the fact, is: "I don't really care whether I perform my duty to you in the best possible manner nearly as much as I care about taking enough chances that my true lord, vanity, may be gratified."

When the Saracen forces are seen approaching, Oliver councils Roland to blow his horn that Charlemagne may return to help them. Roland refuses four times. It is interesting to note that nowhere in this fourfold refusal does he even claim that his decision is based on his duty to Charlemagne. He first states quite boldly that he will not summon help because *his* fame in France would suffer if he did. . . . In his second reply he expands his egotism a little by saying that his family would be shamed. . . . Then he generalizes still further, claiming that the honor of France will suffer. . . . This retreat into abstractions to gild his own vanity is a very human trait. When people are at their silliest or most vicious they always claim to be "representing" something. When Oliver points out the vast size of the Saracen army Roland resorts to another typically human mechanism, the misplaced heroic speech. He says the smallness of their numbers will make the battle still more glorious. This sort of reasoning sounds very noble coming from Henry V at Agincourt, where the "fearful odds" were a necessity. Roland, however, has *chosen* fearful odds. . . . We note that during this argument Roland makes almost no mention of other people. He speaks of Charlemagne only in passing and only as a sort of approving audience. . . . He mentions the men of the French army only as useful aids in his own quest for self-glorification. . . . In choosing pride as lord, Roland has cut himself off from all human contact. He can neither give nor recieve. He is blind to human values. (pp. 573-79)

Interestingly enough, the basic feudal sin is the basic Christian sin: *non serviam*. Roland, of course, is unaware of his own disloyalty and of the fact that he is motivated to it by the same force that motivated Satan, the archetype of felons—pride.

The battle, then, is joined, and continues until the French army is destroyed, only sixty men being left. Roland's lord, pride, has betrayed him. He looks around and sees the slaughter caused by his blind adherence to a false allegiance and for a time his personality is utterly destroyed. He is lordless; he has nothing by which to define his own identity. Roland, as is typical of a man whose ideals have proved untrustworthy, meaninglessly reverses them. He now insists on blowing his horn, turning helplessly to Charlemagne for the protection no longer available. It is at this point that Oliver, with more truth than mercy, points out Roland's total failure as a vassal up to this point. He says: 1) that if Roland blew his horn now he would do so from an ignoble and valueless motive, as he had refused earlier from an equally ignoble and valueless motive; 2) that the failure is Roland's fault *alone,* that his men have died for him and that he has betrayed them and made their deaths purposeless; 3) that Roland has refused service to his lord and prevented others from rendering it; 4) that the friendship between Roland and Oliver is broken, that Roland has in effect cut himself off from any human relationship. . . . Roland is so stunned by the realization that he has betrayed every aspect of the ideal which he sincerely believed himself to be living by that he can only ask in bewildered innocence, "Por quei me portez ire?" ["Why are you angry with me?"] At this point, however, Roland has accomplished the first step in becoming a vassal: he is unarmed, vulnerable.

The Archbishop Turpin, as the representative of God, offers him a meaningful chance to offer service in all truth and, by means of giving himself, to possess himself. It is too late to sound the horn in time to save the French army but Roland can, finally, call upon the protection of his lord to give the men Christian burial and perhaps avenge them. Roland's unquestioning and respectful acceptance of this duty . . . is in a sense an enactment of the second prerequisite of homage, humility. Roland sounds his horn three times with increasing "dolor e . . . peine" ["agony and pain"]. We have seen that previously he cut himself off from human communication by refusing human obligations. He now makes contact at the cost of his life, for the veins of his temple burst with the strain. He re-establishes the feudal bond, the bond with Charlemagne, and from this point on he is a man able to speak to other men.

He turns first to his dead and dying men. This beautiful speech gains a good deal of its power from the fact that Roland has lost his pride but gained, for the first time, self-respect. He is no longer abject, as he was at his first realization of defeat. Blind humility is no more a virtue than blind pride. Either can prevent self-knowledge and, therefore, service. The paradox of vassalage is that to serve and honor another is not humiliating but a sign of one's own worth. Roland pays tribute to the vassals who have died for him in the spirit of one who understands vassalage for the first time. He acknowledges his failure to maintain the feudal contract, to protect his men, but he does so with quiet dignity: "Barons franceis, por mei vos vei morir, / Jo ne vos pois tenser ne guarantir" ["French knights, I see you dying for my sake, / I cannot protect or save you"].

This passage is somewhat confusing because Roland, in the words just quoted, appears to surrender his responsibilities to God, to abandon his command, and yet shortly later he is leading these men to battle with forceful enthusiasm. . . . I would ask whether this surrender is an abdication or an act of homage. It seems to me that Roland surrenders his command to God only to use it henceforth as God's vassal, much as an allodial property is surrendered preliminary to receiving it back as a fief.

The final scene between Roland and Oliver both serves to mark Roland's new acceptance into the human race and curiously re-enacts his previous faults. Oliver, blinded by blood, strikes him. It is as if Roland's earlier blindness of pride were allegorized by Oliver's action, since Roland has likewise harmed those to whom he owed love in a frenzy of blind zeal. Roland, then, forgives his own sin in his friend and does penance for it by accepting a blow which is the result of courage without understanding. This penance, like that of the blowing of the horn which ruptures his veins, is fittingly the result of a difficulty in making human contact. . . . As the two tenderly exchange forgiveness and part, Roland's regeneration is complete.

Roland now, having humbly surrendered himself in homage before God and man, can return in honor and tempered pride to the battle. . . . I cannot agree with those who make of Roland a saint. A saint may, indeed, be defined as "one of the blessed dead in heaven." We generally, however, think of a saint as one who during his life tends to reject worldly values as at best worthless and at worst snares. Roland's spirit, even *after* his regeneration, is very unlike that expressed by Chaucer at the end of *Troilus and Criseyde*. He does not see the joys and triumphs of the earth as "worldly vanyte." A saint, to a degree, renounces humanity. Roland *becomes* human. He redefines his earlier values rather than rejecting them. He is still just as interested in havng Charlemagne know he died a victor, in killing the Saracen who tries to steal his sword, in the many battles he has won. Yet he holds all these things in fief from God; that is, he holds them by right of serving higher ideals first. So Roland returns to the battle and, dying, wins the field. (pp. 579-82)

The story of Roland, then, as I see it, is not the story of a man who lives and dies in an attempt to "enhance his worldly fame." Nor is it the story of a man who comes to realize, through suffering, "that obedience to the feudal code is not enough but must be accompanied by Christian conversion." It is the story of a man who believes himself to be living up to an ideal, the Christian-Feudal ideal, in its very highest sense and yet who is actually, in the blindness of pride, perverting and destroying it. It takes the death of 30,000 men to destroy his illusion but he is at last brought face to face with it. Once his spiritual vision is cleared by vulnerability and humility he is able to understand for the first time the values he has so glibly proclaimed, and by understanding them, to achieve self-knowledge. Roland does indeed undergo a conversion, but his conversion does not lead to sainthood. It leads simply to his becoming a good vassal, a good human being—which is a considerable achievement. (pp. 582-83)

Janet W. Boatner, "The Misunderstood Ordeal: A Re-examination of the 'Chanson de Roland'," in Studies in Philology, *Vol. LXVI, No. 4, July, 1969, pp. 571-83.*

Roland defeats a Pagan in single combat with Charlemagne's army massed behind him.

EUGENE VANCE (essay date 1970)

[In the following excerpt, Vance demonstrates how The Song, *in such sections as the Baligant and Ganelon episodes, relfects changing social and literary premises and presents "established categories . . . [that] appear to be eroding before our eyes."]*

Roland's is a tale of triumph, but is not by itself tragic. True, we are swept with the majesty of his final gestures, but as Roland looks back in time from the edge of death, he never comes to terms with his own human limitations or with the destruction that his pride has inflicted upon the rest of society. Roland achieves a kind of perfection, but it is too autistic. Whatever understanding of mortality he begins to derive from his suffering is quickly offset by the joy of his apotheosis when Gabriel and Saint Michael bear his soul up to heaven. This is exalted Christian comedy.

The poet, however, does not share for long the serenity of his hero, but with an urgent *non sequitur,* deflects the locus of his narrative downward in a single poetic line from the glorious heights of heaven to the ruined community of mortals who must suffer the consequences of Ganelon's treason and—just as importantly—of Roland's pride. The narrative now centers on Charlemagne, who is caught in a tempest of grief and who struggles to grasp the enormity of his loss in ritualized lamentations based on the unanswerable question one must ask about all things of this transitory world: *ubi est?* . . . The center has dropped out of the heroic world. We are left with a man two hundred years old who not only is beyond action but has lost everyone he loved most in the world. Because Charlemagne loves human beings more than heroes, he can find no consolation in Roland's hard-won glory to balance the loss of his nephew. Aside from the personal loss, moreover, there is a severe strategic loss for Charlemagne: "The flower of France" has been ravished, and twenty thousand of his best knights are dead.

As the new hero of the ***Song of Roland,*** Charlemagne represents a perspective of disillusionment with those heroic values for which Roland lived and died. True, this perspective has been latent in the poem since the first council scene, yet neither Charlemagne nor Oliver has been allowed to eclipse Roland's heroic achievement. Though the most powerful man in the world, Charlemagne has remained passive throughout the poem; as for Oliver, he was never granted the stature, necessary for a true hero, of influencing the course of events in the slightest degree. With the new hero—who this time is an old man—comes a shift of emphasis in the narrative. True, the tale almost recovers its earlier narrative tempo when Charlemagne takes revenge upon the Saracens, yet the poet no longer exults in the splendid battle rituals of before. Without the right hero, there is no real action. Instead, the poet miraculously (and conveniently) disposes of the pagan army in the river Ebro and brings the focus of his poem back to Charles, for whom this abbreviated victory brings no joy. . . . As soon as the business of revenge is complete, grief overtakes the Frenchmen in the form of utter exhaustion. Charlemagne lies down to sleep in full armor; even the horses are too tired to stand, but must graze lying down. This nocturnal scene of prostration is the poetic antithesis of those earlier daylight scenes where armies stood eager to attack. . . . A hero is dead, and a poem of energy and action is conspicuously still. Earlier, in Roland's world, life had an eager buoyancy, and death seemed like nothing more than a release of heroic energy as stout souls hurled themselves from this life into the next. Death was everywhere, yet it was nowhere. Now, however, death takes on a more somber dimension. Through their devotion to Roland, whom they have lost, Charlemagne and the French barons learn the full consequences of death as a tragic fact of human existence. Roland's death is now the central event of the world, and the poet has measured the full meaning of this event by bringing the heroic world to an elegiac standstill: day has turned into night, joy into grief, energy into exhaustion, and most significantly, courage into wisdom; as the poet says, "He has learned much who has suffered much." (pp. 64-7)

The moment when Charlemagne discovers Roland's body is perhaps the most moving of the whole poem. Meticulously composed, this scene exploits in vivid and dramatic terms a contrast of perspectives upon the heroic world that has grown out of the presence of two central heroes—one old, one young—in a single tale. Here more than anywhere else the poet concentrates his narrative resources to deepen the meaning of the disaster at Ronceval, and he achieves thereby what might be considered the finest tragic moment in all feudal literature.

No lesser figure is allowed to intrude upon the intimacy of that instant when Charlemagne finds his nephew's body. . . . That the poet should single out Charlemagne to discover Roland's body is important to the unity of his poem: Roland and Charlemagne are supreme in the warrior's ethos and share in a single identity, except that one is young and bold, the other old and wise. Charlemagne alone is worthy both to grasp the full meaning of Roland's final acts and to appraise them in a perspective of tragic wisdom which the young warrior himself could never achieve.

The approach to Roland's body is presented through Charlemagne's eyes, and once again we move in a landscape suffused with human expressiveness:

> While the emperor hunted for his nephew,
> He saw countless flowers in the fields,
> Stained all crimson with our barons' blood.
> He could not stop from weeping out of pity.
> He came to a place beneath two trees,
> And saw the blood of Roland on three stones.
> On the green grass he found his nephew lying.
> It is no wonder that he felt great pain.
> He left his horse and went to Roland running.
> Between his two hands [he clasped his nephew]
> And fainted over him, such was his anguish.

The flowers stained with the blood of his favorite warriors convey in a single image the idea of vernal (and perhaps regenerative) beauty combined with the pathos of youth cut down in its very prime. Our poet has hit here upon an antithesis that has been indigenous to epic poetry ever since the *Iliad;* indeed, this is a permanent truth of the warrior's world. The contradictory aspect of blood on flowers mirrors a contradiction in Charlemagne's own mind, for he is capable, by virtue of his own heroism and his supreme old age, of perceiving both the glory of heroic martyrdom and its tragedy. The association of the bloodied flowers and "our barons" is strengthened by Charlemagne's reference to his barons elsewhere in the poem as the "flower of France," and by his prayer that his barons should rest among the "holy flowers" of the saved in paradise.

When Charlemagne revives from his faint, he begins a complaint (*planctus*) which is sustained through the next five *laisses.* The *planctus* is a conventional resource of French epic and comprises an *ensemble* of recognizable formulas. Of the six complaints uttered by warriors grieving for dead companions in the ***Song of Roland,*** Charlemagne's is the longest and summarizes the motifs of all the previous complaints. Charlemagne's first utterance is short and shows the extent to which he identifies his nephew's heroic glory with his own:

> "Roland, friend, may God have mercy on you!
> Never did a man see such a knight
> Engage in mighty battles, joust, and win.
> My honor is beginning to decline."
> Charlemagne faints; he cannot prevent it.

Though gestures in the ***Song of Roland*** have an irreducible simplicity about them, I am tempted to see the "epic faint" as a symbolic, vicarious death which a hero experiences at the loss of someone he loves as much as himself. Both Roland, who fainted when Oliver died, and Charlemagne, who faints now, proclaim that grief has made of life an unwelcome burden. As the emperor regains consciousness, he contemplates Roland's body—. . . the basis for emotions in a hero is always rooted in the exterior world. Roland in death expresses something he could never express in life: his body retains both the beauty of his youth and the tragic darkness of death. Shadows in the ***Song of Roland*** have repeatedly suggested death, and now the shadows are located in Roland's very eyes:

> Charlemagne the king came out of his faint.
> Four of his barons hold him up by the hands.
> He looks to the ground where his nephew lies.
> His body is splendid, but now is pale.
> His eyes are turned up, and are shadowy.
> Charles weeps for him in faith and love.

Through the mediation of Charlemagne we understand that the triumph of chivalric honor, still discernible in the posture of Roland's remains, is founded upon suffering and death. This is the supreme paradox of the heroic warrior's world, and it now stands revealed with stark but monumental simplicity. What earlier was Christian comedy has veered toward tragedy.

In his second soliloquy, Charlemagne elaborates upon his grief, exclaiming that with Roland, a part of himself has died. He even goes so far as to blame himself for Roland's death—why, we are not told. We may only surmise that he reproaches himself for not having intervened in the course of events to protect his nephew: protection (*warrantia*), after all, is a feudal lord's obligation to his vassal. . . . Charlemagne is a warrior who has inherited all the tragic consequences of the warrior's way of life and death. As king of the Franks, his fate has subsumed that of his vassals. Yet the quality of the world in this poem is such that it can offer him no consolation. He experiences the tragedy of a whole ethos, and perhaps even of a poetic genre. Charlemagne's lament extends not only to the fallen hero, and to himself, but to a whole beloved order that is now irretrievably lost. . . . Nothing meaningful remains in the world, and Charlemagne, like Achilles when he weeps for Patroclus, wants only to die so that he may rejoin his friends in both body and soul. . . . But Charlemagne is denied the tranquility that Roland enjoyed at his death. He seems to be caught in the hell of his own role and cannot die.

The scene of lamentation completes a shift of emphasis between the poem's two major voices, for the ***Song of Roland*** has at last become Charlemagne's. Roland's memory will endure to the end of the poem, but Charlemagne provides a context of wisdom and maturity in which the consequences of Roland's ordeal and passion take on their full meaning. Although with the unfolding of time the psychological outline of neither Roland nor Charlemagne has changed, we of the audience have experienced a profound reversal of perspective, which carries us beyond the arrogant pride of a young knight to the tragic wisdom of supreme old age. A tragedy of personalities is virtually complete now, yet the poet continues. Why? Has the narrative run away with itself? Is there some deeper, unfulfilled purpose which drives the poet to spin new movements, like a symphonic composer? These are questions of poetic intention, impossible to resolve, impossible to resist, and they will preoccupy us next. (pp. 67-71)

Never is the modern reader of the ***Song of Roland*** more likely to fear that the poem is only on arbitrary compilation than when the poet deserts the narrows of Ronceval and the exalted crescendos of passion in Roland and Charlemagne to launch into a phlegmatic and seemingly unrelated episode whch records the demise of Baligant, the Babylonian emir. We hear of Baligant for the first time in *laisse* CLXXXIX, when we suddenly learn that Marsile has been imploring Baligant for aid during the seven years of Charlemagne's campaign in Spain, but that Baligant only now has decided to rally to the support of his defeated ally. Occupying more than a quarter of the total of the ***Roland*** text, the so-called "Baligant episode" includes a long chronicle-like list of battle-corps from both sides (the French have ten, the Saracens no less than thirty), a rather pale description of a combat between them, and a compressed narration of a duel between Charlemagne and Baligant, which can be described as little more than epic shorthand.

To say the least, the Baligant episode inaugurates a wholly different poetic climate in the ***Song of Roland.*** The violent antitheses of the mountain setting in the Pyrenees, so appropriate to the intimate expression of Roland's tragedy, now dilate into a wide-open space where large-scale, impersonal armies conduct the least inventive feudal warfare imaginable. "Broad is the plain, the land is wide open"—such space without contours accommodates a human world similarly without contours; gone is the resounding extravagance of joy and despair which orchestrates the poem's first half. Why, critics ask, should Baligant make what seems to be a gratuitous entry into the ***Song of Roland***? What relationship is there between the Baligant episode and the events that precede and follow it?

Some critics have deemed the Baligant episode the contamination of some lesser poet's hand and have accordingly banished it from their editions of the poem. Other critics, by contrast, vibrating with polemical joy, assert that the Baligant episode and the rest of the ***Roland*** form an altogether harmonious whole. My own instinct as a reader is to feel that neither extreme is justified and that if we stay on middle ground we will discover subtle artistic problems that finally deepen the message of the ***Song of Roland*** more than they confuse it. (pp. 70-3)

[Even] during Roland's half of the epic, the poet sustains a current of *malaise* that counteracts any complacency about the values of the heroic code rooted in the narrative tradition behind the poem. By the time the Oxford version of the poem was composed, shadows were lengthening in the heroic world, and despite Roland's *brio* and magnificence, his tale must have vexed a late eleventh-century audience as well as pleased it. It is as true of the *chanson de geste* as of any art that material inherited from a tradition will inevitably seem problematic and unbalanced to the poet and audience of a new generation. If the oral poem does not adapt itself, it quickly falls into oblivion. Thus, the variants of the *chanson de geste* are to some extent dictated by the perpetual inappropriateness of the material of one age to another. The tenuous relationship of the Baligant episode to the poem as a whole suggests that this poet was highly sensitive to certain crucial complexities of his historical age.

However triumphant it is, the story of Roland's ordeal leaves us with an image of a Charlemagne who is profoundly humiliated as a person, as a leader, and as a Christian. We see him weak and indecisive, even, before the quarrels among his vassals, strategically unwise in assigning his twelve peers and his best knights to the exposed command of the rearguard, and outrageously tricked by a depraved pagan enemy, an enemy of God. Such humiliation almost demands, in literature, that redemption follow, and the existence of the story's second half, which deals with Charlemagne, suggests that such a compulsion was strong in the mind of our poet—at least of *some* poet. This is easily explained. Many of the leaders of later feudalism looked back at Charlemagne with nostalgia and veneration. Not only had he been king of the Franks, but he had represented as well the continuity of imperial Rome, the fourth monarchy prophesied by Daniel (2:39-40) whch was to have endured *in finem saeculi*—that is, until the final struggle with the anti-Christ should usher in the millennium of Christ, the fifth and final monarchy. A memory of the Carolingian Empire persisted as a dream of universalism during those three centuries of political chaos that followed it, during which time (particularly in France) political power became hopelessly fragmented among the feuding nobility. Charlemagne was also celebrated as a tireless defender of the Christian faith, whose conquests were said to have thrown back the boundaries of paganism and to have worked innumerable conversions. During the centuries after his reign, Charlemagne's legend gathered prestige. (pp. 73-4)

The insertion of the Baligant episode in the ***Roland*** may be understood as one poet's commentary on the tale of Roland in the light of later social attitudes. A story of blind temerity, the first half of the ***Song of Roland*** could doubtless still appeal to an eleventh-century audience as a monument to a glorious age still within memory; nevertheless, as an expression of contemporary needs, it fell short and challenged the poet to an extension. Thus the Baligant episode and the trial of Ganelon (which I shall discuss later) may both be regarded as responses to cultural attitudes in Capetian France which inspired men to emphasize those aspects of legendary history that could enhance the hope of achieving some kind of political stability in the world. Even though Roland's death is already avenged before the Baligant episode, the poet probably wished to revive an image of Charlemagne enjoying the full prestige that his memory could still evoke at the end of the eleventh century. Accordingly, a need arose in the poem for an antagonist of Charlemagne's own stature, one who could pretend to the same universalism as Charlemagne himself. With the arrival of Baligant, the ideological axis of the poem no longer involves just France and Moslem Spain, but East and West.

However we may account for it, the poet's decision to revive the image of Charlemagne in the Baligant episode gives rise to some artistic cross-purposes. During the first half of the poem, the tragic contradictions of the heroic world find expression in the dialectic of personalities. Now, however, we have two contrary values expressed in a *single* hero, Charlemagne. The poet asks a figure who is spiritually and physically exhausted to assume a hero's role as Christ's vicar in the struggle against the legions of Satan. Yet this same figure's sole present desire is to leave the burdens of this life and to be united with his barons in Paradise. Needless to say, one side of Charlemagne's character cannot conceivably flourish except at the expense of the other, especially since the poet's narrative resources do not lend themselves well to exploring psychological conflicts in his characters.

The gravity of the poet's artistic cross-purposes becomes all too evident when we analyze the substance of his narrative. The Baligant episode is some 1,228 verses long. Only 190 of these are devoted to the actual battle between the two armies, and only 64 are devoted to the climactic duel between Charlemagne and Baligant, which (like the duel between Aeneas and Turnus in Virgil's epic), is to settle the war. In other words, what ought to have been the dramatic focal point in the second half of the ***Song of Roland*** turns out to be, epically, a narrative flop. The poet devotes a quarter of the whole episode to a mere chronicle-like list of the troops who are to participate. Although an epic "who's who" of the Carolingian Empire could flatter an ancestor-conscious audience in the eleventh century, it brings the narrative to a standstill. Heroes are named everywhere but act nowhere! From the poverty of invention here and the tritely formulaic description of the duel between Charlemagne and Baligant, we suspect that the poet may be as weary of the heroic world as Charlemagne himself. (pp. 75-6)

If the poet nods during the battles of the Baligant episode, there are other moments, nevertheless, when he achieves some remarkably fresh effects. These tend to be clustered in his descriptions of the Saracen people. Nominally, at least, the cleavage of the world in the ***Song of Roland*** into opposing camps dramatizes broad moral conflicts between good and evil, Christianity and paganism, loyalty and treachery, as they were perceived by a pious mind at the end of the eleventh century. Yet there are times when we feel that the poet of the ***Song of Roland*** is more artist than moralist, which is to say that his mind accepts the polarized framework of his cultural world without, however, denying the urge to explore what is taboo. Like Tasso and Spenser, our poet is curious about the operations and attractions of evil, and the forbidden world occasions some of his best poetry. Theologically, of course, there was no place for doubt as a moral tool in the prelogical, crusading mind of the eleventh century; yet curiosity itself (as medieval moralists were well aware) can be a form of doubt and can defy the restraints of moral categories without overtly breaking out of them. The Saracen world satisfies all the direst criteria for evil but seems to satisfy, as well, a taste for the exotic and for sensuous delight. One wonders, indeed, if the ***Roland*** does not betray a certain ambivalence of motive which the crusaders shared—those of them who came back from the East. For the Saracens are most damnably worldly. They love gold, jewelry, fine silk, and gorgeous colors. When Marsile wishes to bribe Charlemagne into returning to Aix, the gifts he proposes are sumptuous: bears, lions, dogs, 700 camels, 1000 freshly molted falcons, 400 mules loaded with gold and silver, 50 wagons full of money. Again, when Marsile decides not to slay Ganelon during the stormy embassy scene, he offers a huge treasure of sables, which Ganelon accepts—the wages of sin can be elegant! Moreover, Arab worldliness includes a strong penchant for the arts of civilization: Marsile sits on a throne of blue marble; Baligant sits on a throne of ivory, before which is spread a great rug of white silk; Abisme carries a shield (given him, as we have noted, by a devil) studded with amethysts, topazes, and carbuncles which "flame" in the light; Anseis's shield is of vermillion and azure. All this Saracen finery is seen at its most brilliant at the instant when it is destroyed. On such instants the poet dwells again and again, as the sword of virtue shatters a precious work of pagan art. . . . But the triumph of morality only highlights the beauty of earthly wealth by destroying it in an explosion of light and color. Does the poet mourn or exult? Consider too the description of Baligant's fleet as it sets sail for Spain in darkness, casting all the while a sinister glow:

> They set sail and row, their rudders on course.
> From atop the masts and from the high bows
> Shine forth many carbuncles and lanterns.
> From above, they cast forward such a glow
> That in the night the sea is beautiful.
> When they come to the Spanish mainland,
> The whole country is lit up, and shines. . . .
> They leave the sea and sail in fresh water;
> They pass by Marbrise and they pass by Marbrose,
> And slink up the Ebro wth all their ships,
> Shining with countless lights and carbuncles,
> Which give great clarity throughout the night.
> At dawn they arrive at Saragossa.

Though passages of such visual beauty are rare in the ***Song of Roland,*** they give rise to an ambivalence that is discernible in other highly charged moral epics, such as the *Aeneid,* the *Gerusalemme liberata,* and the *Faerie Queene:* the artist in the poet often clings to what the moralist must put away.

The poet of the ***Roland*** finds material in Saracen culture to cloy the ear, as well as the eye. Evocative names, like "Escababi," for example, are sometimes marshalled into resonant lists like this inventory of Baligant's battle corps, bristling with French xenophobia but filled with intimations of a world both fearful and inviting. . . . The sensuality of the pagan world is characteristic of its leaders as well. Not once does the poet describe Roland or Oliver, yet Baligant is portrayed in considerable detail and favorably combines the attributes of both age and youth. . . . The poet bestows on Baligant a supreme compliment by wishing what we all wish at times, that evil were good:

> God, what a baron! If only Christian!

The gorgeousness of the Saracens' attire makes them effeminate in appearance, but (as the whole poem shows) they are strong fighters nonetheless. Baligant's shield, for instance, has a buckle of gold and is bordered with crystal. The strap is fashioned of the best silk, embroidered wth circles. His sword's name is "Precieuse," and "Precieuse!" is the cry of his men as they rush into battle.

It is primarily through such contrasts that the Christian and pagan worlds define each other. What a difference between battle cries: "Munjoie!" (Mount-Joy?) and "Precieuse!" One suggests joy won through hardship—perhaps even through crucifixion; the other is absurd and insolent, suggesting vain mockery of virtue. The relation of evil to good here is that of demonic parody, and may well be the poet's extension of fundamental medieval attitudes toward a world created by a benevolent God who nonetheless accommodates evil. (pp. 76-9)

What I find most interesting about the Baligant episode is that the absolute, established categories of good and evil appear to be eroding before our eyes: moral triumph becomes unrewarding and dull, and pretended pagan depravity vibrates with all the colors of life. The moral framework of the poem remains intact, to be sure, yet we can only feel that the impulse to censure is equalled by the impulse to innovate and explore. I am convinced that the ***Song of Roland*** is a poem whose premises change profoundly as continuations are added, and that the outlook imparted at the end is radically different from that at the beginning. It is interesting to observe, moreover, that many of the vices of the Saracen world—the love of finery, of what is sumptuously stylized, even of life itself—become virtues, within a generation or two, in the world of romance. It is dangerous to read history backwards, but I find it interesting to note, as well, that the only woman of consequence in the ***Roland*** is Bramimonde, the wife of Marsile, who is both attractive and loyal, and whom the poet elects to redeem at the poem's end by conversion. Perhaps we would not be wrong to speculate that the Baligant episode, with its unplanned failures and successes, emblemizes an artist's dilemma, a conflict of values, which will be happily resolved only with the new creative outlets of romance.

Whether or not these thoughts capture anything of the true significance of the Baligant episode, I remain convinced that its presence in the ***Song of Roland*** raises problems that are complex but instructive. Weak spots on poetry can provide valuable critical insights, and we sometimes owe them the same kind of consideration that we devote to passages of special artistic merit. True, subsequent versions of the ***Song of Roland*** omit the Baligant episode; but then, none of these later poets achieves anything of the power of this earliest *chanson de geste:* why, therefore, should we accept their authority as censors of the Oxford version of the poem?

Like the Baligant episode, the trial and punishment of Ganelon represents, I believe, the poet's further response (demanded, perhaps, by the sensibility of his eleventh-century audience) to earlier, unresolved problems in his poem. Caught up in the drama of Roland's martyrdom in the first half, he had repressed certain social questions that were raised by the conflict between Roland and Ganelon. Now, in the poem's epilogue, he shows an urge to return to his material, to ponder and interpret it, to deepen it in the light of later feudal ideology.

The ***Song of Roland*** is as much a broad social tragedy—a tragedy of "our barons" and indeed of a whole way of life—as it is a tragedy of individual personalities. The poet leads us to an understanding of this tragedy in social terms by restaging some of the major issues in the form of a traitor's criminal trial. By doing so he translates the significance of the disaster at Ronceval into the publicly intelligible language of judicial process. The poet's consciousness of the burden of history comes close to the surface of his narrative, and with this consciousness comes the poet's role as prophet (within a feudal framework) of social reform.

How to tame the barons? Where does power reside? Where is loyalty due? These questions may well have preoccupied epic narrative from Carolingian times, but they took on burning relevance for the French nobility of the late eleventh century. By this time the Capetian kings had begun to exploit the relationship between lord and vassal as a means of drawing the nobility into a more stable, centralized power structure. . . . The epilogue of the ***Song of Roland*** reflects the . . . trend in late eleventh- and twelfth-century political attitudes: Ganelon must be punished for compromising the interests of Charlemagne, his lord and sovereign.

The trial and punishment of Ganelon take place at Charlemagne's administrative seat in Aachen (Aix), far from the mountains and plains of Spain. The episode is not only spatially and temporally detached from the rest of the action in the poem, but narratively, as well; for the poet formally announces that a new episode is to follow: "Now begins the trial of Ganelon." The dislocation of the trial from the narrative body of the ***Song of Roland*** has encouraged some critics to suspect that this episode is a late interpolation into the story, though not so late as the Baligant episode. Whether or not the trial and punishment of Ganelon figured in the earliest versions of Roland's legend, the poet who composed these episodes remains close to the spirit of revenge which propels so many of the major episodes in the poem. . . . (pp. 80-2)

The charge brought against Ganelon is that he has provoked the personal loss to Charlemagne, his lord and sovereign, of twenty thousand Frenchmen, among whom were Roland, Oliver, and the twelve peers. The poet holds this an act of treason, and in the perspective of feudal ideology, treason was a crime of powerful moral dimensions. Satan, who broke the bond of fidelity to God, is the archetypal traitor, whose crime of treason subsumes all others. Grouped in the ranks of Satan's vassals are all who are not Christian, including the Jews as murderers of Christ, the persecutors of the early Christians (such as Nero), the pagan deities, and of course, the Saracens. Beside these stand Christian traitors to vassalage such as Ganelon and his poetic successor. Ganelon's collusion with the Saracens and his treachery against Charlemagne are one and the same crime, and a crime against God. Thus, when Ganelon proposes Roland as the leader of the rear guard, Charlemagne cries out helplessly in the pain of foreknowledge, "You are a living devil!"; and when Charlemagne charges Ganelon with treason, he lends a Biblical twist to his indictment by tacitly comparing Ganelon to Judas for having betrayed the twelve peers for money. As a crime against God, Ganelon's punishment is both necessary and inevitable.

In Ganelon's case, the specific issue to be decided is whether he was justified in satisfying his honor while compromising, at the same time, the interests of his lord Charlemagne. Bristling with autistic pride, which some critics attribute to an archaic Germanic code of individualism and clannishness, Ganelon replies to Charlemagne's accusations by saying that he acted solely for personal revenge on Roland. . . . Ganelon's account of his actions is factually correct, but he is invoking in his own defense the sanction of an old Germanic custom (*Fehderecht*), whereby retaliation for a crime against an individual remained the responsibility of the private individual and his family. Because his challenge was public and was heard by all, Ganelon insists, he did not commit treason. Interestingly, Ganelon's defense includes what amounts to a countercharge of treason against Roland, for in the medieval mind the need for revenge (which Ganelon cites) was explicitly associated with provocation by treason.

Ultimately, however, the defense of Ganelon's cause will not rest on logic but on brute force: this is the heyday of the champion rather than the lawyer. One of Ganelon's relatives, named Pinabel, readily undertakes Ganelon's defense. Pinabel is a man of formidable strength and skill. . . . The spectacle of

Pinabel rising in Ganelon's defense so intimidates Charlemagne's barons that they hush their voices in fear and agree to urge that Charlemagne drop the whole indictment. . . . When Charlemagne hears the barons' recommendation, he is enraged by their cowardice and exclaims, "You are traitors!" He feels betrayed, no doubt, because his barons are shirking their responsibility of delivering justice, a duty explicitly called for by the bond between vassal and lord. One would have expected Charlemagne's barons to defend Ganelon in order to preserve their honor and political autonomy from Charlemagne, but such is not their motive. They act not out of self-respect but because they are afraid. Is it not possible that the poet is deliberately undermining the cause of political autonomy here by making its proponents seem sleazy and dissolute instead of heroic?

At the moment when justice and authority and leadership seem to have perished from the face of the earth, a dissenting vassal appears before Charlemagne to take up his cause. . . . The poet was generous with Pinabel, Ganelon's champion: well built, handsome, respected by his peers, and forceful of speech, he is a typical heroic warrior. Thierry, by contrast, is a man of modest and even unpromising proportions; courageous, to be sure, but essentially faceless. Unlike Pinabel, Thierry is a subtle man, and his subtlety translates itself into a portrait fraught with qualifications and innuendoes. . . . The contrast between Pinabel and Thierry, between hero and anti-hero, is vividly conceived and serves several purposes. Dramatically, it heightens our suspense; how can justice possibly win out against such odds? Politically, the contrast invites us to re-evaluate the role of the uncomplicated, old-style warrior in society in the light of a less glorious, less attractive man who stands for social order and whose courage takes the paradoxical form of selfless devotion to the interests of his lord. Ethically, the presence of Thierry disputes the fundamental assumption that "might is right," which is implicit in the heroic spirit. Thierry even redefines the goals of dynastic pride and chivalric honor by saying to Charlemagne, "By my ancestors I must uphold your plea."

Thierry is lucid in his formulation of the charges against Ganelon. He recognizes, first of all, what is obvious, that Roland injured Ganelon. Like Oliver, Thierry is both able and willing to consider realities underlying the surface of events. Without trying to vindicate Roland, Thierry claims that Ganelon was wrong to exact revenge on Roland because Roland at the time was in the emperor's service: Roland was not just Roland, in other words, but a representative of Charles; thus, Ganelon's pact of retaliation constituted treason. . . . One suspects, in instances like this, that the premises of the ***Song of Roland*** are changing as the poem progresses. Roland was allowed to die secure in his honor, to be sure, yet retrospectively the barons now seem to acknowledge that Roland bears considerable personal blame for initiating the catastrophe at Ronceval by provoking Ganelon. In any case, Thierry, the man who finally exacts vengeance on Ganelon and who succeeds Roland as Charlemagne's champion, is a far cry from the quick and unreflective hero that Roland was. True, a hundred thousand knights "weep in pity for Thierry for Roland's sake," yet we can only feel that Roland would be out of place in Thierry's brave new world. Roland is dead, and so are the twelve peers. Faceless as he is, Thierry is what some critics have called the "new man," a perfect spokesman for the establishment.

The procedure by which Ganelon is actually convicted takes the form of a judicial duel. A legacy of ancient Germanic and Carolingian custom, the judicial duel remained an instrument of feudal law beyond the twelfth century. The duel is related to the "ordeal" (cognate with the German, *Urteil*), where an accused man would be ordered to grasp a red-hot iron with his hands; if he emerged unscarred, he was innocent. (A literary example of such justice may be found in the tale of *Tristan and Isolde*.) Both the judicial duel and the ordeal were based on a belief that God's will is immanent in terrestrial affairs, and that God, who is the very principle of justice, will intervene in the operations of mankind whenever the cause of justice is in jeopardy. In a large sense, the whole ***Song of Roland*** may be conceived as a judicial duel between the true and false gods, enacted by their respective champions on earth.

Generally, the judicial duel was reserved for extraordinary cases where evidence was insufficient to permit a judgment on other grounds. In Ganelon's case, however, there is no lack of "evidence" regarding Ganelon's actions: the nature of both the deed and the motive is unambiguous to all. The poet seems to wish not only to dramatize the substance of the tragedy of personalities in the judicial forms of society but also to remove the burden of rendering a painful judgment against a powerful vassal from the confused sphere of mortal affairs and to ratify such a judgment against Ganelon with the will of God.

Although the Christian God allows men to be the agents of their own justice, nevertheless "God knows very well what the end will be" before the duel between Thierry and Pinabel takes place. Pinabel is the first to knock down his adversary, and he seizes the occasion to propose a deal to acquit Ganelon. Thierry rejects all discussion and rushes back into action. Next, Thierry knocks down Pinabel, and now *he* is in a position to make proposals. The action is suddenly arrested, and for an instant we witness with emblematic clarity an encounter of perspectives between the old and the new. The "new man" has the upper hand. In a flow of surprising charity, unprecedented in this poem, a victorious warrior openly loves and admires his enemy and exhorts him to put aside his weapons:

> Says Thierry, "Pinabel, you are very brave;
> You are very great and strong; your body is well built;
> Your peers respect you as a noble vassal.
> Give up this battle; put fighting aside.
> I will have you reconciled with Charles.
> Justice will be done on Ganelon,
> Such that men will speak of it forever."

It almost seems as though history itself were hanging in the balance: can a new, benevolent social order encompass the fierce glory of the old guard? Can the ethic of revenge, founded on destruction and even self-destruction, be abrogated, as it was at the end of the *Odyssey*, by a miraculous spirit of reconciliation in the higher order of a just peace? Can the flow of human blood be stanched by an outpouring of human love? These are questions that every society, including our own, must ask and answer for itself. Unfortunately, *we* are the ones, and not the poet, who must formulate such questions here, for they lie beyond the idiom of the poem and perhaps even beyond the conceptual powers of the poet himself. The answer to these questions, whether they are justified or not, is clear: here as everywhere in the poem, the hero remains true to his identity. Pinabel's honor (as he conceives it) can brook no compromise. Thus, there can be no clemency; and the poet returns, at the end of this *laisse* (so pregnant with fresh but undeveloped potential) to the most proven formulas of the epic poet's trade, formulas that summarize with unwelcome finality the heroic warrior's absolute commitment to destruction:

> Pinabel says, "May it not please God!
> I shall uphold the cause of any kinsman,
> And not default for any mortal man.

It is better to die than feel reproach."
With their swords they now begin to strike
Their helmets made of studded gold and gems.
Sparks now brightly fly into the air.
Nothing, now, can separate these men:
Unless one dies, this battle cannot end.

When at last Pinabel's brain is cleft, as it must be, by the sword of divine justice, the French barons all cry out,

"God has shown his power!
It is very right that Ganelon be hanged,
And his kinsmen too, who pleaded for him."

Accordingly, all thirty of Ganelon's relatives are summarily hanged on that "tree of cursed wood." Ganelon himself suffers "marvelous pain" as he is quartered by four horses: such seems to be the traditional form of punishment for treason against one's sovereign. The climate of revenge, however, proffers no relief. On the contrary, three times the poet breaks out of his narrative voice to admonish us directly that traitors must be punished thus. In such urgency may we not perhaps detect a new longing for public order? (pp. 83-8)

With Ganelon dead there is justice, but no joy. If we think back to the first half of the poem, where knights killed and were killed for their lord and where death seemed almost like an excess of life, we now sense that a whole mode of life, a whole system of values, has become exhausted. Evil has been destroyed, to be sure, and revenge is complete: yet, the ethic of revenge has left the world bitter and empty. Along with Roland and the twelve peers and the twenty thousand knights of the rearguard, a heroic order has perished. Even their glory has perished, in a sense, because the men who remain can remember it but cannot inherit it. In short, of all the stuff that epics are made of, nothing remains. There is only Charlemagne, the last survivor of a heroic age, but a hero grown old. To be killed in a heroic poem is not to die but to complete all one has lived for; thus, for Roland, death was an elevation, an apotheosis, anything but the end of life. To be deprived of action and yet to live on in a heroic poem, however, is nothing less than death-in-life, for the true hero lives by action. It is a paradox, perhaps, that the experience of loss and annihilation, which we commonly associate with death, should be conveyed to us by a figure who can*not* die. We should understand, though, that Charlemagne has come to love others more than himself, and by virtue of this love has lost far more life than he could lose by dying himself.

The figure of the old hero is common enough in epic poetry—men such as Nestor, Priam, Romulus, Beowulf, and Calidore come immediately to mind. In most epics that I know of, however, the waning of a life is a theme woven into a broader social fabric which contains, as well, a world that is still vigorous and young. In this poem, the supreme old age of Charlemagne has become the central fact of the world; and his alienation from the time of his own Roland-like youth may be taken as a metaphor, perhaps, for the poet's (and his audience's) sense of remoteness from that age in the tenth century when heroic glory was a possible and honorable goal in life, that violent age where lay the true roots of French oral epic poetry. (p. 89)

Charlemagne does not die. Sick with life ("Lord, such anguish in my life!"), Charlemagne (unlike Beowulf) cannot die until the genre dies. It would not have occurred to the poet to dispatch his hero with a literary *coup de grace* in order to preserve his dignity, as Cervantes did with Don Quixote. Although we sense exhaustion in both hero and poem, the poet nevertheless maintains the conventional cast of his work until the very last lines. Charlemagne is his most characteristic and formulaic self in the final *laisse* as he weeps from his eyes and pulls on his white beard. He has not changed since he entered the poem, but what earlier were hyperboles of grief, which almost seemed unwarranted, have become understatement in the total desolation of the emperor's world. The poet's formulaic language can barely sustain, now, the tragic burden of his conclusion and seems ready to explode with emotion. Charlemagne has fulfilled the potential of his own formulas, and both he and the poet are on the verge, perhaps, of reaching out for new values in life. But these cannot be explored in the idiom of the ***Song of Roland.*** Thus, the poet's style and his material remain intact until the poem's very end. But *barely* intact: the city of Imphe in the land of Bire, both imaginary, seem infinitely far compared with Spain, at least as we see them through the eyes of a two-hundred-year-old warrior. Will Charlemagne resist the mission that his Lord and maker has given him? The question does not arise in the poem, yet it is clear to us that in Charlemagne's tragic vision, the task of life has become far more bitter than the prospect of death. This is the moment when men of the ordinary world would surely yield, yet this is precisely the moment when the epic hero defines himself and reveals, thereby, the distance between his world and our own; of *course* Charlemagne will depart for Imphe in the land of Bire. What is possible will win out over what is probable, and epic art will win out over reality, for this poem—like all epic poems—is an expression of faith (not just Christian faith) in the superbly beautiful and human paradox that man is capable of perceiving the futility of this world and still of struggling for an ideal in life.

To judge by the ending of this poem, in the eleventh century it was possible and perhaps necessary to believe in the myth of Charlemagne, and we may say that a poetic style has stood the test of its own time. But the ***Song of Roland*** is more than a masterpiece of feudal culture. The explicit terms of failure and achievement in life may change with the centuries, yet certain goals remain permanent in man's aspirations. The reader who looks beneath what is distinctly feudal or medieval—or even Christian—about the ***Song of Roland*** will find in it those images of loyalty, courage, and dignity in suffering which are the constant concerns of all epic and which have rightfully earned for this poem a privileged place in Western narrative tradition. (pp. 92-3)

Eugene Vance, in his Reading the "Song of Roland," *Prentice-Hall, Inc., 1970, 118 p.*

ROBERT HARRISON (essay date 1970)

[*Harrison is an American educator who has translated* The Song *into English. In the following excerpt from his comprehensive introduction to the poem, he recapitulates the critical debate over the genesis of* The Song *and explicates some of its historical and social aspects.*]

The ***Song of Roland*** presents one of the most baffling puzzles in the history of French literature. None of the poem's "vital statistics"—its date, its author, its sources—have been established conclusively, and although scholars have labored long and hard over these problems, their solution remains as remote today as it was a half a century ago.

Deeper still, the poem poses another, even more tantalizing riddle which concerns the nature of epic poetry itself. Over three hundred years separate the hard, clear facts in the case of this the greatest and possibly the oldest *chansòn de geste*. At one end there is the historical fact of the battle of Roncesvals on the afternoon of August 15, 778; at the other the literary fact, a bundle of seventy-two small leaves of mediocre-quality parchment catalogued under the name of Digby 23 in the Bodleian Library at Oxford University—and between the two that enigmatic process called epic fermentation, which is somehow able to transform an accident of history into the unique, inevitable expression of a whole people. (p. 7)

Ever since the first printed edition of the ***Song of Roland*** appeared in 1837, literary historians have argued tirelessly over how and why this particular battle should have become the inspiration for France's first great work of literature. By and large, scholars have drawn up their battle lines according to Romantic or Classical sympathies. The nineteenth-century medievalist Gaston Paris, for example, took as his point of departure a fashionable theory which held the *Iliad* and the *Odyssey* to be descended from folklore. He maintained that the ***Song of Roland*** was the product of a new sense of national identity emergent among the French people at the time of the First Crusade, and that its immediate origin was to be found in short folk songs called *cantilènes* which had grown up around the Roncesvals theme through centuries of epic fermentation, finally to appear, in a late, almost decadent stage, as the ***Song of Roland.*** Then, in the early years of the twentieth century, anti-Romantic reaction set in, championed by Joseph Bédier, who refused to accept the poem as a folk-creation and proclaimed it to be the work of a single individual of great artistic genius. According to Bédier, the story of Roncesvals had survived in the form of oral legends circulated along the pilgrimage routes of Europe, especially those of northern Spain. The road to the famous shrine of Saint James at Compostella, for instance, led through the pass of Roncesvals itself; all along this road there were hostels for pilgrims, and at these hostels monks who kept alive the names of local Christian heroes and their great deeds until, finally, spurred by the Crusading fever of the eleventh century, their tales were set down on paper by traveling poets called *jongleurs,* and the gap between folklore and literature was bridged. Finally the poet, working from the songs of the *jongleurs,* created the poem we know as the ***Song of Roland.*** Fairly recently, an eminent Spanish literary historian, R. Menéndez Pidal, has modified Bédier's view somewhat by proposing a traditionalist explanation which sees the poem as the final integer in a long and varied sequence of lost works on the Roncesvals theme.

Although these theories seem at first glance quite divergent, they all possess at least one common element: they assume the necessity of an earlier version of the ***Song of Roland.*** But even within this area of agreement controversies again start to arise concerning the nature and source of the hypothetical proto-***Roland.*** Some scholars think it must have been a spoken legend or folktale, while others see it as a full-fledged literary work written in Latin or Provençal or French and originating in southern France or northern France or even in Norman England. It has been argued that it must have been written in the early years of the twelfth century as a propaganda piece intended to warm up tepid Christian interest in the Crusade and at the same time to praise the dashing hero of Antioch, Bohemond; that it is based on military campaigns carried out by the Franks against Spain in the second decade of the twelfth century and celebrates specifically the capture of Saragossa in 1118; that it was written at the command of Pope Calixtus II, in order to stir the French to action against the Spanish Moors; and even that certain geographical names in the poem, when properly deciphered, show it was composed about 1085 in an effort to obtain Christian reinforcements for Robert Guiscard, who was campaigning at the time against the Byzantine Greeks in Dalmatia. And so the debate goes on.

It seems doubtful that historians will ever reach agreement on the genesis of the poem, but there is a way for the general reader to avoid this impasse, and that is simply to look at the poem itself. For though scholars may engage in endless debate over *fermentation épique* or the *cantilène* theory, one fact remains which vitiates their point of view: they treat the poem as a mine to be worked for the historical data it yields. In the long run, it is not the lack of factual knowledge which creates the riddle of the ***Song of Roland*** so much as it is that habit of mind which, regarding a work of art as nothing more than the sum of its raw materials, considers form and structure and theme and style as elements to be extracted, isolated, and put to nonliterary uses. But if we choose to treat the ***Song of Roland*** as what it is—a unique aesthetic reaction—then many scholarly problems become less compelling. Thus armed, we can now graciously entertain the likelihood that folksongs were composed about Roland and Charles, that the Franks seethed, both individually and collectively, with epic fermentation from 778 onwards, or that lesser poets composed proto-***Rolands*** by the score—as long as it is understood that what we call the ***Song of Roland*** exists only as a work of art justifiable for its own sake. And with this in mind, the reader can defend himself against the insidious influence of centrifugal arguments such as this: "The proto-***Roland*** must have been written before the twelfth century, because there is in it no hint of courtly love, and love is still regarded simply as the feudal duty of woman." Whether this assertion is true or not, it contributes nothing to our knowledge of the poem and is therefore of no literary significance—we already knew from a close reading that the poem contained no elements of courtly love.

Another benefit to be gained from reading the poem as literature concerns the question of its unity. Many early critics, dedicated to seeing the poem solely as a piece of historical documentation, insisted that the entire Baligant episode and the embassy of Blancandrin were late interpolations, and therefore ought to be stricken from the "real" text. Though it is true that these episodes have been omitted wholly or in part from at least one Old Norse and two Latin versions of the poem, the overriding fact is that they are indisputably *there* in the Oxford manuscript and in all other Old French texts.

With these caveats in mind, we may now return to the historical background of the poem and examine it briefly from a literary point of view. All speculation as to date aside, the facts are these: (1) There is no direct reference to the Crusades anywhere in the poem, and hence no absolute need to date it after 1096. (2) Around the end of the eleventh century, hints of the existence of a poem celebrating Roland begin to appear. (3) William of Malmesbury, writing about 1125, says that just before the battle of Hastings a minstrel sang to William the Conqueror's troops of Roland, "so that the warlike example of the hero would enflame those who were about to fight." Taking these facts into account, we might as well assume that the ***Song of Roland*** was written sometime around the beginning of the twelfth century.

Of more immediate interest, however, is the way history and legend are used in the poem. Obviously a skillful, talented writer has shaped from the conglomerate of history, religion, folklore, and earlier literature a compact, highly unified work of art. Take for instance the treachery of the Saracens. An historical precedent can be found in Einahrd's description of the Saxon wars:

> It [the war] might have been over earlier, had the perfidy of the Saxons been exposed. It is difficult to say how often they conceded defeat and offered themselves to the king as suppliants, promised to obey his orders, handed over the required hostages without delay, and received the envoys who were sent forth; how frequently they, so cowed and submissive, swore to give up their worship of devils and to yield themselves to the Christian religion. But even though they were often prone to do these things, they were always prompt to renege, so that it is impossible to say which course they followed more readily, for from the beginning of the war there was hardly a year in which they did not both promise and fail to perform.

This passage need not be read as proof of a direct line of influence from Einahrd to the author of the ***Song of Roland,*** but rather as some indication of the poet's technical skill. Here he has grafted an historical detail of the Saxon war onto the Spanish campaign in order to create an aura of verisimilitude which will lend credence to the necessary fictions of his plot, such as Ganelon's betrayal and the selection of an ambassador to Marsilla.

Another interesting use of an historical source may be found in the stormy relations of France and Spain during the eleventh century. At the beginning of the century Christian power had once again deteriorated in the north of Spain: the shrine of Saint James had been desecrated and plundered, and the Moslems had recaptured Barcelona and moved across the Pyrenees. As the century wore on, however, the French made a concerted effort to push the Moors back, chiefly because of pressure exerted by the zealously Christian wife of King Alphonso VI of Castile. Thanks to her religious fervor, many monasteries were established in northern Spain, and the entire region came back into the European sphere of influence. But this resurgence of militant Christianity so disturbed the Moorish chieftain Yûsuf of Marrakech that he attacked Alphonso and defeated him decisively at the battle of Zalaca in 1086.

At this point the lines of history and epic intersect. According to the ***Song of Roland,*** there were three separate pagan assaults at Roncesvals: first, Marsilla's nephew Aëlroth led an attack and was beaten back rather easily; next, Marsilla himself advanced with the main body of Saracens, and was repulsed when Roland managed to cut off his hand, but only at the expense of nearly all the Frankish knights; and finally, the rear guard was overrun by a wild charge of 50,000 Negro troops under the command of the caliph. Similarly, at the battle of Zalaca a vanguard of Andalusian Arabs made the initial attack on Alphonso, while Yûsuf remained concealed in the hills; when Alphonso succeeded in driving back the Arabs, the main force under Yûsuf attacked. The outcome of the battle hung in the balance for a while, until the pagans were reinforced by a contingent of ferocious Negro guards, and the Christians were routed. At some time during the engagement King Alphonso was wounded in the hand.

Here it would seem that history is being made to serve a literary purpose, but once again it must be stressed that the end-product is our primary concern. The loss of a hand, for instance: an adventitious detail at the battle of Zalaca, in the ***Song of Roland*** it acquires the sort of representational value that we normally associate with symbolism, and becomes much more significant than its literal meaning could possibly warrant. By helping to maintain a scrupulous balance in the military fortunes of the Saracens and the Franks, it contributes to the reader's awareness that there is more at stake at Roncesvals than just another battle, that there is present here an element history usually lacks—*form*. As [Robert S. Picciotto, in a 1965-66 article in *Romance Notes*] has observed, "Roland, who has been depicted as the perfect knight, could not go to his death without first taking his revenge. Had he depended on Charlemagne to even the score, he could hardly be judged perfect by knightly standards. But had he slain Marsile the score would have been far from even, because they were not of equal rank. So he deprived Marsile of exactly the same thing that the Moor was taking from Charlemagne."

In addition, Roland's act has judicial overtones. Mutilation by cutting off the right hand was an accepted punishment for especially heinous criminals, and Roland both symbolically and literally strips Marsilla of his power as a lord and as a man, by rendering him incapable of defending not only his weapons in battle, but his fiefs and chattels as well. By allowing Roland to disgrace him in this way and drive him from the field alive, Marsilla subjects himself to the basest form of humiliation in the eyes of his vassals and his wife. Nor were the subtle social and psychological implications of the act lost on the medieval audience: upon the lintel of the church at Angoulême the sculptor represents with fine ambiguity the retreating figure of Marsilla twisting his body at the last instant to defend himself against Roland.

In the opinion of many scholars, including the German Walter Tavernier, many of the episodes in the ***Song of Roland*** grew out of the events of the astonishingly successful First Crusade into Syria and Palestine (1096-1108). These similarities have been used chiefly to date the poem or to identify its hero with this or that historical figure, but the same data may be applied just as well to literary ends. Although there are close resemblances in subject matter, style, and tone to the early Latin chronicles of the First Crusade, we need not go along with Tavernier and regard the poem merely as a double-barreled propaganda blast directed at the pagan perils in both the Middle East and Spain. The giant Falsaron may owe his existence to the tale of a giant Saracen killed at the siege of Antioch in 1098; the incident of the pagan standard . . . may have been inspired by a similar feat of arms which took place at the battle of Ascalon; and it is quite likely that Turpin's militant theology would have been considered heretical prior to the famous Clermont sermon of Pope Urban II—but interesting as these details are in themselves, and convincing as they may be in arguing for a date after 1100, their importance to the reader lies in what the poet has made of them. This sort of question is more to the point: Why is Falsaron the second pagan killed, and the first killed by Olivier? What use does the author make of the pagan standards? What effect does the character of the archbishop have on the theme and structure of the poem?

In the same way that historical incidents are used in the dating game, so echoes from earlier works of literature are often regarded as veiled hints of the identity of the poet. Yet these same literary influences, when pointed in the proper direction, can shed relevant light on the making of the poem. Take, for instance, the faint echoes of Vergil's *Aeneid*. At the beginning of both poems, the heroes have just completed seven-year campaigns; in both poems envoys are depicted carrying olive branches as tokens of peace, a custom unknown in northern Europe, where the olive tree does not grow; then there is Baligant's mighty spear, which may have been modeled on that of Goliath's brother Lachmi, "whose spear staff was like a weaver's beam," but may equally well descend from Aeneas's spear, which was "huge as a tree"; and, finally, the savage form of punishment meted out to Ganelon, which is found neither in Germanic tradition nor the Carolingian law codes, but has a literary precedent in the execution of the traitor Mettus.

Once again literary considerations should come first. The seven-year campaign—seven years being in the Middle Ages proverbial for a great duration—sets the stage for the widespread disaffection and willingness to compromise in the Frankish camp which will put in motion the machinery of betrayal. The olive branches borne by the pagan messengers, by parodying the practices of antiquity, add the element of travesty to treason. More significant than the literary antecedents of Baligant's spear is its symbolic function; its name, *Maltet,* which probably means "Evil," suggests that it stands for the whole, vast power of the pagan world, locked in deadly struggle with Christendom, here imaged by Charles's sword *Joyeuse*. Even the death of Ganelon is important not because it perpetuates a classical literary tradition, but because it represents a form of retribution peculiarly fitting to the nature of his offense.

Perhaps the most baffling riddle of all appears in the last line of the poem: *Ci falt la geste que Turoldus declinet*. Ambiguous in almost every word, this line may serve as a paradigm of the magnitude of scholarly ignorance. Is the *geste* referred to this poem, or the lost proto-***Roland,*** or is it merely an unknown chronicle the poet used as his source? Does *declinet* mean "compose," "copy down," or, as some have ventured, "grow weak"? And above all, who is this shadowy figure named Turoldus—clerk or *jongleur,* poet or scribe?

As one might anticipate, vast amounts of energy and ingenuity have been expended in hunting down eleventh-century Frenchmen named Turoldus and linking them to the ***Song of Roland.*** Internal evidence throughout the poem suggests that the author was a well-educated clergyman who had some precise, though limited, geographical knowledge of northern Spain, and was familiar with the Bible, the *Aeneid,* and the Latin histories of the Franks. In addition, his name, a variant of the Scandinavian *Thorvaldr,* indicates that he may have been a Norman. The most likely candidate in the Turoldus sweepstakes nowadays is a monk from Fécamp who fought at Hastings, served as abbot at Malmesbury and at Peterborough, and died in 1098. It must be kept in mind, however, that all this speculation rests ultimately upon one single line which bristles with ambiguities, and that there is not a shred of genuine evidence to connect any historical personage with the poem. So until such time as proof may come to light, we are justified in identifying Turoldus only in the manner that we identify Homer—as the man who wrote the poem.

One other scholarly puzzle ought to be mentioned briefly here—the mysterious "AOI." This cryptic signature, most often written in capital letters but sometimes "Aoi" and "aoi" as well, occurs 172 times throughout the poem: 158 times at the end of verse paragraphs, and 14 times in other locations. No other manuscript in the Old French language has anything like it, and none of the later medieval translators of the ***Song of Roland*** show any indication that they understand its purpose. In the early days of ***Roland*** scholarship it was rather casually assumed to be a battle cry or possibly a *jongleur*'s private key to abridgement, but more recently scholars have tended to identify it as a vocalise, an exercise for singers, based probably on the Latin phrase P(A)X V(O)B(I)SCUM, P(A)X D(O)M(I)N(I), "peace be with you, peace of the Lord." This interpretaton suggests that it might have been a musical notation signaling either the uninflected monotone used in some liturgical chants, or perhaps a sustained final vowel sound to mark a close.

But the explanations of AOI only begin here—in the last few years it has been identified as the surviving vestige of an ancient refrain related to the *alleluia,* as a short form of the French (A)INSI S(O)IT (I)L, "so be it," and, most ingeniously, as not AOI at all, but as the scribe's misreading of *Am.*,the standard abbreviation of Amen.

Despite all these theories, there are a few things we may safely say about the elusive AOI. First of all, its function is unquestionably aesthetic—it is almost invariably found at the end of verse paragraphs, where form and rhetorical structure crest simultaneously, and it normally accompanies a shift of scene or of atmosphere. (As a matter of fact, even when AOI is missing from the end of a paragraph, about half the time it follows the first line of the next, suggesting that the scribe may simply have misplaced it through carelessness.) And finally, from a literary point of view, all these varying interpretations amount to about the same thing—whether AOI meant to the poet "so be it" or "*alleluia*" or "Amen," it signals to the reader a moment of heightened significance in the action.

• • • • •

In *Raoul de Cambrai,* a twelfth-century *chanson de geste,* the hero, who has spent a busy day burning down a convent full of nuns, comes home and orders meat to be served at supper. His knights are apalled by this request. "Today is Good Friday!" they remind him indignantly. "Do you want to slay our souls?"

This incident, exaggerated as it is, may serve to point up the narrowly literal attitude toward religion characteristic of the early Middle Ages. To the medieval nobleman piety meant a familiar, almost intimate relationship to the human natures of Jesus, Mary, and the saints of the church, and included not only what we think of as religious devotion, but also unswerving loyalty, national pride, chivalric honor, and a fierce sense of personal dignity. In those days Western Christianity had very little in commmon with the philosophical otherworldliness of the Eastern Church. In fact, it was so unabashedly linked to the mundane and the material that during the Crusades the Byzantine Greeks often suspected their Roman Catholic allies of idolatry. For in spite of the Cluniac reforms of the tenth century, the Frankish knight regarded his obligations to God in very much the same terms as his allegiance to his feudal overlord. But unsophisticated as the faith of the average man may have been, it was nevertheless wholly sincere and zealously militant. It was, in fact, precisely what has since come to be known as the "crusading spirit," that outlook which led eleventh-century Europeans to leave their homes and embark upon a grandiose, idealistic quest in the Holy Land. In the eyes of medieval Christians all non-Christians were despicable worshipers of graven images and false gods, but if awards were to be handed out for heresy, then the nod would have gone to the Moslems. Of course, idolatry has always been specifically forbidden to Moslems, but the Euroepans did not know this, and it was a commonplace among Roman Catholics to see them as fanatical fetishists, and to associate Islam in a vague way with pre-Christian paganism. As a matter of fact, knowledge of the Moslems at the time of the ***Song of Roland*** was still so meager that the Saracens depicted in the poem look less like individuals than hideous imitations of the Christian knights they oppose in battle, and their religion seems to be little more than an obscene parody of medieval Catholicism. The Saracens, like the Franks, have their "trinity" of Apollo, Mohammed, and Termagant (a distant ancestor of Shakespeare's devil Termagant in *Hamlet*), who are represented in the poem as idols alternately worshiped and vilified by the pagans, depending on the fortunes of war.

Even the faint glimpses of Islamic history and culture which appear occasionally in the poem tend to reveal the poet's ignorance rather than his knowledge. The titles given the various pagan champions, for instance, make up a potpourri from four centuries of Arab history: the agnomen *al khalifah,* "successor" (to Mohammed), was in use until the eleventh century; *almodaffer,* "victorious," was the surname of Hakam, a king of Cordova in Charlemagne's time; and *al mansûr,* "victorious," had belonged to the tenth-century Arab hero Mohammed ibn-Ali-Abir, whose fifty-six campaigns against the Europeans apparently had not been completely forgotten even by the time of the ***Song of Roland.*** Evidently the poet was trying to furnish a bit of the exotic local color his countrymen associated with Spain and Islam, while at the same time describing the Moslem world in a fashion both comprehensible to his audience and suitable to the allegorical needs of the poem. Thus the balancing of forces at Roncesvals serves not only to build up the tension finally released in Charlemagne's magnificent single combat with the emir, but it also provides the Saracens with twelve peers to match those of France.

Beneath these surface details lies the unspoken assumption that the pagan world was a mirror-image of the Christian, structured in exactly the same manner yet inverted in every particular. This attitude is revealed by an occasional offhand remark by the poet—when describing an especially valorous Saracen, for example, he says with open admiration that he would have been an ideal chevalier, had he only been a Christian. By the same token, when Roland dies he freely offers his soul to the archangels, while Marsilla's is wrested from him by "lively devils." Nor is this attitude to be found solely in literature: on the west façade of the church at Conques, in southern France, Christ is represented with his right hand raised in a gesture signifying truth, while Satan extends his left hand downward.

Even in the specialized business of waging war, both the Franks and the Saracens seem to observe identical customs. Battles are formally announced by heralds; warriors request their commanders to give them the honor of opening a battle by striking the first blow; knights announce their presence and intentions to the enemy by means of formal boasts; and both sides make use of traditional battle cries to keep up their fighting spirit and to rally their units. In addition, both the Christians and the Saracens carry battle standards or ensigns; here Charles's *oriflamme,* the golden banner of the city of Rome, which, by the way, was actually presented to Charlemagne by Pope Leo III—though years after Roncesvals—is pitted symbolically against Marsilla's dragon and the ensigns of Baligant. It should be made clear that these insignia were not as yet heraldic; what we call heraldry, with its elaborate and systematic representation of family alliances, did not develop until long after the time of the ***Song of Roland.*** In the early Middle Ages knights embellished their shields and carried banners chiefly for identification in the thick of battle when they might easily be mistaken for the enemy. Marsilla's standard should be thought of as much like the one King Harold displayed at the battle of Hastings—a small wooden or metal effigy fixed on a tall pole and carried by a foot-soldier.

In his life of Charlemagne, the Monk of St. Gall writes:

> Then could be seen the Iron Charles, helmed with an iron helm, his iron breast and his broad shoulders defended by an iron breastplate, an iron spear raised in his left hand, his right always rested on his unconquered iron falchion. The thighs, which with most men are uncovered that they may the more easily ride on horseback, were in his case clad with plates of iron: I need make no special mention of his greaves, for the greaves of all the army were of iron. His shield was of iron, his charger iron-coloured and iron-hearted. The fields and open places were filled with iron, a people stronger than iron paid universal homage to the strength of iron. The horror of the dungeon seemed less than the bright gleam of the iron. "Oh the iron, woe for the iron," was the cry of the citizens. The strong walls shook at the sight of iron, the resolution of old and young fell before the iron.

Though the monk may have been carried away somewhat by his imagery, there is nonetheless a measure of truth in what he says. For Carolingian society, as we see it in the ***Song of Roland,*** was based on a primitive unsophisticated form of feudalism not greatly different from the clan society of *Beowulf* and the Old Norse sagas. The division of labor was a simple one: men were classed as warriors or clerics or laborers, and complicating influences such as courtly love had not yet come along to disturb the simple vertical pattern of loyalties which constituted the rationale of social behavior among members of different station. Incidentally, this clear-cut division of labor may help explain why foot-soldiers are practically never mentioned in the poem, even though it was a common practice for feudal lords to require military service from their workers, and Charlemagne's expeditionary force in Spain must have included many thousands of them. The ***Song of Roland*** was intended to present an idealized portrait of warfare, not a realistic one, and any reminder that there were conscripted, nonprofessional troops at Roncesvals would have struck a jarring note.

At the apex of France's pyramidal society stood the emperor. As commander in chief he placed upon his great lords specific military obligations commensurate with their wealth and power; they in turn demanded the same of their subordinates, and so on, down the line of command. Since the nobility all belonged to the miltiary caste, even the humblest fief-holder physically able to take part in a campaign was expected to contribute his services and provide the personal servants—cooks, grooms, foragers, and the like—necessary to maintain him in the field. Thus the Saracens are wrong to speak of Charles's men as "mercenaries." Although there were some mercenary soldiers by the eleventh century, such as the Varangian Guard of the Byzantine emperors, they were unknown in Charlemagne's time, and the very nature of the feudal system made it necessary for every knight to support himself, with only occasional booty to hope for as his reward.

Charlemagne's army was composed not only of vassal lords and their retainers, but included also many men who held no fief and were bound to the person of their overlords. These landless knights who made up the household guard, or *maisnee,* of a great lord, were often taken into his home as children, given training, sustenance, and armament in return for personal allegiance as well as the customary feudal obligations. The members of a *maisnee* were required by oath to fight to the death for their lord; for this reason, it was important for him to lead his men into battle, and to remain alive and in full view of them, so they would know they were still held to their oaths. If a lord was killed or unhorsed, his followers would be likely to interpret their duties as fulfilled, and head for home. This state of affairs may help explain the emphasis placed on single combats throughout the poem—each chieftain in effect represents a sizable contingent of men ready to fight for him just as long as he is successful, but no longer. Thus the entire pagan host, regarded as Marsilla's *maisnee,* deserts the field of battle the moment Roland puts their lord *hors de combat,* and the same thing happens later when Charles kills Baligant.

In the absence of written law it is in the nature of things that men will set great store by symbolic gesture. In the rigidly formal social order of medieval France, the assignment of a fief or an honor was invariably accompanied by a ceremonial transfer of tokens, such as a clod of turf or a staff. But perhaps the most universally recognized emblem of all was the glove, symbolic of personal allegiance; when the dying Roland proffers his right-hand glove to God, he is performing the gesture by which a vassal submitted himself to his lord's rule. Later on, Thierry pledges his faith to Charles in precisely the same manner. Similarly, clasping the hands together, an act which made the suppliant momentarily defenseless, had both religious and feudal connotations of voluntary subservience. And when Charlemagne blesses his knights with an upraised right hand, he imitates not only the usual benediction of the Lord, but at the same time recalls that mysterious force the Germanic tribes called *heil,* which was believed to bring success and health.

As a man's duties to his heavenly and earthly lords were delineated with hair-splitting exactness, so were his responsibilities to his family and himself. In the feudal world honor was a family concern; the relatives who pledged themselves for Ganelon, and Pinable, who put his life on the line for him, were doing no more than what was expected of Christian noblemen. The Saracens, on the other hand, reveal their base natures when they use their own sons as pawns in the treacherous game against Roland.

Relations between social equals were defined with like precision by the Franks. The term "companion," for example, is used throughout the ***Song of Roland*** to designate either a fellow member of one's *maisnee* or, by extension, a member of one's military unit. The twenty thousand Franks in the rear guard thus become companions by virtue of their assignment, while Roland and Olivier were already companions, since both belonged to the king's *maisnee*. Quite different from the companion was the "friend": though companions were often friends as well, the two terms do not overlap in meaning, for friendship was restricted to personal rather than feudal relationships. Two men of equal station might be bound informally to one another in friendship, and a liege-lord might well call a member of his *maisnee* "friend," but under no circumstances would a vassal use the word in addressing his lord.

Social anthropologists have described Roland's world as a "shame" society; that is, one in which moral attitudes and patterns of behavior are based upon the opinions of other people. As evidence they frequently cite the speech Roland makes to his men, when he reminds them that if they do not fight bravely their names will be held up to public ridicule in mocking songs. This, they argue, explains Roland's reluctance to call for help though hopelessly outnumbered, his final walk across the battlefield toward Spain, and, for that matter, the entire ethos of the poem. It is equally possible, however, that an acute sense of personal honor—what one thinks of oneself—gives rise to the idea of shame. Once again it is the question of the chicken or the egg: does Roland behave heroically because he fears the scorn of his countrymen, or because he would share that scorn himself?

Perhaps the better course is to describe it as a "success" society. Inherent in the medieval world-view is the unquestioned assumption that all is for the best, that in the long run truth and justice are bound to prevail in a world created by an all-powerful, benevolent God. In terms of this dictum, success and failure become the modes of good and evil: that is, whatever succeeds is necessarily right, and whatever fails is wrong. This viewpoint so pervades the ***Song of Roland*** that even the pagans share it; interpreting their defeat on the battlefield as a total default of their religion, they renounce their gods and desecrate their images. And, *mutatis mutandis,* the Franks, seeing one of their number overwhelm his Saracen opponent, shout jubilantly, "We are in the right and they are in the wrong!"

Ths pragmatic view of things produces several interesting corollaries. For instance, in a success society there can be no such thing as a "good loser"—the terms contradict one another—and the very fact of defeat imposes a terrible burden of shame upon a knight, his family, and his followers. The language of the poem clearly reflects all this: a common word of abuse such as *caitif,* from the Latin *captivus,* "prisoner," indicates the attitude toward failure, for to be taken alive was a sign of great humiliation, and even to lose one's weapons in the field was cause for reproach.

On the other hand, many of the conventions we associate with honorable behavior seem to be flagrantly disregarded by the Franks. There is no need to look for the modern concept of "fair play" in the single combats of the poem: in a success society sacrificing one's advantage to an enemy is tantamount to disdaining the special favor of God. Though it was considered shameful to attack a foe from behind, this was not due to any obligations to sportsmanship, but simply because a sneak attack could be construed as a tacit acknowledgment of one's inferiority or cowardice. Since a chief goal in battle was to enhance the fame of oneself and one's family, any act that would lessen that fame naturally was to be avoided. Similarly, lines such as "A hundred thousand Franks fall down unconscious" may strike the modern reader as strangely out of place in a story of valiant deeds and dauntless knights. But the stoical acceptance of misfortune which we expect of our heroes grows out of Germanic paganism, and would have been regarded with contempt in medieval France as evidence of a callous, un-Christian nature. Time and again the Franks weep unashamedly, and in moments of great distress even Charlemagne tears wildly at his beard; but reactions such as these, far from diminishing a man's heroism, were taken as evidence of that quality from which heroism derives its significance: sensibility. The greatness of a man's soul was measured largely by his capacity for suffering, and the stiff upper lip would have been interpreted as proof of either brutishness or stupidity.

But perhaps the most anomalous attitude to be found in the poem is the unreserved adulation of riches and the rich man. The Saracens, of course, are the most notorious offenders in this practice, but the Franks, too, in a most un-Christian fashion, often equate virtue with material wealth. Here again, moral conclusions are determined by the psychology of success. Although the word *riche* overlaps in meaning both *Reich,* "realm," and *rex,* "ruler," and in its original sense refers to power rather than to riches, the idea underlying it is still the same—the man who has right on his side succeeds in every way. The wistful lament, "It might have been," has neither force nor meaning to the characters of the ***Song of Roland,*** for it implies a flawed universe and hence an imperfect Creator, a conclusion unacceptable to them. The Bildads of the medieval world prevailed.

Many of the elemental moral precepts which shaped Frankish society are brought to the surface by the trial of the traitor Ganelon. At first the proceedings seem to bear a close resemblance to contemporary trial or, more accurately, court-martial procedure. The king, representing himself and the state he rules, is both the offended party and the convening authority. He summons the *seniores,* the wisest men in his realm, and orders them to serve as judges in the case of the Empire v. Ganelon. This done, he steps down to become from now on merely the plaintiff, and neither presides over the court nor dispenses justice himself. Thus the king has voluntarily relinquished the juridical arm of his authority and bound himself to the verdict of the court, leaving the defendant to be tried by a jury of his peers. It is now entirely up to the *seniores* to decide upon the proper course of action: whether Ganelon should be acquitted of the charges against him, or whether he must pay a penalty commensurate with his offense. Since the grave charge of treason has been made, the death sentence would be mandatory in case of conviction.

Up to now Frankish trial procedure looks very much like our own, but here the resemblances end. It soon becomes apparent that the trial of Ganelon is not what we call a trial, but is rather an appeal. The court makes no attempt to ascertain what happened in Spain; the defendant is never asked to testify about the facts of the case; no witnesses are called. Instead, the judges review the relative merits of the pleas, then hear the formal accusation of Charles and the equally formal denial of Ganelon.

There is no disagreement whatever about the facts; Ganelon freely admits he plotted the deaths of Roland and the entire rear guard in league with the pagans Blancandrin and Marsilla. The question before the court is one of law rather than of equity, namely: did Ganelon's action constitute treason? The king says it did; Ganelon says no, and presents two lines of defense. First, he says he was justified in seeking to avenge himself on his stepson: Roland had committed certain unspecified wrongs against him in the past, depriving him of wealth and possessions, and furthermore had insulted him by nominating him for the embassy to Marsilla. Second, Ganelon reminds the court that he had made a public *defi,* or challenge, to Roland, Olivier, and the Twelve Peers of France in the presence of Charles and his great lords, which automatically clears him of any charge of subterfuge, a *sine qua non* of the crime of treason. In summary, Ganelon claims that his act was one of openly declared, justified vengeance, not treason against his lord and country.

Following each stage of the proceedings, the members of the court withdraw to deliberate the arguments they have heard. According to proper judicial procedure, once all the pleas have been presented and considered, a verdict should be forthcoming, based solely on the merits of the case. But at this point in the trial medieval justice miscarries: because of precisely the same kind of irresolution that caused the Franks in Charlemagne's army to leap at the chance for a truce with Marsilla, the judges, swayed by the men from Auvergne, put expediency and personal safety before principle. Prompted by fear of Pinabel's wrath, they call upon Charles to abandon his suit and let Ganelon go unpunished. The king is understandably infuriated by this display of spinelessness, which leaves both himself and his empire unavenged, and hence disgraced. Yet, since he has given the *seniores* jurisdiction in the case, he is powerless to act in his own behalf.

At this critical moment, a new voice is heard; Count Thierry steps forward to defend the cause of Charles. Acting as a self-appointed judge, he delivers a minority verdict denouncing that given by the court. Thierry argues that Roland, by virtue of the command given him, was an official deputy of the king and should have enjoyed immunity from personal attacks for the duration of his service; therefore, his betrayal by Ganelon amounted to betrayal of Charles himself, and was an act of treason. His verdict is immediately contested by Pinabel; representing both his family and the opinion of the court, he presents a formal rebuttal by calling Thierry a liar.

Suddenly the proceedings have shifted to an entirely different plane. In effect, a new trial has begun, a *judicium dei,* or trial before God, the outcome of which will be determined by the principles of the success theory. The question now, both a legal and moral one, is simply this: who is right, Pinabel or Thierry? The issue will be decided by judicial combat, during which it is assumed that God will intervene personally and uphold the contestant who is right, so that justice may prevail. Because of the gravity of the accusations, this will be a fight to the death; if the defeated man is not killed on the field, he will be hanged afterwards.

Preparations for the battle are carried out with a scrupulous concern for protocol:

1. Both men temporarily hand over their fiefs to Charles, since the holdings of the loser will revert to him.

2. Pinabel offers thirty hostages to vouch for his appearance and proper conduct at the battle, while Charles pledges himself as surety for Thierry.

3. The court sets the time and place of the battle.

4. Servants bring in benches for the combatants and their followers to sit on while the referee, a distinguished nobleman selected by the court to act as *porte-parole* ["spokesman"], carries back and forth the prescibed declarations of innocence, reads aloud the charges, and explains the rules which will govern the battle.

5. The combatants fulfill their religious obligations by attending a special mass for their souls, making generous contributions to their churches, and confessing.

6. They retire briefly to arm themselves, and return ready for battle.

In the combat that follows, the author takes some pains to stress Pinabel's physical superiority to his opponent, even going so far as to say, "when he hits someone his time is up." But though Thierry is hit, his time is decidedly *not* up; he weathers the best Pinabel can offer, is miraculously spared from death, and goes on to win. Divine intervention has proved him, and by extension Charles, to be in the right, and in accordance with God's verdict the court sentences Ganelon to a traitor's death.

Here, by medieval custom, the matter should have ended. What baffles students of the ***Song of Roland*** is the strange decision of the court to execute Pinabel's thirty kinsmen. These men had only warranted that their champion would appear at the prescribed time and place and obey the rules of the battle; when he fulfilled these conditions, they expected to be released. But it would seem that the norm does not apply here, that once again expediency governs the course of Frankish policy, and that the mass execution was occasioned more by fear of retribution than by the imperatives of heavenly or mundane justice. At any rate, this final act of the court does not follow the dictates of medieval justice, and would have been considered harsh and brutal even in the Age of Iron.

A story of men at war, the ***Song of Roland*** was designed to appeal to a predominantly military audience, and many details of equipage and weaponry taken for granted by the poet now need to be explained. Einhard describes Charlemagne's apparel in this way:

> He wore his national—that is, Frankish—dress. He was attired in shirt and underwear of linen, followed by a tunic with a silk fringe and leggings; then his legs were cross-gartered and his feet put into shoes; and in winter he protected his shoulders and chest with a jacket made from the skins of otters or ermine. He wore a blue cloak and always carried a sword with a hilt and belt of either gold or silver. Occasionally he used a jeweled sword, but only at important festivals or when envoys came from foreign nations.

When dressing for battle, the medieval knight added to his everyday clothing a gambeson, a hauberk or byrnie, and a helmet. The gambeson, which was worn over the characteristic Frankish tunic, was a thick jacket quilted with either wool batting or shredded rags. The oldest and most widespread type of body armor known, it was used by ancient Egyptian troops, and is even today the Chinese soldier's first line of defense. Although it offers little protection against a thrusting weapon such as the lance, it is quite effective in warding off swordcuts and arrows fired from a distance. European infantrymen of the Middle Ages normally wore gambesons as their sole defense, while cavalrymen used them beneath their outer armor to cushion the shock of blows.

The knight's principal defensive garment was either a byrnie or a hauberk. The vestlike byrnie was generally made of a material called *cuir-bouilli,* which was leather boiled in oil until it was soft and then molded to fit the torso; when dry it was very tough and resistant to cutting blows. The hauberk was a knee-length cloth tunic made wth slits front and rear, like a riding skirt, and often equipped with an integral coif which had a small opening in it for the face. This garment was reinforced by any of several kinds of metallic armor. The most common variety, called *scale* or *imbricate,* consisted of small plates sewn to the fabric beneath in overlapping rows. Though it was quite serviceable and permitted easy movement, scale armor had one serious drawback: it was immensely heavy. The weight problem was finally solved by the introduction of the more costly chain mail, with its fine mesh of interlocking wire rings. Of Oriental origin, chain mail was first known and imitated in Europe by the Romans, who saw it on Scythian and Parthian cavalrymen, but the time and expense required to make it kept it from being very widely used except by the most affluent.

The conical Norman helmet, or *casque,* was made of four triangular metal plates riveted together in a ring and converging at their apexes. Frequently it was furnished with a *nasal,* a narrow metal flange attached to the front of the helmet and projecting downward in front of the nose, and designed not to stop a right-angle blow but only to deflect the descending path of a sword and thus protect the face.

Evidence of eighth- and ninth-century styles in military apparel suggests that the defensive armor of Charlemagne's time was somewhat less elaborate than that described in the ***Song of Roland.*** The Frankish hauberk, for instance, was probably just a simple jacket reinforced by *pour-pointerie,* metal rings sewn on at spaced intervals, and the casque little more than a plain leather cap. In the relief adorning the church lintel at Angoulême, Christian and pagan cavalrymen are seen engaged in battle, and barring a few minor details such as the shape of the shield and the Christians' fondness for long veils flowing down from beneath their helmets, all the combatants dress very much alike.

The primary offensive weapon of the medieval knight was the lance. Descended from the oriental javelin and originally intended to be thrown, the lance had evolved during the Middle Ages into an exclusively aristocratic thrusting weapon. Its sturdy wooden shaft, commonly of ash, was attached to the head by means of a hollowed-out iron socket about eighteen inches in length. Forged in one piece with the socket, the lancehead was usually leaf- or lozenge-shaped, and was invariably provided with a narrow strip of cloth which served the same purpose as the blood-groove of a sword or bayonet, preventing the head from becoming inextricably lodged in the body of an opponent. In time this little pennant outgrew its utilitarian origin and became the most prized ornament of the medievel knight. As the art of heraldry slowly developed, it became the immediate ancestor of the armorial banners and ensigns which were proudly flown everywhere as guidons and identifying symbols. When an army was on the march, these pennants were kept neatly furled upon the lance shafts—*fermées* is the technical term—but at the first sign of battle they were unrolled and flown with a brave show of color to lift morale and dismay the enemy. They were just as useful in bivouac as in battle; knights planted their lances outside their tents with pennants unfurled as a handy means of recognition, and by analogy flew them from the walls of conquered cities to betoken victory.

Only when a knight was unhorsed or in some way deprived of the use of his lance did he turn to his secondary weapon, the sword. The characteristic Frankish sword, forged from a single steel billet, was about thirty inches long and had a broad, double-edged blade which ran with very little taper to a rather obtuse point. It had short, simple quillons or cross-guards, a straight grip, and a flaring or slightly bulbous pommel. It rode in a metal-lined leather scabbard which was often covered in linen and then painted and hardened with wax to a brilliant luster. The scabbard was hung about the waist by a small cord and worn on the left hip underneath the hauberk. In order that the sword might be quickly accessible, the hauberk was provided with a slit through which the hilt protruded.

Although it ranked second to the lance on the battlefield, the sword always enjoyed a ritual eminence far beyond its actual value as a weapon. Possibly through Oriental influence, ceremonial swords were elaborately damascened and their blades engraved with mottoes and magical symbols and signs of the zodiac. Furthermore, the sword played a significant role in feudal society: knighthood could be conferred only with the sword; together with the scepter and the orb, it was the third major insignia of imperial power; and in solemn processions it was always carried before the sovereign, its blade pointed skyward as a sign of triumphant military power and justice.

Nor was the sword associated only with earthly sovereignty; sanctified by the Church at the time of the Crusades, it became the universal symbol of the union of spiritual and mundane militancy. Of course, ever since the days of Achilles' shield, fine weapons have possessed an irresistible appeal for the men who use them. Roland's Durendal and Olivier's Halteclere and Charles's *Joyeuse* are treated with the same special faith and almost superstitious affection any solider feels for the tools that keep him alive and victorious in battle. The ancient Scandinavian heroes also gave names to their swords, and in Russia as late as the nineteenth century magic spells were still being spoken over swords to enhance their efficacy in battle. But as a Christian symbol the sword acquired even more than ordinary significance. Its shape made it inevitably a makeshift crucifix in times of exigency on the battlefield, and it frequently was used in the last rites of men killed in action. It is therefore not surprising that Durendal should have within its pommel priceless religious relics, or that Roland in his dying speech should address it as the emblem of military and divine power.

A final weapon carried by the Frankish man-at-arms, a large knife which looked much like a scaled-down replica of the sword, was probably used much more in hunting and everyday camp life than in combat. Weapons other than these, especially throwing weapons, were scorned by the Christian nobility, and throughout the ***Song of Roland*** are seen only in the hands of the pagans. Although the early Franks were reputed to favor a heavy, double-bitted throwing ax, by the time of the Crusades such weapons were associated with heathens and the commonalty. The contempt for javelins and bows in particular was a social one, since these had long been infantry weapons; in fact, the feeling against them was so intense that in 1139 the Roman Catholic Church officially banned the use of arrows against Christians.

Unlike most of the implements of warfare, which changed very little in the years between Roncesvals and Hastings, the Frankish shield did show considerable variation. In the ninth century it was modeled closely on the Roman buckler, a small, round metal shield made with a projecting boss or *umbo* in its center. This style predominated in Europe through the tenth century, and was still common well into the eleventh, when it was gradually supplanted by a new model, Oriental in origin, but known in the West long before the Crusades: the tall, almond-shaped shield, constructed of leather or *cuir-bouilli* stretched over a wooden frame, and slung from the neck by a strap called a *guige*. On its padded inner side two leather loops were provided for the left arm and hand to pass through, so that a knight could keep hold of his horse's reins while still protecting his body. Since Homer's time the shield had offered the artist an ideal surface to demonstrate his skill upon, and the shields of all the warriors in the ***Song of Roland,*** both Moslem and Christian, are to be visualized as gaily painted with geometrical designs and fabulous birds and beasts.

The most important item of a knight's equipment was, of course, his horse. Actually, three different kinds of horses were taken along on a military campaign: the packhorse or *sumter;* a smooth-gaited riding horse called the *palfrey;* and a fast, big-boned war horse or *destrier,* so called because he was normally led on the right side of the palfrey. In the early Middle Ages elaborate metal armor had not as yet been developed for horses, and their only protection consisted of a heavy quilted cloth designed to fend off arrows and oblique sword-cuts. (pp. 11-34)

Robert Harrison, in an introduction to The Song of Roland, *translated by Robert Harrison, New American Library, 1970, pp. 7-49.*

JOSEPH I. DONOHOE, JR. (essay date 1971)

[Donohoe is an American educator and critic. In the following excerpt, he addresses the relationship between Roland and Olivier, demonstrating its significance to the poem as a whole.]

In the central panel of the medieval triptych which bears his name, at the heart of the privileged *laisse* which occupies the numerical center of the poem, Roland asks Olivier, who has just dealt him a blow with his sword:

> "Sire Cumpain, faites le vos de gred?"
>
> ["Comrade, sir, are you doing this on purpose?"]

One might conjecture that if Roland considers the question necessary it is because the answer is less obvious than has usually been assumed. And if Olivier declines a direct reply, in the simple yes or no format suggested by the question, it could be that the incident being considered is otherwise delicate and complex. By exploring the motivation underlying both Roland's remarkable question and the curious reticence of his friend, we hope to be able to focus attention on the profoundly human truth of their relationship and on the insightful skill of the poem's maker in portraying it.

When one examines attentively the circumstances surrounding Olivier's action, a certain number of puzzling considerations arise. To begin with, we are told that Olivier's sight had been impaired by the flow of blood into his eyes. . . . But, one notes, he has not been totally blinded, for he is capable of distinguishing a human form, of approaching it, and of launching an attack. Even more significant is the fact that the blow lands directly on target, slicing through the very center of Roland's helmet. . . . How, one is tempted to ask, can Olivier, whose vision has been disturbed to the degree related, deliver a blow of such telling precision—and to a horseman in the unlikely attitude of the unconscious Roland? At the same time, one might bear in mind that, independently of a lifelong comradeship which should have increased his "visibility" for Olivier, Roland is, objectively speaking, the most easily recognizable warrior in the field. Even Grandonie, a pagan, who had never encountered Roland previously, easily recognizes that distinctive figure when they meet for the first time during the rigors of combat. . . . Is it possible that Olivier saw well enough to deliver the blow in question and in the manner described, while he did not see well enough to recognize his friend and peer?

A second matter which offers itself for consideration is that of Roland's reaction to the blow. Aroused by it from his stupor, Roland immediately recognizes Olivier, grasps what has happened, then asks without apparent surprise whether or not the blow was intentional. The fact that he does not treat the matter as an obvious mistake and that Roland feels the need to put such a question to his friends suggests, along with a curious display of emotion ("Si li demandet *dulcement e suef*" ["He asked him softly and gently"]) on the part of the Count, that for him the possibility exists that the attack was not accidental. The following line, as much a protestation of friendship as a matter of self identification—since "Rollant" is qualified by the relative clause "ki tant vos soelt amer!" ["who loves you so!"]—appears to be a reproach touching on the incongruity of the blow in the context of their comradeship—in the absence of any intent on the part of Olivier such a reproach is meaningless. And finally, an element of spontaneous plaintive understanding seems clearly to motivate Roland's third remark:

> "Par nule guise ne m'aviez desfiet!"
>
> ["You haven't challenged me in any way!"]

Elementary logic gives a fair idea of the supposition regarding intent that must have dictated such a reproach: intent is taken for granted. Roland's question focuses rather on Olivier's departure from the sanctioned procedure. Even the black traitor, Ganelon, it will be recalled, remains within the prescribed forms by preparing his act of treachery by the public defiance of Roland. To the disturbing paradox of a blow precisely administered by a man of severely curtailed vision, one must add, it would seem, certain aspects of Roland's behavior which sugggest that for him the action was neither completely a surprise nor wholly involuntary.

Continuing our examination of the exchange between the two warriors it should be noted that Olivier's reply, at best, does little to allay our suspicions:

> Dist Oliver: "Or vos oi jo parler.
> Jo ne vos vei, veied vus Damnedeu!
> Ferut vos ai, car le me pardunez!"
>
> [Oliver said: "I hear you speaking now: I do not see you, may the Lord God see you! I struck you, please forgive me for this!"]

Although one might be inclined to interpret these words as a disclaimer of intent, the truth is that Olivier's reply hedges on the real question; a simple, spontaneous disavowal with perhaps an expression of concern for Roland's well being is curiously lacking—as a matter of fact, Roland will later volunteer the information that he is all right; Olivier will never ask. Looking carefully at what he does say, Olivier's first time: "Or vos oi jo parler" appears to be that of a man regaining contact with reality. Roland, it will be recalled, was an inanimate form at the moment the blow was struck; now at the sound of the familiar voice Olivier is forced, not without discomfort, to reconcile his aggressive act with a returning sense of Roland as a person and as his friend. It is significant, though, that his next line (by the employ of the present tense rather than the past) continues the hedging tactic. (At least, from the point of view of morphology, the forms are sufficiently distinct so as not to have been easily confused and therefore, in context, the choice of present over past could be instructive). To say that he *does not see him* at the moment he is talking is not the same as saying he *did not see him* before the blow was struck. We know, moreover, that Olivier did see Roland before the blow was struck or he could never have struck him—it is whether he *recognized* him or not in the moments before the assault that is disputable. The final line of Olivier's reply constitutes no more a denial of responsibility than the other two. "Ferut vos ai, car le me pardunez!" he says, admitting the fact and requesting pardon while almost pointedly ignoring the matter of intention which, to all appearances, was the point of Roland's question. Why is it that completely innocent Olivier should neglect to refute simply and directly the momentous accusation implicit in the words and manner of his companion? To all of these questions one could conceivably reply that the whole thing is simply accidental: that Olivier, weakened and blinded, had made a regrettable but understandable mistake. This is an objection we shall certainly have to deal with in due course, but let us first pursue another possibility. (pp. 251-54)

In our effort to penetrate the sense of the final moments shared by Olivier and Roland, it is worthwhile to consider carefully what the broader context of the poem has revealed of their comradeship. The dynamics of this relationship have been such, apparently, that previously the divisive tension generated by a marked opposition of life-style (*preux-sage*) has been overshadowed by the cohesive force of affection. It is also probable that this affection has not been tested in the face of an event capable of polarizing completely the disparate styles. But this is exactly what occurs in the events leading up to and culminating in the tragic affair at Roncevaux.

The manner in which affection and latent hostility have coexisted in their relationship is suggested early in the poem by Olivier's reaction to Roland's offer to become the emissary to Marsile. Olivier's action on this occasion is, to be sure, dictated by friendship: the desire to safeguard Roland. At the same time, however, he gives full expression to his critical insight into his friend's character in advancing reasons why he should not be sent, and this appraisal—at least coming from Olivier—cannot be considered entirely flattering:

> "Vostre curages est mult pesmes e fiers:
> Jo me crendreie que vos vos meslisez."
>
> ["You have a very bad temper: I'd be afraid that you would pick a quarrel."]

But, on this occasion, in spite of any undertones of hostility, Olivier's overt behavior is carried out under the sign of friendship. Later, however, the succession of events, shaped by and shaping an increasingly univocal expression of Roland's heroic ego—the spontaneous provocation of Ganelon, which determines the ambush; the refusal of extra support by Charlemagne, which insures the efficacy of the treachery; and, finally, the unwillingness to summon aid which seals the fate of the rear guard—will overturn the equilibrium of this relationship. A curious rearrangement of the moral forces involved is visible in Olivier's angry exchange with Roland over the latter's belated desire to call for reinforcements. This time Olivier's anger clearly dominates his conscious expression while the conscience of friendship is very nearly silenced. His bitter denunciation of Roland's offer to sound his horn breaks off suddenly at the end of the *laisse* and, without transitions, almost by lapsus, becomes a naive expression of concern for Roland's physical condition: "Ja avez vos ambsdous les braz sanglanz!" ["See how bloody both your arms are!"] This intrusion of compassion is only momentary, however, for the renewal of Roland's offer will elicit an undifferentiated expression of anger from Olivier which will culminate in his disavowal of Roland as a "brother."

An added insight into the significance of this reversal of behavior on Olivier's part can be found in the joint consideration of two separate but thematically related moments on the battlefield. The first of these occurs when Roland, deaf to the reasonable advice of his companion, chooses with the ineluctable logic of his heroic mania, for the rear guard to go it alone. Never, perhaps, has Roland been more alone, nor more completely himself. The force of events in conjunction with his own inner dispositions has brought him to an apotheosis of heroism. Detached from the subtleties and complexities of human events, his vision of things has become that of the quintessential simplicity of the man of action: the world exists to be subjugated by his sword; anything else is odious capitulation. Thus, when his friend Olivier, in spite of his reiterated refusals, attempts to demonstrate rationally the difference between discretion and cowardice, the man of action, revealing the now naked antagonism of styles, labels his companion a coward. Conversely, in a later scene, the exact inverted parallel of the previous one, Olivier, having combatted Roland's belated decision to call in the main army, explodes in anger at the Count's continual blindness and does not stop until he has accused him of madness: ''Kar vasselage par sens nen est folie'' [''For heroism tempered with common sense is a far cry from madness'']—the classic reproach of the reflective man against the hero.

Roland's accusation of his friend, it will be recalled, comes just prior to the actual engagement, whereas the angry outburst of Olivier comes in the final moments of the battle. The significance of the time lapse here is that Roland will attempt, during the battle, to escape the solitude occasioned by his starkly heroic decision by attempting to repair the damage to their friendship which had been—in the form of his outrageously simplified appraisal of Olivier's motives—a part of its cost. Olivier, on the other hand, wants more from Roland than an indirect apology for a personal insult. The proud Roland must recognize within himself the insidious pride which is at the base not only of the insult but of the provocation of Ganelon and of the slaughter of their gallant followers. When this insight into himself is not forthcoming from the French commander, Olivier will respond with coldness and sarcasm to his overtures for a renewal of their friendly ties. While the field is still bitterly contested, Olivier will not go beyond this negative expression of his discontent, but when the battle has been all but lost, and in the face of mounting casualties and the unchanging blindness of Roland, he will give vent to his long repressed anger. It is this anger which is in Olivier just moments before the attack on his friend. And, while it is in part dissipated on the enemy, a significant portion of Olivier's infinite rage (''De lui venger jamais de li ert sez'' [''He will never slake his thirst for revenge''], the poet remarks after he has been wounded) must remain intact as he approaches the man whose insufferable pride is the real underlying cause of the tragic occurrence.

To see, even in the circumstances described, Olivier's call for Roland as a trap, is unwarranted—the summons is, on the contrary, in part, an emotional reflex of friendship; but neither can one deny that Olivier's shout has the effect of bringing Roland within range of his sword. Before he faints on his horse, Roland has come close enough to Olivier to distinguish clearly his face; it is doubtful, given Olivier's condition, that without his summons the attack could have taken place. With Roland close by, in response to his request, and with Olivier's anger as yet ostensibly unappeased, it is still difficult to conceive Olivier's blow as consciously directed against his friend. What cannot be denied, however, is that, under the circumstances just detailed, Olivier's use of his sword is a rash act and one in marked contrast to his normally prudent style: angered at Roland, and having just called him to his side, Olivier attacks a soldier whom he is unable to identify. We are inclined, moreover, to see in the impairment of Olivier's vision, not only the physical condition but also the metaphor of a momentary moral blindness which is inseparable from the other: real fuzziness of vision both reflecting and contributing to a fuzziness with regard to intent and responsibility. In his action, under these conditions, we cannot but discern a certain ambivalence and, as in all such acts (like Ganelon's fumbling of the ambassadorial glove) an element, however deformed, of will: an instance, at the level of action, of the familiar ''verbal slip.'' Moreover, this estimate is reinforced by the nature of the blow itself: Olivier's stroke is sufficiently vigorous to cut clear through the protective headdress of Roland but the blade is stilled just as it is about to encounter flesh. If one excludes for the moment, Divine intervention, which is normally referred to explicitly in the poem, and is not in this case, there are only two possible explanations for this detail. Either the blow is ''half-hearted,'' that is to say, an expression of a very human ambivalency comprised of a fusion in action of contradictory anger-love impulses, or it is ''accidental.'' The second alternative, since it implies an interpretation not only of the integral encounter between Roland and Olivier but of the poem *in toto* is worth considering at this point.

To begin with, the sense of ''accident,'' defined as gratuitous event, is hardly applicable to our discussion. An artistic structure may have flaws, a mistaken insight or an irrelevancy, but aside from this the accidents are themselves artistic in nature and suggest meaning. Within the artfully constructed world of the ***Chanson de Roland*** accidents mask meaning either human or divine in its origin. Given the overt presence of Christian ideal and doctrine, one might be tempted to see behind all apparently chance-ordered events the shaping hand of Providence: Roland and Olivier would thus become symbolic figures and the attack on one by the other would signify Divine disapproval of *démesure*. In the context of medieval Christianity, however—or in any other, for that matter—it might be wiser to honor the principle established by Aquinas who forbids the attribution of phenomena to Divine intervention until all human or natural causes have been exhausted. But, as we have attempted to show, there is an ample basis in purely human terms to explain the ''artistic accident'' of Olivier's attack on his friend. The attack, moreover, is essential to the logic of the poem since it alone offers justification for the transposition from anger-engulfed friendship to the undifferentiated love and serenity of the final embrace of the two men.

In the wake of Olivier's attack, with both men conscious of what has taken place, changes are apparent in both of them. As Olivier regains his composure he is without anger, for his anger has not only been expended in a violent act (this is the primitive psychology of the duel) but it has been chilled by the realization that he has gone further than was his intent and was justifiable in reasonable terms. Olivier now experiences guilt as his request for pardon suggests. Roland, on the other hand, has been reached by Olivier's attack in a way that words never could have accomplished; Olivier, one might say, has finally succeeded in touching Roland, by speaking Roland's language. Only after the blow, which must appear to him an incredibly uncharacteristic departure by Olivier, can Roland begin to perceive its justification: in other words, a sense of his own guilt. Such a perception is in fact, paradoxically, suggested by his apparent lack of surprise and, perhaps, even more strongly by his uncharacteristic response, in words, questions, in short, in the willingness to discuss the assault in a reasonable way. Obviously the Roland who replies with searching questions to a sword's blow on the head is, in some manner, a changed man. His willingness, indeed eagerness, to accede to Olivier's request for pardon . . . is in a curious way an admission of his own guilt.

Olivier's attack on Roland involves an irony which to our knowledge has never been set forth clearly but which the present analysis now permits us to grasp: Olivier, the man of clear vision, must become blind to strike the blow that alleviates momentarily the chronic blindness of Roland and permits him

A thirteenth-century stained glass window from Strasbourg Cathedral showing Charlemagne seated between Roland and Oliver. Musee de L'Oeuvre de Notre Dame.

to understand—without which their reconciliation remains unexplained. The implication of this reversal of roles, with its underlying dynamics, is that the *man* has, at least momentarily, bested the *style,* and that the allegorical has been enriched by the artistic imitation of complex human behavior. (pp. 258-61)

Joseph I. Donohoe, Jr., "Ambivalence and Anger: The Human Center of the 'Chanson de Roland'," in The Romanic Review, *Vol. LXII, No. 4, December, 1971, pp. 251-61.*

CHARLES MOORMAN (essay date 1971)

[*Moorman is an American educator and author whose works include* A Knyght There Was: The Evolution of the Knight in Literature *(1967) and* Editing the Middle English Manuscript *(1975). In the following excerpt, he explores several characters and episodes in* The Song *in terms of the way they reflect "a contrast between the individualistic ideal of a heroic society and the corporate values of a later, more organized society."*]

French history from the death of Charlemagne in 814 to the end of the eleventh century was a period of continuing crisis and confusion marked by the collapse of the post-Carolingian kingdoms and the rise of feudalism. There can be little doubt that the French dynasty beginning with the early mayors of the palace and culminating in Charles Martel, Pippin, and finally Charlemagne was politically far ahead of its time in establishing for Europe a common rule and civilization. This it accomplished largely through a skillful use of the one organization common to all Europeans, the Church. By encouraging missions, establishing the parish system in rural areas, and creating a unifying myth, the Holy Roman Empire, to which all Europeans might subscribe, the Carolingian kings were able to overcome, at least for a time, the regional differences which divided the continent and to gather into a single office the major strands of legislative power.

But Carolingian rule could not impose on Europe any sort of economic unity. Communications were slow and untrustworthy, trade between distant cities almost impossible. Thus the progeny of Charlemagne, unfortunately men of no great ability, found it impossible to exact any real influence over local authorities. Unfortunately also, the three grandchildren of Charlemagne divided among them the great empire, thus creating what would in time become the modern states of France and Germany as well as a middle kingdom which itself quickly divided into a number of small warring states. The political confusion caused by the ensuing petty wars was increased, moreover, by the fact that the local lord had also to defend his lands against the predatory raids of the Vikings, Magyars, and Saracens, a task no central government could do for him.

The chief result of the disintegration of the post-Carolingian kingdoms in the ninth century was the emergence of feudalism. As historians have pointed out, the spread of feudalism was not in any way planned; indeed it could hardly be called a "system" of government in any modern sense of the term. It was at best a makeshift scheme, the roots of which extended well back into the Germanic *comites* of pre-Carolingian times, which provided a means of order in a period of threatening chaos stemming from the failure of central government and from the outside attacks. Its chief feature was the mutual responsibility of lord and vassal in a continuous and flexible chain of authority. The vassal, largely autonomous in the governing of his own domain, was obliged to furnish his lord with military service; furthermore, although he was not, as in the *comites,* a member of his lord's household, he owed to him the same sort of personal, as opposed to national, loyalty . . . in the early Germanic societies. The lord, in turn, guaranteed to his supporters protection, justice, and an adequate reward for their services.

Under Charlemagne feudalism was perfectly compatible with the idea of a unified government and, indeed, during the Dark Ages that followed, men still spoke of empires. But during the unsettled days of the tenth century there was nothing that approached, except in name, a feeling for or loyalty to anything above the personal allegiance to a local lord. However, as feudalism developed, particularly through the granting of pieces of land called fiefs in return for services granted a lord, it began to grow more complex and hence more centralized. As his kingdom extended, the feudal lord became more unwilling to leave his vassals completely autonomous in governing their provinces and so created deputies to check the power of his subordinates. And as commerce and industry increased throughout Europe during the eleventh century, the feudal system, which was based on a purely agrarian economy, began to lose control of a serf population which was moving from village to town and could now demand, and receive, more for its services than mere protection. Finally, the religious revival which swept Europe as a result of the Saracen assaults on the holy places of the East did much to bring Europeans together in a cause which transcended their local interests and allegiances.

Hence the rise in authority and power of the Capetian kings in France can be attributed largely to their ability to preserve in even the most troubled times the vestiges of royal authority, and to their good fortune in preserving a direct line of descent. To be sure, by the end of the eleventh century, the time of the writing of the ***Song of Roland,*** France was still ruled for the most part by its great dukes. Even so, the dukedoms of Flanders and Normandy, indeed most of the northern dukedoms, were stable and free from violence and had in fact become feudal states rather than simply feudal lordships. The officers of these dukes were able to supervise the courts and financial interests of their masters and so protect them from rebellious vassals. At every level, then, the decentralized feudalism of earlier centuries had faded, the power of the crown was steadily increasing, and the institutions and indeed the political thought of the West, even within the great dukedoms, had developed far beyond the simple personal loyalties of early feudalism. It was not long before an allegiance to France replaced allegiance to Normandy or Flanders.

By the mid-twelfth century Europe had been reshaped by the emergence of a new culture based on new customs and institutions; one can see everywhere the brilliant effects of new learning, new manners, even, in courtly love, a new relation between men and women. Chivalry emerged from knighthood just as monarchy emerged from feudalism. And although . . . the vast majority of critics see in the ***Song of Roland*** the "social, religious, moral, and imaginative conditions" of this new era, it is also possible to find in its action and ethos remnants of late Carolingian and early Capetian times, of the three hundred years of feudal confusion during which the memory of Roncevaux was preserved, probably in both *cantilenae* and narrative lays, in the courts of warlords throughout France. (pp. 95-8)

In fact, like the Homeric epics and *Beowulf,* the poem contains a mixture of political and social ideas and, like those poems, sees the values of its own time as essentially opposed to those of the more heroic age which it ostensibly celebrates. This contrast between the personalized feudalism of the past and the rising spirit of loyalty to crown and nation is expressed in a number of ways, particularly in the clear-cut opposition in values, upon which the poet insists, between Roland and Oliver.

"Roland is proud [*proz*] and Oliver is wise [*sage*]," the poet says, and their actions plainly bear out this description. They are most conspicuously contrasted in the two horn-blowing episodes, the first of which centers upon Roland's refusal to summon Charlemagne at the beginning of the battle and the second on his final decision, the battle being lost, to call the emperor so that the rearguard's defeat may be avenged. The first episode occupies eight full *laisses. Laisses* 80-82 recount Oliver's description of the pagan host; *laisses* 83-86, Oliver's pleas to Roland to summon Charlemagne's host and Roland's proud refusal; and *laisse* 87, after the statement that "Roland is proud and Oliver is wise," Oliver's reproach to Roland: "You would not sound your horn for pride; . . . now whoever fights today will never fight again."

Like most of the *laisses similaires,* these are incremental, each extending the implications of the total situation. *Laisse* 80 begins with Oliver's climbing a hill to survey the enemy host, whose presence has been announced by trumpets. Oliver's reconnoitering of the enemy forces is, of course, an indication of his prudent, practical nature, but, more important, it allows him to come to two immediate conclusions about the situation, neither of which the proud Roland will accept—that they have been betrayed by Ganelon and that they cannot win the battle. Both of these conclusions are rejected by Roland on the same grounds, personal honor and family pride. He cannot conceive that his stepfather, however much they may disagree within the family, could ever betray the French; and he positively ignores the second warning, his whole concern being with his own conduct in the battle rather than the welfare of the army he commands or its chances of victory.

The wise Oliver, having failed to dissuade Roland from battle, now suggests that Roland blow the olifant to summon Charlemagne and thus insure a French victory. But Roland refuses even this sage advice, again arguing that such conduct would bring dishonor to him and his family forever. Instead he eagerly anticipates the approaching battle, not because it will advance the cause of France or even of Christianity but because it will give him an opportunity to enhance his own reputation. Like Hotspur, whom he greatly resembles, Roland becomes more eager for battle with the news that his force is outnumbered. It is indeed a discouraged Oliver who accuses Roland of sacrificing an army for pride.

The second of the horn-blowing episodes presents a startling contrast to the first. As long as the tide of battle had favored the French, Roland had remained gleeful, urgng his men on and boasting over the slain enemy. But now only sixty of the original twenty thousand Frenchmen remain alive, and the hero is suddenly appalled by the consequences of his first decision. Turning to Oliver, he asks naively why the emperor has not come to aid them and how he may yet summon him.

Oliver's reactions to Roland's late decision to blow the olifant have, it seems to me, been generally misinterpreted. It seems unreasonable that the poet, having insisted on Oliver's prudence and concern for others in the earlier incident, would here present him as an image of stubborn pride. True, Oliver may feel that since their cause is past praying for, personal honor is all that is now left to the French survivors; and there is also something of an "I told you so" tone in his speech. But Oliver in answering Roland echoes almost explicitly the hero's former arguments: they will lose renown and their families will be disgraced if they sound the horn in defeat. Oliver's remarks in this crucial scene are thus consistently and cynically ironic, bitterly mimicking Roland's earlier vaunts; as Roland says, the words are spoken bitterly and in anger. But this is the natural reaction of a man of good will and common sense who has seen an impulsive, irresponsible fool destroy himself and others for the sake of an ill-thought-out set of slogans. Little wonder that Oliver wishes to renounce the chivalric ties, closer even than blood ties, which have bound the warriors since boyhood and that he proclaims Roland unfit to marry his sister. And against this withering attack Roland can defend himself only with a pitiful rationalization—"I have struck many strong blows"—and with a childish attempt, now that it is too late, to repair the irreparable damage—"I will blow the horn and King Charles will hear."

But there is more in Oliver's words here than pique at Roland or bitterness at the inevitability of his own death. His final and longest speech, *laisse* 131, abandons the biting irony of the preceding *laisses* to give plain voice to the real cause of his renunciation of Roland and the values Roland represents:

> There is prudent courage, and there is foolhardiness. These French are dead because of your

> recklessness, and we will never give service for Charles again. If you had heeded me, my lord would have come, we would have won this battle, and King Marsiliun would have been taken or killed. Your prowess, Roland, has proved our undoing. We will never again come to the aid of Charles the Great, a man whose greatness will never be excelled. You will die here and France will be humbled. Now has our loyal companionship been broken, and before nightfall we will have parted in grief.

In substituting rashness for prudent courage, the hero has destroyed not only himself, the *douze* [''twelve''] peers, and the rearguard but the cause of France as well: ''You will die here,'' Oliver says, but more important, ''France will be humbled.'' And it is certainly significant that Archbishop Turpin immediately joins the discussion with the argument that, if summoned, Charles can at least avenge their deaths and procure a national victory.

The contrast in values that separates Roland and Oliver is thus not simply a matter of pride versus prudence but rather individualistic, irresponsible, chivalric pride, the outlook of the tenth-century feudal aristocracy, against the considered, though nonetheless courageous, and at least partly nationalistic prudence of the new age of the Capetian kings. It is certainly clear that Roland's attitude is typically feudal. He regards the rearguard as his vassals, loyal to him personally and subject to his every demand, presumably by virtue of his specific commission by Charlemagne. He is motivated by the desire for personal glory; he cannot endure the thought of personal and family shame. In short, he recognizes no allegiance to any authority except that based on a purely personal commitment. Moreover, Roland's famous *doel,* the powerful emotion with which he views at the very end of the battle the slaughtered French around him, is clearly, as George Fenwick Jones says [see excerpt dated 1963], ''chagrin'' rather than ''grief'' in any Christian sense; it is the despondency into which a feudal hero falls upon realizing ''that he will lose his honor because of his defeat and his inability to protect his men.'' Significantly, in this same *laisse* he refers to his men as ''vassals'' and states that they died for his sake, thus emphasizing even here his feudal point of view toward them.

Oliver, on the other hand, is always motivated by a sense of responsibility toward his nation. Whereas Roland always approaches an issue in terms only of personalities (his whimsical and gleeful nomination of Ganelon to head the embassy to Marsiliun, for example), Oliver always considers the nation. He greets Roland's offer to go as emissary to Marsiliun with a statement to the effect that the tactless Roland would fail the mission by provoking a quarrel. He himself then volunteers but significantly prefaces his offer with ''if the king wishes,'' a meaningful courtesy which Roland had ignored. We have already observed his careful scouting of the enemy forces, his pleas to Roland to recall the main force in order to insure a French victory, and his subsequent bitterness that France should suffer because of Roland's pride.

It is clear that the poet takes special pains to establish the reputation of Oliver as nearly, if not wholly, equal to that of Roland. Although the sources are not available, I think it safe to assume that in the legend as the poet received it Roland was the unqualified hero and Oliver simply his companion. The poet, therefore, may well be responsible for the special attention devoted to Oliver at every opportunity, a treatment which serves to emphasize and elevate the character, and hence the values, of Oliver to an eminence equal to those of Roland. For example, when the names of the two heroes are linked in the early sections of the poem, Oliver's name is nearly always qualified while Roland's is not. When his name is first mentioned, he is ''good, noble Oliver''; Ganelon, who consistently degrades Roland as foolish and prideful, refers four times to Oliver, in *laisses similaires* to be sure, as a brave, courtly knight. At nearly every opportunity, even in the most casual reference, Oliver is singled out for praise, whereas the name of Roland is left unqualified. (Presumably, of course, Roland's character was already well established.) This treatment calls attention to the differences in values which separate the two heroes and give weight to Oliver's point of view. It is a matter of the greatest significance also that in the end Oliver completely renounces the bond of companionship that has united the two heroes throughout their lives. In doing so, he is in fact refuting a personal, and hence feudal, oath of loyalty to Roland, not only because it will result in his own death but also because he has seen that any civilization governed by such oaths is capable of foolishly destroying itself.

This same difference between the personal loyalties of feudalism and the national concerns of a later age may also be observed in the trial of Ganelon, which concludes the poem. Ganelon's defense is based upon a sophistry inherent in the feudal code: injuries to personal honor among nobles may be avenged in a political vacuum without affecting the state to which they all owe allegiance. Thus Ganelon does not deny the fact that he provided Marsiliun with vital information concerning Charlemagne's route of march, but he insists that his action was entirely a family affair: ''Roland tricked me out of gold and possessions,'' he says, ''and for this I sought his ruin and death. But I will not concede treachery.'' Later he adds that in accomplishing his revenge, he was not treasonous.

With such a defense Charlemagne's barons agree. Ganelon's appeal is perfectly valid in feudal terms and the great lords vote for his acquittal. To them it has indeed been a family affair, and Ganelon has acted within his rights in taking revenge on a man who has tarnished his personal honor. That twenty thousand Frenchmen, including the twelve peers, have been slaughtered as a consequence is apparently of little concern to them. His revenge accomplished, Ganelon will now serve the king with love and faith; the barons add that the death of Ganelon will not restore the life of Roland.

Only the knight Thierry comes forward to defend the cause of the grief-stricken king, and his reasons for doing so are instructive. Regardless of Ganelon's relationship with Roland, Thierry argues, the fact that Roland was Charles's officer rendered him sacred. Thus an offense against the king's representative can never be interpreted simply as an attack upon an individual because it is in fact a crime against the state. To be sure, Thierry must settle the issue by personal combat, according to feudal law, but his argument demonstrates clearly the contrast of feudal and national values imposed on the legend by the poet.

The repetition of this major theme in the trial of Ganelon may also help to explain the structure of the poem. (pp. 98-104)

The final episodes [of ***The Song***] have often been thought to be spurious, late additions to both legend and poem. Certainly one's interest tends to flag after the death of Roland. Yet it may well be that the Baligant and Ganelon episodes are as crucial to the action and meaning of the poem, and hence to its structure, as anything that precedes them. The victory over Baligant avenges the deaths of Roland and the rearguard, and the trial of Ganelon completes the action begun with the first lines of the poem. Both are thus necessary to the action of the poem: the deaths of heroes must be avenged and traitors cannot go unpunished.

But this final third of the action (actually almost half the length of the poem) does more than simply provide a denouement. As we have seen, the trial of Ganelon is concerned with the contrast of private and corporate values which so sharply distinguishes Roland from Oliver. It may therefore be that the Baligant episode is introduced not only to provide a fitting vengeance for Roncevaux but also to emphasize the theme of nationalism.

Internationalism, really; or perhaps the whole Church Militant. For suddenly we are no longer dealing simply with the French of the rearguard or the Spanish of Marsiliun's army. Over and over the poet sounds the rollcall and Christian Europe responds; Franks, Bavarians, Normans, Germans, Bretons, Flemings all fight together. And on the other side the whole pagan world is involved; Syrians, Persians, Armenians, and Moors are among the thirty battalions led by Baligant.

The poem thus opens out in the end, and we move from chivalric battle in which man fights man for glory to the world conflict of Cross and Crescent. At last emperor faces emir, archetype against archetype, each more myth than man; but no longer, as at Roncevaux, does mere chivalric prowess or feudal pride settle the issue. Charlemagne's skull is laid bare by Baligant's blows and the emperor staggers. Suddenly Gabriel is at his side, rebuking his weakness: "Great King," the harsh voice demands, "what are you about?" And Charlemagne arises to strike for God the final blow.

Thus the ***Song of Roland*** . . . exhibits a contrast between the individualistic ideal of a heroic society and the corporate values of a later, more organized society. Whatever its first form, the legend of Roland shows its origins in the age of feudalism; its great hero recognizes no values or ties beyond those of personal commitment to an overlord. Like Achilles, he knows nothing of loyalty to the state or even to the cause for which he presumably fights. But in the age of the poet a new spirit, that of the Crusades, and a new concept of French unity and nationalism were in the ascendancy. The Crusades provided knighthood with a cause, and the Capetian kings furnished it with a set of political principles which transcended the older feudal values, however hoeroic those may have seemed in retrospect.

The ***Song of Roland*** holds the two sets of standards in equilibrium. Despite their disagreement and Oliver's denunciation of Roland, the two heroes die reconciled, and Charlemagne's rousing defeat of the Saracen host accomplishes both feudal revenge and national, indeed international, victory. Thierry bases his case against Ganelon on the concept of corporate responsibility but he must settle it by the feudal rite of personal conflict. And Charlemagne's final reluctance to obey Gabriel's command to summon all his forces for yet another war emphasizes the priority of the duties of kingship over the rights and preferences of the individual. (pp. 105-06)

The ***Song of Roland*** is thus no simple battle hymn extolling the virtues of a bygone age. It is rather a stirring of the new France, and indeed of the new Europe, and if Roland is its hero, its final victories fall to Charlemagne. But, like the Homeric epics, it sees the present in terms of the past and weeps for what has gone even as it praises what remains and is to come. (p. 108)

Charles Moorman, "The Song of Roland," in his Kings & Captains: Variations on a Heroic Theme, *The University Press of Kentucky, 1971, pp. 87-108.*

EUGÈNE VINAVER (essay date 1971)

[Vinaver was a Russian-born educator and author who served as editor of Arthuriana *and as president of the Society for the Study of Medieval Language and Literature from 1939 to 1948. Among his works are* The Love Potion in the Primitive Tristan Romance *(1924) and* The Rise of Romance *(1971). In the following excerpt from the latter work, Vinaver discusses atemporal and non-rational narrative elements in* The Song, *pointing out that "the final catastrophe emerges not out of an articulated causal scheme, but, with heightened intensity, out of a series of logically unconnected but emotionally significant events and situations."]*

In describing the ***Song of Roland*** W. P. Ker says that it consists of "separate scenes with no gradation or transition between them" [see 1897 excerpt by Ker]. . . . [Critics] have sensed in the poem the presence of loosely inter-related gestures and scenes, artistically valid as individual moments of great dramatic intensity, and yet dispensing with temporal and rational links and transitions. There is a parallel to this in the visual arts of the same period. Some of the great examples of eleventh- and twelfth-century pictorial narrative in Western Europe show the same concentration on "separate scenes with no transition between them." . . . The narrative function of such a picture can best be described as that of a scene "cut out for the flow of events." Of course, the analogy is not complete: the "flow of events" is never entirely excluded from the ***Song of Roland*** or, for that matter, from any known epic poem; what is excluded is the consistent subordination of each single occurrence to a coherently developed scheme. The ***Song of Roland*** compels us to accept as a legitimate medium of poetic expression a language which dispenses with all the subtle means of coordination which we normally regard as a feature of literary style. The broad sweep of the richly nuanced sentence movement and the carefully structured dramatic dialogue, so characteristic of classical epic, are virtually absent from the epic of medieval France. The assonant strophic pattern in the ***Roland*** gives every line the appearance of an independent unit; each strophe, or *laisse,* is in the words of Erich Auerbach [see Additional Bibliography] "like a bundle of sticks or spears of equal length, with similar points," gathered together, pressed against each other, but never dissolved in a spacious easy-flowng syntactical movement. It is "a paratactic structure consisting of very simple, extremely restricted, and yet often contradictory statements." There is even more to it than that. Parataxis normally means a loose arrangement of sentences; in the classical languages paratactic constructions belong to the low style: they are oral rather than written, comic and realistic rather than elevated. They dispense with the entire apparatus of subordination and sequence and replace syntactic composition by mere juxtaposition of independent verbal units. But within this general definition there is room for two distinct forms of expression. The absence of causal connectives may be merely apparent; they may be there even though they are not expressed; our mind then rushes into the artificially created verbal vacuum to supply by its own cogitations all that the poet has deliberately left unsaid. In such cases parataxis is a mere device, productive of comic or sublime effects as the case may be—sometimes, as in the great examples of biblical narrative, creating a sense of depth and expectancy, the feeling that the unfathomable is there for us to discover, or at least to apprehend. The parataxis used in the French epic is of a different kind: it is genuine, not contrived; it invites simple acceptance, not elaboration; it does not conceal continuity and cohesion in silent intervals, but dispenses with such things, and any exegesis that attempts to supply them results in a distortion of the linguistic and poetic pattern of the work.

This feature of style has its counterpart in the most striking peculiarity of the genre, namely its use of "repetition with variation," to which there is no exact parallel in our modern method of exposition. An event, or a scene, or a speech which forms the subject of a strophe may appear again in the next strophe with certain differences, not only of expression, but of substance; and it may be repeated again and again with variations; not simply with additional details, but with developments which represent departures from earlier statements. (pp. 4-7)

We look nowadays upon a narrative of events as a *temporal* sequence, each element of which moves towards the next as each moment of time moves towards the one that follows; and at the same time we see it as a *rational* sequence so arranged that each phase of it is related in a definable manner to whatever comes before or after. What is so difficult for us to understand is that a great masterpiece such as the ***Song of Roland*** should triumphantly discard the twin principles of rational and temporal motivation. When Roland is appointed, on Ganelon's advice, commander of the rearguard of the French army, Roland's reaction to this is expressed in two consecutive, but seemingly contradictory stanzas. First he replies, addressing Ganelon as his *parastre:* "I must hold you very dear: you have adjudged the rearguard to me. Charles, the king who holds France, shall lose thereby neither palfrey nor charger, neither mule nor hinny, neither hack nor sumpter which has not first been fought for with a sword." And Ganelon says: "You speak true, I know it well." The next laisse is equally brief: "When Roland hears that he will be in the rearguard he speaks angrily to his stepfather: 'You wretch, bad man of ignoble birth, did you think the glove would drop from my hand as the staff did for you before Charles?' "—a reminder of what happened when earlier on in the poem Ganelon, on Roland's suggestion, was appointed to what seemed an equally dangerous mission. This is followed by a third *laisse* addressed this time to the emperor himself and expressing Roland's devotion to him and his determination to serve him. At the emotional level there is no difficulty about this curious sequence: Roland's expression of gratitude to Ganelon stems from his unconquerable, ferocious pride, characteristically conveyed by the enumeration of the various mounts and beasts of burden, not one of which will be surrendered without a fight. But pride and defiance can equally well take the form of hatred and contempt; hence Roland's second speech, every word of which asserts his scornful triumph over the man he despises. The first time he speaks as befits a knight—*a lei de chevalier*—the second time scornfully, angrily, *ireement,* and there is no articulate transition, or suggestion even of a link between the two speeches. Gaston Paris, and many critics after him, thought that there was no room for two such contradictory statements in the poem. . . . (pp. 9-10)

The difficulty increases as we progress from the consideration of individual passages to a view of the poem as a whole. As we follow the progress of the battle of Roncevaux we are tempted, against our better judgement, to forget that we are dealing with a type of poetry which is concerned exclusively with action and statement, not with motives; we are tempted to ask why Roland was chosen for the part he was to play in the disaster, why, when attacked by a superior force of Saracens, he decided to let his men die fighting against insuperable odds rather than ask Charlemagne for help. To these questions there is no adequate answer. The conflict between the reckless courage of Roland and the sound strategy of Oliver is there, but it is not there to be discussed or explained. When it is the poet's turn to speak, he is content to say that Roland is brave and Oliver is wise. Neither on this nor on any other occasion does he attempt to comment on the meaning of the action, and it is an unwarranted simplification to suggest, as critics usually do, that no comment is called for because the motives behind the action are crystal-clear. They are far from clear; and if they are not explained it is not because the poet wishes to leave them to our imagination, nor because he prefers suggestion to analysis, but because he is more interested in the progress of events than in coherent motivation. Not that the ***Chanson de Roland*** has no 'thematic' implications, no 'meaning' apart from its narrative content. It is a theme in movement, but at no point is the movement arrested or suspended in order to make time for a reflection on the theme—for what Northrop Frye calls "the *mythos* in stasis." Nor is there any reason why time should be made for such things. Why indeed should it be part of the poet's—*any* poet's—task to elucidate his narrative in terms of a chain of cause and effect? E. M. Forster asks this very question [in *Aspects of the Novel* (1927)]. While admitting that a rationally devised plot "is exciting and may be beautiful," he wonders whether it is not a fetish borrowed from the drama, "from the spatial limitations of the stage." "Cannot fiction devise a framework that is not so logical, yet more suitable to its genius?"

The ***Chanson de Roland,*** like some other French epic poems, may serve as an example of such a framework. The climax of the battle of Roncevaux, Roland's death, is not the outcome of a series of rationally motivated events. Roland is not even killed in battle: he dies because as he sounds the horn . . . his temples burst, and no one can say that by normal standards of motivation an accident of this kind can justify the death of a hero in whom is vested the glory of his race. What is even more remarkable is that any explanation that we might contribute ourselves would ienvitably detract from our aesthetic appreciation, and consequently from our understanding, of the poem. Karl Vossler observes [in *Langue et culture de la France* (1953)] that the essence of the French epic as represented by the ***Song of Roland*** is "affective and impressionistic" and that the Roland poet works "with affective values and contrasts between affective values." When in *Hérodias* Flaubert makes nine verses in the Gospel according to St. Matthew into a *conte,* he traces the sequence of events that lead up to the execution of John the Baptist, and the story he offers us is a convincing interpretation, marked by deep psychological insight, of the motives that impel the principal characters to act as they do. The sequence is not only orderly, but ordered, and causally ordered; motivation proceeds by logical steps from known causes to unknown but inevitable effects, or from known effects to their hidden but detectable causes. It would be a mistake to think that this is a pattern *unknown* to the Roland poet; all we can infer is that the Roland poet does not seem to think he has to adhere to it *consistently*. When Roland nominates Ganelon as Charlemagne's ambassador to the Saracen king, Ganelon flies into a towering passion and accuses Roland of plotting his death; and he is convinced that by plotting in his turn the ambush at Roncevaux he will only be meeting treachery with treachery. But if this were the real motivation of his behaviour and of the subsequent defeat of the rearguard of Charlemagne's army, it would be a singularly inadequate one. By all reasonable standards Ganelon's mission to Saragossa involves no serious risk for him. Marsile has been defeated by Charlemagne. The only way in which he can avoid disaster is by persuading Charlemagne, through Ganelon, to grant him favourable terms of peace. Ganelon is the bearer of a generous offer, and there is no reason at all why Marsile should commit an act of violence against him. Allusions to the fate of Basan and Basile, two unfortunate messengers sent by Charlemagne to Marsile and beheaded out of hand, have no bearing on the case. All that such allusions suggest is the necessity to accept their irrelevance, however difficult this may be.

What is relevant is the way in which the poet maintains the emotional tone of the narrative, the fact that the final catastrophe emerges not out of an articulated causal scheme, but, with heightened intensity, out of a series of logically unconnected but emotionally significant events and situations. There is no need for the poet to *explain;* as Auerbach has it, "the things which happen are stated with paratactic bluntness: everything must happen as it does happen, it could not be otherwise." The life of the infidel knights seems hardly different from that of the Christians: both sides believe in their deeds of prowess as a road to Heaven, both are graced with the status of knighthood, and in both cases knighthood—*vasselage*—is understood as readiness to die fighting the enemies of one's faith. Why, then, should we believe the poet when he says: *paien unt tort et chrestiens unt dreit* ["pagans are wrong and Christians are right"]? And why, to sum up all such doubts in a single question, why should Roland die a martyr's death at Roncevaux?

When these and other similar questions arise in our minds and we hasten to supply the answers, we do so because we are convinced that it is what the poet intended us to do. A closer view of early French epic poetry would show that the poet's mode of exposition required no such effort on the reader's or the listener's part. It was calculated to produce a reaction of a vastly different kind. It was a mode which sought not to enlighten, but to move and to impress—not a questioning or an explanatory, but a lyrical and a descriptive mode. An exegesis that would reduce the matter of such poetry to questions and answers would distort its very essence; it would be grossly misleading in that it would deal with non-existent issues and ignore the real ones. . . . (pp. 11-14)

Eugène Vinaver, "Roland at Roncevaux," in his The Rise of Romance, *Oxford at the Clarendon Press, 1971, pp. 1-14.*

D.D.R. OWEN (essay date 1972)

[In the following excerpt, Owen comments on The Song *in terms of its qualities as an oral composition and praises its "remarkably sophisticated technique." He also explores the poet's attitude toward several key characters in the poem, concluding that they are treated with a "mixture of approval and disapproval."]*

Then Taillefer, renowned in song,
Urging his rapid steed along,
Before the duke began to sing
Of Roland, of great Charles the king,
Oliver, and those lords beside
Who came to Roncevaux, and died.
(Wace, *Roman de Rou*)

If we are to believe Wace, who was writing in 1160, a certain Taillefer sang a song of Roland to the Normans assembled before the Battle of Hastings. Some thirty-five years earlier William of Malmesbury had mentioned a *cantilena Rolandi* struck up to encourage the same warriors to acts of bravery. William does not give the name of the singer; on the other hand, Gui de Ponthieu, who died no more than eight years after the Conqueror's victory, tells of the minstrel Taillefer's inspiring words at the battle, but does not name the song.

The value of this collective testimony is still debated by scholars. But true or false, it does show that men of the age recognised in the ***Roland*** an admirable palliative for battle nerves and a stimulant for those about to be hurled into the mêlée. Perhaps they were right. What better way to concentrate the knight's mind on his martial duties? He hears the sounds of combat before a blow is struck; he is swept emotionally into acts of firm, even jaunty courage in the face of heavy odds; he is reminded of the obligations of commander to men, men to commander, comrade to comrade; he is fired with the great pride of lineage and nationhood, and shares the spiritual elation of total commitment to a just cause. (p. 9)

The ***Song of Roland*** could have been composed for just such a purpose and occasion, or so one might think after a first hearing. If wars had to be fought, what nobler preparation for, or even accompaniment to, the clash of steel on steel? Yet the vision of the unknown author was less simple than this. The poet in him captured, magnified and reflected back the lurid spectacle of the fight, the bravery and idealism of the heroes. But, and here lies much of the greatness and fascination of the work, behind the epic splendour of his poetry we hear the voice of a man who knows reality for what it is and inclines to question what he most exalts. He feels with Roland, but he thinks with Oliver. Even as he glories in the sights and sounds of court and battle scenes, he is fully aware of the humanity and often the pity and folly of it all. Of course he accepts that "Pagans are wrong and Christians in the right." He recognises that the Franks are the elect of God, fighting in His cause; and he takes for granted that they have a sense of honour ignored by the Saracens. He knows too, however, that in other ways the men of Charlemagne and even the emperor himself have the faults and foibles of ordinary mortals. His very plot is a tale as much of human weakness and error as of unwavering virtue. (pp. 9-10)

Whatever happened to King Charles's rearguard in the pass of Roncevaux and however its slaughter was engineered, it is not likely that the epic recalls much of the true facts; and the fiction may well have been full-fleshed when the poet took it over. Are we then justified in associating the less glamorous side of his story with his own personal vision, or part of it? I think we are. His viewpoint is revealed less in the events themselves than in the small touches, especially certain snatches of dialogue, to which they give rise. The cool-headed Oliver's sardonic exchanges with Roland seem particularly instructive in this respect, as we shall see. The presentation of Charlemagne, too, appears to have about it something more individual than traditional.

Rash though it may be to try to read the mind of a poet vanished for nine hundred years, it is a risk, I feel, worth running, so strong is the impression of a total, yet strangely divided, personality. His double view of things I have already equated with an opposition between the grand poetic concept and the true experience of life. It is expressed constantly in the interplay of antithetical elements: the communal cause contrasting with personal ambition, glorious valour with the working out of petty grievances, firm resolves with doubts and hesitation, Roland the feckless hero with Roland the bewildered companion, Ganelon the betrayer with Ganelon the brave and outspoken supporter of the king, the holy emperor Charlemagne with Charles the muddle-headed old man. There is the whole-hearted idealism of the poet on the one hand, and his implicit criticism, even protest, on the other.

But these are the fruits of reflection. If Taillefer did sing of Roland at Hastings, we should not imagine the Norman knights brooding on tragic flaws of character, or on the moments of spite and self-seeking. For the epic, by its nature, must aim at the immediate impact, must sweep its hearers along on waves of emotion, not thought. The Old French chansons de geste, of which the ***Roland*** is the supreme (and, by chance, earliest) surviving example, were composed for oral performance by the jongleurs, who had to hold the attention of their audience during hours of recitation. Brisk action and direct dialogue set against a rich but easily visualised décor were required, the tension of gripping events and fluctuating emotions, intensity rather than subtlety. This was true audio-visual entertainment in the sense that sound and pictures projected on the screen of the mind played equal parts in kindling the imagination. And it was instant entertainment: there was simply no time for reflection—that could only come later. Taillefer's audience would have seen the action, heard the cries and the fanfares, felt the joy and pathos by turns; they would not have questioned or debated the moral issues implicit in the song.

Compared with theirs, our own appreciation of the ***Roland*** can only be incomplete; and our greatest loss is in the matter of sound. Even if we read the Old French with reasonable ease, no one can now say exactly how it was pronounced at the time of the poet or reproduce the proper resonance of vowels and consonants. It was certainly a full-bodied language, endowed with a wider range of sounds than its modern descendant: of that at least we can be sure. Yet even if we could recapture the quality of the language, we should be unable to discover just how the poem was presented. There was usually some musical accompaniment on an early type of fiddle, it seems; and the voice was probably modulated in a kind of singing or chant, but whether throughout the performance or for certain of the more lyrical passages cannot be told. It is likely that the mysterious AOI, penned so often at the end of lines in our single manuscript, had something to do with the musical presentation, though there is no proof even of this.

The musical accompaniment, then, and the precise phonetic quality of the linguistic elements, are largely if not entirely beyond our powers of recapture today. The marvel is that, even if we quite disregard the meaning of the verse, we can still appreciate and admire so much of its musical texture. The lines have the quality of a score to be interpreted through the instrument of the performer's voice, an art of which the professional jongleur would be and would have to be a master.

In modern terms, the structure of the poem could be called symphonic. It has its distinct movements, and between and within them are the tonal variations: lyrical passages alternate with rousing periods of full orchestra; there are the crescendos and diminuendos, changes of pace and key within the general flow; and of great importance are the continual statements and re-statements of themes and phrases, which bind the whole composition together and strengthen its formal unity.

Whatever acoustic effects are now lost to us, we can still feel the strong pulse of the rhythm of the song. It employs the form most characteristic of the early chanson de geste: the tirades or *laisses* consisting of decasyllabic lines linked by the assonance of their final full vowels, and with the predominant use of the caesura after the fourth syllable, though lines with the main pauses after the sixth are not uncommon. . . . One rather curious feature of our existing copy is that a fairly high proportion of lines contain more or fewer than ten syllables. Why this should be so is not clear, and to call them faulty on this account would be to presume more than our knowledge of the poet's metric standards justifies. In general, then, it can be said that the individual lines have a strongly marked rhythmical element; and this is extended by various devices such as repeated syntactical patterns or formulaic phrasing throughout the *laisses* and beyond them over the whole length of the poem. . . . (pp. 11-13)

Seen always in the context of oral presentation (and, as a corollary, of memorisation by the performer), the form of the song is the product of a remarkably sophisticated technique. It is, moreover, intimately linked to the content. Thus the repeated elements may be used to provide an insistent martial beat, as in the description of the individual encounters at Roncevaux; or to increase the poignancy, as when Charlemagne's lament over Roland's body carries echoes of his nephew's own mourning of the men slain on his behalf; or, in the case of the *laisses similaires* (in which the content of one *laisse* is repeated in the following ones in rather different terms) to heighten the tension or lyrical intensity at crucial moments like the horn-blowing debates, or Roland's death. The *laisses* themselves are not merely convenient compartments for the separate housing of such assonanced groups as entered the poet's head: each one normally presents a self-contained scene or event, while often overlapping and so linking with its neighbours. Every *laisse* is like an individual miniature in an illuminated manuscript: memorably simple and expressive in its stylised manner, where attitude and gesture convey abstract ideas in visual terms—rage or tenderness, dignity or exhaustion. The *laisse* may itself be static or full of movement. But it is no sooner there than it is gone; and we are left with an impression less of the individual "frames" than of a running film-strip synchronised with a resonant, pulsating and evocative sound-track.

If Taillefer did sing at Hastings, no doubt men would have died with their minds still throbbing with the full sound and vision of his song. Only those who lived on, remembering the sordid anguish of the field, might have begun to ponder the poet's deeper meanings. (p. 13)

The figures of Roland and Oliver have been modelled, some would say, on the old rhetorical opposition of *fortitude* ["strength"] and *sapientio* ["wisdom"]: "Roland is valiant, Oliver is wise." This may be so, but it implies a greater degree of stereotyping than is present in their portrayal; or rather it leaves unremarked the darker areas of their characters as revealed by the poet.

"Roland is valiant." Nothing is clearer: no one could deny his eager courage and physical prowess in the field. As a warrior he is obsessed by a triple sense of duty: to his king and country, to his family, and by no means least to himself. It is his total commitment to this ideal that eventually claims his life: even his death-wound is inflicted not by any Saracen, but by his own efforts in blowing his horn to ensure that France's honour is preserved. To Charles he is irreplaceable; to his men a loved and inspiring leader, a commander who deeply respects his troops and secures their own respect by his example: a model epic hero, a figure to whom the poet warms in heart and verse. But see him through Ganelon's eyes.

Ganelon's first speech in the poem reveals his poor opinion of the king's nephew, implying that he is not only arrogant, but a rogue and a fool to boot. To be sure he later freely admits his valour: "A knight unequalled under heaven's fault," as he says to Marsile; and to Blancandrin he speaks of the great love for Roland of his men, though slyly hinting at their pecuniary motives. But in Ganelon's own eyes he is a bombastic braggart, vaunting his prowess before his uncle and showing off before his men: an impossible person to live with, feckless and irresponsible, steeped in the sin of pride. And for Ganelon this *is* a sin: "I marvel that God bears with it so much!" He has even stooped to more mundane wrongdoing, it seems; for at the trial his stepfather asserts that he has tricked him out of gold and possessions; and far from being denied, the crime appears to be tacitly accepted by Thierry, at least as a possibility. The bad blood between them plainly existed before the events of the poem. Should we ascribe it in part to Ganelon's jealousy of a man so dear to the heart of his royal uncle, while his own son Baldwin, also Charles's nephew, lives in the shadows? Such speculation on a fiction is no doubt idle. We should, however, bear earlier rivalry in mind in our judgement not only of Ganelon's initial intemperate outburst but also of Roland's apparently petty and vindictive behaviour when he nominates Ganelon for the embassy.

Oliver, Roland's loyal and loving companion, should see him in a better light. "Oliver is wise," a man of sober common sense, a hero when he has to be, not by pure instinct like his flamboyant friend. The showy heroics are never for him: he concentrates on the job in hand, which should be carried out in the most sensible way; he does not disdain wielding a broken lance-stump when to draw a sword would waste valuable time; he would not have spurned reinforcements, and would have summoned help before it was too late. He is a practical man, not an epic ideal made flesh. What, then, does Oliver think of his companion? When Roland at last wishes to blow the oliphant, he speaks his mind: "We've seen your prowess, Roland, to our cost." The calamity has come about through his friend's reckless self-assurance and folly; deaf to reason, he has for once overreached himself. No starry-eyed adulation, this. But is it just the result of bitter disillusionment when the hopelessness of the situation has become clear?

I do not think so. As we follow the companions through the poem, we are continually aware of a sharp tension between them, for all their mutual affection. Roland has only to offer to go on the mission to Marsile, and Oliver protests: "You are too fiercely proud and violent!" When, in the pass, they await the Saracen attack and Roland has refused to sound the horn, Oliver reproaches him for the king's absence. And again, after his companion's fine prediction of booty to come, he bitterly hints at Roland's responsibility and guilt for their predicament, as well as at the idleness of his boasts. . . . There is sarcasm in the exchange over the relative merits of sticks and swords as weapons, a little more perhaps when, after Roland has exclaimed on Turpin's prowess, Oliver again prefers action to words: "Come then and lend him aid!" But his sarcasm is at its most bitter when Roland suggests that now he will summon aid from Charles, and Oliver hurls his earlier concern for honour back in his teeth:

> 'I'd rather die than see us suffer shame!
> . . . But that would mean disgrace
> And bring reproach on all your family:
> The shame of it would never be lived down!'

It is then that he tells his companion just what he feels about his earlier unthinking conduct. The "quarrel" has not suddenly blown up: we have watched the tension increasing, and Roland's proposal has been enough to bring it to this pitch.

Even so, we might think the quarrel rather one-sided, with Roland meekly suffering his friend's well-merited reproaches. Yet this is not quite the case. Roland had already rebuked Oliver at one point for his suggestion that Ganelon was implicated in the pagan aggression: "He is my stepfather; I'll hear no more!" Here too, of course, Oliver had shown himself the more clear-sighted: Roland's protest seems to have stemmed from a sense of family loyalty that we know all too well to be misplaced. But in the later exchange, Oliver was wrong to taunt his companion for his past concern with his honour, suggesting that to call for aid now would be in conflict with it. For all his perspicacity, he does not realise that Roland sees his duty to himself and his kin as fully performed, and that France's honour now demands the emperor's return and the destruction of the Saracens. In this respect Oliver is wrong and Roland right, as the archbishop confirms.

Despite superficial appearances, then, these two great figures are far from being stereotypes. Even Oliver's wisdom is not absolute. And my interpretation of the quarrel scene appears to be confirmed when the heroes' companionship approaches its end. For then the quarrel is remarkably re-enacted, but this time in physical and surely symbolic terms. The dying Oliver, his sight gone, strikes Roland with his sword, cleaving his helmet but doing him no injury. When Roland makes himself known, his friend begs his forgiveness, which is freely granted. Oliver has made his attack through blindness; Roland has emerged unscathed, and the bond between them has endured. The application to what has gone before needs no more comment. For all his wisdom and prudence, Oliver had not fully recognised his friend's high motives. The tension had built up, but at one final stroke was resolved. Their comradeship survived to become, at the hour of their death, more absolute than ever before.

It is worth asking whether the poet has used Roland and Oliver to express something of his own attitudes to war and knighthood. One might wonder if through Oliver he has not given his own conscience a role in the story. War may be necessary in defence of right and truth, but it should be conducted with prudence. What use is the theatrical gesture if it only brings disaster on oneself, one's comrades, and one's country? Roland was guilty of the sin of *démesure,* which is the pursuance of proper ends in an outrageously exaggerated way, with dire consequences not only to the man who so acts, but also to all those associated with him. The fault is essentially the lack of a sense of proportion; or perhaps it is a virtue exercised in so extreme a fashion as to become a sin. Can one, then, detect a plea for the ordinary man, or at least the ordinary knight, who stands to suffer from his leaders' folly? At one level perhaps one can. Yet, as I suggested earlier, prudence does not make good poetry, and the artist in our composer was aroused by, even if he did not applaud, the very qualities that both exalted and damned Roland's deeds. He was responsive to both the grief and the glory, the human weakness and the sublimity.

The poet's double vision is just as apparent in his treatment of Ganelon. Introduced and finally condemned as a traitor, he nevertheless has admirable qualities. Like the companions, he is no stereotype: only on the rhetorical, poetic level can he be taken as the embodiment of evil within the Christian feudal society. Having been wronged, or so at least he believed, he openly defied Roland and all his party before the emperor in full court. Being forced to treat with the Saracens in their camp, he went even beyond his brief in his vehement presentation of the terms and his unyielding defence of Charlemagne. His outspoken loyalty came near to costing him his life, but he did not flinch. Only then did he propose to Marsile the means of doing away with Roland and the peers, a subject already broached with Blancandrin, it is true, on their ride to Saragossa. But he had performed his duty to Charles first.

Where, then, is the treason? This was what Ganelon asked at his trial. Impressed, perhaps, by his defence as well as by the fierce attitude struck by Pinabel, the judges ask for his acquittal. Charles, despite his wrath, does not refuse it. But there is one dissenting voice, that of Thierry, whose shrewd legal brain has seen the point of feudal law contravened by Ganelon: he had taken his otherwise legitimate revenge when Roland was acting in the king's service. Against Roland no crime has been committed; the treason is against Charles, and it is for this that Ganelon must die.

As with his portrayal of Roland, we discern in the poet's attitude to Ganelon a mixture of approval and disapproval. He approves his courage, loyalty to Charles, and his tender affection for his son and family; he understands his resentment of Roland, violent enough to cloud his judgement as to the manner of his revenge; he can only condemn his crime against the emperor. But his verdict, like that of the court, appears to hang by a thread. His humanity pleaded for a conditional acquittal; his legal sense had to demand the full penalty for treason against the crown.

The king's person must for the poet remain inviolate, symbolising as it does the whole Frankish order and indeed Christendom itself. Patriotism is hardly the right word at this early date, yet it is something very akin that the poet expresses throughout the epic: the greatest dread is that France be put to shame. Charlemagne, then, has a vital symbolic function in the poem; and his vast age and noble appearance are in accordance with his role. Utterly revered and loved by his loyal subjects (only Ganelon has a momentary lapse when the sound of Roland's horn is heard), he is almost equally a figure of awe for the Saracens. Looking back over the centuries, the poet views him nostalgically as the greatest of emperors, God's vice-regent on earth, the ideal monarch, communing with men and angels, the embodiment of French aspirations, whose presence envelops the whole epic like an aureole. Such was the vision of the author as poet: the author as man saw otherwise.

What did he see? A very human, almost crumbling old man. Look at him sitting in state, and one can only admire. Hear him handling the affairs of state, and one can only wonder at his incompetence. "His whole reliance is on those of France": he leans on his baronage like a crutch. All allowance made for his duty as a suzerain to consult his vassals on matters of policy and justice, he lacks even the qualities of a good chairman when he presides over his council. Is it a question of whether or not to treat with Marsile? "Carry on the war," says Roland, and the Franks remain silent; "Accept his terms," says Ganelon—Naimes agrees and the Franks concur, so that is that. Whom shall we send? Each volunteer in turn is rejected by Charles: he needs the wise Naimes, he is too fond of Roland and Oliver, and furthermore none of the twelve peers shall go. Who then is it to be? "Ganelon," says Roland; the Franks concur, so Ganelon it is. This is all no doubt strictly constitutional (except for the unprompted vetoing of the peers), for Charles had asked for a nomination, and Ganelon's was the first he received—the rest had volunteered. But there is an unpleasant partiality and testiness about the king's handling of the matter. It is the same when Ganelon nominates Roland for the rearguard: Charles accepts the judgement, but does not conceal his bitter rage.

One might perhaps think it commendable that despite his strong prejudices, he does not attempt to interfere with the constitutional processes. But there are other occasions when one could legitimately expect some kingly initiative. It never comes, at least in the main part of the poem. His most forthright passions are thwarted by the need to act on the advice of his counsellors; and when he should take the lead, he relapses into passive moods. When all the omens have spoken of imminent betrayal, he makes no move but hides his gloom under his cloak, with the rearguard left to their doom. He hears the horn-blast: "Our men are doing battle!" But Ganelon denies it, implying that Charles is in his dotage. No reply from the king. Fortunately Naimes speaks up: there is a battle, and Charles should go to his men's aid. Only then does the emperor bestir himself, have Ganelon arrested and his troops head back for Roncevaux. When he arrives there, grief overwhelms him. Naimes points out the dust-clouds rising ahead and calls "See . . . the dust-clouds . . . Ride on, and take revenge for our distress!"—"Oh God, they are so far away!" complains the anguished Charles, imploring God's support.

The trial shows him in a very poor light. Even in his capacity as God's temporal justiciary, his continuing obsession with his nephew clouds his judicial vision as he lays the charge against Ganelon: he has betrayed Roland, Oliver and the peers for gain. This of course is the wrong case, and Ganelon has his defence ready. When the Franks ask for his acquittal, Charles again vents his fury in words. It is only Thierry's more percipient intervention that saves the day for him. Sensitivity as well as good sense seems sometimes to desert him. What a tactless and fumbling attempt he makes to console Aude. His own grief for Roland has been real enough, and under its influence his thoughts too have turned to death. Aude's sorrow, however, is deeper still and past all his comprehension: when she speaks of leaving this life, her words are not mere rhetoric. Charles, surprised to find her truly dead, can do no more than supervise her state funeral.

The poet's attitude even towards Charlemagne seems, then, informed by this same dual vision, this blend of approval and disapproval. He pays his homage to the ideal, while probing the human weaknesses of the mortal monarch. Despotism would appear to have no place in his political scheme. He espouses and glorifies the feudal standards of dignity, honour and service, yet at the same time rather blunts the apex of the feudal pyramid. The supreme head is fallible, unreliable, passive, not always in touch with the divine will and only vaguely understanding the signs that are vouchsafed him. The solid core of the system is the nobility, on whom the king must rely. But the nobility must not indulge in reckless extremism: their duty is to safeguard every interest through wise counsel and measured action. It is likely that the poet was composing for noble patronage. His song both set them a stirring example and justified their political role. It would be cynical, though, to suggest that patronage alone determined the poem's ideological content; for if one can speak of a ring of sincerity, then the ***Roland*** has it. More than the political questions it was surely the human ones that most fascinated and inspired its author.

The ***Song of Roland*** is one of the world's great poems; and in these pages I have been able to do no more than hint at some of its qualities. Others, like its much-debated religious values, I have not attempted to define. Like all true works of art it does not diminish but grows with knowledge; and years of study do not suck it dry of interest and surprises. The modern reader may take time to come to terms with some of its features. He may, for instance, initially find the battle-scenes over-extended and repetitious, though less so when the Baligant episode is excluded. At least part of the trouble is the fact that he is a *reader,* not being carried along by the voice of an expert reciter. In purely narrative terms, there is more variety in them than may be seen at a casual glance, and this could be brought out in performance. In musical terms, these *laisses* have a vigorous martial beat that could have an almost hypnotic effect on the listener. And on the visual level there is an element of ritual dance which, however frenzied, has its own aesthetically satisfying patterns. The effects of sound and vision should combine to shift the hearer's reactions from a state of intellectual observation to one of sensual participation, with the exaggerations, simplifications and repetitions of the narrative helping to increase rather than inhibit his involvement.

On the intellectual level, however, there is much in the poem to hold the attention, as I hope I have shown in the preceding pages. The greatness of the ***Roland*** is in fact the product of all its aspects and levels of appeal. Not least important is the fact that the human problems it raises are so easily transferred in the mind from the days of sword and buckler to the present. The basic questions are just as valid now as ever they were and, I believe, could hardly be posed more subtly and provocatively. (pp. 17-24)

D.D.R. Owen, in an introduction to The Song of Roland, *translated by D.D.R. Owen, George Allen & Unwin Ltd., 1972, pp. 9-24.*

R. HOWARD BLOCH (essay date 1973)

[Bloch is an American educator and student of medieval literature. In the following excerpt, he explicates the hostility between Roland and Ganelon in terms of the oedipal archetype, adding that in The Song, *the "father-son motif appears to be almost unique in its reoslution."]*

The death of Roland.

With all that has been written about ***La Chanson de Roland*** the father-son relationship of Ganelon and Roland has not been fully explored. Turoldus is explicit concerning the bond that unites the two vassals, Ganelon having married Roland's mother, Charlemagne's sister. . . . Nephew and maternal uncle, Roland and Charles are bound by ties of blood reinforced by affection. Charles and Ganelon, on the other hand, are linked by marriage through the woman—sister, wife and mother—who is hardly mentioned by brother, husband or son. Nominally, all four belong to the same family unit which is not a real family at all, but an archetype of familial rapports characteristic of parenthood in general. . . . In the absence of the real father, and in the splitting of paternal functions between sympathetic uncle and antipathetic stepfather, we begin to detect the oldest of literary themes: the conflict of father and son. (pp. 3-4)

The specific grounds of dispute between Ganelon and Roland first become apparent in the discussion of political strategy before the walls of Saragossa. When asked to advise Charles whether or not to accept Marsilie's peace offer Roland espouses a hawkish, hard-line «jusqu'auboutisme» ["seeing things through to the end"] of relentless pursuit. . . . Ganelon takes a . . . conciliatory dovish stand, accusing his stepson of foolishness, carelessness and pride. . . . [Their insults] escalate almost immediately into the nomination of Ganelon as ambassador (the equivalent of parricide), the further insult of Roland's offer to replace him, his mocking laughter and open expression of hatred. From mockery, to betrayal, to nomination of stepson to the rear guard (the equivalent of infanticide) the schema follows a systematically irrational course.

Thus the quarrel irrupts suddenly, seemingly out of nowhere. If asked to pinpoint its source, we could trace a scenario of hostility back to the discussion of military strategy. But this is as far as we can go, the military issue a *terminus a quo* of an escalating struggle whose outcome defines the dramatic shape of the poem, yet whose roots lie beyond the text. The author never explains *why* these two vassals confront one another, much less how an apparently abstract debate over policy snowballs so rapidly from a difference of opinion to betrayal of an entire social unit. However flawless the sequence of events leading to Roland's death, the chain still lacks its initial link. In a sense this disregard for ultimate causality characterizes Turoldus' world view; his is a universe of effects—heroic deeds, bright exterior glitter of arms, gesture rather than emotion—with little room for analysis of causes. And yet something more than meets the eye seems to lie buried beneath the well of underlying hatred felt by stepfather and stepson. Their confrontation has the air of fate about it, a fated struggle destined to explode with insufficient pretext and unconscious intent. Viewed as an inevitable clash outweighing the superficial givens of a particular military or political situation, the initial germ of conflict gains added psychological depth as part of an inherent system of father-son rapport.

It is not unthinkable to speak of a predestined or archetypal enmity between Roland and Ganelon in which the actual issues of contention matter less than the psychological make-up of each man's character, character here being equivalent to fate. After all, the two barons remains poles apart temperamentally, one impetuous though loyal, the other calculating and unscrupulous. Their repulsion arises as spontaneously as any «fols amors» ["mad love"] or «amour coup de foudre» ["thunderbolt of love''] in a Tristan and Iseult or Phedre. Hopeless love, love that appears without warning and whose outcome is inevitably tragic, resembles overwhelming hatred to the extent that both are unavoidable. Psychological fate or archetypal representation, Roland and Ganelon's hatred surpasses the limits of individual character to reveal that which remains common to paternity in general (pp. 6-7)

That which seems most universal within the father-son or oedipal archetype is the ambiguity of the rapport, a paradox expressed in many «chansons de geste» by the presence of a hostile true father as opposed to a sympathetic uncle. Terrible, unjust fathers dominate in *Doon de Mayence, Guibert d'Andrenas, Floovant, Aiol* and *Enfances Vivien;* neglectful fathers in *Raoul de Cambrai* and *Huon de Bordeaux*. In contrast, warm uncle-nephew ties characterize ***Roland,*** *Charroi de Nimes, Raoul de Cambrai* and *Gormont et Isembart*.

The nature of paternal bonds is no simple matter in ***Roland.*** Even among the pagans opposing attitudes exist side by side. Blancandrin offers his son as hostage to the French «even at the risk of his life.» . . . Baligant, on the other hand, demonstrates a genuine tenderness for his own son whom he grants the first blow in battle and praises before the Saracen barons. . . . The opposing attitudes of the two Arab fathers reflect, as through a prism in which the integral whole becomes refracted into its distinct component parts, a rounded image of parenthood which seems all the more fearful and seducing because so clearly delineated. Each defines one charactertistic element of all parental ties within Turoldus' poem.

Potentially a negative or positive link, a source of hostility or affection, paternal bonds are portrayed in ***Roland*** through a series of double rapports representing opposite poles of the completed father-imago. Although the French are all in some exaggerated sense the Emperor's children . . . , he has, in fact, two sons: Louis, the real son, and Roland, his spiritual counterpart. The former, despite his higher birth, still plays second fiddle to his favored cousin as seen in Charles' presentation of Louis to Aude as a «faute de mieux» [''for lack of a better''] replacement for her dead fiancé. . . . There is little need to insist upon Charlemagne's affection for Roland, his «right arm,» source of power and filial substitute. Without him the Emperor feels helpless. . . . Through his rejection of all other family relations in favor of the nephew or spiritual son we begin to understand the nature of the nephew-uncle metaphor. Roland represents in Charles' eyes a projection of the ideal son, the son who meets all paternal expectations of loyalty, conscience and prowess. Because their relationship is expressed obliquely as uncle-nephew, or spiritual father-spiritual son, the negative aspects of paternity—rivalry for wife and mother, fear of replacement—are eliminated in favor of the wholly positive elements of affection and support. Roland is the hypothetical son who, willing «to suffer great hardship and pain,» never lets the father down. Louis, however, stands for the threatening son who has stayed at home with mother while father is at war and who will some day take the Emperor's place. Within the paternal archetype a portion of the father's energies is directed towards controlling the menacing side of the son, which for Charlemagne has simply been eliminated through the effacing portrayal of Louis.

With Ganelon's two sons the formula becomes reversed, for here the beloved offspirng, in whom the father places his hopes for the future, stays behind. . . . Evidently younger than his stepbrother, Baldewin represents Ganelon's cherished good child . . . , whereas Roland assumes the negative role of his aggressive brother. This doubling of filial functions—Roland-Louis, Baldewin-Roland—yields a rounded image of filial kinship in which the complementary tendencies of rejection and affection are rendered through evil, innocuous or loving sons. A similar pattern occurs in the paternal realm of wicked and benevolent fathers.

Roland has two fathers in addition to the real one whose identity varies according to legend and who remains completely absent from Turoldus' story. Ganelon, the stepfather, incarnates the degraded, wicked father who punishes and threatens. He has, in marrying the hero's mother, usurped true paternity; and his unpredictable menacing side accounts for the virulence of attack during the political discussion as well as his willingness to betray his stepson. A projection of the negative father-imago, Ganelon provokes an archetypal organically fated hostility within the son who encounters, through the rejection of his proposal, the father as obstacle.

Set in opposition to Ganelon, but no less a part of the total picture, Charlemagne, the oblique spiritual father, provides nourishment and protection. Roland thinks before his death: ''De Carlemagne, sun seignor, kil nurrit'' [''of Charlemagne, his lord, who raised him'']. The Emperor's role is not unusual, for in many epics the uncle, according to the medieval system of fosterage, takes charge of his nephew's training, dubbing and arming. . . . Before departing for France the uncle bestows the bow «drawn by his own hands» as a gesture of paternal solicitude. His shock at Roland's nomination, his concern that his nephew choose sufficient men and arms to form the rear guard, his grief at his death and the determination of his vengeance all support the image of the idealized, loving father «who would rather die than fail his men»: ''Meilz voelt murir que guerpir sun barnet.'' Roland's reluctance as the hypotehtical good son to let the good father down again emphasizes his identification with the principle of benevolent paternity projected upon Charlemagne.

The most essential feature of ideal paternity is the tendency towards absolute moral perfection. In the eyes of the son the good father can do no wrong; it is he, in fact, who defines the boundaries of morality and whose actions are faultless by definition. Charles thus commits errors of judgment—rejection of Roland's «realistic» proposal and trust in Ganelon as ambassador—without incurring the suspicion of the mystified son. Despite his pride, Roland contests neither decision once the Emperor has approved. Charlemagne's perfectionist zeal in pursuing Marsilie, fighting Baligant and his obstinacy during the trial betray an inner necessity of carrying events to their natural conclusion. Charles represents the predictable, accessible father whose love and approval are obtainable. . . . And so for nephew-son the opposing imagos of malevolent and benovolent father remain clearly divided between wicked stepfather and protective uncle. The ambiguity of paternity—the simultaneous attraction and repulsion, love and hate—becomes refracted into absolutely infallible and absolutely hateful figures.

Roland's own attitude towards the distinct paternal functions varies between passive submission and aggressive defiance. His exaggerated respect for Charles, acceptance of the uncle's social aims and overburdening concern for what others will think . . . give some indication of the depth of the son's identification with the all-powerful father. In hopes of appropriating the elder's strength and retaining his love, these ideals have become internalized as part of the warrior's conscience; so that by the time that the Emperor withdraws from Spain, Roland, now a paternal figure in his own right, proceeds to impose upon his men. The hostility that the defiant son feels towards the negative imago, father as obstacle and rival, comes to the surface in the attempt to eliminate Ganelon first by nomination and then by humiliation: offer to replace him, scornful laughter. Despite the feudal ethic of strict group loyalty, which Roland practices to perfection elsewhere, he aggresses freely and without second thought where Ganelon is concerned. Once again, the rapport with the stepfather offers clear evidence of an exceptional psychological state transcending both the warrior's code and the givens of the political situation.

The uncle-stepfather polarity represents an individualized model of the transcendant paternal values of religion and nation, God the Father and Fatherland. Even if we do not accept, as Freud suggests, the source of positive religious sentiment in the memory of the dead (slain) father and the source of negative feelings in his potentially menacing side, the series of religious oppositions in ***Roland*** can still be seen as a projection of the ambivalent Charlemagne-Ganelon pair. (pp. 8-12)

Within medieval literature spatial rapports often express moral or social precepts. Dante's *Commedia* contains a topographic map of abstract human qualities in which virtue and sin determine the geography of heaven and hell. The moral geography of ***Roland*** clearly differentiates two fatherlands, Spain and France, as if each physical region incarnated a distinct moral space with the Pyrenees in-between.

Spain represents the land of potentially wicked paternity where hatred between father and son becomes overt. The situation at the beginning of the poem, the siege of Saragossa, stands for the hostility held in check until such time as the evil father becomes able to dominate his benevolent counterpart. In the absence of the mother, who ordinarily mediates between husband and child, the tension reaches the breaking point, the point at which Roland is willing to commit parricide and Ganelon to betray simultaneously stepson and nation. The negative effects of the absent mother come to the surface in Bramimunde's gift to Ganelon's wife. . . . Here the Saracen Queen purchases the son's death with gifts intended for his mother, as the menacing parents of both sexes enter into unholy alliance. Far from the protective side of woman, Roland finds himself vulnerable to the attacks of the aggressive father, the protective father being helpless in the land of wicked paternity. (p. 13)

The point to which France embodies the principle of gentle paternity is nowhere more evident than in the return of the surviving aggressive parents to the benevolent realm. Ganelon, the obdurate degraded father, cannot survive, his aggression surpassing the limits tolerable to any social unit. The community that supports a father whose unmediated hostility is so overt that intentionally or not it ends in infanticide, cannot long endure. Bramimunde's role, in comparison, seems accessory; and the aggressive woman while in Spain becomes «converted by love» in Aix. . . . The alliance of evil parents—Ganelon, Blancandrin, Marsilie and Bramimunde—in the land of false fathers and gods has thus been neutralized by Charlemagne, the virtuous father of the French and champion (son) of the just Christian God. This triumph of positive paternity and the accompanyng integration of protective femininity has only been accomplished at a price, however, which is the sacrifice of the son.

It has become increasingly clear that the conflict between Ganelon and Roland is neither an isolated psychological phenomenon nor an original literary theme. The double parental and filial imagos (Ganelon-Charles, Roland-Baldewin,Roland-Louis, Bramimunde in Spain-Bramimunde in France) together with the polarized projections of religion and state, correspond to the essential components of the oedipal drama. Thus the mother as a source of ultimate gratification (nourishment, warmth, love) and protection becomes a source of hostility when absent: the good mothers have stayed home in France. Likewise, the father, whose strength the son admires and needs, is potentially a powerful obstacle: Ganelon outwits his younger rival. Through the interplay of these four basic parental functions—good and evil mother, benevolent and threatening father—we are able to situate the confrontation of Ganelon and Roland within the universal father-son motif.

Three features distinguish the ***Roland*** archetype from similar expressions of the common theme. In the first place, the woman as ultimate object of rivalry is excluded from Turoldus' poem. So wholly masculine is the author's world that male-female rapports remain ill-defined, and it is not until the very end that femininity becomes, through Roland's sacrifice and Bramimunde's conversion, assimilated within the closed circle of men. The effects of a new, softer and more flexible mentality—wholly feminine in comparison with Roland's life and death by the sword—can be seen in Thierry's offer to compromise with Pinabel and in Charlemagne's reluctance to accept further crusade. In any case, the epic triangle of dominant fathers, submissive sons and absent mothers will be replaced in Romance by fathers weakened by the strengthened bond between mothers and sons: Marc *versus* Tristan and Iseult; Arthur *versus* Guinevere and Lancelot.

Secondly, the separation of parental imagos remains so clearly defined in ***Roland*** that the unambiguous charge of hatred felt for Ganelon and the affection felt for Charles eliminates the type of interior conflict present when good and evil father are one and the same. . . . [As] long as the positive imago of the father or mother remains distinct from its negative counterpart the son is, like Roland, able to act without hesitation or guilt [unlike such characters as Oedipus, Orestes, Tristan, and Hamlet]. (pp. 14-15)

[Roland] identifies so completely with the good father that he remains capable of killing his negative side without risk to his own sense of self. The two imagos, projected upon separate external objects, at no point occupy the same psychological space and therefore do not contaminate the hero's inner being with the painful seeds of self-doubt.

Finally, the ***Roland*** father-son motif appears to be almost unique in its resolution. There are two traditional outcomes of the oedipal struggle as portrayed in Western literature. Either the son succeeds—like Oedipus, Orestes, Zeus, Hamlet, Dimitri Karamazov (through Smerdiakov)—in killing the father; or, father and son come to some kind of agreement by which the conflict is controlled. This second solution characterizes the Abraham-Isaac confrontation, where a lamb is substituted for the submissive son, the Tristan story, in which Tristan accepts the uncle's pardon but yields Iseult and Gide's *Faux-monnayeurs,* where Bernard, having wrestled with the paternal angel, returns home to the real father. The solution of compromise assumes that negative and positive imagos are in some manner reconciled and that the hostility felt by both parties is somehow mediated.

In ***Roland*** the normal archetype becomes reversed such that Ganelon, the evil parent, actually succeeds in killing the son. . . . ***La Chanson de Roland*** presents the father's elimination of the son in such direct terms that despite the classic disguise of father as uncle or stepfather, we are affected upon a deep psychological level. It is ultimately the directness of the perverted oedipal motif in which the father remains unable to sublimate the hatred experienced towards his younger rival that accounts as much as the slaughter and battles for the brutal impact of Turoldus' poem. (pp. 17-18)

R. Howard Bloch, "Roland and Oedipus: A Study of Paternity in 'La chanson de Roland'," in The French Review, *Vol. XLVI, No. 5, April, 1973, pp. 3-18.*

KARL D. UITTI (essay date 1973)

[*Uitti is an American educator and author of* Linguistics and Literary Theory *(1969) and* Story, Myth, and Celebration in Old French Narrative Poetry, 1050-1200 *(1973). In the following excerpt from the latter work, Uitti examines the way in which the roles of Charlemagne, France, and the Saracens are transformed through "the dynamics of epic binarism" to encompass both historical and symbolic meanings in* The Song.]

Whether one speaks, precisely, of the "poet's art" or of the "voice of tradition"—or of whatever one wishes to stress—the legend, by acquiring poetic and narrative form, hardly loses historical significance. On the contrary, it takes on increased historical value—meanings from which it is impossible to escape, even today. . . . [Such] value is built into the very structure of the poem; to ignore it is to condemn the work to irremediable malfunction. Consequently, one must conjoin the concepts of historical value and poetic function. In a very deep sense the ***Song of Roland*** is history conceived, that is, brought to the light of day, in literary and poetic terms. . . . The history of the poem succeeds in flowing into the mainstream of civilization without, for all that, becoming an abstraction. By reviewing some characteristics of the ***Roland***'s historical and political structure, we might be in a better position to restore, or to render explicit, the *signification historique* that Gaston Paris had thought forever lost. (pp. 67-8)

[An] approach to . . . ***Roland*** ought to be attempted on the basis of the "historical matter" or truth the poem was designed to convey, namely the order that is built around the person of Charles: the empire. . . . [However], caution must be observed. I do not mean to suggest that within the poem lies a political logic that in any significant way resembles the logic of an expository treatise; considered a mere apology for the imperial system, or worse, as propaganda in France for the moribund Carolingian party, the ***Roland*** would soon reveal itself a hopeless maze of seeming contradictions. Something, rather, of imperial doctrine is subsumed into the assumptions of reality made by the poem; the political Augustinianism current in the eleventh century is welded into a work that is literarily coherent despite its seemingly contradictory glorification of the French Royal House. Irreconcilable in themselves as logical proposals, these ideas, as presented in the structure of the poem (e.g., empire, projected against the kingdom of France), complement each other and, indeed, are made to fit into a comprehensive view. The literary artistry of the ***Roland*** poet—of the man, or men, or tradition(s) to which we are indebted for the juxtapositions that make [***The Song***] work out the way it does—is nowhere clearer than in the tensions he creates on the basis of such ideological dichotomies. His empire, it seems to me, is a living institution compared to the nostalgic but intellectualist vision of empire present in Dante and elsewhere in the later medieval tradition.

Charles, king and emperor ("Carles li reis, nostre emperere magnes"), incarnates his empire. But, if the poetic Charlemagne is confronted with what we know "externally" of the historical one . . . , we see that . . . the ***Roland*** is hardly concerned with precise accuracy as we nowadays have come to understand it. Nevertheless, a number of traits are common to both the poetic character and the historical personage. . . . The portrait has been idealized, of course, but does not contradict the (equally literary) sketch given by Einhard (*Vita Karoli*). Moreover, in the poem, Charlemagne is old, very old; his age is patriarchal and would tend to stem the gap separating the time he lived and the present of the poem—a notion further justified by the *trouvère*'s use of the first-person witness, Marsile: "Men escient dous cenz anz ad passet" ["I understand he is over two hundred years old"]. Obviously, the poet took extraordinary liberties in his telling the emperor's *geste*. Although Charles had gone to Spain and had even fought there, the recounting of this adventure in the poem corresponds but slightly to historical fact. Legends and actual happenings blend with no apparent line of demarcation. Now then, Charles' double epithet, *reis* ["king"] and *emperere* ["emperor"], hints at the manner of his construction; he is unique, of course, but he is "king" and "our emperor." Within the poem he is represented on two rather distinct levels as well, though at all times he does remain himself, very much a single person. Thus, on the one hand he is a man of flesh and blood, "historical" and intimate—"Li empereres se fait e balz e liez" ["The emperor jubilant"]—who is, as the line suggests, at times joyful, but who, perhaps even more often, feels himself to be sad and old . . . weeping the loss of his knights, among them Roland, upon his return to Roncevaux. Yet on still other occasions Charles—one is tempted to say Charles the Emperor—is revealed as an almost superhuman personage. It is he who receives the Angel Gabriel's visits, he who has been chosen to hold in trust the vast, virtually supernatural empire upon which rest the hopes of all Christendom. His very slumber is made adjunct to this exalted status; dreams assail him and, in dreaming, he clearly participates in an activity at once mysterious and necessary to the accomplishment of the divine Will. Like Moses and the prophets, Charles retains his humanity, his real "historicity," at the same time he functions as God's spokesman. (Unlike that of the saint, Charles' role is not ostensibly modeled upon an imitation of Christ.) As a man he is more than *primus inter pares,* yet his very designation as God's workman on earth underscores his humanity. Being Charles, both "king" and "our emperor," relates him to us at once of us and over us.

The dual character of Charles in the poem recalls a letter the historical Charlemagne is reputed to have sent Pope Leo III. According to this document, the emperor is entrusted with a mission of combat while "the pope raises his hands toward God, so that, by his intercession, the Christian people might be everywhere and always victorious over the enemies of His holy name." Charlemagne combines both functions: he combats without respite in the defence of the faith, but he is also a spiritual leader, the old king commanded by the Angel Gabriel to lead his armies to the "land of Bire," and, concomitantly in the poem, God's vicar, or spokesman, on earth. The poem's concentration upon the figure of Charles stresses the political rather more than the purely spiritual side of things. Thus, we gather, by declaring fealty to Charles' person, early ninth-century Europe as well as those who similarly respond to the universe of the poem, whether of the eleventh, twelfth, or twentieth centuries, may realize a sense of magical community for the first and last time—or for always, or both—in Western

Christian history. Declaration of fealty is a kind of rite (cf., ''*nostre* emperere magnes'') [''*our* great emperor''] that the narrative of the poem is designed to explain and explore. Note, incidentally, the power here of the adjective *nostre* which, unlike the more common respectful *mes/mon,* was usually applied only to God and the Virgin (*Nostre Dame*). It was such a sense of *community,* or nostalgia for it, during the subsequent degradation into feudal *society,* that, symbolized perhaps in the relationship of Charles and the twelve peers (here, obviously, an image calqued on the New Testament), the ***Roland*** and other poems of the *cycle du roi* bring so poignantly to mind. (pp. 68-71)

Within the world of the ***Song of Roland*** Charlemagne maintains communications between the will of God and human brotherhood, the body politic. In this way he . . . participates, though obliquely, in certain hagiographic patterns. But this is handled in very special ways. During his four appearances before the emperor never once does the Angel Gabriel speak of personal matters; his concern is always political. But when what he says is made over into Charles' concern, then the political is personalized, i.e., transformed into something quite real, as authentic as Charles' feelings of joy and pain, of sadness or delight. Beginning with v. 2525, just after the destruction of the Frankish rear-guard, Gabriel, in a dream, warns Charles of the battle to come. . . . One of the strangest passages in the whole poem follows; Charles is permeated with the supernatural, which he understands only through premonitions and against which, very humanly, he is helpless. In a most magical context he is but a man. . . . It is Charles as emperor, of course, who struggles with the . . . [huge lion in his dream], but it is a Charles whom the poem has humanized by depicting his fear and foreboding. Then, once again, the angelic messenger appears and orders the king to undo his arms and repair to Roncevaux. Later, when Charles, wounded in battle against Baligant, seems to waver, Gabriel encourages him: ''Reis magnes, que fais tu?'' [''Great king, what are you doing?'']. The emperor recovers his strength: ''Fiert l'amiraill de l'espee de France'' [''He strikes the emir with the sword of France''] . . . ; note the very epic double metonymic play: the ''sword'' of ''France,'' identifiable with Charles on two counts—the man and his sword, and himself as France's protector. The fourth time Charles is visited by Gabriel is, of course, at the end of the poem, at which time he is once again summoned to gird his sword and set out for the land of Bire. Although personally unhappy, tired, and weeping, he will, as emperor, perform his duty to God, for such is his condition. He is emphatically not the tragic individual that Roland is and, potentially perhaps, that Ganelon might be, because, though but one man, he is politically also many.

Structurally, then, Charlemagne's role in the poem is unitary: he imposes a logic upon the various events that occur in the work (treason; victory and death of Roland; punishment, vengeance; trial and execution of Ganelon). And the logic derives both from what Charles does within the poem as well as from what he is, i.e., his historical, or real, being. The two sources of this logic are, so to speak, organically blended. Similarly, one might add, the poetic force of Charlemagne's name went a good deal further even than the precise allusions to it in the ***Song of Roland*** or, for that matter, in the bare framework of his biography. In the *Légendes épiques,* Joseph Bédier collected various testimonials of Charles' popularity during the period encompassing the eighth to the twelfth centuries. He recalls Pope Urban II, exhorting the French to arms at the 1095 Council of Clermont (translation mine): ''May your souls be moved and excited by the deeds of your ancestors, by the prowess and grandeur of King Charlemagne and of his son Lewis and of your other kings, who have destroyed the pagan kingdoms and pushed forward the borders of the Holy Church.'' The poetic resonance of Charles' name functions within the new—yet ''traditional''—context of crusade rhetoric. In ''reality,'' then, Charles is also poetic. Other examples quoted by Bédier or by Gaston Paris, for that matter, border upon the marvelous, e.g., nearly defeated Christian soldiers rallying about a miraculously present King Charlemagne, just arrived in their midst to lead them to ultimate victory. Such apparitions are so purely poetic that they seem to be due to, or otherwise incorporated into, the image constructed by the ***Roland*** poet(s).

In the poem, then, the character of Charles is rarely documented, literally authenticated, or even rounded out, because the poet had no need to do so. (It is thus that we must answer those who have criticized the poet for creating in Charlemagne a pale, uninteresting personality.) His double nature, as described above, is immediately related in the minds of those who heard the poem chanted to a tradition either oral or written (probably both) that was known, at least in broad outline, by everyone. King, emperor, old, white-haired, a man spoken to by God and for whom miracles are performed (as when, for example, the sun is commanded to halt its trajectory), yet, at the same time, a being whose humanity is subjected to the pains of this world—these are the elements freely drawn upon and, to a considerable degree, binarily opposed as well as exploited by the *trouvère.* (The connotations, including those of the ''chosen'' Christian people, suggest the patriarchal leaders—Moses, Joshua—of the people of Israel.) Charles' portrait remains selective, however. Thus, his lubricity, though mentioned by Einhard and alluded to in other poems, is never hinted at in the ***Roland,*** unless, perhaps, the episodes concerning Charles' *caitive franche* [''noble prisoners''], Bramimonde, widow of the pagan King Marsile, whom he takes back with him to Aix and whom he has baptized (this term lends itself to *double entendre*), constitute an extraordinarily sublimated reflection of this character trait.

Hard to define, but nonetheless significant in connection with what Charles represents in the poem is the tension between the real political situation of eleventh-century France and the idealized concept of unity present both in the thought of the time and in the poem. Charlemagne's structural role, we observed, is unitary; moreover, he has the same function as a historical referent. Though Hugh Capet's election to the French crown in 987 consummated definitively the political break-up of the Empire that had already advanced quite far by the accession of Otto I to the imperial throne (962), the successors of Robert the Strong considered themselves the heirs of the Carolingians, whom they called in their diplomas ''antecessors'' rather than ''predecessors.'' They wished to perpetuate a kind of ideal link between their state and the imperial principle and past. Charles' story authenticated their own story. Thus they had recourse to the *sacre* [''anointing and coronation of a king''], a Carolingian institution, in order to stress their legitimacy. And constant reference to Charlemagne in their diplomas helped offset accusations of usurpation made by their Carolingian opponents. Moreover, the *sacre* remained symbolically powerful when used to counteract the feudal fragmentation that had been permitted to occur throughout the ninth and tenth centuries. Charles was made to serve the unitary interests of the monarchy in the old Gallo-Roman territories as well as the claims to legitimacy of this monarchy against an empire that had become increasingly Germanic. ''France,'' as a concept, is comparable to the old "empire"—a land whose king endeavored to make his authority felt upon the feudal lords in much the same way as the emperor had done with respect to the *reguli* ["petty kings"] in former times.

Furthermore, the Capetians expended great effort in rendering their rule hereditary; each of the first several kings felt obliged to associate his son . . . with his own reign before his death. Here too the Carolingian *sacre* was called upon to emphasize the legitimacy of the Capetian dynasty and to assure its projection into the future. In this way even a "separatist France" generated a kind of political mystique that, far more completely than any other man or institution, Charlemagne symbolized, indeed incarnated. He constitutes the historical focus of the political myths operative in Capetian France, and . . . this role, both literary and political, became traditionally associated with his person. Through the legitimacy of Charles, Capetian France found itself capable of perpetuating the ideal dimension proper to the medieval view of the body politic as a magical *communitas* ["community"], and, obviously, of articulating this ideal dimension in terms of a distinctly Carolingian heritage or symbolism. As we shall observe, the *petite France* and the *grande France*—"kingdom" and "empire"—of the ***Song of Roland*** were never meant to correspond to precise geographic dimensions; they are rather geographic symbols of spiritual values that the poet endeavors to fuse in his work. Charles as historical referent renders the fusion possible. "France," in the larger, "imperial" sense, is Christendom, led and sustained by Charles in a never-ending journey to virtue and salvation. Within the larger France, the geographical entity "France," a feudal concept and the nucleus of the Capetian kingdom, plays the part assigned to it, leaven to the dough. . . . Despite the separation of Capetian France from the Carolingian Empire, the memory of Charlemagne could be utilized in the political tensions of, say, the tenth and especially of the eleventh century. The ambiguity of these tensions could be exploited: the history or myth of Charlemagne contained a truth that could and did go beyond a mere nostalgia for a golden age of the remote past as well as the considerations of *Realpolitik* indulged by a legitimacy-conscious Capetian dynasty. Enough reality adhered to the myth that it easily became a political ideal whose possible implementation was not to be lightly cast aside.

What might be called the "binary impulse," the force that actualized Charles' meaning in terms particularly appropriate to poetic, or epic, expression, derives, of course, from the crusades: "The pagans are in error [*unt tort*], the Christians are righteous [*unt dreit*]!" There is no need to seek out complicated reasons explaining why the popular imagination of 1070 chose Charlemagne as the prototype of the crusading king. Already in the year 1000 (after a century of minor wars and skirmishes throughout Europe) war between Christians and Muslims broke out in Italy; the struggle was carried on in Spain and, later, was brought to the Orient. The first expedition, organized in large part by Cluny, took place in 1063; it included many French participants. In 1095 Pope Urban II convoked the Council of Clermont at which the crusade policy that was to lead to the conquest of Jerusalem in 1099 was worked out. In these crusades France played a major role: the four principalities that made up, in 1099, the entirety of the conquered territories in the Holy Land were French ("French," Aquitanian, and Norman). Yet frequently men of great importance in the crusading ranks were *adoubés,* i.e., soldiers who had undergone rites of "military consecration." These *chevaliers,* whose allegiance was not to a feudal lord but rather to an international order in which could be found a curious mixture of Roman discipline and German fidelity (*Treue*), multiplied throughout the eleventh century.

This notion of knighthood derived perhaps from the old concept of *miles Christi* ["soldier of Christ"]; it implied, in theory if not always in practice, a hierarchy of values located above the feudal system and the belief that effective action against Islam required political unity rather than feudal separatism. The "dubbed knight" was expected to be the servant of all Christendom, not of any given lord. The sheer size of the Christian military adventure brought poignantly to mind the need for a strong, united front in Europe. No single "nation" could suffice in the task. Though at times given political entities—kinds of "nation"—bore the brunt of the military activity, they usually did so in the name of Christendom or of the empire, as did certain tenth-century Leonese kings, who called themselves "emperors" in their diplomas. The medieval mind never did conceive of the crusades as a "national" venture. Thus, the European dedication to crusade activity involved, on several counts, a truly symbolic identification with the Empire of 800. (This identification occasioned numerous anachronisms in the ***Roland*** itself, which combines in an ideal temporal dimension—an *ævum*—concerns of a "Carolingian past" and of a later era; the literary tradition perpetuates this anachronistic state—the mythology—well into the thirteenth century. (pp. 72-8)

The temporal problem, i.e., Charles' historicity vs. his abstraction out of time ("over two hundred years old"), pervades the complex relationship between Charles and Roland. Roland the nephew is conscious of being his uncle's vassal, i.e., of blood relations and a feudal connection. But it is a feudalism transposed into an ideal *communitas;* both vassal and lord are engaged in the accomplishment of a transcendental mission. Roland the *miles Christi* best serves his task by professing allegiance to Charlemagne. The poem presents the structure of the kind of inspired feudalism in which the ideal Christian knight of every century serves to the best of his ability an ancient, indeed immortal, Charlemagne. There is nothing in Roland with which the eleventh-century feudal knight could not ideally identify himself. And his well-defined place in the social structure would permit proper relative self-identification on the part of listeners and observers of the poem—both "within" (e.g., Aude, Roland's *fiancée,* who dies when she hears the news of his death at Roncevaux) and "without" (the public). Along with Olivier and the other peers, Roland constitutes a link between the *ævum* incarnated by Charlemagne and earthly time. Even today, I venture to say, it is through Roland and Olivier—as well as through Aude and Thierry—that we, as readers of the poem, approach Charlemagne. We approach them all together, of course, through their relationship, i.e., the archetypal construct of lord, twelve "peers," and faithful vassal. (Interestingly, Ganelon—whose punishment is accomplished, thanks to Thierry—advised Marsile to "get at" Charles precisely through the twelve peers; Charles' destruction, he averred, would follow soon upon that of this relational construct. He was, of course, mistaken.)

The emperor's personal mission and the mission of the empire derive from God.Both are sacred, yet both are worked out by and through men. (Another manifestation of epic binarism—from now on I shall refer repeatedly to the mechanics of this binarism.) As the secular arm of the Church, the empire organizes the material and spiritual resources (courage, morale) of the age in the struggle against the Infidel. Because he is Charles' principal support, the knight must impose upon himself a pure and humble morality; this is the lesson implicit in

Roland's personal tragedy and even in Ganelon's destruction. *Corruptio optimi pessima* finds a counterpart in the epic formula—here applied to Baligant, Charles' archenemy—"Deus! quel baron, s'oüst chrestientet!" ["God! What a brave knight, if only he were a Christian!"]. The knight's sword is a gift from heaven; his strength therefore depends on how completely he follows God's will. The empire, Christendom, stands for a strong state, in the medieval sense of "strength," capable of responding to the needs of a Europe launched upon the crusades. The ***Song of Roland*** portrays such an empire. How does it do so?

Although "empire" (*emperie*) appears only once in the Oxford manuscript, a number of terms designating political entities are used with various degrees of frequency. . . . It is curious that whereas Charles is consistently referred to as *reis* and/or *emperere, emperie* is not used to describe his territory. There is no opposition between *reis* and *emperere;* so far as I can see, the titles seem to be rather complementary. Indeed both *reis* and *emperere* are frequently used not only by themselves but also in conjunction as epithets or partial epithets in apposition to *Carles* or to *Carlemagne*. . . . *Reis* being the more familiar and more "French" term in the eleventh century, one might hazard a guess that the poet rendered the word *emperere* a bit more familiar to his audience by such indiscriminate substitution. The similarity of position within the phrase or with respect to *Carles* contributed to a kind of semantic contagion in which the familiarity and loyalty engendered by *reis* spread as well to the grander, more foreboding (and perhaps foreign!) word *emperere*. Charles is thus both king (i.e., French feudal lord) and emperor (above feudal relationships); he is at once subjected to and superior to the laws and uses of feudal political organization. Does not this word-play tend to confirm that the eleventh- or twelfth-century audience probably felt that Charles derived from it and yet surpassed it?

Moreover *emperere,* in constant semantic juxtaposition to *reis,* conferred upon the latter word a special nuance, a grandeur that did not quite correspond to the everyday reality of medieval kingship. The feudal terminology with which the poem is rife undergoes a decided poetic metamorphosis equivalent to the idealism of the political vision expressed in the poem. It cannot be said that the poet is merely groping for a vocabulary that he takes, meekly and gratefully, from whatever source his poverty-stricken language puts at his disposal. The transformations occurring in the poem are too consistent to be the handiwork of chance and happy coincidence. (pp. 79-81)

As has been frequently pointed out, *France* itself is used in several possible meanings; the poet took full advantage of the semantic instability of the terms as well as of the ambiguities present in the dichotomy *France: empire*. Aix-la-Chapelle was never a French city, although it was, certainly, a Frankish one and, moreover, Charlemagne's historical capital. By [a] process of contagion . . . , Aix does indeed become a truly French capital, and, even more important, the French capital becomes Aix; the capital of France acquires values that are "imperial." By the same token, *Franceis* and *Francs* merge: Frenchmen are heirs to Frankish—eventually Roman—imperial universalism. But, thanks to the poetic genius displayed in the ***Roland,*** the *Franceis* do not for that lose their identity which, since Charles' death, they have forged for themselves. . . . And the poem distinguishes between *Franceis* and *Normans,* an invalid, anachronistic distinction for pre-invasion Carolingian times. He is therefore neither consistently historical (eighth century) nor contemporary (eleventh century). (pp. 82-3)

Ferdinand Lot has demonstrated the existence of, and confusion between, a "greater" Frankish *France* and another, smaller, political entity, and has shown that both correspond to equally true political realities. He is mistaken, however, in assigning them definite times and values, since such rigor on his part overlooks the fact that, in the ***Roland,*** the "confusion" was deliberately intended—or at least exploited—since the political vision is expressed here in poetic, not positivistically historical terms.

Neither "France" cancels out the other; the ambiguities, built . . . on the opposition of *France: empire* as well as on the confrontation of *now: then* (for all oppositions are also by definition juxtapositions), constitute a source of richly poetic (and, once again, properly epic) expression. Rendering these ambiguities explicit tends to destroy them, but in what follows here I shall explicate merely in order to illustrate, with these examples, a certain functioning. . . . (pp. 83-4)

If the "confusion" between the words *Franc* and *Franceis* in the year 1080 (or earlier) is linguistically comprehensible, given the poem's context, it is not any more difficult to see that the poet wished also to confuse Charles' empire and contemporary France; a throwback of a century or two would have incurred no difficulty for his audience. The past gives the present greater relief, but also a fusion takes place, quite simultaneously; a past history is dramatized by its narrational resituation in the present time. What then could be more natural than to conceive Charlemagne's empire physically in the geopolitical terms of the eleventh century? . . . The ambiguity of the notion of *France*—a concept floating, so to speak, in the temporal flow separating the year 800 from 1100 (and beyond)—is consequently an artistic *tour de force* of the first magnitude. The ***Song of Roland*** is very much concerned with the here-and-now, but, by constantly identifying France with Charles and his Christian empire, it succeeds in destroying that part of time which might be construed as a limitation. (That is the reason for so much scholarly confusion.)

Both Roland and Olivier are French, from the smaller France. Their prowess as well as the favored position given the *Franceis* in the imperial army exalt French heroism and sense of origin. The poem seldom misses an opportunity to sing the glories of France. . . . Never once does the poem even hint that these men might be used to serve the secular or material advance of the French kingdom, even within the empire. All military conquests are achieved exclusively on behalf of the faith. After the capture of Zaragoza, Charles orders his army to break the idols and heathen images in the pagan temples while his bishops bless the water to be used for the baptism of the vanquished pagans. The French forces, acting as a kind of spearhead with respect to the entire imperial army, are nevertheless completely assimilated into it. . . . The poet of the ***Song of Roland*** constructs a political edifice designed to be at once universal and Christian, but whose spiritual and military center remains clearly France. Thus Charles is both the Christian emperor and the king of France; his political roots remain, so to speak, both Roman-Frankish as well as Germanic-feudal. In no way do these concepts clash in the poem as they so frequently did in medieval and more recent history. The two notions are made to complement one another. (pp. 84-5)

The dynamics of epic binarism also underlie the role played by the pagans in the ***Song of Roland.*** Many debatable, even doubtful, things have been said or written concerning the political, social, and religious institutions of the Saracens. The obvious parallelisms between Charlemagne's empire and the

Saracen nation have been frequently alluded to and described. The pagans are usually "explained away." Thus, the poet—or the tradition—has been blamed for his naïveté calquing the Saracens upon a Christian model. At times he has been justified, but once again on grounds of naïveté: How could he be expected to remain faithful to a political structure of which he had no real knowledge? He did not know enough to be accurate.

It will not do to approach this problem from the standpoint of what we know about the Saracens nor, for that matter, from the assumption of naïveté and folk-like simplicity. The poem itself must orient us. Clearly, the pagan body politic and religious viewpoint can hardly be considered either authentically Spanish or Muslim, except insofar as they, being pagans, ought to be opposed to Christendom. The pagans function as one of the terms of the opposition I alluded to earlier. It is in this context that one must grasp the fact that they worship a Trinity composed of Tervagant, Mahum, and Apollin (names that are epic stock and trade). Like their Christian adversaries, they too speak of *dulce France* ["fair France"] and, amusingly, of *seinte chrestientet* ["holy Christianity"]. Although the poem utilizes foreign words to designate several of their titles (e.g., *amiraill, algalife*)—thereby showing that the poet was hardly averse to a bit of authentic local color when it suited his purpose—the pagans borrow heavily from Christian terminology: Marsile is *reis* and he is aided by his *baruns,* a special group of whom closely resemble the twelve peers. One recognizes here the familiar workings of opposition-juxtaposition and semantic (or structural) contamination. (pp. 89-90)

Baligant, the only character who can be compared to Charles—indeed, in keeping with the notion of the dynamics of the epic binarism, I should say that the presence of Charles required and created a "slot" for Baligant—is introduced rather late in the poem. . . . He is the *amiraill* ("emir"), the head of Islam. Like Charlemagne, he is old. . . . Before helping his beleaguered coreligionary and "vassal," he must summon troops from forty *regnez* (i.e., kingdoms obedient to him), and organize a vast navy to transport them, their baggage, and their animals from Alexandria to Spain. Similarly, of course, Charles had to bring his army from Aix; both rulers are fighting in border country. The poet spares no effort to depict Baligant's grandeur. (p. 91)

We are made to understand over and over again that, in Baligant, Charles has a worthy opponent. At Baligant's command the pagan host bows down before the standards of its gods as do the Christians during prayer. But there is, in this juxtaposition, a striking contrast between Baligant's invocation of *noz deus* ["our gods"] and Charles' previous supplication. . . . Charles' prayer resembles formally the prayers for the dying; it is movingly humble. As a Christian he puts his trust in the Lord, a God whom he can address individually and whom he can exhort in terms of the history of other persons whom He has saved. The harangue of Baligant's priest, on the other hand, implies no god of love or freedom, but rather tyrants exacting a price for their protection. The opposition is many-layered. Essentially, however, what is lacking to the pagan view is any concept of charity, whereas the Christians, though rude warriors too and far from perfect, possess, in their filial relationship to God, a kind of *douceur* or softness born of love. Within the dramatic structure of the poem the pagans are clearly the villains and, of course, cannot be made out to be too sympathetic within that structure. There is no real Homeric sympathy for a Priam or a Hector here, except in that each pagan, including Baligant, may be seen as a kind of "potential Christian." (pp. 92-3)

The pagans serve gods who have promised them money, power, and sensual pleasure—all things of this world to which no magical value adheres. Their régime, externally like the Christian empire, is set up merely to obtain these purely material satisfactions. It is therefore a tyranny. It is against this backdrop of tyranny that Charles' empire is projected. Within the structure of the ***Roland***—a structure based on epic, not novelistic, alternatives—this political dichotomy permits no nuance or shading: The Christian empire is good, the pagans "unt tort" ["are wrong"]. The shading occurs elsewhere, in the very process of contrast. . . . [On] a non-institutional or individual level the poet does stress a certain inherent human merit in persons within the pagan camp; they are corrupt only by virtue of the false gods they serve. And Ganelon too, after all a Christian, is corrupted by his passions and ends up serving false gods as well. Fidelity to Charles, then, is something more than mere feudal homage, although the pattern of showing one's faith is borrowed from the feudal mode. By the same token, pagan tyranny must, I believe, be appreciated here above all as an *internal* danger within Christendom despite the fact that it is ostensibly depicted as emanating from without. On the purely human level Baligant is a man—and, as such, admirable from several viewpoints—irrevocably condemned because not only is he without God, he refuses to receive Him. (And unlike the case of Milton's Satan, the structure of the ***Roland*** does not allow any suggestion of heroism in Baligant's refusal.) It is moreover perfectly logical that Marsile, who dies of chagrin at his ultimate defeat, is snatched away by demons. The point is obvious, perhaps, but its very lack of subtlety underscores the godlessness of the pagan position and the fact that the Saracens are being judged specifically for their godlessness. The point could hardly be lost on an eleventh-century audience.

It is at this juncture that the greatness of the poet's art appears staggering. He uses a symbolic structure—Charles' empire and its struggle—derived both from traditional history and contemporary political theory (at once "imperial" *and* national in direction) in order to depict a *communitas* of Christian heroes. It is this sense of the heroic Christian *communitas,* worked out, as we saw, in specific binary frameworks, that engenders the underlying epic force and value of the ***Chanson de Roland***. . . . The roots of the poem plunge deep into ground its listeners could conceive of as real: France, the crusades, Charles himself, feudal society, the empire, the divine order of creation. Yet by no means can one justify calling it, in the restricted sense of the term, a "French epic." Rather, its universality is such that it both confers upon and extracts from the concept of *France* (a poetic symbol) a value of vital participation in a Christian grand design. Spiritual meanings are imparted to geographical terms in such a way that the reader (or listener) is called upon to recognize the danger of "Saracenism" within himself. Similarly, the audience partakes fully in Charlemagne's endeavor, which, in turn, seems to be a kind of endless journey of penance, an extraordinary pilgrimage. Charles *is* emperor, but an importnat feature of the poem is its telling us what being *nostre emperere* implies.

Whereas it is true that Charles, like Roland and the other characters, is, as Américo Castro put it [in *La realidad histórica de España* (1954)], a "result of the abstract and absolute expression of his being," his being holds our interest—even on the aesthetic plane—thanks to his incessant journey at the head of Christendom. The myth prevails. The abstractness of the imperial ideal and its Saracen counterpart are fully utilized in the poem, but, like the historical Charlemagne himself, they

Aude dies in Charlemagne's arms upon hearing of Roland's death in this fourteenth-century German miniature.

are transfigured. Both are relocated in a new and vital dimension of reality, albeit a magical one, a reality, in short, seeming to have little to do with the bread-and-butter concerns of everyday life. Yet the reality of the poem has so much to do with these petty concerns that it can transform a vulgar border skirmish in a mountain pass into a drama of salvation. The oppositions and juxtapositions that, in conjunction with one another, make up the empire establish it, quite precisely, as a poetic creation in the deepest possible sense of the term. (pp. 98-101)

Karl D. Uitti "The Song of Roland," in his Story, Myth, and Celebration in Old French Narrative Poetry, 1050-1200, *Princeton University Press, 1973, pp. 65-127.*

MINNETTE GRUNMANN-GAUDET (essay date 1977)

[In the following excerpt from a paper read at the University of Western Ontario in 1977, Grunmann-Gaudet examines the concept of time in The Song, *emphasizing that the poem's temporal pattern appears static and illogical, and that "profane time is intimately linked with sacred time."]*

In his well-known work on *Time and the Novel,* Adam Mendilow states that the major characteristics of time are transience, sequence, and irreversibility. Meyerhoff uses similar terminology [in his *Time in Literature* (1968)], attributing to time the qualities of succession, flux, and change.

In ***La Chanson de Roland,*** changes which mark the flow of time go unnoticed. There is no mention of the changing of seasons or of the physical disintegration brought about by old age. Likewise, there is very little mental or emotional development on the part of the epic hero, who seems to be bound by the fatalistic universe in which he lives. Time seems to have suspended its flight, and we are plunged instead into a sort of eternal present.

Aside from the one reference to Baligant's troops embarking in May on the first day of summer, neither the seasons nor the weather is described in the ***Roland.*** One might expect some reference to the change of seasons in the passage describing Ganelon's trial, which supposedly takes place in Aachen on December 31. Yet the grass is still green and there is no mention of snow or frost, a fact which points once again to the poet's lack of concern for verisimilitude. "L'erbe verte" ["the green grass"] presents the necessary contrast to "li cler sanc," or flowing blood, and, therefore, recurs in most death scenes, regardless of the season. Similarly, we witness almost no change in landscape, despite the fact that Aachen is very far north, approximately on the same latitude as Brussels. The rare formulas that do appear to describe the weather or landscape are highly stylized; their principal function is to provide color and create a moral, rather than a physical, climate.

Just as winter has no noticeable influence on the weather or landscape, old age has no appreciable effect on a character's physical capacities or vitality. Although the pagans refer several times to Charlemagne's old age and dependence on his young nephew Roland, Charlemagne is viewed by his Christian followers as strength incarnate. The poet portrays Charles as a vigorous conqueror, and it is this image that the vanquished enemy is finally forced to acknowledge. According to Eginhard, Charlemagne died at the age of seventy-two. Yet in the ***Roland,*** we are told that he is over 200 years old. . . . The Emir Baligant is even older. . . . It is fitting that both rulers have lived many more years than the normal man, for in the Biblical tradition, advanced age is a conventional sign of hierarchic seniority. The old age of Charlemagne and Baligant is a quantitative expression of their dignity and authority, much in the same way that the superhuman proportions of Christ in certain medieval tympana set him apart from ordinary mortals.

The longevity of these two sovereigns may be interpreted in diverse fashions; yet what is most apparent is the element of stasis, the halt of the flow of time. As Auerbach points out, stasis often characterizes that which is legendary [see Additional Bibliography]. Although Charlemagne and Baligant both have white hair and beard, these traits constitute conventional signs of wisdom and in no way indicate physical impairment. On the contrary, the poet consistently stresses their strength and vigor. (pp. 84-5)

It is as if both rulers have each reached a certain optimum age, in terms of wisdom and authority, but remain in a state of suspended animation when it comes to the aging process itself.

As Calin [in his edition of ***La chanson de Roland*** (1968)], Auerbach, and other critics have noted, Charlemagne is an enigmatic mixture of strength and weakness. In spite of his premonitions of Ganelon's treachery, he allows Roland to lead the rearguard. According to Auerbach, the Emperor's position in this scene is unclear, and "despite all the authoritative definiteness which he manifests from time to time, he seems as it were somnambulistically paralyzed. The important and symbolic position—almost that of a Prince of God—in which he appears as the head of all Christendom and as the paragon of knightly perfection, is in strange contrast to his impotence." What Auerbach labels as paralysis may be easily explained by the fact that Charlemagne is graced with an awareness of what is *destined* to take place. His premonitory dreams provide him with a certain omniscience and enable him to share the poet's privileged knowledge of the future. One might call him fatalistic in that he presents no opposition to that which he views as pre-ordained. For Charlemagne, the script has already been written, and all that remains is to play it out, no matter how painful his role may be.

It is this same sense of fatality or inner necessity which seems to motivate Roland. Roland is concerned lest he betray his lineage. He expresses fears that "malvaise cancun" ["bad songs"] might be sung about him, or that he might lose his fame or shame his parentage. Rather than avoid disaster, he welcomes it. When Charlemagne offers to leave his army with the rearguard, Roland refuses. . . . Roland's comments reveal the self-awareness of one who is both actor and spectator, conscious of his role in history and detemined not to disappoint posterity.

As Quinones points out [in *The Renaissance Discovery of Time* (1972)], "Chivalric honor did not derive from any sense of man's exposure to time, but from the sense that within man was an inviolable essence that ought under no conditions to submit to lower contingencies." If Roland's death were bound up with the idea of *malchance* ["bad luck"], that is, of an inept subordination to time, it would lose its quality of grandiose necessity. In the ***Roland,*** the poet makes no effort to create suspense or impart the idea that every minute counts. There is no real concern as to whether Charlemagne will arrive on time to save his nephew, for there is no awareness of time as a force determining events. Instead, there is a heavy sense of fatality which prevents the characters from moving, changing, or exercising their free will. (pp. 86-7)

In the ***Roland,*** this static characterization is reinforced by the use of formulaic epithets which freeze the character in time. Whatever the situation may be, the defining attribute of a person remains constant. Ganelon is labeled from the outset as "traitor" despite the fact that the treason has not yet taken place. Charlemagne calls his men to council to decide how to respond to Marsile's offer of conversion. The poet names the barons and concludes by saying that "Guenes i vint, ki la traïsun fist" ["Ganelon, who committed the act of treachery, come too"]. Such an announcement renders Ganelon the archetypal traitor and precludes the possibility of his experiencing any kind of conflict prior to his decision to betray the rearguard.

Even the language spoken by the characters in the ***Roland*** is marked by a certain rigidity. As Auerbach remarks, dialogue in the ***Roland*** lacks "free-flowing, dynamic, and impulsive movement in expression." Auerbach cites as an example the verses where Charlemagne first hears the sound of Roland's olifant: "'. . . Jo oi le corn Rollant! / Unc nel sunast, se ne fust cumbatant'" ["'. . . I hear Roland's horn! / He'd never sound it if he weren't fighting'"]. In these lines one perceives no violent expression of emotion. Charlemagne states what is happening in a very matter-of-fact way. I should add here, however, that dialogue in the ***Roland*** is not always so static or so colorless. Exaggerated displays of grief, sometimes uttered at inappropriate moments, often appear, but this emotion is always curbed by the formulaic language in which it is uttered and thus lacks the movement or flow characteristic of a more hypotactic syntax.

A lack of emotional flow also emanates from the epic's rigid value scheme. As Auerbach points out, "The subject of the ***Chanson de Roland*** is narrow, and for the men who figure in it, nothing of fundamental significance is problematic. All the categories of this life and the next are unambiguous, immutable, fixed in rigid formulations."

In the ***Roland,*** the poet chooses to emphasize that which is stable and enduring in the universal flux. We are plunged into a sort of atemporal reality where seasons do not change, characters do not grow or age, and the battles which take place are symbolic of the greater eternal struggle between the forces of good and evil.

The second basic characteristic of time as defined by Mendilow and Meyerhoff is sequence or succession. Before analyzing sequence in the ***Chanson de Roland,*** it might be helpful to distinguish between what Genette, Todorov, Ricardou, and others call the "two temporal axes": (1) the "temps du signifié," or the order of events as they actually happened, independent of their disposition in the narrative, and (2) the "temps du signifiant" or the author's arrangement of events in the narrative. If we consider only the first axis, the ***Chanson de Roland*** is not devoid of squence. Events have a beginning, middle, and end which conform to legend. If we consider the second axis, or author's imposition of a pseudo-temporality on the given events, the narrative reveals a lack of linearity. We see that causal relations are seldom expressed and that there is a constant shifting backwards and forwards in time without any apparent design.

The poet brings the future into the present by announcements, prophesies, and other anticipatory remarks. The pagan defeat is implied in the very first *laisse* when the poet says with regard to the Saracen king: "Nes poet guarder que mals ne l'i ateignet. AOI" ["He cannot prevent misfortune from befalling him there"]. The *laisse* introducing the council scene in which Charlemagne accepts Marsile's proposal also terminates with two anticipatory statements: "Guenes i vint, ki la traïsun fist. / Des ore cumencet le cunseill que mal prist. AOI" ["Ganelon, who committed the act of treachery, came too. / Now begins the council that went wrong."]. In this *laisse* the poet alludes to the disastrous consequences of Charlemagne's decision, prior to his description of the deliberations, and labels Ganelon as "the traitor" before the treason is ever conceived.

Illogical tense usage also contributes to the confusion of past, present, and future. Announcements of what is to come are sometimes in the present, as in the examples which I have just cited, sometimes in the preterite, sometimes in the future. In the battle between Marsile's forces and the rearguard, the author intervenes to predict the outcome, using a strange combination of tenses. He begins in the future tense, switches to the present to underscore Charlemagne's grief, then jumps forward into the future and back into the preterite to refer once again to Ganelon's treason and to predict the execution of Ganelon and thirty members of his family at Aix-la-Chapelle. . . . (pp. 87-90)

Succession in a causal sense, that is, as a chain in which each link is conceptually and factually connected with the other, is also weakened by the inconsistent mixture of present and past tenses to express past action. As Buffin points out in the Old Epic the variation in tenses depends to a large degree on the requirements of assonance, number, and cesura. Yet these elements do not always explain the choice of tenses, which often appears to be gratuitous. We are told, for example, that Ganelon "was" so handsome that everyone "looks" at him admiringly and that Roland, when attempting to destroy his sword, "saw" that he could not break it and "begins" to lament. The author wavers indiscriminately between present and perfect, and symbolic significance of the action as expressed by the verb being stronger than the indication of time implicit in the finite form. . . . The symbolic aspect of events is underlined by the historic present which divests them of their temporal contingencies. The tense stresses permanent notions, permanent states of being.

The historical present intensifies imagery by bringing the past into the present and thus abolishing any practical notion of the passage of time. According to Buffin, frequent use of the historical present indicates a lack of concern for time. In any case, it certainly weakens our impression of events succeeding one another chronologically and thus reinforces the enumerative paratactic process found in the ***Roland*** and typical of the Old French epic in general.

In the ***Roland,*** the events of one moment have no propulsive force which demands the next moment. The poem consists of a series of independent pictures, strung together like beads and possessing only a loose causal connection with those that precede or follow. Moreover, the poet gives few analyses or explanations. As Auerbach remarks, "The poet explains nothing, and yet the things which happen are stated with a paratactic bluntness which says that everything must happen as it does happen, it could not be otherwise, and there is no need for explanatory connectives."

As I have already stated, causality is not lacking in the ***Roland,*** since events follow a more or less logical pattern. Yet motives and causes are rarely mentioned because they are not seen as problematic or in need of evidence. The poet simply juxtaposes related moments in time, laying them end to end. The association of contiguities is the job of the reader or listener.

Temporal continuity is also destroyed by abrupt changes in scene, for which the poet provides no transitions. . . . The poet switches without warning from the pagan camp to the French, sometimes even in the middle of a *laisse*. He also moves backwards and forwards in time without providing any temporal signposts. As a result there is sometimes a certain confusion in temporal and spatial sequences. A good example of this is provided in *laisses* 55 and 56. *Laisse* 55 begins with a summary of the action from the Franks' point of view. The poet tells us that Charlemagne has conquered Spain and is heading back towards France, leaving behind him his nephew Roland to protect his army from the rear. In the middle of the *laisse,* the poet jumps to a description of the pagans, as they prepare for battle. The *laisse* terminates with the statement that 400,000 pagans await the dawn when they will ambush Roland's troops. *Laisse* 56 begins with a short leap backwards in time to the setting of the sun and the events occurring in the French camp. In this passage, the temporal relationship between the two *laisses* remains extremely tenuous.

In the ***Roland,*** "reprises épiques" and other parallel structures serve to deemphasize the successivity of narrative elements and thus decelerate the passage of time. The famous verses in which Roland attempts to break his sword on a rock well illustrate the way in which *laisses similaires* create a lyrical pause in time. In *laisse* 171, Roland strikes Durendal ten times against a gray stone, but does not even chip the iron. He then praises his sword and vows that the enemy shall never possess it. In *laisse* 172, Roland smites the rock again, with the same results, then begins an elaborate lament in which he gives the sword's history and names the battles which he has won with its aid. At the end of the *laisse,* he repeats his fears that this weapon may fall into enemy hands. *Laisse* 173 begins with a repetition of Roland's futile efforts to destroy his sword and ends with another long speech in which Roland lists the relics embedded in the hilt and vows that it will never be used by a heathen. As Auerbach remarks, in his analysis of *laisses similaires:* "One intense action is replaced by a repetition of the same action, beginning at the same starting point time and again." Although each subsequent *laisse* presents new elements, there is always a repeated return to the point of departure, and it is this recurrent movement backwards that causes time to appear to be standing still.

The prolonging of the privileged moment through repetitive *laisses* and formulas is echoed on a contextual level in the scene where the sun stands still, allowing Charlemagne to overtake and defeat his pagan adversaries. This passage illustrates another interruption of the normal causal order in which events succeed one another, subject to the contingencies of time. Charlemagne's prayer that the sun stop its course is answered with a miracle. It is a moment of epiphany, when God's grace descends to prolong earthly time and thus to create an unexpected turn of events. Profane time is transcended, and we find ourselves face to face with the eternal. (pp. 90-3)

The third characteristic of time, according to Mendilow, is irreversibility. Since the sequence "earlier" and "later," "past" and "future" can proceed only in one direction, irreversible processes define a unidirectional causal order. Eggs cannot be unscrambled, nor can people return from the dead.

Since irreversibility is a concomitant of sequence, it likewise implies a beginning, middle, and end, the essential component being the end. The horizontal movement towards an end, which reflects the finite quality of secular time, is interrupted in ***La Chanson de Roland*** by frequent reminders of the eternal. The constant intrusion of sacred time into the time of everyday events creates a static vertical element which contributes to the non-linear paratactic structure of the poem.

The question of the irreversibility of the life processes is never really posed in the ***Roland*** because we are dealing with a society indoctrinated with a strong belief in an afterlife. The epic hero is not afraid of death. He does not see himself as moving towards an end, but accepts death as an integral part of time. As Auerbach remarks, "The penance laid upon the Franks when they pray and receive absolution before going into battle is to fight hard," for whoever falls in battle will be considered a martyr and can thus expect a place in Paradise.

In ***La Chanson de Roland,*** symbolic objects and figures enable man to transcend the limited and strictly contingent horizon of his situation. Angels appear and reappear to counsel and aid Charlemagne and to accompany the souls of those who die in battle to Paradise. The Franks also bear swords and armor which contain sacred relics. These religious tokens and angel archtypes remove man from his own time, from his individual, chronological, historical time, and project him, symbolically at least, into what Eliade calls "the Great Time," into a moment which cannot be measured because it has no duration.

In the ***Roland,*** such manifestations of the eternal have their parallel in the pagan world as well. In the course of the first battle, Archbishop Turpin kills Signorel, the wizard who has been to hell and back. Similarly, the pagans bear weapons and armor which were gifts from Satan. The jeweled shield of the Saracen Abisme was first presented to the Emir Galafe at Val Métas by a devil, then transmitted to Abisme.

In the ***Roland,*** objects and events have no autonomous or intrinsic value. They acquire a value, and in so doing become real, because they participate after one fashion or another in a reality that transcends time. Thus, in the poem, temporal events are the images or symbols of unchanging and atemporal truths. (pp. 93-4)

An analysis of time in ***La Chanson de Roland*** reveals a static atemporal pattern. That which is immobile or fixed dominates and is reflected in all aspects of the poem: its rigid value scheme, its archetypal characters and settings, its enumerative, paratactic syntax, and its repetitive use of standard motifs and formulas. There is no historical linear progression, no feeling of change or flow. Temporal connections often seem confused and the choice of tenses illogical, precisely because profane time is intimately linked with sacred time. Charlemagne converses freely with St. Gabriel, and, behind each major event, we sense the hand of God. The ***Roland*** does not reflect our usual sense of the past as different in quality from the present or future. Instead, past fact, present being, and future possibility are fused in a symbolic narrative through which we sense God's eternal present. (pp. 94-5)

Minnette Grunmann-Gaudet, "The Representation of Time in 'La chanson de Roland'," in The Nature of Medieval Narrative, *edited by Minnette Grunmann-Gaudet and Robin F. Jones, French Forum, 1980, pp. 77-97.*

FREDERICK GOLDIN (essay date 1978)

[*Goldin is an American educator and critic whose works include* German and Italian Lyrics of the Middle Ages *(1973) and* Lyrics of the Troubadours and Trouvères *(1973). In the following excerpt from the introduction to his translation of* The Song, *Goldin explicates the poem in terms of "epic necessity"—his theory that "on becoming an audience we know what is going to happen in the tale we listen to: our ordinary knowledge becomes foreknowledge, becomes an analogy of divine providence, and every event in the epic is made necessary . . . by the fact that we know it is going to occur."*]

Many readers of ***The Song of Roland*** . . . are distressed when they try to account for the motives behind certain actions, or to judge their moral value. What lies behind the hostility of Roland and Ganelon? Why does Ganelon explode with such murderous rage when he is named to carry out a plan that he himself had argued for? Why does he threaten Roland before the Emperor confirms the barons' choice? Above all, why does Ganelon commit treason? Or: Roland refuses to sound the olifant and thus ensures the martyrdom of the rear-guard. *Should* he have refused, many ask; was he right, or was he the victim of *démesure,* a term used by many who have written on this poem (but never by the one who composed it) to designate recklessness and inordinate pride? Does he regret the deaths he might have prevented; does he repent before he dies? And soon we find ourselves plagued by questions that arise from the moral uncertainty of everyday life—but not from the poem.

For the poem tells a story purportedly based on history—and in history, too, motives are often obscure and usually held to be less important than events. Furthermore, though the poem is not unconcerned with human motives, it does not—cannot—recognize the values upon which our judgments of our contemporaries are based; and the rash condemnation of Roland's act often expresses nothing more than what we all would think of a man who did the same thing today. Questions such as whether Roland should have acted as he did are out of court. They address themselves to a false issue and raise doubts concerning values regarded in the work itself as beyond questioning; they are alien to the epic world, obscurantist, and anachronistic, for the alternatives implied in such questions belong to another time and to another genre, with another truth to tell. That other genre, in the medieval period, is the romance, a courtly form adapted to the depiction of individual moral experience. (pp. 10-11)

The motives of the epic hero are . . . determined by the action. They conform to a well-known course of events, which the audience is willing to accept as historical fact. The story related in an epic is always a version of some famous and significant historical event, some episode that is crucial, or held to be crucial, in the history of the people among whom the epic arises. Epic action thus has an historical core: it is centered on a past event. Even if the story is fictitious, the events in it are treated as though they had really occurred in the past and engendered the present state of things. For the epic is concerned with "actions irremediably completed."

Since the epic must have an historical core, it must always look back, and its point of view will always be anchored in the presence of its audience. Both the poet and the audience look back to a critical moment in history, the event from which their world emerged, the past they share in every performance. For the epic genre is rooted in the idea of performance; every epic poem needs listeners in attendance. Even if those listeners are utterly alien in time and place, they are bound to the poem. For if the pastness of epic action is essential, there must be a present audience—even if it is an implicit audience—by which that pastness is established and the continuance of its effect realized. Nowadays the old epic poem has an audience of readers, and we look back to other moments in the past to find the roots of our being. But the poem will not modify its demand on us; it insists with ever greater conviction: *Charlemagne is our Emperor*. And so the poem's effect on us depends on our willingness to respond to its words, at least for the time that we play the role of audience, as though we were not alien to this remote part of the human past. For, in fact, this moment too is at the root of our being.

In this one respect we today can identify ourselves with those who heard this poem in the beginning, because we take up a similar position regarding the time in which the action is set. We corroborate its retrospective point of view, we complete its context: with every performance, or with every reading, the presence of the audience establishes the pastness of the action. The audience therefore plays an indispensable role in the creation of the epic world: it calls that world forth by looking back upon it. (pp. 11-12)

The world of ***The Song of Roland*** is ruled by conditional necessity, *necessitas condicionis*. The condition that makes things necessary is "added," as Boethius says, to every event in that world, and it is we, the audience, who add it. Before we become an audience, we know, or are expected to know, what has occurred in history, or in the revered legend that the poem regards as the most authentic history; and so on becoming an audience we know what is going to happen in the tale we listen to: our ordinary knowledge becomes foreknowledge, becomes an analogy of divine providence, and every event in the epic is made necessary (in the Boethian sense) by the fact that we know it is going to occur, by the condition of the audience's knowledge. We know what happened in history; and since this or that event lies entirely in the past, we know further that it is a part of the history of the world thus far, that it participates in a transcendental design: it therefore has to happen, it is *necessary*.

Epic action is set in the past, as required by the genre. The historical event is now viewed within the frame of a narrative; it is integrated into a vast structure, endowed with significance, exempted from chance: the aesthetic form of the epic reflects the transcendental design of history. And since the epic event is thus completely enacted and framed, it is fully present to us in all its moments, we know it from beginning to end. Therefore, we can say, prompted by Philosophy: we know that he will walk, and therefore he *must* walk; for we knew, before the first notes of the song were intoned and we became an audience, that he *did* walk. We know—and our knowledge precedes every event, every cause, every motive—that Roland will refuse to sound the olifant: therefore, his refusal is necessary, for it is accomplished. The witnessed and believed authenticity of his act is all that counts. His motives, whatever they are, are at best secondary causes, completely determined by the action and significant in this poem, not because of what they bring about, but because of what they reveal: the loyal spirit of a true hero. We must regard his great spirit, his proud motives, and his famous act as praiseworthy, exemplary, pleasing to God, because they are necessary, foreseen, exactly as they occurred, in the destiny of Sweet France. For otherwise the *Geste Francor* would be nothing but the history of accidents and whims.

We have no right to ask: *should* he have done what he did? shouldn't he have considered another way? shouldn't he have been more reasonable? Questions like these deny the terrible necessity of history and the monumental dignity of the epic. They are questions brought in from the Age of the Team. Once we view the epic world from a true perspective, that of an audience witnessing the reenactment of an unalterable past, we see a world governed only by providential force. *Within* that world, however, considered only in his nature, the epic hero moves in his own present with undiminished freedom of the will: "I would be a fool to sound the olifant," says he; or "I shall strike a thousand seven hundred blows." The unpredictable present and the immutable past thus wonderfully coincide in an epic poem.

It is the past, or rather the audience's sense of the past, that ennobles these figures and their deeds, as it determines the form and technique of the poem. Because of the double perspective from which we, the audience, view the action—we see it looking back from our present, and looking forward from the hero's present—we experience at once in every figure and event the two forces of a free human will and a transcendental historic purpose. This is obviously true of an epic poem like ***The Song of Roland,*** in which this purpose is revealed as divine Providence: in Charlemagne's dreams, for example, or in the three judicial battles, the will of God announces itself. But even when all the figures and events are the consequences of a mindless causality devoid of purpose, we still recognize the presence of a transcendent design. That is because every epic presents its narrative as history, no matter if it is really a fiction. It demands of us that we regard its action, down to the rightness of the last detail, as a crucial part of the real past—of the *living* past, for the world that surrounds us as we listen derives from it. Even if some event were in its inception completely accidental, it was nevertheless caused, and it produced consequences that led, in turn, to a ramifying pattern of causes; and so, what began as an accident becomes bound by causality and consequence to the ineradicable continuity of the past. For if we were to recreate the fabric of history, we would need this event to weave into our pattern. No matter how it happened, it has led somehow to the present state of things, to the facts we find in our world and the condition of our community, and so becomes, as we look back upon it, a part of the providential past: as things have turned out, it has served a purpose; therefore, it is necessary. (pp. 13-15)

As epic necessity imposes coherence on the past, so it bestows dignity on men and events, for it removes them from the vanity of a personal will and identifies them with a divine intention. Necessity eradicates accidentality and creates, wih its tremendous retrospective power, a need for every moment. The hero's motives are exactly right, even when he appears to a lesser man (like Oliver) to be most willful and undisciplined, for they realize a purpose too great for ordinary men to understand. He desires, with all his character and vitality, to bring about the crucial facts of history. Roland does what he does because he must do it, because the event has already taken place, in our view, and he has no choice. He is the agent of an accomplished action, and we are privileged to witness the true hero's graceful conformity to the rule of necessity.

Because we know the history of these events, we see Roland's acts as part of a pattern; and though we may later force ourselves to change our minds, we first see every pattern as the product of a deliberate will. For the point of view that sees, or projects, an immense design where there is only the welter of blind causality is a religious point of view; and so, even when we reject the substance of religion, we adopt its view of history when we are the audience of an epic poem. Roland's acts are part of an historical pattern, and we perceive them as emanating from the Will that produces history. Because of the ennobling effect of necessity, because his actions are always sanctioned by the demands of that transcendent pattern that we, in our present role as audience, cannot dissociate from the movement of a higher will, the hero can never be denounced as vain, or proud, or lacking in wisdom; nor, it follows, can his enemy ever be dismissed as simply a scoundrel. We must never judge Roland's motives by our common freedom and our common sense, because they are purely epic motives, his personal resolve to bring about what has already been enacted. Thus it is through necessity that the epic hero realizes his greatness and his humility; for he is the agent of providence.

The poet has exploited the effect of the pastness of the action and has arranged the narrative so as to put Roland's eminence beyond doubt; at the very least, if we do not simply admire Roland's actions, we refrain from judging them. But we are meant to admire them. Roland is the only one who knows the right thing to do when the Christians are confronted with Marsilion's offer of peace. The others have every conceivable good reason for accepting that offer. For one thing, nobody in the council knows that it is a trick. And Marsilion does promise to become Christian: his conversion was the object of Charlemagne's expedition. Naimon and Ganelon speak ably from principles—the highest principles. Roland speaks from experience—Basile and Basan had been slain earlier through Marsilion's treachery on a similar occasion: if Marsilion tricked them then, it is likely that he is tricking them now. They must not give up all that they have achieved for a mere promise; the war that Charlemagne came to fight is not over. But the others do not listen, for they are reasonable, and tired. (pp. 17-19)

Roland tells the barons all that they need to know in order to make the right decision. We do not see in this any sign of a moral failing among the barons—they are all men of principle worn out with fighting—and least of all any sign of Roland's *démesure* or bellicosity. What takes place is the revelation of Roland's privileged position in the world. He is right, and all the others are wrong—and that is all: this scene does not show that he is right for the wrong reasons, or that Naimon is wrong for the right ones—two impossible and inconceivable ideas in the Middle Ages; it does not even show that his natural and unaided judgment is better than theirs. It simply shows that he is graced with the right decision. But in the world that this poem celebrates, he cannot be right by accident: not only his decision but his entire attitude is right—his militant response to the pagans, his whole sense of what a Christian knight must do is nearest to what pleases God, for it comes from God.

The massacre at Rencesvals does not begin with Roland's refusal to sound the olifant: it begins right here, in "the council that went wrong," as the poem says. And we are expected to respond to Roland's act at Rencesvals in the light of the grace bestowed upon him in this council, remembering always that he is right, that the perilous position of the rear-guard would never have come about if his voice in council had carried the day, and that after Roland's death Charles ends up doing exactly what Roland had urged; so that the fact of his having been right then confers an authority upon his actions now, at Rencesvals. For judge him as one will, if he was bellicose, impulsive, proud, and foolish in council (that is how Ganelon judges him), he is all of those things now; and he was right then—these qualities led him, completely unaware of Marsilion's plan, to make the right decision. Now the pattern repeats itself at Rencesvals, and Naimon's wisdom is replaced by Oliver's wisdom. We the audience, knew that Roland was right in council because Marsilion's perfidy had been enacted before us. He is doing now what he did then, following the dictates of the Christian vassal's calling with unquestioning faith, though now we cannot see the corroborative light.

Still, it may be there, and the possibility of its presence, the inappropriateness of our moral categories to Roland's act, the very fact that what he does eludes definitive judgment, all indicate that we are not *supposed* to judge. It is an error as well to think that Roland regrets his act and repents before he dies. If he were truly to repent, it would have to mean that his act—his refusal to summon help—was free of all necessity; in that case he could not be an epic hero, and he would become the proper victim of the audience's common sense. For the moment we think that he should have acted otherwise, we deny the force of necessity. If there is no necessity, there is no providence; and if there is no providence, then Roland's heroism becomes an aberration, a state of madness, a terrible display of the private will gone berserk. Only from one point of view—Roland's own—is his choice completely free. From the perspective of the poem's audience, he *had* to do what he did, for the battle of Rencesvals was now locked into the great design of history—the glorious history of France. From that perspective, the action he takes is necessary, pre-established; and Roland's greatness lies in his willingness to carry it out. We are moved by his warrior's rapture as he speaks of the duties of the vassal, not because we share his notion of loyalty, but because we see his notion of loyalty leading him to fulfill the role into which, from the audience's point of view, history has already cast him.

Roland explains why he refuses to summon help: he says that to do so would bring shame upon himself, upon his family, and upon France. He also gives the reasons *why* it would bring shame. He believes that it is his duty to fight alone: that is why the poem makes him twice speak the famous passage on the vassal's duty at this moment. He is also sure that he can win, and it would be shameful to summon help when he and his men can defeat the Saracens alone, for he had sworn that Charles would not lose a single man, not a horse or a mule, as the army made its way through the passes. The concerns that led him to refuse to summon help—honor, lineage, sweet France—are named and praised by Charles, later, in his lament for Roland. These are the lights by which Roland acts. But we, the audience, enlightened by necessity, can see more: if Roland calls for help and Charles returns, the battle will lose its judicial character. Only if there is a victory of the few against the many can the outcome of the battle reveal the will of God. If Roland is right, then God has bestowed upon his outlook a special grace. He is the agent of God's will, the supreme vassal, and God has sanctified his calling, endowed it with a mission. In this we can detect an historical resonance. When the Church, in the interests of the peace movement and the crusade, set about enlisting the warrior class into its service, it did not try to temper the ferocious instincts of these men but rather attempted to train their martial spirit, in all its savage pride, upon a new, universal, Christian goal.

This may be the best moment to warn against importing twentieth-century sanctities into this 900-year-old poem. The Saracens in ***The Song of Roland*** as the fantastic names and the ludicrous creed attributed to them make clear, are the postulated enemies of God, which meant in the Middle Ages that they are the force opposed to all human values. The poem is not, therefore, a genocidal tirade against the civilization of Islam; the Saracens here are demonic reflections, human souls degraded into automatons because they are without God—without reverence and humility. The true faith they lack is the faith of love, the commitment to the human community. Charlemagne naturally looks back to the time of Daniel, his brother-heir; but, except for the fathers who lose their sons, there is no kinship and fidelity among the Sracacen generations—they have no past to look back to. They are agents of discontinuity, mad votaries who trample the idols they worship underfoot, who disintegrate the structures they mimic. Compassion for the enemy would be treason to man's community.

But that does not mean that the human reality of the enemy is obliterated in this great poem. Sometimes vehement hatred of another signifies a greater human commitment than pity, for pity often means that one has given up hope for the other's chances and, amid copious tears, written him off. It is said of Baligant that if he had been Christian he would have been a great man, a remark that is often mistaken as an expression of blind intolerance. But it is really an explicit recognition, in the poem's early feudal idiom, of the secular equality of Christian and pagan, and of the infinitely redeemable humanity of the enemy. The pagans are condemned, not because they are without God, but because they are without God by their own choice. They have used their heroic powers to thwart human value, but to their dying breath they have the chance to be converted by love. That is, as things turn out, a privilege reserved for Bramimunde alone. The others, if they are not killed by the sword, are converted by it. The poem's outlook is thus irreconcilable with the celebration of pluralism characteristic of our enlightenment; but it also excludes the ultimate nightmare, our nightmare, the vision that we dread: the tribalism of the industrial age, which regards those on the far side of the world as alien in essence, morally strange, incapable of our humanity.

Each man in this feudal community finds his place in a hierarchical structure of loyalties that ends in Charlemagne, to whom all are bound, as he is bound to them in the obligation to protect them. Each of the barons holds a position with respect to his own men—the men he brought with him to battle—analogous to that of Charles with respect to the great barons and ultimately to the whole community. The men are bound to the lord, the lord to Charlemagne. The word "man," *hume,* is a technical term here, designating the sworn vassal, one who has done homage to a lord in exchange for protection, nurture, and gifts. The relation that binds man and lord, and man and man, in this way is designated *amur,* love; so that when Ganelon, at the height of his rage, shouts at Roland: *Jo ne vus aim nïent,* "I do not love you," that is no understated and ironical insult but the most terrible thing he could utter. It means: the bonds of loyalty are cut, we are enemies. It is a *desfiance,* a withdrawl of faith, a declaration of war, and, in the feudal age, it legalized revenge. This is a point on which Ganelon pins his life at his trial.

We can see here how the poem depicts Ganelon always as a conscientious follower of the law and of the oldest feudal values. One of the many instances of perfect feudal love (in the sense defined above) occurs in the scene in which Ganelon parts from his men to go on his mission to the Saracens. Here we see the deportment of true vassals and a true lord: they beg to accompany him, he refuses to endanger their lives recklessly and provides for the succession of his son and the peace of his realm in the event of his death. And here we see as well the true Ganelon, the essential Ganelon—the man who, in his whole-hearted obedience to the law, subverts its intention and works the destruction of his community. For the effect of his brave departure is to sow the seeds of discord and to endanger the life of Charles's greatest vassal. Ganelon the traitor is a pure creature of convention: his every word and deed are preceded by a passage indicating how someone regards him and what someone expects of him, and everything he does or says confirms that description and fulfills those expectations. Depending on who describes or observes him, he is a raging malcontent, a faithful vassal, a false counselor, a revered lord of ancient lineage and long service, a liar, a protector. Note the utter inconsequence of his bringing up Basile and Basan after he had argued in favor of accepting Marsilion's offer of peace. In recalling their memory he is restating a point made earlier by Roland. He has completely reversed himself. His successive states of character are bewildering, all the more striking in comparison with the consistency of his effect: he is continually programed and reprogramed, and invariably destructive. Only in the trial is he named and defined forever.

The fact that Ganelon, the traitor, is repeatedly depicted as the perfect lord and vassal is eloquent testimony to the secret, indwelling weakness of the structure over which Charles presides. Ganelon never breaks any rules: he sees himself, and rightly so, as an upholder of the most venerable law, the earliest bonds of human community. In his first outburst against Roland, he denounces his stepson for putting a kinsman in danger and thus breaking an ancient and prefeudal bond. And yet, Ganelon is a traitor. *In fact, it is by following the rules that Ganelon commits his treason.* That is the unspeakable wonder of Ganelon: he betrays his land by conforming to its law.

He denies with his last breath that he committed treason and insists that what he did was legal. This argument is no courtroom trick. His sincerity and the authenticity of his claim are refleted in the truly admiring portrait that the poet inserts at this moment; in the admiration of his peers; in the unwillingness of his judges to condemn him, intimidated as they are by Pinabel, who will fight for him in the trial by battle and whose immense strength reflects the strength of Ganelon's position; in his status as a noble lord of a great and ancient family. He is no outsider, no Sinon, but an authentic member of this society and a passionate believer in its original law. He claims that revenge was his right and that he had fulfilled all of the established prescriptions by which revenge is sanctioned. "I took vengeance," he says; "I'll admit to no treason in that." For the right to take revenge is a basic right in the feudal community ruled by Charles, the oldest sanction of justice. Now the trial must determine whether there is a higher right than vengeance.

In the grandeur, sincerity, and persuasiveness of Ganelon is reflected the weakness of the entire system, for Ganelon, as he sees it, did nothing more than what the system authorized. And he is right; nobody had ever imagined the things their covenant could sanction. It is a fact that Ganelon could never have committed his treason had he lacked what the system provided and his own honored place within it. From his native status and his adherence to the law arises his treason. Without due process, without the prescriptions of custom, without a communal heritage of ethics and rights (as, for example, the right to take revenge), without those conventions that preserve the life of a community, Ganelon would have lacked the means to betray his native land. He is thereforethe arch-traitor, for through him the system betrays itself. Ganelon plays an essential role in this system: he is its traitor. He brings to pass the unsuspected consequences of its fundamental laws, endows it with a shadow. For his presence is as necessary as the shadow cast by a body: if a body exists, its shadow necessarily exists; without the shadow there can be no body. Without the traitor or the traitorous force, there can be no system. In Ganelon we see, not a man who for one reason or another—rage, disaffection, avarice—*becomes* a traitor, but a man who was a traitor from the very beginning, a traitor by necessity, whose destructiveness is uncaused because his essence precedes every cause. For what can be the cause of his treason? It is true that Roland provoked him; one may even believe Ganelon's assertion that Roland cheated him—and these would be sufficient causes if Ganelon were only an avenger. But he is something more—the trial proves it: he is a *traitor,* and no motive conceivable in the poem explains that. His uncaused act can accommodate every cause conceivable in the feudal world. The mystery of his treason is a sign of his elemental being.

Ganelon is the destructive element of every secular structure, the indwelling cause of its instability. In him we recognize the traitorous possibility of every institution. Custom can betray, because it can preserve and reinforce an evil. The law can betray, because it can show the criminal how to commit a crime and be acquitted. Even loyalty can betray, because the object of one's loyalty may obscure higher values: Ganelon keeps faith with his family and his ethical code and just for that reason cannot see the supreme good of the Emperor's mission or the rights of the community sworn to fulfilling it. Praise of one's comrades, the longing for peace, piety itself can betray.

Ganelon's treason reveals that the precious rights and customs of every community will tear it to pieces if they are not hierarchized. Some rights have precedence over others, and the right of the King in fulfilling his God-given role has precedence over all. This is a hard-won principle, for according to the poem, no conflict had brought it down to earth before this, and it is not articulated until the trial, at the very end, by one man—"not too tall, not too short"—a man whose eloquence lies in his lack of personal brilliance and his willingness to stake his life on that principle. And still no one sees the principle, save Charles and his man: the barons do not see it, they are blind and filled with panic before the grandeur of Ganelon's lineage and the strength of Pinabel. They are reasonable, moderate, forgiving, and therefore almost traitors themselves, for they do not know what is at stake—they bear no scars, they cannot see, they did not witness the martyrdom at Rencesvals. It takes the hand of God in the battle between Charles's properly nondescript man and the mighty and beautiful Pinabel to reveal the turth: the right of the King precedes all others.

Through the crime of its native-born traitor, the system has discovered its essential weakness, and a better system has emerged, the system of Charlemagne's great Christian empire. The grave losses caused by Ganelon's treason are redeemed, transformed into the precious suffering of rebirth, the moment he is declared a traitor. For a new state is brought into being by the treason of Ganelon, which appears as a shadow-act of the great treason that inaugurated the salvation of the human race, and by the trial in which he is condemned. For the first time, the reality of *dulce France* is fully established in the poem: sweet France is what he betrayed. For the first time, France is more than the remote and undefined object of the Christian's love and the Saracens' hate. Here, in the trial of Ganelon, it is involved in the action in the way that the other characters are, both as sufferer and as agent. The trial that defines the identity of Ganelon affirms the existence of a coherent political being, a state, whose presence is now immediate and effective. And this dramatic appearance of the state within the frame of the poem's action comes about for this reason: when something can be betrayed, that is proof that it exists, that it is no longer a mass of disunited powers but a defined being capable of engendering obligations. It can be betrayed because it is real and has the right to demand loyalty. And when this being is the community of a people and its king, then the treason committed against them is proof that they have established the institutions that make up a state; for Ganelon has shown that these institutions are the necessary condition of treason. And further, when this being declares itself betrayed, that is proof that it has become aware of its identity, that an act of self-consciousness, a *prise de conscience,* has taken place. And finally, when the state condemns its traitor, it reveals not only its power as an entity but also the ethical basis of its claim to loyalty: the destruction of the state through treason would be an arch-crime because it would threaten the basis of all human community, of human existence itself. Thus in the same act the state declares its identity and asserts its right to exist.

This is the precious moment for which every other moment in the poem was a preparation. We can recall, for example, the "impotence" and "passivity" of the King when Ganelon names Roland to command the rear-guard. Charles's immobility stems from the fact that he is legally paralyzed: Roland has not been chosen for the rear-guard as Charles's vassal, and so Charles is not in a position, even though he is Roland's lord, to order him to stay or go. Roland is chosen by an assembly of the barons, who, in giving the King their counsel, are acting as representatives of the whole state and, in effect, exercising the authority of the state. That is why the King's weakness at this moment is a preparation for the great trial at the end: the King cannot become strong until an act of treason is declared.

Charles's behavior in this scene is usually interpreted as a reflection of the king's historic position vis-à-vis the barons at the time of the poem's composition. There may be something to that idea, but the full effect of this scene is clear only at the end of the poem. If this scene reflects an historical situation, it does not do so directly, for the barons are not shown acting in their own interests against those of the King. They are acting on a state matter, and Roland is named to perform a service to *all*. That is why it is a tremendous moment when Tierri says to Charles: "Roland was acting in *your* service": for the first time the idea is put forth that service to all is identical with service to Charles, and vice versa, that Charles embodies the interests and authority of the state.

Thus it is only after the trial that it becomes possible to define the meaning of "sweet France" and the principle of its unity. Before that, we get only fleeting glimpses of a certain spirit shared by those who fight in that land's name: the courteousness and companionship of Roland and his comrades, the universal love for Charles, the sumptuousness and concord of the Christian camp. But these impressions are obscured by others: the disagreements in council, the sudden revelations of Charles's weakness, the private feuds, the disintegrative allegiances to family and private interests. The French, when they think of their land, remember their wives and daughters, their fiefs and domains. Thus the expression *France* has a certain effect but no clear definition: Baligant and the other pagans speak with perfect ease of "sweet France."

Before the trial, France was defined only by its outer enemies: the hostility of the Saracens proved that France was *dulce,* pleasing to God, for it was locked in combat with the enemies of God. Now, however, through the condemnation of its native-born traitor, France takes on a native character and reveals exactly what it is that pleases God: it is a state in which all men are bound in loyalty through their ultimate obligation to the King, a state whose unity and well-being derive from the subordination of all privileges, rights, and interests to the King chosen by God. At the end of the poem Charles receives a new mission as head of a new born state.

Before the treason, when Roland was still alive, the God-given principle of the supremacy of the King was not yet clear, despite his own exemplary loyalty to Charles. Because of Roland's eminence, the greatest reverence could still be given to horizontal obligations—to family loyalties and the demands of personal honor—until Ganelon revealed the disintegrating effect of these unordered rights. But now all is arranged as it is pleasing to God, in a vertical hierarchy that ends, on this earth, in the King.

In other words: after the trial, as the system expunges its essential traitor, it also makes an end of itself: we do not see emerging from the trial the system that had always existed only now in a healthier condition, but rather a different system, something new and nearer to God's intention. Modern readers may be satisfied with an interpretation of the poem as a justification and celebration of a political and religious order. But for the audience that shared its past and its vision of the future, there was more. The action of ***The Song of Roland*** foreshadows . . . the great apocalyptic battle and the end of time as prophesied in the Book of Revelation. That last great battle will also be caused by treason, and it will end in the Last

Charlemagne grieves for Roland on the battlefield.

Judgment, after which the world will be set right again. Now since Charles's battle against the pagans prefigures that final battle, it must also prefigure that last stage in the restoration of the world: the historical event reveals the eschatological truth. Viewed in this light ***The Song of Roland*** resembles what Dante calls "the allegory of the theologians," setting forth real events—things that really happened—as a revelation of the last things to come. And when the action of the epic is finally completed, when the historical event has taken place, then the condition of the world is in fact closer to the final eschatological perfection that the event foreshadows.

A new state arises from the destruction wrought by treason. The traitor has used to evil purpose all that was good in his society and has thereby served the good: his treason made the King strong. The poem draws a parallel between the crimes of Ganelon and Judas: an immeasurable good arose from both. Therefore this too, this ultimate service of evil to the good, is foreseen. In John 6:70 Jesus says: *Have not I chosen you twelve, and one of you is a devil?* (pp. 19-27)

Thus it is foreseen that the traitor must participate in every structure and be the necessary cause of human amelioration. Here again we see that the poem wants its narrative to be judged in the light of providence; and in that light Roland's death is a great victory, and the cause of great good for all—martyrdom and a place among the flowers of Paradise for those who fell, a new state for those who survive and inherit the earth. Of this new state we are permitted to see only the circumstances of its birth and in Tierri its characteristic man. Its essential traitor has not yet appeared: that belongs to another story. And so we are shown a view of human progress, the providential cycle of treason and rebirth, which will come to an end in the conflict between the last traitor, the Antichrist, and the hordes of heaven—the great battle prefigured in the episode of Baligant. Through this painful cycle a small advance has been won, the foundation of a new state, whose good lies in loyalty, or, in the feudal sense, love. (p. 28)

Frederick Goldin, in an introduction to The Song of Roland, *translated by Frederick Goldin, Norton, 1978, pp. 3-46.*

GERARD J. BRAULT (essay date 1978)

[*Brault is an American educator and author of* Early Blazon: Heraldic Terminology in the Twelfth and Thirteenth Centuries with Special Reference to Arthurian Literature *(1972). A translator of* The Song, *he has written an extensive* laisse-*by*-laisse *commentary on the poem. In the following excerpt from his introduction to that work, Brault examines the depiction of several key characters and groups in* The Song, *noting that Charlemagne "is the most complex figure" and Oliver "without a doubt the most difficult character to interpret."*]

Nowhere is the distance between modern practice and the art of the ***Song of Roland*** greater than in the depiction of characters. . . .

Distinct characterization such as we find in modern literature—often aided by details concerning physical appearance, clothing, gestures, speech mannerisms, and quirks of various sorts—is absent, for the most part, in the ***Song of Roland,*** just as it was in the art of the period. A few scattered indications, notably concerning Charlemagne (deliberateness, fierceness, regal bearing, sensitivity), Ganelon (arrogance, deceitfulness), and the Saracens (diabolism), provide revealing glimpses of personality, but Turoldus does not always rely on such particulars to convey character traits. In fact, individuals tend to look and think a good deal alike and to use the same kind of language. Indeed, personal information rarely imparts meaning in absolute fashion, identical attitudes or features often being subject to widely divergent interpretations.

Characters each have a nature, good or bad, identified from the outset of the poem by an epithet or a phrase . . . , by being Christian or Saracen, or simply by being one of us. . . . (p. 89)

The more important the character, the more his goodness shines forth or his villainy looms large. . . . The character traits one can read in another's face, combined with the advice evildoers receive from Satan, explain how the Saracen messengers are able immediately to identify Charlemagne even though they have never seen him before, and they suggest the reason why Blancandrin, on the road to Saragossa, seems to know that Ganelon will prove to be treacherous.

This categorization . . . governs behavior and outlook to a remarkable degree, for, as a rule, individuals do not change their essences. Good characters learn, acquiring knowledge or experience that edifies or scandalizes them in the etymological sense, that is, builds up or acts as a stumbling block to their faith. Evil characters become more villainous as their despair grows darker. The only exception is the convert, epitomized by Bramimonde, whose complete transformation from evil to good is wrought through the miracle of grace. Other personages simply do not change or develop in the modern acceptation of these terms.

Characterization in the ***Song of Roland*** is often strongly affected by role-playing. Thus while relatively few exterior traits distinguish Charlemagne, Roland, or Ganelon, the modeling of a character after a well-known archetype (e.g., Abraham, Christ, Judas) tends to add the prefiguration's virtues or vices to the individual's portrait. This rubbing-off of pesonality is an important part of the poetic process. Scenic formulas and transpositions produce the same sort of effect upon the protagonists as does role-playing in these figural representations.

A distinction needs to be drawn between conscious and unconscious role-playing. Evil characters, notably when aping, are totally unaware of the image on which they are patterning themselves, and with such derogatory effect upon the audience. On the other hand, as Charles and Roland probe ever deeper into the mysteries of faith and martyrdom, they grow increasingly aware of the archetypal figures whose sublime deeds they reenact.

Turoldus conceived of his characters in medieval fashion, that is, as being motivated by a central virtue or vice, each of these traits being associated or in conflict with corresponding qualities or faults. Although this system of virtues and vices is firmly rooted in biblical and patristic sources, the mundane aspect of moral strengths and weaknesses is also depicted. Thus while Largesse, the chief virtue of the king, is at times viewed as a reflection of divine Largitas, it can also refer to more familiar forms of liberality.

Chivalric virtues, which figure prominently in the ***Song of Roland,*** had not yet been reduced to the rigid code one begins to notice increasingly in the second half of the twelfth century, when the Church's influence also becomes apparent. However, it is a mistake to assume that the only virtue expected of a knight in Turoldus's day was manly courage and that loyalty was merely a contractual obligation between lord and vassal. There can be no denying the fact that the twelfth century witnessed important cultural changes, but the evolution in institutions and in manners and mores was gradual, and sporadic early manifestations of what were later to become highly developed traditions are sometimes noticed. When, in the *Pèlerinage de Charlemagne,* Oliver courts King Hugo's daughter, and when, in the *Pseudo-Turpin Chronicle,* Roland places a pillow under the head of his resting adversary during a truce, these gestures foreshadow the courtesy epitomized by Chrétien de Troyes's knights. One must be careful to distinguish between idealized views and reality, for literature is the province of enhanced images. The fact that the eleventh century may actually have seen little of the heroic stances or of the magnanimity found in the ***Song of Roland*** did not prevent Turoldus from visualizing such behavior. Moreover, in all likelihood, the poet's portrayals helped shape later conceptualizations of ideal conduct.

A character's virtues or vices are chiefly manifested through his actions and words. Physical appearance provides important clues to an individual's nature, but looks can also be deceiving. Impressions of a different sort are gained when the poet himself intervenes, praising or condemning deeds as they occur, or in retrospect. An individual's observations about another—whether in the form of an assertion, an anecdote, or an insult—furnish us with information of yet another kind, for they must always be carefully weighed in light of the fact that the speaker represents a point of view that is not necessarily shared by the author. The stories Ganelon tells about Roland to Blancandrin and later to Charlemagne are intended to vilify his stepson. Oliver's description of his companion's anticipated behavior, when the hero volunteers to go to Saragossa, is self-serving—he himself wishes to go on this mission—and therefore suspect. His characterization of Roland's decisions in the oliphant debate represents a very understandable reaction, but it also constitutes a refusal to come to terms with the deeper meaning of his friend's stand.

Finally, an individual may provide important insights into his own psychological make-up while boasting or talking about others, especially in tense moments.

Self-praise strikes the modern reader as being unseemly in the hero. However, the medieval audience drew a distinction between truthful claims and hollow assertions. Thus Roland's detailing of his past and future accomplishments not only constitutes behavior that is quite acceptable but also provides information which is essential to the narrative. However, the Saracens' *gabs* are repeatedly shown to be vain. Formal laments, which laud a fallen companion's qualities, and insults, which bring out an adversary's villainy, are similarly viewed with suspicion today because each occurs under circumstances notorious for fostering extravagant speech. When reading the ***Song of Roland,*** it must always be assumed that praise for a Christian and scorn for a pagan are well merited, and never the reverse. On the other hand, Ganelon's attempts, in the apple anecdote, to portray Roland as a diabolic seducer and, during the trial, as a felon motivated by greed, unwittingly show his own true colors.

If the battlefield discussion concerning the sounding of the oliphant is viewed as an externalization of an internal debate—the form is identical in each case—Oliver's words can be interpreted as an effort to convince himself that he should assume Roland's stance, or as a reflection of Roland's agony of decision. This explains in part Turoldus's emphasis, in the lines following v. 1093 (Rollant est proz e Oliver est sage [''Roland is valiant and Oliver is wise'']), on the equality of worthiness found in the two companions-in-arms.

One aspect of character depiction, indirect delineation of personality traits, is worthy of special note: Turoldus projects facets of an individual's psychology and spirit on certain objects in his possession.

The praise that Roland lavishes upon Durendal represents a detailing of the hero's own valor and stunning achievements. The sword's brilliance is literally a reflection of the hero's virtues. This radiance corresponds exactly to the shining quality of the gold ground in Emperor portraits of the day. The jewel-encrusted ivory oliphant, like Durendal's priceless ornamentation, symbolizes its owner's matchless qualities, and the horn's ascending voice evokes Roland's undying spirit. Joyeuse plays a similar role in portraying aspects of Charlemagne's character. These emanations link Emperor and nephew in mystical fashion. Conversely, the very name Precieuse is a mocking reflection of Baligant's hollowness, and Murgleis and other sinister names cast an evil glow—like that of the lantern-lit Saracen ships—on the persons with whom they are associated.

Roland and Oliver are brothers-in-arms, but the resemblance between Charlemagne and his nephew goes far beyond community of interest and solidarity of purpose.The hero is the Emperor's right arm, a physical union symbolizing moral and spiritual oneness as well. The lance is an apt symbol for Roland and it is specifically identified with the hero in the first of Charlemagne's dreams. The poet doubtless wishes to suggest that Roland, like his weapon, is straight and strong. But Roland's lance is also an extension of his arm and is thus associated with the right-arm image. Uncle and nephew maintain their separate individualities, but such integration implies remarkable psychological compatibility. Each character's personality reflects various facets of his counterpart's being. Nowhere in the ***Song of Roland*** is the fact that weapons often mirror their owner's moral excellence or depravity more in evidence than in the case of Durendal and Joyeuse, whose brilliance, holiness, and invincibility are virtually indistinguishable, pointing to the poet's similar concept of Charles and Roland. Thus the debate over whether Charles or Roland is the chief hero of Turoldus's poem is pointless: One character is the extension of the other, and the author clearly had no intention of according one precedence over the other. Roland and Alda are also closely linked and reflect each other by virtue of their betrothal, their shared death—including a similarity of phrasing in this respect—and their virginity. (pp. 89-93)

The Emperor is the most complex figure in the ***Song of Roland,*** for aspects of his personality enjoyed an independent existence exceeding by far the limits of the poem. Other personages in Turoldus's epic are historical figures, and legends about a number of these individuals, notably Roland, had doubtless been elaborated before the present work was composed. However, these stories pale beside the Charlemagne myth, which experienced an extraordinary growth throughout Europe, particularly in France and Germany in the centuries following the Emperor's reign. (pp. 93-4)

Biblical associations abound in Turoldus's depiction of the protean figure of Charlemagne, for he is successively—at times simultaneously—Abraham, Christ the Judge, Joshua, the Ancient of Days, Christ the Reaper, Constantine, and Job. First and foremost, however, Charles is a Messianic figure who incarnates Sapientia and plays the role of Abraham. (p. 95)

The narrative of the Sacrifice of Isaac in Genesis mentions no emotion on Abraham's part. Charles evinces the same blind and spontaneous obedience to the strange promptings of the Almighty. However, Turoldus portrays him in a more human light, repeatedly stressing the Emperor's great anguish as the dimensions of his role are gradually revealed to him by the omen of the dropped gauntlet, Ganelon's nomination of Roland to the rearguard, the premonitory dreams, and, finally, the traitor's attempt at deception when the sound of the oliphant is heard.

It has been stated that the vagueness of the warnings received by Charles—he knows who will betray him but not how the deed will be perpetrated—explains the Emperor's inability to stay the onrushing catastrophe. Charlemagne is guided by an inner light that, the poet makes clear, comes directly from God. He may not know all, but this is not the point. In the gospel narrative of the Last Supper, the details of Christ's knowledge of Judas's treachery do not concern us. What matters in the New Testament and in the ***Song of Roland*** is the determination to play the role assigned by God to the bitter end.

Charles survives his nephew, and it is obvious that Turoldus attached a good deal of importance to his serving as a posthumous witness to Roland's edifying death. (pp. 95-6)

For the American scholar Roland's essential virtue is his loyalty, that is, the unswerving allegiance he gives to his friends, his family, his king, his country, and his faith. To sustain him in his fidelity, the poet grants him exceptional courage but also the fault of his virtue, rashness. According to Jenkins [see 1924 excerpt by Jenkins], this tragic flaw, coupled with excessive sensitivity as to his military reputation, brings about the disaster. Roland recognizes his error, has a change of heart, and atones for his misdeed by his suffering and his death. Conversely, Faral considers valor to be the hero's chief quality, and, while he concedes that Roland's bravery borders on recklessness, he insists that Turoldus merely wished thereby to enhance the beauty and grandeur of his heroism. Roland remained true to himself and in no way felt the need to expiate any sin or wrongdoing.

Jenkins points out that it is only Roland's enemies who accuse him of pride and that Oliver's charge of recklessness comes "in the heat of battle and the exasperation of defeat." This distinction, which is not drawn by Faral or by most of the critics in either scholar's wake, is crucial to our understanding of the poet's intention.

Jones has shown that fierceness and justifiable pride (fiertet) are always praiseworthy in the ***Song of Roland,*** as opposed to arrogance and haughtiness (orgoill), which are treated with contempt. "Nevertheless, this professed disapproval of arrogance must have been largely theoretical; for most of the characters of the epic behave arrogantly, especially the most admirable ones. Certainly Roland's braggadocio is the epitome of haughtiness." Jones could not have selected a less suitable passage to support his assertion, for it refers to Roland's apostrophe to his sword. Few words in Turoldus's poem have any absolute value. Applied indifferently to both good and evil characters and situations, terms such as these derive much of their force from a rigid categorization assumed from the start. Superbia in the ***Song of Roland*** is incarnated first and foremost by the Saracens, notably Baligant, and it is symbolized by the mountain citadel of Saragossa. It is also a trait associated with Ganelon. There is no textual support for any *psychomachia* within Roland; there is no evidence that he undergoes any change whatsoever. The view that the hero experiences a conversion or transformation is a lame assertion.

Roland is the ideal knight, his *proece* combining all chivalric virtues, the ability to impart sound advice (consilium) as well as the courage and strength to be of formidable assistance in combat (auxilium). In view of the traditional interpretations of Roland's character, it may seem paradoxical to maintain that, on a spiritual plane, beyond worldly chivalry, the hero personifies Humilitas. In medieval thought true humility consisted in recognizing one's lowly condition compared with God's greatness, one's need to surrender oneself completely to the dictates of the divine Will, and one's total dependence upon grace. Having demonstrated his humility in his speech in Laisse 14, urging Charles to carry on the struggle against Marsile, and in his debate with Oliver, maintaining that Folly is Wisdom, Roland begins his spiritual ascent. (pp. 96-7)

Far too much emphasis has been placed on the negative views of Roland derived from statements made by Ganelon and Oliver. Turoldus's own characterization of the hero is reflected in Charlemagne's perception of his nephew, notably in his lament and in his anecdote recognizing the prophetic significance of the hero's words at Aix.

Another important aspect of Roland's character should be discussed here. Anna Granville Hatcher, in an article [in the *Romantic Review,* 1949] seeking to explain why the heroine of the Old French *Sequence of Saint Eulalia* (ninth century) elects to suffer martyrdom rather than lose her virginity, has equated physical virginity with Christianity. But, as F. J. Barnett has pointed out [in a 1959 essay in *French Studies* and in *Studies in Medieval French Presented to Alfred Ewert in Honour of His Seventieth Birthday* (1961)], the Church never stipulated physical virginity as a condition for salvation. Barnett argues persuasively that what is involved in *Eulalia* is virginity of the heart, mind, or soul, which the Church Fathers, notably Saint Augustine, stressed repeatedly. (pp. 98-9)

In the ***Song of Roland*** Virginitas and the related concepts of intactness (entireness, quality of being uninjured), integrity (quality, state of completeness, of being unimpaired), and inviolability (unassailability) lead inexorably to the hero:

—Roland dies but suffers not a single wound, except that his temples burst from sounding the oliphant. The major threats he overcomes in this respect are Oliver's blow and the Saracen army's assault, but in each case the hero remains unscathed.

—Durendal reflects Roland's many shining virtues, but the fact that it cannot be destroyed, even after repeated attempts by its owner, implies that nothing can break the hero's spirit. Compare the image of the shattered lance in Charlemagne's first dream.

—Roland prays to the Virgin and his sword holds a relic of her clothing.

—Roland carries a white ensign lashed to the tip of his spear; at Roncevaux his heart is placed in a white casket and, later, his body in a white coffin. Whiteness is associated with martyrdom but also with chastity, purity of heart, and virginity. (p. 99)

One may also add that the hero of the ***Song of Roland*** is referred to by Charles in his lament as a *juvente bele* [''noble youth''] and that he is engaged, not married, to Oliver's sister. When Alda learns of his death at Roncevaux, she immediately falls dead at Charles's feet and is buried in a nunnery. Her maidenhood is never in doubt and, because she is linked to Roland, her virginity may be said to reflect his. (p. 100)

It is difficult for present-day readers to accept that a character can be all bad, and there is a tendency—especially since the Romantic period—to view villains as alienated, misunderstood, or, for one reason or another, not entirely to blame for the crimes they perpetrate. Many critics feel a decided sympathy for Ganelon and suggest that he is goaded into his fury and treason by a tactless Roland, shows courage in his dealings with Marsile, and has a strong case when he pleads justifiable homicide during the trial at Aix. The plain fact is that Turoldus and his contemporaries considered Ganelon to be completely evil. Like the Saracens or Satan himself in the ***Song of Roland,*** Ganelon has no redeeming trait whatsoever.

Scholars have long puzzled over the question: Why does Ganelon hate Roland? Turoldus makes it thoroughly clear that the villain *sold* the rearguard. . . . Ganelon's claim that he was cheated out of gold and riches by Roland reveals more about himself than about his stepson, and his claim in v. 3771 that it was the hero who hated him, not vice-versa, should be interpreted in similar fashion. (pp. 100-01)

Most critics, however, are inclined to believe that the real reason for Ganelon's betrayal is the slight he suffers in the scene where Roland nominates his stepfather for the perilous mission to Saragossa. Others suggest that a feud between Ganelon and Roland has been smouldering for some time before the poem begins. At any rate, the allegation of greed is generally viewed as a secondary motive at best, when it is not dismissed out of hand as totally irrelevant.

Such an interpretation reflects modern values, which regard avarice as a lesser vice and a certain amount of acquisitiveness as justifiable and even normal. In Turoldus's day Pride and Avarice were considered to be the root of all evil, a view based on Scripture. . . .

Once Avarice has been placed in its Romanesque setting, one is in a better position to appreciate what Turoldus repeatedly states about Ganelon's essential motivation for betraying Roland. Greed nurtured his hatred for his stepson and, when the poem opens, had already pushed him to the edge of the precipice, over which he falls in the quarrel scene. Each successive episode reveals a new facet of his growing depravity. The affront merely serves as a catalyst for vicious proclivities in Ganelon antedating the poem but successfully masked until that moment. (p. 101)

To sum up, Ganelon is essentially a Judas figure, and it is Avarice that leads him to betray Roland and, by implication, Charlemagne and God. Unable to elude the snares of the devil, a weakness recognized by the Emperor, he resorts to lying in a vain attempt to cover up his misdeeds. His handsomeness is part of the fraudulence traditionally associated with Covetousness (and Satan!), and his alleged courage before Marsile needs to be interpreted in this light. It is Avarice, too, that makes Ganelon jealous of Roland's sway over his companions and over Charles. . . .

In discussions of the various characters in the ***Song of Roland,*** Oliver usually receives the most favorable comment. Most scholars agree that Roland is the central hero, yet they find one aspect or another of his behavior repellent. They either conclude that Turoldus himself disapproved of Roland or assert that he represents a value system that is completely discredited today. Oliver, however, is generally well liked. He is, according to a typical assessment, ''the most lovable of all the characters.'' (p. 103)

The archetypal comrade-in-arms, Oliver simply has a different concept of duty from that exemplified by the hero.

Oliver is without a doubt the most difficult character to interpret in Turoldus's poem. One misconception has confused the issue. *Sage,* in modern French, can mean ''modéré, retenu, maître de ses passions, réglé dans sa conduite'' [''moderate,'' ''cautious,'' ''master of one's passions,'' ''steady in one's behavior''], but this sense was not attested to at this time, or indeed until the seventeenth century. In Old French, *saige* or *saive* refers primarily to unusual understanding of people or situations, judiciousness, or skill. This is not at all the same as the caution as to danger or risk, or the careful weighing of all possible consequences before taking action, which are inherent meanings in the present-day concept.

Modern critics have been unduly influenced by the classical notion that *fortitudo* [''strength''] and *sapientia* [''wisdom''] are the essential virtues of the warrior, and that one quality balances the other in the ideal hero. Valuable as this ideal may have been in antiquity, or may even be for us today, it would be a mistake to assume that Turoldus held it in similar esteem.

Oliver is really very much the same as Roland, and Turoldus makes it clear that both individuals have all the chivalric virtues. Proper balance in no way distinguishes one from the other, Oliver's claim notwithstanding. The crucial battlefield debate is not designed to contrapose Oliver's wisdom with Roland's folly; rather it serves to highlight the nature of the hero's agonizing choice. Oliver is a hero, possessing every human quality; Roland is a super-hero having Sapiential vision as an added attribute, and therein lies a world of difference. In other words, if one considers each character without proper regard for the martyr-ideal Roland incarnates, one misses the author's point completely. The modern reader is free of course to conclude that Oliver's advice should have been followed, but it would be a serious error to believe that Turoldus felt that way. Such a view is out of keeping with clerical values and with what is manifestly the ***Song of Roland***'s central meaning.

The role of Archbishop Turpin as a vigorous, warlike prelate poses no particular problem, for examples of such militancy on the part of contemporary clergymen come readily to mind. Everyone recognizes, too, that Turpin's presence on the battlefield helps to give the struggle a religious character. This is apparent in the Archbishop's intervention in the debate between Roland and Oliver, and in his statements and activities relative to death and its meaning in the poem. (pp. 103-04)

[Bramimonde's] repeated references to Charlemagne . . . are a clear indication that her role is inextricably linked to that of the Emperor. In fact, the notion of winning the hearts of the Saracens in the ***Song of Roland*** usually involves Charlemagne, and it is he whose magnanimous gesture, after the fall of Saragossa, makes the edifying conclusion of the poem possible. But it is Bramimonde's repudiation of her pagan gods and her adoption of Christianity *par amur* [''through love''] that offer the most significant manifestation of the Theme of Conversion in Turoldus's epic. The conquest of foreign lands and Bramimonde's submission at Saragossa play an obvious part in the narrative of defeat turned into victory, but such images also figure in the poem's religious dimension.

Paien unt tort e chrestïens unt dreit [''Pagans are wrong and Christians are right''], asserts Turoldus in a formula celebrated for its glaring simplicity. Turoldus's world view has decidedly black and white characteristics; bad on one side, good on the other. In general the men who make up Charlemagne's army display traditional chivalric virtues, notably bravery and loyalty, and their Christian convictions are unshakable. Their contentiousness, propensity for warfare, and thirst for revenge are doubtless accurate reflections of eleventh-century aristocratic behavior, but they should also be viewed in light of the poem's agonistic theme—the struggle of the virtues and vices for man's soul.

Turoldus nonetheless does ascribe one major weakness to the faceless Franks and even, on occasion, to individuals designated by name or nationality. The Franks vacillate, tend to agree with whoever has spoken last and, above all, cannot be relied upon to give sound advice. This disturbing characteristic is evident in the first French council, when Roland's plea to reject Marsile's proposals, which the audience knows are deceitful, are ignored; whereas Naimes's fateful speech, in effect seconding Ganelon's base counsel, wins immediate general approval. In his initial speech Roland does not hesitate to pillory the advice the Emperor is likely to receive from the Franks, reminding Charles of an earlier parallel occasion involving messengers bearing olive branches, similar proposals, and the ill-fated Basan and Basile. . . . (pp. 106-07)

The Franks are quick to agree with Roland's momentous nomination of Ganelon to carry the Emperor's counterproposal to Saragossa and doubtless misinterpret the significance of the gauntlet dropped by Ganelon. Their untrustworthiness in council is nowhere more apparent than in the trial of Ganelon, where, intimidated by Pinabel, they ask Charles to drop the case against the traitor. Characteristically the Franks agree to another solution—the judicial combat. After Pinabel's menacing presence has been removed, they finally come up with an equitable verdict.

Duke Naimes, Charlemagne's private counselor, is one of the most complicated of the minor French characters in the poem. In the early scenes he recommends mercy when perseverance is called for, and his suggestion that Charles offer half his army to his nephew is brushed aside by Roland. Privileged to share in the knowledge imparted to Charles by a celestial messenger—to be sure, he may only have an imperfect grasp of the meaning of the dream—he plays the mute, until it is too late. In the Emperor's hour of greatest need, he stands by while Thierry champions Charlemagne's cause. Clearly Thierry surpasses Naimes in *auxilium,* Ogier outdoes him in *consilium.*

In the trial of Ganelon fear obviously inhibits the Franks' capacity to offer proper counsel, and, in retrospect, one wonders whether, in the first council, the traitor's commanding and perhaps threatening presence may not have been a factor motivating their prompt concurrence in Naimes's proposal. Militating against this view is the fact that the Franks just as quickly endorse Roland's nomination of his stepfather for the mission to Saragossa. It seems very likely, too, that war-weariness rather than anxiety or lack of courage prompts them to support any proposal that will bring their seven-year involvement in the Spanish campaign to an honorable end in the most expeditious way.

If fear cannot be said to be at the root of the Franks' *legerie,* their constant weeping offers another possible explanation. Emotionalism corresponds to irresolution and often leads to hasty and injudicious decisions. But crying is a conventional expression of concern or grief in medieval epics, and Turoldus's heroes—Charlemagne in particular, who is associated with Sapientia—not infrequently shed tears.

In the final analysis the unreliability of the Franks in council, like the circularity of Oliver's argumentation in his debate with Roland, appears to be a device used by the poet to bring out the vanity of worldly wisdom and the transcendence of Sapientia. Viewed from this perspective, the Franks in the ***Song of Roland*** are the inverted image of Charlemagne. On occasion Christ upbraided his disciples for being men of little faith and for requiring signs and wonders. Similarly, the faith of Charlemagne's men needs constant bolstering with miraculous occurrences, such as Roland's death and Thierry's victory over Pinabel. However, it must be said to their credit that, having seen a sign from Heaven, the Franks take prompt and appropriate action. Also, whatever human failings they may have pale into insignificance when the Franks meet their end in edifying fashion as martyrs.

What few contacts French merchants, soldiers, and travelers had with the Muslim world in the eleventh century contributed little if anything to Turoldus's knowledge of the Saracens. The enemies ranged before the Christians are a strange amalgam of folk beliefs, feudal institutions and practices, scraps of information ultimately derived from classical sources, and stereotypes stemming from the Bible. The conventional portrait of the Saracen, which emerges from a reading of the ***Song of Roland*** as well as other chansons de geste, has been studied in detail by a number of scholars.

What is perhaps most singular is the lumping together of disparate groups from Islam and from other parts of the world, notably from Eastern Europe. The cartographers of Turoldus's day recognized three major geographical areas—Africa, Asia, and Europe—but clerks tended to classify nations according to whether they lived under the Old Law (Jews), the New Law (Christians), or the False Law (Saracens). . . . (pp. 107-08)

The greatest misconception concerns religion. The Saracens are characterized by Turoldus as idolaters and worshippers of the trinity of gods Apollo, Mohammed, and Tervagant. Their land, like Egypt to the Fathers of the Church, is held to be a place of darkness inhabited by hardhearted men given to sorcery and other vile practices. (pp. 108-09)

Although Saracens in the ***Song of Roland*** are at times outwardly indistinguishable in their appearance and behavior from the Christians—certain descriptive adjectives are used interchangeably for either group—the very thought of Saracens triggered a negative reaction in contemporary audiences. The latter considered all pagans to have perverted natures and expected them to be forever engaged in evil activities. The Saracens were universally regarded as being possessed by the devil, a belief that accounts for their impurity, swarthiness, and ugliness in medieval literature. Their pride, that is, their false reliance on their own strength, is underscored . . . , and it is only fitting that such treacherous individuals should consort with the traitor Ganelon. There is some evidence of admiration for the Saracens in later chronicles, but none is to be found in the ***Song of Roland.*** Epithets seemingly implying a favorable opinion of the Saracens belong to the category of terms denoting lying exteriors.

The pagan leaders Baligant and Marsile deserve special note. As to be expected in such a biased account, the Saracens in question are incarnations of every imaginable vice. Baligant appears far more haughty, and his role, which is to oppose Charlemagne in an apocalyptic confrontation, is clearly affected by the image of Antichrist. His behavior, moreover, involves contemptible aping of the Emperor and Roland. Marsile, on the other hand, suffers one indignity after another, and the chronicling of his despair, growing deeper with each succeeding episode—the first syllable of his name . . . is an expression of woe in Old French—constitutes a scathing denunciation of pagan life and worship.

The word *tirant* does not appear in the ***Song of Roland,*** yet Saracens, especially their leaders, were frequently associated with cruel tyrants throughout the Middle Ages. It is safe to assume that such a notion influenced Turoldus's conception of Baligant and Marsile. The medieval iconographic formula for the tyrant—a crowned and enthroned figure often shown in profile rather than frontally—comes particularly to mind when the Saracen chieftains are described by Turoldus as seated. . . . In the Middle Ages tyrant conjured up less the notion of absolutism than that of a monstrous and relentless persecutor of Christians. Religious overtones are clear, for instance, when the individuals who crucified Jesus are referred to as *tiranz* in *Les Chétifs*. It seems reasonable to conclude, therefore, that the poet's idea of Baligant and Marsile is not entirely foreign to that of Herod, murderer of the Holy Innocents . . . , and the succession of diabolic magistrates and rulers who cause the martyrs to suffer unspeakable tortures in the saints' lives. In the end, all are frustrated by the hero's victorious death.

One of Turoldus's most disconcerting habits, insofar as the modern reader is concerned, is to portray Saracens thinking like Christians. The poet goes far beyond showing Muslims wearing Western armor or living under the feudal system, for he also implies they are thoroughly familiar with the Bible. Thus, for example, Marsile has his ambassadors imitate Christ's Entry into Jerusalem; the same messengers presumably grasp the significance of the Last Judgment scene that greets them on their arrival in Charles's camp; and Ganelon, on the ride to Saragossa, expects Blancandrin to understand the allusion to Roland as a diabolic seducer. Such depictions should not be scorned for their lack of realism but viewed in terms of their own esthetic: A biblical reference is a natural and effective way of imparting an aura of blasphemy to foul deeds. (pp.109-10)

Gerard J. Brault, "Character Portrayal," in his The Song of Roland: An Analytical Edition, Introduction and Commentary, Volume 1, *edited by Gerard J. Brault, The Pennsylvania State University Press, 1978, pp. 89-110.*

ANN TUKEY HARRISON (essay date 1981)

[An American educator, Harrison specializes in French medieval literature and language. In the following excerpt, she assesses the significance of The Song's *women characters, emphasizing that while Aude is defined solely in terms of her relationship to male characters, Bramimunde is portrayed as an active, independent individual.]*

Modern students of the humanities in high school, college, and graduate school who study the history of western civilization in a wide variety of disciplines from anthropology to comparative literature and French are currently exposed to the ***Chanson de Roland*** (in English, modern French, or Old French); usually they read short passages of a hundred verses or so, and they are told about the content and emphasis of the work as a whole.

A sixteenth-century depiction of Roland's funeral.

Such readers are led to two conclusions concerning women characters in French epic literature: 1) women are unimportant or even nonexistent in the French epic; 2) the major female character in the ***Chanson de Roland,*** Aude, Roland's fiancée, offers a typical feminine depiction: her appearance is brief, unusually beautiful, and poignant.The first premise does find corroboration in many *chansons de geste,* where women are secondary or tertiary figures, not major protagonists of heroic proportions. The French epic seems to have been written for, by, and about men.

The second premise, asserting the representative nature of Aude and the remarkable beauty of her few verses, continues to be popular, both in French and English-language scholarship. In some ways, this can be seen as a direct response to the intellectual currents of our own time, when women as students and scholars are increasingly interested in the roles of women in literature and in the cultures that produced such writings. Two questions are central to a balanced appraisal and understanding of women characters in the ***Chanson de Roland:*** how important to this work is Aude? are there other artistically interesting women characters in the poem?

Aude is first mentioned during the rearguard battle. When first named in verses 1719-1721, she is a relative latecomer to the story. The poet focuses at once on her relationship or kinship to both of the heroes, Roland *and* Olivier: she is fiancée to one, sister of the other. The two companions have disagreed vigorously earlier, and their debate is renewed at the turning point of the battle, when their heroism is at its apogee. Here the reader first hears of Aude, from Olivier, in the heat of anger. . . . Critics have observed the importance of the whole battlefield debate without much attention to its effect on the characterization of Aude. She is introduced at a privileged moment of high emotion, in a passage that circumscribes four traits essential to her character: her noble family lineage; her passive status therein dominated by their right of bestowal of her person in marriage; her prestigious betrothal; and her discreetly sexual role as bride-to-be. At this point, Aude's possession, within the limits of family and marriage—two of the primary circles of medieval woman's social existence—is a subject of a mild oath, uttered in anger, a corollary to the foremost male pursuit—warfare. It is not an exaggeration, within this context, to equate Aude with royal booty, one of the better prizes of conquest.

Aude's major episode, two thousand verses later, consists of a dialogue with Charlemagne, about Roland, followed by her death and interment. Described only as "une bele damisele" ["a fair damsel"], she meets the emperor on the steps of his palace, to ask: "Ço dist al rei: 'O est Rollant le catanie, / Ki me jurat cume sa per a prendre?' " ["She said to the King: 'Where is Roland, the captain, / Who gave me his solemn word he would take me to wife?' "] Charles, weeping and tearing his beard, tells her she inquires after a dead man, and he then offers her his own son Louis in marriage. Aude finds the offer "estrange," which I interpret to mean "incompatible or inconsistent with my nature and view of my life." Praying that it not please God, his angels, and saints for her to survive Roland, she drops dead. (The same idiom, *aler a sa fin,* is used to describe Roland also, right after his death.) Charlemagne, thinking she has fainted, attempts to revive her, then calls four countesses to carry the body to a convent, where, after a night's vigil, she is buried beside an altar. Finally, Charlemagne endows a convent in Aude's honor.

Aude is faithful, pious, beautiful, a noblewoman whose sacrifice is honored. Her status is thrice indicated: first, by her direct approach to the emperor, which is well received by him; second, by his reactions to her words, his deep concern for her and his marriage offer of his own heir; finally, by his endowment of the convent. Although Aude is here an initiator of action, a woman who speaks and acts, she does so only in relation to male characters. As her introduction as a character was defined by her relationship to Roland and Olivier, her deeds here are directly related to Charlemagne, her soveeign, with full power over her person. The poet implicitly suggests the spatial and legal constraints within which she exists (the palace and the arranged marriage), while explicitly stating the male dominance that circumscribes her life. Charlemagne's actions begin and end the episode, and his words or deeds occupy seventeen of the twenty-nine verses. Aude's life has been one of honor, within the confines of family, betrothal, and church; although she is associated with the major heroic figures of the poem (Roland, Olivier, Charlemagne), she is sheltered, protected, bestowed. She is wholly dependent, and her honor, like her status, is reflected from male characters.

Some critics call her death a martyrdom, and both Réau and Brault associate her demise with the iconographic formula of the Death of the Virgin. As Brault writes: "Like Mary, Alda is a virgin, and her passing, which is so peaceful it completely deceives Charles into believing she has merely fainted, is an awe-inspiring dormition." Scholars have seen her as the last victim of the Battle of Roncevals, the most touching reminder of Roland, the incarnation of ideal love and the most moving of all tributes to Roland's glory, one of Roland's greatest claims to glory. Although her twenty-nine verses are surely not mere decoration, some of these claims on her behalf are hyperbolic and distorted. Her episode is woven well into the epic's action; she does contribute to the character development of both Roland and Charlemagne, but she does not directly reinforce the poem's central theme of Christian supremacy over the pagans. Beautiful Aude is tightly confined, subordinate, and supportive, and if that is typical of unmarried noblewomen of her time, then she can be called representative and, if not mimetic, at least *grosso modo* realistic.

A much more significant female figure is the Saracen queen Bramimunde, wife of Saragossa's King Marsile. By far the most developed woman character in this epic, she is an independent, active participant in four different passages, each of which is strategically located within the poem's action. Bramimunde first appears in the scene of treachery (when the betrayal of the French rearguard is planned by Ganelon and the Saracen leaders to whom he is an ambassador); she is next a central figure during the scenes showing the reactions to Marsile's defeat; she is prominent in three stages of the second half of the poem when Charlemagne as Roland's emperor and Christendom's champion defeats the Emir Baligant, sovereign of Marsile and ruler of Araby; and finally, her conversion to Christianity is reported by the poet as part of the poem's conclusion. In each instance she is directly and explicitly linked with the emperor Charlemagne. She is the sole individualized Saracen survivor, and by her baptism, arranged at Charles' behest, she embodies the primary theme of the *chanson:* the Christians are right, the pagans are wrong.

Laisse 50, within the section of the poem where Ganelon plans the Saracen ambush of the French rearguard led by Roland, contains a description of Bramimunde's gifts to the wife of the French ambassador and traitor. While Ganelon is in council with the enemy Saracens, Bramimunde comes to the gathering, declares her affection for the Frenchman, and states that she is sending two necklaces (with gold, amethysts, and sapphires) to Ganelon's wife. In this her first appearance, Bramimunde concludes with a formulaic, oblique reference to Charlemagne: ''Vostre emperere si bones n'en out unches'' [''Your Emperor never had such fine ones'']. The Queen is not the only pagan to give presents to Ganelon; Valdabrun has already offered his sword and Climorin his helmet, but the men's gifts are to the ambassador directly, and the men exchange kisses as well to seal the gift-giving. Bramimunde's gifts are non-military, for Ganelon's wife (a woman never mentioned again), and the feudal kiss is replaced by a statement that ''Il les ad prises, en sa hoese les butet'' [''He took them, he sticks them in his boot'']. The author of the ***Roland*** is fully cognizant of Bramimunde's femininity, and he depicts actions and statements that are appropriate for women.

Brault finds Bramimunde's words to Ganelon ''bold and suggestive.'' . . . [He] explains that ''the voluptuous and amoral Saracen lady is a stock character in epic literature.'' He also notes that in this passage, as elsewhere in the epic tradition, ''diabolism and eroticism are closely intertwined.'' I find little substantiation for this interpretation, in this section of the text or in other appearances of Bramimunde in the poem. She is a Queen, with a political and religious role; her gifts are to Ganelon's *wife;* and nowhere else in the text does her conduct convey an erotic connotation, much less diabolism.

Bramimunde's second scene takes place in Saragossa, immediately after the defeat of Marsile. In laisse 187, she cries out, along with 20,000 men. They are reported to curse Charlemagne, then proceed to depose their gods while uttering blasphemous shouts and curses quoted by the poet directly. Although Bramimunde is the only individual of the stanza, her appearance is very short (three verses), and the actions and words are attributed to the mob as well. The next stanza, laisse 188, the last before the principal division of the poem (the second part or Baligant episode), is devoted entirely to Bramimunde's outpouring of grief, in deed and word. . . . The Saracen reaction to Marsile's defeat is described in terms of the undifferentiated mob *and* Bramimunde, who is the only individual to speak for the infidel cause. She performs the ritual actions of grief and delivers a carefully balanced, eleven-verse speech of formal lamentation.

The third set of passages in which Bramimunde appears are the three stages of the Baligant section; she is still a part of the Saracen court. Marsile, her husband, was victorious over Roland's rearguard, but Charlemagne's army has destroyed the Saracen troops. Now Marsile's sovereign, the Emir Baligant, comes to do battle with the Emperor Charles, in the ultimate conflict between pagan and Christian. When the messengers from Baligant arrive at Saragossa, at the court of Marsile, his Queen receives them, and she counsels them twice. Neither speech is well received, and both times a male character virtually tells her to be quiet, in so many words. Their refusal to listen to her is, eventually, their undoing, for she has ended each statement of advice with a warning about the power of Charlemagne. . . . (pp. 672-76)

Bramimunde is the official of the court to welcome the Emir Baligant, throwing herself at his feet, as she bemoans her pitiful situation, since she has lost her lord (Marsile being wounded and incapable of protecting her).

And finally, Bramimunde, from a tower, witnesses the Emir's defeat, called the confounding of Araby, and she invokes Mohammed while reporting the shame and death she sees. Upon hearing her words, her wounded husband Marsile turns his face to the wall and dies of grief.

Bramimunde is in evidence and speaks at three crucial moments during the Baligant encounter: the arrival of the messengers, the arrival of the Emir himself, and the defeat of Baligant along with the subsequent death of Marsile. She fills an official role, both as Queen and as witness.

The fourth stage of her role in the ***Chanson de Roland*** is her conversion to Christianity. It is announced by the poet during the sack of Saragossa; each time the reader is told that it is the will of the king that she be converted, but by love and not by force, in France and not in Spain. She is to be taken, as a prisoner, to Aix. This information is conveyed directly twice. The first time, she is the only individual taken, unconverted, from Saragossa home to France. . . . The second reference says that the Emperor wishes her only good.

After the trial of Ganelon and the execution of his kin (among whom there is no mention of his wife, to whom Bramimunde sent the necklaces), Charlemagne's first concern seems to be the conversion of his queenly captive. . . . [In the baptism scene, as] with the gift-giving scene, the poet is conscious that Bramimunde is a woman, and the ritual observed is appropriate for a nun, not a male convert. (pp. 676-77)

The final stanza of the entire poem contains the reiteration of the conversion of Charlemagne's important prisoner; this is the third accomplishment of his mission—he has done justice, assuaged his anger, and given Christianity to Bramimunde. . . . Although converted and baptised Juliana, she is in the last reference known under the old, familiar Saracen name, and she here represents the Saracen community of which she is the sole individualized survivor.

A feminist appraisal of Bramimunde must answer at least three crucial questions: is she a full-fledged member of the society depicted? does she act outside of the love-marriage situation? is she a role model? Certainly Bramimunde's participation in her society is full, if not extraordinary. The gift scene, her role in the formal reception of Baligant's embassy and the Emir's arrival at Saragossa, and finally her conversion, at the singular behest of Charles: the importance of these episodes and her particular behavior in them show her as not only a full-fledged member, but, by the end of the *geste,* as the representative of the Saracen world. On two instances when she is rebuffed by Saracen men, rudely, the poet shows that Bramimunde is right and the pagans are wrong when they do not heed her warnings.

Though the reader would infer that her title Queen of Spain comes to her through marriage with Marsile, the author of the ***Roland*** only twice qualifies her as ''his wife,'' both in stanza 187, in the scene where she sees and understands the severity of her husband's wounds. The poet far prefers to call her by name or royal title. Bramimunde is portrayed as a loyal wife, fulfilling the regal duties of her status, but after the mortal wounding of her spouse Marsile, her activity, prominence, and representative position increase, verse by verse. And long after her king-consort has died, Queen Bramimunde is alive, a worthy convert, far beyond the love-marriage identification of other medieval women in other works of literature, such as Iseut. (p. 678)

The most important facet of Bramimunde's presentation by the ***Roland*** poet is her close association, specifically stated in each instance, with Charles. Every time she appears, without exception, she or the poet makes explicit reference to Charles the Emperor. And this link, forged from her debut as gift-giving queen, to the great king, with a divinely bestowed mission of subduing or converting the pagans, brings Bramimunde into contact with the major theme of the poem. Neither diabolic nor erotic, she is not a romantic foil for Charles, or a feminine counterpart, or a pseudo-consort; she is instead a living example of the most lasting and benevolent side of his assigned earthly task—the flower of the pagan world converted to Christianity, admitted in honor to the very center of Christendom, and the only preoccupation of Charles when the vengeance is over.

Aude and Bramimunde offer an interesting set of opposite characteristics; in some ways they are complementary to one another: Christian/Saracen, virgin betrothed/wife then widow, noblewoman/queen, representative of women left behind/representative of the Saracen political and religious community, inexperienced youth of uncompromising idealism/experienced middle age capable of compromise and conversion. Critics observe a religious association for both (Aude with the Virgin Mary in death, Bramimunde with St. Juliana in baptism), and both are clearly female, depicted as women in actions appropriate to women. Teachers who decide to emphasize Aude at the expense of Bramimunde are choosing to stress Roland's sacrifice as the central event of the epic, since Aude as a character serves, perhaps exclusively, to reinforce Roland's role. Bramimunde as a character is more full, much more active, and woven into the greater theme of the whole epic: Charlemagne's conquest of the pagans, as the champion of Christendom. Although the total number of verses devoted to both women is small (twenty-nine for Aude and one hundred forty-seven for Bramimunde, out of four thousand), these women are integral to the plot, character, and thematic development of the *chanson*. An examination of them both, in measured fashion, is but another way of observing the meticulous artistry of the ***Roland*** poet. (p. 679)

Ann Tukey Harrison, "Aude and Bramimunde: Their Importance in the 'Chanson de Roland'," in The French Review, *Vol. LIV, No. 5, April, 1981, pp. 672-79.*

ADDITIONAL BIBLIOGRAPHY

Allen, John R. "Kinship in the *Chanson de Roland*." In *Jean Misrahi Memorial Volume: Studies in Medieval Literature,* edited by Hans R. Runte, Henri Niedzielski, and William L. Hendrickson, pp. 34-42. Columbia, S.C.: French Literature Publications Co., 1977.

An anthropological study of *The Song,* examining family relationships in the poem.

Ashby-Beach, Genette. *"The Song of Roland": A Generative Study of the Formulaic Language in the Single Combat.* Amsterdam: Rodopi, 1985, 190 p.

A detailed linguistic analysis of the verbal formulae used in descriptions of combat scenes in *The Song*.

Atkinson, James C. "Laisses 169-170 of the *Chanson de Roland.*" *Modern Language Notes* 82 (1967): 271-84.

An explication of *laisses* 169-70, in which the dying Roland is attacked by a lone Saracen. Atkinson postulates that Roland's assailant represents the hero's own pride that must be subdued.

Auerbach, Erich. "Roland Against Ganelon." In his *Mimesis: The Representation of Reality in Western Literature,* translated by Willard R. Trask, pp. 96-122. Princeton: Princeton University Press, 1953.

An analysis of the placement, juxtaposition, and parallelism of the *laisses* in *The Song*.

Borkenau, Franz. "Postscriptum: The *Chanson de Roland*." In his *End and Beginning: On the Generations of Cultures and the Origins of the West,* edited by Richard Lowenthal, pp. 417-33. New York: Columbia University Press, 1981.

A speculative account of the genesis of *The Song* and of its social significance. Borkenau identifies Turoldus as the reciter of the story of Roland for William the Conqueror's troops before the Battle of Hastings in 1066. Borkenau further asserts that as the poem's relevance for its first audience lay in its implicit condemnation of Roland's rashness, *The Song* constitutes the "final break with the aboriginal Germanic tradition of prowess."

Bowra, C. M. *Heroic Poetry*. London: Macmillan & Co., 1952, 590 p.

An extensive and valuable study of the "anatomy of heroic poetry," with scattered references to *The Song*. Bowra states that his aim is to "[compare] many examples and aspects of a poetical form . . . to illuminate the nature of that form and the ways in which it works."

Brault, Gerard J. "The French Chansons de Geste." In *Heroic Epic and Saga: An Introduction to the World's Great Folk Epics,* edited by Felix J. Oinas, pp. 193-215. Bloomington: Indiana University Press, 1978.

A general introduction to the chanson de geste genre and to *The Song,* treating the poem's main themes, images, and techniques of characterization.

Burgess, G. S. "Some Thoughts on Roland and Rodrigue." *The Modern Language Review* 66, No. 1 (January 1971): 40-52.

Compares the concepts of service, honor, and glory in *The Song* and Pierre Corneille's *Le Cid.*

Clark, Cecily. "Byrhtnoth and Roland: A Contrast." *Neophilologus* 51, No. 3 (July 1967): 288-93.

A comparison of *The Song* and the eleventh-century Anglo-Saxon epic, *The Battle of Maldon*. Clark concludes that "*Roland* shows a story very like that of *Maldon* presented from a strongly Christian point of view."

Cook, Albert. "Folk Destinies." In his *The Classic Line: A Study in Epic Poetry,* pp. 3-48. Bloomington: Indiana University Press, 1966.

Describes how both the style and substance of *The Song* exemplify the "mysteries" of the poem's characterization, motivation, and theme.

Cook, William R., and Herzman, Ronald B. "Roland and Romanesque: Biblical Iconography in *The Song of Roland*." In *The Arts, Society, Literature,* edited by Harry R. Gavin, pp. 21-48. Lewisburg, Pa.: Bucknell University Press, 1984.

Identifies stylistic and thematic parallels between *The Song* and Romanesque sculptural art. Cook and Herzman allege that *The Song* evinces "the same solidity, vigor, and forcefulness that form the dominant impression when viewing the stone of the great twelfth-century masons."

Cramer, Marianne. "The Ascendancy of Bramimunde in the *Chanson de Roland*." *Language Quarterly* XIII, Nos. 1-2 (Fall-Winter 1974): 29-34, 41.

Argues for the significance of Bramimunde in *The Song.*

———. "Roland's Heroism." *Language Quarterly* XIV, Nos. 3-4 (Spring-Summer 1976): 37-42, 46.

A reading of *The Song* within a Christian context. Cramer argues that Roland's pride is not "arrogance . . . but the steadfast valiant heroism of the only perfect martyr."

Crosland, Jessie. "The *Chanson de Roland*." In her *The Old French Epic,* pp. 70-91. Oxford: Basil Blackwell, 1951.

Comments critically on *The Song,* asserting that "the poet's psychological instinct never fails him. There is nothing incongruous or inconsistent in any of his characters."

Dorfman, Eugene. *The Narreme in the Medieval Romance Epic: An Introduction to Narrative Structures*. Toronto: University of Toronto Press, 1969, 259 p.

An examination of narremes (defined by Dorfman as structural units of a narrative which are "central or core incidents whose function is to serve as the central focus or core of a larger episode") in *The Song* and in the *Cantar de Mio Cid*. After studying four narremes in the two works—the family quarrel, the insult, the act of treachery, and the punishment and epilogue—Dorfman suggests that "the narremes of the *Cid* show too close a similarity to those of the *Roland* to be the result of coincidence."

Douglas, David. "The *Song of Roland* and the Norman Conquest of England." *French Studies* XIV, No. 2 (April 1960): 99-116.

Speculates about whether *The Song* was of Norman origin.

Duggan, Joseph J. "Virgilian Inspiration in the *Roman d'Eneas* and in the *Chanson de Roland*." In *Medieval Epic to the "Epic Theater" of Brecht: Essays in Comparative Literature*, edited by Rosario P. Armato and John M. Spalek, pp. 9-23. Los Angeles: University of Southern California Press, 1968.

A comparison of the *Aeneid*, the *Roman d'Eneas* and *The Song*. Duggan writes that his purpose is "to examine the *Aeneid* and the *Chanson de Roland* for resemblances in certain thematic and formal aspects, taking the technique of the *Roman d'Eneas* as a controlling element," and concludes that "the medieval product of Virgilian inspiration is the *Roman d'Eneas*, not the *Chanson de Roland*."

———. *The Song of Roland: Formulaic Style and Poetic Craft*. Berkeley: University of California Press, 1973, 226 p.

A study of "the totality of formulas perceivable" in *The Song* and the relationship between the poem's linguistic and thematic formulas and its style.

———. "Legitimation and the Hero's Exemplary Function in the *Cantar de mio Cid* and the *Chanson de Roland*." In *Oral Traditional Literature: A Festschrift for Albert Bates Lord*, edited by John Miles Foley. Columbus: Slavica Publishers, Inc., 1981.

A comparison of the two poems and their "exemplary" heroes. Duggan asserts that the works are similar in that they "both incorporate myths looking back to a foundation, the *Cid* for the Spanish kingdom born of the union of Leon and Castile, and the *Roland* for the Carolingian Empire."

Eisner, Robert A. "In Search of the Real Theme of the *Song of Roland*." *Romance Notes* 14, No. 1 (Autumn 1972): 179-83.

Discusses the integration of conflicting values in *The Song*, focusing mainly on the inconsistency of Charlemagne's character. Eisner concludes that in the poem "individualism clashes with the old, superannuated world of the autocratic emperor," and that "the tragedy at Roncevaux is the result of the breakdown of societal values."

Foulet, Alfred. "Is Roland Guilty of *Desmesure*?" *Romance Philology* X (1956-57): 145-48.

Theorizes that Roland, far from being guilty of *desmesure* in his initial refusal to sound the *oliphant*, knowingly sacrificed himself and his men so that Charlemagne and the army might be motivated by their desire for vengeance to destroy the pagans.

Greene, Thomas. "The Norms of Epic." *Comparative Literature* 13, No. 3 (Summer 1961): 193-207.

An extensive study of the qualities of the epic genre; contains frequent references to *The Song*.

Grégoire, Henri. "The Actual Date and the True Historical Background of the *Chanson de Roland*." *Belgium* III, No. 2 (2 April 1942): 59-64.

Dates the writing of the Baligant episode of *The Song* at about 1085. Grégoire speculates that the inspiration for the episode was an expedition against the Byzantine Empire led by Robert Guiscard, a Norman chieftain, during the years 1081-85.

Guymon, Wayne. "The Structural Unity of *La Chanson de Roland*." *Lingua e Stile* XII, No. 3 (September 1977): 513-36.

Examines the narrative unity of *The Song*. Rejecting Roland as *The Song*'s central figure and viewing the poem "as a mythic work expressive of a collective ideology," Guymon concludes that it "represents an original, universalizing conception of the meaning of the struggle to conquer Spain, a conception which rises above the tale of the tragedy of a single individual to declare the glory of a longed for empire."

Hall, Robert A., Jr. "On Individual Authorship in the *Roland*." *Symposium* 15, No. 4 (Winter 1961): 297-302.

Argues for dual authorship of *The Song*, citing stylistic and thematic discrepancies in the poem.

Halverson, John. "Ganelon's Trial." *Speculum* 42, No. 3 (July 1967): 661-69.

Examines *The Song* as "a Janus-faced poem, at once looking backwards to a basically Germanic tradition and feudal ethos, and forward to the nationalistic development of a coherent French society."

Hanning, Robert W. "The Individual and Mimesis, I: Time and Space in Chivalric Romance." In his *The Individual in Twelfth-Century Romance*, pp. 139-70. New Haven: Yale University Press, 1977.

Analyzes the representation of time in chivalric romance, contrasting it with the treatment of time in *The Song*.

Hart, Walter Morris. "The *Roland*." In his *Ballad and Epic: A Study in the Development of the Narrative Art*, pp. 227-87. Studies and Notes in Philology and Literature, vol. XI. 1907. Reprint. New York: Russell & Russell, 1967.

Discusses various aspects of the poem—including its motives, structure, and narrative method—and compares it with *Beowulf* and with early popular ballads.

Herman, Gerald. "Is There Humor in *La Chanson de Roland*?" *French Review* XLV, No. 3 (Fall 1971): 13-20.

Explores the humorous episodes, which Herman admits are few, in *The Song*.

———. "Why Does Olivier Die before the Archbishop Turpin?" *Romance Notes* 14, No. 2 (Winter 1972): 376-82.

Examines the significance of the order in which the heroes of Roncevaux die.

Hunt, Tony. "The Tragedy of Roland: An Aristotelian View." *Modern Language Review* 74, No. 4 (October 1979): 791-805.

Uses Aristotelian poetics as a standard by which to judge *The Song*. Hunt concludes that "it is possible to discern in the Oxford *Roland* the structure and emotion of the highest form of tragedy, as Aristotle saw it, and this fact contributes to the poem's essential power to move us today."

Huppé, Bernard F. "The Concept of the Hero in the Early Middle Ages." In *Concepts of the Hero in the Middle Ages and the Renaissance*, edited by Norman T. Burns and Christopher J. Reagan, pp. 1-26. Albany: State University of New York Press, 1975.

Contends that Charlemagne, not Roland, is the hero of *The Song*.

———. "Nature in *Beowulf* and *Roland*." In *Approaches to Nature in the Middle Ages*, edited by Lawrence D. Roberts, pp. 3-41. Binghamton, N.Y.: Center for Medieval & Early Renaissance Studies, 1982.

Discusses the description and function of nature in *The Song*, noting that "either details of nature are subsumed into the rhetorical structure of the poem as background and frame for man's actions, or the reality of nature is treated symbolically as a veil through which spiritual reality may be glimpsed."

Hutson, Arthur E., and McCoy, Patricia. "The Song of Roland." In their *Epics of the Western World*, pp. 245-73. Philadelphia: J. B. Lippincott Co., 1954.

A general historical and literary overview of *The Song*.

Jackson, W. T. H. "The Chanson de Geste." In his *The Literature of the Middle Ages*, pp. 160-74. New York: Columbia University Press, 1960.

Considers *The Song* as a Christian and social epic and compares the poem with a German version of the Roland legend, the *Rolandslied*.

Jones, David. "The Roland Epic and Ourselves." In *The Dying Gaul and Other Writings,* edited by Harman Grisewood, pp. 94-104. London: Faber and Faber, 1978.
Reprints a 1938 essay containing a general introduction to *The Song*.

Kay, Sarah. "Ethics and Heroics in the *Song of Roland.*" *Neophilologus* 62, No. 4 (October 1978): 480-91.
Judges Roland's status as *The Song*'s hero through an analysis of the poem's ethics. Kay concludes that "what [Roland] does is accepted as right because he is the hero, rather than that he becomes accepted as the hero because what he does is right."

Kibler, William W. "Roland's Pride." *Symposium* 26, No. 2 (Summer 1972): 147-60.
Argues that Roland, far from being sinfully proud, is "a totally admirable feudal warrior."

———. "Roland vs. the Barons." In *Voices of Conscience: Essays on Medieval and Modern French Literature in Memory of James D. Powell and Rosemary Hodgins,* edited by Raymond J. Cormier, pp. 53-60. Philadelphia: Temple University Press, 1977.
Explores an analogy between the first council scene in *The Song* and the judgment of Ganelon scene.

Knudson, Charles A. "The Problem of the *Chanson de Roland.*" *Romance Philology* IV, No. 1 (August 1950): 1-15.
Examines the unity of *The Song,* its historical allusions and materials, and the origins of the epic as a genre.

Kostoroski, Emilie P. "Further Echoes from Roland's Horn." *Romance Notes* 13, No. 3 (Spring 1972): 541-44.
Discusses the career of the *oliphant* following Roland's death. Regarding it as "Roland's continued symbolic presence," Kostoroski argues that the *oliphant* celebrates Roland's heroic triumph, even in death.

Kunkle, Roberta A. "Time in the *Song of Roland.*" *Romance Notes* 13, No. 3 (Spring 1972): 550-55.
Posits a seven-day "work-rest cycle" as the temporal scheme of *The Song*.

March, Harold. Introduction to *The Song of Roland,* translated by Patricia Terry, pp. xiii-xxxi. Indianapolis: Bobbs-Merrill Educational Publishing, 1965.
A discussion of the style, themes and literary merit of *The Song*.

Martin, June Hall. "The Divisions of the *Chanson de Roland.*" *Romance Notes* 6, No. 2 (Spring 1965): 182-95.
Documents techniques of *laisse* division in *The Song*.

Mickel, Emanuel J., Jr. "Christian Duty and the Structure of the *Roland.*" *Romance Notes* 9, No. 1 (Autumn 1967): 126-33.
Explores the theme of Christian duty in *The Song*.

Nichols, Stephen G., Jr. "Roland's Echoing Horn." *Romance Notes* 5, No. 1 (Autumn 1963): 78-84.
Indicates the importance of Roland's *oliphant* to the narrative structure of *The Song*.

———. "Roncevaux and the Poetics of Place/Person in the *Song of Roland.*" In his *Romanesque Signs: Early Medieval Narrative and Iconography,* pp. 148-203. New Haven: Yale University Press, 1983.
Examines *The Song* as a representative of "a new kind of historiated narrative," or, the making of history into literature.

Niles, John D. "The Ideal Depiction of Charlemagne in *La Chanson de Roland.*" *Viator* 7 (1976): 123-31, 134-39.
Correlates the idealized portrait of Charlemagne in *The Song* with the "hieratic Byzantine concept of the ideal ruler."

Owen, D. D. R. *The Legend of Roland: A Pageant of the Middle Ages*. London: Phaidon, 1973, 205 p.
A lavishly illustrated history of the Roland legend in art and literature.

———. "The Epic and History: *Chanson de Roland* and *Carmen de Hastingae Proelio.*" *Medium Ævum* 51, No. 1 (1982): 18-34.
Shows how the authors of the two works "went about elaborating their primary subject-matter with an eye more to poetic effect than to historical accuracy." Owen also posits that the *Carmen*-poet knew and made use of *The Song*.

Pensom, Roger. *Literary Technique in the "Chanson de Roland."* Geneva: Librairie Droz S. A., 1982, 211 p.
A detailed study of *The Song*. Pensom states in the introduction that his "thesis is that an adequate reading of the poem's meaning must include a consideration of the whole hierarchy of contexts within which the poem's meaning is generated, from the micro-context of the prosodic unit to the macro-context which conditions the poem's ethical perspectives."

Pope, Mildred K. "Four Chansons de Geste: A Study in Old French Epic Versification: Parts I, II, and III." *Modern Language Review* VIII, No. 3 (July 1913): 352-67; IX, No. 1 (January 1914): 41-52; X, No. 3 (July 1915): 310-19.
A scholarly study of the versification of *The Song,* which Pope compares with and declares superior to that of other chansons de geste.

Renoir, Alain. "Roland's Lament: Its Meaning and Function in the *Chanson de Roland.*" *Speculum* 35, No. 4 (October 1960): 572-83.
Focuses on Roland's pivotal lament for his slain men, arguing that *The Song* should be interpreted as a Christian poem. Renoir's conclusions are challenged by Owen and Jones.

Robertson, Howard S. "Blancandrin As Diplomat." *Romance Notes* 10, No. 2 (Spring 1969): 373-78.
Analyzes the scenes between Ganelon and Blancandrin, noting that the latter, "the wisest of the pagans," cunningly exploits Ganelon's jealousy to incite the Frank to treachery.

Short, Ian. "Roland's Final Combat." *Cultura Neolatina* XXX, Nos. 1-2 (1970): 135-55.
Hypothesizes that the Oxford version of *The Song* omits mention of the fact that a Saracen grievously insulted Roland by pulling his beard—a detail necessary to a complete understanding of the scene in which Roland, near death, defeats his last Saracen attacker. Short believes that this incident "seals the debasement of Roland's chivalric honour which started at Roncevaux, at the same time as serving as a necessary prelude to the hero's penance, confession and death."

Simpson, John. "Comparative Structural Analysis of Three Ethical Questions in *Beowulf,* the *Nibelungenlied,* and the *Chanson de Roland.*" *The Journal of Indo-European Studies* 3, No. 3 (Fall 1975): 239-54.
Analyzes the ethics of the epic heroes in the three works not from a Christian viewpoint but "from the perspective of the Indo-European heroic warrior's ethical commitments."

Stern, J. P. "Antecedents and Comparisons." In his *Reinterpretations: Seven Studies in Nineteenth-Century German Literature,* pp. 7-41. New York: Basic Books, 1964.
Includes a comparison of the style and merit of the Oxford version of *The Song* with that of a later twelfth-century German rendering of the story, the *Rolandslied*.

Stranges, John A. "The Significance of Bramimonde's Conversion in *The Song of Roland.*" *Romance Notes* 16, No. 1 (Autumn 1974): 190-96.
Argues that Bramimunde's conversion to Christianity is a symbol of *The Song*'s assertion of the triumph of good over evil and of the Christian faith.

———. "The Character and the Trial of Ganelon: A New Appraisal." *Romania* 96, No. 3 (1975): 333-67.
Presents a case for viewing Ganelon sympathetically, not as a villain but as "a real human being with fears, emotions, despair,

strength, weakness, and all the other attributes that go along with the definition of human being."

Szittya, Penn R. "The Angels and the Theme of *Fortitudo* in the *Chanson de Roland.*" *Neuphilologische Mitteilungen* 72, No. 2 (1971): 193-223.

A detailed explication of the function and significance of the angels Michael and Gabriel in *The Song*.

Thomas, P. Aloysius. "The Structural and Aesthetic Heroes in the *Song of Roland.*" *Neuphilologische Mitteilungen* 81, No. 1 (1980): 1-6.

Differentiates between the poem's structural hero—Charlemagne—and its aesthetic hero—Roland.

Vance, Eugene. "Spatial Structure in the *Chanson de Roland.*" *Modern Language Notes* 82, No. 5 (December 1967): 604-23.

Explores the importance of spatial settings to thematic concerns in *The Song*.

———. "Roland and the Poetics of Memory." In *Textual Strategies: Perspectives in Post-Structuralist Criticism,* edited by Josué V. Harari, pp. 374-403. Ithaca: Cornell University Press, 1979.

Discusses the world of *The Song* as a "commemorative" culture—one which "granted special importance to the faculty of memory"—and speculates about the narrative and ethical implications of such a model.

Van Emden, W. G. "Another Look at Charlemagne's Dreams in the *Chanson de Roland.*" *French Studies* XXVIII, No. 3 (July 1974): 257-71.

A linguistic and thematic analysis of Charlemagne's dreams in *The Song*.

Vitz, Evelyn Birge. "Desire and Causality in Medieval Narrative." *Romanic Review* LXXI No. 3 (May 1980): 213-43.

Considers to what degree the characters in *The Song* achieve their desires.

White, Julian Eugene. "*La Chanson de Roland:* Secular or Religious Inspiration?" *Romania* 84 (1963): 398-408.

Proffers a resolution to the critical dilemma surrounding *The Song*'s fundamental ethos. After considering in turn the theories of Renoir, Jones and Owen, White concludes that *The Song* achieves its unity through a central Christian motif. While a feudal heroic ethic exists in the poem, it operates in conjunction with, and is overshadowed by, a Christian worldview.

Whitehead, F. "The Textual Criticism of the *Chanson de Roland:* An Historical Review." In *Studies in Medieval French Presented to Alfred Ewert in Honour of His Seventieth Birthday,* pp. 76-89. Oxford: Clarendon Press, 1961.

An overview of the editorial treatment given the text of *The Song*. After examining the policies of various editors, Whitehead concludes that the optimum editing of the poem would "combine Bédier's 'structural' approach . . . with the traditional concept of the textual critic as a weigher of probabilities."

Zaddy, Zara P. "The Problem of the Two Ganelons." In *The Medieval Alexander Legend and the Romance Epic: Essays in Honour of David J. A. Ross,* edited by Peter Noble, Lucie Polak and Claire Isoz, pp. 269-88. Millwood, N.Y.: Kraus International Publications, 1982.

A consideration of the correct ordering of the *laisses* describing Ganelon's reaction to being nominated envoy in the council scene. Zaddy compares the Oxford manuscript of *The Song* with other versions of the legend which order this scene differently, concluding that, as the behavior of Ganelon in the Oxford *Song*'s council scene is inconsistent with his character, the Oxford manuscript is faulty.

Zimroth, E. "Grace and Free Will in the *Chanson de Roland.*" *Essays in French Literature,* No. 9 (November 1972): 1-13.

Argues that "although the larger scheme of history encompassed by the *Roland* seems to have been predetermined by God, the individual acting within that scheme has freedom of choice."

Homer
(Iliad)
Circa Eighth Century B.C.

Greek poem.

The *Iliad* is one of the greatest literary artifacts of Western civilization. Over the centuries, it has been admired both for the artistic mastery it demonstrates and for the profound influence it has exerted on all of European literature. Renowned for its clear narrative style, vivid descriptions, and unmitigated realism, the *Iliad* has served as the primary model for most subsequent epics. In addition, Homer's treatment of such themes as fate, honor, and humanity's quest for immortality, along with his delineation of the heroic code, forms the basis of all heroic poetry after his time. Although critics continue to debate the authorship and textual integrity of the *Iliad,* they are unanimous in praising the imaginative and psychological scope of the poem.

Almost nothing is known about Homer, but scholars hypothesize that he was an Ionian Greek (probably from the coast of Asia Minor or one of the adjacent islands), that he was born sometime before 700 B.C., and that he lived in approximately the latter half of the eighth century B.C. According to legend, he was a blind itinerant poet (the Greek word *homēros* means blind man); historians note that singing bards in ancient Greece were often blind and that the legend, therefore, may be based on fact, but that it is also possible that Homer may have lost his sight only late in life, or that his purported blindness was meant to mask his illiteracy.

Internal evidence from the two major works attributed to Homer suggests that the *Iliad* preceded the *Odyssey* and that both were composed in the eighth century B.C. in a dialect that was a mixture of Ionic and Aeolic Greek. Biographies of Homer exist in the form of six early ''lives'' and assorted commentaries by ancient and Byzantine scholars, but the information they contain is considered unreliable and mostly mythical. Some commentators have gone so far as to assert that no such individual as Homer ever lived.

The paucity of information regarding Homer and his relation to the *Iliad* and the *Odyssey* has incited much scholarly inquiry and has brought together the efforts of experts in such fields as archeology, linguistics, art, and comparative literature. As a result of their research, three main theories regarding the composition of the poems have emerged: the analytic, the unitarian, and the oral folk-epic. Until the publication of Friedrich Adolph Wolf's *Prolegomena ad Homerum* in 1795, the notion that Homer was the author of the *Iliad* and the *Odyssey* was largely undisputed. However, citing certain inconsistencies and errors in the texts, Wolf asserted that the two works were not the compositions of one poet, but the products of many different authors at work on various traditional poems and stories. Wolf's argument convinced many critics—who were subsequently termed the analysts—but also inspired the notorious authorship controversy known as the ''Homeric question.'' Although Wolf's view prevailed throughout the nineteenth and early twentieth centuries, it was ultimately challenged by an opposing group of critics, the unitarians, whose primary spokesman was Andrew Lang. The unitarians insisted that a single individual of genius composed the Homeric epics, and they supported that claim by citing a unified sensibility, original style, and consistent use of themes and imagery in the poems.

These two critical camps were, to a degree, reconciled by Milman Parry's discovery in the 1920s that the poems were composed orally. Parry established that Homeric verse is formulaic by nature, relying on generic epithets (such as ''wine-dark sea'' and ''rosy-fingered dawn''), repetition of stock lines and half-lines, and scenes and themes typical of traditional folk poetry. Comparing Homer's poetry with ancient oral epics from other cultures, Parry deduced that Homer was most likely a rhapsode, or itinerant professional reciter, who improvised stories to be sung at Greek festivals. As a public performer, Homer probably learned to weave together standard epic story threads and descriptions in order to sustain his narrative, and relied on mnemonic devices and phrases to fill the natural metrical units of poetic lines. Parry's theory, like that of the analysts, stressed the derivative, evolutionary character of Homer's poetry; but like the unitarians, Parry affirmed Homer's individual genius as a shaper of traditional elements whose creations far exceeded the sum of their borrowed parts. Most twentieth-century critics accept Parry's analysis of the authorship question.

The textual history of the *Iliad,* then, is assumed to have begun with an oral version of the poem which was transmitted by local bards and probably written down on papyri shortly after Homer's death. Although Homeric Greece did not yet have a system of writing appropriate for literary texts, records indicate that a Phoenician alphabet may have been adapted and used in the eighth century B.C. Once set down in writing, the poems most likely became the exclusive property of the *Homeridae,* or sons of Homer, a bardic guild whose members performed and preserved the poems. Scholars believe that in the second half of the sixth century B.C. the Athenian dictator Peisistratus, who ruled from 560-27 B.C., established a Commission of Editors of Homer to edit the text of the poems and remove any errors and interpolations that had accumulated in the process of transmission—thereby establishing a Canon of Homer. The origin of the current title, which means "the poem of Ilios" (the Homeric name for Troy), remains a matter of conjecture. Scholars are uncertain whether Homer ever used it, for the earliest mention of the title yet discovered was by Herodotus in the fifth century B.C. Fragments of papyri, a third century codex, and two other partial manuscripts exist, but the oldest full surviving manuscript of the poem, probably transcribed by a Byzantine scholar, dates from the ninth century. The first printed edition of Homer's poetry appeared in Europe in 1488 and remained in use until the seventeenth century. Many translations, both prose and verse, of the *Iliad* have subsequently been published. Critics agree that the most influential translations have been by George Chapman, Alexander Pope, and the group consisting of Andrew Lang, Walter Leaf, and Ernest Myers; the edition most highly regarded and most often used today is that of Richmond Lattimore.

Approximately 15,000 lines long and divided into twenty-four books (a structure that seems to date from the third century B.C. rather than from Homer's lifetime), the *Iliad* is composed in dactylic, or "heroic," hexameter. The action of the poem takes place near the Hellespont, in northwest Asia Minor, during the tenth year of the Trojan War, which took place in the second half of the twelfth century B.C. In simplest terms, the plot recounts an episode near the end of the war between King Priam of Troy and the kings of Greece, led by King Agamemnon of Mycenae and his brother Menelaus of Sparta. One ot Priam's sons, Paris, has abducted the fabled beauty Helen, wife of Menelaus. The Greek armies, notably the troop commanded by Achilles, prince of the Myrmidons and the bravest and most headstrong of Agamemnon's supporters, have already managed to capture and loot a portion of Trojan territory. However, Achilles and Agamemnon become involved in a personal feud: when Agamemnon is forced to give up Chryseis, a captured Trojan girl and the daughter of a priest of Apollo, in order to avoid the god's revenge, he comforts himself by taking Briseis, another Trojan woman who is Achilles' lover. Achilles withdraws his troops in indignation and wrath, refusing to aid Agamemnon any further. An unsuccessful truce between the Greeks and the Trojans follows, intended to provide the opportunity for Menelaus and Paris to settle their feud by single combat. When fighting resumes, the Greek forces find themselves in the weaker position, and Hector, another of Priam's sons, penetrates their defenses and sets fire to one of the Greek ships. At this point, Achilles relents and sends the Myrmidon troop, with his beloved friend Patroclus in command, to assist Agamemnon in defense of the ships. An exceptionally fine soldier, Patroclus performs gloriously in battle, but is nevertheless killed by Hector. In sorrow and rage, Achilles rejoins the combat, repels the Trojan forces, and kills Hector, mutilating Hector's corpse by tying it to a chariot and dragging it around the city. King Priam, who is overtaken by grief for his son, visits Achilles in his camp and begs for the return of Hector's body. Achilles agrees and the work closes with the description of Hector's funeral.

Over the centuries, critics have been nearly unanimous in praising Homer's handling of the narrative, imagery, structure, and themes of the *Iliad.* They commend his ability to intersperse lengthy descriptions of battle scenes with highly dramatic dialogue, whimsical fantasy about the gods of Olympus, and, at certain key moments, moving lyrical poetry. Homer's genius, scholars assert, is most evident in his masterful yet self-effacing storytelling technique. In a perfectly plain and direct manner, the narrator carries the action forward, examining the events in great detail and occasionally digressing from the main narrative, but always in such a manner that the course of the tale seems completely natural and the end entirely inevitable. Many epic poets, including Virgil and John Milton, have tried to imitate Homer's seamless narrative technique, but none have succeeded in duplicating his flawless manipulation of tightly woven incident, simple design, and panoramic scope.

Homer's imagery in the *Iliad* is also marked by immediacy and crystalline clarity. His frequent employment of similes enhances the realism and enlarges the range of the poem by bringing into its military world parallel images from domestic life, agriculture, and nature. Scholars have marvelled at the degree of accuracy demonstrated by Homer in his portrayal of battle scenes; his knowledge of weapons, battle strategy, and even the medical treatment of wounds has been proven uncannily thorough. Perhaps the greatest testament to Homer's descriptive powers, though, is the fact that his portrayal of Troy in the *Iliad* proved convincing enough to encourage the nineteenth-century explorer Heinrich Schliemann to seek its actual site. The city of Troy was assumed to be fictional until the late nineteenth century. However, in a series of archeological excavations between 1870 and 1881, Schliemann discovered nine layers of the city, establishing that it did exist and that it was indeed sacked in the twelfth century B.C.

Although most scholars praise the narrative impact and brilliant imagery of the *Iliad,* there is a great deal of debate regarding the structural, historic, and thematic unity of the poem. Some critics posit that the unity of the *Iliad* is weakened by Homer's occasional errors and anachronisms. Others admit that Homer's position as an eighth-century B.C. author discussing events that took place in the twelfth century B.C. naturally poses some problems, but they dismiss Homer's historical anachronisms, asserting that his blending the customs of his own era with those of the past contributes to the imaginative force and encyclopedic framework of the poem. Still other commentators divide the *Iliad* into two separate stories—the Acheleid, or the story of Achilles's moral tragedy, and the Iliad, or the tale of the imminent destruction of Troy—and suggest that the structural unity of the poem stems from the interplay of the two parts. According to another theory, the intricate figures and markings on the shield of Achilles provide the main structural clues to the poem. More than any other unifying factor, though, critics cite the comprehensive and cohesive vision of life presented in the *Iliad.* Although Homer presents an extremely harsh view of life in which human beings often seem destined to suffer as mere playthings of the gods and fate, he simultaneously conveys the value of human ideals and the joy of pursuing heroic excellence.

The characterization of Achilles also lends unity to the *Iliad.* The primary subject of the poem, he embodies many of the major themes of the work. For example, in his genuine enjoyment of life and earnest questing for fame and immortality, even at the price of death, Achilles personifies the dual conception of the brevity of life and the eternity of fame. Through Achilles, Homer also delineates a heroic code which all later Western literature imitates: the chief aim of a hero's life is to win renown for his *aristeia* (excellence, courage, prowess). To that end, he uses all the resources given to him through his aristocratic birth, wealth, intelligence, and military and athletic abilities. Furthermore, he fiercely guards his honor and that of his companions, strives to fulfill his *aidos* (duty), and accepts his *Moira* (fate) despite his constant striving for success. In the world of Homeric epic, the effort to gain immortality by adhering to these heroic qualities itself confers a degree of immortality on the hero. Yet the realism of the *Iliad* dictates that this emphasis on heroic glory be balanced by the tragedies of Patroclus and Hector, and that Achilles be revealed not only as the chief proponent of noble heroic behavior but also as vain, intemperate, and boastful. For this reason, critics have often commented on the fullness of Homer's characterizations, emphasizing his keen understanding of human motivation, weaknesses, and strengths.

As one of the best known literary works of the Western world, the *Iliad* has inspired much critical commentary and has wielded an enormous influence on later authors and readers. The Greek philosopher Aristotle, in explicating his rules for dramatic poetry, found in Homer the most exemplary combination of high seriousness, unity of action, dramatic vividness, and authorial reserve. In classical times, Homer's works formed the basis of any educational curriculum and therefore left an indelible imprint on the fields of literature, art, philosophy, and ethics. Medieval Byzantine scholars devoted much time to writing exhaustive commentaries on Homer's poetry and the fourteenth-century Italian poet Francesco Petrarch became the first major writer to attempt to learn Greek specifically in order to study Homer. Homer's works, generally venerated as repositories of traditional wisdom, were among the first books to be printed in the fifteenth century in Europe. However, the vogue for restraint and correctness that characterized the critical thought of the sixteenth century led many scholars to reject Homer's works in favor of those of Virgil. Contending that the *Iliad* possessed a savage, primitive streak evident in its delight in violence and its seeming lack of sentiment, some critics even attacked Homer as immoral. However, Homer's preeminence as an epic poet was reestablished in the eighteenth century by the translations of Chapman and Pope and the essays in praise of Homer by Joseph Addison. Stressing the nobility of Homer's poetry, the nineteenth-century critic Matthew Arnold reaffirmed Homer's mastery by extolling the meter, diction, and themes of the *Iliad*. With the value of the *Iliad* firmly established, twentieth-century critics have focused upon such specialized topics as Homer's narrative technique, use of irony and humor, and development of individual characters. Exploring Homer's philosophical tenets, scholars still grapple with his presentation of death, divine and human justice, and the role of the citizen and the state in society. The concept of *aristeia* and other elements of the heroic code also inspire commentary, with critics attempting to define Homer's attitude toward the heroic code that Achilles celebrates. In addition, studies in such related fields as history, archeology, art, and linguistics proliferate.

There seems no doubt that the *Iliad,* the oldest and in some ways the most formidable work of Western literature, has remained fresh and intriguing for generation after generation of scholars and readers. It impresses as much by its thematic complexity as by its stylistic simplicity, as much by its depiction of tragedy as by its celebration of life, and as much by its harsh descriptions of warfare as by its tender lyric poetry. The many questions regarding its authorship and text have not affected its readers' enthusiasm for the colorful, energetic, all-embracing panorama of life it offers.

PRINCIPAL ENGLISH TRANSLATIONS

The Iliads of Homer (translated by George Chapman) 1611
The Iliad of Homer (translated by Alexander Pope) 1715-20
Homer's Iliad and Odyssey (translated by William Cowper) 1791
The Iliad of Homer (translated by William Cullen Bryant) 1870
The Iliad of Homer (translated by Andrew Lang, Walter Leaf, and Ernest Myers) 1893
The Iliad of Homer (translated by Samuel Butler) 1898
The Iliad (translated by A. T. Murray) 1924-25
Iliad (translated by Emil V. Rieu) 1950
The Iliad (translated by Richmond Lattimore) 1951
Iliad (translated by William H. Rouse) 1954
The Anger of Achilles (translated by Robert Graves) 1959
The Iliad (translated by Ennis Rees) 1963
The Iliad (translated by Robert Fitzgerald) 1974

PLATO (dialogue date c. 4th Century B.C.)

[*Plato was a Greek philosopher and teacher who flourished in the fourth and fifth centuries B.C. Considered by many commentators the greatest master of Greek prose, he is also acknowledged as a seminal influence on the intellectual tradition of the Western world. The pupil of Socrates and the teacher of Aristotle, Plato stressed the role of education in preparing citizens to serve the state; in fact, he believed that social problems would be solved only when philosophers became rulers, or rulers philosophers. Around 387 B.C., he founded the Academy, the prototype of all Western universities and the first known permanent institution whose sole purpose was education and research. His writings, which were largely didactic, are concerned with the preservation and vindication of Socratic doctrine, but also treat such questions as the immortality of the soul, the nature of knowledge, and the role of pleasure in human life. The* Apology, Epistles, *and dialogues contain all of Plato's known writings. Scholars note that his greatest contribution to philosophy is his Theory of Ideas, in which he holds that the only real objects of knowledge are perfect, changeless entities, called Ideas or Forms, which exist outside of time and space. In the following excerpt from his* Republic, *Plato and his brother Adeimantus are engaged in a dialogue about the best way to educate the ideal citizen. Plato criticizes Homer's portrayal of the gods and of Achilles in the* Iliad *as unsuitable because it may foster a mistaken notion of the character of deities and heroes. Since the date of composition of the* Republic *is unknown, Plato's approximate death date has been used to date this excerpt.*]

[Plato: "We] shall begin by educating mind and character, shall we not?"

[Adeimantus:] "Of course."

"In this education you would include stories, would you not?"

"Yes."

"These are of two kinds, true stories and fiction. Our education must use both, and start with fiction."

"I don't know what you mean."

"But you know that we begin by telling children stories. These are, in general, fiction, though they contain some truth. And we tell children stories before we start them on physical training."

"That is so."

"That is what I meant by saying that we must start to educate the mind before training the body."

"You are right," he said.

"And the first step, as you know, is always what matters most, particularly when we are dealing with those who are young and tender. That is the time when they are easily moulded and when any impression we choose to make leaves a permanent mark."

"That is certainly true."

"Shall we therefore readily allow our children to listen to any stories made up by anyone, and to form opinions that are for the most part the opposite of those we think they should have when they grow up?"

"We certainly shall not."

"Then it seems that our first business is to supervise the production of stories, and choose only those we think suitable, and reject the rest. We shall persuade mothers and nurses to tell our chosen stories to their children, and by means of them to mould their minds and characters which are more important than their bodies. The greater part of the stories current today we shall have to reject."

"Which are you thinking of?"

"We can take some of the major legends as typical. For all, whether major or minor, should be cast in the same mould and have the same effect. Do you agree?"

"Yes: but I'm not sure which you refer to as major."

"The stories in Homer and Hesiod and the poets. For it is the poets who have always made up fictions and stories to tell to men."

"What sort of stories do you mean and what fault do you find in them?"

"The worst fault possible," I replied, "especially if the fiction is an ugly one."

"And what is that?"

"Misrepresenting the nature of gods and heroes, like a portrait painter whose portraits bear no resemblance to their originals." (pp. 130-32)

"I entirely agree," said Adeimantus, "that [such] stories are unsuitable."

"Nor can we permit stories of wars and plots and battles among the gods; they are quite untrue, and if we want our prospective guardians to believe that quarrelsomeness is one of the worst of evils, we must certainly not let them be told the story of the Battle of the Giants or embroider it on robes, or tell them other tales about many and various quarrels between gods and heroes and their friends and relations. On the contrary, if we are to persuade them that no citizen has ever quarrelled with any other, because it is sinful, our old men and women must tell children stories with this end in view from the first, and we must compel our poets to tell them similar stories when they grow up. But we can admit to our state no stories about Hera being tied up by her son, or Hephaestus being flung out of Heaven by his father for trying to help his mother when she was getting a beating, nor any of Homer's Battles of the Gods, whether their intention is allegorical or not. Children cannot distinguish between what is allegory and what isn't, and opinions formed at that age are usually difficult to eradicate or change; we should therefore surely regard it as of the utmost importance that the first stories they hear shall aim at encouraging the highest excellence of character."

"Your case is a good one," he agreed, "but if someone wanted details, and asked what stories we were thinking of, what should we say?"

To which I replied, "My dear Adeimantus, you and I are not engaged on writing stories but on founding a state. And the founders of a state, though they must know the type of story the poet must produce, and reject any that do not conform to that type, need not write them themselves."

"True: but what are the lines on which our poets must work when they deal with the gods?"

"Roughly as follows," I said. "God must surely always be represented as he really is, whether the poet is writing epic, lyric, or tragedy."

"He must."

"And in reality of course god is good, and he must be so described."

"Certainly."

"But nothing good is harmful, is it?"

"I think not."

"Then can anything that is not harmful do harm?"

"No."

"And can what does no harm do evil?"

"No again."

"And can what does no evil be the cause of any evil?"

"How could it?"

"Well then; is the good beneficial?"

"Yes."

"So it must be the cause of well-being."

"Yes."

"So the good is not the cause of everything, but only of states of well-being and not of evil."

"Most certainly," he agreed.

"Then god, being good, cannot be responsible for everything, as is commonly said, but only for a small part of human life, for the greater part of which he has no responsibility. For we have a far smaller share of good than of evil, and while god must be held to be sole cause of good, we must look for some factors other than god as cause of the evil.''

''I think that's very true,'' he said.

''So we cannot allow Homer or any other poet to make such a stupid mistake about the gods, as when he says that

> Zeus has two jars standing on the floor of his palace, full of fates, good in one and evil in the other;

and that the man to whom Zeus allots a mixture of both has 'varying fortunes sometimes good and sometimes bad,' while the man to whom he allots unmixed evil is 'chased by ravening despair over the face of the earth.' Nor can we allow references to Zeus as 'dispenser of good and evil.''' (pp. 132-35)

''We must [also] ask the poets to stop giving their present gloomy account of the after-life, which is both untrue and unsuitable to produce a fighting spirit, and make them speak more favourably of it.''

''I agree,'' he said.

''We must begin, then,'' I said, ''by cutting out all passages such as the following—

> I would rather be a serf in the house of some landless man, with little enough for himself to live on, than king of all dead men that have done with life;

and this

> and expose to mortal and immortal eyes the hateful chambers of decay that fill the gods themselves with horror;

and

> Ah then, it is true that someting of us does survive even in the Halls of Hades, but with no intellect at all, only the ghost and semblance of a man;

and this

> he alone has a mind to reason with: the rest are mere shadows flitting to and fro;

and

> his disembodied soul took wing for the House of Hades, bewailing its lot and the youth and manhood that it left;

and this

> the spirit vanished like a wisp of smoke and went gibbering under ground;

and

> gibbering like bats that squeak and flutter in the depths of some mysterious cave when one of them has fallen from the rocky roof, losing his hold on his clustered friends, with shrill discord the company set out.

We must ask Homer and the other poets to excuse us if we delete all passages of this kind. It is not that they are bad poetry or are not popular; indeed the better they are as poetry the more unsuitable they are for the ears of children or men who are to be free and fear slavery more than death.'' (pp. 140-41)

''But when a poet tells or a dramatist presents tales of endurance against odds by famous men, then we must give him an audience. For instance, when Homer makes Odysseus strike himself on the chest, and 'call his heart to order,' saying,

> Patience my heart! You have put up with fouler than this.''

''We must certainly listen to him then.''

''But we must not let him make his characters mercenary or grasping.''

''Certainly not.''

''We cannot let a poet say,

> The gods can be won with gifts, and so can the king's majesty.

We cannot agree that Achilles' tutor Phoenix gave him proper advice when he told him not to desist from his 'wrath,' and help the Achaeans unless they brought him presents. Nor can we consent to regard Achilles as so grasping that he took Agamemnon's presents, or refused to give up Hector's body unless he was paid a ransom.''

''It would be quite wrong,'' he said, ''to commend things of this sort.''

''I say it with hesitation, because of Homer's authority.'' I went on, ''but it is positively wicked to say these things about Achilles or believe them when we hear them said. There are other examples. Achilles says to Apollo,

> You have made a fool of me, Archer-king, and
> are the most mischievous of gods: how much
> I should like to pay you out if I had the power.

He refuses to obey the River Scamander, who is a god, and is ready to fight him, and he sends the lock of his hair dedicated to the River Spercheius as a gift to 'the Lord Patroclus,' who was already dead. We can believe none of this, and we shall regard as untrue also the whole story of the dragging of the body of Hector round the tomb of Patroclus and the slaughter of prisoners at his pyre. We cannot, in fact, have our citizens believe that Achilles, whose mother was a goddess, and whose father, Peleus, was a man of the utmost self-control and a grandson of Zeus, and who had in Chiron the wisest of schoolmasters, was in such a state of inner confusion that he combined in himself the two contrary maladies of ungenerous meanness about money and excessive arrogance to gods and men.''

''You are right,'' he said.

''We must therefore neither believe nor allow the story of the dreadful rapes attempted by Theseus, son of Poseidon, and Peirithous, son of Zeus, or any of the other lies now told about the terrible and wicked things which other sons of gods and heroes are said to have dared to do. We must compel our poets to say either that they never did these things or that they are not the sons of gods; we cannot allow them to assert both. And they must not try to persuade our young men that the gods are the source of evil, and that heroes are no better than ordinary mortals; that, as we have said, is a wicked lie, for we have proved that no evil can originate with the gods.''

''Of course.''

lies are positively harmful. For those who e lenient towards their own shortcomings if this sort of thing is and was always done by e gods,

se kin of Zeus, to whom
ancestral altar high in heaven
Ida's mount belongs,

ns

still runs the blood of gods.

We must therefore put a stop to stories of this kind before they breed in our young men an undue tolerance of wickedness."

"We certainly must." (pp. 146-48)

Plato, "Part III: Education, The First Stage," in The Republic, *translated by Desmond Lee, revised edition, Penguin Books, 1974, pp. 129-76.*

ARISTOTLE (essay date c. 4th century B.C.)

[*Considered the most versatile of the ancient Greek philosophers, Aristotle, who lived in the fourth century B.C., was also a renowned scientist and teacher. He studied at Plato's Academy in Athens and subsequently spent five years researching marine biology on the island of Lesbos. In 342, he received a commission to work as tutor to the young Prince Alexander of Macedon, whom he instructed in political theory and the works of Homer. Aristotle's writings, many of which are lost, exist for the most part in the form of lecture notes that were composed while he taught at the Lyceum, a school modeled on Plato's Academy that Aristotle established in 335. The variety of subjects found in such works as the* Physics, Ethics, Metaphysics, Politics, *and* Rhetoric *attests to the diversity of Aristotle's interests. His two best-known treatises, however, remain the* Organon, *in which he is credited with having created the science of logic, and the* Poetics, *considered perhaps the most influential work of literary criticism ever written. Although he was not widely read in Europe until the medieval period, Aristotle's writings have had an enormous impact on all branches of Western learning, leading Dante Alighieri to deem him "the Master of those who know." In the following excerpt from his* Poetics, *Aristotle discusses the principles of epic composition, praising Homer for his handling of action, characterization, meter, narration, and "the improbabilities." Since the date of composition of the* Poetics *is unknown, Aristotle's approximate death date has been used to date this excerpt.*]

In the Epic, as in Tragedy, the story should be constructed on dramatic principles: everything should turn about a single action, one that is a whole, and is organically perfect—having a beginning, and a middle, and an end. In this way, just as a living animal, individual and perfect, has its own beauty, so the poem will arouse in us its own characteristic form of pleasure. So much is obvious from what has gone before. Putting the thing negatively, we may say that the plot of an Epic must be unlike what we commonly find in histories, which of necessity represent, not a single action, but some one period, with all that happened therein to one or more persons, however unrelated the several occurrences may have been. For example: the Battle of Salamis took place at the same time as the defeat of the Carthaginians in Sicily; but the two events did not converge to the same end. And similarly, one event may immediately follow another in point of time, and yet there may be no sequence leading to one issue. Nevertheless, one may venture to say, most of the epic poets commit this very fault of making their plots like chronicles.

In precisely this respect, therefore, Homer . . . manifestly transcends the other epic poets. Far from taking all the legend of Ilium for his theme, he did not attempt to deal even with the War in its entirety, although this had a definite beginning and end. Very likely he thought that the story would be too long to be easily grasped as a whole—or, if it were not too long, that it would be too complicated from the variety of the incidents. As it is, he has selected a single phase of the war for his main action, and employs a number of the other incidents by way of episode; for example, he diversifies his narrative with the Catalogue of the Ships, and so forth. Of the other epic poets, some take for their subject all the deeds of one hero; others all the events in one period; and others a single action, but one with a multiplicity of parts. This last is what was done by the author of the *Cypria,* and by the author of the *Little Iliad*. The consequence is that the ***Iliad*** and the ***Odyssey*** each furnish materials for but a single tragedy, or at most for two; while the *Cypria* supplies subjects for a number; and the *Little Iliad* for eight or more: an *Award of the Arms,* a *Philoctetes,* a *Neoptolemus,* a *Eurypylus,* a *Mendicant Odysseus,* a *Spartan Women,* a *Sack of Ilium,* a *Sailing of the Fleet*—one might add a *Sinon* and a *Trojan Women*.

Furthermore, there must be the same varieties of Epic Poetry as of Tragedy. That is, an Epic plot must be either (1) Uninvolved or (2) Involved, or the story must be one (3) of Suffering or (4) of Character. . . . The Constituent Parts, also, of the Epic must be the same as in Tragedy—save that the poet does not use the elements of Melody and Spectacle; for there necessarily are Reversals and Discoveries and Sufferings in this form of poetry as in that. And the Intellectual Processes and the Diction must be artistically worked out. These elements were all first used by Homer, who laid the proper emphasis on them severally; for each of his poems is a model of construction—the ***Iliad*** of an uninvolved plot and a story of tragic suffering; the ***Odyssey*** of an involved plot (since there are Discoveries throughout) and a story of character. And in addition to these excellences, each of the poems surpasses all others in point of Diction and Thought. (pp. 77-9)

But Epic poetry differs from Tragedy (1) in the length of the composition, and (2) in the metre. As for the length . . . : it must be possible for us to embrace the beginning and end of the story in one view. Now this condition would be met if the poem were shorter than the old epics—if it were about as long as one of the groups of three tragedies presented for a single hearing. . . . But through its capacity for extension, Epic Poetry has a great and peculiar advantage; for in a tragedy it is not possible to represent a number of incidents in the action as carried on simultaneously—the poet is limited to the one thing done on the stage by the actors who are there. But in the Epic, because of the narrative form, he may represent a number of incidents as simultaneous occurrences; and these, if they are relevant to the action, materially add to the poem. The increase in bulk tends to the advantage of the Epic in grandeur, and in variety of interest for the hearer through diversity of incident in the episodes. Uniformity of incident quickly satiates the audience, and makes tragedies fail on the stage.

As for the metre, Epic Poetry has appropriated the heroic (hexameter verse) as a result of experience. And the fitness of this measure might be critically tested; for if any one were to produce a narrative poem in another metre, or in several others, the incongruity would be obvious. Of all metres, in fact, the heroic is the stateliest and most impressive. On this account, it most readily admits the use of strange words and metaphors;

for in its tolerance of forms that are out of the ordinary, narrative poetry goes beyond the other kinds. The iambic and trochaic measures, on the other hand, are the concomitants of motion, the trochaic being appropriate to dancing, and the iambic expressive of life and action. . . . Still more unfitting would it be to compose an epic in a hotchpotch of metres after the fashion of Chaeremon's rhapsody. Hence no one ever has written a long story in any other metre than the heroic. Rather, nature herself, as we have said, teaches us to select the proper kind of verse for such a story.

Homer, so worthy of praise in other respects, is especially admirable in that he alone among epic poets is not unaware of the part to be taken by the author himself in his work. The poet should, in fact, say as little as may be in his own person, since in his personal utterances he is not an imitative artist. Now the rest of the epic poets continually appear in their own works, and their snatches of artistic imitation are few and far between. But Homer, after a brief preliminary, straightway brings in a man, or a woman, or some other type—no one of them vague, but each sharply differentiated. (pp. 79-81)

Some element of the marvellous unquestionably has a place in Tragedy; but the irrational (or illogical), which is the chief factor in the marvellous, and which must so far as possible be excluded from Tragedy, is more freely admitted in the Epic, since the persons of the story are not actually before our eyes. Take the account of the pursuit of Hector in the ***Iliad.*** On the stage, the scene would be ridiculous: Achilles running after Hector all alone, beneath the walls of Troy; the Grecian warriors halting instead of following, and Achilles shaking his head to warn them not to throw darts at their foe. In the narrative, however, since we do not combine the circumstances into one picture, the absurdity of the situation is not perceived.

That the marvellous is a source of pleasure may be seen by the way in which people add to a story; for they always embellish the facts with striking details, in the belief that it will gratify the listeners. Yet it is Homer above all who has shown the rest of us how a lie ought to be told. The essence of the method is the use of a fallacy in reasoning, as follows. Suppose that whenever A exists or comes to pass, B must exist or occur; men think, if the consequent B exists, the antecedent A must also—but the inference is illegitimate. For the poet, accordingly, the right method is this: if the antecedent A is untrue, and if there is something else, B, which would necessarily exist or occur if A were true, one must add on the B; for, knowing the added detail to be true, we ourselves mentally proceed to the fallacious inference that the antecedent A is likewise true. (pp. 81-2)

A sequence of events which, though actually impossible, looks reasonable should be preferred by the poet to what, though really possible, seems incredible. The story . . . should not be made up of incidents which are severally improbable; one should rather aim to include no irrational element whatsoever. At any rate, if an irrational element is unavoidable, it should lie outside of the story proper—as the hero's ignorance in *Oedipus the King* of the way in which Laius met his death. It should not lie within the story—like the anachronism in Sophocles' *Electra,* where a legendary hero is described as being killed at the modern Pythian games; or like the silence of . . . Telephus in *The Mysians* of . . . Aeschylus, where the man comes all the way from Tegea to Mysia without speaking. Accordingly, it is ridiculous for a poet to say that his story would be ruined if such incidents were left out; he has no business to construct such a plot to begin with. But if he does set out to represent an irrational incident, and if he obviously could have treated it in a way less offensive to our notions of probability, his fault is worse than ridiculous, lying not in his choice of an object to imitate, but in his art as an imitator. In the hands of an inferior poet, how manifest and intolerable would the improbabilities become which we find even in the ***Odyssey,*** at the point where the hero is set ashore. . . . As it is, Homer conceals the absurdity, and renders the incident charming, by means of his other excellences. . . . (pp. 83-4)

Elaborate Diction, however, is to be used only when the action pauses, and no purposes and arguments of the agents are to be displayed. Conversely, where the purposes and reasonings of the agents need to be revealed, a too ornate Diction will obscure them. (p. 84)

Aristotle, "Epic Poetry: The Principles of Its Construction," in Aristotle on the Art of Poetry, *edited and translated by Lane Cooper, Ginn and Company, 1913, pp. 77-84.*

EUSTATHIOS (essay date c. 1150-75)

[A Byzantine scholar, historian, and Metropolitan of Thessalonica, Eustathios is best known for his lengthy commentaries on the Iliad *and the* Odyssey. *In the following excerpt from his introduction to the* Iliad, *he explores the lasting appeal of Homer's verse and stresses his influence on readers throughout history. Eustathios's commentary was written sometime during the third Quarter of the twelfth century.]*

Homer is like Sirens. Perhaps it would be best if you kept clear of him from the start—if you blocked your ears with wax, or steered another course, to escape that magic. But suppose you made your way onward through the range of [the ***Iliad***], you would not easily pass him by, even if you were loaded with chains; and if you did, you would not be glad of it. The Seven Marvelous Sights have long been famous in story, but the *Marvelous Sounds?* If they were ever numbered in the same way, Homer's poetry would be the first of them. I do not think that any of the ancient sages failed to taste of it, least of all those who drew the waters of profane philosophy.

It is an old saying that out of Ocean arise all rivers, all springs, all wells. So out of Homer flooded down to the sages most if not all of the great stream of language. Of all the men one could mention who labored at astronomy, or science, or ethics, or profane literature generally, not one passed by Homer's tent without a welcome. All lodged with him, some to spend the rest of their lives being fed from his table, others to fulfill a need and to borrow something useful from him for their own argument. Among these was the Delphic Priestess, who shaped many of the oracles by the Homeric rule. The philosophers are concerned with Homer . . . so are the orators; the scholars have no other way to their goal but through him. Not one of the poets who have followed Homer works outside the rules which he laid down for the craft. They imitate him, make his goods their own, do anything which will help them to be like Homer. The geographers envy him and marvel at him. The very physicians and surgeons borrow good things from him. This poetry captivates even kings. Witness the great Alexander, who carried Homer's book along with him even in battle, as his treasure, or as provision for his campaigns. On this book he rested his head when it was time for sleep, so that even then he should not be separated from Homer, but should dream well, even while he saw him in imagination.

And in fact Homer's poetry is a royal thing; above all, the ***Iliad.*** The proverb may speak of "an Iliad of evils," but this poem is really "an Iliad of every good." Its arrangement is rather like that of drama because, although the narrative is in one verse form only, there are many characters. It is heavy with good things, which one could describe almost without end: philosophy, oratory, the fine art of generalship, teaching on the moral virtues, and in short every kind of art and science. You can also learn innocent deceptions from this source, and how to construct advantageous falsehoods, besides stinging jests, and the rules for composing eulogies. The good sense that it will bring to any man who cares to pay attention to it is beyond description. No one could deny to Homer's art the qualities that are considered excellent in the art of history: rich experience, or the gifts of making stories interesting, and of educating minds, and of spurring men to nobility, or any other gift that gives fame to the historian.

You may object that his poetry is heavy with myth, and that for this reason he risks banishment from our admiration. I answer, first: Homer's myths are not there for fun. They are shadows, or veils, of noble thoughts. Homer invents some myths to suit his own subject matter, their allegorical sense applying to those particular passages alone. Many of his other myths had been handed down by the men of old time, but he has put them to good use in the texture of his own poetry, although their allegorical sense had no real relation to the Troy-story, but only to the original enigma in the minds of their inventors. Second: even that did not mean that the Master of Wisdom was using myth for his pleasure. Wisdom is contemplation of truth; the wise man has the same goal; and if the wise man, then Homer too. He weaves his poetry with myths to attract the multitude. The trick is to use their surface appearance as a bait and charm for men who are frightened of the subtleties of philosophy, until he traps them in the net. Then he will give them a taste of truth's sweetness, and set them free to go their ways as wise men, and to hunt for it in other places. . . . (pp. 433-34)

Eustathios, "Homer: A Byzantine Perspective," translated by C. J. Herington, in Arion, *Vol. 8, No. 3, Autumn, 1969, pp. 432-34.*

MICHEL DE MONTAIGNE (essay date 1578-80)

[*Montaigne is one of French literature's most important figures and the creator of the personal essay as we know it. Immensely knowledgeable and an insatiable student of human habits and manners, he appears to have conceived his greatest work,* Essais *(1580-88;* Essays*), as a series of assays, or trials, of himself, of his judgment, and of his experience, all designed to probe his emotions, habits, and thoughts as they changed from day to day and year to year. In the following excerpt from that work, Montaigne posits that Homer, along with Alexander the Great and Epaminondas, is one of "three* [men] *outstanding above all the rest" and briefly comments on his poetic legacy. Montaigne's remarks were written in 1578-80.*]

If I were asked my choice of all the men who have come to my knowledge, it seems to me I should find three outstanding above all the rest.

One is Homer. Not that Aristotle and Varro (for example) are not perhaps as learned as he, nor that possibly even in his art itself Virgil may not be compared with him. I leave it to those men to judge who know them both. I who know only the one can say only this according to my capacity, that I do not believe that the Muses themselves could surpass the Roman:

> As sweetly to his artful lyre he sings
> As when the Cynthian god fingers the strings.
>
> PROPERTIUS

However, in making this judgment, we still should not forget that it is principally from Homer that Virgil derives his ability; that he is his guide and his schoolmaster, and that one single detail of the ***Iliad*** furnished both body and matter for that great and divine *Aeneid*. That is not the way I reckon; I bring in several other circumstances that make this personage a source of wonder to me, almost above man's estate. And indeed I am often astonished that he, who by his authority created and brought into credit in the world many deities, has not himself gained the rank of a god. Being blind and poor, living before the sciences were reduced to rules and certain observations, he knew them so well that all those who since have taken it upon themselves to establish governments, to conduct wars, and to write about either religion or philosophy, of whatever sect they might be, or about the arts, have used him as a master very perfect in the knowledge of all things, and his books as a nursery of every kind of ability:

> Better than Crantor and Chrysippus, he points out—
> And fuller too—what's fair, foul, useful, and what's
> not.
>
> HORACE

And as another says,

> From whose perennial spring the poet sips,
> And in Pierian waters wets his lips.
>
> OVID

And another:

> To these add the companions of the Muse, of whom
> Homer alone attained the stars.
>
> LUCRETIUS

And another:

> From whose abundant mouth
> All later poets draw their songs as from their source,
> Draining into their rivulets his torrent's course,
> Rich in the wealth of one.
>
> MANILIUS

It was against the order of nature that he created the most excellent production that can be. For things at birth are ordinarily imperfect; they gain in size and strength as they grow. He made the infancy of poetry and of several other sciences mature, perfect, and accomplished. For his reason he may be called the first and the last of poets, according to that beautiful testimony that antiquity has left to us about him: that having had no one he could imitate before him, he has had no one after him who could imitate him. His words, according to Aristotle, are the only words that have movement and action; they are the only substantial words.

Alexander the Great, having come upon a rich coffer among the spoils of Darius, commanded that it be reserved for him to keep his Homer in, saying that he was the best and most faithful counselor he had in his military affairs. For the same reason Cleomenes, son of Anaxandridas, used to say that he was the poet of the Lacedaemonians, because he was a very good master in the military art. This singular and particular tribute to him has also remained, that in Plutarch's judgment he is the only author in the world who has never sated or palled on men, appearing ever entirely different to his readers, and ever blooming in new grace. That madcap Alcibiades, having asked one who professed to be a man of letters for a book of Homer, gave him a cuff because he had none; as if someone should find one of our priests without a breviary.

Xenophanes was complaining one day to Hiero, tyrant of Syracuse, that he was so poor he did not have enough to feed two servants. "What!" he replied. "Homer, who was much poorer than you, feeds well over ten thousand of them, dead as he is." What did Panaetius leave to be said, when he called Plato the Homer of philosophers?

Besides this, what glory can be compared with his? There is nothing so alive in the mouths of men as his name and his works; nothing so well known and accepted as Troy, Helen, and his wars, which perhaps never existed. Our children are still called by the names he invented more than three thousand years ago. Who does not know Hector and Achilles? Not only certain private families but most nations seek their origin in his fictions. Mohammed, the second of that name, emperor of the Turks, writing to our Pope Pius II, says: "I am astonished how the Italians league themselves against me, seeing that we have our common origin in the Trojans, and that I, like them, have an interest in avenging the blood of Hector on the Greeks, whom they are favoring against me." Is it not a noble drama in which kings, commonwealths, and emperors keep playing their parts for so many ages, and for which this whole great universe serves as a theater? Seven Greek cities fell into dispute over his birthplace, so much honor did his very obscurity bring him:

> Smyrna, Rhodos, Colophon, Salamis, Chios, Argos,
> and Athens.
>
> AULUS GELLIUS

(pp. 569-71)

Michel de Montaigne, "Of the Most Outstanding Men," in his The Complete Works of Montaigne: Essays, Travel Journal, Letters, *translated by Donald M. Frame, Stanford University Press, 1957, pp. 569-74.*

GEORGE CHAPMAN (essay date 1598)

[A successful English dramatist and poet, Chapman is chiefly remembered as a scholar and translator of Homer's works. His rhyming fourteen-syllable translation of the Iliad, *published partially in 1598 and completed in 1611, introduced the poem to English-speaking readers. In addition, he translated the* Odyssey *in 1614-15, and other Homeric works in 1616. While his merits as a translator are often debated by scholars, his* Iliad *remains a landmark in Homer studies. In the following excerpt from his preface to the* Achilles Shield, *a section of the* Iliad *published in 1598, Chapman notes that his inspiration for the translation came from Jean de Sponde, a well-known French poet and translator. In addition, he provides a series of stylistic comparisons between the work of Homer and Virgil.]*

[Jean de Sponde], one of the most desertfull Commentars of Homer, calls all sorts of all men learned to be judicial beholders of this more then Artificiall and no lesse then Diuine Rapture, then which nothing can be imagined more full of soule and humaine extraction: for what is here prefigurde by our miraculous Artist but the vniuersall world, which, being so spatious and almost vnmeasurable, one circlet of a Shield representes and imbraceth? In it heauen turnes, the starres shine, the earth is enflowered, the sea swelles and rageth, Citties are built, one in the happinesse and sweetnesse of peace, the other in open warre & the terrors of ambush, &c.: and all these so liuely proposde, as not without reason many in times past haue beleiued that all these thinges haue in them a kind of voluntarie motion, euen as those Tripods of Vulcan. . . . Nor can I be resolu'd that their opinions be sufficiently refuted by Aristonicus, for so are all things here described by our diuinest Poet as if they consisted not of hard and solid mettals, but of a truely liuing and mouing soule. The ground of his inuention he shews out of Eustathius, intending by the Orbiguitie of the Shield the roundnesse of the world, by the foure mettalles the foure elementes, viz. by gold fire, by brasse earth, for the hardnes, by Tinne water, for the softnes and inclination to fluxure, by siluer Aire, for the grosnes & obscuritie of the mettal before it be refind. . . . Nor do I deny (saith Spondanus) Eneas arms to be forged with an exceeding height of wit by Virgil, but comparde with these of Homer they are nothing. And this is it (most honorde) that maketh me thus sodainely translate this Shield of Achilles, for since my publication of the other seuen bookes [of the ***Iliad***] comparison hath beene made betweene Virgill and Homer; who can be comparde in nothing with more decysall & cutting of all argument then in these two Shieldes. And whosoeuer shall reade Homer thoroughly and worthily will know the question comes from a superficiall and too vnripe a reader; for Homers Poems were writ from a free furie, an absolute & full soule, Virgils out of a courtly, laborious, and altogether imitatorie spirit: not a Simile hee hath but is Homers: not an inuention, person, or disposition, but is wholly or originally built vpon Homericall foundations, and in many places hath the verie wordes Homer vseth: besides, where Virgill hath had no more plentifull and liberall a wit then to frame twelue imperfect bookes of the troubles and trauailes of Æneas, Homer hath of as little subiect finisht eight & fortie perfect. And that the triuiall obiection may be answerd, that not the number of bookes but the nature and excellence of the worke commends it—all Homers bookes are such as haue beene presidents euer since of all sortes of Poems; imitating none, nor euer worthily imitated of any. Yet would I not be thought so ill created as to bee a malicious detracter of so admired a Poet as Virgill, but a true iustifier of Homer, who must not bee read for a few lynes with leaues turned ouer *caprichiously* in dismembred fractions, but throughout, the whole drift, weight, & height of his workes set before the apprensiue eyes of his iudge: the maiestie he enthrones and the spirit he infuseth into the scope of his worke so farre outshining Virgill, that his skirmishes are but meere scramblings of boyes to Homers; the silken body of Virgils muse curiously drest in guilt and embrodered siluer, but Homers in plaine massie and vnualued gold; not onely all learning, gouernment, and wisedome being deduc't as from a bottomlesse fountaine from him, but all wit, elegancie, disposition, and judgement. (pp. 297-99)

George Chapman, "Dedication, &c. of 'Achilles Shield'," in Elizabethan Critical Essays, Vol. II, *edited by G. Gregory Smith, Oxford University Press, 1904, pp. 295-307.*

RENÉ RAPIN (essay date 1664)

[A Jesuit scholar, Rapin was an influential French critic who also composed poetry in Latin. In the following excerpt, he compares the characterizations of Homer's Achilles and Virgil's Aeneas, admitting that Virgil had "an infinitely more noble Groundwork" for his hero, but nevertheless concluding that Achilles represents

"The Epitome of Imperfections and Vices." Rapin's commentary was originally published in French in 1664.]

The Action of Achilles, being somewhat more wonderful and surprizing, than that of Æneas, in regard, that it is wholly manag'd by him himself, without any Assistance or Company, and that his Presence in, or Absence from the Army, occasions all the Advantages and Disadvantages to his Party; every one will be inclin'd at first, to allow the Preference. But upon a Nicer View, it will not be so; and when we have given our selves the Leisure to look more narrowly into things, and shall have strictly examin'd these two Heroes, we shall form a quite different Judgment. The first Observation to be made, in order to the clearing up of this Point, is, that in all probability, it was not the Design and Intent of Homer, to give us in his Hero, the Idea of a great Commander, or of an accomplish'd Prince; but to shew us how prejudicial Discord is to any Party, and so to make a Draught of an Action at the same time terrible and wonderful. This is the Opinion of Tasso, in his *Opuscula*.

In which he has not imitated Xenophon, who in the Description he gives us of his Prince, the great Cyrus, to make an absolutely accomplish'd Person of him, confines himself not to truth of things, but to the Idea in general of a compleat Prince, according to the Rules of Aristotle in his Poetry, who would have the Poet, in the Representations and Descriptions he makes, draw Persons, not as they actually are, but as they really ought to be. And Plato, in the fifth Book of his *Laws*, tells us, that Imitation is not to be made, but from things in themselves most accomplish'd. Besides, as a Picture in a just and regular Imitation, ought to be like its Original; so ought not this Original to be any one Man or Prince in particular; but the Idea of a Prince, or accomplish'd Person in general. According to this Model, hath Plato drawn from the perfect Idea of a just Man, Xenophon of a Prince, and Cicero of an Orator, by attributing to each of these what was most transcendent in the Idea they form'd to themselves of each of them.

And hence it appears, that not only Homer alone, has not follow'd this Maxim, in the framing of his Heroe, by making him subject to great Weaknesses, and notorious Imperfections, instead of inserting into the Idea, he pretends to give of him, the Consummation of all Virtues. . . . (pp. 127-28)

And this is a very considerable Advantage, that Virgil had over Homer. For, whereas the latter had not, for the forming of his Heroe any other Idea, than that of the Virtue of Hercules, of Theseus, or of some other Person of those early times, who were Renown'd in the World, only for their bodily Strength and Vigour; it is no wonder if there be such a Defect, as to Morals, in the Heroe he hath given us, in reference to which he form'd him; there being not to be met with in those Days, either in the Records of History, or in Books, any Idea of Moral Virtue. And as Mankind knew of no greater Enemies to oppose, than Monsters and Wild Beasts, so there needed only good robust Bodies, and good Armour, to give a Man a just pretence to the Title of a Heroe. They were ignorant of, and unacquainted with, in that Age of the World, those more terrible and dangerous Enemies, their own Passions, and their own Desires; and Moderation and Justice were Virtues not known in those dark times in which Homer writ.

Virgil, besides the Advantage he had of forming his Hero, from the two Heroes of Homer, that is, from the Valour of Achilles, and the Prudence of Ulysses, had also the Advantage of intermixing the Gallantry of Ajax, the Wisdom of Nestor, the Indefatigable Patience of Diomedes, and all those other Virtues, of which Homer has drawn the Characters in his two Poems: and of Re-uniting to all these, yet farther, those several Virtues which he had observ'd in all other Illustrious Men, as in Themistocles, Epaminondas, Alexander, Hannibal, Jugurtha, and in a Number of others of Foreign Nations, as also what he had found most remarkable in the Characters of Horatius, Camillus, Scipio, Sertorius, Pompey, Cæsar, and of all the Heroes of his own Country. Had not then Virgil an infinitely more noble Groundwork to raise an accomplish'd Heroe upon, than Homer? (pp. 128-29)

This Inequality in the Subject I am now treating of, will still appear much more evident, if we will but give our selves the trouble of comparing the Character, which [Homer] has left us of Achilles, with that which Virgil has given us of Æneas. Achilles is brave, but withal, Hasty, Impetuous, Furious, Passionate, Violent, Unjust, Inexorable, a Contemner of all Laws, and one that places his Reason in the Sword he wears by his side. . . .

> Impatient, Rash, Inexorable, Proud,
> Scorning all Judges, and all Laws but Arms. . . .

Besides all these excellent Qualities, which certainly are no very great Arguments of a Heroe, he shows a great deal of Cruelty and Barbarity, in relation to the Body of Hector, even to such a degree, as to make it his Diversion, to Exercise his Vengeance upon it; and out of an unparallel'd peice of Covetousness, he Sells, to the Afflicted and Disconsolate Father, the Body of his Son. I shall not say any thing of his quitting, with a Lightness not to be Pardon'd, that great and generous Enterprize, undertaken by a general Combination of all Greece, upon the account of a Female Captive, for whom he gives himself up to Tears and sad Complaints, with all the Demonstrations of Weakness and Folly. In short, this Heroe of Homer, whose Reputation is to Great, and who has been so highly celebrated throughout all Ages, is the very Epitome of Imperfections and Vices.

But on the contrary, Virgil unites and conjoins all the Virtues in the Formation of his Heroe: He gives him Religion towards the Gods, Piety towards his Country, Tenderness and Friendship towards his Relations, and Equity and Justice towards All. He is undaunted in time of Danger, Patient in Labours, Couragious when occasions require, and Prudent in the Management of Affairs. In fine, He is Good, Peaceable, Liberal, Eloquent, Genteel, and Civil: His Air and Mien is all Grandeur and Majesty; and that he may not want any of those Qualifications, which might contribute towards the Accomplishment of a great Person; he is Fortunate. Ilioneus gives Dido a Character of him in these two Verses, which may be oppos'd to those two of [Homer] which are the Portraiture of Achilles. . . .

> Æneas was our Prince, a juster Lord,
> Or nobler Warriour never drew Sword. . . .

These are the three Sovereign Qualities, which make up his Essential Character, Religion, Justice, and Valour, and which were eminently conspicuous in Augustus, and were the Principal Virtues of that good and great Emperour, whom he has so lively express'd in all the Lineaments and Features of the Heroe, whose Picture he has Drawn and Inscrib'd to him. This is one of the most Refin'd and Ingenious pieces of Flattery that was ever known, in which has happen'd to him, what Pliny said some time after, with such a spriteliness of Thought in his *Panegyrick* to the Emperour Trajan: For Ovid tells us, that Piety was one of the Principal Virtues of Augustus, who made it so much his Care to restore the decay'd Honours of the Temples at Rome. . . .

> Under whose Conduct and auspicious Reign,
> Each Temple does its Ancient Worth Retain:
> Nor is h' alone Propitious to Mankind,
> The Gods themselves from him Protection find.

Thus, from the Virtues of Augustus, and a numerous Train of Perfections, distributed and dispers'd amongst divers other Heroes, has Virgil drawn the Portraicture of His: true Heroick Virtue, being a Combination and Complication of all Virtues, as Aristotle affirms in his *Ethicks*. And certainly, if the Pythagoreans would have a Sovereign, not only without the least fault, but also absolutely accomplish'd in, and entirely possess'd of all Virtues in general, that he might deserve to be the Head of the People; with greater Reason should a Heroe, who is the Model by which Kings ought to form themselves, be a Person of the most transcendent and consummate Virtue.

In fine, to conclude this Observation, Homer himself has said more in Commendation of Æneas, than ever was, or indeed can be said in Praise of any great Man; when in the fifth Book of his ***Iliad,*** he tells us, that this great Commander had always a Deity attending on him, for his security, and to preserve him from that Variety of Accidents, to which all other Men are liable to, as if Heaven had interested it self in his Preservation. (pp. 130-33)

René Rapin, an excerpt from "A Comparison of Homer and Virgil," in The Whole Critical Works of Monsieur Rapin, Vol. 1, *translated by Several Hands, H. Bonwicke, 1706, pp. 116-210.*

RENÉ LE BOSSU (essay date 1675)

[*Le Bossu was a French critic best known for his* Treatise on Epic Poetry, *written in 1675. Much discussed in England even before it was translated into English, the* Treatise *was severely criticized by Samuel Johnson and, in France, by Voltaire for its rigid rules concerning epic poetry. In the following excerpt from that work, Le Bossu discusses the structure and themes in the* Iliad, *maintaining that Homer's primary purpose was to show that "a misunderstanding between princes is the ruin of their own states."*]

The fables of poets were originally employed in representing the Divine Nature according to the notion then conceived of it. This sublime subject occasioned the first poets to be called divines, and poetry the language of the gods. They divided the divine attributes into so many persons because the infirmity of a human mind cannot sufficiently conceive or explain so much power and action in a simplicity so great and indivisible as that of God. And, perhaps, they were also jealous of the advantages they reaped from such excellent and exalted learning, and of which they thought the vulgar part of mankind was not worthy.

They could not describe the operations of this almighty Cause without speaking at the same time of its effects; so that to divinity they added physiology, and treated of both without quitting the umbrages of their allegorical expressions.

But man being the chief and most noble of all that God produced, and nothing being so proper or more useful to poets than this subject, they added it to the former, and treated of the doctrine of morality after the same manner as they did that of divinity and philosophy; and from morality thus treated is formed that kind of poem and fable which we call epic.

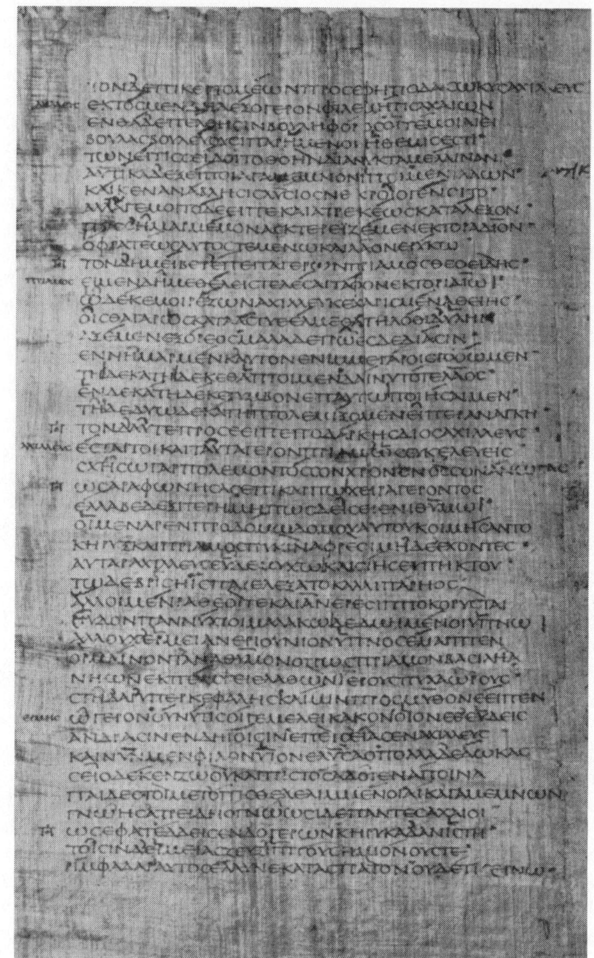

A page from a second-century Homer papyrus.

The poets did the same in morality that the divines had done in divinity. But that infinite variety of the actions and operations of the Divine Nature (to which our understanding bears so small a proportion) did, as it were, force them upon dividing the single idea of the only one God into several persons, under the different names of Jupiter, Juno, Neptune, and the rest.

And on the other hand, the nature of moral philosophy being such as never to treat of things in particular but in general, the epic poets were obliged to unite in one single idea, in one and the same person and in an action which appeared singular, all that looked like it in different persons and in various actions which might be thus contained as so many species under their genus.

The presence of the Deity and the care such an august cause is to be supposed to take about any action obliges the poet to represent this action as great, important, and managed by kings and princes. It obliges him likewise to think and speak in an elevated way above the vulgar, and in a style that may in some sort keep up the character of the divine persons he introduces. To this end serve the poetical and figurative expression and the majesty of the heroic verse.

But all this, being divine and surprising, may quite ruin all probability; therefore the poet should take a peculiar care as to that point, since his chief aim is to instruct, and without probability any action is less likely to persuade.

Lastly, since precepts ought to be concise to be the more easily conceived and less oppress the memory, and since nothing can be more effectual to this end than proposing one single idea and collecting all things so well together as to be present to our minds all at once, therefore the poets have reduced all to one single action, under one and the same design, and in a body whose members and parts should be homogeneous.

• • • • •

What we have observed of the nature of the epic poem gives us a just idea of it, and we may define it thus:

The epic poem is a discourse invented by art to form the manners by such instructions as are disguised under the allegories of some one important action, which is related in verse after a probable, diverting, and surprising manner.

• • • • •

In every design which a man deliberately undertakes, the end he proposes is the first thing in his mind, and that by which he governs the whole work and all its parts; thus, since the end of the epic poem is to regulate the manners, it is with this first view the poet ought to begin.

But there is a great difference between the philosophical and the poetical doctrine of manners. The schoolmen content themselves with treating of virtues and vices in general; the instructions they give are proper for all states of people and for all ages. But the poet has a nearer regard to his own country and the necessities of his own nation. With this design he makes choice of some piece of morality, the most proper and just he can imagine; and in order to press this home, he makes less use of the force of reasoning than of the power of insinuation, accommodating himself to the particular customs and inclinations of those who are to be the subject, or the readers, of his work.

Let us now see how Homer has acquitted himself in all these respects.

He saw the Grecians, for whom he designed his poem, were divided into as many states as they had capital cities. Each was a body politic apart, and had its form of government independent from all the rest. And yet these distinct states were very often obliged to unite together in one body against their common enemies. These were two very different sorts of government, such as could not be comprehended in one maxim or morality and in one single poem.

The poet, therefore, has made two distinct fables of them. The one is for Greece in general, united into one body but composed of parts independent on each other, and the other for each particular state considered as they were in time of peace, without the former circumstances and the necessity of being united.

As for the first sort of government, in the union or rather in the confederacy of many independent states experience has always made it appear that nothing so much causes success as a due subordination and a right understanding among the chief commanders. And on the other hand, the inevitable ruin of such confederacies proceeds from the heats, jealousies, and ambition of the different leaders and the discontents of submitting to a single general. All sort of states, and in particular the Grecians, had dearly experienced this truth. So that the most useful and necessary instructions that could be given them was to lay before their eyes the loss which both the people and the princes must of necessity suffer by the ambition, discord, and obstinacy of the latter.

Homer then has taken for the foundation of his fable this great truth, that a misunderstanding between princes is the ruin of their own states. "I sing," says he, "the anger of Achilles, so pernicious to the Grecians, and the cause of many heroes' deaths, occasioned by the discord and separation of Agamemnon and that prince."

But that this truth may be completely and fully known, there is need of a second to support it. It is necessary in such a design not only to represent the confederate states at first disagreeing among themselves and from thence unfortunate, but to show the same states afterwards reconciled and united and of consequence victorious.

Let us now see how he has joined all these in one general action.

Several princes independent of one another were united against a common enemy. The person whom they had elected their general offers an affront to the most valiant of all the confederates. This offended prince is so far provoked as to relinquish the union and obstinately refuse to fight for the common cause. This misunderstanding gives the enemy such an advantage that the allies are very near quitting their design with dishonor. He himself who made the separation is not exempt from sharing the misfortune which he brought upon his party. For having permitted his intimate friend to succor them in a great necessity, this friend is killed by the enemy's general. Thus the contending princes, being both made wiser at their own cost, are reconciled and unite again; then this valiant prince not only obtains the victory in the public cause, but revenges his private wrongs by killing with his own hands the author of the death of his friend.

This is the first platform of the poem, and the fiction which reduces into one important and universal action all the particulars upon which it turns.

In the next place it must be rendered probable by the circumstances of times, places, and persons. Some persons must be found out, already known by history or otherwise, whom we may with probability make the actors and personages of this fable. Homer has made choice of the siege of Troy, and feigned that this action happened there. To a phantom of his brain, whom he would paint valiant and choleric, he has given the name of Achilles; that of Agamemnon, to his general; that of Hector, to the enemy's commander; and so, to the rest.

Besides, he was obliged to accommodate himself to the manners, customs, and genius of the Greeks his auditors, the better to make them attend to the instruction of his poem, and to gain their approbation by praising them so that they might the better forgive him the representation of their own faults in some of his chief personages. He admirably discharges all these duties by making these brave princes and those victorious people all Grecians and the fathers of those he had a mind to commend.

But not being content, in a work of such a length, to propose only the principal point of the moral, and to fill up the rest with useless ornaments and foreign incidents, he extends this moral by all its necessary consequences. As for instance in the subject before us it is not enough to know that a good understanding ought always to be maintained among confederates, it is likewise of equal importance that, if there happens any division, care must be taken to keep it secret from the enemy, that their ignorance of this advantage may prevent their making use of it. And in the second place, when their concord is but counterfeit and only in appearance, one should never press the enemy too closely, for this would discover the weakness which we ought to conceal from them.

The episode of Patroclus most admirably furnishes us with these two instructions. For when he appeared in the arms of Achilles, the Trojans, who took him for that prince now reconciled and united to the confederates, immediately gave ground, and quitted the advantages they had before over the Greeks. But Patroclus, who should have been contented with this success, presses upon Hector too boldly, and, by obliging him to fight, soon discovers that it was not the true Achilles who was clad in his armor, but a hero of much inferior prowess. So that Hector kills him and regains those advantages which the Trojans had lost on the opinion that Achilles was reconciled. (pp. 307-11)

• • • • •

Aristotle bestows great encomiums on Homer for the simplicity of his design because he has included in one single part all that happened at the siege of Troy. And to this he opposes the ignorance of some poets who imagined that the unity of the fable or action was sufficiently preserved by the unity of the hero, and who composed their Theseids, Heraclids, and the like, wherein they only heaped up in one poem everything that happened to one personage.

• • • • •

He finds fault with those poets who were for reducing the unity of the fable into the unity of the hero, because one man may have performed several adventures which it is impossible to reduce under any one [general and] simple head. This reducing of all things to unity and simplicity is what Horace likewise makes his first rule.

Denique sit quod vis simplex dumtaxat, et unum

According to these rules, it will be allowable to make use of several fables, or (to speak more correctly) of several incidents, which may be divided into several fables provided they are so ordered that the unity of the fable be not spoiled. This liberty is still greater in the epic poem, because it is of a larger extent and ought to be entire and complete.

I will explain myself more distinctly by the practice of Homer.

No doubt but one might make four distinct fables out of these four following instructions.

I. Division between those of the same party exposes them entirely to their enemies.

II. Conceal your weakness, and you will be dreaded as much as if you had none of those imperfections of which they are ignorant.

III. When your strength is only feigned and founded only in the opinion of others, never venture so far as if your strength was real.

IV. The more you agree together, the less hurt can your enemies do you.

It is plain, I say, that each of these particular maxims might serve for the groundwork of a fiction, and one might make four distinct fables out of them. May one not, then, put all these into one single epopea? Not unless one single fable can be made out of all. The poet indeed may have so much skill as to unite all into one body as members and parts, each of which taken asunder would be imperfect; and if he joins them so, as that this conjunction shall be no hindrance at all to the unity and regular simplicity of the fable. This is what Homer has done with such success in the composition of the ***Iliad.***

1. The division between Achilles and his allies tended to the ruin of their designs. 2. Patroclus comes to their relief in the armor of this hero, and Hector retreats. 3. But this young man, pushing the advantage which his disguise gave him too far, ventures to engage with Hector himself; but not being master of Achilles's strength (whom he only represented in outward appearance) he is killed, and by this means leaves the Grecian affairs in the same disorder from which, in that disguise, he came to free them. 4. Achilles, provoked at the death of his friend, is reconciled, and revenges his loss by the death of Hector. These various incidents being thus united do not make different actions and fables, but are only the uncomplete and unfinished parts of one and the same action and fable, which alone, when taken thus complexly, can be said to be complete and entire; and all these maxims of the moral are easily reduced into these two parts, which, in my opinion, cannot be separated without enervating the force of both. The two parts are these, that a right understanding is the preservation, and discord the destruction, of states.

Though then the poet has made use of two parts in his poems, each of which might have served for a fable, as we have observed, yet this multiplication cannot be called a vicious and irregular polymythia, contrary to the necessary unity and simplicity of the fable; but it gives the fable another qualification altogether necessary and regular, namely, its perfection and finishing stroke.

• • • • •

The action of a poem is the subject which the poet undertakes, proposes, and builds upon. So that the moral and the instructions, which are the end of the epic poem, are not the matter of it. Those the poets leave in their allegorical and figurative obscurity. They only give notice at the exordium that they sing some action: the revenge of Achilles, the return of Ulysses, etc.

Since then the action is the matter of a fable, it is evident that whatever incidents are essential to the fable or constitute a part of it are necessary also to the action and are parts of the epic matter, none of which ought to be omitted. Such, for instance, are the contention of Agamemnon and Achilles, the slaughter Hector makes in the Grecian army, the reunion of the Greek princes, and lastly, the resettlement and victory which was the consequence of that reunion.

• • • • •

There are four qualifications in the epic action: the first is its unity, the second its integrity, the third its importance, the fourth its duration.

The unity of the epic action, as well as the unity of the fable, does not consist either in the unity of the hero or in the unity of time; three things, I suppose, are necessary to it. The first is to make use of no episode but what arises from the very platform and foundation of the action, and is as it were a natural member of the body. The second is exactly to unite these episodes and these members with one another. And the third is never to finish any episode so as it may seem to be an entire action, but to let each episode still appear in its own particular nature as the member of a body and as a part of itself not complete.

Aristotle not only says that the epic action should be one, but adds that it should be entire, perfect, and complete, and for this purpose ought to have a beginning, a middle, and an end. These three parts of a whole are too generally and universally denoted by the words *beginning, middle* and *end;* we may interpret them more precisely and say that the causes and designs of an action are the beginning, that the effects of these causes and the difficulties that are met with in the execution of these designs are the middle, and that the unraveling and resolution of these difficulties are the end.

• • • • •

Homer's design in the ***Iliad*** is to relate the anger and revenge of Achilles. The beginning of this action is the change of Achilles from a calm to a passionate temper. The middle is the effects of his passion, and all the illustrious deaths it is the cause of. The end of the same action is the return of Achilles to his calmness of temper again. All was quiet in the Grecian camp, when Agamemnon, their general, provokes Apollo against them, whom he was willing to appease afterwards at the cost and prejudice of Achilles, who had no part in his fault. This then is an exact beginning; is supposes nothing before, and requires after it the effects of this anger. Achilles revenges himself, and that is an exact middle: it supposes before it the anger of Achilles; this revenge is the effect of it. Then this middle requires after it the effects of this revenge, which is the satisfaction of Achilles; for the revenge had not been complete unless Achilles had been satisfied. By this means the poet makes his hero, after he was glutted by the mischief he had done to Agamemnon, by the death of Hector, and the honor he did his friend by insulting over his murderer; he makes him, I say, to be moved by the tears and misfortunes of King Priam. We see him as calm at the end of the poem, during the funeral of Hector, as he was at the beginning of the poem, whilst the plague raged among the Grecians. This end is just, since the calmness of temper Achilles re-enjoyed is only an effect of the revenge which ought to have preceded; and after this nobody expects any more of his anger. Thus has Homer been very exact in the beginning, middle and end of the action he made choice of for the subject of his ***Iliad***. (pp. 314-17)

• • • • •

The causes of the action are also what the poet is obliged to give an account of. There are three sorts of causes: the humors, the interests, and the designs of men; and these different causes of an action are likewise often the causes of one another, every man taking up those interests in which his humor engages him and forming those designs to which his humor and interest incline him. Of all these the poet ought to inform his readers, and render them conspicuous in his principal personages. (p. 318)

• • • • •

As these causes are the beginning of the action, the opposite designs against that of the hero are the middle of it, and form that difficulty or intrigue which makes up the greatest part of the poem; the solution or unraveling commences when the reader begins to see that difficulty removed and the doubts cleared up. Homer has divided [the ***Iliad***] into two parts, and has put a particular intrigue and the solution of it into each part.

The first part of the ***Iliad*** is the anger of Achilles, who is for revenging himself upon Agamemnon by the means of Hector and the Trojans. The intrigue comprehends the three days' fight which happened in the absence of Achilles, and it consists on one side in the resistance of Agamemnon and the Grecians and on the other in the revengeful and inexorable humor of Achilles, which would not suffer him to be reconciled. The loss of the Grecians and the despair of Agamemnon prepare for a solution by the satisfaction which the incensed hero received from it. The death of Patroclus, joined to the offers of Agamemnon, which of itself had proved ineffectual, remove this difficulty, and make the unraveling of the first part.

This death is likewise the beginning of the second part, since it puts Achilles upon the design of revenging himself on Hector. But the design of Hector is opposite to that of Achilles; this Trojan is valiant, and resolved to stand on his own defense. This valor and resolution of Hector are on his part the cause of the intrigue. All the endeavors Achilles used to meet with Hector and be the death of him, and the contrary endeavors of the Trojan to keep out of his reach and defend himself, are the intrigue, which comprehends the battle of the last day. The unraveling begins at the death of Hector; and besides that, it contains the insulting of Achilles over his body, the honors he paid to Patroclus, and the entreaties of King Priam. The regrets of this king and the other Trojans in the sorrowful obsequies they paid to Hector's body end the unraveling; they justify the satisfaction of Achilles, and demonstrate his tranquillity. (pp. 319-20)

• • • • •

We have already observed what is meant by the intrigue and the unraveling thereof; let us now say something of the manner of forming both. These two should arise naturally out of the very essence and subject of the poem, and are to be deduced from thence. Their conduct is so exact and natural that it seems as if their action had presented them with whatever they inserted without putting themselves to the trouble of a farther inquiry.

What is more usual and natural to warriors than anger, heat, passion, and impatience of bearing the least affront or disrespect? This is what forms the intrigue of the ***Iliad,*** and everything we read there is nothing else but the effect of this humor and these passions. (p. 320)

• • • • •

The time of the epic action is not fixed like that of the dramatic poem; it is much longer, for an uninterrupted duration is much more necessary in an action which one sees and is present at than in one which we only read or hear repeated. Besides, tragedy is fuller of passion, and consequently of such a violence as cannot admit of so long a duration.

The ***Iliad*** containing an action of anger and violence, the poet allows it but a short time, about forty days. . . .

• • • • •

The passions of tragedy are different from those of the epic poem. In the former, terror and pity have the chief place; the passion that seems most peculiar to epic poetry is admiration.

Besides this admiration, which in general distinguishes the epic poem from the dramatic, each epic poem has likewise some peculiar passion which distinguishes it in particular from other epic poems, and constitutes a kind of singular and individual difference between these poems of the same species. These singular passions correspond to the character of the hero. Anger and terror reign throughout the ***Iliad*** because Achilles is angry and the most terrible of all men. (p. 322)

René Le Bossu, "Selections from 'Treatise of the Epic Poem'," in The Continental Model: Selected

French Critical Essays of the Seventeenth Century, in English Translation, *edited by Scott Elledge and Donald Schier, revised edition, Cornell University Press, 1970, pp. 307-23.*

JOHN DRYDEN (essay date 1700)

[Regarded by many scholars as the father of modern English poetry and criticism, Dryden dominated literary life in England during the last four decades of the seventeenth century. Through deliberately and comprehensively refining the language of Elizabethan England in all his works, he developed an expressive, universal diction which has had immense impact on the development of speech and writing in Great Britain and North America. Although recognized as a prolific and accomplished Restoration dramatist, Dryden wrote a number of satirical poems and critical essays which are acknowledged as far greater literary achievements. In the following excerpt from his Preface to the Fables, *published in 1700, Dryden compares the temperaments and styles of Homer and Virgil and suggests that, "if Homer had not led the way, it was not in Virgil to have begun heroic poetry."]*

In the works of [Homer and Virgil] we may read their manners, and natural inclinations, which are wholly different. Virgil was of a quiet, sedate temper; Homer was violent, impetuous, and full of fire. The chief talent of Virgil was propriety of thoughts, and ornament of words: Homer was rapid in his thoughts, and took all the liberties, both of numbers and of expressions, which his language, and the age in which he lived, allowed him. Homer's invention was more copious, Virgil's more confined; so that if Homer had not led the way, it was not in Virgil to have begun heroic poetry; for nothing can be more evident, than that the Roman poem is but the second part of the ***Ilias;*** a continuation of the same story, and the persons already formed. The manners of Æneas are those of Hector, superadded to those which Homer gave him. The adventures of Ulysses in the ***Odysseis*** are imitated in the first Six Books of Virgil's *Æneis;* and though the accidents are not the same, (which would have argued him of a servile copying, and total barrenness of invention,) yet the seas were the same in which both the heroes wandered; and Dido cannot be denied to be the poetical daughter of Calypso. The six latter Books of Virgil's poem are the four-and-twenty ***Iliads*** contracted; a quarrel occasioned by a lady, a single combat, battles fought, and a town besieged. I say not this in derogation to Virgil, neither do I contradict anything which I have formerly said in his just praise; for his episodes are almost wholly of his own invention, and the form which he has given to the telling makes the tale his own, even though the original story had been the same. But this proves, however, that Homer taught Virgil to design; and if invention be the first virtue of an epic poet, then the Latin poem can only be allowed the second place. (pp. 251-52)

[Our] two great poets [are] so different in their tempers, one choleric and sanguine, the other phlegmatic and melancholic; that which makes them excel in their several ways is, that each of them has followed his own natural inclination, as well in forming the design, as in the execution of it. The very heroes shew their authors: Achilles is hot, impatient, revengeful—

Impiger, iracundus, inexorabilis, acer, &c.,

Æneas patient, considerate, careful of his people, and merciful to his enemies; ever submissive to the will of heaven—

quo fata trahunt retrahunique, sequanmur.

I could please myself with enlarging on this subject, but am forced to defer it to a fitter time. From all I have said, I will only draw this inference, that the action of Homer, being more full of vigour than that of Virgil, according to the temper of the writer, is of consequence more pleasing to the reader. One warms you by degrees; the other sets you on fire all at once, and never intermits his heat. 'Tis the same difference which Longinus makes betwixt the effects of eloquence in Demosthenes and Tully; one persuades, the other commands. You never cool while you read Homer, even not in the Second Book (a graceful flattery to his countrymen); but he hastens from the ships, and concludes not that book till he has made you an amends by the violent playing of a new machine. From thence he hurries on his action with variety of events, and ends it in less compass than two months. (pp. 253-54)

John Dryden, "Preface to the Fables," in his Essays of John Dryden, Vol. II, *edited by W. P. Ker, Oxford at the Clarendon Press, 1926, pp. 246-74.*

[JOSEPH ADDISON] (essay date 1712)

[A prominent English statesman and man of letters, Addison, along with Richard Steele, is considered one of the most important essayists of the early eighteenth century. With Steele, he founded the influential daily the Spectator, *which was launched with the avowed purpose of improving the morals and manners of the day. Addison's best essays, those in which he adopted the persona of the fictional country squire Sir Roger de Coverley, are trenchant, pointed observations of life, literature, and society. Didactic and moralizing, yet witty and ironic, Addison's style epitomizes the ideals of neoclassical lucidity and moderation; Samuel Johnson remarked that Addison's work is characterized by "an English style familiar but not coarse, elegant but not ostentatious." In this excerpt from a series of articles published in the* Spectator *in 1712 that examined the rules of epic poetry, Addison discusses the* Iliad *in terms of unity, action, and characterization. While he chastises Homer for his occasional lapses in delicacy, he adds that "if there are many Poets who would not have fallen into the Meanness of some of his Sentiments, there are none who could have risen up to the Greatness of others."]*

The first Thing to be consider'd in an Epic Poem, is the Fable, which is perfect or imperfect, according as the Action which it relates is more or less so. This Action should have three Qualifications in it. First, It should be but one Action. Secondly, It should be an entire Action; and Thirdly, it should be a great Action. To consider the Action of the ***Iliad, Æneid,*** and *Paradise Lost,* in these three several Lights, Homer to preserve the Unity of his Action hastens into the Midst of Things, as Horace has observed: Had he gone up to Leda's Egg, or begun much later, even at the Rape of Helen, or the Investing of Troy, it is manifest that the Story of the Poem would have been a Series of several Actions. He therefore opens his Poem with the Discord of his Princes, and with great Art interweaves in the several succeeding Parts of it, an Account of every Thing material which relates to them, and had passed before that fatal Dissension. . . . (pp. 60-1)

Aristotle himself allows, that Homer has nothing to boast of as to the Unity of his Fable, tho' at the same Time that great Critick and Philosopher endeavours to palliate this Imperfection in the Greek Poet, by imputing it in some Measure to the very Nature of an Epic Poem. (pp. 61-2)

The second Qualification required in the Action of an Epic Poem is, that it should be an *entire* Action: An Action is entire when it is compleat in all its Parts; or as Aristotle describes it, when it consists of a Beginning, a Middle, and an End. Nothing should go before it, be intermix'd with it, or follow after it, that is not related to it. As on the contrary, no single Step should be omitted in that just and regular Process which it must be supposed to take from its Original to its Consummation. Thus we see the Anger of Achilles in its Birth, its Continuance and Effects. . . . (p. 62)

The third Qualification of an Epic Poem is its *Greatness*. The Anger of Achilles was of such Consequence, that it embroiled the Kings of Greece, destroy'd the Heroes of Troy, and engaged all the Gods in Factions. (p. 63)

But Aristotle, by the Greatness of the Action, does not only mean that it should be great in its Nature, but also in its Duration, or in other Words, that it should have a due Length in it, as well as what we properly call Greatness. The just Measure of the Kind of Magnitude, he explains by the following Similitude. An Animal, no bigger than a Mite, cannot appear perfect to the Eye, because the Sight takes it in at once, and has only a confused Idea of the Whole, and not a distinct Idea of all its Parts; If on the contrary you should suppose an Animal of ten thousand Furlongs in Length, the Eye would be so filled with a single Part of it, that it could not give the Mind an Idea of the Whole. What these Animals are to the Eye, a very short or a very long Action would be to the Memory. The first would be, as it were, lost and swallowed up by it, and the other difficult to be contained in it. Homer and Virgil have shewn their principal Art in this Particular; the Action of the ***Iliad,*** and that of the *Aeneid,* were in themselves exceeding short, but are so beautifully extended and diversified by the Invention of Episodes, and the Machinery of Gods, with the like poetical Ornaments, that they make up an agreeable Story sufficient to employ the memory without overcharging it. (pp. 63-4)

• • • • •

Homer has excelled all the heroic Poets that ever wrote, in the Multitude and Variety of his Characters. Every God that is admitted into his Poem, acts a Part which would have been suitable to no other Deity. His Princes are as much distinguished by their Manners as by their Dominions; and even those among them, whose Characters seem wholly made up of Courage, differ from one another as to the particular Kinds of Courage in which they excel. In short, there is scarce a Speech or Action in the ***Iliad,*** which the Reader may not ascribe to the Person that speaks or acts, without seeing his Name at the Head of it.

Homer does not only out-shine all other Poets in the Variety, but also in the Novelty of his Characters. He has introduced among his Grecian Princes a Person, who had lived thrice the Age of Man, and conversed with Theseus, Hercules, Polyphemus, and the first Race of Heroes. His principal Actor is the Son of a Goddess, not to mention the Off-spring of other Deities, who have likewise a Place in his Poem, and the venerable Trojan Prince who was the Father of so many Kings and Heroes. There is in these several Characters of Homer, a certain Dignity as well as Novelty, which adapts them in a more peculiar manner to the Nature of an heroic Poem. Tho', at the same Time, to give them the greater Variety, he has described a Vulcan, that is a Buffoon among his Gods, and a Thersites among his Mortals. (pp. 82-3)

There is another Circumstance in the principal Actors of the ***Iliad*** and *Æneid,* which gives a peculiar Beauty to those two Poems, and was therefore contrived with very great Judgment. I mean the Authors having chosen for their Heroes Persons who were so nearly related to the People for whom they wrote. Achilles was a Greek, and Æneas the remote Founder of Rome. By this means their Countrymen (whom they principally proposed to themselves for their Readers) were particularly attentive to all the Parts of their Story, and sympathized with their Heroes in all their Adventures. A Roman could not but rejoice in the Escapes, Successes and Victories of Æneas, and be grieved at any Defeats, Misfortunes or Disappointments that befel him; as a Greek must have had the same Regard for Achilles. And it is plain, that each of those Poems have lost this great Advantage, among those Readers to whom their Heroes are as Strangers, or indifferent Persons. (p. 85)

• • • • •

The Sentiments in all Epic Poems are the Thoughts and Behaviour which the Author ascribes to the Persons whom he introduces, and are *just* when they are conformable to the Characters of the several Persons. The Sentiments have likewise a Relation to *Things* as well as *Persons,* and are then perfect when they are such as are adapted to the Subject. If in either of these Cases the Poet argues, or explains, magnifies or diminishes, raises Love or Hatred, Pity or Terror, or any other Passion, we ought to consider whether the Sentiments he makes Use of are proper for their Ends. Homer is censured by the Criticks for his Defect as to this Particular in several Parts of the ***Iliad*** and ***Odyssey,*** tho' at the same Time those who have treated this great Poet with Candour, have attributed this Defect to the Times in which he lived. It was the Fault of the Age, and not of Homer, if there wants that Delicacy in some of his Sentiments, which appears in the Works of Men of a much inferior Genius. Besides, if there are Blemishes in any particular Thoughts, there is an infinite Beauty in the greatest Part of them. In short, if there are many Poets who would not have fallen into the Meanness of some of his Sentiments, there are none who could have risen up to the Greatness of others. (p. 105)

Nor is it sufficient for an Epic Poem to be filled with such Thoughts as are *natural,* unless it abound also with such as are *sublime*. Virgil in this Particular falls short of Homer. He has not indeed so many Thoughts that are low and vulgar; but at the same Time has not so many Thoughts that are sublime and noble. The Truth of it is, Virgil seldom rises into very astonishing Sentiments, where he is not fired by the ***Iliad.*** He every where charms and pleases us by the Force of his own Genius; but seldom elevates and transports us where he does not fetch his Hints from Homer. (p. 106)

But since several Thoughts may be natural which are low and groveling, an Epic Poet should not only avoid such Sentiments as are unnatural or affected, but also such as are low and vulgar. Homer has opened a great Field of Raillery to Men of more Delicacy than Greatness of Genius, by the Homeliness of some of his Sentiments. But, as I have before said, these are rather to be imputed to the Simplicity of the Age in which he lived, to which I may also add, of that which he described, than to any Imperfection in that Divine Poet. Zoilus, among the Ancients, and Monsieur Perrault, among the Moderns, pushed their Ridicule very far upon him, on Account of some such Sentiments. (pp. 107-08)

I shall give but one Instance of this Impropriety of Sentiments in Homer. . . . Sentiments which raise Laughter, can very seldom be admitted with any Decency into an heroick Poem, whose Business it is to excite Passions of a much nobler Nature. Homer, however, in his Characters of Vulcan and Thersites, in his Story of Mars and Venus, in his Behaviour of Irus, and in other Passages, has been observed to have lapsed into the

Burlesque Character, and to have departed from that serious Air which seems essential to the Magnificence of an Epic Poem. (p. 108)

[*Joseph Addison*], *in three essays from* The Spectator, Vol. IV, *edited by G. Gregory, J. M. Dent & Co., 1898, pp. 60-4, 82-6, 104-09.*

ALEXANDER POPE (essay date 1715)

[*Pope has been called the greatest English poet of his time and one of the most important in the history of world literature. As a critic and satirical commentator on eighteenth-century England, he was the author of work that represents the epitome of Neo-classicist thought. His famous remark, "The Proper study of mankind is man," perfectly illustrates the temperament of his age, a time when influential thinkers altered the theological emphasis in human speculation. All of Pope's work demonstrates his love of restraint, clarity, order, and the classical term "decorum." His greatness lies in his cultivation of style and wit, rather than sublimity and pathos, and this inclination shaped his criticism of other writers. In the following excerpt from the preface to his highly acclaimed 1715 translation of the* Iliad, *Pope praises Homer's plot, characters, description, diction, and versification. Above all, Pope singles out Homer's "Invention" and "unequal'd Fire and Rapture" as the poet's most outstanding traits. Pope also addresses some criticisms commonly levelled at Homer, attributing his faults to his early place in history and adding that, "if* [Homer] *has fail'd in some of his Flights, it was but because he attempted everything."*]

Homer is universally allow'd to have had the greatest Invention of any Writer whatever. The Praise of Judgment Virgil has justly contested with him, and others may have their Pretensions as to particular Excellencies; but his Invention remains yet unrival'd. Nor is it a Wonder if he has ever been acknowledg'd the greatest of Poets, who most excell'd in That which is the very Foundation of Poetry. (p. 323)

Our Author's Work is a wild Paradise, where if we cannot see all the Beauties so distinctly as in an order'd Garden, it is only because the Number of them is infinitely greater. 'Tis like a copious Nursery which contains the Seeds and first Productions of every kind, out of which those who follow'd him have but selected some particular Plants, each according to his Fancy, to cultivate and beautify. If some things are too luxuriant, it is owing to the Richness of the Soil; and if others are not arriv'd to Perfection or Maturity, it is only because they are over-run and opprest by those of a stronger Nature.

It is to the Strength of this amazing Invention we are to attribute that unequal'd Fire and Rapture, which is so forcible in Homer that no Man of a true Poetical Spirit is Master of himself while he reads him. What he writes is of the most animated Nature imaginable; every thing moves, every thing lives, and is put in Action. If a Council be call'd, or a Battel fought, you are not coldly inform'd of what was said or done as from a third Person; the Reader is hurry'd out of himself by the Force of the Poet's Imagination, and turns in one place to a Hearer, in another to a Spectator. The Course of his Verses resembles that of the Army he describes. . . . They pour along like a Fire that sweeps the whole Earth before it. 'Tis however remarkable that his Fancy, which is every where vigorous, is not discover'd immediately at the beginning of [the ***Iliad***] in its fullest Splendor: It grows in the Progress both upon himself and others, and becomes on Fire like a Chariot-Wheel, by its own Rapidity. Exact Disposition, just Thought, correct Elocution, polish'd Numbers, may have been found in a thousand; but this Poetical Fire, this *Vivida vis animi,* in a very few. Even in Works where all those are imperfect or neglected, this can over-power Criticism, and make us admire even while we dis-approve. Nay, where this appears, tho' attended with Absurdities, it brightens all the Rubbish about it, 'till we see nothing but its own Splendor. This Fire is discern'd in Virgil, but discern'd as through a Glass, reflected, and more shining than warm, but every where equal and constant: In Lucan and Statius, it bursts out in sudden, short, and interrupted Flashes: In Milton, it glows like a Furnace kept up to an uncommon Fierceness by the Force of Art: In Shakespear, it strikes before we are aware, like an accidental Fire from Heaven: But in Homer, and in him only, it burns every where clearly, and every where irresistibly.

I shall here endeavour to show, how this vast *Invention* exerts itself in a manner superior to that of any Poet, thro' all the main constituent Parts of [the ***Iliad***], as it is the great and peculiar Characteristick which distinguishes him from all other Authors.

This strong and ruling Faculty was like a powerful Planet, which in the Violence of its Course, drew all things within its Vortex. It seem'd not enough to have taken in the whole Circle of Arts, and the whole Compass of Nature; all the inward Passions and Affections of Mankind to supply this Characters, and all the outward Forms and Images of Things for his Descriptions; but wanting yet an ampler Sphere to expatiate in, he open'd a new and boundless Walk for his Imagination, and created a World for himself in the Invention of Fable. That which Aristotle calls the Soul of Poetry, was first breath'd into it by Homer. I shall begin with considering him in this Part, as it is naturally the first, and I speak of it both as it means the Design of a Poem, and as it is taken for Fiction.

Fable may be divided into the Probable, the Allegorical, and the Marvelous. The Probable Fable is the Recital of such Actions as tho' they did not happen, yet might, in the common course of Nature: Or of such as tho' they did, become Fables by the additional Episodes and manner of telling them. Of this sort is the main Story of an Epic Poem, the Return of Ulysses, the Settlement of the Trojans in Italy, or the like. That of the ***Iliad*** is the Anger of Achilles, the most short and single Subject that ever was chosen by any Poet. Yet this he has supplied with a vaster Variety of Incidents and Events, and crouded with a greater Number of Councils, Speeches, Battles, and Episodes of all kinds, than are to be found even in those Poems whose Schemes are of the utmost Latitude and Irregularity. The Action is hurry'd on with the most vehement Spirit, and its whole Duration employs not so much as fifty Days. Virgil, for want of so warm a Genius, aided himself by taking in a more extensive Subject, as well as a greater Length of Time, and contracting the Design of both Homer's Poems into one, which is yet but a fourth part as large as his. The other Epic Poets have us'd the same Practice, but generally carry'd it so far as to superinduce a Multiplicity of Fables, destroy the Unity of Action, and lose their Readers in an unreasonable Length of Time. Nor is it only in the main Design that they have been unable to add to his Invention, but they have follow'd him in every Episode and Part of Story. If he has given a regular Catalogue of an Army, they all draw up their Forces in the same Order. If he has funeral Games for Patroclus, Virgil has the same for Anchises, and Statius (rather than omit them) destroys the Unity of his Action for those of Archemorus. If Ulysses visit the Shades, the Æneas of Virgil and Scipio of Silius are sent after him. If he be detain'd from his Return by the Allurements of Calypso, so is Æneas by Dido, and Rinaldo by Armida. If Achilles be absent from the Army on the Score of a Quarrel thro' half the Poem, Rinaldo must absent himself just as long, on the like account. If he gives his Heroe a Suit of celestial Armour, Virgil and Tasso make the same Present to theirs. Virgil has not only observ'd this close Imitation of Homer, but where he had not led the way, supply'd the Want from other Greek Authors. Thus the Story of Sinon and the Taking of Troy was copied (says Macrobius) almost word for word from *Pisander,* as the Loves of Dido and Æneas are taken from those of Medæa and Jason in Apollonius, and several others in the same manner.

To proceed to the Allegorical Fable: If we reflect upon those innumerable Knowledges, those Secrets of Nature and Physical Philosophy which Homer is generally suppos'd to have wrapt up in his Allegories, what a new and ample Scene of Wonder may this Consideration afford us? How fertile will that Imagination appear, which was able to cloath all the Properties of Elements, the Qualifications of the Mind, the Virtues and Vices, in Forms and Persons; and to introduce them into Actions agreeable to the Nature of the Things they shadow'd? This is a Field in which no succeeding Poets could dispute with Homer; and whatever Commendations have been allow'd them on this Head, are by no means for their Invention in having enlarg'd his Circle, but for their Judgment in having contracted it. For when the Mode of Learning chang'd in following Ages, and Science was deliver'd in a plainer manner, it then became as reasonable in the more modern Poets to lay it aside, as it was in Homer to make use of it. And perhaps it was no unhappy Circumstance for Virgil that there was not in his Time that Demand upon him of so great an Iinvention, as might be capable of furnishing all those Allegorical Parts of a Poem.

The Marvelous Fable includes whatever is supernatural, and especially the Machines of the Gods. If Homer was not the first who introduc'd the Deities (as Herodotus imagines) into the Religion of Greece, he seems the first who brought them into a System of Machinery for Poetry, and such an one as makes its greatest Importance and Dignity. For we find those Authors who have been offended at the literal Notion of the Gods, constantly laying their Accusation against Homer as the undoubted Inventor of them. But whatever cause there might be to blame his Machines in a Philosophical or Religious View, they are so perfect in the Poetick, that Mankind have been ever since contented to follow them: None have been able to enlarge the Sphere of Poetry beyond the Limits he has set: Every Attempt of this Nature has prov'd unsuccessful; and after all the various Changes of Times and Religions, his Gods continue to this Day the Gods of Poetry.

We come now to the Characters of his Persons, and here we shall find no Author has ever drawn so many with so visible and surprizing a Variety, or given us such lively and affecting Impressions of them. Every one has something so singularly his own, that no Painter could have distinguished them more by their Features, than the Poet has by their Manners. Nothing can be more exact then the Distinctions he has observ'd in the different degrees of Virtues and Vices. The single Quality of Courage is wonderfully diversify'd in the several Characters of the *Iliad*. That of Achilles is furious and intractable; that of Diomede forward, yet listening to Advice and subject to Command: We see in Ajax an heavy and self-considering Valour, in *Hector* an active and vigilant one: The Courage of Agamemnon is inspirited by Love of Empire and Ambition, that of Menelaus mix'd with Softness and Tenderness for his People: We find in Idomeneus a plain direct Soldier, in Sarpedon a gallant and generous one. Nor is this judicious and astonishing Diversity to be found only in the pincipal Quality which constitutes the Main of each Character, but even in the Underparts of it, to which he takes care to give a Tincture of that principal one. For Example, the main Characters of Ulysses and Nestor consist in Wisdom and they are distinct in this; the Wisdom of one is artificial and various, of the other natural, open, and regular. But they have, besides, Characters of Courage; and this Quality also takes a different Turn in each from the difference of his Prudence: For one in the War depends still upon Caution, the other upon Experience. It would be endless to produce Instances of these Kinds. The Characters of Virgil are far from striking us in this open manner; they lie in a great degree hidden and undistinguish'd, and where they are mark'd most evidently, affect us not in proportion to those of Homer. His Characters of Valour are much alike; even that of Turnus seems no way peculiar but as it is in a superior degree; and we see nothing that differences the Courage of Mnestheus from that of Sergesthus, Cloanthus, or the rest. In like manner it may be remark'd of Statius's Heroes, that an Air of Impetuosity runs thro' them all; the same horrid and savage Courage appears in his Capaneus, Tydeus, Hippomedon, &c. They have a Parity of Character which makes them seem Brothers of one Family. I believe when the Reader is led into this Track of Reflection, if he will pursue it through the Epic and Tragic Writers, he will be convinced how infinitely superior in this Point the Invention of Homer was to that of all others.

The Speeches are to be consider'd as they flow from the Characters, being perfect or defective as they agree or disagree with the Manners of those who utter them. As there is more variety of Characters in the ***Iliad,*** so there is of Speeches, than in any other Poem. Everything in it has Manners (as Aristotle expresses it) that is, every thing is acted or spoken. It is hardly credible in a Work of such length, how small a Number of Lines are employ'd in Narration. In Virgil the Dramatic Part is less in proportion to the Narrative; and the Speeches often consist of general Reflections or Thoughts, which might be equally just in any Person's Mouth upon the same Occasion. As many of his Persons have no apparent Characters, so many of his Speeches escape being apply'd and judg'd by the Rule of Propriety. We oftner think of the Author himself when we read Virgil, than when we are engag'd in Homer: All which are the Effects of a colder Invention, that interests us less in the Action describ'd: Homer makes us Hearers, and Virgil leaves us Readers.

If in the next place we take a View of the Sentiments, the same presiding Faculty is eminent in the Sublimity and Spirit of his Thoughts. Longinus has given his Opinion, that it was in this Part Homer principally excell'd. What were alone sufficient to prove the Grandeur and Excellence of his Sentiments in general, is that they have so remarkable a Parity with those of the Scripture: Duport, in his *Gnomologia Homerica,* has collected innumerable Instances of this sort. And it is with Justice an excellent modern Writer allows, that if Virgil has not so many Thoughts that are low and vulgar, he has not so many that are sublime and noble; and that the Roman Author seldom rises into very astonishing Sentiments where he is not fired by the ***Iliad.***

If we observe his Descriptions, Images, and Similes, we shall find the Invention still predominant. To what else can we ascribe that vast Comprehension of Images of every sort, where we see each Circumstance and Individual of Nature summon'd together by the Extent and Fecundity of his Imagination; to which all things, in their various Views, presented themselves in an Instant, and had their Impressions taken off to Perfection at a Heat? Nay, he not only gives us the full Prospects of Things, but several unexpected Peculiarities and Side-Views, unobserv'd by any Painter but Homer. Nothing is so surprizing as the Descriptions of his Battels, which take up no less than half the ***Iliad,*** and are supply'd with so vast a Variety of Incidents, that no one bears a Likeness to another; such different Kinds of Deaths, that no two Heroes are wounded in the same manner; and such a Profusion of noble Ideas, that every Battel rises above the last in Greatness, Horror, and Confusion. It is certain there is not near that Number of Images and Descriptions in any Epic poet; tho' every one has assisted himself with a great Quantity out of him: And it is evident of Virgil especially, that he has scarce any Comparisons which are not drawn from his Master.

If we descend from hence to the Expression, we see the bright Imagination of Homer shining out in the most enliven'd Forms of it. We acknowledge him the Father of Poetical Diction, the first who taught that Language of the Gods to Men. His Expression is like the colouring of some great Masters, which discovers itself to be laid on boldly, and executed with Rapidity. It is indeed the strongest and most glowing imaginable, and touch'd with the greatest Spirit. Aristotle had reason to say, He was the only Poet who had found out Living Words; there are in him more daring Figures and Metaphors than in any good Author whatever. An Arrow is impatient to be on the Wing, a Weapon thirsts to drink the Blood of an Enemy, and the like. Yet his Expression is never too big for the Sense, but justly great in proportion to it: 'Tis the Sentiment that swells and fills out the Diction, which rises with it, and forms itself about it. For in the same degree that a Thought is warmer, an Expression will be brighter; and as That is more strong, This will become more perspicuous: Like Glass in the Furnace which grows to a greater Magnitude, and refines to a greater Clearness, only as the Breath within is more powerful, and the Heat more intense.

To throw his Language more out of Prose, Homer seems to have affected the Compound-Epithets. This was a sort of Composition peculiarly proper to Poetry, not only as it heighten'd the Diction, but as it assisted and fill'd the Numbers with greater Sound and Pomp, and likewise conduced in some measure to thicken the Images. On this last Consideration I cannot but attribute these to the Fruitfulness of his Invention, since (as he has manag'd them) they are a sort of super-numerary Pictures of the Persons or Things they are join'd to. (pp. 324-32)

Lastly, if we consider his Versification, we shall be sensible what a Share of Praise is due to his Invention in that also. He was not satisfy'd with his Language as he found it settled in any one Part of Greece, but searched thro' its differing Dialects with this particular View, to beautify and perfect his Numbers: He consider'd these as they had a greater Mixture of Vowels or Consonants, and accordingly employ'd them as the Verse requir'd either a greater Smoothness or Strength. What he most affected was the Ionic, which has a peculiar Sweetness from its never using Contractions, and from its Custom of resolving the Diphthongs into two Syllables; so as to make the Words open themselves with a more spreading and sonorous Fluency. With this he mingled the Attic Contractions, the broader Doric, and the feebler Æolic, which often rejects its Aspirate, or takes off its Accent; and compleated this Variety by altering some Letters with the License of Poetry. Thus his Measures, instead of being Fetters to his Sense, were always in readiness to run along with the Warmth of his Rapture; and even to give a farther Representation of his Notions, in the Correspondence of their Sounds to what they signify'd. Out of all these he has deriv'd that Harmony, which makes us confess he had not only the richest Head, but the finest Ear in the World. This is so great a Truth, that whoever will but consult the Tune of his Verses even without understanding them (with the same sort of Diligence as we daily see practis'd in the Case of Italian Opera's) will find more Sweetness, Variety, and Majesty of Sound, than in any other Language or Poetry. The Beauty of his Numbers is allow'd by the Criticks to be copied but faintly by Virgil himself, tho' they are so just to ascribe it to the Nature of the Latine Tongue. Indeed the Greek has some Advantages both from the natural Sound of its Words, and the Turn and Cadence of its Verse, which agree with the Genius of no other Language. Virgil was very sensible of this, and used the utmost Diligence in working up a more intractable Language to whatsoever Graces it was capable of, and in particular never fail'd to bring the Sound of his Line to a beautiful Agreement with its Sense. If the Grecian Poet has not been so frequently celebrated on this Account as the Roman, the only reason is, that fewer Criticks have understood one Language than the other. Dionysius of Halicarnassus has pointed out many of our Author's Beauties in this kind, in his Treatise of the Composition of Words, and others will be taken notice of in the Course of the Notes. It suffices at present to observe of his Numbers, that they flow with so much ease, as to make one imagine Homer had no other care than to transcribe as fast as the Muses dictated; and at the same time with so much Force and inspiriting Vigour, that they awaken and raise us like the Sound of a Trumpet. They roll along as a plentiful River, always in motion, and always full; while we are born away by a Tide of Verse, the most rapid, and yet the most smooth imaginable.

Thus on whatever side we contemplate Homer, what principally strikes us is his Invention. It is that which forms the Character of each Part of his Work; and accordingly we find it to have made his Fable more extensive and copious than any other, his Manners more lively and strongly marked, his Speeches more affecting and transported, his Sentiments more warm and sublime, his Images and Descriptions more full and animated, his Expression more rais'd and daring, and his Numbers more rapid and various. I hope in what has been said of Virgil with regard to any of these Heads, I have no way derogated from his Character. Nothing is more absurd or endless, than the common Method of comparing eminent Writers by an Opposition of particular Passages in them, and forming a Judgment from thence of their Merit upon the whole. We ought to have a certain Knowledge of the principal Character and distinguishing Excellence of each: It is in that we are to consider him, and in proportion to his Degree in that we are to admire him. No Author or Man ever excell'd all the World in more than one Faculty, and as Homer has done this in Invention, Virgil has in Judgment. Not that we are to think Homer wanted Judgment, because Virgil had it in a more eminent degree; or that Virgil wanted Invention, because Homer possest a larger share of it: Each of these great Authors had more of both than perhaps any Man besides, and are only said to have less in Comparison with one another. Homer was the greater Genius, Virgil the better Artist. In one we most admire the Man, in the other the Work. Homer hurries and transports us with a commanding Impetuosity, Virgil leads us with an attractive Majesty: Homer scatters with a generous Profusion, Virgil bestows with a careful Magnificence: Homer, like the Nile, pours out his Riches with a sudden Overflow; Virgil like a River in its Banks, with a gentle and constant Stream. When we behold their Battels, methinks the two Poets resemble the Heroes they celebrate: Homer, boundless and irresistible as Achilles, bears all before him, and shines more and more as the Tumult increases; Virgil, calmly daring like Æneas, appears undisturb'd in the midst of the Action, disposes all about him, and conquers with Tranquility: And when we look upon their Machines, Homer seems like his own Jupiter in his Terrors, shaking Olympus, scattering the Lightnings, and firing the Heavens; Virgil, like the same Power in his Benevolence, counselling with the Gods, laying Plans for Empires, and regularly ordering his whole Creation.

But after all, it is with great Parts as with great Virtues, they naturally border on some Imperfection; and it is often hard to distinguish exactly where the Virtue ends, or the Fault begins. As Prudence may sometimes sink to Suspicion, so may a great Judgment decline to Coldness; and as Magnanimity may run up to Profusion or Extravagance, so may a great Invention to Redundancy or Wildness. If we look upon Homer in this View, we shall perceive the chief Objections against him to proceed from so noble a Cause as the Excess of this Faculty.

Among these we may reckon some of his Marvellous Fictions, upon which so much Criticism has been spent as surpassing all the Bounds of Probability. Perhaps it may be with great and superior Souls as with gigantick Bodies, which exerting themselves with unusual Strength, exceed what is commonly thought the due Proportion of Parts, to become Miracles in the whole; and like the old Heroes of that Make, commit something near Extravagance amidst a Series of glorious and inimitable Performances. Thus Homer has his speaking Horses, and Virgil his Myrtles distilling Blood, without so much as contriving the easy Intervention of a Deity to save the Probability.

It is owing to the same vast Invention that his Similes have been thought too exuberant and full of Circumstances. The Force of this Faculty is seen in nothing more, than its Inability to confine itself to that single Circumstance upon which the Comparison is grounded: It runs out into Embellishments of additional Images, which however are so manag'd as not to overpower the main one. His Similes are like Pictures, where the principal Figure has not only its proportion given agreeable to the Original, but is also set off with occasional Ornaments and Prospects. The same will account for his manner of heaping a Number of Comparisons together in one Breath, when his Fancy suggested to him at once so many various and correspondent Images. The Reader will easily extend this Observation to more Objections of the same kind.

If there are others which seem rather to charge him with a Defect or Narrowness of Genius, than an Excess of it; those seeming Defects will be found upon Examination to proceed wholly from the Nature of the Times he liv'd in. Such are his grosser Representations of the Gods, and the vicious and imperfect Manners of his Heroes. . . . When we read Homer, we ought to reflect that we are reading the most ancient Author in the Heathen World; and those who consider him in this Light, will double their Pleasure in the Perusal of him. Let them think they are growing acquainted with Nations and People that are now no more; that they are stepping almost three thousand Years backward into the remotest Antiquity, and entertaining themselves with a clear and surprizing Vision of Things no where else to be found, and the only authentick Picture of that ancient World. By this means alone their greatest Obstacles will vanish; and what usually creates their Dislike, will become a Satisfaction.

This Consideration may farther serve to answer for the constant Use of the same Epithets to his Gods and Heroes, such as the far-darting Phœbus, the blue-ey'd Pallas, the swift-footed Achilles, &c. which some have censured as impertinent and tediously repeated. Those of the Gods depended upon the Power and Offices then believ'd to belong to them, and had contracted a Weight and Veneration from the Rites and solemn Devotions in which they were us'd: they were a sort of Attributes that it was a Matter of Religion to salute them with on all Occasions, and an Irreverence to omit. As for the Epithets of great Men, Mons. Boileau is of Opinion; that they were in the Nature of Surnames, and repeated as such; for the Greeks having no Names deriv'd from their Fathers, were oblig'd when they mention'd any one to add some other Distinction; either naming his Parents expressly, or his Place of Birth, Profession, or the like: As Alexander Son of Philip, Herodotus of Halicarnassus, Diogenes the Cynic, &c. Homer therefore complying with the Custom of his Countrey, us'd such distinctive Additions as better agreed with Poetry. (pp. 333-39)

What other Cavils have been rais'd against Homer are such as hardly deserve a Reply, but will yet be taken notice of as they occur in the Course of the Work. Many have been occasion'd by an injudicious Endeavour to exalt Virgil; which is much the same, as if one should think to praise the Superstructure by undermining the Foundation: One would imagine by the whole Course of their Parallels, that these Criticks never so much as heard of Homer's having written first; a Consideration which whoever compares these two Poets ought to have always in his Eye. Some accuse him for the same things which they overlook or praise in the other; as when they prefer the Fable and Moral of the *Æneis* to those of the ***Iliad,*** for the same Reasons which might set the ***Odysses*** above the *Æneis:* as that the Heroe is a wiser Man; and the Action of the one more beneficial to his Countrey than that of the other: Or else they blame him for not doing what he never design'd; as because Achilles is not as good and perfect a Prince as Æneas, when the very Moral of his Poem requir'd a contrary Character. It is thus that Rapin judges in his Comparison of Homer and Virgil. Others select those particular Passages of Homer which are not so labour'd as some that Virgil drew out of them: This is the whole Management of Scaliger in his *Poetices*. Others quarrel with what they take for low and mean Expressions, sometimes thro' a false Delicacy and Refinement, oftner from an Ignorance of the Graces of the Original; and then triumph in the Aukwardness of their own Translations. This is the Conduct of Perault in his *Parallels*. Lastly, there are others, who pretending to a fairer Proceeding, distinguish between the personal Merit of Homer, and that of his Work; but when they come to assign the Causes of the great Reputation of the ***Iliad,*** they found it upon the Ignorance of his Times, and the Prejudice of those that followed. And in pursuance of this Principle, they make those Accidents (such as the Contention of the Cities, *&c.*) to be the Causes of his Fame, which were in Reality the Consequences of his Merit. The same might as well be said of Virgil, or any great Author, whose general Character will infallibly raise many casual Additions to their Reputation. This is the Method of Mons. de la Motte; who yet confesses upon the whole, that in whatever Age Homer had liv'd he must have been the greatest Poet of his Nation, and that he may be said in this Sense to be the Master even of those who surpass'd him.

In all these Objections we see nothing that contradicts his Title to the Honour of the chief Invention; and as long as this (which is indeed the Characteristic of Poetry itself) remains unequal'd by his Followers, he still continues superior to them. A cooler Judgment may commit fewer Faults, and be more approv'd in the Eyes of One Sort of Criticks: but that Warmth of Fancy will carry the loudest and most universal Applauses which holds the Heart of a Reader under the strongest Enchantment. Homer not only appears the Inventor of Poetry, but excells all the Inventors of other Arts in this, that he has swallow'd up the Honour of those who succeeded him. What he has done admitted no Encrease, it only left room for Contraction or Regulation. He shew'd all the Stretch of Fancy at once; and if he has fail'd in some of his Flights, it was but because he attempted every thing. A Work of this kind seems like a mighty Tree which rises from the most vigorous Seed, is improv'd with Industry, flourishes, and produces the finest Fruit; Nature and Art have conspir'd to raise it; Pleasure and Profit join'd to make it valuable: and they who find the justest Faults, have only said, that a few Branches (which run luxuriant thro' a Richness of Nature) might be lopp'd into Form to give it a more regular Appearance. (pp. 339-41)

Alexander Pope, "Preface to the Translation of the 'Iliad'," in Critical Essays of the Eighteenth Century: 1700-1725, *edited by Willard Higley Durham, Yale University Press, 1915, pp. 323-52.*

VOLTAIRE (essay date 1727)

[A French philosopher and man of letters, Voltaire was instrumental in the development of the Enlightenment, an eighteenth-century European movement which saw the principles of reason and empiricism supersede the long-established reliance on prescription, faith, and religious and monarchical authority. As a man of diverse and intense interests, Voltaire wrote prolifically on many subjects and in a variety of genres, but all his work asserts the absolute primacy of personal liberty—be it intellectual, social, religious, or political. In the following excerpt from his Essay on Epic Poetry, *published in 1727, Voltaire inquires into the question of why Homer has "so many Admirers, and so few Readers." He argues that in the* Iliad, *"the Reader's Imagination is often fill'd with great and noble Ideas, while the Affections of the Soul stagnate," citing historical unfamiliarity, the abundance of battle scenes, and overall length as the main hindrances to enjoyment of the poem.]*

A vase painting depicting Menelaus and Hector fighting over Euphorbus.

Let every Reader consult himself, when he reads [the ***Iliad***], and reflect how that Poem works upon his Mind; then he will judge if Homer hath reach'd to the utmost Pitch of the Art, in any Thing else but in that predominant Force of *Painting* which makes his peculiar Character.

Notwithstanding the Veneration due, and paid to Homer, it is very strange, yet true, that among the most Learn'd and the greatest Admirers of Antiquity, there is scarce one to be found, who ever read the ***Iliad,*** with that Eagerness and Rapture, which a Woman feels when she reads the Novel of Zaïda; and as to the common Mass of Readers, less conversant with Letters, but not perhaps endow'd with a less Share of Judgment and Wit, few have been able to go through the whole ***Iliad,*** without strugling against a secret Dislike, and some have thrown it aside after the fourth or fifth Book. How does it come to pass that Homer hath so many Admirers, and so few Readers? And is at the same time worshipp'd and neglected?

I'll endeavour to give some Reasons for this Paradox. The common Part of Mankind is aw'd with the Fame of Homer, rather than struck with his Beauties. The judicious Reader is pleas'd no doubt with the noble Imagination of that great Author, but very few have command enough over their own Prejudices, and can transport themselves far enough into such a remote Antiquity, as to become the Contemporaries of Homer when they read him: Good Sense bids them to make Allowances for the Manners of his Time, but 'tis almost impossible to bring themselves to a quick Relish of them. The Rays of his Light transmitted to their Eyes through so long a Way, afford them but a feeble glimmering Twilight, and no Warmth. They are like the old Counsellors of Priam, who confess'd without any emotion of Heart, that Helena was a Beauty.

A second Reason of their Dislike, is that Uniformity which seems diffused through all the Work. The Battles take up three Parts of the whole ***Iliad.*** The Reader is more likely to be disgusted by the continual Glare of that predominant Colour which is spread over the Poem, than to be pleased with the Variety of Teints, and Shades, which require a refin'd Sight to perceive them.

Thirdly, the Poem is certainly too long, and 'tis an Exception that all *Epick* Poets are liable to; for there is no *Epick* Poetry without a powerful Imagination, and no great Imagination without over-flowing.

I wave here all the Quarrels rais'd by the Enemies of Homer, to such Parts of his Poems, as may be the Objects of our Criticism, but never the Cause of our Sleep.

His Gods are perhaps at once absurd and entertaining, as the Madness of Ariosto amuses us with a bewitching Delight. And for his other Faults, the Majesty, and the Fire of his Stile, brightens them often into Beauties.

But in my Opinion, the best reason for that Languour which creeps upon the Mind of so many Readers, in Spight of the Flashes which rouse her now and then, is, that Homer interesses us for none of his Heroes. Achilles is too boisterous to inspire us with a tender Concern for him. And suppose his very Fierceness could extort from us that favourable Disposition which the over-powering Idea of Valour generally forces us into, his long Idleness wears away the Thought of him, and as the Poet lays him aside, so does the Reader.

Menelaus, who is the only Occasion of the War, and in whom of Course our Affections ought to center, is very far from being a shining Character. Paris, his Rival, excites our Contempt. Menelaus is in the Poem, but the Brother of Agamemnon, and Paris the Brother of Hector. Agamemnon, King of Kings, shocks us with his Pride, without giving us any great Idea of his Conduct. I do not know how it comes to pass, but every Reader bears secretly an ill Will to the wise Ulysses. The fair Helena, the Cause of so great Mischiefs, is insignificant enough. Nobody cares whose Share she will fall to, since she seems herself indifferent between her two Husbands.

When two Warriors fight in the ***Iliad,*** we are aw'd indeed with the Description, nay often transported with their Fury, but we feel neither Hope nor Fear for any of them.

We are like Juno in the *Æneid, Tros rutulus ve fuat, nullo discrimine habebo.*

We pity indeed the Misfortunes of Priam, nor will I quarrel with the Tears that we give to his Afflictions. I wish only that Homer would have interested us for the Greeks, throughout all the Poem, since he intends to praise them, and since they are the Heroes of the Poem; but I'll go no further than to observe, that if we are mov'd with the Sorrow of Priam, at the very End of the Poem, we are indifferent towards him in the Course of the Action.

Of all the Warriors, the couragious, the tender, and the pious Hector, deserves most our Affections. He hath the best Character, though he defends the wrong Cause; and he is betray'd by the Gods, though he has so much Virtue.

But our Concern for him is lost, in the Crowd of so many Heroes. Our Attention is divided and lessen'd, like a Stream cut into many Rivulets.

Thus the Reader's Imagination is often fill'd with great and noble Ideas, while the Affections of the Soul stagnate; and if in any long Work whatever, the Motions of the Heart do not keep Pace with the Pleasures of the Fancy, 'tis no Wonder if we may at once admire and be tir'd.

If all these Reasons are contested (for what Assertion of our Minds is undisputable?) I must add a further Observation, which is a Matter of Fact out of the Reach of Dispute. Many of the Books of the ***Iliad*** are independent from one another; they might be transpos'd without any great Alteration in the Action. And perhaps, for that Reason, they were call'd Rapsodies. I leave to the Judgement of the Reader, if such a work, let is be never so well written, never so teeming with Beauties (can be interesting) and win our Attention. (pp. 90-3)

Voltaire, "An Essay on Epick Poetry: Homer," in Voltaire's Essay on Epic Poetry, *edited by Florence Donnell White, Bryn Mawr College, 1915, 167 p.*

HUGH BLAIR (essay date 1783)

[*Blair was a Scottish minister, editor, and a distinguished professor of rhetoric at Edinburgh University. His* Lectures on Rhetoric and Belles Lettres, *originally delivered at Edinburgh between 1760 and 1783, were designed to initiate students into the fields of literature and composition. Acclaimed by Samuel Johnson and James Boswell, among others, they remained extremely popular and influential both in Great Britain and the United States until the first part of the nineteenth century. The critic Harold F. Harding has written that "[Blair] did more to interpret and make known the rhetorical theory of the ancients than any other British or American rhetorical writer." In the following excerpt from the* Lectures, *Blair characterizes Homer's style in the* Iliad *as imbued with "Fire and Simplicity" and then analyzes characterization, rhetoric, and descriptions in the poem.*]

Homer claims, on every account, our first attention, as the Father not only of Epic Poetry, but in some measure, of Poetry in general. Whoever sits down to read Homer, must consider that he is going to read the most ancient book in the world, next to the Bible. Without making this reflection, he cannot enter into the spirit, nor relish the Composition of the Author. He is not to look for the correctness, and elegance, of the Augustan Age. He must divest himself of our modern ideas of dignity and refinement; and transport his imagination almost three thousand years back in the history of mankind. What he is to expect, is a picture of the ancient world. He must reckon upon finding characters and manners, that retain a considerable tincture of the savage state; moral ideas, as yet imperfectly formed; and the appetites and passions of men brought under none of those restraints, to which, in a more advanced state of Society, they are accustomed. But bodily strength, prized as one of the chief heroic endowments; the preparing of a meal, and the appeasing of hunger, described as very interesting objects; and the heroes boasting of themselves openly, scolding one another outrageously, and glorying, as we would now think very indecently, over their fallen enemies.

The opening of the ***Iliad,*** possesses none of that sort of dignity, which a Modern looks for in a great Epic Poem. It turns on no higher subject, than the quarrel of two Chieftains about a female slave. (pp. 428-29)

[Afterward] rise all those "speciosa miracula," as Horace terms them, which fill that extraordinary Poem; and which have had the power of interesting almost all the nations of Europe, during every age, since the days of Homer. The general admiration commanded by a poetical plan, so very different from what any one would have formed in our times, ought not, upon reflection, to be matter of surprize. For, besides that a fertile genius can enrich and beautify any subject on which it is employed, it is to be observed, that ancient manners, how much soever they contradict our present notions of dignity and refinement, afford, nevertheless, materials for Poetry, superior, in some respects, to those which are furnished by a more polished state of Society. They discover human nature more open and undisguised, without any of those studied forms of behaviour which now conceal men from one another. They give free scope to the strongest and most impetuous emotions of the mind, which make a better figure in description, than calm and temperate feelings. They show us our native prejudices, appetites, and desires, exerting themselves without controul. From this state of manners, joined with the advantage of that strong and expressive Style, which . . . commonly distinguishes the Compositions of early ages, we have ground to look for more of the boldness, ease, and freedom of native genius, in compositions of such a period, than in those of more civilized times. And, accordingly, the two great characters of the Homeric Poetry are, Fire and Simplicity. (pp. 430-31)

The Subject of the ***Iliad*** must unquestionably be admitted to be, in the main, happily chosen. In the days of Homer, no object could be more splendid and dignified than the Trojan war. So great a confederacy of the Grecian States, under one leader; and the ten years siege which they carried on against

Troy, must have spread far abroad the renown of many military exploits, and interested all Greece in the traditions concerning the Heroes who had most eminently signalized themselves. Upon these traditions, Homer grounded his Poem; and though he lived, as is generally believed, only two or three centuries after the Trojan war, yet, through the want of written records, tradition must, by his time, have fallen into the degree of obscurity most proper for Poetry; and have left him at full liberty to mix as much fable as he pleased, with the remains of true history. He has not chosen, for his subject, the whole Trojan war; but, with great judgment, he has selected one part of it, the quarrel betwixt Achilles and Agamemnon, and the events to which that quarrel gave rise; which, though they take up forty-seven days only, yet include the most interesting, and most critical period of the war. By this management, he has given greater unity to what would have otherwise been an unconnected history of battles. He has gained one Hero, or principal character, Achilles, who reigns throughout the work; and he has shown the pernicious effect of discord among confederated princes. At the same time, I admit that Homer is less fortunate in his subject than Virgil. The plan of the *Æneid* includes a greater compass, and a more agreeable diversity of events; whereas the ***Iliad*** is almost entirely filled with Battles.

The praise of high invention has in every age been given to Homer, with the greatest reason. The prodigious number of incidents, of speeches, of characters divine and human, with which he abounds; the surprising variety with which he has diversified his battles, in the wounds and deaths, and little history pieces of almost all the persons slain, discover an invention next to boundless. But the praise of judgement is, in my opinion, no less due to Homer, than that of invention. His story is all along conducted with great art. He rises upon us gradually; his Heroes are brought out, one after another, to be objects of our attention. The distress thickens, as the Poem advances; and every thing is so contrived as to aggrandize Achilles, and to render him, as the Poet intended he should be, the capital figure.

But that wherein Homer excels all Writers, is the characteristical part. Here, he is without a rival. His lively and spirited exhibition of characters, is, in a great measure, owing to his being so dramatic a Writer, abounding every where with dialogue and conversation. There is much more dialogue in Homer than in Virgil; or, indeed, than in any other Poet. What Virgil informs us of by two words of Narration, Homer brings about by a Speech. We may observe here, that this method of Writing is more ancient than the narrative manner. Of this we have a clear proof in the Books of the Old Testament, which, instead of Narration, abound with Speeches, with answers and replies, upon the most familiar subjects. . . . Such a Style is the most simple and artless form of Writing; and must, therefore, undoubtedly have been the most ancient. It is copying directly from nature; giving a plain rehearsal of what passed, or was supposed to pass, in conversation between the persons of whom the Author treats. In progress of time, when the Art of Writing was more studied, it was thought more elegant to compress the substance of conversation into short distinct narrative, made by the Poet or Historian in his own person; and to reserve direct speeches for solemn occasions only.

The Ancient Dramatic method which Homer practised, has some advantages, balanced with some defects. It renders Composition more natural and animated, and more expressive of manners and characters; but withal less grave and majestic, and sometimes tiresome. Homer, it must be admitted, has carried his propensity to the making of Speeches too far; and if he be tedious any where, it is in these; some of them trifling, and some of them plainly unseasonable. Together with the Greek vivacity, he leaves upon our minds, some impression of the Greek loquacity also. His Speeches, however, are upon the whole characteristic and lively; and to them we owe, in a great measure, that admirable display which he has given of human nature. Every one who reads him, becomes familiarly and intimately acquainted with his heroes. We seem to have lived among them, and to have conversed with them. Not only has he pursued the single virtue of courage, through all its different forms and features, in his different warriors; but some more delicate characters, into which courage either enters not at all, or but for an inconsiderable part, he has drawn with singular art.

How finely, for instance, has he painted the character of Helen, so as, notwithstanding her frailty and her crimes, to prevent her from being an odious object! The admiration with which the old generals behold her, in the Third Book, when she is coming towards them, presents her to us with much dignity. Her veiling herself and shedding tears, her confusion in the presence of Priam, her grief and self-accusations at the fight of Menelaus, her upbraiding of Paris for his cowardice, and, at the same time, her returning fondness for him, exhibit the most striking features of that mixed female character, which we partly condemn, and partly pity. Homer never introduces her, without making her say something to move our compassion; while, at the same time, he takes care to contrast her character with that of a virtuous matron, in the chaste and tender Andromache.

Paris himself, the Author of all the mischief, is characterised with the utmost propriety. He is, as we would expect him, a mixture of gallantry and effeminacy. He retreats from Menelaus, on his first appearance; but immediately afterwards, enters into single combat with him. He is a great master of civility, remarkably courteous in his speeches; and receives all the reproofs of his brother Hector with modesty and deference. He is described as a person of elegance and taste. He was the Architect of his own Palace. He is, in the Sixth Book, found by Hector, burnishing and dressing up his armour; and issues forth to battle with a peculiar gaiety and ostentation of appearance, which is illustrated by one of the finest comparisons in all the ***Iliad,*** that of the horse prancing to the river.

Homer has been blamed for making his hero Achilles of too brutal and inamiable a character. But I am inclined to think, that injustice is commonly done to Achilles, upon the credit of two lines of Horace, who has certainly overloaded his character.

> Impiger, iracundus, inexorabilis, acer,
> Jura negat fibi nata; nihil non arrogat armis.

(pp. 431-35)

Achilles is passionate indeed, to a great degree; but he is far from being a contemner of laws and justice. In the contest with Agamemnon, though he carries it on with too much heat, yet he has reason on his side. He was notoriously wronged; but he submits; and resigns Briseis peaceably, when the heralds come to demand her; only, he will fight no longer under the command of a leader who had affronted him. Besides his wonderful bravery and contempt of death, he has several other qualities of a Hero. He is open and sincere. He loves his subjects, and respects the Gods. He is distinguished by strong friendships and attachments; he is, throughout, high spirited, gallant, and honourable; and allowing for a degree of ferocity which belonged to the times, and enters into the characters of most of Homer's Heroes, he is, upon the whole, abundantly fitted to raise high admiration, though not pure esteem.

Under the head of Characters, Homer's Gods or his Machinery, according to the critical term, come under consideration. The Gods make a great figure in the ***Iliad;*** much greater indeed than they do in the *Æneid,* or in any other Epic Poem; and hence Homer has become the standard of Poetic Theology. . . . Concerning Homer's Machinery, in particular, we must observe, that it was not his own invention. Like every other good Poet, he unquestionably followed the traditions of his country. The age of the Trojan war approached to the age of the Gods, and Demi-gods, in Greece. Several of the Heroes concerned in that war, were reputed to be the children of those Gods. Of course, the traditionary tales relating to them, and to the exploits of that age, were blended with the Fables of the Deities. These popular legends, Homer very properly adopted; though it is perfectly absurd to infer from this, that therefore Poets arising in succeeding ages, and writing on quite different subjects, are obliged to follow the same system of Machinery.

In the hands of Homer, it produces, on the whole, a noble effect; it is always gay and amusing; often, lofty and magnificent. It introduces into his Poem a great number of personages, almost as much distinguished by characters as his human actors. It diversifies his battles greatly, by the intervention of the Gods; and by frequently shifting the scene from earth to heaven, it gives an agreeable relief to the mind, in the midst of so much blood and slaughter. Homer's Gods, it must be confessed, though they be always lively and animated figures, yet sometimes want dignity. The conjugal contentions between Juno and Jupiter, with which he entertains us, and the indecent squabbles he describes among the inferior Deities, according as they take different sides with the contending parties, would be very unlucky models for any modern Poet to imitate. In apology for Homer, however, it must be remembered, that according to the Fables of those days, the Gods are but one remove above the condition of men. They have all the human passions. They drink and feast, and are vulnerable like men; they have children, and kinsmen, in the opposite armies; and bating that they are immortal, that they have houses on the top of Olympus, and winged chariots, in which they are often flying down to earth, and then re-ascending, in order to feast on Nectar and Ambrosia; they are in truth no higher beings than the human Heroes, and therefore very fit to take part in their contentions. At the same time, though Homer so frequently degrades his divinities, yet he knows how to make them appear in some conjunctures, with the most awful Majesty. Jupiter, the Father of Gods and Men, is, for the most part, introduced with great dignity; and several of the most sublime conceptions in the ***Iliad,*** are founded on the appearances of Neptune, Minerva, and Apollo, on great occasions.

With regard to Homer's Style and manner of Writing, it is easy, natural, and, in the highest degree, animated. It will be admired by such only as relish ancient simplicity, and can make allowance for certain negligencies and repetitions, which greater refinement in the Art of Writing has taught succeeding, though far inferior, Poets to avoid. For Homer is the most simple in his Style of all the great Poets, and resembles most the Style of the poetical parts of the Old Testament. . . . I know indeed no Author, to whom it is more difficult to do justice in a Translation, than Homer. As the plainness of his diction, were it literally rendered, would often appear flat in any modern language; so, in the midst of that plainness, and not a little heightened by it, there are every where breaking forth upon us flashes of native fire, of sublimity and beauty, which hardly any language, except his own, could preserve. His Versification has been universally acknowledged to be uncommonly melodious; and to carry, beyond that of any Poet, a resemblance in the sound to the sense and meaning.

In Narration, Homer is, at all times, remarkably concise, which renders him lively and agreeable; though in his speeches . . . sometimes tedious. He is every where descriptive; and descriptive by means of those well chosen particulars, which form the excellency of description. Virgil gives us the nod of Jupiter with great magnificence.

Annuit; et totum nutu tremefecit Olympum.

But Homer, in describing the same thing, gives us the sable eye-brows of Jupiter bent, and his ambrosial curls shaken, at the moment when he gives the nod; and thereby renders the figure more natural and lively. Whenever he seeks to draw our attention to some interesting object, he particularises it so happily, as to paint it in a manner to our sight. The shot of Pandarus' arrow, which broke the truce between the two armies, as related in the Fourth Book, may be given for an instance; and above all, the admirable interview of Hector with Andromache, in the Sixth Book; where all the circumstances of conjugal and parental tenderness, the child affrighted with the view of his Father's Helmet and Crest, and clinging to the nurse; Hector putting off his Helmet, taking the child into his arms, and offering up a prayer for him to the Gods; Andromache receiving back the child with a smile of pleasure, and at the same instant, bursting into tears . . . form the most natural and affecting picture that can possibly be imagined.

In the description of Battles, Homer particularly excels. He works up the hurry, the terror, and confusion of them in so masterly a manner, as to place the Reader in the very midst of the engagement. It is here, that the fire of his genius is most highly displayed; insomuch, that Virgil's Battles, and indeed those of most other Poets, are cold and inanimated in comparison of Homer's.

With regard to Similies, no Poet abounds so much with them. Several of them are beyond doubt extremely beautiful: such as those, of the fires in the Trojan camp compared to the Moon and Stars by night; Paris going forth to Battle, to the war-horse prancing to the river; and Euphorbus slain, to the flowering shrub cut down by a sudden blast: all which are among the finest poetical passages that are any where to be found. I am not, however, of opinion, that Homer's Comparisons, taken in general, are his greatest beauties. They come too thick upon us; and often interrupt the train of his narration or description. The resemblance on which they are founded, is sometimes not clear; and the objects whence they are taken, are too uniform. His Lions, Bulls, Eagles, and herds of Sheep, recur too frequently; and the allusions in some of his Similies, even after the allowances that are to be made for ancient manners, must be admitted to be debasing. (pp. 436-40)

[As] to the comparative merit of [the] two great princes of Epic Poetry, Homer and Virgil; the former must, undoubtedly, be admitted to be the greater Genius; the latter, to be the more correct Writer. Homer was an original in his art, and discovers both the beauties, and the defects, which are to be expected in an original Author, compared with those who succeed him; more boldness, more nature and ease, more sublimity and force; but greater irregularities and negligencies in Composition. Virgil has, all along, kept his eye upon Homer; in many places, he has not so much imitated, as he has literally translated him. The description of the Storm, for instance, in the first *Æneid*, and Æneas's Speech upon that occasion, are translations from the fifth book of the ***Odyssey***; not to mention almost all the similies of Virgil, which are no other than copies of those of Homer. The pre-eminence in invention, therefore, must, beyond doubt, be ascribed to Homer. As to the preeminence in judgment, though many Critics incline to give it to Virgil, yet, in my opinion, it hangs doubtful. In Homer, we discern all the Greek vivacity; in Virgil, all the Roman stateliness. Homer's imagination is by much the most rich and copious; Virgil's the most chaste and correct. The strength of the former lies, in his power of warming the fancy; that of the latter, in his power of touching the heart. Homer's style is more simple and animated; Virgil's more elegant and uniform. The first has, on many occasions, a sublimity to which the latter never attains; but the latter, in return, never sinks below a certain degree of Epic dignity, which cannot so clearly be pronounced of the former. Not, however, to detract from the admiration due to both these great Poets, most of Homer's defects may reasonably be imputed, not to his genius, but to the manners of the age in which he lived; and for the feeble passages of the *Æneid*, this excuse ought to be admitted, that the *Æneid* was left an unfinished work. (pp. 449-50)

Hugh Blair, "Homer's Iliad and Odyssey—Virgil's Aeneid," in his Lectures on Rhetoric and Belles Lettres, Vol. I, *edited by Harold F. Harding, Southern Illinois University Press, 1965, pp. 428-50.*

JONES VERY (essay date 1839)

[*Very, an American poet and essayist, was a prominent figure in the Transcendentalist movement. He is best known for his deeply religious sonnets which deal with the theme of complete submission to God. Such critics as Ralph Waldo Emerson, Margaret Fuller, and Nathaniel Hawthorne considered Very one of the most accomplished poets in the United States. In the following excerpt, Very discusses Homer in historical context and speculates on the possibility of creating a modern epic similar to the* Iliad. *Homer's purpose, Very posits, was "revealing to his age forms of nobler beauty and heroism than dwell in the minds of those around him," and was, therefore, concerned with the "outward world." However, because modern literature is concerned with inwardness, Very notes that a modern epic would be rather different from the* Iliad. *Very's essay was first published in 1839.*]

The poets of the present day who would raise the epic song cry out, like Archimedes of old, "give us a place to stand on and we will move the world." This is, as we conceive, the true difficulty. Glancing for a moment at the progress of epic poetry, we shall see that the obscurity of fabulous times could be adapted to the earliest development only of the heroic character. There is an obvious incongruity in making times so far remote the theatre on which to represent the heroism of a civilized age; and it adds still more to the difficulty, that, although the darkness of fable still invests them, reason will no longer perceive the beings which the infant credulity of man once saw there.

To men in the early stages of society their physical existence must seem almost without end, and they live on through life with as little reference to another state of being as we ourselves do in childhood. To minds in this state there was a remoteness in an event which had taken place one or two centuries before, of which we cannot conceive, and which rendered the time that Homer had chosen for his subject, though not materially differing in character, sufficiently remote for his purpose. If to these advantages possessed by Homer we add those which belonged to him from the religion of his times and from tradition, whose voice is to the poet more friendly than the plain written records of history, we must confess that the spot on which he built up his scenes of heroic wonder was peculiarly favorable. The advance which the human mind had made towards civilization prevented Virgil from making a like impression on his own age. To awaken admiration, he too was obliged to break from the bonds of the present, and soar beyond the bounds of history, before he could throw his spell of power over the mind. Why had he less influence? Because he could not, like Homer, carry into the past the spirit of his times. To the enlarged minds of Virgil's day, the interval between the siege of Troy and their own time did not seem wider than it did to those who lived in the time of Homer. The true distance in time was chosen by each, but the character of Æneas did not possess those great attributes which could render it the Achilles of the Romans. Lucan, while his characters exhibit the true heroic spirit of his age, fails of giving to them their due influence, from the want of some region of fiction beyond the dominion of history in which to place them. He cannot break from the present without violating every law of probability. To escape this thraldom and reach a point from which the heroic character of their age might be seen dilated to its full height, modern poets have fled beyond the bounds of time and woke the echoes of eternity. It was only from this point that the Christian world could be moved; it is only in that region without bounds that the heroism of immortality can be shown in visible action. . . . This new page of the heroic character naturally leads us to inquire whether we are to have no great representation of it, no embodying of this spirit in some gigantic form of action, which shall stalk before the age, and by the contemplation of which our minds may be fired to nobler deeds.

In considering this question, we shall endeavor to show what reasons there are for not expecting another great epic poem, drawn from the principles of epic poetry and the human mind, and that these present an insuperable barrier to the choice of a subject which shall exhibit the present development of the heroic character in action.

In doing this I shall exhibit, by an analysis of the ***Iliad,*** the true model of an epic poem, its origin and peculiarities, and in what manner those peculiarities have been changed, and, at last, lost by succeeding poets, according to the development of the heroic character in their several eras.

I shall thus be led to show that the taking away of the peculiarities of *epic* interest, and the final emerging of that interest in the *dramatic*, is the natural result of the influences to which the human mind in its progress is subjected; and that that influence, while it precludes all former subjects from representing the present development of the heroic character, throws, at the same time, an insuperable barrier in the way of any subject.

Looking upon Homer, at least as regards the ***Iliad,*** as a single man speaking throughout with one accent of voice, one form of language, and one expression of feeling, we leave to the framers of modern paradoxes the question whether this name is a type or not, and proceed to consider what might be the probable origin of the ***Iliad,*** and what it is which constitutes it the true model of an epic poem, a more perfect visible manifestation of the heroic character than can be again presented to the eyes of man. In a philosophical analysis of such a poem as the ***Iliad*** or ***Odyssey,*** made with reference to its epic peculiarities, there is great danger of misconceiving the history and character of early heroic poetry, thus giving to the poet a plan which he never formed, or a moral which he never conceived. The simplest conception of the origin and plan of the ***Iliad*** must, we think, prove the most correct. It originated, doubtless, in that desire, which every great poet must especially feel, of revealing to his age forms of nobler beauty and heroism than dwell in the minds of those around him. Wandering, as his active imagination must have led him to do, in the days of the past, Homer must have been led by the fitness of the materials presented to him in the siege of Troy, by their remoteness from his own time, and the interest with which they would be viewed by the mass of his countrymen as descendants of the Grecian heroes, to the choice of a subject which seemed to present a worthy form in which to manifest the workings of his soul. His enthusiasm would doubtless prompt him to the execution of detached parts before he had completed his general plan, and the various incidents, which constitute so much of the charm and interest of his poem as they suggested themselves to his mind, would also direct him to the great point round which they all revolved. The influence upon the several parts, resulting from the contemplation of the chief character, would thus give all the unity to the subject which we find in fact to belong to the earliest forms of a nation's poetry. "Passion to excite sympathy, variety to prevent disgust flowing in a free stream of narrative verse, not the intricacy and dove-tailing of modern epics, is to be looked for in the ***Iliad;*** for it was not made like a modern epic to be read in our closets, but to be presented only in fragments before the minds of an audience. Thus the single combats of Menelaus and Paris, the funeral games of Patroclus, and the restitution and burial of the body of Hector are generally complete in themselves, yet having an obvious connection as still telling the same tale of Troy." So much for the origin and fable of the ***Iliad.***

The genius displayed in its grand and comprehensive design is only equalled by the judgment manifested in confining the action to the busiest and most interesting period of the Trojan war, in thus uniting in his plan and bringing forward in his details everything which could lay hold of the affections, the prejudices, and vanity of his countrymen. Of his characters we need only say that, like those of Shakespeare, they are stamped with nature's own image and superscription. Though all are possessed of valor and courage, yet they are so distinguished from one another by certain peculiarities of disposition and manners that to distinguish them it is hardly necessary to hear their names. Achilles is brave, and Hector is brave, so are Ajax, Menelaus, and Diomede; but the bravery of Hector is not of the same kind with that of Ajax, and no one will mistake the battle-shout of the son of Atreus for the war-cry of Tydides.

Homer's machinery, as all epic machinery must be, was founded on the popular belief in the visible appearance of the gods; and on account of this belief he was not less favored by the circumstances under which he introduced them than he was by those which enabled him to represent his heroes. It cast around his whole subject a sublimity which it could not otherwise have had, giving occasion to noble description, and tending to excite that admiration which is the leading aim of the epic.

We have made this analysis of the ***Iliad,*** to show in what way all things combined in Homer's age to assist him in giving a perfect outward manifestation of the heroic character of his times. He wrote in that stage of society when man's physical existence assumed an importance in the mind like that of our immortality, and gave to all without a power and dignity not their own. This it was which imparted an heroic greatness to war which cannot now be seen in it. That far-reaching idea of time, which seems to expand our thoughts with limitless existence, gives to our mental struggles a greatness they could not have before had. We each of us feel within our own bosoms a great, an immortal foe, which if we have subdued, we may meet with calmness every other, knowing that earth contains no greater; but which if we have not, it will continually appear in those petty contests with others by which we do but show our own cowardice. The Greeks, on the contrary, lived only for their country, and drew everything within the sphere of their national views; their highest exemplification of morality was patriotism. Of Homer's heroes it may with peculiar propriety be said that they were but children of a larger growth, and they could have no conception of power that was not perceived in its visible effects. "The world," as Milton says of our first parents, "was all *before* them," and not *within* them, and their mission was to go forth and make a material impression on the material world. The soul of Homer was the mirror of this outward world, and in his verse we have it shown to us with the distinctness and reality of the painter's page. Lucan calls him the prince of painters, and with him Cicero agrees, when he says, "Quæ species ac forma pugnæ, quæ acies, quod remigium, qui motus hominum, qui ferarum non ita expictus est, ut quæ ipse non viderit, nos ut videremus effecerit?" It is needless perhaps to say that this state of the mind gives both a reason and excuse for those many epithets, which a false criticism and a false delicacy of taste is so fond of censuring. Such critics would blame the poet for praising the physical strength of his heroes; in short, for representing his gods such as they were believed to be, and painting his warriors such as they were. When we look back upon the pages of their history, we cannot contemplate the greatness there exhibited, without a feeling of sorrow that they had not lived under influences as favorable as our own; without a sense of unworthiness at not having exhibited characters corresponding with the high privileges we enjoy. We respect that grandeur of mind in the heroes of Homer which led them to sacrifice a mere earthly existence for the praise of all coming ages. They have not been disappointed. Worlds to them unknown have read of their deeds, and generations yet unborn shall honor them. They live on a page which the finger of time strives in vain to efface, which shall ever remain an eternal monument of disgrace to those of after times who, though gifted with higher views of excellence, have yet striven to erect a character on deeds like theirs. We reverence not in Hector and Achilles the mere display of physical power, we reverence not the manners of their times, which but too often call forth our horror and disgust; but we do reverence and honor those motives which even in the infancy of the human mind served to raise it above the dominion of sense, and taught it to grasp at a life beyond the narrow limits of its earthly vision.

This state of things gave to the ***Iliad*** and ***Odyssey*** that intense epic interest which we fail to find in later heroic poems. As the mind advances, a stronger sympathy with the inner man of the heart is more and more felt, and becomes more and more the characteristic of literature. In the expanded mind and cultivated affections, a new interest is awakened, *dramatic* poetry succeeds the *epic,* thus satisfying the want produced by the farther development of our nature. For the interest of the *epic* consists in that character of greatness that in the infancy of the mind is given to physical action and the objects associated with it; but the interest of the *drama* consists in those mental struggles which precede physical action, and to which in the progress of man the greatness of the other becomes subordinate. For as the mind expands and the moral power is developed, the mightiest conflicts are born within,—outward actions lost their grandeur, except to the eye, for the soul looks upon them but as results of former battles won and lost, upon whose decision, and upon whose alone, its destiny hung. This is the mystery of that calm, more awful than the roar of battle, which rests on the spirits of the mighty, and which the hand of the Grecian sculptor strove to fix on the brow of his god. Though Homer has given variety to his poem by the introduction of dialogue, and thus rendered it, in one sense, often dramatic; yet we find it is the mere transferring of the *narrative* from his own lips to those of others. The interest is still *without,* it is not the interest of sentiment, but of description. This character of the Greeks, as might be supposed, is shown in their language, and illustrates their tendency in early times to look upon themselves in all reflex acts, whether external or internal, as patients rather than agents; a tendency to use the words of another, which is exemplified in every page of the Homeric poems, and which belongs more or less to every people in an early stage of civilization, before the nation comes of age, and acquires the consciousness along with the free use of its powers. This seems to be the reason why so many of the verbs employed by the Greeks to denote states of mind or of feeling have a passive form. . . . "Men's minds," as Shakespeare has somewhere said, "are parcel of their fortunes," and his age was necessary and alone suited to the mind of Homer. Man viewed himself with reference to the world; not, as in the present day, the world in reference to himself; and it was this state of the mind which then made the taking of Troy the point of epic interest.

We have thus endeavored to show that the manifestation of the heroic character in the time of Homer was perfectly exhibited in outward visible action, and that this reflected from the soul of the poet addressed to a seeing and listening, rather than a reading people, was the poetry of fancy rather than sentiment. Events, characters, superstitions, customs, and traditions, all combined in rendering the ***Iliad*** a perfect embodying of the perfect outward manifestation of the heroic character of that period. The poetry of the senses, the reflection merely of nature and of heroic achievements, is not susceptible of indefinite progress; it must evidently be most perfect when the objects of visible action are noblest, and we view all else only with reference to those actions. The epic poetry of the Greeks corresponds to sculpture, and in the one, as in the other, the outward forms of life and action live and will ever live unrivalled. (pp. 3-10)

We cannot sympathize with that spirit of criticism which censures modern poetry for being the portraiture of individual characteristics and passions, and not the reflection of the general features of society and the outward man. If we want such poetry as Homer's, we must not only evoke him from the shades, but also his times. Purely objective poetry is the most perfect, and possesses the most interest, only in the childhood of the human mind. In the poetry of the Hindoos, of the Israelites, as well as of the Greeks, the epic is the prevailing element. But that page of the heroic character is turned forever;— another element is developing itself in the soul, and breathing into the materiality of the past a spiritual life and beauty. It is in vain we echo the words of other days, and call it poetry; it is in vain we collect the scattered dust of the past, and attempt to give it form and life by that same principle which once animated it. We can only give a brighter and more joyous existence to the cold forms of departed days, by bowing down, like the prophet of old, and breathing into them a purer and more ennobling faith, the brighter flame of our own bosoms. To stir the secret depths of our hearts, writers must have penetrated deeply into their own. Homer found conflicts *without,* to describe; shall the poets of our day be blamed because they would exhibit to us those they feel *within?* (pp. 22-3)

Jones Very, "Epic Poetry," in his Poems and Essays, *revised edition, Houghton, Mifflin and Company, 1886, pp. 3-25.*

THOMAS DE QUINCEY (essay date 1841)

[*An English critic and essayist, De Quincey used his own life as the subject of his best-known work,* Confessions of an English Opium Eater *(1822), in which he chronicled his addiction to opium. De Quincey contributed reviews to a number of London journals and earned a reputation as an insightful if occasionally long-winded literary critic. At the time of his death, De Quincey's critical expertise was underestimated, though his talent as a prose writer had long been acknowledged. Some twentieth-century critics still disdain the digressive qualities of De Quincey's writing, yet others find that his essays display an acute psychological awareness. In the following excerpt, De Quincey criticizes the "immaturity of* [*Homer's*] *metrical art," but praises the poet's depiction of Achilles' "humane and princely character." De Quincey's remarks were originally published in* Blackwood's Edinburgh Magazine *in 1841.*]

[Homeric meter] is certainly *kenspeck,* to use a good old English word—that is to say, recognisable; you challenge it for Homer's whenever you meet it. . . . The fact is, though flowing and lively, it betrays the immaturity of the metrical art. Those constraints from which the Germans praise its freedom are the constraints of exquisite art—art of a kind unknown to the simple Homer. This is a difficult subject; for, in our own literature, the true science of metrical effects has not belonged to our later poets, but to the elder. Spenser, Shakespere, Milton, are the great masters of exquisite versification. And Waller, who was idly reputed to have refined our metre, was a mere trickster, having a single tune moving in his imagination, without compass and without variety. Chaucer, also, whom Dryden in this point so thoroughly misunderstood, was undoubtedly a most elaborate master of metre, as will appear when we have a *really* good edition of him. But in the Pagan literature this was otherwise. We see in the Roman poets that, precisely as they were antique, they were careless, or at least very inartificial in the management of their metre. Thus Lucilius, Ennius, even Lucretius, leave a class of faults in their verse from which Virgil would have revolted. And the very same class of faults is found in Homer. But, though faults as regards severe art, they are in the very spirit of *naïveté* or picturesque naturalness, and wear the stamp of a primitive age—artless and inexperienced.

This article would require a volume. But I will content myself with one illustration. Every scholar is aware of the miserable effect produced where there is no *cæsura,* in that sense of the word *cæsura* which means the interlocking of the several feet into the several words. Thus, imagine a line like this:—

Urbem Romam primo condit Romulus anno.

Here the six feet of the hexameter are separately made out by six several words. Each word is a foot; and no foot interlocks into another. So that there is no *cæsura.* Yet even *that* is not the worst fault of the line. The other and more destructive is—the coincidence of the *ictus,* or emphasis, with the first syllable of every foot. Now, in Homer we see both faults repeatedly. Thus, to express the thundering pace with which a heavy stone comes trundling back from a hill-top, he says,

Autis epeita pedońde kulindeto laaš anaides.

Here there is the shocking fault, to any metrical ear, of making the emphasis fall regularly on the first syllable, which in effect obliterates all the benefit of the cæsura. Now, Virgil, in an age of refinement, has not one such line, nor could have endured such a line. In that verse, expressing the gallop of a horse, he also has five dactyles:

Quadrupedante putrem sonitu quatit ungula campum.

But he takes care to distribute the accents properly,—on which so much even of the ancient versification depended: except in the two last feet, the emphasis of Virgil's line never coincides with the first syllable of the foot. Homer, it will be said, wished to express mimetically the rolling, thundering, leaping motion of the stone. True; but so did Virgil wish to express the thundering gallop of the horse, in which the beats of the hoofs return with regular intervals. Each sought for a picturesque effect; each adopted a dactylic structure: but to any man who has studied this subject I need not say that picturesqueness, like any other effect, must be subordinated to a higher law of beauty. Whence, indeed, it is that the very limits of imitation arise from every art,—sculpture, painting, &c.,—indicating what it ought to imitate, and what it ought not to imitate. And, unless regard is had to such higher restraints, metrical effects become as silly and childish as the musical effects in Kotzwarra's "Battle of Prague," with its ridiculous attempts to mimic the firing of cannon, groans of the wounded, &c., instead of involving the passion of a battle in the agitation of the music. (pp. 77-9)

• • • • •

Once, when I observed to [Wordsworth] that of imagination, in his own sense, I saw no instance in the ***Iliad,*** he replied, "Yes; there is the character of Achilles; this is imaginative, in the same sense as Ariosto's Angelica." *Character* is not properly the word, nor was it what Wordsworth meant. It is an idealised conception. The excessive beauty of Angelica, for instance, in the *Orlando Furioso,* robs the paladins of their wits; draws anchorites into guilt: tempts the baptized into mortal feud; summons the unbaptized to war; brings nations together from the ends of the earth. And so, with different but analogous effects, the very perfection of courage, beauty, strength, speed, skill of eye, of voice, and all personal accomplishments, are embodied in the son of Peleus. He has the same supremacy in modes of courtesy, and doubtless, according to the poet's conception, in virture. In fact, the astonishing blunder which Horace made in deciphering this Homeric portrait gives the best memorandum for recalling the real points of his most self-commanding character:

Impiger, iracundus, inexorabilis, acer,
Jura negat sibi nata, nihil non arrogat armis.

Was that man "iracundus" who, in the very opening of the ***Iliad,*** makes his anger, under the most brutal insult, bend to the public welfare? When two people quarrel, it is too commonly the unfair award of careless bystanders that "one is as bad as the other"; whilst generally it happens that one of the parties is but the respondent in a quarrel originated by the other. I never witnessed a quarrel in my life where the fault was equally divided between the parties. Homer says of the two chiefs . . . they stood aloof in feud; but what was the nature of the feud? Agamemnon had inflicted upon Achilles, himself a king, and the most brilliant chieftain of the confederate army, the very foulest outrage (matter and manner) that can be imagined. Because his own brutality to a priest of Apollo had caused a pestilence, and he finds that he must resign this priest's daughter, he declares that he will indemnify himself by seizing a female captive from the tents of Achilles. Why of Achilles more than of any other man? Colour of right, or any relation between his loss and his redress, this brutal Agamemnon does not offer by pretence. But he actually executes his threat. Nor does he *ever* atone for it; since his returning Briseis, without disavowing his right to have seized her, is wide of the whole point at issue. Now, under what show of common sense can that man be called *iracundus* who calmly submits to such an indignity as this? Or is that man *inexorabilis* who sacrifices to the tears and grey hairs of Priam his own meditated revenge, giving back the body of the enemy who had robbed him of his dearest friend? Or is there any gleam of truth in saying that *jura negat sibi nata* when, of all the heroes in the ***Iliad,*** he is the most punctiliously courteous, the most ceremonious in his religious observances, and the one who most cultivated the arts of peace? Or is that man the violent defier of all law and religion who submits with so pathetic a resignation to the doom of early death?

Enough, I know my fate—to die; to see no more
My much-loved parents, or my native shore.

Charles XII of Sweden threatened to tickle that man who had libelled his hero Alexander. But Alexander himself would have tickled Master Horace for this infernal libel on Achilles, if they had happened to be contemporaries. I have a love for Horace; but my wrath has always burned furiously against him for his horrible perversion of the truth in this well-known tissue of calumnies. (pp. 80-2)

Achilles revolves through . . . the ***Iliad,*** in a series of phases, each of which looks forward and backward to all the rest. He travels like the sun through his diurnal course. We see him first of all rising upon us as a princely councillor for the welfare of the Grecian host. We see him atrociously insulted in this office; yet still, though a king, and unused to opposition, and boiling with youthful blood, nevertheless controlling his passion, and retiring in clouded majesty. Even thus, though having now so excellent a plea for leaving the army, and though aware of the early death that awaited him if he staid, he disdains to profit by the evasion. We see him still living in the tented field, and generously unable to desert those who had so insultingly deserted *him.* We see him in a dignified retirement, fulfilling all the duties of religion, friendship, hospitality; and, like an accomplished man of taste, cultivating the arts of peace. We see him so far surrendering his wrath to the earnest persuasion of friendship that he comes forth at a critical moment for the Greeks to save them from ruin. What are his arms? He has none at all. Simply by his voice he changes the face of the battle. He shouts and nations fly from the sound. Never but once again is such a shout recorded by a poet—

He called so loud that all the hollow deep
Of Hell resounded.

Who called? *That* shout was the shout of an archangel. Next we see him reluctantly allowing his dearest friend to assume his own arms; the kindness and the modesty of his nature forbidding him to suggest that not the divine weapons, but the immortal arm of the wielder, had made them invincible. His friend perishes. Then we see him rise in his noontide wrath, before which no life could stand. The frenzy of his grief makes him for a time cruel and implacable. He sweeps the field of battle like a monsoon. His revenge descends perfect, sudden, like a curse from heaven. We now recognise the goddess-born. This is his avatar—the incarnate descent of his wrath. Had he moved to battle under the ordinary impulses of Ajax, Diomed, and the other heroes, we never could have sympathised or gone along with so withering a course. We should have viewed him as a "scourge of God," or fiend, born for the tears of wives and the maledictions of mothers. But the poet, before he would let him loose upon men, creates for him a sufficient, or at least palliating, motive. In the sternest of his acts we read only the anguish of his grief. This is surely the perfection of art. At length the work of destruction is finished; but, if the poet leaves him at this point, there would be a want of repose, and we should be left with a painful impression of his hero as forgetting the earlier humanities of his nature, and brought forward only for final exhibition in his terrific phases. Now, therefore, by machinery the most natural, we see this paramount hero travelling back within our gentler sympathies, and revolving to his rest like the vesper sun disrobed of his blazing terrors. We see him settling down to that humane and princely character in which he had been first exhibited; we see him relenting at the sight of Priam's grey hairs, touched with the sense of human calamity, and once again mastering his passion (grief now), as formerly he had mastered his wrath. He consents that his feud shall sleep; he surrenders the corpse of his capital enemy; and the last farewell chords of the poem rise with a solemn intonation from the grave of "Hector, the tamer of horses"—that noble soldier who had so long been the column of his country, and to whom, in his dying moments, the stern Achilles had declared (but then in the middle career of his grief) that no honourable burial should ever be granted.

Such is the outline of an Achilleis, as it might be gathered from the ***Iliad;*** and, for the use of schools, I am surprised that such a beautiful whole has not long since been extracted. A tale more affecting by its story and vicissitudes does not exist. . . . Every part implies every other part. With such a model before him as this poem on the wrath of Achilles, Aristotle could not carry his notions of unity too high. (pp. 89-91)

Thomas De Quincey, "Homer and the Homeride," in his The Collected Writings of Thomas De Quincey: Historical Essays and Researches, Vol. VI, *edited by David Masson, A. & C. Black, 1897, pp. 7-93.*

HENRY D. THOREAU (lecture date 1843)

[*An American essayist, poet, and translator, Thoreau is considered one of the key figures in the American Transcendentalist movement. His* Walden; or, Life in the Woods, *a record of two years that he spent living alone in the woods near Concord, Massachusetts, is viewed as one of the finest prose works in American literature. Although critics observe that Thoreau's ideas as presented in* Walden *and his other works do not form a unified system of philosophy, his very way of life, marked by individualism and closeness to nature, embodied the tenets of American Transcendentalism. Thoreau's aphoristic yet lyrical prose style and intense moral and political convictions have secured his place beside Ralph Waldo Emerson as the most representative and influential of the New England Transcendentalists. In the following excerpt, Thoreau commends the simplicity and naturalness of Homer's style and affirms that the* Iliad *is still accessible to the modern reader. Thoreau's comments were originally delivered as a lecture at the Concord Lyceum in 1843.*]

The wisest definition of poetry the poet will instantly prove false by setting aside its requisitions. We can therefore publish only our advertisement of it.

There is no doubt that the loftiest written wisdom is rhymed or measured, is in form as well as substance poetry; and a volume, which should contain the condensed wisdom of mankind, need not have one rhythmless line. Yet poetry, though the last and finest result, is a natural fruit. As naturally as the oak bears an acorn, and the vine a gourd, man bears a poem, either spoken or done. It is the chief and most memorable success, for history is but a prose narrative of poetic deeds. What else have the Hindoos, the Persians, the Babylonians, the Egyptians, done, that can be told? It is the simplest relation of phenomena, and describes the commonest sensations with more truth than science does, and the latter at a distance slowly mimics its style and methods. The poet sings how the blood flows in his veins. He performs his functions, and is so well that he needs such stimulus to sing only as plants to put forth leaves and blossoms. He would strive in vain to modulate the remote and transient music which he sometimes hears, since his song is a vital function like breathing, and an integral result like weight. It is not the overflowing of life but its subsidence rather, and is drawn from under the feet of the poet. It is enough if Homer but say the sun sets. He is as serene as nature, and we can hardly detect the enthusiasm of the bard. It is as if nature spoke. He presents to us the simplest pictures of human life, so that childhood itself can understand them, and the man must not think twice to appreciate his naturalness. Each reader discovers for himself, that succeeding poets have done little else than copy his similes. His more memorable passages are as naturally bright, as gleams of sunlight in misty weather. Nature furnishes him not only with words, but with stereotyped lines and sentences from her mint.

> As from the clouds appears the full moon,
> All shining, and then again it goes behind the shadowy clouds,
> So Hector, at one time appeared among the foremost,
> And at another in the rear, commanding; and all with brass
> He shone, like to the lightning of ægis-bearing Zeus.

He conveys the least information, even the hour of the day, with such magnificence, and vast expense of natural imagery, as if it were a message from the gods.

> While it was dawn, and sacred day was advancing,
> For that space the weapons of both flew fast, and the people fell;
> But when now the woodcutter was preparing his morning meal
> In the recesses of the mountain, and had wearied his hands
> With cutting lofty trees, and satiety came to his mind,
> And the desire of sweet food took possession of his thoughts;
> Then the Danaans by their valor broke the phalanxes,
> Shouting to their companions from rank to rank.

When the army of the Trojans passed the night under arms, keeping watch lest the enemy should re-embark under cover of the dark,

> They, thinking great things, upon the neutral ground of war,
> Sat all the night; and many fires burned for them.
> As when in the heavens the stars round the bright moon

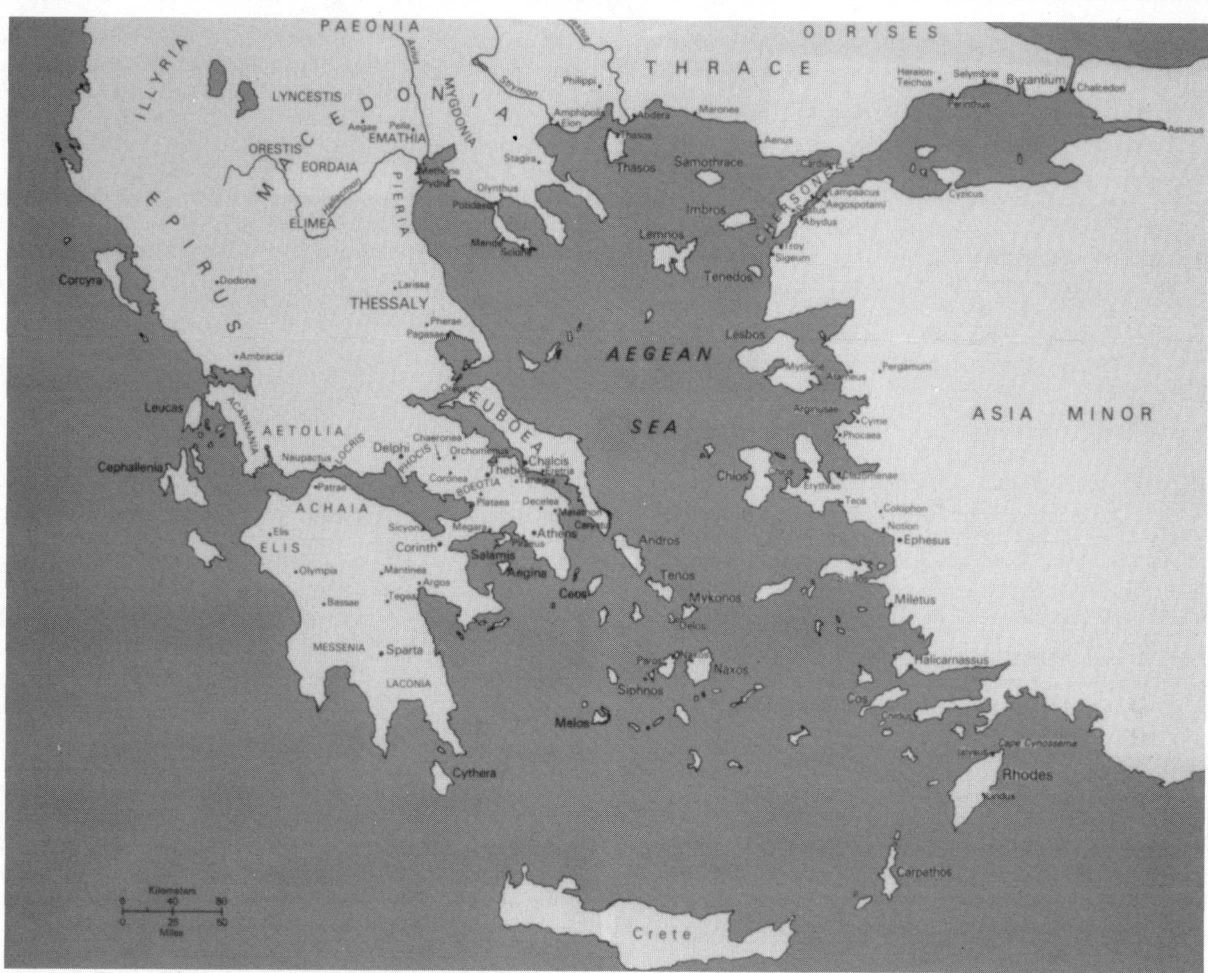

A map of Asia Minor in Homer's time. From A Short History of Greek Literature, *by Jacqueline de Romilly. Translated by Lillian Doherty. The University of Chicago Press, 1985.*

> Appear beautiful, and the air is without wind;
> And all the heights, and the extreme summits,
> And the shady valleys appear; and the shepherd rejoices
> in his
> So between the ships and the streams of Xanthus
> Appeared the fires of the Trojans before Ilium.

The "white-armed goddess Juno," sent by the Father of gods and men for Iris and Apollo,

> Went down the Idæan mountains to far Olympus,
> As when the mind of a man, who has come over much
> earth,
> Sallies forth, and he reflects with rapid thoughts,
> There was I, and there, and remembers many things;
> So swiftly the august Juno hastening flew through the air,
> And came to high Olympus.

There are few books which are fit to be remembered in our wisest hours, but the ***Iliad*** is brightest in the serenest days, and imbodies still all the sunlight that fell on Asia Minor. No modern joy or ecstasy of ours can lower its height or dim its lustre; but there it lies in the last of literature, as it were the earliest, latest production of the mind. The ruins of Egypt oppress and stifle us with their dust, foulness preserved in cassia and pitch, and swathed in linen; the death of that which never lived. But the rays of Greek poetry struggle down to us, and mingle with the sunbeams of the recent day. The statue of Memnon is cast down, but the shaft of the ***Iliad*** still meets the sun in his rising. (pp. 290-92)

Henry D. Thoreau, "Homer. Ossian. Chaucer," in The Dial: Magazine for Literature, Philosophy, and Religion, *Vol. IV, No. III, January, 1844, pp. 290-305.*

W. E. GLADSTONE (essay date 1858)

[In the following excerpt, Gladstone assesses Homer's use of oratory and debate in the Iliad, *stressing that "the intellectual function was no less essential to the warrior-king in Homer, than was the martial."]*

The trait which is truly most worthy of note in the polities of Homeric Greece, is also that which is so peculiar to them; namely, the substantive weight and influence which belonged to speech as an instrument of government; and of this power by much the most remarkable development is in its less confined and more popular application to the Assembly.

This power of speech was essentially a power to be exercised over numbers, and with the safeguards of publicity, by man among his fellow-men. It was also essentially an instrument addressing itself to reason and free will, and acknowledging their authority. (p. 102)

Although it is common to regard the ***Iliad*** as a poem having battle for its theme, yet it is in truth not less a monument of policy than of war; and in this respect it is even more broadly distinguished, than in most others, from later epics.

The adjectives in Homer are in very many cases the key to his inner mind: and among them all there is none of which this is more true, than the grand epithet [kithianeira]. He confines it strictly to two subjects, battle and debate, the clash of swords and the wrestling of minds. . . . Thus with him it was in two fields, that man was to seek for glory; partly in the fight, and partly in the Assembly.

The intellectual function was no less essential to the warrior-king of Homer, than was the martial; and the culture of the art of persuasion entered no less deeply into his early training. How, says Phœnix to Achilles, shall I leave you, I, whom your father attached to you when you were a mere child, without knowledge of the evenhanded battle, or of the assemblies, in which men attain to fame. . . . So he sent me to teach you the arts both of speech and fight. . . . (pp. 103-04)

In a description, if possible yet more striking than that of Phœnix, Homer places before us the orator at his work. "His hearers behold him with delight; he speaks with tempered modesty, yet with confidence in himself . . . ; he stands preeminent among the assembled people, and while he passes through the city, they gaze on him as on a god." From a passage like this we may form some idea, what a real power in human society was the orator of the heroic age; and we may also learn how and why it was, that the great Bard of that time has also placed himself in the foremost rank of oratory for all time. (p. 104)

In full conformity with this strongly developed idea, the Poet places before us the descriptions of a variety of speakers. There is Thersites, copious and offensive, to whom we must return. There is Telemachus, full of the gracious diffidence of youth, but commended by Nestor for a power and a tact of expression beyond his years. There is Menelaus, who speaks with a laconic ease. There are the Trojan elders . . . who from their experience and age chiefly guide the Assembly, and whose volubility and shrill small thread of voice. Homer compares to the chirping of grasshoppers. Then we have Nestor the soft and silvery, whose tones of happy and benevolent egotism flowed sweeter than a stream of honey. In the hands of an inferior artist, Phœnix must have reproduced him; but an absorbing affection for Achilles is the key-note to all he says; even the account in his speech of his own early adventures is evidently meant as a warning on the effects of rage: this intense earnestness completely prevents any thing like sameness, and thus the two garrulities stand perfectly distinct from one another, because they have (so to speak) different centres of gravity. Lastly, we have Ulysses, who, wont to rise with his energies concentrated within him, gives no promise of display: but when his deep voice issues from his chest, and his mighty words drive like the flakes of snow in winter, then indeed he soars away far above all competitors.

It is very unusual for Homer to indulge thus largely in careful and detailed description. And even here he has left the one superlative, as well as other considerable, orators, undescribed. The eloquence of Achilles if left to describe itself; and to challenge comparison with all the choicest patterns both of power and beauty in this kind, that three thousand years since Homer, and all their ebbing and flowing tides, have brought within the knowledge of man. Although he modestly describes himself as beneath Ulysses in this accomplishment, yet in truth no speeches come near to his. But Homer's resources are not even now exhausted. The decision of Diomed, the irresolution of Agamemnon, the bluntness of Ajax, are all admirably marked in the series of speeches allotted to each. Indeed Homer has put into the mouth of Idomeneus, whom he nowhere describes as an orator at all, a speech which is quite enough to establish his reputation in that capacity.

In reviewing the arrangements Homer has made, we shall find one feature alike unequivocal and decisive. The two persons, to whom he has given supremacy in oratory, are his two, his only two godlike heroes . . . , the Achilles and the Ulysses, each of whom bears up, like the Atlas of tradition, the weight of the epic to which he principally belongs.

How could Homer have conceived thoughts like these, if government in his eyes had rested upon either force or fraud? Moreover, when he speaks of persuasion and of strength or valour, of the action of the tongue and that of the hand, he clearly does not mean that these elements are mixed in the ordinary conduct of a sovereign to his subjects: he means the first for peace, the latter for war; the first to be his sole instrument for governing his own people, the latter for their enemies alone.

If, again, we endeavour to estimate the importance of Speech in the heroic age by the degree in which the faculty was actually cultivated, we must take the achievements of the Poet as the best indicators of the capacities of the age. The speeches which Homer has put into the mouths of his leading orators should be tolerably fair representatives of the best performances of the time. Nor is it possible that in any age there should be in a few a capacity for making such speeches, without a capacity in many for receiving, feeling, and comprehending them. Poets of modern times have composed great works, in ages that stopped their ears against them. *Paradise Lost* does not represent the time of Charles the Second, nor the *Excursion* the first decades of the present century. The case of the orator is entirely different. His work, from its very inception, is inextricably mixed up with practice. It is cast in the mould offered to him by the mind of his hearers. It is an influence principally received from his audience (so to speak) in vapour, which he pours back upon them in a flood. The sympathy and concurrence of his time is with his own mind joint parent of his work. He cannot follow nor frame ideals; his choice is, to be what his age will have him, what it requires in order to be moved by him, or else not to be at all. And as when we find the speeches in Homer, we know that there must have been men who could speak them, so, from the existence of units who could speak them, we know that there must have been crowds who could feel them.

Now if we examine those orations, we shall, I think, find not only that they contain specimens of transcendent eloquence which have never been surpassed, but likewise that they evince the most comprehensive knowledge, and the most varied and elastic use, of all the resources of the art. If we seek a specimen of invective, let us take the speeches of Achilles in the debate of the First ***Iliad.*** If it is the loftiest tone of terrible declamation that we desire, I know not where (to speak with moderation) we can find any thing that in grandeur can surpass the passage [in the ***Iliad,*** xvi.]. . . . But if it is solemnity that is sought, nothing can, I think, excel the [passage in the ***Iliad,*** i.].

What more admirable example of comprehensive statement, which exhausts the case, and absolutely shuts up the mouth of the adversary, than in the speech of Ulysses to Euryalus, who has reproached him with looking like a sharper? That speech consists of twenty lines: and I think any one who attempts to give a really accurate summary of it will be apt to find that his epitome, if it be at all complete, has become unawares a paraphrase. Nor is Homer less successful in showing us, how he has sounded the depths of pathos. For though the speeches of Priam to Achilles in the Twenty-fourth ***Iliad*** are spoken privately, and from man to man only, and are therefore not in the nature of oratory properly so called, they are conclusive, *a fortiori,* as to his knowledge of the instruments by which the human affections might be moved so much more easily, when the speaker would be assisted at once by the friendliness and by the electric sympathies of a multitude.

All these are direct instruments of influence on the mind and actions of man. But of assaults in flank Homer is quite as great a master. He shows a peculiar genius for that which is properly called repartee; for that form of speech, which flings back upon the opponent the stroke of his own weapon, or on the supplicant the plea of his own prayer. There was one Antimachus, a Trojan, who had grown wealthy, probably by the bribes which he received from Paris in considertion of his always opposing, in the Trojan Agorè, the restoration of Helen to the Greeks. His sons are mastered by Agamemnon in the field. Aware that he had a thirst for money, they cry, "Quarter, Agamemnon! we are the sons of rich Antimachus: *he* will pay well for our lives." "If," replies the king, "you are the sons of that Antimachus, who, when Menelaus came as envoy to Troy, advised to take and slay him, here and now shall ye expiate your father's infamy." Compare with this the yet sharper turn of Ulysses on Leiodes in the Odyssey: "Spare me, Ulysses! I have done no ill in your halls; I stopped what ill I could; I was but Augur to the Suitors." Then follows the stern reply. "If thou dost avow that thou art Augur to the Suitors, then often in prayer must thou have augured my destruction, and desired my wife for thine own; wherefore thou shalt not escape the painsome bed of death."

But the weapons of sarcasm, from the lightest to the weightiest, are wielded by Homer with almost greater effect than any others. As a sample of the former, I take the speech of Phœnix when he introduces, by way of parable, the Legend of Meleager. "As long as Meleager fought, all was well; but when rage took possession of him—which (I would just observe) now and then bewilders other great minds also—then," and so onward.

But for the great master of this art, Homer has chosen Achilles. As with his invectives he grinds to powder, so with the razor edge of the most refined irony he cuts his way in a moment to the quick. When Greece, in the person of the envoy-kings, is at his feet, and he has spurned them away, he says, "No: I will go home: you can come and see me depart—if you think it worth your while." . . .

Of this passage . . . the following translation may give a very imperfect idea:

> Of fight with Hector will I none;
> Tomorrow, with the rising sun,
> Each holy rite and office done,
> I load and launch my Phthian fleet;
>   Come, if thou thinkest meet,
> See, if thou carest for the sight,
> My ships shall bound in the morning's light,
> My rowers row with eager might,
>   O'er Helle's teeming main.
> And, if Poseidon give his grace,
> Then, with but three revolving days,
>   I see my home again;
> My home of plenty, that I left
> To fight with Troy; of sense bereft!

The plenty of his house . . . is the finishing stroke of reply on Agamemnon, who had thought that his resentment, unsatisfied in feeling, could be appeased with gifts. (pp. 105-10)

If the power of oratory is remarkable in Homer, so likewise is the faculty of what in England is called debate. Here the orator is a wrestler, holding his ground from moment to moment; adjusting his poise, and delivering his force, in exact proportion to the varying pressure of his antagonist. In Homer's debates, every speech after the first is commonly a reply. It belongs not only to the subject, but to the speech that went before: it exhibits, given the question and the aims of the speaker, the exact degree of ascent or descent, of expansion or contraction, of relaxation or enhancement, which the circumstances of the case, in the state up to which they were brought by the preceding address, may require. In the Assembly of the First Book, five, nay, six, successive speeches of Achilles and Agamemnon bring their great contention to its climax. But the discussion with the Envoys deserves very particular notice. Ulysses begins a skilled harangue to the offended hero with a most artful and well-masked exaggeration of the martial fury of Hector. He takes care only to present it as part of a general picture, which in other parts is true enough; but he obviously relies upon it as a mode of getting within the guard of Achilles. He next touches him upon the point, to which Priam afterwards made a yet higher appeal; the tender recollection of his father Peleus, who had warned him how much more arduous was the acquisition of self-command, than that of daring. He then recites the gifts of Agamemnon: and, encouraged perhaps by the kind greeting that, with his companions, he had received, he closes by urging that, however hateful Agamemnon may be, yet, in pity for the other Greeks, both high and low, and in anticipation of their gratitude, he ought to arm. I shall not attempt to analyse the wonderful speech of Achilles which follows, and to which some references have already been made. Suffice it to say, that it commences with an intimation to Ulysses that it will, in the opinion of the speaker, be best for all parties if he tells out his mind plainly: an indirect and courteous reproof to Ulysses for having thought to act upon him by tact and by the processes of a rhetorician. After this follows such a combination of argument, declamation, invective, and sarcasm as, within the same compass, I do not believe all the records of the world can match. But the general result of the whole is the announcement that he will return to Phthia the very next morning; together with an absolute, unconditional rejection of all gifts and proffers, until the outrage of Agamemnon is entirely wiped away: . . .

When he has concluded, all his hearers, abashed by his masculine wrath, are silent for a while. Then Phœnix, in the longest speech of the poem, pours forth his unselfish and warm, but prolix and digressive affection. This speech displays far less of rhetorical resource, than that of Ulysses. Ulysses had conceded, as it were, the right of Achilles to an unbounded resentment against Agamemnon: Phœnix, on the contrary, by parable, menaces him with retribution from the Erinūs, unless he shall subdue the mighty soul within him. But Achilles, touched in his better nature, gives way a little to the more ethical appeal, where he had been inflexible and invulnerable before the intellectual and rhetorical address. He now bids Phœnix come himself, and sleep in his encampment: there they can consider together, in the morning, whether to go or to stay. Still he announces, that nothing will induce him to quit the ships for the field. Next comes blunt Ajax into the *Palæstra;* deprecates the wasting of time; is for taking back the answer, bad as it may be: Achilles has evidently made up his mind; and cares not a rush for all or any of them. "What," says the simple man-mountain, "the homicide of a brother or child is atoned for by a fine, and yet here is all this to-do about a girl. Aye, and a single girl; when we offer seven of the very best, and ever so much besides." Having thus reached the *acmè* of his arts, he now aims at the friendly feeling of Achilles, and in a single word bids him be placable to men whom he has admitted beneath his roof, and whom he owns for as loyal friends as the whole army could find him.

The leverage of this straightforward speech, which is only saved by kindliness from falling into rudeness, again produces an initial movement towards concession on the part of the great hero. He replies in effect to Ajax, "You have spoken well: I like your way of going to work: but my heart swells and boils with the shame inflicted on me before the Greeks by Agamemnon. Tell them then"—there is now no announcement of setting sail; nay, there is no longer any need for debate in the morning whether to set sail or not—"tell them that I fight no more, till Hector, carrying slaughter and fire, shall reach this camp, these ships. Keen as he may be, it will then be time enough for ME to stay his onward path."

Such is the remarkable course of this debate. (pp. 111-14)

W. E. Gladstone, in his Studies on Homer and the Homeric Age, *Oxford at the University Press, Oxford, 1858, 616 p.*

MATTHEW ARNOLD (lecture date 1861)

[Arnold was one of the most important English critics of the nineteenth century. Although he was also a poet and, more significantly, a commentator on the social and moral life in England, Arnold was essentially an apologist for literary criticism. He argued that the major purpose of the critic was to inform and liberate the public at large, and to prepare the way—through the fostering of ideas and information—for his or her country's next creative epoch. Arnold was a forceful advocate of the doctrine of "disinterestedness" in all critical activities—the need for flexibility, curiosity, and a non-utilitarian approach to culture and art. He was severely critical of what he considered the spiritual death of Victorian England; nonetheless, he was optimistic that art, which he considered classless and universal, could save modern society from materialism. Arnold's critical methodology called for the rejection of both the personal estimate and the historical estimate of art; the first assumes the value of something based on subjective criteria; the second distorts the value of a creative work by overemphasizing its influence on historical developments. Instead, he advocated—though scholars point out that he often failed to achieve it in his own writing—the "real estimate" of the created object, which demands that the critic judge a work of art according to its own qualities, in and of itself, apart from the influence of history and the limitations of subjective experience. In the following excerpt from his series of lectures published in 1861 as On Translating Homer, *Arnold offers advice to future translators of Homeric verse. A landmark in Homeric scholarship, Arnold's assessment of Homer's style focuses on four main characteristics: rapidity of meter, plainness of diction, directness of ideas, and nobility, or "grand style."]*

[In] spite of [the] perfect plainness and directness of Homer's style, in spite of this perfect plainness and directness of his ideas, he is eminently *noble;* he works as entirely in the grand style, he is as grandiose, as Phidias, or Dante, or Michael Angelo. This is what makes his translators despair. "To give relief," says Cowper, "to prosaic subjects" (such as dressing, eating, drinking, harnessing, travelling, going to bed), that is to treat such subjects nobly, in the grand style, "without seeming unreasonably tumid, is extremely difficult." It *is* difficult, but Homer has done it. Homer is precisely the incomparable poet he is, because he has done it. His translator must not be tumid, must not be artificial, must not be literary,—true: but then also he must not be commonplace, must not be ignoble. (p. 295)

• • • • •

Homer is neither quaint, nor garrulous, nor prosaic, nor mean: and Mr. Newman, in seeing him so, sees him differently from those who are to judge Mr. Newman's rendering of him. By pointing out how a wrong conception of Homer affects Mr. Newman's translation, I hope to place in still clearer light those four cardinal truths which I pronounce essential for him who would have a right conception of Homer: that Homer is rapid, that he is plain and direct in word and style, that he is plain and direct in his ideas, and that he is noble.

For Homer is not only rapid in movement, simple in style, plain in language, natural in thought; he is also, and above all, *noble*. I have [elsewhere] advised the translator not to go into the vexed question of Homer's identity. Yet I will just remind him that the grand argument— or rather, not argument, for the matter affords no data for arguing, but the grand source from which conviction, as we read the ***Iliad,*** keeps pressing in upon us, that there is one poet of the ***Iliad,*** one Homer—is precisely this nobleness of the poet, this grand manner: we feel that the analogy drawn from other joint compositions does not hold good here, because those works do not bear, like the ***Iliad,*** the magic stamp of a master; and the moment you have *anything* less than a masterwork, the co-operation or consolidation of several poets becomes possible, for talent is not uncommon; the moment you have *much* less than a masterwork, they become easy, for mediocrity is everywhere. . . . [The] insurmountable obstacle to believing the ***Iliad*** a consolidated work of several poets is this: that the work of great masters is unique; and the ***Iliad*** has a great master's genuine stamp, and that stamp is *the grand style*.

Poets who cannot work in the grand style instinctively seek a style in which their comparative inferiority may feel itself at ease, a manner which may be, so to speak, indulgent to their inequalities. The ballad-style offers to an epic poet, quite unable to fill the canvas of Homer, or Dante, or Milton, a canvas which he is capable of filling. The ballad-measure is quite able to give due effect to the vigour and spirit which its employer, when at his very best, may be able to exhibit; and, when he is not at his best, when he is a little trivial or a little dull, it will not betray him, it will not bring out his weaknesses into broad relief. This is a convenience; but it is a convenience which the ballad-style purchases by resigning all pretensions to the highest, to the grand manner. It is true of its movement, as it is *not* true of Homer's, that it is "liable to degenerate into doggerel." It is true of its "moral qualities," as it is *not* true of Homer's, that "quaintness" and "garrulity" are among them. It is true of its employers, as it is *not* true of Homer, that they "rise and sink with their subject, are prosaic when it is tame, are low when it is mean." For this reason the ballad-style and the ballad-measure are eminently *in*appropriate to render Homer. Homer's manner and movement are always both noble and powerful: the ballad-manner and movement are often either jaunty and smart, so not noble; or jog-trot and humdrum, so not powerful.

But so deeply seated is the difference between the ballad-manner and Homer's, that even a man of the highest powers, even a man of the greatest vigour of spirit and of true genius—the Coryphæus of balladists, Sir Walter Scott—fails with a manner of this kind to produce an effect at all like the effect of Homer. "I am not so rash," declares Mr. Newman, "as to say that if *freedom* be given to rhyme as in Walter Scott's poetry"—Walter Scott, "by far the most Homeric of our poets," as in another place he calls him—"a genius may not arise who will translate Homer into the melodies of *Marmion*." "The *truly* classical and *truly* romantic," says Dr. Maginn, "are one; the moss-trooping Nestor reappears in the moss-trooping heroes of Percy's *Reliques*"; and a description by Scott, which he quotes, he calls "graphic, and therefore Homeric." He forgets our fourth axiom—that Homer is not *only* graphic; he is also noble, and has the grand style. Human nature under like circumstances is probably in all stages much the same; and so far it may be said that "the truly classical and the truly romantic are one"; but it is of little use to tell us this, because we know the human nature of other ages only through the representations of them which have come down to us, and the classical and the romantic modes of representation are so far from being "one," that they remain eternally distinct, and have created for us a separation between the two worlds which they respectively represent. Therefore to call Nestor the "moss-trooping Nestor" is absurd, because, though Nestor may possibly have been much the same sort of man as many a moss-trooper, he has yet come to us through a mode of representation so unlike that of Percy's *Reliques*, that instead of "reappearing in the moss-trooping heroes" of these poems, he exists in our imagination as something utterly unlike them, and as belonging to another world. So the Greeks in Shakspeare's *Troilus and Cressida* are no longer the Greeks whom we have known in Homer, because they come to us through a mode of representation of the romantic world. But I must not forget Scott.

I suppose that when Scott is in what may be called full ballad swing, no one will hesitate to pronounce his manner neither Homeric nor the grand manner. When he says, for instance,

> I do not rhyme to that dull elf
> Who cannot image to himself,

and so on, any scholar will feel that *this* is not Homer's manner. But let us take Scott's poetry at its best; and when it is at its best, it is undoubtedly very good indeed:

> Tunstall lies dead upon the field,
> His life-blood stains the spotless shield:
> Edmund is down,—my life is reft,—
> The Admiral alone is left.
>
> Let Stanley charge with spur of fire,—
> With Chester charge, and Lancashire,
> Full upon Scotland's central host,
> Or victory and England's lost.

That is, no doubt, as vigorous as possible, as spirited as possible; it is exceedingly fine poetry. And still I say, it is not in the grand manner, and therefore it is not like Homer's poetry. Now, how shall I make him who doubts this feel that I say true; that these lines of Scott are essentially neither in Homer's style nor in the grand style? I may point out to him that the movement of Scott's lines, while it is rapid, is also at the same time what the French call *saccadé*, its rapidity is "jerky"; whereas Homer's rapidity is a flowing rapidity. But this is something external and material; it is but the outward and visible sign of an inward and spiritual diversity. I may discuss what, in the abstract, constitutes the grand style; but that sort of general discussion never much helps our judgment of particular instances. I may say that the presence or absence of the grand style can only be spiritually discerned; and this is true, but to plead this looks like evading the difficulty. . . . It is no disrespect to Scott to say that he does not attain to this manner in his poetry; to say so, is merely to say that he is not among the five or six supreme poets of the world. Among these he is not; but, being a man of far greater powers than the ballad poets, he has tried to give to their instrument a compass and an elevation which it does not naturally possess, in order to enable him to come nearer to the effect of the instrument used by the great epic poets—an instrument which he felt he could not truly use—and in this attempt he has but imperfectly succeeded. The poetic style of Scott is—(it becomes necessary to say so when it is proposed to "translate Homer into the melodies of *Marmion*")—it is, tried by the highest standard, a bastard epic style; and that is why, out of his own powerful hands, it has had so little success. It is a less natural, and therefore a less good style, than the original ballad-style; while it shares with the ballad-style the inherent incapacity of rising into the grand style, of adequately rendering Homer. Scott is certainly at his best in his battles. Of Homer you could not say this: he is not better in his battles than elsewhere; but even between the battle-pieces of the two there exists all the difference which there is between an able work and a masterpiece.

> Tunstall lies dead upon the field,
> His life-blood stains the spotless shield:
> Edmund is down,—my life is reft,—
> The Admiral alone is left.

—"For not in the hands of Diomede the son of Tydeus rages the spear, to ward off destruction from the Danaans; neither as yet have I heard the voice of the son of Atreus, shouting out of his hated mouth; but the voice of Hector the slayer of men bursts round me, as he cheers on the Trojans; and they with their yellings fill all the plain, overcoming the Achaians in the battle."—I protest that, to my feeling, Homer's performance, even through that pale and far-off shadow of a prose translation, still has a hundred times more of the grand manner about it than the original poetry of Scott.

Well, then, the ballad-manner and the ballad-measure, whether in the hands of the old ballad poets, or arranged by Chapman, or arranged by Mr. Newman, or, even, arranged by Sir Walter Scott, cannot worthily render Homer. And for one reason: Homer is plain, so are they; Homer is natural, so are they; Homer is spirited, so are they; but Homer is sustainedly noble, and they are not. Homer and they are both of them natural, and therefore touching and stirring; but the grand style, which is Homer's, is something more than touching and stirring; it can form the character, it is edifying. The old English balladist may stir Sir Philip Sidney's heart like a trumpet, and this is much; but Homer, but the few artists in the grand style, can do more: they can refine the raw natural man, they can transmute him. So it is not without cause that I say, and say again, to the translator of Homer: "Never for a moment suffer yourself to forget our fourth fundamental proposition, *Homer is noble*." For it is seen how large a share this nobleness has in producing that general effect of his, which it is the main business of a translator to *re*produce. (pp. 296-301)

• • • • •

Homer is rapid in his movement, Homer is plain in his words and style, Homer is simple in his ideas, Homer is noble in his manner. Cowper renders him ill because he is slow in his movement, and elaborate in his style; Pope renders him ill because he is artificial both in his style and in his words; Chapman renders him ill because he is fantastic in his ideas; Mr. Newman renders him ill because he is odd in his words and ignoble in his manner. All four translators diverge from their original at other points besides those named; but it is at the points thus named that their divergence is greatest. For instance Cowper's diction is not as Homer's diction, nor his nobleness as Homer's nobleness; but it is in movement and grammatical style that he is most unlike Homer. Pope's rapidity is not of the same sort as Homer's rapidity, nor are his plainness of ideas and his nobleness as Homer's plainness of ideas and nobleness; but it is in the artificial character of his style and diction that he is most unlike Homer. Chapman's movement, words, style, and manner are often far enough from resembling Homer's movement, words, style, and manner; but it is the fantasticality of his ideas which puts him farthest from resembling Homer. Mr. Newman's movement, grammatical style, and ideas are a thousand times in strong contrast with Homer's; still it is by the oddness of his diction and the ignobleness of his manner that he contrasts with Homer the most violently.

Therefore the translator must not say to himself: "Cowper is noble, Pope is rapid, Chapman has a good diction, Mr. Newman has a good cast of sentence: I will avoid Cowper's slowness, Pope's artificiality, Chapman's conceits, Mr. Newman's oddity; I will take Cowper's dignified manner, Pope's impetuous movement, Chapman's vocabulary, Mr. Newman's syntax, and so make a perfect translation of Homer." Undoubtedly in certain points the versions of Chapman, Cowper, Pope, and Mr. Newman, all of them have merit; some of them very high merit, others a lower merit; but even in these points they have none of them precisely the same kind of merit as Homer, and therefore the new translator, even if he can imitate them in their good points, will still not satisfy his judge, the scholar, who asks him for Homer and Homer's kind of merit, or, at least, for as much of them as it is possible to give.

So the translator really has no good model before him for any part of his work, and has to invent everything for himself. He is to be rapid in movement, plain in speech, simple in thought, and noble; and *how* he is to be either rapid, or plain, or simple, or noble, no one yet has shown him. I shall try to-day to establish some practical suggestions which may help the translator of Homer's poetry to comply with the four grand requirements which we make of him.

His version is to be rapid; and, of course, to make a man's poetry rapid, as to make it noble, nothing can serve him so much as to have, in his own nature, rapidity and nobleness. *It is the spirit that quickeneth;* and no one will so well render Homer's swift-flowing movement as he who has himself something of the swift-moving spirit of Homer. Yet even this is not quite enough. Pope certainly had a quick and darting spirit, and he had, also, real nobleness; yet Pope does not render the movement of Homer. To render this the translator must have, besides his natural qualifications, an appropriate metre.

I have sufficiently shown why I think all forms of our ballad-metre unsuited to Homer. It seems to me to be beyond question that, for epic poetry, only three metres can seriously claim to be accounted capable of the grand style. Two of these will at once occur to every one,—the ten-syllable, or so-called *heroic*, couplet, and blank verse. I do not add to these the Spenserian stanza, although Dr. Maginn . . . pronounces this stanza the one right measure for a translation of Homer. It is enough to observe that if Pope's couplet, with the simple system of correspondence that its rhymes introduce, changes the movement of Homer, in which no such correspondences are found, and is therefore a bad measure for a translator of Homer to employ, Spenser's stanza, with its far more intricate system of correspondences, must change Homer's movement far more profoundly, and must therefore be for the translator a far worse measure than the couplet of Pope. Yet I will say, at the same time, that the verse of Spenser is more fluid, slips more easily and quickly along, than the verse of almost any other English poet.

> By this the northern wagoner had set
> His seven-fold team behind the steadfast star
> That was in ocean waves yet never wet,
> But firm is fixt, and sendeth light from far
> To all that in the wide deep wandering are.

One cannot but feel that English verse has not often moved with the fluidity and sweet ease of these lines. It is possible that it may have been this quality of Spenser's poetry which made Dr. Maginn think that the stanza of *The Faery Queen* must be a good measure for rendering Homer. This it is not: Spenser's verse is fluid and rapid, no doubt, but there are more ways than one of being fluid and rapid, and Homer is fluid and rapid in quite another way than Spenser. Spenser's manner is no more Homeric than is the manner of the one modern inheritor of Spenser's beautiful gift,—the poet, who evidently caught from Spenser his sweet and easy-slipping movement, and who has exquisitely employed it; a Spenserian genius, nay, a genius by natural endowment richer probably than even Spenser; that light which shines so unexpected and without fellow in our century, an Elizabethan born too late, the early lost and admirably gifted Keats.

I say, then, that there are really but three metres,—the ten-syllable couplet, blank verse, and a third metre which I will not yet name, but which is neither the Spenserian stanza nor any form of ballad-verse,—between which, as vehicles for Homer's poetry, the translator has to make his choice. Every one will at once remember a thousand passages in which both the ten-syllable couplet and blank verse prove themselves to have nobleness. Undoubtedly the movement and manner of this,—

> Still raise for good the supplicating voice,
> But leave to Heaven the measure and the choice,—

are noble. Undoutedly, the movement and manner of this,—

> High on a throne of royal state, which far
> Outshone the wealth of Ormus and of Ind,—

are noble also. But the first is in a rhymed metre; and the unfitness of a rhymed metre for rendering Homer I have already shown. I will observe, too, that the fine couplet which I have quoted comes out of a satire, a didactic poem; and that it is in didactic poetry that the ten-syllable couplet has most successfully essayed the grand style. In narrative poetry this metre has succeeded best when it essayed a sensibly lower style, the style of Chaucer, for instance; whose narrative manner, though a very good and sound manner, is certainly neither the grand manner nor the manner of Homer.

The rhymed ten-syllable couplet being thus excluded, blank verse offers itself for the translator's use. The first kind of blank verse which naturally occurs to us is the blank verse of Milton, which has been employed, with more or less modification, by Mr. Cary in translating Dante, by Cowper, and by Mr. Wright in translating Homer. How noble this metre is in Milton's hands, how completely it shows itself capable of the grand, nay, of the grandest, style, I need not say. To this metre, as used in the *Paradise Lost,* our country owes the glory of having produced one of the only two poetical works in the grand style which are to be found in the modern languages; the *Divine Comedy* of Dante is the other. England and Italy here stand alone; Spain, France, and Germany have produced great poets, but neither Calderon, nor Corneille, nor Schiller, nor even Goethe, has produced a body of poetry in the true grand style, in the sense in which the style of the body of Homer's poetry, or Pindar's, or Sophocles', is grand. But Dante has, and so has Milton; and in this respect Milton possesses a distinction which even Shakspeare, undoubtedly the supreme poetical power in our literature, does not share with him. Not a tragedy of Shakspeare but contains passages in the worst of all styles, the affected style; and the grand style, although it may be harsh, or obscure, or cumbrous, or over-laboured, is never affected. In spite, therefore, of objections which may justly be urged against the plan and treatment of the *Paradise Lost,* in spite of its possessing, certainly, a far less enthralling force of interest to attract and to carry forward the reader than the ***Iliad*** or the *Divine Comedy,* it fully deserves, it can never lose, its immense reputation; for, like the ***Iliad*** and the *Divine Comedy,* nay, in some respects to a higher degree than either of them, it is in the grand style.

But the grandeur of Milton is one thing, and the grandeur of Homer is another. Homer's movement, I have said again and again, is a flowing, a rapid movement; Milton's, on the other hand, is a laboured, a self-retarding movement. In each case, the movement, the metrical cast, corresponds with the mode of evolution of the thought, with the syntactical cast, and is indeed determined by it. Milton charges himself so full with thought, imagination, knowledge, that his style will hardly contain them. He is too full-stored to show us in much detail one conception, one piece of knowledge; he just shows it to us in a pregnant, allusive way, and then he presses on to another; and all this fulness, this pressure, this condensation, this self-constraint, enters into his movement, and makes it what it is,—noble, but difficult and austere. Homer is quite different: he says a thing, and says it to the end, and then begins another, while Milton is trying to press a thousand things into one. So that whereas, in reading Milton, you never lose the sense of laborious and condensed fulness, in reading Homer you never lose the sense of flowing and abounding ease. With Milton line runs into line, and all is straitly bound together: with Homer line runs off from line, and all hurries away onward. . . . So chary of a sentence is, [Milton], so resolute not to let it escape him till he has crowded into it all he can, that it is not till the thirty-ninth word in the sentence that he will give us the key to it, the word of action, the verb. Milton says:

> O for that warning voice, which he, who saw
> The Apocalypse, heard cry in heaven aloud.

He is not satisfied, unless he can tell us, all in one sentence, and without permitting himself actually to mention the name, that the man who had the warning voice was the same man who saw the Apocalypse. Homer would have said, "O for that warning voice, which *John* heard"—and if it had suited him to say that John also saw the Apocalypse, he would have given us that in another sentence. The effect of this allusive and compressed manner of Milton is, I need not say, often very powerful; and it is an effect which other great poets have often sought to obtain much in the same way: Dante is full of it, Horace is full of it; but wherever it exists, it is always an un-Homeric effect. "The losses of the heavens," says Horace, "fresh moons speedily repair; we, when we have gone down where the pious Æneas, where the rich Tullus and Ancus are,—*pulvis et umbra sumus.*" He never actually says *where* we go to; he only indicates it by saying that it is that place where Æneas, Tullus and Ancus are. But Homer, when he has to speak of going down to the grave, says, definitely . . .—"The immortals shall send thee *to the Elysian plain;*" and it is not till after he has definitely said this, that he adds, that it is there that the abode of departed worthies is placed: . . .—"Where the yellow-haired Rhadamanthus is." Again; Horace, having to say that punishment sooner or later overtakes crime, says it thus:

> Raro antecedentem scelestum
> Deseruit pede Pœna claudo.

The thought itself of these lines is familiar enough to Homer and Hesiod; but neither Homer nor Hesiod, in expressing it, could possibly have so complicated its expression as Horace complicates it, and purposely complicates it, by his use of the word *deseruit.* I say that this complicated evolution of the thought necessarily complicates the movement and rhythm of a poet; and that the Miltonic blank verse, of course the first model of blank verse which suggests itself to an English translator of Homer, bears the strongest marks of such complication, and is therefore entirely unfit to render Homer.

If blank verse is used in translating Homer, it must be a blank verse of which English poetry, naturally swayed much by Milton's treatment of this metre, offers at present hardly any examples. It must not be Cowper's blank verse, who has studied Milton's pregnant manner with such effect, that . . . he says that Benevolus "reprieves The obsolete prolixity of shade." It must not be Mr. Tennyson's blank verse.

> For all experience is an arch, wherethrough
> Gleams that untravelled world, whose distance fades
> For ever and for ever, as we gaze.

It is no blame to the thought of those lines, which belongs to another order of ideas than Homer's, but it is true, that Homer would certainly have said of them, "It is to consider too curiously to consider so." It is no blame to their rhythm, which belongs to another order of movement than Homer's, but it is true that these three lines by themselves take up nearly as much time as a whole book of the ***Iliad.*** No; the blank verse used in rendering Homer must be a blank verse of which perhaps the best specimens are to be found in some of the most rapid passages of Shakespeare's plays,—a blank verse which does not dovetail its lines into one another, and which habitually ends its lines with monosyllables. Such a blank verse might no doubt be very rapid in its movement, and might perfectly adapt itself to a thought plainly and directly evolved; and it would be interesting to see it well applied to Homer. But the translator who determines to use it, must not conceal from himself that in order to pour Homer into the mould of this metre, he will have entirely to break him up and melt him down, with the hope of then successfully composing him afresh;

and this is a process which is full of risks. It may, no doubt, be the real Homer that issues new from it; it is not certain beforehand that it cannot be the real Homer, as it is certain that from the mould of Pope's couplet or Cowper's Miltonic verse it cannot be the real Homer that will issue; still, the chances of disappointment are great. The result of such an attempt to renovate the old poet may be an Æson; but it may also, and more probably will be a Pelias.

When I say this, I point to the metre which seems to me to give the translator the best chance of preserving the general effect of Homer,—that third metre which I have not yet expressly named, the hexameter. I know all that is said against the use of hexameters in English poetry; but it comes only to this, that, among us, they have not yet been used on any considerable scale with success. *Solvitur ambulando:* this is an objection which can best be met by *producing* good English hexameters. And there is no reason in the nature of the English language why it should not adapt itself to hexameters as well as the German language does; nay, the English language, from its greater rapidity, is in itself better suited than the German for them. The hexameter, whether alone or with the pentameter, possesses a movement, an expression, which no metre hitherto in common use amongst us possesses, and which I am convinced English poetry, as our mental wants multiply, will not always be content to forego. Applied to Homer, this metre affords to the translator the immense support of keeping him more nearly than any other metre to Homer's movement; and, since a poet's movement makes so large a part of his general effect, and to reproduce this general effect is at once the translator's indispensable business and so difficult for him, it is a great thing to have this part of your model's general effect already given you in your metre, instead of having to get it entirely for yourself.

These are general considerations; but there are also one or two particular considerations which confirm me in the opinion that for translating Homer into English verse the hexameter should be used. The most successful attempt hitherto made at rendering Homer into English, the attempt in which Homer's general effect has been best retained, is an attempt made in the hexameter measure. It is a version of the famous lines [translated by Dr. Hawtrey] in the third book of the ***Iliad,*** which end with [the] mention of Castor and Pollux. . . . The passage is short; and Dr. Hawtrey's version of it is suffused with a pensive grace which is, perhaps, rather more Virgilian than Homeric; still it is the one version of any part of the ***Iliad*** which in some degree reproduces for me the original effect of Homer: it is the best, and it is in hexameters.

This is one of the particular considerations that incline me to prefer the hexameter, for translating Homer, to our established metres. There is another. Most of you, probably, have some knowledge of a poem by Mr. Clough, *The Bothie of Toper-na-fuosich,* a long-vacation pastoral, in hexameters. The general merits of that poem I am not going to discuss: it is a serio-comic poem, and therefore of essentially different nature from the ***Iliad.*** Still in two things it is, more than any other English poem which I can call to mind, like the ***Iliad:*** in the rapidity of its movement, and the plainness and directness of its style. The thought in this poem is often curious and subtle, and that is not Homeric; the diction is often grotesque, and that is not Homeric. Still by its rapidity of movement, and plain and direct manner of presenting the thought, however curious in itself, this poem, which, being as I say a serio-comic poem, has a right to be grotesque, is grotesque *truly,* not, like Mr. Newman's version of the ***Iliad,*** *falsely*. Mr. Clough's odd epithets, "The grave man nicknamed Adam," "The hairy Aldrich," and so on, grow vitally and appear naturally in their place; while Mr. Newman's "dapper-greaved Achaians," and "motley-helmed Hector," have all the air of being mechanically elaborated and artificially stuck in. Mr. Clough's hexameters are excessively, needlessly rough; still, owing to the native rapidity of this measure, and to the directness of style which so well allies itself with it, his composition produces a sense in the reader which Homer's composition also produces, and which Homer's translator ought to *re*produce—the sense of having, within short limits of time, a large portion of human life presented to him, instead of a small portion. (pp. 301-09)

If the hexameter best helps the translator to the Homeric rapidity, what style may best help him to the Homeric plainness and directness? It is the merit of a metre appropriate to your subject, that it in some degree suggests and carries with itself a style appropriate to the subject; the elaborate and self-retarding style, which comes so naturally when your metre is the Miltonic blank verse, does not come naturally with the hexameter; is, indeed, alien to it. On the other hand, the hexameter has a natural dignity which repels both the jaunty style and the jog-trot style, to both of which the ballad-measure so easily lends itself. These are great advantages; and, perhaps, it is nearly enough to say to the translator who uses the hexameter that he cannot too religiously follow, in style, the inspiration of his metre. He will find that a loose and idiomatic grammar—a grammar which follows the essential rather than the formal logic of the thought—allies itself excellently with the hexameter; and that, while this sort of grammar ensures plainness and naturalness, it by no means comes short in nobleness. It is difficult to pronounce, certainly, what is idiomatic in the ancient literature of a language which, though still spoken, has long since entirely adopted, as modern Greek had adopted, modern idioms. Still one may, I think, clearly perceive that Homer's grammatical style is idiomatic,—that it may even be called, not improperly, a loose grammatical style. Examples, however, of what I mean by a loose grammatical style, will be of more use to the translator if taken from English poetry than if taken from Homer. I call it, then, a loose and idiomatic grammar which Shakespeare uses in the last line of the following three:—

He's here in double trust:
First, as I am his kinsman and his subject,
Strong both against the deed,—

or in this:—

Wilt, *whither wilt?*

What Shakspeare means is perfectly clear—clearer, probably, than if he had said it in a more formal and regular manner; but his grammar is loose and idiomatic, because he leaves out the subject of the verb "wilt" in the second passage quoted, and because, in the first, a prodigious addition to the sentence has to be, as we used to say in our old Latin grammar days, *understood,* before the word "both" can be properly parsed. So, again, Chapman's grammar is loose and idiomatic where he says,

Even share hath he that keeps his tent, and *he to field*
doth go,—

because he leaves out, in the second clause, the relative which in formal writing would be required. But Chapman here does not lose dignity by this idiomatic way of expressing himself, any more than Shakspeare loses it by neglecting to confer on "both" the blessings of a regular government: neither loses dignity, but each gives that impression of a plain, direct, and natural mode of speaking, which Homer, too, gives, and which is so important, as I say, that Homer's translator should succeed in giving. Cowper calls blank verse "a style further removed than rhyme from the vernacular idiom, both in the language itself and in the arrangment of it"; and just in proportion as blank verse is removed from the vernacular idiom, from that idiomatic style which is of all styles the plainest and most natural, blank verse is unsuited to render Homer.

Shakspeare is not only idiomatic in his grammar or style, he is also idiomatic in his words or diction; and here too, his example is valuable for the translator of Homer. The translator must not, indeed, allow himself all the liberty that Shakspeare allows himself; for Shakspeare sometimes uses expressions which pass perfectly well as he uses them, because Shakspeare thinks so fast and so powerfully, that in reading him we are borne over single words as by a mighty current; but, if our mind were less excited,—and who may rely on exciting our mind like Shakspeare?—they would check us. "To grunt and sweat under a weary load";—that does perfectly well where it comes in Shakspeare; but if the translator of Homer, who will hardly have wound our minds up to the pitch at which these words of Hamlet find them, were to employ, when he has to speak of one of Homer's heroes under the load of calamity, this figure of "grunting" and "sweating," we should say, *He Newmanises,* and his diction would offend us. For he is to be noble; and no plea of wishing to be plain and natural can get him excused from being this: only, as he is to be also, like Homer, perfectly simple and free from artificiality, and as the use of idiomatic expressions undoubtedly gives this effect, he should be as idiomatic as he can be without ceasing to be noble. Therefore the idiomatic language of Shakspeare—such language as "prate of his *whereabout*"; *jump* the life to come"; "the damnation of his *taking-off*"; "his *quietus make* with a bare *bodkin*"—should be carefully observed by the translator of Homer, although in every case he will have to decide for himself whether the use, by him, of Shakspeare's liberty will or will not clash with his indispensable duty of nobleness. He will find one English book, and one only, where as in the ***Iliad*** itself, perfect plainness of speech is allied with perfect nobleness; and that book is the Bible. No one could see this more clearly than Pope saw it: "This pure and noble simplicity," he says, "is nowhere in such perfection as in the Scripture and Homer": yet even with Pope a woman is a "fair," a father is a "sire," and an old man a "reverend sage," and so on through all the phrases of that pseudo-Augustan, and most unbiblical, vocabulary. The Bible, however, is undoubtedly the grand mine of diction for the translator of Homer; and, if he knows how to discriminate truly between what will suit him and what will not, the Bible may afford him also invaluable lessons of style.

I said that Homer, besides being plain in style and diction, was plain in the quality of his thought. It is possible that a thought may be expressed with idiomatic plainness, and yet not be in itself a plain thought. For example, in Mr. Clough's poem, already mentioned, the style and diction is almost always idiomatic and plain, but the thought itself is often of a quality which is not plain; it is *curious.* But the grand instance of the union of idiomatic expression with curious or difficult thought is in Shakespeare's poetry. Such, indeed, is the force and power of Shakspeare's idiomatic expression, that it gives an effect of clearness and vividness even to a thought which is imperfect and incoherent: for instance, when Hamlet says,—

> To take arms against a sea of troubles,—

the figure there is undoubtedly not faulty, it by no means runs on four legs; but the thing is said so freely and idiomatically, that it passes. This, however, is not a point to which I now want to call your attention; I want you to remark, in Shakspeare and others, only that which we may directly apply to Homer. I say, then, that in Shakspeare the thought is often, while most idiomatically uttered, nay, while good and sound in itself, yet of a quality which is curious and difficult, and that this quality of thought is something entirely un-Homeric. For example, when Lady Macbeth says,—

> Memory, the warder of the brain,
> Shall be a fume, and the receipt of reason
> A limbeck only,—

this figure is a perfectly sound and correct figure, no doubt; Mr. Knight even calls it a "happy" figure; but it is a *difficult* figure: Homer would not have used it. Again, when Lady Macbeth says,—

> When you durst do it, then you were a man;
> And, to be more than what you were, you would
> Be so much more the man,—

the thought in the two last of these lines is, when you seize it, a perfectly clear thought, and a fine thought; but it is a *curious* thought: Homer would not have used it. These are favourable instances of the union of plain style and words with a thought not plain in quality; but take stronger instances of this union,—let the thought be not only not plain in quality, but highly fanciful: and you have the Elizabethan conceits; you have, in spite of idiomatic style and idiomatic diction, everything which is most un-Homeric: you have such atrocities as this of Chapman:—

> Fate shall fail to vent her gall
> Till mine vent thousands.

I say, the poets of a nation which has produced such conceit as that, must purify themselves seven times in the fire before they can hope to render Homer. They must expel their nature with a fork, and keep crying to one another night and day: "Homer not only moves rapidly, not only speaks idiomatically; he is, also, *free from fancifulness.*"

So essentially characteristic of Homer is his plainness and naturalness of thought, that to the preservation of this in his own version the translator must without scruple sacrifice, where it is necessary, verbal fidelity to his original, rather than run any risk of producing, by literalness, an odd and unnatural effect. The double epithets so constantly occurring in Homer must be dealt with according to this rule; these epithets come quite naturally in Homer's poetry; in English poetry they, in nine cases out of ten, come, when literally rendered, quite unnaturally. . . . [When], in order to render literally in English one of Homer's double epithets, a strange unfamiliar adjective is invented—such as "voice-dividing," . . .—an improper share of the reader's attention is necessarily diverted to this ancillary word, to this word which Homer never intended should receive so much notice; and a total effect quite different from Homer's is thus produced. Therefore Mr. Newman, though he does not purposely import, like Chapman, conceits of his own into the ***Iliad,*** does actually import them; for the result of his singular diction is to raise ideas, and odd ideas, not raised by the cor-

Achilles dragging the body of Hector around the walls of Troy. Attic B/F water jar, ca. 510 B.C. H: 20 1/2 inches. William Warden Fund, 63.473. Courtesy, Museum of Fine Arts, Boston.

responding diction in Homer; and Chapman himself does no more. Cowper says: "I have cautiously avoided all terms of new invention, with an abundance of which persons of more ingenuity than judgment have not enriched our language but encumbered it"; and this criticism so exactly hits the diction of Mr. Newman that one is irresistibly led to imagine his present appearance in the flesh to be at least his second.

A translator cannot well have a Homeric rapidity, style, diction, and quality of thought, without at the same time having what is the result of these in Homer,—nobleness. Therefore I do not attempt to lay down any rules for obtaining this effect of nobleness,—the effect, too, of all others the most impalpable, the most irreducible to rule, and which most depends on the individual personality of the artist.

Here I stop. I have said so much, because I think that the task of translating Homer into English verse both will be re-attempted, and may be re-attempted successfully. . . . [Poems] like the ***Iliad,*** which, in the main, are in one manner, may hope to find a poetical translator so gifted and so trained as to be able to learn that one manner, and to reproduce it. Only, the poet who would reproduce this must cultivate in himself a Greek virtue by no means common among the moderns in general, and the English in particular,—*moderation*. For Homer has not only the English vigour, he has the Greek grace; and when one observes the boistering, rollicking way in which his English admirers—even men of genius . . .—love to talk of Homer and his poetry, one cannot help feeling that there is no very deep community of nature between them and the object of their enthusiasm. "It is very well, my good friends," I always imagine Homer saying to them—if he could hear them: "you do me a great deal of honour, but somehow or other you praise me too like barbarians." For Homer's grandeur is not the mixed and turbid grandeur of the great poets of the north, of the authors of *Othello* and *Faust;* it is a perfect, a lovely grandeur. Certainly his poetry has all the energy and power of the poetry of our ruder climates; but it has, besides, the pure lines of an Ionian horizon, the liquid clearness of an Ionian sky. (pp. 311-16)

Matthew Arnold, in "On Translating Homer," in his Matthew Arnold: Poetry and Prose, *edited by John Bryson, Harvard University Press, 1967, pp. 287-318.*

WILLIAM CULLEN BRYANT (essay date 1869)

[Bryant is considered one of the most accomplished American poets of the nineteenth century. His poetic treatment of the themes of nature and mutability identifies him as one of the earliest figures in the Romantic movement in American literature. In the following excerpt from the 1869 preface to his translation of the Iliad, *Bryant lauds the poem as "a work of inexhaustible imagination." He also discusses the characterization of Achilles and the gods and speculates that Homer may have intended to write a continuation of the poem.]*

In the intimate acquaintance with the ***Iliad*** which the work of translation has given me, an impression has been revived which was made upon my mind when in my boyhood I first read that poem in an English version. I recollect very well the eager curiosity with which I seized upon the translation of Pope when it came within my reach, and with what avidity I ran through the pages which rendered into our language what was acknowledged to be the greatest production of poetic genius that the world had seen. I read with a deep interest for the fate of Troy, and with a kindly feeling toward Hector, whose part I took warmly against the bloodthirsty Achilles; and great as might have been the guilt of Paris, I read with an earnest wish that Troy might be delivered from its besiegers. When I came to the end of the poem, I laid it down with a feeling of disappointment. I was not told, save in certain dim predictions, what became of Troy, which the Greeks had mustered from so many regions to beseige, nor what was the fate of the mild and venerable Priam, and the aged Hecuba, and Andromache, the gentle and affectionate wife, and her infant son,—personages for whose fortunes the poet had so powerfully awakened my concern and my curiosity. Helen, to recover whom the war was waged, was still in Troy, and Paris, her effeminate husband, was still alive and unharmed. Why the Trojans, who hated Paris—why Hector and the other sons of Priam, who disapproved of their brother's conduct—why Priam himself, who is never said to have approved of it, did not insist that the seducer should restore Helen to her first and proper husband, for whom she seems to have still entertained a lingering regard, I could never imagine. Particularly strange it seemed that Paris was not forced by his countrymen to give up Helen after the combat between him and Menelaus, in which he was clearly overcome, and by the terms of the solemn treaty which preceded the duel was bound to restore his stolen bride and her wealth to thc Grccks. The poet has chosen to leave that circumstance without adequate explanation. The breaking of the truce by Pandarus, and the sudden renewal of the war in consequence, does not explain it, for afterwards, in the Seventh Book, we have Antenor proposing, in council, to restore Helen and her wealth, as a certain way of ending the war,—a proposal which is not adopted simply because Paris objects to it. Paris would not consent to retore Helen, and the Trojan princes and leaders, as if Paris were their absolute monarch, allowed him to have his way, and to prolong a war which Hector foresaw—as he says in the famous interview with Andromache—was to end in the destruction of Troy. The impression to which I refer has been confirmed by the minute study which I have recently made of the poem. I can make nothing of it but a detached chapter of the poetic history of the Trojan war,—an episode in the narrative of that long seige which was to be concluded by a greater event than any recorded in the ***Iliad,*** the taking of the city of Troy;—a work of an inexhaustible imagination, with characters vigorously drawn and finely discriminated, and incidents rapidly succeeding each other and infinitely diversified,—everywhere a noble simplicity, mellifluous numbers, and images of beauty and grandeur; yet everywhere indications that the poem had a continuation. It is full of references to events which are yet to be related, and provokes a desire for further disclosures, which it fails to gratify. There are frequent allusions to the brief term of life allotted to Achilles, and several, one of which I have already mentioned, to the final capture of Troy. Thetis predicts that her son, perishing almost immediately after taking the life of Hector, will not live to see the fall of the besieged city. The audiences before whom the books of the ***Iliad*** were recited by the minstrels would naturally say: "You speak of the capture of Troy; tell us how it was taken at last. Achilles, the mightiest of warriors, you say, was to be slain soon after the death of Hector. Relate the manner of his death, and how it was received by the Greeks and the Trojans. Describe his funeral, as you described those of his friend Patroclus and his adversary Hector. Tell us what became of Andromache, and Astyanax, her son, and all the royal family of Priam." Thus may we suppose that, until Aristotle arose to demonstrate the contrary, the fable of the ***Iliad*** must have appeared to the general mind to be incomplete.

Let me say a word or two of the personage whom the critics call the hero of the ***Iliad.*** Achilles is ill-used by Agamemnon, the general-in-chief of the Greeks,—and so far he has the sympathy of the reader; but he is a ferocious barbarian at best, and as the narrative proceeds, he loses all title to our interest. His horrid prayer that the Greeks may be slaughtered by thousands until they learn to despise a monarch who has done him a personal injury, and his inhuman delight in the havoc made of them by the Trojans under Hector, cause us to turn from him with the horror and aversion due to a selfish and cruel nature which imposes no reserve or restraint upon its own impulses. His warm affection for his gentle friend and companion, Patroclus, partly restores him to our favor; but his pitiless treatment of the Trojans who supplicate him for quarter, and his capture of twelve Trojan youths in order to cut their throats at the funeral pile of Patroclus, as he afterwards does in cold blood, bring back our disgust; and when Hector with his dying voice warns him of his approaching death, the reader has no objection to offer. If Achilles be the hero of the poem, the poet has not succeeded in obtaining for him either our good opinion or our good wishes. In the fortunes of Hector, however, whose temper is noble and generous, who while grieving at the crime of Paris defends his country with all his valor, whose character is as gentle and affectionate as it is spirited and manly, it is impossible for the reader not to feel a strong interest. The last book of the ***Iliad*** relates the recovery of his dead body from the Greeks, and the celebration of his funeral in Troy. In this book, also, the character of Achilles appears less unamiable, since he grants the rites of hospitality to Priam, and is persuaded by his entreaties to restore, for a princely ransom, the dead body of Hector, contrary to his first resolution. It is to be observed, however, that he is moved to this, not by his own native manganimity, but by considerations which indirectly relate to himself,—that is to say, by being artfully led to think of his own father, Peleus, an aged man like Priam, anxiously waiting in his distant palace for the return of his son from the war, and fearing that he may never behold him again. Once in the interview with Priam the fierce and brutal nature of Achilles breaks out in threats, which terrify the old king into silence. Priam is himself warned by the gods that he is not safe in remaining overnight in the tent of Achilles, and, lest he should not be protected from the ferocity of Agamemnon, withdraws by stealth in the darkness and returns to Troy.

I have no answer to make to those who regard it as a blemish in the great work of Homer that he represents the gods in their dealings with men as governed, for the most part, by motives either mean and base, or frivolous and childish. In the Trojan war everything happens by their direction or their prompting. In the system of Homer it is they who stir up men to strife, who bring on the battles, promote the slaughter, and bring it to an end, urge the personages of the fable to ruinous follies and imprudences, and give or withhold victory at their pleasure; and in all this their rule is not one of justice and beneficence, but of caprice. Their favor is purchased by hecatombs, and their hatred incurred by acts which have no moral quality that should give offence to an upright judge. They are debauched, mercenary, rapacious, and cruel; they dwell in a world in which the rules of right and the maxims necessary to the well-being of human society find no recognition. It was for this reason that Plato, the earliest author of an *Index expurgatorius,* forbade the circulation of the writings of the Greek poets in his imaginary commonwealth.

Yet let me say this in favor of my author, that in one part of the poem the absolute rectitude of the Divine government is solemnly recognized. (In the Third Book of the ***Iliad,*** a truce is agreed upon between the Trojans and the Greeks, while Menelaus and Paris are to decide by single combat the quarrel which has occasioned the siege of Troy. A compact is made, according to which the victor is to possess Helen and her wealth, and the Trojans and Greeks are ever afterward to remain friends and allies. The gods are invoked to be witnesses of the treaty, and to pursue with their vengeance those by whom it shall be violated, whether they be Greeks or Trojans. Few passages in the ***Iliad*** are more striking or of graver import than this appeal to the justice of the gods,—this testimony, given by two warring nations, of their confidence—in the equity with which the immortals govern the world. Paris is overcome by Menelaus in the combat; the truce is broken by a Trojan, who wounds Menelaus severely; the treaty is not fulfilled by delivering up Helen; and, as the action of the poem proceeds in the next book, Agamemnon exhorts the Greeks to fight valiantly, in the full assurance that Jupiter and the other gods will never permit treachery to remain unpunished; and accordingly he predicts a terrible retribution already hanging over Troy. And whatever may be our admiration for the amiable and noble qualities of Hector, and our sympathy for the thousands of innocent persons dwelling in his populous city, it cannot be denied that the interference of the gods in the affairs of Troy leads in the end to a great result consistent with substantial justice. Paris, the violater of the laws of hospitality, the adulterer and robber, is sheltered, protected, and countenanced in Troy,—the Trojan people make themselves partakers in his guilt; and in the end they share in its punishment. Hector, the prop of their state, the champion in whom they put their trust, is slain; and we are allowed, by means of predictions, a glimpse of the coming destruction of Troy, and learn that the sceptre of the kingdom will pass from the house of Priam, whose son committed the crime which led to the war, and will be swayed by the posterity of the blameless Æneas. (pp. vii-xiii)

William Cullen Bryant, in a preface to The Iliad of Homer, *translated by William Cullen Bryant, 1870. Reprint by Houghton, Mifflin and Company, 1898, pp. iii-xiii.*

EDWIN ARNOLD (essay date 1869)

[A versatile English poet, journalist, dramatist, translator, and Oriental scholar, Arnold was well known during the second half of the nineteenth century. Though his reputation today has faded, he is still remembered for his The Light of Asia *(1879), a verse biography of Gautama, the founder of Buddhism. In the following excerpt from his* The Poets of Greece, *Arnold discusses characterization and style in the* Iliad, *emphasizing the "savage element" in the poem's depiction of warfare.]*

There is a thoroughly savage element about the actual combats [in the ***Iliad***], which takes us back, indeed, to pre-civilised times; for scarcely a great soldier in the ***Iliad,*** except Hector, comes up at all to the modern idea of "an officer and a gentleman." Achilles, in the opening quarrel of the poem, rails at Agamemnon (his king and general, be it remembered), in this classical Billingsgate:—. . .

Wine-sodden sot, with the face of a dog, and the
  heart of a roe-buck!
Never once into the war, at the head of thy troops, in
  thine armour,—
Never once out on the ambush, along with the lords of
  Achaia—
Darêdst thou to go!

But Achilles is simply a beautiful brutal creature—the apotheosis of animal force and passion—an incarnation of selfish anger, only redeemed by perfect grace and bodily excellence; though his very courage is marred by the knowledge that he has the protection of Athene, and of his goddess-mother, who have made him all but invulnerable. His friendhsip for Patroclus seems of a dubious elevation, and his rage at the death of his friend is rendered more furious, apparently, by personal pique than devotion. It may be said that the words which he exchanges with his horses prove that he foresaw and recognised his fate by the arrow of Paris. If his prowess by rehabilitated by this passage, his ferocity remains at least undefended and indefensible. He is exactly as Horace paints him—

Impiger, iracundus, *inexorabilis,* acer.

No man gets mercy of him in war; valour does not make him respect it, nor youth win him to compassionate it. When he breaks forth at last "like a hungry lion" from his tent, he rages over the plain, inebriate with blood. A lion is not the right simile, for a lion has generosity: Achilles, in his grace and blood-thirstiness, resembles a panther rather, which slays for mere lust of slaughter when peril or appetite are over. Read the passage in which, after endless killing, he encounters and puts to the sword the son of Alastor:— . . .

Nor less unpitied young Alastor bleeds.
In vain his youth, in vain his beauty, pleads.
In vain he begs thee, with a suppliant moan,
To spare a form, an age so like thy own!
Unhappy boy! no prayer, no moving art,
E'er bent that fierce inexorable heart.
While yet he trembled at his-knees, and cried,
The ruthless falchion oped his tender side.
The panting liver pours a flood of gore
That drowns his bosom, till he pants no more.

It is here Homer, his limner, who calls the Greek . . . "nothing sweet-natured," and Homer keeps all his painting consistent and equal, so that wherever we find Achilles we find this same insolent and heartless ideal of a "fighting man," . . . of the ancient pattern. When the unfair gods have given Hector into his hands, and the glorious Dardan lies, with the spear-wound in his neck, bleeding to death, he pleads with Achilles to let his body be buried. "By thy life, by thy knees, by thy father and mother," Hector entreats, "let not the dogs have my flesh. Take what ransom you will; Troy will pay any sum! But as you are brave and victorious, let my remains go to my own people." Whereupon the arrogant conqueror—the cannibal, rather—answers— . . .

No, wretch accurs'd! (relentless he replies:
Flames, as he spoke, shot flashing from his eyes),
Not those who gave me breath should bid me spare,
Nor all the sacred prevalence of prayer.

Could I myself the bloody banquet join!
No—to the dogs that carcass I resign.
Should Troy to bribe me bring forth all her store,
And, giving thousands, offer thousands more;
Should Dardan Priam and his weeping dame
Drain their whole realm to buy one funeral flame:
Their Hector on the pile they should not see,
Nor rob the vultures of one limb of thee.

"Right well," the dying hero sighs, "I knew you were iron-hearted!" Once, truly, the strong and savage nature melts, when the reaction of rage sets in, and he sees Priam kneeling before him, kissing the hands which had killed the hope of Troy, and imploring that the precious body may be surrendered. Achilles softens then, and it is well-nigh the only time in the ***Iliad*** when he is not as hateful as he is fair, and as fierce as he is swift and splendid.

Hector is the "Christian soldier," as far as such a type could exist before the strange doctrine astonished the world that we should "love our enemies." He is even braver than Achilles, for he has no charm against spears and arrows except the favour of the those few Gods who happen to take sides with Troy; yet he sustains the fortunes of his native city from the first to the last with generous and manly valour. The noblest sentiments of the poem come all from his mouth. It is he who laughs at the auguries when they forbid the battle, saying— . . .

Without a bird his sword the brave man draws,
And asks no omen but his country's cause.

It is he who is ever ready to expose himself for the common cause against the most doughty champion offering, and his anger is seldom roused except towards cowardice. For that his patriotic soul has no manner of patience. When Paris, the cause of all the war, turns back from the face of Menelaus in the fight, the great warrior rebukes him very sternly. . . . But when Paris, ashamed and reminded of himself, offers to engage Menelaus in single combat, Hector's heart leaps up for joy to find his brother no poltroon. . . . He is mightily glad, for he harbours no petty feeling, and will fight twice ten years, if necessary, after that, for Paris and Helen. Towards the beautiful Greek who is the cause of such woe to his country, Hector is ever exquisite in manner. The few passages wherein they encounter represent him as gravely courteous, and her as in turn sincerely respectful; and though we must not mistake their age for one of much "morality" in the modern sense, it is plain, from Hector's well-marked deference, and the mild language of King Priam, that Helen was meant to Homer to seem no wanton "light o' love." Obviously

The face that launched a thousand ships,
And sacked the topless towers of Ilium

appeared to the Trojan generalissimo—one of a breed of sea-pirates himself—excuse for a good deal. Yet in his grave and dutiful speeches, and far different estimate of love, as evinced towards Andromache; as well as in Homer's obvious preference for the gallant chieftain, we see the light of a purer principle very clear. Perhaps the most lovely passage of the ***Iliad*** is that oft-cited one in which Hector bids adieu to his wife and child before joining battle. . . . [What] can be finer than the strong soldier's tenderness, the gentle manliness which he displays towards his wife, and that sweet touch of nature, linking the far-off day with all which is soft and loving in human spirits for ever, when he takes off his nodding helmet-plume that the little Astyanax may not be frightened? What can be more eloquent, either, than the . . . "tearful smile" of Andromache? Usage has wrought this noble Trojan much wrong in making the verb "to hector" imply, as it does, "to swagger," "to bluster." The chief talks fiercely and big at times, like the others; but from first to last he is the Bayard of the ***Iliad,*** "sans peur et sans reproche."

This identity in the personal qualities of the Homeric heroes is to a just mind one of the greatest proofs of the unity of the work. It is preserved through all the leading characters. Ajax is ever blunderingly brave—a "heavy" of the Greek foot-guards; a "beef-witted lord," "good at need," in truth, but with muscle somewhat cumbrously overlying mind. Paris is light, womanish, sensitive, graceful, and unstable; Diomed, quick in council and agile in the fight—a Greek Paris without the feminine element. We are nowhere jarred by such inconsistencies as patchwork composition would have brought in. Ulysses, doubly important because he is the hero of the second poem of this duology, never once loses his character. . . . He fights like a cunning man, and plots like a brave one; he has neither any cowardice in him, nor any imprudence—nor, to speak the truth, very much true elevation of soul. He is Common Sense in splendid armour—a mailed *père de famille;* wise, substantial, unvulgar, but as practical as a British tax-payer. The clear, broad lines in which Homer paints this favourite of Pallas—as also the companion portrait of Æneas, the Trojan prince—are almost as strong as proof can be to the careful student that one and the same genius created or recalled to life the grand company of captains amid which these live and move. It may be seen by the *Æneid* and in *Troilus and Cressida* how perfectly easy it was to identify and transfer such vitalised and consistent individualities.

But the women of Homer must have due mention. First in beauty and world-wide fame—not in virtue, alas! comes that fair plague of men . . . , the "*causa terterrima belli*"—Helen. Homer takes care that we shall know how glorious her charms were, and why so many Greeks and Trojans died gladly for their sake. When she passes out upon the wall among the old men of the city, even they chirrup praises at her like grasshoppers. . . . They say, with effusion of admiration— . . .

Sure 'tis no marvel that Troy and the well-greaved men of Achaia
All this while should struggle and bleed for a woman like that one!
Awfully lovely she is, and like the immortals to look on;
Still, it were well she went back in the ships with her terrible beauty,
Rather than tarry, a curse upon us, and our children hereafter.

And Helen—her history notwithstanding, and notwithstanding that she has to look out from the Trojan wall and point below it to Menelaus, her deserted husband—is in Homer no wanton, but a gentle, though sinful, and sorrowful dame. Priam comforts her with pious words about the "power of the gods"; Hector is, as has been said, invariably respectful and polite; Antenor, and all the chiefs—full allowance being made for the laxer morality of the old days—are still particularly tender and pitiful towards her, as if Priam's view of the matter were upon all their minds. . . .

'Tis not you are the cause—the gods are the cause—the gods only.

Her best plea for consideration throughout the carnage which takes place around and on account of her, is, that she never forgives herself. Others may see in her but the victim of the will of Zeus—she for herself is deeply ashamed and penitent; even in her tenderest passages with Paris, she retains enough of the Greek princess in her to upbraid him for his cowardice and to regret her guilt; while before Hector's face she abases herself into the dust with the agony of self-reproach, and pours out all a woman's burning pity for her thousands of bleeding victims. In the ***Odyssey*** these qualities in her, so carefully emphasised by the great artist, have brought her as much peace of mind as the dreadful war can have left. She is discovered to us restored, and not without honour and happiness, to the court of her husband Menelaus—modest, hospitable, but high-serious with her past shame and present forgiveness. Very tender and full of a later wisdom are those last words of Helen in the ***Odyssey*** . . .

> Troy and the Trojan dames were sad. But I then the rather
> Gladdened, because my heart was turned to sail the sea over
> Back to my home—for I mourned the sweet mischief the goddess had done me,
> Aphrodite the strong, in tempting me far from my country,
> Far from my child, my home—far, worst of all, from my lord here,
> Second to no one—ah me! in heart, nor in beauty of body.

But, indeed, if virtue had its rights of precedence, Hector's wife should come first. Andromache, shrined in the very loveliest verses wherever her name occurs, and heroine of that already-quoted passage which breaks the clouds of war like the evening star, is therein sufficiently pourtrayed. Andromache is one of those perfect wives whose instinctive honour and purity taught the world the happy lesson of such words as honour and purity in times when constancy and wedded troth were only being learned. None of the goddesses in the Iliadic heaven are so divine as this Trojan mother and wife, whose grace and goodness, pourtrayed so early, and belonging to an age so far removed, help us to believe that "sweetness and light" were among the most ancient of the possessions of the world, and, above all, of that sex which the other treats as "inferior."

The morality of Homer has been a subject of much discussion in all ages, from Plato down to Mr. Gladstone. The Athenian philosopher, who drove the poets from his republic, makes no exception in favour of the Father of them. He condemns him for a theology where the Gods are of like passions with men; sharing their angers; hot with their foolish factions; fighting in unfair disguise amid their ranks; and even wounded by their spears [see c. 4th century B.C. excerpt by Plato]. This, however, is no fault of the poet. He found the religion of his time anthropomorphic, and he merely turned it into charming verse. Nor is there always wanting an esoteric meaning in his melange of gods and chieftains. If Apollo favours Hector, and Pallas aids Ulysses, this was the old-world way of teaching that "Heaven helps those who help themselves." Judged by the religious thought of later days, of even by the high and clear light of Plato's intellect and conscience, Homer no doubt was but a "heathen-man." The machinery of the blind singer's creed is clumsy—his Jove is overmastered by Fate, and weighs the lives of contending lords against each other with no more power of control than a grocer possesses to make two pounds of one comodity lighter than a pound and a half of another. His heroes fight like Chinese braves for swagger, like cannibals for ferocity; and Diomed and Ulysses, upon a midnight reconnoitring expedition, kill sleeping men without the smallest compunction. But making reservation for the age and the training of Homer, his work is to be unhesitatingly declared as one of a clear and pronounced morality. Horace has not praised him too much in saying that he "teaches the noble and ignoble, the becoming and unbecoming, better than Chrysippus and Crantor." He pourtrays his warriors very much, in truth, *au naturel*—they eat and drink, fight and repose, jest roughly or weep with effusion, like the sons of nature that they were. He is not answerable, however, for them, nor for his uxorious Jove, nor yet for the tiger-like fighting-men who tear the spear from the entrails of their enemy, and deride him as he sobs and dies. But the chivalry of Sarpedon, the patriotic devotion of Hector, the perfect wifehood of Andromache, and the heartfelt repentance of Helen, with many a passage of lofty honour, and much sentiment, rich with the spirit of knighthood before its time, show Homer to have been true to his "divine mission" as a poet. For a real poet is divine, and priest of God by better consecration than any which the churches can confer. St. Basil did very well, therefore, to cite "the blind old man" as one who always upheld virtue and high ends and thoughts in life. To this chief merit must be added his radiant cheerfulness of mind, and simple delight in the world of objects and of actions—the true and glad Greek nature—in itself a virtue. He tells us of the Fates, the Gods, the scenes of camp and city, the joys and troubles, the tears and smiles of his heroes and heroines, with that serene calm which only the best singers have. He will no more be affected by the carnage of his theme than a river will be always stained with the blood from a battle. There is the melancholy, indeed, of early religious thought about him when he speaks of "the races of men falling like the leaves"; and the awe of mankind's eternal wonder at the "for ever" when he describes soul after soul of his fighting men "unwillingly seeking the gloomy shades below." Yet, like the Greek he was, he turns for ever to the light—for ever to the lovely things which are in the world—to this gay, picturesque, sufficing, delightful, many-coloured existence of mankind; and though Jove sports with mortals, and Fate controls Jove, the sense of some . . . more just and potent God above both, is rather felt than read in these his two grand pagan epics.

Their style, as has been said, cannot be conveyed, for the old wine, in this case, truly bursts the new bottles. The study of Greek might well be undertaken were it only for the possession of Homer's music and manner. His Achæan hexameters have the utmost vigour, puissance, and billow-like might and flow of which this powerful metre is capable. It carries itself with such swing and skill, that one forgets the art, which is all the while exquisite, though never finical. Solemn or sweet, majestic or simple, slow as the march of legions, or fiery as the charge of fight, the dactyls and spondees roll along, their very syllables making the music to the sense, as if the verses broke—which doubtless most of them did—straight from the lips of the bard, while his blind eyes worked with the splendour of the vivid vision of each scene. The way in which the spirit of Homer thus drives along the rolling vocables of his Greek in rhythmic flood, is like the action of the wind upon the wide sea. The nature-like power of the poet is, indeed, his central quality; he has so much to tell, and goes the nearest way to tell it, with no apparent art, and no pomp of diction but the glorious language of his race, and the poetry inherent in his theme. He possesses the qualities of a narrator sufficiently to excite and assure attention—but you must sit down and listen;

he will not bribe you with artifices and surprises; when the action demands it, he will tell a message twice over, or repeat a long speech; if one word serves his purpose, he will use it as often as he wants it, not hunting for synonyms. He is the freshest, easiest, serenest, and simplest bard, as he was the first; the colours of his page are clear and strong as those of the dawn; the air of him is like the breath of morning moving over a waking earth; the light upon him lies like the light of heaven upon the highest alpine peaks—white, broad, beautiful, unbroken. (pp. 22-42)

Edwin Arnold, "Homer," in his The Poets of Greece, *1869. Reprint by Books for Libraries Press, 1972; distributed by Arno Press, Inc., pp. 1-54.*

SAMUEL BUTLER (lecture date 1892)

[*An English novelist, satirist, essayist, and translator, Butler is best known for his* The Way of All Flesh, *an autobiographical novel that satirizes Victorian church and family life. As a Homeric scholar, Butler achieved notoriety for his* The Authoress of the Odyssey *(1897), in which he propounded the theory that the* Odyssey *was written by a woman. In the following excerpt, he provides an overview of Homer's use of humor in the* Iliad, *focusing on his treatment of gods and humans, and also notes the objectivity of the poem's narrator. Butler's comments were originally delivered as a lecture in 1892.*]

The leading ideas of the ***Iliad*** are love, war, and plunder, though this last is less insisted on than the other two. The key-note is struck with a woman's charms, and a quarrel among men for their possession. It is a woman who is at the bottom of the Trojan war itself. Woman throughout the ***Iliad*** is a being to be loved, teased, laughed at, and if necessary carried off. We are told in one place of a fine bronze cauldron for heating water which was worth twenty oxen, whereas a few lines lower down a good serviceable maid-of-all-work is valued at four oxen. I think there is a spice of malicious humour in this valuation, and am confirmed in this opinion by noting that though woman in the ***Iliad*** is on one occasion depicted as a wife so faithful and affectionate that nothing more perfect can be found either in real life or fiction, yet as a general rule she is drawn as teasing, scolding, thwarting, contradicting, and hoodwinking the sex that has the effrontery to deem itself her lord and master. Whether or no this view may have arisen from any domestic difficulties between Homer and his wife is a point which again I find it impossible to determine.

We cannot refrain from contemplating such possibilities. If we are to be at home with Homer there must be no sitting on the edge of one's chair dazzled by the splendour of his reputation. He was after all only a literary man, and those who occupy themselves with letters must approach him as a very honoured member of their own fraternity, but still as one who must have felt, thought, and acted much as themselves. He struck oil, while we for the most part succeed in boring only; still we are his literary brethren, and if we would read his lines intelligently we must also read between them. That one so shrewd, and yet a dreamer of such dreams as have been vouchsafed to few indeed besides himself—that one so genially sceptical, and so given to looking into the heart of a matter, should have been in such perfect harmony with his surroundings as to think himself in the best of all possible worlds—this is not believable. The world is always more or less out of joint to the poet—generally more so; and unfortunately he always thinks it more or less his business to set it right—generally more so. We are all of us more or less poets—generally, indeed, less so; still we feel and think, and to think at all is to be out of harmony with much that we think about. We may be sure, then, that Homer had his full share of troubles, and also that traces of these abound up and down his work if we could only identify them, for everything that everyone does is in some measure a portrait of himself; but here comes the difficulty—not to read between the lines, not to try and detect the hidden features of the writer—this is to be a dull, unsympathetic, incurious reader; and on the other hand to try and read between them is to be in danger of running after every Will o' the Wisp that conceit may raise for our delusion.

I believe it will help you better to understand the broad humour of the ***Iliad,*** which we shall presently reach, if you will allow me to say a little more about the general characteristics of the poem. Over and above the love and war that are his main themes, there is another which the author never loses sight of—I mean distrust and dislike of the ideas of his time as regards the gods and omens. No poet ever made gods in his own image more defiantly than the author of the ***Iliad.*** In the likeness of man created he them, and the only excuse for him is that he obviously desired his readers not to take them seriously. This at least is the impression he leaves upon his reader, and when so great a man as Homer leaves an impression it must be presumed that he does so intentionally. It may be almost said that he has made the gods take the worse, not the better, side of man's nature upon them, and to be in all respects as we ourselves—yet without virtue. It should be noted, however, that the gods on the Trojan side are treated far more leniently than those who help the Greeks.

The chief gods on the Grecian side are Juno, Minerva, and Neptune. Juno, as you will shortly see, is a scolding wife, who in spite of all Jove's bluster wears the breeches, or tries exceedingly hard to do so. Minerva is an angry termagant—mean, mischief-making, and vindictive. She begins by pulling Achilles' hair, and later on she knocks the helmet from off the head of Mars. She hates Venus, and tells the Grecian hero Diomede that he had better not wound any of the other gods, but that he is to hit Venus if he can, which he presently does "because he sees that she is feeble and not like Minerva or Bellona." Neptune is a bitter hater.

Apollo, Mars, Venus, Diana, and Jove, so far as his wife will let him, are on the Trojan side. These, as I have said, meet with better, though still somewhat contemptuous, treatment at the poet's hand. Jove, however, is being mocked and laughed at from first to last, and if one moral can be drawn from the ***Iliad*** more clearly than another, it is that he is only to be trusted to a very limited extent. Homer's position, in fact, as regards divine interference is the very opposite of David's. David writes, "Put not your trust in princes nor in any child of man; there is no sure help but from the Lord." With Homer it is, "Put not your trust in Jove neither in any omen from heaven; there is but one good omen—to fight for one's country. Fortune favours the brave; heaven helps those who help themselves."

The god who comes off best is Vulcan, the lame, hobbling, old blacksmith, who is the laughing-stock of all the others, and whose exquisitely graceful skilful workmanship forms such an effective contrast to the uncouth exterior of the workman. Him, as a man of genius and an artist, and furthermore as a somewhat despised artist, Homer treats, if with playfulness, still with respect, in spite of the fact that circumstances have thrown him more on the side of the Greeks than of the Trojans, with whom I understand Homer's sympathies mainly to lie.

The poet either dislikes music or is at best insensible to it. Great poets very commonly are so. Achilles, indeed, does on one occasion sing to his own accompaniment on the lyre, but we are not told that it was any pleasure to hear him, and Patroclus, who was in the tent at the time, was not enjoying it; he was only waiting for Achilles to leave off. But though not fond of music, Homer has a very keen sense of the beauties of nature, and is constantly referring both in and out of season to all manner of homely incidents that are as familiar to us as to himself. Sparks in the train of a shooting-star; a cloud of dust upon a high road; foresters going out to cut wood in a forest; the shrill cry of the cicale; children making walls of sand on the sea-shore, or teasing wasps when they have found a wasps' nest; a poor but very honest woman who gains a pittance for her children by selling wool, and weighs it very carefully; a child clinging to its mother's dress and crying to be taken up and carried—none of these things escape him. Neither in the ***Iliad*** nor the ***Odyssey*** do we ever receive so much as a hint as to the time of year at which any of the events described are happening; but on one occasion the author of the ***Iliad*** really has told us that it was a very fine day, and this not from a business point of view, but out of pure regard to the weather for its own sake.

With one more observation I will conclude my preliminary remarks about the ***Iliad.*** I cannot find its author within the four corners of the work itself. I believe the writer of the ***Odyssey*** to appear in the poem as a prominent and very fascinating character whom we shall presently meet, but there is no one in the ***Iliad*** on whom I can put my finger with even a passing idea that he may be the author. Still, if under some severe penalty I were compelled to find him, I should say it was just possible that he might consider his own lot to have been more or less like that which he forecasts for Astyanax, the infant son of Hector. At any rate his intimate acquaintance with the topography of Troy, which is now well ascertained, and still more his obvious attempt to excuse the non-existence of a great wall which, according to his story, ought to be there and which he knew had never existed, so that no trace could remain, while there were abundant traces of all the other features he describes—these facts convince me that he was in all probability a native of the Troad, or country round Troy. His plausibly concealed Trojan sympathies, and more particularly the aggravated exaggeration with which the flight of Hector is described, suggest to me, coming as they do from an astute and humorous writer, that he may have been a Trojan, at any rate by the mother's side, made captive, enslaved, compelled to sing the glories of his captors, and determined so to overdo them that if his masters cannot see through the irony others sooner or later shall. This, however, is highly speculative. . . . (pp. 59-65)

[There are many] examples of the kind of divine comedy in which Homer brings the gods and goddesses upon the scene. Among mortals the humour, what there is of it, is confined mainly to the grim taunts which the heroes fling at one another when they are fighting, and more especially to crowing over a fallen foe. The most subtle passage is the one in which Briseis, the captive woman about whom Achilles and Agamemnon have quarrelled, is restored by Agamemnon to Achilles. Briseis on her return to the tent of Achilles finds that while she has been with Agamemnon, Patroclus has been killed by Hector, and his dead body is now lying in state. She flings herself upon the corpse and exclaims—

"How one misfortune does keep falling upon me after another! I saw the man to whom my father and mother had married me killed before my eyes, and my three own dear brothers perished along with him; but you, Patroclus, even when Achilles was sacking our city and killing my husband, told me that I was not to cry; for you said that Achilles himself should marry me, and take me back with him to Phthia, where we should have a wedding feast among the Myrmidons. You were always kind to me, and I should never cease to grieve for you."

This may of course be seriously intended, but Homer was an acute writer, and if we had met with such a passage in Thackeray we should have taken him to mean that so long as a woman can get a new husband, she does not much care about losing the old one—a sentiment which I hope no one will imagine that I for one moment endorse or approve of, and which I can only explain as a piece of sarcasm aimed possibly at Mrs. Homer. (pp. 73-4)

Samuel Butler, "The Humour of Homer," in The Humour of Homer and Other Essays, *edited by R. A. Streatfeild, Mitchell Kennerly, 1914, pp. 59-98.*

GILBERT MURRAY (essay date 1907)

[*A British educator, humanitarian, translator, author, and classical scholar, Murray has written extensively on Greek literature and history and is considered one of the most influential twentieth-century interpreters of Greek drama. In the following excerpt from a revised edition of his 1907 work,* The Rise of the Greek Epic, *Murray praises the "intensity of imagination" which enables Homer to succeed in transporting the reader into the ancient world. Murray also discusses the ways in which the Greek epic tradition was preserved and transmitted, concluding that such works as the* Iliad *contain "the spiritual life-blood of a people."*]

[It] is intensity of imagination that makes a poet's work "real," as we say; spontaneous, infectious or convincing. Especially it is this that creates an atmosphere; that makes us feel, on opening the pages of a book, that we are in a different world, and a world full of real beings about whom, in one way or another, we care. And I suspect that ultimately the greatness of a poem or work of imaginative art depends mostly upon two questions: how strongly we feel ourselves transported to this new world, and what sort of a world it is when we get there, how great or interesting or beautiful. Think of the first scene of *Hamlet,* the first page of the *Divina Commedia,* the first lines of the *Agamemnon;* how swiftly and into what wonderful regions they carry you! And if you apply this same test to the ***Iliad*** or ***Odyssey,*** the response is so amazing that you understand at once why these poems have so often and in such various ages been considered absolutely of all the greatest. Open the book anywhere. "So spake he, and the old man trembled and obeyed his word; and he went in silence by the shore of the many-sounding sea, and prayed alone to the Lord Apollo, whom fair-haired Leto bare." Turn the pages. "And a herd he wrought thereon of straight-horned kine. The kine were wrought of gold and of tin, and lowing they wended forth from the byre to their pasture, by the side of a singing river, by a bed of slender reeds." Turn again. "I look upon thee and know thee as thou art. I could never have moved thee, for the heart is iron within thy breast. Therefore beware lest I be to thee a wrath of god, on that day when Paris and Phoebus Apollo shall slay thee in thy valour at the Scaean Gates."

How irresistibly do the chance words bear one away, and to what a world! We can stand apart and argue and analyse, and show that the real world portrayed in the poems was one full of suffering and injustice, and that the poet was sometimes overlax in his moral judgements. Yet the world into which he takes us is somehow more splendid than any created by other men. Where were there ever battles or heroes like these, such beauty, such manliness, such terror and pity and passion, and such all-ruling majesty of calm? There are many strong men and fair women in other stories; why is it that, almost before a word is spoken, we feel in our bones the strength of these Homeric heroes, the beauty of these grave and white-armed women? You remember, in the Old Testament, the watchman who stood upon the tower in Jezreel, when they saw men and chariots approaching in the distance, and sent out one horseman after another to inquire their purpose. "And the watchman answered and said: He came even unto them and cometh not again. And the driving is like the driving of Jehu the son of Nimshi; for he driveth furiously." We knew nothing about the driving of Jehu before. We hear no word more about it afterwards. But the one sentence has behind it just that intensity of imagination which makes thoughts live and vibrate like new things a hundred, or a thousand, or two thousand, years after their first utterance. And that is the quality that one finds in Homer.

Think how the beauty of Helen has lived through the ages. Like the driving of Jehu, it is now an immortal thing. And the main, though not of course the sole, source of the whole conception is certainly the ***Iliad.*** Yet in the whole ***Iliad*** there is practically not a word spoken in description of Helen. As Lessing has remarked in a well-known passage of the *Laokoon,* almost the whole of our knowledge of Helen's beauty comes from a few lines in the third book, where Helen goes up to the wall of Troy to see the battle between Menelaus and Paris. "So speaking, the goddess put into her heart a longing for her husband of yore and her city and her father and mother. And straightway she veiled herself with white linen, and went forth from her chamber shedding a great tear. . . ." The elders of Troy were seated on the wall, and when they saw Helen coming, "softly they spake to on another winged words: 'Small wonder that the Trojans and mailed Greeks should endure pain through many years for such a woman. *Strangely like she is in face to some immortal spirit*'." That is all we know. Not one of all the Homeric bards fell into the yawning trap of describing Helen, and making a catalogue of her features. She was veiled; she was weeping; and she was strangely like in face to some immortal spirit. And the old men, who strove for peace, could feel no anger at the war.

Now this intensity of imagination can be attained by many writers at their most exalted moments. Their imagination can follow the call of their emotions. But one of the extraordinary things in the ***Iliad*** is the prevalence of this intensity all through the ordinary things of life. "As riseth the screaming of cranes in front of the sunrise, cranes that have fled from winter and measureless rain, screaming they fly over the streams of ocean, bearing unto the dwarf-men battle and death." Who that can once read Homer freely, untroubled by difficulties of language, can ever forget the cranes? And not only the cranes, but the swarming bees, the flies about the milk-pails, the wolves and boars and lions and swift dogs, and the crook-horned swing-footed kine? It is a fairly wide world that the poets lay open to us, and every remotest corner of it is interesting and vivid, every commonest experience in it, the washing of hands, the eating of food, the acts of sleeping and waking, shares somehow in the beauty and even in the grandeur of the whole. Mr. Mackail has observed how full the poems are of images drawn from fire: the bright armour flashes like fire, the armies clash, "even as destroying fire that falls upon a limitless forest"; a hero's "hands are like unto fire and his wrath unto red iron"; and the men "fight together, a body of burning fire." The whole poem is shot through with this fire, which seems like a symbol of the inward force of which we have been speaking, a fiery intensity of imagination. Given this force within, and the Homeric language as an instrument for its expression, a language more gorgeous than Milton's, yet as simple and direct as that of Burns, there is no further need to be surprised at the extraordinary greatness of the ***Iliad.***

But now comes a curious observation. We who are accustomed to modern literature always associate this sort of imaginative intensity with something personal. We connect it with an artist's individuality, or with originality in the sense of "newness." It seems as though, under modern conditions, an artist usually did not feel or imagine intensely unless he was producing some work which was definitely his own and not another's, work which must bear his personal name and be marked by his personal experience or character. One element at least in the widespread admiration of such authors as Browning, Meredith, and Walt Whitman, has been, I think, a feeling that their work must somehow be particularly real and spontaneous, because they have insisted on doing it in a way in which, according to most well-constituted judges, it ought not to be done. And conversely, poets like Tennyson or Swinburne have been in certain circles despised as a little tame, conventional, uninspired, because they seemed to be too obedient to the ideals which poetry had followed before them. I do not specially wish to attack this modern prejudice, if it is one. I largely share in it: and its excesses will very likely disappear. But I do very greatly wish to point out that artistic feeling in this matter has not always been the same. Artists have not always wished to stamp their work with their personal characteristics or even their personal name. Artists have sometimes been, as it were, Protestant or Iconoclast, unable to worship without asserting themselves against the established ritual of their religion: sometimes, in happier circumstances, they have accepted and loved the ritual as part of the religion, and wrought out their own new works of poetry, not as protests, not as personal outbursts, but as glad and nameless offerings, made in prescribed form to enhance the glory of the spirit whom they served. With some modifications, this seems to have been the case in Greece, in Canaan, in Scandinavia, during the periods when great traditional books were slowly growing up. Each successive poet did not assert himself against the tradition, but gave himself up to the tradition, and added to its greatness and beauty all that was in him.

The intensity of imagination which makes the ***Iliad*** alive is not, it seems to me, the imagination of any one man. It means not that one man of genius created a wonder and passed away. It means that generation after generation of poets, trained in the same schools and a more or less continuous and similar life, steeped themselves to the lips in the spirit of this great poetry. They lived in the Epic saga and by it and for it. Great as it was, for many centuries they continued to build it up yet greater.

What helped them most, perhaps, was the constancy with which the whole race—to use a slightly inaccurate word—must have loved and cherished this poetry. Amid the chaos that followed [time], when the works of art, the architecture, the laws of ordered society, the very religions of the different centres, were all lost, for the most part never to return, the germs of this poetry were saved. The fugitives left their treasures, their gods, and their wives behind, but the sagas were in their hearts and grew the richer for all their wanderings. They carried their poetry as other nations have carried their religion. How strange and significant a thing, after all, is that which we speak of as either "the Epic style" or "the Epic language." It seems more than a style, though, as we have seen, it cannot quite be treated as an organic spoken language.

For many hundreds of years this wonderful mode of speech was kept alive to serve nothing but the needs of poetry. The ordinary audiences must have understood it as well as, for instance, our audiences understand the authorized version of the Bible, though the differences between Jacobean and Victorian English are utterly trifling compared with those between Homer and the prose speech of classical Ionic inscriptions. And how wonderfully the poets themselves knew it! Even under the microscope of modern philology the Epic dialect appears, in the main, as a sort of organic whole, not a mere mass of incongruous archaistic forms. . . . And this language has been preserved and reconstructed by generations of men who never spoke it except when they recited poetry. It was understood by audiences who never heard it spoken except when they listened to poetry. And not a man among them had any knowledge of the laws of language; they had only a sense of style.

But to meet the special difficulties raised above, let us consider especially the later generations of these bards and the task that lay before them. They were poets, "makers" as well as "singers"; but, much more than that, they were *Homêridae,* or *Homêrou Paides,* the sons and servants of the greatest of the poets. None of them dreamed of vying with Homer; only of exalting and preserving him. Other people no doubt might wish for a new style of poetry, for lyrics, for elegies, for iambic and personal verse. The old Epic language was becoming less known and more remote. The meanings of some of the words were taught in schools, others had been forgotten. And the last bards had before them various books, not very many, it seems, telling the great legends.

I am not looking for the work of any particular compiler or harmonizer; I am merely trying to understand the spirit in which any one of these later poets—how great or how small a poet matters little—seems to have set about his task. He could have written an epic poem himself, of course: but who wanted him to write one? How should he dare to? The world was not yet reduced to such straits as that. There was plenty of the old poetry still in his power. He knew it by heart, and he possessed scrolls of it, poetry of men far greater and wiser than he, voices of those who had talked with gods. Diligently and reverently he wove it together. He had before him—let us imagine—a Wrath in which Agamemnon offered no atonement, and he found besides a lay telling of the Embassy to Achilles; or he had before him some battles around an unwalled Greek camp and found another version with the storming of a wall; or perhaps he merely found fragments of other epics too good to lose and not too firmly rooted in their context to transfer. Diligently and reverently, with a good deal of simple cunning, he arranged his scheme so as to make room for all. He put inconsistent passages far apart; he altered a few words to mask awkwardnesses and get rid of stark contradictions. He added lines, when he needs must, to connect or to explain; always unobtrusive lines, making no dissonance, borrowed word by word, phrase by phrase, from the old poems themselves. And, amid all this gentle and lowly service, when he rehearsed his great recitation, when he went over the lines of some tremendous passage that shook all his being, then, it would seem from the evidence, there came into him the spirit of the ancient men, and a voice as of Homer himself. The lines that he spoke became his own. He had always belonged to them, and now they belonged to him also. And in the midst of them and beyond them he too had freedom to create.

And we critics, we mete to him a hard measure. When he creates, we call it interpolation. When he preserves with careful ingenuity all the fragments that he can save of his ancient Homer, we call attention to the small joints in his structure, the occasional incongruity of a simile which he loved too well to let die. If we knew his name, I suppose we should mock at him. But he has no name. He gave his name, as he gave all else that was in him, to help, unnoticed, in the building up of the greatest poem that ever sounded on the lips of men.

There is, outside and beneath the ordinary rules of art, a quality possessed by some great books or pictures and denied to others, a quality of attracting sympathy and causing the imagination of the reader or spectator to awake and co-operate with that of the artist. It is a quality that sometimes irritates a critic, because it acts fitfully and often depends upon accident. It puts the efforts of art at the mercy of prejudice. Yet, in a clear air, when prejudices can be laid aside and forgotten, this quality is seen to be, despite its occasional connexion with very third-rate things, itself a great thing, like the power of attracting or not attracting love. And in the last analysis, I suspect, one will find that this sympathy, like love in general, mostly goes to the man who both wants it and will duly pay for it. A poet who strikes his reader as perfect—of course none ever are so—who makes the impression of having entirely succeeded in saying what he meant to say, so that he requires no help from others, is apt to be treated with some respectful indifference. If he actually seems self-satisfied, then it is much worse. The reader becomes lynx-eyed for weaknesses, anxious to humiliate, like Ruskin, for instance, in his criticisms of Guido and the later Renaissance painters. And there are other poets or artists whose work has the power of appeal; the nameless charm and wistfulness of a thing not perfectly articulate, which means more than it can ever say, possesses more than it can ever impart, envisages more than it can ever define. It is the beauty of the ruin, suggesting the wonderful building that once was; of the unfinished statue, suggesting the splendour that should have been.

Of course this conception must not be used as an excuse for bad workmanship. It is in the essence of the contract, so to speak, that this appeal to the imagination of others only begins to act when the artist himself has taken all the pains he can. It is only the intensity of his imaginative effort which kindles ours into action. And that intensity will, under normal circumstances, have made him work his best. Only it so happens that the greatest imaginings and desires of the human mind are beyond the greatest powers of words or paintings to utter. And the best artist, when he has used the very utmost of his skill, is left at last dependent on the sympathetic imagination of others. If that fails him, he dies with his meaning unexpressed.

It is in this spirit of sympathetic imagination that we should read most ancient traditional books. And, as a matter of fact, we generally do so. They are all markedly imperfect, but we hardly notice the imperfections. How few of us, for instance, ever noticed that there were two different accounts of the Creation in Genesis before we were compelled? How few scholars were troubled by discrepancies between ***Iliad*** I and II? How little we resent the half-inarticulate quality of ancient vocabulary and syntax? Nay, we admire them. For the best things that these books are trying to express are not to be reached by any correct human words. With all the knowledge in the world at our disposal, we must needs sooner or later throw ourselves on the sea of imaginative emotion in order to understand or express these greatnesses. And the reason why we are willing to do so in these cases, and not in others, is, I think, ultimately the intensity of the imagination behind. The driving of Jehu, the weeping face of Helen: these have behind them not the imagination of one great poet, but the accumulated emotion, one may almost say, of the many successive generations who have heard and learned and themselves afresh re-created the old majesty and loveliness. They are like the watchwords of great causes for which men have fought and died; charged with power from the first to attract men's love, but now, through the infinite shining back of that love, grown to yet greater power. There is in them, as it were, the spiritual life-blood of a people. (pp. 251-60)

Gilbert Murray, "The Iliad as a Great Poem," in his The Rise of the Greek Epic, *fourth edition, 1934. Reprint by Oxford University Press, 1960, pp. 238-60.*

J. W. MACKAIL (essay date 1911)

[Mackail was an English critic, biographer, and educator whose books include The Springs of Helicon *(1909) and* Studies in Humanism *(1938). Primarily devoted to the study of Greek and English poetry, Mackail's work displays the critic's scholarly approach to literature and his belief that the development of poetry is an organic process. In the following excerpt, Mackail pronounces the* Iliad *"probably on the whole the greatest poem ever made" and discusses its characterization of women, fire imagery, and "natural magic."]*

[Like Shakespeare's], Homer's women are . . . remarkable; yet one has the feeling throughout that they are only fragments, sparingly used and jealously scrutinised, of a lost world of poetry that may have held figures as great as those of Gudrun and Brynhild, of Imogen or Cleopatra. In the ***Iliad*** and ***Odyssey*** there are only two women in the foremost plane of the action, Andromache and Penelope. Both are vivid and actual, as fully alive as the men among whom they move; yet in both it seems as if the poet made them live almost against his will, or against the will of his audience; as though he would rather have given, or they would rather have had given them, generalised portraits of the faithful wife and affectionate mother. (pp. 33-4)

Through both the ***Iliad*** and the ***Odyssey*** the figure of another woman moves in a sort of golden mist. Helen of Troy has already in them taken the place which is hers for all time, of one set beyond the bounds of mortality, a thing enskied, from whom a fire goes out that devours many, but on whom the fire cannot take hold. Her words over the body of Hector are the high-water mark of the ***Iliad;*** and it is not of Hector that they leave us thinking, but of her. Even in the domestic surroundings of her regained home in Lacedaemon she moves in the same unearthly calm, the white splendour of the Elysian plain which is destined for her final abiding-place, and whose atmosphere she carries about with her even on this earth. All voices, like those of the Trojan elders on the city wall, fall soft when they speak of her. Only from her own lips is any word of blame allowed to reach her. She is the one instance in which the romance of mediaeval Greece has been left in full play. Except with Helen, there is little in Homer of any feeling for women that we should call romantic, or even chivalrous. There is no morbid sentiment about them; but, on the other hand, there is the beginning of that harshness or chilliness which is a characteristic in developed Greek literature. It is one of the touches which make Patroclus different from all the other Achaean captains, that he had tried, clumsily perhaps, but affectionately, to make poor Briseis happy. It sets him on the same plane with Hector. The perfect tact and courtesy of Odysseus to Nausicaa, when he first meets her, as again when he quietly parts from her, hardly touch the edge of chivalrous feeling; and in contrast with them we have his savage burst of anger at Melantho, when he silences her by threatening to have her cut limb from limb—though no doubt she had provoked him beyond bearing and deserved all she got. But perhaps the most touching of all Homer's women is one obscure and unnamed; the poor maid-servant in Ithaca who was weaker than the rest, and had to go on grinding all night to finish her task when the rest of her fellow-servants were asleep. There seems here a touch of something actual that had come to the poet himself and struck sharply through him the sense of the obscure labour and unsung pain that underlie the high pageant of life, war and adventure, the feats and feasts of princes. Perhaps in some Neleid palace, where at a banquet under the blaze of torches he had been singing to lords and ladies, like Demodocus in Phaeacia, of the glorious deeds of men, he had passed out of the darkened hall into the chill of morning; and there, while dawn was yellowing over Mount Latmus, heard a sharp peal of thunder across the Icarian sea, and then from the mill-house in the palace yard the voice of a tired woman over her quern: "They have loosened my knees with cruel toil to grind their barley meal: may this dinner be their last."

On that island amid unsounded seas the waves washed up rough wreckage as well as treasure. Much of the fighting in the ***Iliad,*** or in such parts of the ***Iliad*** as appear to be extraneous to its essential scheme, is of this kind. But it is unsafe to argue that such passages are later accretions. Generally speaking, we cannot safely call any episode a later accretion which does not bear unmistakeable marks of lateness in its language. The author of the ***Iliad*** dealt prodigally with the whole material of the epic cycle, exulting in his riches, and confident, sometimes too much so, of the fusing and assimilating power of his own genius. But it is just this careless magnificence, guided by a lucid though not always a faultless instinct, that has given to the world in the ***Iliad*** what is probably on the whole the greatest poem ever made. Study of Homer from the point of view not of the scholar or commentator, but of the poet—that inarticulate poet whose presence in us makes us love poetry—shows one more and more that what is put in or left out is in nearly all cases put in or left out for valid poetical reasons. (pp. 35-8)

While we may speak thus of the author of the ***Iliad,*** it is true also that the ***Iliad*** is the work of a nation, just as it has been said that the nameless architect of Westminster Abbey was not this man or that, but the people of south-eastern England. Like a great mediaeval church, the Homeric poems embody the work of whole guilds of artists, of whole ages that appreciated art. In this sense the ***Iliad*** is a more artificial poem than the *Aeneid* or the *Paradise Lost,* as Westminster Abbey is than St. Paul's, because its origin was more complex, and its design lived and grew all the time it was being executed, The architect worked on a ground plan determined by existing building. He incorporated much of the earlier structure into his own. Sometimes he pulled down and rebuilt, sometimes he remodelled into his own style or dialect without pulling down. "The singing masons building roofs of gold" were busy under him and about him, altering, extending, enriching. But the finished work burns throughout with the ardour of a single genius.

This ardour is what sets the ***Iliad*** apart from all other poetry. In the fine phrase of Dryden, Homer "sets you on fire all at once, and never intermits his heat.'' The notes of Homer given by Arnold [see 1861 excerpt by Arnold], that he is rapid, plain, direct, noble, are all exactly true of the ***Iliad;*** but together with these qualities is another of at least equal importance, that the whole poem is at a white heat. (pp. 38-9)

The fire of imagination lifts the height and swells the compass of a subject itself curiously contracted. The Wrath of Achilles is but an episode in a single war, as war itself is but an episode in the whole pageant of life. To this limit the subject of the ***Iliad*** is formally restricted in its opening lines; and lest we should lose sight of it, the restriction is as formally repeated in the speech of Zeus just before the crisis of the action, and emphasised still further by the magnificent image immediately following, of the far-travelled man whose mind ranges with the speed of thought over the whole length and breadth of the world. Even good critics have stumbled here, and insisted that the action ought to be carried on to the death of Achilles. The author of the ***Iliad*** may be trusted to have known his own purpose; he certainly could not have stated it more clearly. And indeed it is obvious, if one takes the pains to think the matter out, that the action stops exactly where it should, and that to continue further would have thrown the whole poem out of scale. Doubtless it might have pleased Homer to choose a better subject than that of the ***Iliad,*** or at least a different one; but it is equally certain that it did not please him to do so.

The Wrath burns in a world which it transforms into fire. Nowhere else, except in Dante, does fire so penetrate the whole structure of a poem. It is perpetually present in single phrases or elaborated descriptions; fire blazing in a forest, fire licking up the plain and scorching the river, fire signalling from a besieged town, fire flashing out of heaven, fire leaping on a city of men while the houses crumble away in the roaring furnace, the fire blazing round the head of Achilles by the trenches, the fire that streams all night from the burning of Patroclus, the constant sense of the day coming when holy Troy itself will flare up in the great doom's image. Idomoneus in his richly chased armour is ''like in his strength to fire.'' The Trojan host follows Hector ''even as flame.'' ''Like flame,'' Hector leads them on. In a splendid reduplication of phrase he declares his resolve to face Achilles, ''yes, even though his hands are as fire, though his hands are as fire and his might as flaming iron.'' Four times over the full fury of battle is summed up in one intense line, ''Thus they fought in the body of blazing fire.'' The curtain falls on the slaking of the burning for Hector, ''as far as the strength of the fire had gone,'' with flame-bright wine under the kindling fires of dawn.

The whole ***Iliad*** moves in this element of intense ardour. Ordinary life is going on its course all the while, but we only catch glimpses of it. The description at the end of Book VII. of the chaffering in the Achaean camp between the soldiers and the provision ships from Lemnos gives briefly but vividly enough a picture of the traffic of the everyday world going on alongside of the tragedies of kingdoms and the feats of heroes. Domestic life is absent from the main action except where, as in the Hector and Andromache episode, it is seen lit up by the lurid light of war. The allusions to it are chiefly in similes, so used as to bring the action into relation with an opener, a wider and less intense life. They are like the little bits of lovely rural or domestic background in old Italian pictures. Such are the vignettes of the poor spinning-woman and her children; and of the boys harrying the wasps' nest; or the many pictures drawn from the life of the herdsman or sailor, the hunter, or smith, or ploughman. One of the most remarkable is that of the man sitting, like a Theocritean shepherd, on a cliff-top and gazing over the purple sea to where the horizon melts in haze. The largest and most highly finished is the set of scenes portrayed on the shield of Achilles. They give a picture of the whole world—a world wider than that of the ***Iliad,*** or even than that of the ***Odyssey,*** inasmuch as it includes the whole of ordinary human life. There were wrought the earth, and sky, and sea; the unwearying sun and filling moon and all the stars; cities of men in peace and war, with their weddings, feasts, and lawsuits, their raids and sieges and battles; ploughing and reaping and vintage, river-meadows and hill-pastures, tillage and hunting. All that *Heimskringla,* that round world encircled by the outer seas, lies in cool daylight; the fighting is not a strife of heroes ''mixed with auxiliar gods''; the Ocean-river is not bordered by the groves of Persephone or approached from a witch's island; there is no word of the purpose of God being fulfilled through woes innumerable, or of destruction being spun for men that there might be a song for times to come.

In the main action of the ***Iliad*** the supernatural element is felt everywhere: it even shapes and colours the physical background. It is a land of thunder and earthquakes, of God-haunted mountains and seas. Twice over the sky drizzles blood. The plain of Troy is like an amphitheatre ringed round with awful faces. Before the city with its God-built walls, swept by the winds of the world, gods charge down upon one another in the mêlée, or sit apart watching the battle. From their cloud-capped towers, Zeus on Ida and Poseidon on Samothrace look down into the arena. Silver-shod goddesses rise, like a mist, out of the grey sea. Lemnos is the home not only of the merchants who supply the camp, but of Sleep, the brother of Death. On the crest of Ida, hidden in a golden could that the sun cannot pierce, is a marvellous sub-tropical paradise, where the dew-drenched lotus, crocus, hyacinth do not merely, as in Milton's colder Eden, ''with rich inlay broider the ground,'' but rush out of the divine earth.

Over this scene passes, too often for us to regard it as accidental, a mystery of darkness. Night, of which as a half-personified Power Zeus himself stands in awe, descends upon and involves the action. In the cooler atmosphere of the ***Odyssey*** night is for sleep, or at most for telling tales in the hall of a king's house, or sheltered in a swineherd's cottage from the wintry wind and driving rain. The cresset borne by Athena in the hall at Ithaca to light it up for the moving of the armour is magical, but with no natural magic. But much of the action in the ***Iliad*** is heightened by this sense of natural magic where it takes place in the dark: the troubled council in the Achaean camp and the embassy of Phoenix; the Doloneia, with its perilous night journey, where the thick-muffled silence is broken by the cry of the unseen heron; the coming of the Winds from Thrace to blow all night round the pyre of Patroclus and sink with the sinking flame just before dawn; the visit of Priam to the camp and his return with Hector's body. Even daylight is often obscured by strange mists and supernatural darkness, that now aid and now hinder flight, within which men struggle blindly and unseen. ''Thus fought they,'' about the corpse of Patroclus, ''in the body of fire, nor would you say that either sun or moon yet endured, for in that battle all the captains were wrapt in mist, while over the rest of the field warriors fought in clear air and sharp sunlight, and not a cloud was seen on the land or on the hills.'' From that ''affliction of darkness and battle'' rose the prayer of Aias: ''O our Father, save us from the darkness; give sight to our eyes, and in the light destroy us if thou wilt.''

On this lurid shifting background, now incredibly clear, now wrapped in a pall of darkness, the action burns. The waves of battle surge backward and forward across the plain. Kings and stately women look on from the battlements of the city. Among the dense ranks of spearmen the princes, like knights at Crecy or Roosebek, move ponderously along the fighting line. They are heavily sheathed in bronze plate-armour, with huge crests and immense leathern bronze-clamped pavises, "like towers," reaching from neck to heel. They tilt at one another with long fifteen-foot spears, with sword and mace and battle-axe. Helenus swings a huge Thracian sword, like Durindana or Morglay, that shears away head and head-piece. From behind the knights' pavises the archers, crouching "like a child by its mother," rain their arrows. Teucer, like Einar in Olaf Tryggvesson's last battle, shoots from the side of Aias, striking down man after man, until his bowstring breaks, and he betakes himself to his heavy armour and long bronze-headed spear. The clatter of weapons on plated helms and cheek-pieces resounds like an armourer's forge. Huge stones are hurled as if from perrières by knights who have lost their spears; where one hits, a prince crashes down with a rattle of armour, "like a tower amid the throng of fight." Above all the clash and din rise the voices of the captains, men of great stature and prodigious strength. Some fight in armour splendidly damascened in gold or silver and inlaid with enamel. Achilles can run at full speed in all his battle-gear, a feat like those told of Richard Cœur de Lion. Aias wields a thirty-foot pike at the defence of the ships. "As when winter torrents flow down the mountains to a watersmeet and join their raging floods through the deep ravine"; "as when angry winds shaking a deep wood in the mountain dells clash and shatter the long boughs," so they fight; "and the iron roaring went up to the vault of heaven through the unharvested sky." Here and there, while winged arrows leap from the bowstring and stones clash upon shields, a mailed figure lies still amid the whirl of dust, great and fallen greatly, his feats of knighthood forgotten, in the sleep of bronze. Behind on both sides rises the clatter of chariots and the continuous shouting of the massed soldiery, close-ranked with shield locked in shield: "the sound of the two hosts went up to the firmament and the splendours of God."

Such is the world of the ***Iliad,*** set before us with incomparable fire and splendour by the genius of a great poet; a world as brilliantly coloured as that of Froissart, as tense and vivid as that of Shakespeare. If we ask what relation it has to reality, we raise the whole question of the relation of art to life. The Homeric world is a world imagined by Homer. It is placed in a past time, evidently thought of as distant, though there are no exact marks of chronology any more than there are in the *Morte d'Arthur*. The destruction of the Achaean rampart, after Troy had been left desolate, is a thing long accomplished; "so were Poseidon and Apollo to do in the aftertime." Helen in the ***Iliad,*** Alcinous in the ***Odyssey,*** speak of the whole war of Troy as ordained for a theme for poets of a remote future. But it was not so distant as to be wholly alien from actual life; it was not uninteresting or unintelligible to the poet's audience.

The life of a nation is partly to be sought in the mirror held up to it by its national poetry. But it has another and larger side. In the ***Iliad,*** as in Froissart, we hear little of the common people who were to become the nation of the future, and nothing at all of the gathering forces which were to sweep away the mediaeval world of romance and chivalry as the nine days' torrential rain swept away the Achaean rampart and laid the sand smooth on the beach. The professional minstrel or guild of minstrels is not concerned with common life. The common people in the ***Odyssey,*** the "princely swineherd," Eurycleia the nurse, Melanthius and Melantho, all the rest upon the crowded living canvas, are only studied in their relation to the principal figures; they are an enriched background. In the ***Iliad,*** but for the single burlesqued figure of Thersites, there are none. Whether the Homeric poems took shape at some feudal court like that of the Neleids of Miletus, or in later and more fully Hellenised surroundings, they are in essence court poetry, adapted to the taste of a court, or of a public which took its taste from that of a court. For the under side of that brilliant tapestry we have to turn to Hesiod. (pp. 40-8)

J. W. Mackail, "Homer and the Iliad," in his Lectures on Greek Poetry, *revised edition, Longmans, Green and Co., 1911, pp. 23-48.*

GEORG BRANDES (essay date 1925)

[Brandes was a Danish literary critic and biographer whose extensive writings on such authors as Henrik Ibsen, August Strindberg, and Sören Kierkegaard helped make their works better known outside of Scandinavia. He was one of the first critics to understand and encourage the innovative drama of Ibsen, and he virtually "discovered" Friedrich Nietzsche, providing the first serious critical attention that the German philosopher received. In his major critical work, Main Currents in Nineteenth-Century Literature, *Brandes viewed French, German, and English literary movements as a series of reactions against eighteenth-century thought. Brandes said of himself that he was more than a critic but less than a philosopher. In a letter to him, Neitzsche called Brandes a "missionary of culture." This is perhaps the best definition of Brandes's function within literature. He possessed the ability to view literary movements and the individuals who contributed to those movements within the broader context of virtually all of nineteenth-century literature. In the following excerpt from his* Hellas, *first published in Danish in 1925, Brandes surveys various aspects of Homeric Greece and enumerates the "qualities and abilities" of the Homeric poets.]*

The primitive Greeks were life-loving, highly endowed children. Yet, their main trait is . . . in the fact that we find clearly illustrated the manner in which at first the heroic figure has here suggested the much tried, widely experienced man, who never loses sight of his object, and later the divine figure, characterized by insight and an all-embracing view, pure, radiant and warlike intelligence, merged together and become the central point in Greek life.

All things finally crystallize about the hero, either the brave and high-minded (like Achilles and Hector) or the inventive, cunning, hard-steeled (like Odysseus): the hero attracts the gods to himself, remakes them in his image, and thus creates the graphic arts, sculpture, painting, as well as poetry.

The hero's fundamental trait is that of independence. In Homer, the hero does not fight in the ranks, but alone, in the chariot, or on foot. Neither among the Hellenes nor among the Trojans do we read of any kind of discipline. The poets have described their western Asiatic kinsmen, under the name of Achæans, and we find that among them independence is the source of a constantly renewed individuality. Never do we find a person in Homer who is completely subordinated to the idea of the state, as are the Spartans or Romans.

The hero dares, like Achilles, to blurt out harsh truths to his lord the king and to refuse to give him assistance. He fights even against gods, as Diomedes against Ares, and inflicts wounds upon the gods. The hero lives in a world that has not had much past history, and that has handed down but few depressing

A reconstructed view of Troy from the north. Reproduced by permission of Peter Connolly.

experiences. He is even less burdened with the prescriptions of a clearly formulated morality.

The ideal of the Ionian hero is that of sitting on one's throne as happy as a god, with the eagle, and of drinking life-giving wine in a richly embellished palace, at a groaning board, while a minstrel with his cithara or his lyre sings the hero's deeds.

The hero is not more than human. He may lose courage at times, though he be brave as a rule. The poet knows men and does not depict his heroes as did the Christian romanticists twenty-five centuries later. (pp. 45-6)

Even the bravest of the brave, Ajax, once loses courage and runs away.

In fact, Hector finally becomes so scared that he runs away, thrice making the circuit of Troy, and not stopping until Athene deceives him, in order to have him slain, by declaring that she is his brother coming to his assistance—whereupon she disappears—an action that would be considered quite shabby in the modern world.—Apollo also, on the other hand, behaves quite shabbily in his method of securing the slaying of Patroklos.

Homer knows mass enthusiasms no less than courage in the individual; but he also understands the phenomenon of panic. When the Atreid is pursuing in the ***Iliad,*** the Trojans flee post-haste over the plains before this single man, in order to find shelter behind the walls of the town.

The heroes of that far-off time did not strike attitudes; they remained men, they loved life and feared death. Not considering the world to be evil, and nature corrupt, the Hellene is fully assured of the fact that life is the source of all joys, and nature holy.

It follows that the Greek is not ashamed of his body, not even of the organs that do not serve the spirit. His comedians make merry with these organs without becoming obscene. And young girls marching in the religious procession bear at the head of the train, without embarrassment, the male symbol of fruitfulness.

The advantages of the Greek character lay in an equilibrium that has been abandoned by modern civilization. They never sacrificed this life for the hereafter; they never (except in the crude primitive days of human sacrifices) sacrificed man to divinity.

They did not feel man to be a mere nothing in the presence of divinity. They knew no dogmas, nor had they even—in Homer's day—any science to speak of.

Their advantage in those remote days was to have been the possessors for three thousand years of the most supple, strong, sound, beautiful bodies, fine senses, ready wit, a bright, proud spirit.

While the chief characteristic of Christianity is its preoccupation with death, the Greek regards the hereafter as a bleak land of shades; so we find it always described in Homer. (pp. 47-9)

The Homeric poems, even when they depict the realm of the dead, are not figments of an over-heated imagination, but of resplendent reason. (p. 50)

The Hellene loves life, even though he be not afraid of that which follows it. The death of Socrates is depicted in Plato's *Phaido* without any sentimentality.

Homer's Greeks had the advantage over us of being much younger. In all their mental clarity and sobriety they had the seriousness and fire of youth, but also its enthusiasm and dash. They were not to create tragedy until four hundred years later. Homeric art compared with ours is like a wild flower compared with a cultivated plant, a babbling brook compared with a tinkling fountain.

The fact that desire is evil, and that nature itself induces us to commit sin, would have been an incomprehensible notion to Homer's Greeks. Never would they have thought of worshiping a god by fasting or by refraining from the drinking of wine, or by confessing their transgressions. They do not take crime lightly; but any crime may be expiated. And the Greeks worship the gods by adorning themselves in their finest raiment, and elevating themselves to the divine level to the best of their ability.

To be sure, in ancient days, when the mind was still crude, the gods were worshiped not with the blood of beasts but with the blood of men. In the myths we still find reminiscences of human sacrifices. Agamemnon's offering up of Iphigenia, for example, is somewhat parallel to the Old Testament story of the offering up of Jephtha's daughter, or of Abraham's offering up of Isaac; or in the New Testament, to the sacrifice of Jesus.

We have human sacrifices also in the ***Iliad.*** But it is important to point out the refinement of manners in the poet's day that is here displayed. Achilles offers up twelve Trojan youths on the grave of Patroklos. So ran the legend, such was the ancient custom. Obviously, the poet, in describing this solemn funeral, was obliged to present more than the sacrifice of sheep, oxen and dogs. But he is somewhat embarrassed and is obviously ashamed of this sacrifice of innocent prisoners. And although he frequently devotes a score of lines to depicting a banquet or a rare beaker, although he never neglects to describe the course of each thrust into the body of an opponent and the nature of each wound, the slaughter of the twelve aristocratic young men gets but a single line. First we are told that Achilles sacrificed two dogs. Then follows the statement:

> And twelve valiant sons of great-hearted Trojans he slew with the sword,

Whereupon the poet adds:

> for he devised mischief in his heart.

This progressive refinement of manners, paralleled by an ennobling in the characters, may be traced in many passages in the Homeric poems.

Very probably the first story was to the effect that Achilles did not drag Hector's corpse attached to his chariot, but the living body of Hector. This would agree very well with his outburst:

> Would that my heart's desire could so bid me
> myself to carve and eat raw thy flesh, for the
> evil thou hast wrought me.

This mode of action on the part of Achilles is still recorded in Sophocles. Later he drags only the dead body. But even this procedure was much condemned by the Homeric poets. His action is called "shameful and shocking." The following disapproving words are also encountered:

> For Achilles had not a heart that was soft and
> easily touched, but his wrath was not difficult
> to arouse.

And yet, Achilles is one of the foremost heroes in the ***Iliad.*** During the many years, however, which elapsed before the ***Iliad*** and the ***Odyssey*** attained their final form, the view of life had changed somewhat. At a very late day we even find the interpolation of a conciliation between Achilles and Priam.

At first, women probably were the passive subjects of purchase, robbery and exchange. The wooer gave *hedna* for the bride. As is indicated by the use of the word *alfesiboia,* the woman's value was expressed in a number of cows; of course, money was unknown. It is a far cry from this condition to the refinement which we encounter in an Andromache, Helen, Nausikaa, or Penelope.

Originally, the divine couples, as well as the princely couples, were brother and sister. Later this condition is felt to be something not to be emphasized in those passages in the poems in which they embrace each other. (pp. 50-4)

Child-like as the poet none the less is, he not only delights in every beautiful object in nature, but particularly in every example of artificial imitation, especially in life-like counterfeits, such as that of the golden dogs before the palace of Alcinous, who know nothing of age of death, or in the automatons in human form, constructed by Hephaistus, on which Hephaistus supports himself as he walks.

Homer knows no real sculpture, but only metal work embossed and chiseled like the shield of Achilles. Casting in molds was not invented until three hundred years later, in 640 B.C. He knows nothing of work in marble, as he knows nothing of money or written characters.

Values were not measured in money but in oxen. When Glaukos and Diomedes learn, in the heat of battle, that their fathers were guest-friends to each other, and when these two adversaries thereupon exchange their armor, we read:

> But now Zeus son of Kronos took from Glaukos
> his wits, in that he made exchange with
> Diomedes Tydeus' son of golden armor for
> bronze, the price of five score oxen for the price
> of nine.

Writing was obviously as little known as money. To be sure, we have found remnants of picture-writing and character-writing on the island of Crete, dating from the pre-Hellenic period, and the Phœnician writing is also quite old. But the personages of Homer know no writing. The only passage in which anything resembling writing is mentioned is found in the much (and later) patched Sixth Book of the ***Iliad*** where Proitus tries to have Bellerophon slain by handing him a sad piece of news:

> graving in a folded tablet many deadly things,
> and bade him show these to Anteia's father,
> that he might be slain.

It could hardly have been a letter, and besides, the passage may have been inserted at a later date. (pp. 56-7)

While we may therefore not definitely infer anything from the fact that the poems themselves do not mention writing, we find that they were left to the mercies of oral tradition for centuries, since memories were then strong, and we know that the Greek alphabet was not finally completed until half a thousand years later, namely, in 403 B.C. And even when not a few were already able to read, preference was probably given to a recitation of the poems, with musical accompaniment, rather than to a reading of them in private.

Dispassionate though the epic mode of presentation may be, we nevertheless find a passion for the art of poetry breaking forth at times. Flaubert saw in all the events of life illusions destined to serve as objects for description. Homer already had this feeling. (pp. 59-60)

It is reasonable to ask what were the qualities and abilities with which the Homeric poets approached their task of representation.

In the first place, we may mention the uniformity of their culture, the clarity and transparence of their language. They were so fortunate as to possess a language without words borrowed from foreign languages, and which therefore was understood by all. Their civilization was original, while ours is a patchwork. A scientific monograph written in a modern language is a hodge-podge of the vulgate tongue, embellished with corrupt Greek and medieval Latin. Furthermore, their art was the product of a uniform civilization, while even the most splendid of the modern arts have declined to be a mere *mixtum compositum*. Michelangelo shapes a Christ who looks like a Jupiter; Correggio's angels are like little pages undressed; Shakespeare's Romeo is at bottom an Englishman; Goethe creates a Ferrara which is more like Weimar; Racine produces an Achilles wearing a Seventeenth Century wig.

In the most ancient Greek art, we already find that uniformity of structure which is a condition for true civilization.

In the first place, these poets have a sober gift of observation, an acute sense of reality. Homer has all the knowledge of his time, being thoroughly acquainted with the working of the soil, the chase, the art of the armorer, navigation, weaving, the construction of houses, strategy and tactics, medicine. We even find mention in the ***Iliad*** of a female physician, the blonde Agamede:

> And she knew all the drugs that the wide earth nourished.

It is characteristic of the high civilization in the ***Iliad*** that we do not find a single treatment of wounds by means of magic incantations. Arrows or darts are drawn out, the flow of blood is stopped, salves are applied, the pain of the victim is appeased with wine or with mixed beverages. There is no trace of superstitious practises. So far had enlightenment advanced among the circles of the nobility. (pp. 60-2)

The vision of these poets, and the great extent of their familiarity with every phenomenon in nature, with the sky, the earth, and the sea, with the entire animal kingdom, with all the vicissitudes of the chase and warfare, are revealed in the celebrated Homeric figures of speech, which are very numerous, particularly in the ***Iliad,*** and which are always developed into complete miniatures, while the element of similarity is relegated entirely to the background, sometimes almost forgotten, in the poet's delight in the process of detailed description. The poets of the ***Iliad*** see far more clearly than they think. In the ***Odyssey,*** comparisons are far more impressive, but relatively few in number.

An example of a figure of the first kind is the following, from the ***Iliad:***

> Even as the harvesters, advancing to meet each
> other over a rich man's land, lay low the grain
> in their course, either the wheat or the barley,
> while sheaf falls after sheaf, even so the Achaians
> and Trojans rushed forth to encounter each other.

The image of the action of the harvester is carried out with care and objectiveness, but the comparison is not a striking one. (pp. 62-3)

The gift of observation in the Homeric poems is combined with an absolutely surprising ability to create individual persons.

In the ***Iliad*** alone, among the women, we have the clearly defined pictures of Andromache, Hekuba and Helen, and among the men, there are splendid objective pictures of Achilles, Hector, Paris, Odysseus, Thersites, and the three brilliantly outlined old men, Nestor, Phoinix, Priam.

Less consistent, in the various books of the ***Iliad,*** is the figure of Agamemnon. In the First and Eleventh he is manly, though unjust and tyrannical; in the Second, Ninth, and Fourteenth, he seems devoid of character. No clearly defined physiognomy may be attached to Ajax of Diomedes. (pp. 65-6)

The action of the ***Iliad*** occupies barely five days; that of the ***Odyssey*** about thirty. The ***Iliad*** contains more than fifteen thousand verses, the ***Odyssey*** more than twelve thousand. With its many interpolations, the ***Iliad*** is rather extensive, and yet, it is quite short as compared with the Oriental epics; the *Mahabharata,* the ancient Indian epic, has one hundred thousand couplets.

There are detached sections in the ***Iliad,*** like the passage containing the list of ships, which are not in their proper places. The description of the shield of Achilles is also an interpolation, drawn with great care, with a delight in nature and in art. In order to afford an occasion for this description, one of the poets was obliged to have Achilles lose the shield, in other words, lend Patroklos his arms, a childish and awkward notion. Patroklos, thus accoutered, is to frighten the Trojans. But Homer constantly emphasizes the closeness with which the cuirass fits the fighter's body. Now Achilles is of gigantic stature; how can his armor fit Patroklos? And Achilles does not state that he recognizes his weapons on Hector's body, which would surely have doubled his rage. Patroklos's borrowing of the weapons is in reality of no significance. It is the subject of a silly masquerade. Patroklos is a deciding element in the conflict because he leads fresh troops to battle, not because he is in disguise, an incident which is introduced merely in order to produce an occasion for inserting a description of the new shield forged by Hephaistus for Achilles.

When I was a young man, and anyone requested me to read aloud something of recent interest, I used to enjoy reading—as a joke—the Ninth Book of the ***Iliad,*** the message to Achilles, which I love and esteem. I was then of the opinion that this book was a portion of the oldest section of the ***Iliad.*** I am no longer of that opinion. The fact that this book was added later is clearly apparent if only from the situation that Achilles is there promised everything which he later, in the Eleventh Book, desires to obtain from Agamemnon, and hopes to get from him in the Sixteenth Book. In other words, Achilles, in these books, is unaware of the fact that he has already definitely rejected the offer of the Atreid.

The Ninth Book presents instructive prospects. Behind the poem concerning the rage of Achilles we glimpse an older, perhaps symbolical, poem on the rage of Meleager.

The fact that the aged Phoinix did not originally participate in this mission is revealed in the no less than six passages, in which the dual form is retained instead of the plural, although there are three messengers. (pp. 66-8)

The famous illustration of the poet's powers of characterization is the celebrated parting scene between Andromache and Hector. It is in the Sixth Book of the ***Iliad,*** having been obviously put in the wrong place in the final arrangement. It should be at the beginning of the Twenty-second Book, in which Hector is slain.

The entire Sixth Book, in spite of many beautiful portions, is merely a piece of patchwork. It is in this book that we suddenly find a temple to Athene, with a seated statue of the goddess, in the castle of Ilion, a temple mentioned nowhere else by either the ***Iliad*** or the ***Odyssey,*** which speak only of altars. In the ***Odyssey,*** Athene helps to get the wooden horse up the mound of Ilion, but no temple is mentioned. The temple is a later addition.

But what a breach this makes in the lovely scene in which little Astyanax, in the arms of his nurse, is frightened by the plumes of Hector's helmet and must put the helmet down on the ground! And how dreadful is an interruption, introduced by the improper placing of the scene, into Andromache's eternal words:

> Nay, Hector, thou art to me father and lady
> mother, yea and brother, even is thou art my
> goodly husband. Come now, have pity and abide
> here upon the tower.
>
> (pp. 70-1)

In Homer, experience is that of an intelligent child, the mode of expression os that of primitive man, the mode of feeling is simply human. We are made to sympathize with the embittered Achilles, with the fleeing Hector, with the irregularities of Helen, and yet do not lose sight of our ideals of courage, mercy, chastity without prudery. The poets seem to have the gift of sympathizing with both sides. For that reason, the Greeks, four centuries later, became the creators of the tragedy. (pp. 72-3)

Georg Brandes, "Homer," in his Hellas: Travels in Greece, *translated by Jacob W. Hartmann, Adelphi Company, 1926, pp. 13-74.*

C. M. BOWRA (essay date 1930)

[Bowra, an English critic and literary historian, was considered among the foremost classical scholars of the first half of the twentieth century. He also wrote extensively on modern literature, particularly modern European poetry, in studies noted for their erudition, lucidity, and straightforward style. In the following excerpt, Bowra analyzes the ways in which Homer both borrowed from and modified the conventions of the past heroic age he depicted in the Iliad.*]*

Homer found the subject of the ***Iliad*** in the doings of an age of heroes. For him the world had changed since those spacious days, and the race of the heaven-born had perished. The world of his similies is different from the world of his story, and he is fully conscious that his contemporaries are weaker than the great men of old. He knows that men . . . cannot do what his heroes did. Between him and them everything has grown more commonplace, and the golden past is dead with Agamemnon in the grave. This gulf between Homer and his subject has often been overlooked, but it is of great importance for a proper appreciation of his poetry. It is, especially, one of the many differences between him and most early poetry. Neither the author of *Beowulf* nor the author of the *Song of Roland* shows any such feeling that his own days were vastly inferior to those of which he writes. Perhaps they thought so, but both are silent on any such sense of inferiority. Even the marvels and miracles which they describe seem to belong to a world which still existed for them. The comet which appeared to the Conqueror would have seemed to Turoldus no less a wonder than the darkening of the earth at Roland's death. And the author of *Beowulf,* full of a newly-discovered Christianity, must have believed that the world was full of things passing his understanding. But Homer, whose story makes horses speak and the gods walk on the earth, avoids all traces of miracle in his similes and seems to have lived in a world not unlike our own. He does not, like Shakespeare, create the heroes of his fancy to match the great men around him. For these he seems to have felt more affection than reverence, and he made his ideal world out of the stuff of story and song.

Homer lived in a generation later than the heroic age, but his creative imagination is so powerful that in his company we are normally among the thoughts and actions which belong to such periods in human history. Nor can we properly understand the ***Iliad*** unless we know something of the thoughts and ideals underlying an age of great, heroic activity. At the back of the ***Iliad*** lies that peculiar notion of honour which is developed in the camp and on the battle-field. This notion has many sides, and in later literature it has been enormously complicated by the notions of medieval chivalry. But in Homer it is comparatively simple in its outlines. The sense of personal honour means that the special reputation of every soldier is of enormous importance to him. He may not and cannot endure slight or insult. His reputation is of the utmost moment, and he will die rather than lose it. This partly explains why Achilles is unable to endure the slights inflicted on him by Agamemnon. His personal reputation is of more account than his loyalty to his colleagues. What holds good of Achilles is true in a lesser degree of several others. Sthenelus cannot endure to be chidden by Agamemnon. Paris refuses to give up Helen, when the Trojans request him. Hector refuses to listen to Priam when he begs him to take shelter in Troy from Achilles. This is the same spirit as that in which Roland refuses to blow his horn, and prefers death with honour to safety and even to victory. So far Homer is in the best traditions of heroic story. The pride of his princes yields in nothing to the pride of Beowulf or Sigurd. But lying as he does outside the actual age of heroes, he has modified the heroic point of view in some directions, and here he is sharply distinguished from the writers of early Teutonic or French epic. In other early epics honour is all that matters, and defeat is nothing compared with it. The result is a magnificent sense of ultimate failure, which is of no importance provided death be found gloriously against overwhelming odds. The *Fight at Maldon* is a glorification of defeat, and the *Song of Roland* ends on a note of unwearying struggle against unconquerable forces. The *Edda* poems are full of the same proud spirit. Sigurd, Gudrun, Brynhild are in turn beaten and brought to disaster. But the ***Iliad*** is not like these. Even in the death of Hector, a theme worthy of early Germanic poetry, we do not feel a savage exultation in death just because it is glorious. Homer feels differently, and he makes defeat more tragic than glorious. Hector's death is an irreparable loss. It means the fall of Troy, the enslavement of Andromache, the misery of Astyanax. The pitiful side of it is what concerns Homer even more than the heroic. Hector dies magnificently, but his glory is no comfort to his defenceless family and friends. Still less has the fate of Achilles the grandeur we find in the death of Roland or the unabating toils of Charlemagne. His heroic prowess is important, but it is not the most important thing about him. Instead of pride in his death we are presented with pity for the shortness of his days and the waste into which his anger leads him. The other old epics are tragic enough in their themes, but they combine their sense of tragedy with a feeling that glory triumphs over death. Homer has no such feeling. His heroes die as heroes should, but their death is an irreparable and uncompensated disaster. We do not even get the comfort, which Shakespeare gives us, that death is peace after the torments of this life. Homer might indeed have felt that "the rest is silence," but to him the words would have meant lamentation and not comfort.

This acute sense of the tragedy of death distinguishes Homer from the age of which he wrote. When battle is an everyday affair and death is always present to their thoughts, men lose their sense of its wastefulness and horror. It is magnified into great glory or reduced to the dull level of common things. But for Homer death was a thing of horror, not "a good end to the long, cloudy day," but the lament of souls leaving their manhood and their youth. This melancholy view was common to most Greeks. Even the most mystical of them found little lasting comfort in the thought of islands beyond the Western Sea or an everlasting spring below the earth. But it is certainly surprising that Homer, writing of an age of heroes, never felt the glamour of defeat and death. The reason for this failure, if it can be called a failure, seems to be twofold. In the first place he is severed from the heroic age, and he views it in retrospect with the eyes of a man used to other things. The heroic view is possible only for men who know the fierce joy of battle and the splendour of looking death in the face. Homer must have lived in quieter times. The great outburst of the Greek peoples over the Mediterranean had spent its force, and the Ionian colonists were settling down to the long task of creating civilization again. Under such conditions much of the heroic outlook would be lost, and its place taken by an outlook more humane and more full of pity. But there is also a second reason. The medieval epics are full of the great struggle between Christians and Pagans. Inspired by the Crusades their writers are full of the overpowering justice of the Christian cause. For it men willingly lay down their lives, because it is of more importance than they are, and to die for it is to go to Paradise. When Roland dies, angels carry him to heaven, but Hector's body is maltreated by Achilles and thrown to the dogs. Christianity provided a consolation such as Homer never knew, abating the tragedy of death, and giving consolation in the worst disaster. Nor can Homer's heroes find a stern Stoic pleasure in dying for a cause of paramount importance. When Patroclus dies, it is for fair-haired Helen's sake. Even Hector, though he dies for Troy, is so great a loss that for the moment Troy seems little beside him. And what is more significant, Homer's fatalism forecasts the fall of Troy, whatever happens, and we know that Hector's death is only part of the foreordained scheme of destruction. Even in the Icelandic poems, which know little of the consolations of Christianity, the view of death is different from this. There is nothing more terrible than the speechless grief of Gudrun over Sigurd's body, but the Icelandic poets do not elaborate the horrors of death as Homer does, and we are confronted only with the bare fact. Homer belongs to a more sophisticated stage of thought, when horror can be abated by lyrical emotion, and a splendour of poetry cast round what is otherwise stark and almost unendurable.

It might be expected that the ***Iliad,*** being cast in a tragic mould, would have no place for comedy, and it is commonly assumed that the high seriousness of a heroic age leaves no room for laughter. But the ***Iliad*** has its moments of comedy, and these have often been thought to represent a later period than most of the poem, when themes once respected are turned to mockery. If this were true, these comic elements would be another of Homer's departures from the true character of the heroic age. But such a judgement certainly needs considerable modification. Though there is no trace of comedy in *Beowulf* or the *Song of Roland,* there are definite traces of it in other heroic poems. The *Song of William,* a French epic as old and in some ways as noble as the *Song of Roland,* has as one of its heroes Rainouart, who is a forerunner of Porthos in his size, simplicity, and engaging naturalness. Nor is heroic humour confined to men. In the *Edda* poems it is applied to the gods. In the *Lokasenna* Loki taxes the gods of Asgard with their weaknesses, and scores good debating points at their expense.

So Homer's humour is not essentially unheroic. He reserves it chiefly for his gods, as we have seen, but he is not above making gentle fun of his heroes. He can only mean us to laugh when Glaucus gets the worst of his exchange of armour with Diomedes. He may even aim at a much grimmer humour in some of his battle scenes, when Mydon, wounded by Antilochus, falls from his chariot and stays standing on his head in the deep sands, or when Cebriones drops and Patroclus compares him to a diver looking for oysters. Such bitter jesting is natural enough in the mouth of a hero. There are, too, the semi-humorous characters, Nestor, with his inopportune garrulity and embarrassment in battle, his sly advice to his son in the chariot race and fuss over the result, or Aias with his obstinate courage and slowness, like the grand fools of the French epic. The humour with which Homer sometimes views his heroes is different both in quantity and in quality from that in which he treats his gods. It is never more than a benevolent tolerance of some amiable human weaknesses, but when he makes fun of the gods he gets very near to farce. . . . They approximate to the spirit in which Loki mocks the Norse gods and belong to the best traditions of a heroic age, which has so high a sense of the dignity of man that it can afford to make fun of the gods. This may seem a paradox, and indeed it is one. But it is none the less true. The heroic standards of honour were so high that they revealed the weaknesses of theologies older than themselves, and the natural result was that the gods were made figures of fun. Such an attitude could only come at the end of a heroic age. The *Edda* poems, despite their simplicity and strength, cannot be earlier than the ninth and tenth centuries. They belong to a time when Icelandic society had standardized its values and was maintaining its stories in the face of a changing world. Such a standardization meant that the intellect was fully and freely at work on old material, and primitive conceptions of the gods were bound to come in for some criticism. In the ages of chivalry and romance, laughter plays little part in poetry. It tends to spoil the elegance of a gesture or to cast doubt on a nice point of honour. But the men of a heroic age are so natural and so sure of themselves that they can afford to laugh, even at what they hold solemn and sacred.

This intellectual honesty and clarity is common both to Homer and to the Icelandic poets, and it is fundamentally a quality of the heroic age. In Greek literature, because of Homer's example, it persists until it is overlaid by rhetoric and sentimentality, but even in the late evening of Greek poetry it is still noticeable and characteristic. It is indeed a heroic quality, and it has its roots in that conception of human dignity which thinks a man too great to need the embellishments of adventitious posturing. It saves Homer from the romantic notions which turned the French epic into the artificial romance of the thirteenth century, and which even in Chaucer sometimes lend unreality to the story. The honesty of the great early epics falls between the childish simplicity of the folk-tale and the artificiality of the chivalrous romances. Homer's intellectual honesty is fundamental to him. He never strains his points or seeks to achieve a melodramatic effect. In the ***Iliad,*** where his theme is tragic, it makes his whole poem entirely serious in tone. The comic intervals are only intervals. They do not affect the fundamental character of the poem. Homer knows nothing of either irony or fustian. His seriousness differs from that of later Greek poetry because it is the seriousness of an age and not of an individual. Sappho and Alcaeus, Aeschylus and Sophocles, have the same candour and sincerity, but they set the impress of their personalities on everything they write, and they achieve their effects because of their remarkable individualities rather than from any qualities held in common with their contemporaries. Even Pindar, who took so much for granted, was more conscious than Homer that his views were the only views that mattered. And Euripides, who lived in doubt, was quite uncertain what he really felt. In particular Homer accepts without any reservations the heroic code of honour, and his view of it is hardly different from that held by other heroic poets. . . . [A man's] life is in battle, and for the risks of battle his whole life must be prepared. Hence all Homer's heroes are brave. Even Paris, idler though he is, is stung into courage by Hector's words. The gods may cry from pain, but men take their wounds without flinching. But courage is not enough. Battle demands that men must stand together, and the central tenet of Homeric morality [*aidos*] is based on this need. . . . Because of it men refrain from excessive cruelty, and help each other in their needs. This quality which Homer gives to his heroes is particularly noticeable in the ***Iliad*** itself. He does not spare us horrors—they are part of his tragic scheme—but he is careful never to condone acts of injustice or of cruelty. The ***Iliad*** is profoundly moral, just because Homer has absorbed the morality of the heroic age. To claim that this singleness of moral outlook is the work of continual expurgation is to misunderstand the temper of an age of heroes. Such an age has its own high standards based on a man's sense of his own dignity. They differ, as might be expected, from other systems of morality, but they are not less exalted. Homer's ethics, though taught by Athenian educators, are not the ethics of Periclean Athens. For him the standard is the individual, but for Pericles it is the city. Of national or racial boundaries he takes little heed. It does not matter that Hector is a barbarian, provided he behaves as a true soldier. Nor has Homer the Athenian view of women, based on their position in an all-absorbing state. His individualism is perfectly logical, and he treats Helen and Andromache with the seriousness and understanding which he gives to Achilles. They have their part in life, and that is enough for him, just as the Icelandic poets were content to portray with complete candour and dignity their tragic heroines, Gudrun and Brynhild. The heroic age honoured its women and gave them power. So Homer was saved from making them too womanly, as Euripides sometimes did, or from raising them to that sublime selflessness to which Sophocles raised Antigone. Still less has Homer any sympathy with those waves of self-denial and puritanism which occasionally swept over later Greece. Such eccentricities are alien to the spirit of an heroic age. The Trojan War was fought for a woman's sake, and over a woman Achilles quarrelled with Agamemnon. The facts of sex are frankly stated, and there is no glorification of purity or self-abnegation. The sword that lay between Tristram and Iseult is unheard of in Homer. But love plays a small part in the story, and though this may be due partly to the exigencies of camp life, it is due much more to heroic standards of conduct. In the *Song of Roland* there is hardly a mention of *la belle Aude,* though she is Oliver's sister and Roland's betrothed, and Beowulf's wife rests on a conjecture made in a single line. Before love became a romantic ideal for which men were ready to undergo any privation and undertake any adventure, it was held below the true dignity of a fighting man. The French romances combined the amatory ideals of Provence with the martial ideals of Normandy by creating the conception of chivalry, which made the beautiful woman the judge of honour and prowess. But in true heroic poetry this combination does not exist, and love is kept out. This is not easy in the story of a war fought about a woman, but Homer's skill is nowhere more apparent than where in a few lines he shows how men can fight about Helen. In the scene on the wall there is no trace of erotic sentimentality such as we might find in the French romances. There is the single wonderful touch of the old men finding it no matter for indignation that men should fight about her. (pp. 234-42)

The dignity which excluded any detailed treatment of love excluded other less interesting themes. Some critics complain that Homer is lacking in those scenes of brutality and bestiality such as we might hope to find in a primitive epic. They are to be found in Hesiod, why not in Homer? We might answer, for the same reason that they are found in the Old Testament but not in the old Germanic or French epics. The audience which likes horrors for their own sake is out of touch with the ideals of martial heroism. Soldiers normally see enough of horrors in their work not to want to hear more about them. But the explanation lies deeper than that. The love of horrors and obscenities lies outside the code of manners common in a heroic age. The great emphasis on personal dignity forbids any lowering of human stature by such concessions to human weakness. This does not mean that poets who write of heroic themes must entirely eschew anything horrible or disgusting. The wide scope of their stories makes such themes sooner or later inevitable. But when they come, they are either treated hastily or made the subject of tragic emotions. The saga no doubt had its crudities, and they were essential to the story, but decency forbade that the audience should be titillated by a detailed exposition of them. When Phoenix tells how he obeyed his mother and slept with his father's concubine, he says [it] simply . . . and leaves it at that. Only an age sure of its standards could achieve such a simplicity with no attempt at palliation or lubricious detail. In the heat of battle it is natural that soldiers should want to strip the dead and even to mutilate corpses. The first of these, however, was not well thought of. Achilles thought it wrong to strip Eetion, and when stripping takes place, the poet hurries over it. Mutilation of the dead was a worse offence. . . . [His] desire to maltreat Hector's body was part of the moral degradation of Achilles, and . . . the poet saves him from putting his threats into effect. But in one place in the saga it seems to have been too difficult for the poet to subdue the horror. When Hector dies, the Achaeans plunge their spears into his body. The scene is full of tragic power and pity. The poet makes no attempt to justify the wanton exultation over the dead. He just describes the scene briefly and passes on to the worse things in store. On the other hand, when such themes were absolutely essential to the main plot, Homer is not ashamed of mentioning them, but he treats them in a moral and even tragic way. In particular this comes out in the account of Achilles, whose every lapse from heroic virtue is a new chapter in his tragedy, and whose failures, though perfectly understood, are never condoned. Apart from him hardly any hero fails in the heroic standards of behaviour. It is true that in the battle scenes there are many incidents which shock the sensitive conscience. But the heroic age felt no disgust at them. To kill your man quickly and well was a warrior's business, and there is no reason to think that Homer did not share the heroic view. Like the great poet that he was, he lamented the loss of life and youth, but he hardly seems to have felt it wrong to kill or be killed in battle. Even the killing of Dolon after he has asked for mercy does not receive his condemnation. Dolon was a spy, and there is no reason to believe that the Homeric age was kinder to spies than the twentieth century. Such an execution might be unpleasant, but Dolon was not entitled to the respect due to an enemy who fought in open battle. His action excluded him from the society of honourable men, and he was killed at once for it. In the same way the traitor Ganelon is torn to pieces by horses for his treachery, and that is the end of him. The heroic code was severe to those who did not accept its standards, and they could expect no mercy.

This code of behaviour seems to have been accepted by Homer without limitations, and it is the common code of all heroic ages. It lauds the virtues of loyalty, generosity, and courage, and it deplores meanness, cowardice, and treachery. In its own way it knows mercy, and Homer's characters are more merciful than those of the Athenian tragedians. Or rather he shrinks from themes which they treated, such as the suicide of Aias or the death of Pentheus. His standards are not theirs, because his audience was stricter in its taste and delicacy than the Athenian democracy, and he shared the taste of his time. This moral responsibility, so often absent from the Old Testament and even at times from Shakespeare, is an aristocratic virtue, derived from a high sense of dignity and decency. It had to cater for men used to privilege and responsibility, not for a Semitic populace trained to suffering, nor for the jaded or primitive tastes of the groundlings whom Shakespeare despised and placated. Hesiod's poor farmers may have liked crude tales, but Homer's audience was bred to better things and had no use for them. If the ***Iliad*** had really been expurgated, as is claimed, we should not have this surprising consistency of moral outlook. We might have in some ways more noble actions, but the morality of the heroic age would have suffered in the process, and it is precisely this which Homer gives us. He himself may well have rejected earlier versions of his story, which revolted his conscience or were unsuited to the ethical taste of his age. It is more than likely that in the old saga Achilles really mutilated Hector's body. But the credit for the far nobler story in the ***Iliad*** must be given not to some anonymous expurgator, but to the creative genius and moral sensibility of Homer.

We have assumed that Homer wrote for an aristocratic class. Such a view needs development and moderation, and is liable to serious misconception. Homer's heroes indeed are all princes. The only member of the populace is Thersites, who is a figure of contempt and scorn. Dolon perhaps may be classed with him, and he too meets a spy's death after a short career of undignified ambition. Of the multitudes who die in battle for their leaders we hear little. Their deaths are as unrecorded as the deaths of the twenty thousand men who died with Roland at Roncesvalles. On the other hand Homer knew and loved humble men and women. In his similes there are many mentions of simple people—shepherds and cowherds, poor women and children. He excluded them from the main current of his poem, not because he was not interested in them but because a heroic age finds its heroes in men who have power and the opportunities of using it. On such men attention is focused, because they alone can fully realize the heroic ideal in adventure and the struggle against great odds. For the poet there is, too, another reason. He has to select his characters, and naturally he selects those whose condition makes them take part in great undertakings. It must not be deduced from this that he only cares for the great. His similes prove the contrary, and, as W. P. Ker well pointed out, in an age like that in the poems there was no essential difference between the activities of a prince and those of his followers. The Homeric king is the type of all his subjects. Like him they pass a large part of their life in the camp or on the sea. Their only pleasures are of the simplest, like his. They share his risks and discomforts, and they share too his ideas and outlook. In Thersites we get the beginning of a new order of things. He is conscious of a gap between the ruler and the ruled, and he has a sense of injury and injustice. . . . Homer, in this as in other ways, comes at the end of the heroic age. He knew that the conventions which sustained it were beginning to be broken, and, though he himself sympathized with the older order, he was honest enough to record the first advent of the new.

Although Homer lived at the end of the heroic age, and perhaps outside it, it was for him perfectly real. Even if he created it out of saga and story, he must have believed that every word they told him was true. He gives us the impression that though things have changed for the worse, the world of his poem is perfectly natural and real. This sense of reality is rare in all poetry, and it is particularly rare in epic poetry. For some reason or other epic poets are seldom wholly persuaded that things are or were just as they describe them. Milton's imagination fails when he creates a cosmogony out of Homer and Virgil, or when he struggles to expound the mysteries of godhead. Virgil, who is so true and intimate in all that concerns the emotions, lacks conviction when he deals with his minor characters or with the heroic prowess of Aeneas in war. The Italian poets of the Renaissance, who understood chivalry and elegance, are frankly cynical in their imitations of antiquity. Nor do even earlier poets always achieve a true and convincing vision of their subjects. The author of *Beowulf* is not quite certain whether Grendel's parent is male or female, and his imagination totters before the description of a waterfall. Only perhaps in Dante and Icelandic poetry do we get that circumstantial reality which carries conviction in every part of the poem. To this select company Homer belongs. He knows his characters and the world they live in. His landscape of Troy may perhaps be less detailed than Dante's vision of Malebolge, but it is perfectly natural and vivid. Even his minor characters have their family connexions and personal histories. He makes us believe in Axylus who lived by the road-side at Arisbe and entertained the passers-by, or Euphorbus, with his peculiar method of doing his hair, or Simoeisius, who was bred on Ida to look after flocks but did not repay his parents for his upbringing. How much more real and convincing these characters are than Virgil's "fortemque Gyan fortemque Cloanthum." They have that personal touch which endears them to us and stirs the curiosity, just as we are interested in the delicate white hands of the Archbishop Turpin, or those friends of Dante whom inflexible Justice put in Hell. This sense of reality comes out particularly when Homer treats of marvels. Here his method differs from Dante's, whose pictorial imagination is so vivid that he creates scenes as if he were really a spectator of them, the man whom his contemporaries thought had been in Hell.

Homer, however, states them with such simplicity that it is impossible not to accept them as facts. . . . Homer and Dante resemble one another in their perfect sincerity in dealing with the objects of their imagination. This sincerity saves them from exaggeration and from vagueness. It is when a poet wants to say something fine and does not quite know what it is, that he lapses into one or the other of these traps. The great Elizabethans, despite their manifold and splendid virtues, sometimes aimed beyond experience and found only chaos. Homer, sure of his traditional material, set down what his clear vision saw and made his marvels credible.

Homer's vivid intelligence found interest in many different things, and this wide curiosity accounts for one of his notable characteristics, his freedom from melancholy. In much early verse there is a brooding sense of futility and despair. The note of *Vanitas vanitatum* echoes through *Beowulf* and even through the *Edda* poems. Nor is such melancholy hard to understand. Heroic life is short and perilous. Its greatest prizes can only be won at the price of death, and for the undistinguished life is full of dangers for which there is not even the consolation of glory. This fundamental melancholy is different from the true tragic temper. For Shakespeare or for Sophocles tragedy helped to enhance the magnificence of the fleeting and defeated present. But the real pessimist feels that even this, too, is futile and purposeless. Such an attitude is not a modern creation. It is as old as *Ecclesiastes* or Theognis, but it owes nothing to Homer. His conception of life is simple and tragic, but not pessimistic. He hardly believes in life beyond the grave, and for this very reason he attaches more importance to life in this world. Generation succeeds generation like the leaves in spring, but the real importance of human life is not affected by this at all. The famous words of Glaucus are only a prelude to a tale of Bellerophon's heroism, and this is the key to Homer's attitude. It is the heroism that matters, and man being mortal has more chance of glory than the immortal gods. The only real pessimist in the ***Iliad*** is Achilles, who doubts the value of heroism, and complains that in the end the brave man and the idler find the same fate. But Achilles is the victim of passion, even of obsession, and his despair is part of his lapse from true nobility. Hector provides the right corrective to him. In the beautiful scene with Andromache he is not deluded by any false hopes of the future. But he never falters in his conviction that what he does is the right thing to do. Even when Achilles pursues him with certain death, in his moment of doubt and indecision he knows that it is best to face his adversary and kill him or be killed. This is not the decision of a desperate man, but of one who knows what his task is and does not shrink from it. What holds for Hector holds for the other heroes. From none of them goes up the cry that their efforts are to no purpose and not worth making. The absence of this note of despair is remarkable. In their different ways both Sophocles and Euripides at times give way to it. It is the burden of some of the

An illustration of Briseis and Phoenix.

finest words written by Shakespeare and by Pindar. It is the cry of Cassandra as she goes to her doom in the *Agamemnon,* and of Macbeth when he hears that his wife is dead. But in the ***Iliad*** for all its sorrow and suffering this despair hardly exists. The heroes themselves do not feel it and the poet himself with his usual self-abnegation passes no comment of this type. The explanation of this lies in Homer's view of life. He knew and loved the heroic world, and he knew quite well that such high deeds meant loss of life and destruction, but he valued them too highly to think that the loss quite outbalanced the gain, and that death made everything meaningless.

From these scattered and diverse indications it may be seen that Homer is well in sympathy with the ideals of the heroic age. At times he reveals that for him the heroic age is already lost, but he still continues to believe that its ideals are the right ideals and that the world is the worse for their loss. The present has its beauties for him, but it is to the heroic past that he looks for all that he holds best in human nature. And the past is not for him entirely beyond recall. He lives in it so intimately and is so absorbed by it that he must have been in some sort of touch with it. Whether his connexion with it is due to its continued survival in his day or to his absorption in the stories of heroic legend is a hard question. Chaucer, coming at the end of medieval romance, understands it perfectly, but inspired by the early Renaissance he sometimes makes gentle fun of it. But Homer hardly makes fun of his heroes, and has hardly any point of view that is not theirs. His perfect sincerity has no sentimental love of the past in it, and the world of the ***Iliad*** is a real world. Such clarity and consistency of outlook could not easily have been based only on legends; they must have been fed on the thoughts of the living men about him. No great poet can live entirely in the past, certainly no poet with Homer's width of understanding and great creative energy. The poet who draws on other poets may create a dream world like that of *The Faerie Queene* of *The Earthly Paradise,* but he cannot create Helen or Achilles. Homer must have lived in a world which still held the ideals of the heroic age, even if on his own admission men were no longer what they once had been. (pp. 242-50)

C. M. Bowra, in his Tradition and Design in "The Iliad," Oxford at the Clarendon Press, 1930, 278 p.

CHARLES ALLEN DINSMORE (essay date 1937)

[*In the following excerpt, Dinsmore comments on Homer's skill as an artist, citing especially his powerful scene descriptions and characterizations. In addition, Dinsmore discusses "the enduring spiritual values which Homer apprehended and enforced."*]

[In the ***Iliad*** there] is no vague impressionism; every scene is clearly conceived, and the characters are so real that they are accepted as historical persons. When a warrior falls we see precisely where the blow struck, we hear the crash of the bronze armor. Sometimes it is almost too vivid for our modern stomachs. When we actually see Patroclus dragging Thestor by his jaw over the rim of his chariot, as a fisherman pulls a sacred fish from the sea, leaving him as he fell, our qualms compel us to ask ourselves whether we are more civilized, or simply more effeminate, than the men of old. The poet makes a scene real by making the details clear. Would he make us see the Greek army, he does not give us a general description, but takes us with Agamemnon as he goes through the host and talks with the different chieftains. Would he make us feel the shining glory of Achilles on the field of battle, he lets us see the glittering armor as the hero puts it on piece by piece.

He reinforces the reader's imagination by the naturalness, abundance, and appropriateness of his similes; they rest the mind in scenes of strenuous action, they furnish a background to make us realize the situation more keenly.

Homer fills his pages with a bewildering variety of men and women, yet he conceives each so clearly as an individual that with an adjective or phrase he makes them live. An epithet flashes a picture—bright-eyed, "well-greaved," "far-shadowing"; or a single sentence reveals a character—"A man who lived by the side of the road and gave hospitality to all": "One omen alone is best, to fight for native land"; "She laughed with her lips, but there was no joy in her face." These lift the veil and we see deep and far. He lived in an age less sophisticated than ours, and looked at the world with young eyes, with a childlike as well as a lucid mind. Like the Old Testament narrators, he takes us to a scene and leaves us. He trusts the reader to see and to feel, and does not, like the writer of today, dim the picture with his private fancies, or linger on its emotional implications.

His skill as an artist, as well as his magnanimity as a man, are revealed in his treatment of Helen. How shall he picture to his reader the most beautiful woman in the world? He is too wise to attempt to describe the

> . . . face that launched a thousand ships,
> And burnt the topless towers of Ilium,

therefore he tells of the effect her glorious beauty has upon others. To the old men of Troy, her natural enemies, she seemed as an immortal goddess, and they ceased to wonder, after they had seen her, that the young men should for her sake suffer hardship.

Neither did he condemn her, for she was but the instrument of Fate. Her lament over the fallen Hector is one of the finest passages in the ***Iliad,*** and goes far to rehabilitate her character in the reader's estimation.

It is a mark of genius that out of meager experience it can open up great spaces of thought and emotion. From a little it gets much. The period covered by the ***Iliad*** is very short—about fifty days; the subject is extremely limited—the prowess of warriors, funeral games, friendship and feasting, the wrath of a man and the beauty of a woman. But with this trivial material the poet portrays most powerfully those emotions which are common to people of all epochs and countries. They are of the stuff of which all timeless literature is made—love and loyalty, courage and fear, gladness in simple things, the tragedy of death. Homer knows the stern joy which warriors feel, but with greater sympathy and with equal power he discloses life's pathos. The parting of Hector and Andromache, and Priam pleading for the body of his son from the bloody-handed Achilles, are high points in literature.

Civilizations change, centuries hurry by, but man's elemental emotions change as little as the sunshine or the sea. Homer has seized the passions of a border warfare between semi-barbarians and has portrayed them so powerfully and in verses so nobly beautiful that they remain an enduring revelation of man and a supreme monument to poetic genius.

In searching for the enduring spiritual verities which Homer apprehended and enforced, we must constantly bear in mind that moral instruction was far from his purpose. These lays were sung at banquets and festivals to give pleasure to the hearers and renown to the minstrel. Their aim was delight, not instruction. Occasionally the poet may utter some favorite conviction, either by way of comment or through the mouth of one of his characters, but primarily he is reciting a story, old in the tradition of his people, and to this he must be true.

This absence of didactic purpose is most fortunate for us, because what one really believes is not what he consciously teaches, but what he assumes as self-evident. We are surer of our assumptions than of our arguments. We proclaim and defend our opinions; we act upon what we really lay to heart. The foundations show what one solidly trusts; the superstructure reveals the quality of one's imagination and understanding. Not only does the lack of a didactic intention disclose the poet's deep convictions, it also brings us near to the confident beliefs of his hearers. He is reciting to please his audience and his tale must conform to their presuppositions. He must do no violence to their instinctive beliefs, if he is to be popular. Therefore in an accepted epic courses the spiritual life blood of a race. In the presuppositions of the ***Iliad*** we have more than the convictions of Homer; we have the ideals and principles of many generations of the most gifted people of antiquity. (pp. 38-42)

The theme of the story seems to be lust and war; nevertheless it plunges immediately into a consideration and solution of one of the world's profoundest spiritual problems. If Homer correctly reveals the principles and dispositions which bring Agamemnon and Achilles together, he throws light on the most insistent spiritual question which has engaged the attention of the Church—the question of the forgiveness of sins. How can there be reconciliation after wrong has been done? The organic idea running through the ***Iliad*** is a deed of sin, its frightful consequences, and the way of reconciliation. Sin, Retribution, Reconciliation, are the theme of the ***Iliad;*** they are the theme of our greatest literature; they are the heart of the message of religion. Homer answered the question of reconciliation between two strong and intemperate men by telling a simple story and by following his own deep instinct. Theologians have formulated the identical principles in terms of philosophic dogma. The moods and the actions which will heal the breach of sin between two persons anywhere will be identical everywhere. No preacher has treated more vividly than Homer the source and nature of evil, the sure retributions which follow wrongdoing, and the constant elements which enter into forgiveness and reconciliation. His theme is Achilles' wrath, to Greece the direful spring of woes unnumbered, which sent to Hades many a valiant soul. The consequences of the wrath were that Achilles sulked, Patroclus was slain, mighty chiefs were untimely killed, and the Greek cause came to the verge of disaster. Reconciliation comes when atonement has been made, the past forgotten, and the two commanders are again allies in the same cause.

Homer assuredly does not think of sin in terms congenial to a modern theologian. Sin, as we meet it in the first instance, is a violation of sacred taboo. Agamemnon has injured the priest of Apollo, and as penalty the god sends his arrows of plague on the army. In the light of his punishment the king sees his folly, repents of it, confesses it, and makes restitution. Then spontaneously the Greeks do two other things which are suggestive: they clean their camp of all pollutions, and they sing a hymn in honor of the offended god. Thus in the very first pages of this most ancient literature, we have a witness to the instinctive feeling that sin is polluting and its stains must be washed away, for the high gods are pleased with cleanliness. Therefore the baptisms and lustrations in all faiths. Then immediately after they have done all they can by way of restitution, the Greeks sing a hymn to Apollo. When we remember how the Church in all her various formulations of the doctrine of forgiveness has ever taken pains to make clear that God in being merciful has also been just, and that in pardoning he has in no way diminished the sanctity of his righteous law, this instinctive act of homage becomes significant.

It is to be observed that the evil thing here is not the inhumanity of Agamemnon in holding Chryseis, the priest's daughter, in foul bondage, but his contempt of the priest. Having made restitution and performed the purifying rites, the King has cleared himself as regards the sun-god. His relations with Achilles are not so easily restored. The methods the poet used to bring about complete reconciliation throw a flood of light on the principles which enter into all atonement, whether human or divine. . . . The root meaning [of the Greek word to express wrongdoing of every kind] is "befooling." Sin is blindness; folly, delusion. And so clearly is punishment bound up with folly that the Greeks included both under the one conception personified as Ate. They were also very human in laying the blame for their folly on the gods, and yet they had a real feeling of human responsibility. When Agamemnon woke to his blindness in alienating Achilles he exclaimed:

> But it is not I who am the cause, but Zeus and Destiny and Erinys that walketh in darkness who put into my soul fierce madness on the day when in the assembly I, even I, bereft Achilles of his meed. What could I do? It is God who accomplisheth all. Eldest daughter of Zeus is Ate who blindeth all, a power of bane: delicate are her feet, for not on earth she goeth, but walketh over the heads of men, making men to fall; and entangleth this one or that.

(pp. 44-7)

If Homer as well as the moderns is confused about the original source of evil, he is perfectly clear in stating what it is that brings a man back to sanity. In the disasters which befell his army, Agamemnon realized the true nature of his folly. Always, both in literature and experience, it is a vivid knowledge of the consequences which brings a man to himself. It is "the woes unnumbered," falling thick upon one's self, which opens eyes blinded by passion. To win back the allegiance of Achilles, Agamemnon acknowledges his fault, sends three friends to offer reconciliation, and promises to restore Briseis pure, and present other gifts in munificent abundance. He not only repents of the wrong; he confesses it. He does more; he renders every satisfaction in his power to atone for his offense. Obstinate pride keeps Achilles stubborn. But the death of Patroclus, his dearest friend, reveals to him his great folly. Renouncing his enmity, he joins the battle and brings victory to the Greeks. He has taken the three steps essential to all complete reconciliation—repentance, confession, fruits meet for repentance or expiation (*confessio, contritio, satisfactio*).

Now let us consider some further assumptions which the great poet makes. Our modern historians lay heavy emphasis on geographical and climatic conditions as affecting the course of history, but in both the Scriptures and in the ***Iliad*** the great man is always the hinge upon which events turn. The Bible interprets history in the light of the character and deeds of significant men. In Homer the fate of nations hangs on the temper of one man. Achilles sulks and the battle goes against the Greeks, the hero takes his proper place, and the cause prospers. The power of the individual looms large in the ancient books.

Because so great a weight of responsibility hangs upon the hero, he must not, like Agamemnon, act peevishly, putting his selfish desires above the interests of the cause, or, like Achilles, nurse his private grievance to the detriment of his comrades. Unity through self-subordination is one of the chief lessons of the ***Iliad.***

To what extent Homer accepted the shining gods of Olympus can never be known. Their names and stories were a common tradition of his times, and he used their dramatic possibilities to the full. But he places them in too many ridiculous positions to have held them in genuine reverence. He could not very well escape being a polytheist. As he looked out over his world, he saw the beautiful and the ugly, the forces which hurt, the forces which help; he saw evidences of freedom and evidences of irresistible fate, of order and caprice. Many wills seemed to be working on human destiny. To personify these forces, the gods and goddesses would be as congenial to his mind as to that of his race. Yet, amid the infinite variety, superior minds discerned a unity, or semblance of order. Zeus, the highest One, prevailed in the councils of the gods. From his rod there was no appeal, and the weight of his government was ultimately for righteousness. He was not indifferent to the deserts of men. He approved of Hector because he was the only man in Troy who never was scornful of Helen; though believing she should be given back to the Greeks, he fought because honor compelled him. Even in those early times, a noble and pondering mind never wholly interpreted the world scheme by what his eyes saw. He instinctively directed the light of his own nature upon what he experienced, and therefore he had faith that valor, justice, and mercy were dear to heaven.

Just here we come to a very significant fact. Although the Greeks, like all primitive peoples, deified the forces of nature, their deities did not take the form of somber monstrosities like the gods of many nations, but were radiant ones, dwelling in ethereal light, graceful, amenable, capable of unquenchable laughter. Thus they shine in Homer, giving to his pages a charm which could not come from Egypt or Assyria. What Homer did believe very sincerely, and assumed as the controlling principle of his epic, was a truth which later emerged as the master conviction of the Greek civilization, a conviction which gave form and glory to Greek art, set the standard of its oratory, gave strength and beauty to its literature, and would have saved the people from the errors which destroyed them, if they had possessed sufficient self-control to put it into practice. The motto, "Nothing too much," comes as near the secret of the glory that was Greece as can any single statement. This sense of proportion gave to their art its severe and graceful beauty, and to their literature its classic restraint. The Greeks had their shrines and rituals for the gods of high Olympus, but their sovereign creed was balance, proportion, the supremacy of reason. This structural faith of the men of the higher consciousness in Greece will later find clear expression in their dramatists. It is interesting to observe that Homer assumes this principle as a matter of course; it moulds the whole fabric of his song, and tempers the glowing energy even of his words.

Achilles might well be angry at the indignity heaped upon him, but his wrath was excessive, and this excess was the source of all the woe which followed. Patroclus would have lived had he obeyed the injunctions of Achilles, but his impetuous valor carried him beyond bounds. Achilles acts as a hero when he avenges his friend, but when in his uncontrolled fury he drags Hector in the dust, he brings reprobation on himself. The cause of every woe from the sin of Paris to the fall of Troy was excess of passion. The poet nowhere explicitly utters this truth, but he assumed it, and it is the organic philosophy of his epic.

A most powerful factor of any drama or epic is the background against which the action is set. This determines the final impression of the whole. In the ***Iliad*** the immediate scene is radiant with the glitter of the ocean, the glory of heroes, the beauty of women, the splendor of gods and goddesses; but the background is Fate, and because Fate dooms most men to sorrow, and all men to death and to the weakness and shadows of the underworld, therefore life is sad and human glory is futile and tragic. Zeus may be the father of the gods and the king of men, but even he is subject to the superior authority of Fate. The most memorable expression of this subordination is found in the issue of the rivalry between Hector and Achilles. Zeus was favorable to the Trojan, but Fate decreed otherwise. The two warriors are confronting each other for the final combat:

> Then the Father hung his golden balances, and set therein two lots of dreary death, one of Achilles, one of the horse-taming Hector, and then held them by the metal and poised. Then Hector's fated day sank down, and fell to the house of Hades, and Phoebus Apollo left him.

In the very years when Homer was painting his brilliant picture of heroic adventure shadowed by impending doom, over in Palestine were men of a loftier spiritual consciousness who saw life against a background that was at once righteous and compassionate. And because their God was good and supreme life had meaning and the future held a great hope.

To Homer life had no ultimate meaning. Man might have a moment of joy, but in the end his soul went to the house of Hades, wailing its doom—Hades, the land of wraiths and weak shadows, of which Achilles said he would rather be a plow boy on earth than rule over the realms of the dead.

The note of hopeless sadness is constantly uttered throughout the ***Iliad.*** Finely has Glaucus expressed this mood: "As is the race of leaves, so is the generation of men, the wind casts some leaves to the ground, others the flourishing forest brings forth when spring has come, so is the generation of men, one is born and another passes away." "There is nothing," declares Zeus, "more wretched than men. Nothing of all things that breathe and move on the face of the earth." Achilles is evidently of the same opinion, for he asserts, "The gods have decreed that wretched mortals should live in sorrow, while they themselves are free from care"; and again: "*Two* urns stand upon the floor of Zeus filled with his evil gifts, and *one* with blessings." How keenly Homer felt the pain and the pathos of existence is revealed in the touching scene between Hector and Andromache. Here he faces life's most perplexing problems—the suffering of the innocent for the guilty, needless sorrow, death to no purpose, the destruction of home and country—and the poet can offer to the weeping wife no consolation save that of duty bravely done. One must carry on. Fortunate is the man, if with inevitable evil he gets some good in life.

Although life is full of sorrow and death certain, Homer does not give himself over to pessimism. He does not wail or whine. Everywhere he strikes the heroic note. Because life is short, live nobly!

> O friends, be men, so act that none may feel
> Ashamed to meet the eyes of other men.

Nowhere is this heroic mood more finely expressed than in these words of Sarpedon: "For assuredly ten thousand fates of death do every way beset us, and these no mortal man may escape or avoid. Let us now go forward, whether we shall give glory to other men or they to us."

The remarkable feature of the ***Iliad*** is that against this dark background of death and futility the poet communicates a zest for life. Generous hospitality, kindness to strangers, heroic valor, are so touched by imagination as to be glorious. This goodness of life is not directly expressed in words but is communicated through the radiancy of the characters. Achilles may be impetuous, but he is magnificent in energy, a god in action, sublime in generosity. The very fact that he chooses to go into the battle for the sake of honor, even though he knows that by so doing he will go early to the eternal shades, makes him appear all the more heroic. The ***Iliad*** leaves the reader not in a mood of pessimism, but with a stouter and more generous heart, inclined to respond to Hector's cry, "Play the man, my friends, and be mindful of impetuous valor." Life is short, death is certain, Hades a land of gloom, yet carry on with high courage.

The poet felt deeply the pathos of life, its brevity, its pain and frustration: he also felt the glory of wisdom and the heroic deed. Homer took a noble view of life because of the essential nobility of his own mind. It is his glory, both as a poet and as a man, that, dealing with a sordid story of lust, bad temper, and savage butchery, he nowhere makes vice attractive, but brings the reader into sympathy with beauty, fortitude, and magnanimity.

Besides the heroic mood there is a virtue which is not explicitly taught but is a spirit of life in the poem itself. This virtue is the inestimable one of sympathetic understanding. Homer was a Greek, singing to a Grecian audience the exploits of their national heroes, yet he so tells his story that his hearers understand and sympathize with Hector; they feel the sorrows of Andromache; they take the part of Priam, pleading for the body of his dead son, as against Achilles. This ability to see events through the eyes of one's enemies is quite characteristic of the Greek genius. We find it in her historians, her dramatists, and her poets. It is significantly absent from early Hebrew literature. The books of Ruth and Jonah stand in lonely isolation in the Old Testament. The first record of sympathetic imagination in the stream of literature which forms our culture appears in Homer, and his subtle and indirect persuasions to toleration form one of the noblest spiritual values of the ***Iliad.***

In this epic we have no lofty insights into the ultimate meaning of things, but we do have our attention focused powerfully on certain virtues of enduring worth, courage, magnanimity, fortitude, moderation, tolerance. Above all we feel the radiant energy of a strong and noble mind unveiling to us unfamiliar beauty, and inspiring our hearts to valor. But of high religion as the modern mind conceives it—communion with the eternal spirit, humility, the spiritual worth of personality, unselfish service in the interests of a high ideal, and a pure heart—of these there is no hint. The good life here is not love of one's enemies, purity, and humility, but beauty, courage, and the thrill of joyous living. (pp. 47-55)

Charles Allen Dinsmore, "Homer: What He Believed and What He Valued," in his The Great Poets and the Meaning of Life, *Houghton Mifflin Company, 1937, pp. 31-63.*

SAMUEL ELIOT BASSETT (essay date 1938)

[Bassett was an influential Greek scholar and one of the foremost Homeric specialists of his time. In the following excerpt, he explores Homer's poetic realism and posits that his idealization of the heroic life "imparts a tragic quality to Homer's poetry."]

In works of the imagination "realism" is the scientific content and attitude. Pure *poiesis* beholds a vision of the mind beyond the reality of its material. In the early epic, too, the material itself was unreal. The past exists in the mind only as an idea. The epic memory views this past as one surveys a great city from a distant point of vantage. Its slums and sewers, the intimate human intercourse in its shops and dwellings, the small tragedies and comedies of its life, are little noticed. The attention is occupied rather with contours and skyline, great buildings and parks, the significant, and, above all, the beautiful. The idealist enjoys the impressions of the distant. . . . [The realist] differs from the idealist in his total disregard for values. Realism is thus the scientific approach in literature, as idealism is the poetic. . . . [The Alexandrian critics'] conclusion that the ***Odyssey*** was closer to reality in its picture of life has been used as an argument by modern chorizonts. The truth seems to be that (1) the theme of the ***Iliad*** requires a more idealistic treatment; (2) in the two poems there are compensations—in certain respects the ***Iliad*** is more "realistic" than the ***Odyssey,*** in certain others the ***Odyssey*** is more "idealistic" than the ***Iliad;*** (3) qualitatively, the same kind of "realism" marks both poems.

The ***Iliad*** deals with matters farther removed from common human experience. War and passion are not so close to life as are peace, common sense, and the use of one's wits. Armies and heroes by the hundreds permit less realism than single families and isolated palaces and settlements. The canvases are too large for much detail: an emotional impression of these extended scenes is more in order than minute description. The national scope of the ***Iliad*** gives more frequent occasion for myth and legend of the remoter past than is offered in its sequel, where the past is limited to the nine or ten years since the War. On the other hand, as if to compensate for this predominance of the ideal, the ***Iliad*** shows a greater attention to facts which are a part of the hearer's life. The more abundant similes relate the ideal and the "heroic" to the real experience and knowledge of the audience. So do the scenes on the shield of Achilles, and the geography of the Catalogues, with its frequent use of the present tense. Even the later obliteration of the Greek wall is more factual than the probable fate of the Phaeacians. In a similar way the ***Odyssey*** offers features far less real than any in the ***Iliad.*** Ithaca itself lies "farthest towards the darkening west," the home of mystery. The unknown lands and seas of the Apologue were farther from reality to the Homeric audience than Troy and Olympus and Ida. Monsters and witches, and even the faery Phaeacians, were not so real as the Olympians, for the latter were parts of a living religion.

But while the isolated and less crowded scenes of the ***Odyssey*** permit—and require—a more realistic treatment, the kind of realism is the same in both poems. At the steading of Eumaeus the hogs squeal and grunt as they get ready for the night; on the Trojan plain the horses stand by their chariots, champing the white barley and spelt. In realistic description there is little to choose between the evening meals in the quarters of Achilles and in the hut of Eumaeus. If the latter is slightly more detailed, the ***Iliad*** has the advantage in the two incidents of the "stirrup cup." It is the importance of the incident that determines the closeness of its approach to reality. Ethos often determines this. The child Eurymachus sitting at dinner in the lap of Odysseus is not so near to life as is the infant Achilles on the knees of Phoenix, drinking from his wine cup, and drenching his tunic as he chokes in his childish helplessness. . . . Thersites is "unknown," since he appears only here; according to the rule of Aristotle, he must be described; the goatherd will become familiar in the sequel. This principle determines the realistic presentation of the two old kings, Priam and Laertes. Laertes appears in a single episode, and both his garb and his occupation are unkingly: wearing a dirty smock, patched and old, with shin guards of leather, and gloves, because of the briars, and a goatskin cap, he hoes his vineyard. Priam likewise is weighed down by old age: he is but a step from the end of his days. . . . He is like the cicada, *vox et praeterea nihil*. (pp. 227-29)

This realism is commonly dismissed with the epithets, "naïve," "primitive"—terms which neither explain nor evaluate, even if they are correctly applied. A narrative and manner marked by

Order, high discourse,
And decency, than which is life less dear,

is hardly primitive; it must be due to the most highly developed taste of an era. The *Nibelungenlied* is far less savage, and includes far less that is revolting, than the Volsung Saga. If this is typical of literary evolution—as Brunetière gives reason for believing,—poetry after Homer showed a tendency to retrogress towards the primitive. Gresham's Law applies to literature as to economics. The public that has tasted [violent imagery], like the man in Plato's *Republic* who has once eaten human flesh, becomes, if not wolfish, at least more animal in his aesthetic likings. The Laestrygonian queen fills the comrades with loathing, but Homer omits the nauseating specifications in which Swift delights. The absence of all revolting details of the plague—which Homer must have known at least by hearsay—is illuminating when compared with the scientific realism of Thucydides and with Sophocles' almost surgical description of the festering foot of Philoctetes. Sophocles permits the spurting lifeblood of Haemon to mar the whiteness of Antigone's dead face. This is not Homerically "primitive," but far less so than a Victorian version of the "heroic" slaying of a knight at the feet of his ladylove:

she saw him bend
Back Robert's head, she saw him send
The thin steel down; the blow told well,
Right backward the knight Robert fell,
And moaned as dogs do, being half dead,
Unwitting, as I deem: so then
Godmar turned grinning to his men,
Who ran, some five or six, and beat
His head to pieces at their feet.

In Homer neither Andromache nor Hecuba sees the slaying of Hector; Penelope does not enter the great hall that has reeked with the Suitors' blood, until all signs of the carnage have been obliterated. Homer describes no cruelty for its own sake. The death of Melanthius is due punishment of a false slave in an age that knew no humanitarianism. There is no instance of prolonged physical torture in the Homeric poems. In battle the outraging of the body of an enemy does not begin till life is extinct. This failed to satisfy the less "primitive" taste of later times: in the later version Achilles dragged the living Hector.

In the action of the poems there is no matricide, parricide, fratricide, or suicide; no friend kills, or plots to kill, a comrade; no woman is ravished. These deeds occur in real life, as Homer knew. But in his picture of Human Life Writ Large they have no place. He refuses to portray the brutally animal in man. The word "primitive," therefore, may label his representation of life; it does not describe it.

"Naïve" is nearer the truth. To the child the outer world is inseparable from life. Its value is not in itself, but in its contribution to the reality of living. This value disappears when nature and fact assume an independent significance, and still more so when they are measured and their parts are related to each other by a norm which the reason abstracts from life. Homer does not count the arrows which Odysseus pours out before him on the threshold. He does not even say that 116 men opposed 4 in the Slaughter; he says 52 + 6 + 24 + 20 + 12 + 2. The listener would hardly have computed the sum, for numerical figures are important historically, not poetically. In seeing in the external only its emotional import in the life which he pictures, Homer reveals the child's mind. But Homer uses this kind of realism with a disciplined restraint which is far from naïve. He always keeps duly subordinate the external appearance and the setting of the larger human life which is his theme. The hundreds of human actors in the two poems are distinguished at least by names. But although Homer knew many kinds of wine and bread, only "bread" and "wine" are served at any Homeric dinner, whether the host is Alcinous or the Swineherd. The poet refrains from particularizing things almost as much as from generalizing human beings.

The degree of the approach to the particular in Homer depends on the poetic demands of the situation. The garb of Thersites would have had much interest for the antiquarian, but Homer mentions rather his misshapen form. The posset in Nestor's quarters, the libation of Achilles, and the harnessing of Priam's horses receive unusual attention partly because they occur in the opening scenes of momentous incidents. . . . Usually, however, the poet is content with a single external detail which vouches for the reality of the whole: *Ab uno disce omnia*. The rim of Hector's shield knocks against his neck and ankles as he strides from the field. Later, as he enters the home of Paris, in his hand is an 11-cubit spear, with its gleaming point and its ring of gold. Still later, Astyanax shrieks with terror at the sight of Hector's plumed helmut. By focusing the mind's eye on a single feature, generalized so that the experience instantly recognizes it as familiar, the object acquired a reality which was felt rather than analyzed. A similar realism is seen in the standing epithets of the sea or the ship: one familiar aspect creates the convincing impression of all the others. But the one feature is made distinct: Hector's shield has a rim of leather that runs all around its edge; his spear has a ring of gold; it is the plume nodding above the helmet which frightens Astyanax.

Homer's realism is thus less naïve than poetic. It calls upon the experience only to accept unquestionably the created picture of life. It never diverts attention from that life to an analysis or weighing of its reality. Even Homer's view of nature is more poetic than naïve. The sun, never wearied, giving delight to mortals, which *goes down,* belongs to the texture of human life, from which science's description is utterly dissevered. The scientific vision is schizopic, separating truth both from beauty and from experienced life. When Homer, like Heraclitus, "wrote the story of nature, dipping his pen into his mind," he was unaware of this dualism. Nature and man were poetically one. His men and women are real and move in a world of reality, which extends as far as the piece of leather from which Eumaeus is cutting a sandal, the salt with which

Patroclus seasons the roast, and the Phaeacian servant's words, "Your bed is ready, Sir." But the mind into which Homer "dipped his pen" saw as clearly as if they were real a more beautiful world and greater men and women, which, because they have been absent from the experience of most of us, we call ideal.

This ideal life, the life lived heroically, imparts a tragic quality to Homer's poetry, for tragedy is "the representation of actions and life" which command deep interest and respect. . . . (pp. 229-33)

Samuel Eliot Bassett, in his The Poetry of Homer, *University of California Press, 1938, 273 p.*

SIMONE WEIL (essay date 1940-41)

[A French writer, mystic, and teacher, Weil was a liberal humanitarian who was deeply interested in literature, science, and Greek and Hindu philosophy. Her writings, most of which were edited and published posthumously, are imbued with her strong Christian faith, belief in human justice, and identification with the underprivileged in society. Weil's best-known works include L'Enracinement *(1949;* The Need for Roots, *1951), an account of a year she spent working in a French automobile factory, and* L'Attente de Dieu *(1950;* Waiting for God, *1951), a spiritual autobiography. In the following excerpt, which first appeared pseudonymously in* Cahiers du Sud *in 1940-41, Weil explores Homer's treatment of force in the* Iliad, *suggestively using the poem to comment on the spread of Nazism in Europe.]*

The true hero, the true subject, the center of the ***Iliad*** is force. Force employed by man, force that enslaves man, force before which man's flesh shrinks away. In this work, at all times, the human spirit is shown as modified by its relations with force, as swept away, blinded, by the very force it imagined it could handle, as deformed by the weight of the force it submits to. For those dreamers who considered that force, thanks to progress, would soon be a thing of the past, the ***Iliad*** could appear as an historical document; for others, whose powers of recognition are more acute and who perceive force, today as yesterday, at the very center of human history, the ***Iliad*** is the purest and the loveliest of mirrors.

To define force—it is that *x* that turns anybody who is subjected to it into a *thing*. Exercised to the limit, it turns man into a thing in the most literal sense: it makes a corpse out of him. Somebody was here, and the next minute there is nobody here at all; this is a spectacle the ***Iliad*** never wearies of showing us:

. . . the horses
Rattled the empty chariots through the files of battle,
Longing for their noble drivers. But they on the ground
Lay, dearer to the vultures than to their wives.

The hero becomes a *thing* dragged behind a chariot in the dust:

All around, his black hair
Was spread; in the dust his whole head lay,
That once-charming head; now Zeus had let his enemies
Defile it on his native soil.

The bitterness of such a spectacle is offered us absolutely undiluted. No comforting fiction intervenes; no consoling prospect of immortality; and on the hero's head no washed-out halo of patriotism descends.

His soul, fleeing his limbs, passed to Hades,
Mourning its fate, forsaking its youth and its vigor.

Still more poignant—so painful is the contrast—is the sudden evocation, as quickly rubbed out, of another world: the faraway, precarious, touching world of peace, of the family, the world in which each man counts more than anything else to those about him.

She ordered her bright-haired maids in the palace
To place on the fire a large tripod, preparing
A hot bath for Hector, returning from battle.
Foolish woman! Already he lay, far from hot baths,
Slain by grey-eyed Athena, who guided Achilles' arm.

Far from hot baths he was indeed, poor man. And not he alone. Nearly all the ***Iliad*** takes place far from hot baths. Nearly all of human life, then and now, takes place far from hot baths.

Here we see force in its grossest and most summary form—the force that kills. How much more varied in its processes, how much more surprising in its effects is the other force, the force that does *not* kill, i.e., that does not kill just yet. It will surely kill, it will possibly kill, or perhaps it merely hangs, poised and ready, over the head of the creature it *can* kill, at any moment, which is to say at every moment. In whatever aspect, its effect is the same: it turns a man into a stone. From its first property (the ability to turn a human being into a thing by the simple method of killing him) flows another, quite prodigious too in its own way, the ability to turn a human being into a thing while he is still alive. He is alive; he has a soul; and yet—he is a thing. An extraordinary entity this—a thing that has a soul. And as for the soul, what an extraordinary house it finds itself in! Who can say what it costs it, moment by moment, to accommodate itself to this residence, how much writhing and bending, folding and pleating are required of it? It was not made to live inside a thing; if it does so, under pressure of necessity, there is not a single element of its nature to which violence is not done.

A man stands disarmed and naked with a weapon pointing at him; this person becomes a corpse before anybody or anything touches him. Just a minute ago, he was thinking, acting, hoping:

Motionless, he pondered. And the other drew near,
Terrified, anxious to touch his knees, hoping in his heart
To escape evil death and black destiny . . .
With one hand he clasped, suppliant, his knees,
While the other clung to the sharp spear, not letting go . . .

Soon, however, he grasps the fact that the weapon which is pointing at him will not be diverted; and now, still breathing, he is simply matter; still thinking, he can think no longer:

Thus spoke the brilliant son of Priam
In begging words. But he heard a harsh reply:
He spoke. And the other's knees and heart failed him.
Dropping his spear, he knelt down, holding out his arms.
Achilles, drawing his sharp sword, struck
Through the neck and breastbone. The two-edged sword
Sunk home its full length. The other, face down,
Lay still, and the black blood ran out, wetting the ground.

If a stranger, completely disabled, disarmed, strengthless, throws himself on the mercy of a warrior, he is not, by this very act, condemned to death; but a moment of impatience on the warrior's part will suffice to relieve him of his life. In any case, his flesh has lost that very important property which in the laboratory distinguishes living flesh from dead—the galvanic response. If you give a frog's leg an electric shock, it twitches. If you confront a human being with the touch or sight of something horrible or terrifying, this bundle of muscles, nerves, and flesh likewise twitches. Alone of all living things, the suppliant we have just described neither quivers nor trembles. He has lost the right to do so. As his lips advance to touch the object that is for him of all things most charged with horror, they do not draw back on his teeth—they cannot:

No one saw great Priam enter. He stopped,
Clasped the knees of Achilles, kissed his hands,
Those terrible man-killing hands that had slaughtered so many of his sons.

The sight of a human being pushed to such an extreme of suffering chills us like the sight of a dead body:

As when harsh misfortune strikes a man if in his own country
He has killed a man, and arrives at last at someone else's door,
The door of a rich man; a shudder seizes those who see him.
So Achilles shuddered to see divine Priam;
The others shuddered too, looking one at the other.

But this feeling lasts only a moment. Soon the very presence of the suffering creature is forgotten:

He spoke. The other, remembering his own father, longed to weep;
Taking the old man's arm, he pushed him away.
Both were remembering. Thinking of Hector, killer of men,
Priam wept, abased at the feet of Achilles.
But Achilles wept, now for his father,
Now for Patroclus. And their sobs resounded through the house.

It was not insensibility that made Achilles with a single movement of his hand push away the old man who had been clinging to his knees; Priam's words, recalling his own old father, had moved him to tears. It was merely a question of his being as free in his attitudes and movements as if, clasping his knees, there were not a suppliant but an inert object. Anybody who is in our vicinity exercises a certain power over us by his very presence, and a power that belongs to him alone, that is, the power of halting, repressing, modifying each movement that our body sketches out. If we step aside for a passer-by on the road, it is not the same thing as stepping aside to avoid a billboard; alone in our rooms, we get up, walk about, sit down again quite differently from the way we do when we have a visitor. But this indefinable influence that the presence of another human being has on us is not exercised by men whom a moment of impatience can deprive of life, who can die before even thought has a chance to pass sentence on them. In their presence, people move about as if they were not there; they, on their side, running the risk of being reduced to nothing in a single instant, imitate nothingness in their own persons. Pushed, they fall. Fallen, they lie where they are, unless chance gives somebody the idea of raising them up again. But supposing that at long last they have been picked up, honored with cordial remarks, they still do not venture to take this resurrection seriously; they dare not express a wish lest an irritated voice return them forever to silence:

He spoke; the old man trembled and obeyed.

At least a suppliant, once his prayer is answered, becomes a human being again, like everybody else. But there are other, more unfortunate creatures who have become things for the rest of their lives. Their days hold no pastimes, no free spaces, no room in them for any impulse of their own. It is not that their life is harder than other men's nor that they occupy a lower place in the social hierarchy; no, they are another human species, a compromise between a man and a corpse. The idea of a person's being a thing is a logical contradiction. Yet what is impossible in logic becomes true in life, and the contradiction lodged within the soul tears it to shreds. This thing is constantly aspiring to be a man or a woman, and never achieving it—here, surely, is death but death strung out over a whole lifetime; here, surely is life, but life that death congeals before abolishing. (pp. 4-8)

Force, in the hands of another, exercises over the soul the same tyranny that extreme hunger does; for it possesses, and *in perpetuo,* the power of life and death. Its rule, moreover, is as cold and hard as the rule of inert matter. The man who knows himself weaker than another is more alone in the heart of a city than a man lost in the desert.

Two casks are placed before Zeus's doorsill,
Containing the gifts he gives, the bad in one, the good in the other . . .
The man to whom he gives baneful gifts, he exposes to outrage;
A frightful need drives across the divine earth;
He is a wanderer, and gets no respect from gods or men.

Force is as pitiless to the man who possesses it, or thinks he does, as it is to its victims; the second it crushes, the first it intoxicates. The truth is, nobody really possesses it. The human race is not divided up, in the ***Iliad,*** into conquered persons, slaves, suppliants, on the one hand, and conquerors and chiefs on the other. In this poem there is not a single man who does not at one time or another have to bow his neck to force. The common soldier in the ***Iliad*** is free and has the right to bear arms; nevertheless he is subject to the indignity of orders and abuse:

But whenever he came upon a commoner shouting out,
He struck him with his scepter and spoke sharply:
"Good for nothing! Be still and listen to your betters,
You are weak and cowardly and unwarlike,
You count for nothing, neither in battle nor in council."

Thersites pays dear for the perfectly reasonable comments he makes, comments not at all different, moreover, from those made by Achilles:

He hit him with his scepter on back and shoulders.
So that he doubled over, and a great tear welled up,
And a bloody welt appeared on his back
Under the golden scepter. Frightened, he sat down,
Wiping away his tears, bewildered and in pain.
Troubled though they were, the others laughed long at him.

Achilles himself, that proud hero, the undefeated, is shown us at the outset of the poem, weeping with humiliation and helpless grief—the woman he wanted for his bride has been taken from under his nose, and he has not dared to oppose it:

. . . But Achilles
Weeping, sat apart from his companions,
By the white-capped waves, staring over the boundless ocean.

What has happened is that Agamemnon has deliberately humiliated Achilles, to show that he himself is the master:

. . . So you will learn
That I am greater than you, and anyone else will hesitate
To treat me as an equal and set himself against me.

But a few days pass and now the supreme commander is weeping in his turn. He must humble himself, he must plead, and have, moreover, the added misery of doing it all in vain.

In the same way, there is not a single one of the combatants who is spared the shameful experience of fear. The heroes quake like everybody else. It only needs a challenge from Hector to throw the whole Greek force into consternation—except for Achilles and his men, and they did not happen to be present:

He spoke and all grew still and held their peace,
Ashamed to refuse, afraid to accept.

But once Ajax comes forward and offers himself, fear quickly changes sides:

A shudder of terror ran through the Trojans, making their limbs weak;
And Hector himself felt his heart leap in his breast.
But he no longer had the right to tremble, or to run away. . . .

Two days later, it is Ajax's turn to be terrified:

Zeus the father on high, makes fear rise in Ajax.
He stops, overcome, puts behind him his buckler made of seven hides,
Trembles, looks at the crowd around, like a wild beast. . . .

Even to Achilles the moment comes; he too must shake and stammer with fear, though it is a river that has this effect on him, not a man. But, with the exception of Achilles, every man in the ***Iliad*** tastes a moment of defeat in battle. Victory is less a matter of valor than of blind destiny, which is symbolized in the poem by Zeus's golden scales:

Then Zeus the father took his golden scales,
In them he put the two fates of death that cuts down all men,
One for the Trojans, tamers of horses, one for the bronze-sheathed Greeks.
He seized the scales by the middle; it was the fatal day of Greece that sank.

By its very blindness, destiny establishes a kind of justice. Blind also is she who decrees to warriors punishment in kind. He that takes the sword, will perish by the sword. The ***Iliad*** formulated the principle long before the Gospels did, and in almost the same terms:

Area is just, and kills those who kill.

(pp. 10-12)

[Violence] obliterates anybody who feels its touch. It comes to seem just as external to its employer as to its victim. And from this springs the idea of a destiny before which executioner and victim stand equally innocent, before which conquered and conqueror are brothers in the same distress. The conquered brings misfortune to the conqueror, and vice versa:

A single son, short-lived, was born to him.
Neglected by me, he grows old—for far from home
I camp before Troy, injuring you and your sons.

A moderate use of force, which alone would enable man to escape being enmeshed in its machinery, would require superhuman virtue, which is as rare as dignity in weakness. Moreover, moderation itself is not without its perils, since prestige, from which force derives at least three quarters of its strength, rests principally upon that marvelous indifference that the strong feel toward the weak, an indifference so contagious that it infects the very people who are the objects of it. Yet ordinarily excess is not arrived at through prudence or politic considerations. On the contrary, man dashes to it as to an irresistible temptation. The voice of reason is occasionally heard in the mouths of the characters in the ***Iliad.*** Thersites' speeches are reasonable to the highest degree; so are the speeches of the angry Achilles:

Nothing is worth my life, not all the goods
They say the well-built city of Ilium contains. . . .
A man can capture steers and fatted sheep
But, once gone, the soul cannot be captured back.

But words of reason drop into the void. If they come from an inferior, he is punished and shuts up; if from a chief, his actions betray them. And failing everything else, there is always a god handy to advise him to be unreasonable. In the end, the very idea of wanting to escape the role fate has allotted one—the business of killing and dying—disappears from the mind:

We to whom Zeus
Has assigned suffering, from youth to old age,
Suffering in grievous wars, till we perish to the last man.

Already these warriors, like Craonne's so much later, felt themselves to be "condemned men."

It was the simplest trap that pitched them into this situation. At the outset, at the embarkation, their hearts are light, as hearts always are if you have a large force on your side and nothing but space to oppose you. Their weapons are in their hands; the enemy is absent. Unless your spirit has been conquered in advance by the reputation of the enemy, you always feel yourself to be much stronger than anybody who is not there. An absent man does not impose the yoke of necessity. To the spirits of those embarking no necessity yet presents itself; consequently they go off as though to a game, as though on holiday from the confinement of daily life.

Where have they gone, those braggadocio boasts
We proudly flung upon the air at Lemnos,
Stuffing ourselves with flesh of horned steers,
Drinking from cups brimming over with wine?
As for Trojans—a hundred or two each man of us
Could handle in battle. And now one is too much for us.

But the first contact of war does not immediately destroy the illusion that war is a game. War's necessity is terrible, altogether different in kind from the necessity of peace. So terrible is it that the human spirit will not submit to it so long as it can possibly escape; and whenever it can escape it takes refuge in long days empty of necessity, days of play, of revery, days arbitrary and unreal. Danger then becomes an abstraction; the lives you destroy are like toys broken by a child, and quite as incapable of feeling; heroism is but a theatrical gesture and smirched with boastfulness. This becomes doubly true if a momentary access of vitality comes to reinforce the divine hand that wards off defeat and death. Then war is easy and basely, coarsely loved. (pp. 16-18)

[The] soul that is enslaved to war cries out for deliverance, but deliverance itself appears to it in an extreme and tragic aspect, the aspect of destruction. Any other solution, more moderate, more reasonable in character, would expose the mind to suffering so naked, so violent that it could not be borne, even as memory. Terror, grief, exhaustion, slaughter, the annihilation of comrades—is it credible that these things should not continually tear at the soul, if the intoxication of force had not intervened to drown them? The idea that an unlimited effort should bring in only a limited profit or no profit at all is terribly painful.

> What? Will we let Priam and the Trojans boast
> Of Argive Helen, she for whom so many Greeks
> Died before Troy, far from their native land?
> What? Do you want us to leave the city, wide-streeted Troy,
> Standing, when we have suffered so much for it?

But actually what is Helen to Ulysses? What indeed is Troy, full of riches that will not compensate him for Ithaca's ruin? For the Greeks, Troy and Helen are in reality mere sources of blood and tears; to master them is to master frightful memories. If the existence of an enemy has made a soul destroy in itself the thing nature put there, then the only remedy the soul can imagine is the destruction of the enemy. At the same time the death of dearly loved comrades arouses a spirit of somber emulation, a rivalry in death:

> May I die, then, at once! Since fate has not let me
> Protect my dead friend, who far from home
> Perished, longing for me to defend him from death.
> So now I go to seek the murderer of my friend,
> Hector. And death shall I find at the moment
> Zeus wills it—Zeus and the other immortals.

It is the same despair that drives him on toward death, on the one hand, and slaughter on the other:

> I know it well, my fate is to perish here,
> Far from father and dearly loved mother;
> but meanwhile
> I shall not stop till the Trojans have had their fill of war.

The man possessed by this twofold need for death belongs, so long as he has not become something still different, to a different race from the race of the living. (pp. 19-20)

To respect life in somebody else when you have had to castrate yourself of all yearning for it demands a truly heartbreaking exertion of the powers of generosity. It is impossible to imagine any of Homer's warriors being capable of such an exertion, unless it is that warrior who dwells, in a peculiar way, at the very center of the poem—I mean Patroclus, who "knew how to be sweet to everybody," and who throughout the ***Iliad*** commits no cruel or brutal act. But then how many men do we know, in several thousand years of human history, who would have displayed such god-like generosity? Two or three?—even this is doubtful. Lacking this generosity, the conquering soldier is like a scourge of nature. Possessed by war, he, like the slave, becomes a thing, though his manner of doing so is different—over him too, words are as powerless as over matter itself. And both, at the touch of force, experience its inevitable effects: they become deaf and dumb.

Such is the nature of force. Its power of converting a man into a thing is a double one, and in its application double-edged. To the same degree, though in different fashions, those who use it and those who endure it are turned to stone. This property of force achieves its maximum effectiveness during the clash of arms, in battle, when the tide of the day has turned, and everything is rushing toward a decision. It is not the planning man, the man of strategy, the man acting on the resolution taken, who wins or loses a battle; battles are fought and decided by men deprived of these faculties, men who have undergone a transformation, who have dropped either to the level of inert matter, which is pure passivity, or to the level of blind force, which is pure momentum. Herein lies the last secret of war, a secret revealed by the ***Iliad*** in its similes, which liken the warriors either to fire, flood, wind, wild beasts, or God knows what blind cause of disaster, or else to frightened animals, trees, water, sand, to anything in nature that is set into motion by the violence of external forces. Greeks and Trojans, from one day to the next, sometimes even from one hour to the next, experience, turn and turn about, one or the other of these transmutations:

> As when a lion, murderous, springs among the cattle
> Which by thousands are grazing over some vast marshy field. . . .
> And their flanks heave with terror; even so the Achaians
> Scattered in panic before Hector and Zeus, the great father.
>
> As when a ravening fire breaks out deep in a bushy wood
> And the wheeling wind scatters sparks far and wide,
> And trees, root and branch, topple over in flames;
> So Atreus' son, Agamemnon, roared through the ranks
> Of the Trojans in flight. . . .

The art of war is simply the art of producing such transformations, and its equipment, its processes, even the casualties it inflicts on the enemy, are only means directed toward this end—its true object is the warrior's soul. Yet these transformations are always a mystery; the gods are their authors, the gods who kindle men's imagination. But however caused, this petrifactive quality of force, two-fold always, is essential to its nature; and a soul which has entered the province of force will not escape this except by a miracle. Such miracles are rare and of brief duration.

The wantonness of the conqueror that knows no respect for any creature or thing that is at its mercy or is imagined to be so, the despair of the soldier that drives him on to destruction, the obliteration of the slave or the conquered man, the wholesale slaughter—all these elements combine in the ***Iliad*** to make a picture of uniform horror, of which force is the sole hero. A monotonous desolation would result were it not for those few luminous moments, scattered here and there throughout the poem, those brief, celestial moments in which man possesses his soul. The soul that awakes then, to live for an instant only and be lost almost at once in force's vast kingdom, awakes pure and whole; it contains no ambiguities, nothing complicated or turbid; it has no room for anything but courage and love. Sometimes it is in the course of inner deliberations that a man finds his soul: he meets it, like Hector before Troy, as he tries to face destiny on his own terms, without the help of gods or men. At other times, it is in a moment of love that men discover their souls—and there is hardly any form of pure love known to humanity of which the ***Iliad*** does not treat. (pp. 20-2)

[A] heaping-up of violent deeds would have a frigid effect, were it not for the note of incurable bitterness that continually makes itself heard, though often only a single word marks its presence, often a mere stroke of the verse, or a run-on line. It is in this that the ***Iliad*** is absolutely unique, in this bitterness that proceeds from tenderness and that spreads over the whole human race, impartial as sunlight. Never does the tone lose its coloring of bitterness; yet never does the bitterness drop into lamentation. Justice and love, which have hardly any place in this study of extremes and of unjust acts of violence, nevertheless bathe the work in their light without ever becoming noticeable themselves, except as a kind of accent. Nothing precious is scorned, whether or not death is its destiny; everyone's unhappiness is laid bare without dissimulation or disdain; no man is set above or below the condition common to all men; whatever is destroyed is regretted. Victors and vanquished are brought equally near us; under the same head, both are seen as counterparts of the poet, and the listener as well. If there is any difference, it is that the enemy's misfortunes are possibly more sharply felt.

So he fell there, put to sleep in the sleep of bronze,
Unhappy man, far from his wife, defending his own
people. . . .

And what accents echo the fate of the lad Achilles sold at Lemnos!

Eleven days he rejoiced his heart among those he loved,
Returning from Lemnos; the twelfth day, once more,
God delivered him into the hands of Achilles,
To him who had to send him, unwilling, to Hades.

And the fate of Euphorbus, who saw only a single day of war.

Blood soaked his hair, the hair like to the Graces' . . .

When Hector is lamented:

. . . guardian of chaste wives and little children. . . .

In these few words, chastity appears, dirtied by force, and childhood, delivered to the sword. The fountain at the gates of Troy becomes an object of poignant nostalgia when Hector runs by, seeking to elude his doom:

Close by there stood the great stone tanks,
Handsomely built, where silk-gleaming garments
Were washed clean by Troy's lovely daughters and
housewives
In the old days of peace, long ago, when the Greeks
had not come.
Past these did they run their race, pursued and pursuer.

The whole of the ***Iliad*** lies under the shadow of the greatest calamity the human race can experience—the destruction of a city. This calamity could not tear more at the heart had the poet been born in Troy. But the tone is not different when the Achaeans are dying, far from home.

Insofar as this other life, the life of the living, seems calm and full, the brief evocations of the world of peace are felt as pain:

With the break of dawn and the rising of the day,
On both sides arrows flew, men fell.
But at the very hour that the woodcutter goes home to
fix his meal
In the mountain valleys when his arms have had enough
Of hacking great trees, and disgust rises in his heart,
And the desire for sweet food seizes his entrails,
At that hour, by their valor, the Danaans broke the
front.

Whatever is not war, whatever war destroys or threatens, the ***Iliad*** wraps in poetry; the realities of war, never. No reticence veils the step from life to death:

Then his teeth flew out; from two sides,
Blood came to his eyes; the blood that from lips and
nostrils
He was spilling, open-mouthed; death enveloped him in
its black cloud.

The cold brutality of the deeds of war is left undisguised; neither victors nor vanquished are admired, scorned, or hated. Almost always, fate and the gods decide the changing lot of battle. Within the limits fixed by fate, the gods determine with sovereign authority victory and defeat. It is always they who provoke those fits of madness, those treacheries, which are forever blocking peace; war is their true business; their only motives, caprice and malice. As for the warriors, victors or vanquished, those comparisons which liken them to beasts or things can inspire neither admiration nor contempt, but only regret that men are capable of being so transformed.

There may be, unknown to us, other expressions of the extraordinary sense of equity which breathes through the ***Iliad;*** certainly it has not been imitated. One is barely aware that the poet is a Greek and not a Trojan. The tone of the poem furnishes a direct clue to the origin of its oldest portions; history perhaps will never be able to tell us more. If one believes with Thucydides that eighty years after the fall of Troy, the Achaeans in their turn were conquered, one may ask whether these songs, with their rare references to iron, are not the songs of a conquered people, of whom a few went into exile. Obliged to live and die, "very far from the homeland," like the Greeks who fell before Troy, having lost their cities like the Trojans, they saw their own image both in the conquerors, who had been their fathers, and in the conquered, whose misery was like their own. They could still see the Trojan war over that brief span of years in its true light, unglossed by pride or shame. They could look at it as conquered and as conquerors simultaneously, and so perceive what neither conqueror nor conquered ever saw, for both were blinded. Of course, this is mere fancy; one can see such distant times only in fancy's light.

In any case, this poem is a miracle. Its bitterness is the only justifiable bitterness, for it springs from the subjections of the human spirit to force, that is, in the last analysis, to matter. This subjection is the common lot, although each spirit will bear it differently, in proportion to its own virtue. No one in the ***Iliad*** is spared by it, as no one on earth is. No one who succumbs to it is by virtue of this fact regarded with contempt. Whoever, within his own soul and in human relations, escapes the dominion of force is loved but loved sorrowfully because of the threat of destruction that constantly hangs over him.

Such is the spirit of the only true epic the Occident possesses. The ***Odyssey*** seems merely a good imitation, now of the ***Iliad,*** now of Oriental poems; the *Aeneid* is an imitation which, however brilliant, is disfigured by frigidity, bombast, and bad taste. The *chansons de geste,* lacking the sense of equity, could not attain greatness: in the *Chanson de Roland,* the death of an enemy does not come home to either author or reader in the same way as does the death of Roland.

Attic tragedy, or at any rate the tragedy of Aeschylus and Sophocles, is the true continuation of the epic. The conception of justice enlightens it, without ever directly intervening in it; here force appears in its coldness and hardness, always attended by effects from whose fatality neither those who use it nor

A vase painting of Hector's farewell with Andromache.

those who suffer it can escape; here the shame of the coerced spirit is neither disguised, nor enveloped in facile pity, nor held up to scorn; here more than one spirit bruised and degraded by misfortune is offered for our admiration. The Gospels are the last marvelous expression of the Greek genius, as the ***Iliad*** is the first: here the Greek spirit reveals itself not only in the injunction given mankind to seek above all other goods, "the kingdom and justice of our Heavenly Father," but also in the fact that human suffering is laid bare, and we see it in a being who is at once divine and human. The accounts of the Passion show that a divine spirit, incarnate, is changed by misfortune, trembles before suffering and death, feels itself, in the depths of its agony, to be cut off from man and God. The sense of human misery gives the Gospels that accent of simplicity that is the mark of the Greek genius, and that endows Greek tragedy and the ***Iliad*** with all their value. Certain phrases have a ring strangely reminiscent of the epic, and it is the Trojan lad dispatched to Hades, though he does not wish to go, who comes to mind when Christ says to Peter: "Another shall gird thee and carry thee whither thou wouldst not." This accent cannot be separated from the idea that inspired the Gospels, for the sense of human misery is a pre-condition of justice and love. He who does not realize to what extent shifting fortune and necessity hold in subjection every human spirit, cannot regard as fellow-creatures nor love as he loves himself those whom chance separated from him by an abyss. The variety of constraints pressing upon man give rise to the illusion of several distinct species that cannot communicate. Only he who has measured the dominion of force, and knows how not to respect it, is capable of love and justice. (pp. 24-7)

Simone Weil, "Homer: 'The Iliad' or the Poem of Force," in The Proper Study: Essays on Western Classics, *edited by Quentin Anderson and Joseph A. Mazzeo, St. Martin's Press, 1962, pp. 3-29.*

MARK VAN DOREN (essay date 1946)

[*Van Doren was one of the most prolific men of letters in twentieth-century American writing. His work includes poetry (for which he won the Pulitzer Prize in 1939), novels, short stories, drama, criticism, social commentary, and the editing of a number of popular anthologies. He has written accomplished studies of Shakespeare, John Dryden, Nathaniel Hawthorne, and Henry David Thoreau, and served as the literary editor and film critic for the* Nation *during the 1920s and 1930s. Van Doren's criticism is aimed at the general reader, rather than the scholar or specialist, and is noted for its lively perception and wide interest. Like his poetry and fiction, his criticism consistently examines the inner, idealistic life of the individual. In the words of Carlos Baker, Van Doren brings to his best work "a warmth of epithet, a crisp precision of definition, and a luminousness of poetic insight." In the following excerpt from his landmark essay on the* Iliad, *Van Doren lauds the energy, variety, and density of the poem. With characters that are "round and clear," and similes "over which action creeps like embroidery," Homer succeeds, according to Van Doren, in making us "take as natural the wonders with which it is filled."*]

Homer, with Shakespeare at his side, is still the sovereign poet. The phrase is Dante's, who is third in this strict company which excludes all others. Only these three—yet Chaucer is a fourth—are masters of the main art a poet must learn: the art of standing at the right distance from his matter, of keeping the right relation to it, and of using, along with the knowledge he brings, the knowledge he gains while he goes. With the poet, as with the historian, the position he takes is everything, and we shall not believe him unless he maintains it. But whereas the historian's distance must be great enough to permit a survey of the event from a point where its limits in time are always visible, the poet must seem to annihilate both time and distance—we enter the action, we are there as these things happen, we believe because we see and hear and touch. The distinction is not pure. The poet without perspective has no meaning, and the historian who cannot move up to the particulars of his choice, to battles and meetings and the sending and getting of messages, will not be read to the end. But as a distinction it will do. And Homer understood it perfectly.

Homer's scenes, and the incidents that fill them, are beheld as if in a long dream, or as if in memory. They are fiercely present, yet they have the brightness of things removed, of things threatened by darkness and only by miracle recalled. The ideas Homer had, and he may have had all possible ideas, were had in the right way: they did not prevent him from being a complete poet. Nothing prevented him from believing and loving the deeds and men that he saw, exactly as he saw them. This is the secret of his constant, surprising, and intimate power, a power that no successor has matched, so that he is still unique, the one, the only epic poet. The higher criticism of him is misguided, or is misunderstood, if it seems to deny the identity of a single artist who twice was capable of measuring the intensity with which a hero felt himself—Achilles burning at the center of his poem, Odysseus swimming or scheming or leaning on a long staff at the center of his. The heroes, like the poems, are as different as night and day, but neither success has been achieved again. No other epic poet is so valuable line by line, so rapid over all and yet so rich in each movement that he follows. No other stories are so clear, so important, or so full of unforgettable persons. We still do not know how these persons were made, because they seem to have been made before the poems were written. Yet they were not. It is poetry, not history, that has rendered them so plain in their differences, so round and solid and simple, so permanently themselves, so endlessly discussable. How did Homer do this? Nobody knows. The conventions about characterization do not apply. The characters of Homer are inseparable from his scenes, as his scenes are from his fables. All is multiple and near, all is one and far away.

Nothing about the ***Iliad*** is more incredible than its power to make us take as natural the wonders with which it is filled—Achilles and his mother, the beauty of the gods, the eloquence of the men. These things are so natural that we are tempted to think them easy, and Homer naïve, a lucky poet who came early to the art. The temptation is soon conquered if we note what happens to us as we read, and to the poem; if we count the things that collect in it as forces collect to make a world, if we study—though it is hard to do this—the massive way in which so many simple units are joined to produce an effect of huge and complex order. The effort required is never mentioned, it is only made, and made with a success that deceives us. Homer may doubt his ability to remember every name that should go into a list of warriors, and he likes to make much of such minor difficulties. The great difficulties he silently solves. And the greatest difficulty of all he solves at the start. The poem, like the world it contains, is first as well as last a single and great thing.

The world of the ***Iliad*** is incessantly and everywhere alive. Energy runs through it like a blood stream, heating it to the high color that shows in wine-dark seas, black ships with vermilion prows, gold and silver and bronze objects, fair women, and one golden-haired hero among a host of swarthy comrades. Nor is this color there for decoration. It is put on, or rather it is put in, to stay; it is what gives each surface its depth, its interior animation, as well as a thousand outward appearances of change; the hue of this life is at once indestructible and disturbed. A storm is going on in Nature, a storm that may engulf all phenomena; but the phenomena are fast, and they survive.

The world of the ***Iliad*** abounds with moving creatures, animal and human, whose images are mixed. The oxen, the sheep, the dogs, the bees, the lions, the boars, the cranes, and above all the horses—the horses, most proud of their capacity to move, most conscious of their necks, their manes, their rippling tails—these share with swarms of men the secret of Homer's life, uttered for them in many a gigantic simile. The men themselves are great and swift, fiery and proud, of exalted stature and magnificent dress; eloquence flows from them like honey, and the epithets by which they are known stream away from them like long hair. It is as if the wind did this, for in such a world the wind is always blowing, as the sea is always heaving, the rivers are always rushing, and the tall trees are trembling to their tops. The gods are in motion too, sliding here from Olympus to show the flash of their eyes before they return along divine tangents; or rising from the grey sea, dripping tears; or slipping again under the waves, which one of them, Poseidon, shows his broad shoulders above, ruling them with his voice and wand.

The landscape of the ***Iliad*** is rich and energetic, as befits its contents. It is deep-soiled and thickly wooded; its mountains have many ridges, and its shining seas are peopled with more islands than men know the names of. Honey bees abound, and cool springs gush in hidden glades which patient kine will seek out even though the danger of lions be what it is. The mountains of the gods are crowned with clouds, and perhaps only there the sound of the world comes faintly. Where we stand it is a strong, unceasing sound, a hum or roar which Homer accompanies with his hexameters. It is a sound we understand as well as hear. It explains for us the power of even inanimate objects to participate in the life of this poem. The goblets, the gold-studded staffs, the shields and swords have biographies, have pedigrees; they came here under their own momentum, and they will go hence likewise.

> And Meriones gave to Odysseus a bow and a quiver and a sword, and about his head he set a helm wrought of hide, and with many a tight-stretched thong was it made stiff within, while without the white teeth of a boar of gleaming tusks were set thick on this side and that, well and cunningly, and within was fixed a lining of felt. This cap Autolycus on a time stole out of Eleon when he had broken into the stout-built house of Amyntor, son of Ormenus; and he gave it to Amphidamas of Cythera to take to Scandeia, and Amphidamas gave it to Molus as a guest-gift, but he gave it to his own son Meriones to wear; and now, being set thereon, it covered the head of Odysseus.

Such an object is not after all inanimate. It glories in its existence as any creature might. It approaches the distinction of being an Homeric animal—as, from the other side of creation, does one of Homer's greatest men:

> And even as when a stalled horse that has fed his fill at the manger, breaketh his halter, and runneth stamping over the plain—being wont to bathe him in the fair-flowing river—and exulteth; on high doth he hold his head and about his shoulders his mane floateth streaming, and as he glorieth in his splendor his knees nimbly bear him to the haunts and pastures of mares; even so swiftly plied Hector his feet and knees, urging on his charioteers, when he had heard the voice of the god.

All the life in the ***Iliad*** is one life.

It is not, however, monotonous or meaningless. If the ***Iliad*** is packed with sound, it is not noisy. If it is restless without end, it is not sick of a fever. Its abundant life is brilliant with form. This is because Homer never forgets the great world he seemed to cut away when he concentrated our gaze upon the small strip of Trojan shore where the crowded action takes place. We are given but a fragment of the world to see, just as we are given but a few days of the war, and just as those few days are subdued to the theme of Achilles' wrath. Achilles, outraged by Agamemnon, withdraws from the fighting, and asks Thetis his mother to intercede with Zeus against the Greeks until they shall have suffered enough to suit his pleasure; but when their sufferings include the death of his comrade Patroclus he returns in a new rage and kills Hector. That is the action of the ***Iliad,*** in one spot and stretch of time. Yet nothing of what Homer knows is missing in the end. The great world is kept. That is the meaning of the catalogue in the second book, the roll call of countries whence these heroes came. They are homesick for Greece, and puzzled as to why they left it. The good past which their present madness has repudiated returns to plague them with many a remembered beauty. The lineage of cups and spears is a life line to normal experience. The gods are shown in their serene dwelling places—but shown, too, leaving them, drawn here by the terrible importance of tragedy. For neither the great world nor the little one is Homer's subject, but the two together, alternating and competing. The little one escapes into the great one when it can, yet often enough the great one bears back upon it, pressing it into place and silence, and all but crushing the strong men who are its inhabitants. So in a steady rhythm the ***Iliad*** oscillates between bustle and quiet, between masses of men in motion and one man making music in his hut, between the din of furious battle and the domestic peace of bedchambers, of weaving rooms, and of walls where old men sit like grasshoppers, weak and lily-voiced. Even the fighting has its variety, its great chords and its pauses. The meaning of the ***Iliad,*** if meaning there must be, is neither in the narrow world it fills nor in the wide one it remembers. It is in the relation between these two—between this much and all.

Nor are the realms confused. Nothing is confused in Homer, because nothing is vague. He gives us one detail at a time, in sharp focus. he is a farsighted poet whose vision penetrates foreground and background with equal ease. He does not run things together as the impressionist, uncertain of his aim, inveterately will. In Homer only one thing at a time is visible, but the others are waiting, silent and apart, to be seen when his attention sweeps to take them in. The ***Iliad*** would be a less tremendous tragedy were this not true.

For it is a tragedy. The emphasis is upon those pressures at the center, those all but intolerable burdens imposed from without, which are the sign that man is trying more than he can do. The little world of war is the world upon which the ***Iliad*** lavishes its art. The other world is there, but this is the one that suffers.

The movement of the poem is compounded of great velocity and great weight. Much is carried, but it is swung with surprising speed. The sense of a burden huge to the point of hopelessness is never lost, yet motion never stops; there is still the lightness that art must have if it is not to encumber the earth. It cannot always be seen how Homer accomplishes this miracle, but it is certain that his repetitions help—his refrains, his never-failing epithets, and his far-famed similes. These stitch his fabric solid, reënforcing every thread to the last corner. Our consciousness is kept always at the full; we are not permitted to forget that Achilles is swift-footed, that Agamemnon is king of men, that Nestor is the Gerenian horseman, that silver-footed Thetis is daughter to the old man of the sea, that Odysseus of the many wiles is also a sacker of cities, that Diomedes is good at the war cry, that Aphrodite loves laughter, that Hera sits on a golden throne, and that Zeus, the son of Cronos, is cloud-gatherer and lord over all. Every mortal, every god, takes the full weight of his identity with him wherever he goes, reappearing in the panoply of his several names as he prepares to speak that which we already know; for Homer's creatures take pleasure in declaring themselves even when there is no novelty to disclose, just as the objects with which he surrounds them grow to be eternal objects, seen in the setting of time. So things that are done are done as in ritual, the same words always coming back: "The wind filled the belly of the sail," "And this plan seemed to his mind the best," "All ungentle was the voice he heard," "But why doth my heart thus hold converse with me?"

The great loom of the similes never pauses in its work of weaving Homer's worlds together. (pp. 1-9)

The similes of the ***Iliad*** are not its ornaments, they are rather the stuff which the fable adorns, they are the basic life over which action creeps like embroidery—gilding it, to be sure, but leaving it no less substantial than it was. No reader in his senses skips them, or misses the significance of their coming at times in flocks and showers, as when the tide of battle rises and wrath grows to a storm; a series of them, one ignited by another, is ever a sign that events of fatal importance are imminent. Nor are they invariably long. When Athene saved Menelaus from death by the arrow of Pandarus she did it quickly, and the words themselves are quick: "She swept it just aside from the flesh, even as a mother sweepeth a fly from her child when he lieth in sweet slumber." The hands of Automedon when he had despoiled Aretus of his armor were "all bloody, even as a lion that hath devoured a bull." And the armor which Hephaestus made for Achilles, though it would have been too much for any other man to wear, fitted his glorious limbs so well that it "became as it were wings to him."

The eloquence of Homer's men, and of his women too, is more than an accident in the ***Iliad.*** It is also a function of the fury with which a vast world drives in upon its center. (p. 11)

[The ***Iliad***'s] is a unique tone, both choked and free. The men and women who speak are full of things they cannot say, and yet they say them. The result is a music at once heavy and clear, like that toward which the tongue of Othello, originally inarticulate, magnificently toils. The heroes of Homer had been taught to deliver themselves of words, but they had not expected that these things would have to be said. They are said under pressures which no man here had imagined far away and long ago in his dear native land.

The density of the ***Iliad*** tends to be absolute. Its passionate beginning is not easily read by one who comes to it relaxed, as one may come to the ***Odyssey.*** This opening is compact of anger, terror, and death. Events are already complex—the wrath now not of Achilles but of Apollo, and the pestilence among the host, so that "ever did the pyres of the dead burn thick." Then in no time at all they become complex beyond cure. Homer has started at the moment most ripe for tragedy. His people are packed into a limited space of earth which nine years have made them loathe. The loathe one another and themselves, in disgust and in despair. Nor is it merely the invading Greeks of whom this is true. They are savage with frustration—the freeing of Helen was not to have taken nine years—but so are the Trojans savage, with fatigue and fear and with a special loathing which they feel for Paris, Helen's abductor and effeminate husband. And both sides hate Helen, even while it is the case that no man who gazes at her can resist her beauty.

Thus the ***Iliad*** begins under the "knotted cord of mighty strife and evil war, a knot none might break nor undo." "Scant is the breathing-space in war," remarks the poet in his seventeenth book, days later than this day when wide-ruling Agamemnon was so sorely vexed, "and with rage was his black heart wholly filled, and his eyes were like blazing fire." This was the day when we met our first god in the poem, and he was nothing like the goddess whose bright charm overspreads the opening of the ***Odyssey.*** "Down from the peaks of Olympus he strode, wroth at heart, bearing on his shoulders his bow and covered quiver. The arrows rattled on the shoulders of the angry god, as he moved; and his coming was like the night." Even of Pallas Athene it was said, when Achilles turned on that day to see who had pulled his golden hair: "Terribly did her eyes flash."

That was the beginning, and all is of a piece thereafter. Achilles has had leisure to reflect that the Trojans never were his enemies; they have harried no kine of his, abducted no wife. He is here for nothing save that Agamemnon's brother shall be avenged. And avenged, ironically, upon a contemptible "ogler of girls,'' a curled and pampered Paris, despised and hated ''of all men like black death''—a ''strange man,'' Hector says, a man of unstable understanding, says Helen. Achilles is here for nothing. But so are all the people of the ***Iliad.*** A vortex has whirled and sucked them into its darkness, and in that darkness where there is so little room their spirits have hardened. ''Ever is thy heart unyielding,'' says Alexander to Hector. ''Thy heart is unbending,'' Patroclus tells Achilles. ''Of iron verily is thy heart,'' cries Hecuba to Priam. The same thing will be said by Telemachus to Penelope, but it will not be true, and it will not be said in a tragedy.

This is a tragedy of strife whose origin can scarcely be remembered, and whose development is altogether out of proportion to that origin. As the sense of disproportion grows, the savagery of what men do increases. The war becomes steadily more abominable. (pp. 13-16)

If Homer is a master of horror, he is also a master of relief from horror. None knows better than he the clean blessing of fire, or the comfort of ''sweet Sleep.'' He does not forget to pause when pause is necessary lest we grow too heavily laden with the terror of his tale. Just when all threatens to be confusion, to be an intolerable heaping up of woe, there comes such a moment of silence as that at the end of the eighth book, when the Trojans rest for the night in their new camp on the plain before the city:

> Even as in heaven about the gleaming moon the stars shine clear, when the air is windless, and forth to view appear all mountain peaks and high headlands and glades, and from heaven breaketh open the infinite air, and all stars are seen, and the shepherd joyeth in his heart; even in such multitudes between the ships and the streams of Xanthus shone the fires that the Trojans kindled before the face of Ilios. A thousand fires were burning in the plain and by each sat fifty men in the glow of the blazing fire. And their horses, eating of white barley and spelt, stood beside the cars and waited for fair-throned Dawn.

Sweet sleep and distant fire. It is a different relief from that brought by Hephaestus as he consumes the stench along the Xanthus. But then Homer is always different. The brawls and magnanimities of the funeral games for Patroclus are another ingredient of change, inserting laughter between the two grimmest moments of this story.

Yet the story remains tragic, its interludes of peace only intensifying the tread of its doom. Its concentration is complete. Difficult to enter, it is impossible to leave. Homer has been praised for his technical triumph in compressing so much of the Trojan war into so small a compass, for his ingenuity in organizing so much history about the wrath of Achilles. But his theme is vaster than any war, and outreaches history. His theme is the world, which here if anywhere is seen, heard, felt, feared, and pitied at its heart. Here, as would be the case with any heart we had entered, all is closeness, darkness, and the terrible beat of the organ. All is urgency. The hatreds of these heroes cannot rest or cease. There seems to be no time for wisdom. Decisions must be made impromptu, against judgment and even against the will. The poem is packed, its atmosphere is thick. Distances dissolve, so that no artist would succeed who set out to make pictures of what he saw. The ***Iliad*** cannot be illustrated. It hums with an energy both divine and diseased, both magnificent and calamitous, both beautiful and terrible. Here is the world of man becoming itself, as it were, in crisis. The morals of existence are being made before us—a nebular creation—and we cannot say that they should not have been so made. This war should never have been, but it is senseless to say so. It has become necessary to our knowledge; man has become most noble, most transparent, through his errors. (pp. 18-19)

The mistakes and the magnificence are telescoped, the landscape of fate is curiously foreshortened. Irony lurks in every line, though we may not know it is there until we have remembered it. Achilles will die young, yet he looks and moves like one who will live forever. This war, bitter to the taste though it is, has so much beauty in it that we cannot glance away. The heroes are subject equally to the gods and to themselves; they are impelled to do what they do, but this does not mean that they lose importance. We watch their war as if we knew it would never end; yet we know it will, and indeed we know that it did. Helen does not love Paris any longer, but she must make love to him when Aphrodite brings him home from battle. Aphrodite, the laughter-loving, cries at her mother's knee because Diomedes has wounded her. Hector is roused to his final wrath, and filled with his final confidence, only because Zeus wishes to hasten the moment when his decree against the Greeks can be recalled; and the Trojans go eagerly in his wake, not knowing that it is to their certain death. When Patroclus returns to the battle which will obliterate him, the only fear of Achilles is that he will do deeds surpassing his, and so lessen his honor. Deiphobus appears outside the walls of Troy as Hector flees Achilles in his last duel and speaks words which seem to be wise: they counsel him to stand his ground and do battle with Achilles man to man. And Hector answers him: ''Deiphobus, verily in time past thou wast far the dearest of my brethren, that were born of Hecabe and Priam, but now I deem that I shall honor thee in my heart even more, seeing thou hast dared for my sake, when thine eyes beheld me, to come forth from out the wall, while the others abide within.'' The irony here is at least twofold. The words are not wise, since Hector has no chance against the man-slayer he has been fleeing; and they are not friendly, because they are spoken in reality by one who knows this. They are spoken by Athene in the guise of Deiphobus, and the real Deiphobus will never learn that great Hector spoke to him thus, using his name in wondrous compliment.

The crowning irony, however, is Thetis' when she rises a second time from the sea, having heard again her dear child Achilles groaning. She had come the first time at the beginning of the story, when the cause of Achilles' grief was the dishonor done him by Agamemnon, and the loss of his fair-cheeked Briseis. Then we were told how she arrived in answer to his prayer:

> So he spake, weeping, and his queenly mother heard him as she sat in the depths of the sea beside the old man her father. And speedily she came forth from the grey sea like a mist, and sate her down before his face, as he wept; and she stroked him with her hand, and spake to him, and called him by name: ''My child, why weepest thou? What sorrow hath come upon thy heart? Speak out; hide it not in thy mind, that we both may know.''

And we were told how he besought her to intercede with Zeus against the Greeks, and how she did so—indeed, all of the action since that day has been determined by Zeus' promises to her. All of the action, including now the death of the mortal whom Achilles loves best, Patroclus of the embattled body, Patroclus who had worn his famous armor and driven his ageless horses. But Thetis does not know this when in the eighteenth book she hears him again:

> Then terribly did Achilles groan aloud, and his queenly mother heard him as she sat in the depths of the sea beside the old man her father. Thereat she uttered a shrill cry, and the goddesses thronged about her, even all the daughters of Nereus that were in the deep of the sea. . . . So saying she left the cave and the nymphs went with her weeping, and around them the waves of the sea were cloven asunder. And when they were come to the deep-soiled land of Troy they stepped forth upon the beach, one after the other, where the ships of the Myrmidons were drawn up in close lines round about swift Achilles. Then to his side, as he groaned heavily, came his queenly mother, and with a shrill cry she clasped the head of her son, and with wailing spake unto him winged words:
>
> "My child, why weepest thou, What sorrow hath come upon thy heart? Speak out; hide it not. Thy wish has verily been brought to pass for thee by Zeus, as aforetime thou didst pray, stretching forth thy hands, even that one and all the sons of the Achaeans should suffer cruel things."

What you wanted has been given you—was it not enough? Too much, Achilles answers. On which irony the entire poem pivots. Thetis and her child who is the best of men have been caught in the net of their success. The success was real, but now success itself has changed its name. (pp. 20-3)

Homer foretells everything, again and again. He knows, or Zeus knows, that the war will last a long time, and that this final year of it will be the most terrible. We are told that Patroclus will die; that Achilles will arm himself again and slay Hector; that the Achaeans will take steep Ilios and sack it; and that the Argives will go back in their ships to their dear native land. We are told all this, and more, because of a greater suspense which we shall then constantly feel. The outcome of a story is one thing to know, but in a great story the outcome is only one thing, if indeed the last thing, in a series. Before it arrives there are a thousand moments on which we hang, suspended in the uncertainty which attends the heartbeat of time. The ***Iliad*** is a great story, and so it is filled with the kind of suspense that matters. It is the kind that can be felt again in the hundredth reading. We know what will happen, yet as we find ourselves once more imbedded in the ironies of the tale it seems that we do not know. The fears, the illusions, the hopes, the despairs come alive again. And the ironies lose none of their crushing weight; mortality still stings. We wait again while Thetis learns that what she has done for Achilles has failed to make him happy. We remember that Achilles will give the body of Hector back to Priam when he comes, but as we watch the old man coming we share his trepidation. Suspense never leaves us in the ***Iliad,*** foreshortened as it is into one complex of dark and sore uncertainty.

Even the gods suffer at times where it hurts gods most to suffer, in their serenity. A world is being made, and it is too much for them. They are very brilliant and beautiful, like shooting stars, or in Zeus' case like all the cloud-capped heaven; but before the poem is finished they have had a war among themselves, and rivalries have developed that will reverberate through eternity. They visit the battlefield in every guise—Aphrodite once as an ancient dame, a wool-comber, though to be sure with beauteous neck and lovely bosom and flashing eyes; Athene once as a heron hard by the way, crying unseen by night to guide Odysseus and Diomedes toward the camp of Rhesus where horses, wondrous like the rays of the sun, are waiting to be stolen. They come and go, restlessly, in animal or human form, and sometimes in their own form, terrible to see. It is not their splendor that suffers. As Poseidon rides the waves the sea-beasts gambol beneath him as they always did, for they know their lord, and the sea parts gladly before his car. As Zeus sits among the peaks of Ida the many-fountained, mother of wild beasts and seat of his fragrant altar, he exults in his glory as he always has, "looking upon the city of the Trojans, and the ships of the Achaeans, on the flashing of the bronze, and on the slayers and the slain." His dalliance on this mountain with Hera, when she beguiles him with dreams, sweet sleep, and herself, could not have been more splendid in any golden age:

> And beneath them the divine earth made fresh-sprung grass to grow, and dewy lotus, and crocus, and hyacinth, thick and soft, that upbare them from the ground. Therein lay the twain, and were clothed about with a cloud, fair and golden, wherefrom fell drops of glistering dew.

It is not the glory of the gods that is disturbed. It is their sense that human life is simple. They too must go their way into the battle: Hera, Pallas Athene, Poseidon, Hermes, and Hephaestus on the side of Agamemnon's men; Ares, Phoebus, Apollo, Artemis, Leto, Xanthus, and Aphrodite on the side of Troy. And the issue is long delayed. Not until the twenty-second book does Zeus hang out his golden scales—"and down sank the day of doom of Hector, and departed unto Hades; and Phoebus Apollo left him." The implication is that Apollo goes reluctantly; puzzled, even, if that is one of the things a god can be.

Yet it must be said again that the ***Iliad*** is not confused. Its people are, and its one grand event; but Homer is always free to separate a scene from its fellows, and in this scene to create a sudden beauty. "The sun was now just striking on the fields" as in the seventh book the two armies set about burying their fallen comrades—it is a short phrase, and a conventional one, but in its place it accomplishes a wonder. The thousand campfires at the end of the eighth book are famous as far as poetry is known; after millenniums they have lost no sparkle of their brightness. The superb episode of the tenth book, the night expedition of Diomedes and Odysseus, is in itself an epic, tough and fearful in its charm; the best friend of Odysseus, Athene of the flashing eyes, is heard this time, not seen; she gives her sign on the right, and the doughty killers go their way "like two lions through the black night, amid the slaughter, amid the corpses, through the arms and the black blood," disappearing from every Greek eye or ear until Nestor catches the sound of horses coming back. (pp. 29-32)

Hector is the greatest man in the poem with the exception of one still greater man, Achilles. More often than others he contemplates the fame which he will some day have. All of them live not only in the conviction that they are doomed but in the clear consciousness that men who come after them will say thus and so. Hector, however, is the most eloquent in his imaginings:

> And some one shall some day say even of men that are yet to be, as he saileth in his many-benched ship over the wine-dark sea: "This is a barrow of a man that died in olden days, whom on a time in the midst of his prowess glorious Hector slew." So shall some man say, and my glory shall never die.

Homer's people know they will be famous, and live in the dusky glow which this certainty kindles about their knees. The lives they expect to lose are valuable to them; they are works of art, each one of them unique. "Even in days to come," says Helen to Hector, "we may be a song for men that are yet to be." Agamemnon knows this too, and Diomedes, and Sarpedon, and of course Achilles. It is as if Homer had no work to do in making them what they are; they mold their own images, carefully building out each part and standing off to scrutinize the whole. Each one of them is round and clear, a sharp detail holding its outline amid a host of others. (pp. 33-4)

Achilles is the refined gold of this world's human wealth. He is supreme in everything, for he is absolutely alive. Among Homer's men he is not only the most wrathful and savage, he is the most loving, the most beautiful, the most splendid, the most inquisitive, the tenderest in filial feeling, the strongest, the most eloquent, and in the end the most courteous. The glory of his utterance—an enitirely personal utterance, piercing and revealing—is like nothing else we hear, and least like the prolixity of Nestor. For Nestor is one thing, but Achilles is many things; his contradictions, his sudden new sides turned fiercely to the light, are the source of some flaming clarity in him which almost surpasses the sun. The poem derives from him; built into it, he is visible at the end of every perspective. We know the most about him because he is reflected in the most minds: in that of Thetis who lives for no one else, in that of Patroclus who can sit so quietly while his great friend sings and plays on a silver harp, in that of Peleus his faraway father, in that of Phoenix who once in Phthia fed him morsels of choice meat, seating him on his knee and giving him wine which he sputtered. And who else is so incessantly in the thoughts of the warriors, Greek or Trojan? For he is an army in himself. He carries unique weapons, he wears at last a shield on which Hephaestus has engraved the world, and he cries out with a trumpet voice which alone turns herds of horses back. His own divine horses, Xanthus and Balius, whose grievous lot it is to live among mortals, and who are so beautiful in their grief for Patroclus, abiding like pillars on a tomb, their heads bowed to the earth, miraculously can speak. "Aye verily," says Xanthus, "yet for this time will we save thee, mighty Achilles, albeit the day of doom is nigh thee. . . . It is thine own self that art fated to be slain in fight by a god and a mortal." And Achilles answers him: "Xanthus, why dost thou prophesy my death? Thou needest not at all. Well know I even of myself that it is my fate to perish here, far from my father dear, and my mother; howbeit even so will I not cease until I have driven the Trojans to surfeit of war."

For the doom of his early death is always in Achilles' ears. Hector's last words to him are of the day "when Paris and Phoebus Apollo shall slay thee, valorous though thou art, at the Scaean gate." And Thetis darkens her first visit to him by reminding him that his span of life is brief—"thou art doomed to a speedy death and withal art compassed with sorrow above all men." He speaks of it himself when he is rejecting the gifts sent to him by Agamemnon in the ninth book; and indeed it is as often on his lips as it is on those of his mother or of Zeus. "Straightway after Hector is thine own death ready at hand," Thetis tells him when she comes again. "Straightway may I die, seeing I was not to bear aid to my comrade at his slaying," cries Achilles. "Seek not then to hold me back from battle, for all thou lovest me; thou shalt not persuade me." His love of life is as great as the amount of it which he has—no man wants less to die—but the knowledge of his doom hangs over his least gesture, deepening the colors with which his person is graced, and accentuating the line of irony which lightens each edge of the wonderful world he lives in.

The poem is his from the moment at the beginning of the eighteenth book when he is told what everybody else knows, and what he himself fears, namely that Patroclus is dead and his body dishonored. The poem has always been his, but now his world is the only one it lives in. Terribly now does he groan, and anger, "sweeter far than trickling honey, waxeth like smoke" in his breast; though the one aim he henceforth has, to kill Hector, he repeatedly insists is the aim to make strife perish and anger itself yield unto peace. His wrath against Agamemnon has been swallowed up in his grief over the best of young men; he will need to be wrathful still if Patroclus is to be avenged, but wrath now will be a ritual, ushering in the end.

The savagery of Achilles which once had slain the father and the seven brothers of Andromache now rages to its height. When his hands grow weary of dealing death in the battle of the Scamander he chooses twelve youths alive out of the river and leads them forth, "dazed like fawns," to be bound with thongs and await their burning on the pyre of Patroclus. When Hector with his last breath pleads that his body be returned to Troy for burial, the answer of Achilles is implacable and monstrous:

> Implore me not, dog, by knees or parents. Would that in any wise wrath and fury might bid me carve thy flesh and myself eat it raw, because of what thou hast wrought, as surely as there lives no man that shall ward off the dogs from thy head; nay, not though they should bring hither and weigh out ransom ten-fold, aye, twenty-fold, and should promise yet more; nay, not though Priam, son of Dradanus, should bid pay thy weight in gold; not even so shall thy queenly mother lay thee on a bier and make lament for thee, the son herself did bear, but dogs and birds shall devour thee utterly.

But dogs and birds do not devour Hector, and Priam's mission will be successful.

Meanwhile the body of Patroclus is burned with a terrible magnificence, on a pyre which measures a hundred feet each way. Many sheep and kine are burned with it, their fat first gathered by Achilles' own hands and used to enfold the corpse from head to foot. He adds jars of honey and oil, four horses with high-arched necks, two of the dead prince's favorite hounds, and at last the twelve valiant sons of Troy, their throats sacrificially cut. The fire does not burn until the North Wind and the West Wind are invoked by Iris to come from Thrace and fall upon the pyre and beat upon the flame.

> And the whole night long swift Achilles, taking a two-handled cup in hand, drew wine from a golden bowl and poured it upon the earth, and

> wetted the ground, calling ever upon the spirit of hapless Patroclus. As a father waileth for his son, a son newly wed whose death hath brought woe to his hapless parents, even so wailed Achilles for his comrade as he burned his bones, going heavily about the pyre with ceaseless groaning.

Then for the first time in many nights sweet sleep can leap upon him as he withdraws a little way from the pyre and lies down in perfect weariness, awaiting the next bright day with its funeral games.

When the games are over, the grief and the wrath of Achilles are still not cured. His companions comfort themselves with supper and sleep, but not so the son of Thetis, who for twelve nights tosses on his side, on his back, on his face, unable to forget the woes he has borne, "passing through wars of men and the grievous waves."

> Then again he would arise upon his feet and roam distraught along the shore of the sea. Neither would he fail to mark the Dawn, as she shone over the sea and the sea-beaches, but would yoke beneath his car his swift horses, and bind Hector behind the chariot to drag him withal; and when he had haled him thrice about the barrow of the dead son of Menoetius, he would rest again in his hut, but would leave Hector outstretched on his face in the dust.

At last his fury becomes a scandal even among the gods. Apollo, the friend of Hector, convinces the rest that Achilles is nowise right in his mind, for his heart is still set on cruelty and he has lost all pity. The gods agree, and Thetis is sent on a third visit to her son; she tells him that heaven is angry with him, and conveys to him the will of Zeus, which is that he shall surrender the body of Hector to whatever man comes from Troy to ransom it. The body all this while has been preserved by Apollo from injury or decay; and the man who is coming is none other than Priam. Achilles, who does not know this as we do, consents—with relief, as if he had been waiting for such instructions, yet still in ignorance that it is Priam who will come.

The journey of Priam across the plain in the company of Idaeus, his old herald, and with the beautiful Hermes for guide, is the last great event of the ***Iliad,*** and no other event is more memorable. The huge poem comes here to a delicate, a genre close. Priam, whom we have seen preparing at home the gear necessary for his trip—horses and a chariot for him to drive, mules and a four-wheeled wagon for Idaeus, with a wicker basket in it to contain the body of Hector—is one of Shakespeare's old men, fussily scolding like Capulet, and contemptuous of the women who would either hinder or help him. Arriving at the hut of Achilles, however, where he astonishes the hero and the friends who sit at table wth him, he goes with a noble straightness to the point which will be of greatest assistance to his cause.

> Remember thy father, O Achilles like to the gods, whose years are even as mine, on the grievous threshold of old age. . . . Nay, have thou awe of the gods, Achilles, and take pity on me, remembering thine own father. Lo, I am more piteous far than he, and have endured what no other mortal on the face of the earth hath yet endured, to reach forth my hand to the face of him that hath slain my sons.

To which plea Achilles, weeping for his father even while he weeps again for his friend, has no resistance to offer. Instead, he heaps courtesies upon the father of his foe as he consents to return the body of Hector. "For this present let us bethink us of supper. For even the fair-haired Niobe bethought her of meat, albeit twelve children perished in her halls, six daughters and six lusty sons." They eat and drink together, marveling at each other's greatness as they munch their mutton and lift their cups. And Achilles asks how many days he should refrain from war while Hector is being buried. Twelve, says Priam; after which "will we do battle, if so be we must."

They must. Nothing in the ***Iliad*** is more dreadful than this prospect, but there it is. As Priam returns across the plain, Cassandra, seeing from Pergamus what he brings, utters a shrill cry and summons the other women to raise their chorus of dirges: Andromache, who can think of nothing but the loneliness in which she will live; Hecuba, to whom Hector had been the dearest of her many children; and at last the bitter, lonely Helen, remembering that Hector had been the only Trojan, who spoke no evil of her, who did not shudder at her, but was gentle and kind. These lament him in the fulness of their grief, and then nine days are consumed in building such a pyre as Patroclus had burned on; whereupon the tenth day comes with its great fire, its golden urn, and its high-heaped barrow; and whereupon with feasting the twelfth day, the day of war again, is awaited by the horse-taming Trojans.

The poem ends there, as if the last courtesy of Achilles were to say: let Hector's buring body be the image that remains. In the ***Odyssey*** we shall hear how his own body burned, and it was a splendid burning as the shade of Agamemnon describes it to the shade of him who was burned:

> And thy mother came forth from the sea with the immortal sea-nymphs, when she heard the tidings, and a wondrous cry arose over the deep. . . . Then around thee stood the daughters of the old man of the sea wailing piteously, and they clothed thee about with immortal raiment. And the Muses, nine in all, replying to one another with sweet voices, led the dirge. . . . Thus for seventeen days alike by night and day did we bewail thee, immortal gods and mortal men, and on the eighteenth we gave thee to the fire, and many well-fatted sheep we slew around thee and sleek kine. So wast thou burned in the raiment of the gods and in abundance of unguents and sweet honey; and many Achaean warriors moved in their armor about the pyre, when thou wast burning, both footmen and charioteers, and a great din arose. But when the flame of Hephaestus had made an end of thee, the morning we gathered thy white bones, Achilles, and laid them in unmixed wine and unguents. Thy mother had given a two-handled, golden urn, and said it was the gift of Dionysus, and the handiwork of famed Hephaestus. In this lie thy white bones, glorious Achilles, and mingled with them the bones of the dead Patroclus. . . . And over them we heaped up a great and goodly tomb, on a projecting headland by the broad Hellespont, that it might be seen from far over the sea both by men that now are and that shall be born hereafter. . . . Thus not even in death didst thou lose thy name,

but ever shalt thou have fair renown among all
men, Achilles.

(pp. 36-44)

Mark Van Doren, "The Iliad," in his The Noble Voice: A Study of Ten Great Poems, *Henry Holt and Company, 1946, pp. 1-44.*

RACHEL BESPALOFF (essay date 1947)

[*In the following excerpt, Bespaloff probes Homer's characterization of Helen in the* Iliad, *asserting that in her, "purity and guilt mingle confusedly" and that her beauty simultaneously elevates and imprisons her.*]

Of all the figures in the poem she is the severest, the most austere. Shrouded in her long white veils, Helen walks across the ***Iliad*** like a penitent; misfortune and beauty are consummate in her and lend majesty to her step. For this royal recluse freedom does not exist; the very slave who numbers the days of oppression on some calendar of hope is freer than she. What has Helen to hope for? Nothing short of the death of the Immortals would restore her freedom, since it is the gods, not her fellow men, who have dared to put her in bondage. Her fate does not depend on the outcome of the war; Paris or Menelaus may get her, but for her nothing can really change. She is the prisoner of the passions her beauty excited, and her passivity is, so to speak, their underside. Aphrodite rules her despotically; the goddess commands and Helen bows, whatever her private repugnance. Pleasure is extorted from her; this merely makes her humiliation the more cruel. Her only resource is to turn against herself a wrath too weak to spite the gods. She seems to live in horror of herself. "Why did I not die before?" is the lament that keeps rising to her lips. Homer is as implacable toward Helen as Tolstoy is toward Anna [in his novel *Anna Karenina*]. Both women have run away from home thinking that they could abolish the past and capture the future in some unchanging essence of love. They awake in exile and feel nothing but a dull disgust for the shrivelled ecstasy that has outlived their hope. The promise of freedom has been sloughed off in servitude; love does not obey the rules of love but yields to some more ancient and ruder law. Beauty and death have become neighbors and from their alliance springs a necessity akin to that of force. When Helen and Anna come to and face their deteriorated dream, they can blame only themselves for having been the dupes of harsh Aphrodite. Everything they squandered comes back on them; everything they touch turns to dust or stone. In driving his heroine to suicide, Tolstoy goes beyond Christianity and rejoins Homer and the tragic poets. To them the hero's flaw is indistinguishable from the misery that arises from it. The sufferer bears it; he pays for it, but he cannot redeem it any more than he can live his life over. Clytemnestra, Oretes and Oedipus are their crimes; they have no existence outside them. Later on, the philosophers, heirs of Odysseus, introduce the Trojan horse of dialectic into the realm of tragedy. Error takes the place of the tragic fault, and the responsibility for it rests with the individual alone. With Homer, punishment and expiation have the opposite effect; far from fixing responsibility, they dissolve it in the vast sea of human suffering and the diffuse guilt of the life-process itself. A flaw in a defective universe is not quite the same thing as a sin; remorse and grace have not yet made their appearance. But it is nonetheless true that this Greek idea of a diffuse guilt represents for Homer and the tragic poets the equivalent of the Christian idea of original sin. Fed on the same reality, charged with the same weight of experience, it contains the same appraisal of existence. It too acknowledges a fall, but a fall that has no date and has been preceded by no state of innocence and will be followed by no redemption; the fall, here, is a continuous one as the life-process itself which heads forever downward into death and the absurd. In proclaiming the innocence of Becoming, Nietzsche is as far from the ancients as he is from Christianity. Where Nietzsche wants to justify, Homer simply contemplates, and the only sound that he lets ring through his lines is the plaint of the hero. If the final responsibility for the tragic guilt rests on the mischievous gods, this does not mean that guilt is nonexistent. On the contrary, there is not a page in the ***Iliad*** that does not emphasize its irreducible character. So fully does Helen assume it that she does not even permit herself the comfort of self-defense. In Helen, purity and guilt mingle confusedly as they do in the vast heart of the warrior herd spread out on the plain at her feet.

Thus Helen, at Ilion, drags her ill luck along with a kind of somber humility that still makes no truce with the gods. But is it really Aphrodite? Is it not rather the Asiatic Astarte who has trapped her? In a certain way, Helen's destiny prefigures that of Greece which, from the Trojan War to Alexander's conquests, was alternately submitting to and repelling the tremendous attraction of the Orient. What the exile misses in Paris' high dwelling is not the blond Achaian, arrogant Menelaus, son of a wild race of Northern barbarians, but the rude, pure homeland—the familiar city, the child she used to fondle.

How tired she gets of the soft, weak ways of Aphrodite's protégé; he is a humiliation and a wound to her. "If the gods have decreed these evils for us, why could not I have had a husband who was capable of a feeling of revolt?" Here in hostile Troy, where boredom makes her despondent, Helen has no one to cling to but Hector, the least oriental of Priam's sons, the most manly, the most Greek. There is a feeling of tenderness between them. Helen's presence is odious to everyone and Hector is her only defender from the hatred she excites. Nobody can forgive the stranger for being the embodiment of the fatality that pursues the city. Innocent though she is, Helen feels the weight of these rebukes; she even seems to invite them, as though courting a just punishment for a crime she did not commit. She is all the more grateful, therefore, to the one person who shows her compassion without importuning her with lust. When Hector comes to scold Paris, Helen is worried about the dangers that threaten her brother-in-law. He is the only one to whom she speaks gently: "Meanwhile, come in, brother, and take this seat. Care assails your heart more than anyone else's, and that because of me, bitch that I am, and the folly of Alexander. Zeus has given us a hard lot, that later on we may be the subject of a song for men to come." These words weave a complicity between Hector and Helen that is something more than fraternal. With an unequalled insight, Homer hears in their talk an accent of intimacy which is attuned to the truth of human relationships. This affection, on Helen's part at least, shields a deeper feeling, which Homer, listening, does to betray.

The exile's lament is the last to echo over Hector's remains; it bathes the end of the ***Iliad*** in the pure, desolate light of compassion. "This is now the twentieth year from the time I came away and left my native land; yet I have never heard a bad or a harsh word from you. So I weep for you and for my unhappy self too, with grief at heart. I have nobody else now in wide Troy to be kind or gentle to me; everybody shudders away from me." This, however, is not the moan of some humiliated creature at the mercy of her tormentors; it is the grief of a mortal at the mercy of gods who have laden her with dazzling graces, the better to balk her of the joy these gifts seemed to promise. No matter who wins in the end, Helen, unlike Andromache and the Trojan princesses, does not have to fear a life of slavery and forced labor "under the eyes of a harsh master." After twenty years, she is still the stake the war is being fought for, and the reward the winner will carry off. In the depths of her wretchedness, Helen still wears an air of majesty that keeps the world at a distance and flouts old age and death. The most beautiful of women seemed born for a radiant destiny; everything pointed that way; everything appeared to contribute to it. But, as it turns out, the gods only chose her to work misfortune on herself and on the two nations. Beauty is not a promise of happiness here; it is a burden and a curse. At the same time, it isolates and elevates; it has something preservative in it that wards off outrage and shame. Hence its sacred character—to use the word in its original, ambiguous sense—on the one hand, life-giving, exalting; on the other, accursed and dread. The Helen the two armies are contending for will never be Paris' any more than she has been Menelaus'; the Trojans cannot own her any more than the Greeks could. Beauty, captured, remains elusive. It deserts alike those who beget, or contemplate, or desire it. Homer endows it with the inexorability of force or fate. Like force, it subjugates and destroys—exalts and releases. It is not by some chance, arising out of her life's vicissitudes, that Helen has come to be the cause of the war and its stake; a deeper necessity has brought her there to join the apparition of beauty with the unleashing of rage. Beside the warriors and above them, Helen is the calm and the bitterness that spring up in the thick of battle, casting their cool shadow over victories and defeats alike, over the living and the thousands of dead. For, if force degrades itself in the insignificance of Becoming (one arrow from Paris' bow puts an end to the might of Achilles), beauty alone transcends all contingencies, including those that brought it to flower. The origins of Leda's daughter are lost in fable, her end in legend. In immortal appearance the world of Being is maintained and protected.

Homer carefully abstains from the description of beauty, as though this might constitute a forbidden anticipation of bliss. The shade of Helen's eyes, of Thetis' tresses, the line of Andromache's shoulders—these details are kept from us. No singularity, no particularity is brought to our notice; yet we see these women; we would recognize them. One wonders by what impalpable means Homer manages to give us such a sense of the plastic reality of his characters. Incorruptible, Helen's beauty passes from life into the poem, from flesh into marble, its pulse still throbbing. The statue's mouth utters a human cry, and from the empty eyes gush "tender tears." When Helen climbs the ramparts of Troy to watch the fight between Paris and Menelaus, one can almost feel the loftiness of her step. By the Scaean gates, the Trojan elders are holding council. At the sight of her, "the good orators" fall silent, struck to the heart. They cannot help finding her beautiful. And this beauty frightens them like a bad omen, a warning of death. "She has terribly the look, close-up, of the imortal goddesses. . . . But even so, whatever she may be, let her set sail and go away. Let her not be left here to be a scourge to us and our sons hereafter." Here—and this is unusual—the poet himself, speaking through Priam, lifts his voice to exonerate beauty and proclaim it innocent of man's misfortunes. "I do not blame you. I blame the gods, who launched this Achaian war, full of tears, upon me." The real culprits, and the only ones, are the gods, who live "exempt from care," while men are consumed with sorrow. The curse which turns beauty into destructive fatality does not originate in the human heart. The diffuse guilt of Becoming pools into a single sin, the one sin condemned and explicitly stigmatized by Homer: the happy carelessness of the Immortals.

A depiction of Achilles and Patroclus.

There follows a scene of starry serenity in which the human accent, however, is still audible. Priam asks Helen to tell him the names of the most famous of the Achaian warriors that he can see in the enemy camp. The battlefield is quiet; a few steps away from each other, the two armies stand face to face awaiting the single combat that will decide the outcome of the war. Here, at the very peak of the ***Iliad,*** is one of those pauses, those moments of contemplation, when the spell of Becoming is broken, and the world of action, with all its fury, dips into peace. The plain where the warrior herd was raging is no more than a tranquil mirage to Helen and the old king.

No doubt this is where Nietzsche listened to the dialogue between Beauty and Wisdom, set above life but very close to it. "Pushed, pressed, constrained, tracked down by torment," come at length to the place where, around him, everything "turned strange and solitary," he had a vision of Helen (or Ariadne), high and inaccessible against the blue sky.

Meanwhile Helen stands helplessly watching the men who are going to do battle for her. She is there still, since nations that brave each other for markets, for raw materials, rich lands, and their treasures, are fighting, first and forever, for Helen (pp. 61-9)

Rachel Bespaloff, in her On the Iliad, *translated by Mary McCarthy, Bollingen Series IX, 1947, 126 p.*

RICHMOND LATTIMORE (essay date 1951)

[Lattimore is a foremost American Greek scholar and is perhaps best known for his highly acclaimed translation of the Iliad. *In the following excerpt from his introduction to that work, Lattimore discusses the characterization of Hector, Achilles, Agamemnon,*

Odysseus, and Aias in the Iliad, *as well as their treatment by later writers.*]

The ***Iliad*** is a story, and the strength of a story, as such, depends to a great extent on its characters. The actions and achievements of the great Homeric characters might have been fixed in tradition, or twisted by *tendenz* [bias], but within the frame-work of fact the personality of the hero might remain plastic. Not the "what", but the "how" and "why", gave the poet some option.

Against the tragedy of Achilleus is set the tragedy of Troy, and the two strands are closely involved. The hero of the Trojan tragedy is Hektor. We looked at him once before, from the Achaian point of view; to them he was a figure of terror even for their bravest, over-rated perhaps, but deadly enough in his actions as well as his menaces. But Goliath of Gath might have looked to the wives and mothers of the Philistines very different from the monster seen by Saul and Abner. It shows a significant difference between epic and chronicle when Homer takes us over to the other side and lets us see Hektor as the Trojans saw him.

In Troy, Hektor was beloved. Homer interrupts his narrative to take him back to Troy and show him with mother, brother and sister-in-law, wife and child, all affectionate and concerned. Priam and Hekabe consider him far the best and dearest of their sons. Helen testifies that where others were hateful (an exaggeration characteristic of Helen) Hektor was always kind. (p. 45)

Hektor's tragedy is that of Troy. He, like it, is destroyed fighting a quarrel unworthy of him. He does not believe in Paris' quarrel, and he does not like to fight. When Andromache beseeches him not to go back into open battle, the beginning of his answer is revealing:

> yet I would feel deep shame
> before the Trojans, and the Trojan women with trailing garments
> if like a coward I were to shrink aside from the fighting;
> and the spirit will not let me, since I have learned to be valiant
> and to fight always among the foremost ranks of the Trojans.

Perhaps one should not stress too much the implications of "I have learned," but the close of Hektor's speech to Paris a little later shows the same tendency:

> Let us go now; some day hereafter we will make all right
> with the immortal gods in the sky, if Zeus ever grant it,
> setting up to them in our houses the wine-bowl of liberty
> after we have driven out of Troy the strong-greaved Achaians.

Not bloodthirsty enough to be a natural warrior, he fights finely from a sense of duty and a respect for the opinions of others, a respect which Paris notoriously lacks.

> Surely now the flowing-haired Achaians laugh at us,
> thinking you are our bravest champion, only because your
> looks are handsome, but there is no strength in your heart, no courage.
> No, but the Trojans are cowards in truth, else long before this
> you had worn a mantle of flying stones for the wrong you did us.

The sneer sticks to Hektor himself. Some hidden weakness, not cowardice but perhaps the fear of being called a coward, prevents him from liquidating a war which he knows perfectly well is unjust. This weakness, which is not remote from his boasting, nor from his valour, is what kills him.

The function of Achilleus in the ***Iliad*** of itself necessitates certain qualities. The necessary man must be a supreme warrior, but in station and as a king he ranks below Agamemnon. As a hero of tragedy, he is great, but human and imperfect. His tragedy is an effect of free choice by a will that falls short of omniscience and is disturbed by anger.

In the ***Iliad*** his supremacy as a warrior is scarcely challenged, and is insisted upon at all times. After Patroklos' death he terrifies the battle-weary Trojans by appearing, unarmed. But his supremacy is powered by gods who favour, strengthen, and protect him. In the scene just mentioned, he is supernaturally attended. When he shouts, Athene shouts with him, and when he appears he is surrounded in a flaming nimbus lit by Athene. Thetis carries his case to Zeus, and it is put through against the will of powerful goddesses. Hephaistos makes him immortal armour. When Hektor at last fights him, he fights at a gross disadvantage, swindled by Athene and deserted by Apollo, with inferior body armour and with no spear. Achilleus goes so well guarded by gods that Aineias, himself a divine favourite, can justly complain; none can meet Achilleus on fair terms. (pp. 45-7)

Nevertheless, Achilleus is not in any sense immortal. The legend of almost complete invulnerability is either unknown to Homer or discarded by him. He is closer to the gods than other heroes, but defers to them generally; one failure to do so, in his fight with the river, almost brings him to an abrupt and undignified ending, from which he is saved only by the intervention of stronger divinities. Achilleus is prescient beyond others, but his knowledge has limitations, and his character can be invaded by the human emotions of grief, fear, a passage which makes plain that he is neither semi-divinity nor superman, and, above all, anger.

It is the anger of pride, the necessary accompaniment of the warrior's greatness, that springs the tragedy of the ***Iliad.*** We see it in the treatment of Hektor's body and the slaughter of captives; we see it motivate the quarrel of the first book, where the fourth word of the first line is "anger." He dares Agamemnon, makes it almost impossible for the latter to act except as he does. Yet as he leaves to pray for the defeat of his friends, though this prayer amounts to outright treason, we feel, as we are meant to feel, that he is in the right. In the ninth book, the burden shifts. Agamemnon has never touched the girl Briseis, and now he will give her back and offers abundant gifts in addition. The offer is conveyed by three of Achilleus' best friends. Odysseus warns him against pride and anger, and appeals to him in the name of friendship, but Achilleus rejects all appeals. Then Aias reproduces him, not with treachery or lack of patriotism, but with bad friendship, and Achilleus answers:

> all that you have said seems spoken after my own mind.
> Yet still the heart in me swells up in anger, when I remember
> the disgrace that he wrought upon me before the Argives.

He has now put himself in the wrong. Anger has clouded a high intelligence, and Achilleus acts uncertainly. Before, he had announced his intention of sailing home, but instead stayed by his ships and watched the fighting, torturing himself and the others by his inaction. Now, again, he threatens to go home; but shifts again, and refuses to fight until Hektor reaches the ships of the Myrmidons. Such a moment is near, when Achilleus at last gives way to Patroklos and lets him go in his place. He is again uncertain:

> still we will let all this be a thing of the past; and it was not
> in my heart to be angry forever; and yet I did say
> I would not give over my anger until that time came
> when the fighting with all its clamour came up to my own ships.
> So do you draw my glorious armour about your shoulders;
> lead the Myrmidons whose delight is battle into the fighting.

There is no reason now why Achilleus should not fight himself. His action makes no sense, and is fatal to Patroklos. So Achilleus admits to his mother. The tragedy is his, the result of his own choice.

Apollo, outraged at the treatment of his friend Hektor, practically describes Achilleus as a brute and a barbarian. He is not. He is a man of culture and intelligence; he knows how to respect heralds, how to entertain estranged friends. He presides over the games with extraordinary courtesy and tact. He is not only a great fighter but a great gentleman, and if he lacks the chivalry of Roland, Lancelot, or Beowulf, that is because theirs is a chivalry coloured with Christian humility which has no certain place in the gallery of Homeric virtues. Above all, Achilleus is a real man, mortal and fallible, but noble enough to make his own tragedy a great one.

Most of the greater Achaian heroes are kings in their own right, but the greatest king among them is Agamemnon. Whether he is emperor of the Achaians, or general of the army, or the king with most subjects, whose friends stand by him in his brother's quarrel (unless he insults them), is a question apparently as obscure to the heroes of the ***Iliad*** as it is to us. But essentially a king is what he is; not the biggest Achaian, says Priam to Helen, but the kingliest; a bull in a herd of cattle; a lord who must be busy while others rest, marshalling his men for ordered assault. In the quarrel with Achilleus, he demands recognition of his kingly stature, as if afraid of losing his position if he lacks what others have, in this case a captive mistress. So he comes off badly, yet even here, while he reviles Kalchas and beats down Achilleus, his first thought is for the army.

Here, in his position, is the key to Agamemnon's character. As brave and effective a personal fighter as one could ask (Achilleus' strictures are manifestly untrue), Agamemnon is a worried, uncertain man. Beyond others, he drifts in his thinking. He invites the Achaians to go home in order to "make trial" of them, but ends up as if he had outwitted himself and believed his own falsehoods. Certainly, he stands helpless in front of the confusion he has caused, and it is Odysseus, backed by Hera and Athene, who pulls the situation around. His panic, when Menelaos is treacherously wounded, causes a similar drift of thought: he begins with the assurance that the Trojans must die for their treachery and ends by visualizing a triumphant Trojan jumping on the grave of Menelaos. He veers between the two poles of thought: that he can take Troy at once, without Achilleus; that he will be lucky if he gets any of his men home alive. Twice after his test of the second book he proposes mass flight, at once. In all moods of despair, he must be rallied and propped up by Odysseus, Nestor, and Diomedes, who are tougher than he. But the uncertainty is that of a king, with whom Homer's aristocratic audience may well have sympathized, and it is his "kingliness," his concern for those he leads, which grounds his uncertainty. Nevertheless, irresolution and consequent anger combine with the anger of Achilleus to motivate tragedy.

Odysseus of the ***Iliad*** foreshadows Odysseus of the ***Odyssey*** not only in his epithets (resourceful, long-suffering, etc.) but in his whole character. I do not know whether this means that the same man composed both ***Iliad*** and ***Odyssey;*** but it does mean that the author of the ***Odyssey*** thoroughly understood the Odysseus of the ***Iliad.*** We can, I think, argue from one work to the other.

Odysseus is crafty, resourceful, daring, and merciless. These characteristics have usually been taken as essentials of his personality from which stem the stop-at-nothing politician of Sophocles, or Dante's treacherous captain (*Inferno,* Canto 26). But guile and unscrupulousness are only secondary characteristics of the Homeric Odysseus.

Essentially, he can be described by the Greek word *sophron* (though the word is not Homeric). This is untranslatable. It means, not necessarily that you have superior brains, but that you make maximum use of whatever brains you have got. Odysseus is the antithesis of Achilleus. Achilleus has a fine intelligence, but passion clouds it; Odysseus has strong passions, but his intelligence keeps them under control. Achilleus, Hektor, and Agamemnon, magnificent as they are, are flawed with uncertainty and can act on confused motives; Odysseus never. So those three are tragic heroes, but Odysseus, less magnificent but a complete man, is the hero of his own romantic comedy, the ***Return of Odysseus,*** or ***Odyssey.***

A single purpose guides Odysseus in the ***Iliad.*** The expedition against Troy must succeed. Whether this motive grows out of personal affection for Agamemnon is not clear. But this is the end toward which the demoralized army must be rallied, Thersites chastised, Achilleus propitiated, Agamemnon braced. A single purpose guides Odysseus through the ***Odyssey*** as well. He must get home and put his house and kingdom in order. To do this, he must drive his men and himself, outwit and outlast trial by danger and trial by pleasure, leave the blandishing goddesses, fight down his joy at seeing home and wife for fear joy might give him away prematurely, fight down, for the same reason, rage at seeing the disorder in his household.

A man who could win through all this is a man supremely adequate, in mind and body; therefore, by corollary, resourceful, much enduring Odysseus can be most eloquent, but he wastes no eloquence on Thersites—who has an unanswerable argument—but beats him up and makes him cry, which is far more effective. He can build a raft and sail it, or build a bed, or plough a field. He has no recklessness, but does have stark courage when that is needed; the Odysseus who makes the plans for others to fight by is post-Homeric. Always equal to the occasion, he startles the Trojans who think he looks like a fool and can be no orator, as he startles the suitors who take him for a broken-down tramp. Not the noblest or stateliest of Homer's heroes, he is the one who survives.

Greatest of the warriors after Achilleus is Aias. Homer is very firm about this, although Diomedes at times seems to surpass anything that Aias can do. Diomedes in his *aristeia* [courage, prowess] fights under the protection of Athene, and Achilleus is constantly attended and favoured by divinities; but Aias carries on, from beginning to end, without benefit of supernatural aid.

A huge man, he is compared to a wall, and carries a great shield of seven-fold ox-hide. He is not the man to sweep the enemy back in a single burst, as Diomedes, Agamemnon, Achilleus, or Hektor can do; rather, his fighting qualities appear in a comparison drawn by Idomeneus:

> Nor would huge Telamonian Aias give way to any man
> who was mortal and ate bread, the yield of Demeter,
> one who could be broken by the bronze and great stones
> flung at him.
> He would not make way for Achilleus who breaks men
> in battle,
> in close combat. For speed of feet none can strive with
> Achilleus.

Lack of inspired brilliance may go with the failure, in Aias' case, of that divine aid lavished on other heroes. He fights as a big man, with no aura of the supernatural about him; best on defence and when the going is worst. With the other great Achaians out of action, he keeps the Achaian retreat from becoming a rout, defends the wall, and then the ships. At the last moment before Patroklos and the Myrmidons come to the rescue, we find him leading the defence of the ships, baffled by Hektor, beaten, sweating, and arm-weary, without hope, but still fighting. Lacking the glamour of others, never the greatest leader, Aias remains throughout the best soldier of them all.

Space will not allow further analysis of Homeric persons, and such a study has in any case frequently been made. My purpose has been to illustrate, briefly, the coherence of these persons as they appear *in the text of the Homeric poems,* particularly the ***Iliad.*** It was necessary to do this, because we too often observe the Homeric hero through a disfiguring mist, and with preconceptions which lead us into error.

The political situation in the Achaian army, as implied in the ***Iliad,*** becomes explicitly developed and exploited in later tradition, until we find something like the following. An unscrupulous king, backed by a little group of politicians, not only leads Hellas into a disastrous, unnecessary war, but consistently slights and outrages his noblest warriors. Homer's story of Achilleus, the analogous, unused story of Philoktetes, the post-Homeric tale of Palamedes—Odysseus' rival, a truly wise man, done to death by chicanery—show the trend. The people of the epic become, in the fifth century, counters for political propaganda and the exploitations of intra-Hellenic hatreds. To Pindar, Aias is an Aiginetan; to Sophocles, an Athenian. Menelaos, the courtly and considerate *grand seigneur* [great lord] (and millionaire!) of ***Iliad*** and ***Odyssey,*** becomes the vulgar villain of Sophocles' *Aias,* the personification of Spartan *machtpolitik* [politics of might] in Euripides' *Andromache*. Euripides can use Kalchas to vent his spleen against soothsayers, Talthybios to convey an almost equally potent aversion for heralds.

Such manipulations passed, of course, as "historical interpretations," and are merely developments, sometimes outrageous, of a situation inherent in the story-pattern of the necessary man. A clear case is the rivalry of Odysseus and Aias. In the ***Iliad,*** it does not exist, or at least goes unrecognized. But in the ***Odyssey,*** we find allusion to the story of how the armour of dead Achilleus was awarded to Odysseus, rather than Aias, and how Aias died as a result. How and why Aias died Homer does not tell us, even in the ***Odyssey;*** but according to the Cycle, he went mad and killed himself.

By the time Pindar and the tragic poets get to work, the opposed heroes have come to represent the man of counsel and the man-at-arms. Odysseus, his valour and devotion forgotten, has stood ever since for the crafty, treacherous politician. Aias does not come off much better. The story of the armour, *in itself,* demands a character different from that of the hero in the ***Iliad,*** for the ***Iliad***'s Aias is as soberly sane as anyone in the epic. The reasoning must be something like this: Aias died as a result of not being awarded the armour. Nobody is known to have killed him, he must have killed himself. If so, he must have been mad; and if capable of insanity over such a point of honour, therefore naturally proud, vain, and choleric. The bare negative fact of the ***Iliad,*** that Aias fought so well without divine protection, becomes twisted into a positive story that he arrogantly despised the proffered help of the gods, particularly Athene, the protectress of Diomedes and Odysseus. Therefore, she wrecked him with delusions which drove him to slaughter cattle in the belief they were his enemies. Here we may have a contamination with Aias' namesake, the Lokrian, who "defied the lightning" and came to so violent an end. At all events, we have the materials for Shakespeare's unbelievably believable caricature in *Troilus and Cressida*. This is an example of tradition, character, interpretation, and new tradition in the life of Homeric figures. (pp. 47-53)

Richmond Lattimore, in an introduction to The Iliad of Homer *by Homer, translated by Richmond Lattimore, University of Chicago Press, 1951, pp. 11-58.*

W. H. AUDEN (poem date 1952)

[*Often considered the poetic successor of W. B. Yeats and T. S. Eliot, Auden is also highly regarded for his literary criticism. He was strongly influenced by the ideas of Karl Marx and Sigmund Freud. As a committed follower of Christianity, he considered it necessary to view art in the context of moral and theological absolutes. Thus, he regarded art as a "secondary world" which should serve a definite purpose within the "primary world" of human history. This purpose is the creation of aesthetic beauty and moral order, qualities that exist only in imperfect form in the primary world but are intrinsic to the secondary world of art. Consequently, it is both morally and aesthetically wrong for an artist to employ evil and suffering as subject matter. While he has been criticized for significant inconsistencies in his thought throughout his career, Auden is generally regarded as a fair and perceptive critic. Auden's 1952 poem "The Shield of Achilles," inspired by the Hephaestos episode in the* Iliad, *appears below.*]

She looked over his shoulder
For vines and olive trees,
Marble well-governed cities,
And ships upon untamed seas,
But there on the shining metal
His hands had put instead
An artificial wilderness
And a sky like lead.

A plain without a feature, bare and brown,
No blade of grass, no sign of neighborhood,
Nothing to eat and nowhere to sit down,
Yet, congregated on its blankness, stood

An unintelligible multitude.
A million eyes, a million boots in line,
Without expression, waiting for a sign.

Out of the air a voice without a face
  Proved by statistics that some cause was just
In tones as dry and level as the place:
  No one was cheered and nothing was discussed;
  Column by column in a cloud of dust
They marched away enduring a belief
Whose logic brought them, somewhere else, to grief.

She looked over his shoulder
  For ritual pieties,
White flower-garlanded heifers,
  Libation and sacrifice,
But there on the shining metal
  Where the altar should have been,
She saw by his flickering forge-light
  Quite another scene.

Barbed wire enclosed an arbitrary spot
  Where bored officials lounged (one cracked a joke)
And sentries sweated, for the day was hot:
  A crowd of ordinary decent folk
  Watched from without and neither moved nor spoke
As three pale figures were led forth and bound
To three posts driven upright in the ground.

The mass and majesty of this world, all
  That carries weight and always weighs the same,
Lay in the hands of others; they were small
  And could not hope for help and no help came:
  What their foes like to do was done, their shame
Was all the worst could wish; they lost their pride
And died as men before their bodies died.

She looked over his shoulder
  For athletes at their games,
Men and women in a dance
  Moving their sweet limbs
Quick, quick, to music,
  But there on the shining shield
His hands had set no dancing-floor
  But a weed-choked field.

A ragged urchin, aimless and alone,
  Loitered about that vacancy; a bird
Flew up to safety from his well-aimed stone:
  That girls are raped, that two boys knife a third,
  Were axioms to him, who'd never heard
Of any world where promises were kept
Or one could weep because another wept.

The thin-lipped armorer,
  Hephaestos, hobbled away;
Thetis of the shining breasts
  Cried out in dismay
At what the god had wrought
  To please her son, the strong
Iron-hearted man-slaying Achilles
  Who would not live long.

(pp. 454-55)

W. H. Auden, "The Shield of Achilles," in his W. H. Auden: Collected Poems, *edited by Edward Mendelson, Random House, 1976, pp. 454-55.*

E. M. W. TILLYARD (essay date 1954)

[Tillyard was an English scholar of Renaissance literature who remains highly reputed for his studies of John Milton, William Shakespeare, and the epic form. In the following excerpt, he praises the complexity and "width of vision" of the Iliad *and explores the thematic and structural importance of Achilles. Tillyard concludes that, although it is the first Western epic, the* Iliad *is an "entirely mature" poem.]*

About the poetic excellence of the different parts of the ***Iliad,*** narrative skill, characterisation, force of style, etc., there is general agreement, and little need be said. However ready-made some Homeric phrases may be, Homer, it is admitted, can put them to effective and, if necessary, new use. He can say just what he wants to say. (p. 25)

If, as has been pointed out, Homer is both a channel for earlier habits of thought and the fountain-head of very persistent and important later ones, he must achieve one kind of variety. But he is ample . . . in that he has an eye for everything: nothing escapes it. And that width of vision, comprehending every detail, in no way impairs the man's concentration on the business he has in hand. Shakespeare, and perhaps no other poet, equals him in this union of concentration and flexibility. The first book of the ***Iliad*** gives in little the prevalent Homeric method. It begins with a display of the most violent passions in the quarrel between Agamemnon and Achilles over the return of Briseis: a scene confined and concentrated in the manner of tragedy. It is followed by a scene of greatly lowered passion but more widely set and pictured with no less intensity, the intensity now concerning the warmth with which the details are apprehended and presented. It represents Agamemnon's two emissaries, coming to Achilles's tent to fetch away Briseis. The details are few, but all necessary, and each stands out with an uncommon clarity like the folds of bare hills lit by the evening sun on a very clear day. The emissaries approach and Achilles was not glad. . . . They stand in embarrassment, till Achilles tells them to get on with their business. They are not to blame, but Agamemnon. And when they leave, Achilles goes apart by the sea, to digest his wrongs and to call his mother from the waters to help him. And the very slight elaboration of seascape beyond one consisting of the bare conventional descriptive phrases serves to suggest the aptness of associating a lonely part of the shore and the digestion of grief. . . . In the picture of the two emissaries, not liking their job and standing embarrassed before Achilles, there is the slightest touch of comedy; and in the subsequent scene on Olympus full comedy emerges. Hera is angry that Thetis and Zeus have been hatching something between them that she knows nothing of; and Zeus replies that there *are* things he means to keep to himself, though she will be the first to hear anything that he thinks fit to divulge. We are in fact in the social world, where folk quarrel yet somehow in the end conform to an agreed standard of conduct, where Zeus has a hard task in controlling his unruly household of deities and just (but only just) succeeds.

But Homer does more than observe and set forth life's many varieties. He recognises incompatibilities and paradoxes, and like the other great poets he can be on both sides at once. The largest paradox has to do with war and peace, and it takes us to the heart of Homer's philosophy and of the scheme of his poem. First, Homer believes that the works of peace are good and that the sacking of cities is terrible. One of the cities Hephaestus represented on Achilles's shield was at peace, and a bridal procession was in progress. In the torchlight they were leading the brides through the streets, while the bridal song was being sung and young men were whirling in the dance; and the women stood on their doorsteps watching and admiring. Homer is in love with his picture as he is with those of ploughing and vintage. He is equally horrified with the foreboding he puts into Hector's mouth of Andromache led to captivity; Hector, uttering it, prays he may be in his grave before he witnesses the sight and hears her cries. But there is another side, as certain and as unescapable. Honour is another value and it can be won only at the expense of the other value. The best men have to sack cities, for only so is the highest vitality achieved and the shortness of life redeemed.

Homer keeps hinting at this double theme, but does not allow it to become very evident till a third of the way through the poem. It is in the ninth book that he shows us Achilles confronted with the two values between which he had made his choice before coming to Troy. There Achilles, though still implacable to Agamemnon and scornful of his gifts, opens his heart to Odysseus and Ajax, the bearers of Agamemnon's offers, whom he respects. He tells how his mother Thetis foresaw that he could choose between two destinies: that of honour and that of domestic happiness. If he joined the Trojan expedition, he would earn the highest honour but lose his life; if he stayed at home, he would inherit his father's wealth and live long. The ordered domestic life and the sanctity of property: Achilles does not underprize these things. But he made his choice, and, having made it, acted on it thoroughly. He slaved for honour, laying waste twenty-three cities in the Troad for little return. And now, as he told his mother when he called her from the sea near the beginning of the poem, Agamemnon has robbed him of his honour. And so he proposed to go back on his choice and return home to live to old age.

There is not space to enlarge further on Homer's variety in the ***Iliad.*** The sum of the matter is that his mind spanned most of life as then experienced.

Spanning so much, he increased the task of shaping his material. He fulfilled it principally in two ways: through his hero and through making his limited plot so pregnant that a few days' fighting implied the whole course of the Trojan War.

Achilles is not a mere fighter; he draws into himself and unifies all the scattered references to the morality of his time. He is a man sinned against, sinning, and repentant. Agamemnon did him a great wrong. But, in the scene where he spoke of the choice offered to him between short life with honour and long domestic joy without, he fell into the great error of refusing Agamemnon's attempt to make amends. He rejected the Prayers, that were the daughters of Zeus, as Homer allegorically put it. From that refusal came Patroclus's entry into battle without Achilles and his death at Hector's hand. That death brings Achilles back to battle but not to his right mind. He kills Hector but insults his body, a dreadful crime which the gods abhor. Only at the very end when Priam goes in person to beg his son's body does Achilles repent. This repentance is invaluable structurally. It exemplifies that reverence for the agreed decencies of life which was central to Homer's morality and for a moment at least it unites the two opposed values of honour and domestic order. To make my point I must go into a little detail. Priam pursues his dangerous quest by night. He goes to Achilles's tent with a ransom and performs the act of a suppliant. In the terms of Homer's earlier allegory, Prayers, the daughters of Zeus, approach Achilles once more. Priam in making his plea reminds Achilles of his father, Peleus. This time Achilles does not fail to reverence the daughters of Zeus. But he does more. The thought of Peleus, old and childless but for himself, who is destined soon to die, stirs his sense of pity, which is extended to Priam, old too and now nearly childless by his own action. At this culminating place in the poem Achilles learns that the two worlds of war and home may be seen in a common light. Though Priam is his enemy, and doubly so because Priam's son killed Patroclus, he applies to him the emotion of pity, an emotion proper to the domestic life. He also gets out of the immediate business of war and bereavement to a position from which he can view all the varieties of experience together. First he describes Peleus's fortune and misfortune, then Priam's early wealth and present plight. . . . For a moment friend and foe are one, as Achilles sees himself the bane of both: of his father by leaving him in his old age, of Priam by killing his sons. Poised on that height, Achilles is the spectator and critic of both the realms between which he had to choose.

The main lines of the structure are majestic and satisfying; and there are signs of the author's bearing the whole in his mind throughout. Homer set himself the difficult task of combining two themes, the whole Trojan War and the personal story of Achilles: difficult, but, if successful, perfect for epic purposes. His method is to begin and end with the two themes intertwined. The anger of Achilles is at once a public disaster and a private passion: the burial of Hector signifies the end of the twelve days' truce which Achilles promised Priam and the end of all Trojan hopes to defend their city—the war is virtually over—as well as the mental regeneration of Achilles. In between, the two themes are often combined, but there are long stretches where one theme (and particularly the first) is to the fore, and the other theme is disengaged, though not absent from the background. The Trojan War was supposed to have lasted ten years, and to give the sense of size and length Homer could not escape including many scenes of fighting. He was interested in military details, but it probably taxed his will-power to the utmost to include so much and yet not to flag. His strategy is to punctuate his fighting with other business, to space it out cunningly; his tactics are to multiply the types of warring acts and to embellish and relieve them by the utmost wealth of simile.

But besides giving in a few days' fighting the sense of a long war, Homer has to imply its course, its beginning, and end. He does so by re-enactment, by prophecy, and by falsification. He re-enacts the beginning of the war at the end of the third and the beginning of the fourth book. There Paris and Menelaus—the two men concerned with the quarrel between Trojans and Greeks—meet in single fight. Menelaus is the stronger and would have killed Paris had not Aphrodite snatched him away. She carries him to Troy, beautifies him, and brings him and Helen together. Paris, in saying that he now loves her more than at any time since he stole her from Sparta, re-enacts his original theft. Then in the next book Zeus asks the gods whether they had not better spare Troy and let Menelaus take Helen back to Sparta; and he re-enacts in imagination the former days of peace. The beginnings of the war are thus summoned up. Prophecy is frequent. We constantly hear that Troy will fall. Hector, dying, prophesies Achilles's death in the Scaean gates at the hands of Paris and Apollo. Hector, parting from Andromache, has a vision of her carried away captive when Troy falls. Most plainly of all, in Book Fifteen Zeus foretells to Hera the deaths of Patroclus and Hector, from which moment the Greeks will attack continuously till Troy falls. Homer falsifies with fine effect in Book Two. The armies muster as if for the first time, regardless of the war being in its tenth year and of all the losses both sides must in actuality have sustained.

The catalogue of the ships and forces, too, is inappropriate to this stage of the war. In Book Three Helen and Priam comment on the Greek chiefs as if they had only just landed. This inappropriateness is no argument for spuriousness or multiple authorship, for it is only factual and not poetical. Homer writes as if the war was in its first year because he wants to create the impression of its whole extent. There is time in twenty-four books for fighters to die or tire, and for the war to grow old. When the fighting begins, forces must be intact and spirits fresh. These are but samples of many touches by which Homer builds up the context of the whole war.

There are many cross-references, and their cumulative effect is very great. One has been cited already, the mention in the last book of Peleus, which links with Achilles's mention of him in the embassy scene in the ninth. And this instance must stand for a great many others I have no room to bring up. (pp. 25-9)

In what I have chosen to say (out of so much that could be said) of the ***Iliad*** I meant to include enough to impress on the readers the mature art of the poem. There is no question of making allowances. The first epic writing in the western tradition is entirely mature, like a great stream that issues straight out of the side of a mountain. There must indeed have been tributaries, but they are invisible. After the ***Iliad*** there can be no question of creating a form, only one of modifying it. (p. 29)

E. M. W. Tillyard, "Homer," in his The English Epic and Its Background, *Oxford University Press, 1954, pp. 21-39.*

CEDRIC H. WHITMAN (essay date 1958)

[*An American classics scholar specializing in Greek literature, Whitman is highly esteemed as a Homer critic. In the following excerpt, he argues that in the* Iliad *Homer imposed a structure "on the loose parataxis of the heroic tradition" by adapting the ring composition technique used in Geometric Greek art of the period. As a result, the* Iliad *is arranged in a circular fashion, Whitman posits, with scenes and books balancing each other through similarity or contrast.*]

[The] typology of the scenes in the poetry of Homer and other oral singers has been the subject of excellent studies, and one does well to keep in mind the warning of Parry not to find "falsely subtle meanings in the repetitions, as meant to recall an earlier scene where the same words were used." And yet, though such echoes would be present in all singers' efforts, one of the traits of Homer's excellence seems to have been the gift to control these echoes more than other oral poets have done. For the fixed elements of the oral style are fixed only in themselves, and out of context. In context they inevitably change color and tone, and it is by no means implausible, on the face of it, that a skilled singer, the scion of many generations of the tradition, should become aware of the subtleties of shifting context and make some effort to use them. Clearly, not every one could be controlled; moreover, it must be assumed that, like so may processes of poetic composition, much of this effort must have failed to reach the level of full consciousness. Yet, insofar as the use of balancing, or echoing, motifs contributes to the broad structure of the poems, conscious intent is probably to be assumed, since the design which emerges bears the unmistakable stamp of the waking intellect. In treating imagery, one had to deal with association and intuition; here, in the matter of structure, one is confronted by a schematized pattern, rationally worked out and altogether consistent with the observable artistic practices of the Geometric Age. (pp. 249-50)

Such a device as ring composition, especially as developed into an architectonic principle, is wholly consistent with Geometric art. The very name "ring composition" arises because such enclosure by identical or very similar elements produces a circular effect, the acoustical analogue of the visual circle; and circles, especially concentric circles, are prime motifs in Protogeometric art. In later Geometric, this design is not so common, but the idea of the circle is carried out in friezes of warriors or mourners running back into themselves, whose moving aesthetic principle is unbroken continuity, perfect and perpetual motion. One may indeed find a similar circularity penetrating all Homeric poetry, especially the ***Iliad,*** not merely in scenes, but in the poem as a whole; and again the root of the principle lies in a practical need. Ever since the time of Cicero, if not before, Homer's habit of returning to things previously mentioned in reverse order has been observed, and sometimes compared to the rhetorical figures of hysteron proteron. This device, doubtless of mnemonic purpose to assist the singer to keep in mind what he had said before, is also pregnant with stylistic possibilities; like ring composition, it returns to its point of origin and effects circularity of design, while the inverted elements may also be spread out to include as a centerpiece a whole scene or scenes, as in a frame. Thus hysteron proteron and ring composition, too, suggest not only circularity, but also framing and balance. (pp. 253-54)

The principle of circularity, including concentricity, or framing by balanced similarity and antithesis, is one of the chief dynamic forces underlying the symmetry of Geometric vase design. In the ***Iliad,*** the old device of hysteron proteron has been expanded into a vast scheme far transcending any mere mnemonic purpose, a scheme purely and even abstractly architectonic. Not only are certain whole books of the poem arranged in self-reversing, or balancing, designs, but the poem as a whole is, in a way, an enormous hysteron proteron, in which books balance books and scenes balance scenes by similarity or antithesis, with the most amazing virtuosity. The very serious question arises, of course, as to whether the audience, listening to an oral presentation of the poem, could possibly have caught the signs of such "fearful symmetry," or whether it would have meant anything to them if they did. Granted that the procedure *abba* is useful in small compass to a singer, and perceptible as a structural unit to the audience, such can hardly be the case when *ba* is separated from *ab* by many thousand lines. Yet two things may be said regarding this point. The human mind is a strange organ, and one which perceives many things without conscious or articulate knowledge of them, and responds to them with emotions necessarily and appropriately vague. An audience hence might feel more symmetry than it could possibly analyze or describe. The second point is that poets sometimes perform feats of virtuosity for their own sakes and without much hope of understanding from their audiences, for one of the minor joys of artistic creation is the secret which the artist buries in his work, the beauty (if such indeed it be) which he has deliberately concealed amid the beauties which he has tried to reveal and express. *Finnegans Wake* and the ciphers and acrostics in late Medieval and Renaissance poetry offer good examples, though an even better one is to be found in the poem which serves as prologue to Dylan Thomas's collected works. This poem, some four pages long, employs perhaps the most imperceptible rhyme-scheme ever invented: the first line rhymes with the last, the second with the second last, and so on until a couplet marks the exact middle. Needless to say, the couplet seems fortuitous to the reader, and the rest of the zealous effort goes by unnoticed, unless it is pointed out by someone who heard it from someone else to whom the author explained it. A poet does such things to please himself, one must suppose. As for Homer, his scheme is at least as evident as Thomas's, and demonstrably serves a more real end. In any case, it should not be dismissed as mere empty virtuosity; for if the oral singer was accustomed to designing scenes, or at least some scenes, by means of hysteron proteron, it is not unnatural that he should seek to give shape to the large epic also in the same way, and especially if he had before him the example of the huge vases of the Dipylon, wherein, with no change of technique, the motifs and proportions of earlier Geometric pottery were expanded and adjusted to monumental dimensions.

There is nothing new in perceiving Geometric design in Homer. His use of polarities as a structural principle has been traced in certain contexts with convincing results. His use of the magic numbers three and nine has been compared, less convincingly, to Geometric circles. Long ago, the *Shield of Achilles* was analyzed as a symmetrically balanced set of opposites, and manifestly a designed balance was intended in the fact that the ***Iliad*** begins with a quarrel and ends with a reconciliation. The men who are reconciled are not the same as those who quarreled, of course; the poem has its own movement and does not end precisely where it began. The formulaic types, Quarrel and Reconciliation, are employed as balanced opposites, while the contextual difference, with all its implications for the character of the hero, creates the poet's meaning. Less meaningful but more surprising is the grouping of the days involved in the poem's action. So far as elapsed, or narrated, time is concerned, the night embassy to Achilles (with the *Doloneia,* if genuine) forms the middle point, flanked on each side by a single day's fighting: namely, the indecisive Interrupted Battle of VIII and the extremely decisive Great Battle of XI to XVIII. These are in turn framed by two groups of three days each, in which the action is not only closely unified but also similar. Books II to VII devote one day to fighting, one to burial of the dead, and one to the building of the wall. The corresponding group includes three days, too: the day of Achilles' *aristeia* [courage, prowess], the funeral of Patroclus, and the Funeral Games. The day groupings of I and XXIV then reverse each other neatly: Book I has first the day of Chryses' appeal, followed by nine days of plague, the day of the council and quarrel, and finally a twelve-day gap till the gods return to Olympus; Book XXIV begins with a twelve-day period during which the gods grow steadily more disgusted with Achilles' excesses, followed by the day on which Iris rouses Priam to go to the Greek camp; nine days are then devoted to gathering wood for Hector's pyre, and on the tenth day he is buried. . . . [The scheme of days] can scarcely have made itself felt to a listening audience; and yet, it can hardly be fortuitous. Homer seems to have been playing with abstract form for its own sake, and basing his conception of it on the hysteron proteron scheme. Its mathematical symmetry would appeal to any artist of the Geometric Age. If it seems farfetched for such a pristine time, we must bear in mind that there is absolutely nothing primitive about Homer except some parts of his traditional subject matter. And if it seems pointless and imperceptible from the point of view of the general public of Homer's period, we should also ask how many of Mozart's original audiences appreciated the extraordinary economy of tonality in *Don Giovanni,* or caught the musical puns on horns in *Figaro* and *Cosi fan tutte*. So too, not all the admirers of *Lohengrin* know that, with the exception of one passage near the end of the first act, the opera is written wholly in 2/4 or 4/4 time, a feature of inner unity of no consequence to the conscious receptivity of the layman, but a token for fellow artists, on the one hand, and an unperceived but effectual device, on the other. Music, indeed, abounds in such abstractions, yet aims at achieving its effect even on those who cannot follow them. To dismiss or judge adversely these technical procedures, however, because they are not readily seen by nonprofessionals, is to assail art and raise the banners of Philistia. The artist hopes, but does not insist, that his technicalities will be universally admired. He can be understood on many levels, and it is only an added pleasure to be caught red-handed in a secret technical virtuosity.

But the ***Iliad***'s Geometric form is not confined to the grouping of days. As said above in connection with the confrontation of the Quarrel and the Reconciliation, the ***Iliad*** presents a vast hysteron proteron of scenes, in which episodes, and even whole books, balance each other through similarity or opposition. In this system, the center is not the Embassy, but the Great Battle, and the responsion of parts is most obvious in the early and late parts of the poem. This fact is not surprising, since the technique is essentially one of framing or enclosing; one might even call attention to the later instinct of the rhetoricians and prose stylists, who paid much attention to the rhythm of the beginnings and ends of sentences, and let the rest be filled in less formally. So too, in Geometric pottery, the greatest tendency toward naturalism, imbalance, and loose design is to be found in the scenes or metopes of funeral or war which sometimes appear toward the center of the vase, while the flanking borders and friezes rely upon the strictest conventionalism and exact symmetry. Furthermore, while the beginning and end of the ***Iliad*** respond mutually throughout the first nine and the last nine books, certain books form separate systems, either singly, or in groups, within the larger system, wherever a section of the narrative achieves a partial self-completeness. Thus the form of Book I, for instance, is not in itself annular, since its action is introductory rather than rounded; but it forms a circle with Book XXIV. Books III to VII, however, whose content intervenes between the adoption and the activation of Zeus' plan, form a perfectly enclosed Geometric system of balancing scenes, framing the *aristeia* of Diomedes.

When one comes to regard the details, they are sometimes surprisingly precise in pattern. The principal scenes of Book I, for instance, are (1) the rejection of Chryses, with the plague and the funeral pyres; (2) the council of chiefs and the Quarrel; (3) Thetis with Achilles, consoling him and agreeing to take a message to Zeus; (4) Thetis with Zeus, where the latter adopts the hero's cause; (5) the disputatious assembly of the gods, where Hera opposes Zeus. Book XXIV takes up this scheme, but reverses it, beginning with (5) the dispute among the gods, with Hera still leading the opposition, though now in a different sense; (4) Thetis with Zeus, receiving notice that the gods no longer support Achilles in his maltreatment of Hector's corpse; (3) Thetis with Achilles, consoling him and bringing him a message from Zeus; (2) Achilles with Priam, where the magnanimous restitution of Hector's body inverts the selfish seizure of Briseis, and the compassion between technical enemies reverses the hostility between technical allies of Book I; and finally (1) the funeral of Hector in Troy, corresponding, though perhaps vaguely to the first funerals of the poem in the Greek camp. Two important episodes cause a slight asymmetry: the Chrysa-scene, and the coming of Priam. Both are journeys, both have propitiation as their purpose, though beyond this they have little in common; also, they do not fit the hysteron-proteron scheme; still, the pattern of the first and last books emerges as essentially Geometric. . . . Here the balanced elements involve identity, or similarity, as in the funerals, or the people involved in the scenes; but the antitheses are actually more important. The case of Quarrel-Seizure versus Reconciliation-Restitution is the most striking, but the two scenes between Zeus and Thetis also offer a subtle contrast. In the first, Thetis is a secret suppliant to Zeus, and Hera regards her with a jaundiced eye. In the second, Thetis comes by invitation to Olympus; Athena yields her own seat to her, Hera offers her pleasant words and a goblet of gold, and this time it is Zeus who has the request. Though his words are couched in the form of a command, he is, in a way, appealing to her, for, as he says, he is bound by his promise to her and cannot allow the body of Hector to be stolen. This reversal of positions between Zeus and Thetis deeply underlines the degree to which Achilles has added cubits to his own stature. He now holds the timeless world in the palm of his hand.

The next pair of books does not show an equal elegance of design. Their responsion is more broad and impressionistic, yet both are fundamentally similar in design, and both are Geometric. Book II is in two parts, the *Assembly* and the *Catalogue,* both of which deploy for the first time in the poem the host at large. Its spirit is panoramic and epic, rather than dramatic, and it offers a glimpse, rare in heroic poetry, of the feelings of the common soldiery in the person of Thersites, who is developed with bitter and rather low humor. The Assembly itself falls into two parts of opposing purport, first where the soldiers, misled by Agamemnon, rush to the ships to sail them home, and second where they are brought to heel by Odysseus with hopes of victory, equally misled, and shout vigorously for war at once. It is a disillusioned picture that Homer paints here, of a people deceived and hypnotized like sheep by leaders who are in turn deceived by Zeus. It is, in Jeffers' phrase, the "dance of the dream-led masses down the dark mountain," and the only person who speaks honestly in it is Thersites, the incarnation of the ugly truth. In the perspective of a society driving to its ruin under magnificent but corrupt leadership, truth shows itself in a warped, repulsive form and is silenced by simple violence—a blow from the lordly but greed-ridden and deceiving scepter of the Pelopids. Thus at the center of this broad and brilliant display of the Achaean power stands Thersites, disgraced and weeping, not a little as Achilles also stands, stripped of his shirt as Achilles was stripped of his prize, by the self-willed decisions of the regime.

The two Assemblies are preceded and followed by two private gatherings of the princes, the first in which Agamemnon reveals his dream from Zeus, which is accepted as true by Nestor, and the second in which the king sacrifices a bull to Zeus for the fulfillment of the dream, and Zeus, accepting the sacrifice, refuses the fulfillment. . . . Incidentally, the first speech of Agamemnon to the people is an important linking motif, for it is repeated in abbreviated form at the beginning of Book IX. The words which Agamemnon first utters in falsehood, leaning comfortably on his scepter, he repeats in a dark hour in deadly earnest, groaning heavily and weeping "like a spring of dark water," when the truth begins to settle on him.

This first section is then followed by the marshaling, with its six fine similes giving the sense impressions of the host, and the *Catalogue,* giving the factual details of it. The *Catalogue* has been most unjustly despised. In its way, it is just as vivid as the famous similes which introduce it. No love is more deeply imbedded in the Greek soul than the love for places in Greece, with their names, the mountains, valleys, nooks, and rivers of the maternal soil. It is more than patriotic; the *Catalogue,* with its recounting of these place names, their leaders and their legends, has a religious love about it; it is a kind of hymnic invocation. When read aloud, its clear and easy stride seems resistless and inexhaustible, like the movement of an army on the march, and each contingent as it goes by is splendid with the retrospect of home, the continuous surprise of the familiar. At the close of each entry, a stock line gives the number of ships attending the leader, and these lines, varying a little, but all echoing each other, have the incantational validity of a refrain. In antiquity, a hymn to a god recounted his deeds; the hymn to an army recounts its constituents. The whole is ballad-like and brilliantly descriptive, freighted, like everything in Homer, with history and tradition, and touched with foreshadowings of the future. A hundred years or so later, Sappho listed an army as one of the things most beautiful in the world, and here we get some idea of what she meant. If the first half of Book II gives an inner view of ugly truth and uglier deceit, the *Catalogue* is a simple vision of the Achaean panorama, seen from without indeed, but seen with clear precise sensibility, and utter mastery of the traditional and formal material.

The twenty-third book again, and for the last time, offers a panorama of the army, and again, its structure is bipartite: *Funeral* and *Games*. Like Book II, it involves a motivating dream, but unlike Agamemnon's dream, that of Achilles is true; that is, the shade of Patroclus appearing in his sleep urges him to do what indeed he should and must do—bury the dead. The pyre scene which follows is in outline the usual formula of such rituals, but enormously inflated with detail, and adorned with symbols of Achilles' devotion, culminating in the offering of the lock of hair, and of his savagery, in the immolation of the captives. It terminates with Achilles again falling asleep exhausted; the gathering and burial of the bones is briefly told, perhaps to balance the scene of the dragging of Hector which opened the book; and then follow the *Games,* linear in design, like the *Catalogue,* with one event following another as the contingents of the army had. Structurally, therefore, it is closely analogous to Book II, though with no reversal of order. . . . In its import, however, the twenty-third book corresponds to and reverses the second book with peculiar subtlety. If the latter had shown the Achaean society deceived and disordered, dreaming of glories that were not to be, and mastered by either violence or fraud, this spirit is quite reversed in the *Games,* where for the last time all the main characters are passed in review. Musterings for war and festival are in themselves social polarities. Agamemnon, wounded and still smarting with humiliation, is somewhat *hors de combat* [disabled]; Achilles is the center of the Achaean scene. In contrast to what Thersites had said of Agamemnon's greed for booty, Achilles is the most lavish of prize-givers and, in pointed contrast to Agamemnon's former behavior, he awards the king a gratuitous prize. This is aristocratic society in order, where magnanimity and *noblesse oblige* operate as they should, and men's true abilities appear. Moreover, where Book II harked back to the portents at Aulis, the panorama of the *Games* foreshadows the future in certain details, and draws into the scheme of the ***Iliad*** hints of the traditional events later told in the *Little Iliad, The Sack of Troy,* and the *Returns*.

The Judgment of the Arms is suggested by the wrestling match of Odysseus and Ajax; Diomedes' safe passage home can almost be foreseen in his easy success in the chariot race. The fate of the brave, but illegitimate, Teucer, who was driven away by his father when he returned without Ajax, seems implied when he is worsted in the archery contest by a lesser man, and comes off second best. Particularly interesting is the slip and fall of Ajax of Locris in the dung of the sacrificed oxen. Athena pushed him, she who later, for his rape of Cassandra, was to blast him with lightning on his return home. The Achaeans all "laugh sweetly at him," the same formula in which they had laughed at the discomfiture of Thersites. These two episodes find their function in the accent they place on two contrasted views of the social order. In the world misled by kings deceived by Zeus and their own self-conceptions, the people laugh at the wrong thing—the vulgar but accurate speaker of the truth. In the world ordered by the law of magnanimity, and *areté* [virtue, merit], they laugh rightly at the indignity suffered by one who is outwardly a prince, but inwardly, as Homer never is weary of showing, a ruffian and a boor.

Thus in a way, Book XXIII offers a true panorama, and one illustrative of the characters of all, where Book II gave a picture at its best external in the *Catalogue,* and at its worst deceptive in the *Assembly,* where authority overrides the truth. Book II is dominated by Agamemnon and Odysseus, a syndicate designed to choose means and achieve ends; Book XXIII is dominated by Achilles and the shade of Patroclus, already an archetypal friendship, an end in itself, and a landmark of being.

As has long been recognized, Book III through VII form a natural group by virtue of the fact that during them the operation of the Plan of Zeus is essentially suspended, and very little notice is taken of the main theme of the Wrath. Only in Book VIII does Zeus forbid the gods their part in the war and begin to encourage Hector. For the space of five books, all that has been put in motion is temporarily set aside, and we find a series of episodes which cannot be regarded as in any sense a sequential narrative of events. The difficulties which arise in the plot are well known. The Greeks, according to plan, are supposed to be defeated in the absence of Achilles; but they are, on the whole, slightly more successful than the Trojans, so that the wall which they build at the end of Book VII to protect their camp seems not very well motivated by the day's events. The deeds of Diomedes, for all their brilliance, lead to no result, nor do the two duels, between Paris and Menelaus, Ajax and Hector. There is much motion, much coming and going, but no one of consequence is slain, except perhaps Pandarus, and the plot is not advanced at all. It has become a truism to point out also that the View from the Walls, where Priam has not yet learned to recognize the enemy leaders, as well as the duel of Paris and Menelaus, and perhaps that of Ajax and Hector, all belong naturally to the first year of the war, and are out of place in the ninth. The same should probably be said of the fortification of the camp, the episode of Glaucus and Diomedes, with its lofty chivalric tone, and of the council wherein a negotiated peace is contemplated in the possible return of Helen. Such attitudes occur when war is not yet a total commitment, and they scarcely accord with the dark and bloody determination of the rest of the ***Iliad.*** Clearly Homer has narrated events out of their natural order, and one must ask both why he did so, and how he dared, before audiences who must have known the tradition and had doubtless heard these episodes sung in their proper places, albeit in perhaps different versions.

If one looks at the structure of the five books as a whole, it is clear that this is no mere case of padding, but a most intricately designed, perhaps the most intricately designed, block of narrative in the whole ***Iliad.*** Homer has deliberately taken these episodes from their original context and rearranged them in the strictest Geometric pattern, which frames the *aristeia* of Diomedes as centerpiece. It is sometimes suggested that this *aristeia* presents Diomedes attempting to fill the gap left by Achilles' retirement. But Achilles' absence is not yet really felt at all, for this whole section belongs to earlier years and different intentions. Diomedes' *aristeia,* packed with bright similes, high-hearted encounters with gods, and all the virtuosity at the command of a great master of the tradition, is a heroic comedy, which corresponds to the heroic tragedy of the *aristeia* of Achilles toward the end of the poem. It is a summary and a type, in part normative for the general view of the characteristic warlike achievements and pretensions of the Achaeans, in part strictly individual in its development of the personal nature of Diomedes, gallant, attractive, but limited. Like so many parts of the Homeric narrative, it falls into four primary phases, each developed with smaller episodes, and these lie symmetrically on either side of the brief meeting of the hero with Apollo. In the first and fourth of these phases, Diomedes is attended by Athena in person, in the second he is extremely successful, until he is thrust back by Apollo, while in the third he is steadily forced to retreat until rejoined by Athena. . . . As an illustration of the singular kinds of inversion the epic motifs are subject to, it might be pointed out that in her first scene with Diomedes, Athena warns him not to fight with any gods except Aphrodite. Diomedes observes this rule with care until it is countermanded by the goddess herself, who urges him to attack Ares.

Books III to IV and VI to VII form a heavy frame around this paradigm of a Greek hero in action, more strict at the edges than elsewhere. Book III has three main episodes: a truce with oaths; the *Teichoscopia* or View from the Walls, where the Trojan elders sit with Helen, and, though their estimate of her is high, wish that she would go home; and the duel between Menelaus and Paris, to which is added the little domestic scene between the latter and his now disillusioned and reluctant mistress, who wishes him dead. Book VII corresponds with some exactness: it begins with a duel, equally indecisive as the former one, between Ajax and Hector, but, in contrast to the other, it ends in mutual respect and a chivalric exchange of gifts. This is followed by a council of the elders of Troy, again though not now in her presence, deliberating about Helen and wanting to send her home. The book ends with another truce, with oaths, for the taking up of the dead to which is added the very brief narratives of the wall-building, the Thracian wine ships, and the nocturnal threat of Zeus' thunder. Books IV and VI correspond a little less exactly, from the external point of view, yet again three motifs seem designed with some parallelism. Book IV begins with an act of treachery on the Trojan side, when Pandarus breaks the truce by shooting Menelaus. At once the Greek army springs to action, and the episode which follows was called in antiquity the Marshaling of Agamemnon. As the battle begins, the gods, Athena and Ares, join in the fight. At the end of Book V and the beginning of VI it is noted that the gods have left the field. The general melee proceeds for a few lines, after which Hector at the instigation of Helenus rallies the beleaguered Trojans and drives back the Greeks somewhat. Presumably this corresponds to Agamemnon's display of generalship in IV. The scene between Diomedes and Glaucus then interrupts the scheme, but connects with the *Diomedeia,* and the book closes with the episode of Hector in Troy, with Hecuba, Helen, and Andromache. This last reveals a very different aspect of the Trojans from that seen in the treachery of Pandarus. The one was the height of irresponsibility and villainy—*anaideia,* in Greek terms—the other offers the complete

A vase detail illustrating the embassy to Achilles, from the fifth century B.C. Krüger-Moessner.

and winning picture of faithfulness, goodness, and *aidôs*. One seems to reflect the justice of the war, the other certainly mirrors its tragedy. But further, the scene of Hector and Andromache, the truly married pair, inverts the picture of the wanton lovers, Paris and Helen, both in the obvious matter of devotion versus lust, and even in some of the details of what they say to each other. Helen rebukes Paris for his lack of valor and wishes he were dead; Andromache fears above everything harm for her husband, and rebukes him for being too reckless. Helen despises Paris for his lack of shame; Hector would be ashamed not to defend his city. Thus the scene of Hector in Troy answers not only to the Pandarus scene, but also to the preceding one at the end of III; and the two latter are thus linked in a way which has further implications. The whole narrative from III to IV—that is, the scenes of Aphrodite, Paris, and Helen, Menelaus in mad frustration hunting for a vanished Paris, and finally Pandarus shooting Menelaus—form a kind of compressed reënactment of the original treachery which caused the war. Pandarus, a garrulous and irresponsible archer, is not entirely different from Paris, and his target is, significantly, Menelaus; the armies move into battle as a result of his act as the Achaean host mobilized at the act of Paris. Aphrodite is revealed as an inward compelling force, and Menelaus is shown, empty-handed, wounded, and raging with humiliation. In opposition to all this are Hector and Andromache, the noble sufferers on the offending side, to whom the war brings unjustified destruction. More than the typology of stock scenes is involved here; Homer has created a montage of the motivating crime under the guise of continuous narrative, and opposed to it a foreshadowing of its ultimate results. For the Hector-Andromache scene also is closely allied with the closing books of the poem, and the lamentation for Hector "while yet alive" pointedly indicates the tragedy to come. (pp. 255-68)

From what has been shown of the structure and import of this group of books, it is clear what the poet's concern must have been. Summary of antecedent events is a regular feature of epic technique; Odysseus' recollection of the portents at Aulis, or the long flashback about the scar in the ***Odyssey,*** and even some of Nestor's remniscences are characteristic examples. But no real account of the earlier years of the Trojan War, or of its motivation, exists in the ***Iliad.*** It could, of course, be assumed that all knew it anyway, and such a deliberate narration would have been intolerable. On the other hand, Homer's intention was not simply to narrate the Wrath of Achilles, but to include a panorama of the war as a whole. To see in the unity of a single episode the summary and the implications of the total action to which it belongs, and somehow to subordinate these to the event selected as central, is one of the first premises of the dramatic instinct. When one considers the skill with which Sophocles reveals the antecedent facts of the story in *Oedipus Rex,* it is obvious that Homer has no such native, supple, and developed gift for structural syntax as that; his style remains, of necessity, bound to the linear parataxis of epic tradition. Events are to be narrated in proper order, or at least they must seem to be. In the ***Odyssey*** the extremely rational and plausible device is adopted of allowing Odysseus himself to narrate the events of the preceding ten years. In Books III to VII of the ***Iliad,*** Homer has selected representative scenes from parts of the story which must have been older, and retold them in the guise of sequential events. So far as the main plot is concerned, they remain static; dramatically they serve to expand enormously the tapestry of the poem and to bring within the scheme of the Wrath of Achilles a total view of the war up to that point. By dint of association of motifs whose typicality allowed them to include wider implications than they have in and of themselves, Homer has created a dramatic inset, a round summary of all the significant emotions, if not all the events, of the earlier part of the war: the crime of Paris, the sorrow and rage of Menelaus, Helen's position in Troy, the reactions of the Trojans to her, the attempt to negotiate peace and Paris' resistance to it, the early efforts to settle the war by duels instead of general bloodshed, the fortification of the beachhead, the misery and fear of the Trojan wives and mothers, and the fresh valor, lit by touches of chivalric generosity, of Diomedes and others, in a time before the action settles down to deadliest earnest. The device by which all this is pulled into the ***Iliad*** is a self-conscious one, and it is a little stiff. But it is Geometric to the core, carefully designed for its place in the poem, and indispensable to the totality which Homer intended. Viewed by the standards of the Geometric Age, it is a triumph of early syntax.

The corresponding group of books at the other end of the poem forms the completest possible contrast. Far from being static plot-wise, Books XVIII to XXII seem at last to put in motion the long-pent-up energy of deeds interminably motivated and anxiously awaited. When Achilles finally takes the field, one has the feeling that all the surge and motion of the ***Iliad*** hitherto has been nothing, so far does the hero's roused vitality surpass all else. More important, as the Group III to VII summarizes the first part of the war, so the *aristeia* of Achilles, as has been noted before herein and also by others, symbolizes the last of it in that it not only foreshadows Achilles' death, but also, in the *Theomachia,* in the surrender of Scamander, and in the frequent images of burning cities, the final fall of Troy. So the ***Iliad,*** ostensibly the tale of an event in the ninth year of hostilities (and not an extremely vital event at that for the general outcome), is made to embrace dramatically and by implication the entire epic tradition about the Achaeans at Troy; and the final touch, as has been suggested, is the foreshadowing, under the guise of athletic contests of Book XXIII, of events after the fall of the city.

Structurally, these books are not quite so elegantly devised as the group to which they correspond. This fact is not surprising in view of the difference in function between the two. The *aristeia* of Achilles advances the plot and must move from point to point, where the earlier group is a self-enclosed inset. Yet the separate phases of Books XVIII to XXII exhibit an attempt to impose the familiar system of balances by similarity and opposition. These phases may be regarded as either three or four in number, of which the first includes Books XVIII and XIX, the preparations for vengeance. When Antilochus brings the news of Patroclus' death to Achilles, the latter's reactions fall into the general pattern of a funeral, which is made more pointed by the great speech, "Let me die at once." This theme of Achilles' death, now a certainty, is indeed touched on lightly by Hephaestus and Thetis, but recurs with heavy emphasis only at the very end of Book XIX, when the horse Xanthus prophesies death to his master as he sets out. Prophecies by horses are calculated to arrest attention, and it is possible that Homer purposely chose to call attention to his motif in this way. It recurs, of course, in the mouth of the dying Hector, echoing both forward and backward. Here it simply rounds off with the knowledge of certain death Achilles' resumption of the war. The principal motif of these two books is perhaps the divine armor. In answer to the speech, "Let me die at once," Thetis points out that her son's armor is lost, and promises him arms from Hephaestus. These he naturally puts on immediately before mounting his chariot when the horse prophesies. But the arms also form the centerpiece of these two books, in the pair of scenes where they are made by Hephaestus and brought to Achilles by Thetis. Before and after this centerpiece fall episodes which group themselves loosely under either Achilles' resolution and the eagerness for battle or the lamentations for Patroclus. These include the shout from the trench, the first laments when the corpse is brought back, the marshaling of the Myrmidons, the official renunciation of the Wrath, with its brilliant confrontation of the demonically possessed Achilles and the wordly-wise Odysseus, and then the further laments, including that of Briseis, over Patroclus. Some asymmetry occurs in two small scenes of the gods, and in the council of Trojans as they camp on the plain for the second time. The latter, of course is a link to Book VIII, and is quite symmetrical in the larger scheme of the whole. (pp. 269-71)

The next two books are very closely unified in action and design. The fight in the plain and the fight in the river actually form two somewhat contrasting phases of the *aristeia,* since Achilles in the second struggles with the river for a time almost as helplessly as his victims do with him in the first; yet since in their broad outlines the two books form a strict annular system, it is better to look at them together. A prelude on Olympus gives the official dissolution of the Plan of Zeus, and the gods are allowed to resume their activities in the war. This forms a link with the renunciation of the Wrath in XIX. The gods then repair to the Trojan plain and line up for hostilities. But no hostilities occur immediately. Apollo encourages Aeneas to meet Achilles, and then presently the gods, who had been so eager to participate, retire upon agreement to two separate vantage points to observe Achilles. There follow two long developed scenes in which Aeneas and Hector both try to stand against Achilles, and both are whisked away to safety, Aeneas by Poseidon, and Hector by Apollo. The book closes with a general melee in which Achilles with the Greeks at his heels slays and drives the Trojans toward the river. This melee (*androktasia*) continues uninterrupted as Book XXI begins, and then two more developed scenes emerge from the confusion. This time the victims, Lycaon, son of Priam, and Asteropaeus, a leader of the Paeonians, are not so fortunate. Both are slain, in contrast to the two previous rescues; and, though it may be coincidental, like Hector and Aeneas, one is a Trojan prince, the other an ally, and at that, they appear in reverse order. And now the divine forces begin to work again: through the natural blocking of the river's flow with corpses, the Scamander first appeals to Achilles, and then overflows and tries to drown him. The rescue of Achilles by Poseidon and Athena perhaps mirrors the former's rescue of Aeneas, but in any case, the subsequent outbreak of hostilities among the gods certainly completes the earlier scene where they had taken up their battle positions and then retired. The issue is now decided: the fire of Hephaestus, which Achilles also carries in his arms, has reduced the local deities of the Trojan rivers, and the city is to fall. In the final scene, the Greek gods defeat the Trojan gods, except Apollo, whose role continues only in a delaying action, betokened by his deception and deflection of Achilles, while the host of the Trojans escape within the walls. The pattern is extremely strict. (pp. 272-73)

Book XXII is linked to the preceding by the completion of the scene of Apollo's deception of Achilles, which subtly reminds one also of the hero's death motif, and thus connects with the last speech of Hector. For the rest, the book is designed rather simply, and is mostly self-enclosed. Priam and Hecuba, seeing Achilles' approach and Hector standing outside the gate, utter their appeals; then comes Hector's famous soliloquy. These three speeches are balanced at the end by the three laments of Priam, Hecuba, and finally Andromache; here all mere formality is transfigured by the inevitability of the speakers, and one may observe how perfectly the poetic economy is devised to fit the given material. As Achilles gets close, Hector flees, and the chase around Troy begins, to be balanced by the dragging of the body later. The poet in both connections emphasizes that these horrors were happening to Hector on his own home soil, a feature of special poignancy. The next scene, that of the scales, the arrival of Athena, and the departure of Apollo, might be called asymmetrical, but the divine scenes frequently are mere extensions, either before or after the human ones, and this should probably be looked upon as part of the duel, which forms the center of the book. (p. 273)

In another way, perhaps, it could be said that Book XXII corresponds to Book III, in that the latter offers the first glimpse of Hector, and this narrates his death. To a degree also, the disgraceful and indecisive duel of Paris and Menelaus in III is balanced by this grave and catastrophic one, and the escape of the transgressor is somehow tragically answered by the fall of the unoffending hero. But one need not press matters too far. The correspondences and antinomies are clear and precise in any case.

After the compressed, "dramatic" time of Books III to VII, Book VIII returns to the original time level, or what might be called the "real" time of the ***Iliad.*** The Plan of Zeus is at last implemented, and the victory begins to go to the Trojans. Functionally, this book serves chiefly to motivate the *Embassy* to Achilles by bringing the Greek pride low, but it is also a masterly deployment of character and dramatic issues. The purport of Achilles' retirement from the war was simply that without him the Greeks could not withstand Hector. Yet the fact that the Greeks ultimately were victorious, and without Achilles, was a complication which somehow had to be reckoned with; that is, this temporary but frightening defeat was not the final truth, and for that reason it appears in the light of peculiar unreason, especially to the pro-Greek gods and to that incarnation of success, Diomedes. Diomedes in retreat is almost a reversal of nature, and Hera's resentful anger reflects and enlarges this feeling of unaccustomed and almost inexplicable frustration. The Trojan victory must be seen, therefore, on two levels, as both natural and unnatural—natural, because Achilles' boast would be idle if the Greeks could perfectly well have done without him, and unnatural because the heroes whose valor in the end did take the city must here be flung into confusion and despair. It would have been possible to tell the story simply on the first level, but Homer chooses to keep the perspective of the gods before our eyes, and to dramatize the passing moment against the background of events in their totality, which is Moira, or Fate. Diomedes' frustration and disgust, together with the seething rage of Hera and Athena, convey the responses of the long view; so also does the eagle which Zeus sends in answer to Agamemnon's prayer, an omen which recurs in the Great Battle with precisely the same meaning, that the despair need not be permanent. The other level, which views Hector's triumph as a natural result, seems to be suggested in the symbol of the scales which Zeus holds up at noon when the battle is raging. The scales, indicating here as elsewhere what is organically true in any situation, shift the causal responsibility away from Zeus; he consults the facts, so to speak, and the answer which the scales give puts a special coloring on the lightning with which the god proceeds immediately to encourage Hector and confound the Achaeans. The lightning is not a mere external miracle, but a miraculous emblem of what must be inevitably the case under the circumstances—Trojan victory if Achilles retires.

The individual reactions of the chiefs are wonderfully characteristic: Diomedes horrified and unable to believe that he is really being defeated; Nestor, though in grave danger, quite detached and ready to wait for victory on another day; Odysseus so concerned to save his own life that he leaves Nestor helpless; Agamemnon desperate and in tears; Ajax and Teucer grim, but steady and coolheaded, the nucleus of the brief resistance which the Greeks make. Hector, however, is the real masterpiece, as he gradually awakens to the fact that this is, unexpectedly, his day. His modest but sanguine temperament soon recognizes the lightning's import; he urges his men forward, and then calling to his horses, he reminds them of the grain which Andromache has given them in abundance. This rather surprising mention of Andromache, recalling Hector's own scene with her and his warm intense loyalties, somehow poignantly prevents the mind from identifying the man too wholly with the delusion which, beginning at this point, leads him presently to grandiose expectations—the capture of Nestor's shield or Diomedes' breastplate, and finally total victory.

The delusive hope, loyalty, frustration, and dismay which attend the activation of Zeus' plan make up the spirit of the book. From the point of view of scenic structure, it is self-enclosed. It opens with a council of the gods, in which Zeus begins by boasting of his supreme strength, and then forbids the gods to participate in the war. As shown elsewhere, this mood in Zeus is not his natural one in the ***Iliad;*** it reflects the supremacy and absolutism of Achilles. In turn, its tone of arrogant self-assurance is echoed by Hector at the close of the council of Trojans, when they camp for the night on the plain. Two perhaps inconsequential passages seem to balance each other, where the armies take their meals before and after the battle. Then come the lightning scenes. With some difficulty, Zeus drives Diomedes back with flash after flash, and he finally yields, thinking of the Trojan taunts and wishing the earth would swallow him up. This scene of direct frustration by Zeus finds its counterpoise in the one where he stops Hera and Athena halfway to the battlefield and sends them back with furious threats to maim them with lightning. Later, Zeus seems to point the correspondence neatly when he tells Hera that she too (like Diomedes) may plunge into the depths of the earth in helpless rage, and he still would not care. When one remembers that these two goddesses were the ones who attended Diomedes in his *aristeia,* the connection becomes even clearer. In the center of the book is the attack and victory of Hector, interrupted by a short scene in Heaven, Agamemnon's prayer with the omen and the brief resistance of the chiefs, especially Ajax and Teucer. At the outer verges of the book are two images of Dawn.

As observed earlier, there is a stricter tendency in the early books of the ***Iliad*** toward Geometric composition than in the later ones, Book XVII, the positional counterpart of VIII, shows no very clear-cut symmetry of outline. Itself a continuation of the Great Battle, it follows the general design of that section in having phases and episodes which bring matters to where they must be plotwise, but, since its action is not self-contained, it seeks no self-contained order. On the other hand, the implications of this book partly reflect and partly invert those of VIII. The atmosphere of frustration is now pervasive, as both Trojans and Greeks strive vainly to possess the body of Patroclus. Still deluded by over-high hopes, Hector tries to secure the horses of Achilles. Moreover, his delusion is reaching its climax, as Zeus reflects when Hector puts on the arms of Achilles. Most important of all, XVII reverses the Plan of Zeus which began to operate in VIII. It is not, of course, formally renounced until Book XX, but in XVII Zeus' mind reflects Achilles' partly abated anger, and begins to waver. He envies Hector the arms, pities Patroclus, and sheds mist over the battle to obscure the sorrowful sight. The other gods, who had been banned from the field in VIII, begin to reappear: at least, Athena appears, sent by Zeus himself to help the Greeks; "his mind changed," says Homer. But presently he changes it again, and for the last time, corresponding to its first appearance in VIII, the lightning comes back to hearten Hector. Zeus is indecisive and so is the battle. The decisive end can come only when Achilles learns what has happened; and one of the prominent motifs of the book, a token of its vain effort and helpless striving, is the reiterated fact that Achilles does not yet know, and that someone must tell him. The whole episode ends only in the next book, when Achilles shouts from the rampart, the Trojans reel back, and the Achaeans rescue the body. Thus part of XVIII must be taken as the counterpoise to VIII, and here indeed one finds a pronounced circularity. As in VIII, the Trojans camp again on the plain, and Hector reiterates his boasts, in very similar terms. The irony is obvious, of course, since now the Plan of Zeus no longer exists, Achilles is aroused, and only Pulydamas perceives where matters really stand. The responsion with its reversed import is clear, and the slight inconcinnity of position is necessitated by the plot which is now becoming imperious and putting difficulties in the way of perfect symmetry. (pp. 274-78)

If Book XVII lacks extreme elegance of design, it nevertheless is extremely rich, as are all the battle books, in handsome similes. Compositional procedure here somewhat resembles also that in Book V, where four sequential phases of the *aristeia* were set off against each other by rather slight surface devices to produce contrast; in addition, Book V also abounds in dazzling imagery. Here the recurrent motifs, which set off to a degree the parts of the book, and lend a little order to the general melee and *androktasia,* are primarily: Achilles' arms, put on by Hector toward the beginning of the book and noted as lost by Ajax near the end; the theme of Achilles' ignorance of the tragedy and the need to tell him; Zeus shaking his head mournfully over the miseries of men; and the theme of mist. These motifs mark off somewhat vaguely four stages of the fight, in the first two of which the Achaeans have a slight advantage in spite of Apollo's presence on the other side, and in the last two of which the case is reversed in spite of Athena's presence on the Greek side. This is indeed the book of confusion, the dark hour before dawn, but such symmetry as it possesses might be analyzed as shown on the opposite page.

These parts can scarcely be called clearly articulated, and it remains that the chief elements which connect this book with VIII are the disappearance of the Plan of Zeus, and the Trojan council on the plain, which actually is reserved for Book XVIII.

The ninth and the sixteenth books of the ***Iliad*** are so obviously linked to each other as focal points of the main narrative that it is unnecessary to point out how the latter completes and in a way reverses the former. Achilles' rejection of the embassy, or at least of Agamemnon's offer, is here answered by his yielding to Patroclus. Yet in a sense he had yielded to Ajax also when, in contrast to his former threat to go home, he stated that he would fight when the battle reached his ships. His further modification of his stand here continues to express the force of Achilles' sense of humanity, but also brings into final conflict the two irreconcilables which are rending his will. This conflict is felt and discussed in Book IX; in XVI it must be acted out, partly because the real urgency is now greater, but chiefly because the human demand comes home to Achilles much more closely. Perhaps the most beautiful and clearly significant repetition of a motif in the whole ***Iliad*** is the one of the "dark-watered spring" which occurs at the beginning of both IX and XVI. When it first occurs, it is Agamemnon who weeps like a dark-watered spring when he cries failure and proposes abandonment of the war. His words are identical, though in abbreviated form, with those in which he had made the same proposal in Book II, but then speciously, himself deceived by Zeus. Now it is Patroclus who weeps like the dark spring in Achilles' presence, and the image, now weighted with its former associations and future implications, does more than link the two books together. It also reflects Achilles' torn emotions, his sense of grief, to which wrath has now given place. In Book IX, even to Ajax, he had said that his heart swelled with rage when he remembered the insult. To Patroclus, he calls his feeling "pain," and confesses that he cannot maintain ceaseless rage. Accented by the repeated simile, the altered context gleams the more dramatically, and there is a close union between Achilles' mood and the tears of Patroclus.

Both IX and XVI are approximately of tripartite construction, though in the latter case, the traditional features of a battle scene lend themselves less readily to Geometric balance than does a series of speeches. Book IX is quite orderly, with its councils at the beginning and end, and the *Embassy* proper in the middle. Agamemnon's first speech is a link, as already noted, to Book II, and falls outside the design. Diomedes' brave retort to him, a paradigm of the simple valor which had been found wanting in the preceding day's fight, is echoed by that hero's restatement of his own value and intentions at the very end of the book. For the rest, the council speeches do not balance precisely, since three by Nestor and one by Agamemnon are answered by only one each of Agamemnon and Odysseus. The symmetry, however, makes itself felt. The *Embassy* proper is extremely formal, both in atmosphere and design. At the center lies the speech of Phoenix, the pattern of *sophrosyne,* to which is opposed, before and after, two speeches of Achilles which eloquently, if with some confusion and indirection, express the absolutism of his position, and his search for its appropriate expression. Phoenix is the only one of the envoys who understands the real and dangerous inner forces in Achilles, and these three speeches, the core of the *Embassy,* are the only ones relating to those forces. The appeals of Odysseus and Ajax are diametrically opposed, the one based on gain (*kerdos*) and self interest, the other on humanity, the claims of others, and *aidôs*. Achilles' answer to Ajax, with its partial acquiescence and at least theoretical approval of the claims of *aidôs,* is typical of his whole reception of the envoys, whom upon arrival he receives with all the formalities proper to the occasion, and, what is more, with real friendship. The reception of the envoys, therefore, and the answer to Ajax have the common denominator, friendship, which, though set aside by the superior claims of absolute honor for the moment, becomes in Book XVI a force no longer to be denied. (pp. 278-80)

The design of Book XVI is somewhat simpler, but again with three main parts: the first extending to the departure of Patroclus, the second through the Sarpedon episode, and the last from Apollo's first opposition to the death of Patroclus. The centerpiece is the fight with Sarpedon, flanked by two scenes on Olympus having to do with the burial of the Lycian prince. The whole piece is enclosed by two scenes of general melee, the first by the ships and in the plain, the second where Patroclus tries to ascend the walls of Troy. Here Apollo intervenes, and Patroclus' star begins to set as the god first urges Hector on him and then attacks him in person. The last part may not seem very analogous to the first, yet both are full of heavy foreshadowing, and both emphasize powerfully the defection of Achilles. The scene which Homer has inserted between Achilles' speech and the arming of the Myrmidons, the scene of Ajax battered but still struggling faithfully, can only be intended to accent the desperate straits to which Achilles' retirement has reduced his friends. The death of Patroclus is, of course, the nadir of this defection, the point at which it becomes impossible even for Achilles himself to remain inactive. In a sense, therefore, Ajax' desperate hour prepares for that of Patroclus. Prophetic foreshadowings also frame the book, both in Patroclus' own speech, where Homer abandons his anonymity long enough to remark that he was begging for his own doom, and in the prayer of Achilles for his safety, which Zeus rejects. These foreshadowings of course come to fulfillment in the final scenes, but not without a recurrence of prophetic motifs, as the dying Patroclus warns Hector of the vengeance of Achilles. Hector's lighthearted reply is, in keeping with his present delusion of victory, a kind of inversion of prophecy. (pp. 281-82)

So by [a] series of frames we are brought to the five books of the Great Battle which is the center of the ***Iliad.*** These battle scenes do not, apparently, fall into any particular system of balances; the hysteron-proteron technique makes its appearance in passages of small compass, but these seem to imply no attempt to spread the device into a principle of large design. In treating battle scenes, Homer relies on the unity of tone in the formulae themselves; the echoes are less planned, more chaotic thus, more suitable to the confusion of war. Yet even here, there is a touch of framing: the battle begins with the shout of Eris, and ends with the shout of Achilles. Moreover the placement of Patroclus' scenes offers the possibility that these also were intentionally drawn toward the extremities of the battle: Patroclus might have been sent out by Achilles at any point, but actually he is sent fairly near the battle's beginning; and he does not return until near the end—strange behavior for a man who was expected to hurry. But aside from these touches, the battle goes simply through its necessary phases, none of which provides sufficient contrast to balance another amid the general similarity of mood, except the Beguiling of Zeus, which forms a single relieving interlude.

The patterned regularity of the nine opening books and the nine closing ones might be pressed in more minute detail; but the object here has not been such detail; it has rather been to demonstrate how the native oral devices of hysteron proteron and ring composition, involving the balance of similarities and opposites, have been enlarged to provide concentric design for an enormously expanded heroic poem. Two special points must be noted. First, it will be recognized that this analysis of the ***Iliad*** assumes that the books of the poem, as we have them, existed in Homer's own time. As a rule, they are regarded as the arbitrary divisions of the Alexandrine scholars, but there is no reason to retain this view. They are clearly the natural divisions of the poem, and most of them have very marked beginnings and ends, even when the narrative is continuous between them. Also, it has been recently estimated that these books average about the number of lines which it is possible for a singer to perform on a single occasion. It is reasonable therefore to assume that the poem was conceived in terms of the books as we have them, and that the canonical division is not late. Secondly, the problematical Book X obviously does not belong to the Geometric structure as analyzed here, and this fact perhaps should be taken as an indication of its later insertion in the poem. Neither part of the battle, nor of the elaborate rings which enclose the battle, the *Doloneia* corresponds to nothing formally, and leads to nothing dramatically. It is the one part of the ***Iliad*** which can be omitted with no damage to the poem at all; the rest is from every point of view profoundly organic. On the other hand, the *Doloneia*'s lack of any place in the Geometric pattern, though it creates a strong supposition, hardly seems sufficient proof for unauthenticity. Inconcinnities exist in the design in any case, even though none are so glaring as this would be; and in the last analysis the ***Iliad,*** coming from a tradition where parataxis, both in sentence and in scenic structure, was the rule, need not have departed from it so completely as to exclude all inorganic material. Moreover, Book X bears some significant resemblances to the rest of the ***Iliad,*** notably in its conception of the relationship between characters, such as Agamemnon and Menelaus, and in the continuation of the fire image. And yet, where everything else is so finely organized, this one episode does introduce a false note, a less mature procedure, with peculiar disregard for a symmetry which must have cost the poet some pains. Though the matter is hardly clear, it seems perhaps best to accept the dictum of the Townley *Scholia,* that this book was added later, perhaps even by Pisistratus.

For the rest, the scenic structure, when laid out entire in a chart . . . , offers an extraordinary analogue to the rhythm and balance of the Dipylon vases. In the simple grouping of books, omitting X, one finds the relationship 2 : 5 : 2 : 5 : 2 : 5 : 2, a relationship frequently found also in the alternations of narrow and wide elements in Geometric ware. Within this basic rhythm, if the details seem enormously complex, so are the works of the Dipylon, and their ornamentation depends similarly upon the deployment of traditional motifs in accordance with the first ripe development of the Hellenic sense of form. The underlying psychology of that sense in this early period has already been discussed, and it could only have been such a psychology, and such a conception of what form is, that led Homer to design the ***Iliad*** as he did, and to seek in his own materials of oral composition the means to impose order, suitable to a monumental work, on the loose parataxis of the heroic tradition. It is the spirit of the Geometric Age which is at work here, and the form which it produced would have been all but impossible in any other time. (pp. 282-84)

Cedric H. Whitman, "Geometric Structure of the 'Iliad'," in his Homer and the Heroic Tradition, *Cambridge, Mass.: Harvard University Press, 1958, pp. 249-84.*

JOHN COWPER POWYS (essay date 1959)

[A versatile English educator, critic, novelist, and poet, Powys wrote prolifically and published widely. His critical commentary is considered perceptive, accessible, and always personal; in fact, Mark Van Doren has written that Powys' Autobiography *(1934) is still his best book. Motifs that most often recur in his works include myths, cosmic fantasies, elemental forces of nature, and human sexuality. In the following excerpt, Powys commends Homer's treatment of women, gods, family, and sex in the* Iliad,

claiming that it surpasses other masterpieces by being "more realistic and more natural." Powys maintains, however, that the poem's best feature is "the magical, bewitching, irresistible, intoxicating sweep of music" of its meter.]

[The ***Iliad***] is not nearly as imaginative as Dante. It is not nearly as dramatic as Shakespeare. It is not nearly as eloquent as Milton. It is not nearly as philosophical as *Faust*. And yet it is a greater poem than the *Inferno* or *King Lear* or *Paradise Lost* or *Faust*! Why is this? In what way can it possibly surpass these masterpieces?

I will tell you at once. By being more realistic and more natural. In other words, it is more like what has happened, is happening, and will happen to us all, from the very beginning in our history in this world until the end of human life upon this earth. (p. 10)

[What] has made Homer for three thousand years the greatest poet in the world is his *naturalness*. We love each other as in Homer. We hate each other as in Homer. We are perpetually being interfered with as in Homer by chance and fate and necessity, by invisible influences for good and by invisible influences for evil, and we see the unconquerable power that Homer calls *keer* leading our parents, leading our uncles and aunts, leading our grandparents to a particular death; and there do exist among us those who even feel this implacable destiny propelling themselves to a definite end, actually indicated as inescapable when some particular date in the calendar is reached or when some particular event has occurred. Thus Achilles assures his horse Xanthus, who is dragging his chariot, and who turns his head to remind him that if he kills Hector his own end will shortly follow, that he needs no reminding of this *keer,* for he knows it well, but "all the same for that"—*alla kai empees,* as Homer puts it—he intends to drive on to the end.

What is so particularly natural about the ***Iliad*** and what is such a daily inspiration to me in my ordinary life is the place he gives to women. First of all are the beautiful mistresses of the houses and halls of Homer's warriors, such as Argive Helen, carried off from Menelaus by Paris, *alias* Alexander; such as Hector's mother, Hecabe, and his wife, Andromache, and his half-sister, the beautiful prophetess Cassandra, whom Agamemnon takes captive and conveys to his home. Then there are the women who are taken captive by the conquerors who have slain their parents, husbands and sons. These women are treated at first as if they are slaves. In fact we are told in one place that their value is equal to the value of four oxen. But when once they enter the dwelling of their conqueror and take up their abode there, they very quickly dominate the whole house.

The beautiful Lady of the House may go off on her own and leave her lord as Helen did Menelaus, but these women brought into the Homeric hall as "worth four oxen" very quickly by their wisdom, beauty, tact and competence became either the housekeeper, whom Homer calls "the *Tamiee*" and who always is praised by the guests for the delicious things to eat and drink "which she brings out of her store," or, if the Lord is an old man, as Nestor was, without any Lady, become in that old man's dwelling a beautiful handmaid like Hecamede, daughter of Arsinoös of Tenedos. Homer certainly describes with reverential relish the lovely meal she once arranged upon old Nestor's table, and how ready she would be, as Nestor told them himself, to give Doctor Machaon, the son of the greatest of all doctors, Asclepius, a beautiful cleansing and healing warm bath. (pp. 11-12)

There are many scenes in the ***Iliad*** where we touch the reality of our life as it is today when it is transformed for us by our own private thoughts; as for example when we struggle with certain forces of nature. Consider, for instance, the passage in Book XXI . . . where the River Scamander calls upon his brother, the River Simoïs, to help him in his battle with Achilles. Here we have a perfect example of that element in life where the sub-human wrestles with the human and they both are compelled in some strange way to appeal to the super-human to decide their strife. Here the burden of our oldest ballads seems anticipated by Homer, and all those ancient market-town quips and proverbs and all those immemorial fairy-tales and roadside legends reaching us from forests long ago cut down, and from moorlands long ago built over, find their parallel. There is something about the rhythm of the Homeric hexameter that is more able to catch and absorb into its current, as it rolls along, these familiar human situations that are always recurring, than any other form of poetic rhythm except the simplest of our best-known old ballads. (p. 13)

Many of the most appealing passages in the ***Iliad*** consist of prayers; and it is impossible sometimes not to associate these prayers, such as "O Sun that beholdest all things and hearest all things, O Rivers, O Earth, O all ye lost ones of our race who, weary of life, rest forever in peace below it all," with the calm, majestic resignation of so many of the Collects in the Book of Common Prayer of the Church of England "as by Law established."

My own favourite book in the whole of the ***Iliad*** is Book XXI, wherein the gods and goddesses fight among themselves, some taking the side of the Greeks and some the side of the Trojans; and nothing is more perfectly characteristic of Homer as a poet than the fact that the chief of all the immortals, the great Zeus himself, Heavenly Father of both gods and men, regards this fighting among the gods with humorous amusement. I implore . . . Homer's readers . . . to ask themselves whether they can imagine the author of *Hamlet* and *Macbeth* and *Othello* and *King Lear* and *The Tempest,* however shrewdly he may hint that the Power above us all laughs at lovers' quarrels, going so far as to suggest that the behaviour of angels and devils, as they contend for the victory in our hearts, is to that great Power a matter for hilarious amusement. Does the Deity in Dante's *Divine Comedy* even for a moment look down upon it all as if it were a comedy in *our* sense of the word? Can we imagine for a moment Milton's "Heavenly Muse" who "with mighty wings outspread dove-like satst brooding on the vast Abyss and mad'st it pregnant," chuckling with ribald amusement at the silly quarrels going on in both Heaven and Earth?

What we get as we follow Homer through the ***Iliad*** is not at all the feeling that "all the world's a stage and all the men and women merely players," nor is it the feeling that there is what Wordsworth, my own favourite poet, calls

> . . . something far more deeply interfused,
> Whose dwelling is the light of setting suns,
> And the round ocean and the living air,
> And the blue sky, and in the mind of man:
> A motion and a spirit that impels
> All thinking things, all objects of all thought,
> And rolls through all things.

Without any of these exalted emotions, derived from the contact of our human souls with the colours and forms and substances of our planetary Earth, dominated by Sun and Moon, as it swings through infinite Space—yes, without any of these emotions, we who love Homer in the way the immortal Aether loved him may find ourselves by degrees learning, without effort, without any particular concentration of will, to enjoy the natural, ordinary course of our daily life with all its shocks, stresses, quarrels, rivalries, frustrations, surprises, desperations and heavenly quiescences, just in the sort of way Keats felt when he wrote that perfect fragment of an ode which begins:

> Mother of Hermes! and still youthful Maia!
> May I sing to thee
> As thou wast hymned on the shores of Baiae?

and which breaks off with the words:

> Rounded by thee, my song should die away
> Content as theirs,
> Rich in the simple worship of a day.

(pp. 14-16)

I have been swept away by a fascinating wave of excitement in observing how this stupendous poem, that may easily have been recited by some reciter with my own mania for it three thousand years ago, still embodies the life of men, women and children as it is lived upon this earth. And the exciting thing is that Homer treats his Divine Beings in exactly the same way that he treats us ourselves, his Human Beings. Over and over again, we find ourselves awed and hushed in the presence of his Divine Beings and aware of a natural feeling that their ancient altars must be respected and their legendary ritual upheld; but at the same time there is absolutely nothing of that peculiar atmosphere of unctuous solemnity and oily gloom that some of us find so hard not to associate with our Christian Sunday.

How interesting it is that the peculiar shiver of terrified awe which our great religious prophets and teachers and preachers and saints have, by degrees, ever since the year one of our calendar, forced us to associate with the word God, doesn't enter for a moment into Homer's conception of Zeus, any more than it does into Vergil's conception of Jupiter or Jove. How Satisfactory it is to be able to worship Zeus or his daughter Pallas Athene or his sister-wife Hera, without having to think of a God that we have been taught for nearly two thousand years to associate with the "bowing and scraping" of a Hush-a-bye Heaven and the infernal cruelties of a diabolical Spanish Inquisition Hell, not to speak of the Presdestination doctrines of Knox and Calvin and the fiery stakes of Bloody Mary.

The essential thing with Homer—and most especially is this true of the ***Iliad***—is the magical, bewitching, irresistible, intoxicating sweep of music of his metre. There is no metre in the world, there never has been, that can equal the hexameter of Homer. (pp. 17-18)

Every lover of Homer will I think agree that the most significant and characteristic thing about his gathering, accumulating, enlarging, thickening, expanding, deepening story of human life—of human life as it has been in every age, from the beginning and as it will be to the very end—is his emphasis upon the family. He does not, as so many poets since his time have done, talk a great deal about tribes and groups and clans and sects and varieties of idealistic associations, whether pacific or belligerent. What Homer does is to confine himself to the immediate family of the warrior in question. In the speeches they make to each other, in the appeals they make to the people, every single one of them will invariably refer to the father by whom he was begotten; and Homer himself is concerned with this paternal link to such an intense degree that if the two names can possibly be united into one single name he will unite them.

But now let us pause to consider the Homeric attitude to sex love. I think everyone will agree with me that in the passionate love of Achilles for Patroclus there is not a trace of homosexuality. Their love is like the love that existed in historic cases all down the ages between man and man while both men can at the same time have their women. Indeed it is an interesting and remarkable thing that it is impossible to avoid noticing in Homer the complete absence of the least suggestion of homosexuality or of Lesbianism. Considering the emphasis laid upon these erotic eccentricities in this modern age of ours what are we to make of their complete absence in Homer? I would even be inclined to go a little further and to emphasise the absence from the ***Iliad*** of any mention of those two sexual aberrations connected with cruelty, namely, what we have come to call Sadism and Masochism. There are several familiar historic cases of tyrants obviously addicted to sadism, and several prehistoric myths and legends whose cruelties can easily be connected with these two sexual aberrations. But there is not, as far as I can discern, a trace of either of them in the ***Iliad.*** Is the reason for this the fact that in the ***Iliad*** we are dealing with a desperate war, a war that so exhausts everyone's energy that there is no energy left over to indulge in erotic sensations except the most natural and ordinary ones? Or is the reason simply that the lovers of and composers of poetry all the way down human history are so absorbed in the normal current of human life that they instinctively tend to avoid abnormalities, whether erotic or otherwise?

There are those who instinctively prefer the neat Greek tragedians, Aeschylus, Sophocles and Euripides to Homer. Why, I ask you, do they? The answer is simple. Because they are full of intellectual Ideas and Theories and Interpretations of Life, full of creative Visions and moral Principles as to how human existence upon earth could be improved. Matthew Arnold, one of my own favourite poets, tells us that Sophocles "sees life steadily and sees it whole." O what a pure delight it is to return to Homer after "seeing life whole!" Why, I ask you, *is* it such a relief and such a comfort? Because Homer has the reality of our natural feeling about life, and Sophocles has an intellectual vision of things that may turn out to be . . . no reality at all, *in fact a lie*. Sophocles may see life as "steadily" and as "wholesale" as he likes, but real life, as all men and women and children soon discover from personal experience, is the extreme opposite of anything you can see "steadily" or as "a whole." It is a wild, chaotic series of exhausting contradictions. When is Shakespeare at his greatest? When his characters are philosophizing? Not a bit of it! All the supreme scenes in Shakespeare are when his people are transported by ecstasies of love and hate. . . . But none of the passionate defiances and challenges of Shakespeare's stage, nor any of the pandemoniacal eloquence of Milton's angels and archangels, nor the most contorted twist of Browning's tipsy piety with its belching outbursts of county council optimism, really expresses, as we all know well, the actual experience of life which we poor mortals from childhood to manhood and womanhood have fled from or endured, have fought against or submitted to, ever since we were born. But Homer does express precisely this. We may be put off by the Greek words or annoyed by the conventional or slang translations. But now and again, as we go struggling on, there come glimpses and murmurs . . . of a natural and wonderful reality that the sweeping tide of these tremendous hexameters has caught up from the simplest human lives. Let us therefore listen to it rolling on with all its multifarious cross-currents, as it has done from the beginning, if there was a beginning, and will do until the end, if there will be an end, suffering and enjoying at the same time what "*is all,*" as Keats said, "*we know on earth* and all we need to know." (pp. 18-21)

John Cowper Powys, in a preface to his Homer and the Aether, *Macdonald, 1959, pp. 9-21.*

ROBERT GRAVES (essay date 1960)

[A highly versatile man of letters, Graves was an English poet, novelist, translator, and critic. He was first associated with the Georgian war poets during World War I, but afterward followed a less traditional yet highly ordered line, being influenced during the 1920s and 1930s by the American poet Laura Riding. Working outside the literary fashions of his day, Graves established a reputation which rests largely on his verbal precision and strong individuality as a poet. He is also considered a great prose stylist and is well known for such historical novels as I, Claudius *(1934) and* Wife to Mr. Milton *(1943). Witty, imaginative, and seldom concerned with the ordinary, Graves's novels are considered eccentric, but scholarly, and his characters larger than life. He was influenced by classical literature—some of which he translated—and used classical and mythological themes as points of departure in both his fiction and his critical works. In the following excerpt from his introduction to his translation of the* Iliad, *Graves focuses on satire in the poem, speculating that its cynicism probably contributed to its popularity.]*

[The] original High King of the Achaeans was a living god; his palace, a temple; his courtyards, holy ground. He corresponded on equal terms with the High King of the Hittites, a fellow-god. But by Homer's time this religious High Kingship had perished, all the great cities had fallen, and the semi-barbarous princelings who camped on their ruins were ennobled by no spark of divinity. It is clearly these iron-age princes—descendants of the Dorian invaders who drove his own ancestors overseas—whom Homer satirizes in Mycenaean disguise as Agamemnon, Nestor, Achilles and Odysseus; and of whom Hesiod, a late contemporary of Homer's, was thinking when he wrote, in a lugubrious vein, that the divine race of men had been destroyed at ancient Thebes and Troy.

The Homeridae, being sacrosanct servants of Apollo, could risk satire, so long as they remained serene and unsmiling throughout their performances, pointed no finger, cocked no eye, tipped no wink. Homer's wit is at its most merciless in *Book II,* when Agamemnon calls a popular Assembly and tests his troops' morale by offering to abandon the siege of Troy. Members of the Privy Council have been warned to shout protests and demand a vigorous assault; but Agamemnon so over-acts his defeatist part that he convinces even himself, and the war-weary soldiers at once rush cheering down to the ships. A fiasco! The Goddess Athene is obliged to intervene. Homer makes Agamemnon superbly ridiculous again in *Book IV,* when the armistice has been broken and he addresses his wounded brother Menelaus:

> Alas, my poor brother! I fear that the oath which pledged you to single combat in no-man's-land has proved your ruin: the Trojans have broken the armistice and transfixed you with an arrow. . . . I am more than ever assured that Troy's doom is sealed, also that of King Priam the Spearman and his subjects. Zeus, Son of Cronus, indignant at this outrage, will shake his shield threateningly at them from the Olympian throne; thus the armistice will not have been concluded in vain. Nevertheless, I should be most unhappy, brother, if you succumbed to your wound.

Agamemnon does not send for a surgeon at this point, but continues self-pityingly and once more in a defeatist strain:

> Your death, by removing the cause of war, might set my men clamouring for home—how ashamed I should be to find myself back on the thirsty plains of Argos, having allowed Priam's people to make good their old boast of keeping Helen. Your bones would rot in Trojan soil, and the proud Trojans capering on your tomb would scoff: "I pray the gods that ill-tempered Agamemnon will have no greater success in his other ventures than in this! He has sailed away empty-handed, and noble Menelaus lies here beneath our feet, his mission unaccomplished." Rather let the earth swallow me alive than that they should say such things!

Menelaus has, however, only been scratched. Battle is resumed, and Agamemnon stalks from contingent to contingent of his army, encouraging the commanders; but merely succeeds in setting their backs up by his ill-chosen phrases. Idomeneus is barely civil; Diomedes preserves a resentful silence; Odysseus and Sthenelus are downright rude to their High King.

In *Book IX,* Agamemnon's flood of tears and thunderous groans, after a severe defeat due to his own stupidity, introduce further comic scenes. He wakes Nestor, with the odd excuse that he must no doubt be suffering from insomnia. Nestor, courteous though sarcastic, revenges himself by waking everyone else of importance. But for what? He has no idea. Nor has Agamemnon. They solemnly call a council, and decide to send out a small patrol. Diomedes leads this, and when asked to choose a partner, picks Odysseus as the bravest present; yet he remembers Odysseus' cowardly desertion of him in battle, and Odysseus knows that, unless he redeems his good name, a spear will be driven between his shoulders. He offers Diomedes a half-apology.

Homer is utterly cynical about the Olympian gods. Zeus rules them by fear and cunning, not love, and must keep on constant guard against a palace revolution. In most myth-making societies, what is alleged to happen in the courts of Heaven reflects what happens in the royal palace below; but Homer lets his gods behave far worse than the one royal family to whom he introduces us, namely the Trojan. Priam, in *Book XXIV,* may rage at his surviving nine sons as malingerers and playboys who have dared outlive their forty-one heroic brothers; but his curses are doubtless intended to avert Nemesis, and so protect them. On all other occasions the domestic atmosphere in the Trojan palace is irreproachable, despite the presence of Helen, prime cause of their continued sufferings.

Zeus, on the other hand, hurls horrible threats at his wife Hera and the rest of the Olympian family, too well aware of their jealousies, grudges, deceptions, lies, outrages, and adulteries. Hera is a termagant, so cruel and sly that she manages to convert her only virtues, marital chastity and an avoidance of direct lies, into defects. She would like to eat the Trojans raw—and all because, long ago, Paris rejected the bribe she offered for a verdict in her favour, and instead gave Aphrodite the prize of beauty. We are left wishing that Hera would commit adultery with some River-god or Titan, to be taken in the act, and thus compel Zeus to chain her down for ever in the Pit of

Hell. Zeus' spoilt daughter Athene shares Hera's grudge against Paris—she also entered for the beauty prize—and Homer does not ask us to approve of her mean behaviour when the lovable Hector at last faces Achilles, a far stronger champion than himself, and she robs him of his advantage. Athene shines in comparison only with the foolish and brutal Ares. Of the three Olympians who come pretty well out of the tale, Apollo the Archer was the Homeridae's patron; Hephaestus the Smith ruled Lemnos, one of the Ionian Islands; and Hermes the Helper had invented the lyre and protected travellers. Then there is Poseidon, whom Homer clearly despises for not standing up to Zeus, and for being so touchy about his reputation as a master-mason; but abstains from ridiculing him because the Pan-Ionian Festival falls under his patronage.

Homer's audiences burned sacrifices to the gods, and celebrated annual festivals; yet they felt, it seems, no more and no less religiously sincere than most cradle-Catholics and cradle-Protestants do today—though supporting their Churches for the sake of marriage and funerals, keeping Christmas and Easter holidays, and swearing oaths on the Bible. Libations and sacrifices, the Ionians agreed, might be useful means of placating angry gods—a splash of wine and the thighbones of the victims on which one feasted cost little—and in the interests of law and order one should never swear false oaths, nor break the sacred bonds of hospitality. But they appear to have lacked any spiritual sense, except such few of them as had been admitted to the Eleusinian, Samothracian, Orphic, or other soul-stirring Mysteries. That Demeter and Persephone and Iacchus, the main figures in these mysteries, are kept out of Homer's Divine Harlequinade, suggests that he, and his sons after him, were adepts—hence their poor view of official religion.

Perhaps it was the very cynicism of the ***Iliad*** and ***Odyssey*** that made them acceptable Holy Writ in Peisistratus' day, when the Greeks were already practising free philosophic speculation—Thales was an old man by 560 B.C. Homer soon became the basis of all Classical Greek culture and, when Rome conquered Greece, of all Roman culture too. Nobody could be thought educated who had not studied him under a "grammarian," and many bright youths knew both his epics by heart. (pp. xiv-xviii)

The ***Iliad,*** though popular throughout Greater Greece in the sixth century, as vase paintings and other works of art prove, earned little reverence until jurists and grammarians treated it as a Bible: for instance, Xenophanes of Colophon (about 500 B.C.) complained of Homer's "imputing to the gods all that among men is shameful and blameworthy." But Thucydides, writing about 420 B.C., already discusses Homer as a reputable theologian, if sometimes inclined to figurative language; and it is odd to find the later grammarians of Rhodes, Athens and Alexandria commenting ponderously on passages which were no less satirical, in their tragic way, than Mark Twain's *Huckleberry Finn.*

When I "did" *Book XXIII* at my public school, the ancient classroom curse forbade me to catch any of the concealed comedy in the account of Patroclus' funeral games, which distinguishes them from Anchises' tedious funeral games in Virgil's *Aeneid*. Thus: Nestor, too old to compete in the chariot-race, gives his son Antilochus advice before he drives the Pylian team, confessing that the horses are slow and hinting that the race can be won by gamesmanship alone. Antilochus dutifully spurts to overtake Menelaus in a bad part of the track which, as they both know, will soon become a bottle-neck, and declines to slacken his pace. Menelaus, rather than be involved in a crash, lets Antilochus drive ahead, and cannot afterwards retrieve the lost ground. When Menelaus complains of a deliberate foul, Antilochus voluntarily forfeits his prize, though he has recently saved Menelaus' life in battle. Achilles, as President of the Games, thereupon awards Nestor a consolation prize. Nestor, in a gracious speech of acceptance, tells a long story of how, when young, he won all the events at King Oedipus' funeral games—or all except the chariot-race, in which Actor's sons scandalously jockeyed him. Homer leaves his audience to grasp that Achilles sympathizes with Antilochus, and that Nestor means: "Yes, we cannot blame my son for boldly putting Menelaus to a test of nerves. It was a different matter at Thebes, long ago, when a rival chariot deliberately crossed my lane and headed me off. Yet my rivals were the Moliones who, though putative sons of Actor, claimed Poseidon, God of Charioteers, as their real father; so, of course, I could make not protest."

In the subsequent foot-race Antilochus, the fastest runner of his age-group—the early twenties—is outdistanced by Odysseus, a man old enough to be his father, but makes a polite comment on the athletic pre-eminence of veterans. In fact, Antilochus purposely lost, to rehabilitate himself as a true sportsman—and this becomes clearer when Achilles shows gratitude by doubling the value of his third prize. Agamemnon then sees an opportunity of winning a prize himself: he enters for the javelin-throw, confident that Meriones, his sole opponent, will have the politeness to scratch. Achilles does not even give Meriones the chance, but sarcastically announces that Agamemnon, the best warrior in the world, may as well take both first and second prize—a contest would be sheer waste of time!

Nestor, Homer's favourite butt after Agamemnon, can never refrain from boasting of his youthful prowess and, though rated the sagest councillor among the Greeks—as Polydamas is among the Trojans—consistently gives bad advice which Agamemnon always adopts; whereas Polydamas consistently gives good advice, which Hector always rejects. Thus the Greeks would never have suffered such a heavy defeat on the plain if Nestor, instead of encouraging Agamemnon to act upon the false dream sent by Zeus, had done as Priam later did—tested its truth by demanding a sure augury. Again, the Trojans would never have been allowed to break into the Greek camp, if Nestor had not advised Agamemnon to build a grandiose defence system of rampart and fosse—without also suggesting a sacrifice to placate Poseidon's jealousy. Nor would Patroclus have been killed, had Nestor not advised him to borrow Achilles' armour and fight in it.

When a Trojan arrow wounds Machaon, and Nestor agrees to drive him out of danger, Homer's humour is at its dryest. Once back at the Greek camp, they settle down to a refreshing beverage of onion-juice, honey and barley-water in a great golden beaker, or tureen, to which the slave-girls add wine flavoured with cheese; and Nestor embarks on a long story of his own youthful adventures at Pylus. He makes no attempt to remove the arrow still protruding from Machaon's shoulder, though after fifty years of warfare he can hardly have avoided picking up a little simple surgery; nor does he send for Patroclus, a competent surgeon who, we know, was not busy at the time; nor does he even return to the battlefield and encourage his hard-pressed troops. He is still droning on when the Trojans swarm over the rampart. Then he hurriedly excuses himself: "Pray continue drinking, and one of my slave-girls will wash the blood off your shoulder." Nestor later dishonestly explains his absence from the field as due to a wound; and the ***Iliad*** ends with no further mention of Machaon who, for all Nestor cared, may have succumbed.

Menelaus, although despised by his brother Agamemnon, comes well out of the story. Conscious that this bloody war is being fought to avenge the wrong which Paris did him, he shows commonsense and dignity, keeping up a steady average of kills in various battles, and has even on one occasion decided to spare a suppliant prince—when Agamemnon, bustling up, officiously murders him. Moreover, Menelaus does not protest against Achilles' usurpation of the army command which, when Agamemnon gets wounded, should be his. Nevertheless, (*Book XIII*) Homer jokingly makes him rage against the Trojans as insatiable in their love of war—as though he had not himself been attacking them for the past ten years—and then plunge back into battle.

Homer treats Achilles with irony rather than humour. Though we are enlisted at the start as this ill-used hero's partisans, Achilles is soon discovered to be the real villain of the piece, who heartlessly watches the massacre of his comrades, just to spite Agamemnon. We believed his assurance to the Assembly that whenever he sacks cities and adds their treasures to the common stock, Agamemnon awards him only a trifle and takes the lion's share himself; later, we find Achilles' hut chock-full of loot—he has been selling captured prisoners as a side-line and pocketing the proceeds. We also believed his assurance to the Assembly that he was sincerely enamoured of Briseis; but when Agamemnon at last repents and offers to surrender her, untouched, together with an enormous compensation for his insults, Achilles tells the envoys that he does not really want the girl—she means nothing to him—and that he despises treasure. (Of course, Agamemnon also lied by pretending to have done no better out of the war than Achilles.)

Achilles' famous love of Patroclus, the kindest-hearted and most unselfish soldier in the Greek camp, proves to be pure self-love which grudges his comrade pre-eminence in battle. Patroclus dies, and Achilles, leaving his body unburied, announces that when he can get a new suit of armour, he will kill Hector and collect twelve Trojan prisoners for a human sacrifice at the pyre. Homer emphasizes Achilles' real object—which is to show that he can outshine Patroclus—when the miserable ghost appears in a dream, altogether uninterested in these barbarous works of vengeance, and complains of the delay. Until his body is duly burned, the Infernal Spirits are refusing him entry to Hades' kingdom, and he must wander from gate to gate, a homeless exile. Achilles answers brusquely that he is doing everything possible to make the funeral a success, and resents having his elbow jogged. Eventually Achilles gets Briseis back, accepts Agamemnon's heavy compensation—though not destined, he knows, to enjoy it—and also insists on Priam's paying a tremendous ransom for Hector's corpse: a transaction which he dishonestly hides from the Privy Council. Nor does he respect Patroclus' wishes by honourably marrying Briseis, but continues to treat her as a convenient bed-fellow and chattel.

Homer the satirist is walking on a razor's edge and must constantly affirm his adherence both to the ruling aristocracy, however stupid, cruel or hysterical, and his belief in auguries and other supernatural signs. The most sensible and telling speech at Agamemnon's Assembly, in *Book III,* is made by the antimonarchical commoner Thersites, whom Odysseus thereupon flogs. To dissociate himself from Thersites' sentiments, Homer presents him as bow-legged, bald, hump-backed, horrible-looking, and a general nuisance; but the speech and Odysseus' brutal action stay on record. And Homer's real feelings on the subject of auguries are put into Hector's mouth—he thinks birds are simply birds and fly about on their own lawful business without divine instruction—for Hector, having Zeus' direct promise, can be pardoned this cynicism. An inveterate hatred of war appears throughout the ***Iliad;*** and Homer smuggles into *Book XXIII* a bitter comment on the monstrous slavery it entails, by awarding the winner of the wrestling match a copper cauldron worth twelve oxen, and the loser a captive Trojan noblewoman valued as highly as four, because she is skilled at the loom. (pp. xix-xxiii)

Robert Graves, in an introduction to The Anger of Achilles: Homer's Iliad, *translated by Robert Graves, Cassell, 1960, pp. xi-xxxiv.*

ALBERT B. LORD (essay date 1960)

[*A professor of Slavic studies and contemporary literature at Harvard University, Lord has written extensively on folklore and folk epics. In the following excerpt from his* The Singer of Tales, *a study of the methods oral poets use to "compose, learn, and transmit their epics," he examines several key thematic patterns in the* Iliad.]

The essential pattern of the ***Iliad*** is the same as that of the ***Odyssey;*** they are both the story of an absence that causes havoc to the beloved of the absentee and of his return to set matters aright. Both tales involve the loss of someone near and dear to the hero (Patroclus and Odysseus' companions); both contain the element of disguise (the armor in the ***Iliad***); in both is the return associated with contests or games and followed by remarriage (Achilles with Briseis, Odysseus with Penelope), and, finally, in both a long period of time is supposed to elapse, or to have elapsed.

The story of the Trojan War is a simple one of bride-stealing and rescue. It belongs primarily to Menelaus, Paris, and Helen, and might have remained uncomplicated even if the struggle did call forth the armada of Achaeans and a host of Trojan allies. But bride-stealing in epic was mythic before it became heroic and historical. The rape of Persephone in all its forms as a fertility myth underlies all epic tales of this sort, and until the historical is completely triumphant over the mythic, all such tales are likely to be drawn into the pattern of the myth.

I believe that it was the element of the length of the Trojan War, itself apparently an historical fact, which drew unto its story the bride-stealing theme. Once thus sanctified, the war became the setting for tales of absence and return, the mythic death and resurrection, associated with fertility myth and ritual. The story of Odysseus is one form of these tales; that of Achilles is another. In the former the length of time causes no difficulty (even though it is doubled by the addition of another form of the story, a form involving wanderings), because the lapse of time coincides with the absence from home. In the ***Iliad,*** the length of the war is not conceived of as coincident with the absence of Achilles from battle. The reason for this is that the death of the substitute for Achilles, Patroclus, is stressed in the ***Iliad,*** whereas it is only vestigial in the ***Odyssey***. . . . (p. 186)

The story pattern of the god who dies, wanders for a period of time in the other world, and then returns, requires the element of length of time because this element has seasonal significance. It is kept and stressed in heroic tales that follow this pattern, such as the ***Odyssey.*** But the death of the substitute is final unless he is considered to be wandering in the lower world

A fifth-century B.C. vase illustration showing the fight between Achilles and Memnon. The British Museum.

in need of rescue, in which case we enter into another complex of themes of search and rescue, the complex in which the Telemachus part of the ***Odyssey*** belongs. In these cases, however, the substitute is not really a substitute but a form of the god himself. The substitute is a ritual figure, a sacrifice, and his story is terminated by his death. With this ritual figure the element of length of time has no meaning; his absence is forever. Even when the human substitute is really killed or really dies (rather than simply being lost or wandering) and is sought and found in the lower world by a loved one, he cannot be brought back. And if he returns, as significantly enough Patroclus does, it can be only as a ghost or in a dream.

The emphasis on the death of the substitute, Patroclus, in the ***Iliad,*** in the framework of a story of absence and return, has deprived that story of the element of length of absence. Yet the element is kept as vestigial. It belongs to the story of the war, and hence events are told that we should expect to find at the beginning of the war and not in its tenth year; it belongs with the story of Achilles' absence, the duration of which, together with the duration of the war, has been telescoped into a much shorter period of time. In the Dictys version, in which the death of Patroclus occurs long before Achilles' withdrawal, point is made of two truces, one of two months' and the other of six months' duration, between the withdrawal of Achilles and his return to battle. In the ***Iliad,*** the story of the substitute's death has been placed at the point of return, and so the entire tale of the war thus far is concentrated between Achilles' withdrawal and return.

Thus in Book II when Agamemnon makes trial of the army we are in the last year of the war, but when the army reassembles and we enter into the Catalogues, a theme properly belonging to the beginning of the war, but yet not out of place here either, we find ourselves in a series of events that are logical only or chiefly in the beginning, but questionable after nine years of fighting. Helen's pointing out the Greek leaders to Priam is scarcely sensible if the Greeks have been battling before his eyes for nine years. The single combat between Paris and Menelaus in which Menelaus claims the victory and nearly ends the war is surely better placed somewhere nearer its beginning. Zeus' plan as just announced is not working out very well, but this is because the events immediately following its announcement really belong earlier.

It is true that we might explain the presence of these incidents merely by saying that Homer went off the track in the reassembly theme and inadvertently went back to the beginning of the war. We might argue that in his desire to lengthen the story he has included everything he knew of the war up to this point. Such an argument and such an explanation would be consistent with oral composition. The trial of the troops and the reassembly are bound together by association of themes. The assembly and the single combat are also bound together by association. The singer has unwittingly, or wittingly, modulated backward. All this is true. But I believe that there is a more significant reason for the return to the beginning. This material belongs with the story and is fitting. It is not mere background, not a scenic and artistic backdrop for the staging of the tale of Achilles. It has meaning in the larger tale of the war and in the tale of Achilles' absence, the kind of essential meaning that makes epic song effective and draws multiforms together into a concentrate.

The events leading up to the wrath of Achilles in Book I follow a pattern similar to that of the poem itself. The daughter of Chryses is captured and given to Agamemnon; her father seeks her release, offering ransom; Agamemnon refuses the offer and sends Chryses away. Chryses prays to Apollo; the plague is sent; Agamemnon returns the girl to her father. Interlocking with the last theme, the pattern begins again in another form: Agamemnon's concubine is taken from him with the consent of the Achaeans and under the protection of Achilles; Agamemnon asks them to replace her with another as his due; they refuse, and, following his prerogative, he takes Achilles' concubine. With the appeasing of Agamemnon the first repetition of the pattern seems to be broken, but in reality the refusal of the Achaeans leads to the quarrel between Agamemnon and Achilles (parallel to the plague, in the pattern). Thus, whereas from one point of view the taking of Briseis satisfies Agamemnon's anger (parallel to the return of Chryseis), from another point of view the acknowledgment of error by Agamemnon and the embassy mark, or should mark, the end of trouble, corresponding also to the last scene of the pattern, the return of Chryseis.

The difference of the working out of the basic pattern in these two cases is caused by the fact that in the first instance Apollo is a god who must be appeased when wronged or hurt, but in the second instance Agamemnon, divine king though he be, cannot really demand restitution when hurt, especially when that hurt is the result of an offense against the god. The story pattern fits the actions of a god, but when a mortal replaces the god, the pattern itself seems to condemn him on the grounds of *hybris*. The only possible outcome is either death or capitulation.

The taking of Briseis starts the pattern again for the third time. The wrath of Chryses-Apollo caused the wrath of Agamemnon, which caused the wrath of Achilles-Thetis-Zeus, the main tale of the ***Iliad.*** The third pattern is like the first, but since Achilles is mortal, though the son of a goddess, and not, like Chryses, the representative of a god, the pattern of his story has affinities to that of Agamemnon's wrath. Achilles acts both as god and as mortal. When Achilles' pleas that Briseis not be taken from him prove vain in spite of his threats to sail back home, Achilles, like Chryses, goes to the shore and prays. This is obviously parallel to the Chryses pattern. But Achilles has also, like Agamemnon, taken things into his own hands by his action of withdrawal from the fighting. The plan of Zeus to give victory to the Trojans and defeat to the Achaeans corresponds to the plague sent by Apollo in the Chryses pattern. The withdrawal of Achilles has the same effect in the Agamemnon pattern. Thus the defeat for the Greeks fits into the same place in the three patterns of the story; (a) in Agamemnon's wrath, (b) in Achilles' wrath as god, and (c) in Achilles' wrath as mortal.

There are three devastations and three returns because Achilles' actions follow three patterns. The complexity of the ***Iliad*** and some of its apparent inconsistencies come from the working out of all three patterns in this one song. The hurt caused by the taking of Briseis would have been satisfied by the embassy, but by then two other patterns were operative; it would have been satisfied by a possible return of Briseis in Book XVI, a vestige of which we see in Achilles' conversation with Patroclus when Achilles shows an almost-willingness, and allows Patroclus to enter in his stead as a compromise. But another pattern is still left in operation, the most powerful pattern in the ***Iliad,*** the pattern which began with the withdrawal of Achilles. This pattern is the tragedy of Achilles, but the art and irony, the *hybris* [hubris] of Achilles, arise from the fact that all three patterns are interlocked in the song.

The embassy should have been the final scene, parallel to the return of Chryseis to her father and to Apollo, in all three patterns. When Athena restrained Achilles from drawing his sword, in Book I, during the quarrel with Agamemnon, she intimated that this would be so. She told him: "Some day three times over such shining gifts shall be given you by reason of this outrage." Yet this is not the case. In terms of story patterns, there are two possible explanations of Achilles' refusal to accept the terms of the embassy. In order to understand them we must note that the element that would have been omitted by Achilles' acceptance is the death of Patroclus. It is possible that in the Chryses pattern the return of Chryseis implied her sacrifice to Apollo. This would mean that before the final appeasement there must be sacrifice of a human life. Although we know that Apollo did not disdain such sacrifices (at the Leucadian rock maidens were sacrificed to Apollo), this solution does mean reading something into the ***Iliad*** that is not there.

On the other hand, the refusal of the embassy is parallel to Agamemnon's refusal of the ransom of Chryses (still within the Chryses pattern, before the Agamemnon pattern begins). The difference is that whereas up to this point we have seen Achilles playing Chryses to Agamemnon, now we find him playing Agamemnon to Chryses. In other words, he was the bereaved seeking restitution, the god seeking retribution, but now he is the mortal refusing to accept just return. And by slipping into the role of Agamemnon he brings further disaster upon the Achaeans and on himself, thus prolonging the story until the final reconciliation with Agamemnon and the return of Briseis to Achilles. This suggestion of a move from one pattern to another is one possible solution, made even probable by the thematic correspondences (a) of Achilles-Chryses praying to the god and (b) of Achilles-Agamemnon refusing an embassy offering ransom. However, although this might suffice to renew the fighting and to take us back to war (the plague), it would not be sufficient, I believe, to lead to the death of Patroclus, without recourse to the idea of the sacrifice of the maiden Chryseis. Of course, from Agamemnon's point of view, Chryseis was sacrificed.

There may be truth in all of this, but if so, I think it is subsidiary to and supporting the other possibility: that by his withdrawal from the fighting Achilles has brought another powerful pattern into play, that of death and return. The story pattern of the wrath, the one that we have been considering, leads to the troubles of the Achaeans, even to the duplication of those troubles before and after the embassy. But it does not in itself seem to include the death of Patroclus. This appears to belong to another pattern into which the story of the wrath has modulated.

That the pattern of the wrath is really a pattern of bride-stealing and rescue is clear in the case of Chryses and Agamemnon quarreling over Chryseis, because Agamemnon has stolen Chryseis and Chryses seeks to rescue her. But it is equally true of Agamemnon and Achilles quarreling over Briseis; for Agamemnon steals her from Achilles, who wishes to rescue her. We are reminded that the Trojan War is also a tale of bride-stealing and rescue. The pattern of the wrath, however, would not by itself lead to the killing of Hector. It should lead after the reconciliation with Agamemnon to the victory of the Achaeans with Achilles at their head. The killing of Hector is part of the feud begun by the death of Patroclus, another feud which is ended by the reconciliation with Priam. Feuding patterns have a tendency to recur. Achilles' return to battle should mean the end of the Trojan War according to the pattern of the story of wrath. But the wrath is introductory. The withdrawal of Achilles is the key; for by it we modulate from the wrath pattern to a pattern of death and return, which in turn evokes the complex of death by substitute. And that death, Patroclus', leads into another feud, between Hector and Achilles.

Captivity and rescue tales, of course, are closely allied to stories of captivity and return. . . . They are sometimes combined, as . . . in the ***Odyssey***. . . . The relationship between them is close because of the captivity theme itself. But the coincidences are even greater when the captivity is of long duration and is pictured as causing devastation at home. In the wrath patterns at the beginning of the ***Iliad*** the duration is not specified as long, but rather presented as short. Hereby we have seen a difficulty arising in the poem, a difficulty involving the apparent return to the beginning of the war. But the second element, devastation at home, links them clearly with the captivity-return pattern.

Agamemnon plays the part of captor in the first two cases in the ***Iliad,*** first as the captor of Chryseis, who is rescued by Chryses, and then of Briseis, who is "rescued" by Achilles. But by the time of the embassy his role has changed; we find him offering ransom as would either a rescuer or a captive. Achilles, when he prays to Thetis, is the rescuer (note again the parallel with Chryses), but by the time of the embassy he refuses ransom, and here he acts as captor. This is because we have modulated via the withdrawal to another, closely related, story pattern.

The idea of withdrawal is, of course, inherent in the idea of captivity. But there is another sense of withdrawal, that of return home, withdrawal from the war, which appears in the first book of the ***Iliad.*** Chryses wishes the Greeks victory and a happy return homeward. Achilles, at the beginning of the assembly of the Achaeans, suggests that they will have to return home if both war and pestilence ravage them. At the beginning of the quarrel Achilles threatens to depart for Phthia if his prize is taken from him; for this is not his war. Agamemnon tells him to go ahead home. The subject does not come up again until Book II, and then in a controversial and important incident, when Agamemnon makes trial of his men. We must consider this incident with some care. For one thing, it has been said that it does not follow logically from what precedes it, the baneful dream. Secondly, it is here that we learn for the first time that we are in the ninth year of the war. Until now we might very well have been at the beginning of the war. Thirdly, it is the start of the modulation back to events at the beginning of the war. In short, there seems to be something seriously wrong here. Except for the intervention of Athena in Book I and her speech, which would seem to indicate that the death of Patroclus was not in all singings of the wrath of Achilles, this is the first real difficulty in the ***Iliad.*** Her intervention is also inconsistent with the statement by Thetis later, that all the gods are on vacation in Ethiopia, whence they return twelve days later for the ***Iliad***'s first scene on Olympus.

The sequence in which the testing of the troops occurs is as follows: after twelve days the gods return to Olympus and Thetis plots with Zeus; Zeus sends the deceptive dream; Agamemnon tests the troops. Restated in terms of essential ideas, this gives us return after long absence, deceptive story, testing (the number twelve is significant as twelve months, although sometimes we find it as days and sometimes as years also: cf. the nine days of the plague and the nine years of the war). We recognize this sequence as belonging to the return story. True, the characters are different and the shift from the gods to Agamemnon is puzzling. But the sequence that Homer is following is a well-established one. In the inner logic of oral song the testing of the troops belongs with what precedes it, namely, deceptive story and return. The idea of return has haunted Book I, as we have seen.

The shift to Agamemnon, which has come about by his repetition of the deceptive story of the baneful dream, has occasioned Homer's reference to a long period of time, and for him the nine years of the war properly provide that reference. By it, we have moved from an event, the withdrawal of Achilles, which belongs at the beginning of a period of troubles, to the culmination of a period of troubles and to return home. The modulation back to the beginning of the war is accomplished, as we have noted, by the assembling of the troops, leading to the catalogues. The return of the gods from their twelve-day vacation started a sequence in which the testing was in place, but in the larger sequence of the story beginning with the withdrawal of Achilles, a sequence in which return and all its associated ideas have played a part, the testing was out of place and premature, as was the return itself.

In the books which follow (II-VII) the war begins, and the Achaeans, perhaps contrary to our expectations, are almost victorious. At the end of Book VII and the beginning of Book VIII we reach a complex of themes that throws us back again to the end of Book I and the beginning of Book II and to the story of Achilles, who has been almost forgotten in the intervening episodes.

Book I ended with the feasting of the gods and their going to sleep. Book VII ends with the feasting of the Achaeans after the building of the wall, and their going to sleep. At the beginning of Book II we find Zeus wakeful, plotting the destruction of the Achaeans; at the end of Book VII Zeus plots their destruction all night long. The results of his scheming are different in each case. In Book II the result is the baneful dream; in Book VIII the result is an assembly of the gods at dawn, when Zeus tells them to refrain from fighting. After this he repairs to Ida and watches the battle resumed, until at midday he balances the scales and things go worse for the Achaeans. Hera and Athena band together to stop the carnage, but Zeus intervenes and recalls them. He tells them that nothing they can do will change the fate which has been decreed:

For Hektor the huge will not sooner be stayed from his fighting
until there stirs by the ships the swift-footed son of Peleus
on that day when they shall fight by the sterns of the beached ships
in the narrow place of necessity over fallen Patroklos.

This is the first we hear about the death of Patroclus. This plan is different from the earlier one in Book II. But the general sequence here is the same as that in the earlier passage: feasting, sleep, a sleepless, plotting Zeus, and action proceeding from his plot.

What follows has also a parallel in Book II, and is germane to our previous considerations. Night falls and the Trojans keep watch after a speech by Hector. Meanwhile, Agamemnon, at the beginning of Book IX, summons an assembly, as in Book II. Now he suggests to the Achaeans, and not in a testing mood, that they return home. The similarity to events in Book II is striking. The interchange following this suggestion is reminiscent of what follows the threat of Achilles during the quarrel to return home to Phthia. It is now Diomedes, who in words like those of Agamemnon, says that Agamemnon, indeed all the rest of the Achaeans, may return home, but he will stay and fight until Troy is taken. Nestor intervenes here, as he did in Book I, and suggests a meeting of the council. At that meeting he urges Agamemnon to appease Achilles, and the embassy is the result.

Agamemnon's suggestion for returning is fully in place in Book IX, whereas, although we can trace the singer's thinking in Book II, I believe, it is there out of place. The words are the same in both books:

> Zeus son of Kronos has caught me badly in bitter futility.
> He is hard: who before this time promised me and consented
> that I might sack strong-walled Ilion and sail homeward.
> Now he has devised a vile deception and bids me go back
> to Argos in dishonour having lost many of my people.
> Such is the way it will be pleasing to Zeus who is too strong,
> who before now has broken the crests of many cities
> and will break them again, since his power is beyond all others.
> Come then, do as I say, let us all be won over; let us
> run away with our ships to the beloved land of our fathers
> since no longer now shall we capture Troy of the wide ways.

(pp. 186-93)

The Chryses pattern, we saw, instructed us that the return of Briseis should mean the end of the wrath. Athena promised Achilles, when she restrained his hand, that he would receive threefold payment for the rape of Briseis. This promise, too, would lead us to believe that Achilles would accept the return of the girl with additional gifts as appeasement for his wrath. But the words of Zeus shortly before have notified us that this embassy is doomed to failure because Patroclus first must die. The Chryses pattern is completed formally, but we have been occupied wth another pattern (that of death and return) since the withdrawal of Achilles. Now for the first time we can state this with assurance. Zeus has told us so himself. Achilles' anger was godlike (cf. Apollo) and its effects were godlike (cf. the plague). Achilles the bereaved, the hurt, has been satisfied. The return of Briseis was all that was asked for in the Chryses pattern. The new pattern demands human sacrifice. And so Achilles, prolonging his withdrawal in the role of his own captor, refuses the inadequate ransom, and thus insists on Patroclus' death. So far, then, in the new pattern we have an absence that causes devastation and requires human sacrifice for return. The quarrel of Agamemnon is of no import after the embassy. The devastation of the Achaeans, however, is of significance after the embassy, and must continue until Patroclus' death. Now all hinges upon that.

But the action of the ***Iliad,*** almost in consternation, as it were, that the embassy has not turned out as envisaged from the beginning of the song, comes to a stop at the end of Book IX, and takes a rest before continuing. Book X, the Doloneia, could be omitted without anyone being the wiser; many feel that the ***Iliad*** would be better without it. Yet it is there and we have no evidence that justifies our eliminating it, since it does not contradict anything in the song. I am not sure that we can find a satisfactory answer at the present time to the question of why the Doloneia is included in the ***Iliad,*** but we can indicate its relationship in respect to thematic patterns with other parts of the song. And this knowledge may lead us in the direction of possible solutions. Book X opens with the scene of all the Achaeans asleep by the ships except for Agamemnon, who is worried about the fate of his forces. And associated with his worry is a simile of a storm. With this opening we are thrown back to the beginning of the previous book (IX) which discovers the Achaeans in panic, their panic emphasized by another storm simile; here, too, Agamemnon is singled out as wandering about among his captains. In fact, we are reminded of a still earlier scene, the opening of Book II, where we find all the gods and men asleep except for Zeus, who hits upon the plan of the baneful dream, which he sends to the sleeping Agamemnon in the form of Nestor. There is a kinship in the opening of these three books, a kinship made closer by the fact that each of these books presents particular problems in the structure of the ***Iliad.***

After the opening, the pattern in each case continues with the calling of an assembly, although the technique employed is not the same in all three books. In Book II Agamemnon orders the heralds to summon an assembly, while he holds a council of kings by Nestor's ship. In Book IX Agamemnon orders the heralds to summon every man by name, and he himself assists. There is no meeting of the council of kings, but the assembly gathers immediately. In Book X the pace is much more leisurely, Agamemnon's worries are described, and then Menelaus'; the latter goes to seek his brother and they exchange ideas about a plan; then Agamemnon seeks out Nestor. Menelaus has alerted Odysseus and Diomedes, and soon we find that a council of the kings has been summoned. These are all multiforms of a favorite theme, that of the assembly.

It seems that either Book IX or Book X could follow immediately upon the action of Book VIII. This would perhaps point to the fact that they are in some sense duplications, or that one is an intruder. As a matter of fact, Books IX and X are possibly interchangeable; at any rate their order could be reversed. It may be that we are dealing with two versions of the story, which have been amalgamated, one in which there was a *successful* embassy to Achilles, thus having a different ending to the tale; the other without an embassy but with a Doloneia leading into the Patroclus episode. I am inclined to feel that the mixing of a story of Achilles without a Patroclus substitute and one with Patroclus has again caused difficulty in the structure of the ***Iliad.*** But whatever the answer may be, we shall undoubtedly reach it by way of a careful analysis of the repetition of thematic patterns.

The story of Patroclus really begins in Book XI, but it is interrupted at the very beginning of Book XII and does not reappear until the middle of Book XV, briefly, and at the beginning of XVI, where it is fully resumed. After this there seem to be no further interruptions.

It might be said that there is some vestige of a return after the embassy; for it is in Book XI that Achilles shows interest in the fate of the Achaeans and sends Patroclus to find out what is going on. Patroclus' entrance on the field of battle, first as a messenger, and then in the stead of Achilles into the battle itself, is Achilles' return by proxy. In fact, Patroclus' mission to spy out the situation for Achilles is strangely like the mission of Diomedes and Odysseus in the Doloneia.

Patroclus' entrance into the battle parallels that of Achilles, for whom he is a double. He enters in disguise in Achilles' armor (not quite complete, for the spear is lacking) and with Achilles' horses. The disguise is soon forgotten, to be sure, but it is there, and it is operative at the point of his victory over Sarpedon. Glaucus' words to Hector seem first to ignore it. Zeus takes from Sarpedon his protection, as Apollo does from Hector. Even as Achilles was almost overcome by the river, so Patroclus was almost overcome by Apollo, at the wall of Troy. Disguise, recognition, a struggle with an opponent (supernatural) who almost overcomes him, link Patroclus' fighting with that of Achilles. Only their ultimate fates in the battle are different, although Patroclus' death in Achilles' armor and in his stead is also Achilles' death by proxy. The laments for Patroclus by the Greeks in general, by his friend Achilles, and by Briseis, as well as his funeral games all form part of the complex. (pp. 193-95)

We would not be inclined to see any similarity between the withdrawal of Achilles and the absence of Odysseus, between the devastation caused by that withdrawal and the destructiveness of the suitors, certainly not between the death of Patroclus and that of Anticleia, nor between the role of Thetis-Zeus and that of Athena-Zeus, were it not for the character of Achilles' return to the fighting. Achilles' return is portentous. If he has been "disguised" as Patroclus before, he now appears as himself to the Trojans, unarmed, but glorified by Athena.

> But Achilleus, the beloved of Zeus, rose up, and
> Athene
> swept about his powerful shoulders the fluttering aegis;
> and she, the divine among goddesses, about his head
> circled
> a golden cloud, and kindled from it a flame far-
> shining . . .
> so from the head of Achilleus the blaze shot into the
> bright air.
> He went from the wall and stood by the ditch, nor
> mixed with the other
> Achaians, since he followed the close command of his
> mother.
> There he stood, and shouted, and from her place Pallas
> Athene
> gave cry, and drove an endless terror upon the
> Trojans. . . .
> The charioteers were dumbfounded as they saw the
> unwearied dangerous
> fire that played above the head of great-hearted Peleion
> blazing, and kindled by the goddess grey-eyed Athene.
> Three times across the ditch brilliant Achilleus gave his
> great cry,
> and three times the Trojans and their renowned
> companions were routed.
> There at that time twelve of the best men among them
> perished
> upon their own chariots and spears.
>
> (pp. 195-96)

This is a mystical and magic passage, and we realize here that Achilles is more than a human hero, that he is a symbolic figure. It seems to me important that Achilles cannot wear his own armor nor is his new armor ready—though in the divine economy, I suspect, it might have been possible, had it been fitting for Achilles to be seen in it at this point. (p. 196)

He must be recognized and for that reason he must be recognizable. The similarity to the appearance of Odysseus, beautiful and transformed by Athena before his son Telemachus, is, I think, not forced. There is something mystical and otherworldly in both these returns and recognitions.

The ashen spear of Achilles, too, has its counterpart in the bow of Odysseus. It is noteworthy that this spear is not carried by Patroclus, for only Achilles can wield it. It is an heirloom, like the bow. It, not the armor of Hephaestus, is the distinguishing mark of Achilles.

Achilles' fight with the river, however, corresponds to the near death of Odysseus in the sea before his landing at Phaeacia, when he is saved by the intervention of Ino. A struggle which almost ends in disaster for the hero is regularly found in connection with return songs; hence, the fight with the river is thoroughly at home in this tale of Achilles. . . . Beowulf's battle with Grendel's mother belongs in the same category with the fight with the river, as does the battle between Charles and Baligant in the *Roland*. An excellent parallel can be found in Jacob's striving with the angel in *Genesis*, chapter 32, a portion of the Scriptures rich in latent folklore meanings with duplication of incident. There is evidence in older traditions that it was not an angel with whom Jacob struggled but a river spirit whom he had to overcome before the river could be passed.

By the killing of Patroclus a feud has started in this heroic society, and according to its rules Hector must in turn be killed, Hector or one of his kin. The element that makes the situation somewhat different in the ***Iliad*** is that Patroclus has been killed by decree of Zeus or of fate. The gods have here been the aggressors. Patroclus is a sacrifice. It is Apollo who has killed Patroclus, and now one of Apollo's men, Hector, must pay.

This is no ordinary feud, indeed. The parallel with the return complex has been fruitful and helpful in understanding some of the developments in this part of the ***Iliad,*** but it is not enough. For the closest parallel to Patroclus we must turn to the epic of Gilgamesh. It seems more and more likely that the Near Eastern epics of ancient times were known to the Greeks of Homer's day or that they had some effect upon Greek epic before his day. In the epic, Gilgamesh and his friend Enkidu have broken the taboos of the gods. The gods decide that Enkidu shall perish and not Gilgamesh. And Gilgamesh, when told of this decision by Enkidu, to whom it has been revealed in a dream says: "Me they would Clear at the expense of my brother!" Here as in the ***Iliad*** it is the decree of the gods that the friend be killed for the hero. Gilgamesh, like Achilles, is part divine, "two thirds of him is god, [one third of him is human]." Enkidu's death is followed by the lament of Gilgamesh over his friend. Thus far is the parallel between Achilles and Gilgamesh clear. But here the correspondence seems to end; for now Gilgamesh departs over the steppe, and sets out for the island of the blest to visit Utnapishtim to learn the secret of eternal life. Only in the peaceful ending of the two poems, the reconciliation of Gilgamesh with his failure to learn that secret and with his loss of the plant of eternal youth, and the reconciliation of Achilles with Priam, is there a similarity of spirit. (pp. 196-97)

Albert B. Lord, "The Iliad," in his The Singer of Tales, *1960. Reprint by Atheneum, 1965, pp. 186-97.*

GEORGE STEINER (essay date 1962)

[Steiner is a French-born American critic, poet, and fiction writer. He has described his approach to literary criticism as "a kind of continuous inquiry into and conjecture about the relations between literature and society, between poetic value and humane conduct." A central concern of his critical thought is whether or not literature can survive the barbarism of the modern world, a barbarism embodied by the Holocaust. Steiner's work encompasses a wide range of subjects, including social and literary criticism, linguistics, philosophy, and chess. Though some commentators have found fault with his sometimes exuberant prose style, Steiner

is generally regarded as a perceptive and extremely erudite critic. In the following excerpt from an essay that originally appeared in 1962, Steiner compares the tone and characterizations of the Iliad *with those of the* Odyssey *and finds that the two poems exhibit "contrasting qualities of mind." He further suggests that the* Iliad *is an early and the* Odyssey *a later work of the same author.*]

By far the greater part of recent Homeric scholarship deals with the ***Iliad.*** Excavation and decipherment seem to lead to Troy rather than to Ithaca. The ***Odyssey*** accords neither with the search for a Mycenaean tradition nor with the theory of a geometric style. This is revealing. It points to a conviction which many readers have held from the start. The two epics are profoundly different; different in tone, in formal structure, and, most important, in their vision of life. The Homeric question, therefore, goes beyond problems of authorship and text. It must deal with the literary and psychological relations between the ***Iliad*** and the ***Odyssey.*** What happens when we read the ***Iliad*** through the eyes of Odysseus?

Archaeologists differ on the way in which the world image of the ***Iliad*** was put together. Some assert that the narratives of battle are realistic and that efforts have been made to bring archaic details up to date (the classic instance being Homer's awkward treatment of Ajax's body shield, a piece of equipment which went out of use in the tenth century). Others regard the world of Homeric Troy as a "visionary structure" in which elements ranging from the Bronze Age to the eighth century are woven together by the set formulas and conventions of the heroic style. But one thing is clear: the ***Iliad*** expresses a specific view of the human condition. In no other work of world literature, with the possible exception of *War and Peace,* do we find the same image of man. And certainly not in the ***Odyssey.***

The poet of the ***Iliad*** looks on life with those blank, unswerving eyes which stare out of the helmet slits on early Greek vases. His vision is terrifying in its sobriety, cold as the winter sun:

> "So, friend, you die also. Why all this clamour about it?
> Patroklus also is dead, who was better by far than you are.
> Do you not see what a man I am, how huge, how splendid
> and born of a great father, and the mother who bore me immortal?
> Yet even I have also my death and my strong destiny,
> and there shall be a dawn or an afternoon or a noontime
> when some man in the fighting will take the life from me also
> either with a spearcast or an arrow flown from the bowstring."
> So he spoke, and in the other the knees and the inward
> heart went slack. He let go of the spear and sat back, spreading
> wide both hands; but Achilleus drawing his sharp sword struck him
> beside the neck at the collar-bone, and the double-edged sword
> plunged full length inside. He dropped to the ground face downward,
> and lay at length, and the black blood flowed, and the ground was soaked with it.
>
> (pp. 178-79)

The narration proceeds with inhuman calm. The sharp directness of the poet's vision is never sacrificed to the demands of pathos. In the ***Iliad*** the truth of life, however harsh or ironic, prevails over the occasions of feeling. This is strikingly illustrated in the crowning moment of the epic: the night encounter of Priam and Achilles. There is a stillness in the midst of hell. Looking upon each other, the bereft king and the slayer of men give voice to their great griefs. Their sorrows are immeasurable. Yet, when they have spoken they feel hungry and sit down to an ample meal. For as Achilles says of Niobe, "She remembered to eat when she was worn out with weeping." No other poet, not even Shakespeare, would have run the risk of so humble a truth at such an instant of tragic solemnity.

But this magnificent clearheadedness derives not from bitter resignation. The ***Iliad*** is no lament over man's estate. There is joy in it, the joy that burns in the "ancient glittering eyes" of the sages in Yeats's "Lapis Lazuli." The poet revels in the gusto of physical action and in the stylish ferocity of personal combat. He sees life lit by the fires of some central, ineradicable energy. The air seems to vibrate around the heroic personages, and the force of their being electrifies nature. Achilles' horses weep at his impending fall. Even insensate objects are kindled by this excess of life. Nestor's drinking bowl is so palpably real that archaeologists claim to have dug it up three thousand years after the event.

Pure energy of being pervades the ***Iliad*** like the surge of the wine-dark sea, and Homer rejoices at it. Even in the midst of carnage, life is in full tide and beats forward with a wild gaiety. Homer knows and proclaims that there is that in men which loves war, which is less afraid of the terrors of combat than of the long boredom of the hearth.

In the sphere of Agamemnon, Hector, and Achilles, war is the measure of man. It is the only pursuit he has been trained for (in the shadow of death, Hector worries who will teach his son how to throw a spear). Beyond the shadow, moreover, gleams the light of returning dawn. Around the ashes of Patroclus, the Greek chieftains wrestle, race, and throw the javelin in celebration of their stength and aliveness. Achilles knows he is foredoomed, but "bright-cheeked" Briseis lies with him each night. War and mortality cry havoc, yet the center holds. That center is the affirmation that actions of body and heroic spirit are in themselves a thing of beauty, that renown shall outweigh the passing terrors of death, and that no catastrophe, not even the fall of Troy, is final. For beyond the charred towers and brute chaos of battle rolls the tranquil sea. Elsewhere dolphins leap and shepherds drowse in the peace of the mountains. Homer's famous similes, in which he compares some moment of battle to an episode from pastoral or domestic life, act as an assurance of ultimate stability. They tell us that the waves will race to the shore when the location of Troy is a disputed memory.

It is a specific and unique portrayal of man. Truer, says John Cowper Powys, than that given by any other poet: "it is more like what has happened, is happening, and will happen to us all, from the very beginning, in our history in this world until the end of human life upon this earth" [see excerpt dated 1959]. This may well be; but the truth of the ***Iliad*** is not that of the ***Odyssey.***

To the "ancient glittering eyes" of the ***Iliad,*** Odysseus opposes a roving and ironic glance. The war epic is hewn of great solid blocks; the story of the long voyage home is a cunning weave. Like the sea water which laps its every page, the vision of the poem is swift, changing, exploratory, prone to odd shallows and sudden depths. "This novel," said T. E. Lawrence. A marvel of design and variousness, but difficult to get into focus. The old fires of the heroic are banked, and the muscular simplicity of life around Troy has yielded to all manner of irony and complication. The work was revered by its ancient readers, but it put them ill at ease. Papyrus fragments of the ***Iliad*** far outnumber those of the ***Odyssey.***

The geography of the tale is a riddle. It appears to include Greece and Ionia, Crete, Lycia, Western Sicily, Egypt, and even a hint of Mesopotamia. At times, it is clearly a geography of the imagination, bristling like medieval maps with fabled beasts and wind daemons blowing out of every quarter. Certain elements in the ***Odyssey*** correspond to the period of the decline of Mycenaean feudalism (the fact that the societies shown are illiterate, the vague status of kingship in Ithaca, the queer economics of Penelope's marriage settlement). But other aspects of the poem seem to reflect the values of the new city-states as they began to emerge in the very late eighth century. What there is in the ***Odyssey*** of Mycenaean culture, moreover, appears to derive from those outposts and colonies of Mycenae which long survived in Asia Minor. For what is inescapable in the ***Odyssey*** is a sense of the Oriental.

That the poet knew the Babylonian *Gilgamesh* epic is probable. That very ancient Asiatic and African myths are echoed in the Wanderer's saga is almost certain. Consider one of the most haunting touches in the entire ***Odyssey.*** Speaking out of death, Tiresias prophesies to Odysseus that another voyage awaits him beyond Ithaca:

> go forth under your shapely oar till you come to a people who know not the sea and eat their victuals unsavoured with its salt: a people ignorant of purple-prowed ships and of the smoothed and shaven oars which are the wings of a ship's flying. I give you this token of them, a sign so plain that you cannot miss it: you have arrived when another wayfarer shall cross you and say that on your doughty shoulder you bear the scatterer of haulms, a winnowing-fan. . . .

Where is that saltless land, and what does the confusion between oar and winnowing-fan signify? We do not know. But in his remarkable study *Genèse de l'Odyssée,* the French anthropologist Gabriel Germain has shown that the tenor of the myth is profoundly un-Greek. To find the motif of a landlocked kingdom in which men know neither salt nor ships, we must look to the legend world of pre-Islamic North Africa.

Dante learned of Tiresias' prophecy through Seneca (he had no direct knowledge of the Homeric ***Odyssey***). He gave it a grim Christian reading. Making of Odysseus a Faustian man, too grasping of life and hidden science, he launched him on a last fatal voyage past Gibraltar (*Inferno,* XXVI). The mariner's ghost, however, would not stay put. It rose from damnation to assume countless shapes in Western art and literature. Most of these shapes—even those given it in our time by Joyce and Kazantzakis—are already implicit in the first Odysseus. The characters of the ***Iliad*** are of a rich simplicity and move in a clear light. The hero of the ***Odyssey*** is elusive as fire. He has enjoyed an afterlife even more various and fascinating than that accorded to an Achilles or a Hector precisely because his initial adventures comprise areas of thought and experience undreamed of by the bronze warriors before Troy.

Twice, at least, the winds that drive Odysseus blow out of Araby. He seems to come to Nausicaä straight from *A Thousand and One Nights.* The entire episode is an Oriental fairy tale. The afflicted beggar is washed up by the sea. Invisible powers guide him to the royal palace, and there he reveals his true splendor. He departs laden with riches and falls into a magic sleep. Woven into this romance of beggar and caliph is the theme of a young girl's nascent love for a much older man. Again, there is in the thing a flavor which has little in common with the classic Greek sensibility. It foreshadows the romances of Alexandrine Hellenism.

Or take the only fully explored relationship in the ***Odyssey,*** the friendship of Athene and Odysseus. The goddess and the Wanderer delight in virtuosities of deception. They lie to each other in a gay rivalry of falsehood. They bargain like street merchants of Damascus, seeking to outwit one another with affectionate larceny. More than two thousand years before Shakespeare's Beatrice and Benedick, Homer knew that there can be between men and women affairs of the brain as well as of the heart. (pp. 179-82)

Once more, we are at a great distance from the tone and vision of the ***Iliad.*** The quarrels and lusts of the Olympians are, at times, satirized in the ***Iliad.*** But more often, the deities are seen as random and malignant forces destroying or favoring men at their caprice. Nowhere do we find the crafty, amused, deeply feminine amity which binds Athene to Odysseus. The flavor is Oriental. (p. 183)

But if the ***Iliad*** and ***Odyssey*** differ so notably in tone and in their view of human conduct, what is the relation between them?

Whitman contends that the "vast and obvious" change occurring between the composition of the two epics corresponds to a change in the style of Greek ceramics. In contrast to the geometric, the proto-Attic style is "breezy, open and slightly orientalizing." The proto-Attic vase painter handles his subjects as a series of fluid episodes, as does the ***Odyssey.*** We are no longer in the rigid, concentric world of the ***Iliad.*** Many scholars have rejected Whitman's entire thesis, arguing that poetry and ceramics cannot be compared. But Whitman has made one arresting observation. The physical appearance of personages in the ***Iliad*** is stylized. The descriptive epithet is a stock formula; thus, women are almost invariably "white-armed." In the ***Odyssey,*** flesh tones appear; Odysseus is darkly tanned and Penelope's skin is like cut ivory. The same change occurs in vase painting.

The two works may not only have been written at different times but in different places. Professor Denys Page insists that their vocabularies are so different that one cannot assign them to the same locality. The ***Iliad*** might have been composed in Attica; the ***Odyssey*** in Ionia, or even Sicily (as Robert Graves argues). This thesis has come under fire. Critics point out that an epic which deals with land warfare must necessarily use a different vocabulary from one mainly concerned with navigation. Nevertheless, it is hard to believe that the same ground was native to both. The Homer of the ***Odyssey*** seems to have verified with his own eyes certain settings and activities which the poet of the ***Iliad*** had only imagined.

Readers of Homer who are themselves writers or men of war nearly always reject the idea of a single authorship. Samuel Butler and Robert Graves discern in the ***Odyssey*** a woman's hand unraveling the ancient web of heroic action. John Cowper Powys states that the two poems "had different authors or originals" and that there is "an historic gap of three or four hundred years between them" [see 1959 excerpt by Powys]. T. E. Lawrence characterized the poet of the ***Odyssey*** as a "great if uncritical reader of the ***Iliad***" and guessed that he was not much of a practical soldier. We seem to be dealing with contrasting qualities of mind.

Consider the image we get of the ***Iliad*** when looking at it through the ***Odyssey.*** It is exceedingly complex. We get nearest to it in Book VIII, when Demodocus, the minstrel, sings of the fall of Priam's towers in the hidden presence of Odysseus. This is one of the great moments of divided focus in all literature (it reminds one of the performance of an air from *The Marriage of Figaro* in the last scene of *Don Giovanni*). To the audience of the blind singer, the quarrels of Agamemnon and Achilles are remote. They have the muted radiance of legend. To Odysseus they are unbearably close. He draws his purple cloak around him and weeps. His position is ambiguous, for he is both within and outside the saga of Troy. Hearing himself sung about, he knows that he has entered the realm of the legendary dead. But he is also a living man seeking return to Ithaca. Thus, he looks upon the Trojan War both in tragic remembrance and refutation. This is the crucial point. There is in the ***Odyssey*** a critique of the archaic values of the ***Iliad*** in the light of new energies and perceptions.

This critique is made dramatically explicit in the brief dialogue between Odysseus and the shade of Achilles:

> "How I envy your lot, Achilles, happiest of men who have been or will be! In your day all we Argives adored you with a God's honours: and now here I find you a Prince among the dead. To you, Achilles, death can be no grief at all." He took me up and said, "Do not make light of Death before me, O shining Odysseus. Would that I were on earth a menial, bound to some insubstantial man who must pinch and scrape to keep alive! Life so were better than King of Kings among these dead who have had their day and died." . . .

The Achilles of the ***Iliad*** would not have said quite this, even in death. He has his moods of harsh gloom, and carps at the predestined imminence of his fall. But he never rejects the excellence or necessity of the heroic ideal. Had he done so, there would have been peace before Troy. That Achilles should prefer to be alive as a poor man's slave rather than king of the immortal dead is to query the very impulse of the ***Iliad.***

Though it is conceivable, it seems unlikely that the same poet should have articulated both conceptions of life. I find no other example in literature of a writer producing two masterpieces that look to each other with that mixture of awe and ironic doubt which the ***Odyssey*** displays toward the ***Iliad.*** And yet, time and again, a single voice seems to resound through the differences of narrative technique and world view. Certain glories of the ***Iliad*** are fully visible only in the mirror of the ***Odyssey.*** When Achilles laments over Patroclus, he is compared to a father mourning the death of his newly married son. The exact converse of this simile expresses Odysseus' joy at seeing land after the destruction of his raft. Both similes, in turn, are hinted at in Penelope's recognition of the Wanderer. Subtle but tenacious strands relate the two poems. How can we reconcile the sense of contrast to that of unity?

I believe that the Homer whom we know, the poet who continues to shape many of the principal forms of the Western imagination, was the compiler of the ***Iliad*** and the inventor of the ***Odyssey.*** He assembled and ordered the fragmentary battle sagas of the Mycenaean tradition. He had the insight to group them around the dramatic and unifying motif of the rage of Achilles. He treated the ancient material and folk legends with profound respect. At times, he misunderstood the language and technical circumstances of the remote action. But he chose to retain what was obscure rather than improve upon it. He grasped the austere symmetries inherent in the archaic mode of narrative and saw life through the harsh, glittering eyes of battle. To the brief intensities of oral poetry, he made available the new amplitude and elaboration of the written form. The compiler of the ***Iliad,*** like the men who wove together the sagas of the Pentateuch, was an editor of genius; but the gold and the bronze lay ready in the crucible.

I imagine that he completed his task in the first powers of maturity. The ***Iliad*** has the ruthlessness of the young. But as he richened in experience and sensibility, the vision of the ***Iliad*** may have struck Homer as incomplete. One can readily conceive of him as a constant and observant voyager. "He had sailed upon and watched the seas,"says T. E. Lawrence. In particular, I would suppose that he grew familiar with the complex, Orientalized civilizations of the Eastern Mediterranean. The part of the Orient in the ***Iliad*** has the stiffness of ancient legend. It is traditional material dating back to the commerce of the Bronze Age. The Orient of the ***Odyssey*** is more modern, more immediately observed.

In the afternoon of his life, this much-traveled man may have turned back to the world of the ***Iliad*** in order to compare its vision of human conduct with that of his own experience. From that comparison, with its delicate poise of reverence and criticism, grew the ***Odyssey.*** With marvelous acumen, Homer chose for his protagonist the one figure out of the Trojan saga nearest to the "modern" spirit. Already in the ***Iliad,*** Odysseus marks a transition from the simplicities of the heroic to a life of the mind more skeptical, more nervous, more wary of conviction. Like Odysseus, Homer himself abandoned the stark, rudimentary values inherent in the world of Achilles. When composing the ***Odyssey,*** he looked back to the ***Iliad*** across a wide distance of the soul—with nostalgia and smiling doubt.

This view of Homer does, at least, match the few facts available to us. The ***Odyssey*** is younger than the ***Iliad,*** but not, I think, by very much. The one poem is intensely alive in the other. The two epics express judgments of man's condition which differ considerably. But a related craftsmanship is at work in both. Behind each lie remote, partially misunderstood legacies from the Mycenaean past; in the ***Iliad*** they are more obtrusive. In the ***Odyssey,*** on the other hand, gleam the first dawn lights of the Socratic future. The bridge between Troy and Ithaca could be the personal life of an incomparable editor and poet.

We shall never really know. But the ***Iliad*** and the ***Odyssey*** remain as the unassailable fact. And although there are many books by which men have ordered their lives, I wonder whether any can do more than the Homeric poems to make us understand the relationship of man to time and to the necessary outrage of the death we carry within us. (pp. 183-87)

> *George Steiner, "Homer and the Scholars," in his* Language and Silence: Essays on Language, Literature, and the Inhuman, *Atheneum Publishers, 1967, pp. 171-87.*

G. S. KIRK (essay date 1965)

[An English professor of Greek, Kirk is the author of numerous critical works on classical authors, including several books on Homer. In the following excerpt, he examines the oral techniques

A detail showing Patroclus taking leave of Achilles.

of "the singer of the Iliad,*" analyzing such issues as the building of reality in the poem, the Homeric simile, expansion, and dramatic impact upon the audience. Kirk stresses that, although Homer worked with traditional themes, it is important to acknowledge the degree to which he "extended and deepened" them.*]

For the modern taste, and for continuous reading, the ***Iliad*** may seem too long. It would have greater dramatic impact if the battle-poetry were cut by about a third, and if some of the reversals of fortune which delay the required Trojan success were omitted or drastically curtailed. Yet one cannot say that such a contraction would seem desirable by the completely different canons of oral poetry—in particular by those of monumental oral poetry, which remain to a large degree obscure. In any case Homer's ***Iliad*** was shorter than the 5th-century ***Iliad,*** which our text not too distantly resembles. There is little reasonable doubt that our poem contains at least two or three sizeable expansions and elaborations. Many other passages, most of them quite short, probably accrued after the main act of monumental composition had been completed. Yet the first substantial ***Iliad*** must still have been on a vast and quite unusual scale and must still have contained broad tracts of battle-poetry. And it was this poem that was thought successful enough, and brilliant enough in its scope and construction, to be the pattern for another *tour de force* in a slightly different genre, the ***Odyssey,*** which set out to emulate precisely the scope and scale and fullness of the great new poem on Troy. Nor did the Greeks from the 6th century onwards find fault with its length and structure or the apparent similarity of many of its descriptions of warfare.Their criteria, it is true, were no longer those of the original oral audiences; but they confirm that any judgement of redundance and excessive length tends to arise from a modern literary taste—a taste which may still have some value, and reveal characteristics of the poem that the Greeks themselves ignored, but which must be clearly recognized as extraneous and academic.

A poem of the length of the ***Iliad,*** even if we imagine it stripped of post-Homeric excrescences and elaborations, must have taken several days in the singing. That in itself involves different standards of cohesion and dramatic effect from those applied either to a written work of literature or to a poem designed for continuous single recitation. In the monumental poem, unless the main themes are allowed to drop altogether out of sight—which they never are, even in our expanded ***Iliad***—it does not matter that they are diffused and separated by masses of other and secondary material. The wrath of Achilles did not need to be often mentioned between the second and the fifteenth books (of course it reasserts itself strongly in the Embassy in IX); his absence from the fighting must have been conspicuous all through, and must have reminded an audience which knew from other poetry, or from Homer himself, that Achilles was the greatest warrior on either side, that the wrath-theme was there in the background, waiting for its inevitable development and conclusion. This being so it mattered less, from the standpoint of structure, how often the battle raged to and from the Achaean ships. Eventually one of those ships had to be fired, Achilles had to be drawn back into the fight. The audience on the first or second day of singing was not, in any case, going to hear of those things. They lay in the future; meanwhile the question was whether the intermediate episodes, the advances and retreats, the digressions and all the incidents of camp and city and battle, were brilliant and compelling in themselves; or whether their scale and complexity, together with the remoteness of their known outcome, were likely to prove tedious and confusing to a possibly shifting audience.

Certainly they were not found tedious. If they had been, our ***Iliad*** would not exist. A true poetical impression of such a war, fought out brilliantly through ten whole years between the greatest heroes of the Achaean world and an enemy not unworthy of them, positively demands a treatment massive in scale, detail and depth. To convey this kind of impression, as much as to tell of Achilles's quarrel, seems to have been Homer's aim. His poem was an ***Iliad,*** a summation of all the years of fighting in front of Ilios. His choice of the wrath of Achilles as main theme was acute, since apart from being intensely dramatic in itself it served as an effective skeleton for the whole organism. It promoted radical changes of fortune within a limited period; it involved the gods; it emphasized the pre-eminence of Achilles and the underlying dangers of the whole expedition, yet gave a foretaste of the ultimate fall of Troy. It subjected the heroes on each side to exceptional emotional stresses and showed their reactions to abnormal events, which allowed the poem to explore and reveal the whole heroic idealism of pride, loyalty and courage. Finally the wrath-theme enabled the veering progress of battle, under the interested guidance of the Olympians, to maintain some special relevance to the development of the central plot.

In fact it is only at three or four points that unrelieved descriptions of the fighting are protracted for long enough to run the risk of excess. The first occasion is the fifth book, which for most of 900 lines describes the triumphant foray of Diomedes. Here, however, there is little doubt that post-Homeric expansion has taken place; some of it in the rhapsodic stage, some probably by other singers in the fully oral period. Certain passages, not least in the descriptions of Diomedes's encounters with gods, contain an unusually high proportion of untraditional language; they misuse established formulas and show many signs of an extravagant taste. Expansion would be particularly tempting in episodes that were most often sung or recited. This explains what otherwise seems puzzling, that there are many short anomalous passages even in books essential to the main structure of the ***Iliad,*** which consequently have special claim to be considered as part of what was sung by the main poet. Important among these are the books that composed the "original ***Iliad***" or *Ur-Ilias* that was once a standard and misleading concept of Analytical scholarship: I, XI, XVI, XXII, which describe respectively the beginning of the wrath, the first and crucial Achaean defeat, the sally and death of Patroclus, and the vengeance of Achilles on Hector. Even these sections of the poem have suffered sporadic elaboration; yet their richness in essential narrative content, together with their outstanding literary quality, prevented large-scale interpolations or very widespread later interference. An episode like the Diomedeia of book V was different. It is not essential to the main plot, indeed like most of the first half of the poem it delays its development. It was worked into the poem to give breadth and scale and to increase the effect of omnipresent war. It must often have been chosen for special performance, since it contains many felicities, concentrates on the exploits of a single hero and thus possesses an obvious unity of its own, and makes a powerful impression of heroic invincibility and Achaean triumph. In addition its nucleus of divine encounters, expanded as it may have been, must have given the whole episode a special appeal.

The Diomedeia has often, indeed, been taken as a supreme example of Homer's art as a poet of battle, and many critics have failed to recognize the degree of later elaboration to which it was probably subjected. In fact the concentrated descriptions of fighting in the twelfth book (after the probably added opening) or the sixteenth—the former describing the fight to break through the Achaean wall and ditch, the latter the *aristeia* [courage, prowess] and death of Patroclus—are more magnificent and more typical of Homer at his best. The fighting of V is better paralleled by that of the seventh and eighth books, or the seventeenth. The last, which describes the long-drawn-out tussle for Patroclus's body, resembles the Diomedeia in its unevenness, and perhaps for a similar cause: it is a more or less self-contained episode which was probably often chosen for special recitation and thus for post-Homeric exaggeration.

It is possible to feel that books V or XVII are too long, but most of the descriptions of warfare do not run a serious risk of this effect. That is largely because of the force and variety of Homeric detail and digression. The accounts of battle are far more than mere lists of victors and victims, though even the unadorned sequence of victims has its use at times: not as a mere resource for filling out a few more lines, but rather to drive home the savagery and invincibility of a great hero in a moment of inspired rout, and the confused and almost anonymous mass of those he slaughters.

Usually, though, the devices that bring reality and life to the scenes of warfare are not so simple. The two main ones are the lapidary sketch of the minor victim—for it was a difficulty that most of the victims *had* to be insignificant figures, almost unknown to the rest of the poem—and the elaborate slow-motion account of the fatal wound. Hundreds of otherwise obscure Trojan and Achaean warriors are brilliantly illuminated at the moment of their death. A vignette of three or four lines describes how one of these lesser fighters came to Troy, or gives the name of his homeland and father or wife, or describes some special quality or skill that he possessed in his lifetime, or combines all these elements: he came to woo a daughter of Priam, or to win glory with the Achaean army, his father had lost two sons already and was now to lose a third, his wife was newly married and had hardly known him, he was faster at running than his friends—but now this did not avail him, for he was face to face with the god-like Hector, or Patroclus, or Diomedes. And then the manner of death: anatomical, often fantastic, stereotyped in the dark cloud that comes over the eyes or the clatter of armour about the falling corpse, but curiously pathetic, and, even more surprising, producing a feeling of variety and freshness rather than the satiation and sterility one might expect.

There can be few parts of the body that were not pierced or shattered in the myriad different deaths of the ***Iliad.*** I once read a remark by a continental scholar of the old school that went something like this: "Homer's knowledge of the human anatomy was so profound that a Surgeon-General of the Imperial German Army did not hesitate to salute him by the name of colleague"—an endearing comment which is as inaccurate as it is absurd. The description of wounds must have been an established theme of oral heroic poetry, and successive singers brought their own particular observation or imagination to extend the range of possible alternative formulations. It was not just one singer, Homer, who thought up all these different deaths; though it could be that he first used them in such profusion and variety and as a deliberate stylistic element. He and his predecessors may have seen some of the disagreeable things that spears can do to flesh and bone, and these things must have been a commonplace of experience in any of the more martial periods of Greek history before his time. There is a strong element of accurate description in these accounts of wounds; but there is often, too, a strong element of fantasy and exaggeration. We know for a fact that human eyeballs do not drop on the ground when heads are shattered, that marrow does not spurt out of the spinal column when it is severed, that spear-shafts do not vibrate under the action of the heart when their points pierce into it. Sometimes the course of the spear-head is minutely described as it penetrates first neck, then jaw, and so on; and sometimes too this course is impossible to reconcile with the arrangements of human anatomy, a fact which has needlessly worried many an Analytical critic. Sometimes these excesses of inaccurate fantasy are probably due to the tasteless and inept ambitions of rhapsodic elaborators, but in their less extreme forms they reflect simply the vagaries of the poetical imagination working on the basis of distant or indirect observations.

The result, nearly always, is brilliant. It is both horrifying and, whatever the actual and surgical imprecisions, vividly realistic in its effect; and it stresses over and over again the brutal finality of war, the feebleness of human aims and ambitions and delusions, the harshness and dynamism of the hero in action, and the pathos, cruelty and completeness of human mortality. (pp. 101-06)

These are the basic ways in which the singer varies and enlivens that necessarily recurrent theme, the death of a minor figure. Different resources prevent the battle scenes from being a mere succession of such encounters, however brilliant some of them may be in themselves. Often the greatest heroes do combat with each other, meeting either by chance or because one sets out to track the other through the mêlée of battle. Then a more elaborate duel takes place—more elaborate, at least, in its preliminaries and consequences, for the fighting itself never lasts for long and the alternation of spear-cast and sword-stroke is never fully developed. The elaboration consists in an initial conversation, a challenge or threat or boast on one side met by a determined reply and an affirmation, perhaps, of race or prowess; and then perhaps in a dying speech, a detailed stripping of the arms, and the capture or rescue of the body. Sometimes the duel does not result in a death, but the weaker participant is saved by a divine protector, as Aeneas is saved by Aphrodite, Apollo or Poseidon; sometimes he is merely wounded and manages to retreat to the safety of his companions. The gods provide other forms of diversion: often the description of battle is suddenly interrupted, and the scene shifts to Olympus or Ida where the gods plan to help their favourites or where Zeus weighs fates in his scales. These divine scenes successfully avert the threat of monotony, because they provide a total change of atmosphere and behaviour—domesticity and humour and all sorts of not very heroic qualities are allowed to enter the lives of the gods. Yet such scenes are not objectionably irrelevant or structurally heavy-handed; and they usually lead to a reversal in the progress of battle, or to some relieving factor like the personal intervention of Hera or Apollo, disguised or invisible, to chide a favourite or make his limbs lighter and fill him with might, or deflect a spear by catching it or blowing it aside, or rescue a damaged warrior by covering him in a cloud or flicking him over the heads of his companions to a place of safety, or removing him, in the case of Paris, to his wife and bedchamber.

These different kinds of individual intervention or encounter are occasionally broken by scenes of mass fighting: armies preparing or moving against each other, slowly and inexorably, packed tight like stones in a wall, or armies in panic and pursuit like deer before a ravening lion. These generic scenes are used sparingly, because in themselves they tend to be uninteresting; they are synoptic glances at the whole battlefield, the whole Trojan plain, designed to emphasize and define a movement which has so far been suggested in terms of individuals. Even so they are invested with some specific life, because these mass movements are nearly always illuminated by an image or a group of images. The use of imagery, of course, is one of the basic resources of the poet of the ***Iliad:*** regularly the developed simile intervenes to vivify the actions of armies or individuals, or of deities as they tread like doves or dart downwards like sea-birds or plummets. The expanded simile, in which the details of the image are developed far beyond the point of comparison, and for their own sake, is one of the chief glories of the ***Iliad.*** The simile is a deliberate and highly wrought stylistic device, as careful in its language—which is often untraditional in appearance, because the subject-matter is often untraditional too—as in its variety and its placing in the narrative. Some similes have a complex or a changing point of reference:

> They advanced like the blast of grievous winds, which descends to earth under father Zeus's thunder, and with marvellous din mingles with the salt sea, and in it are many foaming waves of the boisterous ocean, arching and crested, some in front, others behind; so the Trojans were ranged, some in front, others behind. . . .

Others are more abstract in point of comparison: the Danaans defend their wall and the Lycians cannot dislodge them,

> but as two men quarrel about boundaries, holding measures in their hands, in a common field, and they in a narrow space strive about a fair division; so then did the battlements keep them apart. . . .

The similes have a double purpose: to crystallize, in a sphere close to the listener's own understanding, a sight or a sound or a state of mind; and to give relief from the harshness and potential monotony of warfare by suddenly actualizing a quite different and often peaceful, even domestic, scene—the shipwright who fells a tall pine-tree to make a ship's timber, or the shepherd who from his watch-point sees a dark cloud growing over the sea.

Grouped in profusion such images can create a new effect of massive and complex movement or appearance, as when the Achaean forces move out in II or as in the fighting at the end of XVII. Sometimes, too, a simile fills a simple structural need by serving as transition from one scene or one manner of narrative to another: to lead back to individual fighting after a generic description . . . , for instance. Not all these comparisons are peaceful ones; but even the many variants of the ravening-lion motif, which is the commonest of all Homeric images and must have been long established in the epic tradition, depend upon violence *in a peacetime context.* In these cases the intention is less to relieve a surfeit of horrors than to emphasize and colour the rage, determination or invincibility of a great hero. In the lion-similes and some of the nature-similes there is an occasional danger of monotony. Not all examples are successful, though most are, and a few are ponderously vague or muddled in their detail:

> Such as is the dark mist that appears from clouds, out of heat when an evil-blowing wind arises, such did brazen Ares appear to Diomedes as he went together with clouds into the broad sky. . . .

No doubt lesser singers than the monumental poet, and then in their turn the rhapsodes, played their part in introducing or elaborating such confused or conflated images.

The singer of the ***Iliad*** had many other ways of varying his story, apart from essential devices like the switch to Olympus, the simile, or the brief biography of a lesser victim, and apart too from stylistic variants like apostrophe and rhetorical question. The warfare itself can be diversified by descriptions of movement by chariot, or of irregular kinds of fighting like the hurling of vast stones or the shooting of arrows. A greater relief was achieved by the reminiscence of heroic events before the Trojan war. Nestor indulged in such reminiscences at inordinate length, and it was hard, too, to stop Diomedes from bringing up the deeds of his father Tydeus in the Seven against Thebes. The doings of Heracles were often recalled, for example in Dione's list of outrages perpetrated by mortals against gods. These Heracles stories seem to be based on earlier—though not very early—poetical accounts, just as the Pylian reminiscences of Nestor summarize some kind of independent Pylian saga. Nestor also gives the oddest kinds of tactical advice, which were probably the prized invention of a particular singer. Longer versions of earlier stories are exemplified by Glaucus's tale of his ancestor Bellerophon in VI and Phœnix's recital of the paradigm of Meleagros and his wrath in IX; but even these passages show signs of condensation from fuller poems. Events from the earlier years of the Trojan expedition are occasionally mentioned—Achilles's expeditions against Thebe and Lyrnessus, the omen when the fleet was delayed at Aulis—but no doubt many Trojan episodes were reserved for incorporation in the action of the ***Iliad*** itself, and historical digressions in this poem, unlike the ***Odyssey,*** are concentrated on the experiences of earlier generations.

Sometimes, again, the whole tenor of the narrative is broken or transformed by some unique and fantastic occurrence: not so much by standard portents, birds or thunderclaps, which are less frequent though more convincing in the ***Iliad*** than in the ***Odyssey,*** but by special signs of divine emotion or heroic transfiguration, like showers of bloody rain or sudden darknesses which enclose a part of the battlefield, or a bellow from Ares or Achilles that frightens men out of their wits or their lives, or Agamemnon waving a red banner, or the prophecy of Achilles's horse Xanthus. These odd occurrences derive their power from their uniqueness; they are not traditional, but there is no need to claim them as later elaborations for this reason alone, and often they make a powerful climax which could have been planned by the monumental poet himself. His, too, must be the subtle observation that diversifies the egregious heroic personalities of many of the chief figures—for instance in the hysterical pride and intermittent defeatism of Agamemnon, the tetchiness of Priam, Hector's unfairness to Polydamas and the resentment towards him shown by Aeneas or Sarpedon; not to speak of the complexities and introspections of Achilles which give solidity to the main theme of the poem.

To consider these and other variations of style, subject and feeling as mere mechanisms for keeping monotony at bay is clearly wrong. They prevented monotony, but they did much more too. Yet the monumental singer was aware of the dangers of so long a poem; so much is clear from the care he took in arranging the larger structural elements of his song. The ***Iliad*** is constructed so as to provide variation and colour in the background action while the central plot moves intermittently towards its climax and the great battle makes its massive impression, swaying to and fro across the plain. After the opening book and the setting of the plot the first half of the poem consists largely of a series of special episodes, which conceal the truth that Zeus's promise to Thetis, to drive back the Achaeans to the ships, is not being fulfilled. It is in this part of the poem that the poet's work of expansion, magnifying and diversifying a few independent themes so as to represent a whole war, is most apparent—to those who look. It is not *obtrusive* in the way in which the effort to draw out a scene, apparently for the sheer sake of length, is occasionally obtrusive in the ***Odyssey.***

The dream of Agamemnon and his curious testing of morale is followed in II by the long catalogues, themselves justified by the march-out of the two contingents. The expected clash is prevented by the arranged duel between Paris and Menelaus in III and by the viewing from the walls, in which Helen identifies for Priam some of the leading Achaean warriors—a procedure, as is well known, which properly belongs earlier than the tenth year of war. Danger of a premature armistice is prevented by Pandarus's treacherous wounding of Menelaus, and this leads in IV to Agamemnon's inspection of his contingents. Battle is at last joined, and the triumph of Diomedes occupies V; in the next book variation is achieved first by the encounter with Glaucus, then by Hector's withdrawal to Troy and his meetings with Andromache, Helen and Paris—all of which enlarges sympathy for the Trojan side. VII presents another duel, a truce for burial, and the construction of the Achaean wall and ditch which are often ignored later in the poem; these events show signs of strain, and VIII, too, consists mainly of rather meaningless advances and retreats. It leads, however, to the embassy to Achilles in IX, an episode of a new kind and one which, while it is inessential to the main plot, deepens the hearer's interest in Achilles and his motives and contains some of the most careful poetry in the ***Iliad.***

Next comes the night expedition of Odysseus and Diomedes in X—a post-Homeric insertion according to most modern scholars and some ancient ones, and such it must certainly be. It was probably made for separate recitation; it is untraditional and inconsistent with the ***Iliad*** at many points in respect of weapons, clothes and behaviour, and its language is strained or anti-traditional in the rhapsodic manner. It can be removed from the ***Iliad*** without a tremor of disturbance and could be inserted just as easily. It is quite exciting, though, and so long as I am not required to associate it with the monumental composer I am happy to accept it as part of that ***Iliad*** to which we have grown accustomed. Its irrelevance to the progress of the main plot is no greater than that of much which preceded, and the audience remains happily unconscious of any strong deception.

Book XI for the first time effectively advances the promise of Zeus to Thetis by putting many of the Achaean chieftains out of action, and XII sees the Trojan penetration of the camp. XIII delays the expected crisis, for Poseidon rallies the Achaeans; and in the next book, with the help of Hera who lulls Zeus to sleep in a splendid digression, he inspires a revival in which Hector is wounded. Zeus awakes and restores the Trojan fortunes in XV, and at the beginning of the following book Patroclus is allowed by Achilles to wear his armour and fight in his place. The wrath-plot is firmly in hand again: Patroclus is killed, his arrmour stripped, and the struggle for his body forms the content of a long set-piece in XVII. Achilles mourns and awaits new armour; the making of the shield by Hephaestus is described in charming detail. In XIX Achilles is formally reconciled with Agamemnon; the next book contains the prelude to a battle between the gods, and some inconsequential and not very effective human fighting. Hector must be killed in revenge for Patroclus, but first comes Achilles's fight with the river in XXI. In the following book Hector is lured to death, his body is misused, and he is mourned in Troy. That is an obvious climax of the wrath and its consequences; but Patroclus has yet to be duly burned, and the games at his funeral are elaborately described in XXIII. The last book of all describes the divine displeasure at the mutilation of Hector, and Achilles's relenting, and his return of the body unharmed to Priam, who travels through the night to retrieve it and prepare for the funeral with which the ***Iliad*** ends.

Thus the main events of the ***Iliad,*** as well as its detailed treatment, are solid and various enough to accommodate the masses of battle narrative and to cover all necessary gaps between different phases of the central theme. The result, as is obvious, is a poem of acceptable unity and great dramatic force. A close examination—which the poem was not designed to withstand—soon shows that it has been swollen to its present length by the incorporation of all sorts of material which does not particularly suit the main thematic structure. Much of this material must have existed in embryo, at least, in the repertoire of many Ionian singers; and it demanded to be incorporated in a poem that aimed at presenting the Trojan war in all its magnitude. Some elements, like the second formal duel in VII—which by its hopeless ending suggests itself as a doublet of the duel in III—or the frenzied sequence of events in VIII, or the futile argument in XIX about whether or not Achilles will take food, are not really successful. In general, however, the process of inflation, most drastic in the first half of the poem, is inconspicuous and technically well accomplished.

Leaving aside technical matters of composition, what kind of dramatic impact did the ***Iliad*** make on its more assiduous and sensitive listeners? It was obviously more than a great anthology of battle-poetry or a great compendium of heroic conduct, though it was these things too, and Plato, for one, sometimes treats it as little else. It is also much more than the working out of the wrath-theme—in the sense that the ***Odyssey*** is mainly the working out of the theme of a hero's return and vengeance. Rather it is the exploration of a wrath-theme supplemented and made more profound, and set against a monumental background of the whole Trojan war concentrated into the action of a few days. Admittedly the wrath of Achilles, properly so taken, is only part of the whole dire and dramatic aspect of the poem. Yet it possesses a complexity and a profundity that is quite absent from the rather prosaic anger of Meleagros, which was recited to Achilles as a cautionary tale in book IX and which some critics believe to have been the thematic basis of the ***Iliad.*** That seems unlikely: it was probably just another and much simpler example of a well-known theme that underlay many epic songs. The important thing to recognize is the degree to which the monumental composer extended and deepened this kind of theme. The withdrawal of Achilles entails not just the loss of prizes but the loss of his closest friend. This in its turn increases the rage and infatuation of Achilles, diverting it now to Hector. Achilles returns to the fight and saves the Achaeans, but this is almost incidental; he lives for the moment when he can slay Hector in return for Patroclus, and when he has done so he maltreats Hector's body and commits yet another atrocity by cremating twelve Trojan prisoners on the pyre of his friend. By these actions he half-expurgates his grief, and is ready to accept, though at first with bad grace, the divine instruction to abandon his infatuation and return the body of his enemy. It is the addition of these other consequences that sublimates the prosaic motif of heroic sulking into the complex, touching and tragic plan of the ***Iliad.***

It would be falsifying the balance of the poem to claim that it is the mental and emotional history of Achilles that chiefly matters; but the transformation of his pride and anger, first in the Embassy into doubt of the whole heroic code, then into indecision and the compromise that leads to Patroclus's death, then into self-reproach and grief, then into obsessional madness, and finally into some sort of reluctant acceptance of the basic laws of society and at least a similitude of generosity—all this is the moral core of the whole poem, and that which raises it beyond the level of reiterated cruelty and death to a more universal plane of pride, purgation and divine law. There is little doubt in my mind that this deepening of the themes of war is the work of Homer, the main composer of the poem. So much of the ***Iliad*** presents the heroic way of life with implied approval: that was the tradition which had descended from the heroic age itself, and in a sense the first questioning of the ultimate perfection of heroic standards was, as well as its consummation, the beginning of the epic's decline. It is in the Embassy, in Achilles's rejection of the offers of the Achaeans, that the new and profounder attitude to the old ideology reveals itself most clearly. Probably this episode was subjected to minor alterations and conflations; certainly it must have been one of the most popular parts of the whole poem for rhapsodic performance; yet the portrayal of Achilles there must surely belong to Homer and to the original form of the great poem. The last book, too, has been subjected to post-Homeric rehandling, yet again the reactions of Achilles must belong to Homer's conception of how the whole poem should develop. That conception finds no real parallel either in the ***Odyssey*** or in identifiably earlier elements of the ***Iliad*** itself, and is the supreme justification for the development of the monumental epic form. (pp. 106-13)

G. S. Kirk, "The Iliad," in his Homer and the Epic: A Shortened Version of "The Songs of Homer," *Cambridge at the University Press, 1965, pp. 101-13.*

CHARLES MOORMAN (essay date 1971)

[Moorman is an American educator who specializes in medieval literature. In the following excerpt, he defines Homer's purpose in the Iliad *as the exploration of the individual's relation to the state and discusses the way various characters in the poem illuminate each other and their historic context.]*

It is not at all necessary, or even very profitable, to approach the ***Iliad*** as a heroic type and to bring to it our accumulated knowledge of the poet's tradition and age. For while such knowledge can be tremendously helpful and revealing once we have read the poem, it can also be misleading if we first read the ***Iliad*** in its reflected light. It is certainly true that the often repeated stock epithets—the "bright-eyed Athenes" and "rosy-fingered dawns"—were a part of the poet's working tradition and an enormous aid to the kind of oral composition he was expected to produce, but if, forearmed with such knowledge, we regard them *only* as inherited formulas, we are liable to miss the particular literary effects they have upon the poet's audience, ancient or modern: the individualization and particularization of characters in terms of specific traits, the expression of a pervasive and intuitively accepted faith in the permanence of the essential characters of men and in the abiding qualities of nature, the occasional irony which arises from a startling discrepancy between epithet and action, the suggestion of the importance of the daily rituals by which men live—all of these help to form the richly colored backdrop, the established world picture, before which the swift action of the poem takes place.

The ***Iliad,*** then, makes its first impression simply as story, as sheer narrative excitement, rather than as any particular type of literature for which preparation is demanded. It opens with an invocation, a prayer for inspiration, but this invocation is so presented that it hardly seems a prayer at all but, more to the poet's immediate purpose, a forceful presentation of theme. The "wrath of Achilles" and its effect, the suffering of the Achaeans, are the poet's stated subjects, and true to his word he plunges immediately and, more important, dramatically into the causes of the wrath. The poem does not begin, because it cannot dramatically afford to, with a lengthy exposition of the military situation or of the characters involved in the quarrel. There will be time for that later, but at the very outset we must observe (and not simply be told about), even without fully understanding it, the beginning of Achilles' wrath. Thus we have a few sentences devoted to the crisis at hand. An elderly priest of Apollo, Chryses, has come to King Agamemnon—and note how the epithet here serves as an introduction—to rescue his daughter Chryseis captured in war; immediately follows a highly charged scene in which Agamemnon, ignoring the expressed wishes of his army, summarily refuses, threatens, insults, and dismisses Chryses. Within a few lines Chryses has returned home and prayed for help to Apollo, who responds by sending a devastating nine-day plague upon the Achaeans. In desperation Achilles, at the prompting of Here, does what Agamemnon is patently unwilling to do: he calls a full meeting of the assembly and in what seems to be a prearranged action calls upon the prophet Calchas to explain the cause of the plague. Calchas, having secured Achilles' protection from Agamemnon's spite, reveals Apollo's displeasure with the king. Agamemnon (ironically here "noble son of Atreus") turns first on Calchas, insulting him as a false prophet and refusing to return Chryseis. Achilles in turn takes up the argument, and immediately what purportedly began as a fact-finding inquiry becomes a bitter, public, mudslinging squabble between the noble sons of Atreus and Peleus. Achilles accuses Agamemnon of profiteering, of committing the whole of Greece to war to satisfy a personal vendetta, and of malingering, and threatens to withdraw from the field. Agamemnon in turn calls Achilles a brawler and a deserter and threatens to take from him his prize of war, the beautiful Briseis. The whole argument is punctuated by slanders of "unconscionable cur" and "drunken sot" and is saved from violence only byAthene's command that Achilles sheath his half-drawn sword. Despite the pleas of old Nestor, the council ends in a shambles, and Agamemnon, though agreeing to return Chryseis, makes good his threat by claiming Briseis.

In a matter of some three hundred lines the quarrel is over and the wrath has begun. It is a brilliant beginning—swift, dramatic, yet also suggestive in establishing the nature of the characters and the themes to come. Our initial sympathies lie with Achilles. Agamemnon is peremptory with Chryses; he obviously cares nothing for the opinions of either army or council; he ignores the sufferings of his army which his action has caused; he insults his soothsayer and dismisses his best warrior without a second thought. He is obviously in the wrong from start to finish and seems totally incapable of the leadership entrusted to him.

Achilles, on the other hand, is, in the beginning at least, calm and responsible. He obeys the prompting of the goddess and calls the council, probably in full knowledge that such action will infuriate Agamemnon. He carefully uses Calchas, and Calchas's position and authority, as a means of persuading Agamemnon to return Chryseis. True, he gives way to anger at Agamemnon's insults, but he obeys Athene's entreaties to sheath his sword and later politely turns Briseis over to Agamemnon's heralds, who are afraid even to approach him.

The argument, moreover, is broken by Athene's intervention and by Nestor's brief speech (brief at least for Nestor) urging that Achilles yield to Agamemnon's authority, on the grounds that it is god-given and embraces them all, and that Agamemnon refrain in turn from misusing that authority by taking Briseis. The old king's remarks, replete as usual with allusions to his own heroic past, define clearly the real issue which underlies the debate. For the disposition of Chryseis and Briseis cannot account for the bitterness of the quarrel or the enduring wrath that follows. The actual issue here is the authority of Agamemnon, its limits and responsibilities, and, more particularly, the proper relationship between individual warrior and group commander in a time of crisis. For Athene and Nestor are right: *aidos,* the mutual responsibility of leader and subordinate—the one to command intelligently, the other to obey unquestioningly—has indeed been violated on both sides. The ultimate authority, however ill used, by divine commission lies with the king; Achilles has not the right to kill him nor should he act contentiously toward him. Paradoxically, however, the rebellious, individualistic Achilles has here shown much more concern for the welfare of the army than has Agamemnon, who by virtue of his office is entrusted with his men's safety, and so has some measure of right on his side. The poem thus begins not simply with an argument over a girl but with a complex question of the disposition and use of power and authority.

In short, aside from the use of epithets and speeches and actions of the gods, there is nothing in the opening of the ***Iliad*** to demonstrate that it conforms to the epic type as we have been taught to envision it. Instead of heroes performing superhuman deeds and playing out their fated, nationalistic roles, against a setting vast in scope, in "a style of sustained elevation and grand simplicity," we have the vituperative tongue brawling of two most unheroic warriors engaged in a power struggle occasioned by the disposition of a slave girl. It is . . . an undignified spectacle at best and, honestly read, not at all what we should have expected of the archetype of the epic poem.

There is ample evidence, however, that this is Homer's calculated effect. For even without entering into a detailed discussion of the "Homeric question," the great debate over single or multiple authorship, one can demonstrate in the poem the kind of careful structure and thematic unification that one expects only in a poem composed by a single man; nowhere does literature, or any other art, demonstrate that either mere accumulation of traditional materials or corporate writing by a committee, however skilled, can produce the unity of structure, theme, and characterization that the ***Iliad*** everywhere manifests. As C. M. Bowra has shown, the first three books provide an introduction to the action by presenting the audience first with the wrath of Achilles, then with the first great war council of the Achaeans, and finally, in Book 3, with the Trojans and the first duel, that of Paris and Menelaus. The last three books complete the frame by treating the same three subjects in reverse order: Book 22 dramatizes the final duel, that of Achilles and Hector, and the lamentations of the Trojans; Book 23, the assembly of the Greeks at the funeral games of Patroclus; and Book 24, the appeasement of the wrath which began in Book 1. In Books 4-21, the Aristotelian middle, the account of the battle which ranges from the walls of Troy to the sea and back again is divided precisely into thirds by the two appearances of Achilles in Books 9 and 16.

Structure, moreover, here outlines and enforces the theme of authority with which the poem begins and with which it everywhere deals: we begin and end with the anger of Achilles, which is always kept in the thematic center of the poem. And though the structure demands that Achilles be absent from the battlefield in most of the poem, the effect of his absence is constantly felt in the waning fortunes of the Achaean army as it is inexorably forced toward the beaches by the Trojan host, led by Hector. Moreover, by restricting our view of Achilles in the middle books to the scene in which he receives the embassy sent by Agamemnon to appease him and the one in which he grants Patroclus permission to wear his armor into battle, Homer is able to record precisely the stages of the hero's descent into *hubris;* he moves from righteous indignation to cold, unyielding fury to blind vanity, and finally, after the death of Patroclus, to bestiality.

Agamemnon, on the other hand, rises above his initial anger even as Achilles sinks beneath his. At first completely negligent of the welfare of his command, then tactless and peremptory in his efforts to urge his unit commanders into battle, after the first disastrous engagements he overcomes his impulse to give up the siege and responds to the advice of Nestor, admitting his "blind folly" and offering handsome amends to Achilles. Rebuffed by Achilles, he cannot sleep for fear that his army will be destroyed by the Trojans, who for the first time have dared to spend the night outside their impregnable walls and whose nearby campfires he can see. He personally leads the next morning's charge and is wounded, and following the death of Hector, at Achilles' request he orders wood gathered and Patroclus's funeral pyre prepared. We last see him yielding without demur to Achilles' decision to cancel the javelin-throwing contest and to award equal prizes to Agamemnon and Meriones, the only two contestants, though Agamemnon would certainly have won had the contest taken place. Agamemnon thus moves from selfish wrath and *hubris* to a sense of the responsibility of his office and an involvement in the war to a willingness to forgo a personal victory by accepting an equal share of the prize. While Briseis certainly is not to be equated with the new cauldron which Agamemnon receives, the king in his willingness to share with his men the spoils of war on equal terms displays at the end of the poem a far different concept of his office than he had held a month before.

What little is known of the antecedents of Agamemnon and Achilles throws some light on their actions in the ***Iliad*** and hence on their roles as the chief representatives of authority and the individual. Here a few fundamental distinctions have to be made. It is clear that three kinds of source material were involved in the tradition of the Trojan War inherited by Homer: history—the remnants of actual persons, places, and events of the struggle, doubtless distorted by time but still in the main discernible, if not wholly accurate; legend—"primitive history . . . unconsciously transformed and simplified" beyond recognition by an accretion of folktales and wonders; and myth—the stories of the gods, ultimately derived from ritual—expressing in its simplest, though most illusive, form "primitive philosophy, . . . a series of attempts to understand the world, to explain life and death, fate and nature, gods and cults." There was doubtless an actual Trojan War involving allied Greek forces, but in the centuries during which this unusual war was talked and sung about, its leaders and events became aggrandized by the natural tendency of primitive people to glorify and magnify their past heroes and history, and its causes and meaning came to be attributed to supernatural forces, the gods who continually oversee and in the long run control human history.

Unfortunately for the critic, the ***Iliad*** itself is, like *Beowulf,* our chief historical document for the period it represents, though indeed it contains even less "pure" history than does *Beowulf.* Avoiding for the moment the tangle of technical arguments surrounding the time of composition, it seems clear that the ***Iliad*** was put into very nearly its present form in the eighth or ninth century B.C. and that its dramatic date, according to Greek tradition, is the late twelfth century, 1184 to be precise, some three to four hundred years earlier. There can be very little doubt that there was a siege of Troy; certainly the Greeks themselves regarded Homer's account as based on historical fact, and the archaeological work at Troy corroborates the possibility that an engagement took place somewhere around 1230. On the other hand, our knowledge of Bronze Age chronology is so scanty as to make any speculation about the actual circumstances of the war extremely risky. Since there are no early Greek accounts of the period, no one can say whether the war was caused by the abduction of a Greek queen, whether it resulted from the colonizing expeditions of the Aeolian tribes into Asia, or whether it was an attempt to break Troy's economic stranglehold on Greek shipping in the Hellespont.

Even so, some general conclusions about the period of the late twelfth century are possible. Whatever the relationship between Crete and the cities of the Greek mainland had been in earlier years, the Achaean sronghold of Mycenae had been from the time of the fall of Knossos in 1400, and probably for 150 years before, the greatest of the Greek kingdoms and remained so until well into the twelfth century. Her art, which shows during the early centuries of her dominance a strong Cretan influence, her tombs, fortifications, and palaces all evidence that Mycenae was the center of a great commercial empire which extended throughout the Peloponnesus and spread outward into Asia Minor and Cyprus and even into Egypt and Sicily. It was probably also the chief military power of the period, dominating its neighbors by "an elaborate system of gift-giving, which imposed reciprocal obligations without formal alliances or the necessity for a hierarchy of states." As the tablets which have survived from Pylos and Mycenae show, the social and economic life of the early Mycenaean period was organized minutely; the scrupulously kept accounts show a tightly controlled, though cumbrous, system of economic control over a vast area.

In time, however, a kind of decadence at home and aggressive restlessness abroad set in as Mycenae's trading empire was threatened by political and trading difficulties in Asia Minor and Egypt and by the decreasing wealth of Crete, from which she had long drawn a great part of her income. Egyptian and Hittite records dating from the late fourteenth century downward record a change in the relations between the Achaeans and their overseas neighbors. At first the allies of the Hittites, to whom they may have been related, against the Egyptians, by the middle thirteenth century Achaeans had become "sea raiders" fighting for the economic life of their empire against the Hittite colonies in Asia Minor as well as against Egypt. There are records of broken treaties and coastal raids, all evidencing the vigor with which the Mycenaeans pursued new trade routes and areas for colonization. In 1225 and 1194, together with other tribes, the Achaeans attacked Egypt unsuccessfully, but the cumulative effect of these campaigns was the destruction of the Hittite empire in Asia Minor and the beginning of political divisions among the Greeks. The wealth and influence of Mycenae apparently continued to decline until the great waves of Dorians in the twelfth century put an end to a civilization already crippled by economic failures, dynastic feuds and internal struggles, and a long and costly series of wars. The centuries following were in every way the "dark ages" of Greece.

It is during the last period of Mycenaean domination, the period of aggression and the struggle to survive, that Greek tradition placed Greece's "heroic age." Hesiod interposes an age of heroes between the age of bronze of early Mycenae and the prosaic age of iron in which he considered himself to live. The two great events of the heroic age, he tells us, were the sieges of Thebes and Troy. The Greeks themselves envisioned the heroic age as closing with the Doric invasions, and Homer's genealogies indicate that he thought of the period as encompassing some two hundred years, a period roughly coinciding with the restless, aggressive activities of the Achaeans, a time in which the whole Mediterranean world was marked by wars and confusion and the restless migration of its peoples.

It seems probable that while the epics of Homer reflect the warlike spirit of these later centuries, they occasionally in spirit if not in fact look back even further, to the tradition of the power and influence of early Mycenae. Certainly Homer had no accurate knowledge of life in the Mycenaean ages nor of the historical causes or conduct of the Trojan War; his picture of the period was likely a distorted one shaped by a long and probably at times a weak oral tradition. Almost every element in Homer is thus an amalgam. His geography, his language, his poetic technique, his descriptions of armor, of battle procedures, architecture, customs, and beliefs—all derive both from the Ionic uses of the dark ages and of his own time and from the Mycenaean period, remnants of which were retained, though distorted, in the historical and poetic tradition which survived, probably through the descendants of Achaean refugees in Asia Minor. But the Achaean Confederacy is seen in the poem not as a desperate and decaying civilization, nor as one fighting for trade and colonization opportunities, but as the world's greatest established power in its heyday of unification and influence. The great catalog of ships demonstrates the range and might of its domain; the power of Agamemnon to keep a united expeditionary force in the field for ten years, the dominance of Mycenae in its organization.

The use of the term *Achaean* in Homer as a general name for the Greek force gathered at Troy is in itself puzzling. Certainly we are not to gather from it that there was ever anything resembling a single Mycenaean kingdom, much less a single people; but considered along with the Hittite records, the use of the term in Homer demonstrates that the Mycenaeans were indeed the dominant military group as well as the most prosperous people of the age. This fact throws considerable light on the position of Agamemnon and hence on his role in the poem. He is clearly commander in chief: he has the sole power to continue or abandon the siege, and the strategy and tactics of the war are his; he has in his power the disposition of the booty; he presides at council by virtue of the scepter; and he has, as Nestor says, a divine commission to command. But it is clearly the power to command rather than to rule absolutely. He may rebuke the stormy Achilles but not punish him, and although his decisions are final, he is constantly open to the criticisms of his officers and even of the common Thersites. His real power lies in his scepter rather than his person: Achilles can also use the scepter to call together a council, the purpose of which is to condemn an action of Agamemnon; and Odysseus can restrain the Greeks from leaving Troy only because he holds the scepter.

Agamemnon's position in the field as military commander of a conglomerate, though unified, expeditionary force seems to indicate the limits and degree of his authority as well as the place of Mycenae in the Achaean empire. Nestor clearly states that Agamemnon's authority is based on the wide extent of his kingdom. And not only does his kingdom, joined with that of Menelaus, encompass almost the whole Peloponnesus, but he is clearly the political overlord of some of his subordinates as well as their military superior. Yet, as the catalog makes clear, the Achaean leaders are for the most part kings in their own right and have merely delegated to Agamemnon the military authority necessary for efficient command. Like the Hittite commands of the same period, the Mycenaean military force was a confederacy of kings organized for efficient military action.

Such a position as that held by Agamemnon thus seems to be based on a confederacy of kings in the Mycenaean period rather than the disposition of the Ionian aristocracy in Homer's own time. Homer is portraying a historical reality, a portrait of military kingship drawn from the past. Whether or not an actual Agamemnon directed the operations at Troy is outside the sphere of debate; there is historical evidence neither for nor against his existence. Yet certain names appearing in the Hittite records may verify the existence of an Eteocles and an Atreus, and certainly some Achaean king directed the siege of Troy, whatever his name was.

To summarize briefly, the figure of Agamemnon is drawn from history, and his position reflects the extensive, though in some ways limited, power held by the Achaean commander in chief at Troy. The mixed nature of the authority delegated by the Achaean kings, moreover, does much to explain Agamemnon's dramatic role in the poem. According to the legend, the Greek rulers were called into service because of an agreement among them, made years before during their courtship of Helen, to protect the marriage of Menelaus and Helen should it be threatened. Having with some difficulty gathered the army at the port of Aulis, Agamemnon was unable to launch the expedition because of the enmity of the goddess Artemis, Apollo's sister. In desperation he agreed to sacrifice his daughter Iphigenia in return for favorable winds and so finally set sail.

But nine long years of frustration and deprivation have gone by. The Achaean kings, who were never eager to leave their homes to honor a long-forgotten, boyish agreement to protect Menelaus's wife, have become testy; a hoax designed by Agamemnon to test their loyalty reveals their eagerness to abandon the expedition. It is little wonder, therefore, that Agamemnon both resents and reacts hotly against any challenge to his authority, even one by the god Apollo. The general council of the Greeks clearly wishes him to return Chryseis; Achilles calls a meeting of the council without his consent; he is accused of personal cowardice; even the army soothsayer speaks against him. He is clearly in the wrong and probably knows it, but the circumstances are such that a proud man, pushed to the limits of his patience and fearful of his position, can react in no way except to bully his way through.

It should be remarked also that no question of romance or of a lady's honor is involved. Indeed Homer, especially in the ***Odyssey,*** creates a striking number of intelligent, sympathetic women, but Chryseis and Briseis have no real personalities in the poem, and it is clear that their captors care little for them.

The captured girls are thus only the excuse for the quarrel among the chieftains. The real issue is *aidos,* the relationship between the commander in chief and his best warrior, and it is an issue which has presumably been simmering for a long time, needing only a catalyst to set it boiling.

Although Agamemnon reflects in his position, if not necessarily in his personality (which is almost purely the invention of Homer and/or an inherited tradition), a historical situation, Achilles does not seem to have been drawn at all from history but instead from myth. There is, in the first place, some confusion regarding his inclusion in the expedition at all. He is not really an Achaean but is said to come from Phthia in Thessaly rather than from any of the Peloponnesian centers from which the other heroes are called. His people, the Myrmidons, are unknown to historians. He is thus to some degree an outlander, distinguished even by his speech from his compatriots. Throughout the ***Iliad*** he is a lonely figure; we never see him in close association with the other Greek leaders. He is, moreover, the only major hero to be killed during the war.

There are also an unusual number of tales associated with his birth and *enfance* [childhood]. He is of semidivine origin; according to myth, his mother, Thetis, attempts to secure immortality for him by dipping him either in the river Styx or in fire. He is reared by Cheiron the centaur on Mount Pelion, and his weapons and horses are miraculous. He is, moreover, doomed either to live a long, though pedestrian, life or to fall in glory at Troy.

His actions and powers also are different not only in degree but also in kind from those of the other heroes: his armor is forged by the god Hephaestus; a magical fire blazes about his head on the eve of battle; in his ire he fights the swollen Xanthus. Homer throws about Achilles, as about none of the other characters, an aura of the superhuman and the mythical. Even the gods seem to respect and shun him; unlike the other heroes, he is free from their tricks and deceits.

Scholars have pointed out a number of similarities between the careers of Achilles and Siegfried, those of Achilles and Cuchulain, and those of the Greek hero and Gilgamesh. Like Achilles, Siegfried is entrusted to an outsider, the dwarf Regin, to be reared and is given a magical bath, in dragon's blood, to gain invulnerability. He inherits a miraculous sword, as Achilles does a spear, from his father, and he too rides a horse which has supernatural powers. Cuchulain's horses, like Achilles', shed tears of grief, and the Irish hero also possesses a magical spear and is surrounded in battle by a supernatural aura. As T. L. Webster points out, the relationship between Gilgamesh and his companion Enkidu is very like that of Achilles and Patroclus, especially in the violent grief which the heroes show for the death of their companions; and there is a remarkable similarity between the heroes in scenes in which their mothers appeal to the gods for help. While there is little point in assigning to the tales of these heroes a common origin, it does seem at least plausible to conjecture that they stem from the same type of source—myth rather than history, or history enlarged by legend.

The origins of these four heroes, moreover, have at least one factor in common: they all seem to be intimately associated with the sun gods of the mythic traditions from which they are derived. Although solar myth is in general discredit today, the solar mythologists were almost certainly correct in seeing Siegfried's penetration of the magic fire to awaken the sleeping Brunhild as a symbolization of the sun awakening the sleeping dawn. Among the traditions associated with Cuchulain, one maintains that he never rose later than the sun and another that "the intense heat generated by his body melted the snow round him for thirty feet." His head is surrounded by "a diadem of gold," his shining, yellow hair; and his contortions suggest "the transformation of the sun-god into the fire-shooting thunder cloud." It may well be that the signs of the Zodiac, through which the sun runs its yearly course, "gradually evolved in Babylonia from the twelve incidents in the life-story of the hero Gilgamesh." Greek mythology also bears witness to the importance of solar myth in the history of religion: "Helias, Kronos, Zeus, Apollo, Phaethon, Talus, Hercules, Phoebus, Admetus, Ixion, Aesculapius, Hyperion, Hades, Ares, Hippolytus, Janus, all had their solar aspects, and our post-Frazerian habit of thinking only in terms of vegetation myths should not obscure the awe in which primitive man held the sun, and the central place of the sun in his religion.

The fact that Achilles seems descended from a solar myth—though he may well have connections with other myths as well—helps to explain his role in the ***Iliad,*** though I should be unwilling to interpret the whole poem, or even any single episode in it, as being mythical, as distinct from historical or legendary, in origin or conception. Certainly, however, his unrelenting fury and the aura which surrounds his head seem vestiges of his mythic past, as does his appearance at dawn on the last day of battle after his long sojourn in his tent. I would not insist on this point, but it may well be that Achilles' retreat in isolation reflects also, at least in part, the withdrawal-return pattern which is an essential part of the myth of the questing hero. For although most of the familiar stages in the withdrawal-return—the call to adventure, the crossing of the threshold, etc.—are not to be found in the ***Iliad,*** Achilles does indeed return to his people to bring victory out of defeat.

But my central point is that the figure of Achilles is the only one derived from myth and that his mythic origin explains his individuality, his isolation from others and from their common cause. Never after the initial quarrel with Agamemnon does he exhibit the slightest interest in an Achaean victory. He is perfectly willing, therefore, to sacrifice the whole mission to justify his own position and to salve the wound of a personal assault. All the efforts of Odysseus and Phoenix to appeal to his sense of duty or his responsibility to their common cause fail simply because he has no conception of such a role. When he finally does emerge, it is to avenge a personal wrong, the death of Patroclus, and even here he fights as an individual; his killing of Hector is prompted not by Hector's position as leader of the enemy forces but by the fact that Hector killed Patroclus. When at last his fury is abated and his wrath assuaged, it is not because he realizes that his actions have been irresponsible and his brutality unreasonable but because Priam's grief moves him to think of his own father and his father's sorrows.

Thus the ***Iliad*** poses as antagonists king and captain: the historical Agamemnon, whose sense of the responsibility of leadership steadily grows until it overcomes the egotism and personal pride that originally inspired his quarrel with Achilles; and the mythical Achilles, whom fury and pride send raving into alienation until he becomes more beast than man. The other characters of the poem, moreover, illuminate various aspects of this central clash in authority. As C. M. Bowra has pointed out, the minor characters tend to "fall into two classes, the soldiers and the statesmen. In the first class are Aias, Diomedes, and Menelaus, and in the second are Nestor and

Odysseus.'' Like Achilles, Aias and Diomedes are essentially individualistic warriors, fierce and aggressive in combat; neither has any use for the councils of the wise. Diomedes, in fact, will not accept Agamemnon's grief-stricken decision to abandon the siege and deplores Agamemnon's having humbled himself in attempting to make amends to Achilles.

But neither Aias nor Diomedes can match Achilles. Aias is compared by Homer to both a lion and an ass; he has a stubborn natural courage, but he is essentially slow-witted, a great, hulking brute whose ultimate fate is frustration, dumb rage, and suicide. He thus differs from Achilles, whose intelligence immediately pierces Priam's flattery. Diomedes has a good deal of Achilles' dash and brilliance in the field, but he lacks the fury that makes Achilles ''godlike'' in battle. The scene in which Diomedes and Glaucus courteously exchange armor on the battlefield sharply contrasts with Achilles' refusal to spare the unarmed and suppliant Lycaon. Both Aias and Diomedes, however, help to define the essential quality that sets Achilles apart from the others: an unswerving and unalterable faith in the rightness of his own conduct, a prideful self-assurance capable of destroying an army for the sake of personal honor.

The true foil to Achilles is, of course, Hector, his Trojan counterpart and, at least to modern readers, the most sympathetic of the heroes. Unlike Achilles he fights only to protect his home and country, and his prowess and heroism stem from necessity rather than, as with Achilles, the fury of personal insult. The famous scenes with Andromache show him at his best, kind and loving, yet thoroughly responsible, a conscientious soldier and a wise leader. Yet the fire of the gods never burns about his head, nor in the end can he understand the nature of the man whose ire he has incurred. He decides to press the Trojans' hard-won military advantage by opposing Achilles and later to stand alone against his fury. But at the sight of Achilles brandishing the spear of Pelion, his armor glowing ''like a blazing fire or the rising sun, he no longer had the heart to stand his ground; he left the gate, and ran away in terror.'' In the end Hector is duped by Athene into fighting and dies charging into Achilles' lance. Deliberate courage and prowess and a cause to defend have failed to stand against the wrath of the godlike Achilles.

The characters of Nestor and Odysseus throw light in much the same way upon that of Agamemnon. For if Agamemnon struggles to understand the nature of authority and command, Nestor is surely past understanding it. A man of great experience, he has come to live only in the past and its glories, and therefore his experience is of little use to the Greeks. His advice is nearly always ineffective and at times almost disastrous. It is he who on the basis of a false dream counsels the building of the wall, which soon crumbles under theTrojan assault, without offering the necessary sacrifices to Poseidon. The futile embassy to Achilles is his idea as is the plan to have Patroclus appear on the battlefield dressed in Achilles' armor. In Nestor Homer portrays the uselessness of mere experience as a basis for authority and wise decision, and though Nestor can in his interminable yarns suggest a heroic standard of conduct, the appeals to valor by the high-spirited Diomedes are much more effective in rallying the army.

Odysseus, on the other hand, is (in the ***Iliad,*** at least) so totally involved in the affairs of the moment that he lacks the breadth of judgment great authority demands. He operates always at the level of advice and stratagem and is thus always the man called upon to deal with the immediate problem by the most practicable means. He can be trusted to return Chryseis to her father with perfect tact; he manages to cope with the panic that follows Agamemnon's announcement that the army will embark for home; he can worm information from the unsuspecting Dolon; he wins the wrestling contest with Aias by a trick; and he even talks the bloodthirsty Achilles into allowing his soldiers to eat before battle. But he fails in the greatest, the only crucial mission assigned him: he cannot dent Achilles' determination to refrain from battle; his subtlest arguments cannot match Achilles' prideful determination. He is in every way a man of the greatest intelligence and charm, but he lacks Agamemnon's stature and honesty and, ultimately, his sense of the responsibilities of power.

The gods also reflect, in their eternal bickering, the theme of the nature of authority that so occupies the heroes below. Zeus rules by sheer power rather than intelligence and is reduced all too often to shouting and threatening. The other gods, wary of his thunderbolts, must take advantage of their father in whatever devious ways they can: Here by nagging and eventually by seduction, Athene by argument, Aphrodite by flattery, Thetis (not even a close relative) by wheedling. Whatever Homer may have thought of the gods, it is clear that they present no proper model for government among men.

Because of the scantiness of biographical and historical information, it is difficult to ascertain with any hope of exactitude Homer's ultimate purposes in the poem. He almost certainly lived in the late ninth or early eighth century, apparently in Ionia in Asia Minor, and was thoroughly trained in the usages of formulaic poetry. He was, moreover, an inheritor of a long tradition of lays concerning the Trojan War, a tradition which he might well fabricate into a single brilliantly conceived and executed poem but which he could not basically change. The major causes, events, and characters of the tradition were beyond alteration; similarly, one could not today write a poem, however heroic, in which the South won the Civil War and Lincoln appeared as a drunken scoundrel. But Homer, by selection and emphasis, might well use his tradition to shape a theme. He might not alter a received character, but he might, by the addition of detail, shape that character to fit his own purpose.

It is this sense of purpose that everywhere distinguishes the ***Iliad*** from the imitations and continuations of the so-called epic cycle that follow it. Obviously Homer did not recount the ancient stories simply for their own sakes; in fact he leaves out the most exciting among them, that of the Trojan Horse. Nor are they told historically; the full chronology of the war is not only ignored but often, as in the engagement of Menelaus and Paris in Book 3, actually violated. Nor are they told, as men often tell stories of the past, either reminiscently or, despite Robert Graves's interpretation [see excerpt dated 1960], satirically; the poet is neither a Nestor nor a Mark Twain.

Some help in determining Homer's attitude toward the past, and hence in defining his purpose, may be gleaned from the bits of history that have come down to us. The Greek world of Homer's own time was emerging from over two hundred years of civil chaos and cultural disruption, the so-called dark ages. Undeniably, however, the Ionian colonies had prospered as a result of the new trade and maritime ventures that followed the dark ages, and by Homer's time they must have enjoyed considerable social stability. More important, Ionia had by then completed, as had most of the Greek kingdoms, the shift from a monarchic to an aristocratic and federal form of government, a change caused primarily by the shift in population from the land to well-defined cities, what are later to emerge as the great city-states of the golden ages. These new aristocratic republics such as that under which Homer must have lived were governed for the most part efficiently, though rather narrowly. The governing class was trained in the business of ruling, and they passed their knowledge and skill along from generation to generation.

There is little doubt that the new form of government rescued the Greek cities from the anarchy and poverty which followed the collapse of the Mycenaean empire. Colonization began anew throughout the Aegean area and eventually beyond, and under the careful direction of the new republics it became systematic and profitable. The colonies had to be supplied both with agricultural goods such as wool and with manufactured articles and so provided the republics with new markets as well as sources of raw materials. The new age might well have been, as Hesiod complained, an age of iron in which the practices of the ages of silver and gold had fallen into disuse, but it also created social conditions in which a poetry celebrating the glories of those former ages might be composed; furthermore, it provided through its commerce with Phoenicia an instrument, the alphabet, which could preserve those glories forever.

I would maintain that Homer, looking back from the point of view of a romanticized tradition, saw the great legend of the Trojan War not merely, like Hesiod, as the record of an adventurous and golden time; more important, he saw it as raw material for a commentary on the life of both ages, gold and iron alike, and on the great problem common to both—the individual's relation to the state, and the values involved in the conflict between ruler and ruled, between loyalty to the state and the rights of the individual.

To frame this great commentary Homer selected from the oral tradition of history and legend and myth which had kept alive the memory of the war at Troy a single incident, the quarrel of Agamemnon and Achilles, and by arrangement and emphasis built into his account of that incident all his reflections upon his own time and the heroic past. Not that the poem is a personal judgment and commentary in the sense that a Romantic poem is, for Homer observes scrupulously the objectivity of the great classical artist. He narrates and shapes the action, but he never imposes his own voice on it. To do so would have been to sacrifice universality and to reduce the poem to something less than heroic in scope. But a judgment is there, nevertheless, implicit in the actions and speeches of the characters and in the development of the conflict between the two great antagonists. (pp. 1-20)

Charles Moorman, "The Iliad," in his Kings & Captains: Variations on a Heroic Theme, *The University Press of Kentucky, 1971, pp. 1-29.*

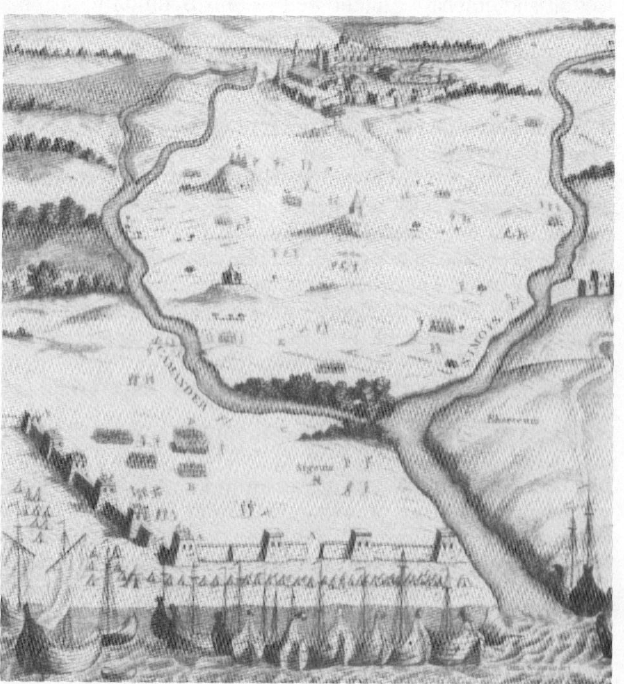

A map prepared by Pope in 1714 for his edition of the Iliad.

ERIC A. HAVELOCK (essay date 1973)

[Havelock is an English-born American classics scholar who has written extensively on Greek history and literature. In the following excerpt, he acknowledges the difficulties that the Iliad *poses for the modern reader; he goes on to demonstrate Homer's sophistication, however, through an analysis of Helen's "divided heart" and her relation to other characters in the poem.]*

It is difficult for a poet who composed in one of the dead languages to gain much success in winning the attention of our present culture. He will enjoy that unsubstantial esteem which is due to a great and ancient name, but only the scholars are likely to spend pains upon him. Most of us seem to have more important things to think about, like a voyage to the moon. If he is read in his own tongue he becomes a task, a theme at school. If he is read in translation he virtually ceases to be a poet at all. These barriers, that interpose between the modern mind and its classical past, are in Homer's case raised higher by special difficulties. He is the most ancient of European poets, which for practical purposes means the oldest poet we have. Not only is he a Greek poet, but also in some sense a pre-Greek poet. Even to the men of his own race who came after him, and who in the classical period memorized his poems with affection and respect, his splendor was slightly archaic. They revered him, but did not always understand him, a fact sufficiently betrayed by their attempts to allegorize his tales, to censor his morals, or to correct his theology. His work takes its place along with portions of the Old Testament as not just a poem, but as a massive milestone in the history of human culture. It is a monument hewn in a curious shape. It is a likeness of the pattern of the human mind not as it exists today, but as it existed in those immense pre-literate epochs when the common man did not read or write. Man's thoughts and his speech were different then, different even from what they became in the age of Pericles, and far removed indeed from ours. Homer therefore addresses us, if at all, across a great gulf of literate experience and abstract habit.

It is no use trying to leap the gulf impatiently. Modern taste has first to be reconciled to those qualities in his style and substance which seem alien to modern literature. There is for example the diffuseness of the epics. The ***Iliad*** begins, promisingly enough, by announcing as its theme a quarrel between two chieftains with fatal consequences for the Greek host. For the space of a book the setting is then developed with the rapid economical strokes of an artist with an eye to coherent effect. But as the reader then continues the saga, he finds it well nigh impossible to hold the thread of the promised drama, so frequently is it interrupted. Books two through seven constitute an enormous pause, giving us to be sure a great deal of background material, but nothing more about the announced theme which is not resumed until books eight and nine. Homer then inserts book ten which reads like a separate episode of night operations, after which the Greeks and Trojans trade blows for six more books. There is a lot of hard fighting of which the reader grows rather weary and which has no direct bearing upon the quarrel between Achilles and Agamemnon, until, at book sixteen, Patroclus, the friend of Achilles, complicates the issue by taking his friend's place in the forefront of battle and getting himself killed. By his death he at last involves Achilles in the main action. The reader's patience, if it has lasted this far, will now be rewarded, but at the cost of feeling that the whole tale would have been more effective if boiled down to half its present length.

Diffuseness itself is not a fatal defect in a work of art. The hero of a picaresque novel may become involved in episode after episode, but he remains the hero. Yet so much of Homer is not even episodic. The materials which clog his narrative exhibit the quaintness and confusion of an ill-assorted musuem. From the point of view of epic artistry, who would not gladly scrap the catalogue of Greek and Trojan contingents contained in the ***Iliad***'s second book? What modern reader does not grow impatient with the endless reminiscences of other sagas, about other wars and other cities; the genealogies and histories of clans; the topographies of districts; the catalogues of properties and precious materials; itemized lists of armour and ornament; detailed descriptions of rituals and sacrifices; and a great farrago of wise saws and instances?

Then there is Homer's diction and idiom. It is tautologous and repetitious. His heroes are never allowed to just speak or act or fight or sleep. They "speak and answer and utter winged words"; they "make covenant and swear"; they "are gathered together and meet in assembly"; they "consider and take thought"; and so forth. Lines and half lines recur like entries in a ledger. His characters are always "sailing over the unharvested sea" or "the wine-dark deep," "setting in order goodly hecatombs," "putting from them the desire of meat and drink" and the like. Most of them are encumbered with a variety of ornamental titles. Achilles is always son of Peleus or noble or swift of foot. Agamemnon is always son of Atreus or wide-ruling or king of men, Hera is white-armed or golden-throned, even when her behavior is anything but regal. These are all symptomatic of a general economy of vocabulary, a rigidity of idiom, which strikes us as archaic and even primitive, and recent Homeric scholarship has tended to confirm this judgement. This is the vocabulary and style of a pre-literate poetry composed of formulaic units hoarded in the poet's memory, a vast storehouse of verbal expressions of fixed metrical shapesuited for fixed positions in the hexameter line. These formulas resist change, even when the contemporary speech is changing. So linguistically they constitute a hoarded amalgam of survivals from successive dialects preserved and embalmed in the bardic diction. Homer's Greek was never spoken in daily speech by any existing Greek tribe of any given epoch. It was never a vernacular, but always archaic in relation to contemporary speech, the product of a poetic economy which sought to mitigate the strain on the oral memory by preserving the traditional at the expense of the novel.

It has become equally clear that this archaism of language is matched by a similar degree of archaism in content. Whatever Homer's own date may have been, the tales he tells, the topographies, dynasties, wars, go back to a vanished Achaean culture identified from the site of Agamemnon's palace as the "Mycenaean Age." The inhabited sites, the architecture, the armour, the art uncovered by the archeologists all have their counterparts in the Homeric tales. The inscribed records of the Hittites and Egyptians may even preserve names which roughly correspond to Homer's Achaeans and Danaans. This culture by 1100 B.C. had been swept away and a new and very different Greece, the Greece of the historical period, emerged slowly from the ashes of the old. Homer lived in this new Greece or at the edge of it. But once more, as in his language so also in his content, Homer contrives an amalgam of preserved memories. He reports the Greece not only of the Mycenaean age but of the post-Mycenaean migrations. He remembers the Achaean confederacy which warred against Anatolia. But he also recalls the Phoenicians, their voyages and their art in the period when Mycenae was becoming a memory. His material like his diction illustrates that law of oral communication whereby the collective memory slowly receives and blends successive deposits of experience and fuses them incongruously in epic structures which take on the quality of a dream, a historical fantasy belonging to no fixed time or place.

For these very good reasons, the Homeric critic, however sensitive he may grow to the presence in the poems of a reflective genius, who somehow has placed a unique stamp upon this material, falls easily into the habit of picturing Homer, whether he was author or editor, as an itinerant bard of primitive resources who recited at the command of a rude aristocracy. Were not Agamemnon, Achilles, and their like princes who commanded the uncertain allegiance of barbarous retainers? Does not Homer himself sometimes represent the minstrel as their servant, obedient to praise the exploits of princely patrons, eating at the table in the great hall, sleeping maybe on the rushes which strewed the floor? Was the Greek community which he celebrated really a community, rather than a set of scattered cantons, each dominated indeed with an edifice which passed for a palace, but united only in a confederacy of freebooting, with the loosest sort of social structure? There are no thronged city streets (except in Troy), no docks and wharves (except in Phaeacia), no parliaments, no commercial exchanges and not much in the way of domestic affluence and leisured conversation. On the plains of windy Troy, as in the island manor of Odysseus, the atmosphere of the Mycenaean age predominates. Its values can be read as those of Greek "Vikings," men of shrewd but uncultivated instincts, and we may fall into the unconscious habit of picturing their poet as a man himself of rude genius with unkempt beard, blind perchance, and led by some boy to the site of the great hearth. While the cups clink he bends to tune his lyre and waits for boisterous laughter and rude jest to subside before beginning some song of the great deeds of heroes.

From such a poet we might expect what indeed we get in Homer, tales of battles, duels, cities, voyages, genealogies of great families, tribal customs, and acccumulated lore. We might expect crude dynamic power, vivid similes recalled from nature and art, portraits of princes, queens, and serving men; heroic virtues, heroically portrayed. These too we get in Homer. We can even concede the existence of an oral genius powerful enough to impose some loose dramatic unity on his lays, grouping them round a chosen theme, the anger, the prowess, the deeds, the frustration, the self-discovery and the predicted death of a single chieftain, an Achilles. This too we get in Homer. The ***Iliad*** is indeed, as Aristotle divined, not just a heroic tale, but also the prototype of a Greek tragedy.

But is even this the sum of the Homeric equation? So far, the virtues of the poem are seen to be monumental, they are attained by a great act of comprehension rather than by isolation and analysis of minute situation. The vision of life is direct and in a sense uncomplicated, or at least its complexities are felt and conceived within the value system of the heroic age. But are there any traces in the ***Iliad*** of a rather different perspective on the human scene, one which we might identify as cultivated and even complex, not to say ironic and detached—a perspective in short in which we might discern the urbanity characteristic of a leisured culture? (pp. 259-63)

[Comic] portraiture relies on an intimacy between the artist and his human material, and this intimacy can repeat itself at a second and more serious level of sympathy when the same artist turns from comedy to consider the human heart and its affections. Possibly an appreciation of this fact lay behind the Socratic proposition that the composer of comedy is also the composer of tragedy. Homer at any rate can deal with Helen and her tragic situation with a degree of sophistication which recalls his powers of comic observation. Her name and role as the stolen wife for whose sake the war is fought recur formulaically in some twenty-six contexts in the poem, none of which go further than the formula. But on three occasions and only three she intrudes into the story in her own right, in the third, the sixth and the twenty-fourth books. The contexts are so dispersed that a close comparison between them may evade the critic's attention. But in what they explicitly tell us, and still more in what they implicitly reveal, they are both congruent and cumulative in their effect and in the information that is communicated to us. They occur wholly within Helen's Trojan context. Menelaus is present only as a memory, and poignant memory at that, of what has been abandoned and lost.

The personalities who successively are brought into conjunction with her are her lover-husband (so he is prefigured in ambivalent status), her lover's father, and her lover's brother: Paris, Priam and Hector. At each conjunction, the poet has contrived that rare effect of portraying a woman herself passive yet the respository of some latent force which impinges upon the men she meets, a magnetic pull to which they respond, and in responding reveal their respective natures. In the contexts thus prepared for her she is indeed presented as a man's woman.

The third book discovers Paris leading the Trojans to battle against the Greeks, till he unexpectedly confronts Menelaus from whom he had stolen Helen. He retreats precipitately with the involuntary fear of a man who has stumbled upon a snake. This provokes his brother Hector to assail him with reproaches. The lover of Helen, he exclaims, who brought wanton disaster on his own country by stealing her away is only a lover, not a fighter. "Why cannot you confront Menelaus, and realize what a warrior is he whose lovely wife you have taken. Little use your lyre would be to you then, and those gifts of Aphrodite, your flowing hair and good looks, when you make your bed in the dust!"

Paris attempts no retort nor on the other hand is he abashed by these reproaches. He replies with equanimity that Hector's mind is ever keen, like an axe that cleaves a beam. "Cast not in my teeth the lovely gifts of golden Aphrodite. The gifts that the gods may choose to give a man cannot be discarded, any more than they can be got just because he wants them."

Already the poet has used a brief dialogue to etch two contrasted types: the responsible elder brother, obedient to the call of duty, ever mindful of what is at stake for others, with a touch of Puritanism in his character which comes out as he confronts his younger brother, the Absalom of Homer's story, no mean fighter as it turns out, but a gay irresponsible figure who gets what he wants because of his god-given charm.

Paris straightway offers to meet Menelaus in single combat, on terms that the winner shall take all and the war between Greeks and Trojans ended. At once Hector is relieved and his heart gladdened. Preparations for the duel are set in motion; the epic stage is cleared as it were, for the two men in Helen's life, the wronged husband and the successful lover. At this point, the news of the impending contest and the issues at stake is conveyed to Helen herself. The audience at the epic recital are allowed to see her for the first time. Homer's touch here is sure; there is nothing wrong with his sense of timing. Her reaction to the news is simple and profound: "It put sweet longing into her heart for the man she had before, and for her city, and for her parents." She has then not forgotten, and in her adopted city is aware of isolation.

She hastens to the Scaean gate of Troy and over the gate are sitting the Trojan elders, and Priam with them. These are old men and frail; their days of love and fighting are spent. Yet the woman they now see provokes from them no senile imprecations, no conventional denunciation. Rather they feel a faint stirring of the blood, a warming of instincts long disused: "Now when they saw Helen coming to the tower, they spoke the winged words in whispers to each other: 'What a woman! No good blaming the Trojans and well-greaved Achaeans for suffering all these years on her account! She is incredibly like the deathless gods to look upon. Yet for all her beauty, better she take ship and go with them, rather than be left behind to our sorrow and our children's sorrow.'"

Here is the eternal tribute of man to woman released by the immortal power of sex and acknowledged with an objectivity which is characteristically Greek. Equally characteristic is the sense of danger lurking within the embodiment of beauty. The tribute is all the more forceful as it is conveyed not in the impulsive rhetoric of the young and lusty, but by the considered testimony of the old, from whom any hope of seduction has been emptied away. As Helen herself becomes the instrument of revealing others, so also it is the old men who are used to reveal Helen. The poet intends her as the living symbol of passion, and as the focus of gallant response to passion, but the method by which this quality of hers is conveyed to his audience is oblique. Let others, even the old, by their reactions, tell us what Helen was like. She also as she passes will reveal to us what they are like. This two-way system of revelation by mutual reaction is typical of Homer's technique.

From this setting, the aged Priam then emerges into sharper focus. He lifts up his voice and calls to her: "Dear child, come and sit in front of me so that you can see the husband you had before, and your kindred and friends. I do not hold anything against you. It is the gods I hold responsible for bringing dolorous war upon me." She has been the instrument of his sorrow, but he has no reproaches for her, only affection. And he realizes, with the insight of age, that she is thinking of her own people on the other side of the battlements. So she proceeds to mark the Greek host, telling him the names of those she recognizes, and the chief warriors of the Greeks pass in review before us.

The duel is the next event, and it ends summarily and unsatisfactorily, for the poet still has business to finish with Helen and Paris. His intentions in this book are not directed upon the heroic themes of battle. Paris is worsted in the contest, but his luck stays with him. He slips from under the avenging sword, and is translated by Aphrodite's help, as in a flash, to his bedchamber, unruffled, relaxed, laughing, the darling of fortune. Helen has watched the tournament, and now at her elbow an affectionate retainer of hers, an old woman from the cherished past when she lived in Sparta, plucks at her sleeve: "Come with me. I have a message form Paris. He wants you to go home. Yes, Paris is in the bedroom. He looks just beautiful. You would never think he had just been fighting another man. It is as though he was on his way to a dance, or maybe resting in one of the intervals."

She is the voice of seduction sly but tender, prototype of the affectionate nurse of Euripides and Shakespeare, and she stirs response in Helen. But the response is complex, wayward and finally bitter. Beneath the old woman's disguise she recognizes the physical splendour of the goddess of love herself: "My divine dear, why do you persist in seducing me like this? Are you going to lead me a dance from city to city—through Phrygia or Maeonia maybe? Do you have a favorite man waiting there for me, now that Menelaus has beaten Paris, and wants to hale me home in disgrace? Is that why you are here at my side with your proposition?"

This is her point of release of all the pent bitterness which her destiny self-chosen has brought upon her. Homer for once omits all connection in his verse as she bursts out: "Go and sit beside him yourself. Abandon the primrose path of the gods. Never mind returning to Olympus. Stay around him, keep agonizing over him, keep your eyes on him! Wait for him to make you into a wife—no—into a slave. Go to him I will not, nor get his bed ready. It would be too shameful. All the Trojan women will whisper about me behind my back. I have grief enough and untold in my heart." Love's only answer is a stern warning: "You are going too far. Provoke me, and I will abandon you. I have lavished my affection on you. Just as surely I can cast you off. I can arrange for you to be hated by both sides at once."

Love is her *daimon,* the second self that now controls her as she silently and secretly returns to Paris' arms. To reject her role would be to reject her sex, and the magic of her name and nature would vanish. But as she greets Paris, the mood of revulsion is still upon her: "Here you are back from battle. I wish that mighty man had beaten you—the husband I used to have. Why not challenge him again? But no! Perchance his spear may overcome you. Don't be rash and fight him again."

The formulaic not to say ceremonial style in which Homer is compelled to clothe this intimate confrontation makes it hard to be sure whether her closing sentence is inspired by sarcasm or by a revived and protective affection for her lover. At any rate, he answers her with the same equanimity with which he had earlier replied to his brother's reproaches: "I have lost today. Tomorrow I will win. But as for now, O! let us go to bed. My senses are overpowered by you. It is like when I first took you, on Lemnos, after I had snatched you away from Sparta. Only now, the tide of my desire is so much stronger!"

Thus is the tribute to immortal sex renewed, this time from the young and lusty. His fascination for her, and her magic for him, jointly prevail as she follows him to bed. But how complex and even bitter has been the revelation of her own mood and destiny!

There, at the close of the third book, Homer leaves them. Unforgettably, and at some length, he has delineated Helen's divided heart. When she reappears, it will be to fill in and confirm the portrait already presented. The next two books are filled with the noise of dolorous war, till we come to the sixth. This book, in which Hector leaves the battle to summon further aid from Troy, is memorable for the scene of parting between himself and his wife Andromache. Her tears and entreaties, his own resolute affection, and the moment when both parents dandle the little boy and play with him, denominate a domestic relationship as simple as it is profound.

But there is a brief preface to this scene. Hector, on his way to his own house, calls at his younger brother's house to summon him back to battle. The domestic interior is one of surface dignity and repose: "He found Paris in the room looking after his armour, shield, breastplate, and trying his bow. Helen was seated surrounded by her domestic staff supervising the maids in their handicrafts." It is a tranquil and civilized scene; Helen and Paris enjoy no vulgar relationship.

On this scene impinges Hector. In the third book we saw Hector with Paris and then Helen with Paris. Now here the three of them are conjoined as Hector confronts Helen. The poet has created an opportunity for a further revelation of Hector's character, a marginal revelation, irrelevant to his epic role. We see him through Helen's eyes. She, his sister-in-law, furnishes footnote to his official character, as husband, father, and protector of Troy, and in so doing further reveals herself.

He begins the dialogue with an appeal to Paris to return to battle. In effect, he seems to be saying "Let bygones be bygones between us." Paris replies that he need not worry: "It's not that I am angry. That's not why I am staying here. I just wanted to give way to my own bitter feelings." However, Helen, he adds, has already been gently urging him to reenter the combat. "Just give me time to don my armour" he concludes, "or else let me follow you later."

Hector makes no reply. But Helen fills in the silence. "Oh my dear," she says to Hector, "my brother, vile creature that I am—horrible instrument of woe," and overcome, she bursts into passionate self-reproach. Hector has power to break her down because of his affection for her: "Would that on the day when my mother bore me at the first an evil storm wind had caught me away to a mountain, or a billow of the loud-sounding sea." Then, recovering herself, she thinks of Hector and the burden he carries, and the contrast with Paris; if only she could do something for him: "However, since these sorrows the gods saw fit to assign, O! would that then I had been mated with a better man who knew what it is to feel respect and to realize the reproach of his fellows. Paris here is so unstable. Please come in and take this chair, brother. It is you that have to bear the anxiety and responsibility, and all because of me, bitch that I am, and Paris, who began it all. Fate is too much for him and me. So Zeus decrees, that hereafter we become a song on the lips of mankind." There is no hint of coquetry, nor taint of rhetoric, in this dialogue. The poet has distanced it, by giving Helen the power to foresee her own role in his epic. In the bitter dilemma of her troubled spirit, it is to Hector she has turned for confession, if not for strength.

All he can do is to ask her not to entreat him to stop: "I realize how you feel about me, Helen, but it's no good. The Trojans miss me when I am away. Just encourage Paris. He can bestir himself to join me. I must go on to my own house, perhaps for the last time.'' And so he leaves her, in order to have his last meeting with his own wife and child.

Yet once again, at the very end of the long tale, in the conclusion of the twenty-fourth book, the poet adds a postscript on this relationship, and as he adds, he underlines the inferences we have drawn. Hector is dead now: his corpse has been dragged round Troy; abused and mutilated; until at length ransomed for burial and brought back to Troy. The formal lamentations, in keeping with ceremonial requirements, are performed by Andromache and Hecuba, the widow and the mother, with appropriate sentiments. The end of the epic is at hand. But now that the pride and vain glory, the conquest and killing, the fate of Troy, the public destiny of Hector, his city, his parents, his home, are all spent and fulfilled, Helen, for whom, one would think, space could scarcely be found in such a setting, is nevertheless allowed the last word, a private footnote:

> Hector of all my brethren of Troy far dearest to my heart
> My mate I know is Paris of the divine form
> Who brought me to Troy land—and would I had perished first.
> I have now seen nineteen years go by
> Since I left my own country
> Yet never yet from you in all that time have I heard an evil or despiteful word.
> Yes, and if any other man in these halls would upbraid me,
> Whether brother or sister of yours, or brother's favorite wife
> Or your mother—but not your father; he has always
> been so gentle with me, as if he were my own father—
> Why, then you would divert him and stop him
> By the loving kindness of your spirit and the loving kindness of your words.
> Therefore do I now weep for you, and in weeping for you, I weep for myself, a castaway in my heart's grief.
> For none other now remains in all wide Troy
> That is to be my friend and kind to me, but they all shudder and shrink from me.

Readers of those reminiscences of Arnold's Rugby which Thomas Hughes incorporated in *Tom Brown's School Days* may recall how one day in Homer class the pathos of this passage was too much for one brilliant pupil, the future Dean Stanley, who broke down in tears as he construed it, to the enormous embarrassment of his shuffling schoolmates. The speech is indeed charged with emotional revelation, of Helen herself and the waste spaces in her proud and passionate heart. As in the third and sixth, so also in the twenty-fourth book she speaks still as an exile, enslaved by her passion for Paris, yet utterly alone. But how vividly in her despair does she also illuminate the character of her brother-in-law! It is before him once more, before his mute corpse, that her composure breaks. And once more, with her aid, we can see that streak of romanticism, that touch of imaginative affection, which had made Hector something more than either a warrior, husband, or parent. It was the same man who, when he abode Achilles' onslaught beneath the walls of Troy in the last crisis of his career, could debate within himself whether it were worth while to offer terms to his antagonist and try and bargain for Troy's sake, to bring peace: ''But it is no time now to dally with him from oak tree or from rock, like youth with maiden, as youth and maiden hold dalliance, one with the other. Better to join battle at once.'' Only Hector the chivalrous romantic would have allowed himself that kind of simile at such a time.

Helen, Hector, Paris and Priam emerge in joint relation only in these three widely scattered contexts. Yet the contexts are not only congruent, they supplement each other with a fine economy. On their first appearance, the poet arranges them in three separate but overlapping pairs: Hector with Paris, Priam with Helen, Helen with Paris. The sixth book follows this up by combining Hector, Paris and Helen in a trio. In the twenty-fourth, all four are finally brought together within the compass of Helen's last retrospective pronouncement. What kind of genius was it, that was capable of such subtleties, operating on the margin of his main plot?

His vehicle to be sure is still the oral saga, and though he laid it on the anvil of intellectual artistry, this artistry is muted, because it speaks with the archaic, formulaic intonation of the oral minstrel. That is why, as hero challenges hero to primitive combat and genealogy piles on genealogy and the terrific hexameter repeats its hoarded refrains, we have to attend closely, bending our ear, if we are to catch the note of urbane irony concealed in the domestic comedy on Olympus, or perceive the romantic chord which vibrates gently in Hector's gallant affection, or listen to the muffled pain of Helen's divided heart. (pp. 268-75)

Eric A. Havelock, ''The Sophistication of Homer,'' in I. A. Richards: Essays in His Honor, *Reuben Brower, Helen Vendler, John Hollander, eds., Oxford University Press, 1973, pp. 259-75.*

ERIC A. HAVELOCK (essay date 1978)

[*In the following excerpt, Havelock explores the Homeric concept of* dikē, *''an oral prototype of what later was to become 'justice' in the conceptual sense in which we now use the word.'' Tracing the way in which* dikē *functions in the Achilles/Agamemnon and Antilochus/Menelaus feuds, Havelock determines that justice in the* Iliad *''is a procedure, not a principle or any set of principles.''*]

[The] Greek epic, so far from being an oral improvisation, is a compendium of social and personal conventions, as these become illustrated in an appropriate mythos—one that is told in a way and with a style that will continuously provoke their utterance. On the face of it, the culture that is being both reported and supported in this way by the enclave of contrived speech is self-regulating. No individual can stand outside it and criticize it on the basis of principles independent of the culture. Personal ''alienation'' from society is impossible because unthought of. What becomes law in a literate society remains custom and usage; morality is not easily definable except as conformity to custom.

Yet conformity is surely not automatic. The behavior of the human being . . . is not confined within the limits set by herd instinct. Whether his society is oral or literate, his individuation will interrupt and disrupt the web of custom and precedent by the self-motivated arrogance of personal decision or desire, anger or ambition, or even mere eccentricity. From time to time, the general rules will be broken: and very often their correct application in given cases will be doubtful, because of uncertainty created by competing claims. The nomos and ethos continually recalled and illustrated in Homeric narrative and rhetoric are normative. They state and restate the proprieties of behavior as these are assumed and followed. But the oral medium, in order to fulfill its complete function as the verbalized guide of the culture, will also be required to describe situations and frame statements which are corrective rather than merely normative, which, describing how the mores are abrogated, therewith describe also the means and manner whereby they are restored. The master symbol of this corrective process, which is also a procedure, is the Homeric *dikē* and its plural *dikai,* in which we encounter an oral prototype of what later was to become "justice" in the conceptual sense in which we now use the word.

An epic mythos could not come into existence if it limited itself to reporting a culture that was self-regulating. The memorizable story must exploit the tensions of a conflict. Such a situation creates itself when the mores are subjected to disturbance or abrogation; they are defied in part or whole by at least some of the protagonists. A Sarpedon, a Diomede, an Aeneas, an Odysseus, a Nestor, a Priam, even a Hector are examples of characters whose roles as played in the ***Iliad*** are by and large normative and "normal." These roles could never of themselves create an ***Iliad.*** What the listening audience wants and expects from the singer is a story of a collision provoking the excitement of vigorous action and speech. This the mythos will supply, and then to fulfill its didactic function, it will proceed to narrate the corrective process which restores the proprieties. Both epics conform to this pattern, but it is particularly in the ***Iliad*** that restoration can be seen to depend upon the application of a set of rules recognized by the community present in the story, and recognizable by the modern reader, as a form of "justice."

The action of the plot grows out of a Greek raid on a neighboring town which is pillaged. The booty, in accordance with custom, is distributed through the army, Agamemnon receiving a captive girl, who turns out to be a priest's daughter. His rejection of her father's plea to return her involves the army in a disastrous plague, for which the required remedy is that he comply with the plea, which he does. But he then pulls rank on Achilles, and compensates himself by abstracting from him a substitute girl, hitherto Achilles' property. What have now been provoked as a central factor in the story are a contention and a feud (*eris* and *neikos*) between two powerful men. The preface to the epic carefully identifies these as the subject of the story, for their concomitant is a rage which, as it seizes on Achilles, has the effect of gravely damaging the Greek army. He expresses his feelings by withdrawing himself and his force totally from combat. The Greeks in due course confront a second crisis as they are pressed by superior opponents to the point of near defeat.

It did not take Agamemnon long to regret the "contentions and feuds" which he confesses he himself had initiated, and if resolution of the impasse had depended on him, it would have been resolved without critical consequences. As the Greek army suffers reverses, Nestor proposes that Achilles be conciliated and offered compensation. Agamemnon readily agrees, accepting the fact that he has erred. The burden he carries, and confesses to Nestor that he carries, is symbolized in the word "Disaster" (*Atē*), capitalized as a demon that afflicts mankind. She destroys both wits and fortunes; she infatuates and ruins. "You have accurately recounted my disasters. I have been disastered, no denying it." "Disastered as I have been, through giving way to wits pestilential, I desire in return to conciliate and give enormous gifts." Ten books later, after further prolongation of the crisis (for Achilles remains obdurate), as settlement of the feud is at last achieved, Agamemnon converts the occasion into a second opportunity to descant upon the operation of this demon. On that fatal day when he took Achilles' girl, "Zeus and Fate and Erinys cast into my wits savage Disaster." "Eldest daughter of Zeus is Disaster, she who disasters all men . . . she passes over the heads of men disabling them . . . Yes, once on a time even Zeus was disastered." Hera had tricked Zeus into giving her a solemn promise on false pretenses, "and then was he much disastered." When he found out the truth, "straightaway he seized Disaster by the hair . . . and swore that never again would Olympus and starry heaven be entered by Disaster, she who disasters all men. So he threw her out of heaven and she descended on the works of men." "So I too, when Hector began to slay the Greeks at their ships' sterns, could not evade Disaster, she by whom I first was disastered. But disastered as I have been, robbed of my wits by Zeus, I desire in return to conciliate and give gifts unlimited." The reiteration within each context, and between two contexts so widely separated, is compulsively formulaic.

Agamemnon need not stand in the pillory alone. This demon can distribute her favors impartially. Earlier in the story, at the point where Achilles had declared his continued obduracy, he had received a solemn address from his tutor, Phoenix:

> Supplications are daughters of great Zeus,
> lame and wrinkled and blear-eyed,
> moving cautiously on in the rear of Disaster;
> Disaster is strong and fleet-footed and so
> she far outruns all of them and gets in front all over the earth,
> disabling mankind; and they follow in the rear to heal.
> If a man is gracious to the maids of Zeus as they draw near,
> they greatly prosper him, and as he prays they listen;
> if a man refuse and stubbornly say "No,"
> then do they, even they, go to Kronian Zeus and supplicate
> that Disaster go in that man's company, that he be disabled and pay back.

The predicted comes to pass. Achilles, still obdurate, makes only one small concession, which, precisely because of its niggardliness, proves his undoing. For when it is implemented by allowing Patroclus to go into battle to rescue the ships, Patroclus is killed. Achilles by his own action—or lack of action—has lost his best friend, and in a crisis of revulsion, aside from vowing vengeance on Hector, he formally pronounces against that Contention (Eris: she, like Disaster, is capitalized here) around which the plot to this point had been built:

> O, that Contention from among gods and human beings might perish
> and anger which sets even the prudent to make trouble—
> (anger) which, sweeter far than honey spilled over,
> in the hearts of men waxes as smoke.

This statement announces the beginning of the termination of the mythos announced in the opening lines of the poem: "which of the gods was it that set these two together in contention to fight?" Confronting the contrite Agamemnon, Achilles recalls the "contention spirit-devouring" . . . and, speaking for the poet, pronounces that the story of "this contention, mine and yours, will long be commemorated." It is the poem's own definition of what the story has been all about and what its claim will be upon the memory of posterity.

A perceptive critic noted over forty years ago that the ***Iliad,*** though of oral composition, is an epic with psychological overtones, exhibiting a sophistication uncommon in the genre. The account so far summarized of the plot, to the conclusion of Book 19, confirms this judgment. The action is so described as to be explicitly governed by the passions and decisions of two men of power: the controlling symbols are those of feud and hatred, pride and blind anger, honor and arrogance, rash decision and rueful regret, pleas and reproaches, defiance and confession, as these distribute themselves on both sides of the argument. Even though the Homeric idiom can sometimes objectify these facts of psychology as forces external to man, we feel their operation within men as they speak and act. For the literate reader the epic is probably easiest to enjoy and sympathize with if understood in these terms.

But those in search of justice in the ***Iliad*** must take a different tack, focusing their inquiry on the political and social context. What precisely are the procedures that are followed in the story at those few occasions where the feud, its causes, its effects, and possible amendment are directly in question? Though the initial error was Agamemnon's, trouble first erupts when the aggrieved father appeals not just to him (and also his brother) but to the entire Greek company. He offers to buy his daughter back, a reasonable proposal, and the Geek audience shouts its approval, which is overridden by Agamemnon. To deal with the consequences, which fall on the Greeks as a body, they meet in an agora summoned by Achilles. This is not a casual event. The formulaic hexameters which describe the initial summons and the final dismissal, the succession of debaters as they get up and sit down, offering proposals or rebuttals, defiance or mediation, are carefully programed. We are watching a town meeting in session, and it is a fair inference that it was at a previous session that the priest had first appeared. As in the ***Odyssey,*** anyone can call a meeting (in this case Achilles), and when he speaks he holds the "scepter." The word *agora* can denote either a "speaking" or (in the plural) speeches, or an assembly where speaking occurs, or the place where the assembly is held (which later in Athens and perhaps elsewhere also became the marketplace). It is a "parliament" in the literal sense of that word. The Greeks for fantasy purposes are an army in the field besieging Troy. More realistically, they are behaving as the "parliament" of a polis, thereby furnishing a paradigm of civic procedure as an item of oral storage.

The truth of this becomes clearer in the second book. Agamemnon has a dream which instructs him to marshal the troops: clearly a preparation for the catalogue of the ships. Unaccountably, he then instructs the heralds to announce an agora, which accordingly meets, as described in regulation formulas. Then it is left in suspense while Agamemnon "holds a session of the council of elders," proposing to them to marshal the troops. They approve and the session then "rises," and the scene reverts to "the people," now buzzing about like bees, but there are also "many nationalities drawn up in file on the foreshore," who then proceed "en masse into agora," an event which has already been stated. The next 306 lines are a narrative of the parliament and its proceedings. At one point it is interrupted, as the members leave their seats and make for the ships, but order is restored and the session resumed. Formulas appropriate to the occasion are reiterated. The assembly is seated in orderly fashion in rows of seats; heralds (whose duties are omitted in Book 1) have the task of arranging the seating, keeping order, calling for silence as a speaker rises. The scepter, though described in antiquarian terms as the inherited property of Agamemnon, is at the realistic level appropriated by Odysseus (as previously by Achilles) when he wants to speak or use it to enforce discipline. The whole account, confused as it is, to the point where the catalogue begins, is a blend of antique fantasy and contemporary political reality. It leaves the impression that for the transaction of public business and the formation of important decisions a parliament was essential, assisted by a council which met separately, something which the narrative of Book 1 gives no opportunity to mention. Aristotle, in a later age, tacitly accepted the fact that such functions were indeed vested in the Homeric agora, when he remarks, apropos of this same scene in Book 2 of the ***Iliad,*** that "Agamemnon (regularly) sustained verbal attacks in the meetings of the ecclesia," a term he would use only on the assumption that the agora was in fact the prototype of the parliamentary machinery employed in Athens. In drawing a sharp distinction between Agamemnon's role in the ecclesia and his power as a commander-in-chief on a campaign, he appears to assume that the agoras of the ***Iliad*** were in fact not military but civilian, like those held in the ***Odyssey,*** where in Ithaca the agora at times seems to be in continual session, its proceedings being supplemented by a council who have reserved seats in it. There are several other agora sessions in the ***Iliad,*** on both Greek and Trojan sides, in one of which it is noted as an exception that the members are standing. Procedures are wholly oral. Aside from the debating process itself, all communications, motions, and decisions are framed and implemented by oral formula.

This does not mean that the agora is a legislative body. It can only accept or reject leadership supplied by the "top men" (*aristoi, basileis*). But acceptance or rejection can be decisive. Agamemnon by rejecting the priest's plea rejected a "vote" of the agora, and the results proved painful. The second meeting produces a debate in the face of which his reluctance is overcome. The pressure on him emanates not only from the speakers but from the silent listening audience. The plea he then makes to the agora discloses its powers. "You all are looking on as my prize is divested from me." "So furnish me with a prize at once." It is the prerogative of the assembly to do so, even as it controlled the original distribution of the loot, a fact which Achilles is quick to point out. Propriety would be violated by opening up the process again. Agamemnon will have to wait for the army to seize more booty elsewhere. Yet the issue is dubious, precisely because it involves the commander-in-chief. Should not his superior rank take precedence? This is also a propriety: the two are discovered in collision. A personal decision to appropriate Achilles' girl as a substitute offers no solution; it only provokes a confrontation, which might be settled by direct action between the parties, murder, in fact. Such a solution lacks divine sanction, and it is abandoned. Achilles will wait for remedy and bring pressure by withdrawing himself and his men from battle.

It is as he announces this decision that the notion of Homeric "justice" enters into the debate. The decision takes the form of an oath and a vow sworn before the assembly and involving the audience and not just Agamemnon in the consequences. They had assigned Achilles Briseis; they are witnesses to the cancellation of that assignment; in effect, they are responsible for the act. Holding up the scepter before them, he describes how it was once a living tree, and is now become forever lifeless wood.

Now just as surely the sons of the Achaeans
carry and handle it, the managers-of-justices [*dikaspoloi*] who also the formularies
under Zeus do conserve. So shall this oath be great to you

He then promises disaster for the Greeks, which Agamemnon will be powerless to avert. Having said which, he dashes the gold-studded club on the ground. *Dikai* in the plural are not principles of justice, but events involving justice which become procedures because they are subject to ''management'' by officials, who, however, do not manage the ''formularies'' but protect them.

But procedural justice in this case has not been put to work. Its task would have been to prevent the insult to a member of the army whose services were indispensable. The agora is a necessary partner in the procedure, for it has the responsibility for allotting not only spoils but the honors that accompany them. It has failed in the present case by acquiescing in Agamemnon's act of individuation. Achilles dramatizes the failure by dashing the club to the ground. The gold-studded scepter, honored in this case as the insignia of judicial rather than monarchical power, has been dishonored. The agora is so told, and is warned that it must share the consequences. The debate, however, continues with an attempt at mediation, appropriately undertaken by Nestor in the character of elder statesman, proposing the kind of solution that will in fact be followed in the end, but the case for the present is hopeless. The two parties are still contestants ''fighting each other with counterviolent words.'' They rise and dismiss the agora.

Yet the meeting has achieved one positive result. Nomos and ethos, violated by the capture of a priest's daughter, are remedied by a decision taken in the course of the proceedings. The offender arranges for the girl to be ceremoniously restored to her father, and this ceremony as it is carried out is carefully and repetitively described, for it is required to complete the ''legalities.'' One item of justice as orally managed has been implemented, though the poem does not use the term.

As already noted, Agamemnon's repentance is not long delayed, and it is noteworthy that it is stated in Book 2 before a fresh meeting of the agora. What he says is an expression of personal feeling which offers no legal solution. The business at this meeting is preparation for combat without Achilles. Only after the Greeks have suffered serious reverses is an agora summoned to deal formally with the crisis created by the fulfillment of his vow. It is formulaically convoked and seated. Addresses by Agamemnon and Diomede are followed by a speech by Nestor, who states in axiomatic form the communal danger created by the personal confrontation:

> Out of clan, out of law, out of hearth stands [*estin*] that one whose lust is for war internecine within the demos

This is a judgment upon both contestants. He then proposes that the army recoup morale by eating a meal, and while they are doing so Agamemnon can convoke the elders in his own quarters for a meal. For practical purposes, this is a meeting of the council, at which Nestor ceremoniously notes that in Agamemnon's hands ''lie scepter and formularies given by Zeus'' to assist his leadership in counsel; it is therefore his duty both to speak and to listen to what others have to say. This recollection of what happened in Book 1, or rather did not happen, is continued as Nestor reviews his previous abortive attempt at mediation. The remedy proposed at that time being no longer applicable, he proposes instead adequate compensation from Agamemnon for injury inflicted. This suggestion, accepted by Agamemnon, in effect emanates from the council, and it proves ineffective. A final solution will require the renewed presence of the agora which had witnessed the original rupture.

If the ***Iliad*** were limited to being a psychological epic, Achilles' revulsion at the news of his friend's death would be enough to cancel the past without more ado. The epic itself, however, is well aware that the functions of the story it is telling are not primarily psychological but legal, social, and political. At the point where Achilles has become eager to abandon the feud in order to join battle and kill Hector, his mother admonishes him that he must first call an agora and formally renounce his wrath. Formal and formulaic summons is then issued for the meeting of all concerned; the attendance of noncombatants is specifically mentioned. Achilles as summoner gives the opening address renouncing his wrath, and the assembly applaud. Agamemnon, speaking from his seat, announces that he has something to say if the agora will stop interrupting and give him a hearing. At the beginning of the lengthy apology that follows, he observes that the savage demon which had destroyed his judgment was inflicted on him ''in agora.'' The apology concluded, he signifies readiness to pay lavish compensation, as already offered. The call to battle the enemy is urgent, but wait, he says to Achilles, till the compensation is brought here for your inspection. Achilles courteously declares his indifference: he is impatient to begin fighting. Odysseus, assuming Nestor's role as the voice of propriety, admonishes . . . that the army should disperse and eat a meal if they are to fight. But first, a settlement between the two erstwhile antagonists should be ceremoniously performed. The goods constituting the compensation should be conveyed ''into the middle of the agora so that all may view with their eyes,'' not just Achilles. Agamemnon must then ''rise and give solemn oath'' that he is able to restore Briseis in her original condition. He is also to play formal host to Achilles at a feast of reconciliation. Then Odysseus adds:

> You [Achilles] will not be left holding anything that
> falls short of ''justice,''
> and you [Agamemnon] thereafter ''more just''
> [*dikaioteros*] on any other ground as well
> shall stand [*esseai*], since it is no matter of reproach
> that a *basileus* should appease a man in a case where
> one has been the first to make trouble.

Agamemnon readily complies and prepares the formalities necessary to the completion of the negotiation: the intention to pronounce oaths is repeated three times; he will produce the gifts of compensation in full view. Achilles, still indifferent to the ceremony, will fast, he says, till he kills Hector; not so the army, says Odysseus. But before the meal is eaten, the ceremony is completed: the gifts are brought into full view, an animal is solemnly sacrificed, and a solemn oath is sworn, after which Achilles in brief but formal reply acknowledges for his part the disastrous effect of the demon of ruin upon Agamemnon personally and upon the body politic as well. So the agora is at last dissolved. It has been witness to, and, we may add, guarantor of, the termination of a *neikos,* achieved under the superintendence of an arbitrator who has functioned as a ''manager of justices,'' though the narrative does not award him the title. The terms of Homeric justice, honored in the breach when the feud erupted, have emerged as decisive, pronounced in the settlement over which they may be said to preside as symbols of what has happened. Achilles receives an adequacy of justice, almost as though it were a quantity. His opponent also becomes ''more just,'' so that his ''justice'' too may be said to be increased, in the sense that he is ''justified'' in apologizing (despite his superior rank) because (as he himself admitted in Book 2) he was the inciter of the *neikos*. Justice, whatever it is, can be seen as something exchanged between two parties, or added to both, in the course of a settlement; or, alternatively, as symbolizing the process of exchange itself. It is certainly not a principle which when applied excludes its opposite.

To achieve proper result, certain conditions have to be met. Though the feud which calls for such procedure occurs between two parties, justice can be applied only with the participation of the agora, functioning as a forum for rhetoric addressed to the issues that have arisen. The performance of judgment is also a function of rhetoric: the one is achieved through the other, so that the scepter is both a judge's symbol and a speaker's symbol. The settlement is likely to involve a reassignment of goods both material and moral, that is, of money and of honor. Since no documentary evidence of the settlement is available to be exchanged, the witness of a mass audience who will remember what they have heard and seen is vital. Equally, the procedure must include not only the material compensation placed on view but appropriate vows, promises, and confessions orally pronounced and heard.

Aside, therefore, from the substratum of nomos and ethos which is discovered incidentally as it lurks in Homer's verse, the mythos of the epic itself as announced in the preface and terminated in the nineteenth book is a paradigm of oral "justice," that is, of legal procedure as conducted in the early city-state. The didactic purpose of the storage epic emerges in the way the story is told. It may be objected that the *dikē* language actually present is scanty, and further that the epic after nineteen books has not completed itself. Action is transferred from the agora back to the battlefield, and the succeeding course of the story is dominated by the theme of Achilles' onslaught and its aftermath.

In the twenty-third book, however, the scene once more becomes an assembly of the Greeks, in the form of an *agōn,* or race meeting, which, however, is "seated."

The chief sporting event is the chariot race. Homer's extended description includes an account of some cheating that occurred during the race. The poet narrates how the teams of Antilochus and Menelaus ran almost neck and neck till Antilochus by a trick got ahead, and how Menelaus at the prize-giving ceremonies then blocked the award to Antilochus. Neither was placed first, but they had conducted a private and fierce competition for second place. Antilochus, behind Menelaus, lashed his horses to overtake his rival and draw close to him; he observes that they are approaching a narrow point in the course, where there is not room for two chariots to pass; he is just behind Menelaus; he swerves his team off the course to bypass him. Menelaus exclaims: "You fool! Wait! The way is narrow here, it will soon widen to allow your team to pass; otherwise, you will smash up both of us." Antilochus ignores the warning, Menelaus slackens pace to avoid the collision, Antilochus gets ahead, followed by the curses of Menelaus: "You dastard, damn you, you haven't any sense, as we Achaeans said; but don't think that you can carry off the prize (he means for second place) without swearing oath." Seventy-five lines later, the race ends, with Menelaus closing in on Antilochus; if the course had lasted longer, says Homer, "he would have bypassed him."

Diomede was first. The rest of the field in order of arrival are Antilochus, Menelaus, Meriones, and Eumelus. Achilles awards the prizes; there is no dispute over the winner, but Eumelus, who came in last, is judged by Achilles to have deserved second place, which an accident had prevented him from winning. Antilochus protests, and proposes instead a consolation prize for Eumelus, himself taking the second, to which Achilles accedes; whereupon Menelaus gets up in anger and presents a formal accusation against Antilochus of cheating, in support of his own claim to second place.

"Before them Menelaus stood up . . . and the herald placed the staff in his hand, and commanded silence upon the Argives. And Menelaus then addressed them." "You disabled my horses by casting yours in front"; this is his accusation. Then, turning to the audience and addressing them formally as "lords and leaders of the Achaeans," he invites them to intervene: "Apply justice to this," he says to them, using the verb *dikazō,* "in between both parties without favor"; he adds that he does not want any Greek to be able to say that Menelaus, pulling rank on Antilochus, used false statements to take the mare from him. Then he substitutes a second method: "No, I will do the justicing [*dikasō*] myself, without, I think, any risk of criticism; the justice [*dikē*] will be straight. Come here, Antilochus; take your stand as the formulary has it [*themis esti*]; stand in front of your horses, take the whip in your hand, touch the horses, and swear oath by Poseidon that you did not deliberately use guile to cripple my team."

Antilochus promptly gives in quite gracefully, saying in effect: yes, I did; I admit I was ignorant and rash, and I could not swear such an oath. Whereupon not only are the two reconciled, but Menelaus replies in effect: I forgive you, your youth prevailed over your senses; and he invokes the testimony of those present: "I am a man of kind heart, never arrogant." (pp. 123-35)

The episode conspicuously dramatizes the settlement of a dispute carried out orally in public and rendered effective because it is witnessed by the community acting as a body. Its "legality" depends upon an oath uttered by one party (or in this case declined) and heard by the other, in public, before witnesses. Equally, the episode illustrates how the procedure can be taken over by one of the litigants who himself becomes the utterer of a "justice" which is not less so because he speaks it. He does not pronounce a verdict, he demands one. The equity of his management is guaranteed in this case not only by the agreement of the opposite party but by the assent of the audience who would otherwise protest. Both parties know that what they say and do is "public."

A "justice," singular or plural (*dikē, dikai*), is something spoken aloud. This can be seen from an episode familiar to historians who have explored the origins of Greek law. The life-style of the city at peace as described on Achilles' shield is symbolized by two civic situations, a wedding ceremony and also a legal trial described as follows:

> The people were assembled en masse in agora. There a feud [*neikos*]
> had arisen; two men were feuding over penalty
> for a man killed. One claimed to have paid all of it,
> explaining to the demos; and the other said, no, he had taken nothing.
> Both parties were eager for a "knower" [*histōr*] to make a determination [*peirar*];
> the people were shouting for both, supporting this side and that;
> heralds were seating the people; and the elders
> sat upon polished stones in a sacred circle;
> and the staff of the heralds clear voiced they held in hands.
> They then rushed up to them and alternately argued the justice of it [*dikazon*];

there were placed in the midst of them two gold talents
to give to him who among them should speak justice
most straightly.

Oral law (themis) had forbidden Achilles to murder Agamemnon. Here too the same rule holds. Causing the death of a man in civil life can be redressed by payment of compensation in money, probably to a surviving relative. But there is no written record to attest such an act; the memories of the two parties concerned are the sole source of knowledge, and this situation can give rise to doubtful claims on one side or the other. A feud (*neikos*) is the result, to be settled by a comparison of oral statements, for which there is a proper procedure. For guidance, both parties resort to the "knower"; what he "knows" are "justices and formularies": his memory is stored with relevant information to guide the parties in their argument. The case, however, has to go before the seated agora of the "demos," where the oral machinery for settlement consists of two parts: the agora itself and the committee of elders,who have special seats (in front?). Their duty is that of regulating the order of speakers and listening to them. Do they vote, or simply preside over an agreement reached by the agora as to which side of the case wins, that is, is preferred? The "justice of it" is pleaded by the litigants in person, as it was by Menelaus; the decision will go to the rhetorician who can "state his justice most directly." The audience, previously divided, will be supposed to acclaim the winner; perhaps the elders address them before this happens. The award is placed on view, to be witnessed by the agora. Court discipline, if that is the best word, is regulated by heralds in charge of the seating and by the sight of the staff held in the hand held up to command silence; what is not stated, but may be inferable, is that the litigants receive the staff alternately from the elders before speaking. This kind of justice is not a set of preexistent principles or a set of rulings imposed by judges in the light of such principles. It is a symbol or a process achieved through oral persuasion and oral conviction.

One might expect that such legal proprieties might occasionally be encapsulated more explicitly in aphoristic or proverbial form. The ***Iliad*** contains one such example. Characteristically, it is occasioned by a simile. Describing the headlong rush of Hector's horses as they carry their owner away from Patroclus' onslaught, the poem compares it to a cloudburst resulting in a destructive flood which carries away the works of men; it is a hazard typical of valley settlements in mountainous country and therefore typically Greek. A cloudburst, however, is the work of Zeus, and so the verse supplies a motive for his intervention. The god acts in this way

when in anger with men he inflicts severities upon them
who by violence [*bia*] in agora adjudicate formularies
[*themistas*] crookedly
and drive out justice, regarding not awe of gods

The latter two lines propound the role which nomos requires by describing its negation. In oral citation the formulas of the tradition guarded in memory can be twisted or bent "crooked," that is, misquoted, or misapplied, to suit the interest of one party or the other. This is the error which in Homer's formula is stigmatized as "adjudicating" or perhaps "selecting" them "crookedly." The legal situation places the litigant before the agora where he and presumably his opponent have pleaded the case; he receives an adverse ruling based on precedents incorrectly used. He insists on arguing against it; his argument has "the justice of it" on its side; he has to be physically removed by force so that his "justice" is "expelled" from the agora; this is the concrete sense of the language employed. Nothing in the formula is inconsistent with the way *dikē* has operated elsewhere in the epic.There is no need to look for a late or post-Homeric source; the only difference is that elsewhere the procedure is memorialized by describing how it is applied, whereas here it is recommended by describing what happens when it is not applied. Both types of definition are conveyed by indirection, but less so in this negative example.

In sum, the "justice" of the ***Iliad*** is a procedure, not a principle or any set of principles. It is arrived at by a process of negotiation between contending parties carried out rhetorically. As such, it is particular, not general, in its references, and can be thought of either in the singular or in the plural—the "right of it" in a given case or "the rights" as argued and settled in one or more cases. There is no judiciary conceived as an independent state authority, but there are experts on oral "law"—men with specially equipped memories, one would guess. Judicial functions are mainly confined to presiding, listening, speaking, and sensing a consensus in the audience; they are shared or passed around indifferently between the experts, acting as "managers of justices," the elders or the contestants themselves, according to circumstance. The procedure takes place in public, because in a preliterate society the memory of the public is the only available attestation as to what is promised or agreed to. However loose or vague the procedure may appear from the standpoint of literate practice, it worked effectively to preserve "law and order" (*eunomia*) in the city-states of early Hellenism. It supplied those directive formulas which

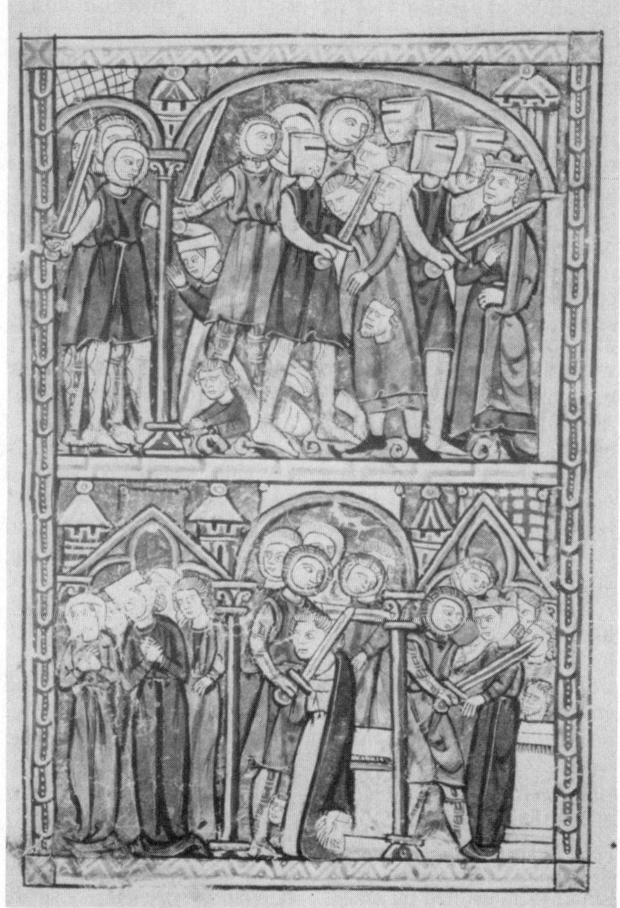

A seventeenth-century portrayal of the second sack of Troy.

were also corrective, a necessary supplement to the nomos and ethos as normatively taught and accepted. Such procedures may have been of immemorial origin, invented to control the impact of individuation upon nascent human communities.

But for disputes between competing city-states, the procedure was not available, because no common agora was available to allow it to function. Between Greeks and Trojans, "justice" cannot exist, only the inaction of peace or the activity of war. So *dikē* vanishes from the epic when Achilles takes the field, returning only when confrontation with the enemy is replaced by a fresh assembly and a fresh dispute between the Greeks themselves. (pp. 135-38)

Eric A. Havelock, "The Justice of the 'Iliad'," in his The Greek Concept of Justice: From Its Shadow in Homer to Its Substance in Plato, *Cambridge, Mass.: Harvard University Press, 1978, pp. 123-38.*

JASPER GRIFFIN (essay date 1980)

[*In the following excerpt, Griffin asserts that the* Iliad *is a poem meant to explain "the greatness and fragility of the life of man" and discusses the characteristics of the gods and the attitude toward battle and glory presented in the work.*]

With small exceptions, the serious poetry of Greece is concerned with the myths; and the subject of Greek mythology is the heroes. These are two obvious facts. Epic dealt with the "deeds of gods and men," and so did the choral lyric, while even the personal lyric is full of mythical narratives and excursions. Tragedy, too, tended to restrict itself to the mythical period, although the *Capture of Miletus,* by Phrynichus, and the *Persians,* by Aeschylus, show that this was not actually a rule. The mythical period was quite a short one, two or three generations about the time of the Theban and Trojan wars; the rest of the past, however vivid or striking in the memory, was felt to be different, and inappropriate for serious poetic treatment. Hence no tragedies about Pisistratus or Periander, the colonizing period, or the Lelantine War.

There was something special about that time. Heroes, we read, were bigger and stronger than we are—a hero of Homer could pick up and throw a rock which "nowadays two of the best men in a city could barely hoist on to a waggon"—but that is not the important thing. In that time gods intervened openly in human affairs, and it is their passionate concern and personal participation which marks heroic events as possessing significance. Aeschylus, brooding upon the morality of war and conquest, writes about King Agamemnon; Euripides, brooding upon the relation of the sexes, writes about Jason and Medea. An event like the murder of a husband by his wife, or a question like that of civil disobedience, is raised to the level at which it can be "seen" and taken seriously, when a poet writes of Clytemnestra or Antigone. In the epic, the divine presence and concern ensure that the story of Paris and Helen is a tragedy, not a mere spicy tale, and that the fall of Troy is not just one more disaster but an event of moral significance. The gods find nothing so enthralling as the spectacle of human heroism and suffering; their attention marks its importance, but equally their superiority marks its smallness in another perspective. The heroes were nearer to the gods than later men. "Born of Zeus," "nourished by Zeus," "honoured by Zeus"; these are standard epithets for Homeric kings and princes, and not less interesting are "loved by Zeus" and "god-like." "Like Zeus in counsel," "the equal of Ares," "a man equal to the gods," "god-like," "resembling the immortals," "divine," "with the appearance of a god," "honoured by his people like a god"—no reader of Homer needs to be told that these and other such epithets are among the commonest in the poems. Heroines, too, "have beauty from the goddesses" or "look like a goddess in face," and can be compared to Artemis or Aphrodite. A hero may be compared to several gods at once, as when Agamemnon is said to be "in eyes and head like Zeus who delights in thunder, in girdle like Ares, in chest like Poseidon." Priam says of his son Hector that "he was a god among men, and did not seem like the son of a mortal man but of a god." But these passages suggest complications, for Agamemnon is being led to disaster by Zeus, while Hector is dead, his body in the power of his ruthless enemy. What is it to be "god-like"?

There is one great difference between gods and men. Gods are deathless and ageless, while men are mortal. When Apollo thrusts Diomede back into the limits of his mortality, he shouts, "Reflect, son of Tydeus, and fall back; do not try to be the equal of the gods. Never is the race of immortal gods on a level with earthbound men." When Achilles is misled into attacking Apollo, the god says, "Son of Peleus, why do you pursue me, when you are a mortal and I a deathless god?" He declines to fight with Poseidon "for the sake of mortal men, wretched creatures, who one day flourish and another day are gone." The heroes who are "god-like" are subject to death, and we see them die. The epithets which belong to them as heroes contrast poignantly with their human fate. Sometimes the effect seems so light that it is not certain whether it is meant to be felt at all: as when in the boxing match the only challenger for the formidable Epeius is "Euryalus, that man equal to a god"—who is promptly knocked out and helped off by his friends, "with feet dragging, spitting out thick blood, with his head lolling to one side." Similarly light is the stress in a passage like that where Briseis tells the tragic story of her life: Achilles slew her husband and destroyed "the city of divine Mynes." The attentive listener is aware of a certain faint resonance, in the first case of irony, in the second of pathos.

More positively striking, perhaps, are such passages as those where old Nestor indulges himself in reminiscences of his great exploit in youth: "Would that I were young, as I was when I slew god-like Ereuthalion," and "Ereuthalion was their champion, a man the equal of gods . . . he was the biggest and strongest man I ever slew." Ereuthalion was a Goliath-figure whom nobody but the youthful Nestor dared to face; his great stature and terrifying power are dwelt upon by his slayer, who adds "He lay sprawling, far in both directions." He was like a god—but I slew him. The emphasis becomes, I think, clearly deliberate when we read of Paris, when he has gaily challenged any Achaean champion and Menelaus has appeared to fight him, that "When Paris, beautiful as a god, saw him appear, his spirit was dashed, and he slunk back into the ranks to avoid his fate. . . . So did he slip back into the body of the haughty Trojans, Paris as beautiful as a god, in fear of Atreus' son." For the poet makes it very clear that the beauty of Paris is what characterizes him, and is at variance with his lack of heroism: Hector at once rebukes him as "Evil Paris, great in beauty, woman-mad, seducer. . . ." and adds that "Your music and your gifts from Aphrodite, your hair and your beauty, would not help you when Menelaus brought you down in the dust." (pp. 81-4)

But the poet can find deeper notes of pathos and significance in this way. When "the god-like Sarpedon" is dead, his body fought over by the two armies, "then not even a discerning man would have recognized god-like Sarpedon, for he was covered with weapons and blood and dirt, from his head right down to his feet." Zeus, his father, keeps his shining eyes fixed on the struggle over the body of his son, unrecognizable in blood and dirt; that is all that remains of the handsome warrior Sarpedon, who in life was like a god. The epithet helps to bring out the human pathos, and also to underline the contrast of the human, even at its greatest and most attractive, and the really divine. When Achilles has killed Hector, he starts a paean of triumph over his body: "We have won a great victory: we have slain the god-like Hector, whom the Trojans adored like a god in Troy." Here the epithet, and the idea of adoration by one's fellow citizens, become a triumphant taunt, in which what was largely left implicit in the boasts of Nestor is fully developed. It becomes pathetic explicitly when Hecuba laments her son: "You were my pride night and day, and you were the defender of all the men and women of Troy, who hailed you like a god. Alive, you were their great glory; but now death and fate have caught you." The greatness of his fall and her loss emerge in this touching claim.

In the light of these passages I think it is clear that we are also to see force in the epithet "god-like" when it is used in the context of Hector's body being dishonoured by Achilles. Thus the poet tells us that after Achilles' triumphant paean "he wrought acts of humiliation on god-like Hector," piercing his ankles and dragging through the dust of his own country "his head that before was comely." The immediate juxtaposition of "god-like Hector" and "acts of humiliation" enables the poet to bring out, without sentimentality, the pathos of the greatest possible fall for a man, from god-like stature to humiliation and helplessness. I find the same technique repeatedly in the last book of the ***Iliad.*** "Achilles in his rage was abusing god-like Hector, and all the gods, looking on, felt pity for him." "He has tied god-like Hector to his chariot, having robbed him of his life, and is dragging him round the tomb of his friend. That is not right or good for him; we gods may grow angry with him, for all his strength; for he is abusing dumb earth in his rage"—so says Apollo, and we see in the speech of the god the full nature of man, at once capable of being "god-like" and also doomed to be "dumb earth." A last and rather different example: when Patroclus is called by Achilles to go on the mission which will lead to his return to battle and to his death, the poet, with unequalled economy and power, presents him in one line: "He came out, the equal of Ares; and that was the beginning of his doom." His greatness and his fragility emphasize and reflect upon each other.

The love of the gods for men is not less capable of bearing a range of emotional overtones. That great gods "loved" great kings was an age-old part of the belief of Egypt and the kingdoms of the Levant. There it was a simple and unambiguous conception. The god would be on our side and would frustrate the knavish tricks of our enemies; our king was the special favourite of mighty forces, and rebellion against him was as wicked as war against him was futile. Such an idea is to be found in Homer, as when Odysseus warns the Achaeans not to provoke their king Agamemnon: "Great is the anger of kings nourished by Zeus: their honours come from Zeus, and Zeus the Counsellor loves them." But the subject of the epic is not a simple and one-sided narration of "our" king's career of conquest, like an Assyrian or Egyptian historical inscription. Zeus honours Troy, he tells us himself, more than any other city under the starry heaven, and he loves Hector and his own son Sarpedon, on the Trojan side, no less than he loves Achilles and Patroclus, their slayers. And he loves Achilles, the opponent of Agamemnon, more than he loves the sceptred king himself, as Agamemnon is forced to learn.

Zeus loves Hector and Sarpedon, Patroclus and Achilles; but by the end of the ***Iliad*** three of the four are dead, and the fourth is to be slain very soon. He loves Troy, yet Troy will fall. He loves Agamemnon, but he sends a lying dream to him to deceive and defeat him. Odysseus, indeed, loved by Zeus and Athena, will survive, but that is the exception rather than the rule in the Homeric poems, and even he reproaches his patron goddess bitterly for her failure to protect him in his sufferings. Aphrodite claims that she has "loved exceedingly" the Helen whom she forces against her will into the shameless embrace of Paris:

> "Do not provoke me, wretch, lest I be angry and forsake you, and hate you even as I have exceedingly loved you; between both sides, Trojans and Achaeans, I shall devise bitter suffering for you, and you will come to a miserable end." So she spoke, and Helen, daughter of Zeus, was afraid. She followed in silence, shielding her face with her shining robe, and none of the Trojan women saw her; the goddess led the way.

That is what it might be like to be loved by a god.

Even the greatest of the sons of Zeus, Heracles himself, "who was the dearest of men to Zeus," did not for that escape suffering and disaster. Peleus, Hera tells us, was dear above all men to the immortal gods and all the gods attended his wedding to Thetis, but now he is alone and miserable, far away from his only son, who will never come home. Amphiaraus was "loved exceedingly by aegis-bearing Zeus and by Apollo, with all kinds of love; yet he did not reach the threshold of old age, but died at Thebes by reason of a woman's gifts"—betrayed to death by his wife for a bribe. The poet of the ***Odyssey*** tells us with inimitable objectivity that the singer Demodocus was blind: "the Muse loved him exceedingly, and she gave him both good and evil; she robbed him of his sight, but she gave him sweet singing." The ancients believed that Homer was a blind man, and that belief adds to the poignancy of his representation of another singer, his counterpart in his epic.

Zeus is a father to men, and Athena sometimes looks after a favourite "like a mother"; Zeus is said to "care for and pity" Priam in his misery. It has often been emphasized that the gods of Homer love the strong and successful, not the weak and poor, but it is wrong to think that means a straightforward idealizing of successful power and force. The gods love great heroes, but that love does not protect them from defeat and death. The heroes who engross the attention of the poet of the *Iliad* are those who are doomed—Sarpedon, Patroclus, Hector, Achilles; they it is whom the gods love, and who will exchange their strength and brilliance for the cold and darkness of death. As they come nearer to that terrible transition, the shining eyes of Zeus are fixed on them all the more attentively; he loves them *because* they are doomed. They in their mortal blindness cannot know, as the god allows them temporary triumph, that in his long-term plan they must die; the victories of Hector and Patroclus, which show Zeus' love for them, are in that perspective only a stage in their planned defeat and death.

The hero who is most often compared with the gods is Achilles. But not only is he said to be "god-like," but also we observe in action how like the gods he is, and above all how like Zeus himself. He has sacked twenty-three cities in the Troad, he boasts, and he numbers "Sacker of Cities" among his formulaic titles: Zeus "has brought down the towers of many cities and will bring down many more." His quarrel with Agamemnon over his "honour" . . . is reflected in heaven when Poseidon resents the claim of Zeus to higher rank. Zeus rubs in his quelling of Hera's attempted mutiny by saying, "In the morning, if you wish, you will see the paramount son of Cronus destroy the Argive host yet more, ox-eyed Lady Hera." In the same words Achilles tells the envoys of Agamemnon that despite all their pleas he will go home: "Tomorrow . . . you will see, if you wish, and if you are interested, my ships sailing at dawn on the Hellespont." He possesses a special cup, from which no man drinks but himself, and libations are poured to no god but Zeus. He is urged to "be like the gods," whose prepotent power does not prevent them from relenting and giving way to suppliants, but his nature is god-like in a different sense. Patroclus, who knows him better than any other man, says "You know what he is like; he is terrible. He may well blame the innocent." We remember what Iris says that Zeus will do, if his will is crossed: "He will come to Olympus to cast us into confusion; he will seize in succession on the guilty and the innocent." The poet even creates a parallel between the bringing of the mourning figure of Thetis before the gods on Olympus and the appearance of the mourning Priam before Achilles. In both scenes the incomer emerges from the darkness, dressed in mourning, and finds the other in the light, sitting at ease and drinking; the gods press a wine-cup into Thetis' hand; Achilles insists that Priam eat and drink with him.

But above all it is in being irresponsible and arbitrary that kings resemble gods. Achilles, we have seen, is apt to blame the innocent. The conduct to be expected of a king is viewed in the same light, and with the same apprehension, in both epics. Calchas asks in advance for a guarantee of protection before he names Agamemnon as the cause of the plague, "for a king is too powerful when he is angry with a man of lower rank: even if he digests his wrath for a time, yet he keeps his anger in his heart thereafter, to pay him out." In the same way we hear of Zeus: "if the Olympian does not bring it to pass at once, he brings it out in the end, and men pay for it dearly." Penelope describes the normal kingly behaviour, to which Odysseus was such an exception: "This is the custom of god-like kings: one man he will hate, another he will love—but Odysseus never did violence at all to any man." The gods, in their superior power, can be arbitrary. Kings, placed on the pinnacle of mortal power, try to emulate them. Agamemnon tries to treat Achilles with mere force, as he tried with the suppliant Chryses. In both cases a greater force defeats him. Achilles is asked to be like the gods and yield; he might have replied that he emulated the gods at least as well in refusing to yield to prayer. We see in the ***Iliad*** Zeus accept the sacrifices but reject the prayer of the Achaeans for an early victory, reject the prayer of both sides for a negotiated peace, disregard the passionate prayer of Asius, and plan disaster for the Achaeans though they pour anxious libations to him all night long; and we see Athena reject the prayers of the women of Troy. The motives which impel the gods to intervene in human affairs are personal and arbitrary, all-too-human in fact. Men try to act in the same way and come to grief, for Achilles, god-like beyond any other hero and indulging his passionate and arbitrary will in rejecting prayers which he knows to be right, causes the death of Patroclus and wishes only to die himself. While he lives, the hero is god-like and loved by the gods. In his martial rage, the high point and essence of his existence, he is like a lion, a wild boar, a storm, a river in flood, a raging forest fire, a bright star from a dark cloud; his armour blazes like the sun, his eyes flash fire, his breast is filled with irresistible fury, his limbs are light and active. The mere sight of his onset and the sound of his great battle-cry are enough to fill enemy heroes with panic. Encouraged by gods, even "thrust on by the mighty hand of Zeus," he mows down opponents like a reaper in a cornfield, like a wind scattering the foam of the sea, like a great dolphin swallowing little fishes. Men fall and are crushed under his chariot wheels, and he drives on, his chariot rattling over them. He challenges his opponent to single combat with insults and exults over his body, so that the defeated must die with the taunts of the victor in his ears. He then aims to strip off his armour and abolish his identity by depriving him in death of burial, and leaving his corpse to be mauled by scavenging animals and birds.

"To be alive and to see the light of the sun" is in the Homeric poems a regular phrase, along with "while I have breath in my lungs and my knees are active." To die, conversely, is to "leave the light of the sun" and to "go into the dark," or to have one's knees or limbs "undone." The ***Iliad*** is full of detailed accounts of the moment of death of the warrior. The poet dislikes any account of men being gravely wounded but not dying; a wounded man either dies quickly or recovers and fights again. The incurable Philoctetes is left far from Troy, groaning on the island of Lemnos; the Achaean chieftains wounded in Book II are healed and will return to battle. This works with the removal of chance as a possible cause of a hero's death (no arrow at a venture can kill a Homeric hero as Ahab or Harold were killed), and the virtual suppression of trickery and treason, and the fact that, in the poem, prisoners are no longer taken, all suppliants being killed. The effect of all this stylization is to concentrate attention as exclusively as possible on the position of the hero, face to face with his destiny at the hands of another hero: either he must kill or be killed, dying a heroic death.

When a hero dies, dark night covers him, he is seized by hateful darkness; he is robbed of his sweet life, his soul rushes forth from the wound; it goes down to Hades bewailing its fate, leaving behind its youth and strength. The doom of death covers his eyes and nostrils, his armour rings upon him, he breathes out his life in the dust, hateful fate swallows him up, he gluts the god of war with his blood. Stabbed in the back, he lies in the dust, stretching out his hands to his friends; wounded in the bladder, he crouches breathing his last, and lies stretched out on the earth like a worm. With a spear driven through his eye he collapses, arms spread wide, and his killer cuts off and brandishes his head; he lies on his back in the dust, breathing his last, while all his guts pour from his wound to the earth; he dies bellowing with pain, clutching the bloody earth, or biting the cold bronze which has severed his tongue, or wounded between the navel and the genitals, "where the wound is most painful for poor mortal men," writhing like a roped bull about the spear. His eyes are knocked out and fall bloody before his feet in the dust; stabbed in the act of begging for his life, his liver slides out and his lap is filled with his blood; the spear is thrust into his mouth, splitting his white bones, and filling his eye sockets with blood which spouts at his mouth and nose; hit in the head, his blood and brains rush from the wound. Wounded in the arm and helpless, he awaits his slayer, seeing death before him; his prayer for life rejected, he crouches with arms spread out waiting for the death-stroke. After death his corpse may be driven over by chariots, his hands and head may be lopped off, all his enemies may surround his corpse and stab it at their leisure, his body may be thrown into the river and gnawed by fishes, or lie unrecognizable in the mêlée. His soul goes down to a dark and comfortless world, to a shadowy and senseless existence, for ever banished from the light and warmth and activity of this life.

That is what the hero faces every time he goes into battle. It is clear in Homer that the soldier would, in general, prefer not to fight. Not only do the Achaeans rush for the ships and home, the moment they see a chance, but the rank and file need constant and elaborate appeals and commands to keep them in the field, and even heroes have at times to reason themselves into a fighting mood, and at others to be rebuked by their superiors or their comrades. Women attempt to hold them back from the battlefield, as we see in Book 6, where Hecuba, Helen, and Andromache in turn try to detain Hector in the safe and comfortable women's realm, but the true hero, like Hector, must reject the temptation and go. We are not dealing with berserkers in the pages of Homer, whatever Mycenaean warriors may have been like in reality. Self-respect, respect for public opinion, the conscious determination to be a good man—these motives drive the hero to risk his life; and the crowning paradox of the hero, the idea of inevitable death itself. "If we were to be ageless and immortal once we had survived this war," says Sarpedon to Glaucus, "then I should not fight in the fore-front myself, nor should I be sending you into the battle where men win glory. But in fact countless dooms of death surround us, and no mortal man can escape or avoid them: so let us go, either to yield victory to another or to win it ourselves." If the hero were really god-like, if he were exempt, as the gods are, from age and death, then he would not be a hero at all. It is the pressure of mortality which imposes on men the compulsion to have virtues; the gods, exempt from that pressure, are, with perfect consistency, less "virtuous" than men. They do not need the supreme human virtue of courage, since even if they are wounded in battle they can be instantly cured; and since they make no sacrifice for each other, as Hector does for his wife and child and Odysseus for his, their marriages, too, seem lacking in the depth and truth of human marriage. We see no union on Olympus which has anything of the quality of those of Hector and of Odysseus.

Death is constantly present in the hero's thoughts. Hector knows that Troy will fall, and hopes only that he will be dead and buried first. Before his duel with Ajax he makes careful provision for the burial and memorial to be allotted to the man defeated. Achilles describes his life, fighting and ravaging the Troad, "constantly exposing my own life in battle," and in his speech to Lycaon he says "I too am subject to death and cruel fate: there will be a morning or an evening or a noonday, when someone will take my life in battle, hitting me with a spear or an arrow from the bow-string." No hero, not even the greatest, is spared the shameful experience of fear. Hector runs from Achilles; Ajax is put to flight, "trembling and looking at the crowd of men like a wild beast"; Achilles himself is alarmed by Agenor's spear, and later, reduced by the attack of the River Scamander to seeing a miserable death apparently unavoidable, he is told by Poseidon, "Do not tremble too much nor be afraid." We have seen that in some ways the fighting described by Homer is highly stylized, and that it omits some of the characteristic horrors of war. Yet the audience remains convinced that in fact the poet has done full justice to its nature, that its frightfulness has not been palliated or smoothed over. That effect is achieved, in great part, because the poet insists on presenting death in its full significance as the end, unsoftened by any posthumous consolation or reward; in depicting it dispassionately and fully in all its forms; and showing that even heroes fear and hate it. The hero is granted by the poet the single privilege of dying a hero's death, not a random or undignified one, but that death haunts his thoughts in life and gives his existence at once its limitations and its definition.

It is in accordance with this overriding interest in human life, in its quality as intense and glorious yet transitory, and its position poised between the eternal brightness of heaven and the unchanging darkness of the world of the dead, that the Homeric poems are interested in death far more than they are in fighting. Homeric duels are short; heroes do not hack away at each other, exhausting all their strength and cunning, as do the heroes of Germanic epic or the knights of Malory. Recent work has emphasized the brevity and standardized character of these encounters. When a hero's time of doom has arrived, his strength is no use to him. The armour is struck from the shoulders of Patroclus by a god; Athena secretly gives back to Achilles the spear with which he has missed Hector, "and Hector, shepherd of the people, did not notice"—while as for his doomed opponent, when his death was foreshadowed by the Scales of Zeus, then "Phoebus Apollo abandoned him." In many killings the victim seems rather to wait passively for his death than to be killed fighting. The most powerful descriptions of death in battle are like that of Hector, recognizing that "the gods have called me to my death . . . now my destiny has caught me," and resolving to die fighting; Patroclus, disarmed and exposed helpless to death; Lycaon, arms outstretched, seeing death before him. Achilles, too, though the poem does not show his death, accepts and faces it; for this is what interests the poet very much, the sight of a hero succeeding in facing his own death. It is to produce and emphasize this situation that Homeric fighting is stylized as it is, when it might for instance have been developed much more as blow-by-blow accounts for the expert, interested in the technical details of fighting. The chariot race in Book 23 is treated much more in that manner. Walter Marg called the ***Iliad*** "the poem of death." I think it will be more appropriate to call it the poem of life and death: of the contrast and transition between the two. This is what the poet is concerned to emphasize, and on this he concentrates his energies and our gaze. It is part of the greatness of Achilles that he is able to contemplate and accept his own death more fully and more passionately than any other hero.

The reward of the warrior is glory. It has been argued recently that we can reconstruct with confidence some features of a very early Indo-European heroic verse lying behind Homer, and that phrases such as "deathless glory" and "widespread glory" are the most certain examples of expressions which can be traced back to that poetry. Whether or not these speculations are correct, it seems clear enough that the great themes of epic poetry, Germanic as well as Greek, go back far into the past. Heroic anger, revenge, pride, and suffering, are themes of many other stories in Greek, and of other Indo-European heroic literatures. Phoenix knows of many stories of heroic . . . anger and withdrawal, and is able to tell Achilles that when a hero of former time was seized, like Achilles himself, by a violent fit of anger, "they were prevailed on with gifts and won over with words." Achilles consoles himself in his enforced inaction by singing "the glorious deeds of men." We hear of some of these tales: of Heracles, Jason, Tydeus, Oedipus, Nestor, Bellerophon, Meleager. Already for Homer's characters their stories are paradigms for their own conduct: "You are not the man your father Tydeus was," "Do not make the same mistake as Meleager." "Even Heracles had to accept death." This status of being memorable and significant after death, the status which Homer's own characters have for him, is achieved by great deeds and great sufferings. Oedipus and Niobe remained in the memory for their terrible disasters, the others for their great achievements, although some, like Bellerophon, suffered greatly too.

Hector, in confident mood, hopes to kill an Achaean champion who answers his challenge: if he does, he will allow his body to be buried by his friends and a tomb raised over it, by the shore of the sea, so that passing sailors in time to come may say, "That is the grave of a hero of olden time, whom bright Hector slew in single combat." That is what they will say, says Hector, "and my glory will never die." The shooting of Menelaus brings glory to Pandarus. Hector's last words as he nerves himself for his despairing attack on Achilles are these: "At least let me not die unheroically and ingloriously, but achieving something great for men hereafter to hear." Achilles chose a heroic fate, short life, and deathless fame, rather than long inglorious existence, and when Patroclus is dead he accepts his own death—"but now let me win fair fame," by slaughtering Trojans and making their wives shriek as they wipe away their tears.

But in the Homeric poems glory is not a simple and straightforward thing, won by heroic deeds and consoling the hero for his death. We are far from the unreflective heroism of the Germanic lays. Helen sees herself as a character in history, whose sin has produced suffering for everyone. She invites Hector to sit down, "Since you above all are involved in trouble, because of me, bitch that I am, and the sin of Paris; Zeus has imposed an evil destiny upon us, so that in later times we may be a theme of song for generations to follow." It is surely a symbol for this that in Book 3, when she is fetched to watch the duel between Paris and Menelaus, she is discovered "weaving at the high loom, at work upon a crimson double cloth, and in it she was weaving many ordeals of the horse-taming Trojans and the Achaeans corseleted in bronze, which they were undergoing for her sake at the hands of the god of war." The detail, the description of what it was that Helen was weaving, is there because it is significant; when Andromache, by contrast, is discovered at her loom, we are told only that "she was weaving in many decorations." The point in the case of Andromache is that she was told by her husband, the last time we saw her, to attend to her housewifely work, her loom, and her servants; the faithful wife obeyed her husband, and we find her carrying out his instruction. The pattern of her weaving is not important. In the case of Helen, on the other hand, it is important, because it shows her as aware of her own role in causing all the distress. What she makes in Book 3 is exactly what she says in Book 6. This Helen is the same conception as we find in the ***Odyssey,*** when she unexpectedly produces a present of her own for the departing Telemachus, a woman's garment which she has made herself. Placing it in his hand she says, "I too give you a present, a keepsake of the hands of Helen, for your bride to wear on the joyous day of your wedding." She is aware that the dress will have special value because of its maker, and refers to herself in the third person, as a figure in history; any bride will be flattered to wear what the legendary Helen made. And Helen is a legendary figure not for her great achievements, not even for her womanly virtue, like Penelope, but for her guilt and suffering.

The whole disaster of Achaeans and Trojans at Troy, says Alcinous, was devised by the gods, so that out of the destruction of men there should be a theme for song in later generations. The disastrous return of the Achaeans from Troy is the theme of a song, and Telemachus tells his mother that she should listen to it and realize that many others besides herself have had suffering decreed for them by Zeus. Achilles says the Achaeans will long remember his disastrous quarrel with Agamemnon, and we see in the ***Odyssey*** that a comparable quarrel, between Achilles and Odysseus, was the subject of an epic lay. Demodocus the singer is blind; the lyre on which Achilles accompanies himself as he sings of the "glorious deeds of men" is one which he captured when he sacked Thebe, the city of Eetion. There, as we know from Andromache, he slew her father and her seven brothers, and left her alone in the world. Suffering produces song, and by song we understand that suffering is universal for men, comes from the gods, and must be accepted. And glory is attached particularly to the tomb of the dead, while the glorious death which Hector finally achieves is no comfort to his defenceless family and friends, upon whom the emphasis falls.

Such a treatment of the idea of glory is a sophisticated one. Not only general probability, and the evidence of such simpler epics as *Beowulf,* force us to believe that behind Homer there lay a tradition in which it was seen far more simply; the fact that in the epics themselves no fewer than twenty-four persons, male and female, bear names which are compounds of . . . "glory," points strongly in the same direction. The parents who bestowed such names on their children meant to associate them with an unambiguously splendid thing. But the poet, who transforms a story of the sack of a city, a perfectly ordinary event common in the Dark Ages, into the vast and tragic tale of Troy, and who develops the heroic theme of revenge with the same sort of moral complexity, allows his hero to brood upon glory, too. Achilles has been told that the price of glory for him is a short life; he will not return from Troy, if he chooses the heroic path. The straightforward heroic choice can be illustrated by the great hero Cúchulainn of the Ulster cycle. As a boy he learned that he who took up arms for the first time on a certain day would be a mighty warrior, "his name would endure in Ireland . . . and stories about him would last forever." He seized the opportunity. "'Well,' Cathbad said, 'the day has this merit: he who arms for the first time today will achieve fame and greatness. But his life is short.' 'That is a fair bargain,' Cúchulainn said. 'If I achieve fame I am content, though I had only one day on earth.'" But Achilles, who has duly chosen the heroic path, is filled with bitterness as he broods on Agamemnon's treatment of him. Agamemnon tries to persuade him by the offer of enormous presents and the promise that he will "honour him like his only son"; the presents are marks of honour (not merely a bribe), as we see clearly when Phoenix says, "If you return to battle without the presents, you will not be so highly honoured, even if you repel the attack."

But for Achilles the gifts have lost their symbolic value and become mere objects, in the light of the humiliation he has suffered at the hands of the king. If that is the way he is to be treated, when he has been acting as a true hero, risking his life and fighting with men defending their women-folk, then there is no honour to be won; coward and hero are given the same honour, man of action and man of sloth must both alike die. And from this point of view the thought of inevitable death ceases to be the stimulus to heroism: why should Achilles not toddle safely home and die in bed? As for the gifts, mere things can be no compensation for the loss of a man's life, so that Achilles is perfectly logical to demand infinite, impossible quantities of them before he will change his mind—"not even if he gave me ten and twenty times as much, all that he has and more, as much as makes its way to Orchomenus or to Thebes in Egypt . . . even if he gave me as much as the sand of the sea and the dust of the earth, even so would Agamemnon not change my purpose." And in fact Achilles does not return for gifts, to which in Book 19 he remains indifferent, nor does he really regain his belief in heroism. Sitting with Priam in the last book he still sees the war in an unheroic light. As in Book 9 he spoke bitterly of "fighting with men who are defending their women-folk," and in Book 19 of "waging war for the sake of hateful Helen"—an intensely unheroic view of the struggle—so here he speaks of himself yet more movingly. "My father Peleus was happy once and honoured by the gods, but he had only one son after all, doomed to an untimely death; and I am not even looking after him as he grows old, since I have been sitting here by Troy, far from home, causing grief to you and your children." At the point from which Achilles speaks now, glory is shrunk to an inconsiderable thing. Priam reminds him of his own father, old and unhappy, and he sees himself making pointless war, no good to either side. Priam asks for a truce of eleven days for the funeral of Hector, and says, "Then on the twelfth day we will fight, if we must." For both Priam and Achilles the war has become an endless process, unrewarding and meaningless, from which they cannot extricate themselves.

The ***Odyssey*** develops similar ideas, but in a rather different manner. In the ***Iliad*** Achilles expresses profound disenchantment with glory as the reward of the hero, but heroic he still remains. To the last he is a fighter, even when he has by suffering attained a perspective like that of Zeus, who "has sacked many cities and will sack many more." In the ***Odyssey,*** Odysseus meets him among the dead, and congratulates him on his felicity: honoured like a god in life, he is mighty among the dead thereafter. Achilles rejects the compliment. There is no consolation for death; he would prefer to be in the lowest position in the world, the servant of an impoverished master, than to be king of all the dead. Agamemnon himself, the sacker of Troy, of whom Odysseus says that "his glory is now the greatest under heaven, so great a city he has sacked and destroyed many people," and to whom his son Orestes built a tomb "so that his glory might be inextinguishable," asks bitterly, in the lower world, "What joy have I in it, that I have endured the war to the end? Zeus planned a cruel return home for me at the hands of Aegisthus and my accursed wife." Menelaus, happily home with Helen and his accumulated treasures, tells his guests that he would give up two-thirds of his possessions to undo the effects of the Trojan War and to have alive again all the men who perished there, far from home; often does he sit in his palace and weep for them. Nestor can say only that the tale of Troy is a tale of woe, . . . "all that we suffered by land and sea"; "there all the best of us were slain: there lies war-like Ajax, there lies Achilles, and Patroclus, and my own dear son. . . . Not even if you were to sit by me and question me for five years and for six years, could I tell you all the sufferings of the god-like Achaeans at Troy."

This passive view regards heroic achievement and endurance in the light of mere suffering inflicted, and looks back on it with self-pity, not with pride. Odysseus himself, when he begins his narration of his career to the Phaeacians says "Your heart has inclined to ask me of my grievous sufferings, so that I may mourn and lament yet more. What first then shall I tell of, what last? The Olympian gods have given me woes in plenty. . . . I am Odysseus, Laertes' son; men know of me for my many wiles, and my fame has reached heaven." To Agamemnon he says flatly that "for Helen's sake many of us were slain," the least heroic description of the Trojan War as a whole. When he and his Penelope are finally united, they each tell the other their experiences: "They took delight in the tales they told each other. The queen told of all that she endured in her house from the suitors . . . and Odysseus, sprung from Zeus, told of all the griefs he had brought upon men and of all his own travail and suffering. And she listened with delight. . . ." The Phaeacians, too, are held spellbound by Odysseus' recital of his "sufferings" and beg him to go on, receiving from him the reply that "I should not grudge telling you even more moving sufferings of my companions."

From suffering comes song, and song gives pleasure. In the ***Odyssey*** it is presented with a rather more plaintive tone, in the ***Iliad*** the light is rather more robust, but the picture is not really different. Without his "woes in plenty," the fame of Odysseus would not have reached heaven. Without the accursed wrath of Achilles, which made many noble heroes into food for scavenging dogs and birds, there would have been no ***Iliad.*** The Homeric hero is anxious for glory, and he faces the full horrors of death. But as there is no posthumous reward for the brave man in the other world, so the consolation of glory is a chilly one. Odysseus, sacker of cities, "brought many griefs upon men" in his wanderings; as he tells us himself, at the very beginning of his recital, "from Troy the wind took me to Ismarus: there I sacked the city and slew the men." But by the end of his wanderings he has lost all the booty he gained, his own men are all dead, and it all seems to have been as futile as the raids he tells of in his false tales. Achilles "sits by Troy, causing grief to Priam and his sons." These terrible events produce glory, but we are not dealing with heroes for whom that is an adequate reward. . . . The hero dies, not so much for his own glory, not even so much for his friends,

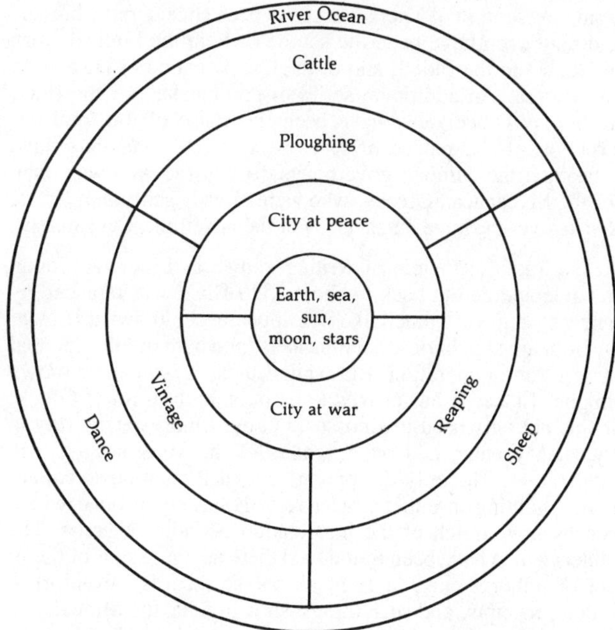

A chart of the pattern of images portrayed on the shield of Achilles. From A Companion to the Iliad, *by Malcolm M. Willcock. The University of Chicago Press, 1978. © 1976 by The University of Chicago. All rights reserved. Reproduced by permission of the publisher.*

as for the glory of song, which explains to a spellbound audience the greatness and fragility of the life of man. (pp. 84-102)

Jasper Griffin, "Death and the God-like Hero," in his Homer on Life and Death, *Clarendon Press, Oxford, 1980, pp. 81-102.*

DENISON BINGHAM HULL (essay date 1982)

[In the following excerpt from the introduction to his translation of the Iliad, *Hull, an American Greek scholar, discusses the history of the Trojan War.]*

The real history that lies behind the legends of the Trojan War, might be said to begin some time around 2800 B.C. when invaders speaking an Indo-European tongue called Luwian invaded the Troad, and, pushed on by a second wave in 2500 B.C. settled the western coast of Asia Minor. About 1900 B.C. two other invasions of Asia Minor occurred: one was that of the Hittites, who came from the northeast, perhaps in the area of the Pontic steppes, and spoke another Indo-European tongue, and Greek-speaking peoples from the northwest, possibly from Bulgaria, who not only settled in northern Greece, but also occupied the Troad, and pushed the Luwian-speaking peoples still farther south. The Greeks brought the horse with them.

The Hittite kingdom expanded rapidly, and in about 1600 their king, Hattushili I, built his first capital at what is now known as Bogasköy. The Greek speaking people were expanding even more rapidly, and had already reached the southern end of the Peloponnesus, and had begun to settle in Crete. Then, in about 1520, came the first of a series of disasters. The volcanic island of Thera erupted with a force much greater than that of any eruption ever known to man: it was nearly four times as great as that of Krakatoa in August, 1883, which laid waste large parts of the East Indies, and killed 36,000 people; tidal waves rising to over 120 feet were recorded. The tidal waves resulting from the eruption of Thera must have been considerably higher, and may even have been the source of both the biblical story of Noah and the Flood, and of the Greek legend of Deucalion and Pyrrha. An additional series of earthquakes, or the flood itself may conceivably have been the cause of the final destruction of the palace of Knossos in Crete, and thus have weakened the Minoan government so that the way was open for the Mycenaean Greeks, who were already settling in Crete, to take over the huge bureaucracy of the government in Knossos.

At any rate the system of writing known as Linear A, found in Crete and dating back to about 1570 B.C., was replaced by a new system very much like it in appearance, known as Linear B. Both are syllabaries, not alphabets, and both use the decimal system for enumeration. But while Linear A is in an unknown tongue, Linear B has proved to be in an early form of Greek. It was not only used in Knossos, but even more extensively in Pylos, Mycenae, and other centers of the Mycenaean Greek civilization. The only disappointment, if it must be so called, is that nothing in either Linear A or B has been found which can by any stretch of the imagination be called literary. The tablets which have been found (and there are thousands of them) are of unburnt clay, and are all palace records, inventories, orders, receipts, and such things, showing that the Minoan and Mycenaean governments were run by heavily staffed bureaucracies that kept an eye on everything that went on in their realms. As far as the Homeric poems are concerned, the decipherment of Linear B throws absolutely no light on them, a fact which is a sad disappointment compounded by the fact that even Linear B seems to have faded out some time soon after the final destruction of the palace of Knossos, and the alphabet was not introduced into Greece before the first Olympiad, 776 B.C., at the earliest.

Meanwhile both the Hittite Empire and the power of the Mycenaean Greeks were growing. Politically the world of the Homeric epics was divided like a sandwich: on the west was Mycenae and its Greek city-state associates; on the east was the Hittite Empire, which covered the parts of Anatolia which in classic times would be called Phrygia, Cappadocia (except the seacoast), Cilicia, Syria and Phoenicia. In the middle was Arzawa, a loose confederation of states which included all but the seacoast of Lycia, Lydia, and Caria; and another federation farther north, Assuwa, which the Greeks called Asia; it included states on the seacoast between Lydia and the Troad. Boundaries are nowhere given, and are almost impossible to define. The Mycenaean Greeks had established a colony in Miletus, and had settled the island of Rhodes, which the Hittites called Ahhiyawa, confusing the part with the whole, which was, of course, Achaea, or Mycenaean Greece.

The Achaeans had been trading with Troy—though we must bear in mind that trading was by means of barter, as money had not yet been invented—for centuries, and since the apparently peaceful conquest of Crete, had continued the Cretan trade with the southwest coast of Asia Minor, although for some reason not quite clear, had never been able to do any business with the coastal cities of Assuwa. But, in spite of that fact, the Achaeans, led by Mycenae, continued to expand.

The Hittite Empire, however, in spite of outward signs of prosperity, was on the verge of disaster, and one of the agents of its collapse was a trouble maker named Madduwattas, who would probably have been unable to cause as much havoc as he did if the empire had not already become shaky. Madduwattas wrote to the Great King of the Hittites to complain that he had been driven off his land by an Achaean named Attarssijas, whose name might conceivably be Atreus, although there is no reason to believe he was the father of Agamemnon and Menelaus. Anyway Madduwattas wanted help. The Hittites gave him a small place of his own, Zippasla, and made him swear he would not make war on the Hittites' friends. But Madduwattas attacked the ruler of Arzawa, the strongest state in southwest Asia Minor, was defeated, and had to be rescued again. Next the Achaean, Attarssijas, threatened him, and fled. Again the Hittites rescued him by defeating Attarssijas. After a period of quiet, the towns of Hinduwa and Dalawa offended the Hittites. The Hittite general, Kisnapilis, was sent to punish them. Madduwattas saw another chance, and proposed that while the general attacked Hinduwa, he, Madduwattas, would attack Dalawa to prevent its coming to the aid of Hinduwa. But instead, he persuaded the Dalawans to join him and the Hinduwans in defeating the Hittite general. They did, and Madduwattas then took Dalawa for himself.

Next Madduwattas asked the ruler of Arzawa to come to his house to discuss marriage with his (Madduwattas') daughter, and to talk about a new treaty. The ruler of Arzawa came, and was never seen again, so that in about 1385 Madduwattas was able to take control of Arzawa. Yet, in spite of the erosion of its western boundary, the Hittite state seemed to be expanding.

At the same time the Mycenaean state was enlarging its bureaucracy. Tablets in Linear B, in Greek, were in use for clerical purposes in Crete, Pylos, Mycenae and Thebes, all dating from this time. We are sure of our dates here, because in 1335 there was a solar eclipse during the reign of the Great King Murshili II.

Before the end of the reign of Murshili II had ended, the Hittites had another trouble maker on their hands. A certain Tawagalawas, whose name some scholars equate with Eteocles (Etewokleweios), although there is some evidence that he was not an Achaean, wished to become a vassal of the Hittite king, and was accepted on condition that his troops would not fight against the Hittites. Yet in the very next town the king found them fighting his troops, and so he defeated them, and took 7000 prisoners. A Hittite, Pijamaradas, stole the prisoners, and took them to Miletus. The Hittite king then wrote the Achaean king in Rhodes about it, but got a surly answer and no prisoners. So the Hittite king entered Miletus and found Tawagalawas and Pijamaradas already gone. When asked to return Pijamaradas, the Achaean king refused. The Hittite king then offered to send a relative of his own wife as hostage in return for Pijamaradas.

Yet this same king could have taken by force the very things he is begging for. His timidity is shown also by the fact that he had moved the capital of his empire from Hattusha to Dattashshash the same as if he felt in danger. Yet only fifteen years later he was to claim that he had defeated the Egyptians in the battle of Qadesh (the Egyptians claimed otherwise), and the next Hittite king, Murshili III, was to move the capital back to Hattusha again three years later. Alternating fear and boldness seem to indicate signs of weakness in the Hittite Empire, particularly when the next king, Tuthalija, put on a campaign in Assuwa in 1250. At any rate the signs of weakness were real indications of the condition of the Empire, for it collapsed in 1210, and disappeared completely.

The political power structure in western Asia Minor had been built on the principle that was followed so often in western Europe later: keep on friendly terms with the state on the far side of your next door neighbor, so that, in case of war, he will be faced by enemies on two fronts. The Mycenaeans had kept on reasonably good terms with the Hittites, but could not open up Assuwa to trade, in spite of the fact that they had been trading with Troy for centuries, and that their colony at Miletus and their settlements on Rhodes had been trading with the other coastal cities farther south for years. The Hittites had been an influence for peace as long as they were able to control the policies of Arzawa. With Madduwattas at the helm, Arzawa was unpredictable, and the leadership of the coastal cities fell to Assuwa. Almost any incident might start trouble, and there had been a series of incidents all through the centuries of the Heroic Age, if we may put any trust in legends.

Legends, of course, are not as reliable as Hittite inscriptions, for the Hittites could, and did, write at that time. But when they fit the situation, they are plausible if not solid evidence. The first legend was that of the abduction of Io, daughter of Inachus, king of Argos, by Phoenician traders. Whether she went unwillingly, or, as Herodotus says, willingly, in order to conceal her pregnancy, the episode was an insult to the Argives. The second incident was the abduction of Europa, daughter of Agenor, king of Tyre, by Cretans who, so Herodotus believes, were Greeks. The bull which carried her across the sea was obviously a bit of fantasy, but the abduction may have been historical. Her name is supposed to be nothing more than the eponym of the continent of Europe, for the Greeks were fond of inventing people for whom places were named. But it may have been a nick-name, ''Broad-face,'' or ''Wide-eyes,'' just as Plato's name is said to have been derived from his broad shoulders.

The abduction of Europa evened the score. But then Jason in the good ship Argo reached Colchis at the eastern end of the Black Sea, and ran off with Medea, daughter of Aeetes, the king. None of these episodes can be dated, but the Argo had sailed past Scylla and Charybdis before Odysseus did, and was therefore at least a generation before the Trojan War. The score was again evened by the abduction of Helen, wife of Menelaus, king of Sparta and richest man in Greece, as well as brother of Agamemnon, king of Mycenae, the most powerful of the kings in Greece. It was Menelaus' status that made this abduction so humiliating. An expedition against Troy to bring her back was planned and launched, but when the Achaean fleet arrived at Troy, and demanded the return of Helen, she wasn't there, and nobody knew where she was. Herodotus tells us that Paris' ship had been blown off course, and had landed in Egypt, where the Egyptians compelled him to leave her with them until the war was over. When there are contradictory legends, one or both may be fantasy, but in this case if she had been taken straight to Troy, neither Priam, the king, nor Hector, the heir to the throne and best of the Trojan fighters, is likely to have wanted to risk a war against the huge army Agamemnon brought, over a woman. But Achilles and many of the other Achaeans began raiding the countryside for food, loot, and prizes such as Chryseis and Briseis, and the neighboring state of Assuwa, which was the victim of many raids, objected. In common interest Troy and Assuwa became allied, and as the Achaeans refused to believe that Helen was not in Troy, and as they would have lost face, as well as chances to raid for loot, if they had turned around and gone home after all the preparations and publicity, they did not want to lose face by going home again. This, then, is one way the war may have started. (pp. xvii-xxii)

Denison Bingham Hull, in an introduction to Homer's Iliad, *translated by Denison Bingham Hull, N.p., 1982, pp. xiii-xxx.*

SETH L. SCHEIN (essay date 1984)

[In the following excerpt, Schein provides an overview of Homer's attitude toward heroism and death in the Iliad. *He focuses on the concept of* aristea, *''the main compositional unit of battle narrative'' in the poem, and particularly on its meaning for Achilles. Noting that the view of death presented in the* Iliad *is a complex and balanced one, Schein deems the epic a poem about mortality in which ''to be fully human . . . means to kill or be killed for honor or glory.'']*

The ***Iliad*** has been called ''from beginning to end a poem of death.'' This description is obviously accurate in a literal sense: the poem begins with an invocation to the muse to sing the *mēnis,* the ''wrath,'' of Achilles, ''which hurled forth to Hades many strong souls / of heroes and made them [the heroes] prey for dogs / and all the birds''; it ends with a description of the burial of Hektor. More generally, most of the action of the epic consists of Greeks and Trojans killing one another. By the end, Hektor, the main figure on the Trojan side, has been killed and his city symbolically sacked; Achilles, the chief figure on the Greek side and the central character in the poem, has lost and buried his beloved comrade Patroklos and, by killing Hektor, has in effect brought about his own death, which has been repeatedly prophesied and prefigured. The funeral games of Patroklos in Book 23 and the mourning and burial of Hektor in Book 24 are, in a sense, not only for these two heroes but for everyone in the poem. They form a ritually appropriate, aesthetically and spiritually satisfying conclusion to the relentless killing and dying; they help us, as well as the Greeks and Trojans, to endure the pain and loss entailed in being mortal.

Yet one could also argue that "from beginning to end" the ***Iliad*** is a poem of life, or, as E. Vermeule has suggested, a poem "of mortality and mortal accidents, and of the kinds of behavior only mortals need have to confront these." In the world of the poem, war is the medium of human existence and achievement; bravery and excellence in battle win honor and glory and thus endow life with meaning. Heroes affirm their greatness by the brilliance and efficiency with which they kill. The flashing action of a warrior's triumph represents the fullest realization of human potential, despite the pain and loss for the victim, his family, and his community. And even for the victim, death that "yields glory to another" can be more than simply pain and loss. Some glory can be won, too, by dying bravely, in an act that sums up and puts a seal on a life lived in accordance with the generally acknowledged standards of heroic "excellence" (*aretē*). Thus when Hektor realizes that Athene has tricked him and that he is about to die at Achilles' hands, he says, "At least let me not perish without a struggle, ingloriously / but after having done something great, for future generations to learn of." (pp. 67-8)

Homer's descriptions of killing and dying are traditional and formulaic in action and style, but as always he selectively reworks the tradition in accordance with the characteristic themes of his poem and achieves a depiction of human existence that is distinctively Iliadic. The main reason why winning honor and glory in war can endow life with meaning is that in the world of the ***Iliad*** there is no significant afterlife. For Homer, as Vermeule says, "The realm of death is more a series of standard expressions and a few deliberately pointed contrasts [with life] than a serious focus of imagination." The word *psuchē,* usually translated "soul," has none of the intellectual or spiritual significance that it came to have for later Greeks and for the West. Etymologically, *psuchē* seems to mean "wind-breath." In the ***Iliad*** it is simply an entity that, when it is in a human body, makes that body alive, and that, when a person is killed, departs to Hades; there it is a ghost, with no significant physical or mental existence. The *psuchē* is not particularly important for Homer, who contrasts to the "souls" (*psuchas*) hurled forth to Hades the "selves" (*autous*) left as prey for dogs and birds. This conception of the body as the "self" both accounts for Homer's much greater concern with what happens to bodies than with what happens to "souls" and explains his characters' sense that what counts is what one can do and win and suffer in the only life there is for a mortal.

This was not always the case in the poetic tradition. In Hesiod's *Works and Days,* for example, after death the mortals of the golden race live on as good "divinities" (*daimones*) above the earth, watching over mortal men, keeping evil away from them, and rewarding them with prosperity; those of the silver race survive death as "blessed mortals below the earth," that is, as heroes with hero cults. In the ***Odyssey*** Menelaos, because he is Helen's husband and Zeus' son-in-law, will not die but will be sent to the Elysian plain to live "the life that is easiest for mortals"—a life like a god's. But in the ***Iliad,*** regardless of what the audience may have expected from their familiarity with the traditional conceptions of an afterlife, Homer suppresses all mention of any continued or posthumous existence for mortal warrior-heroes.

Homer's attitude toward heroism can be seen in the very word *hērōs,* which elsewhere denotes a figure worshipped in hero cults, but in the ***Iliad*** signifies a warrior who lives and dies in the pursuit of honor and glory. *Hērōs* seems to be etymologically related to the word *hōrē,* "season." Although a "hero" might originally have been "seasonal" in the sense of going through the cycle of seasons and being, as it were, reborn when the cycle begins anew—that is, as an immortal "hero" to be worshipped in cult—in Homer *hōrē* means in particular the "season of spring," and a "hero" is "seasonal" in that he comes into his prime, like flowers in the spring, only to be cut down once and for all. [The] Greek army is compared in numbers to the leaves and flowers that arise "in the season," and in a famous passage Glaukos, speaking to Diomedes, compares the generations of leaves to those of men: the wind pours some down to the ground, and the living stock puts forth others when the season of spring returns. As befits an aristocrat boasting of his family tree in a passage that ends with an affirmation of ancestral guest-friendship between the two opposing fighters, Glaukos puts his emphasis as much on the stock that survives to put out new leaves as on the leaves that bloom and are poured to the ground like dead warriors. Still, we can see that the vegetal imagery expresses the ***Iliad***'s conception of a hero as a mortal who fights and dies with no afterlife as his reward other than the glory of celebration in epic song.

In the ***Iliad,*** although death can be a source of anxiety for mortals, it "is not the enemy of creativity but its cause, since the contemplation of death is the single factor that makes us long for immortality." As Sarpedon says to Glaukos, "If . . . we two were going to be unaging and immortal forever, / neither would I myself fight in the front ranks / nor would I send you into the battle where men win glory. / But as it is, since the spirits of death stand over us / numberless, which it is not possible for a mortal to flee or avoid, / let us go—either we will give glory to boast of to someone else, or someone will give it to us." (pp. 68-70)

[Since] the gods by definition are "unaging and immortal," they can neither win nor lose significant glory. Since they cannot die, they risk nothing; for this reason their existence, compared with that of mortals, is trivial. They emphasize by contrast the seriousness of the human condition, in which winning honor and glory alone makes a brief life meaningful and enables an individual to stand out in his own and in others' eyes.

Winning honor and glory, however, makes life meaningful not only because humans are mortal but also because of the social value system that is normative throughout the poem. This value system is most clearly stated earlier in the same speech of Sarpedon to Glaukos:

> Glaukos, why, then, are we two especially honored
> with a seat of honor and with meats and with full wine goblets
> in Lykia, and all look at us as at gods
> and we are assigned a great estate by the banks of the river Xanthos,
> a fine one of vineyard and wheat-bearing plowland?
> Therefore it now is right that among the front ranks of Lykians
> we stand and encounter the blazing battle,
> so that someone of the Lykians who wear thick armor will say:
> "By no means without glory do they rule Lykia—
> our kings—and they eat fat sheep

and drink exquisite, honey-sweet wine; but their
strength, too,
is good, for they fight among the front ranks of
Lykians.''

This same code of values is illustrated by the dispute between Agamemnon and Achilles in Book 1, which turns on Achilles' sense that in violation of the societal norm he has been robbed of the honor he has earned.

This ''honor'' is not merely an abstraction. The basic meaning of *timē,* ''honor,'' is ''price'' or ''value'' in a tangible sense. The word can be used of a woman like Briseis, who was a *geras* or special ''gift of honor'' from the army to Achilles, as well as of the seat of honor, full wine goblets, meats, and fertile land mentioned by Sarpedon as rewards for prowess in battle and reasons for continued bravery and achievement. Those who win such tangible honors also receive honor conceived abstractly; from this comes their *kleos,* ''glory and reputation,'' what is said about them near and far, even when they are dead. To be sure, in the course of the ***Iliad*** Achilles comes to question and contradict the validity of the normative social value system. This disillusionment enhances Achilles' tragedy and constitutes part of Homer's critical exploration of the nature and conditions of heroism and of human life. Nevertheless, for Achilles and for everyone else in the poem, there is no real alternative. Life is lived and death is died according to this code of values: to be fully human—that is, to be a hero—means to kill or be killed for honor and glory.

The human situation in the ***Iliad*** might well be called tragic, because the very activity—killing—that confers honor and glory necessarily involves the death not only of other warriors who live and die by the same values as their conquerors, but eventually, in most cases, also of the conquerors themselves. Thus, the same action is creative or fruitful and at the same time both destructive and self-destructive. Odysseus states the situation well and plainly when he says to Agamemnon, ''Would that you were giving signals to some other, vile army, / and were not lord over us, to whom Zeus / has given from our childhood even to our old age to wind up the thread / of difficult wars, so that finally we perish, each of us.''

The fact that ''each of us'' will perish through the very warfare that makes life meaningful indicates the cost as well as the rewards of the heroism Homer celebrates. When a warrior dies, limbs which have been warm and active become cold and still. Darkness prevails where eyes had previously been bright. Feelings of love for and solidarity with comrades, family, and native land are suddenly ended. Though Homer's account of the war may appeal to different emotions at different places in the poem, he never becomes naively sentimental or thoughtlessly brutal about death. He balances equally the greatness of the slayers and the pathos of the slain.

The Homeric attitude toward death is especially clear in the descriptions of the fates of numerous minor warriors, the little heroes who exist merely to be killed, whose deaths are the occasions for brief remarks or vignettes about their lives and manner of dying. As Jasper Griffin has demonstrated, these ''lesser heroes are shown in all the pathos of their death, the change from the brightness of life to a dark and meaningless existence, the grief of their friends and families. . . .'' Certain motifs recur in their ''obituaries'': a man's life was brief; he died far from home and family; his comrades or parents or wife and children were bereaved; they were unable to help him and could not make good his loss. When the husband or son is young or newly married, the description of the death is especially moving; when emphasis is placed on the victim's ignorance of what was in store for him, or on his beauty and potential cut short, we are even more affected. Clearly, many of these motifs were traditional, but they are integrated with important themes of the ***Iliad*** itself. For example, as Griffin points out, ''The bereaved father is a dominant figure in the plot from Chryses to Priam, who appeals to Achilles in the name of another tragic father, Peleus.'' And all the young warriors who fall far from their parents and wives, whose comrades can do nothing for them, who die even as their ignorance of destiny becomes certain knowledge, culminate in Hektor. The descriptions of the deaths of the minor heroes help to create by their content and tone the consistent, unsentimental view of death and of life, that we think of as Homeric. They help us to interpret the overall dramatic situation and main story of the poem in a particular way. Homer never lets us forget that the minor warriors really are minor compared with the greater heroes who kill them, but the pathos he endows their deaths with makes us see what is lost in the glory of these greater heroes.

One passage that well illustrates Homer's attitude toward death is the description of the death of the Trojan warrior Simoeisios. This is one of the richest and most exquisite of many passages that recapitulate a central theme of the ***Iliad:*** the cost in human terms of heroic achievement. The death of the Trojan youth is analogous on a small scale to the death of Hektor and the destiny of Troy as they are portrayed and prefigured elsewhere in the poem. Simoeisios' death makes a particularly strong impression on us also because he is only the third character killed in the ***Iliad;*** the description helps to establish a pattern of meaning that prevents us from simply becoming habituated to or dulled by the many later reports and descriptions of killing and dying:

Then Ajax son of Telamon killed the son of Anthemion,
unmarried, blooming Simoeisios, whom once his
mother
coming down from Ida beside the banks of the Simoeis
gave birth to, when she followed along with her parents
to see the flocks.
Therefore they called him Simoeisios. Nor did he give a
return
to his dear parents for rearing him, but his life was
brief,
conquered beneath the spear of great-hearted Ajax.
For as he was moving in the front ranks, Ajax hit him
in the chest beside
the right nipple; straight through his shoulder the bronze
spear
went, and he fell to the ground in the dust like a black
poplar
which has grown in the lowland of a great marsh,
smooth, but its branches grow at the very top;
and which a man who makes chariots cuts down with
the shining
iron, so he can bend it into a wheel for a beautiful
chariot;
and it lies hardening beside the banks of a river.
Such then was Anthemion's son, Simoeisios, whom
Ajax
sprung from Zeus killed.

The passage is framed by statements that Ajax killed Simoeisios. It is notable that Ajax is described as son of Telamon and merely as ''sprung from Zeus,'' a standard epithet of kings in the ***Iliad,*** while Simoeisios in each case is called the son of Anthemion. In the case of Ajax the patronymic merely tells us which Ajax is in action; there is no reason to repeat it. In Simoeisios' case the repeated patronymic calls attention to itself. It suggests the word *anthos,* ''flower,'' thus associating the youth with natural growth.

This botanical association is reinforced by the comparison of Simoeisios' fall beneath Ajax's bronze spear to that of a tree cut down by the ''shining iron'' of a chariotmaker. Just as the chariotmaker puts an end to a living poplar, which then lies hardening, so Ajax ends the life of the youth, whose body, as corpses do, will grow rigid in death. That the chariotmaker cuts down the tree for a productive purpose, to make an instrument of war, a chariot, is ironically appropriate to Simoeisios' own effort to be a hero in war: he is killed ''moving in the front ranks.''

Simoeisios, as befits the son of Anthemion, is called ''blooming,'' an etymologically botanical word used elsewhere in the ***Iliad*** of young men, especially husbands. But he is also ''unmarried.'' We get an idea of a youth both blooming and potentially a husband, of warmth and energy that might have been directed toward a peaceful, fruitful life but were instead turned to war, where death put an end to warmth, flowering, and potential. This sense of unfulfillment is strengthened by the statement that Simoeisios did not repay his dear parents for rearing him.

The vignette about Simoeisios' birth is as moving as the details of his death. Like many other vignettes and similes in the ***Iliad,*** it moves from the realm of battle and death to a contrasting world of peacetime and everyday life. His mother had been visiting flocks with her parents on Mount Ida, an activity no longer possible during the war, and gave birth to him by the banks of the Simoeis river: one feels the rhythm of a normal, peaceful pastoral life. There is a particular significance, too, to the river as birthplace. As a source of fertility for the Trojan plain and a landmark associated with the city, the Simoeis, like the Skamandros, serves as a landscape symbol for Troy itself. Simoeisios' death is felt, indirectly and on a small scale, as the death of Troy.

The poplar's ''hardening by the banks of a river,'' though in itself not an especially significant detail, echoes ''beside the banks of the Simoeis,'' thus associating the fall of the tree more closely with the death of the youth. It almost makes us see the gradual stiffening of his body. Similarly, one can associate the description of the poplar, ''smooth, but its branches grow at the very top,'' with the appearance of Simoeisios. We visualize the smooth body of an adolescent, entirely without hair except that on his head. This vividness makes the whole scene more poignant; so also does the moving detail that Ajax's spear struck beside the right nipple. The bronze spear, passing straight through the shoulder, coldly destroys what is tender, warm, rooted in life like the poplar. Yet the youth is destroyed by the highest Homeric excellence, heroic *aretē,* both his own (''moving in the front ranks'') and that of Ajax, whose status and glory are based on just such killing of lesser warriors. And the chariot for the sake of which the poplar is cut down is ''beautiful.''

As I have said, the Simoeisios passage is but one of many such vignettes and similes about young men whose deaths Homer narrates. None of the others is so carefully wrought, but each to some extent makes us aware of what the war with its splendid killing costs in human terms. It is significant that almost all of the young victims are Trojans, for the greatest cost of the war is to Troy itself, whose eventual destruction is most clearly prefigured by the death of Hektor. Indeed, Hektor's visit with Andromache and Astyanax in Troy in Book 6 is set in the action of the poem as an expanded vignette of how a man had gone to war leaving his wife and child whom he was never to see again. Homer achieves a similar effect by the description of how Achilles pursued Hektor past the twin springs of Skamandros and the washing troughs ''where the wives and beautiful daughters / of the Trojans used to wash their shining garments / before, in peacetime.'' Homer suspends an image of the normal, domestic life of Troy ''before the sons of the Achaians came'' in the midst of the climactic episode of the war and of the poem. The effect of this juxtaposition is to remind us of the cost of Achilles' supreme heroic act. Hektor dies fighting not only for glory but also for the life of tender domesticity, characteristically Trojan in the ***Iliad,*** of which he and Andromache are the poem's prime exemplars.

The description of the death of Simoeisios, like all of Homer's battle narrative, is conventional in style, form, and content; Homer's achievement is the meaning that emerges from this and other such descriptions. . . . [Poems] about heroes killing and dying for their own imperishable glory and the sake of their communities seem to be very old in the Indo-European poetic tradition. The formulaic style of the ***Iliad***'s battle scenes, as of the rest of the poem, is derived from this tradition. . . . [Not] only descriptions of individuals killing and dying but also the various sequences of Greek and Trojan deaths, and of kinds of wounds, are patterned. In other words, the battle scenes are thematically as well as linguistically formulaic, and they share several other important formal features that would have made them readily intelligible and meaningful to an audience schooled in the conventions of the oral poetic tradition.

For our understanding of the nature and significance of war in the ***Iliad,*** perhaps the most important shared feature of the numerous scenes of killing and dying is that the combats are generally decided quickly, by one fatal blow. Rarely does a warrior need as many as two moves to finish off an opponent. Correspondingly, those who are hit, with a couple of exceptions, are killed immediately; Homer describes very few nonfatal wounds other than those dealt to the Greek kings in Book 11, when he is motivating the entry of Patroklos and the Myrmidons into the battle. This emphasis on killing rather than wounding shows that Homer is interested not so much in the technique of battle or the detailed, anatomical description of wounds—vivid as this is—as in questions of death itself. Descriptions of warfare are essentially descriptions of death.

On the other hand, the fighting among the gods, and between Diomedes and the gods in Book 5, always results in wounding and never, of course, in a god's death. In contrast to human conflict, which is literally a matter of life and death, divine warfare is a game without serious consequences, a game that, as W. Marg says, can always be replayed. For mortals, death is the end, death is everything.

Just as interesting as the almost universal fatality of wounds inflicted by Homer's heroes are the verbal threats, boasts, and taunts made by warriors to their opponents before and after individual combats. The threats and battle mockery are intended primarily to deny or reduce the opponent's bravery and warcraft; as Vermeule says, ''The aim [of a warrior's taunts] is to turn the opposing soldier into a female, or into the weaker animal role.'' She has pointed out, too, that often the vocabulary of these taunts exploits semantic ambiguities in such words as *meignumi,* "mingle," which is used of mingling in battle or in sex, and *damazō* or *damnēmi,* "subjugate" or "dominate," verbs used of taming an animal or raping a woman or killing a man. A warrior who is killed has become in effect a subdued animal or a subjugated woman. It is no accident that the phrase *krēdemnon luesthai,* "to loosen a veil," can mean either to sack a city or to breach a woman's chastity.

In different battles and different books of the ***Iliad*** there is a striking variety in the wounds inflicted and in the tone and details of the verbal threats, boasts, and mockery. Some scholars, not realizing that every battle scene is traditional and formulaic, have suggested that these differences might serve as refined criteria for the "analysis" of the ***Iliad*** into various historical layers on stylistic grounds. Rather than drawing such historical conclusions, we should recognize that differences in the kinds and details of killing, dying, threatening, and boasting reflect Homer's varying poetic emphases, since in different places in the poem he stresses different consequences of war for mortals. For example, Book 13 is remarkable for the gruesomeness of the wounds described and for frequent, rather baroque boasts, especially by victorious warriors over their victims. These grotesque wounds and boasts should be connected with the fact that in Book 13, though there is a great deal of killing, neither side makes any progress in the battle. The controlling image of the book is the "knot of powerful strife and of war equal for all" which Zeus and Poesidon "drew tight for both sides, / unbreakable and unable to be loosened, but which loosened the knees of many men." There is a strong sense that mortal effort is futile because of this conflict of wills between the older and younger divine brothers; that strife on a cosmic level parallels the quarrel between Agamemnon and Achilles. The words "unbreakable and unable to be loosened" are particularly effective because they occurred earlier in the same book in the idyllic description of Poseidon's chariot ride over the sea on his way to Troy, but there is nothing idyllic about the knot of war. Books 13 and 14 are a study of what makes war seem primarily futile and painful for mortals, especially when, as in these books, the gods intervene directly. The characteristically Homeric play on words, "unable to be loosened, but which loosened the knees of many men," is of a piece with the humor of the deceitful seduction of Zeus by Hera in Book 14. The gruesome wounds, grisly taunts, and lack of progress in Book 13 are the other, mortal side of this humor. Together, the two sides add up to a meditation on warfare that remains for a reader's or listener's consideration and enjoyment alongside the imagined sight of war. There is no contradiction between the fact that Homer and his audience could aesthetically enjoy as mere performance the skillful narrative of warfare in the traditional style and the fact that scenes of battle in the ***Iliad*** can be appreciated intellectually and be thought-provoking in a variety of ways.

One mark of the traditional nature of Homeric battle descriptions is the way they make use of "formal patterns long used for animal combats and hunting scenes" in visual art. Such "animal art" typically "expressed valor and pathos in duels between a predator and a grass-eater, usually a lion attacking a bull or a deer. . . . On the battlefield of Troy the duel between enemy heroes is handled in precisely the same formal patterns as the animal fight." Just as in the visual art "the lion was . . . the image of success in both war and hunting," so in the ***Iliad*** the greatest of heroes at the peak of their prowess are compared to lions. Such comparisons, like those to wild boars and other animals, show Homer's self-consciousness of his artistic tradition. He not only arranges his individual combats like the animal combats in art, but he says over and over to his audience in lengthy similes how his human warriors act or feel like wild animals. These similes make explicit the implied predatory animality of the poem's heroes; they testify that the psychological connection between hunting and warfare, so well known in many ancient and modern cultures (including our own), is present in the minds of Homer's audience as well as those of his characters.

There is, to be sure, a certain decorum in Homer's comparisons of his heroes to wild animals and in the heroes' own animalistic behavior. Although on a couple of occasions we hear that one or another mortal would like to hack an enemy to pieces and eat him raw, such "cannibal impulses and . . . animal language stay in the realm of rhetoric, like almost all 'ugly actions' in the ***Iliad.***" This is a major difference between Homeric epic and other traditional Greek oral poetry, which told such stories as that of Tydeus' punishment by Athene for eating the brain of a dead enemy during the campaign of the seven against Thebes. The greatest lapse into savagery in the ***Iliad*** is Achilles' sacrifice at the pyre of Patroklos of twelve Trojan youths captured near the river Skamandros for that purpose. Such deliberate savagery, however, really is not animalistic but distinctively human in its planned brutality and its perversion of an activity (sacrifice) that is supposed to bring humans closer not to animals but to the gods. Clearly Homer is portraying Achilles at this stage of the poem as beyond a boundary that humans in the ***Iliad*** normally do not cross. As we shall see in more detail, he is at once superhuman and subhuman, almost like a god in his power and a force of nature in his destructive savagery. Yet in thus "having made savage his great-hearted spirit" and temporarily losing his civilized sociability, Achilles in fact acts like a deranged human, not like an animal; it would eat its victims raw, not sacrifice them alive.

Another important traditional feature of Homer's description of war in the ***Iliad*** is the *aristeia. Aristeia* is a word used in later Greek for "excellence" or "prowess," including, in particular, the excellence or prowess of a Homeric warrior when he is on a victorious rampage, irresistibly sweeping all before him, killing whomever of the enemy he can catch or whoever stands against him. *Aristeia* is an abstract noun, closely related to the verb *aristeuō,* which in the ***Iliad*** means "to be (or try to be) the best and bravest in battle." This verb is used by Glaukos when he tells Diomedes that his father sent him to Troy and told him "always to be best and bravest and to surpass all others, / and not to disgrace the line of my fathers, who were / much the best." It also is the word used by Odysseus when he reminds himself that while cowards may flee, whoever "is best and bravest in battle" must stand strongly and either himself be hit or hit another. In Greek of all periods, the adjective *aristos,* "best," is the superlative of *agathos,* "good," but in the ***Iliad,*** whose world is a world of war, "good" and "best" mean "good [or: best] in battle."

In the ***Iliad*** the *aristeia* is the main compositional unit of battle narrative. One can distinguish five sections of a normal *aristeia*. First there is a description of the hero arming himself, including an especially detailed description of his triumphantly gleaming armor. Next the hero turns the tide of a dead-locked battle by killing an opponent who stands against him. Thirdly, the hero breaks into the grouped ranks of the enemy and wreaks havoc among them. Thereafter the hero is himself wounded (which causes a temporary setback for his side), but he prays to a god, is healed or strengthened, and reenters the battle to kill an important enemy. Finally, there is a fierce battle over the corpse of this enemy, until it is taken (often with divine aid) from the clutches of the hero. Although not every *aristeia* in the poem has all these sections in identical sequence and form, the normal *aristeia* would have been present in the minds of both poet and audience, since it was a major element of the oral poetic tradition; the audience would have been able to appreciate both the fulfillment of the norm and artful, meaningful variations on it. Thus, a description of a hero arming would have raised in their minds the expectation that he would stand out in the ensuing battle, and nuances of the description would foreshadow the precise degree of his success.

The different sections of the *aristeia* were characterized by particular kinds of similes. Each kind was associated with a certain type of event or action. An audience schooled in the tradition would have been prepared by the similes for the associated event or action and, conversely, would have expected a given kind of simile in a given narrative context. The fact that five-sixths of the similes in the ***Iliad*** occur in scenes of battle indicates the close connection of similes to the *aristeia,* the typical form of Homer's battle narrative. The similes were one means by which Homer, and presumably every poet in the tradition, could both control the expectations of his audience regarding descriptions of warfare and, by breaking the narrative flow, adjust their attention to his own poetic performance.

Achilles is the main hero of the ***Iliad,*** and his *aristeia,* concluding with the killing of Hektor and the eventual return of his body at the gods' behest, is the culmination of the poem. But there are three other Greek heroes, Diomedes in Book 5, Agamemnon in Book 11, and Patroklos in Book 16, whose *aristeiai* prepare the way for Achilles': in contrast to them Achilles is absolutely outstanding. Some scholars have spoken of these heroes as surrogates or substitutes for Achilles, as if the original form of the poem had been a story of Achilles and the other *aristeiai* were directly modeled upon his. Such a supposition fails to recognize the traditional formulaic nature of the *aristeia.* While Achilles is the real hero of the poem, we can appreciate his uniqueness only through juxtaposition and contrast with other heroes and *aristeiai*. For instance, while each of the others is wounded by a human opponent and/or rescued by a helper-god to whom he prays, Achilles is threatened by the river god Skamandros himself, reassured by Athene and Poseidon, and rescued by Hephaistos at Hera's request. His status as a hero beyond all others is enhanced both by his divine opponent and by his multiple divine helpers. Likewise, while the victims of the other *aristeia*-heroes are taken from them by divine aid on the battlefield (Aineias in Book 5, Sarpedon in Book 16), Achilles drags Hektor's body to the Greek camp and only restores it to Priam at Zeus' request. As T. Krischer says, by this variation on the usual final element of the *aristeia,* the gods show Achilles not the limits of his power as a hero (as is the case with Diomedes, Agamemnon, and Patroklos) but the limits of the human condition itself.

That the ***Iliad*** tells the story of a war for a city is central to Homer's conception of war and to our understanding of the poem. Although war in Homer is . . . a socially validated way of life, it is at the same time supremely antisocial. The tragic situation that became clear in the case of Simoeisios—that the only way for an individual to achieve greatness and meaning in life is by the destruction of other individuals engaged in the same pursuit—is clear also on the level of society. The aim of the war is to destroy a socially evolved human community just like the community that each Greek left behind him when he set sail for Troy. The price of individual self-assertion and self-fulfillment is social annihilation. From the point of view that sees human beings as by definition social, the Greeks, cut off from their homes and families, are in effect less human than the Trojans. From a point of view that sees war as the only way for a human being—or rather, a human male—to exist meaningfully, the Greeks are more successfully, and therefore more fully, human than the Trojans.

Despite the poem's unsentimental, realistic, and complex portrayal of war, several critics have interpreted the ***Iliad*** as simply an antiwar epic. In various ways these critics have held "that Homer's values were ultimately spiritual," and that the violence depicted in the poem must be viewed in a larger context within which, and only within which, it "can be understood in the poet's terms." Undoubtedly the most eloquent and influential of these interpreters is Simone Weil in her essay *The Iliad or the Poem of Force*. This was written in occupied France and displaces onto the ***Iliad*** Weil's emotional and moral repugnance to the atrocities Nazi Germany inflicted on its victims [see 1940-41 excerpt by Weil]. (pp. 70-82)

We inevitably distort and misread the ***Iliad*** when we foist the values of another time and culture upon its objective, internally consistent presentation of and attitude toward war and death. Of course, we all bring our preconceptions, prejudices, values, and beliefs to whatever we read. Still, there is a difference between evaluating a work of art in personal terms and finding our personal terms in the work. Warfare in the ***Iliad*** has a complexity which eludes one-sided interpretations, spiritual or otherwise. As Rachel Bespaloff has written, Homer has a "virile love of war and a virile horror of it"; he presents war as it is, with no illusions, without condemning it. This is only to be expected. In the poem, war and death *are* life itself—the medium in which life is lived and through which it amounts to something. The ***Iliad*** is filled with what J. G. Gray has called "the enduring appeals of battle": "the delight in seeing, the delight in comradeship, the delight in destruction." Indeed,

A reconstruction of the shield of Achilles. Ashmolean Museum, Oxford.

''delight'' (*charmē*) is Homer's word for the joy of battle which warriors ''remember'' (*memnēmai*) and call on their comrades to ''remember'' in the uttermost stress of the fighting. To be sure, this delight is tempered by Homer's full recognition of the self-defeating nature of war, of the contradictions that make human life in the poem, and the poem itself, tragic as well as joyful. As Bespaloff says, ''[I]n the ***Iliad*** force appears as both the supreme reality and the supreme illusion of life. Force, for Homer, is divine insofar as it represents a superabundance of life that flashes out in the contempt of death . . . ; it is detestable insofar as it contains . . . a blind drive that is always pushing it on to the very end of its course, on to its own abolition and the obliteration of the very values it engendered.''

The ***Iliad*** is both a poem of death and a poem of life: in other words, it is a poem of mortality. With unwavering and unsentimental realism it presents the necessities and opportunities of human existence, tragic limitations that are at the same time inspiriting and uplifting to live with and to contemplate. Its depiction of war and death is thoroughly traditional, but the tradition is transformed by Homer's characteristic artistry into a comprehensive exploration and expression of the beauty, the rewards, and the price of human heroism. (pp. 83-4)

Seth L. Schein, in his The Mortal Hero: An Introduction to Homer's ''Iliad,'' *University of California Press, 1984, 223 p.*

WALLACE GRAY (essay date 1985)

[*In the following excerpt, Gray explores Homer's attitude toward the epic hero and the Greek heroic code in the* Iliad. *In Achilles, Gray points out, Homer portrays ''a new and different epic hero [who] breaks rules, forswears oaths, is moved by compassion for the enemy.''*]

The ***Iliad*** is not about the Trojan War; that war lasted ten years and the central actions of the poem occupy only a few weeks. War brutalizes men and women, wounds their bodies and minds, enslaves and kills them. This is Homer's message as he focuses on one hero, Achilleus, to demonstrate wrath's destruction of self and others. Achilleus' moral journey in the ***Iliad*** brings him face to face with his own humanity, leading him to a startling and essentially unheroic act of generosity toward his enemy. When he gives Priam the dead and mutilated body of Hektor, Achilleus stands for a few moments on the threshold of a different civilization, as Homer shows wrath dissolved through compassion, and human feeling overcoming the stringent heroic code of conformity.

A hero is one who willingly and eagerly confronts death, and three Greek words embody the heroic code: *áristos, aretē,* and *aristeía. Áristos* is being the best at whatever is called for by the situation: in wartime, killing; in peacetime, husbandry; in seamanship, steering. To be known as the best requires *aristeía*—exploits which gain for the warrior the prestige of having comrades consider him possessed of *aretē*, merit. *Aretē* can only be bestowed by others, not by self. In the world of the ***Iliad*** what the world thinks of you is far more important than what you think of yourself. Indeed, it *is* what you think of yourself. Fame and glory, *kléos,* can only be achieved through action. This is why the withdrawal of Achilleus from the battle is such a devastating decision: without exploits he has no identity and can only sit in his shelter singing about fame and glory instead of achieving it. Achilleus is no longer *áristos,* the best of the Achaians, when Agamemnon succeeds in depriving him of Briseis. The girl, along with tripods, spears, and other paraphernalia of war, is war booty, a symbol of *aretē*. And so he has to sing of *kléos:* without exploits no poet is going to sing about him. In a pitiful and ultimately tragic attempt to regain *aretē,* he sends Patroklos into battle as his *therápōn,* a ritual substitute clad in the armor of Achilleus.

By permitting his beloved friend Patroklos, whom he knows to be a lesser warrior than himself, to reenter the battle, Achilleus is consequently responsible for the death of this gentle warrior.

However, according to a widely accepted theory, Achilleus feels no guilt, as this Homeric society is not a guilt-culture, but rather a shame-culture in which man does not consider himself responsible for his own behavior. Shame-cultures attribute human imperfection to external causes, such as failure to make proper sacrifices, or accidentally slighting the gods in some other way. These heroes do not yet understand that character is fate, and they project onto external forces whatever ills happen to them. Guilt and a sense of sin (a word not in the Homeric vocabulary) develop as societies grow older and men replace gods as the instruments of cause and effect.

But Achilleus is undoubtedly displaying all the signs of guilt in his behavior after the death of Patroklos, and he does feel responsible. Perhaps the most reasonable attitude to take is that shame-cultures and guilt-cultures are not mutually exclusive, and that it is possible for a Homeric hero, as well as for a contemporary person, to feel both shame and guilt in varying proportions.

Because these men are called heroes, the sensibility of the modern reader is often shocked and disturbed by behavior considered unheroic today. Achilleus stabs and kills Priam's naked and defenseless young son, who has taken off his armor and sword in weariness after escaping the river. On the nighttime spying expedition to the Trojan camp in Book 10, Odysseus and Diomedes capture Dolon, a Trojan sent to spy on the Achaians. After assuring him they will do him no harm if he gives them information, they lop off his head, which falls, still speaking, to the ground. Proceeding into the Trojan camp, they do not hesitate to slaughter the sleeping warriors. Victory, Paris says, goes first to one man and then to another: it's not how you play the game in the Homeric world, it's whether you win or lose.

Sarpedon's speech to Glaukos in Book 12 is the clearest expression of what it means to be a hero. He wonders aloud: Why are we given the best places at the banquet table, served the best meat and wine, given the choicest land, and why do men look upon us as being immortal? We deserve these benefits because we show our bravery by fighting in the forefront of the battle. If we were able to live forever, to be immortal, then there would be no need to fight in order to win glory. Now, however, the battle is upon us, we cannot escape it, so let us plunge in and win glory for ourselves or, by dying, give it to the enemy.

Glory, eternal fame, *kléos,* can only be achieved by killing or being killed in battle; either way one becomes a subject of epic poetry and lives forever in song. He is right, of course; Sarpedon dies, but lives forever in the ***Iliad.***

This inflexible heroic code does not permit choice, and the fact that Achilleus chooses distinguishes him from the other warriors and makes him the hero of this epic. Knowing that he is endangering his status as *áristos,* the best, he chooses to disengage himself from the battle and retire to his shelter. Odysseus tells Achilleus of Agamemnon's offer of gifts if he will return to the battle. In response, Achilleus rejects the heroic code once again. We are all going to die, he says, both the brave and the weak, so it matters little whether you do a great deal or nothing. Look at me, how I've fought harder than anyone, and how I have nothing. And what was I fighting for, why are the Argives fighting the Trojans? For Helen? What is so special about Helen? (pp. 1-3)

In a dramatic rejection of the heroic code, Achilleus questions the sexual cause of the war, finding it unworthy of dying for. He has alienated himself from the war and has had time to question the standards of his society. Returning to the battle only after the death of Patroklos, Achilleus slays Hektor and then mutilates the body. That behavior is properly heroic. But then, in another brave defection from the heroic code, Achilleus takes a stance of compassion toward his enemy: he gives the body of Hektor to Priam for proper burial, a rite that will not only ensure the eternal peace of a spirit Achilleus has reason to condemn to a restless eternity, but will also give the body a continuing temporal fame in a burial marker. Achilleus ceases his erasure of the identity of Hektor.

In this first great work of Western literature, Homer shows war destroying not only cities and civilizations but the souls of men. War turns men into things, objects without pity. What difference does it make? Achilleus asks. We are all going to die. And he plunges his sword through the neck of the naked and defenseless young son of Priam.

Hektor, prince and defender of the city of Troy, becomes for the reader a more complete human being than does Achilleus. The latter deals primarily with other warriors, whereas Hektor is seen responding to his mother, Hekuba, his sister-in-law, Helen, and his wife, Andromache. Hektor is revealed through these three women, and they reveal themselves, especially by their positions when, in Book 6, Hektor returns to the city for respite from the fighting. These scenes gain for Hektor a sympathetic response from us that might otherwise have been reserved solely for Achilleus.

Hektor's first encounter is with his mother (the present Queen of Troy); this woman does not bury herself deep within the palace, but, herself a fierce warrior who can cry out that she would like to eat the liver of Achilleus raw, she comes rushing to greet her son. However, her first words to Hektor are not of comfort but of reprimand: she demands to know what he is doing behind the city walls, away from the fighting. No mother to coddle her children, she immediately commands Hektor to offer a libation of wine to Zeus for victory in battle, and only then does she suggest that Hektor may drink some of the wine himself. But only to restore his energy for battle. This stern Queen of Troy is equal to the Spartan enemies besieging the walls of her city. How different she is from Thetis; Achilleus' mother treats him like a little baby before his final battle with Hektor. (pp. 3-5)

Hektor continues on to the palace of his brother, where he finds Paris and Helen (the former Queen of Sparta) in a most appropriate place, her bedroom. Paris is polishing his battle gear rather than fighting with it, and Helen is berating him, projecting the blame for the war on the gods, and referring to herself as a vile bitch. When she suggests that future poets will, as they indeed have done, make songs about her and perpetuate her fame, one wonders whether she really does resent her "misfortune." The lady protests at great length, and she responds to Hektor with much more tenderness and regard than she does to Paris. And Hektor, for all the ten years of suffering Helen has caused, treats her with the respect due a former Queen of Sparta. (To be fair to Helen, it must be remembered that women of this period had no more control over their fate than did those in the male-dominated Athenian "Golden Age.")

When Hektor goes searching for his wife (whom destiny will prevent from becoming Queen of Troy in the future), he finds her in a place that reveals her character as the wife of a prince who is slated to be the future King of Troy: she is standing on the city wall, from which she can watch the battle. There she reminds Hektor that Achilleus had killed her father as well as her seven brothers, and was responsible for the death of her mother. Hektor, then, she tells him, is both father, brother, mother, and husband to her. Indeed, when she loses Hektor to the sword of Achilleus, she loses everything in the world. Both she and Hektor know Achilleus is the greater warrior; they realize Hektor is going to die. He knows the city of Troy will perish and that Andromache and his son will be lost. Although he may at times deny it, Hektor returns to the battle knowing that he will die; this is his heroic grandeur. But, before he goes, he reaches out for his baby son, who, not recognizing his father in plumed helmet and battle gear, cries out in fear and terror. Homer shows that war is not just glorious action bringing fame and honor to the participants; it is also a mechanism turning men into creatures from whom even their children draw back in fright. There are neither good men nor bad men in the ***Iliad;*** this is the humanity of Homer, who, Hellenic himself, doesn't favor Hellenes over Trojans.

Homer is given credit for anthropomorphism, for providing the gods and goddesses with human traits. He endowed them with richly human characteristics, turning Ares into the blood-thirsty young god of war, Aphrodite into the "flighty" goddess of love, Hera into a jealous and conniving wife, and Athena and Apollo into grandiose, superhuman beings. To Homer's listeners, as well as to many in the following generations, these divine gods and goddesses constituted their religious beliefs, and their participation in the two Homeric poems was real—the gods controlled and directed the events. The modern reader, however, can choose among a variety of ways of reading the poem: the gods and goddesses are actually real and present; they are external symbols for the internal emotions, desires, and drives of men and women, of their good and bad luck; or, they are both at the same time.

In the first instance the reader can suspend his disbelief in ancient Hellenic religion and enter into the spirit of the times. In the second—the symbolic reading—the reader can consider that everything that happens to the heroes in the ***Iliad*** could have happened *without* the actions of the gods, since they are personifications of the fears and aspirations of the heroes. If a hero is suddenly filled with courage, or overcomes his opponent, or has good luck, or lets out a war cry that terrifies the enemy, then a god or goddess is given the credit. Even Apollo's stunning of Patroklos, and Athena's return of a spear to Achilleus—two occurrences often cited as indisputable evidence of divine intervention—can be considered as symbols for human actions.

However, in reading imaginative literature it is possible to have the best of both worlds: the imaginative reader need not consider the two readings mutually exclusive, need not choose between the actually divine and the symbolically divine. Indeed, this dual function is expressed by Diomedes when he is speaking about Achilleus' rejection of the embassy: "He will fight when the heart in his breast urges him, and the god arouses him.'' The single combat between Menelaos and Paris and its aftermath illustrate this dual role of the Olympians in Homer.

After ten years of battle it has been decided to resolve the conflict through single combat between Menelaos, Helen's first husband, and Paris, Helen's second husband. (This is one of a number of incidents in the poem which seem likely to have occurred earlier in the war.) In the first moments of the contest Menelaos throws his spear at Paris and misses the body. He then grabs Paris by the helmet, spins him around until Paris falls, and begins to drag him away by the helmet. Aphrodite, however, the protectress of Paris, breaks the chin strap holding the helmet, and Menelaos strides on, carrying only the helmet. Thus, what was accident, a worn chin strap breaking and saving Paris, is attributed to the intervention of a goddess. Paris escapes through a cloud of dust, carried off by Aphrodite and deposited gently in the bed of Helen. The goddess is given credit for spiriting Paris away from the battle, whereas it could also be read as an act of apparent cowardice on his part. Aphrodite leads Helen to the bedroom—or perhaps she is led by her own lust. What happens next in that bed is a startling precursor of the link between sex and death in succeeding literature. Paris, turning to Helen, tells her he has never before felt such passion for her. Although this may be a formulaic statement always uttered at each instance of lovemaking in epic poetry of this period, it appears Homer is suggesting that the exciting stimuli of danger and imminent death have served to increase Paris' sexual excitement. (pp. 5-8)

At this early stage of Greek civilization, the concept of *díkē,* justice, is inconsistent and rudimentary. Although the ***Iliad*** has been read by some as a poem about divine justice—Zeus' punishment of Troy in retribution for Paris' abduction of Helen—the gods and goddesses themselves are all too humanly fickle, wrathful, inconsistent, and ambiguous in their behavior for a reading of the poem as one concerned primarily with divine justice; the poet, after all, opens by telling the listener that his poem is about the ''wrath of Achilleus.''

Díkē in the ***Iliad*** consists of getting one's own fair share of war booty, food, or land—the share due a hero who risks his life. And the wrath of Achilleus is first stirred when he is deprived of part of his ''fair portion,'' the captive Briseis. Among men, brute force determines justice: Agamemnon has more warriors than Achilleus and can thus have his way, and Achilleus can only resort to withdrawing from the war and thus causing vital losses to Agamemnon.

Divine justice seems to be based on favoritism and whim, and Judeo-Christian concepts of an all-knowing God must be set aside for a Zeus who seems not always to know the future. In order to determine which of two battling warriors will die, Zeus places their death portions on the scale; the heavier one will die that day. In spite of teaching at one point that the gods listen to those who obey them, the ***Iliad*** shows Zeus granting some prayers and denying others. Zeus has two urns, one of evils and one of blessings, and he mingles gifts from the two urns to be distributed to an individual without regard for merit. The definition of human life seems to be that it is always a mixture of both good and bad experiences for every human being, that those experiences are not always merited, and that all must die. Heroes who forget their human nature and begin to act like deathless gods are soon reminded of their mortality.

In the Homeric poems two kinds of *díkē* exist side by side; one for wartime and another for peacetime. In wartime a hero's experiences are usually the result of force or chance; in the city at peace on the shield of Achilleus, the poet presents a different concept of justice. When two men disagree, they go to arbitrators, elders of the city who listen to the men's cases as well as to the voice of the people; two talents of gold are given to the judge who speaks the best opinion. Homer portrays justice and love and dancing in the city at peace, but only destruction and death in the city at war. There is no arbitration in war, no peaceful solution, no restitution through the payment of a blood price, but only desecration by dogs and vultures. Deliberation and arbitration result in recompense for the killing of a man in the city at peace, whereas the victorious warrior on the battlefield always rejects the payment promised by the defeated warrior for his proper burial. In the ***Odyssey,*** Odysseus conquers the suitors through cunning rather than brute force, and his victory over them, as we shall see, is one that rights a civic injustice. In the two Homeric poems it appears that war is a time when justice is subject to irrational, arbitrary, and hasty determinations, and peace a time for reflection and rational deliberation. (pp. 9-10)

Homer seldom relents in showing the brutality of war. Within a hundred lines at the beginning of Book 5, various fighters are struck in the back by a spear that drives on through the chest; pierced by a spear through the right shoulder; struck in the right buttock by a spear that plunges in under the bone and through the bladder; struck in the back of the head by a spear that drives on through the teeth and under the tongue until the spearhead sticks out through the warrior's mouth and he falls, gripping the spear between his teeth; struck by a spear that severs the arm, which then drops bleeding to the ground.

By using similes from experiences common to everyone at that time, Homer succeeds in making battle vivid to those in his audience who may never have been to war. He likens combat to lions attacking sheep, to the fury of thunderstorms, to lightning and raging forest fires: the comparisons are always to destructive elements or to violent animals. Heroes may achieve glory and fame on the battlefield, but war itself is brutal and degrading. On the point of death, a warrior pleads pitifully for mercy he knows is not forthcoming, while the hero stands crowing and vaunting over him, spearhead pointed at the sprawled warrior's chest.

Striking illustrations of Homer's technique of using familiar comparisons occur in Book 2. He first shows the visual aspects of war: the battle is like a raging forest fire running across mountaintops whose glorious bronze light dazzles all the way up to the heavens. He next compares the sounds of battle to flying geese and cranes, to the throated sound of swans and their wings as, when they are settling, meadows echo with their clashing swarms. The sound is also like horses' hooves thundering. Next he presents the kinetic movement, the impetus of thrusting armies, comparing them to swarming insects frantically buzzing around the milk pails in a sheepfold. The leaders of the armies are compared to goatherds separating and organizing goats, to the strongest ox of the herd, to a chief bull who stands out among the cattle. A touching comparison occurs when Apollo leads the Trojans in their destruction of the ramparts of the Achaians; Homer sings that they do this as easily as a little boy at the seashore amuses himself by trampling his carefully built sand towers with his feet. (pp. 11-13)

Homer frequently employs what we would call a cinematic approach in dealing with large battles, photographing from a distance, then moving to the foreground, and only at the last showing a close-up of two specific warriors. At the beginning of the battle, . . . [in] Book 4, he gives an overview of two armies surging toward each other, and the comparison is to sea surf pounding in toward the shore, driven by the wind. The cries of the oncoming army sound from a distance, and the cries are compared to those of sheep waiting to be milked and yearning for their lambs. . . . [Later] the camera moves in closer to show still-unidentified men killing and being killed, and, Homer sings, blood running along the ground like rivers rushing down from mountain streams. The sound of armies clashing is like thunder. Having provided a long view followed by a move to the foreground, the poet is now ready for a close-up of a distinct individual: "Antilochos was first to kill a chief man of the Trojans."

One of the chief men of the Achaians is Patroklos, the dearly beloved friend of Achilleus. Patroklos is so youthful, so guileless, so saddened by the sufferings of others, that, given Achilleus' protective attitude toward him, it is necessary to remind ourselves that Patroklos is the older of the two: *he* has been sent along to protect *Achilleus*.

Patroklos initiates the final climactic scenes of the story. Moved by the sight of his wounded comrades, Patroklos—his name means glory to the fathers—pleads with Achilleus to allow him to reenter the fighting. Thus, clad in the armor of Achilleus, he goes forth only to be killed by Hektor. In an ironic foreshadowing of the final battle between Hektor and Achilleus, Patroklos, wearing the armor of Achilleus, is surrogate for that greater warrior. In larger terms, Achilleus experiences his own death, as well as that of his dear friend. "Die all," Achilleus shouts at a later point. And they *will* die all, including Achilleus, as he symbolically dies in the ***Iliad*** when he kills Hektor, a warrior clad in the armor of Achilleus that he stripped from Patroklos. Achilleus knows the prophecy that he is to die shortly after the death of Hektor; he thus embraces his own death when he kills Hektor, especially so since the armor makes that warrior another surrogate Achilleus. Like Patroklos, Achilleus also requires three instruments of death—in his case, Patroklos, Hektor, and finally, Paris—the actual killer.

Odysseus is a different breed of Iliadic warrior. The skill of the hero of Homer's second epic is not in brute force but in crafty strategies. Odysseus is intelligent and resourceful, descriptions not applied to other warriors. From the very beginning, in Book 2, he seems to take charge through speech and persuasion when decisions are to be made. And when Agamemnon finally gives in to the fact that he needs Achilleus, it is Odysseus who is put in charge of the embassy to persuade Achilleus to return. This embassy in Book 9 consists of the wily Odysseus, the older and respected Phoinix, and Ajax, that plain-spoken, tough, honest warrior. Each has his own approach to the unyielding Achilleus.

Odysseus speaks first, repeating the speech Agamemnon has delivered to him, promising numerous gifts to Achilleus if he will come to their aid. Odysseus cleverly omits the one part of Agamemnon's speech that would have much offended Achilleus: Achilleus should yield to him because he is the kinglier of the two. Achilleus is unpersuaded; there is a standoff between the *mêtis,* cunning, of Odysseus and the *bíe,* might, of Achilleus. Both *mêtis* and *bíē* are needed to win the Trojan War. In the ***Iliad*** they are represented by the characters of Odysseus and Achilleus, whereas in the ***Odyssey,*** melded as they are into one hero, Hellenic awareness takes a sophisticated step forward in the realization that man needs to have both *mêtis* and *bíē* to be *áristos,* the best.

Phoinix next recounts a somewhat lengthy but pointed story about a warrior, Meleagros, who also withdrew from battle and, in spite of the failure of the army without him, refused the entreaties of mother, sisters, and friends to return to the fight. He succumbed only to the pleas of his wife, Kleopatra. Phoinix is being even more subtle than he perhaps realizes. He knows Patroklos is Achilleus' dearest friend, that only Patroklos could possibly persuade him, and he has chosen this particular story because the name Kleopatra is Patroklos in reverse, and he hopes the echo will set up some kind of emotional response in Achilleus. Kleopatra is the only one who is successful in persuading her husband, Meleagros, to put on his armor and return to the battle: Homer is here brilliantly foreshadowing Achilleus' return to the war because of Patroklos: the dead body of Patroklos becomes the ultimate persuasive force.

Finally, . . . the blunt Ajax speaks, and doesn't try to be psychologically clever or wily; he is incapable of either. He speaks directly: We're not getting anywhere with this stubborn and proud man, he is so hard that he doesn't even listen to his friends, and he is being selfish. This short, direct appeal succeeds more than the others—at least enough for Achilleus to promise to return to the battle should the Trojans fight their way up to the ships.

Achilleus is a new and different epic hero; he breaks rules, forswears sacred oaths, is moved by compassion for the enemy. The partially successful embassy to Achilleus is a stage in his development which reaches a climax in Priam's own embassy to Achilleus to plead for the mutilated body of his son.

The war and the world have come to a halt with the death of Hektor. Following the funeral games for Patroklos, Achilleus spends twelve days without sleep, alternately rolling in the dirt, weeping over the death of Patroklos, and tossing and throwing the body of Hektor in the dust as though it were some despoiled rag doll. Even the gods are upset by his behavior: Apollo complains that Achilleus doesn't even feel helpful shame about what he is doing, and that he has destroyed pity by tying Hektor's body to horses and dragging it around the tomb of Patroklos. Thetis, Achilleus' immortal mother, descends and urges him to return the body. Although this external appearance can be interpreted as the internal promptings of Achilleus' spirit to give up his wrath, he does say that he will, for ransom, turn over the body. The emotional scene in which he offers Hektor's corpse to Priam shows that this action is for reasons other than ransom.

Within the walls of Troy, Priam prepares for his journey to Achilleus, much against the fears of Hekuba, who argues . . . that Achilleus cannot be trusted, will show no pity, and is an "eater of raw meat." Despite her warnings, Priam sets out on a strange, eerie, frightening journey past the great tomb of Ilos, alongside a river, and into the darkness. Zeus sends Hermes down to guide him, and even though Hermes appears to him as a young man, Priam is so frightened that his hair stands on end. Hermes questions him, asking why he is traveling through the immortal black night. Conducting him to the barricades protecting Achilleus' dwelling, Hermes casts sleep on the sentries. (pp. 13-16)

All of the components of a fearful journey to Hades are here, as Priam travels past tombs and rivers through an immortal black night in which Hermes, who guides souls to Hades, casts sleep on watchdogs. This can only be a symbolic journey to Hades to visit Achilleus, who has truly become King of the

Dead. And his dwelling is no ordinary battlefield shelter, but an imposing structure worthy of this symbolic King of Hades.

Priam enters alone, falls to the ground, clasps the knees and kisses the hands of Achilleus. Moved by the tears of the groaning father, the hero of the ***Iliad*** weeps at the thought of his own father's devastation had the body of Achilleus lain on a battlefield to be ravaged by wild dogs and vultures. As Priam and Achilleus shed tears of sadness and loss in recognition of their common human condition, Achilleus, in a heroic thrust *through* the heroic code, agrees to return the body of Hektor, slayer of his dear friend and companion Patroklos. The days of wrath thus end with a compassionate human rather than heroic gesture. (p. 16)

Wallace Gray, "Homer: 'Iliad'," in his Homer to Joyce, *Macmillan Publishing Company, 1985, pp. 1-16.*

ADDITIONAL BIBLIOGRAPHY

Adkins, A. W. H. "Values, Goals, and Emotions in the *Iliad.*" *Classical Philology* 77, No. 4 (October 1982): 292-325.

Discusses "the interplay of values, goals, and emotions in the behavior of Homeric characters" and "the relationship between the respective values of the characters, the poet or poets, the original audiences or readership, audiences or readers in the fifth and fourth centuries B.C., and readers in the twentieth century A.D."

Allen, Thomas W. *Homer: The Origins and the Transmission.* London: Oxford University Press, 1924, 357 p.

A detailed overview of the origins, evolution, and transmission of Homeric poetry. Contains many scattered references to the *Iliad.*

Anderson, Warren D. "Achilles and the Dark Night of the Soul." *The Classical Journal* 51, No. 5 (February 1956): 265-67.

Argues that Achilles suffers "terrible isolation . . . , [barred] from communion with his fellow men" as a result of his relentless adherence to the heroic code. He is "restored to humanity," according to Anderson, only after he shows pity toward Priam.

Apfel, Henrietta V. "Homeric Criticism in the Fourth Century B.C." *American Philological Association Transactions and Proceedings* LXIX (1938): 245-58.

Cites and examines the reactions of such fourth-century B.C. critics of the *Iliad* as Isocrates, Xenophon, Plato, Zoilus, and Aristotle.

Atchity, Kenneth John. *Homer's "Iliad": The Shield of Memory.* Carbondale and Edwardsville: Southern Illinois University Press, 1978, 352 p.

Focuses on the shield of Achilles and other artifacts in the poem "which serve as signposts in the vast but coherent landscape that shapes character, action, and symbolism into a clear expression of Homer's instructive theme"—"the relationship between order and disorder, on all levels, from the most personal to the most widely social, from the human to the divine."

Austin, Norman. "The Function of Digressions in the *Iliad.*" *Greek Roman and Byzantine Studies* 7, No. 4 (1966): 295-312.

An important assessment of verbal digressions in the *Iliad.* According to Austin, they serve "not . . . [as] a release from tension but a concentration of tension" in the text.

Bassett, Samuel Eliot. "The Pursuit of Hector." *Transactions and Proceedings of the American Philological Association* LXI (1930): 30-149.

Analyzes the pursuit of Hector episode, positing that it "adds a novel and exciting preliminary to the encounter [of Hector and Achilles]" and increases the emotional tension "so that we participate more freely in the pathos of the tragic outcome."

———. "Achilles' Treatment of Hector's Body." *Transactions of the American Philological Association* LXIV (1933): 41-65.

Explores the ramifications of Achilles' mutilation of Hector's corpse in the context of "the Greek Age of Chivalry."

Beckwith, Guy V. "Technology and Myth in the Homeric Age." *The South Atlantic Quarterly* 86, No. 2 (Spring 1987): 135-50.

Contains a discussion of the shield of Achilles as both a technological and mythological object. Beckwith writes that "the 'brazen' world of the *Iliad* is undergirded by the craft-magic of the smith."

Benardete, Seth. "Achilles and the *Iliad.*" *Hermes* 91, No. 1 (January 1963): 1-16.

Focuses on three paired relationships in the *Iliad*—between human beings and heroes, Trojans and Acheans, and Agamemnon and Achilles—and their shifting valuation in the poem.

Beye, Charles Rowan. "The *Iliad.*" In his *The "Iliad," the "Odyssey," and the Epic Tradition,* pp. 111-57. Garden City, N.J.: Doubleday and Co., Anchor Books, 1966.

Examines the roots and techniques of oral epic poetry as they relate to the *Iliad.*

Bolling, George Melville. "The Interpolations in the *Iliad.*" In his *The External Evidence for Interpolation in Homer,* pp. 57-204. London: Oxford University Press, 1925.

A detailed analysis of textual variations and additions to the *Iliad.*

Bonnard, André. "The *Iliad* and Homer's Humanism." In his *Greek Civilization,* pp. 30-58. London: George Allen and Unwin, 1957.

Discusses Homer's humanistic tendencies in the *Iliad.* Bonnard notes that, "Above all else, this poem in which death seems to reign tells of the love of life, but also of man's honour which is higher than life and stronger than the gods."

Bowra, C. M. "The *Iliad*: Its Shape and Character." In his *Homer,* pp. 97-116. Classical Life and Letters, edited by Hugh Lloyd-Jones. London: Duckworth, 1972.

A general appraisal of the structure and style of the *Iliad.*

Camps, W. A. *An Introduction to Homer.* New York: Oxford University Press, 1980, 108 p.

An overview of the poem which includes sections on historical background, characterization, performance, translation, and style.

Carpenter, Rhys. "Folk Tale and Fiction in the *Iliad.*" In his *Folk Tale, Fiction and Saga in the Homeric Epics,* pp. 68-89. Berkeley and Los Angeles: University of California Press, 1946.

Comments on the traditional literary components that make up the *Iliad* and examines patterns of magic and elements of dramatic form in the poem.

Clader, Linda Lee. *Helen: The Evolution from Divine to Heroic in Greek Epic Tradition.* Leiden, The Netherlands: E. J. Brill, 1976, 83 p.

Explores the role of Helen in the *Iliad, Odyssey,* and other poetry, and seeks to establish both a human and a divine identity for her.

Clarke, Howard. *Homer's Readers: A Historical Introduction to the "Iliad" and the "Odyssey."* Newark: University of Delaware Press, 1981, 327 p.

A historical survey of Homeric criticism from the medieval period to modern times. Clarke presents a concise but inclusive summary of various critical attempts to respond to the "Homeric question."

Clarke, W. M. "Achilles and Patroclus in Love." *Hermes: Zeitschrift fur Klassiche Philologie,* Heft 3, Band 106 (1978/3. Quartal): 381-96.

Examines the evidence for the contention that Achilles and Patroclus were homosexual lovers.

Coffey, Michael. "The Function of the Homeric Simile." *American Journal of Philology* LXXVIII, No. 2 (1957): 113-32.

A detailed study of the simile and its functions in the *Iliad* and the *Odyssey*.

Coleman, Arthur. "*Iliad.*" In his *Epic and Romance Criticism,* Vol. II, pp. 178-91. New York: Watermill Publishers, 1974.
A bibliography of *Iliad* criticism from 1940 to 1973.

Combellack, F. M. "Contemporary Homeric Scholarship: Sound or Fury?": I, II, and III. *The Classical Weekly* 49, Nos. 2, 3, and 4 (October 24; November 14; November 28, 1955): 17-26, 29-44, 45-55.
Surveys Homeric scholarship up to 1955, examining the state of studies on such topics as orality, archeology, literary merit, sources, transmission, and editions of the poems.

Dodds, E. R. "Agamemnon's Apology." In his *The Greeks and the Irrational,* pp. 1-27. Berkeley and Los Angeles: University of California Press, 1951.
Discusses the "divine temptation or infatuation . . . which led Agamemnon to compensate himself for the loss of his own mistress by robbing Achilles of his."

———, Palmer, L. R., and Gray, Dorothea. "Homer." In *Fifty Years (and Twelve) of Classical Scholarship,* edited by Maurice Platnauer, pp. 1-49. New York: Barnes & Noble, 1968.
Three bibliographic essays focusing on the analytic, unitarian, and oral schools of Homer criticism, respectively.

Donnelly, Francis P., S. J. "The Secret of Homeric Simile" and "Homeric Litotes." In his *Literature: The Leading Educator,* pp. 26-50, 51-72. New York: Longmans, Green and Co., 1938.
Focuses on the nature and function of similes and litotes in the *Iliad,* examining their narrative and oral qualities.

Duethorn, Guenter A. *Achilles' Shield and the Structure of the "Iliad."* Amherst, Mass.: Amherst College Press, 1962, 30 p.
Argues that "the shield [of Achilles] represents, like the chorus in fifth-century drama, the universalizing element in the poem; as an interlude of clarity it reflects the emotion of Achilles during his moment of revelation, and relates it to the world in general."

Ebel, Henry. "Homer." In his *After Dionysus: An Essay on Where We Are Now,* pp. 68-85. Rutherford, N.J.: Fairleigh Dickinson University Press, 1972.
Comments on several key aspects of the *Iliad*'s structure. Ebel contends that the poem "is about human relation and disrelation."

Foerster, Donald M. *Homer in English Criticism: The Historical Approach in the Eighteenth Century*. New Haven: Yale University Press, 1947, 133 p.
Traces historical and scientific approaches to Homer's works from the late seventeenth century to Robert Wood and the German critics.

Greene, Thomas. "The *Iliad.*" In his *The Descent from Heaven: A Study in Epic Continuity,* pp. 26-51. New Haven: Yale University Press, 1963.
Emphasizes the elements of continuity and the transformation of epic form in the *Iliad*. Greene concludes that the poem "was to be so healthy an influence on later poetry because it maintained so finely divided an interest between the outer and inner worlds."

Griffin, Jasper. *Homer*. Past Masters, edited by Keith Thomas. Oxford: Oxford University Press, 1980, pp. 16-45.
Griffin writes that he "sets out to explain the thought which underlies [the *Iliad*] and is conveyed by [it], with some indication of its significance for posterity and for us."

Groten, F. J., Jr. "Homer's Helen." *Greece and Rome* 2d Series XV, No. 1 (April 1968): 33-9.
Assesses the role of Helen in the *Iliad,* focusing on the issue of her responsibility for the Trojan War. Groten stresses that, "throughout the Homeric portrayal of Helen there exists no one consistent point of view about her actions."

Grube, G. M. A. "The Gods of Homer." In *Studies in Honour of Gilbert Norwood,* edited by Mary E. White. *The Phoenix,* Journal of the Classical Association of Canada, supplementary vol. 1. Toronto: University of Toronto Press, 1952, pp. 3-19.
Discusses the "insoluble paradox" of the characterization of the gods in the *Iliad*. Grube warns that in the poem, "men have only just begun to feel the need to impress upon the gods the essentials of their own moral code."

Gwinup, Thomas, and Dickinson, Fidelia. "*Iliad.*" In their *Greek and Roman Authors: A Checklist of Criticism,* pp. 107-11. Metuchen, N. J.: Scarecrow Press, 1982.
A bibliography of modern criticism of the *Iliad*.

Hoare, F. R. "The Epics of Homer." In his *Eight Decisive Books of Antiquity,* pp. 95-119. London: Sheed and Ward, 1952.
Explores the historical and cultural significance of Homer's epics, providing general background information for understanding their rise and character.

Ingalls, Jeremy. "Structural Unity of the *Iliad.*" *The Classical Journal* 42, No. 7 (April 1947): 399-406.
Ingalls analyzes the structure of the *Iliad* and hypothesizes that its "ordering and disposal of emotional stresses . . . may be analogous to the ordering and disposal of emotional stresses in the larger form of musical composition."

Jebb, R. C. *Homer: An Introduction to the "Iliad" and the "Odyssey."* 1894. Reprint. Port Washington, N.Y.: Kennikat Press, 1969, 201 p.
An early, important assessment that includes discussions of the *Iliad*'s style, historical background, and the influence of the poem from antiquity to the late nineteenth century.

Jensen, Minna Skafte. *The Homeric Question and the Oral-Formulaic Theory*. Opuscula Graecolatina, edited by Ivan Boserup, vol. 20. Copenhagen, Denmark: Museum Tusculanum Press, 1980, 226 p.
Argues that the *Iliad* was composed orally during the sixth century B.C. on the directive of the Greek emperor Pisistratus.

Kakridis, Johannes Th. "The Rôle of the Woman in the *Iliad.*" *Eranos* 54 (1956): 21-7.
Stresses that "it is the main poetic mission of a woman in the *Iliad* to consciously exert [a] restraining power over men, trying to avert them from doing their duty as they feel they should."

Kirk, G. S. *The "Iliad": A Commentary*. Volume I: books 1-4. Cambridge: Cambridge University Press, 1985, 409 p.
A line-by-line textual commentary on the first four books of the poem, including an introduction to its composition and style.

Knight, W. F. Jackson. *Many-Minded Homer: An Introduction*. Edited by John D. Christie. New York: Barnes & Noble, 1968, 224 p.
Includes commentary, originally written in 1938-39, on the literary and historical influences on Homer's poetry, its myth and legend, and its unity and greatness.

Kott, Jan. "Ajax Thrice Deceived, or The Heroism of the Absurd." In his *The Eating of the Gods: An Interpretation of Greek Tragedy,* translated by Boleslaw Taborski and Edward J. Czerwinski, pp. 43-77. New York: Random House, 1970.
Compares the treatment of Ajax in the *Iliad* with that in Sophocles's trajedy *Ajax*. Kott notes that "Ajax must first be despoiled of greatness and heroism before Sophocles will give him a moment of cold clear-sightedness and restore to him a gloomy greatness, so different from the Homeric . . . heroism."

Kullmann, Wolfgang. "Gods and Men in the *Iliad* and the *Odyssey*." *Harvard Studies in Classical Philology* 89 (1985): 1-23.
Highlights "the differences between the ways the [Homeric] epics represent relationships between gods and men." According to Kullmann, the *Iliad* exhibits "the tragic fate allotted to man by the gods," whereas the *Odyssey* shows "that correct behavior toward the gods may save man from coming to harm."

Lang, Andrew. *Homer and His Age*. 1906. Reprint. New York: AMS Press, 1968, 336 p.
A detailed study of Homeric history and culture. Lang, one of the most prominent defenders of unity in Homeric poetry, ad-

dresses "the fallacy . . . [of the analyst critics] of disregarding the Homeric poet's audience."

Lattimore, Richmond. "Man and God in Homer." *Proceedings of the American Philosophical Society* 114, No. 6 (December 1970): 411-22.

Includes a discussion of the treatment of various characters in the *Iliad.* Lattimore concludes that "Homer was not, like Hesiod, a didactic poet. His stories were told to delight and inform an audience. But in telling of persons, divine or human, every storyteller must be implicitly something of a moralist."

Lee, D. J. N. *The Similes of the "Iliad" and the "Odyssey" Compared.* Victoria, Australia: Melbourne University Press, 1964, 80 p.

A textual comparison of similes in the two poems. Lee's main interest lies in distinguishing older and newer parts of the *Iliad.*

Lloyd-Jones, Hugh. "The *Iliad.*" In his *The Justice of Zeus,* pp. 1-27. Sather Classical Lectures, vol. 41. Berkeley and Los Angeles: University of California Press, 1971.

An inquiry into "what part, if any, is played by justice or righteousness in the *Iliad,* and if it does play a part there, what kind of justice or righteousness it is."

Long, A. A. "Morals and Values in Homer." *The Journal of Hellenic Studies* XC (1970): 121-39.

Analyzes the system of morality embodied by the *Iliad,* stressing that its ethics are "complex and often difficult to describe in modern terminology." Long points to "a standard of appropriateness which condemns excess and deficiency" as paramount in Homeric poetry.

Lorimer, H. L. "Homer's Use of the Past." *The Journal of Hellenic Studies* XLIX, Part II (5 February 1930): 145-59.

Traces the various historical layers embedded in the *Iliad*'s narrative by analyzing material and stylistic evidence.

MacKay, L. A. *The Wrath of Homer.* Toronto: University of Toronto Press, 1948, 131 p.

Focuses on the structure and composition of the *Iliad.* MacKay's hypothesis is "that there was a Trojan war, and that Homer wrote about it a poem into which he introduced myths and legends from other sources, including his own invention."

Macleod, C. W. *Homer: "Iliad," Book XXIV.* Cambridge Greek and Latin Classics, edited by E. J. Kenney and Mrs. P. E. Easterling. Cambridge: Cambridge University Press, 1982, 161 p.

A detailed analysis of Book XXIV of the *Iliad* in terms of its "spirit," structure, style, and prosody.

McNamee, Maurice B., S.J. "Proud Achilles, the Noblest Achean of Them All." In his *Honor and the Epic Hero,* pp. 8-39. New York: Holt, Rinehart and Winston, 1960.

Focuses on the character of Achilles as hero of the *Iliad.* Arguing that, despite his ultimate fate, Achilles is not a tragic figure, McNamee points out that "he had lived gloriously; he had fought gloriously; he died gloriously and was gloriously honored after death; and he had the assurance that his glorious reputation would live on in the ears of men forever."

Michalopoulos, Andre. *Homer.* Twayne's World Authors Series, edited by Sylvia E. Bowman; Greece, edited by Mary P. Gianos. New York: Twayne Publishers, 1966, 217 p.

A general introduction to Homeric poetry and "the purpose, the ideals, and the beauty of the poet." Includes sections on history, structure, and characterization in the *Iliad.*

Moulton, Carroll. "The *Iliad.*" In his *Similes in the Homeric Poems,* pp. 18-116. Hypomnemata, vol. 49. Göttingen, West Germany: Vandenhoeck & Ruprecht, 1977.

An extensive study of similes in the *Iliad,* with sections on simile sequences, the role of similes in narrative structure, and the relation of similes to characterization.

Mueller, Martin. *The "Iliad."* Unwin Critical Library, edited by Claude Rawson. London: George Allen & Unwin, 1984, 210 p.

An overview of the history, style, and plot of the poem. Mueller also includes chapters on fighting in the *Iliad,* the simile, the gods, and composition of the work.

Nagler, Michael N. "The 'Eternal Return' in the Plot Structure of 'The *Iliad*'." In his *Spontaneity and Tradition: A Study in the Oral Art of Homer,* pp. 131-66. Berkeley and Los Angeles: University of California Press, 1974.

Explicates the structure of the poem in terms of the mythic pattern of "withdrawal," "devastation," and "return" of the hero. Nagler notes that while Achilles "merely returns to socially acceptable behavior in external terms, . . . he has grown in spiritual depth."

Owen, E. T. *The Story of the "Iliad" As Told in the "Iliad."* Toronto: Clarke, Irwin & Co., 1946, 248 p.

Examines the *Iliad* from the point of view of story-telling. Acknowledging that its plot "has held its listeners spellbound," Owen inquires into "how it works its spell."

Packard, David W., and Meyers, Tania. *A Bibliography of Homeric Scholarship: Preliminary Edition,* 1930-1970. Malibu, Calif.: Undena Publications, 1974, 183 p.

A bibliography based on yearly listings under "Homer" in *L'Année philologique,* a prominent classics journal.

Page, Denys L. *History and the Homeric "Iliad."* Berkeley and Los Angeles: University of California Press, 1963, 350 p.

A study of the historical background of the *Iliad.* Page examines the facts surrounding Troy and Mycenean Greece, with additional sections on documents and relics from the period of the Trojan War.

Parry, Adam. "The Language of Achilles." *Transactions of the American Philological Association* LXXXVII (1956): 1-7.

Focuses on the nature of Achilles' language in the poem and concludes that "Achilles is . . . the one Homeric hero who does not accept the common language, and feels that it does not correspond to reality."

———. "Have We Homer's *Iliad*?" *Yale Classical Studies* 20 (1966): 175-216.

Discusses the ways in which the origin and transmission of the *Iliad* have influenced its text as we have it today.

Pomeroy, Sarah B. "Women in the Bronze Age and Homeric Epic." In her *Goddesses, Whores, Wives, and Slaves: Women in Classical Antiquity,* pp. 16-31. New York: Schocken Books, 1975.

Focuses on the social and political roles of women in Greek Bronze Age culture and in Homeric poetry, concluding that classical depiction of women is "filled with inconsistencies."

Post, L. A. "The Moral Pattern in Homer." *American Philological Association Transactions & Proceedings* LXX (1939): 158-90.

Includes an analysis of the system of values and morals embodied by the *Iliad.*

———. "The Tragic Pattern of the *Iliad.*" In his *From Homer to Menander,* pp. 27-55. Berkeley and Los Angeles: University of California Press, 1951.

Explores the tragic elements in the *Iliad* and theorizes that the "double tragedy of Achilles and Hector is . . . unique in Greek literature" and ultimately teaches pity.

Prendergast, Guy Lushington. *A Complete Concordance to the "Iliad" of Homer.* Edited by Benedetto Marzullo. 1875. Reprint. Hildesheim: Georg Olms Verlag, 1983, 427 p.

A comprehensive concordance to the *Iliad.*

Redfield, James M. *Nature and Culture in the "Iliad": The Tragedy of Hector.* Chicago: University of Chicago Press, 1975, 287 p.

Deems Hector the hero of the *Iliad,* considering his story "as a self-contained and partly detachable whole."

Reckford, Kenneth J. "Helen in the *Iliad.*" *Greek Roman and Byzantine Studies* 5, No. 1 (Spring 1964): 5-20.

Focuses on the treatment of Helen in the *Iliad.* Reckford studies the way she is described through traditional formulas, individual characterization, and through her encounter with Aphrodite in Book 3 of the poem.

Rousseau, G. S. "Seven Types of *Iliad*." *English Miscellany* 16 (1965): 143-67.
Discusses the problems inherent in translating the *Iliad* by examining the ways in which several different scholars have translated a particular passage from the poem.

Rubino, Carl A., and Shelmerdine, Cynthia W., eds. *Approaches to Homer*. Austin: University of Texas Press, 1983, 275 p.
A collection of critical essays that includes commentary on the *Iliad* by such critics as Mabel L. Lang and Gregory Nagy.

Segal, Charles. *The Theme of the Mutilation of the Corpse in the "Iliad."* Mnemosyne: Biblioteca Classica Batava. Leiden, The Netherlands: E. J. Brill, 1971, 82 p.
Analyzing the incident of Achilles' mutilation of Hector's corpse, Segal demonstrates "how Homer manipulates his formulas for special effects and how contrasts and parallels between analogous scenes enlarge the range and significance of the action."

Shannon, Richard Stoll, III. *The Arms of Achilles and Homeric Compositional Technique*. Mnemosyne: Biblioteca Classica Batava. Leiden, The Netherlands: E. J. Brill, 1975, 108 p.
Emphasizes the role of armor in Homer's compositional technique in the *Iliad*.

Sheppard, J. T. *The Pattern of the "Iliad."* 1922. Reprint. New York: Barnes & Noble, 1969, 216 p.
Interprets the *Iliad* as a work of art, positing that "the pattern of its poetry, like the vision which the poetry interprets, is symmetrical, clear-cut, and simple."

Simpson, R. Hope, and Lazenby, J. F. *The Catalogue of the Ships in Homer's "Iliad."* Oxford: Oxford University Press, 1970, 191 p.
Presents an overview of the history of each kingdom mentioned in the *Iliad*'s catalogue of ships section.

Smith, Robinson, ed. *The Original "Iliad": Text and Translation*. London: Grafton & Co., 1938, 245 p.
Hypothesizing that "additions to the Original *Iliad* represent about three-fourths of the whole poem," Smith here presents an uninterpolated text of the poem.

Snodgrass, W. D. "Gods of the *Iliad:* Memoirs of a Brainpicker." In his *In Radical Pursuit: Critical Essays and Lectures,* pp. 320-64. New York: Harper and Row, 1975.
Presents an anecdotal account of his teaching of the *Iliad*.

Stawell, F. Melian. *Homer and the "Iliad": An Essay to Determine the Scope and Character of the Original Poem*. London: J. M. Dent and Co., 1909, 331 p.
An attempt to ascertain and describe the original text of the poem.

Steiner, George, and Fagles, Robert, ed. Twentieth Century Views, edited by Maynard Mack. *Homer: A Collection of Critical Essays*. Englewood Cliffs, N.J.: Prentice-Hall, 1962, 178 p.
Includes several essays on the *Iliad* by such critics as Cedric H. Whitman, Albert B. Lord, and Rachel Bespaloff.

Stoll, Elmer Edgar. "Art and Artifice in the *Iliad:* Or the Poetical Treatment of Character in Homer and Shakespeare." In his *Shakespeare and Other Masters,* pp. 362-93. Cambridge: Harvard University Press, 1940.
A discussion of characterization in the *Iliad* through a comparison of Homer's methods with those of Shakespeare.

Tait, Marion. "The Tragic Philosophy of the *Iliad*." *American Philological Association Transactions & Proceedings* LXXIV (1943): pp. 49-59.
Tait argues that, because it constantly depicts the conflict between life and death, "the scope of the *Iliad* is tragic rather than epic, and the two figures in whom the elements of conflict are made explicit, Achilles and Hector, are tragic rather than epic heroes."

Thornton, Agathe. *Homer's "Iliad": Its Composition and the Motif of Supplication*. Hypomnemata, 1984, vol. 81. Göttingen, West Germany: Vandenhoeck & Ruprecht, 182 p.
A reading of the *Iliad* that emphasizes the motif of supplication—its nature, its role in four key textual sequences, and its implications for the characterization of Agamemnon and Achilles.

Trypanis, C. A. *The Homeric Epics*. London: Aris and Phillips, 1977, 114 p.
Includes a general introduction to the authorship, structure, technique, and influence of the *Iliad*.

Versényi, Laszlo. "The *Iliad*." In his *Man's Measure: A Study of the Greek Image of Man from Homer to Sophocles,* pp. 1-42. Albany: State University of New York Press, 1974.
Comments on the view of man presented by the *Iliad*. Versényi posits that the main organizing principle of the poem is "the heroic image and heroic conception of life" it embodies.

Vivante, Paolo. *The Homeric Imagination*. Bloomington: Indiana University Press, 1970, 215 p.
A detailed study of the depiction of reality in Homeric poetry. Asserting that "Homeric poems are tantamount to a full-scale representation of reality," Vivante suggests that, "by abstracting it from everything else and becoming familiar with his language, we may learn to look with Homeric eyes."

———. *Homer*. New Haven: Yale University Press, 1985, 218 p.
An analysis of Homer's poetic style. According to Vivante, "we find in Homer not so much narrative as drama, or events in the making."

Wace, Alan J. B., and Stubbings, Frank H., eds. *A Companion to Homer*. London: Macmillan and Co., 1962, 595 p.
A comprehensive collection of critical essays on Homeric poems and their authorship, history, and archeology. Contributors include Sir Maurice Bowra, J. A. Davidson, and Carl W. Blegen, among others.

Webster, T. B. L. *From Mycenae to Homer*. London: Methuen and Co., 1958, 311 p.
Provides a description of Mycenean civilization and a discussion of its influence on Homer's poetry.

White, James Boyd. "Poetry and the World of Two: Cultural Criticism and the Ideal of Friendship in the *Iliad*." In his *When Words Lose Their Meaning: Constitutions and Reconstitutions of Language, Character, and Community,* pp. 24-58. Chicago: University of Chicago Press, 1984.
Analyzes language in the *Iliad* and its relation to Homer's "clearly defined and understood world" in the poem. Asserting that uncertainty, opposition, and tension are built into its language, White argues that the *Iliad* teaches the reader the reality of a universal vision, but also that such an ideal "is imperfectly attainable by man."

Willcock, M. M. *A Commentary on Homer's "Iliad," Books I-VI*. London: Macmillan, St. Martin's Press, 1970, 220 p.
A close textual and stylistic examination of Books I-VI of the *Iliad*. Includes a general introduction to the history, language, mythology, formulas, themes, and scansion of the work.

———. *A Companion to the Iliad*. Chicago: University of Chicago Press, 1976, 293 p.
Commentary intended for the first-time reader of the *Iliad*. The volume includes several explanatory appendices on transmission of the text, methods of warfare, and mythology.

Wright, John, ed. *Essays on the "Iliad."* Bloomington: Indiana University Press, 1978, 150 p.
A selection of contemporary essays on various topics relating to the *Iliad* written by such critics as Adam Parry, Norman Austin, and Martin Mueller.

Lady Murasaki

Genji monogatari (The Tale of Genji)

Circa Eleventh Century

Japanese novelist.

Written at the beginning of the eleventh century, *Genji monogatari* (*The Tale of Genji*) is considered the first novel in world literature and the greatest, most influential work of Japanese literature. The lengthy and detailed portrait of medieval aristocratic society found in the novel represents a major landmark in Japanese prose fiction, achieving a degree of narrative coherence and psychological depth which far surpasses that of similar works from the same period. The stylistic elegance and sophistication of this novel are still considered the supreme achievement of Japanese literature, and while *The Tale* is greatly valued for the insights it provides into the Heian period, it is most highly revered for its purely aesthetic qualities.

Even after centuries of investigation, the origins of *The Tale* remain somewhat obscure. Scholars have ascribed its composition with some degree of certainty to an aristocratic woman identified only as Murasaki Shikibu (Shikibu is usually translated as ''Lady'' and Murasaki is the principal female character of the novel; the author's real name is unknown). The few available facts concerning Murasaki's life and the creation of *The Tale* have been obtained primarily through the correlation of her cryptic diary with other equally cryptic documents of the period.

While the date and place of Murasaki's birth are not known, researchers have ascertained that she was born sometime between 970 and 979, with the majority favoring 978. As a member of the powerful Fujiwara clan and the daughter of a classical scholar of some note, she ranked in the highest stratum of Japanese society, a tiny elite whose concerns did not generally extend beyond the innumerable social and aesthetic intricacies of life in the emperor's court. In 996, Murasaki traveled with her father to the Echizen province, where he was to serve as governor. She married an elderly, wealthy nobleman named Fujiwara Nobutaka in 999; within one year she had given birth to a daughter, Kaneko, and within two years she became a widow. Nothing is recorded of Murasaki's subsequent life until her appearance in the court of the Empress Shoshi, known familiarly as Akiko, around 1005. Some scholars suggest that Murasaki had already written much of *The Tale* by that time, possibly to alleviate her grief and loneliness, and that she was summoned to the court because of the enormous popularity of the novel. An alternative theory maintains that Murasaki began *The Tale* after entering Akiko's entourage, composing the work as entertainment for the empress, whose activities were greatly circumscribed by custom and left her dependent largely upon her ladies-in-waiting for diversion. Although there is no documentation to support or discredit either opinion, most scholars accept the former, while noting that no matter when *The Tale* was begun, its extreme length seems to indicate that its composition required several years.

The events of Murasaki's first years at court are described in her diary, a brief document which has been attributed to her

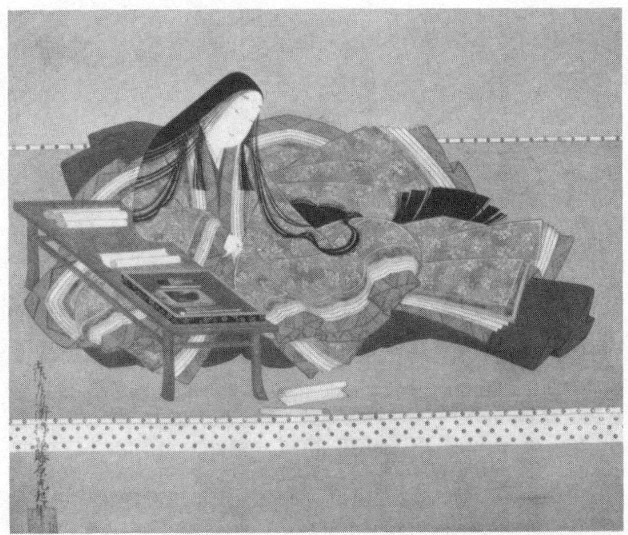

as the result of several references to *The Tale* that appear in the text. It is clear that she was present at the birth of the imperial prince Go-Ichijo in 1008 and that she enjoyed the special favor of both the empress and the powerful regent Michinaga. While some scholars believe that Murasaki became one of Michinaga's several concubines, they admit that evidence for such a relationship is inconclusive. One particularly significant passage in the diary describes Murasaki's central role in a book-binding project that is widely assumed to be the assembly of original manuscripts of *The Tale*. Although a series of poems bearing dates from 1010 to 1015 have also been attributed to her, nothing is known of Murasaki's life after the completion of her diary in early 1010. Commentators have attempted to construct an account of her final years based on the activities of her father, her brother Nobunori, and the empress, whose life was well documented, but their conclusions remain unsubstantiated.

Similarly, facts concerning *The Tale* itself are virtually nonexistent for the period during and immediately following Murasaki's lifetime. The diary's last reference to the novel occurs in a passage dated 1009: Murasaki complains that Michinaga has stolen a manuscript copy from her room and fears that her inferior calligraphy will disgrace her. Some scholars maintain that this passage suggests *The Tale* had been completed at that point. As a matter of traditional humility, Murasaki makes no further mention of the novel or its popularity. It is assumed that, according to the custom of the period, she sent portions of the work to a number of calligraphers to be copied and later supervised the assembly of the pages into a series of small booklets, one volume for each chapter. None of these original copies still exist and it is not known how many such versions ultimately circulated. Scholars do know, however, that the novel was widely read, for it is frequently mentioned in surviving documents from the late eleventh and early twelfth centuries. In the diary of a young girl from 1022, for example, a complete set of the fifty-four chapters is described as her most cherished possession. Arthur Waley, who first translated *The Tale* into English, believes this diary reference suggests that there were not many complete copies of the novel available at the time. The earliest surviving version of the novel was transcribed by the poet Fujiwara Teika at the beginning of the twelfth century; while variant texts exist, Fujiwara's version is regarded as standard. The language of the Heian period (794-1184), however, bears little resemblance to modern Japanese, so most contemporary Japanese readers must rely upon one of the several modernized versions of *The Tale*.

Written in a classic Japanese form known as the *monogatari,* or prose tale, *The Tale* nevertheless represents a radical departure from its predecessors in both content and style. Donald Keene has noted that *monogatari* written prior to *The Tale* lacked continuity and were, as a result, no more than collections of short episodes featuring an assortment of hyperbolic characters drawn from supernatural folk legends. In relating the numerous amatory adventures of Prince Genji, Murasaki created a lengthy but unified narrative using realistic characters and events, thoroughly modernizing the *monogatari* and in effect fashioning a new narrative form. Critics have frequently noted the surprising sophistication of Murasaki's literary techniques. They stress that the actions of her characters are not explained as results of such metaphysical forces as fate or deities, as in earlier *monogatari,* but in terms of such human motivations as passion, altruism, and jealousy. Murasaki's perceptive portrayal of various characters' emotional states is considered one of the chief strengths of the novel. In addition, she subtly achieves narrative coherence through recurrent patterns of action and symbolic motifs, creating a story which, according to W. C. Aston, "flows on easily from one scene of real life to another, giving us a varied and minutely detailed picture of life and society at Kiōto such as we possess for no other country at the same period."

As the hero of *The Tale,* Prince Genji, called "The Shining One," has been the focus of much popular and critical attention. Possessed of human virtues and failings, he is considered such a realistic character that a historical analogue has been sought. The critic William J. Puette has observed that Genji is also "the quintessential manifestation" of Heian ideals. Puette adds that, because these ideals differ so radically from those of the modern West, it is difficult for occidental readers to comprehend Genji's reputation among the Japanese people. Chief among Genji's virtues is his sensitivity to beauty and sadness, a quality that the eighteenth-century critic Motoori Norinaga termed *mono no aware*. Indeed, the reason Genji becomes involved in so many romantic liaisons during the course of the novel is that he is completely unable to resist the charm of a beautiful woman and is frequently overcome by compassion for an unfortunate one. Genji's own physical beauty and artistic sensibilities serve to indicate the emphasis placed on aesthetic factors in the aristocratic society of Heian Japan: in an atmosphere where conversations were conducted in the form of poetry and an incorrect color combination in garments was a shocking reflection on the dignity of the wearer, the heroic figure was one whose tastes were irreproachable and whose appearance was flawless.

Analysis and exegesis of *The Tale* began within one generation of its composition: initially, commentators concentrated on interpretation of the text and on such matters as the family relationships of the many characters. By the early fourteenth century, the language spoken by educated Japanese had become so different from that of *The Tale* that the greatest work of Japanese literature was rapidly becoming unreadable. In response, scholars compiled a special dictionary of words used in the text and devoted much commentary to simple explanation of the plot. Later in the medieval period, the focus of scholarship shifted to complex textual analysis, with rival schools developing secret and carefully guarded solutions to classic exegetical difficulties. Since that time, the amount of textual criticism and explication has grown steadily and an estimated ten thousand books have been devoted to various aspects of *The Tale*. The most renowned commentary was written by Motoori, who disputed the two most widely accepted interpretations of his time. From its appearance, the novel had been viewed by Buddhist scholars as a lesson in the impermanence of physical reality, and by Confucians as a series of biographies of virtuous, enlightened women. Motoori asserted that *The Tale* was not intended as an illustration of any philosophical or religious doctrine, but that it was concerned with "the goodness of those who are aware of the sorrow of human existence." The strength of Motoori's argument was immediately perceived, and his interpretation of the novel continues to be the basis for all scholarship on *The Tale*.

While a few chapters of *The Tale* were translated into English late in the nineteenth century, a complete English edition was not available until 1933, when Waley published the final volume of the six-part translation he had begun in 1925. Critical response was unanimously favorable, with some commentators ranking *The Tale* among the finest novels ever written. Although several critics noted that Murasaki's concentration upon the emotional life of her characters resulted in a lack of narrative depth, and others lamented the novel's extreme length, their objections were always balanced by an appreciation of the beauty of Murasaki's language and the perceptiveness of her characterizations. Many readers were also delighted by the opportunity to become acquainted with an exotic culture so far removed from their own. When Edward Seidensticker published his two-volume translation of the novel in 1976, scholars noted that Waley had evidently performed what Ivan Morris called "the freest possible type of translation," embellishing the narrative where he thought best and deleting portions he considered too obscure. Conversely, Seidensticker chose to follow Murasaki's text as closely as possible, even when that method resulted in equivocal passages. Nevertheless, critics value both versions of *The Tale,* and revelations concerning Waley's textual manipulations have not reduced critical esteem for the novel itself.

Despite its critical reputation, *The Tale* still enjoys only limited popularity in the West, due in part to cultural barriers. In Japan, however, the novel is widely read and universally revered. Much of its renown stems from the fact that, like such Western classics as Homer's *Odyssey* and Dante Alighieri's *Inferno, The Tale* has inspired countless drawings and paintings, as well as other literary works. As a result, even those Japanese who have never read the novel are familiar with its plot and characters. Nevertheless, the unrivalled importance of this work remains its purely literary merit; according to Nobel laureate Yasunari Kawabata, *The Tale* represents "the highest pinnacle of Japanese literature."

PRINCIPAL ENGLISH TRANSLATIONS

The Tale of Genji (translated by Arthur Waley). 6 vols. 1925-33
[The six volumes were subtitled and issued in the following manner: *The Tale of Genji,* 1925; *The Sacred Tree,* 1926; *A Wreath of Cloud,* 1927; *Blue Trousers,* 1928; *The Lady of the Boat,* 1932; *The Bridge of Dreams,* 1933.]

Diaries of the Court Ladies of Old Japan (translated by Annie Shepley Omori and Kochi Doi) 1935

The Tale of Genji (translated by Edward Seidensticker). 2 vols. 1976

Murasaki Shikibu: Her Diary and Poetic Memoirs (translated by Richard Bowring) 1982

MOTOORI NORINAGA (essay date 1801?)

[Motoori was one of the most prominent literary scholars and philosophers of eighteenth-century Japan. His nine-volume interpretation of The Tale *is considered a watershed in the history of* Genji *scholarship, since, unlike his Buddhist and Confucian predecessors, he considered the novel's realistic portrayal of eleventh-century court life to be its chief literary merit. In the following excerpt, Motoori explains that Murasaki's conception of human goodness is based on "awareness of the sorrow of human existence." Since the date of composition of this essay is unknown, Motoori's death date has been used.]*

There have been many interpretations over the years of the purpose of [***The Tale of Genji***]. But all of these interpretations have been based not on a consideration of the nature of the novel itself but rather on the novel as seen from the point of view of Confucian and Buddhist works, and thus they do not represent the true purpose of the author. To seize upon an occasional similarity in sentiment or a chance correspondence in ideas with Confucian and Buddhist works, and proceed to generalize about the nature of the tale as a whole, is unwarranted. The general appeal of this tale is very different from that of such didactic works. (pp. 532-33)

Good and evil as found in this tale do not correspond to good and evil as found in Confucian and Buddhist writings. . . . Good and evil extend to all realms. Even with the human being good and evil are not necessarily limited to his thinking and his conduct. Rank and position imply good and evil; thus, the noble person is regarded as good, the lowly as bad. In the ***Tale*** persons of high rank are spoken of as good, while in common parlance there are such expressions as "of good family" and "of good or bad standing." Thus it is too that we speak of good or bad features of one's face. Again, longevity, wealth, and prosperity are all good things, while short life, poverty, failure, loss of material things, illness, and disaster are all bad things. In addition to these strictly human aspects of good and evil, there is good and evil in such things as dress, furniture, housing, and in fact in all things. Thus, it is not only in the psychological and ethical realms of life that we find good and evil. Again, good and evil are not constant—they change according to time and circumstance. For example, an arrow is good if it penetrates its object, while armor is good if it is impenetrable. In the heat of a summer day coolness is good, while in the cold of winter heat is good. For the man who treads the road at night darkness is bad, but for the one who seeks to conceal himself moonlight is bad. In such a way all things may be good or bad. Thus too the good and bad in man's mind and in his acts may not be as opposed to each other as they seem: they differ according to the doctrines one follows. What Confucianism deems good Buddhism may not; and what Buddhism considers good Confucianism might regard as evil. Likewise, references to good and evil in the ***Tale*** may not correspond to Confucian or Buddhist concepts of good and evil. Then what is good or evil in the realm of human psychology and ethics according to the ***Tale of Genji?*** Generally speaking, those who know the meaning of the sorrow of human existence, i.e.,those who are in sympathy and in harmony with human sentiments, are regarded as good; and those who are not aware of the poignancy of human existence, i.e., those who are in sympathy and not in harmony with human sentiments, are regarded as bad. Regarded in this light, good and evil in the ***Tale*** may not appear to be especially different from that in Confucianism or Buddhism. However, if examined closely it will be noted that there are many points of difference, as, for example, in the statement about being or not being in harmony with human sentiment. The ***Tale*** presents even good and evil in gentle and calm terms unlike the intense, compelling, dialectical manner of Confucian writings.

Since novels have as their object the teaching of the meaning of the nature of human existence, there are in their plots many points contrary to Confucian and Buddhist teaching. This is because among the varied feelings of man's reaction to things—whether good, bad, right, or wrong—there are feelings contrary to reason, however improper they may be. Man's feelings do not always follow the dictates of his mind. They arise in man in spite of himself and are difficult to control. In the instance of Prince Genji, his interest in and rendezvous with Utsusemi, Oborozukiyo, and the Consort Fujitsubo are acts of extraordinary iniquity and immorality according to the Confucian and Buddhist points of view. It would be difficult to call Prince Genji a good man, however numerous his other good qualities. But the ***Tale*** does not dwell on his iniquitous and immoral acts, but rather recites over and over again his profound awareness of the sorrow of existence, and represents him as a good man who combines in himself all good things in man. . . .

For all that, the ***Tale*** does not regard Genji's misdeeds as good. The evil nature of his acts is obvious and need not be restated here. Besides, there is a type of writing which has as its purpose the consideration of such evils—in fact, there are quite a few such writings—and an objective story therefore need not be used for such a purpose. The novel is neither like the Buddhist Way which teaches man to attain enlightenment without deviating from the rightful way, nor like the Confucian Way which teaches man how to govern the country or to regulate one's home or one's conduct. It is simply a tale of human life which leaves aside and does not profess to take up at all the question of good and bad, and which dwells only upon the goodness of those who are aware of the sorrow of human existence. The purpose of the ***Tale of Genji*** may be likened to the man who, loving the lotus flower, must collect and store muddy and foul water in order to plant and cultivate the flower. The impure mud of illicit love affairs described in the ***Tale*** is there not for the purpose of being admired but for the purpose of nurturing the flower of the awareness of the sorrow of human existence. Prince Genji's conduct is like the lotus flower which is happy and fragrant but which has its roots in filthy muddy water. But the ***Tale*** does not dwell on the impurity of the water; it dwells only on those who are sympathetically kind and who are aware of the sorrow of human existence, and it holds these feelings to be the basis of the good man. (pp. 533-35)

Motoori Norinaga, "Good and Evil in the 'Tale of Genji'," translated by Ryusaku Tsunoda, in Sources of Japanese Tradition, *Ryusaku Tsunoda, William Theodore de Bary, Donald Keene, eds., Columbia University Press, 1958, pp. 532-35.*

W. G. ASTON (essay date 1899)

[*In the following excerpt, Aston discusses the style of* The Tale *and addresses several common criticisms of the work.*]

The ***Genji Monogatari*** is a novel. There is nothing remarkable, it may be said, in a woman excelling in this branch of literature. But Murasaki no Shikibu did more than merely write a successful novel. Like Fielding in England, she was the creator in Japan of this kind of fiction—the prose epic of real life, as it has been called. In the quality of her genius, however, she more resembled Fielding's great contemporary Richardson. Before her time we have nothing but stories of no great length, and of a romantic character far removed from the realities of daily life. The ***Genji Monogatari*** is realistic in the best sense of the word. Here we see depicted men and women, especially women, as they are, in their everyday lives and surroundings, their sentiments and passions, their faults and weaknesses. The author does not aim at startling or horrifying her readers, and she has a wholesome abhorrence for all that is sensational, unnatural, monstrous, or improbable. Such a hero as the nineteenth-century novelist Bakin's Tametomo, who has two pupils to his eyes and one arm longer than the other, and who, after falling over a cliff many thousand feet high, presently picks himself up and walks home several miles as if nothing had happened, would have seemed to her as ridiculous as he does to ourselves. There are few dramatic situations in the ***Genji,*** and what little of miraculous and supernatural it contains is of a kind which might well be believed by a contemporary reader. The story flows on easily from one scene of real life to another, giving us a varied and minutely detailed picture of life and society at Kiōto such as we possess for no other country at the same period.

The hero is the son of a Mikado by a favourite concubine, whose colleagues are all jealous of the preference shown her, and are continually annoying her in a petty way. She takes this so much to heart that she falls ill and dies. Her death is related with much pathos. Genji grows up to be a handsome and accomplished youth of a very susceptible disposition, and his history is mainly an account of his numerous love affairs, and of his ultimate union with Murasaki, a heroine in all respects worthy of him. It continues the story up to his death at the age of fifty-one. The last ten books, which relate chiefly to one of Genji's sons, are by some considered a separate work.

The style of the ***Genji*** has been called ornate. The writer who applied this epithet to it was probably thinking of the courtly honorifics with which it is in many places burdened. But there is much excuse for this. The ***Genji*** is a novel of aristocratic life. Most of the characters are personages of rank, in describing whose sayings and actions a courtly style of speech is indispensable. To a Japanese it would be simply shocking to say that a Mikado has breakfast—he augustly deigns to partake of the morning meal, and so on. The European reader finds this irritating and tiresome at first, but he soon gets accustomed to it. In truth, such language is in entire consonance with the elaborate ceremonial, the imposing but cumbrous costumes, and much else of the rather artificial life of the Japanese court of the time. Apart from this the style of the ***Genji*** is not more ornate than that, let us say, of *Robinson Crusoe,* and incomparably less so than that of many Japanese books of later date. It is free from any redundance of descriptive adjectives or profusion of metaphors such as we are accustomed to associate with the word ornate.

Others have objected to the style of the ***Genji*** as wanting in brevity. It must be admitted that its long, involved sentences contrast strongly with the direct, concise manner of the *Ise Monogatari*. But, as Motoöri points out, a brief style may be a bad one, and lengthy sentences full of detail may best fit the subject. Murasaki no Shikibu's fulness is not prolixity. On close examination it will be found that there is nothing superfluous in the abundant details of her narrative. That is her method, and is essential to the effect she aims at producing.

The ***Genji*** is not intrinsically a very difficult work, and no doubt the author's contemporaries found it quite easy to understand. But since then the language, institutions, and manners and customs of Japan have changed so much as greatly to obscure the meaning, not only to European students, but to the Japanese themselves. Piles of commentary by native editors have been accumulated over it, and their interpretations are often so blundering and inadequate that Motoori found it necessary to devote to its elucidation a critical work in nine volumes, mostly taken up with correcting the errors of his predecessors.

The enormous bulk of the ***Genji*** will always remain another obstacle to its just appreciation by European readers. It is in fifty-four books, which in the standard (but not very satisfactory) Kogetsushō edition run to no less than 4234 pages. The genealogical tree alone of the personages which figure in it, comprising several Mikados, a crowd of Princes, Princesses, and Imperial consorts, with a host of courtiers, occupies eighty pages.

Japanese critics claim for the ***Genji*** that it surpasses anything of the kind in Chinese literature, and even deserves to be ranked with the masterpieces of European fiction. None, however, but an extreme Japanophile (the species is not altogether unknown) will go so far as to place Murasaki no Shikibu on a level with Fielding, Thackeray, Victor Hugo, Dumas, and Cervantes. On the other hand, it is unjust to dismiss her summarily with the late M. George Bousquet as "cette ennuyeuse Scudéry japonaise" [that boring Japanese Scudéry]. . . . There are in the ***Genji*** pathos, humour, an abundant flow of pleasing sentiment, keen observation of men and manners, an appreciation of the charms of nature, and a supreme command of the resources of the Japanese language, which in her hands reached its highest point of excellence. Though never melodramatic, she gives us plenty of incident, and is seldom dull. A scholar, she abhorred pedantry and fine writing, the bane of so many of the modern novelists of Japan.

It is unnecessary to discuss here the opinion of some Japanese writers, that the ***Genji*** was written to inculcate Buddhist doctrine, or the notion of others, that the teaching of Confucian morality was its aim. Nor need we trouble ourselves with the suggestion that it is a novel *à clef,* and that the personages are to be identified with real persons who were alive at the time when it was written. As Motoöri very justly observes, all these ideas show an ignorance of the true object of novel-writing, which is to excite our sympathies, and to interest and amuse by the presentation of a picture of real life.

Another subject much dwelt on by native critics is the morality of the ***Genji,*** some denouncing it, as it deserves, while others strive to defend what even from the Japanese point of view is indefensible. Truth to say, the laxity of morals which it depicts is deplorable. It is a satisfaction to add that it belongs to the age and country in which the author lived, and that her own private life is admittedly free from any stain of this kind. Of coarseness and pruriency, moreover, there is none in the ***Genji,*** or indeed in the literature of this period generally. The language is almost invariably decent, and even refined, and we hardly ever meet with a phrase calculated to bring a blush to the cheek of a young person. (pp. 93-8)

W. G. Aston, "'Genji Monogatari'," in his A History of Japanese Literature, *1899. Reprint by Johnson Reprint Corporation, 1966, pp. 92-103.*

AMY LOWELL (essay date 1920)

[Lowell was the leading proponent of Imagism in American poetry. Like the Symbolists before her, some of whom she examined in Six French Poets, *Lowell experimented with free verse forms. Under the influence of Ezra Pound, Lowell's poetry exhibited the new style of Imagism, consisting of clear and precise rhetoric, exact rendering of images, and greater metrical freedom. Although she was popular in her time, standard evaluations of Lowell accord her more importance as a promoter of new artistic ideas than as a poet in her own right. In the following excerpt, she discusses the importance of* The Tale *in Japanese literature, stressing that its realism, Murasaki's principal innovation, was "the flash from a mind of genius."]*

[Murasaki] had made herself famous, not only for her own time, but for all time, by writing the first realistic novel of Japan. This book is the ***Genji Monogatari*** or "Narrative of Genji."

Hitherto, Japanese authors had confined themselves to stories of no great length, and which relied for their interest on a fairy or wonder element. The ***Genji Monogatari*** struck out an entirely new direction. It depicted real life in Kioto as a contemporary gentleman might have lived it. It founded its interest on the fact that people like to read about themselves, but this, which seems to us a commonplace, was a glaring innovation when Murasaki Shikibu attempted it; it was, in fact, the flash from a mind of genius. . . . It is an enormous work, comprising no less than fifty-four books and running to over four thousand pages—the genealogical tree of the personages alone is eighty pages long—but no reader of the ***Diary*** will need to be convinced that the ***Genji*** is not merely sprightly and captivating, but powerful as well. The lady was shrewd, and if she were also kindly and very attractive, nevertheless she saw with an uncompromising eye. Her critical faculty never sleeps, and takes in the minutest detail of anything she sees, noting unerringly every little rightness and wrongness connected with it. (pp. xxi-xxii)

Amy Lowell, in an introduction to Diaries of Court Ladies of Old Japan, *translated by Annie Shepley Omori and Kochi Doi, 1920. Reprint by Kenkyusha Co., 1935, pp. ix-xxix.*

RAYMOND MORTIMER (essay date 1925)

[In the following excerpt, Mortimer compares The Tale *favorably with several classics of Western literature. For additional commentary by Mortimer, see the excerpt dated 1928.]*

It is amusing to wonder which are the twelve finest novels that the genius of man has so far produced. The other day I was stimulated to make a list—no one is likely to agreê with it, especially as it includes no novel the interest of which is not chiefly psychological. Here it is: *La Princesse de Clèves, Clarissa Harlowe, Les Liaisons Dangereuses, Persuasion, Adolphe, Les Illusions Perdues, La Chartreuse de Parme, War and Peace, L'Education Sentimentale, The Brothers Karamazov,* and *A la Recherche du Temps Perdu*. If one started to discuss the reasons for such a choice and the other strong candidates, there would be room for nothing else upon this page. But some mathematically minded person may have noticed that only eleven books are included. I suspect that the name of the twelfth is ***The Tale of Genji;*** and it was reading it which made me attempt this list of its Occidental rivals. . . .

[He] is a Prince, the son of an Emperor, this Genji whose life Lady Murasaki invented in a novel so long that the present volume is only the first of six [of Waley's translation]. But you must not imagine that the tale is one of those picaresque novels, including a hundred other tales, all packed with ingenious incident, which have found favour in the East. ***The Tale of Genji*** resembles *The Arabian Nights* infinitely less than it does Proust. Smart contrivances and curious accidents—the stock-in-trade of the Eastern story-teller—are neglected by Lady Murasaki to an extent unparalleled in Europe till quite recently. She describes the state of mind of her characters when faced with the possibility of an event, and the state of mind resulting from it; but the description of the event itself is dispatched in a few sentences, or written only between the lines. Almost all the qualities which the European novel has been slowly gathering through the three hundred years of its existence are here already. The character-drawing is achieved by the most delicate touches, wrong attributions of motive, for instance, by one personage to another: these people are always wondering what impression they are making and what is going on in other people's minds. The little ways of children and servants are caught to perfection. And, above all, the authoress writes with profound understanding of the passion of love in its various and most sophisticated forms; of the way the image of the beloved is created by the lover's imagination; and of the attraction of the exotic, the bizarre, the unresponding, and the unexplored.

The sensibility of the characters is, indeed, uncannily like our own. I do not think our Victorian grandfathers would have cared for the book at all. There are, of course, touches of local colour, chariots drawn by bulls, perfumed clothes, paper windows, fireflies, and verandahs. But the translator has evidently made these as little insistent as possible, and it is something of a shock when one realizes, for instance, that these ladies, whose feelings are so like those of the more civilized of our contemporaries, follow the fashion of their time by blackening their teeth. There are moments curiously reminiscent of Proust; take the scene where Genji with his mistress hears the various street-cries and sounds of the early morning; and then, a year later, hearing them again, is suddenly overwhelmed with sorrow for her loss. Again, the passionate feeling for nature, and the longing for the companion who would share one's appreciation of its beauties, are carried to a point hardly known in Europe before the Romantic Movement. And in her use of atmosphere, her description of overgrown gardens and dilapidated country houses, of snowy desolation and terrifying storms, Lady Murasaki positively reminds one of the Brontës.

The civilization that makes the setting for the tale is intensely æsthetic. The personages never meet or correspond without quoting or extemporizing poems to express their sentiments. Good breeding is shown not only by tactful behaviour but by accomplishment in music, verse-writing, and, above all, calligraphy; and the young bloods rival each other in dancing, as they would to-day in tennis or shooting. Good taste is a matter of the first importance, and though some of the characters lament "these latter and degenerate days," the younger ones demand that everything, from clothes to verses, should be quite "up to date." Society is in some ways like that of Europe in the days of Chivalry; the hierarchy of class is sharply defined, and religious observances are continual. Two of the characters die by a sort of unconscious witchcraft as a result of the jealousy they inspire. "It is a fundamental thesis of the book," says Mr. Waley, "that hate kills." But the Buddhism of the time appears, on the whole, an unembarrassing creed. . . .

[It] is clear that Lady Murasaki has every quality that goes to make a great novelist—imagination, humour, uncommon good sense, a lively phrase, a command of narrative on a large scale, and a sympathetic, observant regard for human character. . . .

Whether Mr. Waley's translation is good in the sense of being accurate, I cannot say. But certainly the style he has found for it is beyond praise: tact when carried to such a point amounts to an act of creative imagination. The resulting work fascinates me so much that I have read it twice. And without a second reading to confirm my opinion, I should hardly dare to suggest, as I most definitely do, that, when completed, ***The Tale of Genji*** will probably prove one of the twelve great novels of the world.

Raymond Mortimer, "A New Planet," in The Nation and Athenaeum, *Vol. XXXVII, No. 12, June 20, 1925, p. 371.*

VIRGINIA WOOLF (essay date 1925)

[A British novelist and essayist, Woolf is considered one of the most prominent literary figures of twentieth-century English literature. Like her contemporary James Joyce, with whom she is often compared, Woolf is remembered for her innovative use of the stream of consciousness method. Concerned primarily with depicting the life of the mind, she revolted against traditional narrative techniques and developed her own highly individualized style. Woolf's works, noted for their subjective explorations of characters' inner lives and for their delicate poetic quality, have had a lasting effect on the art of the novel. Her critical essays, termed "creative, appreciative, and subjective" by Barbara Currier Bell and Carol Ohmann, cover almost the entire range of English literature and contain some of her finest prose. In the following excerpt, Woolf discusses the effect of Murasaki's cultural milieu upon the style and content of The Tale. *Woolf's comments were originally published in* Vogue *magazine in July 1925.*]

[Readers] will scarcely need to be reminded that it was about the year 991 that Ælfric composed his Homilies, that his treatises upon the Old and New Testament were slightly later in date, and that both works precede that profound, if obscure, convulsion which set Swegen of Denmark upon the throne of England. Perpetually fighting, now men, now swine, now thickets and swamps, it was with fists swollen with toil, minds contracted by danger, eyes stung with smoke and feet that were cold among the rushes that our ancestors applied themselves to the pen, transcribed, translated and chronicled, or burst rudely and hoarsely into crude spasms of song.

Sumer is icumen in,
Lhude sing cuccu

—such is their sudden harsh cry. Meanwhile, at the same moment, on the other side of the globe the Lady Murasaki was looking out into her garden, and noticing how "among the leaves were white flowers with petals half unfolded like the lips of people smiling at their own thoughts."

While the Ælfrics and the Ælfreds croaked and coughed in England, this court lady, about whom we know nothing,. . . was sitting down in her silk dress and trousers with pictures before her and the sound of poetry in her ears, with flowers in her garden and nightingales in the trees, with all day to talk in and all night to dance in—she was sitting down about the year 1000 to tell the story of the life and adventures of Prince Genji. But we must hasten to correct the impression that the Lady Murasaki was in any sense a chronicler. Since her book was read aloud, we may imagine an audience; but her listeners must have been astute, subtle minded, sophisticated men and women. They were grown-up people, who needed no feats of strength to rivet their attention; no catastrophe to surprise them. They were absorbed, on the contrary, in the contemplation of man's nature; how passionately he desires things that are denied; how his longing for a life of tender intimacy is always thwarted; how the grotesque and the fantastic excite him beyond the simple and straighforward; how beautiful the falling snow is, and how, as he watches it, he longs more than ever for someone to share his solitary joy.

The Lady Murasaki lived, indeed, in one of those seasons which are most propitious for the artist, and, in particular for an artist of her own sex. The accent of life did not fall upon war; the interests of men did not centre upon politics. Relieved from the violent pressure of these two forces, life expressed itself chiefly in the intricacies of behaviour, in what men said and what women did not quite say, in poems that break the surface of silence with silver fins, in dance and painting, and in that love of the wildness of nature which only comes when people feel themselves perfectly secure. In such an age as this Lady Murasaki, with her hatred of bombast, her humour, her common sense, her passion for the contrasts and curiosities of human nature, for old houses mouldering away among the weeds and the winds, and wild landscapes, and the sound of water falling, and mallets beating, and wild geese screaming, and the red noses of princesses, for beauty indeed, and that incongruity which makes beauty still more beautiful, could bring all her powers into play spontaneously. It was one of those moments . . . when it was natural for a writer to write of ordinary things beautifully, and to say openly to her public, "It is the common that is wonderful, and if you let yourselves be put off by extravagance and rant and what is surprising and momentarily impressive you will be cheated of the most profound of pleasures." For there are two kinds of artists, said Murasaki: one who makes trifles to fit the fancy of the passing day, the other who "strives to give real beauty to the things which men actually use, and to give to them the shapes which tradition has ordained." How easy it is, she said, to impress and surprise; "to paint a raging sea monster riding a storm"—any toy maker can do that, and be praised to the skies. "But ordinary hills and rivers, just as they are, houses such as you may see anywhere, with all their real beauty and harmony of form—quietly to draw such scenes as this, or to show what lies behind some intimate hedge that is folded away far from the world, and thick trees upon some unheroic hill, and all this with befitting care for composition, proportion, and the like—such works demand the highest master's utmost skill and must needs draw the common craftsman into a thousand blunders."

Something of her charm for us is doubtless accidental. It lies in the fact that when she speaks of "houses such as you may see anywhere" we at once conjure up something graceful, fantastic, decorated with cranes and chrysanthemums, a thousand miles removed from Surbiton and the Albert Memorial. We give her, and luxuriate in giving her, all those advantages of background and atmosphere which we are forced to do without in England to-day. But we should wrong her deeply if, thus seduced, we prettified and sentimentalised an art which, exquisite as it is, is without a touch of decadence, which, for all its sensibility, is fresh and childlike and without a trace of the exaggeration or languor of an outworn civilisation. But the essence of her charm lies deeper far than cranes and chrysanthemums. It lies in the belief which she held so simply—and was, we feel, supported in holding by Emperors and waiting maids, by the air she breathed and the flowers she saw—that the true artist "strives to give real beauty to the things which men actually use and to give to them the shapes which tradition has ordained." On she went, therefore, without hesitation or self-consciousness, effort or agony, to tell the story of the enchanting boy—the Prince who danced "The Waves of the Blue Sea" so beautifully that all the princes and great gentlemen wept aloud; who loved those whom he could not possess; whose libertinage was tempered by the most perfect courtesy; who played enchantingly with children, and preferred, as his women friends knew, that the song should stop before he had heard the end. To light up the many facets of his mind, Lady Murasaki, being herself a woman, naturally chose the medium of other women's minds. Aoi, Asagao, Fujitsubo, Murasaki, Yugao, Suyetsumuhana, the beautiful, the red-nosed, the cold, the passionate—one after another they turn their clear or freakish light upon the gay young man at the centre, who flies, who pursues, who laughs, who sorrows, but is always filled with the rush and bubble and chuckle of life.

Unhasting, unresting, with unabated fertility, story after story flows from the brush of Murasaki. Without this gift of invention we might well fear that the tale of Genji would run dry before the six volumes [of Mr. Waley's translation] are filled. With it, we need have no such foreboding. We can take our station and watch, through Mr. Waley's beautiful telescope, the new star rise in perfect confidence that it is going to be large and luminous and serene—but not, nevertheless, a star of the first magnitude. No; the lady Murasaki is not going to prove herself the peer of Tolstoi and Cervantes or those other great storytellers of the Western world whose ancestors were fighting or squatting in their huts while she gazed from her lattice window at flowers which unfold themselves "like the lips of people smiling at their own thoughts." Some element of horror, of terror, of sordidity, some root of experience has been removed from the Eastern world so that crudeness is impossible and coarseness out of the question, but with it too has gone some vigour, some richness, some maturity of the human spirit, failing which the gold is silvered and the wine mixed with water. All comparisons between Murasaki and the great Western writers serve but to bring out her perfection and their force. But it is a beautiful world; the quiet lady with all her breeding, her insight and her fun, is a perfect artist; and for years to come we shall be haunting her groves, watching her moons rise and her snow fall, hearing her wild geese cry and her flutes and lutes and flageolets tinkling and chiming, while the Prince tastes and tries all the queer savours of life and dances so exquisitely that men weep, but never passes the bounds of decorum, or relaxes his search for something different, something finer, something withheld. (pp. 424-27)

Virginia Woolf, "'The Tale of Genji'," in Literature East and West, *Vol. XI, No. 4, December, 1967, pp. 424-27.*

ROBERT LITTELL (essay date 1925)

[*An American journalist and critic, Littell was associate editor of* The New Republic *from 1921 to 1927 and later served as the dramatic critic for the* New York Evening Post *and the* New York World. *In the following excerpt, he praises the subtlety and sensitivity of Murasaki's characterizations in* The Tale.]

About nine hundred years ago, Murasaki Shikibu became lady-in-waiting to the Empress Akiko. . . . While at court she wrote the ***Tale of Genji,*** in some fifty-odd chapters . . . , and the novel was apparently thought well of by the Emperor. And that is about all we know of this novelist, so ancient, so very modern, and of her novel, which Mr. Waley thinks not only "by far the greatest novel of the East," but "one, which, even if compared with the fiction of Europe, takes its place as one of the dozen greatest masterpieces of the world." On the strength of this first volume—we hear five more are yet to come—we feel very much like agreeing with him, but we wonder if he has not helped to bridge the gap between the near-great and the great by one of the most charming translations ever made from any language into English.

Prince Genji was the Emperor's illegitimate son, and his favorite. He was beautiful, young, gifted beyond belief, he could write the most delicate and difficult Chinese poems, when he danced tears came to the eyes of all who beheld him, and he was allowed to do almost anything he pleased. Occasionally we find him attending state functions where some unmentioned, and possibly important business was being transacted, but most of the time he lived in freedom and idleness, spending the bright currency of his jeunesse dorée. "At his age it was inevitable that he should cause a certain amount of suffering." Many were the ladies who caught his fancy, and few resisted him. There seem to have been no gaps between these ladies, and often he was in love with, or paying court to two or three at the same time. Genji sought, as have so many great lovers since, the only and perfect one, the final conclusive dream. Now and then he thought he had found her, only to see her slip from him, into inexplicable coldness, as in the case of his first wife, Aoi, or into equally inexplicable death, as with Yugao.

But the story of Genji, which in later hands, using the bare skeleton of the same incidents, might strike one as not much more than long and complicated intrigue, becomes, through the skill of this mediæval chronicler, something far superior to intrigue, something, indeed, not like any other love story in the world. Lady Murasaki had a happy forgetfulness of the details and consistencies of time, place, event, which lend her story the lightness and the poignancy of a dream. The framework of what happens seems so unimportant, so little insisted upon by comparison with the changing colors and the half-seen faces which flit in and out and airily fix themselves in our memory, there to grow and haunt us. We have to turn to the dramatis personæ in the front of the book, and pay close attention to Mr. Waley's useful footnotes, in order to be sure of where we are and of what has already happened. But this vagueness is general, and does not rob her characters or her incidents of the little touches which make every incident and most of the important characters wonderfully distinct, like bright faces floating on a cloud. An unconscious artist perhaps—or one of the most conscious, it is impossible to tell which—Lady Murasaki tells her story and makes it real with almost no use of the furniture or detail, or any of the most convenient raw materials of realism. She barely describes a house, she hardly mentions food, she refrains from detailed accounts of externals such as clothing—

> A complete description of people's costumes is apt to be tedious, but as in stories the first thing that is said about the characters is invariably *what they wore*, I shall once in a way attempt such a description. Over a terribly faded bodice of imperial purple . . .

She describes people, to be sure, but it is not this physical accuracy which makes her characters live. They live through what they say and do, and through what they feel, and by what effect others have on them, and they on others. Some of her characters she never quite focuses, perhaps intentionally, leaving them to move, remotely, tenderly, just behind a light haze of emotion, or not quite sharply seen in the most discreet, the most revealing of moonlights. Others she suffers to appear in the full light of day. Of these, little Murasaki, age ten or twelve, is by far the best, and one of the most touching, living characters in any fiction. She is made captive by her creator, watched over and listened to, but forever free, unapproachable, inscrutable and altogether heartbreaking in her shy young loveliness. No short passage could be quoted to make her live but for a reader of her whole story, she comes to life slowly, in half-phrases, in words unsaid, in overtones remembered from the last page.

All these characters move against a background of the country, against a landscape which is indissolubly bound to them by a magic dome of words. One thinks of Japanese paintings, the economical grace of the best of them, but Lady Murasaki's writing is something more. Instead of the mute faces, the arrested landscape, the outlines overclear, a sky of excessive candor, we have lips parted, trees waving faintly in the wind, a dream landscape, not sharp to the eye, but deep and blurred with imagination, rich with the vague thrill that childhood feels in places and before things which it could not exactly name. Lady Murasaki's own poetry is part and parcel of nature, and not to be isolated by any analysis from the substance of day and night and air, from a land dripping early, or hidden in green or quiet with mysterious stir and change. A poetry it is that lies nearest to the core of life, not remote, fantastic, but reasonable, humorous, earthly, a poetry compounded not only of its own intangible essence but of warm good-manners, wise good-will. One longs to have lived in those times and among such people, to return home and find that the servants, like Genji's servants, "were at his pains to improve the view from his windows, for example by altering the course of certain rivulets," or to be met as the revellers were met by Chujo's father "who usually pretended not to hear them when they returned late at night," and "on this occasion brought out his flageolet, which was his favorite instrument, and began to play very agreeably."

As we look down this vista of nine centuries, at people who are not like us, yet hauntingly familiar, at feelings and places immobilized in another language so many years, yet still so green, we find, along with the antique freshness which is not of our time, which we could never recapture, a strangely modern soul. A soul that is naturally, easily aware of all human inward divisions, of the many cross currents which we had supposed were explored by novelists only in the last few decades. Now Lady Murasaki's people are children, direct, naïve, untortured, and the next moment she shows us layers and layers within each of them with as sure an instinct as any Russian, any "psychological" novelist. While Genji loved Yugao, he went to see her in a poor quarter of the town, with workmen's hovels all about, and it saddened him on such visits to hear the unbearably noisy pounding of the cloth-beaters' mallets, and to think he could not carry her away to peace and beauty. After Yugao died Genji thought of her many many times, and "even the din of the cloth-beaters' mallets had become dear through recollection." The Princess Fujitsubo regretted her relations with Genji, "as something wicked and horrible," and the memory of it "was a continual torment to her." When Genji came to see her "she met him with a stern and sorrowful countenance, but this did not disguise her charm, and as though conscious that he was unduly admiring her she began to treat him with great coldness and disdain. He longed to find some blemish in her, to think that he had been mistaken, and be at peace."

Probably few people will be born of our fiction for whom we shall feel the affection we do for Genji and his ladies. Few characters are likely to drop from twentieth century novels real and charming enough to make us forget Lady Murasaki. . . . (pp. 324-25)

Robert Littell, "'The Tale of Genji'," in The New Republic, *Vol. XLIII, No. 558, August 12, 1925, pp. 324-25.*

MARK VAN DOREN (essay date 1925)

[Van Doren was a distinguished American man of letters whose work includes poetry (for which he won the Pulitzer Prize in 1939), novels, short stories, drama, criticism, social commentary, and the editing of a number of popular anthologies. Van Doren's criticism is aimed at the general reader, rather than the scholar or specialist, and is noted for its lively perception and wide interest. In the following review, he maintains that while The Tale *is clearly the product of Oriental culture, its perceptive portrayals of human nature reveal affinities with* Tom Jones *and other works of Western literature.]*

One of the reasons why Arthur Waley may be right in claiming that . . . ***The Tale of Genji*** belongs among "the dozen greatest masterpieces of the world" is that while the manner of the story is strange its matter is familiar. If there were only a manner to consider, one might call the book quaint and be done. And it is quaint enough. The decorum is that, presumably, of a medieval Japanese court. The clothing, the houses, the flowers, the morals are as "different" as such things may be. The people, as they talk, fall into beautiful verse, so that the scene becomes at times a veritable field of blossoms suddenly blown:

> Then unlike the lovers in the "Everlasting Wrong" who prayed that they might be as the "twin birds that share a wing" (for they remembered that this story had ended very sadly) they prayed "May our love last till Maitreya comes as a Buddha into the world." But she, still distrustful, answered his poem with the verse: "Such sorrow have I known in this world that I have small hope of worlds to come." Her versification was still a little tentative.

Not thus, surely, are lovers in our longitude heard to speak.

Yet it is easy, as one reads on, to slip into the conviction that this story of Prince Genji and his innumerable mistresses is but accidentally different from stories one has read of other lovers in other courts. There is the nearer world, for instance, recorded so brilliantly and so endlessly by the French memoir-writers of the seventeenth and eighteenth centuries. Might not most of these events have taken place at Paris, Fontainebleau, or Versailles? Was not Whitehall dimly like this for a time? And if the events are credible when transferred to a familiar background, are not the emotions credible and familiar too? Granted the premise of a society whose sole occupation is with the refinements of love, is there anything essentially strange—by the world's testimony—about ***The Tale of Genji***?

It is easier still to forget decorums and courts altogether. The triumph of Lady Murasaki after all is that she has made a man, and that although she made him a thousand years ago he is alive in every nerve today. It was inevitable that someone should have compared ***The Tale of Genji*** with *Tom Jones,* as I understand someone has. The comparison carries with it a greater compliment than is involved in the mere merit thereby implied. For it is a long way from the Emperor to Squire Allworthy, from Omyobu to Mrs. Honour, from the Lady of the West to Molly Segrim, from Genji to Tom. One book is as precious as the other is plain; the material at hand in the two cases would seem to have made comparison impossible. Yet there it is: Genji, like Tom, growing up among persons who in their various ways teach him a little wisdom and much love. The two authors are alike simply in that they know a great deal about human beings, and know also how to bring their learning to bear upon the career of an impulsive, sensitive, and not too intelligent boy. Lady Murasaki, like Fielding, prefers to say that she is writing "history"; on a greater scale than Fielding's, and with a vastly greater delicacy, she pursues the reality which she was privileged to see.

Mark Van Doren, "First Glance," in The Nation, *New York, Vol. CXXI, No. 3141, September 16, 1925, p. 305.*

ARTHUR WALEY (essay date 1926)

[*Waley, an English critic and author, composed the first English translation of* The Tale. *Until Edward Seidensticker's translation in 1976, Waley's six-volume work (1925-33) was the only complete version of the work available to English-language readers. In the following excerpt from his introduction to* The Sacred Tree, *the second volume of his translation of* The Tale, *he discusses Murasaki's narrative skills.*]

Most critics have agreed that [***The Tale of Genji***] is a remarkable [book] and that Murasaki is a writer of considerable talent; but few have dealt with the points that seem to me fundamental. No one has discussed, in anything but the most shadowy way, the all-important question of how she has turned to account the particular elements in story-telling which she has chosen to exploit. The work, it is true, is a translation, and this fact prevents discussion of Murasaki as a poet, as an actual handler of words. But it has for long been customary to criticize Russian novels as though Mrs. Garnett's translation were the original; nor is there any harm in doing so, provided actual questions of style are set aside.

One reviewer did indeed analyse the nature of Murasaki's achievement to the extent of classifying her as "psychological" and in this respect he even went so far as to class her with Marcel Proust [see Mortimer excerpt dated 1925]. Now it is clear that, if we contrast ***Genji*** with such fiction as does not exploit the ramifications of the human mind at all (the *Arabian Nights* or *Mother Goose*), it appears to be "psychological." But if we go on to compare it with Stendhal, with Tolstoy, with Proust, the ***Tale of Genji*** appears by contrast to possess little more psychological complication than a Grimm's fairy tale.

Yet it does for a very definite reason belong more to the category which includes Proust, than to the category which includes Grimm. Murasaki, like the novelist of to-day, is not principally interested in the events of the story, but rather in the effect which these events may have upon the minds of her characters. Such books as hers it is convenient, I think, to call "novels," while reserving for other works of fiction the name "story" or "romance." She is "modern" again owing to the accident that medieval Buddhism possessed certain psychological conceptions which happen to be current in Europe to-day. The idea that human personality is built up of different layers which may act in conflict, that an emotion may exist in the fullest intensity and yet be unperceived by the person in whom it is at work—such conceptions were commonplaces in ancient Japan. They give to Murasaki's work a certain rather fallacious air of modernity. But it is not psychological elements such as these that Murasaki is principally exploiting. She is, I think, obtaining her effects by means which are so unfamiliar to European readers (though they have, in varying degrees, often been exploited in the West) that while they work as they were intended to do and produce aesthetic pleasure, the reader is quite unconscious how this pleasure arose.

What then are the essential characteristics of Murasaki's art? Foremost, I think, is the way in which she handles the whole course of narrative as a series of contrasted effects. Examine the relation of Chapter VIII ("The Feast of the Flowers") to its environment. The effect of these subtly-chosen successions is more like that of music (of the movements, say, in a Mozart symphony) than anything that we are familiar with in European fiction. True, at the time when the criticisms to which I refer were made only one volume of the work had been translated; but the quality which I have mentioned is, I should have supposed, abundantly illustrated in the first chapters. That to one critic the ***Tale of Genji*** should have appeared to be memoirs—a realistic record of accidental happenings rather than a novel—is to me utterly incomprehensible. But the first painted makimonos that were brought to Europe created the same impression. They were regarded merely as a succession of topographical records, joined together more or less fortuitously; and Murasaki's art obviously has a close analogy with that of the makimono. Then there is her feeling for shape and tempo. She knows that, not only in the work as a whole, but in each part of it there is a beginning, a middle and an end, and that each of these divisions has its own character, its appropriate pace and intensity. It is inconceivable, for example, that she should open a book or episode with a highly-coloured and elaborate passage of lyrical description, calculated to crush under its weight all that follows. Another point in which she excels is the actual putting of her characters on to the scene. First their existence is hinted at, our curiosity is aroused, we are given a glimpse; and only after much manoeuvring is the complete entry made. The modern novelist tends to fling his characters on to the canvas without tact or precaution of any kind. That credence, attention even, may be a hard thing to win does not occur to him, for he is corrupted by a race of readers who come to a novel seeking the pleasures of instruction rather than those of art; readers who will forgive every species of clumsiness provided they are shown some stratum of life with which they were not previously familiar.

How finally does Murasaki achieve the extraordinary reality, the almost "historical" character with which she succeeds in investing her scenes? Many readers have agreed with me in feeling that such episodes as the death of Yūgao, the clash of the coaches at the Kamo festival, the visit of Genji to the mountains, the death of Aoi, become, after one reading, a permanent accession to the world as one knows it, are things which have "happened" as much as the most vivid piece of personal experience. This sense of reality with which she invests her narrative is not the result of realism in any ordinary sense. It is not the outcome of those clever pieces of small observation by which the modern novelist strives to attain the same effect. Still less is it due to solid character building; for Murasaki's characters are mere embodiments of some dominant characteristic; Genji's father is easy-going; Aoi, proud; Murasaki, long-suffering; Oborozukiyo, lightheaded. This sense of reality is due rather, I think, to a narrative gift of a kind that is absolutely extinct in Europe. To analyse such a gift would require pages of quotation. What does it in the last resort consist in, save a preeminent capacity for saying the most relevant things in the most effective order? Yet, simple as this sounds, I believe that in it rests, unperceived by the eye of the Western critic, more than half the secret of Murasaki's art. Her construction is in fact classical; elegance, symmetry, restraint—these are the qualities which she can set in the scales against the interesting irregularities of European fiction. That such qualities should not be easily recognized in the West is but natural; for here the novel has always been Gothic through and through. (pp. 30-3)

Arthur Waley, in an introduction to The Sacred Tree: Being the Second Part of "The Tale of Genji," *translated by Arthur Waley, George Allen & Unwin Ltd., 1926, pp. 15-33.*

L. P. HARTLEY (essay date 1926)

[*Hartley was an English novelist, short story writer, and literary critic. In the following excerpt, he finds* The Tale *aesthetically pleasing but lacking perspective.*]

To the Western mind much oriental art seems under-emphasized, or else the accent, obeying a law unfamiliar to us, falls on an unexpected place. In those exquisite poems, for instance, which Genji exchanges with the ladies of the court [in ***The Tale of Genji***] notepaper and penmanship are rated little less highly than substance and style. Moreover the slenderest message is valued as a contribution to literature and calligraphy apart from its effectiveness as the intercommunication of two minds. It is by no means easy to realize that, for the people about whom Murasaki writes, self-expression is an art; it must do more than answer the need of the moment, it must satisfy an exacting standard of gracefulness and elegance. And although Genji is himself the glass of fashion and the mould of form and to some extent *arbiter elegantiarum,* he is only *primus inter pares;* he is no pioneer of culture. He found it all about him. There may have been societies more civilized than Japan at this epoch, but few (certainly not ours) can have worn their civilization so naturally or so becomingly. They drew in beauty as simply as a breath; aesthetic appreciation was a condition of their lives. Genji stops to admire a view just as the ordinary modern man stops to admire a motor-bicycle.

(This omnipresent sense of beauty is the great delight of Murasaki's novel. It makes up for dull passages, for a certain tenuousness in the character-drawing, for a tendency to repetition.) Mr. Waley, whose introduction one cannot praise too much [see excerpt above dated 1926], affirms that the novel is classical in construction. The major part of the book being still unpublished, we are in ignorance of its final shape: but we confess to finding portions of the narrative difficult to follow and, although *The Sacred Tree* does certainly enlarge our knowledge of Genji's character, we do not feel that it proceeds on any but a roughly biographical plan. Before, we had always seen Genji in the heyday of success; now we see him in exile, almost in eclipse, depressed, other-worldly, with hardly enough energy to begin a new love affair. But presently his old temperament reasserts itself: he pays court to the Lady of Akashi and has a child by her. This is how he breaks the news to Murasaki, his second wife:

> "I had far rather that this had not happened. It is all the more irritating because I have for so long been hoping that you would have a child; and that, now the child is come, it should be someone else's instead is very provoking. It is only a girl, you know, which really makes it rather a different matter. It would perhaps have been better from every point of view if I had left things as they were, but this complication makes that quite impossible. I think, indeed, of sending for the child. I hope that when it arrives you will not feel ill-disposed towards it." She flushed. "That is just the sort of thing you always used to say," she answered. "It seems to me to show a very strange state of mind. Of course I ought to put up with it, but there are certain things which I do not see how I can be expected to get used to. . . ." "Softly, softly," he answered, laughing at her unwonted asperity, "who is asking you to get used to anything?"

Imagine this scene treated by a modern novelist! What tears, protestations, vows, recriminations, would there not have been! Or, supposing the novelist to have sympathized with Genji's point of view, how cynical, how cruel, how shocking the interview would have seemed. In either case there would have been an impression of vivid disunion, the man taking the high line, the woman knuckling under. But here, though none of the elements of disagreement is omitted, though Genji regrets the incident, and his wife is annoyed by it and both feel that it is in some sense "wrong," the effect is totally different. The characters are more pliable; they have less stake in themselves than we have, they can give way gracefully. They feel less; but they feel less not because they are undeveloped or insensitive organisms, but because they are unwilling to disturb the calm surface of behaviour. They learned submission not at a hard school but from a tradition which found little beauty in eccentricity and the glorification of the individual.

Murasaki's taste is not unerring; there is a streak of snobbery in her and she sometimes writes like a lady's maid rather than like a great lady. But as a novelist she is remarkably well equipped. She is equal to anything she undertakes; her sympathy rarely fails her, nor does the delicacy and sureness of her touch. Like Jane Austen, she had few general ideas, but a novelist is often better without them. She was absorbed in her subject and seems to have had few interests outside it. She saw her characters, generally, in relation to their circumstances and environment; it is only rarely that she sees them in relation to life. That is why her work lacks perspective. She makes little distinction between the trivial and the important; she takes things as they come and deals with them consummately. Her work owes its unity to the mature unchanging civilization of which she is the mirror, not to a complete imaginative conception of her theme. (pp. 481-82)

L. P. Hartley, in a review of "The Sacred Tree," in The Saturday Review, *London, Vol. 141, No. 3676, April 10, 1926, pp. 481-82.*

RAYMOND MORTIMER (essay date 1928)

[*In the following excerpt, Mortimer assesses* Blue Trousers, *the fourth volume of Waley's translation of* The Tale. *For additional commentary by Mortimer, see the excerpt dated 1925.*]

When the first part of the ***Tale of Genji*** appeared I suggested in *The Nation* that when the translation was completed it would probably prove one of the twelve great novels in the world [see excerpt by Mortimer dated 1925]. With *Blue Trousers* the ***Tale*** ends, though there are two further volumes dealing with Genji's son. And I believe my prophecy has been justified. But what can be said against the book? First, that it is too long: that is to say that there is in it neither the epic sweep nor the variety in feeling necessary to a book longer than *War and Peace*. Secondly, that the intellectual content is slight: the author accepts her world without questioning. Stated so barely, this objection appears very Philistine. For most of us profess to believe that the intellectual content of a work of art is, if often important, at any rate inessential. But I believe that to its absence is due the slight malaise which many people feel in the presence of ***Genji***, and of the civilization it depicts. These courtiers, we obscurely feel, lived too exclusively for beauty. Developing their æsthetic sensations to a point which escapes us, like the cry of the bat or the high notes of a Chinese singer, they neglected the activities which, since the Greeks, have given European civilization its character. They wondered why a prince was too sad to enjoy the maple leaves in autumn, but never why some trees are deciduous and others not. They argued for hours about the significance of a scent, but hardly for an instant about the meaning of good. We Europeans are all infected with the malady of thought: compared with these Japanese, Oscar Wilde appears a Herbert Spencer. It is also our Western tradition which makes it difficult for us to accept such low relief on so extensive a monument. We are used to bold perspective and strong chiaroscuro. We are not ready to collaborate with the artist: we expect him to impose himself upon us. And much of the beauty of ***Genji*** springs from Murasaki's horror of the explicit. The most important events happened between the chapters, the most telling comments we must read between the lines. To appreciate ***Genji*** to the full, we need to shed a skin and respond actively to the lightest stimulus. There is a nervous condition known to doctors as hyperæsthesia: it seems to have been endemic in tenth-century Japan.

It is really impossible to distinguish between the art of Murasaki and the beauty of her subject-matter. We can make no comparisons: she is the first to reveal to us this delicate world, rivalled in loveliness only by the mythic Greece of Botticelli and Piero di Cosimo. It is a world at once eloquent and fresh, dewy as Aucassin's meadows, subtle as the Court of the Princesse de Clèves. Every detail is laden with significance—the cord with which a box is tied, the frost on a branch of blossom, a change in the tuning of a zithern, an incense devised for a particular season to mix with the prevailing scent of the air. Nothing escapes the curious eyes of these courtiers, who consume the leisure left over from ceremonial, love-making, and the arts, in speculations upon each other's hidden thoughts. Rumour runs wild, as in the pages of Saint-Simon; and tact is elevated to a cardinal virtue. Everyone is concerned about what the servants may hear or think; "embarrassing" and "inconsiderate" are the usual epithets of blame. But in the background there is ascetic Buddhism. At the Festivals and Processions there is a bustling of equipages, filled with ladies flowering in silks—the Auteuil, you would say, of the Empress Eugénie; but at the first grey hair, or should they fall sick, these beauties hasten to shave their heads and take their vows. Of such grim contrasts this volume is particularly full. Blue trousers are a sign of mourning, and the characters are falling into middle age. Genji, the Shining One, gives his son the useless advice his own father once had given him; and he, who had once got his father's consort with child, has another's child fathered on him. Madness and disease are menacing, irony and disillusionment prevail. Jealousy racks the adoring and adorable Murasaki, Rokujo still visits vengeance from beyond the grave. And time passes.

Beside the desolation and the sensuous beauty, there is the constant flow of familiar life, shrewdly observed by a woman of experience. "In their relations with women, people who show the utmost good sense in other matters seem constantly to get into the most inextricable messes. One of the difficulties is that we tend to be attracted precisely by those people with whom it is most impossible that we should be permanently connected." "But unfortunately, Genji reflected, people who do not get into scrapes are a great deal less interesting than those who do." "He had, indeed, charged her with not 'understanding' love; but so far as it meant anything at all, the phrase seemed to imply merely a readiness to yield oneself at demand, irrespective of one's own principles or inclinations." "What sort of man can he have been (Yugiri asked himself) who started the notion that love was an agreeable business?" Might not Jane Austen have written thus if she had lived in the circle of Julie de l'Espinasse?

I have used many European comparisons because I believe that Murasaki can take her place as an artist with the finest whom the West has produced; and also to suggest the variety of tones which she commands. Mr. Waley's translation is in itself a masterpiece. I have little doubt of its accuracy, because I happened to see an attack upon it by a Japanese scholar who, with the best will in the world, could discover only infinitesimal details to find fault with. Its beauty as English prose seems to me very great. I believe fragments from it will be found in the anthologies of the future, but it is not so much isolated passages as the rhythms which inform the whole work which excite my admiration.

Raymond Mortimer, "A Masterpiece," in The Nation and Athenaeum, *Vol. XLIII, No. 7, May 19, 1928, p. 211.*

CONRAD AIKEN (essay date 1928)

[*An American man of letters best known for his poetry and considered a master of literary stream of consciousensss, Aiken was deeply influenced by the psychological and literary theories of Simund Freud, Havelock Ellis, Edgar Allan Poe, and Henri Bergson, among others. In reviews noted for their perceptiveness and barbed wit, Aiken exercised his theory that "criticism is really a branch of psychology." His critical position, according to Rufus A. Blanshard, "insists that the traditional notions of 'beauty' stand corrected by what we now know about the psychology of creation and consumption. Since a work of art is rooted in the personality, conscious and unconscious, of its creator, criticism should deal as much with those roots as with the finished flower." In the following excerpt, Aiken expresses his admiration for the structure and characterization in* The Tale, *and stresses its remarkable evocation of medieval Japanese culture. Aiken's essay on Murasaki was written in 1928.*]

The Tale of Genji . . . takes a place with the great "stories" of the world. One says "stories" more or less advisedly. For it is primarily as a story that one reads it: it falls, in a sense, somewhere between the epic and the novel: somewhere between the mere collection of episodes (loosely surrounding the history of one particular hero) and the careful delineation and charting of a character: but it is obviously nearer to the *Odyssey*, or the *Arabian Nights,* than to *Swann's Way*. It is really a compilation of stories, a compilation managed with an extraordinary skill. If Prince Genji is the principal character, and is more often on the stage than off it, there are also (especially in the later chapters of the book) almost as many episodes which do not concern him at all, or only very obliquely. Of at least half a dozen people we get the more or less complete life history. A half century of time is covered, roughly, and in the course of it we are given an astonishingly complete survey of the entire "court" life of the period. The country, of course, is Japan, although no names are mentioned. And incidentally, but importantly, we are presented with as complete a view of Japanese civilization, in the year 1000, as the *Odyssey* and *Iliad* give us of early Greece, or *Beowulf* of early Britain.

This, apart from the story, will be the feature of this remarkable book which will most impress, one imagines, the majority of readers. At a time when our English forbears were just emerging from savagery, two thirds of a century before the Norman conquest brought Latin refinement to England, Lady Murasaki, in Japan, wrote a masterpiece of fiction in which one of the most striking things is the sophistication and culture of the *milieu* described. Of superstition there is a certain amount of evidence: ghosts, or fox-spirits, figure importantly in several of the death scenes, for example, and it appears that Lady Murasaki subscribes to the current belief that hate may actually be a destroyer of human life. But of barbarism, unless one is very niggling with one's definitions, there will scarcely be found a trace. This is an extraordinarily civilized society. It is as rich in conventions as the court life of France from 1650 to 1790; and far richer in aesthetic conventions than the only parallel in European culture which one easily thinks of—the period of the troubadours. Every courtier was, if one wants to put it invidiously, an aesthete. Every man or woman who belonged to the privileged stratum of society had to be an expert in the "forms" of social behavior. Social life was simply a long series of ceremonies, and of the most elaborate description. Every occasion demanded its special form, whether of dress or decorum; and for every encounter, even of the most casual description, the individual was expected to be prompt with a poem improvised for the moment, a poem packed with reference and cross-reference. It is no exaggeration to say that everyone who in the least participated in court life, or who belonged in the remotest degree to the upper classes, had to be an accomplished poet.

In short, one is compelled to accept the Japan of the year 1000 as representing one of the high-water marks of human civilization. It was one of those moments when the genius of a race comes to flower. That very few "great" works of art were produced in Japan in this period—comparable for example to Chinese art in the Sung or Tang dynasties, or to Greek art in the age of Socrates—does not materially alter this fact. It seems simply to have happened that Japanese genius went for the most part into an elaboration of life itself, an elaboration almost to the point of ritual. Was there ever a people so conscious, for instance, of the beauty of nature, so steeped in it or so close to it? One doubts it. The whole racial attitude to life was a poetic one: sentimental, perhaps, but none the less exquisite and imaginative in the highest degree.

It is this background that Lady Murasaki gives us for her ***Tale of Genji.*** And one could not have conceived an author better fitted for her task. It is clear, in Mr. Arthur Waley's admirable translation, that she had a poetic genius of the finest order: for the whole of this enormous four-volume novel is simply soaked, simply opalescent, with poetic beauty. One suspects that in no other single literary work in the world could one find so marvelous and delicate and various an interpretation of every mood of nature. In this world of plum-blossom and dewfall, of frost on the grass-blade and moonlight on the pine-needles, this world in which the peculiar beauty of every season received intimate reverence, Lady Murasaki sets her tale in motion. It has been compared to the *Arabian Nights*—and in sheer inventive power it is indeed not far behind it. The scene is a crowded one, an extraordinary number of people are deployed for us, the complications are endless: but the author keeps complete control of her complex narrative and manages even the time-element with consummate skill. Not only this, but also, as Mr. Waley points out in his excellent preface to the third volume, *A Wreath of Cloud,* Lady Murasaki has employed contrast, between chapter and chapter or section and section, with a nicety in sense of value for any parallel to which one must go to music. Humor follows and sharpens pathos, the most poignant and searching of realisms alternates with farce, the succinct and graphic gives way to the leisurely reflective or the idyllic. Everything is in its place, nothing is disproportionate, the intricate narrative moves forward as harmoniously as a tone-poem. And gradually we become aware that in addition to the fascination of the tale itself, with all its by-paths and retrogressions and momentary cul-de-sacs of intrigue, we are also in the presence of a series of psychological portraits which are as astonishingly modern as they are unforgettable.

There has, apparently, been some disagreement among the critics as to this matter of Lady Murasaki's "psychology." One critic has maintained that there is more than a mere surface resemblance between Murasaki's compendium and Proust's great "autobiography" [see excerpt by Mortimer dated 1925]. Other critics have challenged this assertion, and have felt, rather, that Lady Murasaki gives us a keen psychological perception of "moments," but not of that other and profounder affair which we might vaguely call the "dynamics of character." On the latter point we are accustomed to hearing a great deal of cant: the textbooks on the novel are full of it. For example, we are assured again and again that no "character" is worth the name if he doesn't "evolve" under our eyes. We must see him emerge from the chrysalis of some complex, and then, in accordance with the laws of that complex, take a predetermined and inevitable course of development. This strikes the present critic as a very limited view—or, at the very least, as a view which may lead to serious misunderstandings of the matter. Why should we object to the presentation of a character *a priori,* a character who does *not* especially change or evolve, a character who in a sense remains fixed, except for those minor deviations or modulations which are sufficiently explainable and natural in *any* human being? Why, indeed, so long as this character is made vivid and recognizable and identifiably individual for us? And this, precisely, is what Lady Murasaki has done for us. Her "Murasaki" of the novel, Genji's chief concubine, is a patient Griselda of flesh and blood. She is an extraordinarily moving figure, she behaves exactly as we expect her to behave, she dies as we expect her to die. She is a tragic figure as convincing as she is beautiful. Her death, and its effect on Prince Genji, is one of the half dozen great things in the book. Aoi, Genji's first wife, is another figure almost as good; and so is Yugao. These women do not, in any useful sense, "evolve": they are stationary; but they are none the less real for that. We know them and believe in them.

That Murasaki should have made vivid her female characters for us is perhaps not so surprising, however, as that she should have given us, in Prince Genji himself, perhaps the most sympathetic and humane and, *ipso facto,* the wisest, portrait of a Don Juan that can be found in literature. Genji is, without exaggeration, one of the great figures given to the world by the art of letters. That a woman should have succeeded in understanding a man of this type is surprising enough; but one would rather naturally have expected such a portrait to be somewhat contemptuous, or grudging, or bitter. Of these things, however, there is here not a trace. Murasaki is in love with Genji, as indeed she is in love with life itself. Never minimizing his weaknesses, making fun of them deliciously, she nevertheless *sees* him perfectly, with the maximum of poetic divination; and she ends by achieving through her creation of him that enhancement of our valuation of the world which is the gift of only the greatest artists. (pp. 311-14)

Conrad Aiken, "Lady Murasaki," in his Collected Criticism, *Oxford University Press, 1968, pp. 311-15.*

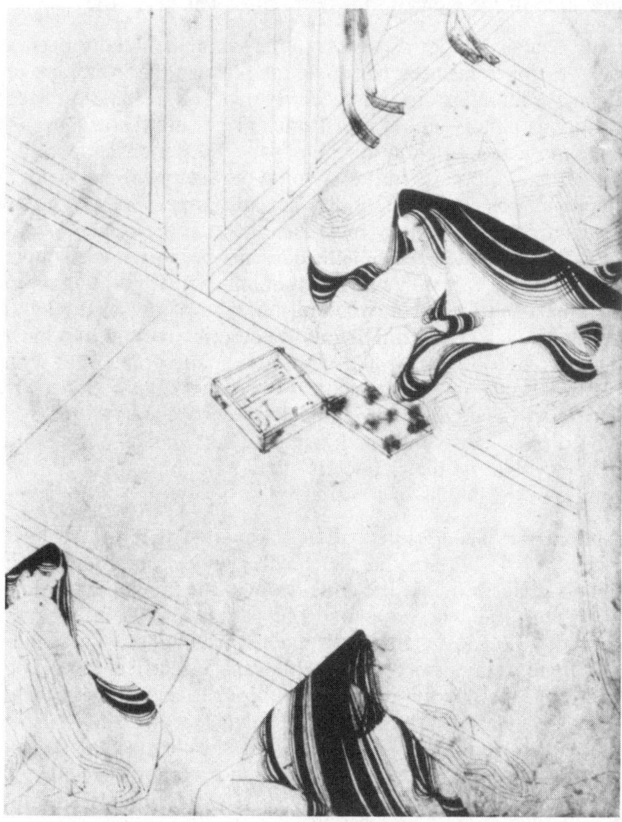

A thirteenth-century illustration of a scene from the Ukifune section of The Tale.

LIFE & LETTERS, LONDON (essay date 1933)

[*In the following review of* The Bridge of Dreams, *the final volume of Waley's translation of* The Tale, *the critic challenges the widely espoused view that Murasaki's novel is essentially "modern" in nature.*]

With the publication of [*The Bridge of Dreams*] . . . , Mr. Arthur Waley brings to a close his magnificent translation of ***The Tale of Genji.*** The great novel breaks off rather than ends; it "fades out," says the translator, "like a Chinese landscape-roll. . . ." *The Bridge of Dreams,* down which the last of Genji's descendants, those exquisite courtiers of the Heian period, those unhappy gracefully languishing court-ladies, are observed on their ceremonious yet passionate way, "leads nowhere" and seems to melt into the void. Kaoru, whose character is studied at some length in Volume V, finds Ukifune, the Lady of the Boat, half-sister to Agemaki, whom he had loved and lost, then is robbed of her by his less scrupulous acquaintance, Niou. Ukifune attempts suicide and disappears. Kaoru discovers that she is still living, but, haunted, as always, by the dread of failure, assumes that once again he has missed his chance, and the narrative ends sadly, vaguely and quietly.

On the whole it is an appropriate conclusion. English critics, when discussing the earlier episodes of Lady Murasaki's immense book, made much—rather too much we now realize—of the novelist's affinities with modern writers. Actually, as Mr. Waley points out in an excellent critical Foreword, Murasaki's genius was part and parcel of the period in which she lived. She shared its delicacy, the fineness of its perceptions; she was also limited by the outlook of her time and place. The fine flower of an aristocracy, more exclusive, more fastidious, more brilliant perhaps, that any that has existed in the Western world, she had absorbed its tenets, accepted its point of view, and gave no sign of attempting to cross its spiritual frontiers. Thus, the mention of Proust or of Jane Austen—both names introduced by English reviewers—does not help us, except as a digressive footnote towards an understanding of Murasaki's gift. ***The Tale of Genji*** includes elements both archaic and extremely "modern"; the novelist's sense of character, with certain obvious lapses, is modern, while her methods of construction—her somewhat inconsequent and easygoing manner of adding episode to loosely connected episode, and allowing her personages to drop behind and vanish for good—are the antithesis of methods now employed. A "well-constructed" novel, in the current phrase, ***The Tale of Genji*** is not and could never have been. It is processional, pictorial, poetic, a frieze of brightly coloured figures, moving to subtle rhythms across a stage, of which neither end can be distinguished by the audience. It marks the passage of a doomed civilization—the Heian culture, so brilliant and soon to fall—across the phantom bridge of which the last volume gives us a hint. (pp. 379-80)

A review of "The Bridge of Dreams," in Life & Letters, *London, Vol. IX, No. 3, September, 1933, pp. 379-80.*

J. M. MAKI (essay date 1940)

[*Maki is an American political scientist and literary critic who has written extensively on Japanese society. In the following excerpt, he praises the depth of Murasaki's characterizations and of her portrayal of Japanese culture in* The Tale.]

Nine hundred years ago the Japanese Imperial Court at Kyoto was the setting for the most magnificent culture Japan has ever known. As rich in great men and women, in pomp and pageantry, color and costume as it was delicate in its aesthetic pursuits, it was the perfect *milieu* for the development of a great literature. Fine poetry and novels and fascinating diaries make this period the greatest in all the centuries of the history of Japanese literature and towering above all these works is Lady Murasaki's novel, ***Genji Monogatari.*** This masterpiece is perhaps the greatest Japanese literary creation and is certainly the one, above all others, that strikes a responsive chord in Western readers. Its supreme position has been recognized in Japan almost since the day it first appeared and after its translation into English it has won a secure position as one of the truly great novels in world literature.

Lady Murasaki took the incredibly rich environment of the Imperial Court of which she was a member and molded it into a background for her story. No one who has read the tale of the life and loves of Prince Genji has failed to be fascinated by her description of the great and vanished culture of Heian Japan; but the ***Genji Monogatari*** is remarkable as much, if not more, for its psychological realism as for its descriptive realism. If she has succeeded in creating in words all the magnificence of the Heian court, she has also been successful in the far more difficult task of peopling her novel with men and women who experience the emotions common to all human beings, no matter what their race or what the period in which they live.

The novel owes much of its vitality to the unchanging nature of the human emotions that are to be seen in Lady Murasaki's characters. The love, hate, fear, joy, hope, anxiety, sorrow and other emotions that flow through Prince Genji, Murasaki, Yūgiri, Tamakatsura, Kaoru, Niou, Agemaki and all the wealth of characters that appears in the book are the same as those that many people today, Occidental and Oriental alike, have experienced.

It is fitting that such a great cultural period as the Heian age of about 1000 A.D. should have been described by one who knew it as a part of her own daily life. Her picture of her times was transformed by her literary art into the crowning literary achievement of her age and with this one novel she added immeasurably to the stature of Japanese literature. (pp. 120-21)

In the Heian court of that time there was abroad a spirit which was probably more purely aesthetic than any that can be found anywhere in the world at any other period of history. That spirit was an aestheticism that was something more than a pose, something more than a cult, something more than a philosophy, something more than refinement for refinement's sake, something more than we can re-create even in our imaginations in this twentieth century. It perhaps had all the weaknesses that we are prone to attribute to a culture that fails to take into what we would deem proper consideration the more material aspects of life; yet it had all the brilliance that Murasaki gave it in her novel. It was a society which most certainly appreciated to the full all that Murasaki wrote for it. In other words, Murasaki was not forced to attempt to create a novel out of thin air. She had before her a brilliant, though circumscribed, society which was ideal subject matter for a novel and which was eager to read about itself. On the other hand, Murasaki, as an individual belonging to that society, was possessed of the spark of genius that made her work transcend the limitations of time and an environment foreign to the modern world so that it speaks today as clearly to us as it did to the audience for whom it was written. (pp. 131-32)

Every student of Japanese literature knows that in the Heian period Japanese was not regarded as being a fit medium of literary expression for men. Except in the field of Japanese poetry, men did not condescend to write in Japanese, but expended their literary energy on attempts to create gems of Chinese verse and prose. Murasaki, however, was not tied down by the literary conventions that bound the men so tightly and consequently was able to use her native Japanese in composing her novel. She used it as it had never been used before and as it has been used but a few times since. But even her prestige was not enough to establish Japanese as a true literary style in Japan at that time.

Apparently the ***Genji Monogatari*** was written for the delectation of the court ladies—very likely it was originally intended only for the members of the small circle of which Murasaki was a part. In the light of the male attitude toward composition in the Japanese style, it is highly improbable that Murasaki had male readers in mind while she was writing. Yet it seems that Murasaki's novel soon captured a goodly number of readers among the men. From references in her diary it is clear that both the Emperor Ichijō and Fujiwara Michinaga were familiar with the work. If two such outstanding men placed their stamp of approval on the novel by reading it, it is certain that not a few men of the Court followed in their wake. (p. 133)

Lady Murasaki's art as a story teller has undoubtedly been a great factor in insuring her novel the place in the front rank of Japanese literature that has been its own for so long. Viewed simply as a story, the life of Prince Genji and the account of the experiences of Niou, his grandson, and Kaoru, supposedly his son but really the fruit of a union between Nyosan, Genji's wife and Kashiwagi, the eldest son of his best friend, are as fascinating today as they must have been in the eleventh century. The story achieves its greatness not because it is a simple chronicle of interesting and entertaining events, building up to a climax and then gently fading off to a happy ending, but because it is a successful attempt to describe the life of a most happily endowed individual with no climatic points, but with periods, some long, some short, of happiness, misfortune, joy and sorrow. The lives of Genji and his descendents are neither wholly good nor wholly bad; neither wholly happy nor wholly unhappy. Nor do the characters attain a final idyllic happiness or end in the depths of tragedy.

Although Prince Genji dominates the first part of the tale, Murasaki did not smother her readers under a multiplicity of details concerning his life. She devoted much attention to the stories of those who came into contact with him. Tamakatsura, Tō no Chūjō's lost daughter, is the heroine of one of the stories within the main story. As a child she is carried far off to Western Japan by her nurse and is brought back to the capital many years later after a series of adventures that must have seemed tremendously exciting to the cloistered court ladies. She is brought to Genji's attention and becomes the center of one of his most fascinating intrigues. Tō no Chūjō's search for her is another secondary story and assumes comic proportions when he discovers the uncouth Lady of Ōmi whom he believes to be his lost daughter. The story of the young Yūgiri, Genji's son, is another tale that moves along with the story of the hero. The affair between Nyosan and Kashiwagi is a story within itself and yet it is indispensable to the novel as a whole. It exposes Genji to a fate that he had inflicted on another and it lays the foundation for the entire latter part of the book.

Nevertheless, through the entire first forty-four chapters of the book, it is Genji who commands the interest of the reader. His brilliant youth when he pursues one woman after another; his lonely days in stormy Suma where he has gone into voluntary exile as a result of an indiscreet affair; his return to greater glory and more honors; his middle years which find him involved in a struggle between his reason and his emotions; his loss when Murasaki, who was the one great love of his life, died, all form unforgettable incidents in the story of the great Prince Genji.

His death is not described in the book. The last section of the story opens with the poignant sentence, "Genji was dead, and there was no one to take his place." Indeed, the entire mood of the last part of the book, with Genji missing, is different. No longer does one great figure dominate the story; interest is divided between Niou and Kaoru. Neither is the great figure that Genji was, Niou being too impetuous and Kaoru too reserved. Much of the pageantry of the early part of the book is also missing. Furthermore, the very setting of much of the action in this part of the book serves to alter the mood as the scene is no longer primarily in the capital but in the rural region of Uji which gives its name to this section.

The rivalry between Kaoru and Niou is the central theme of this last section of the book. Niou by his impetuosity wins the ladies whom Kaoru wishes to make his own but whose fatal inability to push anything to a decision ruins his chances. The emphasis in this part of the book is even more on the psychological lives of the characters.

Murasaki's genius encompasses more than skill, no matter how great, as a story-teller for, fascinating as the story is, the greatness of the novel lies in something far more than that. There is, for example, her realism in the sketching of court life. This realism must have made her tale all the more enthralling to her readers and for us it has the fascination which must be a part of any picture of a great and beautiful culture which is today non-existent. The characters move in an environment that was rightfully theirs because they were a part of the Imperial Court.

Lady Murasaki gave her characters depth and they move from inner compulsion rather than as a result of mere wooden manipulation on the part of the author. Indeed, it is because of the fact that their lives share in that great pool of human emotions which remains substantially unaltered, even though the environment in which they are expressed may change and the stimuli which waken them may differ, that her characters can speak to us across a gap of some nine centuries.

The author lavished much of her art as a psychological realist on Prince Genji. If one considers all his talents, Genji apparently could be nothing more than an uninteresting prodigy. He was the most beautiful man at the Court—in his case "beautiful" was a better adjective than "handsome." He was also a great lover; but "Don Juan" could not be applied to him, for he was a much more sensitive person than Byron's famous hero. Genji was also possessed of every talent that would go to make up the perfect courtier of the Heian period; he was a fine painter, an excellent poet, and outstanding scholar in the Chinese classics, a superb dancer, a great musician and well-versed in government. He was so superbly endowed, however, that instead of arousing feelings of enmity or jealousy among his fellows he commanded their respect and admiration. His character, too, helped insure his popularity. Murasaki says, "Unlike most occupants of the exalted position which he now held, Genji was entirely devoid of pomposity and self-importance. Whatever the rank of those whom he was addressing, under whatever circumstances he met them, his manner remained always equally kind and attentive. Indeed, by that thread and that alone hung many of his oldest friendships."

If Genji had been possessed of only his manifold talents, he would be a terrific bore and with as little appeal for the modern reader as a Prince Charming; but for all his beauty and talents Genji had fatal human weaknesses in his character, weaknesses that make him a human being understandable to human beings. He brought about his own downfall, the exile to Suma, simply by continuing to involve himself in a love affair when he knew that discovery would mean disaster; his principles often run a bad second to his actions; he is not satisfied with easy conquests, but almost deliberately sets himself to win those who, for one reason or another, are inaccessible; when he becomes a cuckold and discovers it, he suddenly realizes that he is now in the same position he had placed others in; he tries to be paternal toward a beautiful young lady and discovers his paternal feeling lapsing into something that is anything but paternal. He has defects in character which make him not a great individual involved in a struggle with himself that makes his story a tragedy, but simply a human being, although one most favored by the gods, who sets himself certain goals and then defeats himself by being all too human. Murasaki did not create a great tragic character in Prince Genji, but she did depict him as a human being with great skill through the use of a psychological realism that only a few in the history of the world's literature have possessed.

Genji by all odds, stands out head and shoulders above the rest of the characters in the book, yet Murasaki did not exhaust her art in portraying him. In the ***Genji Monogatari*** there is probably the most remarkable galaxy of feminine characters that has ever appeared in any literary work. They range from the great Lady Murasaki who is generally accepted as embodying all that a woman should be according to the standards of the Imperial Court of the Heian period to the incredible Lady of Ōmi who most certainly had all the qualities that a lady should not have. However, all of the female characters are of Court circles by birth; even the maids are of good lineage. Murasaki could not bring herself to write of the common creatures whom some of the men pursued; on the rare occasions she mentions them it is with the deepest disgust.

The magnificently lovely Murasaki, the heroine of the novel, is more than a mere beauty—she is a woman in love with a man who is not as faithful as he might be; Tamakatsura, Tō no Chūjō's lost daughter, beautiful and cultured in spite of her rural upbringing, was possessed of a singularly open and fresh character until her unfortunate love affair with Higekuro made her gloomy, irritable and short-tempered; the mad Lady Makibashira who was filled with the strangest impulses to harm Higekuro, her wandering husband, even though she loved him; Fujitsubo whom Genji's forbidden and impetuous love filled with terror and fear, but who was also noted for her kindness to those around her; the vindictive Kōkiden who is probably the least sympathetic character in the book; the self-sacrificing Agemaki who was a model of filial piety; the old Lady of the Bedchamber who was the embodiment of kittenish, middle-aged love; Suyetsumuhana, possessed of an inordinate shyness and an almost appalling lack of beauty (her huge red-tipped nose is a comic touch, but Murasaki tempers her description by giving Suyetsumuhana surpassingly beautiful hair which was a *sine qua non* for the beauties of the court of Heian Japan), who, however, awakened a kind of pity in Genji's breast which led him to take her under his protection; Nyosan, Genji's second wife, who was so innocent and childish that she slipped into an illicit love affair hardly knowing what had happened; and the young Kumoi who revealed the first awakening of an adolescent love, are all a part of Lady Murasaki's great gallery. This brief listing of some of the principal female characters indicates the variety of women that may be encountered in the book and the author's wide knowledge of feminine psychology.

Murasaki's male characters generally do not attain the high artistic level of the psychological portraiture of the female characters. The general criticism that can be made is that we look in vain for out-and-out masculine elements in them. Those who are what we would call ''masculine'' were quite evidently characters that would not appeal to Murasaki's readers. Yet we cannot charge Murasaki with being unable to create a psychologically sound portrait of a male character because the ideal for the men of the Heian period was feminine rather than masculine. A man to be accepted at the Court had to be refined and gentle and skilled in many delicate arts which by their very nature called for the feminine touch. In the eyes of the modern world many of the pastimes of the men in the Heian period verge on the psychopathic—the sort of thing that only peculiar males would indulge in. Murasaki's male characters are more the realistic reflections of what was supposed to be the ideal male of the time rather than weak individuals whose weakness springs from the author's inability to create masculine personalities.

Kaoru, central figure of the last part of the book, is perhaps one of the greatest portraits of a weak, vacillating, effeminate character in the world's literature. Murasaki's art as a psychological realist is at its greatest in her development of Kaoru's personality. He is far from being a person to command our respect and in almost everything he falls short of Genji, yet he emerges as one of the outstanding characters of the entire book.

Lady Murasaki's psychological realism is, beyond a doubt, the one thing in the story that has contributed most to its freshness. Strange as their costumes and customs are, most of Murasaki's characters are men and women whose emotions are understandable today. If Murasaki is such a great master of psychological realism it goes almost without saying that she was also masterful in her treatment of the environment in which the characters move. She has many passages in which she describes the brilliance of the costumes of both the men and women—passages that must have been avidly read by the Court ladies and which today add much to the color imagery of the book. She has also left us many unforgettable pictures of the pageants, processions, meetings, religious observances that filled the days of the courtiers.

Murasaki is also a master at the description of landscapes. Her travels with her father in her early years apparently did much to sharpen her powers of observation and to store in her mind many scenes which she must have drawn on when she wrote. She made abundant use of the effect of physical environment on her characters. Particularly striking is her use of gloomy weather or dark, forbidding scenery to create melancholy moods in her characters.

Music also plays a tremendously important part in the story—both as music itself and as a means by which the characters either express themselves or reveal something of their personalities in playing their instruments. Murasaki's knowledge of music is really astounding. Many passages are devoted to it—music as it influences her characters' actions; music as merely a part of a brilliant party; judgments as to the skill of those who play on no matter what instrument; abstruse points of musical history and technique; and music simply as a part of the aesthetic environment of the Heian age.

That the olfactory sense was far from being neglected in the complex system of Heian aesthetics is also abundantly illustrated in the ***Genji Monogatari.*** Incense and perfumes apparently played an important part in the daily lives of the courtiers. Reference must also be made to the famous passage describing the incense competition.

Murasaki ranges as freely in the intellectual sphere as she does in the world of the senses. As I have indicated above, she was a great music critic. Her views on the novel, as was pointed out earlier in this paper, were singularly advanced. In the famous chapter entitled ''The Picture Competition'' which is one of the most brilliant of the entire book Murasaki writes at length of the art of painting. Indeed, judging by her remarks on the arts, Murasaki must be given a ranking in aesthetics almost as high as that which is hers in the history of the novel.

It is almost superfluous to state that Lady Murasaki had a detailed knowledge of Japanese poetry which is reflected on almost every page of her novel. This knowledge was not, perhaps, extraordinary in Murasaki's day. Poetry played an extremely important part in the social intercourse of the times and the average courtier or court lady had to be as familiar with poetry as he was with the gossip of the hour. Japanese scholars do not have a very high opinion of Murasaki as a poet but they are almost unanimously agreed that she had no equal, let alone superior, in the art of incorporating apt verses into a novel. The reader of these times when poetry has been rudely elbowed into untouched library shelves by the pastimes, professions and pursuits of the twentieth century cannot but marvel at the intimate role poetry played in the life of the Heian period courtier.

But Murasaki did not let herself become preoccupied in the arts to such an extent that she neglected a problem that must have indeed been pressing in the minds of all Heian period courtiers, that of the security of their positions. It was struggle enough for men to attain ranks that would give them both prestige and a good income, but it was a constant concern of parents to see that their daughters were properly placed either through marriage or by court appointment. According to the picture that Murasaki has left us, intrigue was as rampant in the Imperial Court of Japan around the year 1000 as it has been in every other court the world over. For all its aesthetic refinement, the Heian court was not without its undercurrent of material insecurity.

Modern readers will find in the ***Genji Monogatari*** many superstitions, the belief in possessions with power to kill, an undue deference to omens and portents and an uncritical acceptance of a necessary connection between human actions and natural calamities. While all these things cannot be accepted by the modern reader he perhaps should remember that they were all a part of the mental environment of the courtiers of the Heian period. It is not unreasonable to believe that there are many contemporary beliefs which in A.D. 2800, granting that man-kind will not have succeeded in annihilating itself by that time, will appear to be just as superstitious and just as uncritical as do the beliefs of Heian Japan today. That Murasaki did not rise above those beliefs is not to be held against her, for she would have been something more than superhuman had she been able to anticipate some nine hundred years of Western thought and present a point of view that we could accept today as "modern." Not only that, but if she had had such an outlook she undoubtedly would have had far fewer readers in her own time. (pp. 137-43)

J. M. Maki, "Lady Murasaki and the Genji Monogatari," in Monumenta Nipponica, *Vol. III, No. 2, July, 1940, pp. 120-43.*

RICAREDO DEMETILLO (essay date 1955)

[Demetillo is a Filipino poet and critic. In the following examination of Murasaki's literary objectivity, Demetillo analyzes characterization in The Tale *as well as Murasaki's views on the art of fiction.]*

The Tale of Genji, which strictly speaking is not a novel in the usual Occidental sense, is rather a family chronicle and is, in the Occidental translation made famous by Arthur Waley, divided for convenience into six books, each book roughly comprising a novel by itself. Offhand, the only Western writer that would parallel this literary achievement of a sequelized narrative through several books is Proust, where there is some effort made to unify the narrative pattern by the method of centering all the actions around one dominant character and by the fluidity of narration, enabling the author to work back to certain incidents occuring in the past with the least awkwardness or vagueness and to mention certain characters who would not appear until later on in the narrative. Psychologically, the achievement of Murasaki is astonishing, for it is to be remembered that she lived and wrote in the tenth century A.D., when depth psychology was not yet to be thought of systematically for another thousand years. Both Proust and Lady Murasaki succeed in giving us superlative exposés of their own times by a microscopic analysis of human motives; although Lady Murasaki herself, unlike Proust, does not start out to expose bourgeois failings but is interested purely in the sophistication of romance, which was the *elan vital* of Japanese fiction at the time. In this respect, her objective is a more purely aesthetic one than that of Proust.

The age in which Lady Murasaki lived was a supremely literary and artistic age. The society in which she moved cultivated poetry, painting, flower arrangement, the tea ceremony, and the other rituals of both religious and court life. At the court lived Fujiwara No Kinto, another kinsman of Lady Murasaki's. So did Lady Izumi Shikibu, one of the greatest poets that Japan ever produced. Apparently, even in that far-off age, poets and poetesses were keenly jealous of one another, for in the diary of Lady Murasaki, she states, concerning Lady Shikibu: "It does not seem to me that in herself she is really a poet at all."

The diary also mentions the fact that it was common to dash off impromptu poems, of which Lady Murasaki and Lady Shikibu were experts. Indeed, the ***Tale of Genji*** owes its charm partly to the fact that in every chapter, one comes across references to this interesting literary practice, now lost to the world, though it once flourished in the Chinese and Japanese classical ages. These poems, it must be said, were brief, strict affairs, far more constricted than the sonnet. The modern descendant of the poem is the Japanese *hokku* or *haiku,* which is a purely Japanese achievement, a further condensation of the brief *tanka*. These poems recorded the most flitting moods and the subtlest (sometimes obscurest) ideas. The marvel is that so much grace and profundity could be sometimes captured in such narrow limits, as in the anniversary poem written by Kaga No Chiyo on the death of her child:

> Today, how far
> May he have wandered:
> The brave hunter of dragon-flies!

The novel itself was a widely cultivated art form in Lady Murasaki's time. The romancers and tale writers of the period had found much excellent apprenticeship in the writing of histories and annals, often of a romanticized or glamorized form. But as the ***Tale of Genji*** itself shows, by the time of Murasaki the falsification of emotion and characterization inevitable in the romanticized version of a story had given place to the most accurate and sophisticated art of psychological characterization, so that the classical novel of the Japanese invariably is marked by the very breath and movement of life. As the Chinese and the Japanese themselves would say about their great novels (say, the *Dream of the Red Chamber* or *All Men Are Brothers*), the readers would be able to identify immediately the character concerned just by listening to bits of conversation in the narrative. This means only two things: first, that the novelists did a thoroughly workmanlike job; and second, that the common people themselves had been so saturated by the literary spirit as to be themselves, as the English in the time of Shakespeare or the Athenians in the time of Sophocles, a critically sympathetic audience, demanding of their artists only the superlative in the fictive art.

We are told, historically, that the ***Tale of Genji*** is the greatest single achievement in the Japanese novel. Lady Murasaki, like Dante, found in her country a medley of dialects, none of which had been welded into an artistic vehicle by any writer of repute. But by writing her novel, Lady Murasaki showed the great aesthetic possibilities of the dialect used in court circles. She found that tongue a dialect but she bequeathed it to her people, a flexible language.

The ***Tale,*** on one level, shows that the greatest literary achievement must be national: that is, it should be expressive of the life of a people, breathing their spirit, fed by their hopes and fears, watered by their tears. In its pages, one sees the mysterious landscapes of Japan: the forest, fields, and valleys and mountains with their gusty rains and sudden storms, their lightning and thunder and winds that sough the trees. Here are the desolate moors and weed-grown *patios* of old ancestral homes, many going into decay, as their occupants did into decrepitude or senility, to objectify the decadence Murasaki indirectly reveals. The exquisitely designed interiors are here, decorated with precious scrolls, jade ornaments and bells. Here also are the boudoirs of the wives and concubines of the princes and emperors of old Japan, ladies fragile and slim and graceful, sometimes doll-like, always patient because they are forced to their social position to be so. In the novel, one encounters the teeming court life, with its intrigues for power, its favoritism, its sudden changes in favor or disfavor, the banishments and exiles, the recalls and disgraces; here also are the literary examinations, the reverence paid to letters and paintings, to calligraphy and music. Here is portrayed, without any disapproval but with complete matter-of-factness, the social stratification of Japan, the nobles living luxurious lives in their houses and those lower down serving as cushions for the princes and princesses and court favorites. Lady Murasaki takes for granted that such an order is the right, the only imaginable one.

One is also impressed by the fact that women in these pages accept their lot as begetters of children and bearers of sorrow; they meekly believe that they cannot enter into the kingdom of the blessed, for such it is ordered through all time by Amitabha, the Infinite One. Sex is apparently without much social or Puritanical taboo, comparable to that existing in the decadent periods of the Roman and Greek civilizations. Sexual licence is widely accepted, with only certain aesthetic and partly social prohibitions in certain special cases.

Obviously, the ***Tale*** is aristocratic, with the interest focused on the amative relationships. But so carefully delineated is the characterization in terms of the actual social background that the work has become a monumental achievement as indirect social criticism: a criticism not intended by Lady Murasaki. As a novel of love, it presents the amatic adventures of Genji and of his cousins and children; as a chronicle of family life, it objectifies the loves, the petty jealousies, the intrigues, and the interplay of passions in a family; as a picture of aristocratic life, it shows the old aristocracy of Japan being corroded slowly but definitely by the luxury, the license, and the careless leisure of the nobles; and, therefore, it becomes also a moral exposé of universal human weaknesses. In fact, it might well be entitled "Original Sin" or "The Sins of the Fathers Visited Upon the Children to the Seventh Generation."

The Tale of Genji is not only an objectification of the way a great novel may be written but also contains direct ideas on the art of writing fiction. Prince Genji, the hero of the novel, in a conversation with one of the young court ladies whom he had discovered reading avidly a romance, says:

> I too have been studying these books and have, I must tell you, been amazed by the delight which they have given me. There is, it seems, an art of so fitting each part of the narrative into the next that, though all is mere invention, the reader is persuaded that such things might easily have happened and is so deeply moved as though they were actually going on around him.

Clearly, the implication of this passage is that the realistic novel was already, by the beginning of the tenth century fast becoming an established art form in Japan. Here is no art-for-social-progress theory of the novel, but of mimesis in the strictly Aristotelian meaning, the imitation of life for the sake of enjoyment and the purgation of the emotions. Genji, in the same section where I have extracted the passage just cited, speaks of the mind "burning with indignation at the wrongs endured by some wholly imaginary princess" and by the readers being "dazzled by sheer splendour of language." What are the greatest literary works in the world (Dostoyevski's novels; the dramas of Aeschylus, Euripedes, Sophocles, Shakespeare and Racine; the *Divina Commedia* by Dante) if not the works that supremely enable us to arrive at the fiercely illuminating moment of catharsis through the vehicle of dazzling language?

Genji goes on to delineate his theory (Murasaki's) of the art of fiction in the following words:

> But I have a theory of my own about what this art of the novel is, and how it came into being. To begin with, it does not simply consist in the author's telling a story about the adventures of some person. On the contrary, it happens because the storyteller's own experiences of men and things, whether for good or for ill,—not only what he has only witnessed or been told of—has moved him to an emotion so passionate that he can no longer keep it shut up in his heart. Again and again, something in his own life or in that around him will seem to the writer so important that he cannot bear to let it pass into oblivion. There must never come a time, he feels, when men do not know about it. That is my view of how this art arose.

These words ring with complete modernity. T. S. Eliot may find in it not a complete summing up of the art of fiction or of poetry, but he will agree to it as a precise analysis of the nature of poetic vision or inspiration, the literary imperative which writers all over the world feel when confronted by the reality impinging on their consciousness.

The imitation that Lady Murasaki has expressed through Prince Genji obviously is not just the imitation of external action. (This, incidentally, is the point where the great Aristotle bungled, for he totally misunderstood the nature of the source of the tragic emotion when he based it on action.) By the practice of Lady Murasaki, we know that she was completely aware that imitation does not stop at the external mimesis, but in the capturing of the powerful, driving emotions springing from the wells of the sub-conscious. Time and again, we are startled into assent at the sensitive insights of Lady Murasaki into the compulsiveness of certain desires in her characters. Not a few of her characters are scourged by their feelings, but there is no evidence of over-writing, or melodramatizing, or of sentimentalizing. Kauro, for example, is, to our thinking, a split personality, who yearns for the love of woman but who can never feel the depth of attachment for any person and allows his desires to be uncomfortably restricted by uncertainty, never taking the initiative to take the occasion, as it were, by the horns; until he himself and those he loves are victimized by his apparent neglect. Terror and guilt form part of the subtle chiaroscuros in ***The Tale of Genji,*** making for narrative density and enabling the action to achieve intense purgative power. As in Shakespeare or the Greek dramatists, there is no shying away from the evil that pervades the world or the social order. Lady Murasaki belongs to the rare group of artists who have looked on human evil and never shrunk from the contemplation or desired to falsify the impression through her art. It is part of her greatness that makes her objectify nervous breakdowns in her characters with fidelity, a fidelity deceptively artless.

One is impressed by the muting of the Oedipus pattern in human behavior in the ***Tale of Genji.*** It comes in the most surprising, though natural, moments, pivotal to the action of the story. The interesting thing is that in each case, the Oedipus-feeling is largely unconscious on the part of the characters involved, manifesting itself in the most intimate and dearest possessions of the father—his favorite wife or concubine. Genji himself succeeds in seducing his father's consort, Fujitsubu, who bears a son to Genji, a son who later became emperor, having been brought up as heir to the throne. Ordinarily, this would not have happened, for the sons of Genji would, in the old system of reckoning, be nothing but commoners. But since his child by Fujitsubu was brought up as a son of the Emperor, not of Genji, he came into the direct line of succession.

Yugiri, the son of Genji, by his own legal wife, also falls in love with Murasaki, the heroine of the story, (not to be confused with the author) the most beautiful woman of her age, worthy consort to Genji. Yugiri saw one stormy day, a glimpse of his father's favorite concubine:

> Without thinking what he was doing, he paused and looked in. Numerous ladies in waiting were passing to and fro just inside, and had he made a sound they would have looked up, seen him, and necessarily supposed that he had stationed himself there on purpose to spy upon those within. He saw nothing for it but to stand dead still. Even indoors the wind was so violent that screens would not stand up. Those which usually surrounded the high dais were folded and stacked against the wall. There, in full view of anyone who came along the corridor, reclined a lady whose notable dignity of mien and bearing would alone have sufficed to betray her identity. This could be none other than Murasaki. Her beauty . . . was wafted towards him, suddenly imbued him, as though a strong perfume had been dashed against his face. . . . Now he understood why it was that Genji had always taken such pains to keep him away from her.

That last sentence is a masterly one to convey Yugiri's feeling, which is of understanding, tinged with a slight resentment at his father, a feeling that carries with it a sense of shame and of guilt. "What view would his elders take if they should discover that he spent his leisure in thinking of Genji's wife? He tried hard to think of other things; but after a moment or two the recollection of what he had seen that morning sprang back into his mind."

But the literary power is not just in this searching psychological insight; but in the objectification of feeling in terms of concrete symbols. Thus, in the earlier passage quoted, we feel that the emotions of Yugiri are best symbolized by the perfume image and also by the dramatic use of the storm.

It is in this particular power of rendering emotion superbly that most of the appeal of Lady Murasaki consists of. It is not just in one or two isolated instances, but it pervades the narrative. This explains why one can read through the whole story, which in fairly readable print, takes a thousand pages, without letdown in interest. Of only one or two other long masterpieces can such a claim be justly made.

There is another passage, or rather a whole large section, which fascinates me because of its unusual handling of symbolism. This is found in the fourth book, which tells of the guilty passion of Kashiwagi for Genji's latest wife, Nyosan, whom he had taken into his household when he was already past forty and she only about fourteen. Before the marriage, Kashiwagi had been corresponding with Nyosan occasionally, with the knowledge of her father, the Emperor Suzaku. Now, however, she was Genji's legal wife and was well-guarded by the walls, screens, and draperies of decorum that surrounded such personages. But one day, Kashiwagi was invited by the young Yugiri to play a game of football near the quarters of Genji, in fact, just below the wing where Nyosan was housed. Kashiwagi was not prepared adequately for the incident that would happen then; for "suddenly a large cat leapt between the curtains in pursuit of a very small and pretty Chinese kitten."

Nothing is more within the bounds of fictive probability, and nothing could be so unusual as the use of this animal for conveying the narrative purpose. Here is no god out of the machine legerdemain that disturbs one's credulity in reading Greek plays. Here is no over-straining at devices, but the delineating of the most natural thing.

> The big cat, it soon appeared, was a stranger in the house, and lest it should escape had been provided with a leash, which was unfortunately a long one, and had now got entangled in every object in the room.

The figure of the cat becomes a marvelous symbol for Kashiwagi and his passion. He is the stranger in the house, let in though some breach of loyalty and carelessness, so that he should force his desires upon Nyosan and create disorder in Genji's household, getting himself entangled in the meshes of his passion. . . .

Later on in the story, we are told again about the cat when he lay by the side of Nyosan, upon whom he had forced his attention:

> For suddenly there appeared before him the cat which he had once contrived to steal from her. It advanced towards him purring loudly, and wondering in his dream how it had got there, he supposed that he might have brought it with him. What had made him do that?. . . So he was asking himself in his dream, when he woke with a start. There was of course no cat anywhere to be seen, and he wondered why he should have had so curious a dream.

Already, the seeds of guilt are evident in the dream. When we further learn that the Japanese interpret the dreaming of a cat's entrance into a room as presaging the birth of a child, we realize with what deep wisdom Lady Murasaki uses that particular symbol to invest her story with a hierarchy of meanings.

The delineation of Kashiwagi is indicative of the rich art of characterization practised by Lady Murasaki. Kashiwagi, who comes closest to being the villain in the narrative, is presented in a highly sympathetic manner. In fact, he would fill the requirement for the tragic hero in Greek plays, for he is high born, brilliant in promise as public servant, handsome and highly accomplished. There is also in his passion to be first in everything what amounts to the tragic flaw, a passion which makes him want that which is legally and morally taboo, in his case made acute by his excessive pride. This is no melodramatized presentation of the evil in men, for it is as factual as one could make it.

There is something in all this which is highly courageous and essentially moral, in the best sense of that unfortunate word. Lady Murasaki presents characters, not as they would like to be, which invariably is the purpose of certain propagandistic-didactic writers, who falsify human nature and, therefore, the whole moral nature of life itself, by presenting man better than he really is. Instead, she has taken the far more difficult, the only way open to genuine art, which is to present man as he is. This is essentially the classic view, which has hard objectivity about it. This view Lady Murasaki has to an unusual extent. Her objectivity is bolstered up by her Buddhistic proclivities, for she finds authority in the art of depicting the noble or good side by side with the imperfect and the evil in the doctrine of Upaya, extracted from the Mahayana, where the actual mixture of truth and error is the condition of being. Thus, Lady Murasaki concludes her views on the art of fiction, thus;

> But the purpose of these holy writings (the Buddhist Scriptures), namely the encompassing of our Salvation, remains always the same. So, too, I think, may it be said that the art of fiction must not lose our allegiance because, in the pursuit of the main purpose to which I have alluded (the setting down of the moving emotion or thought or experience for all time), it sets virtue by the side of vice, or mingles wisdom with folly. Viewed in this light the novel is seen to be not, as is usually supposed, a mixture of useful truth with idle invention, but something which at every stage and in every part has a definite and serious purpose.

Clearly then, it is no part of the fictionist's craft to describe only what is good or beautiful; for if he must be true to reality, of which his work is the symbolic or verbal objectification, the novelist will not only show the lineaments of virtue but of numerous examples of vice and folly in the world around him; and if the writer has the aesthetic distance, as Joyce or Murasaki has upon her characters, she will give the illusion of god-like objectivity, neither blaming nor praising, but only limning the action or feeling.

I have emphasized these words spoken by Prince Genji, the mouth-piece of Lady Murasaki, because I think that here lies the core of the art of that Japanese master; here also is the key to the understanding and appreciation of the ***Tale*** itself. The novel itself is her objectification of her difficult ideal, which is all the more astonishing when we consider that eight hundred or more years is the gap between her own achievement and the first brilliant masterpieces in the English novel.

There are critics who complain that the novel is unwieldy, that it contains too many characters. Viewed from the prejudices of the Western novel this may be true. But when understood in terms of the theory of art expounded by Lady Murasaki, we find that the creation of characters who appear and disappear and appear again becomes a fundamental aesthetic necessity—for more than any Occidental novelist, she has objectified the very flow of life itself, than which there is hardly any greater achievement.

But her work, viewed even by our own rather artificial Western standards, is no stringing of incidents or of characters, but is the meaningful presentation of the moral ideal she has expressed: that life is neither more nor less good or bad than what it is; that the novelist should suspend judgment on his characters but should, like God, let the sunshine and the rain of his creativity fall on the just and on the unjust. This is what Shakespeare does in his dramas: aware of the constant tug of war between good and evil, he nevertheless has the objectivity (Keats called it the negative Sensibility), to make no moral judgments. The result is the creation of a universe full of people of infinite variety, moving in which one finds occasion for delight and purgation of emotions. Beyond this literary achievement, the literary artist cannot go. This is what, in her way, Lady Murasaki achieved. (pp. 57-68)

Ricaredo Demetillo, "The Art of Lady Murasaki," in The Diliman Review, *Vol. III, No. 1, January, 1955, pp. 56-68.*

DONALD KEENE (letter date 1958)

[Keene is one of the foremost contemporary translators and critics of Japanese literature. In the following excerpt, he remarks upon the historical dimension of Murasaki's novel, while admonishing readers to remember that the work was intended primarily as a work of fiction. Keene's comments were first presented at the Conference on Oriental Classics in 1958.]

The greatest glory of Japanese literature is unquestionably ***The Tale of Genji.*** It has been recognized as such ever since the early eleventh century when first it circulated in manuscript, and no one has ever suggested that it might be the second-best Japanese classic, or one of several equally great masterpieces. Scholars of both ancient and modern times have devoted the major part of their lives to commenting on and elucidating the text; its themes and incidents have furnished the material for innumerable novels and plays; it has inspired some of the loveliest works of Japanese art. In our day Junichirō Tanizaki, the outstanding modern novelist, has sacrificed years of his own career in order to make two complete translations of ***The Tale of Genji.*** Arthur Waley's English version, over which he labored ten years, is considered by many to be the finest translation of this century, and ranks by the beauty of its expression as a classic of English. It is a work of inexhaustible riches, to which we may return again and again with pleasure and enlightenment. (p. 186)

The Tale of Genji is an extremely Japanese book, unmistakably so, and to read it is to learn much about the Japan of its time and today, but it would be a terrible mistake to read it for information or, in the current phrase, to gain a better understanding of Asia. It is one of those rare books which can heighten our enjoyment of life by revealing new possibilities of beauty. It chronicles the triumphs of the aesthetic ideals of what was probably the most exquisitely cultivated society ever realized on earth, and though it suggests that ultimately these ideals were not enough, they can add an extra dimension to our experience of life. Who can ever forget after reading ***The Tale of Genji*** the love letters folded carelessly but elegantly, the page-boy in bewitchingly baggy trousers, the pine-tree, so jealous of the attentions paid to an orange-tree that it shook billows of snow from its heavily laden branches? The loving detail given to the descriptions of nature, to the appearance, manners and clothes of the characters, to the delicate hesitations expressed in the countless exchanges of poems, may at first irritate the undergraduate more accustomed to the stronger stuff of European novels, but it may also, to paraphrase Flaubert, give him an education in sentiment and beauty.

The Tale of Genji, however, is certainly not merely a series of charming vignettes. It tells a story which, if wanting in the scenes of physical violence and bloodshed which commonly merit the adjective "exciting," has its own unflagging interest, whether read as the love adventures of a handsome and supremely accomplished prince, or as one of the most subtle and penetrating expositions of the varieties of love. It is hard to think of any other novel which has in particular so many female characters who remain unique and unforgettable. ***The Tale of Genji*** can and should be read like any other novel, but it carries with it also the personality of a whole culture.

It is noteworthy that a novel should be considered the glory of Japanese literature. In most other parts of Asia the writing of novels was unknown before the arrival of the influence of European literature. Even in such countries as China and Korea, where the novel has had a long history, it was considered to be an idle pastime, the amusement of women and semiliterates, and not a form of serious writing. The excellence of ***The Tale of Genji*** was partly responsible for the novel being considered to be a dignified literary medium by the Japanese, but it was chiefly the Japanese belief in the importance of the emotions—even of physical passion, so deplored by the Confucian scholars—which gave this sanctity to the novel. The author of ***The Tale of Genji,*** Murasaki Shikibu, in a famous passage described her theory of the origin and importance of the novel:

> To begin with, it does not simply consist in the author's telling a story about the adventures of some other person. On the contrary, it happens because the storyteller's own experience of men and things, whether for good or ill . . . has moved him to an emotion so passionate that he can no longer keep it shut up in his heart. Again and again something in his own life or in that around him will seem to the writer so important that he cannot bear to let it pass into oblivion.

This view of the novel may not seem so startling to us after all the modern developments in our literature, but it is extraordinary that in the year 1010 or so there should have been so cogent an explanation of why people write novels. In the insistence on the importance of preserving and transmitting the author's most deeply felt emotions, we may be reminded of Proust's discovery of his life's work in the search for and recollection of time past. Despite Murasaki Shikibu's clear statement, however, later men preferred to find in ***The Tale of Genji*** a didactic intent of Buddhist or Confucian nature, depending on the commentator. It was declared variously to be a lesson in the vanity of the things of this world, an account of the workings of retribution, or a series, of biographies of model women. Even today such views retain a surprising currency. Many well-educated Japanese think of ***The Tale of Genji*** as a novel which demonstrates how Genji because of his affair with Fujitsubo, his step-mother, is punished when his own wife is unfaithful to him. The novel has also been interpreted by Marxist critics, who insist that it is an exposé of the corrupt aristocratic society of Murasaki Shikibu's day, and that she was a disgruntled member of the lesser nobility anxious to assert the claims of her class. Certainly none of these interpretations accords with what Murasaki Shikibu herself wrote, and as early as the eighteenth century the great scholar Motoori Norinaga declared that such interpretations were based not on a consideration of the nature of the novel itself, "but rather on the novel as seen from the point of view of Confucian and Buddhist works. . . . To seize upon an occasional similarity in sentiment or a chance correspondence in ideas with Confucian and Buddhist works, and proceed to generalize about the nature of the tale as a whole, is unwarranted" [see excerpt dated 1801]. Motoori's comment still stands today as a model of good sense.

Motoori declared that ***The Tale of Genji*** was a novel of *mono no aware,* a term which is difficult to translate, but means something like "a sensitivity to things" or, to translate one untranslatable phrase by another, *lacrimae rerum.* It is a novel in which people who are sensitive to the innate sadness of things, their brevity, the passage of beauty, the impossibility of love meaning everything in life, are treated sympathetically despite their lapses from moral standards. Their punishment is in their own hearts, in their growing old, and is not marked by the arrival of a chastising lightning bolt or by the flames of a burning hell. There is certainly no attempt to indict the society for the failings of the individual. The characters of ***The Tale of Genji*** are people who devoted themselves entirely to the cultivation of the senses, who created a world of marvelous grace and beauty, and who were often extremely unhappy. This unhappiness—or perhaps "melancholy" would be a better word—comes from their awareness of the sorrow of things, from their appreciation of the implications of the moment of parting or of the fall of a leaf. The novel darkens in tone as it goes on, and pessimistic Buddhist doctrines, often enough in the mouths of the characters earlier in the book, begin to acquire conviction, but there is no attempt made in Buddhist fashion to describe the world as a place of dust and ugliness. The world is lovely, the people in it are lovely, and though this is not sufficient for lasting happiness, the world is worth remembering and chronicling in the details which Murasaki Shikibu has summoned up. Its sorrow as reflected in the novel may lead to a Buddhist awakening, but the novelist's purpose was to depict *mono no aware,* and not to preach a sermon. It is up to the reader to supply the rest.

The emphasis on aesthetic matters in ***The Tale of Genji*** is a notable characteristic of Japanese culture. There is hardly an aspect of Japanese life untouched by a love of beauty. In religion, for example, the complex Buddhist doctrines taught in India and China tended to be simplified in Japan to artistic formulae. The Zen Buddhist insistence on sudden intuition—so congenial to the Japanese—rather than on intellectual attainment, shares the same aesthetic bias. A belief in intuitive experience, in the preferability of the emotions to cold logic, in the necessity of presenting thought and experience in an elegant and pleasing form, avoiding the harsh edges of more direct expression, has accounted for many of the finest things in Japanese arts and letters as well as some of their shortcomings. The exquisite poetry in thirty-one syllables (the *tanka*), for example, is one pure lyrical impulse, devoid of intellectual content and prevented by its brevity from becoming explicative, perfect of its kind but lacking the vitality and content of less polished forms. One of the supreme triumphs of Japanese aestheticism, of course, is ***The Tale of Genji,*** and the sign of its triumph is our willingness to accept as a whole world, the only possible world, what we objectively know to be only a very small part of the world. Within its bounds ugliness is the greatest crime, and ignorance of a poetic allusion or a mediocre penmanship cause enough for derision and even ostracism. There is no place here for starving farmers, sweating laborers, corrupt officials, and the other people of eleventh-century Japan whose numbers, we know, must have far exceeded those of the court society Murasaki Shikibu described. The element of coarseness, which Western writers have consciously injected into their works so as to give the illusion of a complete world, is virtually absent. (pp. 188-92)

The fact that ***The Tale of Genji*** is a novel and not a diary or court chronicle is too obvious to require explanation, but because of the remoteness of the world it treats, there is a tendency on the part of some to forget that it is fiction, that Genji never existed, and that the author had to devise and control a plot and characters, just like any other novelist. Its techniques are not those of the Western novel, but they are consciously employed. For example, the first chapter states most of the principal themes of the work in a seemingly casual manner. The death of Genji's mother, brought about mainly on account of the jealousy of the other court ladies, is a foreshadowing of the famous death scenes of Yugao and Aoi. The emperor's love for Fujitsubo, for the resemblance she bears the dead lady, is echoed again and again in the novel in Genji's search for new loves, and has its final tragic statement in Kaoru's love for Ukifune. Again Genji's love even as a child for Fujitsubo, and his coldness toward Aoi, though briefly stated, here prepare us for their fuller exposition later on. The general mood of the opening chapter, the sensitivity to things of the emperor, sets the tone of the entire novel, and with the second chapter, the famous discussion of the different categories of women, tells us as clearly as the overture to *Don Giovanni* the kind of work which is to follow.

Like any great novel, ***The Tale of Genji*** is interesting from page to page. We want to know what will happen to Yugao or to the princess with the red nose or to the girl Murasaki. But it is the character of Genji himself which properly claims our greatest attention. He is not only described as being peerless but convinces us of his attributes in a manner rare in literature, and though seemingly perfect from the very outset, he develops as he tastes sorrow and as he becomes "sensitive to things." His capacity to love, his beauty, wit, and talent mark him as a hero, though he performs no heroic deeds. Such a hero stands apart from our traditions, and even from later Japanese ones, as is witnessed by the fact that in the recent Japanese film version of ***The Tale of Genji*** it was felt essential to enhance Genji's qualities by having him overcome barehanded three sworded adversaries. The imagination boggles at this "improvement" of the original, as much as it would at a scene inserted in *Macbeth* in which Macbeth debates the proper choice of stationery before penning a letter to Lady Macbeth. Genji has no need of his fists to prove his status as a hero; he moves a whole world as surely as the most powerful men of fiction. He is a superman who breathes no fire. I am reminded by him of the music of Mozart, perfect in the details as in the whole, growing always a little faster than we ourselves grow; and as a taste for Mozart's music is likely to follow rather than precede one for Wagner's, Genji may continue to claim us when we find ourselves exhausted by more strenuous heroes. (pp. 193-94)

Donald Keene, "'The Tale of Genji'," in Approaches to the Oriental Classics: Asian Literature and Thought in General Education, *edited by William Theodore de Bary, Columbia University Press, 1959, pp. 186-95.*

IVAN MORRIS (essay date 1961)

[*An American critic and translator, Morris was renowned for his numerous, highly esteemed studies of Japanese literature, history, and culture. In the following excerpt, he outlines various aspects of daily life in Heian Japan.*]

The Tale of Genji, so far as we know, is the first full-length psychological novel produced in any country. To examine how this monumental work came to be written, some fifty years before the Norman Conquest, by a lady belonging to the Court of a remote and, in some ways, remarkably backward island kingdom in the Pacific is a fascinating study. These notes are chiefly concerned with one aspect of the background, namely, the physical setting in which Murasaki Shikibu lived and worked.

By the time that Murasaki was born, in the seventies of the tenth century, official relations with the outside world, that is to say, with China and Korea, had been in a state of abeyance for almost one hundred years. After her feverish importations from the Continent during the seventh and eighth centuries, Japan was going through one of those long periods of relative isolation that in the course of the island's history have followed the "borrowing" phases, like the reverse swings of a pendulum.

This is not to suggest that the Japanese had lost their interest in learning from China. Long after the lapse of official relations, priests, scholars and merchants continued to risk their lives on the arduous ocean voyage to the Continent; and they

A mid-sixteenth-century illustration from the Ukifune section of The Tale of Genji.

returned to the islands with the material and cultural treasures of the Middle Kingdom. Indeed, by Murasaki's time an educated Japanese gentleman was in a position to acquire a rich fund of knowledge—though often rather patchy and out of date—about Chinese culture and even, indirectly, about Central Asia. A catalogue of Chinese books in Japan, compiled at the end of the ninth century, mentions some 1,500 titles; and this was only a partial list.

Yet, from the time of the decline of the T'ang dynasty in the ninth century, there seems to have been a progressive change in the Japanese attitude to importations from China. The Nara Period in the eighth century had been a period of wholesale borrowing and adaptation. From the ninth century, the approach became increasingly selective and critical. For Japan was now evolving her own characteristic forms in government, economic organization, religion, art, literature, architecture, dress and many other fields. China, for all its power and riches and cultural tradition, was no longer regarded as the great cornucopia from which all knowledge must be derived.

By Murasaki's time, at the end of the century, this process of emancipation from foreign tutelage had gone very far indeed. Contemporary terms like *Yamato-damashii* (the spirit of Japan), *Yamato-e* (Japanese-style paintings) and *Yamato-uta* (Japanese-style poems) reflect a self-conscious effort on the part of the islanders to assert the identity of their own culture as distinct from that of China.

In examining the setting of ***The Tale of Genji,*** then, the first point is that tenth-century Japan was in many ways more self-sufficient, more independent from the Continent, than at any time since the first flood of Chinese imports half a millennium earlier. Chinese continued to be used for state documents, scholarship and written communication between men. In a sense, however, it had the marks of a dead language: few of the men who wrote Chinese for official, or even for literary, purposes had ever heard it spoken by a native of the country; and even their written models were taken not from contemporary Sung, but from the T'ang period or before.

The insularity of tenth-century Japan is reflected in the scarcity of foreigners. Whereas the T'ang capital of Ch'ang An had been a great cosmopolitan city, crowded with travellers from every part of Asia and highly responsive to foreign influences, Heian-kyō, the Japanese capital, had few visitors from the outside world. ***The Tale of Genji*** gives a realistic and fairly complete picture of the cultural life in the capital. Yet the only foreigners to appear in the course of the immense work are the Korean astrologers in the opening chapter; and Murasaki clearly had little interest in these exotic gentlemen. Sei Shōnagon's *Pillow Book,* a meticulous record of life in Heian-kyō, does not (so far as I can recall) contain a single mention of a foreigner in the capital, although that is where all Chinese influences in Japan were concentrated.

If Murasaki and her circle were comparatively uninterested in the present state of their great neighbour, China, we can imagine how little concern they had with points farther west. In *The Tale of the Hollow Tree,* another late tenth-century work, the hero, who is on his way from Japan to China, is shipwrecked on the Persian coast—an impressive feat of navigation. India (*Tenjiku*) is occasionally mentioned, but as a semi-mythical place where none but strange hermits or magicians would dream of going.

Many important aspects of the world of ***The Tale of Genji*** are bound up with the "Continent Isolated" frame of mind that had developed by Murasaki's day. On the negative side, her world had a closed and rather parochial character, not infrequently verging on the claustrophobic. Yet the fact that for so many centuries the Japanese were able to develop peacefully, and without outside interference, allowed them to devote their energies and resources to the perfection of a highly specialized, intense, indigenous culture, a culture marked by the particular aesthetic approach that Sir George Sansom has described as "the rule of taste." Both in literature and in painting, the greatest works of the Heian Period, notably ***The Tale of Genji*** and the Genji picture scrolls, are those in which Chinese influence is indirect and relatively unimportant.

Murasaki's Japan was virtually identical in territory with the present archipelago, except that the great northern island of Hokkaidō was still the preserve of the Ezo aborigines, the putative ancestors of the "hairy Ainu." These aborigines had originally been spread over all the islands; but they had been driven steadily northwards, and in Murasaki's age they no longer represented a military problem.

The country was divided into sixty-six provinces and two islands, essentially the same division that the Westerners found when they arrived a millennium later. By far the most important area for Murasaki and her cultured contemporaries was the five home provinces round the capital. The remaining provinces were grouped in seven circuits; of which the most famous has always been the Tōkaidō, extending north-east from the home provinces.

In Murasaki's day, the provinces were administrative units, each under the authority of a governor who was appointed by the central government for a term of four years. Murasaki's father was the governor of one of the northern provinces on the Japan Sea; and many other women writers of the time were the daughters of provincial officials.

The governor's main duty was to collect the various taxes, notably the riceland produce tax, on which the central administration depended for its revenue. By the end of the tenth century, however, this was becoming increasingly difficult, because of the mushroom-growth all over the country of great tax-free manors, to which more and more farmers on the public estate were commending their land in order to escape the burden of taxes. This process would soon have had a disastrous effect on central government, but for the fact that the administration was now virtually in the hands of a single family, the Fujiwaras (to a minor branch of which Murasaki herself belonged), and that the Fujiwara leaders, as well as occupying all the principal posts in the government, were the greatest manor-holders of the time. Though the Imperial Treasury was being starved of tax revenue from the provinces, the dominant political group in the capital was amply provided with funds to carry out the essential tasks of administration.

It was, none the less, a precarious state of affairs; and, although the system continued to work during Murasaki's lifetime, making possible the peaceful and elegant life depicted in ***The Tale of Genji,*** there were already portents of the collapse that occurred about a century later, involving the downfall of the Fujiwara aristocratic government and the growth of a Japanese form of feudalism under a warrior class.

The provinces were the source of economic power, and they were also steadily becoming the centre of military power. But we should hardly guess this from reading ***The Tale of Genji*** or other contemporary literature; for Murasaki and her friends in the capital looked on the provinces as harsh, dreary, backward places—as, no doubt, they were.

To be appointed governor of a remote province, however economically profitable such a post might be, was regarded as a form of exile. For, like the aristocratic denizen of Versailles who had been banished to his "*terres,*" in Heian Japan the provincial governor was cut off from cultural pursuits and from the other pleasures of polite society; besides, he stood little chance of being promoted while *en poste*. When Murasaki refers to a girl as having been brought up in "undesirable surroundings," it usually means that she is the daughter of a governor, and that she has spent her childhood in the provinces. In ***The Tale of Genji,*** when the Lady of Akashi learns from her grandmother that she was brought up in the provinces—actually a mere sixty miles from the capital—her reaction is one of unmitigated horror: "Never had she imagined that she could have been born in a place so cut off from the world." And the daughter of the Governor of Kazusa, a province near present-day Tokyo, starts her famous *Sarashina Diary* with the following doleful entry: "I was brought up in a remote part of the country—so remote that it lies even beyond the end of the Tōkaidō. I expect that people [in the capital] will think of me as hopelessly outlandish."

The few provincials who figure in ***The Tale of Genji*** are usually pictured as boorish upstarts, utterly devoid of good taste and standing in exaggerated awe of their "betters"—that is, of the inhabitants of the capital. No harsher pejorative existed in Murasaki's vocabulary than *inakabitaru* ("countrified"). Yet is was precisely these despised provincials who, once they were armed and fully conscious of their own strength, were to bring Murasaki's world down in ruins.

For the cultured inhabitants of Heian-kyō, the only mitigating aspect of the provinces was the varied beauty of the magnificent Japanese countryside. *The Sarashina Diary,* for instance, contains some splendid descriptions of Mount Fuji and of the other natural wonders that the author witnessed on her journey back to the capital. Yet, even in this respect, Murasaki and her contemporaries preferred the more familiar environment of the home provinces, where nature seemed less raw and savage. The capital itself was situated in the most beautiful country, encircled on three sides by thickly forested hills and mountains, often delicately wreathed with trails of mist; the landscape abounded in streams and waterfalls and lakes; and into its pleasant slopes and valleys the countless shrines and temples blended as if they too had been a part of nature.

The countryside and climate of Japan are certainly one of the most important influences on its literature; and the rôle that nature plays in Murasaki's writing can hardly be exaggerated. Japan is a country of marked seasonal changes, a country in which, even now after a century of relentless industrialization, it is particularly hard to be *unaware* of nature. It is a country, too, in which an awesome variety of natural disasters has combined to make people highly conscious of the influence of nature on their lives. For Murasaki and her circle, sensitivity to the subtle moods of nature was an essential attribute of "good people" (*yoki hito*); without such sensitivity it was impossible to understand the "emotional quality of things," which was regarded as the basis of aesthetic, and even of moral, awareness.

From the earliest times, Japanese poetry was overwhelmingly concerned with the lyrical evocation of nature in all its varied aspects. The core of the poem was almost invariably a natural image, used to symbolize some human emotion or experience. This tradition was carried over into prose literature of the Heian Period, especially that written by women. Murasaki's diary (1007-10) starts with a short and most effective description of autumn, the favourite time of year in most contemporary literature. . . .

In ***The Tale of Genji,*** the nature of Heian-kyō and its environs is no mere static background. It is a vital force exerting a constant influence on the main characters; and it is in terms of this nature that Prince Genji and the others perceive and express their emotions.

In view of the prevailing attitude towards the provinces, it is hardly surprising that ***The Tale of Genji*** and other contemporary literature should have been concerned almost exclusively with life in the capital city and its immediate surroundings. In Murasaki's eyes, as in Genji's, only those who were urbane—in the original sense of the word—could be regarded as really civilized.

Heian-kyō was constructed during the last decade of the eighth century, its official buildings being completed in 806. As at Nara, the previous centre of government, the general plan was copied from the huge western capital of China, Ch'ang An, which had reached its heights during the eighth century, at a time when numerous admiring visitors from Japan had travelled to the Continent. Heian-kyō, which remained the capital for over one thousand years (later being known as Miyako and Kyōto), was conceived on a very much larger scale than Nara; and it had a completely different atmosphere. The great Buddhist centre of Nara represented antiquity and calm; Heian-kyō, at least during its early centuries, stood for all that was new and lively in the country. *Imamekashi* (up to date) was the keynote of the new age, and the highest term of praise for Murasaki and her friends.

The city of the world of Genji was a rectangle about three and a half miles from north to south, and two and a half miles from east to west. Unlike most modern Japanese cities, it was planned in a perfectly systematic fashion, being divided at regular intervals by parallel streets and avenues crossing each other at right angles. Some of the streets were extremely wide, as in the model city of Ch'ang An: the great central street ("Red Sparrow Avenue") had a width of nearly three hundred feet. Between the avenues were narrow streets and still narrower alleys, almost all running parallel or perpendicular. Most of the houses, except for those of the nobility, lay close together, permitting an urban population in Murasaki's time of close on 100,000.

Directly in the north centre of the city was the Greater Imperial Palace, which contained both the palace buildings themselves and the government offices, and which, as in China, faced the auspicious southern direction. It was surrounded by a very low wall; and the bare grounds were strewn with gravel, in typical Japanese style.

The site of the new capital was ideal from every traditional point of view. Hills lay to the north, west and east; and in the north-east—the unlucky direction—the great mountain range of Hiei, on which Buddhist temples and monasteries clustered in almost endless profusion, protected the city from evil influences. Along the foot of the eastern hills flowed the Kamo River, which curved round at the south, again as topographical tradition demanded; the Katsura River to the west of the city provided the second of the two essential "female" elements. To the north-east Lake Biwa provided ample water supply for the artificial streams in the noblemen's gardens, as well as for more prosaic purposes.

Although far more elaborate than anything that had existed previously in Japan, the "City of Peace and Tranquility" (as the name Heian-kyō so aptly denoted) was of the utmost simplicity when compared to its Chinese model; and, seen next to Imperial Rome or Versailles, the dominant impression of its Court life would be one of almost Spartan restraint. References in contemporary literature to the pomp and glory of Genji's world must not be allowed to obscure this aspect, which was dictated both by Japanese canons of taste and, to a lesser extent, by economic necessity.

The same simplicity characterized the domestic architecture of the period. The type of mansion occupied by Murasaki and those of her class was known as *shinden* ("sleep pavilion"). Although originally influenced by Chinese concepts and by Buddhist temple architecture, the *shinden* style had by Murasaki's time assumed a distinctively Japanese air, having bark-shingled roofs, deep eaves and open wooden piling to raise the buildings from the ground.

Constant fires and earthquakes have deprived us of authentic examples of the Heian house; but fairly reliable reconstructions have been made. The typical *shinden* mansion consisted of a number of rectangular buildings, joined by long covered corridors—similar to the cloister colonnades of Buddhist temple complexes—forming a large rectangle open to the south. Here there would be a formal landscape garden, usually comprising an artificial lake with a pine-dotted island, one or two miniature hills and two parallel streams, along which elegant verses would be floated during the frequent poetry parties; and the earth would be strewn with very fine white sand to reflect the full beauty of the moonlight.

The main building, the master's quarters, was flanked by eastern and western pavilions, which were occupied by relations, friends, secondary consorts or children. Each pavilion in the *shinden* complex consisted basically of a single large room, which, as we can see from the Genji scrolls, could readily be divided by screens and curtains into sections or cubicles as circumstances required. The building to the north was traditionally inhabited by the principal wife, who accordingly was known as the "northern person." New buildings and corridors could, when necessary, be added behind the main complex. Prince Genji's mansion in the Sixth Ward, where he brought his numerous women friends to live together, must have been a maze of detached pavilions and connecting corridors.

The main mood of *shinden* architecture, however, was one of restraint and tranquillity. A characteristic Japanese desire for understatement and avoidance of ostentation discouraged the use of the bright colours associated with Chinese architecture. From reconstructions of the Imperial residence—on which the *shinden* mansions were based—we may judge that it was one of the most austere palaces in the world.

In Heian times, as today, the furnishings of the typical Japanese house could scarcely have been more sparse. The wooden floor was bare, except for the individual straw mats on which people sat. Chairs had been imported from China in an earlier period, but never gained much popularity. In Murasaki's day, they were used mainly on ceremonial occasions in the Palace and in Buddhist temples; elsewhere, life, both waking and sleeping, was mainly spent on the floor.

The emptiness of the room was, as a rule, relieved only by an occasional chest, brazier, screen or other movable object. One piece of furniture that plays an important part in the literature of the time was the *kichō,* a wooden frame supporting movable silk hangings, which Arthur Waley translates as "screen of state." When receiving male visitors, women normally ensconced themselves behind these curtains, where, at the best, they could be seen only in dim outline; and one of the main aims of the Heian gallant was to insinuate himself behind the *kichō*. Readers of ***The Tale of Genji*** will recall the passage in which Prince Sochi, seated outside Tamakazura's *kichō,* has been making an impassioned declaration to the girl, only to be informed by a lady in waiting that Tamakazura has long since retired to the inner room.

A significant aspect of the *shinden* mansion, and of traditional Japanese architecture in general, is the way in which the inside of the house merged into the world outside. Apartments were separated from the open verandas by a series of shutters; in the warm weather, these could be removed, and the split-bamboo blinds rolled up, so that the room would become almost a part of the garden. The separation between "out of doors" and "indoors" has never been so strong in Japan as in the West; and Buddhist influence helped to combat the idea of a solid, permanent dwelling-place that might provide a barrier against the outside world of nature.

Japan is a country of climatic extremes; and the insubstantial character of traditional architecture made the Japanese more than ever conscious of nature and its changing moods. Thus, in the illustration of the heroine's death scene in the Genji scrolls, there is no visible demarcation between the room and the wind-swept garden with its desolate clover bushes; and the poems that she, Genji and the other characters exchange are all built about images taken from the surrounding world of nature to which their emotions are so closely attuned.

Not only did the Heian house provide little defence from the outside world; it offered scant protection indoors. No architecture could have been better suited to the eavesdropper or the Peeping Tom; and many of the plots in contemporary fiction revolve about conversations that are overheard, or about ladies who are spied through a lattice by some enterprising gentleman. Readers of ***The Tale of Genji*** will recall the ubiquitous ladies-in-waiting who hear and see everything that is happening in the house, and who are forever commenting on the doings of their unprotected superiors. Certain apartments in the Imperial Palace were provided with "singing" floorboards, to give warning of eavesdroppers and other interlopers; but for most of Murasaki's contemporaries privacy would have been a meaningless term.

Another practical consideration that had an important effect on Heian life was the difficulty of transport. Even in the vicinity of the capital, the roads were unbelievably poor; and in many of the provinces they were virtually non-existent. Travel by sea was risky, uncomfortable and hard to arrange. Tamakazura is obliged to languish some fifteen years in the wilds of Kyūshū, before she is able to make the sea journey back to the capital. The speediest method of travel was, of course, on horseback. This, however, was hardly appropriate for the decorous personages of Genji's world; and for members of the aristocracy the standard mode of transport was the unwieldy ox-drawn carriage that lumbered along the streets at about two miles an hour.

It is not surprising, then, that people avoided any unnecessary expeditions from the capital, and that even a visit to a nearby temple was regarded as an arduous journey, requiring days of preparation and rest. When we read of Prince Genji's distress at being banished to Suma, we have the impression that he has been relegated to the antipodes; in fact, his place of exile was so near the capital that it can now be reached by train in less than two hours. Even Uji, the setting of most of the action in the last part of the novel, is viewed as being hopelessly remote and inaccessible, although it is actually only some ten miles from the centre of the city. "Even our deep bond of affection," writes Prince Niou to a girl who lives at Uji, and whom he is shortly to bring to the capital as his secondary consort, "can hardly survive the rigours involved in visiting you [at Uji]. How on earth could you have chosen such a place?" And when the young lady sits in the Prince's ox-drawn carriage, having finally brought herself to make the journey to the capital, she is appalled to observe the hardships that her lover has had to undergo on his visits: "As she travelled down the long arduous mountain road, she began to see how reasonable had been [the Prince's] hesitations which previously she had regarded as the marks of a cold heart."

The slow pace of ***The Tale of Genji,*** and of most contemporary literature, is undoubtedly related to this problem of locomotion. Life, in many ways, was attuned to the speed of the ox-carriage; and, whereas a leisurely approach may encourage a delicate, polished and subtle type of writing, it may also result in a certain monotony, especially for readers who are used to more rapid movement.

The general lack of interest and knowledge concerning other parts of the country—as well as the almost obsessive fear of being sent to the provinces—are related to this same problem. Indeed, it might be argued that the backwardness of internal communications was one of the factors that indirectly helped to bring about the downfall of Murasaki's world. For by losing control over the provinces, the source of economic strength in a rice economy, the central government under the Fujiwara aristocracy was eventually to forfeit all real power in the capital city itself. (pp. 527-35)

Ivan Morris, "The World of Genji: Japanese Civilization in the Eleventh Century," in History Today, *Vol. XI, No. 8, August, 1961, pp. 527-35.*

IVAN MORRIS (essay date 1964)

[*In the following excerpt from* The World of the Shining Prince, *which is generally considered the definitive study of the Heian period in Japanese history, Morris discusses the structure, unity, language, and world view of* The Tale.]

The first psychological novel in the literature of the world is also one of its longest. In its original form ***The Tale of Genji*** consisted of fifty-four books or chapters, which were separately bound and which . . . often circulated independently. Arthur Waley's translation, which does not expand the original (and from which one of the books is missing), has some 630,000 words; this makes Murasaki's novel about twice as long as *Don Quixote, War and Peace,* or *The Brothers Karamazov,* though only two-thirds the length of *A la recherche du temps perdu.*

The action is spread over three-quarters of a century and involves four generations. There are about four hundred and thirty characters, not counting messengers, servants, and anonymous members of the working class. Most of these characters are related to each other, and early commentators devoted years to the sisyphean task of producing genealogical tables in which almost every character in the novel was included. The tradition has been maintained by modern scholars: Ikeda's recent *Encyclopaedia of the Tale of Genji* has over seventy closely-printed pages of genealogy. Murasaki belonged to a rigidly stratified society in which family connexions were all-important, and while working on the novel she must have kept her own charts to show how her huge cast of characters were related. For never once is she inconsistent about the relationship of even the most obscure people in her book.

This methodical approach is even more striking in Murasaki's time scheme. There is hardly a passage in the entire novel that we cannot identify in terms of year and month and in which we cannot determine the exact age of each of the important characters. Occasionally Murasaki will depart from straight chronological order in telling her story. The events in one chapter, for example, may occur before those in the previous chapter ("flashback"), or two chapters may overlap. But such deviations are deliberate and there is never any confusion. Commentators have subjected the time scheme of the novel to the minutest scrutiny. They are, one feels, almost hoping to find some inconsistency; until now they have been unsuccessful.

This precision is one aspect of Murasaki's talent for organizing her voluminous material in the most effective way. It immediately puts her work in a different category from *The Tale of the Hollow Tree,* the only extant precursor in the field of lengthy prose fiction. For one of the things that makes *The Tale of the Hollow Tree* so hard to read, and ultimately so unreal, is its disorganized construction and its chaotic time scheme.

The Tale of Genji does not ramble on amorphously as a haphazard sequence of loosely connected episodes. It is true that the books tend to be more independent than the chapters of most modern novels, especially since there is often a gap of several years between them; yet to view the work as a series of vaguely related short stories (as some critics have done) seems to me completely off the mark. Like the individual books of which it is composed, ***The Tale of Genji*** is an artistic unit whose shape has been carefully and deliberately designed. It is so constructed that the entire work can be resolved into certain general divisions, which represent its beginning (Books 1-12), its middle (Books 13-41), and its end (Books 42-54), and into a number of signficant sub-divisions whose various chapters are closely bound together by the coherent development of character and event.

Above all, ***The Tale of Genji*** is constructed about a set of central ideas or themes, the historical theme of Fujiwara power, for example, and the human theme of impermanence, which combine to give it an artistic unity. This is one of the aspects (the use of realistic psychological detail is another) that allow us to describe Murasaki's work as a "novel," a term that cannot be applied to any of its exact precursors.

One device that Murasaki uses with particular effect is anticipation or build-up. Frequently she will hint at the existence of some character long before that person enters the action of the novel, or she will adumbrate some sequence of events that is to take place many years in the future. There is a scene in one of the early books, for example, in which Prince Genji and a young friend stand on a hill and discuss the beauties of the countryside in the distance. "If one were to live in such a place," exclaims Genji, "one could really ask for nothing more in this world!" Here Murasaki anticipates, not without irony, the events that are to happen eight years (and seven books) later. For the landscape at which Genji gazes so fondly is to be the place of his forlorn exile from the capital. His friend then tells him the story of the strange old lay priest of Akashi and of his attractive little daughter. This arouses the young prince's curiosity, as well as the reader's, and paves the way for Genji's love affair with Lady Akashi and for all the complications that this entails in later years.

Sometimes Murasaki will speak about a character never mentioned before as though the reader already knew all about him. In the hands of a skilful writer this device can produce a curiously realistic effect and, as Arthur Waley has pointed out, it was used by Proust. Murasaki's more usual method of build-up, however, is to make different characters speak about someone from their respective points of view long before the person in question actually appears on the scene. For example, Kaoru hears various reports about Ukifune, the tragic heroine of the last five books, many years before he actually meets her. It is not until we have formed a fairly clear picture of the girl that she enters the action.

By far the best-known case of anticipation in ***The Tale of Genji*** occurs in Book 2 when Genji and his young friends meet on a rainy night to discuss the different types of women they have known and to compare their merits. This passage, with its detailed comments on various sorts of women that are to figure in the novel, has often been regarded as a key to the organization of the entire work, not unlike the first movement of a symphony in which the composer may suggest the themes that he intends to develop later. In fact the "discussion on a rainy night" does not have nearly such a mechanical function as this might suggest. Of the many types of girl that the young gallants describe, only one can be identified with a specific character in the novel. This is Yūgao, the simple young woman whose love affair with Genji and whose weird death are described in the following two books. One of Genji's friends mentions that he has had an illegitimate child with Yūgao; mother and child have both disappeared and he has been unable to track them down. Here is another case of anticipation; for the child in question turns out to be Tamakazura, who enters the action of the novel seventeen years later.

Another aspect of Murasaki's style that serves to tighten the structure of her narrative is the deliberate repetition of situations, settings, and relationships between characters. ***The Tale of Genji*** contains certain patterns of action that occur with variations at widely separated points of the narrative, not unlike the motifs in a musical composition. Here again we are reminded of *A la recherche du temps perdu* with its subtle use of internal "rhythms."

One of the best ways to understand the carefully balanced architecture of Murasaki's novel is to note how she places different characters, or sometimes the same character, in successive situations that "correspond" with each other. Thus, when Genji finds out that his young wife, Princess Nyosan, has been seduced by Kashiwagi and that the little boy (Kaoru) whom everyone takes to be his own son and heir is in fact the result of this affair, he realizes that history has repeated itself to an uncanny degree. For some thirty years earlier Genji himself had seduced his father's new consort, Lady Fujitsubo, and she had given birth to a boy (Reizei), who was accepted as the Emperor's son and who as a result came to the throne illegitimately. As Genji holds the little child in his arm, it occurs to him that the old Emperor may secretly have known and suffered about Fujitsubo's unfaithfulness, in much the same way that he himself is now tormented by what Nyosan has done. The same pattern continues to unfold in later years. Just as Reizei was racked with doubts about his paternity, to the extent that he eventually resigned the throne, so when Kaoru grows up he is obsessed with the feeling that there was something strange about his birth, and this serves to intensify the neurotic aspect of his character.

There are many cases like this in which a pattern that has been developed in the early part of the novel, when Genji is the hero, is repeated with variations in the Kaoru books. For example, the relationship between Genji and Yūgao finds its echo, as it were, in the love affair between Kaoru and Ukifune some fifty years later. In each case the hero's interest is aroused by hearing about an attractive girl who belongs to a far lower social class than himself. It is only after careful anticipation that Murasaki puts her on the scene. The hero meets her by chance and is almost immediately captivated (Books 4 and 49). The love affair begins in the lady's humble town dwelling; and in the morning the hero lies listening to the unfamiliar street noises. He abruptly decides to move his mistress to some more isolated place and despite the protests of her attendants he takes her in his carriage to a gloomy country house. In both cases the relationships are marked by a sense of strangeness and end in tragedy. It is not surprising that such closely parallel situations should contain what Waley describes as "balancing scenes," like those in Books 4 and 50 when Murasaki describes the sounds of the peasants and the pedlars. The emphasis in the two scenes is on the unfamiliarity of the common surroundings in which the hero suddenly finds himself. Both men are fascinated by the street sounds, which in Genji's case are able years later to evoke the memory of his love. These are the scenes:

> (Book 4) . . . the dwelling, so different from those to which Genji was accustomed, seemed strange to him. It must have been nearly dawn. From the neighbouring houses he could hear the uncouth voices of workers who were just waking up: "Oh, how cold it is!" "We can't count on much business this year. It's a poor look-out for our hauling trade." "Hey, neighbour, wake up!" With such remarks they set out noisily, each to his own pitiful job.
>
> (Book 50) Soon it appeared to be dawn, but instead of the song of birds, Kaoru heard the raucous and unintelligible cries of pedlars calling out their wares from near the main street while they passed by in large groups. As he looked out at them staggering past in the dawn light with their loads, they appeared like phantoms. The experience of having passed the night in this simple dwelling seemed most strange to Kaoru.

Murasaki's deliberate repetitions are never as obvious as this may suggest. Nor are they exact. Psychological realism demanded that different types of people react differently in the same situation; however parallel the patterns may be, it is unthinkable that we should, for example, find a resolute character like Genji handling a love affair with the diffidence and deviousness of a Kaoru.

The use of "sustained imagery" (the repetition, that is, of a single central image in both the narrative passages and the poems) can also serve to connect different parts of the novel that are widely separated in time, or to tighten the structure of a particular series of books. Throughout the novel, for instance, Murasaki rings the changes on the image of dreams and thereby evokes one of her central themes—the nebulous, unreal quality of the world about us, and the idea that our life here is a mere "bridge of dreams" (the title of her final book), over which we cross from one state of existence to the next.

Another example of sustained imagery is the river at Uji, which figures prominently in the last ten books. This section (commonly known as the "Ten Books of Uji") occupies a special place in the writing of ***The Tale of Genji.*** It is marked by tightly-knit narrative and by a most effective use of psychological detail and of imagery. In almost every sense, indeed, it represents the climax of Murasaki's style. (pp. 265-71)

It has sometimes been suggested that the modern Western reader is so divorced from Murasaki in time and space, in patterns of thought and expression, in custom and in sensibility, that she might as well have belonged to a different planet, and that what we derive from the work of this court lady of tenth-century Japan can be only the palest approximation of what she intended to convey. According to this argument, even the modern Japanese reader, the child of Westernized industrial society, is hardly less cut off from the world of the shining prince than we in the Occident.

I do not subscribe to this view. Indeed, it seems to me, one of the remarkable things about this novel of a millennium ago is how readily we can enter into the thoughts and feelings of its characters and respond to the total vision of life that its author communicated. The more we know about the times—social organization, religious ideas, marriage customs, literary conventions, and so forth—the greater our understanding will be. Yet, even with the most elementary knowledge of the Heian background, the sensitive reader can grasp the psychology of a character like Kaoru, for example, and appreciate the close connexion between beauty and sorrow that is an underlying theme of the novel.

Many things that seemed important to Murasaki (calligraphic skill, for instance, or the court hierarchy) have little relevance in the present day; yet, when it comes to vivifying a character by psychological detail, or using imagery to evoke the feelings that death can inspire, she seems close to us and ''modern'' in a way that no previous writer of prose fiction can approach.

But is our present text of ***The Tale of Genji*** what Murasaki actually wrote? It is a complex matter and this is not the place to discuss it in any detail. The earliest extant manuscript dates from the middle of the twelfth century, over one hundred years after Murasaki was writing; it could hardly be more inaccurate and incomplete. Our first full text of the fifty-four books belongs to the fourteenth century, and varies in many ways from the manuscripts on which most modern texts are based. The rival schools of medieval ***Genji*** scholars had their own texts, which they guarded like military secrets. It was not until relatively recent times that the various manuscripts could be correlated and compared for accuracy.

Considering this rather confused history and the difficulties of producing reliable copies of Japanese ''grass writing'' script, we might expect the most bewildering discrepancies between the different versions. In fact a study of Ikeda's textual correlations suggests that they are remarkably close and that most of the differences are matters of detail which have little bearing on the overall content or signficance of the novel. Of course such correlations do not tell us how faithful the texts are to the sentences that Murasaki committed to paper one thousand years ago. Failing a monumental literary discovery, this is something we shall never know. The consensus among modern Japanese scholars, however, is that the printed texts of ***The Tale of Genji*** may for all literary purposes be regarded as quite close to the original.

The real barrier between the modern reader and ***The Tale of Genji*** is not any corruption of the text, nor any confusion of theme. It is a far more direct one: the difficulty of the language in which the novel is written. Since this language is virtually pure Japanese, one might expect that at least for Murasaki's countrymen it should present no insuperable hardships. The trouble is that during the past seven centuries both the literary and spoken languages of Japan have become so thoroughly impregnated with Chinese vocabulary and constructions (not to mention the recent flood of linguistic imports from the West) that Heian Japanese has become quite as remote as the Anglo-Saxon of *Beowulf* is for the average Englishman. Most people in Japan who read ***The Tale of Genji*** nowadays use the modern-language version by the eminent novelist, Tanizaki Junichirō; and some, including as prominent a literary man as Masamune Hakuchō, find Arthur Waley's translation more comprehensible than the original text.

The main trouble does not arise from the length and complexity of the sentences, nor from the massive agglutinative verb forms, the involved honorific usage, and the host of obscure particles. With a certain amount of patience we can work all this out systematically and remember it. What we can never hope to surmount is the fantastic lack of specificity in Heian writing. The Japanese language in general lacks the precision of which Chinese is capable and which is the glory of some Indo-European languages. But in the *kanabun* literature of the Heian period—including, alas, the work of Murasaki Shikibu—this obscurity can reach nightmare proportions. Proper names are rigorously avoided. Direct speech is common, but the speaker hardly ever indicated. As often as not we have to guess at the subject of the sentence, and sometimes the subject will change half-way through without any warning. The mutually exclusive categories that we take for granted in European languages—past and present tense, affirmation and question, singular and plural, male and female (as identified by personal names and pronouns), doubt and certainty—have little relevance in Heian Japanese; sometimes it is not even clear whether the sentence is positive or negative.

This reluctance to be specific, which has given so much trouble to commentators and readers of Heian literature, results partly from the intimate connexion between this literature and classical Japanese poetry—a poetry that is marked by extremely laconic wording and an overwhelming reliance on imagistic suggestion. It also results from the ''closed'' nature of upper-class Heian society. The members of Murasaki's society always preferred the allusion to the statement, the hint to the explanation. This applies most conspicuously to poetry and poetic quotations, but it also affected their everyday speech, their occasional writings (diaries and notes), and the vernacular literature in which their lives were described. For people who live in a small, closed society, like that of the Heian court, the entire range of experience will be so familiar that the briefest hint will suffice to convey one's meaning, and any systematic exposition of one's thoughts is regarded as otiose, even boorish. Language becomes a sort of shorthand, immediately understood by those who are ''in,'' vague and slightly mysterious to the outsider. The same phenomenon can be found in almost any small, closed group, but in the court society of Heian Japan this economy of expression was carried to extraordinary lengths and profoundly influenced the literature, which was an intimate part of that society.

Another reason that Heian writing impresses the modern reader as being so vague is the poverty of the vocabulary that Murasaki and her colleagues had at their disposal. Like many languages in an early stage of development, tenth-century Japanese was endowed with an extremely rich grammatical apparatus but a relatively limited choice of words. This applies especially to abstract adjectives. The result is that certain words tend to be greatly overworked and to lose all precision of meaning. Modern English, of course, has its share of such words (''interesting,'' ''nice,'' ''good''), but the conscientious author uses them with the greatest caution. Heian writers, on the other hand, almost seem to revel in the repetition of the same emotive words, whose range of meaning is so widely and thinly spread as to make accurate communication impossible. In [one] sentence . . . , for example, the word *ayashi* is used no less than three times, with the successive meanings of ''remarkable,'' ''outlandish,'' and ''disagreeable.'' This by no means exhausts the possible translations of the word. Among its many other senses is ''absurd,'' and it is quite possible that this, rather than ''distasteful,'' is what Murasaki intended here—a typical example of how lack of verbal specificity can obscure meaning for readers of a later age. (pp. 278-81)

One question that has engaged the many generations of ***Genji*** scholars is the extent to which Murasaki derived her material from actual life. Should her novel be read as a *roman à clef* in which the characters represent people with whom she was personally acquainted or about whom she had heard? Successive commentators have had their pet theories about the models on whom Genji and the other principal figures are supposedly based. At least twenty people have been named as the source for Prince Genji alone. They include Ariwara no Narihira (the famous ninth-century poet, Adonis, and lover), Emperor Murakami, Sugawara no Michizane, and even such improbable candidates as Po Chü-i and the Duke of Chou.

The main contender for the honour, however, is Michinaga's nephew, Korechika, the attractive young nobleman whose rapid rise in the world was followed by sudden disgrace and exile owing to the machinations of his Fujiwara enemies. (p. 285)

In discussing the art of fiction with Tamakazura, Genji makes a remark that throws some light on this question of models: "I am quite sure," he says, "that the author does not write about specific people, giving all the circumstances of their actual lives." The trend among modern scholars has been to move away the simple type of correlation, according to which each character in the novel represents a single historical figure, and to substitute a more complicated system of sources. The character and life of Prince Genji, for example, are shown to be based on those of numerous eminent exiles of the Heian period: his good looks and attractive personality relate him to Korechika; his artistic skill, to the great Michizane; his family name, to Minamoto no Takaaki. In the later books the principal model for the hero may well have been the resplendent figure of Fujiwara no Michinaga himself. (p. 286)

There is a more important question than that of specific models for characters and events: does ***The Tale of Genji*** as a whole present a reasonably faithful picture of Heian society? If we are using Murasaki's novel as a source of social history, the question becomes crucial.

The first point is that the people in ***The Tale of Genji*** represent only a minute percentage of the inhabitants of tenth-century Japan. With few exceptions they belong to the aristocracy, who numbered a few thousand out of a population of several million. Their lives were as remote from those of the common people as is a Maharaja's from that of an untouchable. A modern scholar (a Russian as it chances) has emphasized the contrast between the elegant luxury in the urban court circles and the poverty and barbarism that prevailed elsewhere in Heian Japan. He compares the flourishing, beautifully planned city of Heian Kyō with the primitive settlements in the provinces, the glittering mansions with the squalid huts, the lofty learning and the exquisite works of art with the bestial ignorance and the primitive household utensils, the magnificent tree-lined avenues with the rough tracks that served for transport in the countryside. He has no doubt exaggerated the splendour of life in the capital by accepting the contemporary idealizations at face value. Yet on the whole his contrast is valid, and we must never forget that what Murasaki describes in her novel was almost totally inapplicable to the vast majority of the population.

Besides, even the aristocratic world is not fully described. Hardly anything is said about affairs of state and politics, let alone about the economic activities that permitted this class to maintain its power. (In exactly what form did they extract income from their land, for instance, and how much did they pay their retainers?)

In short, Murasaki's interest is almost exclusively focused on the private, emotional, and aesthetic lives of a select group of aristocrats. She would no more have thought of entering into the feelings of a peasant than would a novelist nowadays try to describe what a horse or a cow was thinking; and to discuss the economic life of her people would have seemed as preposterous as for a modern writer to give details about his characters' thymol turbidity.

Far from regretting this, however, we should be grateful that in her novel she did not venture into realms about which she and her female contemporaries could have little reliable information. Murasaki wrote about the sides of life that she knew from her own direct experience; and, if the result is a one-sided representation of a period, so is that of a great modern author like Proust.

Making allowance for a certain measure of idealization, especially in the depiction of a character like Prince Genji, we can be fairly confident that what ***The Tale of Genji*** does describe it describes realistically. There is no discrepancy between the image that the novel gives us and what we know of contemporary conditions from chronicles, diaries, and other sources. With immense care and detail Murasaki depicts the world as she saw it. She tells us, for instance, exactly what it was like to be a jealous woman in a polygamous society where jealousy was the most scorned of all emotions, and what a sensitive man might experience when confronted with the demands of his various wives. Her novel does not attempt to give a full picture of a period (few successful novels do); but it does provide an authentic picture of a beautiful and most intriguing world. (pp. 287-89)

Ivan Morris, "Aspects of 'The Tale of Genji'," in his The World of the Shining Prince: Court Life in Ancient Japan, *Alfred A. Knopf, 1964, pp. 265-89.*

KENNETH REXROTH (essay date 1968)

[Rexroth was one of the leading pioneers in the revival of jazz and poetry in the San Francisco area during the 1940s and 1950s. However, it was as a critic and translator that Rexroth gained prominence in American letters. As a critic, his acute intelligence and wide sympathy allowed him to examine such varied subjects as jazz, Greek mythology, the works of D. H. Lawrence, and the cabala. As a translator, Rexroth was largely responsible for introducing Chinese and Japanese classics to the West. In the following excerpt, Rexroth provides some cultural background for The Tale, *focusing on its "concealed drama" and the characterization of Genji.]*

Murasaki Shikibu, the authoress of ***The Tale of Genji*** and lady-in-waiting to the Empress Akiko, was born about A.D. 978 and died about 1031. Japanese civilization as far as the general populace was concerned was at a lower level than the contemporary Polynesian. Almost all Japanese lived lives of squalid, laborious poverty. Set apart from the brutalized mass was a tiny aristocracy, a few thousand people at most, whose culture had been transmuted into a way of life of a peculiar refinement so intense, subtle, and delicate as to constitute a utopia of exquisite sensibility and hyperaesthesia.

Nothing like it has ever existed before or since. The records that have survived from other remotely similar ruling castes—of the Egyptian Old Kingdom, Persia, or India, for instance—are crude, impersonal, stereotyped by comparison. From the eleventh century Heian court of Japan we have a number of imaginative and complex records of the most intimate interpersonal relations, diaries and novels and poems, many of them written by women. Not only does ***The Tale of Genji*** far surpass all of these, but most people who have read it agree that it is probably the world's greatest novel.

There is a huge and extraordinarily contradictory literature on ***Genji*** in modern Japanese. Some liberal critics consider it a suffragist denunciation of male promiscuity. Marxists have called it a satire on the evil ruling class. Mystical Buddhists see Prince Genji as a Bodhisattva. Westernized literary taste compares Lady Murasaki to Marcel Proust. The overt plot of the novel is simple enough in principle and infinitely complicated in detail. It is the story of the erotic relationships of Prince Genji, called *Hikaru,* The Shining One; of his friend and brother-in-law To no Chujo; and of their descendants, to the second and even third generation, with an illimitable number of women—wives, mistresses, and wives of others. The story is told entirely from the woman's point of view. The men have titles of generals, administrators, but nothing is ever said of any work they might do beyond writing love notes, playing musical instruments, and climbing over balconies. The Japanese court had already become non-functional and parasitic, but even its symbolic activities are reduced by Lady Murasaki to the basic complexities of sexual refinement.

This is only the superficial plot. Underneath it runs a profound concealed drama: the working-out, reduction, and final redemption of an evil *karma*—the consequence of a moment of irresponsible jealous anger. Early in the book and offstage, as it were, the elaborately decorated bullock cart of Lady Rokujo, Genji's mistress, is scratched by the cart of his wife. She gives way to a spasm of wrath, and a being, an incarnation of her anger, "takes foot," as the Japanese say, and struggles throughout the book with the grace that emanates from Genji gratuitously.

Lady Murasaki in her descriptions of Genji gives many clues to his character. "The Shining One" is a Bodhisattva epithet, and his body has the unearthly perfume that distinguishes such a savior, but she presents him as an unconscious as well as an indifferent Bodhisattva—a profoundly original religious notion. A Bodhisattva is a being who turns away from the bliss of Nirvana with the vow that he shall not enter ultimate peace until he can bring all other beings with him. He does this, says mystical Buddhism, indifferently, because he knows there is neither being nor non-being, peace nor illusion, saved nor savior, truth nor consequence. To this Lady Murasaki adds the qualification that he does it without knowing it—an idea derived from Chinese neo-Taoism, Shingon Buddhism, and rationalization of primitive Shintoist animism and from the philosopher Wang Ch'ung, from whom also comes the clearest statement of the personalized, subsisting embodiment of evil emotion, act, or thought.

Lady Murasaki grew into her novel. The most profound and subtle writing occurs in the later half, after Genji is dead. As the generations go by, the *karma,* the moral residues, of the lifetimes of Genji and his beloved friend To no Chujo cross and recross in their descendants and are at last resolved when a young girl, beloved by descendants of both, struggles with the demon and destroys it forever in a series of gratuitous acts as indifferent and unconscious as the original grace of which she is the re-embodiment.

The story that seems on superficial reading to be only an endless kyriale of philandering turns out to be an unbelievably complicated web of moral tensions and resolutions. Modern Japanese, even more than Western readers, find this outlandish and incomprehensible. The *hannya,* the devil that speaks through the mediums called in when the girls it is killing are dying, is almost always accepted by the critics as the ghost of Lady Rokujo, although at the beginning of its career she not only is still alive but has forgotten the incarnating episode and left the court to become a priestess of the national shrine of Ise, where she eventually dies in what we would call a state of grace. Although the *hannya* speaks in her name, it is only the personalized subsistent moment of hate which grows by feeding on the souls it destroys.

A similar situation surrounds Genji's birth, the death of his mother, and his first love affair. The plot is stated in a kind of overture at the beginning of the novel, as it is resolved in a recapitulation of all the principal motives at its end. Strung on the skein of this subtle plot are any number of subplots of like nature. The episodes, with an ever-receding profundity, are encapsulated one within another like Chinese boxes, or they are reflected one within another like a universe of mirrors and diamonds—the universe of universes of the *Kegon-kyo,* the *Avatamsara Sutra,* the most visionary of all Buddhist documents.

When in the Sutra the complex of universes is revealed to the historic Buddha Sakyamuni, he bursts into laughter. I have never known anyone to read ***The Tale of Genji*** who was not thrown into a state of aesthetic joy, a kind of euphoria of response which very few other works of art can produce—the state of being that Marcel Proust sought in the paintings of Vermeer or the *Jupiter Symphony* and that he tried to reproduce in his readers at the most crucial episodes in his novel. ***The Tale of Genji*** communicates this ecstatic revery and joy, like Genji's perfume, with unconscious, effortless indifference. (pp. 136-40)

Kenneth Rexroth, "Lady Murasaki, 'The Tale of Genji'," in his Classics Revisited, *Quadrangle Books, 1968, pp. 136-40.*

JAMES R. NICHOLS (essay date 1970)

[*In the following excerpt Nichols argues that in* The Tale, *Murasaki created "a novel of manners" centering on the relationship between individual and society.*]

Due largely to Arthur Waley's fine translation, Lady Murasaki's ***The Tale of Genji*** is recognized today as a masterpiece both in the Occident and the Orient. It is strange, therefore, that modern critics have so persistently neglected the work. The very abundance of structures and techniques within Lady Murasaki's novel should not only invite but demand scholarly interest.

As early as 1899, W. G. Aston self-assuredly pronounced that while ***Genji*** was a fine work, it did not compare with the works of Fielding, Thackeray, Hugo, or Cervantes [see excerpt dated 1899]. Only the most avid Japanophile would have insisted on such a comparison, observed Aston. Aston's comment was mildly insular; but, the remark itself is not without value. ***Genji*** cannot compare with *Vanity Fair* or *Don Quixote*. It does not differ qualitatively from these works, however, but thematically. Ever since its discovery by a few Western critics, ***Genji*** has labored under the disadvantage of being unfairly compared to works which bear only surface relationships to it. Recently, Saburō Ienaga correctly praised the realism of ***Genji,*** but attempted to compare it to *Don Juan* and *The Decameron*. Perhaps, the early date of a work of such obvious sophistication has led to so many inadequate comparisons, but this should not mislead us. Aston himself recognized that while ***Genji*** was, like *Tom Jones,* a "prose epic of real life," like Richardson, Murasaki emphasized sentiments and emotions of individuals and characters. Above all, even to Aston, the work was "realistic in the best sense of the word."

Genji is doubtless realistic. Importantly, however, the realism of ***Genji*** is specifically related not to the robust qualities of epic or satire, but to the humor and tension of the novel of manners. Indeed, Murasaki's work is a novel of manners, a novel in the realistic tradition which deals with the relationship between individuals and a stable, precisely defined society. In its subject matter, objective style, humor, drama, and point of view, ***Genji*** easily fits the pattern of a manners novel. ***The Tale of Genji*** is an objective, dramatic narrative of personal interrelationships within a closed social grouping. Genji is the novel's hero, and the tension between the society and the protagonist is the novel's subject. The manners and customs of Genji's society are the means by which both the individual and the society are tested and evaluated.

The subject matter of a novel of manners might well be considered its most distinguishing characteristic, and Murasaki's subject bears little difference from Austen's or Wharton's. Jane Austen's characters are the English country gentry and Edith Wharton's the ruthlessly indifferent New York élite. Murasaki's semi-feudal and frivolous aristocracy is only superficially different. In all three instances, it is the interrelationship of society and the individual that is the real subject of the novel. Parallel material and supporting themes within the narrative should not obscure this fact. When Donald Keene distinguishes ***Genji*** by its "tone of stoic sadness," he mistakes the cultural background of the novel for its subject. The Buddhistic conception of life as essentially pain and disappointment is one of the basic assumptions of the book and of Genji's society. But, it is only the moral ethic beneath the society, just as Christianity is beneath Jane Austen's country gentlemen. In ***Genji*** this may seem more important only because Murasaki is depicting a society which upon the religious and secular level is almost completely fused.

Genji himself is "The Shining One," the very paragon of his society. Throughout his life Genji searches for the perfect woman, a theme which is introduced in Chapter II, Book I, as the famous *Shina-Sadame* or "critique" of women. Abstracted, Genji's search is for perfection within a hopelessly imperfect world. Structurally, however, Genji's search leads to a tension between the protagonist and his society which quickly becomes the center of the narrative's action. Genji's lovers range from Fujitsubo, a beautiful young mistress of his father; to the Akashi Lady, a lovely but awkward country girl; to Aoi, his first cold and proud wife; to Murasaki, the most abiding and sufficient of Genji's women. In his search for perfect beauty, Genji must break many of the rules of his society and is often punished for his extravagance. As Genji's father notes, however, his son's major fault is not immorality but "reckless and inconsiderate conduct." Murasaki never suggests, nor does Genji suggest, that the society does not have a right to judge Genji by its own principles.

In Book II, Genji is exiled to Suma because of another particularly ill-timed illicit amour with Oborozukiyo, a maid destined to be consort to the young emperor Suzaku. When Genji finally returns from exile, he has not given up his search, but he has gained wisdom and prudence. Genji has learned not to flout, but to use society's rules. His final rejection of life as disappointing and inadequate is both a conception of the culture and a culmination of the novel's theme. When Murasaki dies, Genji finds that all beauty has left the earth. His own youthful dreams and hopes fade as if illusions, while the values and prejudices of his society come to seem trivial and childish. Genji dies merely because he no longer wishes to live. The Shining One's death does not condemn his society; it merely evaluates it and defines its limits. Thus, both Genji and his society are implicitly judged.

Finally, Genji's rejection of society is all the more pathetic because of his initial immersion within that society. Genji could, for instance, play a number of musical instruments with great skill and he had excelled at letter writing, producing a distinctive script, dancing, and the ability to compose short poetic pieces with quickness and facility. Interesting and colorful though he may be, Kaoru, the image of Genji's cuckoldom and failure during the final two books of the novel, is but a slight counterpart of his magnificent foster father. "Genji was dead, and there was no one to take his place," begins Book V. Kaoru, a bastard as was Genji, attempts to find the same perfection. There is no more dramatic scene in the novel, however, than at its end when Kaoru tells himself that Ukifune, his love, must surely come back from her hermitage to him and to his world. In reality Ukifune has taken the final vows of a nun and with her hair completely shorn, she has renounced Kaoru and society forever. Kaoru fails to gain enlightenment and remains a slave to his social existence.

Earlier in the novel Kaoru had watched some work which was taking place upon a nearby river. He had thought: "Down the stream strange rafts were now passing loaded with timber. All along the river were people busy in one way or another with the humble tasks that kept them alive. How strange an existence it must be, day in and day out, to live thus frailly supported above the peril of those tossing waters! And yet how often had he, amid his terraces of jade, felt that he too was perilously afloat—was drifting from uncertainty to uncertainty, with no solid ground beneath his feet!" Kaoru here recognizes the ephemeral quality of his society, but foolishly and inevitably continues to depend upon that society throughout the novel. In fact, only death can divorce man completely from his social existence.

Through the use of varying points of view, then, Murasaki is able to depict quietly and dramatically the tension that exists between the individual and his society. Throughout the first four books the predominant point of view is Genji's, while Kaoru controls the last two. When the dramatic and objective structure of the novel demands it, however, Murasaki unhesitatingly enters the consciousness of any of her characters. In the following passage we enter the consciousness of a comparatively minor servant: "Lady Murasaki was now almost twenty-eight, but never (thought the old woman when she arrived) had she looked so handsome. It seemed indeed as though her full charm had only just matured . . . There was indeed an undeniable difference between this splendid princess and the shy girl from Tsukushi. But it was only the difference between obscurity and success; a single turn of fortune would quickly redress the balance." Aston has stated that there are few dramatic situations in Genji, yet here we have the essence of the dramatic narrative. Maintaining a rigid objectivity, the author changes the point of view to that of an old and trusted servant Ukon. In reality there is no competition at all between Murasaki and Tamakatsura. Ukon's judgment, however, shows us how the situation appears to those within and around the household. This is the essence of drama. Characters create themselves, no authoritarian judgment is made, and the reader is left to decide the truth for himself. Such technique is the heart of the realistic tradition within which the novel of manners exists.

Of course in any objective depiction of the actual world there must be humor as well as pathos. The comedy of the novel of manners, however, is not satire, and Murasaki's realism is thus different from Swift's or Fielding's. Meredith notes that "... you must be receptive of the idea of comedy. And to love comedy you must know the real world." "The laughter of satire is a blow in the back or the face. The laughter of comedy is impersonal and of unrivaled politeness, nearer a smile—often no more than a smile." How easily this definition applies to the humor and realism of ***Genji,*** an objective and humanistic acceptance of an imperfect world. Even Genji is not above this spirit. At the end of the *Shina-Sadame,* supposedly the most serious and explicitly philosophical section of the novel, Genji finds that he cannot return to his palace because the stars are against him. "'But my own palace is in the same direction!' cried Genji. 'How vexing! where [*sic*] then shall I go?' and promptly fell asleep." Even the beautiful "Shining One" is capable of childish petulance and youthful innocence.

Nor is Murasaki quite as femininely delicate as Bersihand would have us believe. While her sense of decorum is beyond question, Lady Murasaki faces sexual matters without hesitation and often with a sly and knowing smile. Late in the novel Niou, Genji's grandson and heir to the throne, succeeds in conquering the beautiful and shy young girl Ukifune (all this is unknown to Kaoru). As dawn arrives, Niou must make his escape, for old Ukon is coming toward the room. "Niou," remarks Murasaki, on the verge of a dirty joke that would have appalled Austen or Howells, "needless to say, would much rather have stayed where he was." Ukon, of course, cannot alert the household to Niou's presence because she is worried about decorum, how such an uproar would look to the lower servants.

Customs, traditions, and manners are important in ***Genji*** and much of the novel's comedy is drawn from the incongruity between social background and character action. Ukon is caught in a comic paradox. If she reveals Niou, she brings shame upon her mistress. If she hides him, she allows a sin to go unpunished. In either case she soon rationalizes away her inaction without once realizing the importance of the incident. Ukifune has now not only betrayed her maidenhood to Kaoru, but she has betrayed her first lover by sleeping with another. Here, one of the crucial incidents in the last two books (it leads to Ukifune's rejection of the world) is treated with a comic objectivity almost unbearably direct. Truth becomes isolated within the actual world, hidden from all but the most introspective consciousness. Murasaki sees the absurdities of life and adds to them a pathos which approaches tragedy in its completeness.

In its structure and assumptions, then, ***Genji*** is essentially a novel of manners. It is concerned with customs, traditions, and the actual world. It is objective and dramatic, often exploiting the inner and subjective visions of its various characters to obtain this objectivity. The narrative grows largely through the actions of its characters and the tensions that are built up between the individual and his society. Irony asks as the essential pathos of the work. It is both an attitude and emotion which penetrates beneath the surface of the subject matter without explicitly attacking the contradictions which are thus discovered.

But perhaps the best proof that ***The Tale of Genji*** is a novel of manners in fact and in intent is a passage in the novel which is universally accepted as Murasaki No Shikibu's vindication of her art. While discussing fiction, Genji states:

> Sometimes, of course, virtue will be his [the novelist's] theme, and he may then make such play with it as he will. But he is just as likely to have been struck by numerous examples of vice and folly in the world around him, and about them he has exactly the same feelings as about the preeminently good deeds which he encounters: they are important and must all be garnered in. Thus anything whatsoever may become the subject of a novel, provided only that it happens in this mundane life and not in some fairy-land beyond our human ken.
>
> So too, I think, may it be said that the art of fiction must not lose our allegiance because, in the pursuit of the main purpose to which I have alluded above, it sets virtue by the side of vice, or mingles wisdom with folly.

Throughout this section, Murasaki makes a definite distinction between reading "romances" and "novels." The novels of Austen or James rest easily within Murasaki's restrictions. Indeed, Lady Murasaki's novel is of common life and a mixture of the wisdom and folly of that life. Its ultimate appeal is always to the conventions of its society. This is not far from comedy and even closer to the novel of manners. (pp. 178-81)

James R. Nichols, "'The Tale of Genji': A Novel of Manners, 1020 A.D.," in Japan Quarterly, *Vol. XVII, No. 1, January-March, 1970, pp. 178-82.*

MARY DeJONG OBUCHOWSKI (essay date 1976)

[In the following excerpt, Obuchowski explores the influence of Japanese religious eclecticism on The Tale.*]*

In the lengthy and complex Japanese novel, ***The Tale of Genji,*** Buddhist priests attend court ceremonies, women disappointed in love become nuns, jealous spirits possess the bodies of Genji's wives and mistresses, and folk superstitions work their way into the most dramatic of adventures. These varied and apparently conflicting religious elements pose some questions about the dominant religious attitudes in the story. Are the various practices exclusive, and are they ever at odds with each other? How do knowledge of religious rites and understanding of the associated beliefs illuminate both the plots in the novel and the themes that dominate it?

In order to approach these questions, one may look at religious practices in Japan to illustrate the eclectic nature of the general attitudes toward Buddhist, Shinto, folk, and even Christian beliefs. A historical context shows them most clearly. The folk religions, indigenous to Japan, came first, before history. The mythological beginnings of Japan, imbedded in folk tales, were transmitted, preserved, and undoubtedly transmuted by storytellers until they were permanently committed to writing in the *Kojiki* and *Nihongi* in the eighth century as the official history of Japan. Shinto priests kept the manuscripts for many centuries more, and the myths solidified into part of the Shinto orthodoxy. Folk legends outside these documents still hover around shrines and landmarks, especially in rural areas, and recently anthologists have compiled amazing numbers of such stories and variations of them. Shinto became the national religion and remains in its "pure" form at the state shrines at Ise and elsewhere. After 1945, however, the government declared state and religion separate. It denied the belief in the emperor as divine in heritage and act, though many adults today still consider Hirohito to be ordained by the gods. The role of religion nationally remains controversial.

"Then they all moved onto the bridge and started their drunken racket yet again."

Buddhism arrived in Japan in the eighth or ninth century through China and Korea. At first a threat, it merged into the established religion by a creed known as *Ryobu,* or two-way Shinto. The practices mingled, and Buddhism became increasingly Japanese as new sects such as Zen groups and followers of Nichiren emerged. Christianity first came via Portugese Jesuits in the fifteenth century. Tokugawa Hidetada declared it illegal in the seventeenth, and his son, Tokugawa Iemitsu, who also closed Japan to outsiders, had Christians pursued and persecuted. They went underground, and preserved their icons in disguise; artifacts purportedly Buddhist but containing secret Christian symbols appear from time to time. Missionaries arrived again in the nineteenth century when Japan reopened itself to foreigners.

Rather than maintaining distinct identities, these religious beliefs and their related customs tend to come together in Japan. Of course, they exist officially in relatively pure forms, but many supposedly Shinto Shrines bear decorations in Buddhist style. A wedding may have both Christian and Buddhist ceremonies, and when a baby is born, his parents might take him to a Shinto shrine for a ritual visit. Legally, funerals must proceed according to Buddhist conventions. Even young Japanese consciously or unconsciously maintain respect for their ancestors as well as for family honor. Most homes keep small altars which display pictures of deceased parents, often with incense burners beside the portraits. A missionary at a theological seminary told me about a Christian student who, after his ordination, went directly to a cemetery to "tell" his ancestors.

In the eleventh century, when Murasaki Shikibu was writing ***The Tale of Genji,*** Christianity had not yet reached Japan, but *Ryobu* Shinto had already assimilated much of what was Buddhist in ritual and architecture as well as belief, and folk superstitions were only more present than they are today in the intensity of their reality to the Japanese. Therefore, when one examines religion in the novel, he must consider its eclectic nature. In the novel, most of the religious ceremonies at the court appear to be Buddhist. The installations, coming of age rites, purifications, and prayers for success or prevention of trouble seem to follow these conventions. Exorcisms, though Shinto in origin, are performed by Buddhist priests. On the other hand, a religious conflict occurs when Lady Rokujo's daughter becomes Vestal Virgin at Ise. Rokujo accompanies her to that royal Shinto shrine. When she returns, however, Rokujo feels a definite struggle, even a sense of guilt at having violated the Buddhist faith by observing the Shinto rites, and decides to become a Buddhist nun. (pp. 185-87)

Lady Rokujo is also a primary figure in one of the most complicated tangles of religion and superstition and the occult that occur in the story. With her, Genji has his first adult affair of consequence. As the liaison progresses, she becomes irritable, demanding, and jealous, the last with some reason. While Genji is trying to disentangle himself from this "older" woman (she is in her middle twenties, he in his teens), he meets a mysterious girl. She is called Yugao, after a flower translated as "evening face," because of her lovely, fragile appearance, their nocturnal meetings, her shadowy background, and the terrifying nighttime circumstances which bring about her death. As this affair proceeds in great secrecy, neither party revealing name or history, a spirit suddenly possesses Yugao and kills her. Since the whole situation is so clandestine (the body is disposed of quickly and silently), and Genji is prostrated by grief for weeks afterward, no one investigates the cause of Yugao's death. Twice on the night of the disaster, however, Genji has seen at their bedside a dreamlike figure of an angry woman who is undoubtedly responsible.

Some years later, Genji's proud and estranged wife, Aoi, develops the symptoms of a similar possession after she gives birth to Genji's only legitimate son. Because the circumstances of her illness are more public, unlike the secrecy with Yugao, Aoi is subjected to prayers and incantations to remove the spirit which is debilitating her, although no one is absolutely certain that she is really possessed. She dies, and Rokujo seems to be the only person jealous enough of Genji to be responsible. Rukujo acknowledges that on occasion her body and spirit do feel detached from each other, and though she emphatically intends Aoi no harm, she may not be able to control the hatred she cherishes toward Genji's wife. She admits to herself that she has retained a deep sense of injury against Aoi since that lady's servants rendered Rokujo an unintentional insult during

Aoi's pregnancy. In Japanese folk literature, spirits of the jealous, both living and dead, may enter the object of that hatred and kill that person: this belongs to the most ancient of recorded beliefs. Still later in the novel, Genji's beloved consort Murasaki falls prey to an identical malady (though she is not pregnant), and Genji again calls in quantities of priests to force the spirit out. At length, a medium induces the spirit to identify itself as Rokujo, who has died several years before, and it answers that it had caused the deaths of both Yugao and Aoi. It tries unsuccessfully to persuade Genji to call off the priests. Murasaki partially recovers for a while but later dies anyway, and Genji follows soon after. It is interesting in this context to note that the beliefs regarding possession are folk beliefs, the priests are Buddhist, and the acts of exorcism are Shinto: nowhere is there any indication that those beliefs and practices should be exclusive, nor, in spite of the failure of the rites, that any is more powerful than the others.

Both folklore and Buddhism subscribe to the theory that a spirit of a person longing for a loved one at the time of his death will not be able to rest. Hence, Rokujo's spirit remains active after she dies. Similarly, in Book Five, Hachi no Miya, a half-brother of Genji, is urged to stop mourning his wife in order that he, a priest himself, might be at peace after his own death. He dies, still longing, mourned by his two daughters. The story proceeds in a different direction, enhanced by more folk superstitions. One of the girls, Agemaki, is courted by Genji's supposed son, Kaoru. She resists all of his advances and offers, and she tries to turn his affections toward her younger sister, Kozeri. Genji's grandson, Niou, however, begins an affair with Kozeri first, and carries her off as his mistress. Worn out by resisting Kaoru and worrying about the future of her sister, Agemaki wastes away and dies. Heartbroken by the loss of both girls, Kaoru locates a half-sister of theirs, Ukifune, becomes intimate with her, and prepares to set her up near him. Niou, singleminded and voraciously competitive in regard to women, again moves faster and visits her secretly. When Ukifune finds that Kaoru has learned about her infidelity, she attempts suicide by jumping into a rushing river, and her household gives her up as dead. A group of travellers find her and nearly run away because they fear that she is a fox-spirit. According to folklore, foxes are notorious shape-changers. They may assume the form of beautiful maidens and seduce men, or they may perpetrate other kinds of mischief. Apparently a good deal of trouble had occurred in the locality where Ukifune appeared, for an old man reported,

> "Oh yes, it's a fox that has done that . . . They're always doing odd things just here. It's their favorite tree. Only last autumn one of them carried off a child or two and brought it to this very spot. And when I came running up, do you suppose that fox took any notice of me? Not at all." "What a dreadful thing!" said one of the priests. "The child, I suppose, was dead?" "No, it wasn't," said the old man rather testily, "it was alive. Fox isn't a fellow to do any real harm. He just likes to give people a bit of a fright sometimes; that is all."

Nevertheless, the travellers decide Ukifune is really human and nurse her, though she lies half-conscious for months, not revealing her identity. Her rescuers feel, of course, that she must be possessed, and request a priest to exorcise her. The spirit he contacts makes a significant admission:

> "I, too, in my day was a master of magic such as yours. But I died with something on my mind. Not much—a trivial resentment; but it was enough to hold me back, to keep me drifting hither and thither, back and forth between this world and the next. I walked into a house. It was full of beautiful women. One of them [Agemaki?] I destroyed. Then I bided my time, and presently this girl here gave me the chance I sought. Day after day, night after night, she lay moaning and weeping, and calling for death to come. At last, one evening when it was very dark, I saw her get up and leave the house. I followed her, and when she was alone, I did my work."

Later, the priest states an additional theory of his own: that because she was found in a clump of trees, Ukifune may have been a *tengu,* or tree-spirit. *Tengu* are also shape-changers and causers of mischief, and even as recently as 1860, official documents contained warnings against them. Ukifune, still pursued by Kaoru and yet another suitor, retreats from these complications by becoming a nun. The story, then, incorporates a number of folk myths and creatures as well as possession and exorcism.

Many of the superstitions and folk beliefs have bases in common sense, as a matter of fact. Possession explained many illnesses that medical science has more clearly defined in recent years. Custom dictated, however, that a person weakened by sorrow or guilt was more vulnerable to wandering spirits than a happy and stable one might be, as in any illness. The possessing spirit was generally one of an unhappy, grieving, or jealous individual, as is the case with Rokujo and with the spirit that worked upon Agemaki and Ukifune; hence the concern that a person be done with worldly attachments before he dies. Themes of the damage caused by jealousy, shame, and guilt run through the novel like threads of different colors but of similar texture. Genji and his descendants alike compromise their happiness and that of their offspring by repeating mistakes engendered by passion or wilfulness.

The cluster of stories surrounding Rokujo establishes one dominant theme: that hatred kills, directly or indirectly. The jealousy in her destroys the three most important women in Genji's life, and his death is surely linked with that of Murasaki. It works inversely in the case of Rokujo's final illness; her hostility may well have provoked it. Genji has tried desperately to placate her, even to arranging the marriage of her daughter to the heir apparent. She finally seems to accept his attempts to make amends and his apologies at her deathbed, but her spirit still runs its destructive course afterward.

In fact, it becomes increasingly clear through the novel that one is fundamentally responsible for his feelings and desires as well as for his acts, and that religious belief has firm grounding in common sense. In Buddhist as well as Christian thought, the sins of the father are visited on the sons, and the corruption may affect or express the condition of his country. For example, Genji has an affair with his beautiful stepmother, Fujitsubo, who has a baby, Ryozen. The child is apparently Genji's stepbrother but really his son. The boy becomes Emperor while still a small child and comes painfully to find that he was born out of divine succession. The priest tells him, ". . . the Powers Above are manifesting their displeasure; for, as you have been taught, it frequently happens that the sins of one generation are visited upon the next." He knows that by continuing as

Emperor he is violating religious and ancestral traditions. According to Waley's note, "In sacrificing at the Imperial tomb (as if in honor of his father), etc., he was committing an outrage upon the dead." Moreover, this time is one of political and astrological unpleasantness. Public dismay coupled with irregularities in astronomical and weather conditions seem to portend displeasure on the part of the Sun God, from whom the Emperor of Japan is supposed to descend. Now that Ryozen is of sufficient age to understand the problem of his birth and its possible consequences, he worries about whether or not to resign. Genji feels acutely his own guilt in the matter, but attempts to persuade his son to continue as Emperor, because if the reason for his resignation became known, it would appall the Japanese people, who had never known the line of succession to be broken before. The political effects might be drastic. Nevertheless, after some years Ryozen quietly resigns with the excuse of poor health. Thus, the religious belief in divine succession is intertwined with issues of practical responsibility and the consequences of guilty knowledge.

Further links between the effects of sexual misconduct, the physical ravages of guilt or shame, and the kind of understanding that leads to forgiveness come up in a parallel situation. In his later years, Genji takes on an unwelcome marriage of convenience with a niece, Nyosan, in whom he (surprisingly, for Genji) has little interest. He neglects her outrageously. A nephew of his, Kashiwagi, falls in love with Nyosan and seduces her, and she bears his son, Kaoru (mentioned earlier in connection with Agemaki and her sisters). Kashiwagi, a young man who makes heavy demands on himself and who is anxious to be right and perfect in whatever he does, breaks down completely, overwhelmed by grief and guilt at having betrayed his friend and idol, Genji. When Genji finds that Nyosan is pregnant, knows that the child is not his, and suspects Kashiwagi, he is angry only at first. Remembering that he behaved in an almost identical fashion toward his father and that his child by Fujitsubo had been a constant source of discomfort and guilt, he regains his compassion. Consequently, Genji acts kindly toward his nephew, but Kashiwagi feels terrible remorse and imagines that Genji must be justly angered at both himself and Nyosan, and declines rapidly in health. Moreover, he feels that death would remove his "treachery" from Genji's memory, and in his last days confesses to Genji's legitimate son, Yugiri, "for if I died with it on my conscience I should be held back from Salvation in the life to come." His self-hatred finally destroys him. As Fujitsubo had done before her, Nyosan becomes a nun: her shame, too, drives her out of the world.

Genji is a character of sufficient magnitude and intelligence to sustain successful affairs with a score or more women; to seduce his father's wife and to father an emperor out of succession; to survive exile (provoked because of still another affair with another emperor's prospective consort) and return to political prominence; and to develop enough self-knowledge and conscience to forgive the nephew who philanders with his wife. He is a gifted musician, dancer, calligrapher, poet, and diplomat, among many other accomplishments. With every woman he seduces or even desires, he maintains a gentle consideration for the remainder of her life; he even employs or grants places in his household to several former favorites (who get along amazingly well), and he never forgets one or deliberately treats any unkindly. Genji's descendants inherit a number of his physical assets but lack, however, his self-consciousness and moral strength. As the story about Agemaki and her sisters indicates, Genji's grandson, Niou, and supposed son (really his great-nephew by two routes), Kaoru, expend themselves on affairs with women without putting similar energy into other accomplishments. Nothing particularly distinguishes either young man except charm and good looks. Niou stands out only in his appetite for new affairs, from which he quickly tires: he may have more than Genji, but he does not exhibit the concern that Genji has lavished on his ladies, even the old and unattractive ones. He vies with his more serious cousin, Kaoru, trying to reach first any woman Kaoru might have been courting. (Genji and his cousin, To no Chujo, Kaoru's real grandfather, had carried on a lighthearted rivalry as youths: Yugao, for example, attracted them both.) Kaoru, indeed, inherits some of the moral sensitivity that appears in both Genji and Kashiwagi, his real father, but he finds himself unable to act upon it and wastes his time in ceaseless worry and indecision. After his successive failures with Agemaki, Kozeri, and Ukifune, he, too, wants to leave the world and take up the religious life, but he never manages to decide to do so.

In religious as well as practical terms, a person not only bears the responsibility of his own acts and inclinations, he also passes on those predilections and their consequences. For example, Genji's affair with his father's consort grants him understanding when his own wife is seduced. Genji's grandson, Niou, inherits his ability to carry on numerous affairs, and they both have liaisons with women who are really possessed or supposed to be. Though Genji passes on his charm and beauty to his descendants, he cannot prevent them from repeating his errors; though he can understand Kashiwagi, he remains unable to extricate him from the consequences of his affair; and though Genji's relationship with Yugao is one of the most profound in his life, that of Niou (and Kaoru as well) with the lady Ukifune dwindles off into nothingness.

Thus, the religious elements of court ritual, exorcism and folk superstition, and themes of jealousy, guilt, and responsibility turn out to be so closely intertwined as to be inseparable. Possession and other folk beliefs work together with the practical realities of jealousy and hatred and the destruction they work on both the object and the source of those emotions, as in the stories about Rokujo. They point up the physical as well as the spiritual consequences of anger and depression. Adherance to Shinto and Buddhist ritual becomes intimately connected with politics in the case of the Emperor Royzen's tenure. Belief that crosses religious boundaries, as in the recurrent emphasis that a man's errors affect his children, is Buddhist in the context of ***The Tale of Genji*** but universal in its implications. (pp. 187-94)

Mary DeJong Obuchowski, "Religious Threads and Themes in 'The Tale of Genji'," in CLA Journal, *Vol. XX, No. 2, December, 1976, pp. 185-94.*

D. J. ENRIGHT (essay date 1977)

[*Enright is an English man of letters who has spent most of his career abroad, teaching English literature at universities in Egypt, Japan, Berlin, Thailand, and Singapore. The author of critically respected works in a variety of genres, he is best known for his poetry, which is conversational in style and often reflects his humanistic values through portraits of Far Eastern life. In the following excerpt from an essay written in 1977, Enright discusses Murasaki's characterization of Prince Genji and contrasts Seidensticker's translation of the novel with that of Arthur Waley.*]

Since practically every reader is on occasion a common reader, perhaps the reviewer may venture upon a few common and possibly vulgar observations. The hero of Lady Murasaki's

[***The Tale of Genji***], or of the larger part of it in that Genji dies two-thirds of the way through, is that not uncommon fictional character, the Great Lover—potent, gifted, irresistible, and nice with it. Genji *is* too good to be true, until sadness sets in. But that ***The Tale of Genji*** is not a "romance" in the pejorative sense, that it is not simply a Heian fantasy of an earlier and better Heian world, a more sophisticated opposite number of England's Restoration comedy at its most sophisticated, can be seen by reference to other tenth- and eleventh-century Japanese women writers. In particular, Murasaki's contemporary, Sei Shōnagon, whose *Pillow Book* (a generic term, Ivan Morris suggests, describing an informal notebook kept in a drawer of its owner's wooden pillow) reveals her as an astringent, forthright and unromanticizing witness while also testifying to the general authenticity of Murasaki's more dreamlike impressions.

The impression of reality, as opposed to fantasy, is assisted in ***Genji*** by the author's periodical cool interventions; for instance, at the end of Chapter 4:

> I had hoped, out of deference to him, to conceal these difficult matters; but I have been accused of romancing, of pretending that because he was the son of an emperor he had no faults. Now, perhaps, I shall be accused of having revealed too much.

And more humorously: "Though no one has asked me to do so, I should like to describe the surprise of the assistant viceroy's wife at this turn of events," she writes in concluding Chapter 15, "but it would be a bother and my head is aching." In Chapter 25 there occurs a passage reminiscent of Jane Austen's spirited defence of novels in *Northanger Abbey* ("performances which have only genius, wit, and taste to recommend them"). After teasing Tamakazura about her fondness for romances—"Women seem to have been born to be cheerfully deceived"—Genji changes tack:

> I have been rude and unfair to your romances, haven't I? They have set down and preserved happenings from the age of the gods to our own. *The Chronicles of Japan* and the rest are a mere fragment of the whole truth. It is your romances that fill in the details . . . to dismiss them as lies is itself to depart from the truth. Even in the writ which the Buddha drew from his noble heart are parables, devices for pointing obliquely at the truth.

No more than Jane Austen did Murasaki approve of running down the very activity she was engaged in.

Heian Japan was "a man's world"—though apparently less overwhelmingly so than Japan (and the world at large) has been at much later dates—and it was left to the women to write about it. The men were busy with more pressing things, such as governing the country (or in the case of the ***Genji*** males serving at court), being accomplished and noble, writing "seriously" or stodgily in Chinese—and seducing women. Women, it has been suggested, were less confined by convention than men, and had more time and licence for scribbling in their native tongue. Murasaki Shikibu was the most remarkable of a group of remarkable females: she has no male counterpart in her own country, indeed no male or female counterpart in any country. Proust is her nearest of literary kin.

None the less, her admiration for her hero is likely to stick in feminist gullets. One would say that she doted on Genji, were it not that such crude, barbarous emotions as that verb implies are never found in her. An attempt on the reader's part to enumerate Genji's love affairs would be incongruously loutish, and in any case frustrated by uncertainty in many cases as to whether the protagonists exchanged only poems or something more besides. Lack of privacy often seems to rule out the latter in these overcrowded compounds: people who live in paper houses should stay in their own rooms, especially when their silk robes rustle so loudly. (Though against this consideration one should perhaps set the Japanese ability to remain blind or deaf to those things it would be incorrect or inconvenient to see or hear.) Murasaki shows not the faintest interest in the physical act of sex. Desire or curiosity on the man's side is indicated, willingness (sometimes but by no means always) on the woman's, a relatively secret meeting has to be contrived, and there we leave them: "let us not look in too closely upon their dalliance." We take up the story again with the next morning's exchange of poem-notes or bed-and-butter letters. But Genji's affairs are indisputably many. "He went on thinking about whatever woman he encountered. A perverse concomitant was that the women he went on thinking about went on thinking about him."

Genji is not merely good at everything that counts, he is the best at everything that counts: poetry, painting, music, perfumes, dress, bearing, conversation, attentiveness. . . . And of course he is the best-looking of all the good-looking nobles who throng the scene. The words of the imperial consort's attendant refer to more than the perfume he happens to be wearing: "He brings everything all together in himself, like a willow that is all of a sudden blooming like a cherry. It sets a person to shivering." For Murasaki, Genji is "the shining one of whom the whole world talks"; and at times it strikes the reader that the whole of this world has precious little else to talk about, and precious little to do except to talk. Admittedly Murasaki does chide the prince now and again, if fondly. "It continues to be his great defect that his attention wanders." We note with some amusement that when Genji becomes convinced that a current liaison is illicit, his attention at once wanders to a new liaison in which he anticipates unadulterated joy. Thus, when the fruits of his affairs with his stepmother begin to show under her robe, his thoughts turn to a ten-year-old girl, although he knows he is taking risks: "People would say that his appetites were altogether too varied." But, Murasaki insists, one of Genji's great qualities is that he never forgets his women, he does the right thing by them as far as is in his power. "The result is," someone remarks, "that he has a large collection."

Not that the prince is a carefree Lothario. Oh no, he is Japanese after all, and a sense of the transitoriness of things is never far away, a tear never far from his eye. With a sensibility like his, a little suffering can go a long way: you barely need anything as uncouth as a reason. However, Genji does have his troubles. One unsuitable intrigue leads to his banishment for a period; the effect on his retinue reminds us of the defeated Antony's ability to make his followers weep. Another intrigue scars his soul permanently. Early on, he fell in love with the second wife of his father the Emperor, and the child he had by her is generally believed to be the Emperor's: his supposed brother is actually his son. A form of retribution arrives later, when Kashiwagi, son of Genji's closest friend, gets Genji's wife, the Third Princess (and Kashiwagi's sister-in-law incidentally) pregnant. When this comes to light, there is no duel, no recrimination, no overt recognition of the matter. Kashiwagi has been guilty of a lapse in taste, of bad manners, above all (the cynic might say) the bad manners to be found out. At least he has the good manners to die soon afterwards, just as Enobarbus dies after deserting his master Antony, and the Third Princess becomes a nun. This sequel, it may be felt, is necessary in Murasaki's eyes because it is the shining Genji who is the offended party: he himself didn't die when he got his father's wife with child.

What matters is manners rather than morals, or so it must seem to us, who distinguish more sharply between the two. The aesthetically pleasing way of doing a thing is of more consequence than the thing itself. And shame lies less in being naughty than in being so maladroit as to be discovered. Telling lies or inventing plausible stories in the cause of avoiding trouble and loss of face for either the offender or the offended is quite in order, even *de rigueur*. For worrying over "what people will say" is almost incessant here: to be laughed at is a fate worse than death. Yet this delicacy of feeling is general, not solely self-directed. Having learnt that his elder brother Genji is really his father, the new emperor is fearful of embarrassing Genji by hinting at his knowledge. And when suffering from malaria, Genji takes care to consult a sage in secret—because, he explains, "such is his reputation that I hated to risk marring it by failing to recover."

The exquisiteness and precision of manners, broken on occasion by outbursts of animal spirits and a somewhat brutal disposing of other people's lives, intimates a social precariousness. Yet—and for all the rather mechanical readiness to shed *lacrimae rerum*—what does most to save ***Genji*** from brittleness and shallowness of soul is the pervasive sense of evanescence, of the fleeting insubstantiality of this world. If a child is intelligent and beautiful, everybody sighs: it cannot be expected to live long. That Genji lasted just into his fifties is a mark of the author's unwillingness to let go of him; even so his ladies muse, "it is true—the cherry blossoms of spring are loved because they bloom so briefly." Nor are thoughts of past or future particularly cheering. A "stupid, senseless affair" is accounted for by "a bond in some other life," and unsuccessful undertakings or actions injurious to others are put down to "the disabilities we bring from other lives." Karma can be thought a useful device for saving face or releasing from responsibility—or, more generously, a tactful and in some cases stoical admission of and allowance for human weakness. There is something of *Rasselas* here: "Human life is everywhere a state in which much is to be endured, and little to be enjoyed." Genji's philandering, like the conduct and attitudes of others in the story, can be traced without exercising undue charity to the hunger for human contact in a highly formalized society, for something beyond prescription and propriety, for love and companionship. This hunger is movingly expressed in a poem alluded to in Chapter 47, "Trefoil Knots," and given by Seidensticker in a footnote:

> A loose thread here to joint to a loose thread there.
> If it cannot be so with us, what use is life?

Truly speaking, it is futile to compare Seidensticker's ***Tale of Genji*** (1976) with Arthur Waley's translation (1925-33) since the two versions differ both in the material worked with and (more important) in their intentions. But it is also irresistible. We shall at times find it hard to believe they are concerned with the same original, even allowing for the work done on the Japanese text since Waley's day. For one thing, Seidensticker's version is complete, whereas Waley abridged, omitted a whole chapter, and frequently elaborated. The effect of his elaboration is generally to help the Western reader by weaving an element of explanation into the narrative. And when we come across a textual crux indicated by Seidensticker, and hence an annotation, the chances are that Waley has quietly skipped the passage—with no apparent loss, it must be said, as far as the general reader is concerned. Seidensticker is scholarly, enormously conscientious and (the lay reader feels confident) accurate. He is much brisker too (which in general is to be welcomed), as may be deduced from the fact that despite Waley's bold abridgements the new translation is actually shorter. This briskness, this economy in words, Seidensticker states, are characteristic of the original. At the same time he pays a handsome tribute to Waley when he tells us that the power of that pioneer version "has continued to be so great that the process of preparing a new translation has felt like sacrilege."

Much more than "nuance" is involved. The difference between their priorities can be indicated, concisely, crudely, but without too much overstatement, by saying that Waley has the reader in mind whereas Seidensticker has Murasaki in mind. Where Seidensticker has the somewhat rebarbative "Prajñapāramita Sutra," Waley softens with "Spring Devotions," referring to the Buddhist nature of the ceremony in passing. Waley has "Lady Murasaki" (the character, not the author) where Seidensticker more allusively and elusively gives "the lady in the east wing." The dramatis personae are many indeed, and Waley's habit of identifying them by name makes for smoother reading than Seidensticker's (no doubt literal) "he" or "she." In Chapter 21 Sachūben, a master of poetry reading, is annotated by Seidensticker as "otherwise unidentified"; Waley refers to him not by name but by office, "the Under-secretary to the Council," a neat though perhaps unauthorized way of investing him with a little substance. A page later, however, the personage reappears as "the Chief Secretary of Council."

When a father is reflecting on his daughter's future, Seidensticker translates thus:

> If he is still interested when he is a little older, she would be better off in his hands than at court. I know his Lordship well. Once a woman has attracted his attention he never forgets her.

Waley's version is:

> There's this comfort about it, that if Prince Yūgiri is anything like his father he will continue to show an interest in her when he grows up. You know I have always told you that once Prince Genji takes a fancy to people, he never forgets them, come what may.

Waley has spelt out the pronouns and distinguished between the son and the father, thus assisting the reader to keep his bearings. Seidensticker writes elliptically, presumably in accord with the original, and in fewer words. Immediately afterwards he has the advantage in ready comprehensibility with "I know that people are calling me the unpromoted marvel, and I don't enjoy going to court" over Waley's "Why should I go to Court if I do not choose to? As a matter of fact, it is very unpleasant to be only in the Sixth Rank. People notice it and make remarks."

Very occasionally Seidensticker's expressions strike one as obtrusively slangy where Waley's language is bland and timeless, though it may be that some readers will welcome little modern jolts. "When they are side by side, my husband seems rather short on good looks'' comes jarringly from the second daughter of the Eighth Prince; Waley has ''When they are together I sometimes think that Niou comes out of it none too well.'' And surely Seidensticker's sentence ''He sought to dismiss it as an ordinary marital spat'' offends by mixing two quite contrary modes. When young men are discussing the wiles of women and one remarks that ''The fact is not up to the advance notices,'' the anachronism shocks more than it enlivens; at the same place Waley gives ''But when we take steps to test their statements we are invariably disappointed,'' which is long-winded and a shade pompous for the gilded youth who is speaking.

In making these spot-checks, much of the time one is conscious less of inferiority or superiority than of difference, and more to the point would be to suggest that the average reader (who is unlikely to be all that dumb) might still welcome a résumé offering a ready reminder of the story's tangled relationships and its more important events. This is scarcely a book to be knocked off in a couple of winter evenings and the list of ''Principal Characters,'' though helpful, doesn't go far enough.

Just as Proust is the only Western writer I can think of as bearing any resemblance in manner or preoccupations to Murasaki Shikibu, so the comparison of Waley's ***Genji*** with Scott Moncrieff's *Remembrance of Things Past* (before Terence Kilmartin's revision) is the only possible one—in respect of inaccuracies and liberties taken, and of triumphs scored—although it would need someone of surpassing scholarship and literary sensibility to assess the implications. At all events, the reader coming fresh to the Japanese novel will meet with very few obstacles in Seidensticker's version that Seidensticker himself can be held responsible for. The reader acquainted with Waley's version will do well to banish it to the back of his mind while engaged on Seidensticker. My guess is that the two translations are going to co-exist peacefully, neither ousting the other. (pp. 81-8)

D. J. Enright, ''The Tale of Genji' and Two Women Diarists,'' in his A Mania for Sentences, *Chatto & Windus/The Hogarth Press, 1983, pp. 81-93.*

SHUICHI KATO (essay date 1979)

[*Shuichi is a Japanese scholar and critic. In the following excerpt, he discusses the central unifying elements in* The Tale, *addressing Murasaki's handling of language, Buddhism, and the passage of time.*]

The narrative of the ***Genji monogatari*** is made up from the author's objective descriptions, the words and poems of the characters of the novel, and records of what they were thinking. However, these basic ingredients are not always sharply differentiated and quite frequently are mixed up in one sentence or paragraph. Thus, often the subject changes even within a sentence and sometimes this is not specifically stated so that the reader has to judge the subject from the context.

With such a literary style, the thoughts and impressions of the author self-identifying with the hero and the thoughts and impressions of the hero himself can be extremely close together. It is a style which, despite the inclusion of many stories amounting to almost independent entities and an ever changing *dramatis personae,* gives a strong feeling of the author's presence. This provides continuity to the novel as a whole and creates a kind of intimacy, rather as if the tale were being told as gossip.

Another special feature of the style of the ***Genji monogatari*** is the constant repetition of a comparatively limited range of vocabulary, indicating both the narrowness of the world of the novel and the tendency to convey suggestions indirectly or by hints rather than explicitly. Both the above-mentioned features of Murasaki Shikibu's style heighten the effectiveness of the description of the psychological relationships between characters. The reader was able to direct his attention onto the characters and how their minds were working, without being distracted by a wealth of detail concerning the complex world in which they lived.

It goes without saying that these stylistic features made the ***Genji monogatari*** very difficult to interpret by later generations of readers, but it should not be thought that contemporary readers had any such problem. Murasaki Shikibu wrote her novel for the limited number of aristocrats and court ladies who lived in the same world as she did and with whom in most cases she was even personally acquainted. There can be no doubt they were thoroughly familiar with the background which provided the setting for the novel, that they probably had a fair idea of the identity of the actual people on whom the characters of the novel were modelled, and that they perfectly understood the subtle nuances of the limited vocabulary.

Of course, Murasaki Shikibu omitted the subject of sentences because this is permitted by Japanese grammar and perhaps because what she was saying was perfectly clear to her readers anyway. A long novel which needed scholars to interpret who was saying what would not have been popular. The style of the ***Genji monogatari*** succeeded only under the conditions of an extremely small and closed society into which author, readers and the characters of the novel alike were thoroughly integrated where one (although by no means all) of the possibilities of the Japanese language could be explored to the uttermost.

Buddhism provided the philosophical background to the ***Genji monogatari.*** Naturally, the influence of Confucian morality can also be detected. . . . The career advancement of the characters is described, but power struggles at court are hardly mentioned and still less is there any indication of influence of Confucian political philosophy. There are two aspects to the role played by Buddhism—first, the anticipation of the magical efficacy of Buddhist ceremonies performed in this world, and, second, the desire for salvation in the next world. The first of these stems from traditional, conventionalized and institutionalized practices from earlier court society, and the second from the influence of Pure Land Buddhist beliefs as summarized in the *Ōjōyōshū*.

''This-wordly'' Buddhism is typically manifested in the prayers and incantations repeated over and over again with the purpose of ensuring recovery from illness, safe delivery in childbirth and exorcising the ''demons.'' These prayers and incantations involved numerous monks and impressive ceremonial to the point where it may even have been that the magnificence of the ritual was an end in itself. For example, when describing in detail the prayers which were recited by many priests for Murasaki (Genji's wife) when she fell sorely ill, the author writes: ''As it was the tenth of the third month, the cherry blossoms were in full bloom . . . It seemed precisely like the land of the Buddhas.''

This line puts one very much in mind of the viewpoint of the author of the *Eiga monogatari* who equated the magnificence of this world with Paradise. Taking the tonsure and secluding oneself into a temple was frequently practised by both men and women as a convenient means of escaping from the problems of this world and seems to have been a kind of institutionalized form of "retirement."

Of the ten women with whom Genji was deeply involved two met untimely deaths, five became nuns, one wished to become a nun but was not allowed to do so; only two (apart from those who died suddenly) did not become nuns. However, since the ultimate ends of these two women are not described in the novel, they too may well have entered a temple. It is easy to believe that in this age becoming a nun at a certain time in their life was part of the custom of the female aristocracy.

On the other hand, however, there are passages which indicate the author's belief in "next-worldly" Buddhism. For example, the word *sukuse* (*karma* or "fate") is frequently used when explaining the inevitability of a character's destiny (a fate which cannot be avoided). Since *sukuse* is a concept used to explain present effect in terms of the "cause" of a previous existence, naturally it must also imply that the deed of the present will bring reward or retribution in a future existence. This is the principle on which the Pure Land Sect's "desire for the afterlife" is based. In these terms, the act of becoming a nun is not a question of convention, but of aspiration for the next world. That Murasaki Shikibu apparently believed that the desire to become a nun in this sense was a vital attribute of the ideal human being is clearly shown by the fact that her most idealized character (Murasaki) expressed such a desire. Unlike Fujitsubo who became pregnant after her adulterous affair, Murasaki had not encountered problems difficult to solve in the context of this (secular) life. That she expressed the desire to become a nun was not because she had a pressing reason to do so, but because, from the author's viewpoint, she was an ideal character.

Murasaki Shikibu's Buddhist ideals may also be judged from her description of the "High Priest of Yogawa," said to have been modelled on Genshin. This monk, overcoming the opposition of his disciples, saved Ukifune when she tried to commit suicide and fainted, and caused her to become a nun. When his disciples said that it was a fuss to leave their mountain (Hieizan) and damaging to their master's reputation in the world when only one woman was involved, the monk replied that even though it was the life of only one woman, "The Buddha will surely save her." As for his reputation in the world, that did not matter to him. He said, "Now I'm already over sixty, it doesn't matter to me if people criticize me for that." ("Tenarai") Ukifune, for her part, captivated by two men and attempting suicide, had ample reason for desiring the Pure Land, while the monk, in persuading her to become a nun, had a force which was derived from his transcendental beliefs.

In his own attitudes towards Buddhism, Prince Genji was divided between these two aspects. After the death of his beloved wife Murasaki, he "kept desiring the afterlife earnestly." This is not merely a conventional expression and clearly at this point Genji was profoundly concerned with the next world. However, unlike the case of the "High Priest of Yogawa" who did not care about his worldly reputation, Genji's interest in the next world was not strong enough to enable him to transcend such worldly concerns as his reputation in this world. Almost in the same breath as expressing his desire to enter holy orders, he wondered what people might think of his motives for doing so. Readers will not witness their hero becoming a priest. Genji's attitude here corresponds to Murasaki Shikibu's own as expressed in the ***Murasaki Shikibu nikki.*** She herself was clearly identifying not with the "High Priest of Yogawa," but with Genji.

The Buddhism of the ***Genji monogatari*** went beyond simple convention and formed an integral part, at least, of the author's field of vision, probably being a major reason for the objectivity of her observations and descriptions. Here, Buddhism is an inherent part of the structure of the whole novel giving it a cause and effect order as can be seen from the fact that the novel begins and ends with two adulterous love affairs. The novel's obsession with the portrayal of the *minutiae* of everyday life was a direct manifestation of the "this-worldly" nature of the indigenous world view, while the maintenance of structure and order throughout such a long tale was a reflection of the comprehensive discipline of the Buddhist world view. In this sense one might say that the ***Genji monogatari*** was a work born of a Buddhism which had undergone native transformation.

However, the most lasting impression left by the ***Genji monogatari*** has nothing to do with Buddhist philosophy, the Buddhist interpretation of fate as typified by the concept of *sukuse,* or even the idealized characterization of the beautiful men and women who people the novel. The psychological relationships between the men and women who come and go in the pages of the novel are skilfully told and have considerable charm, but they are not what provide the hallmark of the novel. What is it then which only the ***Genji monogartari*** has and sustains throughout its fifty-four chapters? In my view it is an awareness of the reality of the passage of time; a feeling for the reality of time as something which cannot help but make all the activities and emotions of human beings relative. The ***Genji monogatari*** is a presentation of the emotional condition of human beings conscious that they tread this earth but once: "Life is not long, but make the most of it even if only one or two days are left." ("Tenarai") What is expressed here is the mortality of man as well as eternity caught within "only one or two days."

With the exception of the last thirteen chapters, the ***Genji monogatari*** can be read as the biography of its hero. We have already seen how the life of Genji—his birth, upbringing, his loves, his exile, his promotion, and, in old age, his desire for the afterlife—is a connecting thread running throughout the novel. We have already seen also how through the literary style of the book the author is always with us and provides continuity despite the inclusion of many independent anecdotes and stories. However, it is not solely these two factors which provide the sense of the reality of time in the ***Genji monogatari.***

In the course of the ***Genji monogatari*** the natural and social environment change and the various characters (not only Genji) change. Sensitivities to the changes in the four seasons nourished since the age of *Kokinshū* are clearly apparent and many events (mostly trivial events) are closely related to shifts in human emotions occasioned by the changes of the seasons. For example, Genji's exile to Suma begins at the end of the third month "when the days are long," and when he has become a little more settled there, "the rainy season comes" and he thinks of the women of the capital, his endless memories of the women overlapping and harmonizing remarkably with the never-ending rain. There are innumerable similar examples of emotions and natural conditions being attuned in this way. The social background is provided by the court where changes are denoted by the accession of different Emperors. The novel covers the reigns of four Emperors and the rule of three Regents and one of these summons Genji from Akashi back to the capital. Almost overnight the position of Genji and his family at court is changed completely.

Many other characters, both men and women, also follow their own ''destinies'' from childhood to adulthood and reveal their personalities in the process. As a child the beautiful Murasaki is put into the care of Genji, then when she grows up she marries him, falls ill and eventually dies tended by Genji. She is a character who represents a unifying thread in the novel from the very beginning. Then there is the undying love which Fujitsubo has for Genji even after she has become a nun. Again there is the boy Kaoru who grows up after Genji's death and plays a leading role in the final thirteen chapters. In all these instances one feels an acute awareness of the passage of long periods of time.

However, the course of time is clearly accentuated not only by the world changing even as it continues, but also by the different reactions of the characters when, after the passage of years, they are confronted by similar circumstances to those they had previously experienced.

Murasaki Shikibu displayed truly great skill in constantly resurrecting situations resembling each other with which to face her characters. This is one of her characteristic methods of dealing with time, as is typically represented by the two adulterous affairs; one is Genji's affair with Fujitsubo and the other is that of his wife Onna Sanno Miya with Kashiwagi. As a result of the first of these affairs Fujitsubo suffers and becomes a nun, but Genji himself does not feel any particular remorse or responsibility. On the contrary, even when Fujitsubo's child becomes Emperor and he himself as a father of the Emperor rises to the state of ex-emperor and lives in great splendour, he does not feel any doubt whether it is right or not. Therefore, when his own wife commits adultery, it does not have the effect on him of being a retribution for his own transgression. The re-occurrence of similar circumstances is not a matter of cause and effect, but gives the impression of a change of Genji's role within those circumstances and makes the reader sharply aware of the fact that it is the passage of time which has brought about that change in role.

The second method which Murasaki Shikibu uses to bring home the passage of time is her emphasis on the influence of the past on the present. Impressions of characters from the past are overlapped with the impressions of present characters and operate in a special way on any given character. For example, the reason Emperor Kiritsubo loves Fujitsubo is that she reminds him of his dead wife, Lady Kiritsubo. Genji was captivated by Murasaki because she reminded him of Fujitsubo. The reason he was attracted by Tamakazuna was that she was a living image of her mother Yūgao who died an untimely death. Kaoru loved Uji no Ōigimi and when he met her stepsister Ukifune who put him in mind of her, he came to love Ukifune. In the case of these men, they found in one woman what they had loved in another, with echoes of the love past mingling with the anticipation of the love to start. Thus, by overlapping the past, present and future into the emotion of one moment, the author demonstrates the flow of time vividly.

By skilful use of such fictional devices, Murasaki Shikibu succeeded in conveying the intensity of time. The truth about humanity which the ***Genji monogatari*** reveals to us is not the destiny, nor the transiency of human life but the passage of time which is so ordinary and at the same time so fundamental a condition to all of us. To present or to reveal this truth indeed demanded a long novel. (pp. 181-88)

Shuichi Kato, ''The Age of the 'Genji monogatari' and the 'Konjaku monogatari','' *in his* A History of Japanese Literature: The First Thousand Years, *translated by David Chibbett, Kodansha International Ltd., 1979, pp. 137-206.*

V. S. PRITCHETT (essay date 1980)

[*Pritchett is a highly esteemed English novelist, short story writer, and critic. Considered one of the modern masters of the short story, he is also one of the world's most respected and well-read literary critics. Pritchett writes in the conversational tone of the familiar essay, approaching literature from the viewpoint of a lettered but not overly scholarly reader. In his criticism, Pritchett stresses his own experience, judgment, and sense of literary art, rather than following a codified critical doctrine derived from a school of psychological or philosophical speculation. In the following excerpt, Pritchett comments on several significant events and characters of* The Tale.]

When Arthur Waley's translation of ***The Tale of Genji*** came out, volume by volume, in the late Twenties and early Thirties, the austere sinologue and poet said that Lady Murasaki's work was ''unsurpassed by any long novel in the world.'' If we murmured, ''What about *Don Quixote* or *War and Peace*?'' we were, all the same, enchanted by the classic of Heian Japan which was written in the tenth and eleventh centuries, and we talked about its ''modern voice.'' What we really meant was that the writing was astonishingly without affectation. Critics spoke of a Japanese Proust or Jane Austen, even of a less coarse Boccaccio. They pointed also to the seeming collusion of the doctrines of reincarnation or the superstition of demonic possession with the Freudian unconscious—and so on.

Arthur Waley admitted a remote echo of Proust, for there was a nostalgia for *temps perdu* in a small aristocratic civilization; but he was quick to point out that the long and rambling ***Tale*** was hardly a psychological novel in the Western sense [see excerpt dated 1926]. The Chinese had excelled in lyrical poetry, but despised fiction outside of legend and fairy tale; in Japan, Lady Murasaki's contemporaries were given only to diarizing. What she had contrived was an original mingling of idealizing romance and chronicle, but a more apt analogy was with music: the effect of her classical and elegant mosaic suggested the immediate, crystalline quality of Mozart. Evocations of instrumental music and also of things like the music of insects occur on page after page: at one point Genji floods a garden with thousands of crickets. The more one thinks about this, one sees that Waley's insight contains a truth: it is music that steps across the one thousand years that separate us from Lady Murasaki. (pp. 195-96)

It is impossible to do more than point out a few of the 800 characters of the story which passes from episode to episode. The main dramas move among the large number of Genji's love affairs, which are as various as those in Boccaccio. Princes and their trains move from the capital, where all is ambition and court gossip, to the country, where mysterious girls, usually of noble connection, have been hidden, protected only by corruptible or sentimental nuns or servants. There are soldiers but they do not fight. There is no violence. There are no crimes of passion. There are a few rather unpolished provincial governors—a despised caste. Lady Murasaki is as sensitive as Jane Austen is to rank and status, noting drily the pretentious who have come to nothing and the common who have risen. There are priests in their temples, soothsayers, exorcists who are called in to throw out demons, which are, as a rule, projections of jealous passion.

We see a society ruled by ceremonies and rituals and checked by taboos. Ill-luck, bad behaviour, tragedy may be caused in one's life by influences from a previous incarnation for which one cannot be held responsible. Lady Murasaki's temperament is not religious: for her, religion is a matter of proper observances and manners. She has a taste for funerals properly conducted.

The sexual act is never described; the ecstasies of physical love are not even evoked conventionally as they are rather tiringly in *The Arabian Nights*. We see the lovers meet with a screen between them. They strike the string of the koto or exchange short poems to show their artistic skills. The touching of an embroidered sleeve causes alarm and desire; when the lover is admitted or breaks in, the servants retire and we have a full description of the lady's clothes and her hair, but not her body. A coverlet is removed and the next thing we know is that night has passed and the lover is required to leave at dawn under cover of the perpetual mist, his sleeves washed by the dews. He hands the lady a sprig of blossom and sends her a two-line poem with a conversational postscript. The book is almost entirely concerned with the interplay of feelings, joyful, sorrowing, and longing. All is rendered with classical restraint.

The magnificent and always engaging Genji dominates two-thirds of the book and then with little explanation fades out of it. (Perhaps the manuscript has been lost.) He is incurably susceptible and unfaithful, but he makes amends to his conscience by behaving generously. Society deplores but forgives what are called ''his ways.'' He is the illegitimate and favourite son of the emperor—''a private treasure''—and he is scarcely more than a boy when he falls in love wth his stepmother, the emperor's second wife, who seems, in this incestuous society, to be an ideal. She has a child by him, but that is nothing. He is married off to Aoi, another woman years older than himself. They do not cohabit and she treats him like a schoolboy but in time he will love her deeply. Meanwhile he takes Lady Rokujō, his uncle's wife, also many years older than himself, as his mistress.

Lady Rokujō's violent jealousy of Aoi leads to one of the great dramatic scenes of the book, for if she is resigned to Genji's casual love affairs, she finds his love of Aoi intolerable. The drama comes to a head at the Festival of Kamo. An enormous crowd of all classes comes to see the nobility ride by on horseback. There is a great traffic jam of fine carriages, among them Aoi's. Lady Rokujō has gone incognito to the festival in a simple curtained carriage, to get one last glimpse of Genji, but her carriage and her attendants collide with Aoi's. There is a brawl between the rival servants and Lady Rokujō is pushed into the background.

The affront is devastating. From now on the evil spirit of jealousy becomes a demonic entity. Aoi is pregnant, indeed about to give birth, and is found to be dying. The evil spirit has indeed entered her, and when the demented Genji speaks to her, she answers in the voice of Lady Rokujō. Powerless to control herself Lady Rokujō has projected her voice into the dying woman. It is an instance of possession. Such scenes are not uncommon in romance, but this one is so well done that we believe it and feel the horror. A wild emotion has been transmitted and is recognizable as an emanation of the unconscious, for Lady Rokujō, who has not consciously willed this act, nevertheless feels remorse. It drains her of all desire to continue her powerful life at court: to annul the magic that possesses her she enters a nunnery. Had the scene been done in the high manner of romance it would be as unreal as a fairy tale; in fact the writing is restrained and therefore frightens us.

Genji's ''ways'' continue rashly until he sins against protocol and is obliged to go into exile in the mountains. The whole court, even the offended emperor, is upset. There are many rough journeys over muddy tracks, in fog, snow, freezing winds, across flooded rivers. The amount of rain that pours down in the ***Tale*** must be about equal in volume to the floods of tears, whether of joy, grief, longing, or remorse, which so easily overcome the characters. The tears themselves are a kind of music, a note of the koto. In exile, Genji thinks of his new wife, Murasaki—she seems unlikely to have been the authoress—and of his other ladies. But Genji cannot really repent. He thinks of old lovers:

> He went on thinking about whatever woman he encountered. A perverse concomitant was that the women he went on thinking about went on thinking about him.

A cuckoo calls—it is a messenger from the past or the world beyond death, not the mocking creature of Western culture.

> It catches the scent of memory, and favours
> The village where the orange blossoms fall.

Even the sinister Lady Rokujō is forgiven. She had been a woman of unique breeding and superior calligraphy. She replies in a long letter:

> Laying down her brush as emotion overcame her and then beginning again, she finally sent off some four or five sheets of white Chinese paper. The gradations of ink were marvellous. He had been fond of her, and it had been wrong to make so much of that one incident. She had turned against him and presently left him. It all seemed such a waste.

The lady of the orange blossoms, an older mistress, writes:

> Ferns of remembrance weigh our eaves ever more,
> And heavily falls the dew upon our sleeve.

A Gosechi dancer, a wild girl, writes:

> Now taut, now slack, like my unruly heart,
> The tow rope is suddenly still at the sound of a koto.
> Scolding will not improve me.

Genji spends his time among the fishermen of the wild Akashi coast and here, of course, temptation comes and he is sending messages to a girl hidden in one of the houses, a rustic, whose parents have ''impossible hopes.'' Her father is a monk, but soon stops his prayers when he sees Genji may raise her fortunes. Genji admires beyond the protecting screen:

> Though he did not exactly force his way through, it is not to be imagined that he left matters as they were. . . . The autumn night, usually so long, was over in a trice.

No hope of a respectable marriage for her. All the same, Genji will install her in the capital later in the story and she will have her influence on his life. As usual, he is guilty about this secret. The girl had enhanced his love of his wife, to whom he confesses.

> It was but the fisherman's brush with the salty sea pine
> Followed by a tide of tears of longing.

His wife replies gently but ironically, in words that have a bearing on the Calderón-like theme of the novel, i.e. that life is a dream:

> That you should have deigned to tell me a dreamlike story which you could not keep to yourself calls to mind numbers of earlier instances.

And politely adds to her poem:

> Naïve of me, perhaps; yet we did make our vows.
> And now see the waves that wash the Mountain of Waiting.

She knows that Genji will not stand jealous scenes for one moment. Everyone knows it. His lasting defence of his adding new loves to old is that he never forgets, and he adds: ''Sometimes I feel as if I might be dreaming and as if the dream were too much for me'': it is an attempt to define what life itself, with all its happiness and disasters, feels like.

Genji's early love of mother figures perhaps necessarily accounts for the incestuous strain in him. His second wife (i.e. Murasaki) was taken into his mansion as a child and he has brought her up to think of him as her father. He flirts with the little girl; then, when she reaches puberty, he can't control himself and gets into bed with her. It is a kind of rape. The girl is shocked and sullen. The silent aftermath is plainly and delicately shown; but ritual saves the situation. The required offerings of cakes are pushed through her bed curtains. Marriage follows and, in time, she adores him. She has after all married the ruler of the country; however, in years to come, she will find him playing the father game again. He has by this time installed his chief concubines in apartments in his mansion; each has her own superbly made garden. He is getting on—probably in his forties—and he likes dropping in for a chaste evening chat with some of the older ones. There is some discreet bitching among the women, disguised as two-edged gardening presents. One older lady sends the younger Murasaki an arrangement of autumn leaves with the words:

> Permit the winds to bring a touch of autumn.

Murasaki's garden is without flowers at this time. She replies with an arrangement of moss, stones, and a cleverly made artificial pine, with the words:

> Fleeting, your leaves that scatter in the wind.
> The pine at the cliffs is forever green with the spring.

The pine is a symbol of hopeless longing and Genji tells his wife she has been ''unnecessarily tart.''

> What will the Goddess of Tatsuta think when she hears you belittling the best of autumn colours? Reply from strength, when you have the force of your spring blossoms to support you.

The magnificent man is fortifying because he is not only benevolent by nature, but also astute.

After the deaths of Genji and his second wife, the novel is dominated by a new generation: Yūgiri, Genji's pompous son, and the young heroes and courtiers, Niou and Kaoru. These two are friends, who laugh and drink together, and also rivals. The important thing is the marked difference of their temperaments, and on this Lady Murasaki becomes searching. Niou is the handsome and dashing Don Juan or playboy who lacks Genji's powers of reflection. Kaoru has a startling physical quality. In a story where the men are known by the scent they use, Kaoru has a body that needs none: its natural fragrance can intoxicate 200 yards away like the smell of some powerful flower. (It can of course betray where he has been!) If this perfume allures it does him no good: he is a neurotic, tormented, indecisive, and self-defeating Puritan who botches his feelings and escapes to the fuss of court administration at the decisive moment. Responsibility is his alibi and curse. The explanation of his insecure character is that he is a bastard incurably depressed because he does not know who his father is.

The rivalry between Niou and Kaoru begins with a long intrigue with two orphaned sisters who live in the Uji country, a solitude of howling winds and sad rivers. Elsewhere we hear the cheeping of the crickets, the songs of birds, but at Uji the music is the mournful, deafening, maddening music of waterfalls. Niou quickly conquers one of the sisters but only to make her his concubine and not his wife. Kaoru, who is in love with both girls, in his way, loses both. His trouble is that he is an intellectual whose real interest is religion. He will eventually take the vows of Buddhism.

The ''novel'' has by now almost ceased to be a work of worldly and poetic comedy and, in its last part, becomes a fast moving drama of intrigue and passion and dementia in which lying servants and old women play their part. (The analogy is extravagant, I know, but it is as if we had moved from, say, Jane Austen to an Oriental version of *Wuthering Heights*.) This final section, along with the opening one of the ***Tale,*** is by far the most gripping. It excited Arthur Waley! The drama arises from one more adventure of the rivals. Niou and Kaoru are this time in love with a simple, hidden girl of mysterious parentage called Ukifune. Kaoru loves her because she reminds him of the one he had lost earlier—memory, or being reminded of earlier loves, is a continuous musical theme—Niou is out for yet another rash seduction.

The girl is too young to know who of the two she loves and who is her friend; and in her misery decides to drown herself as girls always do, Lady Murasaki remarks, in the romances she has read. The girl attempts this and disappears, and is generally supposed to be dead. Indeed the servants arrange a false funeral in order to avoid scandal. They go out with a coffin containing her bedding and clothes, and burn them on the funeral pyre; the country people, who take death seriously, are suspicious and shocked by the hurry. They watch the smoke: it smells of bedding, not of a burning corpse. In fact, unknown to Niou and Kaoru and ourselves, Ukifune has been rescued and hidden once more in a temple. We see Niou shocked by grief for the first time in his life. (Lady Murasaki is remarkable in scenes of wild grief.) The extraordinary thing is her account of Ukifune's loss of memory and speech after the ''drowning'': it is done with astonishing realism and could be a clinical study.

Lady Murasaki is almost too inventive. She is, as I have said, properly class-conscious, quick to detect the vulgar, and is therefore capable of refreshing bits of farce. Pushing, common provincial governors or tomboys with bad accents are neatly hit off: ''Pure, precise speech can give a certain distinction to rather ordinary remarks,'' she notes like any lady in a Boston or London drawng room, *circa* 1910. Girls who talk torrentially become ''incomprehensible and self-complacent.'' Still, eventually there is a chance that being in good society will cure them. On the other hand, don't imagine that there is any deep difference between the aristocrat and the lowborn: the sorrows of life afflict all. Life is short, time swallows us up; old palaces fall into ruins, new ones take their place. Our life is a dream and, like the ***Tale*** itself, fades away. (pp. 197-205)

V. S. Pritchett, "Lady Murasaki: 'The Tale of Genji'," in his The Tale Bearers: Literary Essays, *Random House, 1980, pp. 195-205.*

MARGUERITE YOURCENAR (conversation date 1980)

[*Yourcenar is a Belgian-born American novelist and critic who writes primarily in French and who, in 1981, became the first woman to be elected to the prestigious Académie française. She is best known for her novel* Mémoires d'Hadrien *(1951;* Memoirs of Hadrian*), which is considered a masterpiece of historical fiction. Displaying a vast knowledge of philosophy, history, and myth, Yourcenar seeks in her fiction to link the past wth the present, and thus to provide a deeper understanding of the human condition. She has also written a number of esteemed critical works. In the following excerpt, Yourcenar praises Murasaki's literary achievements. Because the exact date of her comments is not recorded, the date used is that of the original French publication of these conversations.*]

[***Genji monogatari*** is] one of the richest novels I know, for the complexity of its female characters and for the extraordinary subtlety of Prince Genji's portrayal in his relationships with several women and in his awareness of how varied those women and his feelings for them are. . . . [I distinguish] between love-as-compassion, love-as-sympathy, and love-as-play: play of a very high order indeed, the play of a civilization that blends love with all the arts—poetry, painting, calligraphy—other than those of the bedroom. The novel offers us a wonderful mix of fragrances as well as contact with the invisible. (p. 86)

The book is written with incredible subtlety, not only as to the psychology of relations between men and women but, more profoundly, in the manner of depicting the ambiguity of life, the passage of time, the way love has of combining tragedy, delight, and a certain fugitive quality in all its episodes. The opening is admirable. The emperor, having lost his mistress (who, because she was not a member of one of the court's powerful clans, was subjected to mental torture by palace intriguers and rivals), sends a lady-in-waiting to find out what has become both of the child he had by the former mistress and of the woman's elderly mother. The lady-in-waiting returns and describes a more or less abandoned house, open to the rain, a deserted garden, a tearful old woman, mother of the former mistress, who is unable to explain anything, and a child who is, on the contrary, gay, lively, and very handsome. The feeling this gives of the transition from generation to generation, of the solitude of each generation along with the ties that bind one generation to another through life and death, is magnificent.

Whenever I'm asked what woman novelist I admire most, the name Murasaki Shikibu comes immediately to mind. I have extraordinary respect, indeed reverence, for her work. She was truly the great writer, the great novelist, of eleventh-century Japan, which is to say, of the period when Japanese civilization was at its height. In a word, she was the Marcel Proust of medieval Japan: a woman of genius with a feeling for social gradations, love, the human drama, and the way in which people will hurl themselves against the wall of impossibility. Nothing better has ever been written in any language. (pp. 86-7)

Marguerite Yourcenar, "From the Orient to Politics," in her With Open Eyes: Conversations with Matthieu Galey, *translated by Arthur Goldhammer, Beacon Press, 1984, pp. 85-91.*

EDWARD SEIDENSTICKER (essay date 1982)

[*Seidensticker is an American critic and the translator of numerous Japanese works, including a 1976 edition of* The Tale. *In the following excerpt, he surveys Murasaki's critical reputation, disagreeing with certain views expressed by other commentators.*]

On the whole the English have had more interesting things to say about the ***Genji*** than the Americans. I refer not to specialized scholars, but to critics and writers of the wide-ranging sort. Americans have tended to be petulant and somewhat too clever, as when Marvin Mudrick called me Koremitsu G. Seidensticker [see Additional Bibliography] with reference to a faithful but occasionally censorious servant in the ***Genji.*** One chuckles, without quite knowing why. It is not so with the

"The senior courtiers, led by the two First Secretaries, came up in turn to receive their gifts."

British. When they produce chuckles, one *does* know why. Of specialists a thing may be said, briefly. They make mistakes. Translators do too, and whether or not they are glad to have their mistakes pointed out, most of them are aware of vulnerability. I have a list of mistakes made by scholarly reviewers. They are not mistakes of opinion. It is arrogant to aver, and difficult to establish, mistakes of opinion. They are rather mistakes of fact, having to do with chronology and the number of children the characters have and who is whose cousin and the like. It is a considerable list, a growing and interesting list, and some day it may be published.

Pritchett speaks of Murasaki Shikibu's "modern voice," and continues: "what we really meant was that the writing was astonishingly without affectation. Critics spoke of a Japanese Proust or Jane Austen, even of a less sparse Boccaccio. They pointed also to the seeming collusion of the doctrines of incarnation or the superstition of demonic possession with the Freudian unconscious—and so on" [see excerpt by Pritchett dated 1980].

Pritchett insists on the modernity of the ***Genji,*** which is another way of saying that it seems near and immediate. A similar insistence runs through most British and American discussion of the ***Genji.*** Pritchett is also representative in his way of remarking upon the characters as if they were real people. It is an attitude a critic might take towards a realistic or psychological novel of the West. Again like most Western critics, he seems better at secondary characters than at the major figures. Here is he talking of Kaoru, who is reputedly Genji's son but actually the grandson of his best friend, who is known for his fragrance (which is what Kaoru signifies), and whose knack for making people unhappy dominates the last ten chapters: "If this perfume allures it does him no good: he is a neurotic, tormented, indecisive, and self-defeating Puritan who botches his feelings and escapes into the fuss of court administration at the critical moment. Responsibility is his alibi and curse."

Genji, the dominant character until his death, upwards of two-thirds of the way through the book, is more elusive. D. J. Enright finds him "too good to be true" [see excerpt dated 1977]. Frank Gibney is of the view that "Casanova, Don Juan, the Earl of Rochester, Humbert Humbert, and Hugh Hefner's *Playboy* fantasy-life pale by comparison. . . . Nothing was safe from Genji's roving eye."

These remarks are interesting but not entirely to the point. The young Genji may be idealized but the aging Genji is not; and philandering becomes philandering only when it goes beyond what is reasonably and conventionally expected of a fellow. Compared to his best friend, Kaoru's natural grandfather, Genji is not at all promiscuous. He may even be a little prudish. The important point is, however, not that these views are at fault, but rather that two themes, modernity and the strength and subtlety of the characterization, dominate British and American writing about the ***Genji.***

Marguerite Yourcenar, perhaps the most distinguished continental writer to comment at length upon the ***Genji,*** is fascinated with Genji, and it may be that she does him better justice than the English and the Americans. She remarks upon the complexity of his nature, his rapport with his several ladies, his sense of the differences among them, and his willingness to partake of the several varieties of love, to one of which she gives the interesting name "charitable love" [see excerpt dated 1980]. Her example of this last is his willingness to favor the red-nosed Hitachi princess. Dissatisfied with Genji's abrupt disappearance from the scene, she did what more than one Japanese has done: she wrote a new chapter. It is called "The Last Love of Prince Genji." The last love is the most self-effacing and self-sacrificing of Genji's ladies, the one whom I call the lady of the orange blossoms and Waley calls the lady from the village of falling flowers. It is a better supplemental chapter than any the Japanese have done. Mlle. Yourcenar found the orange-blossom lady "an exemplary personage." This seems remarkable and admirable in our feminist age.

"When someone asks me who is the *romancière* I admire most," Mlle. Yourcenar said in an interview, "I always think of Murasaki Shikibu, with extraordinary respect and reverence. . . . She was the Marcel Proust of medieval Japan, a woman who had genius, a sense of social variety, of love, of the human drama, of the way in which we encounter the impossible. No more can be done in any literature."

The comparison with Proust is probably the one most commonly made by people who compare things. To some of us it may seem to go too far, and some of us may have trouble knowing what it means. Formally, the two great works by two writers could scarcely be further apart. Had Proust stopped writing somewhere along the way, we would have known it. What we already know of his relentless and vigorous mind would inform us that he could not have meant to leave things thus. Whether or not the ***Genji*** is finished is among the problems that will be debated forever.

The formal comparison is not often made, and it is not much to the point. More pertinent by far is the matter of characterization. Murasaki Shikibu is seen, like Proust, as an explorer of states of mind. Here the comparison is certainly not pointless, although differences between the two writers are considerable. There is not a great deal of psychological exploration in the ***Genji.*** The major characters, of whom there are perhaps fifty or sixty, stand out most remarkably as individuals, but there is little dialogue; nor is there much by way of soliloquy or overt analysis of states of mind.

There is more as the story moves to a conclusion, if indeed it can be called a conclusion, and so it is possible that Murasaki Shikibu was moving in a direction which would have made her a Proust far in advance of her time. She had not yet arrived there.

The ways in which Murasaki Shikibu succeeded in giving the illusion of individual life are mysterious. The novelist Kawabata Yasunari once said that the fiction of Japan is peopled by ghosts ("spooks" might be a better translation for the word he used). He held this to be most certainly true of his own work. I know what he meant, I think. He meant that the characters in most Japanese novels flicker onto the stage, and while there seem on the point of flickering off again. It is so with the ***Genji*** too. The characters seem to emerge only a short distance from the natural background, which is always there as if about to claim them again for its own. They are all of them like the new-born infants in the ***Genji*** itself, so beautiful and so fragile that everyone expects them to be reclaimed by the powers that allowed them brief life.

The matter of characterization probably brings us close to what the critics mean when they call the ***Genji*** "modern." In this too they may have outdone themselves. In some respects the nineteenth-century scholars who saw Murasaki Shikibu as a romancer may have been nearer the truth than twentieth-century critics who see her as a novelist. "Romance" and "novel" are complex and elusive words, but we may here take them to signify respectively a story remote from the ordinary and centered upon remarkable events and a story of the familiar, even commonplace, centered upon character. The one is pre-modern, the other modern. There is a strong element of the pre-modern in the ***Genji.*** Attempts to explain it away can never be completely successful.

The problem of ''demonic possession'' mentioned by Pritchett is a good instance. We cannot be sure whether or not Murasaki Shikibu believed in it. We may detect evidence in at least one of her poems (not in the ***Genji***) that she did not quite. There is genuine horror, and an element of what seems like the inevitable, in the death of Aoi, Genji's wife, in a fit of possession, but the remarkable story in the last chapters of Ukifune's gradual recovery from amnesia begins with a possession so offhand as to be almost frivolous. A malign spirit happens to wander by and comes upon the kind of case he likes best. It is as if Murasaki Shikibu could not commence a story the likes of which her readers cannot possibly have had before without the lure of something which, far from realistic, would excite them without outraging them. While we do not tend to admire her as a spinner of yarns, especially now that we have grown accustomed to the comparison with Proust; but here she does seem to be a spinner of yarns, a romancer.

These points are worth making because fixed ideas, accepted notions, tend to edge away from reality. Here, however, the ideas are more interesting and important than the edging away. Murasaki Shikibu is seen in the West as modern. She is seen as one of us, speaking to us across a millenium with astonishing immediacy. (pp. 50-2)

Edward Seidensticker, '' 'The Tale of Genji': Here and There,'' in Yearbook of Comparative and General Literature, *No. 31, 1982, pp. 47-53.*

RICHARD BOWRING (essay date 1982)

[Bowring is an English critic who specializes in the study of Oriental literature. In the following excerpt from the introduction to his translation of Murasaki's diary, he clarifies the nature and significance of that text, relating it to her writing of The Tale.*]*

Given that we are dealing with such a fragmented text, parts of which are clearly written in the mode of private communication and parts of which are public record that remains in a fairly raw state, how are we to approach [the diary of Murasaki Shikibu]? What is it? Should we look upon it as a renegade, a miscellany that in the normal course of events would, but for the fame of its author and its scarcity value, be consigned to her *Nachlass*? Or do we treat it as a coherent text, a work fully deserving its place in the literary canon? How, in other words, are we to read it?

It is usual in such cases to invoke the concept of genre. A sense of genre is critical to understanding because it puts into operation a whole series of shared responses that help the reader in his initial voyage of discovery through any given text. If the unread text can be thought of as having a high degree of entropy, reading can then be defined as the process by which that entropy is reduced. Any clues that help us to reach this goal are welcome, especially when we are dealing with something so remote in both time and place as the work in question.

One place to go to for a sign of genre might well be the title—not that this would be true of the majority of literatures, but Japanese have always had a penchant for using taxonomic labels. The complication here, however, is that those titles which appear to contain explicit information about genre often prove to be less useful on a closer look. One of the reasons for this may well be that a need to classify works by means of this kind of label never arises until a particular genre is already well developed. Indeed, it could be argued that a sense of genre becomes *necessary* only when the text in question begins to seem remote, generic definitions being based on pairs of oppositions that only later become apparent. As far as [works classified as] nikki are concerned, most of them seem to have remained without titles (they may even have remained unread) until the time of the classical scholar-poets Shunzei and Teika, some two hundred years later. The notorious vagueness of boundary lines between monogatari, nikki, and kashū, and the fact that some works share more than one of these titles, is to be laid at the door of this later period; it does not mean that the original authors had no clear idea of what they were writing.

At first sight men like Shunzei and Teika seem to have been somewhat cavalier in their use of titles, and the task of discovering the rationale behind their choice is not an easy one. One look at those works entitled nikki, for instance, will reveal differences that almost outweigh similarities. The *Kagerō nikki* and the *Sarashina nikki* are memoirs which pattern personal history in such a manner as to approach fully fledged autobiographies, but the *Izumi Shikibu nikki,* on the other hand, is clearly a fiction and indeed the majority of manuscripts entitle it a monogatari. Perhaps different scholars used different methods of classification; some may have considered those texts which dealt with people who had actually existed were nikki, leaving monogatari for those works which dealt with fictional characters, or it may have been more subtle, having to do with the presence or lack of the narrative marker *keri*. The ***Murasaki Shikibu nikki*** itself comes closer to the usual meaning of diary than any of these works, and yet it is obviously a hybrid. That it is not overtly fictionalized, however, should not exclude it from consideration as a literary text. To read it correctly, then, we must approach it for what it manifestly is, a combination of a traditional court lady's diary and a private letter. The generic classification ''diary'' does not prove to be of much use in this case and should be ignored for the present purposes.

So why is this text of such importance over and above its value as historical record? Is it just the cast-off notes of a genius of fiction? The fact that it was written by the author of the ***Tale of Genji*** is, of course, of major importance, but the diary does have its own significance. It represents a unique combination of those two elements which give the best of Heian prose its ''modern'' feel: ''realism'' and confessionalism. It serves to place Murasaki in direct literary descent from the mother of Michitsuna and reveals much about the conditions that made the creation of such a fictional masterpiece as the ***Genji*** possible. It helps us to ''explain'' the ***Genji.***

Let us deal with these two elements in turn. For realistic description we must look primarily at Parts A and D. Despite the presence of the author within the text and the existence of a number of inaccuracies, the record sections of the diary are clearly not fiction but history. The driving force behind them is a will to record factual information, bearing witness to an apparently obsessive fascination with the concrete details of life, a concentration of fact that cannot be explained away as being merely part and parcel of her role at court. But this drive leads Murasaki in what is for an artist an unusual direction. Anyone who writes does so partly to order experience, to reduce the chaos that is reality, but the author of a fiction strives to go further, to design and present a world that will produce meaning when reconstructed in the reading.There is an effort to project a particular vision of the world that may be quite personal, and is often very difficult to extract, but is intended. The same process of choosing and ordering the world is at work in a historical text, but the extra step of investing that description with ulterior meaning is missing. The ordering itself is considered to provide sufficient meaning. The facts become their own justification. And this is precisely why Parts A and D are so "opaque," that is, resistant to any attempt to extract meaning from them. On the one hand, this bears witness to a belief in the significance of historiography, a belief in the ability of the written word to hold reality, to reduce it to manageable proportions and hence to preserve it for memory, but by the same token the acceptance of the temporal progression given by the chronological nature of events as they occur in a preordained order and the refusal to employ reality gives the impression that Murasaki is somehow running away from the significance of what she is describing, using language not to "mean" but to block meaning. The more detail one is given, the less one is able to grasp the significance of what is being described, and in a paradoxical sense this can be interpreted as a veiled attempt to reduce it all to triviality.

The usual view of the world as revealed in the diary is basically that, apart from some personal melancholy, all was well in a golden age. Murasaki's vision is, as one might expect, highly restricted. There is no mention of the floods and famine that afflicted the whole country throughout the summer and autumn of 1008, and the attitude towards Imperial-Fujiwara relations seems particularly askew. Contrary to the picture one receives from reading the diary, Emperor Ichijō chafed under the oppressive yoke of Michinaga, and tried more than once to supplant Shōshi as a favorite, only to find that the choice was not his to make. . . . For Murasaki, however, the world outside was basking in the beneficient light of imperial, and hence Fujiwara, rule, and there seems to be little indication that she saw Shōshi's position as anything but fortunate. She was absorbed in her own small world, and it is purely through her genius and that of her contemporaries that it takes on such color for us.

And so it may seem on the surface. But the simple fact that a writer of such superb fiction, a fiction that defined her age for all later ages, felt moved to produce such an opaque record demands an explanation. There are, of course, moments when she takes exception to certain court figures, Michinaga's wife in particular, and the claims of the Fujiwara to magnificence are essentially undercut by the very presence of her own personal distress. But one can, I think, go much further and explain the very existence of such a record as an act of covert opposition. The production of such a text was in itself an act of revenge, and as a writer of fiction Murasaki could hardly have been unaware of the deadening effect such prose would have. The tendency the text has of slipping into personal anecdote and self-analysis reveals a fundamental distrust of such a mode of writing. For the author of the ***Genji*** it could hardly have been very stimulating, and its very opaqueness betrays a lack of commitment, a sense of resistance. One would not want to take this too far and argue that Murasaki had an active dislike of the court, but such an interpretation goes a long way towards explaining how one person could create two such different works as the diary and the ***Genji,*** and it would also allow us to see Murasaki as a much more positive figure. All fiction is essentially subversive, and the act of producing such a work as the ***Genji,*** which implicitly criticized the world as it was by comparison and which took as its hero a taboo-breaker, was the subversive gesture par excellence. Ultimate revenge lay in Murasaki's ability to produce a text that came to have more significance, more power, than the reality from which it was engendered, an ability not given to or even sought by the historian.

And whence the interest in concrete detail in the first place? Perhaps she began recording these events because she was asked to. It is, in any case, part of the same mentality that drove the men of the court to write endless records of their daily doings to ensure that a knowledge of precedent and ceremonial would be kept in the family. Such factual records were safe and became a mode of self-definition. In itself this is not a very significant procedure, and only in the ***Genji*** was it to be put to more subtle ends.

The second element that demands our attention is confessionalism, for which we have to look no further than Part B, where the truly autobiographical nature of this diary becomes explicit. It is an oft-repreated statement that classical Japan knew no real sense of self and had no use for the concept of individuality. Buddhism, which expressly denied the self, combined with native Shinto attitudes to produce a culture where the world was not seen in terms of subject and object. So, for instance, the idea of rights never occurred because the Japanese lacked a sense of the necessary distinction beween individual and society. Japan, of course, was not unlike the majority of traditional societies in this. But we are faced with the fact that much of Heian prose is autobiographical in nature. There is a willingness, indeed an insistent drive, to subject oneself to analysis and to broadcast the results of this curiosity, and it is in great measure this obsession that laid the foundation for the production of works of prose fiction that have, for their time, an astonishing degree of psychological maturity and penetration. It may be argued that as time went on the restrictions of conventionalized expression took all the life out of them, but in the beginning with, say, *The Gossamer Years* or Murasaki's diary, it is an anomaly. How, one might ask, in a traditional society, and a Buddhist one at that, could there be such a manifestation?

Georges Gusdorf, in his now classic formulation of the conditions of autobiography, argues that the form emerges only with Augustine at the juncture of the classical and Christian traditions, and that it was, until modern times, restricted to the Western world. "This conscious awareness of the singularity of each individual life," he writes, "is the late product of a specific civilization. Throughout most of human history, the individual does not oppose himself to all others; he does not feel himself to exist outside of others, and still less against others, but very much *with* others in an interdependent existence that asserts its rhythms everywhere in the community. No one is rightful possessor of his life or his death; lives are so thoroughly entangled that each of them has its center everywhere and its circumference nowhere." Autobiographical writing occurs only when a sense of history is fully developed, and where there has taken place an "involution of consciousness," a diversion of the usual outward gaze, a shift that goes against some of the oldest taboos of primitive cultures—veneration of the mirror being a prime example.

How are we then to explain the emergence of self-consciousness among women at such an early date in Japan? It may not be a modern self that was discovered and opened up to the world, but it was a self. It is often assumed that because Buddhist teaching brands the self as a pernicious illusion that a sense of self was never developed, but the opposite might also be argued, namely that such emphasis was placed on the evils of the rift between the self and other that the concept was very much alive and readily available to anyone who felt like using it. One need not, it seems, appeal to a putative secularization of court society to explain this. And, although the ties between confession and salvation cannot be said to be as strong as in the case of Christianity, the connection was nevertheless made. Priests and nuns made vows; attachment to the world was a sin that could be atoned for in the form of *sange* or *keka;* and Amidism was already stressing the personal nature of salvation. It is no accident that it is Amida to whom Murasaki appeals when thinking of salvation, nor that such an appeal should come at the end of the confessional Part B.

What of court society? The position of women like Murasaki at court was hardly conducive to a sense of belonging. Transported into the midst of a highly artificial society, totally at the mercy of the whims of the elite, and cut off from the world in a kind of harem, Murasaki shows in her diary an acute sense of what can only be called alienation. The enforced seclusion and the overwhelming artificiality bred an introverted consciousness that fed on itself. Self and society are very clearly distinguished, and the recurrent topoi of *kaimami* and *nagaame* which saturated the literary personae of such women could have done nothing to alleviate such a situation. It was a special kind of hot-house whose conditions were never really to occur again, and it played a decisive role in the genesis of the ***Genji.*** Here again, Murasaki, in a confessional mood, is in direct descent from Michitsuna's mother. The impulse of memoir sharpens the analytical faculties and whets the appetite for the explanation of motives, which is in turn the prime element in successful characterization; and it is in characterization that we see the greatest difference between the ***Genji*** and its precursors, and indeed its successors.

One of the central concerns of a diary, by its very form, is the nature of time. In *The Gossamer Years* and *The Diary of Izumi Shikibu* time is organized internally; it is a process that refers not to the outer world of society with its dates and ceremonies, not even to the way one specific year follows the next, but rather inward to the feelings and perceptions of the individual at the center. Murasaki's diary, however, is somewhat different and contains both kinds of time. As a figure in the public arena recording a series of ceremonies, she is the slave of external time not only physically but also in the sense that the diary itself is largely organized according to such principles. And, a point that she shares with many of the *kanbun* diaries of the period, this external time stresses not so much change, or development, as a simple procession of discrete events. As an individual with her own personal thoughts and emotions, however, Murasaki lives in a very different kind of time, governed by entirely different principles: those of mood, of internal rhythms, and above all of memory. Given these two conflicting kinds of time and the two conflicting worlds they represent, Murasaki proves to be remarkably successful in combining them, and the result is an unrivalled presentation of Heian court life from outside and from within by someone who is at once participant and observer.

Whenever she is drawn to contemplation or self-analysis, the discussion seems to emerge from a description of the external world and is invariably tied to natural time and to seasonal change. The inner world and the outer are therefore linked by a series of points where they intersect. The selection of these points is governed not by accident or personal whim but by a whole set of conventions common to her culture. It is the sight of birds on the lake, of fading chrysanthemums, of snow in a dilapidated garden, that trigger such responses. All these are moments sanctioned and sanctified by literary tradition. They are therefore in essence not real moments at all but literary moments drawing their significance from language itself. More than anything else it is this which marks her as a Heian woman, and which marks the diary as a Heian work.

The inner life is governed to a great extent by memory, especially with such a literary form as a diary written in retrospect. Indeed this work can also be understood as actually being "about memory," about the effect that time and mind has on events. The careful use of essentially tenseless descriptions, which helps to deemphasize the past nature of particular events; the continual presence of the literary past in the midst of the linguistic present through the manipulation of poetic allusion; and the fact that the work seems to have been written in a number of stages, stages which are themselves often referred to directly within the work,—all these serve to create an eternal present in which the past lives, in other words memory in action. And this aspect of the work is specifically referred to in the remark at the end of section 4: "Strange how a little incident like this suddenly comes back to one, whereas something that moved one deeply at the time can be forgotten with the passage of the years." This is the key to the diary: the process of remembering and forgetting is itself an eternal fascination, and the diary is to be an illustration of that process.

One of the best aids to memory is attention to detail, and it is no accident that Murasaki's interest in accuracy almost amounts to an obsession. Indeed in eight places she goes out of her way to record that she was not actually present at the events described (*e-mihaberazu*), or did not have a very good vantage point (*kuwashiku mizu*), and the verb forms *beshi* and *kemu* are often used to suggest varying degrees of uncertainty. The same mentality is seen in the lengthy passages describing women's dresses. Apart from the way they function as a symbol of the magnificence of Shōshi's entourage, they assume enormous importance as a major device whereby the past can be recreated in all its concreteness; they form a bulwark against forgetfulness. The act of writing such a work becomes an attempt to stop time, to recreate the past within the present, and the irony of this attempt is the irony of all such endeavors: the present is immediately cast into the past by time itself.

To attempt such a recreation, to test the memory, is also to test the self, and clearly much of the diary is devoted to such an end. Murasaki achieves a high degree of self-awareness. The main question in her life would seem to be the uneasy balance between desire for worldly honor and success on the one hand, and the knowledge that all these matters were at root illusory on the other. She is at her most poignant when she gives voice to her ambivalence in a way that often seems to echo the breadth of vision that we see in the ***Tale of Genji.*** In part such balance is achieved by observing herself very much as a third person, and this is done by clearly differentiating between the "I" of narration and the "I" of action. By stressing the difference between the time of event and time of narration through the use of a verb form like *haberi* and the other memory "markers" mentioned above, she manages to maintain a distinct personality for the narrating "I" while at the same time merging the acting "I" into the impersonality of the other ladies-in-waiting. Time, in its personal and public aspects, is also made to serve the same purpose. (pp. 30-9)

Richard Bowring, "The Diary: Introduction," in Murasaki Shikibu: Her Diary and Poetic Memoirs, *translated by Richard Bowring, Princeton University Press, 1982, pp. 19-41.*

ANDREW PEKARIK (essay date 1982)

[Pekarik is an American critic who has written numerous studies of Japanese literature. In the following excerpt, he describes attitudes toward sexual liaisons, particularly as they are revealed through vocabulary, in The Tale.*]*

The Tale of Genji is an extraordinarily complex work with multiple purposes, but it is certainly not neutral to the behavior of its characters, and the narrator, perhaps speaking for the author, comments critically at times. The very vocabulary of descriptions frequently implies judgments of right and wrong that are presumably shared by author and readers, and reflects the standards governing the relations between the sexes.

The Suzaku Emperor, concerned about the future of his daughter, the Third Princess, says, "Upon mentioning such matters I have been told of promiscuous, dissolute behavior in our own time. I have heard of many cases of daughters who once were treasured and carefully raised in the homes of their important parents, but who now are deceived and led into scandal by low-class, low-ranking gallants."

The words translated here as promiscuous (*sukizukishi*) and gallants (*sukimonodomo*), share a root (*suki*) that is found in a number of words used in ***Genji*** to describe and criticize the relations between men and women. *Suki* derived from the verb *suku* ("to be attracted to") which primarily described a strong interest in the opposite sex. The verb form is used only once in ***Genji,*** when Koremitsu thinks of Genji: "Although he is in a position where he should have a reputation for seriousness, in view of his youth and the way that women are drawn to him and admire his beauty, it would be a cruel shame if he were not interested in love" (*suku*).

Some *suki*-related words in ***Genji*** refer only to relations between men and women. *Sukiwaza* (*suki*-act) and *sukigoto* (*suki*-event) simply refer to a love affair of casual liaison. *Sukigokochi* (*suki*-feeling) and *sukigokoro* (*suki*-mind) describe the innate inclination to have such affairs. These words have only mildly negative connotations in the many contexts in which they appear in ***Genji.*** True censure is reserved for such words as *sukigamashiki* (unpleasantly *suki*) and *sukizukishi* (intensely *suki*).

Lower-ranking courtiers who devote themselves to having secret affairs are called *sukimono* (*suki*-person). The guards officer and man from the Ministry of Rites in the second chapter, Genji's attendant Koremitsu, and the errant Kashiwagi are the only named characters called *sukimono*. Koremitsu's enthusiasm for romantic intrigue is the catalyst in a number of Genji's youthful escapades, such as the affair with Yūgao. Such amorous behavior, although it may distress the parents of seducible girls, is apparently not surprising in a youth of middle rank who does not bear the illustrious background, and hence the responsibilities, of a man like Genji.

Genji envies such men their freedom. When by accident he first spies the young Murasaki he thinks, "How lovely she looked! This is why those gallants [*sukimonodomo*] are always on such expeditions discovering women one would not expect to find." The young Genji shares the romantic inclinations (*sukigokoro*) of his lesser friends and attendants, but he must be more careful how he realizes them. Position and influence in Genji's world depended on family background, wealth, appearance, and status. Since it is difficult for Genji to move about without attracting attention, any indiscretion is likely to become the subject of rumor and therefore potentially harmful. When Genji officiously lectures his son Yūgiri he claims, "I was raised in the palace where I was restricted and could not do as I pleased. I was careful because I knew that even the slightest indiscretion would lead to a charge of frivolousness. Nonetheless it seems that I was criticized as promiscuous [*sukizukishi*] and held in disrepute."

The word *sukizukishi* is used as a strong criticism in ***Genji*** although examples in Sei Shōnagon's *Pillow Book* indicate that the intense devotion it describes can have a favorable connotation when applied to such nonromantic pursuits as the study of poetry. It does not refer to the number of one's amorous relations, nor simply the enthusiasm with which they are pursued, but rather is determined by the appropriateness of one's liaisons.

In addition to marriage to several wives, a man's options in the Heian period included any number of secret affairs and both occasional and live-in lovers. The apparent guiding principle of all these relationships was that the status of a particular attachment was supposed to correspond approximately to the position of the woman in society. A woman of influential family and very high rank (for example, the daughter of an emperor) would properly be the object of a formal marriage. Secret affairs were appropriate for noblewomen of middle rank, while the women least important socially would not expect to be much more than live-in lovers.

As with so much else in Heian court life, hierarchy was dominant even when it was not explicit. The sensitive courtier was expected to balance such factors as birth, family, and political influence in his treatment of a woman he loved.

For the most part Genji manages to keep his marriages, secret affairs, and mistresses within the bounds of propriety. But from time to time in his youth he gave cause for vague rumor.

> There was doubt about the extent of Genji's secret loves and although it was his nature to disfavor insincere and unusually sudden promiscuity [*sukizukishisa*], there were times when he recklessly defied his own inclinations and set his heart on some impossible affair. This was an unfortunate tendency and there was a certain amount of impropriety in his behavior.

The two most improper loves in Genji's life are Fujitsubo and Rokujō. Genji admits this after both of them are dead.

> "In the past, even in relationships that should have been free of any particular torments there was still suffering because of my own promiscuous behavior [*sukizukishiki koto*]. There were many unfortunate results of these improper affairs and two of them continue to distress me and refuse to go away. The first is my affair with your late mother, Lady Rokujō."

The other, unmentioned and undiscovered affair was with Fujitsubo. The affair with Rokujō was improper because Genji refused to make her his wife. He kept her as a secret affair although her background and position required that she be treated better. When Genji's father first learns of his relationship with Lady Rokujō he scolds his son.

> "The late crown prince thought very much of her and it is a shame for you to treat someone who has been so favored as casually as if she were an ordinary person. And I think of her daughter, the high priestess, as one of my own children. For both of these reasons you should be considerate of her. You will be severely criticized for having such an affair [*sukiwaza*] and letting yourself be ruled by emotional whims."
>
> He was very displeased. Genji realized that his father was right and listened respectfully.
>
> "Don't give any woman cause for resentment by embarrassing her or being difficult," his father went on.
>
> Genji wondered what his father would think if he knew of his worst indiscretion. . . .
>
> For both Genji and the Rokujō lady it was a scandal [*sukigamashiku*] and a pity that the former emperor had heard of their affair and spoken of it that way. But although Genji felt very sorry for her, he had no intention of making their relationship public.

By refusing to take her as his wife and to publicly acknowledge their relationship, Genji demeans the lady's position in the eyes of the court. This neglect would cause resentment in most Heian women, but it is even more painful for the proud Rokujō lady. The battles of the carriages in the "Aoi" chapter illustrates the type of embarrassment that arises from his public indifference to her. Their affair is about five years old when Genji's father discovers it. Though we are told in "Yūgao" that Genji tired of her almost immediately, his visits must have continued with enough regularity to give rise to rumor. She is six years older than Genji and reportedly very sensitive of that difference. But it would seem from the carriages scene that she would gladly accept Genji's public attentions. His insensitivity to her is in obvious contrast to the devotion he shows his other women.

Genji's improprieties toward the Rokujō lady are matters of unkindness and neglect rather than passion. It would seem that Genji feels himself somewhat inferior in her presence. Her age and exquisite taste intimidate him in a way that is impossible with his other loves who are either younger, inferior, unattractive, or trained by himself. Genji punishes Rokujō for her superiority by continuing to visit her when he no longer loves her. The visits aggravate her resentment and frustration and cause embarrassment by occasioning rumor.

He is cruel to Fujitsubo too, but in her case his improper behavior is fueled by passion. The distress he causes her is due to his attentions, not his indifference. Fujitsubo is not the proper candidate for a romantic liaison of any sort. She belongs to his father who is, in addition, the emperor. Their child aggravates the crime. Genji risks everything and forces Fujitsubo to do so too.

Fortunately for Genji, his most terrible secret is never publicly revealed, or even suspected. Genji's greatest known indiscretion remains his treatment of Rokujō, and she makes him pay in her own way. Genji keeps most of his secret affairs properly secret, marries those he should, and keeps the rest handy at home. Only the aunt of the Safflower Lady, in a clearly malicious exaggeration, accuses Genji of bad behavior. "He has always been promiscuous" [*sukizukishiki migokoro*], she said, "and I've heard that he has broken off with all of the women he casually made love to here and there."

The *sukizukishi* person thinks only of himself and his desires and fails to treat the object of his passion as she deserves to be treated. Genji's love life is a busy one, yet not as busy as it could easily have been. Even so there is a falling off of romantic activity after Genji's return from Suma andAkashi, when he is presumably more mature.

Genji's friend and competitor, Tō no Chūjō, is presented as a strong contrast to Genji in romantic attitude. Whereas Genji is basically considerate, Tō no Chūjō is introduced as "a wanton trifler" (*sukigamashiki adabito*). This is about as strong a criticism as one could make of a man's romantic attitudes. The word *adabito* is particularly negative. Like *suki* the root *ada* is the basis for a number of related words. *Ada* is used to describe something that is fickle, faithless, unreliable, and fundamentally insubstantial. A person inconstant in love is called *ada naru,* or, more strongly, *adaadashi*. The verb *adaku* and noun *adake* describe such behavior, and *adameki* tells us when someone seems to be that way. But the most critical word is *adabito,* an *ada*-person, someone so thoroughly undependable in love that his unreliability is his chief feature.

A certain amount of inconstancy could be expected in a society that permitted so many simultaneous loves. The Suzaku Emperor, in considering Genji as a potential husband for his daughter, worries about Genji's "never-ending inconstancy" (*furisenu adake*). Genji's interest in so many women at the same time means that any wife of his would be forced to compete for his attention.

Correct behavior is a matter of degree. A man with a number of loves must leave some of them disappointed some of the time. If he is to avoid criticism he must give each her due to a relatively satisfactory degree. The Suzaku Emperor may be exaggerating Genji's case, but beside some others, such as Yūgiri, Genji could seem to have spread his affections somewhat thin.

We are told so little of the love life of Tō no Chūjō that the contrast with Genji that was established in the beginning of the novel is never fully worked out. They independently share Yūgao, compete over the Safflower Lady, and scuffle comically over the aged Gen no Naishi, but this is simply the romantic extension of the general competiton between them. At this point in her story Murasaki Shikibu does not seem to be particularly interested in investigating the emotional and social implications of different approaches to love. This is a question she reserves for the period after Genji's death, when the tone of the novel in general becomes more thoughtful and penetrating.

The subject is investigated ultimately by the contrast of the friends and competitors, Niou and Kaoru. Niou is the only character in ***Genji*** besides Tō no Chūjō who is called an *adabito,* and the manner of his inconstancy is described and illustrated frequently. Kaoru is drawn as an almost exact opposite. He is frequently referred to as a *mamebito* (*mame*-person). *Mame,* meaning sincere and serious, is the exact antonym of *ada,* and even implies a certain stiffness.

Kaoru's faithfulness does not mean that he loves only one woman or that he is uninterested in secret affairs. It means that he takes the duties of love seriously. "Because of the attentions of the Emperor and Empress, Kaoru had a splendid, unimpeded reputation despite his being a commoner, but in his own mind there were things he perceived about himself that caused him maturely to avoid carefree and self-indulgent love affairs [*sukigoto*] even when he was deeply moved."

Kaoru's deep concern for his public image leads him to conduct his love affairs in the proper manner. It is almost as if by his strict propriety and self-control he were attempting to atone for the carelessness of his mother and the rashness of his true father, Kashiwagi.

The women involved in secret affairs with Kaoru are protected from scandal by his caution. Since a secret affair by its very nature is likely to give rise to rumor and potential criticism sooner or later, Kaoru converts these affairs into more stable, less risky relationships. Unwilling to marry any of them, he offers them positions as attendants in his mother's house, where they would be likely to see him frequently. A woman employed in a household and as a mistress at the same time was called a *meshiudo,* literally, "a person who is summoned," in contrast to a secret love, who is visited in her own home. These women seem to have been treated slightly better than the other attendants, but they did not generally receive the attention or privileges of a wife or secret lover. On the other hand, they might have the most frequent opportunity to see their man. Murasaki Shikibu does not seem to have been especially interested in this level of romance. There are only two explicit references to *meshiudo* in ***Genji.*** The first is in a remark by Genji: "Prince Hotaru is unmarried but I've heard that his character seems to be very inconstant [*adamekite*] and that he is conducting numerous secret affairs. I've also heard that he has a number of mistresses [*meshiudo*] as well as women whom we would describe with unpleasant names."

Higekuro is also identified as having two mistresses, named Moku and Chūjō, who advise him against divorcing his wife, Prince Hotaru's daughter. After Murasaki's death we learn that Genji too had a mistress named Chūjō.

For a lady of lower rank this was an acceptable form of romance. Ukifune's attendant Jijū thinks of Niou, "I certainly wouldn't be able to sit here reading of such affection if I were the one he was interested in. I would go to serve his mother and see him regularly."

This does seem to be the sort of plan that Niou considers for Ukifune when he wonders how she would look in the service of his sister. Ukifune is the daughter of a prince, and although her father has not publicly recognized her, she is nevertheless in a position somewhat above that of an ordinary woman. If she were to go to live in the household of one of Niou's family as a lady-in-waiting, she would, like Kaoru's women, be accepting a position beneath her potential. Niou's intentions with respect to Ukifune are never entirely clear. He already has two wives and is known to be carrying on all sorts of secret affairs, some of which are considered improper. His wife Nakanokimi thinks of him, "Whenever it occurs to him to have a brief affair with one of the women in service, he will even go visiting her in her home, where he ought not to be." In other words Niou would improperly treat a woman of the attendant level as a true secret love, instead of as a *meshiudo.*

Niou is so fond of women that he has little regard for established custom. He is criticized not just for his behavior, but for his state of mind and character as well. He is called innately unreliable (*tanomishige naki*), inconstant (*adaadashi*), faithless (*adamekitaru*), promiscuous (*sukizukishi*), wanton (*sukigamashiki*), and a trifler (*adabito*). This criticism is brought upon him not by his sexual drive itself, but by the disregard he shows for the positions and feelings of the women who are the objects of his desire, as well as for his own reputation.

Because he is a prince, like Genji he can get away with behavior that would be unforgivable in a man of lesser position (and charm). The spoiled son of indulgent parents, he thinks only of his own emotion. It is typical of him that immediately after raping Ukifune he cries as he thinks of how hard it will be to see her again soon. This disregard for convention allows him a spontaneity that Ukifune comes to find exciting, and despite the problems he causes her, she falls in love with him.

Ukifune is repeatedly called immature. Although she is not particularly young (in "Ukifune" she is about 21 and Niou 27), she is often described as a person with "youthful feelings" and "childlike." Women of that sort are themselves held to be at fault if they are victimized. In this respect Ukifune resembles the Third Princess at the time of her affair with Kashiwagi. Genji philosophized, "When a woman is weak and docile, the man, perhaps because people despise her, is suddenly drawn to where he shouldn't be, and ends up losing control."

By contrast, Tamakazura represents the ideal, mature woman who is able to keep men under control. Genji admires such skills in a woman under his charge but is frustrated by them in a woman he would pursue, such as Asagao. If Ukifune were a more experienced and clever woman she could conceivably have saved herself from Niou. Instead she acts at first as if he were a newly discovered playmate who has come to draw her pictures and innocently amuse her. Between the time of Niou's first visit to Uji and Kaoru's visit, Ukifune comes to realize that she may, after all, be in something of a predicament. She starts to consider consequences. The gradual maturation which begins at that point is aided by frequent comparisons of Kaoru and Niou, a process imitated by the reader following her thoughts. The two are further contrasted in a continuing series of parallel episodes and meetings.

The contrast in character and the rivalry between Niou and Kaoru are important in the chapters from "Yadorigi" through "Kagerō." The competition over Ukifune is presaged by their contest over Nakanokimi. Ultimately the fact of rivalry becomes more important to them than the women they fight over, as each strives to bring the other disappointment. The bitterness and deception behind their competition is well-known to the reader, who is afforded glimpses of their thought, but to those around them they represent the pinnacle of civilization. They are special principally by virtue of their birth. Ukifune's mother, for example, echoes the sentiment of the times when she generalizes that "looks and character accord with inferiority and superiority, with low and high status."

The experience of Ukifune's mother is a demonstration of the importance of social status. Despite her high birth (she is a niece of Prince Hachi's late principal wife) she had been in service. This marked her as one who could not properly hope for more than the favor of the Prince as his mistress (*meshiudo*). Her plight is made worse by the Prince's regret and rejection of her daughter. But Ukifune's status is, ironically, somewhat better than her mother's. Although, as the Prince's unrecognized daughter she is relatively inferior, her mother manages to keep her from becoming an attendant. Her rural upbringing has prevented her from having the proper ladies-in-waiting and experience appropriate to her age, but the accident of birth and the gift of inactivity have made her theoretically marriageable to even the highest courtier.

If it were not for her attentive mother, Ukifune would probably have been forced to find employment. She would have been faced with the fate of Miyanokimi, a minor character introduced in "Kagerō" to further illustrate the rivalry between Kaoru and Niou. Miyanokimi is the daughter of a prince and a niece of Genji, but since her father is dead and her stepmother uninterested in her, she is forced to enter the service of the First Princess. This is considered a very unhappy decline in status. Kaoru thinks of her, "It seems as if it were only yesterday that her father considered marrying her to the crown prince and he made overtures to me too. Considering the declines that occur in this insubstantial world, one cannot even criticize those who drown themselves."

Status was almost everything at the Heian court and Ukifune's uncertain position makes her particularly vulnerable. Ukifune's mother is very aware of her daughter's position and the suffering that plagues women of all levels "both in this world and the next." She is convinced that men love best the women of highest birth. Nonetheless, when she sees Niou and Kaoru, reason gives way to something like adoration. Despite their different personalities they are both—again mostly by virtue of birth—paragons of all that is worth admiring in a nobleman. In the opinion of Ukifune's mother, just to see them, even if only once a year, would be worth sacrifice. Such an annual event she even compares to the annual meeting of stars across the milky way. Even reducing oneself to the level of a lady-in-waiting would, she thinks, be worthwhile if it brought occasional access to such examples of beauty and refinement. We might expect Ukifune's mother to feel that way, as this is the course she chose for her own life.

In dealing with men like Kaoru and Niou, a woman's risks and rewards were greater. Ukifune, too immature to make an informed choice, is directed by her mother, who hopes Ukifune will be able to avoid a decline in status like her own.

We are not told directly what Niou or Kaoru intend to do with Ukifune once they have brought her to the capital from Uji. The clearest statement of intentions concerns Kaoru, always the careful planner: "If he were to bring her to his house and seriously establish her there in the near future, the rumors would be inconvenient. At the same time he probably did not intend to include her in an ordinary way among that group that he kept here and there."

This probably means that Kaoru did not want to take Ukifune immediately as a second wife, nor did he want to make her a mistress (like Azechi or Kosaishō . . .) by bringing her as an attendant into his mother's house. Since he has been married less than half a year, it would seem politic not to take on another wife of lesser status so soon. The only alternative is to establish Ukifune independently in a place where he can have a secret affair with her, until something more serious is possible.

To head off the potential resentment of his wife, he announces to her that he would like to bring back into town a secret love he has had "for years" and whom he had abandoned in the country. His excuse is that his recent marriage has caused him to give up his old plan of rejecting the world to lead a religious life. Although he claims that this old friend is of too low a status to occasion significant gossip, the fact that he bothers to discuss the issue indicates that he intends more for Ukifune than a casual liaison of his usual sort.

Once Ukifune is presumed lost, Kaoru's rationalizing mind reviews her importance. After marveling that she has had the fond affection of Niou, a prince, he thinks of himself,

> "Despite my own position and the fact that I have the daughter of a reigning emperor, I thought Ukifune no less charming. Now that I know she is gone I am even less able to quiet my heart. This is ridiculous."

As a proper courtier Kaoru studies his problems in the light of relative rank and precedent. With Ukifune he ran a certain risk.

> "Certainly my connection to Ukifune's family is nothing special, but hadn't even emperors taken the daughters of women no more important than Ukifune's mother? How could anyone have criticized me if I were to have shown favor where it was inevitable? Frequently commoners like myself took women of inferior status or those experienced in love. Even if people were to have called Ukifune a governor's daughter, I intended from the beginning that my treatment of her would not have sullied me."

Niou's intentions for Ukifune are unclear because he has so little interest in planning or propriety. He considers that Ukifune would do well in his sister's service, but his principal concern is simply to win her from Kaoru and then to hide her. He would carry on his affair whatever her status. It is characteristic of his "promiscuous" personality to disregard the consequences.

His true affection for Nakanokimi, strengthened by their son, would have put him in a difficult position if he were to have done enough for Ukifune in the capital to have made his wife jealous of her. When Niou compares the two he admits that Nakanokimi is superior, and we are led to speculate that Ukifune would have been little more than a brief affair. (pp. 217-30)

Andrew Pekarik, "Rivals in Love," in Ukifune: Love in "The Tale of Genji," *edited by Andrew Pekarik, Columbia University Press, 1982, pp. 217-30.*

WILLIAM J. PUETTE (essay date 1983)

[*In the following excerpt, Puette relates* The Tale *to the salient features of Japanese culture during the Heian period.*]

Genji Monogatari is, many agree, the world's oldest novel, written a thousand years ago, but almost totally unknown to Western readers until the appearance of the fine translations of Arthur Waley and Edward G. Seidensticker in this century.

Before launching into a reading of this momentous work, it is important to have some grasp of the historical and cultural climate of the period of Japanese development that produced it. Ivan Morris makes the following crucial observation in his treatise, *The World of Shining Prince:*

> If the informed Westerner was asked to enumerate the outstanding features of traditional Japan, his list might well consist of the following: in *culture* Nō and Kabuki drama, Haiku poems, Ukiyoe colour prints, samisen music, and various activities like the tea ceremony, flower arrangement, and the preparation of miniature landscapes that are related to Zen influence; in *society* the two-sworded samurai and the geisha; in *ideas* the Zen approach to human experience with its stress on an intuitive understanding of the truth and sudden enlightenment, the samurai ethic sometimes known as

A scene from The Tale of Genji *handscroll, created in the twelfth century.*

> *Bushidō,* a great concern with the conflicting demands of duty and human affection, and an extremely permissive attitude to suicide, especially love suicides; in *domestic architecture,* fitted straw matting (*tatami*), large communal baths, *tokonoma* alcoves for hanging *kakemono;* in *food,* raw fish and soy sauce. . . . The list would of course be entirely correct. Yet not a single one of these items existed in Murasaki's world, and many of them would have seemed as alien to her as they do to the modern Westerner.

Indeed, the greatest barriers to the modern reader's appreciation of this novel are the stereotypes and invalid preconceptions or expectations that we are likely to impose upon it. Heian Japan (A.D. 794-1186) was a period so unlike modern Japan, and so unlike any other periods familiar to us, that we are obliged to sweep away all of our preconceptions and try to understand the world on its own terms, as we see it in the novel.

The period is called Heian after the name of the capital which in 794 had been moved from the old site at Nara to eventually occupy the area which today is known as Kyōto. The word "heian" . . . means "peace and tranquillity" and was adapted, as was the plan of the city itself, from the Chinese Tang capital at Chang-an . . . , occupying a six-thousand-acre mass of land approximately three and a half miles long and three miles wide.

The move, it is believed, was made because of the political grip that the Kegon sect Buddhist monasteries had obtained at Nara (then called Heijō . . .). Emperor Kammu, a Confucianist at heart, simply moved out from underneath them and established his court at Heian Kyō. There he enfranchised the less ambitious, more ascetic Tendai and Shingon sects, who were inclined to keep to their monasteries in the surrounding mountains outside of the city.

As the capital, the city was designed and built to accommodate almost exclusively the emperor and the ranked hierarchy of his court. Consequently, the world of ***The Tale of Genji*** is not really the world of Heian Japan at large; it is more accurately the refined world of the inner circle of the highest class in the land. In Chapter 2, for instance, when reference is made to the three classes, we should not make the mistake of supposing the reference was in large terms to the nation's aristocracy, its middle-class merchants, and its peasant farmers. Rather, as John Whitney Hall describes:

> The aristocracy as a whole . . . fell into three general divisions. The first three ranks were especially privileged and were available to only a few of the families closest to the imperial house.

The great majority of people, not of the aristocratic class at all, were barely considered human, their appearance and language being so disparate. Conversely, at the top of the pyramid was the emperor and his immediate family whose majesty was so distinguished as to have them commonly known as "cloud-dwellers" (*kumo-no-uebito*). In fact, whenever the emperor was depicted in drawings or picture scrolls, it was an artistic convention to showonly the lower extensions of his robes descending from a heavenly mantle of clouds.

So centralized was this aristocracy at Heian Kyō that it became a kind of Mecca; indeed, for the privileged few, it was the only place of any worth. Throughout the ***Tale*** there abound references to the primacy of the capital. To a Heian patrician the worst possible fate was exile from its compound, and the worst possible stigmas on an aspiring aristocrat's pedigree would have been a vulgar origin in the provinces (i.e., anywhere but the capital) and countrified (*inakabitaru*) manners or speech. Unlike the previous Nara period, all that was worthy, noble, and beautiful was believed to reside exclusively in the capital. It was, then, truly a brilliant city and the focal point for all national development.

In the centuries just preceding this period, as a result of what is called the Taika Reform, the court had been involved in a wholesale absorption of practically all aspects of the illustrious Chinese Tang culture. At the Nara court all that was Chinese was so much in vogue that even the language was being conscientiously studied. Yet in the Heian period portrayed in ***The***

Tale of Genji, these Chinese systems and beliefs, having been digested, were in the process of essential modification to accommodate native Japanese sensibilities.

Confucianism was still the mainstay of formal education and so influenced the atmosphere at court that all formal edicts and even court poetry were composed in Chinese, as we see in Chapter 8, "Hana no En." Unfortunately, this Confucian-Buddhist culture was primarily a male preserve. Women were deliberately excluded. Yet the political structure of Heian Japan was such that considerable influence and power were accorded to women of the aristocracy. So, while the men learned Chinese and studied the Confucian classics, Heian women were left to amuse themselves by mastering their native Japanese via the newly devised phonetic writing system and the Nara-period poetry anthologies. Of course, the men needed to know all these things as well so that they could deal socially with the women. As a result, the influence of Chinese began to wane, becoming more and more a specialized, exclusively masculine indulgence, less and less related to the realities of political connivance in court life.

On the other hand, women were important particularly because they were used to extend and infiltrate, by marriage, family- or clan-power cliques. The most famous and successful practitioner of this technique was the Fujiwara family, which had managed to be the prime supplier of imperial consorts during most of the Heian period. Before long, almost all of the emperors had Fujiwara mothers and Fujiwara wives, until the Fujiwara family was practically in control of the throne.

It is no surprise, then, to see the tremendous concern in the novel with marital alliances, for practically the only way of climbing the Heian social ladder was by securing a good match for one's offspring. Note how often fathers seem to throw their daughters at Genji's feet, hoping to match their fortunes with such an obviously promising prince, who was on the one hand clearly a member of the imperial family and, on the other, owing to his placement in the non-royal Gen clan, not beyond the reach of a reasonably well-bred aristocrat. To further simplify matters, polygamy was an accepted part of the social web. Though a single major marriage was usually arranged early in childhood, later, on the basis of personal preference, valid lesser marriages could be effected simply by mutual consent upon the third successful connubial visitation. However, for political reasons, a courtier with a wife whose family was powerfully connected at court, such as the Fujiwara, was less likely to enjoy a second or third marriage. Indeed, even an emperor's designs could be thwarted by the intrigues of the Fujiwara.

In ***The Tale of Genji,*** as a matter of fact, the Fujiwara clan is represented in the persons of Lady Aoi and Tō-no-Chūjō. It is interesting to chart the fortunes of their family in this powerful position as it moves through the three generations depicted; though we must be careful to remember that this is, after all, a novel focusing on manners and the high society of the Heian court. The political events are generally peripheral to the plot.

For the denizens of the capital, the actual world of daily activities was, by comparison to ours, largely nocturnal, where time was solely governed by the flow of events. People slept, ate, and committed their other quotidian duties around their social activities, which more often than not were conducted at night, till just before dawn. Even the design of the buildings and furniture required that, for the most part, the courtiers lived out their lives in a state of semi-darkness, which certainly increases the significance of Genji's reputation as "the shining prince."

Indeed, so much was the woman's world shuttered and protected from the light of day, that simple identification could often be a difficult feat (note the "Oborozukiyo" episode in Chapter 8 as just one example). Women of the upper classes were scrupulously sheltered from public view by a plethora of screens and curtains, as well as by a retinue of ladies-in-waiting and attendants. Hence, eavesdropping and voyeurism, far from being considered perverted indulgences, were raised to a fine art.

There were, however, more artful means by which identification was possible. First, women of the court wore very elaborate and distinctive robes, layered and arranged tastefully so that color gradations and combinations could be admired in the long, dangling sleeves which were often allowed to project beneath their protective screens or from their carriage doors in transit, in a style referred to as *idashi-guruma*.

Second, as their robes were worn and slept in for extended periods of time, they were delicately incensed and perfumed with distinctive fragrances, especially created by the wearer, which could easily be recognized by anyone of good breeding. In fact, these garments could be so formidable that, as in the case of Nyōsan, the Third Princess of Suzaku, they might outweigh the inhabitant. (pp. 23-30)

Little emphasis was placed on the physical features in judging the beauty of a lady. Her teeth would normally be blackened, and her generally plump face would be powdered white and artificial eyebrows painted over her real ones. Like classical European tastes, a slight corpulence was believed to enhance one's natural beauty. The only important physical trait that was admired and praised in poetry was a lady's hair, which was groomed to be at least as long as she was tall. (p. 32)

In Heian Japan of the time that the ***Genji Monogatari*** was written, there existed a curious blending of several religious strains.

To begin with, the native religion of Japan is Shintō . . . , literally "the Way of the Gods," according to which all the beautiful and vital manifestations of nature are deified. Furthermore, the living souls of departed ancestors were believed to pass into nature, thereby linking man and nature in a mystic union. Life and the forces of life in nature were glorified. Likewise, death and its forces of decay were abhorred and regarded as pollutants. At the top of the Shintō hierarchy, then as now, is the emperor who, as living descendant of the Sun Goddess and, therefore, grand ancestor of all the Japanese, is the high priest of Shintō and purest representative of the Way of the Gods on earth. In fact, the overwhelming concern of Shintō is with purity. Most of its rites deal with purification and lustration. Taboos, known as *mono-imi,* result when people or things are defiled by such negative forces as death, disease, and even menstruation, requiring elaborate rituals to restore their purity.

Very early, though, from China and Korea came three major modifications to Shintō. The first of these was Confucianism (Jukyō . . .) which had a vast political impact from about A.D. 645 with the issuance of various imperial edicts that came to be known as the Taika Reform. Though superficially Confucianism shaped the Japanese bureaucracy and even the map of the capital, its severe ethics had little permanent effect on Heian religious tenets. It is true that the Doctrine of Filial Piety, which dictates strict observance of the loyalty and honor that should exist between members of a family, did become especially popular as it tended to fit into the Shintō sense of ancestral sanctity, but the cool logic of the Doctrine of the Mean and the relentlessly dispassionate concept of "the virtuous bureaucrat" did not flourish in Japanese soil.

Taoism, pronounced *dah oh ism,* (Dōkyō . . .) on the other hand, did make a strong impression. The magical formulas of Taoist rituals, in particular, were so similar to the familiar Shintō ceremonies that the Japanese readily adopted the Taoist obsession with astrological and numerological codes, adopting as well the *in-yō,* or yin-yang, explanation of nature's dualism. The yin-yang, visually symbolized in the *tomoe* crest, expresses the notion that reality exists in the dynamic tension or balance struck between passive (yin) and active (yang) forces. Taoism further teaches that there is no true purity, that opposites tend to converge, for in the midst of yin there is always yang (note the little white circle in the black comma), as in the midst of yang there is always yin. Although this seems to run against the grain of Shintō belief, as ever the Japanese have happily accommodated paradox when the truth is keenly felt or intuited.

Perhaps the best example of this penchant for accepting the incongruous can be seen in the third and most influential import from China: Buddhism or Bukkyō. . . . While it is true that Buddhism originated in India, the Buddhism that had found its way to Japan by the tenth century was clearly a Chinese product. When we talk about Heian Buddhism, we must be careful not to confuse it with the well-known Zen Buddhism, which did not develop in Japan until long after the Tale was written. The primary sects, as seen in the ***Genji Monogatari,*** were Tendai and Shingon (esoteric) Buddhism.

If some of the other religious ideas introduced to Japan had non-Shintō elements, Buddhism seemed its very antithesis. While Shintō had almost a phobia about death and decay, Buddhism seemed determined to encourage morbid reflection. The way of the Buddha is to seek salvation by enlightenment, that is, by realizing that the beauties of nature and the physical pleasures of life are illusory and transient (a concept known as *mujōkan*). Man's material and emotional desires only tie him to a continuous cycle of rebirths. To seek enlightenment, man must put aside the things of this world and concentrate on the holy word of the scriptures, primarily the Lotus Sutra. All efforts made to achieve enlightenment can, even if enlightenment itself is not achieved, benefit one in the next incarnation, and, conversely, evil deeds will assuredly follow one as a curse from one existence to the next. This concept of moral causality is known in Sanskrit as *karma* (a term used often in the Waley translation, but scrupulously avoided by Seidensticker). To the Heian mind *karma* neatly accounted for the apparent inequities in the world: why one man, despite his virtue, seemed to have nothing but troubles to live with, or why another was blessed with continuous satisfaction. It was also employed to explain such strong emotional affinities as when one falls in love at first sight, for people once bonded together in a previous life were likely to be pushed together by the force of *karma*. In fact, the term is often translated as "fate" because the Japanese were very fatalistic about the inevitable workings of *karma*.

Thus, in Buddhism all people are encouraged to put aside their family attachments (violating precepts of filial piety), divorce themselves totally from their material possessions, and take holy orders, so that upon their deaths they may be reborn as Buddhas on a lotus petal and escape forever the ignorance and desire of earthly existence. In ***The Tale of Genji,*** therefore, when reference is made to nuns and priests, we must remember that these were not a special caste or vocation as they are in Christian churches, but ordinary members of the court who, feeling that their lives or careers had come to an end, were preparing themselves for the final step by renouncing the world and trying to sever their karmic bonds.

Perhaps the most alien aspect of ***The Tale of Genji*** is the tremendous preoccupation of its characters with artistic pursuits. It is, in fact, impossible to exaggerate the importance of aesthetics in general, and poetry in particular, to the plot, theme, and character development of the novel. We might be familiar with other cultures in which virtues such as spiritual integrity, a ready wit, or simply military prowess figured so highly as to advance the esteem we would have of characters so endowed. But in ***The Tale of Genji*** the most important of all virtues, the aristocratic touchstone by which men and women at court were ultimately measured, was essentially their sensitivity to the inherent pathos of things, especially in the traditional arts.

This aesthetic was known as *aware* and is as difficult a term to translate as can be found. It has been variously defined:

> . . . a word frequently used in ***The Tale of Genji*** and other classical literature. Among its wide range of meanings are "pathetic," "moving," "beautiful." The phrase *mono no aware* corresponds to *lacrimae rerum,* "the pity of things," which is often taken to be the underlying theme of Murasaki's novel.
>
> Morris

> . . . exclamation of sympathy or distress.
>
> Waley

> . . . an ejaculation of vague and undefined sadness.
>
> Seidensticker

> In old texts we find it first used as an exclamation of surprise or delight, man's natural reaction to what an early Western critic of Japanese literature called the "ahness" of things . . . elsewhere it expressed a gentle sorrow, adding not so much a meaning as a color or a perfume to a sentence.
>
> Tsunoda, Keene, De Bary

> The term suggests an anguish that takes on beauty or a sensitivity to the finest—the saddest—beauties. Both the condition and the appreciative sensibility are implied.
>
> Miner

> . . . that which stirs cultivated sympathies by touching them with beauty, sadness, and the awareness of ephemeral experience.
>
> Miner

> . . . "an emotional awareness." *Aware* has a long history, from its origins in an exclamation expressive of admiration, surprise, or delight, to its modern meaning of "misery." In the Heian Period its most characteristic use was to express a feeling of gentle, sorrow-tinged appreciation of transitory beauty.
>
> Cranston

> Originally an interjection ("Ah!" "Oh!"). From the Heian period on, it was used to express controlled feeling. As an aesthetic concept, it stands for elegance, or, at times, for pathos.
>
> Hisamatsu

> . . . an emotion of tender affection in which there is both passion and sympathy . . . in such moments the sentiment is instinctively felt, for in them joy mingles with a kind of agreeable melancholy.
>
> Anesaki

It is also possible to understand this sentiment as an outgrowth of the religious conflict between the nature-worshiping creed of Shintō and the Buddhistic abhorrence of natural phenomena; the conflict between a philosophy urging oneness with nature on the one hand, against a philosophy urging transcendence of nature on the other. Caught in this ideological vise, the Japanese of the Heian period blended to their needs a sentiment which commanded a pathetic appreciation for illusory beauty.

As an aesthetic, it touched all of the arts and all of nature, but we see its most perfect expression in poetry. There are nearly eight hundred poems woven into the Tale, representing not the formalistic Chinese poetry composed by the males at court competitions, but the native Japanese *tanka* or *waka* (not *haiku*) form, consisting of thirty-one syllables. As is surely the case in all literatures, the linguistic peculiarities of the language largely determine the possible verse forms. We cannot expect sonnets to spill out of every tongue, nor was Chinese poetry particularly successful in the completely different character of Japanese speech, which is neatly described here by Amy Lowell:

> Japanese is a syllabic language like our own, but, unlike our own, it is not accented. Also, every syllable ends with a vowel, the consequence being that there are only five rhymes in the whole language. Since the employment of so restricted a rhyme scheme would be unbearably monotonous, the Japanese hit upon the happy idea of counting syllables. Our metrical verse also counts syllables, but we combine them into different kinds of accented feet. Without accent, this was not possible, so the Japanese poet limits their number and uses them in a pattern of alternating lines. His prosody is based upon the numbers five and seven, a five-syllable line alternating with one of seven syllables with, in some forms, two seven-syllable lines together at the end of a period, in the manner of our couplet. The favourite form, the "tanka," is in thirty-one syllables, and runs five, seven, five, seven, seven.

This poetry was usually composed in momentary flashes of inspiration. Most frequently, it was used as a subtle means of communication between lovers and friends, and was, therefore, an important part of daily life. Relying heavily on suggested meaning rather than overt expression, the images in these poems were used to hint at very subjective emotions, as people were often associated with flowers, trees, or other aesthetically acceptable images.

Furthermore, *waka* was composed according to accepted conventions that are difficult to discern even in the best translation. There was an extensive body of poetry from the Nara period already anthologized and circulated, and often a poet would use a well-known epithet, called a "pillow-word" or *makura-kotoba,* to describe a common subject or emotion. Or the reference might be more specific and allude directly to a famous poem, subtly changing a word or two to relate it to the new circumstances. This device was known as "allusive-variation" (*furu-kotoba* or *honkadori*) and was much admired when skillfully handled. Its recognition in the more obscure cases of its use was a sure test of breeding and discrimination, and Seidensticker's frequent notes attest to its popularity.

Finally, a poem might employ an elaborate pun or sophisticated double entendre, called a "pivot-word" or *kake-kotoba.* Careful manipulation of such a device could provide a way for courtiers to suggest a more explicit word which, by itself, might be considered indelicate. . . . [In] Chapter 13, "Akashi," as the newly exiled Genji is at last able to see the remote island of Awaji, the island's name becomes a literary nexus, and the beauty of the acclaimed coast now mixes with the sting of his banishment in this *waka:* . . .

> Oh, foam-flecked island that wast nothing to me, even such sorrow as mine is, on this night of flawless beauty thou hast power to heal.
>
> Waley

> Awaji: in your name is all my sadness,
> And clear you stand in the light of the moon tonight.
>
> Seidensticker

As Seidensticker's note informs us, there is a three-way *kake-kotoba* with the word *awa,* "foam," touching the name of the island, Awaji, and the sentiment, *aware.* Here is also an allusion to the *Shinkokinshū* poem number 1513:

> Awaji in the moonlight, like distant foam:
> From these cloudy sovereign heights it seems so near.
>
> Seidensticker

For Genji the foam is no longer distant. Remembering that *Shinkokinshū* poem, but seeing the cloudlessness of this night by contrast, Genji is painfully but sweetly reminded that he is now banished from the court.

In all things, therefore, a sensitivity to the delicacy and subtlety of beauty was most admired. Not only was a courtier expected to compose delicate poetry, but the way each poem was written, the shading of the ink, the selection of the paper, and more were also meticulously scrutinized for evidence of courtly sensibility.

Western readers often wonder in what respect Genji could be the object of so much admiration, not only in the novel itself, but as an idealized character throughout the history of Japanese literature. We must look for the answer not in our own concepts of heroic action, nor even in existing Japanese codes of stoic nobility, but in the Heian ideals of aristocratic sensibility, of which Genji is the quintessential manifestation. (pp. 37-49)

William J. Puette, in his Guide to "The Tale of Genji" by Murasaki Shikibu, *Charles E. Tuttle Company, 1983, 196 p.*

DORIS G. BARGEN (essay date 1986)

[*In the following excerpt, Bargen considers the social implications of the episodes of spirit possession in* The Tale, *suggesting that they can be viewed "as a female protest against the polygyny of Heian Society."*

The Japanese national classic, Murasaki Shikibu's ***Genji monogatari,*** is chiefly valued for its exquisitely drawn psychological character portrayals and detailed realistic descriptions of tenth-century Heian court life. Yet the work also contains highly dramatic episodes and animated scenes of spirit possession. One of the most memorable scenes occurs in a minor episode in which Higekuro's wife dumps ashes on her husband's head. She is violently enraged by the prospect of being ousted from her position as principal wife by a new mistress, and she is possessed. According to the Heian practice of polygyny, she was expected to tolerate another woman joining the household, and therefore her indignant and undignified behavior is perceived as that of a madwoman:

> Suddenly she stood up, swept the cover from a large censer, stepped behind her husband, and poured the contents over his head. There had been no time to restrain her. The women [in attendance] were stunned.
>
> The powdery ashes bit into his eyes and nostrils. Blinded, he tried to brush them away, but found them so clinging and stubborn that he had to throw off even his underrobes. *If she had not had the excuse of her derangement* he would have marched from her presence and vowed never to return. It was a *very perverse* sort of spirit that possessed her.

Higekuro's wife's case is the exception to the rule which takes spirit possession seriously and requires that it be treated with respect. Inasmuch as spirit possession "permits the expression of things that cannot be said ordinarily or directly," it is, as a technique of communication, eminently suited to the general cultural preference for elegant indirections and subtleties in Heian Japan (A.D. 794-1185). Thus it is the very directness of the distraught woman's physical attack on Higekuro that renders her blunt action comic. Precisely because her behavior is undisguised and straightforward, and thereby unconventional, it paradoxically appears as an instance of the infuriated lady's "derangement." This particular madcap version of possession is counterproductive; direct action defeats its own purpose.

The relative simplicity of this comic possession contrasts with the extraordinary complexity of a series of possessions which involve the eponymous hero of ***The Tale of Genji.*** In the first of them, Genji's affair with Yūgao is suddenly terminated when Yūgao is possessed. Her death puzzles Genji and his puzzlement leads us to speculate about the phenomenon of spirit possession and its relation to gender and courtship conventions at the peak of the Heian period (c. 950-1050). These speculations enable us to understand spirit possession as a female protest against the polygyny of Heian Society.

A few readers have begun to speculate about ***The Tale of Genji***'s four major possession cases. William H. McCullough has pointed to "the havoc wreaked upon Genji's lovers and wives by the possessing spirit of the very possessive Lady Rokujō," whose spirit he sees as "one of the principal unifying elements" in the ***Genji.*** McCullough draws several useful conclusions. First, the victims of spirit possession in Heian times—indeed in most cultures, and especially in polygynous societies—are women. Second, the spirit who attacks is most typically that of a dead person, and third, the spirit's motive is jealousy. These insights are valuable, but, in light of the questions raised by anthropologists, they merely lay the foundation for an investigation into the very complex interaction between the possessed, the possessor and society.

The phenomenon of spirit possession is an old and universal one, but anthropological research into the subject is relatively new. The opinion that spirit possession is *not* simply a primitive, pathological practice of superstitious peoples is even more recent. Since the pioneering work of Oesterreich (1921), the many varieties of spirit possession have been divided into two basic categories: voluntary (self-induced) and involuntary (spontaneous). Similarly, the response has been twofold: spirit possession is either thought to be desirable or undesirable. In the latter case, exorcism is deemed necessary. In the most problematic case, then, someone involuntarily enters an "altered state of consciousness" that is considered undesirable or is feared by society at large. It is important to note that spirit possession is not merely a conflict between the possessed and the possessor; it is also a test of the values of the whole society. These values are usually, but not always, represented by exorcists who employ a medium to approach the possessed and drive out and identify the spirit. With identification of the spirit and the promise to meet its wishes, the spell is broken, the victim and the spectators are relieved and, curiously, life goes on much as it had, until the next seizure occurs. Unlike witches, the possessed are not persecuted or punished.

When such dramatic occurrences are placed in the realm of fiction, they must be understood within their literary context. While in reality altered states of consciousness can have purely physical causes, as, for example, the hardships of pregnancy, nutritional deficiencies or the use of drugs, the literary manifestations of possession can usually be traced to grave psychological disturbances or conflicts.

Certain peculiarities about the phenomenon of spirit possession—such as the elements of ecstasy and self-enhancement in the state of dissociation or speaking in different voices—have raised important questions about the meaning of spirit possession. Who are the possessed in relation to the possessor and the witnesses? What public statement does the intensely private and esoteric experience of spirit possession make about the society in which it occurs? In other words, what do the spirits' complaints and wishes, voiced either directly through the possessed, or indirectly through a medium, say about the values of the society? How successful is possession as a psychological strategy?

It is mainly women who are possessed because they and other peripheral groups oppressed by the dominant group release their tensions and frustrations in this way. Their protest, however, is not directed straightforwardly at the dominant group, but indirectly, through the mysterious esoteric language of spirit possession. Joan M. Lewis has aptly described the nature of this protest as "oblique aggressive strategy."

Jealousy is traditionally regarded as the major force behind spirit possession in the ***Genji*** because female grievances are revealed to be rooted in the polygynous system which constantly threatens women's status and lowers their self-esteem in the very sensitive matter of sexual relations. Thus it is a conspicuous fact that the mainly female authors of Heian tales and diaries voice complaints that are universal to polygynous societies, namely, that competing wives, concubines and mistresses become the agents or victims of jealousy. And to the extent that Heian aristocratic women enjoyed exceptional freedom and economic independence, they made bold to express psychological conflicts in a varity of ways. However, from a pool of diverse grievances, scholars have singled out jealousy as the symbol—or source—of women's rebellious rejection of their assigned role in society.

As the case of Higekuro's wife demonstrates, openly violent, aggressive behavior was viewed with contempt in an elitist society that prided itself on its refined esthetics and an exquisite code of manners in harmony with the society's hierarchical structure. Therefore hostile and aggressive feelings could not easily find expression. They must be repressed or find their own culturally accepted idiom. Higekuro's wife's behavior was not respectable because of the violation of options available to women under intense psychological pressures. These options encompassed a wide range of activities, such as religious austerities or devotion to the arts. Spirit possession was a woman's most dramatic strategy.

Yūgao's possession is the first of the major possession cases. It is prototypical and symptomatic of the cause and purpose of possession, even though its technical apparatus is minimal: there are no exorcists, no mediums and consequently no public ritual. The only spectator, aside from a lady-in-waiting who merely confirms but does not perceive the possessing spirit, is Genji, the woman's lover. Although spirit possession constitutes the climax of an intensely private love affair, its larger social implications cannot be ignored. What especially distinguishes this possession from the others is its direct termination in death.

For many critics of the ***Genji,*** spirit possession is virtually synonymous with death. Yet between the first and the last case a remarkable progression takes place. While possession and death are practically synchronic events in the first case, in the next three cases the fatal consequences of spirit possession are postponed or avoided completely. Consequently, a note of hope is sounded in the last case: a suicide attempt is converted into spirit possession, which is transformed in turn into an act of artistic affirmation. Ukifune, the last of the heroines in the ***Genji,*** sublimates her self-destructive desires into spirit possession and then resolves her psychological crisis through the therapeutic composition of poetic memoirs.

Yūgao, however, is seized by a spirit, and dies. The mystery of the sudden possession and its tragic end challenges the witness's analytic powers. The events before and after the climax of the affair—the possession—are viewed mainly from Genji's male perspective. His biased interpretation complicates and psychologically charges this famous episode.

Crucial to an understanding of the affair between the son of an emperor and an aristocratic lady of relatively low rank are the lovers' secretive motivations that lead to the mysterious, supernatural event of spirit possession. The mystery of this affair is largely due to the lovers' sustained incognito. One singular aspect of Heian courtship ritual was that the lover frequently had no inkling of his or her sexual partner's physical appearance and identity before the consummation of the affair. Esthetic responsiveness was all that mattered and furtive glimpses of the prospective lover were ever so much more enticing than full visibility. In the case of Genji and Yūgao, however, the couple's tantalizing secretiveness continues beyond their initial encounters and into the phase of intimacy. Why? The lovers' previous adventures determine their response to each other, and provide a clue to the tragedy that results from their departure from courtship routines.

Yūgao's unhappy love affair with Genji's best friend Tō no Chūjō bears directly on her subsequent relations with Genji. An orphan without the parental backing necessary for marriage, Yūgao was at the mercy of her former lover and had no choice but to forgive him for his frequent neglect. However, after three years of mistreatment, her patience was exhausted. When Tō no Chūjō's wife dealt the last blow by humiliating her, Yūgao resolved to disappear, to live without her lover's support, and to take with her the daughter she had borne him—a strategy that contained elements of self-assertion, protest and self-sacrifice. Her inaccessibility revives Tō no Chūjō's interest. In the famous "Rainy-Night Discussion," he confides to Genji the story of his lost love. Genji is intrigued and, through a fortuitous turn of events, begins to court Yūgao, whom he does not initially recognize as the lost lady described by his friend. She is caught in a psychological conflict between lovers which provokes her to terminate the new relationship with a strategy that is the logical, forceful extension of the first: spirit possession and death.

Genji's discovery of Yūgao is serendipitous. He is attracted by a humble flower whose name is the sobriquet of the woman of lower rank with whom it is symbolically associated: Yūgao. When Genji comes upon the woman, he is captivated by the Yūgao flower, its mystery deepened by the poem penned on the fan that accompanies it. Genji pursues this enticing flower-woman despite the fact that he is married to Aoi (Tō no Chūjō's sister) and is still interested in his first passion (Lady Rokujō) and in other ladies of high rank. Much later when Genji has taken not only the flower but also the woman, he fully realizes what he had merely suspected: he has coveted his best friend's love.

While Yūgao sees herself in two triangular situations—as a rival of Tō no Chūjō's wife for his love and as the object of an implicit rivalry between Genji and Tō no Chūjō—Genji perceives quite a different triangle. Aware of his own promiscuity, he imagines his neglected ladies consumed by jealousy over the new mistress. From his perspective, the figural constellation seems initially to involve several females and one male. Genji's subsequent awareness of Yūgao's identity complicates matters considerably. The ominous thought crosses Genji's mind: "Might she be the lady of whom Tō no Chūjō had spoken that rainy night?" The possibility of identifying Yūgao with Tō no Chūjō's unassertive lady is so disturbing that it is, at first, entirely repressed: "Genji did not know who the lady was and he did not want her to know who he was." (pp. 15-19)

As his love becomes like "madness," Genji grows increasingly reflective about his fascination with Yūgao: "What was there about her, he asked himself over and over again, that drew him to her?" The lady, in addition to her profound excitement, is unduly worried and through her anxiety betrays the fact that she is experiencing this affair in the traumatic context of the previous one: "She was frightened, as if he were an apparition from an old story." While the bittersweet memory of the "old story" with Tō no Chūjō causes her to repress the source of her pain, the mystery of her new incognito lover evokes once more the half-forgotten past which casts its ominous shadow on the present and well into her daughter's future. It is unacknowledged triangular complications of this kind that trigger spirit possession.

Genji alludes lightheartedly to the uncanny mystery of their bond. The metaphor used for their reciprocal seductiveness is the fox: "Which of us is the mischievous fox spirit?" As the fox in Japanese folklore induces sexual passion by taking either male or female shape, the image is appropriate and occurs in other possession scenes. Approaching the height of his passion, Genji is again reminded of Tō no Chūjō's unassertive lady. Although he intuitively recognizes a strong resemblance between his friend's lost love and Yūgao, his behavior indicates that he still resists identifying the two.

It is at this point that the first crisis in their love affair occurs. During their harvest-moon love-making at Yūgao's residence, Genji is fascinated at first, but soon exasperated, by the epitome of lower-class life, the "plebeian voices in the shabby houses down the street," which he finds "genuinely earsplitting." Such a difference in the lovers' sensibilities would ordinarily have been unthinkable in Heian court life, but here dark romantic passion overpowers conventional etiquette. Genji manages to resolve the crisis. Inspired by a pious old man, he makes a modest vow to Yūgao and takes her, against her wishes, to a desolate, isolated villa. This forced move triggers their second crisis, and it is lethal for her.

Yūgao may seem unreasonably "frightened, and bewildered," but the fears that she experiences as she approaches the climax of the relationship concern a power no less than nemesis. Of lower rank than her former and her present lovers, she must consider herself fortunate to be favored by such high-ranking courtiers. At the same time, she has learned to be distrustful of uneven matches. Yūgao, whose self-confidence the earlier affair has already impaired, suffers from anxiety about a similarly abrupt end to passionate love.

The move to Genji's desolate villa is an ambiguous statement that both threatens and elates Yūgao. On the one hand, Genji's earlier plan to establish her at Nijō, his main residence, was rather quickly abandoned in order to avoid all risk of public scandal. In this sense, Yūgao interprets the isolation of their affair as her lover's refusal to acknowledge her and as an omen of inevitable rejection. On the other hand, "Memories of past wrongs quite left her" when she considers how much she must mean to a disguised lover willing to risk his own peace of mind at a neglected residence where "devils" might come forth. The lovers oscillate between psychological stress and the joys of passion, but the trauma of her first love intensifies Yūgao's conflicts to a degree not experienced by Genji.

At the deserted villa, in the dead of night, Yūgao becomes possessed. It is important to note that the phenomenon is described from Genji's perspective. Because of his successful repression of all thoughts concerning Yūgao's affair with Tō no Chūjō, he interprets the possession as an expression of *his* imagined triangular conflict, i.e., simply as the result of female jealousy. However, for Genji's other women to have been jealous of the new mistress required their knowledge of her existence. Since the affair had been kept a secret, none of them knew of the new affair and each of them had reason to attribute Genji's neglect to attentions paid to one of the others rather than to the unknown Yūgao. Yet critics have unanimously adopted Genji's preliminary interpretation of jealousy. In fact, in their exclusive focus on Lady Rokujō, they have been more definite than he. And they have ignored the function of the possession and its meaning for the afflicted female protagonist.

Time and setting help induce Yūgao's extreme mental and physical agitation: "The girl was trembling violently. She was bathed in sweat and as if in a trance, quite bereft of her senses." Genji too is entering an altered state of consciousness—albeit on a quotidian scale—that of sleep. While sleeping, he has a nightmare of "an exceedingly beautiful woman" who berates him for neglecting her in favor of Yūgao. Genji awakens just as this specter of one of his neglected ladies is turning to snatch his beloved away from his bedside. He has been jolted from sleep by Yūgao's violently restless possession trance. His first thought is for himself: he does *not* at once conclude that *Yūgao* is possessed: "He awoke, feeling as if he were in the power of some malign being." This moment has gone virtually unnoticed by scholars because Genji reaches for his sword, symbolic of male power, and quickly dispells his fears for himself. Nonetheless it is important to see that the drama of Yūgao's possession is so powerful that Genji feels compelled to share her altered state and continues to do so, in a form of "possession once removed," even after she has died.

While Genji's waking, dozing and sleeping during that fateful night are minutely described in reference to Yūgao's crisis, the heroine's perspective is dramatized in far less detail. It is through Genji's feverishly involved perspective, at crucial times bordering on the hallucinatory, that Yūgao's rapid psychological and physical decline are first assessed. Genji's frame of mind is, therefore, at least as pertinent to our understanding of Yūgao's tragedy as her own history of anxieties. In fact, the violent dénouement of the love affair forces the hero into the role of interpreter. Due to the suddenness of Yūgao's death and the absence of an exorcist who might have lent the seal of authenticity to the mysterious, Genji must psychologically master his lover's possession and death without the aid of esoteric magic rituals.

It is only when Genji's "rationalizations" include his role in the drama of spirit possession that he gradually learns to come to terms with Yūgao's death. With a certain amount of self-pity, Genji acknowledges his share of guilt: "He was being punished for a guilty love, his fault and no one else's . . . he would gain immortality as the model of the complete fool." Torn between the conflicting emotions of grief for the lost lover and a terror akin to that of a murderer who must dispose of a dead body, Genji's breakdown seems inevitable. His suffering does not end when his confidant Koremitsu takes care of practical matters. Indeed, he further implicates himself by lying to the suspicious Tō no Chūjō about the cause of his absence from court and his present inaccessibility. Not surprisingly, emotional distress is accompanied by psychosomatic symptoms, such as headaches, lack of appetite and fever. Again, only his confidant can help him by suggesting practical ways of doing penance, instead of passively "torturing" himself.

Although Genji risks discovery of his involvement in Yūgao's fate, he feels compelled to pay his last respects to his departed lady. At a mountain temple he overcomes some of his own grief by commiserating with her lady-in-waiting. Yet, exhausted from guilt and shame, and perhaps from a momentary sense of relief at having completed this tragic affair, he falls from his horse, like a fool. It is as if this accident were the worst fate liable to afflict a courtier who has been romantically involved with a woman of lower rank.

Back at Nijō he must endure the aftereffects of stress in a twenty-day crisis. His readjustment is slow and painful: "For a time he felt out of things, as if he had come back to a strange new world. . . . He spent a great deal of time gazing into space, and sometimes he would weep aloud." Since "gazing into space" was a common expression of Heian women's "immobile existence," Genji's form of suffering gives him the appearance of a woman possessed. In short, Genji now reenacts a milder version of Yūgao's trauma which the court, despite their ignorance of Yūgao's tragedy, diagnose as akin to possession: "He must be in the clutches of some malign spirit, thought the women."

From Genji's standpoint, Yūgao's tragedy can be traced back to his offenses against several women, thus evoking the possessing spirit of jealousy, the stock explanation for female hysteria. That this spirit might attack him as well as any preferred lover is vaguely sensed by the female public's assessment of Genji's psychological state. Yet males in Heian culture generally fancied themselves not only aloof from but even immune from the untidy, specifically female emotion of jealousy. Hence Genji remains fixed on the "exceedingly beautiful woman" of his nightmare as the victimizer of Yūgao.

Although the possessing spirit is never named, a significant detail (foot)noted by one reader, most critics have identified the "exceedingly beautiful woman" as Rokujō. But the image of the beauty is a collective image, an allegory of Genji's betrayed ladies. To single out Rokujō "whose sense of rivalry" becomes a serious threat only in the second possession case, or to speculate about others such as Aoi, is equally beside the point.

The emphasis of the author is not on solving the riddle of the spirit's identity but on analyzing the male response to the complex phenomena. The critics have neglected the role which Tō no Chūjō plays in Yūgao's possession and in Genji's guilty reaction to it. While the affair with Rokujō is over as far as Genji is concerned, Yūgao's affair with Tō no Chūjō lies in the immediate past and is, moreover, the very affair confided to Genji in the "Rainy-Night Discussion." As accomplices in love, Genji and Yūgao have both, each in his or her own way, betrayed Tō no Chūjō. It can plausibly be argued that this betrayal contributed to Yūgao's possession and death and to Genji's profound misery. The wrong done to Tō no Chūjō is, after Yūgao's death, followed by Genji's continuing offenses. Not only does the hero dishonestly cover up the affair, but he also blocks Tō no Chūjō's paternal rights until Chūjō's daughter by Yūgao is nearly grown. Genji is, in fact, claiming to be doing penance by caring for Yūgao's child, but his charitable intentions appear rather selfish in the light of his friend's frustrated natural privileges. No wonder, then, that Genji develops a painful conscience. After the 49th-day services for Yūgao, Genji is in a bad way: "His heart raced each time he saw Tō no Chūjō." He concludes that the secret affair with Yūgao was actually an "unfortunate contest of wills." Once again, Genji is haunted by the nightmarish dream "of the woman who had appeared that fatal night." This dream had originally functioned to repress Genji's guilt toward Tō no Chūjō, and it continues to do so.

The problem, however, is that Genji's initial interpretation of the nightmare and the possession, *and* his subsequent guilt about his betrayal of Tō no Chūjō, ignore the one person who suffers firsthand from the casual behavior of both men: Yūgao. Genji's other women and his best friend are all quite unaware of Yūgao's affair with Genji. In short, only Yūgao, the most vulnerable of all the people involved, had been in a position to know all the relevant facts. If anyone had a motive for the oblique aggressive strategy of spirit possession, it was she, the otherwise helpless woman who had been victimized once and was fearful of a second victimization by a second lover. Unfortunately for Yūgao, her feverish attempt at spirit possession fails because Genji is simply unable to realize that she, a woman made vulnerable by her lower rank, is the person most likely to use the only psychological weapon available to her in her unequal position vis-à-vis Genji, Tō no Chūjō, and their high-ranking aristocratic wives and concubines. Ironically, then, after a moment of fear that he himself might be possessed, he interprets her possession and death neither as an obliquely hostile act nor as an appeal for sympathy and reassurance; he can do no better than to assume egoistically that Yūgao's trauma is the result of female rivalry over him. His halting efforts to fathom Tō no Chūjō's and his own complicity in Yūgao's fate cease. His perceptions are too gender-bound to see that the complex relations between men and women in polygynous Heian society are reflected in the superimposed triangular constellations of his affair with Yūgao. Consequently, his guilt remains diffuse. In later years, it intensifies. When his wife Aoi and his favorite concubine Murasaki become possessed, Genji's sympathy for his women grows, but his intellectual response remains clouded by the mores of the times. Finally, spirit possession cannot change the social structure, and male-female relations remain as they were.

Yūgao, the female heroine, is doomed to lose in her nonverbal oblique aggressive strategy; in her case, spirit possession is a self-destructive protest. Yet at the end of the Yūgao chapter, the author of the ***Genji,*** herself a lady at the Heian court, verbalizes the heroine's grievance against the hero by making a direct appeal to the reader. *Monogatari* conventions, which required the hero of a romance to be an idealized prince, are flouted. In short, Murasaki Shikibu refuses to make concessions to public taste: "I had hoped, out of deference to him [Genji], to conceal these difficult matters; but I have been accused of romancing, of pretending that because he was the son of an emperor he had no faults. Now, perhaps, I shall be accused of having revealed too much." Yūgao's case of spirit possession is an oblique criticism of male behavior toward women in polygynous society. Unlike subsequent possessed heroines, who are more eloquent, this unassertive lady has, quite literally, no voice to express her fears. Her spirit possession neither castigates the men who toyed with her nor does it calm her agitated mind. She may nonetheless have scored a victory. The shock of her spirit possession left Genji vaguely, uncomprehendingly, uneasy. In the attempt to penetrate the mystery of his dream and her possession, he is compelled to rehearse—again and yet again—the drama of her death. (pp. 19-23)

Doris G. Bargen, "Yūgao: A Case of Spirit Possession in 'The Tale of Genji'," in Mosaic: A Journal for the Interdisciplinary Study of Literature, *Vol. XIX, No. 3, Summer, 1986, pp. 15-24.*

JIN'ICHI KONISHI (essay date 1986)

[*In the following excerpt, Jin'ichi details the narrative techniques and imagery Murasaki used to express her themes in* The Tale.]

The three themes of the ***Genji***—reality and clear insight, karma and predetermined suffering, piety and spiritual blindness—are not simply contiguous elements. When the ***Genji*** consisted of only Part One, its theme was reality and clear insight. When Part Two appeared, the theme of Part One was enveloped by Part Two and was dissolved to form an element in creating the theme of Part Two, karma and predetermined suffering. This is the theme of Part Two, but it is also a comprehensive theme held in common with Part One. The completion of Part Three led to its theme, piety and spiritual blindness, enveloping the earlier themes, which become elements of a theme for the entire ***Tale of Genji***. . . . The ***Genji*** as a whole can be explained in the light of the theme of piety and spiritual blindness, but when

An illustration of a scene from The Tale of Genji *dated 1650.*

only the first two parts are considered the theme of karma and predetermined suffering obtains. The theme of reality and clear insight regains its effectiveness when Part One is read on its own.

What methods did Murasaki Shikibu employ to express these themes? Her use of waka [Japanese court poetry] technique is immediately noticeable. One such technique is the use, in narrative prose sections, of expression resembling pillow words and prefaces; but this is a trivial matter. We would do better to address the question of why Murasaki Shikibu dared to experiment with poetic expression. In the famous discussion of monogatari [Japanese prose tales] in "Fireflies," Murasaki Shikibu has Genji say, "'But the beginning is when there are . . . things that happen in this life which one never tires of seeing and hearing about, things which one cannot bear not to tell of and must pass on for all generations'." This narrative passage is reminiscent of a passage from the Japanese Preface to the *Kokinshū:* "Because human beings possess interests of so many kinds, it is in poetry that they give expression to the meditations of their hearts in terms of the sights appearing before their eyes and the sounds coming to their ears." Motoori Norinaga (1730-1801) may have been influenced by this resemblance when he wrote,

> Murasaki Shikibu profoundly understood deep emotion [mono no aware]. She wrote . . . about the profound meaning of varied circumstances in this world, and the hearts and actions of both good people and bad, as grounded in the sights appearing before her eyes, the sounds coming to her ears, and the experiences she shared. All the deep emotions of our world are contained in this monogatari.

Therefore, Norinaga asserts, "This monogatari expresses in various ways all the feelings people are likely to experience, and evokes deep emotion."

This excellent opinion has long been upheld by scholars of Japanese literature. To be sure, Norinaga's attempt to solve all the problems of the ***Genji*** by means of his ideas, and his refusal to consider any interpretation based on Confucian or Buddhist perspectives, are indicative of his occasional lapses into excessive logicality. Nevertheless Norinaga pinpoints Murasaki Shikibu's intent, to acknowledge that monogatari are of equal worth with waka. Of course, Murasaki Shikibu did not expect that the fictional monogatari, up to her time a mere diversion, would gain immediate recognition as a premier art equivalent to waka. One of her characters speaks for her when he says, "'The *Chronicles of Japan* and the rest are a mere fragment of the whole truth.'" That is her only comment on the subject. If, however, we assume that Murasaki Shikibu wrote with an awareness of the premier arts, then her use of expression resembling pillow words and prefaces is, despite their insignificant bearing on monogatari, noteworthy as indicating the presence of such an awareness. (pp. 333-35)

The monogatari was not made into a premier art equal to waka simply by introducing waka techniques. The monogatari has its own techniques, which needed refinement if monogatari expression was to rise to the level of waka. One such refined technique is the sōshiji, or narratorial intrusion. The term itself is first used in the fifteenth century, but the technique appears frequently in the ***Genji*** as well as in other monogatari. With intrusion, the narrator of, say, the ***Genji,*** briefly makes her presence known and offers explanations or opinions from a first-person perspective. Consider, for example, the passage from "Suma" in which Genji, about to leave for Suma, writes to his various ladies.

> He did write to certain people who should know of the event. *I have no doubt that there were many fine passages in the letters with which he saddened the lives of his many ladies, but, grief-stricken myself, I did not listen as carefully as I might have.*

The italicized area represents the narratorial intrusion. The Western technique of authorial intrusion corresponds to it and frequently appears in modern Japanese fiction. In the ***Genji,*** the calculated effect of the narrator's intrusion is much like that of a zoom lens: its use extends or shortens the psychological distance between the audience and circumstances and characters in the work. Murasaki Shikibu's experiment is surprisingly original for the eleventh century.

Her experimentation is noticeable above all in the multilayered narration of the ***Genji.*** The narrator who speaks to the audience from within the ***Genji*** will be termed the primary narrator. In this setting, the primary narrator has not directly witnessed the events from the story: she has been told them by another, a secondary narrator.

> Though no one has asked me to do so, I should like to describe the surprise of the assistant viceroy's wife at this turn of events, and Jijū's pleasure and guilt. But it would be a bother and my head is aching; and perhaps something

> will someday remind me to continue the story.
> This is what I heard.

The narratorial intrusion ends with the words "to zo" ("this is what I heard"), an indication that the story has been told to the primary narrator by someone else. "This is what I heard" is spoken by the primary narrator, and the secondary narrator speaks the rest of the passage, from "Though no one has asked me to do so" through "to continue the story." Secondary narration is performed by more than one person.

> The story I am about to tell was heard at second-hand from certain obscure *women* discharged from Genji's family after his death. They found employment in Higekuro's house, where they lived into old age, and there volunteered this story. It may not seem entirely in keeping with the story told by Murasaki's *women*; but those at Higekuro's house say that there are numerous inaccuracies in the accounts we have had of Genji's descendants, and distrust Murasaki's women, who they say were so old that they had become forgetful. I would not presume to say which story is right.

The primary narrator has gathered and recorded accounts by several secondary narrators, the "obscure women" (warugo-tachi, noblewomen of relatively low origin) of the text. The ladies are clearly fictional narrators; the setting of primary and secondary narrators establishes considerable distance between the readers and the characters and events of the ***Genji.*** When a secondary narrator does not appear, the reading audience draws proportionately closer to the characters and events. At times the audience is even unaware of the primary narrator's existence, and at such times it directly experiences situations described in the work and feels as if it is entering into the characters' innermost hearts. Then a narrator's statement will suddenly appear: "What a fainthearted fellow!" The audience is thereupon pulled back to a scene in which the primary narrator is speaking. The technique of varying an audience's proximity to situations and characters in the ***Genji*** is somewhat reminiscent of the manipulation of a cinema lens, which shows an audience a close-up of a scene and then recedes from it.

Such techniques are extremely effective in portraying the psychologies of the characters. Immediately after a character's thoughts or feelings have been described, the narratorial intrusion is introduced. Because early medieval fictional monogatari are without exception told from an omniscient point of view, they run the risk of appearing shallow and monotonous by comparison with modern psychological novels. These unwelcome characteristics can sometimes be modified by employing the technique of a narratorial intrusion. In "Suetsumuhana" ("The Safflower"), Genji spends his first night with the safflower princess but must wait until dawn to see her face for the first time:

> Though his face was politely averted, Genji contrived to look obliquely at her. He was hoping that a really good look might show her to be less than irredeemable.
>
> *That was not very kind or very realistic of him.*

Genji's thoughts are told by an omniscient narrator, and the result is a sense of excessive directness. Once the audience is exposed to the primary narrator's criticism of Genji's incorrigible ways, though, it is pulled back from an intimate view of Genji's mind to the narrator's point of view. This provides a perspective from which to observe Genji's character more or less objectively and avoids overly direct narration.

Murasaki Shikibu is not only adept in her use of the narratorial technique. She also seems to have mastered the technique of achieving the proper distance in psychological portrayal. Consider, for example, the scene from "Yūgiri" ("Evening Mist") in which Yūgiri pursues the Second Princess into a large closet and has his first glimpse of her face.

> It was dark inside, but the morning light somehow came seeping in, dimly revealing her form. He pulled away the quilts and smoothed her tangled hair. She was very graceful, delicate, and ladylike.

Formally speaking, the last sentence is the narrator's comment. It may in effect be seen, however, as Yūgiri's own feelings. We know this from an earlier passage, in the second "Wakana" chapter ("New Herbs: Part Two"), in which the narrator notifies the reader that the princess is not a great beauty: ". . . although she was quite attractive compared to the general run of women." When the same narrator pronounces the princess "very graceful, delicate, and ladylike" in "Evening Mist," she is not voicing her own opinion but narrating Yūgiri's observations and impressions of the princess at this moment. If Yūgiri's feelings had been entered into and explained—"He found her very graceful, delicate, and ladylike"—the result would be excessively direct and explicit narration. The purpose of this sentence is to link the audience's consciousness to the primary narrator's viewpoint; the technique also effectively transmits Yūgiri's emotions.

Explicating a character's emotions from the narrator's position is a technique frequently found in fictional monogatari written from an omniscient point of view. Murasaki Shikibu attempts a new technique in touching on a character's emotions while maintaining some distance from the individual. This signals a movement toward a yet more complex technique, that of suggesting the characters' innermost thoughts rather than stating them outright. This is reminiscent of novels written from a limited point of view, including the later works of Henry James. When, in "New Herbs, Part One," Genji is asked by his brother, the abdicated Suzaku, if he will marry the Third Princess, he agrees with little demurral. Up to then, Genji has shown no great interest in the girl, and the reasons and motives underlying his decision are not explained. The Third Princess's marriage is the major event of Part Two. An omniscient narrator would be at liberty to describe Genji's emotions at length, as he arrives at his decision. Murasaki Shikibu does not allow her narrator this freedom, instead choosing to hint at Genji's motives in a speech made by a minor character, a certain middle controller. He hears from his sister, the Third Princess's nurse, of Suzaku's intent to marry the girl to Genji; the controller observes that as long as Murasaki is alive, things will be difficult for the princess. He adds,

> "Yet I have heard him say, without making a great point of it, that his life has been too well favored in this degenerate age, and that it would be greedy and arrogant of him to want more; but that he himself and others too have thought that in his relations with women he has not been completely successful. I think he truly feels this way."

The precise nature of Genji's lack of success with women is left unstated. But the controller, noting that none of Genji's ladies is of the highest birth, thinks the Third Princess would make "the most suitable wife" for Genji. Of course, this is only the controller's interpretation of Genji's speech. The audience naturally feels confused about the extent to which it can rely on a minor character's opinion. On the other hand, facts supporting the controller's interpretation appear somewhat earlier in the chapter:

> "It would seem that Genji still has the old acquisitive instincts and that he is always on the alert for ladies of really good pedigree. I am told that he still thinks of the former high priestess of Kamo and sometimes gets off a letter to her."

This, too, is only an opinion spoken by one of the Third Princess's nurses. There is no other mention in the text of Genji's conscious longing for an alliance with a woman of superior lineage. The abdicated Suzaku, who has solicited the nurse's opinion, comments that his only worry is Genji's well-known weakness for women. He does not touch Genji's desire for "ladies of really good pedigree," but neither does he deny it.

Absorbing all these remarks, the reader is given to believe that Genji's desire to marry the Third Princess stems from a desire—whether he is aware of it or not—for a lady of superior lineage. Henry James excels in the technique of casting light on the hidden recesses of a protagonist's heart by portrayal through the eyes of secondary or minor characters. Such characters serve as "reflectors," or "centers of consciousness." Although the controller and his sister, the Third Princess's nurse, do not necessarily have an identical function, there are similarities in Murasaki Shikibu's use of minor characters to reflect a protagonist's own thoughts.

Full psychological portrayal first appears with Part Two of the ***Genji.*** A work that does not employ the narrator to explain the characters' thoughts, but that instead has the reader follow carefully placed clues that will eventually lead to their discovery, presents a text made comprehensible only through repeated, careful reading to oneself. Such comprehension is impossible through hearing, in which a lector reads the text to an audience. I do not mean to deny that Part Two was probably aurally received. Aural reception would have been quite acceptable to those interested only in enjoying the plot development. Yet the kind of reception Murasaki Shikibu seems to have anticipated most as a writer would have been possible only through reading by oneself. This would also have been true for Part Three, especially as concerns its use of symbolism.

As we have seen, the theme of Part One is reality and clear insight, that of Part Two is karma and predetermined suffering, and that of Part Three is piety and spiritual blindness. Spiritual blindness, an inability to understand the truth, is linked to the imagery of darkness. Avidyā, the Sanskrit term for "spiritual blindness," can be literally translated as "inability to see." This explains the opening sentences of Part Three: "The radiant Genji was dead, and there was no one to take his place from among his many descendants." Genji, the protagonist of Parts One and Two, is a being whose superiority is manifested by the sobriquet "radiant" (hikaru). No one can rival him. Of course, it is only in Part One that he appears as an idealized, superior being. In Part Two the radiant hero experiences a series of disappointments, and although his superiority still illumines the heavens, it begins to take on sunset colors. Nonetheless, it continues to be radiant.

The characters in Part Three, by contrast, experience only disappointment. Nothing goes as they expect; they are plagued by unwelcome results. There is no radiance here. Part Three is a world of darkness. Thus it is no accident that the male protagonists of Part Three are called "Niou" (Perfume) and "Kaoru" (Scent). Contemporary readers of the ***Genji*** knew that even in the dark one could appreciate fragrance; this was thought especially true for plum blossoms, as one famous waka attests.

Haru no yo no	On the spring night
Yami wa ayanashi	The darkness fails in its ends:
Mume no hana	For the flowering plum
Iro koso miene	May have its colors kept from us,
Ka ya wa kakururu.	But its fragrance cannot be concealed!

This is why both Niou and Kaoru are frequently associated with plum blossoms. There are too many instances to enumerate, but a few might be mentioned: Kōbai sees "a rose plum in full bloom" and is reminded of Niou. When Kaoru's natural fragrance is first described, an image is evoked of "his sleeves brushing a spray of plum blossoms." . . . There is also a scene in which Niou and Kaoru play the thirteen-stringed zither and chat, as "the scent of plum blossoms," drifts in. It is perhaps reasonable that the more energetic Niou is associated with the rose plum and Kaoru with the white.

When Murasaki Shikibu wrote Parts One and Two, she probably did not envision them as symbolizing a world of light. A tradition, dating back to the Ancient Age, dictated that a superior being be described in luminous terms; hence Genji's epithet. Before her death in "Minori" ("The Rites"), Murasaki bequeaths her rose plum and cherry trees at the Nijō Palace to Niou, as a remembrance of her. This is the origin of Niou's association with rose plum blossoms, but it is not an underpinning for Part Three. As soon as Part Three was completed, however, all these elements came to possess symbolic significance. Genji's epithet no longer denotes the radiance of the ancient hero and heroine whose "dazzling countenances illumined their villages." It has been transformed into the glory of worldly success, behind which is darkness, the Buddhist symbol of spiritual blindness. The relationships among the three parts have been given above, and now we can add their symbols.

Other thematic aspects of Part Three cannot be satisfactorily symbolized by the imagery of darkness. Piety, the search for truth in the midst of spiritual blindness, cannot be summed up by the image of darkness alone. Two more images may serve to symbolize, respectively, piety and spiritual blindness: mountains and the river. Most of the action in Part Three takes place at Uji, an evocative landscape of mountains and river. The Uji mountains represent piety to characters in the ***Genji.*** The mountains are mentioned in "Hashihime" ("The Lady at the Bridge") in connection with the profoundly pious Eighth Prince, who can find serenity only at a mountain monastery: "There happened to be in those Uji mountains an abbot, a most saintly man." The prince considers his temple "a quiet place," since his secular residence is near the Uji River with its constant sound of coursing water. "The roar of the fish weirs was more than a man could bear, said the Eighth Prince as he set off for the abbot's mountain monastery, there to spend a week in retreat." The sound of rushing water signifies more than physical noise: it frequently appears in connection with spiritual suffering. Whenever the characters of Part Three are lost in grief, the sound of the river comes inevitably to their ears. The coursing river is compared, moreover, to the evanescent world:

> Strange, battered little boats, piled high with brush and wattles, made their way up and down the river, each boatman pursuing his own sad, small livelihood at the uncertain mercy of the waters. "It is the same with all of us," thought Kaoru. . . . "Am I to boast that I am safe from the flood, calm and secure in a jewelled mansion?"

The conceit may be partially due to a waka convention, in which the "u" of "Uji" is used homophonically to signify "misery." It might also have originated from the Buddhist convention of employing river and sea imagery as metaphors for the world of love-torments.

Perhaps the most outstanding metaphorical use of river and sea imagery to suggest the world of men, replete with worldly attachments and suffering, appears in a chapter of the *Lotus Sūtra,* "The Former Affairs of the King Fine Adornment." One of the king's sons says that "'A Buddha is as hard to encounter . . . as it would be for a one-eyed tortoise to encounter a hole in a floating piece of wood.'" The tortoise and the piece of wood are metaphors for all living things, who have little likelihood of coming to know the truth, and the sea on which they drift represents the human world. This metaphor evokes the epithet "ukifune" (floating boat) accorded to one of the heroines of Part Three. She is never actually called Ukifune in the ***Genji.*** Readers probably drew her "name" from a poem and the chapter title derived from it, "Ukifune" ("A Boat upon the Waters").

Tachibana no	Leaves of the orange tree
Kojima wa iro mo	On Little Orange Island
Kawaraji o	Hold fast in color
Kono ukifune zo	But this boat drifting on the waters
Yukue shirarenu.	Does not know her destination.

It is of little importance that the character is not named Ukifune in the text. What is significant is that the readers who gave her the appellation fixed on the image of a boat floating on the river as fitting to the heroine's life. In that boat loose in the current, Ukifune, who is already Kaoru's mistress, crosses the Uji River by boat with Niou and spends the night with him there in a cottage. During their river crossing, she recites her waka about the little isle with its orange trees. She is indeed a small boat drifting on the river of love, this woman torn between Kaoru and Niou and carried off by the course of events. The title of the final chapter of the ***Genji,*** "Yume no Ukihashi" ("The Floating Bridge of Dreams"), may also be considered boat imagery. A "floating bridge" (ukihashi) is a pontoon bridge: the hulls of small boats are lashed together and planks put on top of them to provide a temporary crossing. If the ropes that hold the boats break, each craft will drift off, its destination unknown. Part Three must be symbolized by the image of a boat adrift on a river that flows between darkening mountains.

The world of Part Three is symbolized by four images: the mountains for piety, the river for spiritual blindness, the boat for those drifting between piety and spiritual blindness, and growing darkness as a comprehensive image. Strictly speaking, this imagery applies only to the Uji chapters, the ten chapters from "The Lady at the Bridge" through "The Floating Bridge of Dreams." It does not appear in the three preceding chapters, "His Perfumed Highness," "The Rose Plum," and "Bamboo River." It is only when these three chapters are considered together with the Uji chapters that this imagery has meaning for the former group.

The Uji chapters abound in imagery. In addition to the repeated images of mountain, river, and boat that are linked to the themes of Part Three, there is also symbolic significance in images appearing infrequently, or even once. Some examples are mist, winter rain, and the bridge. I call them symbols, which leads one to conceive of them in terms of modern Western symbolism; this might precipitate some misunderstanding. The difference between the imagery of the Uji chapters and modern symbolism is that, in the former case, there is no strict relationship between the image and its corresponding tenor, no fixed relation between signifier and signified. My proposal that the river symbolizes spiritual blindness is intended to deepen the significance of Part Three, but its function as a signifier is not limited to this signification; and a different one might well provide a more profound meaning. Murasaki Shikibu would not mind which signification is chosen, and a reader is free to determine its nature providing some kind of meaning is grasped from within the ***Genji.***

I approach the imagery of the Uji chapters in this fashion because of the peculiar nature of Buddhist figural imagery. The kind of imagery found in the Uji chapters does not appear in Chinese shih [a verse form sometimes used in Japan] or in other Chinese works. Murasaki Shikibu's only point of reference was the Buddhist scriptures. Buddhist imagery can be interpreted in various ways, however, depending on the ability of the person receiving instruction. In the introductory chapter of the *Lotus Śūtra,* for example, Śākya emits light from the tuft of white hair between his eyebrows, and illuminates eighteen thousand worlds to the east. This light is the central image of the entire sutra, but there is no definitive interpretation of its significance. One of the many interpretations made over the centuries is highly plausible. But other interpretations, including those just occurring to oneself, are correct if they deepen one's own religious experience. Murasaki Shikibu applies this to literature: she presents us with only an outline within her work so as to force us to discover meanings beyond those given in the text. It can be interpreted in accordance with the individual reader's abilities, and so is seen to have multiple correct interpretations. What I have attempted here is only one relatively accurate interpretation. (pp. 336-46)

Jin'ichi Konishi, in his A History of Japanese Literature: The Early Middle Ages, Vol. II, *edited by Earl Miner, translated by Aileen Gatten, Princeton University Press, 1986, 461 p.*

ADDITIONAL BIBLIOGRAPHY

Abe, Akio et al: eds. *Murasaki Shikibu: The Greatest Lady Writer in Japanese Literature*. Japanese National Commission for Unesco, 1970, 424 p.

An exhaustive genealogical and biographical study of Murasaki.

Carter, John. "Perfumed Pages." *The Saturday Review of Literature* IX, No. 49 (24 June 1933): 661-64.

Judges *The Tale* "a gem of literary portrayal of human character."

Daisaku Ikeda and Makoto Nemoto. "The Portrait of Prince Genji" and "*The Tale of Genji* and the Lotus Sutra." In their *On the Japanese*

Classics: Conversations and Appreciations, pp. 114-34, pp. 135-52. New York: Weatherhill, 1979.

Some general commentary on *The Tale* recorded in the form of conversations.

Field, Norma. *The Splendor of Longing in the Tale of Genji*. Princeton: Princeton University Press, 1987, 372 p.

A study of female characters in *The Tale* which is based on the premise that "the eponymous hero, far from being the controlling center of the work, is as much constituted by his heroines as they are by him."

Gatten, Aileen. "A Wisp of Smoke." *Monumenta Nipponica* XXXII, No. 1 (Spring 1977): 35-48.

Discusses the central importance of scent and scent preparation in *The Tale*.

———. "The Order of the Early Chapters in the *Genji Monogatari*." *Harvard Journal of Asiatic Studies* 41, No. 1 (June 1981): 5-46.

An examination of the numerous problems surrounding the ordering of chapters in *The Tale*. Gatten argues that the order in which scholars usually place the early chapters might not be that intended by Murasaki and that an alternative arrangement results in a more satisfactory narrative sequence.

Haruo Shirane. "The Aesthetics of Power: Politics in *The Tale of Genji*." *Harvard Journal of Asiatic Studies* 45, No. 2 (December 1985): 615-47.

Proposes that "in highly allusive, poetic, aesthetic, and less than apparent ways, the *Genji* is concerned with imperial succession and political power."

Herrick, Robert. "The Perfect Lover." *The New Republic* LVI, No. 723 (10 October 1928): 214-16.

Discusses Murasaki's portrayal of polygamy.

Janeira, Armando Martins. "The Classic Novel." In his *Japanese and Western Literature: A Comparative Study,* pp. 54-74. Rutland, Vt.: Charles E. Tuttle Co., 1970.

Examines the historical context of *The Tale* and discusses its impact upon the primary elements of the novel.

Keene, Donald. "The Japanese Novel." In his *Japanese Literature,* pp. 67-87. London: John Murray, 1953.

An introductory discussion of *The Tale* in which Keene admonishes: "We should not . . . be misled into imagining that Lady Murasaki has given us a realistic portrayal of contemporary conditions. Rather, her novel is the evocation of a world which never quite existed."

Lin Wen-yueh. "*The Tale of Genji* and *The Song of Enduring Woe*." *Renditions,* No. 5 (Autumn 1975): 38-49.

Compares portions of the text of *The Tale* with similar passages in *The Tale of Enduring Woe,* a classic Chinese poem.

Masao, Miyoshi. "Translation as Interpretation." *The Journal of Asian Studies* XXXVIII, No. 2 (February 1979): 299-302.

Compares the Waley and Seidensticker translations.

Meletinsky, Elzar M. "The Typology of the Medieval Romance in the West and in the East." *Diogenes,* No. 127 (Fall 1984):1-22.

Compares *The Tale* with Western medieval romances. Meletinsky concludes that the "psychological skepticism and impressionist aesthetics" of the Japanese romance "find no correspondent in European consciousness except in much later historical stages."

Miner, Earl. "The Rise of the Radiant Prince." *The Times Literary Supplement,* No. 3907 (28 January 1977): 98.

Praises Seidensticker's translation for its syntactic simplicity and clarity.

Morris, Ivan. "Translating *The Tale of Genji*." *Orient/West* 9, No. 1 (January-February 1964): 21-4.

Describes the difficulties of interpreting and translating *The Tale*.

Mudrick, Marvin. "Lady Murasaki: *The Tale of Genji*." In his *On Culture and Literature,* pp. 49-68. New York: Horizon, 1970.

Discusses Prince Genji's life as presented in *The Tale*.

Noguchi Takehiko. "The Substratum Constituting Monogatari: Prose Structure and Narrative in the *Genji Monogatari*." In *Principles of Classical Japanese Literature,* edited by Earl Miner, pp. 130-50. Princeton: Princeton University Press, 1985.

Examines the function of traditional unifying devices in *The Tale*.

Pritchett, V. S. "A Great Japanese Classic." *The Christian Science Monitor* XXV, No. 178 (24 June 1933): 6.

An essentially positive review in which Pritchett states that "it cannot be said that [*The Tale*] is a great epic; but to go to the other extreme and to put it below Jane Austen is equally futile."

Rimer, J. Thomas. "Source Books I: *Tales of Ise, The Tale of Genji*" and "*The Tale of Genji* as a Modern Novel." In his *Modern Japanese Fiction and Its Traditions,* pp. 82-96, pp. 200-44. Princeton: Princeton University Press, 1978.

Explains the importance of *The Tale* in Japanese fiction and explores elements of modernity in the narrative.

Rohlich,Thomas H. Review of *Murasaki Shikibu: Her Diary and Poetic Memoirs,* by Richard Bowring. *Journal of Asian Studies* XLIII, No. 3 (May 1984): 539-41.

Discusses the importance of Murasaki's diary as a historical document.

Seidensticker, Edward G. "Murasaki Shikibu and Her Diary and Her Other Writings." *Literature East and West* XVIII, No. 1 (March 1974): 1-7.

Discounts the value of Murasaki's autobiographical writings in illuminating the text of *The Tale,* concluding that "there is a kind of biographic critic for whom the [diaries] might . . . be her most important writing. One would not wish to be that sort of critic, really."

———. "The Free Ways of Arthur Waley." *The Times Literary Supplement,* No. 4100 (30 October 1981):1279-80.

Assesses Waley's translation of *The Tale*. While Seidensticker commends Waley's skill as a translator, he notes that his stylistic amendments resulted in some rather serious semantic distortions.

Snow, C. P. "Shining One." *Financial Times,* No. 27, 199 (17 February 1977): 28.

Expresses his preference for the Seidensticker translation of *The Tale,* praising it as "tauter, more economical and restrained" than Waley's.

Ury, Marian. "The Complete Genji." *Harvard Journal of Asian Studies* 37, No. 1 (June 1977): 183-201.

Compares the Waley and Seidensticker translations, finding the latter preferable.

———. "*The Tale of Genji* in English." *Yearbook of Comparative and General Literature,* No. 31 (1982): 62-7.

Assesses the fidelity to the original of the two English translations of *The Tale*.

Slovo o polku Igoreve (The Igor Tale)

Twelfth Century

Russian poem.

Slovo o polku Igoreve is the greatest extant work of medieval Russian literature. Variously translated into English as "The Song of Igor's Campaign" and "The Lay of Igor's Host," among other titles, the work commonly known as *The Igor Tale* recounts a battle led in 1185 by a minor prince of Kievan Russia, Igor Svyatoslavich, against the nomadic Polovetsians (or Kumans) of the Russian steppe. Combining epic narrative, political oratory, and lyrical reflection, the work is valued both as a historical record and portrait of feudal life and as an individualistic expression of its anonymous author's political and artistic vision. Distinguished by its literary complexity, *The Igor Tale* is considered unique among works of Old Russian literature for its highly symbolical, allusive style, which stands in sharp contrast to the simplicity of other surviving works of the Russian Middle Ages and which has prompted favorable comparisons to the greatest medieval epics in world literature.

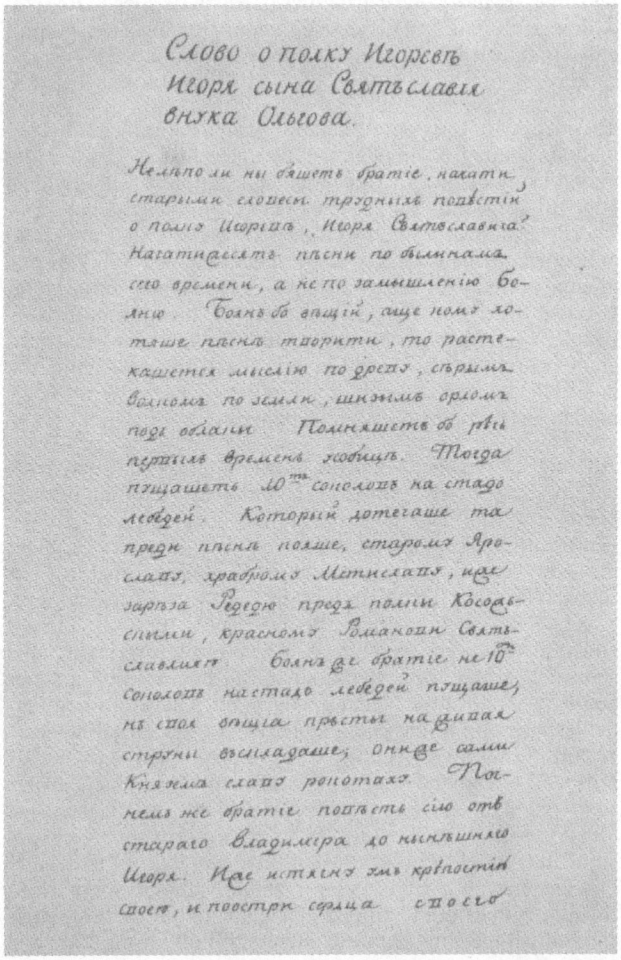

Between the ninth and eleventh centuries, the city of Kiev served as the economic and political center of Russia. By the twelfth century the city's hegemony was in decline, primarily due to the increased prominence of other trading centers and to the political fragmentation caused by internecine wars between various Russian princes. These factors were exacerbated by the attacks of the Polovetsians, cattle herders and warriors of the steppe who made frequent, devastating raids into Kievan Russia. Igor Svyatoslavich, prince of Novgorod-Seversk, was active both in the internecine wars and in the repeated campaigns waged by coalitions of Russian princes against the Polovetsians. In April 1185, shortly after a victorious campaign led by the Grand Princes Ryurik and Svyatoslav against the nomads, Igor impetuously launched a campaign of his own into Polovetsian territory without consulting the senior princes. Undeterred by a solar eclipse, which his companions took to be an evil omen, Igor led his troops to initial victory over a small detachment of Polovetsians; however, the Russians' subsequent confrontation with the full Polovetsian army ended in disaster. In the course of a three-day battle, the majority of Igor's retinue was killed, while Igor, his son Vladimir, and his brother Vsevolod were taken prisoner. The Polovetsians were inspired by their victory to launch renewed attacks into Russian territory, causing widespread devastation and jeopardizing the survival of the principality of Kiev. Igor remained captive for five weeks, but escaped with the help of a Polovetsian guard in June 1185.

Six centuries later, in 1795, a single manuscript copy of a poem recounting Igor's campaign, capture, and escape was discovered by Russian archaeologist A. Musin-Pushkin. This manuscript was destroyed in the Moscow fire of 1812, and the poem survived only in copies of a first edition published by Musin-Pushkin in 1800 and in a handwritten copy discovered in the library of the empress Catherine some years later. Since that time, critical controversy has raged over the authorship and authenticity of *The Igor Tale*. The poem's detractors, seeking to prove it a forgery perpetrated or unknowingly promoted by Musin-Pushkin, base their arguments on a number of chronological and textual peculiarities, including modernisms of orthography and punctuation; anachronistic concepts, such as the advocacy of pan-Russian unity in an era of feudal separatism and overt paganism in an era of Christian literature; the absence of references to *The Igor Tale* in literature of the twelfth through eighteenth centuries; and explicit correspondences of content and style between *The Igor Tale* and the *Zadonshchina*, a chronicle dating from the fourteenth or fifteenth century. Defenders of the poem's authenticity locate its origins between 1185, the year of the events it relates, and 1187, the death date of a Kievan prince mentioned in the poem as still living. While these critics acknowledge that *The Igor Tale* contains seemingly anachronistic details, they attribute these to the poet's individuality of thought, and counter the skepticism of the poem's detractors with the following arguments: the modernisms of orthography and punctuation were introduced by Musin-Pushkin and his fellow editors, who altered the twelfth-century text in an attempt to make it comprehensible to modern readers; the text contains archaisms of such obscurity that they have only recently been deciphered by philological researchers and could not have been utilized by scholars of earlier centuries; *The Igor Tale* is more likely the source of the *Zadonshchina* than its imitation; and finally, that the artistry of *The Igor Tale* far surpasses the poetic capabilities of any of its alleged forgers. Although a significant dissenting minority remains, most critics today acknowledge the poem as a genuine creation of the twelfth century.

The identity of the poem's author remains the subject of speculation, although commentators do agree that *The Igor Tale,* unlike many medieval epics, was the creation of an individual poet. In the words of Vladimir Nabokov, "The structure of *The Song* shows a subtle balance of parts which attests to deliberate artistic endeavor and excludes the possibility of that gradual accretion of lumpy parts which is so typical of folklore. It is the lucid work of one man, not the random thrum of a people." Critics have speculated that the author was an itinerant court poet, a chronicler associated with the monastic houses, a courtier of Igor, or was either an eyewitness to or a participant in the prince's campaign.

Although designated a "slovo"—translated as song, lay, ballad, oration, or discourse—and commonly referred to as a poem, *The Igor Tale* does not adhere strictly to any of these genres. Printed (in its original form) in lines of continuous text, the work comprises rhythmic yet flexible prose which has defied the efforts of scholars to reduce it to a metrical pattern. *The Igor Tale* demonstrates the influence of both the literary and oral traditions, combining elements of folk poetry and spoken language with stylistic features traceable to contemporary works of history and poetry. Critics have devoted particular attention to the poem's profusion of technical devices. According to N. K. Gudzy, "The *Slovo* is distinguished by profound saturation with imagery and symbolism. Poetical personification, metaphor, simile, parallelism: with all these the *Slovo* is full to overflowing." The poet eschews direct exposition in favor of symbol, allusion, and complexes of frequently obscure metaphors, presenting reality, in the words of Dean S. Worth, "in brief, almost cinematographic flashes, interspersed with lengthy authorial digressions into other times and places."

The poem's imagery, symbolism, and metaphors are most often drawn from nature, which is portrayed animistically. George P. Fedotov has noted that "nature and its phenomena occupy in *Igor's Tale* at least as important a place as human society," as natural elements mourn and rejoice in sympathy with humanity and play an active role in events. After Igor's defeat, for example, "the grass drooped in pity"; upon his escape, "the nightingales herald the dawn with their merry songs"; and during his flight, the River Donets "caressed the prince on its waves, spread out green grass for him by its silvery banks, clothed him with warm mists beneath the shade of the green trees." Related to this animism is the mythological and pantheistic worldview informing the poem, which is replete with demons, ancient Slavic gods, mythological creatures, and supernatural occurrences. Critics consider this pantheism an anomaly of the late twelfth century, an era in which remnants of paganism were retained by the majority of the people but the influence of the newly established Russian Orthodox Church dominated most works of literature. Gudzy, among others, attributes the pagan elements in the poem to literary traditionalism, maintaining that the author "was so steeped in poetry that . . . he could not, and did not wish to, depart from that attitude toward the world about him which went with paganism and which still had a very powerful hold at that time among the general masses."

In contrast to this literary traditionalism stand the author's progressive political convictions. Throughout *The Igor Tale,* the poet condemns Igor's campaign as an impetuous quest for personal glory which ultimately endangered the security of Russia, and utilizes the disastrous consequences of Igor's action as an admonition to the Russian princes to renounce personal ambition and unite for their own survival in the face of external danger. This concept of Russian unity has received a great deal of attention from critics, who consider the poet's political strategy particularly astute in an era dominated by the factionalism of petty principalities. Focus on the issue has yielded a number of assessments of *The Igor Tale* as political commentary, with Soviet critics in particular stressing the nationalistic aspects of the poem.

However, the images of Russian unity that pervade the poem extend beyond the political realm to the land itself, in its geographic, natural, and spiritual manifestations, and Dmitry Likhachov cautions that "the task of the *Lay* was less the military unity of the Russian people than their moral unity around the idea of a single Russian land." Nabokov dismisses the political aspects of the work entirely, noting that the poem's "political and patriotic slant pertaining to a given historical moment is . . . of small importance in the light of its timeless beauty." Similar assessments of the poem's artistic value have been put forth since the discovery of Musin-Pushkin's manuscript in 1795. Calling *The Igor Tale* "the greatest poetic monument Kievan Russia has handed on to us through the ages, and . . . a magnificent testimony to its culture," Renato Poggioli praises the universality achieved by the poem's anonymous author: "It is not only to an elite, either of our time or of his, that the poet of the *Slovo* appeals, but to all men able to understand poetry as a song of the tribe as well as a song of man."

PRINCIPAL ENGLISH TRANSLATIONS

"The Tale of the Armament of Igor," A.D. 1185: A Russian Historical Epic (translated by Leonard A. Magnus) 1915

"The Song of Igor's Campaign": An Epic of the Twelfth Century (translated by Vladimir Nabokov) 1961

"The Tale of the Campaign of Igor": A Russian Epic Poem of the Twelfth Century (translated by Robert C. Howes) 1973

GEORG BRANDES (essay date 1888)

[Brandes was a Danish literary critic and biographer whose extensive writings on such authors as Henrik Ibsen, August Strindberg, and Søren Kierkegaard helped make their works better known outside of Scandinavia. In his major critical work, Hovedstrømninger i det 19de Aarhundredes Litteratur *(1872-90;* Main Currents in Nineteenth-Century Literature*), Brandes viewed French,*

German, and English literary movements as a series of reactions against eighteenth-century thought. Brandes said of himself that he was more than a critic but less than a philosopher. In a letter to him, Nietzsche called Brandes a "missionary of culture." This is perhaps the best definition of Brandes's function within literature. He possessed the ability to view literary movements and the individuals who contributed to those movements within the broader context of virtually all of nineteenth-century literature. In his Impressions of Russia, *first published in Danish in 1888, Brandes combined personal observations based on a three-month visit to that country with a survey of Russian history and literature. In the following excerpt from that work, he discusses the epic qualities of* The Igor Tale.]

Russian literature possesses in ***The Story of Igor's Campaign*** an old epic of art of very high rank, corresponding to what the *Song of Roland* is for the French, and the *Niebelungenlied* for the Germans, but which, nevertheless, has the fault, which would be very serious in the eyes of the Germans, of being much shorter. (pp. 153-54)

When we mentally compare the ***Story of Igor*** with the heroic lays of the Edda, which are probably of greater antiquity and, at any rate, describe a rougher and wilder form of national life, the Russian poem, no doubt (in contradistinction to the Niebelungennôt), has the inequality and lyrical form as well as the predilection for a vivid dramatic representation in common with the Norse poems, but the essential feature of the Slavic epic is still entirely distinct. In the first place, the latter possesses an individuality. We do not know the author's name, but his entity stands out very distinctly before the reader, rich as it is in enthusiasm and piety. He speaks in his own name, stands as an individual responsible for his words, is conscious of a personal style of composition which is less flighty and fantastic than the style of the older seers and bards, whom he in other respects admires. In the next place, you feel that his love for the poetic art is not less strong than his admiration for the deeds of the princes of his day. He is an enthusiast for poetry. It is, as he expresses it, his intention to free himself from the poetic traditions; he does not wish to borrow from his predecessors "the old words." From the *bîlinî* [epic folk songs] we can see what he meant by this. There is found in them, just as in the Homeric poems, a standing supply of descriptive epithets. The mountains are always *gray,* the sea always *blue,* the sun always *red.* The earth is *our mother, the damp earth.* They always run on their *swift* feet, always take another by his *white* hand, etc. The unknown poet has plainly wished to adopt as little of that as possible. Nevertheless, we meet in him certain constantly recurring expressions which are evidently inherited, as, to drink the Don dry with his helmet, to set ten falcons on a flock of swans, to sow the earth with human bones, and certain constantly recurring epithets, as, Vsevolod, *the wild bull,* the *falcon* Igor, and his son the *young falcon,* and others.

As a man, the author of ***Igor's Campaign*** is far milder in his emotions than the author of even the mildest of the heroic poems of the Edda, "The Songs of Helge." The style in which, in his poem, Yaroslávna expresses her longing for Igor during his absence in the war, and her fear for the life of her lover, is more like Ingeborg's languishing lamentations in Tegner's poem than it is to Sigrun's loss of Helge in the Edda. And the whole life of emotion and nature, which the nameless poet has spread out before us, makes an entirely characteristic impression, by the grand, childlike simplicity with which the association between man and nature is interpreted and described. The whole of nature is alarmed when Igor starts upon his unfortunate ride to the Don: the sun is darkened, the night groans, the beasts howl in anticipation of the impending danger. Both Yaroslávna and Igor, on their part, address winds and streams as if they were men; nay, give them titles and complimentary words just as plainly as it is done in the *Iliad* two thousand years before. And the river Donyets gives Igor an answer. The living naturalism, the transfer of human qualities and emotions to nature, is so prominent here that it is noticed as the expressive personal naïveté of the characteristic poet.

Finally, the patriotism of this epic and of its author is characteristic in the highest degree. Patriotism permeates and constitutes its motive; a love for the Russian land, which breaks forth not only in mourning over the triumph of the heathen Polovtsians, but even more vehemently in wrath and laments on account of the discord between the Russian princes who, at the close of this pregnant period, rent the land asunder with civil war. (pp. 154-56)

This written epic is unique in Russian literature. It differs from the *bîlinî* of the Kief-circle by its purely historical character, since none of its leading actors are demi-gods, but all the heroes who figure there are men, who conquer or suffer in a purely human manner. In the next place, this epic is characteristic from its stamp of aristocratic culture, since it was evidently written with the purpose in view, like the old Norse laudatory poems, of being recited before the body guard of a prince. Therefore it does not extol the masses in the person of a popular hero, but sings of the chiefs and leaders of the army as the leading men. Still, however patriotic the poem is, it is nevertheless inspired by the patriotism of the princely power and of the highest culture. (p. 159)

Georg Brandes, "The Song of Igor—Its Characteristics, and Extracts from It," in his Impressions of Russia, *translated by Samuel C. Eastman, 1889. Reprint by Thomas Y. Crowell, 1966, pp. 153-59.*

K. WALISZEWSKI (essay date 1900)

[*In the following excerpt, Waliszewski discusses the authorship and plot of* The Igor Tale *and assesses the poem's artistic qualities.*]

Is [the ***Slovo***] the work of a single author who has failed to leave his name behind him? Or does it, like the *bylines* [epic folk songs], represent the conjoint labour of several generations of poets? These questions afford matter for cogitation. At the present day, the hypothesis of an individual authorship prevails, coupled with the admission of the existence of an ingenious grouping of elements, common to all the popular poetry of that period. . . . The very form of the poem seems to indicate it as the work of an individual. The author is constantly speaking in the first person, sometimes to invoke the memory of some forerunner of his own—whom he calls Boïane, and our knowledge of whose existence we owe to him—and sometimes to express his own admiration or sorrow, for he has not a touch of the Homeric calm.

He tells us the story of the expedition led by Igor, Prince of Novgorod-Siéviérski, charged by Sviatoslav, Prince of Kiév, to drive back the Polovtsy. Up to the time of the Tartar invasion, the Polovtsy were the greatest enemies of Russia. Igor begins with a victory, but, in a decisive battle, he is utterly beaten and carried into captivity. This event is attributed, in the chronicle known as that of Ipatiev, to the year 1185, and in that of Lavrentiï, to the following one. Both chronicles agree with the poet in ascribing the responsibility for the disaster to a quarrel between the princes. The poet adds some inventions of his own. Sviatoslav, who has not left Kiév—these Kiév princes are stay-at-home fellows, and generally send some one else when there is fighting to be done—sees the awful disaster in a dream. He hears the moans of the vanquished, mingled with the croaking of the ravens. Waking, he learns the facts, does not bestir himself, but sends messengers to the other neighbouring princes beseeching them to rise, "for the sake of the Russian soil and the wounds of Igor." Meanwhile, Iaroslavna, the wife of Igor, shut up in the castle of Poutivl, mounts the walls, and "mourns like a lonely cuckoo at sunrise." She is ready enough to go forth! "I will fly like a bird towards the Danube. I will dip my sleeve of otter-skin into its waters, and I will lave the wounds on the mighty body of Igor!"

The denouement is a triumph, though not of an over-heroic nature. Igor escapes from his prison. The Polovtsy pursue him, but Nature herself abets his flight. The woodpeckers, tapping on the tree-trunks, show him the way to the Doniets; the nightingales warn him of the approach of dawn. He reaches his home, and the Danube bears the voices of the daughters of Russia, singing the universal joy, across the sea to Kiév.

Though this arrangement of the episode is weak enough, both historically and geographically, it proves great wealth of imagination, and a tolerably intense poetic feeling. Certainly there has been an exaggeration as to the sentiments of a higher order—the love of the Russian Fatherland, the aspirations towards national unity—which some have chosen to discover in the work. Yet I cannot share the absolute scepticism of certain commentators as to these points. Surprising as the idea that such conceptions and emotions should have existed round about Kiév and Novgorod, towards the year 1185, may now appear to us, we are forced to admit that the *Chronicle* of Nestor shows us something of the same nature, at a much earlier date.

And apart from this, the poem, whether its authorship be individual or collective, is a work of art, and occasionally of very subtle art. Its methods of expression are classic; in the descriptive portions similes are frequent. The rolling *telegas* (waggons) of the Polovtsy scream in the darkness like a flight of wild swans. The invading army is likened to a cloud, which pours a murderous rain of arrows.

Another favourite poetic artifice is the personification of the elements. After Igor's defeat, the grass withers, the trees bend under the weight of the mourning that overshadows Russian soil. Iaroslovna confides her grief to the sun, to the wind, to the Dnieper. There is a fine lyric flow in her lament. (pp. 25-8)

I agree with the majority, as to the authenticity of the ***Slovo,*** though it has been greatly tampered with by copyists, translators, and commentators. Like Biélinski, and contrary, this time, to the majority, I refuse to regard the [***Slovo***] . . . as a second *Iliad*. I do not even place it, as a work of art, on a par with the poems of the Round Table Cycle. This work, as it stands at present, excels them in that simple wildflower freshness, full of colour and perfume, which made so great an impression on Biélinski. It is behind them too—far behind, especially as regards the principal figure, that of Igor, which is utterly lifeless and dim. On the whole, it shows great wealth of form, and an absolute poverty of idea. Russian life in the twelfth century could furnish but little of that. (p. 29)

K. Waliszewski, "The Epic Age," in his A History of Russian Literature, *William Heinemann, 1900, pp. 8-46.*

LEONARD A. MAGNUS (essay date 1915)

[Magnus's Tale of the Armament of Igor, *an English translation with critical and historical commentary, was the first extensive study in English of* The Igor Tale. *In the following excerpt from that work, Magnus presents the history of* The Igor Tale *manuscript, relates the events recounted by the poet, and examines the structure, style, authorship, and pagan elements of the poem. Line references in the text are to Magnus's translation, cited below.]*

In 1795 Count Musin-Puškin, a distinguished archaeologist, bought from the archimandrite of the Spaso-Yaroslávski monastery a bound volume of manuscripts, amongst which was the original of [the ***Slóvo***]. In 1800 he published the *editio princeps* under the title of "A heroic song of the foray against the Pólovtsy of the hereditary Prince of Nóvgorod-Sěverski, Ígoŕ Svyatoslávič." There were 1200 copies printed, a few of which survived the fire of Moscow in the year 1812 in which the original MS. and most of the printed copies perished.

Thus this printed book of 1800 was the only original, until Pekárski discovered a second modern copy amongst the papers of the Empress Catherine II, an account of which appears *infra*.

The *editio princeps* contains the text with a modern Russian translation, historical and other notes, an abstract of the action of the poem, and a preface giving the facts of the discovery. The text is printed as continuous prose, and there is a long list of *errata* at the end of the volume. The preface provides no sufficient detail as to the style, conditions or date of the lost original; nor to what extent, if any, the editors had adhered and followed it literally, or emended the orthography in conformity with the standards either of Russian or Church-Slavonic. From all accounts, Musin-Puškin was an ardent collector, but an indifferent critic; and, from contemporary evidence it has been gathered that only six of the learned men of the time ever had the opportunity of seeing this vanished MS.: amongst them Bantyš-Kamenski, A. F. Malinovski, A. I. Ermoláev, N. M. Karamzín, R. F. Timkovski and G. N. Boltin.

In the preface Musin-Puškin says:—"The original MS. is in very ancient handwriting. It belongs to the editor who, through his own endeavours and help received from experts in the Russian language has, in the course of some years brought this translation to the degree of clearness desired, and is now at the request of his friends publishing it to the world at large. But, in despite of all this, there remain some passages which are unintelligible; so, I beg my kindly readers to submit their suggestions to me. . . ."

Since that date there has been a deluge of editions and criticisms. . . . Evidently Musin-Puškin underrated the interest of his casual purchase.

It appears from the criticisms of Barsov and Tikhonrávov, as well as from contemporary statements, that the lost MS. was in a sixteenth century hand unpunctuated and with the words undivided, and Barsov impugns the handwriting of Musin-Puškin as a contributory cause of error.

For some years controversy raged on the genuineness of the poem; but the drift of opinion confirmed authenticity. This poem was flashed on the world very soon after MacPherson had roused all the scepticism of London with his Ossian; but the historical exactitude of the ***Slóvo,*** the fact that it had been vouched by a few but notable and responsible persons soon allayed the doubts.

No other ancient copy has been traced. Petrúševič very plausibly opines that the reason of the rarity is that the author was a layman with a strong inclination towards Pagan superstitions:—as is plain from the constant references to Slavonic deities—and that, for this reason, the poem was anathematized by the Church, which in medieval Russia, even more than in the rest of Europe was the sole custodian of written records and the art of writing. . . . [Double] faith lingered on throughout the hastily converted immensities of the Russian Continent for a very long time; and certainly this poem betrays no religious horror of the gods of olden time.

The poem must have been written and completed after 1185 and before 1187; and probably suffered in various transcriptions leading up to the XVI century original, which fell into Musin-Puškin's hands. Indeed I suspect that this lost text must have been in two hands; otherwise I cannot explain the variants in [certain] terminations, the relative clarity of some parts and the utter corruption of others, e.g. the passages referring to Svyatopólk and Tugorkán, the digression on Vséslav of Polotsk. . . . (pp. i-ii)

However, in 1864, Pekárski, whilst burrowing among the private archives of Catherine II, lighted on six folios of manuscript, consisting of chronological and historical notes, many of them in autograph. The Empress was a keen student of medieval Russia, and, as appears from the autobiography of Musin-Puškin, very much interested in his collections of original records. She graciously allowed the Count to lend her some of his treasures, and, in return gave him access to papers in her own cabinet, asking him to elucidate manuscripts she found hard to decipher.

It follows that he must have been her chief informant on ancient Russian history: a fact confirmed by the discovery of a second copy of the ***Slóvo*** from the lost original, together with a special abstract of its contents, special notes, and a new manuscript translation into modern Russian for her use. She evidently conned this with great attention, as some of her pencil notes on the margins go to prove. This text is known as . . . the Archive copy, and is designated "E" . . . in this edition, the printed text of 1800 being called "P" (Musin-Puškin). In the same folio the Empress inserted in her own hand a number of genealogies of the princes of Kíev.

The variants in these two copies are important and significant. First, the vocalization of E is generally more in accordance with Russian than Church Slav usage; in the second place, in a number of corrupt passages, E supplies a better reading; in fact I take it that in E we are spared the additional mistakes of the printing house. . . . The explanatory documents—the translation, commentary etc.—also differ very slightly. Thus Yaroslávna is made out to be the wife of Vladímir Ígorevič, instead of Ígoŕ's; the abstract is shorter and more concise; the grammatical forms . . . regular, though still pointing to an original confusion in the lost MS. The numerals in E are marked with the modern Arabic symbols, not with the old Slav letters with numerical values, a difference of some considerable critical value. . . . In other cases, where words occur, probably derived from Eastern sources, already unintelligible to the sixteenth century copyist . . . E gives us a better, if more difficult reading; probably leaving the original as it stood, uninterpreted.

Obviously, in all these uncertainties and this hopeless field of conjecture, it would be ridiculous to attempt to fix on an author. But . . . the date of composition is fixed by the eclipse of the sun, by the reference to Yaroslάv of Galicia as alive, and by the appeal for help to contemporary princes, and must have been in 1185 and 1186; in the latter year the jubilant conclusion celebrating Ígoŕ's escape (uncontemplated in the first two parts of the poem) was added to the first draft.

Furthermore, the author must have been an eye-witness; for his account of the battle confirms and corroborates the tales of the Chronicles, supplying other detail; he had strong sympathies with the faction of the Ólgoviči and the independent house of Polotsk, and shows little kindliness towards the branch of the ruling family of whom Vladímir II was the greatest and the best. Lastly, the author has a strong and markedly individual style, avoiding exaggeration and grotesque figures (such as are found in the folk-tales, e.g. as extraordinary magic, many headed monsters etc.); and is also free from the loose and inchoate profuseness of the Ballads, with their rather sploshy and irregular metre.

Lastly, to hazard a guess, the headings in the Ipatíevski Chronicle for the years succeeding the events of 1185, often fall into a poetical style, not altogether dissimilar; and as the writer of the ***Slóvo*** shows accurate acquaintance with the records of the past and often repeats almost *verbatim* the expressions used in these Chronicles, it is not improbable that he may have been associated with the production of them. (pp. ii-iv)

The ***Slóvo*** falls into three distinct parts, each of them subdivisible. The episode eternized by the author is very slight, one of the many forays against the nomad foes, with whom, for the rest, these Russian princes never scrupled to ally themselves in their perpetual dynastic and territorial quarrels. But Ígoŕ, to judge by the space his exploits occupy in the Chronicles, seems to have been a romantic and impulsive figure, and this particular raid receives very much more than the usual allowance of space. Still, to eke out the tale, the author in true epic style introduces a mass of material, incidental and illustrative.

In the first section of Part I, (l. 1-28) the poet opens by hesitating whether he shall tell the weary story of Ígoŕ's expedition in the old-world style of Boyán (or Yan), or in contemporary manner, probably like the ballads, (a diffuse method of narration with many repetitions, and couched in a loose metre of long lines with four or five accentual beats). He passes on to a eulogy of Boyán the wizard, whose fingers made the harp-strings live, in recording the feats of the princes three and four generations back.

The next section (ll. 29-37) states the scope of the invention of the author from Vladímir I to his contemporary Ígór; and passes on to the third (ll. 38-58) where in words almost identical with the Chronicles, Ígoŕ, despite the evil omen of an eclipse of the sun (astronomically verified to the hour) summons his men, he being fierily eager,—as the Chronicles tell,—to avenge the imagined slight that he had taken no share in the victory of the previous year 1184.

At l. 38 the action begins in words very nearly identical with the Chronicles.

The author, in the fourth section (ll. 59-78), characteristically interrupts the narrative, this time with an invocation of Boyán, whose inspiration extended back to the legendary days of Troyán, probably representing the founders of the Scandinavian dynasty. He quotes some of Boyán's lines, and composes a sequel in the same style, but applicable to his own day.

In the fifth section (ll. 79-99) the action of the poem is resumed. Vsévolod in a spirited speech,—which points a moral against others' indifference,—announces his readiness to help his brother;

and the following division (ll. 100-112) relates how they start, how evil were the portents.

But (ll. 113-135) the enemy are making their preparations and the Russian force is cut off from its base.

Section Eight (ll. 136-148) describes the first day of battle, and the Russian victory, the looting of the Polovsk tents; followed by a night of ill-judged repose (149-155).

The tenth sub-division gives a brief narrative of the second day's fight (156-189) and the countless re-inforcements of the barbarian enemy.

Again (section XI, ll. 190-208) other matter is interposed; the panegyric of Vsévolod who showed such valour; and in section XII (ll. 209-249) there follows a reminiscence of the days of Rurik and Yarosláv the Great and of Olég of Tmutarakáň, the ancestor of the Ólgoviči, the house ousted from Kíev by Vladímir II. The exploits of Olég and his associate Borís Vyáčeslavič, the battle on the Nežátin are mentioned: the author deplores that the children of the civilizing Sun, the Russians were and are wasting their blood in internecine strife.

Section XIII (250-284) describes the battle during the next night, and the morning of the next day; the language is powerful and poetic; the calamity expressed in words of striking simplicity and pathos, Ígoŕ has fallen; his banners are the enemy's prize; the brothers are separated.

So the first part ends: and the second, the longest, touches on the woes of Russia consequent on this defeat, and the misery inflicted on her by her disunion.

The first section (ll. 284-308) is a gruesome account of how Discord arose, and Ignominy walked abroad. So, too, after this disaster; when Končák the Polovsk leader used the Greek fire against the cities of Russia, (ll. 309-331) and the women of Russia wept, and Kíev was oppressed with grief. The cause is ever the same; civil strife, whilst the Pagan gathers tribute. But this was Russia's secular bane; under the Tatar rule, those immense territories could not combine for defence; only the iron hand of Moscow could enforce union and despotism.

The third movement of this part (ll. 332-360) continues in the same strain; that Ígoŕ and Vsévolod have courted disgrace and contrasts Svyatosláv III, the reigning prince at Kíev, who had in 1184 gained such a glorious victory. And, all the nations rang with his praise.

At this point (section IV. ll. 361-389) the poet interposes another subject, the Dream of Svyatosláv, and its interpretation by his *boyárs*. He had dreamed he had been given wine mixed with dust; that the mainstays of his house had been sapped; for on that fatal Third day two such mighty princes had been defeated, and the Lights of Russia extinguished (Section V. ll. 390-413) on the Kayála river; whilst the maidens rejoiced on the shore of the Black sea.

After this lyric interruption, the poet (section VI. ll. 414-452) resumes the lament of Svyatosláv. This "golden word" is terse and moving. Ígoŕ and Vsévolod are valiant, but headstrong. Yet Svyatosláv sees no aid approaching from his powerful Galician ally Yarosláv Vladímirkovič who could summon the mercenaries from beyond the Carpathians. Nor is there any relief going out to the city of Rim which the Pólovtsy have sacked and gutted.

At section VII (l. 453) the poet leaves Svyatosláv and addresses the principal territorial rulers of his time, who are backward in offering assistance. First of all, he adjures Vsévolod Yúrevič, the sovereign of Suzdal (the Northern state which had already gained practical supremacy (ll. 453-464). Vsévolod had in 1182 conducted an expedition against the Bolgars of the North; if he would help, slaves would be cheap again!

Next (ll. 465-476) he demands succour of Ruric and David Rostíslavič, princes of Smolénsk.

Thirdly (ll. 477-494) he directs himself to Yarosláv of Galicia, a wise and circumspect ruler over an immense territory bounded by the Carpathians for all their length, and bordering on Poland. Yarosláv was also Ígoŕ's father-in-law.

Fourthly, Roman and Mstíslav Rostíslavič (ll. 495-516) of Smolénsk are besought for aid. These campaigned beyond the Tátra range of the Carpathians, and amongst the Lithuanians; will they not turn their arms nearer home to the frontier rivers of the East?

Next, the poet requests help (ll. 517-530) of Ingváŕ and Vsévolod Yaroslávič of Lutsk, another branch of this prolific house . . . , and joins with them the three Mstíslaviči, their first cousins. Of all these the poet records no good done; will they not bestir themselves?

Now the writer prepares the way for suggestive reminiscences of chieftains of the past. He recalls (ll. 531-587) the heroic death of Izyasláv Vasíl'kovič of the house of Polotsk, fighting alone and unaided of his brothers against the Lithuanians. It is curious that this is one of the few references for which no authority can be found in the Chronicles. The tone of these lines carries conviction of their factual truth and is strong evidence of contemporary authorship. The same expressions of ceremonial mourning are used of this Izyasláv, as of Ígoŕ (ll. 555-557).

After this long section of the poem, we find a general imprecation against the sluggishness of the princes of the day, addressed to the cowardly brother of Svyatosláv III, Yarosláv Vsévolodovič, and to all of the descendants of the great Vséslav of Polotsk (ll. 558-568). The writer, whose sympathies are entirely with what the historians regard as the rebellious houses of Polotsk and the Ólgoviči, still accuses these princelets of degeneration from ancestral valour, and of utilizing barbarian mercenaries, rather than fending off the national foe. With this introduction of Vséslav who revolted so successfully against Vladímir II, he enters on the ninth section (ll. 569-611).

This is one of the difficult and corrupt passages in the text; full of references which have been the standing puzzles of all interpreters.

The author selects the episode of the battle on the Nemíga, after Vséslav had sacked Nóvgorod and Pskov, when Vséslav was treacherously imprisoned at Kíev. For nine months he was chosen Grand Prince of Kíev, whilst his enemy Izyasláv, the reigning prince, was in exile in Poland; on Izyasláv's approach he fled secretly by night to Bělgorod and thence home to Polotsk. Vséslav in the ballads was turned into a wizard, and in these passages the writer of the Slóvo accumulates a perplexing detail of mythological and superstitious lore, with incidental mention of those riddling persons Boyán and Troyán.

From Vséslav (ll. 611-620) the poet passes on to a brief mention of Vladimir I, whose energy was never abated.

A new section opens (ll. 621-662) the lament of Evfrósyna Yaroslávna, Ígoŕ's wife. It is not too much to say that this portion of the poem is one of the most beautiful heroic lyrics known. It is no doubt based on some pagan incantation of the four elements and splits up into four sections, her resolve to bind her hero's wounds, her appeals to the Wind, the Water and the Sun.

The third great division of the poem opens at line 663. It is very short and has the appearance, (as has been suggested by Sederholm and others) of being a subsequent addition. This poem must have been written immediately after the disaster, as the appeals for help go to show. When Ígoŕ escaped, this jubilant appendix was added.

The first section (ll. 663-693) describes how Ígoŕ escaped at night from captivity, during a drunken feast. He had to be persuaded against his will, and removed by his fear of being murdered before he would adopt this course of breaking parole. His groom Ovlur, Vlur or Lavor obtained him the means of evasion.

There follows (ll. 694-718) a curious dialogue between Ígoŕ and the river Donéts, in which the clemency of the river-god to Ígoŕ is contrasted with the cruelty of the Stugná to young Rostíslav Vsévolodič at the battle of 1093 against the Pólovtsy.

Still more remarkable is the following section (ll. 719-744), a conversation between Gzak and Končák, the Polovsk leaders: the good omens cease and these two discuss what will be the outcome of the escape. They say that Ígoŕ's son will marry a daughter of one of their chieftains during his captivity, but this will not be to the advantage of the nomads.

The fourth section (ll. 745-753) contains a reference, possibly a quotation, from Boyán, probably an outline of the history of the princes whom he celebrated; and the quotation is made to bear upon the Ígoŕ of 1185.

The fifth section (751-770) concludes the poem and mainly consists of an account of Ígoŕ's return, the joy it spread, and a conventional ending not unlike that of the later ballads: some of this conclusion might be spurious.

Allusions and historical references are very aptly introduced, and serve to make, out of the bard's commemoration, a little epic in which the life of medieval Russia is faithfully and appositely illustrated; one, too in which much poetry of very high quality abounds. (pp. xxxv-xxxix)

To enquire for the name of an author of this poem is a hopeless quest; there is only one original; and other medieval writings of Russia must likewise remain nameless.

But it is still possible from both internal and external evidence to localize and individualize the poet.

This poem is a little epic, to celebrate an event of merely passing interest, to invoke aid to release a minor prince of the House and revenge an unimportant defeat,—almost a broadsheet which was also a work of genius. It is narrowly and strictly historical. The date of composition is fixed by the reference to the eclipse of 1185, the adulation of Yaroslav of Galicia who died early in 1187, and also by the evident manner in which the first two sections were written as an appeal for help, without any anticipation of Ígoŕ's escape which is poetized in the third part.

Thus the poem is absolutely topical; and its accuracy in enhanced by its close connections with the contemporary Chronicles in style, grammar and matter. The historical invocations and reminiscences are not only in conformity with the records, but in many cases borrow their phraseology with the very slightest modifications.

The account of the battle, as many of the commentators have observed is so sharp, and contains corroborative details, which would almost make it appear that the poet was an eye-witness or a combatant. . . .

The style is strongly marked. There is a recurrence of animal similes, a very evident love of nature, not the modern lyrical worship, but shown in an intense faith in Nature's cooperation and sympathy with mankind, a genuine survival of the old Pagan pantheocracy.

The style is terse and powerful. There is no waste of effort, no empty verbiage such as mars the longer and more intimate passages in the Chronicles; nor again any of that wearisome reiteration and loose metre that makes the *bylíny* [epic folk songs] so formless, turgid and unschooled. In fact, the writer seems to take his resolve "not to follow the school of the ballads of his own day" so seriously, that at the crises of his story, his narrative becomes almost telegraphic in its compression, e.g. the parting of the brothers Ígoŕ and Vsévolod, the recital of Ígoŕ's escape and rescue; whilst in the invocations to the princes there is hardly one word that does not serve to explain their boundaries, their exploits, or their patriotic record.

This exactitude and conciseness, combined with poetic presentation, and a wealth of imagery drawn from the forests and the heavens, is broadly speaking the determinant feature of the style of the ***Slóvo***; and it is not inapposite to remark that the Ipatíevski Chronicle, in the years succeeding the events of 1185, contains snatches of verse reminiscent of the ***Slóvo***. . . . (pp. xlii-xliii)

Probably, if not certainly, the close correspondence of the Chronicles and this poem tends to prove that the writer must have been connected with the monastic houses, which, year by year set down so faithfully the little incidents in Russia's anarchic history, and yet so often were able to discern and insist on the bigger events, e.g. the taking of Kíev by Mstíslav Andréyevič of Súzdal' in 1171, the first approach of the Pečenegs, the Pólovtsy and the Tatars.

But all we have is the poem, and it is only from its style that any guess should be hazarded as to who the author may have been. He is a sincere patriot who has exact acquaintance with his country's history and deplores the petty selfishness of the numberless princes, between which the wide territories were being parcelled up; his ambition was a united Russia, and, it is perhaps for this reason that he coined the word Russichi, sons of Russia, an affectionate patronymic not used since or before to designate the Russian people.

This poem must have enjoyed some fame, for it was woefully and unintelligently plagiarized in the *Zadónščina* to celebrate the great and unique victory of Dmítri Donskóy over the Tatars,—this copy is occasionally useful to enable us to restore a text earlier than that of Musin-Puškin's MS.—and passages from the ***Slóvo*** are quoted in some of the XV or XVI century *bylíny*. . . . Its semi-pagan tone and the comparative triviality of the history it celebrates must have contributed to its neglect.

So much has been made of the heathendom of this poem, so full a construction has been put on the passage from Strabo . . . that it becomes hard to see what is stated, or omitted,—apart from what modern critics delight to read into it.

One fact stands out, in the strongest contrast with the Chronicles—even those for 1185, where Ígoŕ is presented as a devotee—and with other more or less contemporary productions such as The Virgin's Visit to Hell, Daniel the Prisoner, Abbot Daniel the Palmer, that this poem is conspicuously non-Christian, non-pietistic in tone; the one or two references to churches impress me as conventional and insincere, and are, I think, interpolations made between the date of the original Manuscript of 1186 and the sixteenth century copy which was burned in the conflagration of Moscow.

At the same time the poem is not Pagan; it seems to reflect the mind of a sincere patriot, with no marked disbelief either in the lingering superstitions, or in the world-faith superimposed on them.

The attitude is what the Russians call . . . double-belief.

When Pagan gods go down before the intolerant and exclusive banners of Christianity, the former sovereigns of the empyrean are dethroned, anathematized and soon forgotten, whilst the meaner local, deities of the rivers and the way-side are left in possession, as before the great change; perhaps, clandestinely.

Incantations and ideas of witchcraft linger on; and, in Russia especially voluminous collections have been made of the formulas.

But, in the ***Slóvo*** these ordinary conditions are reversed; there is frequent and specific mention of the great gods, such as Stribog, Veles, Khors, Div, Dažbog; the Virgin of the primitive Slavs (recorded in Herodotus IV 9; poetized by Euripides in Orestes as Artemis of Tauris; and geographically certified by Strabo) reappears as the personification of Strife, counterbalanced by the figure of Glory. And, be it noted, in all of these passages both texts agree in using the old Bulgarian vocalization (which is replaced in E by more Russian forms). It is also observable that the principle god of the Russian pantheon, Perun, the Thunderer, is never so much as mentioned: he was the Jupiter who had been dethroned.

The beautiful wail of Yaroslávna is based on some primitive incantation of the four elements, but has been transfigured far beyond the model,—to judge by the examples compiled by Sakharov.

Where the great gods are mentioned, it is always to ascribe to them metaphorical descendants: thus the winds are the scions of Stribog, the Russians the descendants of Dažbog, the fertilizing sun,—possibly also some Saturn who founded a Golden Age (cf. the Chronicles for 1114)—whilst Boyán, the great poet of the past epoch, is the inspired grandson of Véles the god of cattle, a phrase, which in the complete absence of other contemporary evidence, it is impossible to explain.

Div, some kind of malignant bird who screeches disaster from the tops of the trees, scarcely comes in the same category. He possesses more reality than these other semi-metaphorical beings. He must be ranked with the numerous omens of the natural phenomena, which play so live a part in the elaboration of the unimportant foray, the subject of the poem. The crows, the magpies and daws, the nightingales and the wild beasts are all credited with superstitious relevance to human happenings; in these lines there is no trace of convention or effort after style. After all such ideas are rife even in latter-day England.

The sun is, if not worshipped by the writer of this poem, regarded as a person of great influence. In the Chronicles every eclipse of sun and moon is narrated with the greatest detail; and the highest compliment that can be paid to virtuous and vigorous princes is to compare them with the sun, to treat them, literally, as the sources of enlightenment. So, too, in this poem Ígoŕ and his brave brother are called two suns who have been extinguished, his infant children, two moons that have waned. One of the real survivals of heathendom in this poem is to be traced in the passionate attention paid to Nature and her manifestations.

The rivers and wells of Russia have always been peopled with spirits. This fact emerges throughout all of the balladry and the folklore of Russia and, indeed, all the Slav nations. The rivers consciously protect or destroy their favourites; they are powers who must be appeased. The story in this text, of the malicious Stugná that drowned young Rostíslav Vsévolodič, whilst the Donéts smoothed its waves to facilitate the escape of Ígoŕ; the conversation between our hero and the Donéts; all of these are real beliefs, the outcome of heathendom, that can be parallelled voluminously in the later ballads (e.g. in the account of the death of Vasíli Buslávič, and in the *bylíny* of the mystic river Smoródina).

In this poem every form of nature has active power to help, to sympathize or to thwart. When the heroes of Russia falter, all nature literally droops, the trees weep, the grass withers. These expressions are real, the live relics of the old nature worship of the Slavs; of which Rimbaud has said:—"Les Grecs se sont bien plus vite dégagés de la matière; ils sont allés aussitôt au polythéisme. . . . Chez les Slaves le panthéisme est partout à fleur de terre; cette matière cosmique, les Slaves l'ont aimée comme elle était, l'ont chérie, sans éprouver le besoin de lui donner forme humaine . . ." ["The Greeks became much more quickly disengaged from matter; they went immediately to polytheism. With the Slavs pantheism is everywhere level with the earth; this cosmic matter the Slavs loved as it was, cherished it, without feeling the need to give it human form."]

To sum up; it seems to me that in this poem the author was expressing his inmost convictions, and therefore indulged in no conventional religious outbursts such as disfigure his plagiarist in the *Zadónščina,* and pall on the reader of the monastic Chronicles; but, he was well acquainted with the Chronicles and imported images from them of the ancient Pagan gods, without transliterating them into his own dialect; perhaps it was an assertion of the longing for a united Russia to fight the infidel nomads, a literary asseveration of nationalism.

I cannot hold, with Vyázemski and Petrúševič that there is any Greek influence on his form, still less any adaptation of classical models. In the passages dealing with that remarkable figure Vséslav whose reputation for Pagan practices must have had some foundation in history, there are probably records of what was told of him; though most of the direct allusions to episodes that would only suit a fairy-tale are certainly misreadings of a text unusually corrupt. The principal survival of Pagandom is the vivid presentation of the active part which every natural growth and phenomenon,—from the stars in heaven down to the grass of the steppe—takes in the affairs of humanity, to forward the right and deplore the wrong. (pp. xliii-xlvi)

Leonard A. Magnus, in an introduction to The Tale of the Armament of Igor: A Russian Historical Epic, A.D. 1185, *edited and translated by Leonard A. Magnus, Oxford University Press, London, 1915, pp. i-lv.*

PRINCE D. S. MIRSKY (essay date 1927)

[*Mirsky was a Russian prince who fled his country after the Bolshevik Revolution and settled in London. While in England, he wrote two important histories of Russian literature,* Contemporary Russian Literature *(1926) and* A History of Russian Literature *(1927). In 1932, having reconciled himself to the Soviet regime, Mirsky returned to the USSR. He continued to write literary criticism, but his work eventually ran afoul of Soviet censors and he was exiled to Siberia. He disappeared in 1937. In the following excerpt, Mirsky discusses elements of* The Igor Tale *that distinguish it from poetry of its own and subsequent eras.*]

There existed in Kievian times a secular oral poetry, the preservers of which were singers belonging to the upper military class of the prince's companions, and similar to, but less professional than the Norse scalds. This poetry flourished in the eleventh century; some of the poems were still remembered in the end of the twelfth. They were associated with the name of a great singer, Bayan, whose songs are quoted by the author of the ***Slovo.*** But it is not clear that at the time of the composition of the ***Slovo*** this oral poetry was still alive. ***The Campaign of Igor*** itself is a purely literary work, *written,* and not sung. Its title ***Slovo*** (which, however, may be an addition of a later scribe) is the translation of the Greek *logos,* and like *logos* means originally *word,* and secondly "discourse, sermon, oration"; it was used to describe a great variety of literary works of not strictly narrative character. On the other hand the ***Slovo*** speaks of itself as a *song*. The author, though anonymous, has a powerful individuality. He was a layman, probably the companion of some prince. He was steeped in books and in oral tradition. The great originality of his work was that he used the methods of oral poetry in a work of written literature. There is no reason to believe that he had had any literary predecessors in this manner of writing. But he has also roots in the literary tradition. The similarity of some turns of phrases and expressions with the Russian Josephus . . . is very striking, and there are more distant associations with the style of the ecclesiastical orators, and with that of the Annals. The rhythmical structure of the poem is not that of verse. Russian scholars have spent great pains in trying to reduce it to a metrical pattern, but they have not succeeded in arriving at a satisfactory solution. They have always been guided by the preconceived idea that a work of such great poetic beauty must be in verse and have overlooked the existence of such a thing as highly organized rhythmical prose. The rhythm of prose is different in *kind* to the rhythm of verse, for it lacks the essential element of the latter—*the line*. It must be remembered that the parts of the Slavonic liturgy that are sung are nevertheless couched in prose, and that consequently even if the ***Campaign of Igor*** was actually a song (which is very unlikely) it need not necessarily have been in verse. A rhythmical analysis of the ***Slovo*** reveals (as a first impression suggests) that it possesses a very real and efficient rhythm, but a rhythm far more flexible, varied, and complex than that of any metrical pattern. It is perhaps not an exaggeration to say that in this respect it is a thing *sui generis:* no rhythmical prose I know of in any language can so much as approach it for infinitely varied flexibility.

It is not only the nature of its rhythmical prose that makes ***The Campaign of Igor*** a work unique of its kind. It is altogether difficult to classify. It is neither a lyric, nor an epic, nor a piece of political oratory, and it is all these blended into one. (pp. 17-19)

The spirit of the ***Slovo*** is a blend of the warrior spirit of the military aristocracy as reflected in the Chronicle of 1146-1154, with a wider patriotic outlook, that is more akin to that of Monomakh and of the patriotic clerics and which regards self-sacrifice for Russia as the noblest of virtues. It is also distinctly secular in spirit. Christianity appears only incidentally and rather as an element of contemporary life than as part of the poet's inner world. On the other hand reminiscences of an older nature-worship are part of the most intimate texture of the poem.

The style of the poem is the reverse of the primitive and barbaric. It is curiously, disconcertingly modern, all suggestion and allusion, full of splendid imagery, subtly symbolic and complex. (pp. 19-20)

Nature symbolism and nature parallelism play a large part in the poem. The movements of men have their "correspondences" in the movements of the "vegetable universe." This feature has been adduced as proof of the kinship of the ***Slovo*** to "popular poetry." A vague kinship there certainly may be, but no similarity of detail with later Great-Russian or Ukrainian folk-song. Besides, a nature parallelism of a very similar kind was a time-honoured form of expression in Byzantine sacred oratory.

The Campaign of Igor, alone of all Old Russian literature, has become a national classic, which is familiar to every educated Russian, and often known by heart by lovers of poetry. The quality of its poetry is entirely different from the quality of the poetry of the Classical Age of Pushkin, but it cannot be regarded as inferior. If Pushkin is Russia's greatest classical poet, the author of the ***Slovo*** is the greatest master of ornate, romantic, and symbolical poetry. His work is a continuous succession of purple patches, the least of which has no counterpart in modern Russian poetry. (p. 20)

Prince D. S. Mirsky, "'The Campaign of Igor', and Its Family," from his A History of Russian Literature: From the Earliest Times to the Death of Dostoyevsky (1881), *Alfred A. Knopf, 1927, pp. 17-25.*

N. K. GUDZY (essay date 1941)

[*A Russian literary historian, Gudzy was among the most prominent twentieth-century scholars of Old Russian literature. He also wrote studies of modern literary figures, including Nikolai Gogol, Alexander Pushkin, and Leo Tolstoy. In the following excerpt from a study originally published in 1941, Gudzy discusses the historical raid by Igor against the Polovetsians and examines literary influence, authorial intent, and poetic technique in* The Igor Tale.]

The clash between Russians and Polovcians described in the ***Tale of Igor's Expedition*** was by no means the first nor would it be the last. Rus had been subject to Polovcian attacks for a hundred years, since 1061, and the raids stopped only with the Tartar invasion itself, when the Polovcians were vanquished and partly amalgamated into the Horde.

At the beginning of the twelfth century, Rus took the offensive against the nomads of the steppe and dealt them a series of crushing blows. Vladimir Monomakh won particular distinction for his campaigns against the Polovcians. Between 1103 and 1116 he mounted four expeditions, as a result of which the Polovcians were thrown back across the Don, part of them into the Caucasus. Monomakh's work was continued by his son Mstislav. But with the death of Mstislav (1132), the Polovcians are seen gathering strength again.

In two centuries there were more than forty devastating Polovcian raids into Russian territory, without counting innumerable minor raids. Rus was severly shaken by the attacks. No sort of treaties or agreements insured safety from sudden

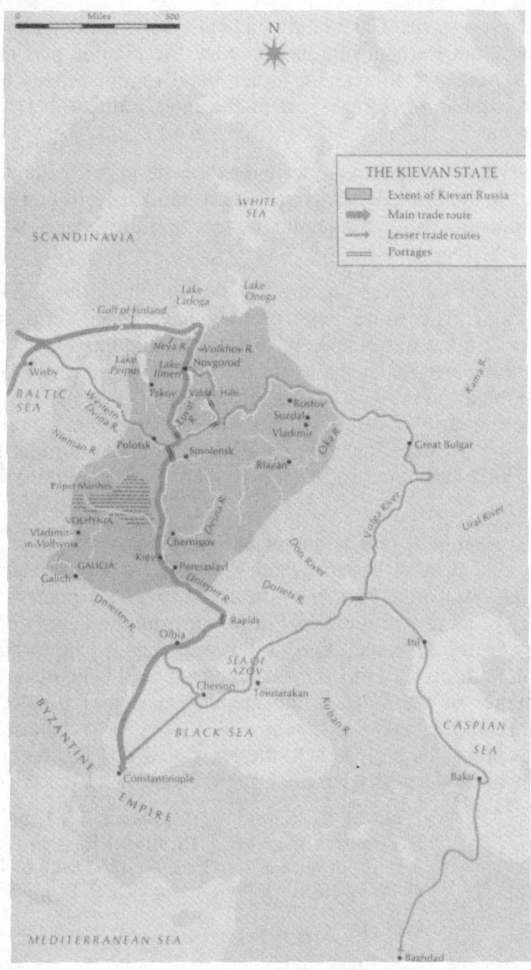

A map of Kievan Russia. Rafael D. Palacios.

incursions by the restless nomads. Even marriage alliances between Russians and Polovcians were of no use.

From the middle of the twelfth century, the Polovcians began to assail the Russian lands with particular violence. In 1170, fifteen years before Igor's expedition, a congress of South Russian princes talked of joining forces to fight the enemy. Prince Mstislav Izyaslavich, calling upon the princes to mourn for the land of Rus and for their heritage from their fathers and grandfathers, said of the Polovcians, who were constantly breaking their oaths: "They have already deprived us of the road to Greece, and the salt road [to the Crimea] and the gold road [to the Danube]."

The gravity of the situation was aggravated by perpetual quarrels between the princes, during which they frequently sought help of the Polovcians in settling their personal accounts.

All this was the chief contributing factor in the decline of the principality of Kiev, which, from the second half of the twelfth century, was clearly on the way toward political and economic collapse, so that by the time of the Tartar invasions its glory had long since faded. Ever since the ravaging of Kiev in 1169 by the forces of Andrew Bogolyubsky the great-princely throne and the principality of Kiev had lost their political preeminence. Kiev continued to impress the Russian princes actually only by the conventional semblance of being the traditional center of the Russian state and of Russian culture. In political influence and military might, Kiev was now definitely surpassed by the principalities of Suzdal and of Galicia-Volynia.

The failure of Igor's expedition, both in itself and in terms of the immediate historical setting of the campaign, must have been felt as an occurrence of especial gravity, out of all comparison with previous fiascoes of the Russian princes in their struggle with the steppe. Igor's defeat was unexpected not only to himself but also to his contemporaries. He had acquired a reputation as a Polovcian hater and as the lucky winner in several campaigns against them. Igor's first victory took place in 1174, when he killed many Polovcians and took many captive. In 1183 Igor vanquished the steppe tribes for a second time. In March, 1185, he made ready to assist Svyatoslav, Prince of Kiev, in his campaign against the Polovcians, saying: "God grant we may never refuse to fight the pagans: the pagans are the common enemy of us all." But ice conditions unexpectedly prevented his carrying out his intention.

Two months later, however, Igor and his allies set out against the Polovcians without consulting Svyatoslav of Kiev. The plans of the Severian princes were very far-reaching: the hope was, apparently, to win lost Tmutorakan back from the Polovcians. At least the boyars in the ***Tale of Igor's Expedition*** who interpret Svyatoslav's "troubled dream" speak of two falcons (that is, Igor and Vsevolod) having flown down from the golden throne of their fathers to seek the city of Tmutorakan or drink of the Don from their helmets.

And all these proud hopes were doomed to be cruelly dashed. The first impact of Igor's troops with the steppe, as we know, ended in victory for the Russians. But close on its heels came a grievous reckoning for them. The Polovcians gathered their forces and attacked. The three-day battle ended in the full rout of Igor's troops. The author of the ***Slovo*** recalls past battles of the Russian princes with hostile forces but can recall none so bloody as this one.

The defeat suffered by Igor in 1185 was really very serious: all four princes were taken captive, the greater part of their retainers were killed and the rest taken captive like themselves. Never yet, to judge by the chronicle accounts, had one of their campaigns against the Polovcians ended so disastrously for the Russians; never before had Russian princes been taken captive by Polovcians.

After their victory over Igor, the Polovcians rushed in to ravage Russian territory. Not without reason does the author of the ***Slovo*** say that the seeds sown by Igor sprouted sorrow for the land of Rus. The *Hypatian Chronicle* tells how, after routing Igor, the Polovcians were filled with self-confidence and made ready to invade the land of Rus. A dispute arose among them as to which direction they should move in. Khan Konchak voted for Kiev, where the Polovcians had been defeated, and Khan Bonyak and the other Khan, Gza, insisted upon attacking Posemyo where only women and children remained. This town was ripe for capture by the Polovcians and they could take it "without risk." Failing to come to an agreement, the Khans set out in different directions. On his way to Kiev, Konchak attacked Pereyaslavl and besieged the city. The prince of Pereyaslavl, Vladimir Glebovich, defended himself bravely, but was seriously wounded. From Pereyaslavl Konchak marched upon the city of Rimov, sacked it, took a large number of prisoners, and returned to his own country. Gza attacked Putivl, took it, set fire to villages, even burned down the jail at Putivl, then he too went back to the Polovcian steppes.

Like the chronicle, ***The Tale of Igor's Expedition*** tells of the shock sustained by the land of Rus following Igor's defeat. After this the "pagans" came victoriously into the land of Rus from all sides. Kiev groaned with sorrow and Chernigov groaned over its calamities. Anguish flooded the land of Rus, sadness flowed full across it. The princes were busy quarreling, and the "pagans" scoured the land of Rus. Svyatoslav of Kiev mourns the destruction of Rimov and the wounds of Vladimir, son of Gleb.

The gravity of Igor's fiasco was accentuated for Rus by the fact that this failure rendered meaningless beyond belief the brilliant victories over the Polovcians by the coalition of Russian princes headed by Svyatoslav of Kiev the year before. The long-awaited reconciliation between the sons of Oleg and the sons of Monomakh had finally taken place, and with their combined forces they had administered a crushing blow to their worst enemies.

Judging from the *Hypatian Chronicle,* Svyatoslav, in alliance with the other princes, had immediately won two more great victories over the Polovcians. After this it might have seemed that the enemy had been rendered powerless, and that the principality of Kiev, which had suffered from ceaseless forays by the nomads, been weakened and deprived of political prestige, might now entertain hopes of a political revival. But these hopes were rudely dashed by the rout of Igor's army, which gave new impetus to Polovcian expansion. This explains the energetic attempt of Svyatoslav to unite several Russian princes for the purpose of liquidating the consequences of Igor's fiasco; it explains also the quick reaction to events that we get in the author of the ***Slovo,*** who purposes by his talent and the force of his civic loyalty to be of service to the interests of his native land. He had a passionate patriotism for Kiev, was afflicted by her misfortunes, and dreamed of restoring her former authority and her former position as center of the Russian commonwealth. The still recent quarrels between the sons of Oleg and the sons of Monomakh were now a thing of the past to him and he was summoning these and the rest to support a common cause, the defense of the land of Rus, under the leadership of the Kievan prince of the line of Oleg, who had surmounted his former family sympathies and prejudices and was fighting for the common property of the "grandson of Dazhbog," the Russian people.

However, the well-being of the principality of Kiev was for the author of the ***Slovo*** inseparable from the well-being of the land of Rus as a whole, of the whole Russian people. His patriotic feelings for his native South were combined in him with a patriotism for all Rus, and fed this patriotism. For the defense of Rus against the Polovcians, he called not only upon those princes whose lands were immediately threatened by Polovcian inroads, but also upon those who were safe from these inroads, Vsevolod III of Suzdal, and Yaroslav of Galicia.

As affecting the fortunes of the Kievan principality at the end of the twelfth century, the military catastrophe which overtook Igor must have been regarded by the most farsighted of his contemporaries as a bitter trial, as a sort of final warning to the princes who had been following a policy of isolation and even at times striking up quarrels. The ***Tale of Igor's Expedition*** was an act of intervention on the part of a poet-citizen in affairs which might, he realized, prove fatal for the land of Rus. Consequently it is with trepidation and with passion that he cries out upon the grievous manifestations of princely separatism which had been the undoing of Rus before, and now threatened it with incalculable misfortune. The seriousness and tensity of the political situation of Kievan Rus, in view of the recrudescence of a danger which had but a moment before seemed past, thus evoked immediately after Igor's expedition, and in striking poetic form, what constituted, to use the words of Marx, "a summons to the Russian princes to unite, on the very eve of the Mongol invasion."

The ***Tale of Igor's Expedition*** gives a vivid picture of feudal life in Rus in the eleventh and twelfth centuries, especially in its characterization of princes and retainers. Igor and Vsevolod come before us as knights for whom honor and fame are the principal motives of conduct. Igor says to his retinue: "Brothers and retainers! It is better to fall in battle than to fall into captivity. I wish to break a lance at the edge of the Polovcian plain; with you, Russians, I wish either to lay down my head or drink my fill of the Don from my helmet." In the words of Svyatoslav, Prince of Kiev, the hearts of the two brothers were "forged of hard steel and tempered in daring." Knightly daring, bravery, warlike courage distinguish Igor, his brother the wild-aurochs Vsevolod still more, and likewise the princes Boris, son of Vyacheslav, and Vseslav of Polotsk. Of Román, Prince of Vladimir-Volynia, Svyatoslav says: "You fly high at heroic deeds, like a falcon soaring in the air, rushing boldly to strike at a bird." Igor's retinue is characterized as an army not interested in the material results of battle alone. It is seeking honor for itself, glory for the prince. And this is twice brought out in the ***Slovo.*** Vsevolod speaks thus of his retinue: "My men are experienced warriors, they were swaddled to the sound of trumpets, cradled to the sight of helmets, fed from the point of a spear. The paths they know, the ravines are familiar to them, their bows are taut, their quivers are open, their sabers sharpened: they leap like gray wolves in the field, seeking honor for themselves and glory for the prince." When addressing Rurik and David, Svyatoslav says: "Have you not a brave retinue who bellow like aurochs wounded by sabers tempered in the unknown plain?"

In the ***Slovo*** we find vivid and inspired portraits of historical figures of Old Rus, struck off upon occasion with uncommon success, and literally in but a few words. It required great historical and psychological acumen to sketch a whole group of historical portraits in such a masterly way as the author of the ***Slovo*** has done, and not portraits of his contemporaries alone but of personages who lived and made their name long before the poet's time. It would be difficult to point to anything in the history of the heroic epos in any country that equals the ***Slovo*** in the degree to which it reflects actuality.

The author of the ***Slovo,*** judging from the content of the monument, was a warrior, a retainer, presumably of the Kievan prince Svyatoslav, but he has immediate understanding of more than the warlike deeds of battle-hardened soldiers: he understands a brother's feeling of pity for a war-worn brother, and the sorrow of a mother mourning for a young son drowned, and the devoted love of a wife invoking the forces of nature to aid her husband's return to his own land. He is stern when he speaks of the enemies of his country and when he censures princes who start quarrels, and lyrically tender and compassionate when he speaks of those dear to him, the objects of his very real human interest.

Maintaining a viewpoint well in advance of his time in championing broadly national interests, the author of the ***Slovo*** surrounds the prince of Kiev with the aureole of political authority over all Rus. He looks disapprovingly on Igor's ruinous undertaking and, with Svyatoslav, grieves over the failure that had cost the Russian people so dear. But since he is aiming not at dissociation of their forces, not at disunion among the princes, but at solidarity in a common aim, he speaks of Igor and Vsevolod in such a way as to call forth the sympathy of other princes with respect to the fate of colleagues who had already paid so heavy a price for not tempering their martial fervor. He gives the courage and daring of both princes their due, emphasizes their knightly intrepidity and the warlike quality of their retainers, and in everything that he says about Igor and Vsevolod and about their fate, strives to inspire sympathy and good will for the ill starred unfortunates and to unite the princes all the more firmly for repulsing the Polovcians. And when Igor succeeds in escaping from captivity, the author rejoices over his return to Rus. It is a satisfaction to the poet's patriotic sense that the brave though unfortunate warrior should have returned from bondage to the princely fold, that, as the ***Slovo*** says, he should have come straight to Kiev, to Svyatoslav, instead of stopping at his own appanage, and thereby had, as it were, atoned for his highhanded behavior with respect to the senior prince.

The distinguishing marks of the ***Tale of Igor's Expedition*** as a work of art are graphically demonstrated when we compare it with the *Hypatian Chronicle*'s account of the campaign of Igor Svyatoslavich against the Polovcians. The chronicle narrative gives seriatim all the principal facts about Igor's campaign, the destruction of Russian cities by the Polovcians following the rout of Igor's army, and the return of Igor from captivity. It is informed to a considerable degree by the pious Christian attitude, and this piety distinguishes Igor himself first and foremost. Seeing an eclipse of the sun when already on the way, Igor consoles his retinue with the observation that the secrets of God no man knows, but that every portent comes from God, creator of the universe. The victory of the Russians over the Polovcians in the first encounter Igor attributes to divine aid, and the defeat that follows victory he explains as God's punishment for the acts of murder and bloodshed that he has perpetrated in the land of Rus.

The ***Slovo*** does not aim to give a recital of consecutive moments in Igor's campaign and his return from captivity but primarily at awakening emotions of pity and sympathy for Igor's misfortune and explaining everything that happened in terms of a definite political situation. With this aim in view, the author of the ***Slovo*** presents a series of shifting lyric scenes in which the factual element is relegated to the background and prominence given to picturesque descriptions of the most dramatic moments in the fate of Igor and his army. The ***Slovo*** bespeaks a Christian author, but that author does not assign to anyone of his personages specifically Christian, let alone pious, feelings and attitudes of mind. It contains more elements of pagan mythology than any other Russian monument.

After hesitating as to how to begin his account of Igor's campaign—whether "according to events of our time," that is, in accordance with the historical narratives of his time, or "Boyan's way," as it might have been sung by a poet now unknown who lived in the second half of the eleventh century and the beginning of the twelfth—the author of the ***Slovo*** decides to choose the former method rather than aim to keep pace with the bold fancy of Boyan, who, when he wanted to compose a song, "set his thought running up a tree, or along the ground like a gray wolf, or flying under the clouds like a gray-blue eagle." But though verbally refusing to follow Boyan, the author in point of fact does follow in his footsteps, and instead of the traditional war story produces what is simultaneously a passionate lyric ballad and a rousing publicistic pamphlet, constituting himself judge not only of present but of past Russian history, repeatedly digressing from his narrative to lapse into reasoning and reflections. Exact facts do not interest him; he finds it more important to give a general impression of events and make the reader relive and really experience them emotionally. The account in the *Hypatian Chronicle* tells exactly what transpired during the first encounter of the Russians with the Polovcians and, just in passing, indicates that the Russians took prisoners. In the ***Slovo,*** as in the *Laurentian Chronicle,* we find no details of this first encounter, yet here, described in sumptuous hyperbole, are the fruits of Igor's victory, its rich trophies: pretty Polovcian girls and, with them, gold and all manner of costly textiles, seized in such abundance that bridges of them might have been laid across the marshes and swampy places. Following the notice of their first success against the Polovcians, the *Hypatian Chronicle* gives a fairly detailed description of the battle which ended in defeat for the Russians. The ***Slovo*** provides almost no exact facts about the battle, but conveys with the utmost artistic expressiveness all the drama, all the extraordinary intensity of the action: "The earth hums, the rivers are muddied, dust covers the fields. . . . From morning until evening, from evening until dawn, the tempered arrows fly, swords clang on helmets, steel lances crash in the unknown field, in the land of the Polovcians." (pp. 158-64)

For the sake of comparing the *Hypatian Chronicle* account with the ***Slovo,*** let us also study a narrative moment that is common to both. The chronicle account in very realistic, albeit not entirely unlyrical, detail, tells how Svyatoslav was informed of Igor's defeat: he had got as far as Severian Novgorod, with the intention of spending the whole summer attacking the Polovcians on the Don, when he first learned that his cousins Igor and Vsevolod had set out against the Polovcians by themselves, and it was not pleasant news to him; then, upon reaching Chernigov, he heard of the rout of the brothers, from Byelovolod Prosovich, evidently a participant in Igor's campaign, and with a sigh, as he wiped away the tears, began reproaching the princes whose youthful impetuosity had opened the gates of the land of Rus to the enemies whom he had himself laid low the year before. "But God's will be done in all things," he ended by saying. "I now feel sorrier for Igor, my brother, than I before felt vexed with him." Then Svyatoslav sent word of Igor's rout to the neighboring princes, calling upon them for help against the Polovcians.

This literal account, adhering to the actual facts in the case, takes on under the pen of the ***Slovo*** poet new poetic and publicistic details. Svyatoslav, though as yet he knows nothing of Igor's defeat, is already oppressed by evil forebodings. He has a troubled dream which presages him no good, though the meaning of this dream is as yet not clear to him. The ***Slovo*** author employs a device as old as the Bible, one which had been used both in oral poetry and in literary monuments, among them the *Adventures of Digenis,* where the prophetic-dream motif, as we have seen, figured twice—with Amir, then with his wife—and where one dream was interpreted by Amir's "knights" (as in the ***Slovo*** by Svyatoslav's suite, his boyars), the second by soothsayers. In accord with the whole style of the ***Slovo,*** Svyatoslav's dream is interpreted not through literal realistic equivalents, as in the *Adventures of Digenis,* but metaphorically: "Behold, two falcons have flown from the golden throne of their fathers to reach the city of Tmutorakan or drink of the Don from their helmets; already the falcons' wings have been clipped by pagan sabers and themselves been enmeshed in iron fetters," and so forth. Then follow Svyatoslav's reproaches against Igor and Vsevolod, in spirit and in purport closely resembling the reproaches which Svyatoslav addresses to these princes in the *Hypatian Chronicle*. But the next brief statement in the chronicle, telling how Svyatoslav urged the Russian princes in Igor's neighborhood to aid in checking the Polovcians, is transformed under the pen of the ***Slovo*** author into the impassioned "golden word" addressed by Svyatoslav to all the most powerful Russian princes, and thrice interrupted by the lyrical refrain: "for the land of Rus, for the wounds of Igor, bold son of Svyatoslav."

Immediately after Svyatoslav's "golden word" come the author's historical recollections. By analogy, the quarrels of the present princes, who have brought ruin upon the land of Rus, recall to his mind the princes of Polotz, who were guilty of the same sin. First the author speaks of the destruction of brave Izyaslav, son of Vasilko, who, unsupported by the other princes, had fallen two years previously in battle with the Polovcians, then his thought turns to Izyaslav's grandfather, Vseslav, warrior and adventurer, energetic participant in interprincely clashes and quarrels, about whom Boyan composed the refrain: "Neither a crafty man nor a clever man nor a clever bird can escape the judgment of God." And this whole part of the ***Slovo*** ends with the author's sorrowful exclamation: "Oh, groan for the land of Rus, remembering the olden times and the princes of old!" He regrets that old Vladimir Monomakh, terror of the Polovcians, could not have been kept forever on the hills of Kiev, that the princes of Rus have now divided his banners, and that their standards stream separately to the breeze.

This historical reminiscence and that which accompanies the description of Igor's ill starred second battle with the Polovcians, splitting the description itself into two parts, are, like the author's lyrical outpourings, very characteristic of the composition of the ***Slovo.*** They illustrate the author's habitual intrusion of his personal evaluation into events as he narrates them. The figure of the author thus never leaves our field of vision throughout the tale.

To turn to the title, one naturally wonders why our monument should be designated a *slovo,* or discourse, when farther on the author calls it a "song" and a "tale." The first interpreters of the ***Slovo,*** who were in bondage to classical poetics, called it a "heroic ballad." The monument's title of ***Slovo,*** however, is very organic to it, being in the tradition of those typical old Russian titles where *slovo* may be taken to mean an oration, an address to listeners and readers. The ***Slovo*** too begins as an address. The author calls his listeners or readers "brothers"; that is, just what any Old Russian *slovo* would call them. "Would it not be well for us, brothers, to begin in the old-fashioned way our story of the expedition of Igor son of Svyatoslav?" And this form of address occurs five times more. Having begun the ***Slovo*** with a salutation, the author also ends it with a salutation, proposing, since the fame of oldtime princes has been sung, to sing that of the young ones, and concluding the whole work with the "amen" common to all Old Russian *slovos*. Thus the author maintains throughout the position of an orator speaking in the first person.

He places so little importance on the literal agreement of his narrative with the historical facts as sometimes purposely to arrange events counter to the order in which they occurred, or might have occurred, but in accord with his poetic design. Thus, in the *Hypatian Chronicle* the eclipse occurred at the Donets, when Igor and his army were already on the march, and when to return home would have been inexpedient from the military point of view, but in the ***Slovo*** it comes when Igor is still only in process of launching the campaign and consequently when he could easily have let the projected undertaking await more favorable portents. As a result of this shifting of the eclipse, the figure of Igor gains in knightliness. His fearlessness, his scorn of threatening danger, are thereby emphasized. It is not faith in Divine Providence, as in the *Hypatian Chronicle,* that makes him go in spite of evil omens to meet the Polovcians, but his knightly desire to break a lance at the edge of the Polovcian plain, to see the blue Don and to draw water from it in his helmet. At the same time an important artistic advantage is also achieved: the augury of disaster opens the account of the campaign like an overture, to recur in various forms up to the time when Igor's fate takes a more favorable turn.

But if our author moved the solar eclipse ahead of the date given in the *Hypatian Chronicle,* he did just the opposite with the lament of Igor's wife Yaroslavna, whom the chronicle does not mention, postponing it from the time when it would actually have taken place. Yaroslavna laments not at the point in the course of events when it would have been natural for her to lament, not immediately after Igor's capture, when the women of Rus began mourning for their husbands, but considerably later, just before Igor's escape from captivity, and thus the lament becomes a magical incantation evocative of Igor's escape itself. One of the most remarkable creations in all literature for beauty of poetical expression, this lament gains special artistic effect from its precise position in the general structure of the ***Slovo.*** Igor is saved and brought back to the land of Rus by the all-conquering and victorious power of love as embodied in the person of his grieving wife, lamenting for him on the walls of Putivl like a cuckoo for its mate. (pp. 165-68)

The ***Slovo*** is distinguished by profound saturation with imagery and symbolism. Poetical personification, metaphor, simile, parallelism: with all these the ***Slovo*** is full to overflowing. The most important underlying characteristic of this wealth of poetical embellishment is the indissoluble bond existing between the world of nature and the world of man. Nature here takes a very active part—as friend or as foe—in all the events that occur; the animal and the vegetable kingdoms, the earthly and the heavenly elements, are very animately evoked, now to the sorrow, now to the joy of Igor, of his army, and of everybody mentioned in the ***Slovo.*** (p. 168)

Nature in the ***Slovo*** is not dumb, not speechless, but vocal and even talkative: the magpies chatter, the Donets converses with Igor; even inanimate objects utter sounds: the carts screech, the battle standards talk. The whole ***Slovo*** is filled with sounds, ringing, singing: fame rings out; there is a ring of battle, the spears sing.

The rich and abundant epithets and similes in the ***Slovo*** are without exception from the world of nature. Boyan is a nightingale, Vsevolod a wild aurochs, the pagan Polovcian a black raven. Boyan runs like a gray wolf along the ground, darts like a blue-gray eagle beneath the clouds. To the gray wolf are also compared the princes, the retinue, and Konchak. The princes are in addition compared to the sun, to the moon, to falcons; the retainers, to those same falcons and to flocks of jackdaws; Yaroslavna, to a cuckoo; Igor, to an ermine, a white goldeneye; Vseslav, to a wild beast; the Polovcians, to a nest of snow leopards. The prophetic fingers which Boyan lays upon the living strings that he may sing a song in praise of the princes are compared to ten falcons released by a hunter upon a flight of swans, and the screeching carts, to a flock of frightened swans.

By the complete organic harmony between the author of the ***Slovo*** and the elemental forces of nature is explained the presence in the ***Slovo*** of pagan gods. In giving a general description of the ***Slovo,*** K. Marx noted that "the whole ballad has a Christian-heroic character, though pagan elements also stand out very prominently." The ***Slovo*** portrays the Old Russian pagan gods, Veles, Dazhbog, Stribog, Khors, introduces the mythical Div, Deva-obida with the wings of a swan, and Karna and Zhlya, evidently personifications of lamentation and woe. Boyan is called the grandson of Veles, the winds, the grandsons of Stribog, the Russian people, the grandson of Dazhbog. There is no reason to consider these gods of the Slavic pagan Olympus a literary expedient which the ***Slovo*** author resorted to as eighteenth century poets habitually brought in the names of classical gods; nor is there any basis for thinking that he believed in them as his pagan ancestors had done. It is more correct to suppose that the author was so steeped in poetry that, notwithstanding his connections with Christianity, he could not, and did not wish to, depart from that attitude toward the world about him which went with paganism and which still had a very powerful hold at that time among the general masses. The author of the ***Slovo*** was under the influence of that animistic perception of nature which characterized not only the culturally backward strata but at times the highest cultural levels as well, especially where they had not lost touch with folk poetry.

In harmony with the general character of the poetic style of the ***Slovo*** is its varied and graphic symbolism. Symbolical equivalents are a favorite means of figuratively disclosing facts and events in the ***Slovo.*** The movement of the Polovcian troops is here symbolized by the image of black clouds striving to hide the four suns; that is, the four princes who participated in the campaign. The battle is symbolically likened now to the sowing, now to a wedding feast, now to the threshing: "The black earth under the horses' hoofs was sown with bones and watered with blood, and it sprouted a crop of sorrow for the land of Rus. . . . Then the bloody wine gave out; then the brave sons of Rus brought the feast to an end: they gave the wedding guests to drink and laid themselves down in behalf of the land of Rus." Thus is the rout of Igor's army at the river Kayala given poetic interpretation. (pp. 169-70)

Indissolubly linked with symbol is metaphor, which attends the exposition of events every step of the way: Igor "armed his mind with fortitude and whetted his heart with courage"; calamity "drives the birds to the trees"; "the song of the nightingale is stilled, the chatter of the magpies starts up"; "bloody rays announce the break of day"; "sadness flowed full through the land of Rus"; "the princes forged sedition against themselves," and so forth.

Another factor in the ***Slovo***'s saturation with imagery is its wealth of epithet. One of the author's favorite epithets is "golden," with its derivatives: "gold-tipped," "gold-forged," "gilded." Some of the combinations in which this epithet occurs in the ***Slovo*** have their parallels in oral poetry; for example: "golden saddle," "golden throne," "golden helmet," "golden stirrup." The epithet "silver" also appears frequently in the ***Slovo,*** in combinations, however, which are not encountered either in other written monuments or in oral poetry: "silver spear," "silvery hair," "with silver streams," "on its silvery banks." Of particular interest for us are combinations of noun and modifying epithet which are paralleled only in works of oral literature, and are not encountered in written monuments contemporary with the ***Slovo*** or of earlier date; for example: "blue-gray eagle," "blue sea" "green grass," "tempered arrows," "fair maidens," "bloody wounds," "sharp swords," "cool dew," "gray wolf," "brave retinue," "black raven," "black cloud," "open plain." The author of the ***Slovo*** also makes use of metaphorical epithets: "prophetic fingers," "iron ranks," "golden word," "pearly soul," "living strings."

The poetical style of the ***Slovo*** shows the influence both of written and of oral literature. In many cases it is hard to draw a line between the two. In defining the bookish influences, however, it will not do to go to any such lengths as did V. Miller, who vastly overemphasized the presence of borrowed elements. None the less, the attitude of regarding the ***Slovo*** as a monument reflecting certain peculiarities of style found in book literature of the author's own time or earlier is not to be dismissed. On this theme we find much of value in existing literature on the question, all the way from Tikhonravov's book to the studies by P. V. Vladimirov, A. S. Orlov, and V. N. Peretts. Suffice it to quote the following parallels. A counterpart to the ***Slovo*** image: "But Boyan, brothers, would lay his prophetic fingers on the living strings" is found in the *slovo* on the Resurrection of Lazarus: "David would say . . . laying his learned fingers on the living strings. . . ." Corresponding to the images, "darting . . . like a blue-gray eagle" and "flying in thought beneath the clouds," we find in Clement the Slovene: "Like an eagle he soared aloft in thought"; in the "***Slovo*** on the Life": For he is young in body but old in mind and lofty in thought, flying in thought beneath the clouds like an eagle"; in the *Testament* of Cyril the Philosopher: "Fly in thought like an eagle through the air," and so forth.

In style the ***Slovo*** still more closely resembles, particularly in its description of martial episodes, the *Account of the Destruction of Jerusalem* by Josephus Flavius. Thus we read in the ***Slovo***: "He armed his mind with fortitude," while in Josephus, Vespasian "possessed his mind with fortitude and stood firm." The ***Slovo*** continues: "And whetted his heart with courage," and Josephus says: "Whet your souls for vengeance"; in the ***Slovo***: "Filled with martial spirit," in Josephus: "Fulfilled with martial spirit"; in the ***Slovo***: "There was a rain of arrows"; in Josephus: "And the arrows pelted them like rain"; in the ***Slovo***: "They roar like aurochs wounded by tempered sabers"; in Josephus: "They fell to groaning like wounded beasts." (pp. 170-71)

The author of the ***Slovo*** was undoubtedly well versed, too, in Russian oral literature, and this exercised an almost greater influence on him than did learned literature, but unfortunately we cannot precisely define the extent of this influence since we do not know exactly what the oral literature of the eleventh and twelfth centuries was like. In any event it is quite clear that the profound saturation of the ***Slovo*** with animistic concepts was the result of the author's organic connection with the creative works of oral poetry. Then, as we saw above, we meet in the ***Slovo*** noun-and-epithet modifier combinations not encountered in corresponding works of written literature, another circumstance which unquestionably attests to a connection between the ***Slovo*** and the products of folk poetry. (p. 173)

As to the problem of our author's connection with the literary and with the folk-poetry tradition, it must be emphasized that he was completely independent and original in his use both of learned and of oral poetry material. The ***Slovo*** reveals such a high degree of artistic originality that there can be no question of imitation even in separate passages.

In speaking of the poetical style of the ***Slovo,*** it is necessary to touch upon one of the most complicated questions in its study; namely, the question of rhythmic structure. A number of students (Zhitetsky, Tikhovsky, Abikht, Korsh, Shchurat, Zivers) have thought that the ***Slovo*** was written entirely in meter and have attempted to divide it into lines. Zhitetsky and Tikhovsky considered the verse structure of thc ***Slovo*** similar to the verse system of the Ukrainian ballad; Abikht compared it to that of the Scandinavian skalds, Korsh, with Russian *bylina* verse; Birchak, with Byzantine church song. Professor Sievers takes Korsh's point of view in the main (***Das Igorlied,*** *metrisch und sprachlich bearbeitet*).

Frankly, however, none of the attempts to divide the ***Slovo*** throughout into lines can be recognized as successful. First of all it must be borne in mind that the ***Slovo*** has come down to us in a very much mutilated copy, which no doubt in large measure destroys its rhythmic structure. But even apart from this, it is doubtful whether the ***Slovo*** was wholly written in verse: in the first place the large amount of purely historical information that it gives, involving the mention of a great many princes, can hardly have been entirely arranged as lines of verse. The presence in many instances of complex sentences also points to the absence of any continuous poetic rhythm. It would almost be more correct to suppose on the basis of its song phrases that the ***Slovo,*** like the Scandinavian sagas which, incidentally, it resembles in its wealth of alliteration, is an alternation of prose and verse. (pp. 175-76)

The profound political purpose of the ***Slovo,*** prompted by the very pressing interests of the historic moment, in conjunction with the fact that it is organically connected with the richest strata of folk creation, set it apart as a work of genuinely national character.

The greater part of the ***Slovo*** cannot have been written later than April, 1187, since it mentions as alive Prince Vladimir Glebovich of Pereyaslavl, who died on April 18 of that year. But taking into account that it was presumably written in connection with the Kievan prince Svyatoslav's preparations for his campaign against the Polovcians in 1185, immediately after he had received the news of Igor's crushing defeat, there is every reason to suppose that the main part, ending with Yaroslavna's lament, was written in 1185. Some students, Kallash among them, have very astutely called attention to the fact that the account of Igor's escape and his return to the land of Rus, written in triumphant and joyous tones, is out of keeping with the whole preceding exposition, in which the fate of the land of Rus and of Igor himself is depicted in gloomy and pessimistic colors. Therefore the thought quite naturally suggests itself that when the rest of the ***Slovo*** was written, describing in sorrowful pictures the ill fortune of Rus and of Igor, wounded and in captivity, Igor's escape had not as yet taken place. As soon as Igor reached Rus, however, in that same year, 1185, the author wrote, in honor of him and of the princes who had not yet returned but who were expected; the concluding section of the ***Slovo,*** calculated to offset the mood of dejection induced by the telling description of the military fiasco. This concluding section may have been written at the end of 1185 or somewhat later.

If we agree with those scholars who think that the inclusion of Vladimir Igorevich among the eulogized princes could have taken place only after his return from captivity, and this was in the autumn of 1187, then the date of the completion of the ***Slovo*** must be moved forward to the closing months of that year or the early months of 1188. In this case it is natural to suppose that originally Yaroslavna's lament was placed alongside the lamentations of the wives of the Russian warriors who had been in the rout, and that later on, after writing the concluding section of the ***Slovo,*** the author shifted Yaroslavna's lament closer to the episode of Igor's escape and thus attained the artistic effect above mentioned.

In the history of Russian literature previous to or contemporary with the ***Slovo*** we do not have a single monument which either equals it artistically or even in any measure approaches it. This does not mean that the ***Slovo*** was necessarily the only thing of its kind in our early literature, however. We have no assurance whatever that there did not exist other monuments which, even if not its equal artistically, were perhaps in some degree similar to it. The fact that the ***Slovo*** has come down to us at all is, as we have seen, to a great extent the result of chance. It is known in only one copy earlier than the beginning of the nineteenth century. How can we be sure that comparable works of the time have not been lost?

However that may be, even by itself the ***Slovo*** is a striking index to the height of cultural development and of national consciousness already attained by the Russians at that far distant time, in the first centuries of their existence as a state. The ***Slovo*** is in any event not inferior in artistic quality to the best examples of heroic epos that the world has produced. Originating as it did in Kievan Rus, common cradle of Great Russians, Ukrainians, and White Russians, it by right belongs equally to all three of these brother peoples. (pp. 176-78)

N. K. Gudzy, "'The Tale of Igor's Expedition'," in his History of Early Russian Literature, *translated by Susan Wilbur Jones, Macmillan, 1949, pp. 149-81.*

GEORGE P. FEDOTOV (essay date 1946)

[Fedotov is a Russian-born American critic. In the following excerpt, he analyzes the religious perspective of the Igor *poet, examining the poem's combination of Christian, pagan, and secular ethical systems.]*

The ***Tale of Igor's Campaign*** stands unique in ancient Russian literature. It is the only work of purely secular content and of intentionally artistic form. It could be styled a poem and would deserve the title but for its external form which reads like rhythmic prose rather than verse. In artistic value it looms like a mountain over the flat plain of contemporary literature. The anonymous author, living at the end of the twelfth century, was undoubtedly a poet of genius. One has to wait until the nineteenth century, until Pushkin, to find his equal. In western poetry the ***Tale*** can be compared to the *Chanson de Roland* and the *Niebelungenlied;* to the Russian taste it might even excel these in poetic value. (p. 315)

In analyzing the religious tenor of ***Igor's Tale*** one must keep in mind its stylistic form. The tale deals with the same feudal society as the contemporary chronicles, but it belongs to quite a different literary school. Stepping from the ecclesiastical air of the chronicles—not to speak of the rest of contemporary literature—into the secular and even slightly heathen world of ***Igor's Tale*** is no little surprise. Without its miraculous preservation, one would have quite a different idea of the strength of the Christian and Byzantine impact upon the pre-Mongolian Russia.

With regard to the religious and moral world-outlook of ***Igor's Tale,*** three strata can be discerned in its artistic tissue: Christian, heathen, and purely secular. Measured by mere verbal criteria, the Christian element is the scantiest of all. (p. 317)

Incomparably richer is its heathen counterpart, the interpretation of which, however, presents many difficulties. The general skepticism of modern scholars towards the problems of Slavic mythology was reflected in their appraisal of the heathen world of ***Igor's Tale*** as a simple poetic convention. A distinguished student compared the paganism of the ***Tale*** to the mythological names in the classic poetry of the eighteenth century. The exaggeration in this view is obvious. The medieval poet lived in a time when Christianity in Russia had to wage a serious struggle with the survivals of paganism; when, after the acknowledgement of ecclesiastical preachers, the folk were still devoted to the "double faith." This historical situation, on the borderline between the two religious worlds, requires the most accurate investigation of the poet's religious background.

The pagan elements of the ***Tale*** can be found in the names of the great gods of the Russian Olympus, in a number of minor divine entities or personifications and in the poet's general attitude to nature and life.

Among the great pagan gods known from other sources, the poet names four, three of them in an indirect way, as the ancestors or masters of men and elements. The formula is always the same: the grandsons of Stribog, the grandsons of Dazhbog, the grandson of Veles. The poet likes to designate the relation of descent by employing the expression "grandson" rather than son. Striborg's grandsons are the winds; Veles' grandson is Boyan, the poet,—on what particular ground, we do not know. Veles (or Volos), together with Perun, is one of the greatest of the Russian gods; very often he appears as god of cattle and of riches; here he is a patron of the poet, a "magic" poet. Perhaps for a wizard the protection of a pagan god, or the descent from him, is not unfitting. We do not know who are the grandsons of Dazhbog, the sun god; the context permits conceiving of them as Russian princes, or Russian folk in general, or even the whole of mankind. The poet says that during princely feuds "the life (or wealth) of Dazhbog's grandson was being ruined." The fourth god Khors, who is also a solar god, probably of Iranian origin, is named directly but obviously as the synonym of the sun itself. The prince Vseslav "raced, as a wolf, across the way of great Khors." The word "great" reminds us again that the divine meaning of Khors is not forgotten: he is more than the luminary itself. In what spirit, with which emotional strain are these names used by the Christian author?

As poet, the disciple of Boyan, he was the inheritor of a poetic tradition going back to pagan times. This tradition probably transmitted the names of gods who once were full of life and glamour and who, certainly, were dimmed by the victory of the new faith. But even for the official spokesmen of Christianity the ancient gods did not turn into nonentities. Unlike modern theologians, the ancient Church did not deny the existence of gods. The medieval theology considered them either as demons or as deified men. The second theory, that of Euhemerism, was very popular in Russia. Thus, one finds in the Ipatian *Chronicle* (1114) which transcribes the Greek chronicle of Malalas, the history of Egyptian kings who became gods. The king Feost "was called the god Svarog. . . . After him reigned his son, by the name of Sun, who is called Dazhbog. . . ." It is noteworthy that the chronicler gives to Egyptian king-gods Slavic names. Like the author of these lines, the poet of Igor could believe in the historical existence of the gods. But, whereas for the Christian preachers their names were an abomination, he treated them with the veneration of a son or grandson. Perhaps he had no theological theory at all about the gods: whether they were demons of nature, such as the Sun or Wind, or human ancestors. Christian theological ideas among the Russian folk were very confused, even in the nineteenth century. Essential is the fact that these names conveyed to him great and magical associations. He used them as symbols; but as realistic symbols, necessary for his mythical world-outlook.

His *Weltanschauung* is indeed mythical. It is very interesting for a scholar of religion to observe in him a living process of mythical creation. Most of the great poets have mythical elements in their world-outlook; but in primitive poetry it is quite impossible to draw the line between religious mythology and the creation of poetic fictions. The poet of ***Igor*** is no primitive, but he stands near the primitive world of paganism. He blends popular mythological tradition with his own more or less pantheistic symbolism. There is hardly one abstract idea which could not be turned by him into a living being or living symbol. Such is, for instance, *Obida,* Outrage, one of his favorite symbols, and a symbol necessary for a mourner, for a poet of woe. According to the recent discovery by Professor Jacobson the image of Outrage was borrowed by the Russian poet from a translation of a Greek work by Methodius of Patara. . . . Outrage to him is a maiden. "Outrage arose among the hosts of the Dazhbog's grandson, stepped as a maiden on the Troyan land near Don, and splashing with her swan wings in the blue sea, she chased away the happy times." But Russian folklore always knew Woe (*Gore*) as a being who pursued an accursed man, sitting on his neck, accompanying him to the grave. Fever, or rather Fevers, were, to a Russian, demonic females of whom he tried to rid himself by the aid of magic spells and incantations.

The maiden Outrage does not stand alone in the poem. Together with her, one finds personified Woe, Lie (*Lozh*), and two female beings *Karna* and *Zhlia* who, according to the probable meaning of their names, must be interpreted as incarnate Lamentation and Mourning: "Karna shouted and Zhlia rushed over the Russian land shooting forth fire from a flaming horn."

Among these demonic entities who originated as personifications of fate and destiny there is one being of quite a different origin and unclear significance. It is *Div,* whose nature has not yet been fully explained. "Div is crying at the top of a tree," foreboding the misfortune. The same Div rushes to the land when the catastrophe is fulfilled. Most of the commentators take him for a demonic bird-like being, of Slavic or Iranian mythology, who is ominous, evil-bearing, and, consequently, close to the symbolic Woe and Outrage.

All these divine or demonic beings are represented as dwelling and acting within a nature setting which is more than scenery for their action. In fact, nature is living and animated through and through. It can be said without exaggeration that nature and its phenomena occupy in ***Igor's Tale*** at least as important a place as human society. Nature, of course, is not quite independent from the latter: it embraces human life with love but also challenges it with threats; it sends its warnings; it shares human woe and joy. That the narrative of the Igor's expedition is opened by the eclipse of the sun—an evil omen—has nothing peculiar about it. The Russian *Chronicles,* not unlike those of the western Middle Ages, are full of astronomical events to be interpreted in the same providential sense. But in ***Igor's Tale*** nature is not the organ of God's revelation. It is a living essence by itself. When Igor leads his warriors to the fatal campaign, "the sun with darkness barred his way, the night groaned with the thunderstorm . . . the whining of the wild beasts arose. Div cries at the top of the tree: he bids the unknown land hearken.'' Foreboding the bloody battle, ''the wolves conjure the storm from the ravines; the eagles, with their shrieking, call the beasts to a feast of bones; the foxes yelp at the red shields.'' After the Russian defeat—''the grass drooped in pity, and in grief the tree bowed low to earth.''

In conformity with the general tragic character of the ***Tale,*** nature reveals itself chiefly in the quality of mourner. Yet it can rejoice as well, in sympathy with human happiness. At Igor's escape from captivity ''the woodpeckers show him the way to the river with their tapping, the nightingales herald the dawn with their merry songs.'' Nature is not only the witness of human destinies. It can be either a mighty helpmate or the enemy of man. During Igor's flight, the Donets river ''caressed the prince on its waves, spread out green grass for him by its silvery banks, clothed him with warm mists beneath the shade of the green trees.'' Igor himself gives thanks to the Donets, his savior, in a poetic dialogue with the river. But the river can be malicious and evil, like the Stugna whose bad temper is mentioned in contrast with the mild Donets. ''Quite another was the Stugna river; it has an evil current, it had swallowed strange brooks and scattered the barges among the bushes. It had closed the Dnieper to the youth, Prince Rostislav (who was drowned in Stugna in 1093).''

Igor enters into conversation with a river. His wife, Iaroslav's daughter, on the walls of the town Putivl', in lament over her captured husband addresses the Wind, the Dnieper River, and the Sun with complaints and incantations which read like heathen prayers. It is worth noticing that the elements are addressed with the title ''lord,'' which suggests not so much sympathetic intimacy with nature as awe and reverence towards it.

> O Wind, mighty Wind! Why dost thou blow so violently, O lord? Why dost thou hurl the Huns' arrows with thy light wings against my beloved's warriors? Why hast thou, O Lord, scattered my joy over the feathery grass? . . . O Dnieper Slovutich (son of the Glorious)! . . . bear fondly my beloved one to me, O lord, that I should not send him my tears toward the sea at the dawn. O bright and thrice-bright Sun! Thou art warm and beauteous towards all. Why didst thou, O Lord, spread thy burning rays upon my beloved's warriors?

Thus far we have seen in ***Igor's Tale*** nature personified or acting. But the instances are countless where nature gives substance to similes and poetical figures. Prince Vsevolod's constant surname is ''aurochs.'' Warriors are compared with wolves, princes with hawks, musicians's fingers on the strings with ten hawks loosed upon a flock of swans. In the human and even in the political world the poet does not abandon the world of nature. He lives by its recollections, images, by its inspiring spirit. There is probably no other poem or work of art belonging to the European sphere of culture in which the unity with nature is so complete and so religiously significant.

Most of the Russian literary historians envisaged the world of ***Igor's Tale*** as a purely poetic fiction. A strong pantheistic feeling permeates modern Russian poetry both literary and oral, cultivated and popular. Reared in this poetic tradition, Russians pay no attention to it nor question its roots. In the oral poetry of Russian peasants, artistic pantheism lives hand in hand with the remnants of ancient paganism. The literary Russian poetry of the nineteenth century was strongly influenced by the art of the people, though often ignoring its pagan sources. In the twelfth century, when sacrifices to the gods were still offered in the countryside, the impact of the imaginative and emotional pagan world upon popular art must have been immensely stronger than nowadays.

We certainly do not think that the poet of ***Igor's Tale,*** still less Igor himself and his wife, worshipped ancient gods. They were good Christians in their conscious minds. But, the poet, at least, in the subconscious depths of his soul where he communicated with the soul of the people, lived in another, hardly Christian world. It is true that most of his images of nature are purely poetical. But in speaking of nature he can not help feeling it as a living being, and his imagination immediately enters upon mythological creation. In this natural-supernatural world the names of ancient gods, preserved probably by the poetic tradition, find the place which is refused at that early stage of Russian poetry to the saints and spirits of the Christian heaven. The poet feels that the name of the Archangel Michael or Saint George would spoil the poetic form which requires the names of Veles and Dazhbog. This is the function of the paganism prevailing in ***Igor's Tale.***

If we do not know how far Igor's poet shared the pagan beliefs and superstitions of the Russian folk we can be certain, at least, of his belief in magic. Moreover, magic is treated by him without any repulsion and even with a certain reverence. Several times he calls Boyan, his master poet, *veshchy*. This word which in later Russian has acquired the meaning ''wise'' with the nuance of ''clairvoyant'' and ''prophetic,'' has, in ancient documents, only the sense of ''wizard.'' (pp. 319-26)

If nature in ***Igor's Tale*** is saturated with pagan elements which can hardly find their parallels in the Russian *Chronicles,* in the attitude to society, in social or political ethics, the ***Tale*** and the *Chronicles* come nearer to each other without reaching, however, a full identity. The main difference consists in a complete secularization of the poet's social ethics. It is purely laic, or neutral, neither Christian nor pagan, at first glance, whatever may be the secret sources nourishing it from the two religious world. Let us consider first of all its face value, without heeding its religious significance. (pp. 326-27)

Three main social ethical streams flow through ***Igor's Tale***—the same which can be distinguished in the lay section of the *Chronicles* as well: the ethics of clan or charity of blood; the ethics of class, or feudal and military virtues; and the ethics of mother country or patriotism of the Russian land. Clan or family consciousness in ***Igor's Tale*** is perhaps not stronger than in the *Chronicles,* but it is strong enough and finds eloquent emotional forms for its expression. Prince Vsevolod addresses his brother as they start on the campaign: ''My only brother, my only bright light, Igor! We are both Sviatoslavichi (Sviatoslav's sons).'' The patronymic names are used by the poet very often instead of first names: Iaroslavna, Glebovna—speaking of women, or ''the brave sons of Gleb.''

Prince Igor and his brother, the unfortunate heroes of the ***Tale,*** belonged to the great Chernigov line of the Russian princely dynasty, descending from the famous Oleg Sviatoslavich who died in 1116. The poet is conscious of the common destiny and the common honor of this clan: ''In the field the Oleg's valiant brood is slumbering: afar has it flown. It was not born to stand an insult,'' says he of the Russian camp in the steppe. He dedicates some touching lines to the memory of Oleg, the unfortunate but glorious ancestor. We have seen also how the clan feeling of the poet induced him to use patronymic names even for the elements of nature: winds as grandsons of Stribog, Dnieper-Slovutich; Russian princes are grandsons of Dazhbog or, otherwise, Rusichi, the favorite patronymic commonly used by the poet and coined, perhaps, by himself.

This clan ethics is linked with and overshadowed by the feudal or military ethics. . . . Here all the facets of the warlike virtues are glorified without any restraint: courage, bravery, boldness. In the style of the historic tales (and the *Chronicles*) the poet begins his praise of Igor: ''He strengthened his mind and sharpened his heart with manliness; and, filling himself with warlike spirit led his brave hosts to the land of the Polovtsi.'' This is still a reasonable courage, the dutiful way of a Christian prince. ''Igor said to his druzhina: Brothers and druzhina! It is better to be slain than to be captured.'' This can also be parallelled in the *Chronicles,* but, signficantly, in the tenth century records of the great pagan warrior Sviatoslav. Even an imprudent, impassioned boldness, beyond the reason of war, is glorified. Such was, indeed, the whole campaign of Igor, which is justified in these words by the prince: ''I wish to shatter a spear on the farthest borders of the Polovetsian land. With you, O Rusichi, I wish to lay down my head, or to drink of the Don in my helmet.'' (pp. 327-29)

Nowhere in Russian literature, written or oral, can be found such a pitch of warlike intensity, such superhuman or subhuman fierceness as in this portrayal of Vsevolod's warriors, the men of Kursk:

> My men of Kursk are skillful fighters, nursed amid trumpets, rocked in helmets, fed at the spear-blades; well-known to them are the paths; familiar the ravines; their bows are strung; their quivers open; and their sabres whetted. Like grey wolves in the field, they gallop seeking honor for themselves and glory for their prince.

This last motive of ''honor'' and ''glory'' reveals the other side of the same feudal ideal. Glory for real greatness, particularly after death, and honor on a lesser scale, constitute a moral good, the fruit and privilege of the military virtue, valor. Glory is given not by success or political might, but by intrepid conduct. That is why the poem ends with a ''glory song'' to Igor and his kinsmen, although from the political point of view their campaign was a failure and defeat. (p. 329)

The third source of social ethics for the poet of ***Igor*** is his strong patriotism which embraces not any one of the Russian principalities, but the whole of the Russian land. This pan-Russian consciousness . . . was in its decline at the end of the twelfth century and few traces of it can be found in the contemporary *Chronicles.* In ***Igor's Tale*** it is as vital as in the eleventh century; its poet is, in fact, a true inheritor of Boyan's age. There is no phrase repeated as frequently in the ***Tale*** as ''the Russian land.'' This expression is taken not in the narrow sense of Kiev and its surrounding lands as it usually was at that time, but in the large sense of all the principalities and countries inhabited by the Russian people. Igor's foray, in itself a very insignificant episode of frontier fighting, is treated as a national tragedy. Igor marches on for the ''Russian land,'' he fights for the ''Russian land.'' His defeat produced a national mourning. The poet goes so far as to complete the sentence of Boyan: ''It is heavy upon thee, O Head, without the shoulders; evil is it to thee, Body, without the Head,'' by the daring conclusion: ''the Russian land without Igor.'' It looks as if, for him, Igor were the real head or leader of all Russia. That the ''Russian land'' is not only a hyperbole serving to enhance Igor's glory appears from the general political outlook of the poet. Spokesman of the poet's political ideals is Prince Sviatoslav of Kiev, the head of the Olgovichi house. In a grand and poignant call to all princes of Russia, Sviatoslav urges them to intervene for the Russian land, ''for the wounds of Igor, fierce Sviatoslavich.'' Smolensk and Polotsk, Galich and Suzdal, the remotest border lands of Russia, are included in this impassioned call. In the panegyrical enumeration of Russian princes the poet makes no discrimination between the branches of the Rurik house. The Monomachovichi, the traditional enemies of the Olgovichi, even take predominant place because of the political importance of their seats. On the contrary, one of the strongest representatives of the Olgovichi clan, Iaroslav of Chernigov, is rebuked for his dishonorable conduct: he abstained from all common expeditions against the Polovtsi.

Here the national consciousness of the poet crosses that of his clan. But it crosses also his feudal ethics of unbounded honor. The poet, as patriot, could not help seeing the fatal effects of princely feuds and he condemns them in a most unambiguous way:

> Brother spoke to brother: ''This is mine and that also is mine.'' And the princes began to say of a paltry thing ''this is great''; and amongst themselves to forge feuds; and the heathen from all sides advanced with victories against the Russian land.

Here is avarice rather than pride, the political original sin, a view which is not incompatible with feudal ethics. But ''this is great'' points to the exaggerated sensitivity of personal honor. The poet fully acknowledges the national reverse resulting from the search for glory while speaking of his great hero, the ancient Oleg:

> That Oleg forged feuds with his sword and sowed arrows over the earth. . . . Then, in the time of Oleg Gorislavich, feuds were sown and grew apace; the fortune of Dazhbog's grandson was wasted in the factions of the princes, and the life of men was shortened.

This political condemnation of Oleg does not diminish the poet's admiration for his ''glory'' and bravery. The same dualism of appreciation is found even for the person of Igor. Speaking for himself, the poet dare not utter any word of blame for the adventurous and inconsiderate foray which ended with calamity for the ''Russian land.'' But the political lesson is put into the mouth of Sviatoslav of Kiev who, amidst tears and lamentations, sends the words of rebuke to his captured cousins:

> O my nephews, Igor and Vsevolod! too early have ye begun to harass the land of the Polovtsi with your swords! But ingloriously were you defeated, ingloriously have you shed the blood of the heathen. Your brave hearts are forged of cruel steel and tempered in fierceness. What have you wrought to my silvered hair!

One is here in the presence of an ethical conflict which the poet does not resolve. His heart is equally responsive to the call of ''glory'' and to the call of suffering Russia. He is obviously not in sympathy with domestic feuds. He prefers to see his admired military valor exercised in the war against the common foes of Russia, the heathen. In this he stands on common ground with the best traditions of the *Chronicles*. (pp. 331-33)

Both the chronicles note the motive of honor in Igor's conduct, but they deal with it in quite different ways. The Lavrentian has no sympathy with this motive, ridicules it, and sees in it the reason of the catastrophe. The Ipatian tries to mitigate and merge it into the general strain of a deep piety which transfigures the character of Igor into that of a saintly Christian hero.

The poet of ***Igor's Tale*** has no words of blame for his prince; he himself is highly enthusiastic about honor and glory. He needs no religious mitigation for, nor limitation of it. He only dares, through the lips of Sviatoslav, to point at the fatal consequences of Igor's bold imprudence for the Russian land.

Coming back to the poet's warlike ardor one finds another restraint for its display—and this not of a social, but rather of an emotional, nature. The poet manifests such a degree of kindness, sensitivity, and delicacy that it is positively incompatible with joy in killing. He likes the audacity, the impetus, even the intoxication of a fight. But he obviously dislikes the act of killing, of bloodshedding. This can easily be seen in his treatment of combat. The fatal battle at the Kaiala river is the main subject of his epic. It forms the first, the longest part of it. But the battle itself is depicted rather indirectly. At first a series of omens, presentiments, forebodings. After follows the mourning, the picture of the fatal consequences of the defeat. Concerning the fighting itself, a few lines suffice. (pp. 336-37)

The mildness and gentleness of the Russian poet can be tested by still other criteria. The whole composition with its tragic tension and joyful solution seems to require, after the hell of the dark defeat, the compensation of revenge or, at least, the final victory. But the poet—and the reader as well—is satisfied with the escape, the flight. From the point of view of strict feudal honor, that is not compensation. Without revenge the hero would feel dishonored. But for some reason the idea of revenge does not come into the reader's mind. It was Igor, and not the Polovtsi, who began the fighting, in the frame of the epic, and Igor himself caused his misfortune. The Polovtsi committed no cruel deeds and one of the heathen helps the prince in his escape. From the lips of the pursuing khans we are informed of the plan to marry young Vladimir, Igor's son, to a Polovtsian princess. So, the Polovtsi may not be so bad, after all. The poet seems to have pardoned them from the joy of seeing his prince free again. (p. 338)

With this tenderness of heart is linked the particular attention paid by the poet to woman. He is certainly not a poet of love, least of all of romantic or chivalrous love, though he likes the epithet "fair" applied to the maidens, even to those of enemy nations: "fair maidens of the Polovtsi," "fair maidens of the Goths." He likes the words designating different nuances of love and friendship: *lado, khot'*, (lover, beloved, espoused, friend, and so on) but he uses them mostly in metaphors. "The beloved maiden" of Vseslav is his ambitious dream: the princedom of Kiev. But where the poet really appreciates woman is in the beauty of her suffering. If the whole ***Tale of Igor*** is a poignant lament its best organ is the voice of woman. All the Russian women share in the lament over Igor and his warriors: "Now can we no longer imagine our dearests in our thoughts, nor see them with our eyes, nor play with gold or silver. . . ."

The climax of the ***Tale***—the second one—is the lament of Iaroslavna, Igor's wife. Poetically it has always been considered the best part of the epic. We are acquainted already with her impressive incantations addressed to the elements of nature: Wind, Dnieper River, and Sun. Is it mere chance that, immediately upon the half-magical incantations of Iaroslavna, the poet shows prince Igor in the midst of flight? It is as if the incantations of the woman wrought their effect upon the elements, which return to the princess her deplored husband. Indeed, the next part—the flight—begins with the stir of elements: "The sea spurted at midnight; waterspouts move in mists. God shows the road to prince Igor from the land of the Polovtsi. . . ." By this artistic effect the poet gave the woman—side by side with old Sviatoslav—a predominant place in his ***Tale***. She is, or can be, the savior. Sviatoslav tried to save Igor with political speeches. His call sounded in vain. Iaroslavna—with cries from her heart and with the power which a passionate desire gives over the elements—succeeded.

Mildness and tenderness of heart, limiting warlike ardor, do not yet exhaust the sensibility of Igor's poet. There is in him a trait which perhaps gives a key to the deepest strata of the Russian soul. It is linked with the general tragic tone of the poem; yet it needs a closer examination.

Tragic is almost every great epic of any historical nation: the *Iliad*, the *Chanson de Roland*, the *Niebelungenlied*. It is not irrelevant that great epic poets, representing the deepest poetic tradition of a primitive nation, choose for their song of glory some tragic event: a defeat, the ruin of a realm, the death of a young hero. A general law of moral life as well as of artistic creation reveals that the greatest in man is awakened not by happy life but by heroic death. ***Igor's Tale*** is not an exception. Yet in it there are some particular traits which are uniquely Russian. First, one can easily notice that the accumulation of tragic impressions is not sufficiently motivated by the subject. ***Igor's Tale*** is a drama with a happy ending. Thus, the richness of ominous spells is somewhat gratuitous. Secondly, the tragic effect is achieved not by the death of a struggling and doomed hero (the idea of Achilles, Roland, Siegfried) but by suffering and humiliation: in ***Igor***, the suffering and humiliated being is the Russian land itself, oppressed by the Polovtsi.

Especially striking and unexpected is the return of the tragic theme before the happy end. Prince Igor is riding to his homeland; escaping from captivity, he praises the Donets River for his salvation; and just at this moment, by a strange association the poet remembers another evil river, the Stugna, which drowned in its waves the young Prince Rostislav. This event has nothing to do with Igor. It took place about a hundred years before. But the poet dedicates the whole stanza to this irrelevant association. He introduces—a favorite device of his—a lamenting woman, the prince's mother, and lets all nature participate in the mourning: "The flowers drooped for pity and the trees bowed low to earth in grief." The poet repeats one of his best refrains, used previously for Igor's defeat, in this passage where it is out of place from the point of view of composition. The poet simply could not help pouring some drops of sorrow into the final cup of triumph. Both the absence of final revenge or its promise, and the insertion of the superfluous theme of mourning are highly revealing. The evaluation of suffering as a superior moral good, as almost an end in itself, is one of the most precious features of the Russian religious mind. Here, it is found, in an esthetic transposition, with a bard of military valor and honor in whom one would least of all expect to find it: the poet who abhors Christian symbols and Christian vocabulary.

This discovery forces us to return to the question of religious elements in ***Igor's Tale***. . . . If it was legitimate to trace the influence of paganism in the poet's sense of nature it is only fair to ask for the Christian influence in his general ethical attitude. The question is easier to pose than solve. In this domain one is guided by intuition rather than factual data.

As a rule, all deeper ethical or social norms and attitudes, even merely secular in appearance, have some religious origin and are supported by religious beliefs or their survivals. It is possible, then, to suppose behind Russian clan ethics, with its strong and tender feeling of blood-kinship, the pagan roots, or pagan sanctification of primitive tribal institutions. In Christian times they were reinterpreted in terms of evangelical charity and remained for ever one of the main bases of Russian social ethics. It is also legitimate to suppose some pagan connections for warlike ethics of bravery, though they were socially necessitated by the feudal institutions of Christian times. (pp. 339-42)

Conceding a place to the pagan sway in war ethics, one is the more obliged to look for Christian influences in accounting for the mildness and tenderness of Igor's poet. Two centuries of evangelization could not pass in vain; it had gradually transformed the general moral attitude of people, and even their sensibility. The poet of Igor feels no longing for revenge; but for a pagan Russian princess (Saint Olga), before her conversion, revenge, of a most cruel pattern, constituted an important part of her glorious tradition. It was related calmly and objectively by the monk-annalist and probably belonged to the epic store of ancient times.

Yet, while Christianity accounts for the mildness of the Russian epic, it may also have had its pagan antecedents. From all the scanty records of Russian paganism, it appears to have been much milder than that of many other tribes, for example, the Teutons. The charity of the Gospel found a particularly fertile soil in Russia. Indeed, the Byzantine interpretation of Christian ethics was not marked by any particular mildness. Nor was the Western doctrine or life of the early Middle Ages. In Russia itself this charitable spirit is felt strongly in the literary documents which are less colored by the Byzantine culture; often in the laic, and rarer in official ecclesiastical works.

Yet, after all is said, one must keep in mind that the mildness of Russian paganism can only have been relative. Not only Princess Olga, but also Vladimir (both canonized saints) are depicted as cruel before their conversion. Acts of cruelty are reported of the pagan magicians in the eleventh century as well. And the pagan Viatichi killed a Christian missionary, Saint Kuksha, about 1100. So the Gospel really did transform, or was transforming, the coarse hearts of the heathen; and to it, in great part, are due the most touching and morally the finest features in the only preserved work of the ancient epic tradition of Russia. (pp. 342-43)

George P. Fedotov, "The Tale of Igor's Campaign," in his The Russian Religious Mind: Kievan Christianity, the Tenth to the Thirteenth Centuries, *1946. Reprint by Harper & Brothers, 1960, pp. 315-43.*

AVRAHM YARMOLINSKY (essay date 1949)

[*Yarmolinsky was a Russian-born American translator, biographer, social historian, and critic who edited numerous anthologies of and wrote extensively on Russian literature, especially works by Fedor Dostoevsky, Anton Chekov, and Alexander Pushkin. In the following excerpt, he surveys early English-language criticism of* The Igor Tale.]

In the articles on Russian literature which found their way into London magazines during the twenties of the last century there is occasional mention of the poem. Thus, in the volume with which the *Westminster Review* made its bow before the public in 1824 one comes upon this:

> Among the poetic names which have been preserved out of the ruins of old times, there is one which though but a name, is religiously venerated in Russia. *Boyan,* the nightingale (*Solovei*), whom tradition has cherished as the bard who led the old Russian warriors to battle, and enabled them to work miracles of valour by the magic excitement of his strains, still lives in the universal mind, though not a single breath of his lyre has found its way to the existing generation. In a warlike and anonymous fragment, the hymn used in the campaign of Igor in the twelfth century, written in the dialect of southern Russia, in measured prose, a fine spirit of heroism is mingled with the obscurity of a forgotten mythology.

There seems to be no earlier English reference to the ***Slovo.***

A paragraph on the ***Expedition of Igor against the Polovtzi*** occurs in the initial volume of *The Foreign Quarterly Review,* which appeared in 1827. Here "the poem" is described as one that "merits particular attention for its originality, its bold imagery, and that richness of imagination which characterizes the poetry of all young nations." The reader is told further that "the name of the author has not survived, but he has transmitted to us that of Bojane, a still earlier poet, whose works have also unfortunately perished." The reader of *The Foreign Review and Continental Miscellany* for 1828 learned that the ***Slovo*** recorded "the military exploits of Igor against the Poles (!)" and that a fragment of it was discovered in 1796 and published in 1800.

These remarks in the London magazines are mere second-hand reports, embroidering confusedly on passages from Emile Dupré de Saint-Maure's *Anthologie russe, Vzgljad na staruju i novuju slovesnost v Rossii* by Alexander Bestužev, with which the St. Petersburg miscellany, *Poljarnaja zvezda* for 1823 opens, and *Opyt kratkoj istorii russkoj literatury,* by Nikolaj Greč.

To the United States belongs the distinction of having produced the first English comment on our text by one who actually perused it. This comment came from the pen of a German-American lady, at once a remarkable linguist and an erudite student of literature. This Thérèse Albertine Louise von Jacob Robinson, who wrote under the pseudonym of Talvj, learned Russian at an early age and eventually became proficient in all the Slavic vernaculars, as well as in many other tongues. . . . In 1834 she contributed to the review, *Biblical Repository,* founded by her husband, an extensive essay, written in English, on the Slavic languages and literatures. Here she had this to say about the ***Slovo***:

> That . . . the genuine old Russian had its poets, was, until the close of the last century, only known by historical tradition, no monument of them seemed to be left. But at that time, A.D. 1794, a Russian nobleman, Count Mussin-Pushkin, discovered the manuscript of an epic poem, ***Igor's Expedition against the Polovtzi,*** apparently not older than the twelfth century. It is a piece of national poetry of the highest

Illustrations from the fifteenth-century Radziwill Chronicle depicting Polovetsian raiders carrying off Russian prisoners and livestock (top) and a Kievan army pursuing the invaders.

> beauty, united with an equal share of power and gracefulness. But what strikes us even more than this, is, that we find in it no trace of that rudeness, which would naturally be expected in the production of a period when darkness still covered all eastern Europe, and of a poet belonging to a nation, which we have hardly longer than a century ceased to consider as barbarians. There hovers a spirit of meekness over the whole, which sometimes seems to endanger the energy of the representation. The truth is that the Russians enjoyed at this early period a higher degree of mental cultivation than almost any other part of Europe.

When the essay was expanded into a book, which was published in 1850, the author deleted the sweeping final sentence, and added the following paragraph:

> The genuineness of this poem, has, as far as we know, never been questioned, but it is indeed a very surprising feature, that during the recent diligent search through all the libraries in the country after old manuscripts, not a single production has been discovered, which could in any way be compared with it. This remarkable poem stands in the history of ancient Russian literature perfectly isolated; and hence exhibits one of the most inexplicable riddles in literary history.

Mrs. Robinson was unaware of the controversy over the authenticity of the poem, which broke out in the Russian press during the eighteen-thirties. Sooner or later, however, the "skeptical" point of view was bound to become known abroad. A commentator on several French histories of Russian literature in the *Westminster Review* for 1877, in referring to "the ***Song on the Expedition of Igor***," observes: "Some consider it to date as early as the twelfth century, others that it is a modern forgery. . . . With many Russian scholars it seems a point of national honour to believe in this composition, but to a foreigner the whole piece appears bombastic, and not without signs of modern falsification."

It was not until the publication, under the auspices of the Society for Promoting Christian Knowledge, of another survey of Slav literatures, by an English scholar, William R. Morfill, nearly half a century after the first appearance of Mrs. Robinson's monograph, that a few extracts from the ***Slovo*** became available. The quality of the translation leaves much to be desired. Thus Jaroslavna—her lament is the longest passage cited—is made to dip in the river Kajala her "*gloves* of beaver-skin." The author characterizes the epic as "a kind of prose bîlina" and notes its resemblance to "the Irish prose-poems, such as the description of the Battle of Clontarf in The War of the Gaedhill with the Gaill, and the Battle of Magh Rath."

Several extracts from the ***Slovo,*** including the lament of Jaroslavna, in a fairly commendable translation, illustrate the rather ample discussion of the tale in Georg Brandes's *Impressions of Russia* [see excerpt dated 1888]. . . . A rendering of that part of the text which precedes the Dream of Svjatoslav was contributed to *Stories from the Classic Literature of Many Nations* (New York, 1898), by J. A. Joffe, who had a hand in the preparation of the volume, *La Geste du Prince Igoŕ,* brought out fifty years later under the auspices of Ecole Libre des Hautes Etudes à New York as vol. VIII of Annuaire de l'Institut de philologie et d'histoire orientales et slaves. Even that fragment is not given in its entirety, several passages and not a few phrases having been omitted. Nor can it be said that the wording, for which Bertha Palmer, the editor of the volume, is partly responsible, is impeccable.

Prince Sergei Volkonski in his Lowell Lecture on Russian history and literature touches upon the ***Slovo*** and so does an English author, Hector H. Munro. While narrating "the feuds of the House of Rurik" in his history of Russia, he mentions as one of the Russian sources, "an epic poem of great beauty," namely, ***The Song of the Expedition of Igor***. This work, he writes, "one of the earliest Slavonic folk-songs that has been handed down from the dead past, has been translated into many languages, but never before into English, so that it is well worth reproducing in part in a history of Russian development." There follows a brief summary of the poem, based on H. von Paucker's German rendering and on "a modernized Russian reproduction of the Slavonic text" (the author seems to have had some Russian).

Munro's book was published both in England and the United States in 1900. Two years later there appeared the first English translation of the poem, complete except for the more obscure passages. It was an American contribution. The rendering was included in an anthology of Russian literature compiled by Leo Wiener, a native of Russia who was then a professor of Slavic languages and literatures at Harvard University. The text is preceded by a translation of the narrative of Igor's campaign of 1185, taken from the Hypatian Chronicle, and by a general introductory note, detailing the circumstances under which the manuscript of the poem was discovered and containing a word of appreciation. To Wiener, as to Munro, the poem was a piece of folklore. "The superior value of the ***Word [of Igor's Armament]*** lies in its being a precious relic of popular poetry of the twelfth century, such as no other nation can boast of. The *Nibelungenlied* and the *Chanson de Roland* are chiefly productions of a literary character, while the ***Word*** bears every evidence of representing the untutored labour of a popular bard." The translator does not indicate the editions which he followed. It may be assumed that they were among the best available at the time and that he was competent to interpret them. If he failed dismally to do justice to the ***Slovo,*** it was because of his insufficient mastery of the English language, and because too, like most of the other translators who were to try their hands at the task, he had a deficient sense of poetic values.

The studious reader could gain some shreds of information about our poem from the several English histories of Russian literature which soon began to appear on the market. There are two or three pages on ***The Ballad of the Band of Igor*** in Waliszewski's volume [see excerpt dated 1900], and a page in *A Survey of Russian Literature* by Isabel Hapgood, who emphasizes "a curious mingling of heathen beliefs and Christian views" in ***The Word (or Lay) Concerning Igor's Raid*** and quotes the opening of the poem in a free translation. Peter Kropotkin's book, made up of lectures he delivered at the Lowell Institute in 1901, offers a garbled and helpless version of Jaroslavna's lament and a few lines of comment. *A Literary History of Russia,* by Alexander Brückner, contains little besides a rapid, competent summary of the "peculiar little work," as he describes the poem.

The Lament reappears in Maurice Baring's *Outline,* but in a readable, somewhat free rendering. Unlike Brückner, this author is warmly appreciative of the ***Slovo.*** It is, we are told, "not only one of the most remarkable memorials of the ancient written language of Russia, but by virtue of its originality, its historical truth, its vividness, it holds a unique place in the literary history of Europe, and offers an interesting contrast to the *Chanson de Roland.*" A stimulating and rather ample discussion of the poem may be found in Mirsky's history [see excerpt dated 1927]. "The style of the poem," this author tells us, "is the reverse of the primitive and barbaric. It is curiously, disconcertingly modern, all suggestion and allusion, full of splendid imagery, subtly symbolic and complex." The work, he writes, is couched in a highly organized rhythmical prose of "infinitely varied flexibility." The ***Slovo***'s other claim to uniqueness lies, according to him, in the fact that "it is neither a lyric, nor an epic, nor a piece of political oratory, and it is all these blended into one." It might have been the better part of valor for him not to have succumbed to the temptation of giving some excerpts in translation.

Some echoes of the poem reached the public in England and America, at least the opera-going section of it, via Borodin's *Prince Igor,* the libretto of which is, of course, based on the ***Slovo.*** (pp. 203-08)

Avrahm Yarmolinsky, "The 'Slovo' in English," in Russian Epic Studies, *edited by Roman Jakobson and Ernest J. Simmons, American Folklore Society, 1949, pp. 203-23.*

ROMAN JAKOBSON (essay date 1952)

[*A Russian-born American linguist and Slavicist, Jakobson was one of the most influential figures in twentieth-century philology. Best known as the founder of modern phonology and structural linguistics, he was the author of over five hundred books and articles treating a wide range of linguistic and literary subjects. Among his first scholarly studies was a reconstruction of the text of* The Igor Tale, *and the poem remained one of Jakobson's preoccupations throughout his career. Between 1943 and 1946 he organized, with H. Grégoire, a series of seminars devoted to the study of the poem, with participants including Samuel Hazzard Cross, George Fedotov, Karl Heinrich Menges, and George Verdansky. Several pioneering studies of* The Igor Tale *were published as a result of this association. Notable among these is* "La geste du Prince Igor": Epopée russe du douzième siecle *(1948; Grégoire, Jakobson, Marc Szeftel, and J. A. Joffe, eds.), a collection of translations and commentaries that is widely considered the definitive Western study of* The Igor Tale. *In the following excerpt from an essay originally published in* Speculum *in 1952, Jakobson discusses scholarship devoted to* The Igor Tale *since its rediscovery in 1795, stressing the confusion resulting from attempts by the poem's earliest editors to render it comprehensible through modernization. An unexcerpted portion of this essay contains a detailed explication of what Jakobson considers the errors in André Mazon's* Le Slovo d'Igor *(1940)—the most extensive and influential argument against the authenticity of* The Igor Tale.]

The greatest difficulties face the student approaching the literary monuments of the final phase of the pre-Mongol period—the late twelfth and early thirteenth centuries. All works of this epoch—be they sermons, epistles, panegyrics, tales such as that of Lazarus in Hell, supplications such as that of Daniel the Exile—are rich in intricate puzzles, according to the trend of the time, which required speaking in riddles (*gat''kami besědovati*). It is the so-called parabolic-figurative (*pritočno-inoskazatel'-nyj*) style developed during the twelfth century in Russia, and puzzling only for literary historians who treat Kievan Russia in splendid isolation from the rest of the world. Otherwise the synchronic international correspondences are strikingly obvious. It is enough to evoke the Golden Age of the French medieval literature under Louis VII and Philip Augustus with its meridional *poésie recluse* (Provençal *trobar clus*) of Raimbaut d'Aurenga and Arnaud Daniel de Ribérac, or the German *blüemen* in Wolfram's epics and the refined symbolism and hermetism cultivated in the skaldic poetry of the late twelfth century, as exemplified by the *kenningr* of Snorri Sturluson. Similar tendencies appear in the Irish poetry of the time; enigmatic speech (*significatio*) and *ornatus difficilis* in general was advocated in the contemporary Latin textbooks of *ars poetica,* especially by Gaufredus de Vinosalvo; a flowering of the metaphoric style has been pointed out by E. R. Curtius in the international Latin poetry after the First Crusade (*Europäische Literatur und lateinisches Mittelalter . . .*); and finally, in the Byzantine literary art of the same period, students note the high-flown, "factitious" manner, the brilliance and abundance of metaphors and metonymies, the excess of adornments, the intricate chains of symbols and the multi-level semantic structures. In the light of comparative literature the allegedly scattered and isolated phenomena of single national literatures prove to be links of a world chain, and particularly interesting is C. H. Haskins' statement that the literary movement of the twelfth century "owed its beginning to no single country" (*The Renaissance of the Twelfth Century*).

The typical epics of this world style are far from being epic in the usual sense of this term. Instead of narrating, they allude to facts that they presume to be familiar to the reader and link them by fanciful associations of contiguity, resemblance, and contrast with various levels of reality, with events close and distant in space and time. This spatial, temporal, and thematic multiplicity and condensation is naturally supplemented by a skillful combination of diverse and even contrasting styles of bookish and oral provenience and of diverse and contrasting attitudes—secular and clerical, popular and seignorial, Christian and semi-pagan.

Just as the Russian literature of the late twelfth and early thirteenth centuries is one of the typical manifestations of the contemporary international poetic current, so the ***Tale of the Raid of Igor' (Slovo o p''lku Igorevě),*** composed during that period, belongs to the representative epics of the type described. What is its subject? It is the adventurous and unfortunate raid of Prince Igor' against the Polovcians, the rout of his army, his imprisonment and escape, and an appeal to the Russian princes for a new common front against the foe. This matter, however, is multiplied by metaphoric references to such various fields as agriculture, falconry, revelry, and love, by focusing not only on Igor's rout but also on the whole of Russia and surrounding countries, by wide digressions into the historical past and glimpses into the future. Every event, every image, dream and reported speech in the ***Igor' Tale*** foretells, portends, prophesies. This epic is far from any psychologism, any subjective lyric attitude, any sentimentalism. The author represents and appeals, but none of his personal emotions is directly expressed: at the tragic events, he does not mourn: he only reports the verbalized passions of the *dramatis personae*—the laments of the women and the grief of the men—and, finally, sorrow as well as joy fully embodied in the transparent imagery of the ***Tale.***

Melchior de Vogüé was right: at the end of the eighteenth century when the ***Igor' Tale*** was discovered, there was no one in Russia able to understand it. In the atmosphere of the declining classicism and of the dominant pre-romantic trend, the appealing medieval poetry was the sentimental, descriptive, and univalent hoax of Macpherson, the opposite of the absolutely non-sentimental, non-descriptive, and deliberately ambiguous ***Igor' Tale.*** To make the ***Slovo*** accessible to the taste of the epoch, its first editors and commentators were faced with the necessity of Ossianizing it, and one must confess they did their job cleverly. Their reshaping of the twelfth-century epic through punctuation, translation, and explanation brought it as close as possible to the esthetic demand, and the nearly unanimous assertion of the "spirit of the Russian Ossian" appears triumphantly both in the first, and obviously related, reports of Xeraskov and Karamzin on the discovery (1796) and in the preface to the *editio princeps* (1800), and even in the bookstore's advertisements of the new publication. In vain did the learned German expert in the Old Russian monuments, L. von Schlözer, recognizing the ***Igor' Tale*** as "eine ehrwürdige russische Antiquität" ["a venerable Russian antiquity"], express as early as 1801 the wise doubt "ob wirklich Ossianischer Geist in dem ***Slovo*** wehe" ["whether the Ossianic spirit truly blows through the ***Slovo***"]. Most of the retouchings committed by the first editors, critics, and emendators of the ***Igor' Tale*** remained decisive for the further interpretation of the epic. The critical apparatus to this text was elaborated and to a high degree standardized by scholars adhering to the esthetic bias of Russian realism. The quoted judgment of Repin is one of the innumerable examples of the complete incompatibility of this tenet with the artistic values of the Russian Middle Ages. The hermetic style and the intricate symbolism of the final chapter of the pre-Mongolian epoch was unreadable through realist glasses. Hence the process of modernizing the ***Igor' Tale*** continued, and it must be stated that sometimes the results were no less distorting than the notorious "restorations" of Old Russian frescoes, icons, and buildings in the nineteenth century. The exegesis was as far from the original wording as the illustrations of Viktor Vasnecov and other realist painters were from the poetic world of the ***Slovo*** and from the Old Russian pictorial pattern.

When, on the eve of the last war, André Mazon grappled with the puzzles of the ***Igor' Tale,*** this French philologist, deeply rooted in the esthetic and scholarly tradition of the nineteenth century and educated in Gončarov's and Turgenev's language and literary art, naturally felt much more at ease with all these recent linguistic and artistic interpretations of the ***Slovo*** than with the ***Slovo*** itself and its literary ambiance of the twelfth century. Hence it is not surprising at all that the observant Frenchman grasped some of the Ossianisms and modernisms super-imposed on the ***Igor' Tale*** by its editors and commentators and doubted whether they could be of ancient date. It would, however, be asking too much from a foreign specialist in modern Russian literature to accomplish the task of cleansing the ***Slovo*** of this disturbing modern superstratum. Instead of analyzing the ***Slovo*** itself, it was much easier to take the modernisms injected by its popularizers for genuine ingredients of the ***Tale*** and subsequently to launch what Mazon calls the "legitimate hypothesis" of the ***Slovo*** as a forgery of the late eighteenth century: *Le Slovo d'Igor.*

A group of students of Slavic and comparative medieval literature and of its historical background were linked with the Institut d'Histoire et de Philologie Orientales et Slaves, which during Hitler's occupation of Belgium was transported from Brussels to New York. They undertook a systematic study of the ***Slovo*** to liberate it from the prejudices and retouchings accumulated since its discovery, and the results were printed under the title *La Geste du Prince Igor', Epopée russe du douzième siècle* in New York in 1948 as the eighth volume of the *Annuaire* of the Institute under the editorship of H. Grégoire, M. Szeftel, and myself. Further works connected with this collective research appeared as *Russian Epic Studies,* edited by E. Simmons and myself [see Additional Bibliography] . . . ; the monograph by K. Menges, *The Oriental Elements in the Vocabulary of the Oldest Russian Epos, the Igor' Tale (Slovo o P''lku Igorevě)* appears as a publication of the Linguistic Circle of New York.

Our basic device was quite simple. In 1813 Count Musin-Puškin, the discoverer, owner, and publisher of the manuscript of the ***Igor' Tale,*** which in 1812 (during Napoleon's occupation of Moscow) perished with his entire renowned library and house, acknowledged in a letter to the philologist Kalajdovič that the manuscript was written in rather clear characters, but that nevertheless it was very difficult to decipher it because there was no orthography (comparable to the modern one), no punctuation, and no divisions between words. As he stated, a multitude of these words themselves were unknown and obsolete, so that first and foremost it was necessary to introduce divisions and then to sift out the meaning, and this was extremely perplexing. The Count adds that he did not even dare to print his results, for fear of repeating the notorious mistakes of the Prince Ščerbatov, who, in deciphering a Novgorod charter, rendered the words *zajač'imi lovcy* as *zajač' i Milovcy*. In fact, the *editio princeps* of the ***Igor' Tale*** teems with such errors, distorting the sense; and many of them have slipped into the later editions. In spite of the clear warning quoted, most of the critics tried to eliminate the obscurities of the text by changing letters and words, while the most natural way was to rewrite the text as, according to Musin-Puškin, it looked in the manuscript—that is, without divisions into words and phrases—and then to read these lines as we read the numerous Old Russian manuscripts of this type, dividing the text into lexical and syntactic units in the light of the abundant philological data we now possess. In applying this device we obtain a version nearly free of the alleged obscurities and the imaginary modernisms.

It is startling to what extent erroneous punctuation distorted the sense and style of the ***Slovo.*** The *editio princeps* reads in verse 30 (we follow *La Geste* in the enumeration and translation of the "verses"): "Their carts [those of the fleeing Polovcians] scream at midnight like startled swans. Igor' leads his warriors toward the Don. . . ." This reading, repeated by the later editors, including the recent ones of the Academy, gave full right to Mazon to detect a "retouche moderne"; but when we eliminate the period inserted by the first editors and replace it by a colon (in accordance with the style of the ***Tale,*** for which any descriptive image is but a presage, omen, announcement) we obtain a perfectly clear twelfth-century text: "Their carts scream at midnight like startled swans: Igor' leads his warriors toward the Don!" (according to S. H. Cross's accurate translation in *La Geste*). In other words, the strident sound of the fleeing Polovcian carts in the darkness of the night announces that Igor''s attack is close; and by the way, the comparison of the Polovcian carts with startled swans is based not only on an external resemblance, but on the totemic link of the swans with the Turkic hordes, as Menges points out in his monograph. This construction was no longer understood either two centuries later by the imitator of the ***Slovo***—the author of the *Zadonščina*—or by the first editors of the ***Slovo***; hence the *Zadonščina* and the translation of the ***Igor' Tale*** in the *editio princeps* quite naturally replace the unusual "scream" (*kryčat*) by the purely descriptive "squeak" (*skrypjat, skripěli*). In the same way the *editio princeps* reads in verse 50: *stjazi glagoljut, Polovci idut'* . . .

and translates "the banners rustle, the Polovci come . . ." (although this verb does not mean "rustle," but "say, announce"); and again Mazon is right in having some doubt whether it is not a modernism imputable to Musin-Puškin: the comma and the subsequent translation are indeed such. But for the ***Slovo*** we must once more substitute a colon as Jungmann, Erben and Barsov already did, contrary to most of the editors who still follow the blunder of 1800. Then the translation becomes "the banners announce: the Polovcians come." . . . Again neither the author of the *Zadonščina* nor the first editors understood the construction they found in the ***Slovo.***

Mazon's book and the American response provoked a considerable series of articles and critical notes both in American and in European academic periodicals. (pp. 382-87)

Except for A. Vaillant, who prefers to "circumvent" the ***Slovo*** with its "strange problems", all of the international philologists and literary historians who have touched upon the recent discussion reject any suspicions and recognize "the final proof for the genuineness of this remarkable monument of early Russian secular literature" (K. H. Menges). . . . (p. 388)

Roman Jakobson, "The Puzzles of the Igor' Tale on the 150th Anniversary of Its First Edition," in his Selected Writings IV: Slavic Epic Studies, *Mouton & Co., 1966, pp. 380-410.*

DMITRIJ ČIŽEVSKIJ (essay date 1960)

[*Čiževskij is a Russian-born critic and educator. In the following excerpt, he analyzes various stylistic and technical devices in* The Igor Tale *and discusses the poem's structure, ideology, authorship, and place in world literature.*]

The Tale of Igoŕ's Campaign (Slovo o polku Igoreve) is the [twelfth-century] monument to which most research has been devoted and which to this day is still obscure in many respects. Not because the authenticity of the work may be doubted . . . , its manuscript having been burned during the Moscow fire of 1812. The great number of unsolved questions linked with the ***Tale*** arise from the fact that it is in many respects an exceptional monument. Its language and, to a considerable extent, its style can—with a great degree of probability—be included in the history of the development of Kievan literature. The style of the ***Tale*** can be linked with the culture and art contemporary with it. But the ***Tale*** is the only example of a genre of which (with the exception of the ***Tale*** itself) we have only insignificant remains included in works of another type (the chronicles) and which undoubtedly have suffered great changes. Moreover, the ***Tale*** is a monument of such high poetic standing that it is impossible to suppose that it may be considered *typical* of its genre—the secular historical epos. Thus, in spite of the undoubted links of the ***Tale*** with the preceding, contemporary and subsequent literature, we are forced to study it as a work *sui generis,* and we shall dwell with special attention on its original traits. (p. 112)

The subject-matter of the ***Tale*** is simple in the main; it is the campaign of the Novgorod-Seversk Prince Igoŕ Svjatoslavič in 1185 against the restless nomads—the Polovtsians. The campaign ended, after an initial victory over the Polovtsians, in the cruel defeat of Igoŕ's army. The army was almost entirely destroyed; Igoŕ himself fell into captivity from which he later succeeded in escaping. One of his sons, who also found himself in captivity, married a Polovtsian princess and returned home even later. We are familiar with this campaign in sufficient detail from the Hypatian and Laurentian Chronicles.

The basic scheme, in accordance with which this factual material is distributed, is quite clear; the ***Tale*** begins with a short introduction and ends with a brief conclusion. The main content can be divided into four parts. 1) To begin with, the history of the campaign is expounded, up to the final defeat of Igoŕ. 2) Then the narrative takes us to Kiev where Prince Svjatoslav tells the boyars of his ominous dream and, learning of Igoŕ's defeat, pronounces a speech, "The Golden Word," addressing himself to various appanaged princes and exhorting them to fight against the Polovtsians. This "Word" of Svjatoslav merges imperceptibly into a speech by the author himself. 3) The following section is clearly distinguished; it is the "lament" of Igoŕ's wife, Jaroslavna, over her husband. 4) Then follows the story of Igoŕ's escape from captivity. The ***Tale*** has a brief conclusion. The whole story is not very long—about sixteen pages of modern print.

If the plan of the entire work is clear, in the individual parts a truly poetic "disorder" reigns; this was probably intentional. The "lament" alone is divided into four separate "stanzas" beginning with the same words, "Jaroslavna weeps. . . ." In the remaining parts the author continually proceeds from one theme to another, from the description of contemporary events to reminiscences of the past, or to representation of scenery, or to the expression of his own feelings, or even to quotations from the 11th century poet Bojan, or to allusions at times obscure to us. All the attempts to "correct" the vagueness of the plan by various transpositions of parts of the text are questionable and unconvincing. Scholars of recent times have refrained from such attempts.

The obscurity is further intensified by the main stylistic peculiarity of the ***Tale,*** a peculiarity which is found but rarely in the chronicles of the 11th-13th centuries. Instead of an exposition, a rendering of events, the author presents the reader with complexes of metaphors. Moreover, the real significance of the metaphors is rarely explained (and then usually after the metaphor), and is often revealed only by an allusion, or not at all. Thus Bojan "recalling . . . the fights of olden times, it was his wont to loose ten falcons on a flock of swans; and the one swan whichever was overtaken was the first to sing a song." The explanation follows: "Bojan did not loose ten falcons on a flock of swans, . . . but laid his own magic fingers upon the living strings, and they would of themselves sound forth the glory of the princes."

More often the meaning of the metaphor is revealed only by an allusion: Igoŕ addresses the army—"I wish . . . to break a lance on the edge of the Polovtsian land. . . . I wish to lay down my head, or else to quaff of the Don from my helmet." It is clear to the reader that Igoŕ is exhorting the warriors to a campaign the issue of which is unknown. Or the reminiscences about the battles of bygone years: "On the [river—D.Č.] Nemiga they threw sheaves of heads and thresh with chain flails of Frankish steel; on the threshing floor they lay down life and winnow soul from body." Here only the words "life" and "soul" show that this complex of metaphors denotes battle and the death of soldiers. "Alone"—it is said of a prince—"thou didst let fall the pearl of thy soul out of the valiant body through thy golden necklace": the word "soul" shows that death is indicated.

But very often the metaphors are not elucidated at all. Of another prince's death during battle, it is said, "He fell under scarlet shields upon the bloody turf as it were upon the couch with his beloved"—the image of death as a marriage or a wedding is found in the epics of various nations. "Prince Igoŕ dismounted from his golden saddle, but only to a captive's saddle"—a metaphor of defeat and captivity. "Vladimir stopped his ears in Černigov morning after morning,"—even in the context of memories about discussions of former times, the metaphor is not quite clear, and has been explained in various ways. Or, "Vseslav cast lot for the coveted maiden. Craftily leaning on his spear, he leaped to the city of Kiev, and touched with the spear-shaft the golden Kievan throne"—from the Chronicle story of Vseslav we know that in 1068 he had for a short time seized the Kievan princely throne. The metaphor "city = maiden" can be found in the folk-lore of various peoples. Quite obscure is yet another excerpt devoted to memories of Vseslav. "In Polock the bells of St. Sophia's would ring in the morning for him, but he already heard the matin-bells in Kiev." Though we know that Vseslav was a Polock prince, it is difficult to give a satisfactory explanation of this metaphor.

In some ways the metaphors of the ***Tale*** remind us of those verbal riddles which we occasionally find in the chronicles. . . . They also recall a special device of Scandinavian poetry, the so-called *kenningar,* i.e., conventional metaphors in which the very mysteriousness of the obscurity is valued; notwithstanding the considerable bulk of extant Scandinavian poetry, some of the *kenningar* remain enigmatic to this day. The similarity of the metaphors of the ***Tale*** with the *kenningar* of Scandinavian poetry does not reside in the individual figures of speech, but rather in the very principle of using conventional, obscure and unexplained metaphors. Like the *kenningar,* the metaphors of the ***Tale*** are frequently composed of two terms and replace definite nouns: for example, "ten swans"—fingers; "steel chains"—swords; "scarlet wine"—blood; "coveted maiden"—town; and so forth. Also frequent are verbal metaphors, of this kind: "to winnow soul from body"—to kill; "to touch the throne with a spear"—to ascend the throne, etc. But at the end of the 12th century, any influence of Scandinavian poetry was hardly possible. Citing quotations and sayings from Bojan, the ***Tale*** thus reveals that this device had *already* been used in the 11th century (probably all the memories of Vseslav are linked with the poetical works of his contemporary Bojan). The metaphors of the ***Tale*** continue this old tradition.

The Tale of Igoŕ's Campaign also uses omens, dreams, and forebodings as metaphors. Svjatoslav's dream reminds us even more of verbal riddles and the *kenningar*. Here is the beginning of this dream, as narrated by Svjatoslav: "Early this night . . . they were clothing me in a black shroud upon a couch of yew, they poured me blue wine mixed with sorrow. They dropped upon my chest large pearls out of the empty quivers of the pagans. And they caress me, and the beams of my gold-domed hall are already without roof-girder. . . ." The meaning of further omen-metaphors have remained obscure to this day. Nature is full of auguries; for instance, before the campaign Igoŕ's army sees an eclipse of the sun—an evil omen. In reality, this took place on May 1st, 1185, *during* the course of the campaign. The ***Tale*** transposes it to the eve of the campaign, in this way stressing the heroic determination of Igoŕ to undertake the campaign despite the evil omens. Before Igoŕ's defeat: "The next day, very early, bloody dawnings announce the break of day. Black clouds come up from the sea; they would fain veil the four suns,—and within them blue lightnings quiver"; and "The earth groans, the rivers flow turbid, dust covers the fields." And after the news of the defeat is received, "and trees have shed their foliage for evil!"

The metaphors of the ***Tale*** are not always so involved. Very often the metaphor simply consists in replacing an ordinary word, the name of an object, by its symbol. Bojan is a nightingale, the Polovtsians are crows or jackdaws, the heroes of the ***Tale*** are falcons, and so forth. The whole of Nature is symbolically portrayed: animals, sun, moon, mist, dust, dawn, and twilight. The ***Tale*** also uses equivocal metaphors, based on the dual function of the Slavonic instrumental case—the latter denoting both a real attitude and a comparison. For instance, we are told of Prince Vseslav: . . . "he leaped secretly like a wild beast"; "at night he coursed like a wolf"—these sentences may be understood as an assertion that Vseslav was a werewolf and turned into various animals, but they may also be interpreted as a comparison of the rapid campaigns of Vseslav with the leaps of a "wild beast" or "wolf."

The metaphors and the symbolism of the ***Tale*** are sometimes difficult to elucidate, as we often have no knowledge of the real facts which the author communicates merely by a metaphor (cf. the examples above about Vseslav). In other cases, for instance before the campaign, when Igoŕ "proved his mind with firmness and sharpened it by the courage of his heart," the metaphor hints at two processes of preparation of arms for the battle: "proved" and "sharpen," the basic metaphor being the "mind" (*um*) = sword.

Hyperbole is another favourite device used in ***The Tale of Igoŕ's Campaign.*** The author represents princes as cosmic forces. Prince Svjatoslav "with his powerful hosts . . . set his foot upon the land of Polovtsian, trod down hills and ravines, muddied their rivers and lakes, dried up torrents and swamps; like a whirlwind, he snatched the infidel Kobjak . . . from the great Polovtsian iron hosts, and Kobjak fell in the city of Kiev, in the hall of Svjatoslav." Or Prince Vsevolod of Suzdal' "can stir up the Volga with oars, and pour out the Don with helmets." The regiments of the Černigov prince "vanquish hosts with war-whoop, sounding the glory of their grandsires." The soldiers of other princes "swam in blood in their gilded helmets"; this is an intensification of the usual in the military tales—"blood filled the valleys." And here too, as in the metaphors, reality is hidden behind imagery.

The same function of replacing reality by an image is performed by the mythological elements of the ***Tale.*** In other monuments mythological elements appear only incidentally and are at once either rejected by the authors or incorporated by them into the system of Christian *Weltanschauung*. Thus, the pagan gods are mentioned in the sermons, though these latter are directed against faith in them. . . . In the Chronicle, prophetic predictions and omens are narrated, and parallel examples from Christian literature are quoted. According to the Chronicle only "ignorants" . . . believe that during an eclipse "the sun will devour" some mythological creature (serpent or wolf). In the ***Tale*** we more than once find representatives of lower mythology: Div, Deva-Obida; Prince Vseslav is a Proteus, a werewolf. Beside these the Slavs are "grandchildren of Dažbog," Bojan is the "grandson of Veles," sun—"Chors," etc. The use of the names of pagan gods in the poetry of the Christian era has an analogy, it is true, in Scandinavian poetry and in the Latin poetry of the Middle Ages. But, most probably, the expressions "*grandchildren* of Dažbog," "*grandson* of Veles" point to the author's euhemerism—a popular conception in Christian literature that the pagan gods are the product of superstition, and are, in fact, simply ancient kings and heroes mistakenly regarded as gods. (pp. 113-17)

Metaphor and hyperbole represent only the most striking feature of the ***Tale***'s style. But we also encounter in it the use of diverse tropes and figures of speech. Some of them are striking in their richness. Thus, an extraordinary role is played in the Tale by euphonic devices: alliterations and the harmony of sounds within words. (p. 117)

The choice of words is quite often . . . determined by euphonic considerations. Harmonies of rhyme (*homoioteleuton*) are rare and probably accidental.

One must also add to the euphonic elements of words a certain syntactic rhythm of the language. However, all attempts to find in the ***Tale*** some kind of verse measure have failed: it is not, of course, verse, but a somewhat rhythmic, cadenced prose.

If we turn our attention to the imagery used in ***The Tale of Igoŕ's Campaign,*** the first thing that strikes us is the considerable amount of auditory and colour imagery.

The author himself, as well as Bojan, ''sings'' songs of Gothic maidens in the Crimea; songs of virgins on the Danube are also mentioned; the author refers to the laments of wives of dead soldiers and to the lament of the drowned Prince Rostislav's mother; the lament of Jaroslavna is one of the component parts of the work. There are mentioned the war-cries of soldiers and the cries at the beginning of the battle—the Polovtsians with their war-cry even ''barred the fields,'' whereas the Černigov soldiers with one war-whoop ''vanquish hosts.'' Before the campaign ''praises ring''; during the battle the soldiers ''roar like aurochs''; the inhabitants of the town of Rimov ''wail'' under the blows of Polovtsian sabres; during the battle ''spears clatter,'' sabres and swords rattle when banged against helmets, trumpets blow before the campaign and emit a ''mournful sound'' after the battle, horses neigh, carts creak. The author hears even the peal of ''Russian gold'' in the hands of Gothic maidens in the Crimea; he depicts the peaceful life recalling the cries of the ploughmen; church bells are also mentioned. Especially remarkable is the frequent mention of the voices of nature. Animals and birds appear very often (mention of animals and birds is frequent in the Chronicle from the end of the 11th century): nightingales, crows, jackdaws, the cuckoo, eagles, woodpeckers, river birds, wolves, foxes, aurochs, horses—every animal has its own voice, and for every voice there is a special verb. The whole of nature resounds: ''the night moans with thunder,'' ''the earth drones'' or ''knocks,'' clouds draw near with lightning and thunder. To these are further added mythological and metaphorical sounds: ''Div'' cries from the top of the three, ''*Děva-Obida*'' splashes her swan's wings in the sea, Russian earth (here personified) groans, glory ''rings'' (''glory'' or ''praise'' here means not only a song of praise but also, for instance, ''glory of the forefathers''). The author and the *dramatis personae* ''hear'' the sound of events remote in space and time. In this context, the abundant usage of euphonic and onomatopoeic stylistic devices is not surprising.

The colours are also very vivid; they are partly real and partly symbolic. The epithets ''golden'' and ''silver'' are very frequent; everything referring to princes is connected with gold—their helmets, saddles, stirrups, arrows, thrones, the roof of the castle, and so forth. The epithet ''red'' is also frequent; the shields of the Russian army and the standards are red. The variant—blood-red—gives the epithet a horrific shade: a blood-red dawn presages defeat, ''blood-red grass'' is an indication of a bloody battle, ''blood-red wine'' is a metaphor for blood; other variants are ''purple'' and ''fiery.'' The black colour is used in connection with obscure and evil things: crows are black, so are clouds, the soil after battle, loosened by the horses' hooves, and the shroud in Svjatoslav's ominous dream. Blue is, of course, employed in connection with the sea, but sometimes it appears as an ominous symbol: ''blue wine'' and ''blue lightning.'' ''Silver'' is again a positive symbol: the ''silver shores'' of the river Donec, which helped Igoŕ in his flight, the venerable silver hair of Prince Svjatoslav. . . . The grey colour (like its variants *sizyj* and *busyj*) has no special significance; the wolf and the eagle are grey.

The art of psychological characterisation is worthy of mention. It is true, psychological experiences are in most cases conveyed in terms of their external manifestations; the protagonists sing, shed tears, moan and cry. But the author includes in his work three lyrical monologues: Prince Svjatoslav's speech, with an appeal for peaceful relationships between the princes, and a united struggle against the Polovtsians; the thanksgiving speech of Prince Igoŕ to the river Donec; but especially Jaroslavna's lament, original for the fact that she is not lamenting the deceased prince but complaining of separation from him and that her address to the sun, wind, and the river Dniepr bears rather the character of ''amorous incantation.'' The Princess turns to the river Dniepr with the words: ''float back to me my beloved, that I may not at morn send him my tears down to the sea.'' The author was able to fill these three lyric monologues, quite different in tonality with a vividly expressed emotional content.

By the use of metaphors, taken from military life or from nature, the author can represent not only the external but also the psychological aspect of his heroes. Of such are the soldiers' hearts ''tempered in turbulence,'' or Prince Igoŕ's spirit ''sharpened his mind by courage of the heart,'' or the designation of Igoŕ's brother who took part in the campaign of Prince Vsevolod as *buj tur* (courageous aurochs). Or, in the mouth of Prince Vsevolod, the characterization of his Kursk soldiers: ''And my men of Kursk are glorious warriors: swaddled under trumpets, cradled under helmets, nursed at the spear's point. To them the roads are known and the ravines are familiar; bent are their bows, open their quivers, sharpened their sabres. Like grey wolves in the fields they roam, seeking honor for themselves and glory for the Prince.'' And the very composition of the ***Tale*** comprises elements of similar artful psychological characterisation. Let us recall, for instance, that the author transposed the eclipse of the sun—an ominous presage—to the eve of the campaign in order to stress in this way Igoŕ's intrepidity and his thirst for military feats. The author says himself, ''The Prince's mind was ablaze with eagerness and the omen was dimmed by his craving to taste the great Don. . . .''

The Tale of Igoŕ's Campaign has a number of features in common with the style of the Chronicle. The main feature is the use of aphorisms and set formulas. Some of these are repeated in the ***Tale*** as ''refrains.'' To these belongs the formula ''seeking honour for themselves and glory for the Prince''; then ''and the Russian land is already beyond the hill''; or in two variants of the ***Tale*** about nature's compassion for human sorrow ''the grass bends in sorrow, and the tree is bowed down to earth by woe'' (on another occasion the first part of the formula is replaced by another—*unyša cvěty* (flowers have grown), probably because the word *unyša* harmonises with the preceding word *unošu* (to the youth). Some of these formulas are introduced with the patriotic ideology in Svjatoslav's speech, exhorting to vengeance against the Polovtsians ''for the Russian land, for Igoŕ's wounds.''

A few proverbs are ascribed to Bojan: "Neither a crafty man, nor a clever man . . . can escape God's doom"; "If it be hard for thee, head, without the shoulders, it is bad for thee, body, without the head." But we find also proverbs which are not ascribed to Bojan, for instance, "*Koli sokol b mytěch byvajet, vysoko ptic vzbivajet*"—here the rhyme is characteristic too, linking both parts of the two-term formula ("When a falcon moults, high does he smite the birds").

The ***Tale*** is linked with the style of the Chronicle also by the frequent introduction of speeches. Besides the already mentioned monologues, one notes Igoŕ's address to the army; his conversation with Vsevolod before the campaign; the mention of the princes' conversation among themselves ("This is mine, and this is mine, too"); the reporting of women's laments in direct speech; the Polovtsian khans, while pursuing Igoŕ, speaking among themselves (their conversation is typical speech in riddles).

In spite of the originality of the ***Tale***—the only extant monument of the historic epos—it does not stand isolated either lexically or phraseologically. Only a very small number of words used are not to be found in other monuments of the same (or a close) period, and, moreover, a number of such words are completely *normal* derivatives of popular roots. A whole range of turns of phrase finds exact parallels not only in ecclesiastical literature, but even in the translation of the Bible, in which so many passages are devoted to military events. Quite a number of parallels has been found also in the contemporary East Slavonic folk-lore, primarily in the Ukrainian and Byelo-Russian. The similarity with contemporary folklore, however, is explained rather by the fact that the old historical epics contributed to its stylistic formation.

Various hypotheses have been advanced concerning the author of the ***Tale*** and, especially, concerning his origin. No one of those has been proved: neither the excessively high appraisal of the Kievan Prince Svjatoslav and the Galician Prince Jaroslav (Jaroslavna was his daughter), nor the great space devoted to Vseslav, the appanaged Prince of Polock (Svjatoslav's wife belonged to the family of Polock princes) allows us to link the poet *definitely* with any of these principalities. It must be borne in mind that it was very typical of the medieval "bards" to wander from the court of one ruler to another. The fact that the poet knew military and hunting life well, and that he was perfectly acquainted with the genealogy and inter-relations of princely families allow us to consider him most probably "a court poet." The ***Tale*** is indeed a work of "court" poetry. But it reflects also the ideal of peaceful life among princes, an ideal which found no reflection in the political practice of the rival princes. From this point of view the author of the ***Tale*** rose above the typical ideology of the princes of his time, as expressed for instance in the chronicles of the 12th-13th centuries. At a time when every annalist is chiefly preoccupied with the interests of his prince and his principality, the author of the ***Tale*** is conscious of the community of Eastern Slav tribes and their common political interests. In this respect the ***Tale*** is an ideologically important monument, though this ideology reflects rather that of a great Eastern Slav power. Not for nothing does the author of the ***Tale*** mention the two princes Jaroslav and Valdimir Monomach, who came closest to the realisation of this ideal. In general there are in the ***Tale*** elements of "historic romanticism," of attraction to the past, which appeared in the 12th century in the period of political and economic decadence in many fields of life; by this attraction can be explained also the names of pagan gods (euhemeristically interpreted). Here belongs, too, the appearance of Varangian names in princely families: *Rjurik, Ingvar, Rogvolod Malfred*. By this same fascination with the greatness of the past are explained the unsuccessful military enterprises such as Igor's campaign; almost at the same time the Novgorodians made a successful raid on the Swedish commercial town of Sigtuna, which brought, however, no further effects; also, the attempt by Prince Jaroslav of Galič to intervene in Eastern politics is mentioned in the ***Tale***. In general, mention of foreign countries is very frequent in the ***Tale***—beside Polovtsians we meet Greeks, Moravians, Germans and Venetians (as Prince Svjatoslav's guests).

Typical of the ***Tale***, too, is the ideology of chivalry, which is also vividly represented in the Kievan Chronicle. Interesting as well is the appearance in a literary work of a feminine figure, Jaroslavna, though not endowed with individual features. Mention is also made of Prince Vsevolod's "love and caress of the fair daughter of Glěb, his dear wife." A number of feminine figures, real and metaphoric, are scattered throughout the entire ***Tale***. This fact, too, though in a small degree, causes the ***Tale*** to resemble the typical works of "court literature" of other nations.

Attempts have been made to find points of similarity between the ***Tale*** and the epic works of Western Europe. Only minor resemblances have been noted. This is not surprising, as the ***Tale*** stands on a quite different *genetic* step from comparable works of other nations. This is an epic whose historical content closely reflects reality. On the other hand, the Greek epos, and the songs of Icelandic *Edda*, as well as the *Nibelungenlied* and other German epic works, and the French *Chanson de Roland*, being all based on historical material, are separated from the events depicted by several hundred years and the historical occurrences therein are therefore distorted and enveloped by the trappings of the saga. Their form also belongs to an entirely different stage of development: they are either more archaic (*Edda*) or, on the contrary, are products of a very lengthy stylistic evolution resulting in a vast exposition of the content. Closer to the ***Tale*** in some respects are works in a more concise though florid style—*Beowulf* or, even more so, songs about the journeys of Charlemagne to Jerusalem, but these too are not "historical" in the same sense as the ***Tale***. In the ***Tale*** only the prophetic omens and dreams are unreal; only the stories about Vseslav could be a basis for the development of epic fantasy out of the material of the ***Tale***, and possibly also the metaphors in the description of Igor's flight, who, having overstrained his horse, runs "like a wolf," . . . "like an ermine," . . . *swims* "like a species of duck" . . . across the river, bolts like a falcon. . . . But owing to the scarcity of written epic works, we do not know whether such development was achieved later. Some hint at such development is given by the contemporary epos . . . and partly by fables. (pp. 119-23)

Dmitrij Čiževskij, "The Tale of Igoŕ's Campaign," in his History of Russian Literature from the Eleventh Century to the End of the Baroque, *Mouton & Co., 1960, pp. 112-24.*

VLADIMIR NABOKOV (essay date 1960)

[A Russian-born American man of letters, Nabokov was a prolific contributor to many literary fields, producing works in both Russian and English and distinguishing himself in particular as the author of the novels Lolita *(1955) and* Pale Fire *(1962). Nabokov was fascinated with all aspects of the creative life, and his works frequently explore the origins of creativity, the relationships of*

artists to their work, and the nature of invented reality. Considered a brilliant prose stylist, Nabokov wrote fiction that entertains and sometimes exasperates readers in its preoccupation with intellectual and verbal games. The following excerpt is taken from an introduction to Nabokov's English translation of The Igor Tale, *entitled* The Song of Igor's Campaign: An Epic of the Twelfth Century, *and line references in the text are to this translation. Nabokov examines technical aspects of the poem—noting in particular how the reiteration of themes, motifs, and poetic formulas contributes to the artistic unity of the work—and discusses the poem's authenticity.*]

The original text of ***The Song*** as published in 1800 consists of 14,175 letters or about 2850 words. . . . Its first sections are devoted mainly to an account of the unfortunate foray. The facts tally with those of the Ipatiev Chronicle but they are grouped and illumined according to the poet's own views and needs. That there was some exchange of information between the original chronicler and the author of ***The Song*** is evident from a few bizarre coincidences . . . , but who was influenced by whom is far from clear. The chronicle is the work of a learned monk adept at pious formulas, a conscientious writer with a shapeless style and little originality of thought. ***The Song,*** on the other hand, is a harmonious, many leveled, many hued, uniquely poetical structure created in a sustained and controlled surge of inspiration by an artist with a fondness for pagan gods and a percipience of sensuous things. Its political and patriotic slant pertaining to a given historical moment is, naturally, of small importance in the light of its timeless beauty, and . . . I am not interested in considering ***The Song*** as a corollary of history or a birch-stump speech.

The structure of ***The Song*** shows a subtle balance of parts which attests to deliberate artistic endeavor and excludes the possibility of that gradual accretion of lumpy parts which is so typical of folklore. It is the lucid work of one man, not the random thrum of a people. From the extraordinary prelude, where the tenacious shadow of Boyan is used by our bard for his own narrative purpose, to the conclusion of the work, where Boyan is once more invoked to preside over the happy end, there is a constant interplay of themes and mutual echoes. The entire composition neatly divides itself into five parts: 1. Exordium (lines 1-70); 2. Narration (lines 71-390); 3. Conjuration (391-730); 4. Liberation (lines 731-830); 5. Epilogue (lines 831-860). In Part 2, Vsevolod's speech to his brother before they set out (lines 71-90) forms a companion piece to the description of Vsevolod in action on the battlefield (lines 211-230); the bright sun which is eclipsed in 91-110, when Igor addresses his warriors before the campaign, later rises in gory grandeur over the battlefield (181-183), is addressed by Euphrosyne from the rampart (722-730), and finally sheds a gay and benevolent radiance on Igor's homecoming (841). In another ingenious arrangement of nicely fitting pieces, the Winds, which in Part 2 drive enemy arrows against Igor (197-199), are conjured by Euphrosyne in Part 3 (699-708), and in answer to her prayer brew up a diversionary storm (731-732) to assist Igor's liberation. Especially satisfying to one's sense of inner concord and unity is the ample treatment of the theme of the Rivers, among which the Great Don plays a leading role. Igor's urge to take a look at it (100) and drink a helmetful of it (110), expressed in a stylistically perfect refrain at the beginning of Part 1, is repeated with a symmetrical intonation at 180 and 190, in the beginning of the great battle, when the resounding, redoubtable Don is felt to be on the side of the Kumans. Throughout ***The Song*** that river is mentioned a number of times in terms of terror and disaster (131, 194, 205, 309, 741) as well as in terms of passionate desire (100, 110, 416, 503, 567), with the subtheme of the "helmetful" repeated at 416 and 503. Igor does not attain the blue mirage of the Don (which will be reached two centuries later in the *Zadonshchina,* a vulgar imitation of ***The Song*** concocted in celebration of a great victory over the Mongols), but in a perfect structural move the artist substitutes for the Great Don its tributary, the Lesser Don, the "little" Donets, with which, or rather with whom, the prince in the Liberation part of ***The Song*** indulges in a charming colloquy (771-802), contrasting the kind Donets with a much less amiable stream, the Stugna, in a passage (791-802) which resolves itself in a last echo of danger and misfortune. Igor's speech of thanks to the Lesser Don is beautifully duplicated by his wife's prayer to the Dnepr (711-719): the great Kievan river transmits as it were the power of intercession and assistance to the prairie stream, and Igor's historical recollection of a less fortunate lady's weeping on the Dnepr's banks is a necessary element of rhetorical harmony to balance, at the close of the entire movement, Euphrosyne's initial apostrophization of that river. And finally there is the river Kayala, near which the disastrous battle is fought. The reiteration of its name with emblematic allusions is a haunting presence throughout ***The Song*** (194, 251, 292, 380, 431, 694).

An array of animals, resembling the stylized fauna of rich-hued rugs, and marginal designs of delicate plants play a changeful double role in the structure of ***The Song.*** They give its circumstances a touch of local reality, and they participate in the general theme of magic, prophecy and conjuration, a theme bespeaking a singular freedom of thought and distinguishing this pagan poem from the pallid and rigid compositions of routine Christian piety which by that time had begun to direct and to drain literary art. It will be noted that here again the diverse expressions of the theme enter into a subtle arrangement of calls and recalls, with every step having its reverberation and every echo its arch. Thus, the colorful prairie creatures participating as agents of doom and as the Kumans' allies in the excitement of the eclipse (115-126, 132-139) or taking cruel advantage of the dead (263-266, 602-604), or reveling in tragedy (406-407, 422-443), are replaced and responded to, within the work's plural melody, by the antiphonal pro-Russian birds (787-790, 806-813), assistants of the river gods conjured by Euphrosyne and, in the case of the nightingales, representatives of Boyan.

In what may be termed a more feminine strain, flowers and trees by their drooping movements express their choral compassion for the misfortunes of the Russians. Besides an allusion at 562, the formula of their participation occurs as a refrain at 299-301 and again at 801-802: it comes here during that triumphant homeward trek where, seemingly, nothing but elation could be experienced by Igor, but where, by an artistic device, the pathetic refrain lends a poetically needful support to the symmetry of the over-arching theme of melancholy; which melancholy is now transformed into a remembered event referring to a long-dead prince and thus brings out, in vibrant contrast, among the light and shade of riverside willows, the lucky fate of the live hero.

The all-pervading sense of magic so vividly conveyed by flora and fauna, demon peacocks and fairytale ducks, waters and winds, auroras and thunders, is introduced by our bard's descriptions of Boyan's enchantments (especially 11-18 and 35-38) and is further illustrated by a series of thematic panels such as the Eclipse (91-119), the Portentous Storm following it (132-139 and 181-190), the Arrival of the Antivirgin (306-310), the King's Dream (391-410), the Spells of Vseslav (651-690),

Euphrosyne's Incantation (691-750) and Igor's Escape (especially 731-733, 751-760, 781-790, 806-810).

Among other elements of our author's technique the good reader will note his art of transition and preparation. Thus, interrupting with a dramatic aside the account of the battle which starts with the "Vsevolod Wild Bull" movement (211-230), our bard, in preparation of the political centerpiece of ***The Song*** (that magnificent section, 497-686, where old feuds are recalled and contemporaneous princes implored to help Igor), contrives a first digression beginning at 231, "There have been the ages of Troyan" (which in itself is a companion intonation to the Boyan apostrophe at 51-60), and continuing to 270, after which we return to the Kayala battlefield. In this long digression the feuds of Oleg Malglory (233-238), the death of Boris son of Vyacheslav (245-250) and that of Izyaslav I (251-254) are recalled, and the image of a dissension-torn Russia (255-268) is projected from there into another section (311-350) where a clamor of lament rises after Igor's defeat. The transition from that defeat to the recent victories of Svyatoslav III leads to the great scene in Kiev, while the various evocations, pictorial in brightness and dramatic in sonority, of Oleg, Vyacheslav and Izyaslav have now prepared eye and ear for the brilliant glimpses of princes who are rallied to Igor's assistance: Yaroslav of Chernigov (466-478), Vsevolod of Suzdal (497-510), the brothers Rurik and David (511-522), Yaroslav of Galich (523-541), Roman later of Galich and his brother Mstislav (542-559) and Mstislav's brothers Ingvar and Vsevolod (571-582), after which a historical recollection, the recent death of Izyaslav son of Vasilko (591-610), leads to the admirable evocation of the enchantments and misfortunes of Vseslav, Izyaslav's grandfather (631-678).

Within these ample surgings of interlinked themes we can mark such smaller elements of inner unity as intonational refrains and recurrent types of metaphor. Among the refrains are such striking repetitions of euphonious formulas as "seeking for themselves honor and for their prince glory" (89-90, 149-150), "O Russian land, you are already behind the culmen" (140-141, 195-196), the double formula of "drooping" pertaining to grass and trees (299-301), to ramparts and merriment (387-390), to voices and merriment (611-614) and, in perfect structural symmetry, to the flowers and the tree at 801-802. Another refrain is the plea to avenge Russia and Igor (519-523, 539-541, 580-583); and "Yaroslavna early weeps in Putivl on the rampart, repeating" in an especially musical reiteration recalling Western European ballads (697-698, 709-710, 720-721). Finally, I leave to the students of generic style to notice the various categories of metaphor which adorn ***The Song*** and add the pleasures of connotation to those of direct imagery. These metaphors can be classified mainly as belonging to the vocabulary of the hunt, to the domain of agriculture and to that of meteorological phenomena.

Throughout ***The Song*** there occur here and there a few poetical formulas strikingly resembling those in Macpherson's *Ossian*. . . . Paradoxically, these coincidences tend to prove not that a Russian of the eighteenth century emulated Macpherson, but that Macpherson's concoction does contain after all scraps derived from authentic ancient poems. It is not unreasonable to assume that through the mist of Scandinavian sagas certain bridges or ruins of bridges may be distinguished linking Scottic-Gaelic romances with Kievan ones. The curious point is that if we imagine a Russian forger around 1790 constructing a mosaic out of genuine odds and ends with his own mortar, we must further imagine that he knew English well enough to be affected by specific elements of Macpherson's style; but in the eighteenth century, and well into the age of Pushkin, English poetry was known to Russians only through French versions, and therefore the Russian forger would not have rendered, as Letourneur did not render them, the very special details of that curious "Ossianic" style. . . . (pp. 5-13)

The eleventh and twelfth centuries were marked in Kievan Russia by amazing artistic achievements, but the making of diadems, frescoes, ikons, and marvellously lovely churches, such as the Cathedral of St. Sophia in Kiev (built in 1036) or the Uspenskiy Cathedral in Vladimir (1158-1189) or the Dmitrievskiy Cathedral in the same town (1193-1197), does not necessarily imply a contemporaneous development of literature; and similarly, great poetry is known to have been produced at periods when the (on the whole more primitive) arts of painting and architecture did not exactly flourish. Despite the Marxist scholastics and nationalistic emotions which tend to transform modern essays on ***The Song*** into exuberant hymns to the Motherland, Soviet historians are as helpless as earlier Russian scholars were to explain the striking, obvious, almost palpable difference in artistic texture that exists between ***The Song*** and such remnants of Kievan literature as have reached us across the ages. Had only those chronicles and sermons, and testaments, and humdrum lives of saints been preserved, the Kievan era would have occupied a very modest nook in the history of medieval European literature; but as things stand, one masterpiece not only lords it over Kievan letters but rivals the greatest European poems of its day.

Considerations of historical perspective prevent one from believing that ***The Song*** was composed around 1790 by an anonymous poet endowed with a degree of genius exceeding in originality and force that of the only major poet of the time (Derzhavin) and possessing an amount of special erudition in regard to the Kievan era which none in his time possessed Suggestions to the effect that a forger gave up a future of personal fame in order to glorify the past of his country, or that he was able to avail himself of documents which are now lost, immediately provoke new questions requiring new conjectures to deal with them. But after all this has been said, and the possibility of fraud contemptuously dismissed, and the entire burden of its proof shifted onto the frail shoulders of insufficient scholarship, we still have to cope with certain eerie doubts.

We are faced by the unnatural combination of two generically different notions: we are forced, first, to assume that at a singularly precise point in historical reality, namely in the early summer of 1187, somewhere in Kievan Russia a person describes—pen in hand or harp in lap—a series of events which started only two years before and are still in a state of live flux and formlessness; and second, we are forced to combine in our mind this political, local, actual, journalistic reality with the impact of such poetical imagery in ***The Song*** as is usually associated with the maturity of fondly manipulated impressions and with a long period of time—a decade, a century—elapsing between the event and the metaphor. In other words, it is very difficult to imagine the author of ***The Song*** singing the actual dew with which Igor's cloak was still wet as he rode into Kiev, or echoing Euphrosyne's sobs while she was actually rushing down from her wooden tower in Putivl to embrace her prince; or turning into a mannered dialogue the panting messenger's news of Vladimir's bringing home a wife from the Kuman steppe. (pp. 13-15)

Vladimir Nabokov, in a foreword to The Song of Igor's Campaign: An Epic of the Twelfth Century,

Igor's troops attack the Polovetsian leaders.

translated by Vladimir Nabokov, Vintage Books, 1960, pp. 1-20.

RENATO POGGIOLI (essay date 1965)

[*Poggioli was an Italian-born American critic and translator. Much of his critical writing is concerned with Russian literature, including* The Poets of Russia: 1890-1930 *(1960), which is one of the most important examinations of that literary era. In the following excerpt, Poggioli discusses* The Igor Tale *as a continuation of and departure from the epic tradition.*]

The first question to be asked by any student of the ***Slovo*** is how to place its anonymous author within history and time. Actually the question quite simply answers itself: there is enough internal evidence to prove that the work was undoubtedly composed by an eyewitness, if not by one of the actors of the events it retells. As for the external evidence, it comes to us from the Hipatian Chronicle, which gives historical authority to the narrative, the more so since it seems to have been written shortly afterward, but without apparent knowledge of the ***Slovo***'s report of the same facts. The comparison between these two reports, one poetic, the other historical, confirms the authenticity and the validity of the ***Slovo***'s testimony also in matters of detail, to a point which leads one to infer that the author must have actually taken part, at least as a follower, in Igor's campaign. It would not be an exaggeration even to reverse the usual argument, and to maintain that it is the ***Slovo*** which confirms the historical report of Igor's exploit in the Chronicle version: and that it does so not merely because of its temporal precedence, but also because of the effect of authenticity produced by the poet's account. There is, for instance, no better proof of the ***Slovo***'s exactitude than the perfect chronological sequence whereby the various phases of the campaign are marked by datings which are often indirect but always precise, starting with the first of the three decisive days, identified by its name within the week: "early on Friday."

The first paradox of this epic is the evocation of a historic fact belonging to a past which is recent rather than remote. And if it is true, as it has been claimed, that the ***Slovo*** was written and recited two years after the event, on the occasion of the marriage of the son of Igor, which coincided with the latter's return from captivity, as the happy outcome of an unhappy undertaking, then we may say without fear of error that the past events which are the ***Slovo***'s subject belong to the historical present. Such contemporaneity of historical experience and of poetic inspiration is exceptional in the history of epic literature, or at least in most of its surviving monuments. It is only met with in the heroic poetry of the Serbs or in some of the later Russian *byliny,* where, however, the historical experience becomes almost unrecognizable. As for the great epic poems of the classical world, there is no doubt that the heroic events they celebrate are centuries distant in time, while for the medieval epics the interval must be measured at least by several generations. Thus, for example, the *Chanson de Roland,* which was composed less than a hundred years before the ***Slovo,*** is more than three centuries removed from the defeat at Roncevaux, and the *Poema de mio Cid,* which precedes the ***Slovo*** by more than half a century, is separated from the death of the Campeador by the same lapse of time.

If Mnemosyne is the true muse of epic poetry, then it must be said that the ***Slovo*** was dictated by a memory which was individual and direct, whereas most of the other epics were dictated by a memory which was indirect and collective. In other words, what occurs in the ***Slovo*** is that a historical recollection, immediate and still alive, transmits at once the legendary traditions of times gone by. Yet history, refusing to be turned into a mere fable, re-emerges almost unchanged while transcending itself into epic representation and heroic vision. The extraordinary quality of all this will become even more evident if we recall that the story was known in all its particulars not only to the poet, but also to his listeners, who must have taken part, either as actors or as spectators, in Igor's undertaking.

What is even more extraordinary is that the poet is clearly aware of this particular feature of his own work. He thus establishes from the very opening a distinction between himself as a poet "of these times" and the legendary Boyan, "nightingale of the times of old." Such an opposition may be understood not as a contrast between two historical epochs different in spirit and temper, but as an antithesis between a legendary era and a historical one. Since the antithesis is made in terms of two kinds of poets and poetry, it may be translated on the plane of aesthetic psychology into a contrast between imagination and memory or, as the poet himself says, between the actual events ("happenings of these times") he reports and the artful fancies ("contriving") of Boyan. Thus, at least in intention, the poet would seem to deny himself that fabulous evocation and legendary transfiguration of the narrated events which is the aim of every genuine epic inspiration. But in reality such is not the effect of the work, much less its intention.

The complex and apparently contradictory attitude of the author toward his mythical predecessor and his own creation by no means implies that he intended to compose a historical work, while Boyan had intended to compose a purely poetic one. What such an attitude implies is rather the awareness on the part of the author of the ***Slovo*** that the time has finally come for a new kind of epic poetry: for a kind of epic poetry more suitable to an epoch which could be defined, in terms of Vico's cyclical theory, as more of an "age of man" than an "age of the gods." It is such a view that, notwithstanding the poet's sharp distinction between past and present or between history and legend, ultimately helps the author of the ***Slovo*** in bringing together the various contrasting elements to form a harmonious and organic creation. This means that he succeeded in evoking, with the proper poetic distance, a chronicle of current events.

It is in this, and in no other sense, that the poet seems to be conscious of the originality of his own work, a consciousness which is neither negated nor impaired by the fact that the opposition between his own method and the manner of Boyan is essentially a literary device, a formal convention, a poetic reminiscence. In fact, as Roman Jakobson has shown, the entire proem of the ***Slovo*** is an imitation, not only in the general phraseology, but even *in ipsis verbis,* of the preamble to an account of the Trojan War which can be read in the Chronicle by Constantine Manasses, a Byzantine writer of the first half of the twelfth century. The author of that preamble contrasts his own "true" stories to the poetic fables of Homer, whereas the poet of the ***Slovo*** substitutes the wizard ("vatic") Boyan for the Homer of his model. And to Boyan he attributes the very gifts of prophecy and magic that the Byzantine and medieval Latin traditions attributed respectively to Homer and Virgil.

The poet of the ***Slovo*** seems to realize the diversity of his own work not only from the standpoint of the novelty of its attitude and content, but also, paradoxically, from the standpoint of its stylistic archaism. In this respect he knows himself to be indebted to the tradition established by the ancient Boyan, even though he hardly mentions this fact. It is only by keeping this in mind that the reader can understand the rhetorical question that opens the ***Slovo,*** the aim of which is to anticipate and offset the objections of anyone wanting to call into question the appropriateness or the convenience of an archaic style ("the diction of yore") for a work of this kind: or of the very fact that it resumes and revives the ancient manner of speech marking the heroic songs which had preceded it. In the lines that follow the opening question the poet seems, however, to react against some of the surviving conventions of the archaic heroic style, as if the metaphorical and mythical idiom had lost all prestige for him. It is the obvious duty of any critical inquiry to find the rationale of all these contradictions, and to reconcile them.

Such contradictions are due to the complicated relationship of the ***Slovo*** to the main traditions of its poet's culture, which are on one side heroic poetry, which coincides with oral literature (*slovesnost, ustnaya slovesnost*), and on the other historical or religious prose, which coincides with written literature (*pismennost*). The ***Slovo*** differs from the first of these traditions through the radical antithesis of the technique of written composition and the methods of oral creation. There is no doubt that the ***Slovo*** is not only a written work, but that it is exquisitely literary. This is indirectly and partially proven by the fact that it was handed down in written form, even though it reached us only through single and rather late manuscript; and that no parts or fragments of it have come to us through oral transmission. Even from this standpoint, the ***Slovo*** must be considered a product of *Kunstdichtung* in the simple as well as in the complex sense of this expression. This is not to say that oral poetry, to which the ***Slovo*** is both related and opposed, and which by taking other forms will even survive it, was in its time, despite its ethnographic roots, a product of *Volksdichtung* in the narrow sense of the term. Almost all recent scholars think that the oral poetry which preceded the ***Slovo*** must have been the slow and mature fruit of a secular tradition handed down from master to disciple through generations of professional singers. The essential difference, then, is that the ***Slovo*** is the expression of a cultural situation more advanced and complex, as well as subtler and richer: one that differs more in degree that in essence from the poetic culture that preceded it.

This is why, notwithstanding all his declarations to the contrary, the poet of the ***Slovo*** ends by taking toward the old heroic poetry represented by Boyan the attitude of an unavowed disciple. One of the paradoxes of the ***Slovo*** is indeed that of being a written work that up to a point was led to follow the methods of oral poetry, as may be seen for example in the constant use of the vocative "brothers," by which the poet means the comrades at arms of his *druzhina* or guard, which is proper only if addressed to an audience of listeners rather than to a reading public. The fitness of the example cannot be denied even by considering that the spoken tone of the work might partly derive from the oratorical conventions of any sermon or *slovo*. At any rate, only a deliberate repatterning after the models of oral poetry can explain why the poet feels obliged to cite Boyan and to evoke in the climaxes of the story the proverbs and oracles attributed to his fabulous predecessor; or why he imitates the magniloquent, metaphorical, and imaginative language of the latter. To prove this point it may suffice to mention the passage where the poet feigns to feel defeated in a kind of ideal competition with the forgotten master, introducing two preludes which he pretends are not his own, the one supposed to represent the manner of Boyan, and the other that of a presumed disciple.

But the ***Slovo,*** though very literary, is distinguished even more sharply from the written literature of its age. Whereas *slovesnost* was secular and profane in inspiration, cultivating as its only genres the epic and the lyrical, and making use of popular speech, or at least of a language which was neither erudite nor learned, the *pismennost,* moralistic and religious in inspiration, developed preferably the edifying genres of the sermon and the treatise, using as its unique vehicle a prose overburdened by the artificial diction of the liturgical tongue. Yet, while his work seems far more alien to this tradition than to the folk poetry of the former heroic culture, the poet of the ***Slovo,*** who was certainly a man of letters, underwent in his turn the influence of a bookish culture.

The very fact that it was the product of written composition, affected in other ways by its relationship with a bookish culture, resolves the problem of whether the structure of the ***Slovo*** is metrical or not. Being a *slovo,* it belongs to *pismennost:* it could not have been composed except in *sermo solutus.* This is now the opinion of most scholars, who consider all the metrical reconstructions tried up to now as groundless. We do not know, however, whether the ***Slovo*** was intended to be sung from its written text, with or without the accompaniment of music. What seems certain is that it was meant to be recited, in a scanned and modulated reading voice, as if it were a "prose" in the medieval sense of the term. The individual units or phrases may sound to the ear of the modern reader like Biblical versicles, even though endowed with a clearer rhythmical ring. During moments of epic emphasis or of lyrical ecstasy, the ***Slovo*** gives the illusion of song. There is no doubt that such passages re-echo Russian popular poetry, which, in the later forms we are acquainted with, follow the accentuative system, in patterns that seem to anticipate some of the more melodic variants of modern free verse.

It is perhaps because of this wavering between the opposite poles of the *cursus* of prose and the rhythm of verse that the poet gives his own work the different names of *povest* or "tale" and of *pesn* or "song." It is probably also in the terms of this ambiguity or polyvalence that he opposes his own conception of poetry to that of Boyan. As the etymological tie between the Latin *carmen* and the French *charme* easily shows, all ancient and primitive cultures consider poetry an incantation, and view the vehicle of such magic power in the main poetic instrument, which is rhythm itself. The author of the ***Slovo*** is obviously acquainted with this notion, which, however, he attributes to Boyan and treats not without an indulgent irony. Thus, for example, in the famous opening passage he pretends to take seriously the legendary wonderworking of Boyan, only to reduce it afterwards to purely verbal and magic portents. But these in their turn are literally described, in a most beautiful image, as that specialized witchcraft which consists of the dominion of the spirit over the technique and the instruments of art, by themselves deaf and dumb: hence the pathetic metaphor of the live strings that "twanged out by themselves" a praise to the princes. In this regard the author of the ***Slovo*** seems to be acquainted with the ancient fable of Orpheus, which attributes to the poet the power of taming and soothing the brutes, as shown by his comparison between poetry and the art of falconry, as well as the power to give life and the faculty of speech to inanimate things, as shown in the image of the quivering and singing strings. But the author reveals an understanding of the Orphic myth in a sense quite different from the literal. As a man no longer primitive, he knows that poetic sorcery is an incantation not of things but of words: yet he seems to imply that this makes it not a lesser but a greater wonder.

All this suggests that the ***Slovo*** operates at once both within and outside the framework of tradition. This is not rare in great poetry. What this means in the case at hand is that the difference between an oral and a literary epic is cultural and technical, rather than aesthetic and formal: and that the interval between a spontaneous epic and a literary one can be overcome by a smooth transition. In other terms, it shows that in moments of particularly creative bliss it is not impossible to reconcile in a new synthesis these opposing extremes, in the recurring cycles of the history of poetry, which are conventionally called primitivistic and Alexandrian. Such reconciliations, though always rare, took place frequently in the very age which Vico designated as *barbarie ricorsa,* that is, the Middle Ages. It is perhaps more than a mere coincidence, as has already been observed, that the plant of the ***Slovo*** grew in the Byzantine garden of Kievan Russia just when the arts and the letters of the West were blooming anew: at the very moment to which an American historian gave the glorious name of "the Renaissance of the Twelfth Century."

Like all heroic poetry, of any age or land, the ***Slovo*** is based on an aristocratic conception of the social order and of life itself. Though the author takes a stand of opposition toward the figure of his legendary forerunner, he still acts as a court bard, no less than Boyan or the type that Boyan represents, as we see in the work's valediction. He thus plays the same role as any member of the school of professional singers who preceded him, and whose traditions he must have embodied, at least in part. That such a school did really exist is no longer seriously doubted. And since the Russian princes were of Scandinavian origin, descending from the Norman stock of the Varangians, that school of singers must have been related to the poetry of the Scalds, as can be proved by the stylistic archaisms of the ***Slovo,*** in which we encounter in petrified form those stereotyped formulae or metaphorical periphrases replacing the names of the objects they refer to, and which in Scaldic poetry are given the name of *kenningar* (*kenning* in the singular).

Rich as it is with a broad and deep sense of real life, the ***Slovo,*** like Scaldic poetry, shows no interest or liking but for the moral and social values of the military caste, which was after all the ruling and dominant class. Thus, for example, the work abounds in references to valuable objects and rare commodities, like that booty of "gold, and brocades, and precious samites" which the Russians seize in the tents abandoned by the Kumans; or in frequent allusions to gold in the form not only of ingots or jewelry but of coins as well: yet, in spite of all this wealth, there never appears the figure of a single merchant. Likewise the poet often speaks of the various objects produced by the skilled and laborious hands of armorers and goldsmiths, but without ever once mentioning the trade of a single artisan. We meet frequent allusions to country life and agriculture, as well as to sowing and reaping: yet we do not see any peasant, except in the collective vision of the plowmen stunned by the fratricidal wars that since the time of Oleg have turned Russia into a wasteland. In brief, all the ***Slovo***'s characters, even the minor and nameless ones, are princes, boyars, and knights, all belonging to the nobility by right of blood or office, because they wield the sword and own the land. From this standpoint the ***Slovo*** differs considerably from the popular *byliny* that celebrate the merchant and the sailor in *Sadko,* and raise to heroic stature the peasant Mikula Selyaninovich.

The warrior class is not only the ideal object or subject, but also the natural audience of this kind of poetry. As in the case of the Scandinavian Scalds, this anonymous Russian poet of the twelfth century addresses himself to a public as limited as it is compact, since it coincides with the retinue of his own lord: a retinue made more of warriors than of courtiers, practically identical with the *druzhina* of the prince, with the men who are his table-companions, his blood-brothers in hunt and war, as the poet often directly hints. In such a circle the prince is little more than *primus inter pares,* according to the rule of the Round Table; yet this does not mean that in the case of the Russian and Scandinavian lords the tie should be understood as chivalric in the Western sense of the word. The old aristocracy of Kievan Russia was a society of the heroic type, if not barbaric, intent upon conquest and plunder, inclined to raids and adventures, and as such they were aliens to the ethical ideas of medieval Western nobility, from vassalage to courtesy.

To prove this it will suffice to show how the poet of the ***Slovo*** treats the theme of love. He treats this theme in a manner totally different from that of the romances of chivalry, and also from that of the epic poems of France and Spain. In the latter, love appears only as a family tie or conjugal bond, as in the *Poema de mio Cid,* in which the only female characters are the wife and the daughters of the protagonist. In the *Chanson de Roland* there are only two women, and we see them all too briefly. One is the hero's chaste fiancée, Aude the Beautiful, who appears only to lament for the untimely end of Roland, in a complaint uttered in a scene of some thirty lines, which stands in sharp contrast to the far longer lamentation of Yaroslavna in the much shorter ***Slovo.*** The other female figure, also the only wife to appear in the *Chanson de Roland,* is the pagan queen Bramimonde, widow of the Saracen king Marsilius, whose destiny is not the shameful and painful slavery of an Andromache, but peace of the soul, since she is converted to the religion of the victors and takes the veil of a nun.

Thus the ***Slovo*** does not seem to share that Christian ethos which marks the *Poema de mio Cid* and the *Chanson de Roland,* and contrasts them with the barbaric epics of the Germanic world. The attitude of the ***Slovo*** toward woman and love reminds us more of the Homeric poems, where there is place for the slave and the concubine beside the young bride and the loyal wife. To prove this point it will suffice to recall on the one hand that cynical and vividly realistic scene in the ***Slovo*** where the Kuman maidens are abducted as booty, just like the precious goods seized from the enemy, in a scene which has no parallel except perhaps in *Digenis Akritas;* and on the other, the tender passages by which the poet evokes the fidelity and devotion of the spouses of the warring princes, the wives of Vsevolod and Igor.

If the ***Slovo*** seems unaffected by the moderating influence of the Christian ethos, it seems equally indifferent to Christian-national pathos in its conception of war. Yet, like the Byzantine *Digenis Akritas* (in which the very surname of the hero indicates the duty of guardian of the border); like the *Poema de mio Cid;* or better still, like those epic-lyric compositions which in English and Spanish take on the names of *border ballads* and *romances fronterizos,* the ***Slovo*** is an epic of reconquest. This is easily proved from internal evidence, since Igor repeatedly declares to his companions from the very beginning of the ***Slovo*** that the aim of their undertaking is to "take a look at the blue Don" or to "drink a helmetful of the Don." This means, as George Vernadsky has remarked, that the political and military intent of Igor's enterprise was to reopen the great river route to the South, as far as the Black Sea. In another passage, precisely in the boyars' speech, the campaign and its objectives, one a major and the other a minor one, are likened to the unsuccessful flight of two falcons who had set off "in quest of the town of Tmutorokan—or at least to drink a helmetful of the Don." The maximum limit of Igor's ambition was then to include in his domains this remote city, which formerly had been part of his ancestors' domain up to the time when Oleg abandoned that outpost, or, as the poet says, "he set foot in the golden stirrup in the town of Tmutorokan" to go back to the North, where he "forged feuds with the sword" in an attempt to conquer the central principalities and to seize the hegemony of all the Russian lands. This implies that Igor's war of reconquest is conceived not only as a patriotic duty, but also as a dynastic necessity. When Igor starts to retrace in the opposite direction his grandfather's footsteps, he seeks to redeem a fief as well as a marque. The spirit of his enterprise is, then, not that of a national and religious undertaking, of a crusade or holy war, of *gesta Dei per Russos.*

It is true that the Kumans, like the Saracens of the Carolingian cycle, are here constantly called "pagans" in the sense of unbelievers. It is also true that the poet once addresses the "pagan Kuman" with the formula "black raven," which recalls the similar formula, "infidel dogs," by which the paladins refer to the Moorish warriors, when challenging them to personal duels, in the Italian chivalric romances. Actually the ***Slovo***'s appellation for the enemy differs little from the Greek designations of all aliens as barbarians. It is evident that the author of the ***Slovo*** considers the Kumans barbarians in a similar sense, as shown by the way in which he continuously compares and contrasts the martial behavior of the Russians with the military conduct of the nomads. So, for instance, while the former await the attack in silence, the latter move in to assault them with stentorian cries, a custom which the poet attributes also to the Turkish mercenaries in the Russians' service. In other words, "pagan" is in the ***Slovo*** little more than a synonym for "foreigner" or "enemy": its poet opposes the Kumans with the "sons of Russia" rather than with the "Christians." As a matter of fact, the word "Christian" never appears in the text. From this standpoint the Lithuanians (who up to that time had not yet been converted to Christianity) do not differ in any sense from the other enemies of the South and East, except that they threaten Russia from another side and that at this moment they are inactive. Whereas the Kumans are once called "fiends," or "Fiend's sons," the Russians on the other hand are never treated as chosen children of the one and true God, but rather as the "sons of Dazhbog," that is, as the offspring of an ancient god of the pagan Slavs. But it would be wrong to attach excessive importance to a formula such as this, since it is merely a conventional metaphor, a traditional *kenning.*

In conclusion, the relationship between believers and infidels which obtains in the ***Slovo*** differs little from that between Christians and Turks as treated in Serbian epics, especially in the Marko Kraljević cycle, or from that between Arabs and Byzantines in *Digenis Akritas*. The contest is between two neighboring peoples rather than between two opposing creeds. The proximity of two populations determines two equal and contrary necessities, now hostility, now coexistence. The enemy may even be viewed as a neighbor and relative to whom one is bound by ties of blood, in peace as well as in war. As in the case of the Greek hero Digenis, whose name means "of two races," enemy or infidel blood runs through the veins of the Christian warriors. We learn that Igor was born of a Kuman mother, and that the Kuman Vlur, who delivers him from captivity, is the son of a Russian mother. The poet of the ***Slovo*** does not emphasize these facts; yet in a famous passage he designates the enemy with the epithet "in-laws," which can also have the meaning of "wedding guests," an expression that would have sounded false and blasphemous to the ears of a Western contemporary of the author's, even if understood merely as a figurative term.

Yet that very term may well allude to the frequent matrimonial alliances which bound the families of the Russian princes to the Kuman khans. As a matter of fact, it is with just such a reference to another of these alliances that the ***Slovo*** ends. The reference itself enhances the uniqueness of the ***Slovo***'s finale, which . . . has no equivalent in the epic literature of medieval Christianity. In this finale, the marriage between the son of Igor and the daughter of Konchak, the foremost of the enemy leaders, is announced, or rather, hinted at, as a future event, which will follow at some distance in time the outcome of the tale, that is, the return of Igor. It is possible that the poet and his audience looked at the wedding between the Igorevich and the Konchakovna as the result of abduction or as the fruit of an act of seduction—an erotic motive exploited in the nineteenth-century opera which Borodin composed after the ***Slovo,*** entitled *Prince Igor*. Such a circumstance might explain how and why the allusions to such a wedding, the celebration of which was seemingly the very occasion of the composition, are so rare and brief, so evasive and elusive. It is perhaps the silent suggestion of such a fact that makes even more comic the dialogue between the father of the girl and the other Kuman leader, especially Gza's anticlimactic remark, "if we entoil him by means of a fair maiden," which seems to confirm the hypothesis suggested above.

It is from this view of the enemy as a close relative that the author of the ***Slovo*** looks at war, an outlook that finds magnificent expression in the epic metaphors by which the poet compares the battle to a banquet and to a wedding. The image of the bloody encounter of war as a wedding seems to confirm the conjecture that the word *druzhina* also had the meaning of "wife," "companion," and "friend," as it seems suggested in one of Boyan's oracles. On the other hand, the singular duels between heroes and knights which abound in the chivalric romances are replaced by the slaughter of anonymous victims, by mass murders and merciless exterminations; hence the vision of the battlefield as a plowed ground "sown with bones and irrigated with gore"; hence the splendid simile likening martial operations to the work of threshing and winnowing.

If the ***Slovo*** is an epos of reconquest, like the *Poema de mio Cid,* it is also, like the *Chanson de Roland,* an epos of defeat, which it contemplates in a spirit of serenity, free from any rancor or fanaticism. The poet does not feel the need to evoke in its turn, like the author of the *Chanson,* the *revanche* which will follow the rout. Such a serenity was possible only to a heroic, rather than purely epic, inspiration, though even here the theme of defeat is dictated not so much by a sense of patient suffering of the destinies of war as by the muse of pride and hope, certain of a not too distant upturn. For this very reason the poet was naturally led to exaggerate the importance of the undertaking and the gravity of the rout, which after all involved only a handful of men, even though, probably because it was a historic event still fresh and alive in everyone's memory, he avoided magnifying it out of all proportion as did the author of the *Chanson de Roland* in regard to the engagement lost by Charlemagne's rear guard at Roncevaux.

The similarities and differences between the *Chanson de Roland* and the ***Slovo*** are not limited, however, to the common theme of defeat. Another similarity is that the heroes of both epics are in part responsible for the defeat itself. Roland refuses to listen to the voice of reason when the cautious Olivier tells him to blow the horn and call for help from the main body of the Franks, so as to avoid being cut to pieces by the Saracen army in the pass of Roncevaux. In a similar manner, Igor launches his expedition without adequate preparations or proper aid, and refuses to withdraw, not only in the face of evil omens, but even when seeing himself assaulted by overwhelming forces, simply because he and his brother want to "be heroes on their own" and to win for themselves an unrivaled glory, even at the cost of their lives. But the similarities end here, for, whereas Igor acts like Roland, Vsevolod, who is ready to sacrifice himself like Olivier, not only fails to dissuade his brother from a hopeless enterprise; he even incites him with foolhardy audacity to adventure and risk.

Several critics have compared the *Chanson de Roland* to a Greek tragedy. The protagonist, just like a tragic hero, is the victim of a weakness or folly (*desmesure*) acting as the nemesis of his character, and thus becoming his destiny. In Christian terms one could say that he commits a sin of pride and is punished for it. But the hero of the ***Slovo*** escapes all retribution in spite of his *hubris* or *hamartia:* Igor does not pay the penalty for his own crime or suffer the consequences of his own error. This very fact deprives the ***Slovo*** of tragic pathos; and it may even check the heroic sweep of its inspiration. The return home of the embattled and defeated warrior is an ending less than heroic, especially when we consider that he returns as a fugitive, if not from the field of battle, at least from the enemy camp.

Whereas the *Chanson de Roland* ends in the death of the hero and of all his companions in a hecatomb that is also a deliberate self-sacrifice, the ***Slovo*** ends with the flight of the protagonist, who survives not only the public shame of defeat but also the private shame of imprisonment, even though he had in the beginning declared to his men that "it is better . . . to be slain than to be enslaved." The ***Slovo*** is perhaps the only epic in which the hero is not only defeated but made a prisoner, and wins praise for acting more like a fox than like a lion, outsmarting the enemy whom he had failed to conquer. The poet actually celebrates the escape of Igor as though it were a victory, as he does in the words which he has the river Donets say: "not small is your triumph," as well as in the triumphal song which closes the work.

A case of this kind is indeed more unique than rare in the annals of epic poetry. In *Rabinal,* a heroic drama of the Quiché, a tribe of Guatemala Indians, the hero is conquered and made prisoner. But the protagonist represents the enemy tribe of Rabinal, while the Quiché are represented in the person of the antagonist. The drama ends at any rate with a feigned duel, which is in reality an execution, and with the immolation of the captured prince on the sacrificial altar. A hero who escapes or evades, then, is inconceivable in epic and tragic terms: yet the situation becomes acceptable and possible when heroic deeds turn into chivalric adventures or knightly feats. Cervantes could afford to have Don Quixote so often defeated, or even made prisoner, only because he found precedents for this in the very chivalric romances of which he wrote the parody. In brief, the routed and fugitive hero belongs primarily to the realm of fiction, to that fiction which triumphs so easily in the epic narratives fashioned by the flowery fantasy of the Near and Far East, as, for example, in the *Knight of the Leopard Skin,* a work of the great Georgian poet Shota Rustaveli, who is almost contemporaneous with the author of the ***Slovo.*** The inspiration of fiction, as well as the theme of the fugitive hero, appears fleetingly even in such a poem as the *Odyssey,* where Ulysses, like Igor, and indeed after longer and harder sufferings, returns to his home and his country without any of his companions. Like Igor, too, Ulysses saves himself by flight and cunning; rather than fighting men and heroes like himself, he confronts gods and monsters who represent the same natural elements which challenge Igor on his flight, and which the poet of the ***Slovo*** portrays by means of direct personifications rather than mythical metamorphoses.

The romanesque quality of the story, while failing to turn the ***Slovo*** into a courtly or a sentimental work, supplies it with a modicum of pathetic interest, exemplified in the tender solicitude the poet feels for the person of the protagonist, for the sake not only of his ultimate safety, but even of his health or well-being. The concern of the poet for the anxiety and the pain of the hero reflects itself in the praise which the poet has Igor himself address to the river Donets for having given him care and shelter. Yet, despite such pathetic concern, the ***Slovo*** recalls the romances of late Greek antiquity rather than the Western romances of the Middle Ages. The very quality of the romanesque elements, as well as of the epic or heroic ones, shows once again the absence of a truly Christian spirit within the ***Slovo.*** This does not mean that the poet was a pagan, as some have thought; or that after baptism he remained a false convert, like a Spanish *marrano.* Either alternative is a historical and cultural impossibility, as well as a psychological absurdity. There is no doubt that, if only to be a man of letters, the poet of the ***Slovo*** must have actually been in form and substance a Christian. To prove this it may suffice to recall that he has the services for the dead celebrated in the sanctuaries of the new creed, and not in the ruins of pagan temples, as when the body of Izyaslav is borne to the cathedral of Saint Sophia, or that he closes the final song with the vision of Igor going up to another church in Kiev to give thanks to the Lord.

Yet notwithstanding this final thanksgiving, neither the hero, nor Igor's wife, nor the poet himself had till that moment implored the help of Providence and called on the God of the Christians, who, for his part, seems to remain as indifferent to the trials of the hero as he is remote, or even absent, from the ordeal of the faithful. Such indifference and remoteness are, however, not absolute. For instance, there is at least a simple, literal intervention of God's hand, and that is when the Lord points to Igor the way of salvation and escape, though the hero had not even deigned to call on him for help. On the other hand, one could maintain that the final thanksgiving is merely an edifying but incongruous interpolation, rather than the natural ending of such a work; and that it may seem as alien to its spirit as the Amen which traditionally closes all old Russian *slova* and which was tacked onto the text of the ***Igor Tale*** by the scribe of the only manuscript in which it was ever known.

The princes fallen on the field of battle may be buried in consecrated ground according to Christian rituals, while prayers are being said for the rest of their souls: yet despite this, and without fear of contradiction, the poet of the ***Slovo*** insists on referring at the same time to religious ceremonies and funeral rites pagan by origin or nature. This fact attests the survival of the ambiguous phenomenon known under the name of *dvoeverie* or double faith, or of the persistence within the cultural life of Kievan Russia of pre-Christian traditions and beliefs side by side with the liturgy and doctrine of the new creed. A negative proof of such a persistence may be seen also in the demonology of the ***Slovo,*** which is both Christian and pagan. The first, to be sure, limits itself to the verbal image of the Kumans as "fiends" or "Fiend's sons," while the second unfolds itself a little more fully in the appearance of the inhuman monster, Div.

Yet it is not this religious parallelism or cultural syncretism that explains the frequent allusions in the ***Slovo*** to the deities of the Slavic pantheon. The gods of the ancient national mythology perform here a high literary function: they act as local equivalents of the classical divinities of the Homeric poems, probably known to our poet second hand through the Byzantine tradition, as shown by the proem and by such an allusion as that to the "Troyan affrays." In this respect the ***Slovo*** is just the opposite of *Beowulf,* which is a genuine pagan epic coated over with a late and thin Christian varnish. In the use of myth the ***Slovo*** is much closer to the *Inferno* of Dante, where, however, a total and absolute faith makes it possible on the one hand to call the God of the Christians "Great Jove," and to treat on the other the "false and lying gods" of the pagans as imaginary monsters or creatures of fancy. The difference is that the ***Slovo,*** though the work of a Christian hand, is neither religious nor edifying: the secular and heroic character of its inspiration renders the use of mythology at once more symbolic and more literal.

This is to say that the poet of the ***Slovo,*** while employing myth in a manner which is not too different from that of the author of a literary epic, is yet able to do so with a sense of temporal and spiritual proximity to an earlier mythmaking age, which was impossible to such poets as Virgil, Camoens, Tasso, and the like. That is why the appearance of such divinities of the pagan pantheon as Dazhbog and Stribog, Veles and Chors, never gives the impression of a *deus ex machina;* even though one should remember that such apparitions take place on a metaphorical plane, a fact which prevents those gods from becoming personnages and from taking part in the action. They act only within the framework of an emblematic imagery. Yet, by a new wonder, they do not play merely a decorative or ornamental role: even though they never act, so to speak, on the stage, we feel their poetic if not their mystical presence. (pp. 6-22)

[It] is in the lament of Yaroslavna and in the scene of Igor's flight that we note the peculiar relationship that the poet of the ***Slovo*** establishes between the emotional climates of the story and what one might call the sympathy of nature. Such a relationship must not be understood in the sense of Ruskin's pathetic fallacy, which designates the eminently modern tendency to humanize animals and plants, or even nature itself, not by means of mythical metamorphoses but rather of psychological analogies, as if all things were but shadows or copies of human archetypes. The anthropomorphism of the ***Slovo*** is not anthropocentric, that is, sentimental: instead of considering the universe a reflection of the human situation, the poet seems to consider it a mirror wherein man contemplates a destiny greater than his own.

This special affinity between man and nature is a bond at once positive and negative, generating the polarities of attraction and repulsion, of sympathy and antipathy. Creatures and elements are now active and now passive, at one moment friendly and at another hostile. Yet they are never indifferent to the ordeals of the Russian warriors, especially to those of the epic hero. Their moral participation in reported happenings may often take the form of an evil omen, as in the classic example at the beginning of the campaign, when the sun envelops itself within its own eclipse as in a veil of mourning. All manifestations that precede and follow Igor's disaster have the same prophetic or symbolic meaning, from the nocturnal awakening of the birds terrified in their nests by the storm and the wailing of the wild beasts, to their seeking a daytime hiding place under the clouds where they are threatened and frightened by rapacious animals, eagles, wolves, and foxes. And the same significance must be seen in the clouds' turning black in the sky or in the sunrise horizon's taking on a blood-red glow.

When the calamity strikes, the moral participation of nature's realms takes the form of pity and sorrow: the grieving grass and trees are likened to a human being kneeling and bowing his head. But just at the moment when the men are about to succumb to their fate, the forces of nature enter the scene as actors, to play the role that in the Homeric poems belongs to the pagan gods, who descend on the field to sustain this or that group of warriors or to help a beloved hero. It is, for instance, a series of marine cataclysms that assist Igor and make possible his escape. During the flight itself Igor is aided by personified elements, beginning with the river Donets, which, as we have seen, serves and protects the prince with the generous loyalty of a knight, and ending with all the flora and fauna living in the domain of which that river is lord. If the Donets bears Igor on its waves just as Yaroslavna had beseeched the Dnieper to do, so the trees and the grasses on its banks provide him with a friendly shade and a soft couch. And whereas the water birds keep watch like sentinels on the winds, the marshland fowl sacrifice themselves to sustain the exhausted body of the fugitive. (pp. 35-6)

[It] is perhaps in order to emphasize the exceptional quality of the favor which nature grants to Igor, through the help of the Donets, that the poet refers to the contrary action, once performed on a similar occasion by another river, the insidious and evil Stugna. This stream did the very opposite of the majestic Donets, playing the role of a traitorous vassal or, like Scamander of old, acting as an ally of the enemy, when he vilely drowned another ardent and young prince in a huge, sudden flood of its otherwise shallow waters. As has already been pointed out, the reference to this long past incident softens the adventurous and romanesque temper of the flight episode, and acts as a kind of tragic warning. The hero's good fortune persists notwithstanding: Igor is able to count on the faithful allegiance of those things and beings, which help him even more than the companion of his flight. Thus, for instance, the woodpeckers show him the way to safety by beating their beaks on the tree trunks: this help the poet considers far from useless, even though the same aid has been given him by God's pointing finger. (p. 36)

An element of special importance in the composition of the ***Slovo*** is the use of allegory, which performs a formal function as well as a structural one, determining what has been called its "parabolic-figurative style." The functions hinted at by these two epithets derive equally from the eschatological allegory of Byzantine literature, where allegory is not only a vehicle of mystic vision but also of trope or figure. If we may use two terms Bernard Berenson introduced into the criticism of the visual arts, we may say that allegory works in the ***Slovo*** as both "decoration" and "illustration." It thus often takes the form of personified abstractions, always and only of the female sex and the feminine gender, without however destroying the reality of the object, acting as a parallel or synthetic image, which accompanies the action as a mute sign or silent comment.

Sometimes allegory anticipates the course of the story, as prophetic vision or divinatory dream. Thus the defeat and capture of the two princes, first foreshadowed by a literal and real eclipse are then symbolized by an ideal or figurative one which in a sort of sympathetic magic produces similar natural phenomena in the surrounding landscape. In the same way, the allegorical figure of the lamenting woman and the abstract personification of the lament immediately precede, as already remarked, the actual complaint of the warrior's wives, and act as a distant prelude to the threnos of Yaroslavna. That such visions and prefigurations become an integral part of the work's structure and texture is proved by the rhetorical excursus, in which every phrase is an augury or auspice, every sentence an annunciation.

Allegory and the parabolic-figurative style have a compositional task which tends to create linear and geometric effects. The formal and imaginative originality of the work is, however, evident not only in the simplicity of the design but also in the richness of the coloring. The chromatism of the ***Slovo***'s imagery is without precedent in other epics. (pp. 41-2)

The Homeric poems give the impression of clear sunlight, of a pure and serene air, of lively and transparent colors. The Nordic epics are dominated by a gloomy darkness foreshadowing the northern mists of the Ossianic mystifications. Menéndez y Pidal was forced to admit the grayness of the *Poema de mio Cid.* As for the *Chanson de Roland,* it seems painted by an austere Gothic hand, shunning the temptations of the picturesque: its atmosphere is opaque, and seems to know no other hue than that of burnished iron. But the ***Slovo*** gives the impression of a dazzling and vivid painting, enameled and shining, striking the eye by the variety and the opulence of its polychromy. The dominant color is the yellow of gold, in which are forged numberless objects, great and small, from the roof of the royal palace of Kiev to the thrones of princes; from the helmets, stirrups, and saddles of the warriors to the necklace of the grand prince and the bracelets that the maiden of the Goths makes clink in cadence. (pp. 42-3)

Almost as frequently the color red appears in the ***Slovo,*** the color of wine, which turns blue in one famous passage, and the color of blood, which stains the grass or earth of all the battle fields. The very color of human life, it affects even nature, of which it conveys the wrath in the glows of sunrise and sunset. In the famous image of the "red pillars of light," it clothes the entire Russian army, gives shine to their "vermilion shields," flows through their banners and pennons. The landscapes sparkle with emerald green, the prime color of nature, from the blades of the steppes to Igor's rustic couch of grass, from the banks of the peaceful Donets to the tree with its shady and gentle branches. Blue triumphs in the mists, in the waves of the Don, and in the vast spaces of the sea, whereas the waters of the Sula vanish in shades of silver. (p. 43)

If the *Chanson de Roland* is dominated by dark glimmers of burnished iron, the ***Slovo*** is pervaded by the dazzling glitter of steel, which once flashes as "blue lightning" in the enemy lances. Whereas silver appears but rarely, white is always present, taking on an almost blinding purity in the immaculate mantles of such animals as ermines, geese, and swans, or in the splendid spot of the "white-footed" wolf. And like red, white triumphs in banners and standards. The gray of dust and the mud of stormy rivers stand in opposition to this purity. As a more obvious contrast to white we have black, the color of mourning and death, properly clothing the raven, a bird of ill omen; and it suddenly dyes stormclouds, the sod marked with horses' hooves, the riverbank where Rostislav was trapped, and other and greater phenomena of nature.

This emphatic and hyperbolic chromatism, often used conventionally, is ornamental without being decorative. Its real function is often symbolic: a fact which, along with the already observed predominance of the color of gold, suggests a fitting parallel with the mosaics or icons of Byzantine art. Nothing proves the Byzantine quality of the ***Slovo***'s chromatic symbolism more than the role played by the colors representing darkness and shadow, which transcend the normal sphere of night and obscurity to invade the dream world of the spirit. Think, for instance, of a storm which is at once literal and figurative, or of that real eclipse haunting the whole campaign, thus outlasting its physical duration as an astronomical phenomenon. (pp. 43-4)

The sound in the ***Slovo*** should be studied as stylistic instrument rather than as acoustic material. Any inquiry into the phonetic structure of the ***Slovo*** could only be made by constant returns to the original language. Suffice it to say here that onomatopoeia and alliteration occur with great frequency, even if at irregular and intermittent intervals, in accord with the nature of the medium, which is prose. Since the sonority of the diction is not subordinated to the pre-established harmony of a metric scheme, the effect is that of a modulation at once spontaneous and deliberate. This shows that, even in the matter of verbal music, the ***Slovo*** is ruled by a unique fitness of form and content. Just as color does not have merely a decorative function, so sound fulfills more than a purely suggestive task. They are both equally compositional, joining together the visual and musical elements in the same images, as in that which turns into blue lightning the enemy lances flashing and resounding from afar.

This very example brings us to examine the problem of epic formulary, which plays an important part in the ***Slovo***'s diction and imagery. The ***Slovo*** abounds in traditional heroic metaphors, fully unfolded, as in the elaborate sequence by which Vsevolod praises his Kursk warriors: "swaddled under the war-horn, nursed under the helmet, fed from the tip of the spear"; or briefly hinted, as in the fixed metaphor in which banners stand for whole armies. We frequently encounter epithets or appositions in the heroic manner: such as the formula of "bold aurochs" often accompanying Vsevolod's name, a formula to which a few scholars attribute totemic origins and in which they see remote traces of the cult of Thor. It is easy to find the deliberate use of epic exaggeration in all the passages that exalt warlike deeds. . . . Such exaltation of war culminates in the hyperbolic metaphors of the warriors navigating a sea of blood, and of the grand prince Vsevolod scattering in drops with his oars, and drinking with his helmet, the waters of the Volga and the Don, the great rivers of Russia.

Some of the stylistic formulae are analogous to those of the popular epos, especially those following the universal model: "it is not this (which is seen, felt, or believed), but it is that." Such a model was made universally known by the famous beginning of the Serbian song of Hasan Aga, so much admired by Goethe. It is significant that such a formula, which the poet of the ***Slovo*** uses in two places, appears first in the prelude in which the author pretends to imitate the manner of a Boyan disciple—"this is no storm sweeping falcons"; and later in the passage imnmediately preceding the dialogue between the two Kuman khans—"no chattering magpies are these." Since the prelude is meant as a parody, and the dialogue of the khans is the only comic situation in the work, it seems as if the poet uses the formula with a caricatural intent, as if to distinguish his own work in this respect from oral epic. (pp. 45-6)

Repetitions and refrains, being devoid of any metrical scheme, fulfill in the ***Slovo*** a task quite different from that of those fixed phrases or of those metrical and verbal formulae which, according to Milman Parry and Albert Lord, prove without doubt that a composition is the product of oral creation. A more direct proof that the ***Slovo*** is a written work is offered by the internal evidence of its language and diction. The ***Slovo***'s language is ecclesiastical, or rather bookish, as it happens so often in the medieval literature of Christendom: meaning that it was composed by a man of letters, or by a man of clerical education, which is the same thing. . . . It is just because of this tie with the religious tradition of the written word that the ***Slovo*** abounds in Biblical images, such as that of times which have turned inside out or that of the grieving walls. If not taken from the Bible, the mystical and eschatological images come from other edifying writings, thus showing on the part of the poet a direct or indirect knowledge of Byzantine literature. (pp. 46-7)

This religious and spiritual imagery, applied to secular themes, proves again the complexity of the ***Slovo***'s stylistic and symbolic structure. Despite this complexity, the ***Igor Tale*** is far from being an eclectic product: it is rather the creation of a talented poet who was at once sophisticated and naive, Hellenized in taste and yet medieval in temper. This unique combination is evident chiefly in the rapport in both harmony and tension between the ornamental style and the oracular tone. The reader will ultimately realize that the ***Slovo***'s inspiration, though solemn, is not hieratic; that its attitude, though ritualistic, is not liturgical; that its tone is not that of a sacred hymn, but of a secular song.

The nobility of the material and the symmetry of the design, far from oppressing the narrative, help to throw the action into sharper relief. Likewise, the suggestive obscurity of the evocation gives the drama greater intensity and significance. The ***Slovo*** indeed may be recondite, but it is not hermetic. Thus, although related to Scaldic poetry, it avoids the pitfalls of that school, which makes one sometimes think of Provençal *trobar alus*. The ***Slovo*** is full of meanders, but not of ambiguities. Though an aristocratic and courtly production, it speaks to princes and of princes with a voice which is public and civic. Thus there is little reason to compare the ***Slovo*** with modern poetry, except with regard to its verbal sorcery. Nothing proves this point better than such a poem as the *Anabase* of St.-John Perse, in which even the heroic becomes an almost private concern. It is not only to an elite, either of our time or of his, that the poet of the ***Slovo*** appeals, but to all men able to understand poetry as a song of the tribe as well as a song of man. (pp. 47-8)

Renato Poggioli, "The Igor Tale," in his The Spirit of the Letter: Essays in European Literature, *Cam-*

bridge, Mass.: Harvard University Press, 1965, pp. 3-49.

M. ISENBERG AND T. RIHA (essay date 1967)

[*In the following excerpt Riha and Isenberg counter readings of* The Igor Tale *that consider the poem an excoriation of Igor and a call for unity among Russian princes, noting instead that praise of Igor is the principal theme of the poem.*]

Despite the immense amount of critical labor expended on ***The Song of Igor's Campaign***; most readers have found this work difficult to understand and, thus, to appreciate. The beauties of language, the romantic intensity, and the deep melancholy of the work evoke an immediate response in the hearts of all lovers of poetry, but what it is the poet is saying and what the main theme of the work is, has left many a reader puzzled and at a loss.

The purpose of the present paper is to suggest a way of reading this poem which will highlight its main theme and enable the reader to understand its basic thought. In this way, we hope that one's appreciation and pleasure in the work will be heightened and that the merit of the work will be shown to be commensurate with its reputation as a gem of world literature. (p. 105)

[We] may clarify our thesis by citing an extreme interpretation of the ***Song*** which most critics would now reject. Marx has said, "The ***Slovo*** is a summons to the Russian Princes to unite on the very eve of the Mongol Invasion." The late Professor Gudzii, on one occasion, made a publicist of the poet when he said, "The author of the ***Slovo*** . . . purposes by his talent and the forces of his civic loyalty to be of service to the interests of his native land." It may be helpful to keep in mind this interpretation as the opposite of our own point of view. We shall return to this opposition after we have presented our poetic interpretation. To this purpose we now address ourselves.

The first twelve lines of the poem merit the reader's close attention.

> Might it not become us, brothers,
> to begin in the diction of yore
> the stern tale
> of the campaign of Igor,
> Igor son of Svyatoslav?
>
> Let us, however,
> begin this song
> *in keeping with the happenings*
> *of these times*
> and not with the contriving of Boyan.
> For he, Vatic Boyan,
> if he wished to make a *laud* for one . . . .

Now, what our author is saying appears to be quite clear. He intends to tell the "stern tale" of the Prince, Igor, and, furthermore, to give us a laud or to praise that Prince. Yet, he has a problem. He cannot praise him as Boyan praised former princes. Our author must tell his story "in keeping with the happenings of these times." We are to expect, then, a new kind of praise, a strange kind of praise, which, apparently, will not have the directness nor the swiftness which characterized Boyan's praise of princes. As we shall see, there will be an indirectness and obliquity in our author's praise of Igor which is the very stuff of poetry.

Since we believe that the "praise" of Igor is, in truth, with all its obliquity, the main theme of the poem, we would like to follow this theme of "praise" through the poem. In doing so it will be necessary to neglect the obvious well-demarcated parts of the poem and the numerous digressions. As we follow the theme of "praise," it will become clear that the parts of the poem only become parts because they hang together on this theme or thread of "praise." Furthermore, as we follow this theme, it will become evident that it goes along and comes to an end in a full circle. From "praise" the author proceeds to "blame," and comes full circle about to end with "praise" again. But let us trace this theme, keeping in mind that the above statements about "praise" still await their full development and the full working out of it strange obliquities in the rest of our paper.

At the beginning, Igor is praised for his fortitude.

> So let us begin, brothers,
> this tale—
> from Vladimir of yore
> to nowadays Igor,
> who girded his mind
> with fortitude,
> and sharpened his heart
> with manliness;
> (thus) imbued with the spirit of arms . . . .

What Igor has undertaken to do, he does for honor and glory.

> themselves, like gray wolves,
> they lope in the field,
> seeking for themselves honor
> and for their prince glory.

But, despite the bravery of Igor and his brother, Vsevolod, they are defeated in the field of battle and their "banners fell." Igor is taken prisoner and the Russian land is indeed "already behind the culmen."

The "praise" of Igor now turns into a series of lamentations for the anguish that has now seized the Russian land. But even more to the point, Igor is now directly "blamed."

> Now the Germans,
> and the Venetians,
> now the Greeks,
> and the Moravians
> sing glory
> to Svyatoslav
> but *chide*
> Prince Igor . . . .

This is a curious turn-about of our poet. Certainly, if he intends to "praise" Igor, it is strange that he should openly "blame" him. But this he does through a whole series of charges. Igor has earned disgrace rather than glory as the Boyars point out.

> "Already disgrace
> has come down upon glory.
> Already thralldom
> has crashed down upon freedom . . . ."

Igor has not acted honorably as Svyatoslav says,

> "O my juniors, Igor and Vsevolod!
> Early did you begin
> to worry with swords the Kuman land,
> and seek personal glory;

but not honorably you triumphed
for not honorably you shed
pagan blood . . . ."

And more, Igor and his brother have acted selfishly.

"But you said:
'Let us be heroes on our own,
let us by ourselves grasp the anterior glory
and by ourselves share the posterior one.'". . .

From this point in the *Song* the princes of the day are apostrophized so that they may avenge the defeat of Igor and the wrongs of the Russian land. But, note well, they are not urged to unite and to compose their discords. This would hardly be possible as we shall show later. And, too, other princes of old are mentioned in one of the typical and beautiful digressions of our poet.

However, this whole theme of "blame" now undergoes a complete transformation. With the introduction of Yaroslavna, Igor's wife, who now sings incantations from the ramparts of Putivl, the brave prince Igor becomes again a hero, a hero worthy of "praise." Not only does Yaroslavna express her love and longing for him, but Igor, himself, manages to escape from the Kumans in a most heroic manner. He returns to Kiev and rides up the Borichev (slope). As the poet remarks:

After singing a song
to the old princes
one must then sing to the young.

This is the way to praise the heroes of our times, if, as a poet, one must sing praises of our contemporary princes. This is the way to praise them "in keeping with the happenings of these times." Thus, with true poetic dash, even, perhaps, with tongue in cheek, and, certainly, with bitterness in his heart, our poet can end his poem on a note of glory and glorification for his hero.

Glory to Igor son of Svyatoslav;
to Wild Bull Vsevolod;
to Vladimir son of Igor!
Hail, princes and knights
fighting for the Christians
against the pagan troops!
To the princes glory, and to the knights (glory)—Amen.

The "praise" has come around in a full circle. Starting with praise, our poet has gone to "blame" and, with many digressions, has ended with fulsome "praise." The circle, as it were, is complete.

But there is need of another outer circle to do justice to the *Song.* Not only is Igor praised, obliquely and indirectly it is true, but all of Nature has participated in the glorious adventure of Igor. Thus, with the risk of being tedious, we shall trace this outer circle, so to speak, of Nature with respect to the inner circle of "praise and blame."

At the beginning, Nature is completely out of sympathy with the venture of Igor. An eclipse takes place, Night moans ominously, and the animals forfelt his misfortunes.

Igor leads Donward his warriors.
His misfortunes already
are forfelt by the birds in the oakscrub.
The wolves, in the ravines,
conjure the storm.
The erns with their squalling
summon the beasts to the bones,
The foxes yelp
at the vermilion shields.

Bloody effulgences "herald the light."

Contrary to the tone of praise with which the *Song* begins, Nature hardly shares in Igor's glorification. But with the defeat of Igor, Nature becomes more sympathetic.

The grass droops with condolements
and the tree with sorrow
bends to the ground.

This note of sympathy continues through many digressions until Yaroslavna enlists the active aid of Nature by her incantations. She summons the wind.

"Wind, Great Wind!
Why, lord, blow perversely?" etc.

Igor can now address the Donets as a helper in his escape.

"O Donets!
Not small is your magnification:
you it was who lolled
a prince on (your) waves; etc.

Even the animals, who before were unsympathetic, now actively aid him.

No chattering magpies are these:
on Igor's trail
Gzak and Konchak come riding.
Then the ravens did not caw,
the grackles were still,
the (real) magpies did not chatter;
only the wood peckers, in the osiers climbing,
with taps marked (for Igor) the way to the river.

And at the end, when Igor arrives in Kiev, Nature is in full sympathy with the hero. The eclipse is in the past.

The sun shines in the sky
Prince Igor is on Russian soil.

Again, our poet, obliquely and indirectly, but with true poetic feeling, has brought in Nature to accompany the hero, Igor, in his adventures. The outer and inner circles, with many omissions, are now complete, as it were.

At this point, the following objection may be raised against our interpretation: "If the *Song* according to your interpretation is an indirect and oblique 'praise' of Prince Igor and Nature, too, has reacted both unsympathetically as well as sympathetically to the venture of the hero, where do all the passages about princely feuds and discords and the anguish of the Russian land come in?" There are many such passages.

In the Lamentations section, the poet says:

The strife of the princes
against the pagans
has come to an end,
for brother says to brother:
"This is mine,
and that is mine too."
and the princes have begun to say
of what is small:
"This is big,"

while against their own selves
they forge discord,
(and) while from all sides with victories
the pagans enter the Russian land. . . .

There are many such passages.

But the point of such passages can be very easily misinterpreted. It will, perhaps, be helpful to recall the opposite interpretation, which we cited at the beginning of this paper, in order to clarify our own point of view.

Nowhere in all these passages does the poet say that, since the princely feuds and discords are the cause of Russia's troubles, then the princes should cease quarreling and unite to repel the pagans. As T. S. Eliot, another oblique and indirect poet, would say:

That is not it at all.
That is not what I meant, at all.

Our poet knows the political realities of 12th century Kievan Rus. He looks at these political realities, points them out, and sees that they are the cause of all Russia's woes. But that is a far cry from inducing the reader to suppose that the poet is commending political nostrums and panaceas. He is too much of a poet for that. So in the center of our "praise and blame" of Igor and in the center of our concentric circles, we must place the central point and cause of the poet's bitterness and melancholy. At the center are the princely discords and the woe of the Russian land. From this center radiate out all the lines which make it so difficult for him to praise his hero directly as Boyan probably did in the past. The 12th century poet must write.

in keeping with the happenings
of these times
and not with the contriving of Boyan.

But as a poet he still must sing a laud of the heroes:

After singing a song
to the old princes
one must then sing to the young.

His whole poem is an attempt, a highly successful one, to demonstrate how a hero such as Igor can be praised. ***The Song of Igor's Campaign*** is the concrete fulfillment of such a laud. If the poet is bitter, if he is melancholy, that attitude of his is the very essence of poetry. He sees the life about him, its realities, and its despairs and, yet, can still sing a laud as all poets have done from time immemorial. (pp. 105-11)

Thus, we may summarize our interpretation of the poem in the following manner. The poet wished to sing a praise of Igor. To do so in times such as these demands an indirect and oblique manner of presentation, full of digressions and artful transitions. The Russian land is overcome by princely discords and feuds, the cause of all Russia's woes. One must be bitter, one must be melancholy, if one is to praise any prince at all, especially a prince like Igor, who is a prime example of the cause of all these discords. But, then, such are the political realities of Kievan Rus. One must still praise heroes. Therefore, our poet seems to be saying, "Here is my laud of Igor. Let him make what he will of it. At least I, the poet, have written as a true poet of my times can only write." Such a poem is the ***Song***—a true gem of world literature—and a fitting monument to poetic truth. (pp. 111-12)

M. Isenberg and T. Riha, "'The Song of Igor's Campaign': A Poetic Interpretation," in Canadian Slavic Studies, *Vol. 1, No. 1, Spring, 1967, pp. 105-12.*

ROBERT C. HOWES (essay date 1973)

[*Howes is an American critic who has translated* The Igor Tale *into English. In the following excerpt from an introduction to his translation, he presents a historical account of the events related in* The Igor Tale, *detailing the history of antagonism between the Russians and the Polovetsians and recounting Igor's campaign, capture, and escape.*]

In the second half of the twelfth century Russia was ruled by various members of the princely family that would later trace its origin to Ryurik the Varangian (or Viking), who, according to tradition, came to rule the Slavs of the Ladoga and Novgorod region in 862. The veracity of this tradition and the real role of Ryurik remain uncertain and continue to be topics of both serious research and heated debate among Russian historians. It is quite clear, however, that by about 880 one of Ryurik's successors, the powerful and energetic Viking warrior-merchant Oleg the Wise, had imposed his control—and a semblance of unity—upon a number of the Slavic peoples living along the great trade route (known as the Great Water Route) between the Baltic Sea and Constantinople. Oleg and two of his successors, princes Igor and Svyatoslav, warred with their neighbors, on several occasions even forcing the haughty Byzantines to enter into trade agreements with the barbarians of Rus'.

In the latter part of the tenth century the unity of the eastern Slavs was strengthened through the adoption of Byzantine Christianity by the ruling class of Rus' under the leadership of Grand Prince (later Saint) Vladimir. With the reign of Yaroslav the Wise (1015-1054) the unity and prosperity of Kievan Rus' seemed secure. Yaroslav, a strong, able, and reasonably enlightened prince, maintained order along the Great Water Route from the Varangians to the Greeks, defeated the principal enemy from the steppes (the Pechenegs), and furthered the development of the city of Kiev as one of the leading European cities of the time. Before he died, Yaroslav wrote a will in which, apparently hoping to avoid such a conflict as that which preceded his own accession to the throne, divided Rus' among his five surviving sons and one grandson. This action unfortunately had the opposite result; contention among the princes was renewed, the prize being the "golden throne of Kiev," the senior city of Rus'.

Kiev, on the Dnieper near the border of forest and steppe, was the most important city of Old Russia. The prince of Kiev was considered the senior prince of the House of Ryurik; he usually had at his disposal a strong military force, and his control of the middle Dnieper and much of the Great Water Route added to his importance. It was his duty to defend all Rus' against invaders and to keep open the trade route.

Kiev dominated Russia from the ninth century until about the middle of the twelfth century. By this latter date the political and economic fragmentation of Rus' had reached such proportions that new centers of power were beginning to emerge, centers that would eventually replace Kiev in power and importance. These were the Vladimir/Suzdal' Land in the northeast between the Volga and Oka rivers, the great northern trading city of Novgorod with its vast territories, and the Galich/Volynya Land to the west. Yet the idea lingered that all Rus' was one and that it was the common patrimony of all the

A fourteenth-century depiction of the battle between Igor's army and the Polovetsians.

princes of the House of Ryurik. Moreover, the fiction of Kiev as the dominant city of Rus'—the Mother of Russian Cities—was long in dying.

If the lack of princely unity weakened Kievan Russia from within, the steppe nomads threatened her from without. The Polovetsians (called Polovtsy, Cumans, or Kipchak Turks) had been moving into the steppes north of the Black Sea since the 1050s, replacing the older enemies of the Russians, the Pechenegs, who had been decisively defeated by the Russians during the reign of Yaroslav the Wise. The *Ipat'yevskaya Chronicle* reports that in 1055: ''That same year came Bulush' with the Polovetsians and Vsevolod made peace with them and they returned to their own land.''—This incursion was into the Pereyaslavl' Land and probably as far as the Dnieper River. In 1068 the Russians were defeated by the Polovetsians on the Al'ta (L'to) River.

In the late eleventh and early twelfth centuries Kiev was threatened by a powerful alliance of Polovetsians under the leadership of two khans, known to the Russians as Bonyak the Mangy and Sharukan the Old. This threat was so great that, under the leadership of the brilliant Vladimir Monomakh (d. 1125) and his son Mstislav the Great (d. 1132), the princes of Rus' temporarily set aside their differences and dealt the Polovetsians several serious defeats. But with the death of Mstislav and the apparent subsidence of the danger from the steppes the princes of Rus' returned to their bickering and internecine wars, while the feudal fragmentation of Kievan Russia continued apace. The enmity between two of the most gifted and energetic of Russian princely lines—the descendants of Vladimir Monomakh and the descendants of his cousin Prince Oleg of Chernigov—well illustrates the irreconcilability of the antagonisms among the princes.

Between 1136 and 1170 several events took place that illustrate the danger Kiev faced. In 1136 a serious uprising in Novgorod foreshadowed the establishment of a republic dominated by boyars and wealthy merchants, in that great city near the northern terminus of the Great Water Route. The uniting of the Black Cowls (Chernyye klobuki, a Turkic people) in the region of the Ros' River southwest of Kiev, and the organization of two Polovetsian political units in the steppes—the Western and Eastern alliances—also boded ill for Kiev. Furthermore, Kiev was being weakened by the gradual decline of the Great Water Route, a result of the reorientation of Byzantine trade to the West during the Crusades. From about 1170 the Eastern alliance of the Polovetsians, under the leadership of Khan Konchak, renewed its pressure on the southeastern border of Rus'.

The Polovetsians were nomads. Living in movable camps, they were cattle raisers and warriors. The enmity between them and the Russian farmer, artisan, and trader was similar to the classic enmity between the Chinese and the nomadic peoples living beyond the Great Wall. But in the case of Russia there was no Great Wall and there was no strong emperor standing at the head of a highly developed, centralized state apparatus. In Russia there were only open plains and warring princes.

A curious entry in the *Ipat'yevskaya Chronicle* for the year 1159 indicates that as early as that date the lands along the middle Dnieper were already becoming deserted as a result, at least in part, of the ravages of the Polovetsians. When Prince

Izyaslav Davidovich of Chernigov succeeded to the Golden Throne of Kiev in 1157, he granted the city of Chernigov and seven other towns to his cousin, Prince Svyatoslav Vsevolodovich of Novgorod-Seversk. When, in 1159, Grand Prince Izyaslav planned a campaign against Galich, he called upon Prince Svyatoslav for aid. When Svyatoslav refused, Izyaslav replied: "If God grants that I succeed in Galich, then do not complain to me when you go crawling from Chernigov [back] to Novgorod." The Chronicle reports that Svyatoslav, greatly angered by these words, said: "My lord, you see my humility. How much of that which is mine have I foregone, not wishing to spill Christian blood or bring my patrimony to ruin. I received Chernigov and 7 empty cities: Moravsk, Lyubech, Orgoshch, Vsevolozh, and in them are [only] dog keepers and Polovetsians."

Excellent horsemen and experienced fighters, the Polovetsians would make yearly forays into the southeastern borderlands of Kievan Russia. Burning villages and grainfields, besieging and sacking towns and carrying off captives to be sold as slaves to Arab, Greek, or Italian merchants, they menaced the peaceful population of Rus' for almost two centuries. Their very name must have struck terror in the hearts of Russians.

Yet the Polovetsians never completely defeated the Russians: they seemed to be satisfied with the booty from their raids against Rus'. On the other hand, the Russian princes could not unite to bring an end to the Polovetsian threat. Although it is true that by about 1200 there had developed an uneasy truce among the Russians and the nomads of the steppes, the Polovetsian threat did not completely disappear until it was replaced by the much more serious threat of the Mongols. But the discord among the princes of Rus' remains the darkest page in the history of Kievan Rus'.

In 1185 *two* Russian princes were referred to in the chronicles as Grand Prince of Kiev. The first and most powerful was Prince Ryurik Rostislavich of Smolensk. The great grandson of Vladimir Monomakh, Ryurik neither resided in nor reigned in Kiev. (Seven times during his life he gained Kiev for himself; twice he returned it voluntarily to its former prince.) The other Grand Prince of Kiev was Svyatoslav Vsevolodovich. A grandson of Oleg of Chernigov, Svyatoslav was a member of the princely family that had contended so stubbornly with the Monomashichi (descendants of Vladimir Monomakh) for supremacy in Kiev. He had ruled in Novgorod-Seversk and then in Chernigov. In 1178 he moved to Kiev, where he ruled in collaboration with Prince Ryurik of Smolensk and other Rostislavichi.

Now at this time a junior prince, Igor Svyatoslavich, ruled in Novgorod-Seversk, a lesser city on the Desna, northeast of Chernigov. Igor, born in 1150, was the grandson of the famous Oleg of Chernigov and the cousin of Grand Prince Svyatoslav of Kiev. Prince in Novgorod-Seversk since 1178, Igor was an active participant in the internecine wars of his time. In 1180 he and other Ol'govichi (Oleg's descendants), with Polovetsian allies, invaded Smolensk and fought against Prince David Rostislavich. Then, with Khans Konchak and Kobyak, Igor moved against Kiev in support of Grand Prince Svyatoslav, whose claim to the throne of Kiev was not secure. Although successful in driving Grand Prince Ryurik from Kiev, Igor and his Polovetsian allies were defeated subsequently. The chronicler, reporting the battle on the Chertoryya (a tributary of the Dnieper, near Kiev), writes: "Now the Polovetsians were fleeing before the Russian troops [of Grand Prince Ryurik and] many were drowned in the Chertoryya, and others were captured, and others were slaughtered. Now seeing the Polovetsians defeated, Igor and Konchak forthwith leapt into a boat and fled to Gorodets [and] to Chernigov."

Three years later, in 1183, Prince Igor and Prince Vladimir Glebovich of Pereyaslavl' undertook a campaign against the Polovetsians. But there was a disagreement between the two princes as to whose forces should lead the way, and Vladimir, angered, turned and plundered Igor's principality of Novgorod-Seversk.

In 1183 Grand Prince Svyatoslav inflicted a serious defeat on the Polovetsians, taking prisoner Khan Kobyak. The Ol'govichi did not participate in this victory. But Igor and his brother Vsevolod, Prince of Trubchevsk and Kursk, hearing of the Polovetsians' defeat, undertook a campaign of their own against the Polovetsians, toward the Donets River. This undertaking was a failure.

Early in 1185 the "accursed and godless and thrice-cursed Konchak, with a multitude of Polovetsians" invaded Rus'. Grand Princes Ryurik and Svyatoslav met the invaders on the Khorol River and on March 1 "God . . . gave the victory to the Russian princes." (pp. 1-5)

According to the Chronicle Igor had wanted to participate in the campaign to the Khorol but was unable to do so because of the tardy arrival of the runner with the news of the campaign. But on April 23, 1185, Prince Igor, without having consulted the senior princes, Svyatoslav of Kiev and Ryurik of Smolensk, set out with his son Vladimir (who was fifteen at the time), his brother Vsevolod, and his nephew Svyatoslav of Ryl'sk, on a campaign into the Polovetsian steppes intending to "lay down my head or / Drink with my helmet from the Don." (It is true that Igor did consult Prince Yaroslav of Chernigov, who contributed his boyar Olstin Oleksich and some Turkic mercenaries to Igor's army.)

There was apparently opposition to this campaign among members of Igor's retinue. On May 1, 1185, there was an eclipse of the sun, which the *Nikonovskaya Chronicle* describes: "A Portent. That same year, in the month of May, on the 1st day, there was a portent in the sun; it was very dark, and this was for more than an hour, so that the stars could be seen, and to men's eyes it was green, and the sun became as the [crescent] moon, and from its horns flaming fire was emitted; and it was a portent terrible to see and full of horror." Although the Russians interpreted this phenomenon as an evil omen, Igor insisted that the campaign continue, saying, "No one knows the mysteries of God. God is the maker of this sign and of the whole world. And whether that which God does to us is for good or for ill, this too we shall see" (*Ipat'yevskaya Chronicle*).

In the first battle, on Friday, May 10, 1185, the Russians were victorious over what was apparently merely a rather small scouting detachment of Polovetsians. Igor now urged retreat, saying, according to the Chronicle: "Lo, God with His strength has inflicted a defeat on our enemies and [has given] us honor and glory. Lo, we saw the Polovetsian armies that were many. But were they all gathered here? Let us ride the night. . . ." Igor may well have sensed the impending disaster. But his nephew Svyatoslav (who was only nineteen) objected, noting that his men were tired and that if the main body of Russians were to retreat, some of his men would be left behind on the road. Igor's brother, "Wild Ox" Vsevolod, the most dashingly heroic personage in ***Prince Igor,*** sided with Svyatoslav, and the Russians pitched camp for the night.

Prince Igor's estimate of the situation had been correct. The following morning, Saturday, Polovetsian troops "began to appear like a forest." The Russians, alarmed, held a council of war. Some argued for retreat, but now Igor insisted that they stand their ground, saying: "If we flee we shall ourselves escape, but we will leave the black people [the common foot soldiers]. That will be a sin against us from God, having betrayed them. Let us go: we shall either die or be alive in one place." So the princes and voivodes (officers) dismounted and went into battle against the Polovetsians.

All day they fought and into the night. When Sunday morning dawned the battle was still raging. And then the Turkic mercenaries, the Koui, panicked and began to fall back. Igor, who had been wounded in the arm and was on his horse, set out at a gallop to rally them. Thinking that they, having caught sight of him, were indeed returning to the battle, Igor galloped back toward his own men. Unfortunately, the Koui did not return to the fight but continued their retreat; only one man, according to the Chronicle a certain Mikhalko Georgiyevich, turned back. When Igor was within an arrow's flight of his own men he was taken prisoner. At this moment—one of the most dramatic in the story—Vsevolod was seen by Igor, surrounded by the enemy and fighting fiercely. Believing all was lost, Igor "asked for his soul's death that he might not see his brother fall."

But neither prince was killed. The Polovetsians carried the day and decisively defeated the Russians, taking many prisoners, including Igor, Vsevolod, and Igor's son Vladimir.

Following their defeat of the Russians, the Polovetsians decided to counter the Russian attack with an invasion. They entered Rus' with two armies: the one commanded by Khan Gza struck into the Posem'ye (the area along the Seym' River in the Chernigov Land); the other, under Khan Konchak, invaded the Principality of Pereyaslavl', southeast of Kiev. Although both armies caused much destruction and laid waste many Russian districts, the result, typical of all the Polovetsian raids, was not conclusive. Konchak besieged Pereyaslavl', where Prince Vladimir Glebovich—grandson of the terrible Yuriv Dolgorukiy of Suzdal' and apparently a favorite of the chronicler—was seriously wounded in a heroic defense of his city. Unable to capture Pereyaslavl', Konchak retreated, sacking the town of Rimov on his way back to the steppes.

Grand Prince Svyatoslav did not hear of Igor's campaign until he chanced to stop at Novgorod-Seversk on his way to Kiev from Karachev, where he had been raising men for another campaign against the Polovetsians. Displeased that Igor had undertaken such a campaign, Svyatoslav proceeded to Chernigov; here he learned of Igor's defeat and capture. The Chronicle relates that Svyatoslav, upon hearing the news, wiped away his tears and said: "O my beloved brothers, and sons, and men of the Russian Land! God has given it to me to weaken the power of the pagans; but you, not restraining your youthfulness, have opened the gates to the Russian Land. May the Lord's will be done in all things. As I have grieved for Igor, so now I lament for Igor, my brother, even more."

Grand Prince Svyatoslav had taken measures to counter the impending Polovetsian invasion of Rus'. He sent his sons Oleg and Vladimir into the Posem'ye, the area along the Seym' River that was especially open to attack from the steppes. He sent word to Prince David of Smolensk, who had apparently intended to participate in the campaign, calling upon him to come immediately with his army. David started down the Dnieper but halted at Trepol', a town south of Kiev near Pereyaslavl'. The grand prince's brother, Prince Yaroslav of Chernigov, did nothing. The Chronicle reports that he, having gathered his troops, waited in Chernigov. It was at this time that the two-pronged Polovetsian invasion began. Vladimir, the valiant defender of Pereyaslavl', appealed to Svyatoslav and to Ryurik and David: "Lo, the Polovetsians are at my gates. Help me!"

David and his Smolensk men turned back, refusing to go farther; but Svyatoslav and Ryurik set out against the Polovetsians, who retreated, sacking Rimov as they went. The Russians did not pursue them into the steppes but returned home. Igor and his fellow Russians remained in captivity.

According to the Chronicle Prince Igor, early in his captivity, became deeply troubled by feelings of guilt. The prince, blaming himself for the disastrous campaign, said: "I remembered my sins before the Lord my God: how I caused many killings and [much] bloodletting in a Christian land; how I showed no mercy to Christians, but took by storm the city of Glebov. . . . I was not worthy to live. And lo, now I see the vengeance of the Lord my God. Where now is my beloved brother? Where now is the son of my brother? Where is the child to whom I gave birth? Where are the boyars of my council? Where are my brave nobles? Where are my men of the line? . . . Lo, the Lord has repaid me for my lawlessness and for my evil. This day my sins have descended upon my head. . . . But O Master, O Lord my God, do not reject me utterly! But as Your will is, O Lord, so is Your mercy toward us, Your servants" (*Ipat'-yevskaya Chronicle*).

Igor felt that it would be dishonorable for him to try to escape: "For the sake of glory I did not flee then [during the battle] from my retinue, and now I shall not flee ingloriously." But at least two of Igor's counselors, the son of a chiliarch (commander of a thousand men) and the prince's groom, advised otherwise, feeling that the Polovetsians, returning unsuccessful from their campaign, might in frustration kill the prisoners, especially the princes and voivodes for whom sufficient ransom had not been forthcoming. (The eighteenth-century Russian historian Tatishchev wrote that because the chiliarch's son was the lover of Khan Toglyy's wife, he heard from her of plans to kill the Russians and thereupon alerted Igor's groom. According to the *Ipat'yevskaya Chronicle,* both the chiliarch's son and the groom warned Igor of the danger.)

Fortunately for Igor, a Polovetsian named Lavor (or Ovlur)—Tatishchev says he was a Christian—offered to help Igor escape. One evening when Igor's guards were drinking koumiss (fermented mare's milk), the prince stole from his tent to meet Lavor, who had two horses ready on "the other side of the Tor [River]," and made his escape. Khans Gza and Konchak pursued Igor but failed to recapture either him or Lavor. Crossing the Donets River, the two men arrived at the town of Donets. Igor then went to Kiev, where he was greeted with great joy by the two grand princes, Svyatoslav and Ryurik.

Such, in brief, is the account of the campaign, captivity, and escape of Prince Igor of Novgorod-Seversk. The campaign had not been decisive; in fact, it was much less important historically than a number of similar campaigns undertaken by Russian princes (including Igor himself) in the twelfth century. Yet this comparatively insignificant campaign was to be immortalized by an epic poem, probably written in the year 1187 by a contemporary, perhaps one of Igor's retinue. (pp. 5-8)

Robert C. Howes, in an introduction to The Tale of the Campaign of Igor: A Russian Epic Poem of the

Twelfth Century, *translated by Robert C. Howes, W. W. Norton & Company, Inc., 1973, pp. 1-26.*

JOHN FENNELL (essay date 1974)

[*An English educator and critic, Fennell has written extensively on Russian literature and history. In the following excerpt, he surveys the principal arguments in the debate over the authenticity of* The Igor Tale.]

No work of pre-nineteenth-century [Russian] literature has had so much research devoted to it as the ***Slovo o polku Igoreve* (*Tale of the Campaign of Igor'*)**. Up to 1940 more than seven hundred works connected with the ***Slovo***—commentaries, editions, translations—had appeared in a wide range of languages. Since that date the number has probably doubled. As virtually every possible literary and historical aspect of the work has been discussed, it would serve little purpose here merely to reiterate the views of countless literary critics and historians. Better to limit ourselves to a brief outline of the main arguments which divide those who believe that the ***Slovo*** was written in the twelfth century and those who don't—a topic which has received relatively little attention in English. (p. 191)

During the first half of the nineteenth century doubts as to the authenticity of the ***Slovo*** as a twelfth-century work were frequently expressed by scholars of varying political hues and literary reutations. They were evoked in the main by the absence of references, direct or indirect, to the ***Slovo*** in early Russian literature and by the fact that only one MS of the work was said to have survived, a MS moreover which few specialists had seen and which none could examine after the fire of 1812. Such doubts bred other doubts. The narrative appeared illogical; there were seemingly evident historical and linguistic anachronisms; furthermore, for a work which purported to stem from the twelfth century, there were a disturbing number of what looked like polonisms, gallicisms and even traces of Ossianisms. Most of the sceptics considered it to be a work of the fifteenth or sixteenth centuries, in other words of the period which it was commonly believed that Musin-Pushkin's original MS dated from; only one, Count N. P. Rumyantsev, thought it a forgery of the eighteenth century.

The discovery and publication in 1852 of the *Zadonshchina,* the epic work of the late fourteenth or early fifteenth century glorifying Dmitry Donskoy's victory over the Tatars at the battle of Kulikovo (1380) . . . , was one of the main factors which led to a temporary silencing of the sceptics. The striking similarities between whole passages of the two works made it hard for anyone to doubt that the ***Slovo*** preceded the *Zadonshchina;* for if the *Zadonshchina* was unknown in the eighteenth century, how could the author of the ***Slovo*** have copied it? No one, however, could actually prove that a version of the *Zadonshchina* could not have been read or studied by someone before it was officially discovered. But to assume that it was known before its discovery necessitated the existence of a hypothetical forger, and a forger who had destroyed or concealed his MS of the *Zadonshchina.*

The thesis that the *Zadonshchina* was in fact the source of the ***Slovo*** was first adumbrated by the French scholar Louis Léger at the end of the century, but it was not until the 1930s that a serious attempt to re-open the whole question was made by his compatriot, A. Mazon. In Mazon's opinion, the ***Slovo*** was an eighteenth-century pastiche ("une oeuvre récente en forme de pastiche" ["a recent work in the form of a pastiche"] . . .), based on a late version of the *Zadonshchina,* which, of course, the imitator had been obliged to destroy in order to conceal the source of his falsification. Mazon's main arguments are based on what he calls his "rehabilitation" of the *Zadonshchina.* There were, he argues, two main redactions of the work. The first of these, represented solely by the earliest surviving MS, consisted merely in what he calls the "primitive" *zhalost'* (sorrow, lament) (i.e. the description of the first phase of the battle and the lament of the wives); the second, represented by all the remaining (and later) MSS, consisted in the *zhalost'* and the *pokhvala* (encomium)—the second attack of the Russians, the defeat of the Tatars and the religious coda.

In Mazon's opinion, the first redaction (*zhalost'*) is primary—i.e. it is not the prototype of the *Zadonshchina* but reflects it closely: alone, the earliest MS gives us an idea as to what the original work was really like. The second redaction, on the other hand, is secondary and clearly stems from the first, the *pokhvala* being an easily-discernible later addition to the *zhalost'*. Now as the ***Slovo*** shows most striking similarities with the second redaction of the *Zadonshchina,* and with later (seventeenth-century) versions at that, Mazon conjectured that the compiler of the ***Slovo*** had before him a late variant of the *Zadonshchina,* which closely resembled one of the late MSS of the second redaction.

Such was the textological basis of Mazon's main argument. In order to bolster his theories, still further "evidence" pointing to the late provenance of the ***Slovo*** is adduced. All must fit in with the atmosphere of the late eighteenth century, hence the pseudo-classicisms, the florid *griseries verbales,* the blatant pantheism and deliberate neglect of Christianity, the gallicisms, modernisms, even the Americanisms, the echoes of Ossian, the modern embellishments, the subtle hints of approbation for Catherine II's imperialistic designs. And, at the same time, Mazon compares the incoherence, the awkward "joints," the frequent suspicious *hapax legomena* with what he calls the freshness, the grandiose nature, the irreproachable cohesion and the "typical fifteenth-century mentality" of the early *Zadonshchina.*

Not surprisingly Mazon's views caused a violent reaction in the Soviet Union. They were met with incredulity and contempt and, along with those of his *"epigony"* (imitators), treated as little short of heretical. But they also obliged scholars, both inside and outside the Soviet Union, to reconsider the whole problem of authenticity. The most important of the works written in defence of the ***Slovo*** as a twelfth-century monument were undoubtedly the articles on the *Zadonshchina* written by V. P. Adrianova-Peretts in vols. V and VI of the *Trudy Otdela drevnerusskoy literatury* (1947, 1948), and *Slovo o polku Igoreve—pamyatnik XII veka* (1962), a collection of articles written by leading Soviet specialists with the aim of summarizing recently discovered evidence concerning the ***Slovo*** and confounding any sceptics there might still be.

Slovo o polku Igoreve—pamyatnik XII veka, however, far from stilling dissenting voices and settling the question once and for all, seems to have acted as a catalyst for still further questionings and doubts; for it was its appearance that first led the Soviet medievalist A. A. Zimin to question the main theses of the defenders of the ***Slovo***'s authenticity and to examine the whole problem—particularly the problem of the interdependence of the ***Slovo*** and the *Zadonshchina*—afresh. His conclusions, which he outlined to an astonished audience at the Institute of Russian Literature (Academy of Sciences) in Leningrad on 27 February 1963, amounted to the following: the ***Slovo*** was based primarily on a late redaction of the *Zadonshchina,* was written in the 1770s by Archimandrite Ioil' Bykovsky, and was published as an original twelfth-century work by Musin-Pushkin, who added three interpolations.

Zimin's lecture had immediate repercussions in the learned world. Indignant scholars leapt to the ***Slovo***'s defence in the Soviet Union, Europe and the U.S.A. A three-day symposium was held in Moscow (May 1964) to destroy what was considered by most of those present but not all, to be a frivolous and impertinent theory; a strong team of literary specialists and medievalists produced *"Slovo o polku Igoreve" i pamyatniki Kulikovskogo tsikla* (1966), which constitutes the greatest collection of "evidence" so far assembled in favour of the ***Slovo***'s authenticity and easily the weightiest attempt to confound the sceptics; a number of distinguished scholars wrote learned articles attacking Zimin's theories; an Ilchester Lecture was delivered at Oxford University by D. S. Likhachev on the subject (February 1967) [see Additional Bibliography]; there were even articles in the "popular" Soviet press (e.g. *Pravda, Izvestiya, Soviet Literature*), some of which crudely belaboured "that amateur detective," as Zimin is called on one occasion. Zimin, himself, although he prepared sufficient material for a large volume, never succeeded in publishing his work in book form. Instead most of his theses have appeared piecemeal in articles widely differing in accessibility and printed in journals ranging from *Istoriya SSSR* and *Russkaya literatura* to such remote publications as *Uchenye zapiski Nauchno-issledovatel'skogo instituta pri Sovete Ministrov Chuvashskoy ASSR*. (pp. 192-95)

Undoubtedly it is the textological question which separates most sharply the serious sceptics from their serious opponents. And, of course, it is a question on which there can be more than one opinion. Not surprisingly the two sides attack each other both on methodology and on details: what constitutes proximity of readings? Which readings are primary and which secondary? But inevitably the sceptics' textological arguments and their opponents' refusal to accept them lead to further problems and pose further questions.

One of the major bones of contention on the non-textological level is the problem of ideology. Now the sceptics argue that the ***Slovo*** is impregnated with the idea of Russian unity, of the "Russian land" (*Russkaya zemlya*), while the chroniclers of the period (i.e. of the twelfth century) show that this was the age of extreme "feudal separatism" (*feodal'naya razdroblennost')*, and an age of "indifference" to national unity. Furthermore, they claim that the out-and-out paganism of the ***Slovo*** is, to say the least of it, unexpected in a period in which the Church was still struggling with relics of heathenism; and why, they ask, was the ***Slovo*** never included in the lists of books proscribed by the Church from the fourteenth century onwards? Their opponents have produced few, if any, convincing arguments to counter their claims that ideologically the ***Slovo*** does not fit in with what we know of the twelfth century. "Common-Russian patriotism," they maintain, *did* exist in the twelfth century, but the only evidence adduced for this "patriotism" is the *Tale of the Destruction of the Russian Land (Slovo o pogibeli Russkoy zemli)* . . . of the *thirteenth century*, which was written under very different circumstances. As for the heathen elements in the ***Slovo,*** while conceding that "paganism is more strongly expressed in the ***Slovo*** than in any other extant monument of the twelfth century," they claim that these elements are entirely in keeping with the spirit of the age. Art and archaeology, indeed, have shown that paganism was widespread in the twelfth century amongst not only the common folk but also the nobility; there was nothing anachronistic about the author of the ***Slovo***'s appeal to heathen deities: "the author of the ***Slovo*** was a man of his own sharply-defined age, and his pagan romanticism was indissolubly linked with the life of the twelfth century." Furthermore, the concept of Old Russian paganism in the eighteenth century was quite different from that displayed in the ***Slovo.***

As far as the language of the ***Slovo*** is concerned, Zimin considered it to be the result of stylization. It is, he considers, lexically and grammatically based on Old Church Slavonic of the eighteenth century with an admixture of the lexis of the *Zadonshchina* and the Hypatian Chronicle. At the same time it contains Ukrainisms, Belorussisms and polonisms, as well as a number of orientalisms which could not have been known in pre-fifteenth century Russia. In an article dealing exclusively with Turkic elements in the vocabulary of the ***Slovo*** ("K voprosu o tyurkizmakh") he claims that of nineteen orientalisms which do *not* occur in either the *Zadonshchina* or the Hypatian Chronicle account only two can be found in Russian sources dating from the eleventh or twelfth centuries: all the remainder are either not mentioned in pre-fourteenth-century Russian monuments or are absent from Russian sources altogether.

Zimin's opponents deny most of his propositions. They point out that numerous distinguished philologists have stressed the indubitably archaic nature of the grammar and syntax of the ***Slovo*** as compared with that of the *Zadonshchina*. Nearly all the lexis and phraseology of the ***Slovo,*** they claim, is paralleled in works of the eleventh or twelfth centuries. Zimin's so-called "Ukrainisms, Belorussisms and polonisms" are all part and parcel of the Russian language; what is more, the "overwhelming majority of them can be found in Old-Russian monuments of the pre-Mongol era." Even the Turkisms—although it is admitted that Turkologists usually fail to agree on such matters—are held to be part of the Turkic linguistic milieu of the pre-Tatar age, and no reputable orientalist is said to doubt the antiquity of words of eastern origin found in the ***Slovo.*** One of the strongest linguistic arguments against Zimin, however, concerns the question of orthography. It is pointed out that the ***Slovo*** contains clear traits of the orthography of the twelfth and thirteenth centuries at the same time as idiosyncratic Bulgarisms which result from the so-called "Second South Slav Influence," . . . are peculiar to Russian of the fifteenth and sixteenth centuries, and are quite untypical of late Old Church Slavonic. How, asks the Soviet philologist Filin, could Ioil' have known about orthographical peculiarities of the "Second South Slav Influence," which has only recently been discovered by linguists? His known writings contain no such elements.

On a more theoretical and abstract plane, but none the less important for that, are the arguments concerning what Likhachev calls the "poetics of imitation." Likhachev, himself, outlined them in the first two articles on the conflict to appear after Zimin's lecture of February 1963. His "poetics" are based on the assumption that artistically the ***Slovo*** is vastly superior to the *Zadonshchina* and that, as imitators only use an outstanding work for their model, it is illogical to claim that the author of the ***Slovo*** used the inferior *Zadonshchina* as his source. Furthermore, literary imitators are never creative in their reproduction of the style of others. They tend to borrow mechanically, making use of separate phrases and formulas which happen to please them, and making use of them in entirely new contexts. This leads, in the case of the *Zadonshchina,* to "monotonous" and "inconsistent" borrowing from the ***Slovo,*** and to the watering down or omission of the ***Slovo***'s complex images. The *Zadonshchina* is typical of an age of imitation such as the fourteenth and fifteenth centuries in Russia: it is a mosaic containing a variety of styles, repetitions of borrowed phrases and impoverished imagery, whereas the ***Slovo*** contains no elements of imitation. Indeed, he asks, how would it have been possible for the author of the ***Slovo*** to have been so selective in his borrowing from the *Zadonshchina,* for the latter contained three distinctive stylistic layers, one of which, the "official prose" (*delovaya proza*) layer, he would have had to have purged and omitted from his "imitation"?

If Likhachev's arguments cannot be considered conclusive, neither can Zimin's counter-arguments. In the main he attacks Likhachev for picking whichever MS of the *Zadonshchina* best suited his purposes: indeed all Likhachev's examples of the "imitative" *Zadonshchina* are taken from this or that MS of the "expanded redaction." Many of Likhachev's selections from the *Zadonshchina* give the impression of monotonous and inconsistent borrowing—this Zimin is prepared to concede. But it is merely the "expanded redaction" he is dealing with, and this itself *is* a repetitive borrowing, a borrowing, however, from the "short redaction" and not from the ***Slovo.*** Likhachev's *delovaya proza* is not to be found in *KB*—only in the later MSS which reflect a redaction influenced by the *delovaya proza* of such works as the *Skazanie* and the Nikon Chronicle.

These arguments, however, are merely an extension of his, Zimin's, insistence on the rightness of his textological hypothesis (just as Likhachev's in a way reflect *his* refusal to accept the primacy of a "short redaction"). Zimin counters his opponent's arguments more directly by claiming that such a borrowing technique as Likhachev assumes the author of the *Zadonshchina* employed was an impossibility at the time of the emergence of the *Zadonshchina*. Certain passages of the ***Slovo,*** he maintains, consist of a number of micro-readings taken from separate passages of the *Zadonshchina,* while certain passages of the *Zadonshchina* consist of fragments occurring in different parts of the ***Slovo.*** Now it was, he considers, impossible for a writer in fourteenth- or fifteenth-century Russia to have treated his main source in this way—i.e. he would have been incapable of creating a unified passage out of disparate fragments or of scattering fragments of a whole phrase or passage from his model throughout his own work. Why, however, anyone at the end of the eighteenth century would have been any more capable of doing both these operations is not made clear by Zimin.

As a final argument, Zimin points to the highly developed euphonic, rhythmic and rhyming devices, which few commentators have failed to note in the ***Slovo,*** and what he calls the complete absence of such devices in the *Zadonshchina* (with the exception of folkloric alliteration). Such deliberate and selective destruction of the artistic fabric of the ***Slovo*** could hardly have been carried out by the author of the *Zadonshchina,* whereas the reverse process—the introduction of euphony, rhythm and rhyme into an imitative work—is in his opinion perfectly feasible.

Of all the theories which the sceptics have had to elaborate in order to claim that the ***Slovo*** is not a work of the twelfth century, that which has always been attacked most savagely—and often most effectively and convincingly—is the hypothesis that the ***Slovo*** was written in the late eighteenth century. The reasons for postulating so late a date are obvious: for the sceptic who accepts the view that the author of the ***Slovo*** used a copy of the *Zadonshchina* close to late extant versions, any date prior to the seventeenth century seems most unlikely; while if he considers that such works as the Nikon and Koenigsberg Chronicles (first brought to light in 1767), or for that matter the relevant volumes of Shcherbatov's and Tatishchev's *Histories,* were used as sources for the ***Slovo,*** then the date must be pushed still further forward.

Whoever is claimed by the sceptics as the author, be it Musin-Pushkin (as Mazon originally thought) or Archimandrite Ioil', his credibility is undermined by the seemingly incontrovertible arguments of the defenders of the ***Slovo***'s authenticity. Why, they ask, should Ioil', or any other eighteenth-century falsificator, wishing to glorify the success of Russian arms, write a poem about a *defeat*? Why not publish the hitherto unknown *Zadonshchina,* which after all sang of the magnificent victory of Catherine's predecessors over the Tatars? But why indeed should anyone have felt the need for justifying Catherine's policy of expansion on the northern shores of the Black Sea? Zimin had held up to Ioil'—in view of his links with west Russia, his interest in the princely families of Polotsk and Chernigov, his intelligence, his liberalism—as the ideal author of this "bookish bylina" (*knizhnaya bylina*): but what evidence is there to show that he really possessed the necessary knowledge or that he was a "cassocked Voltairian" (*Vol'ter'yanets v ryase*)? How could this limited monk have manipulated the subtleties of the ***Slovo***'s phraseology? Even a superficial analysis of the language of his sermons shows no outstanding skill and certainly no lexico-stylistic similarities with the ***Slovo.***

Perhaps the strongest of the arguments brought to bear by those who refuse to see in the ***Slovo*** an eighteenth-century work is that contemporary knowledge was simply not up to the production of a monument of such scholarship as the forgery of the ***Slovo.*** After all, the 1800 edition of the ***Slovo,*** which was carried out by three of the leading scholars of the day, betrayed extraordinary ineptitude and ignorance, or so it seems to-day—words misread and wrongly divided . . . , mistranslations, misinterpretations in the commentary. If these men represented the flower of philological, historical and literary knowledge of the age, can we imagine the existence of a man so far ahead of his time in knowledge, skill and experience as to be able to produce a work, the true complexities of which only *future* generations of scholars were to be able to unravel and understand?

In the final analysis we are left with the question: who in the last two decades of the eighteenth century could possibly have done it? For whether we consider the ***Slovo*** a work of brilliant imagination and dazzling imagery or "factice, incohérente et médiocre" ["factitious, incoherent, and mediocre"], we must admit that if it was written in the eighteenth century, its creator was a man of singular genius and almost superhuman knowledge.

The problem of the authenticity of the ***Slovo*** is not yet solved. Perhaps it only will be if and when a further copy of the *Zadonshchina* is discovered, or if ever a manuscript of the work itself comes to light. (pp. 201-06)

John Fennell, "'The Tale of Igor's Campaign'," in Early Russian Literature *by John Fennell and Anthony Stokes, University of California Press, 1974, pp. 191-206.*

DMITRY LIKHACHOV (essay date 1980)

[*Likhachov is the foremost contemporary Soviet scholar of Old Russian literature. In the following excerpt from a study first published in Russian in 1980, he discusses elements of medieval folk poetry in* The Igor Tale *and examines the poem's central theme of Russian unity.*]

The *Lay* does not relate the events in Igor's campaign in sequence. It evaluates them poetically and appraises their importance: it speaks of them as if these events were already well-known to readers. It is addressed to Prince Igor's contemporaries. The work is a fiery narrative by a Russian patriot and lover of the people—passionate and excited, not strictly sequential, but organised poetically—telling of events in the recent past, then in the distant past, alternately angry and sorrowful, but always filled with faith in the Russian land, proud and confident of its future.

The *Lay* opens with the author's reflections on the manner in which his narrative should be told. He rejects Boyan's old-fashioned manner, deciding instead to closely follow the "deeds" of his own time and to stick to real events. This is a lyrical introduction typical of the beginning of many Old Russian works (from sermons to hagiographical works), and it gives the narrative an appearance of spontaneity; it persuades the reader that he is reading an improvisation, free of the strictures of literary tradition—including works as powerful as Boyan's. And, in fact, everything that follows is so spontaneous and so closely linked to living speech and folk poetry, so sincere and fervent in tone that, despite the *Lay*'s traditional beginning, we believe it.

In fact, ***The Lay of Igor's Host*** contains a keen sense of broad, free, spoken language. . . . [This] can be felt in its choice of expressions—ordinary expressions taken from oral speech, military and feudal terms; it can also be sensed in the choice of images, which lack literary refinement. It can be felt in the very rhythm of the narrative, which would seem to be aimed at a verbal rendering. The author of the *Lay* constantly addresses his readers as if he sees them before his very eyes. He calls them "brothers" and addresses them individually by name. Among his imaginary listeners he includes his contemporaries, as well as men from the past. He speaks to Boyan: "O Boyan, nightingale of old! Were you to sing this warfare." He addresses Vsevolod: "O Vsevolod, you fearless bull! You stand at bay, you spray with arrows the host of the foe, your swords of steel clang upon their helmets." He addresses Igor, Prince Vsevolod of Suzdal, Rurik and Davyd Rostislavich, and others. He even asks lyrical questions of himself: "What clamour is that far away, so early, before dawning?" He interrupts himself with exclamations of grief: "O Russian land! Far are you now beyond the hills!" All this creates an impression of direct contact between the author of the *Lay* and his readers. The same closeness exists between an orator and his audience. The author seems to be speaking, rather than writing.

A prince's iron and silver war helmet from the early thirteenth century. The Armoury of the Kremlin.

However, we would be mistaken in assuming that this is a typical oratorical work. It may be that the author of the *Lay* intended his work to be sung. In any event, there is more lyricism, spontaneity, and mood in the *Lay* than one would expect in an oratorical work. [The work's] rhythmical quality is also extraordinary. Finally, we should keep in mind that the author, although he defines his work somewhat vaguely—as either a "lay," a "song," or a "tale"—refers, in choosing his poetic manner, not to any of the famous 11th- or 12th-century orators, but to Boyan—a singer and poet who performed his works to the accompaniment of a string instrument, probably a dulcimer. Although the *Lay*'s author contrasts his style to that of Boyan (the author promises to begin his "song," "after the deeds of this time, not after the fancies of Boyan"), nonetheless this contrast is only possible because he regards Boyan as his predecessor in the same field of poetry into which his own work fits. We can find oratorical devices in any Old Russian literary work. They exist everywhere to a greater or lesser degree. That is why it is important to turn to folk poetry in searching for a generical definition of the poem. ***The Lay of Igor's Host*** is not folk poetry, and yet folklore is directly linked to the question of the genre of the *Lay* as we shall see further on.

The link existing between the *Lay* and oral folk poetry can be most clearly felt in the two genres most often mentioned in the *Lay*: laments and eulogies intended to be sung, although it is by no means limited to these two genres. The author introduces laments and eulogies directly into his work, and he follows them most of all in his narrative exposition. Their emotional contrast provides him with the broad range of feelings and shifts in mood so typical of the *Lay* and serving to distinguish this work from oral folk literature, where each work is subordinated to one basic genre and one underlying mood.

The author of the *Lay* mentions laments several times: the lament of Yaroslavna, the lament of the wives of the Russian warriors who were killed during Igor's campaign, and the lament of Rostislav's mother. The author has laments in mind when he speaks of the groans of Kiev, Chernigov, and the whole Russian land after Igor's campaign. The author provides the texts of these laments for us twice: the lament of Yaroslavna and the lament of the Russian wives. He interrupts his narrative many times with lyrical exclamations typical of laments: "O Russian land! Far are you now beyond the hills!"; "Thus was it in those battles, in the days of that warfare. But such a battle as this has never been heard of yet!"; "What clamour is that?

What clang is that far away, so early, before dawning?''; ''And the valiant host of Igor shall never rise again!''

Svyatoslav's ''word of gold'' is also similar to a lament if we take only the passage ending with the mention of Vladimir Glebovich—''woe and sorrow to the son of Gleb.'' The ''word of gold'' is ''mingled with tears'' and Svyatoslav addresses it, as Yaroslavna also does, to absent listeners: Princes Igor and Vsevolod Svyatoslaviches.

The author of the ***Lay*** follows Igor's host and laments it in his thoughts, interrupting his narrative with lyrical digressions reminiscent of laments. ''Oleg's brave brood slumbers on the battlefield. Far, far has it flown! It was not born to be worsted by the falcon, nor by the gerfalcon, nor by you, o black raven, pagan Polovets!''

The link between laments and lyrical songs is especially noticeable in Yaroslavna's lament. The author creates the impression that he is quoting Yaroslavna's lament, recording a large excerpt from it or composing it for Yaroslavna, but in a style that would be appropriate to her.

Eulogies (songs of praise) are no less a part of the ***Lay*** than are the laments. The work begins with mention of the eulogies sung by Boyan and ends with eulogies to Igor, Vsevolod, Vladimir, and the host. A eulogy to Svyatoslav is sung by the Germans, Venetians, Greeks, and Moravians. A eulogy resounds throughout Kiev, and is sung by maidens on the Danube. It flows across the sea and travels to Kiev from the Danube. Individual excerpts from ''eulogies'' are woven into the ***Lay***: when the author speaks of Boyan, when he composes a song in honour of Igor's campaign, and at the end of the ***Lay,*** when he greets the princes and the *druzhina*. Hints of a eulogising tone are to be found in the addresses to the Russian princes and in Igor's dialogue with the Donets River (''O Prince Igor, no small glory is yours . . .''; ''O, Donets, no small glory is yours . . .''). Finally, the concluding part contains a eulogy: ''The sun lights up the heavens—Prince Igor is in the Russian land!''

Thus, the ***Lay*** is very close to the form of a lament or a sung eulogy. Both laments and eulogies are frequently mentioned in 12th- and 13th-century chronicles. The ***Lay*** has some similarities to them in form and in content, but as a whole, it is neither a lament nor a eulogy. Folk poetry allowed for no mixture of genres. The ***Lay*** is a work of written literature, but close to these genres in folk poetry. It was evidently a special type of written poetry, perhaps a genre that was still in a fluid state. (pp. 172-76)

The ***Lay*** is permeated from beginning to end with an appeal to unite in the face of external danger. The author shows the need for this unity by using Igor's campaign as an example, proving the need by many historical comparisons, as well as by depicting the consequences of wars between the princes, creating a mighty image of the Russian land, its cities, rivers, and many inhabitants, and a panorama of Russian nature with its endless expanses.

Igor's campaign and defeat serves to illustrate the unfortunate consequences of disunity. Igor is defeated only because he undertakes the campaign alone. He acts in accordance with the medieval formula: ''We take care of ourselves, and you take care of yourselves.'' The words spoken by Svyatoslav of Kiev to Igor characterise the author's attitude towards Igor: ''O my nephews, O Igor and Vsevolod! Too soon you began to smite with your swords the Polovets land, to seek glory for yourselves! No glorious victory have you thus gained, for not in victory have you spilt pagan blood! Your valiant hearts are forged of steel tempered with daring. But what have you done to my silver locks. . . . But you have said, 'Let us dare this alone! We two will grasp the glory of old, we two will share the fame to come!'—Is it a marvel, my brethren, for the aged to regain youth? When a falcon has moulted, he pursues the wild fowl high up into the air, he lets no harm come near his nest! But here is evil indeed: the princes are now no help to me. These are evil times!''

The essence of the ***Lay***'s entire narrative about Igor's campaign is contained in this explanation by Svyatoslav: Igor unwisely embarks on this campaign despite the fact that it is doomed from the very beginning. He sets off despite ill omens. His only motivation is his desire for personal glory. Igor says: ''O brethren and warriors! Better be slain than taken captive! Let us mount, my brethren, our fleet-footed steeds, and let us behold the blue Don!'' and ''I will break my spear to splinters at the far end of the Polovtsian plains with you, O Russians! I will either lay low my head, or drink a helmetful of Don water!'' (Compare Igor's and Vsevolod's brag in the Laurentian Chronicle's account of Igor's campaign: ''Are we not princes? Let us go, then, and win glory for ourselves.'') The desire for personal glory ''obscures the omens.'' Nothing can stop Igor on his fatal path. (pp. 180-81)

Throughout the whole of the ***Lay,*** the author is sympathetic to Igor. However, while sympathising with Igor, he condemns his actions, and he places this condemnation in the lips of Svyatoslav of Kiev, as well as stressing it through all the historical parallels drawn in his work. The stance he adopts is thus not that of a courtier. He is independent in his judgements.

The author's attitude towards Igor is that historical events are stronger than he is. On his own, Igor is neither good nor bad: he probably has more good than bad in him, but his actions are bad, and this is because he is dominated by the prejudices and erroneous ideas of his time. Thus, the general and the historical are of primary interest in the ***Lay,*** rather than what is individual and transient. Igor is a typical product of his time. He is an ''average'' prince: courageous, bold, he loves his country, but he is also unwise and short-sighted; he is more concerned for his personal glory than for the glory of his country.

The events of Igor's campaign are shown against a broad historical background in the ***Lay.*** The author constantly resorts to comparisons between the past and present. And these are by no means lyrical digressions by the author. He does not offer us simply ''poetic chaos,'' but broad historical generalisations on the basis of historical comparisons. The author turns to Russian history in order to understand contemporary events and as a source of material for artistic generalisation.

This use of the past in order to understand the present was best expressed in the two figures who stood at the source of the feudal disturbances, the two founders of the most turbulent princely lines—Oleg ''Gorislavich'' and Vseslav of Polotsk.

The ***Lay*** gives the reader not only portraits of these two princes, but also brief characterisations of their disobedient and petty descendents—the Olegoviches and the Vseslaviches. In fact, in the author's view, princes and principalities always bear the ''glory'' of their ancestors, the creators of their independence: the men of Chernigov, armed only with boot-knives, routed whole armies with their battle-cries, ''making their forefathers' fame resound again.'' Izyaslav Vasilkovich struck his sharp swords against Lithuanian helmets, ''bringing to naught the fame of Vseslav, his grandfather,'' the Yaroslaviches and all of Vseslav's grandsons had ''far fled'' from their ''forefathers' glory''; Vseslav, having taken Novgorod, ''shattered Yaroslav's glory,'' and so on. These were not empty words: from the author's point of view, the glory of his contemporaries and principalities was created by their ''forefathers,'' and therefore the ''forefathers'' of the present Chernigov and Polotsk princes—Oleg Svyatoslavich and Vseslav Bryachislavich—were alive in their descendents' deeds. The author of the *Lay* did not casually provide a description of these princes: he speaks of their unfortunate fates in order to urge their restless descendents to make peace with each other and act jointly against the steppe nomads.

The description of Oleg ''Gorislavich'' precedes the account of Igor's defeat. Igor's defeat is regarded as a direct consequence of the feudal quarrels which began during Oleg's reign. After discussing Oleg's internecine wars, the author proceeds to tie these in with Igor's defeat: all our misfortunes arose from these battles and campaigns, but Igor's battle surpassed even Oleg's feuds by its consequences. The tale about Vseslav in the *Lay* also directly precedes the appeal to Vseslav's descendents and their enemies, the Yaroslaviches.

The description of the ambitious prince Oleg ''Gorislavich'' is given in light of the consequences of his wars for the Russian people. He is described less as an individual than as a political figure, in terms of the consequences of his activity. His wars are regarded as a whole epoch in the life of the Russian people: ''The age of Troyan is gone, the days of Yaroslav are past. Gone are the wars waged by Oleg.''

The author of the *Lay* mentions Oleg, however, not only because he was the first of the line of the Chernigov clan. It was Oleg who laid the foundation for the ensuing web of feuds which arose out of the patrimonial system of Old Rus. In addition, Oleg's use of the Polovtsy created the basis for the continuation of this policy by all the later Olegoviches.

The entire description of Oleg's destructive activity is founded on a contrast between it and the constructive labour of farmers and artisans: ''For he, that Oleg, forged feuds with his sword, sowed his arrows over the earth,'' ''Then, in the days of Oleg, the Son of Woe, discord was sown and throve. Then perished the birthright of the grandsons of Dazhbog,'' and finally, ''Then was the voice of the husbandmen seldom heard . . . but often, indeed, the ravens croaked feasting on the dead. . . .'' This image of a peaceful tiller of the soil, whom the princes should protect by fighting the Polovtsy, is employed in *The Tale of Bygone Years* as a reproach against the greedy princes in a similar historical situation. ''When the peasant begins to till the soil,'' Vladimir Monomakh, Oleg's chief opponent, said in 1103, appealing to the princes to join forces for a campaign against the Polovtsy, ''then the Polovtsy come to kill him, take his horse, and go to his village, abducting his children, wife, and all his possessions.'' The *Lay*'s author held Oleg responsible for the failure of Monomakh's cause, and he pointed this out using Monomakh's own metaphor, thus showing that Monomakh's hopes for protecting peaceful labour remained unrealised. (pp. 181-84)

The description of another trouble-maker prince, Vseslav of Polotsk, agrees with the facts about him provided by *The Tale of Bygone Years*. These facts are interpreted poetically in the *Lay*. The author of the *Lay* draws on them not only to create a poetic image of Vseslav, but also to give an historical evaluation of his activity. This historical evaluation, skillfully made to conform to the entire structure of ideas in the *Lay*, is striking in its penetrating grasp of Russian history.

The author of the *Lay* presents his reflections on Vseslav's unfortunate life. Vseslav is depicted critically, but warmly and lyrically: a restless prince dashing about like a baited animal, cunning ''sooth-sayer,'' but still a failure. His was a vivid portrait of a prince from the period of Rus's feudal dismemberment.

The swiftness of Vseslav's raids and his ''restlessness'' are verified by his true biography. Monomakh says in his *Instructions* that in 1078 he and his Chernigov horsemen pursued Vseslav, but Vseslav was faster than they were: Monomakh could not catch him. Vseslav did in fact dash around Rus, one minute appearing outside the walls of Novgorod, the next in distant Tmutorokan on the shores of the Black Sea. He was captured by Yaroslav's sons and taken in captivity to Kiev, where he next found himself on the throne, having been proclaimed prince by the rebellious people of Kiev. Seven months later he was forced to flee from these very same people at night.

His feuds, like those of Oleg ''Gorislavich,'' are contrasted by the author of the *Lay* to peaceful, constructive labour: ''On the Nyemiga River heads lie strewn like sheaves of corn, the threshers thresh with flails of steel. On that threshing-floor lives are laid down, the soul is winnowed from out of the body. The Nyemiga's gory banks were sown not with good seed—they were sown with the bones of Russia's sons!''

Thus, the descriptions of Oleg and Vseslav occupy a strictly defined, central position in the *Lay*'s structure of ideas. These were neither casual insertions nor lyrical digressions. They are organically linked to the author's own historical views and serve as a means of artistically embellishing the author's main theme—his appeal to the Russian princes for unity.

The *Lay*'s central image—the Russian land—also serves as an appeal for unity. The author creates this image by mentioning extreme geographical points: Novgorod in the north, Tmutorokan in the south, the Danube and the Volga, the Western Dvina and the Don rivers. Simply listing the Russian cities named in the *Lay* gives us a fair notion of the Russian land's breadth: Kiev, Chernigov, Polotsk, Novgorod the Great, Novgorod-Seversky, Tmutorokan, Kursk, Southern Pereyaslavl, Belgorod, Galich, Putivl, and Rimov; we also read of the Princes of Vladimir Zalessky and Vladimir Volynsky, of Smolensk, and Rylsk.

During the feudal period, the ''Russian land'' or ''twelfth-century Rus'' was often understood to mean the Kievan land and its immediate neighbours. To ''go to Rus'' in the 12th century often meant to set off for Kiev. Unlike Pereyaslavl Zalessky, Southern Pereyaslavl was called ''Russian Pereyaslavl.'' In Novgorod, the road to Kiev was called the ''Russian road.'' This narrow conception of ''Rus'' as lying within the boundaries of the Principality of Kiev was a typical consequence of the feudal divisions, when only Kiev could claim to represent Rus as a whole.

In contrast, the author of the *Lay* does not limit his notion of the Russian land to the Principality of Kiev. He includes Vladimir-Suzdal, Vladimir Volynsky, Novgorod the Great, and Tmutorokan. The inclusion of this last principality is especially interesting: the author is thus including among the Russian lands even those which had lost their political independence by the latter half of the 12th century. For the author of the

Lay, for instance, the Don River, where the Polovtsy had their nomad camps, but where there were also many Russian settlements, is a Russian river. The Don calls Prince Igor "to victory." The Donets helps Igor flee from the Polovtsy. Maidens "on the Danube," where there were also many Russian settlements, sang praises of Igor upon his return to Kiev. Yaroslavna's lament is also heard there. Even the Principality of Polotsk, which in the 12th century was constantly opposed to the rest of the Russian land, was included in the list of Russian principalities by the ***Lay***'s author. He appeals to the princes of Polotsk to defend the Russian land together with all the Russian princes, and urges them to put an end to their "strife" with the sons of Yaroslav. Consequently, the Polotsk land is regarded as part of the Russian land in the ***Lay.***

This same conception of the Russian land as a single whole is felt clearly when the author speaks of defending its frontiers. The enemies of Rus to the south—the Polovtsy—are the main enemies for him, but not the only ones. The defense of the Russian borders should be a united defense, in his view: he speaks of the victories won by Vsevolod of Suzdal on the Volga, that is, against the Volga Bulgars, of the war between the princes of Polotsk and the Lithuanians, of the Danube "gates" to the land of Galich, and of the struggle waged against the countries on the Danube subordinated to Byzantium.

The author also regards Russian nature as a single whole. The wind, the sun, storm clouds containing dark-blue thunderbolts, evening dusk and morning sunrises, the sea, ravines, and rivers make up the unusually broad canvas against which the ***Lay***'s action unfolds and convey a sense of the country's open expanses. The ***Lay***'s landscape seems to be viewed from on high. The horizon of this landscape takes in whole countries; the edges of this landscape are pushed back to enable us to see not just local scenery, but a whole province or country.

This far-ranging landscape is especially visible in Yaroslavna's lament. Yaroslavna addresses her lament to the wind wafting the clouds along and rocking the ships on the blue sea, to the Dnieper River cutting its way through stone mountains in the Polovets land and rocking Svyatoslav's galleys all the way to Kobiak's camp, to the sun, which warms and brings joy to all, but which scorched the Russian warriors in the parched steppe, tormenting them with thirst and wearing them out with exhaustion.

Nor is nature excluded from historical events. The ***Lay***'s landscape is tied in closely to man's life. Russian nature takes part in the Russian people's joys and sorrows. The more of the Russian land the author takes in, the more tangible and lifelike its description becomes—its rivers, which converse with Igor, and its animals and birds which are endowed with human reason. The work's sense of space and expanse is enhanced by many images drawn from hawking, and the participation of birds which fly over long distances (geese, golden-eyes, crows, jackdaws, nightingales, cuckoos, swans, and gerfalcons) in the action ("No storm is this that has blown the falcons beyond the rolling plains. The daws are fleeing in flocks towards the great Don!").

This joining of the entire Russian land into one tangible, living, and deeply affecting image, these scenes of Russian nature are essential elements in the author's appeal for unity. We see here how the idea underlying the ***Lay*** is joined inseparably to its embodiment. The appeal for unity is freely and naturally joined to the ***Lay***'s central image—that of a single, splendid, but suffering homeland. This image produces a sense of compassion for the Russian land on the part of the reader, makes him love its natural landscape, feel proud of its historical past, and makes him aware of the indefatigable strength possessed by this land.

How does the ***Lay***'s author understand this unity which he urges all Russian people to create for the Russian land.

The unity of Rus is conceived of by the author not as an ideal alliance between the Russian princes on the basis of goodwill, nor as the chronicle's idea of the need to observe good fraternal relations between princes. The author's conception of unity is based on notions inherent in the feudal era. He does not reject feudal relations, but in these feudal relations he constantly insists on the need to observe obligations between feudal lords, not on their rights. He stresses the disobedience of Igor and Vsevolod to their "father," Svyatoslav, and criticises them for this. He urges feudal loyalty to Prince Svyatoslav of Kiev for the good of the whole Russian land.

Disregarding the known historical facts about Prince Svyatoslav Vsevolodovich of Kiev, who was a weak ruler, the author of the ***Lay*** describes him as mighty and "terrible." In reality, Svyatoslav was not "terrible": he ruled only Kiev, sharing his authority with Rurik, who dominated the rest of the cities in the principality of Kiev.

We should not think that the ***Lay*** is simply a courtier's flattery. The author places the prince of Kiev among the leading Russian princes only because Kiev was still regarded as the center of the Russian land—if not the real center, then at least the theoretical, ideal center. He did not see any possibility for a new center in north-east Rus. For the author of the ***Lay,*** the prince of Kiev was still leader of all the Russian princes. He regarded the strict and absolute observance of feudal obligations to the declining throne of Kiev as a counterweight to the internecine wars and a means by which Russian unity could be preserved. He endowed Svyatoslav with the ideal qualities of a leader of the Russian princes: he is "terrible" and "grand." The word "grand," which was frequently applied to the senior princes, was starting to be used at this time by the princes of Vladimir: Vsevolod the Big Nest took the name "Grand Prince" for himself, thus laying claim to seniority among all the Russian princes. The word "terrible" was often used as part of the official address to the senior Russian princes right up until the 17th century, although it did not enter their official title (it became a nickname for Ivan III and Ivan IV, stressing their strong leadership in a positive sense). The word "terrible" as a synonym for the might of princely rule was often used in the 13th century. For the author of the ***Lay,*** the "terrible" prince of Kiev was an ideal, not a reality. There can be no doubt that he regarded Svyatoslav, whose strength he hyperbolises, as the legitimate prince of Kiev. Nonetheless, ignoring Svyatoslav Vsevolodovich's patrimonial right to Kiev, he writes, addressing Vsevolod the Big Nest—a prince who belonged to a branch of the Monomakh line of Russian princes hostile to Svyatoslav, one of the Oleg clan: "O Grand Prince Vsevolod! Is it not in your thoughts to come flying from far off to guard your father's golden throne? . . . If you were here (i.e. in Kiev)—slave-girls would be a *nogata* each, bondmen—but a *riezan*" [Likhachov explains in a footnote that the "nogata" and "riezan" were small coins in medieval Russia]. This appeal to Vsevolod shows the author of the ***Lay*** to be a man with his own independent stance, by no means a courtier. He addresses Vsevolod as "Grand Prince," recognises the throne of Kiev as Vsevolod's "patrimonial throne," and appeals to him go to the south: how can we make this conform to the author's support of the Olegoviches? The main point is that the author evidently regarded Vsevolod's new policy—of non-participation in southern Russian affairs—more dangerous than his interference in the struggle over the Kiev throne. Unlike his father, Yury Dolgoruky, Vsevolod tried to establish himself in the north-east to replace the hegemony of Kiev by the hegemony of Vladimir Zalessky; he therefore refused to make any claims on Kiev and strove to direct Russian affairs from Vladimir Zalessky. To the author of the ***Lay,*** Vsevolod's position seemed too local, too self-contained, and therefore dangerous.

Similarly, the narrow policies of Yaroslav of Galich also seemed dangerous to the author of the ***Lay,*** and he stressed his power over Kiev itself: "He opened the gates to Kiev," he said of Yaroslav of Galich. This might seem incompatible with his notion of the might of Svyatoslav of Kiev, an impossible assertion for a "courtier" poet of the Olegoviches, but is simple and understandable for a man who regarded Kiev as the center of the Russian land.

The author of the ***Lay*** could not reject the idea of Kiev as the single center of Rus. It would indeed be unfair to expect this of him. He is a fervent supporter of Russian unity, but he conceives of this unity in terms of 12th-century ideas. He sees the importance of firm authority in Kiev, but he still believes in the need to strictly observe feudal rights, on which both suzerains and vassals relied in their struggle. However, in these feudal rights the author stresses the rights of the suzerain, not the vassal. He recognises the strength of the prince of Vladimir-Suzdal, but he would rather see him in the south—in Kiev, the traditional center of Rus.

The author of the ***Lay*** draws the ideas he needs to support Russian unity from the accepted ideas of his time. To develop entirely new political conceptions was a task for the future. The author of ***The Lay of Igor's Host*** is a brilliant man of his time: he thinks in 12th-century terms, but he infuses them with a progressive content.

The entire narrative exposition of the ***Lay*** is permeated with the notion of Kiev as the center of the Russian land. The accuracy of the expressions used to describe the consequences of Igor's defeat is striking: "Then Kiev, my brethren, moaned in sorrow and Chernigov moaned beneath these disasters." The land of Chernigov was, in fact, stricken with misfortune. Kiev and the towns in the Principality of Kiev were not destroyed, but, as the center of Rus, they grieved for the entire Russian land; Kiev thus suffered not for its own misfortunes, but for the misfortunes of Rus as a whole.

Kiev's role as center of the Russian land is especially keenly felt in the concluding section on ***The Lay of Igor's Host.*** According to the chronicle, Igor goes to Chernigov to see Yaroslav Svyatoslavich after his return from captivity to Novgorod-Seversky, and then goes to Kiev to see Svyatoslav Vsevolodovich. The ***Lay*** does not mention his stay in Novgorod-Seversky, nor his trip to Chernigov: Igor goes directly to Kiev to the Church of Mother of God of Pirogoshch. The fact that Igor goes to Kiev immediately to see Svyatoslav reflects the author's belief that Igor is a Russian prince first and foremost: thus it is his return to Kiev that is important, not his return to Novgorod-Seversky. His praise is sung not in Novgorod or Putivl, but on the Danube—in the distant Russian settlements, which the Polovtsy have cut off from the rest of Rus—for all Rus rejoices in his return: "The lands rejoice, the cities make merry." The singing of these praises reaches Kiev from the Danube. Igor's return produces a response in all Russian hearts.

Thus, the author of the ***Lay*** regards Russian unity as centred in Kiev. This unified land is headed by the Prince of Kiev, who is represented as a powerful and "terrible" prince.

Appealing to the Russian princes to defend the Russian land, the author of the ***Lay*** created a composite picture—in his characterisation of various princes—of a strong and mighty prince: one who has many fighting men ("lord of many hosts"), strong by force of law, ("sitting in judgement even as far as the Danube"), able to inspire fear in the lands neighbouring on Rus ("you are able to splash away the Volga with your oars, to scoop up the Don with your warriors' helmets," "pressing back the Hungarian hills with your iron hosts, barring way to the king, making fast the gates to the Danube"), extending his rule over an enormous territory centered on Kiev, and praised in other countries ("the Germans, Venetians, Greeks, and Moravians sing Svyatoslav's praises").

This, then, is a prince who embodies the idea of strong princely rule. This notion of princely power, by which the Russian land was meant to be united, only came into being in the 12th century. This same ideal of a "terrible" grand prince was later also created in *The Tale of the Ruin of the Russian Land.* It is reflected in the *Life of Alexander Nevsky,* the *Supplication* of Daniel the Exile, and other 13th-century works. The only change is that behind this image of a "terrible" grand prince, Kiev is no longer posited as the center of Rus. The relocation of Rus's center to the north-east and the decline of the Kiev throne was by then entirely obvious.

At the time of the writing of the ***Lay*** strong princely rule had only just begun to emerge. Its future development still unseen, the author had already defined its most typical features and had pinpointed future tendencies in it.

Thus, Russian unity is seen by the author not as an alliance between the Russian princes based on their goodwill, nor as the chronicle's idea of the need for all the princes to maintain good fraternal relations (all princes are "brothers" and "grandsons of one grandfather"), nor as some future idea of single rule, but as an alliance of Russian princes based on the strict observance of feudal obligations towards the powerful and "terrible" prince of Kiev.

Appealing to the Russian princes to defend the Russian land, the author of the ***Lay*** proceeds from their real capabilities, and evaluates the qualities that would enable them to defend Rus. The author thus emerges as a sensible politician, and his work provides a picture of the Russian political situation during his time.

Did the appeal by the author of the ***Lay*** reach the ears of those for whom it was intended? We can assume that to some extent it did. Igor Svyatoslavich did not undertake any further solitary expeditions against the Polovtsy.

In 1191 he builds a coalition against the Polovtsy. Apart from Igor, the other participants included Vsevolod Svyatoslavich, Vsevolod, Mstislav and Vladimir (the three sons of Svyatoslav Vsevolodovich of Kiev), Rostislav Yaroslavich (son of Yaroslav Vsevolodovich), and the son of Oleg Svyatoslavich—Davyd. This campaign was unsuccessful, but its large-scale organisation was significant.

However, the real meaning of the author's appeal was perhaps not its attempt to organise a given campaign, but a broader and bolder task—to rise public opinion against feudal warfare, to condemn harmful feudal conceptions, and to mobilise public opinion against the princes' seekings after personal glory, honour, and vengeance for "offences" committed against them. That is why this public opinion occupies such an enormous place in the ***Lay.***

Druzhina notions of "honour" and "glory" can be very clearly perceived in ***The Lay of Igor's Host.*** The entire work is permeated with such notions. All the Russian princes, warriors, cities, and principalities are represented in the ***Lay*** in a halo of "glory" or "shame."

That is why the author only briefly mentions various details in question form, as if they are well-known to everyone: "Were not those warriors yours whose gilded helmets sailed a sea of blood? Are those brave men-at-arms not yours that roar like wild bulls, wounded with swords of tempered steel, in the unknown plains?"—he says of the *druzhina* of Rurik and Davyd Rostislaviches. We would say today that this question is rhetorical, for it only recalls scenes to remind the reader of the glory enjoyed by Rurik and Davyd's *druzhina*. Igor's defeat is also evaluated in terms of public opinion: "Dishonour has vanquished glory. . . ."

In telling about the Russian princes, the author of the ***Lay*** mentions first of all their glory. The ***Lay*** presents public opinion about each of the Russian princes and their *druzhinas*.

These descriptions of the princes are based on a keen sense of public opinion ("your terror flows through the lands," or "far, far have you fled from your forefathers' glory").

This same "glory" is also possessed by individual cities (Novgorod is famed for "Yaroslav's glory") and by lands which are given their glory by local *druzhinas*.

The author of the ***Lay*** often appraises events from the point of view of the "glory" or "praise" (the Russian word *slava* means both "glory" and "praise"—Doris Bradbury) that spread across the Russian land about them. Just as the chronicler evaluates historical events on the basis of public opinion which says "never before has such a thing happened," so the author of the ***Lay*** writes of Igor's defeat: "Thus was it in those battles, in the days of that warfare. But such a battle as this has never been heard of yet!"

The notions of honour and glory are reflected in the ***Lay*** even when they are not directly mentioned. Igor says to his *druzhina:* "Better be slain than taken captive!" or "I will break my spear to splinters at the far end of the Polovtsian plains, with you, o Russians! I will either lay low my head, or drink a helmetful of Don water." Thus he is referring to the personal glory he hopes to win.

The glory won by the princes' grandfathers is constantly mentioned in the ***Lay***—the glory of their family line: Izyaslav Vasilkovich, the Yaroslaviches and all Vseslav's grandsons have "far fled" from their forefathers' glory, and Vseslav of Polotsk "shattered Yaroslav's fame"—the glory of Novgorod. Finally, ***The Lay of Igor's Host*** repeatedly mentions the singing of this same "glory"—a song of praise which gave concrete meaning to the ideal of "glory" as public opinion. Boyan's songs were songs of praise—"lays" ("he laid his wise fingers upon the living chords, and they themselves sang out glory to princes") devoted to various heroes and their feats.

"Praise" is sung by the neighbouring peoples on Rus's borders. They sing this praise not in Svyatoslav's reception hall as some students of the ***Lay*** have mistakenly thought, but in their own countries. We thus have an example of the same worldwide praise of the Russian princes also to be found in Hilarion's *Discourse,* in Daniel the Exile's *Supplication,* in the *vitae* of Alexander Nevsky and Dovmont Timofei of Pskov, in *The Tale of the Ruin of the Russian Land,* and in *The Eulogy to the Princes of Ryazan:* "The Germans, Venetians, Greeks, and Moravians sing Svyatoslav's praises." Here the conception of "praise" as "fame" and as a "song of praise" are poetically fused, but the ***Lay*** also mentions the singing of "praise," the reality of which we have no grounds to doubt. Upon Igor's return from captivity, "maidens" on the Danube sing his praises. The author of the ***Lay*** also concludes his work with traditional praises of the princes and their *druzhinas:* "Glory to Igor, son of Svyatoslav, to Vsevolod, the furious bull, to Vladimir, son of Igor! Health to the princes, to their men-at-arms standing up for Christiandom against the pagan hosts! Glory to the princes and to their men-at-arms! Amen!"

Thus, the author of ***The Lay of Igor's Host*** recreates events which took place in his own time, evaluates them, and provides appraisals of the princes—his contemporaries—on the basis of public opinion and the notion of glory, which had its own special features in the 12th century, associated with the ideology of class-based feudal society. The author does not divide his own views from that of public opinion. He acknowledges himself to be a medium for public opinion as he tries to present his evaluation of events and the current situation in Rus as that of the whole people. The public opinion which he expresses, however, was that of the best Russian people of his time.

The author of the ***Lay*** isolates the best aspects of feudal conduct, the codes of *druzhina* notions of honour and glory, and the ideology of the upper circles of feudal society, and poeticises them. He fills out the notions of "honour," "glory," "praise," and "dishonour" with his own broader, more patriotic content. He criticises Igor Svyatoslavich and his brother Vsevolod, Boris Vyacheslavich, and other Russian princes, for seeking personal glory. However, when "glory" in its broader sense is under discussion, the author adopts a positive stance towards it. Honour and glory surmount their feudal limitations in the ***Lay.*** For the author, these notions with their marked class bias acquire a more general meaning. The honour and glory of the country, of Russian arms, and of the prince as a representative of the entire Russian land stir the author of the ***Lay*** more than anything else.

Thus, the task of the ***Lay*** was less the military unity of the Russian people than their moral unity around the idea of a single Russian land. That is why the author appeals to public opinion so frequently and insistently. This was not a task to be performed in one or two years' time. Unlike the appeal to organise a military campaign against the Polovtsy, its mobilising influence affected an entire period in Russian history, continuing right up to the Tatar-Mongol invasion. Karl Marx very rightly wrote of the ***Lay*** that its main theme was its appeal to the Russian people to unite "just before the Mongol invasion." (pp. 184-95)

Dmitry Likhachov, "The Lay of Igor's Host," in his The Great Heritage: The Classical Literature of Old Rus, *translated by Doris Bradbury, Progress Publishers, 1981, pp. 155-225.*

ADDITIONAL BIBLIOGRAPHY

Besharov, Justinia. *Imagery of the "Igor Tale" in the Light of Byzantino-Slavic Poetic Theory.* Leiden: E. J. Brill, 1956.

Attempts to interpret *The Igor Tale* by means of "a complex scheme of literary devices inherited by the Church Slavonic civilization, especially in Kievan Russia, from Byzantium."

Bida, Constantine. "Linguistic Aspect of the Controversy over the *Tale of Igor's Campaign*." *Canadian Slavonic Papers* I (1956): 76-88.
Asserts the authenticity of *The Igor Tale* on the basis of linguistic evidence.

Čiževska, Tatjana. *Glossary of "The Igor Tale."* London: Mouton, 1966, 405 p.
Attempts "to record all the words of the monument, to cite all their occurrences in all the grammatical forms in which they appear," and "to identify these instances."

Cooper, Henry R., Jr. *The Igor Tale*. White Plains, N.Y.: M. E. Sharpe, 1978, 130 p.
A comprehensive annotated bibliography of non-Soviet scholarship on *The Igor Tale* from 1900 to 1976.

Cox, Gary. "Toward a System of Poetic Parallelism in the *Slovo o Polku Igoreve*." *Ulbandus Review* 1, No. 2 (Spring 1978): 3-15.
Analyzes the "elements of a poetic system based on thematic and syntactic parallellism" in *The Igor Tale* in an attempt to determine the poetic character of the work.

Emerson, Caryl. "Rilke, Russia, and the *Igor Tale*." *German Life and Letters* n.s. XXXIII, No. 3 (April 1980): 221-33.
Discusses Rainer Maria Rilke's German translation of *The Igor Tale*. Emerson proposes "possible reasons for his attraction to the poem" and examines in detail "Rilke's treatment of two sections which he judged 'most beautiful'—the opening exordium to Boyan, and Jaroslavna's Lament."

Fennell, J. L. I. "The *Slovo o polku Igoreve:* The Textological Triangle." *Oxford Slavonic Papers* n.s. I (1968): 126-37.
Discusses the interrelationship of *The Igor Tale,* the *Zadonshchina,* and the Hypatian Chronicle. Fennell disputes the assertion of D. S. Likhachev (see the 1967 Likhachev Additional Bibliography entry below) that the Hypatian Chronicle influenced *The Igor Tale,* which in turn influenced the *Zadonshchina*; he argues instead that *The Igor Tale* is a later work which demonstrates the independent influences of both the Hypatian Chronicle and the *Zadonshchina*.

Hordynsky, Sviatoslav. "The Poetic and Political Aspects of *The Tale of Prince Ihor's Campaign*." *The Ukrainian Quarterly* V, No. 1 (Winter 1949): 20-8.
Stresses the poem's Ukrainian origin.

———. "English Resume." *Slavistica,* Nos. 46-7 (1963): 87-94.
English synopses of ten essays appearing in Russian in this issue, which is devoted to the influence of Ukrainian folk poetry on *The Igor Tale*.

Jakobson, Roman. *Selected Writings IV: Slavic Epic Studies*. The Hague: Mouton, 1966.
Contains fourteen essays on *The Igor Tale* in English, French, and Russian, including "The Vseslav Epos," "The Archetype of the First Edition of the Igor Tale," and "The Puzzles of the *Igor Tale* on the 150th Anniversary of Its First Edition" (see excerpt dated 1952).

———, and Simmons, Ernest J., eds. *Russian Epic Studies*. Philadelphia: American Folklore Society, 1949.
Contains eight essays on *The Igor Tale* by critics including Andre von Gronicka, Clarence A. Manning, and Avrahm Yarmolinsky (see excerpt dated 1949); also includes Rainer Maria Rilke's previously unpublished German translation of the work.

Kuskov, Vladimir. "*The Lay of Igor's Host*." In his *A History of Old Russian Literature,* pp. 109-35. Moscow: Progress Publishers, 1980.
A comprehensive discussion of the poem.

Likhachev, D. S. "The Authenticity of the *Slovo o Polku Igoreve:* A Brief Survey of the Arguments." *Oxford Slavonic Papers* XIII (1967): 33-46.
Summarizes principal arguments for and against the authenticity of *The Igor Tale*, concluding that the work's fabrication remains unproven and is highly improbable.

———. "Further Remarks on the Textological Triangle: *Slovo o polku Igoreve, Zadonshchina*, and the Hypatian Chronicle." *Oxford Slavonic Papers* n.s. II (1969); 106-15.
A rebuttal to J. L. I. Fennell's 1968 essay (see Additional Bibliography entry above) concerning the interrelationship of the three works.

Mann, Robert. "A Note on the Text of *The Igor Tale*." *Slavic Review* 39, No. 2 (June 1980): 281-85.
Maintains that previous reconstructions of the poem's opening passage have been inadequate and suggests an alternative reading.

———. "Is There a Passage Missing at the Beginning of *The Igor Tale*?" *Slavic Review* 41, No. 4 (Winter 1982): 666-72.
Asserts that as much as a page of the original manuscript may have been lost or omitted in the copying process.

Monas, Sidney. "Boian and Iaroslavna: Some Lyrical Assumptions in Russian Literature." In *The Craft and Context of Translation: A Critical Symposium,* edited by William Arrowsmith and Roger Shattuck, pp. 165-85. Garden City, N.Y. Anchor Books, 1964.
Cites examples from *The Igor Tale* in a discussion of English translations of Russian literature.

Moser, Charles A. "The Problem of the *Igor Tale*." *Canadian-American Slavic Studies* 7, No. 2 (Summer 1973): 135-54.
Considers *The Igor Tale* an eighteenth-century fabrication. Moser summarizes the principal arguments against the work's authenticity and builds a case for Nikolai Aleksandrovich L'vov as its probable forger.

Picchio, Riccardo. "On the Prosodic Structure of the *Igor Tale*." *Slavic and East European Journal* 16, No. 2 (Summer 1972): 147-62.
A technical analysis of the work's metrical organization.

Pritsak, Omeljan. "*The Igor Tale*." *International Journal of Slavic Linguistics and Poetics* XXVII, supp. (1983): 30-7.
Discusses Roman Jakobson's contribution to scholarship on *The Igor Tale*.

Tartak, Elias L. "Prince Igor in America." *The Russian Review* 8, No. 3 (July 1949): 230-33.
Discusses the discovery, publication, and critical history of *The Igor Tale*.

Ward, Dennis. "On Translating *Slovo o polku Igoreve*." *The Slavonic and East European Review* 36, No. 87 (June 1958): 502-12.
Presents what the author considers the most critical principles of translation to be followed when rendering *The Igor Tale* into English and illustrates these principles with examples from the text.

Worth, Dean S. "*Slóvo o polkú Ígoreve*." In *Handbook of Russian Literature*, edited by Victor Terras, pp. 425-27. New Haven, Conn.: Yale University Press, 1985.
Examines the historical background, content, style, and imagery of *The Igor Tale*.

Appendix

The following is a listing of all sources used in Volume 1 of *Classical and Medieval Literature Criticism*. Included in this list are all copyright and reprint rights and acknowledgments for those essays for which permission was obtained. Every effort has been made to trace copyright, but if omissions have been made, please let us know.

THE EXCERPTS IN CMLC, VOLUME 1, WERE REPRINTED FROM THE FOLLOWING PERIODICALS:

Agōn, v. 1, 1969. Copyright 1970 by Agōn. Reprinted by permission of the publisher.

Arion, v. 3, Autumn, 1964 for "The Comedy of Evil in Apuleius" by William E. Stephenson; v. 4, Autumn, 1965 for "The Sin of the Golden Ass" by L. A. MacKay; v. 8, Autumn, 1969 for "Homer: A Byzantine Perspective" by Eustathios. Copyright © by the Trustees of Boston University. All reprinted by permission of the publisher and the respective authors.

Blackwood's Edinburgh Magazine, v. L, October, November, and December, 1841.

The Bookman, London, v. 5, March, 1894.

The Bookman, New York, v. LXVIII, December, 1928.

Canadian Slavic Studies, v. 1, Spring, 1967. Copyright © 1967 by Charles Schlacks Jr., Publisher. All rights reserved. Reprinted by permission of the publisher.

CLA Journal, v. XX, December, 1976. Copyright, 1976 by The College Language Association. Used by permission of the College Language Association.

The Dial: Magazine for Literature, Philosophy, and Religion, v. IV, January, 1844.

The Diliman Review, v. III, January, 1955.

The Edinburgh Review, v. 94, October, 1851; v. CLIII, April, 1881.

ELH, v. 36, December, 1969. Copyright © 1969 by ELH. All rights reserved. Reprinted by permission of the publisher.

English Studies, v. XXIX, December, 1948.

Fraser's Magazine, v. VIII, October, 1873.

The French Review, v. XLVI, April, 1973; v. LIV, April, 1981. Copyright 1973, 1981 by the American Association of Teachers of French. Both reprinted by permission of the publisher.

History Today, v. XI, August, 1961. © History Today Limited 1961. Reprinted by permission of the publisher.

Japan Quarterly, v. XVII, January-March, 1970 for "'The Tale of Genji': A Novel of Manners, 1020 A.D." by James R. Nichols. © 1970, by James R. Nichols. Reprinted by permission of the author.

Life & Letters, v. IX, September, 1933.

The Modern Language Review, v. XVI, April, 1921.

Modern Philology, v. XLIV, November, 1946.

Monumenta Nipponica, v. III, July, 1940.

Mosaic: A Journal for the Interdisciplinary Study of Literature, Special Issue on LITERATURE and ALTERED STATES OF CONSCIOUSNESS, XIX/3 Summer 1986, 15-24. © MOSAIC, 1986. Acknowledgment of previous publication is herewith made.

The Nation, New York, v. CXXI, September 16, 1925.

The Nation and Athenaeum, v. XXX, October 22, 1921; v. XXXVII, June 20, 1925; v. XLIII, May 19, 1928; v. 40, July 29, 1950.

The New Republic, v. XLIII, August 12, 1925.

The Phoenix, v. X, 1956. Reprinted by permission of the publisher.

Poet Lore, v. VI, November, 1894.

Politics, v. 2, November, 1945.

Proceedings of the British Academy, v. XXII, 1936.

Ramus, v. 4, 1975. © Aureal Publications 1975. Reprinted by permission of the publisher.

The Review of English Studies, v. XIV, October, 1938.

The Romantic Review, v. LXII, December, 1971. Copyright © by the Trustees of Columbia University of the City of New York. Reprinted by permission of the publisher.

Saturday Review, v. XLVIII, April 10, 1965. © 1965 *Saturday Review* magazine. Reprinted by permission of the publisher.

The Saturday Review, London, v. 141, April 10, 1926.

The Sewanee Review, v. XIX, January, 1911.

The Spectator, n. 267, January 5, 1712; n. 273, January 12, 1712; n. 274, January 19, 1712; v. 198, April 5, 1957.

Speculum, v. XXVII. January 1952; v. XXXVII, July, 1962. Copyright 1962 by the Mediaeval Academy of America. Reprinted by permission of the publisher.

Studies in Philology, v. LXVI, July, 1969. © 1969 by The University of North Carolina Press. Reprinted by permission of the publisher.

Traditio, v. 24, 1968 for "Roland's Christian Heroism" by Constance Hieatt. Copyright © 1968 by Constance Hieatt. Reprinted by permission of Fordham University Press.

Yearbook of Comparative and General Literature, n. 31, 1982. Copyright 1982, Comparative Literature Program, Indiana University, Bloomington, IN. Reprinted by permission of the publisher.

THE EXCERPTS IN CMLC, VOLUME 1, WERE REPRINTED FROM THE FOLLOWING BOOKS:

Adams, Henry. From *Mont-Saint-Michel and Chartres*. N.p., 1904.

Adlinton, William. From an introduction to *The XI Bookes of the Golden Asse, Conteininge the Metamorphosis of Lucius Apuleius*. By Lucius Apuleius. Translated by William Adlington. Henry Wykes, 1566.

Anderson, George K. From *The Literature of the Anglo-Saxons*. Princeton University Press, 1949. Copyright, 1949, by Princeton University Press. Renewed 1976 by George K. Anderson. Reprinted with permission of the publisher.

Apuleius, Lucius. From a preface to *Apuleius, the Golden Ass: Being the Metamorphoses of Lucius Apuleius*. Translated by W. Adlington. Revised by S. Gaselee. The Macmillan Company, 1915.

Aristotle. From *Aristotle on the Art of Poetry*. Edited by Lane Cooper. Ginn and Company, 1913.

Arnold, Edwin. From *The Poets of Greece*. Cassell, Petter, and Galpin, 1869.

Arnold, Matthew. From *On Translating Homer*. Longman & Co., 1861.

Arnold, Matthew. From an introduction to *The English Poets, 4 Vols*. Edited by Thomas Humphry Ward. Macmillan and Co., 1880.

Aston, W. G. From *A History of Japanese Literature*. D. Appleton and Company, 1899.

Auden, W. H. From "The Shield of Achilles," in *W. H. Auden: Collected Poems*. Edited by Edward Mendelson. Random House, 1976. Copyright 1952 by W. H. Auden. Reprinted by permission of Random House, Inc.

Bassett, Samuel Eliot. From *The Poetry of Homer*. University of California Press, 1938. Copyright, 1938, renewed 1966, by The Regents of the University of California. Reprinted by permission of the publisher.

Bespaloff, Rachel. From "Helen," in *On the Iliad*. Translated by Mary McCarthy. Bollingen Series IX, 1947. Copyright 1947 by Bollingen Foundation. Renewed 1975 by Princeton University Press. Reprinted by permission of Princeton University Press.

Blair, Hugh. From *Lectures on Rhetoric and Belles Lettres, Vol. I*. W. Strahan, T. Cadell, 1783.

Bonjour, Adrien. From *The Digressions in Beowulf*. Basil Blackwell, 1950.

Bowra, C. M. From *Tradition and Design in "The Iliad."* Oxford at the Clarendon Press, Oxford, 1930.

Bowring, Richard. From *Murasaki Shikibu: Her Diary and Poetic Memoirs*. Translated by Richard Bowring. Princeton University Press, 1982. Copyright © 1982 by Princeton University Press. All rights reserved. Reprinted with permission of the publisher.

Brandes, Georg. From *Impressions of Russia*. Translated by Samuel C. Eastman. Thomas Y. Crowell Co., Inc., 1889.

Brandes, Georg. From *Hellas: Travels in Greece*. Translated by Jacob W. Hartmann. Adelphi Company, 1926.

Brault, Gerard J. From "Character Portrayal," in *The Song of Roland: An Analytical Edition, Introduction and Commentary, Vol. 1*. Edited by Gerard J. Brault. The Pennsylvania State University Press, 1978. Copyright © 1978 The Pennsylvania State University. All rights reserved. Reprinted by permission of the publisher.

Brodeur, Arthur Gilchrist. From *The Art of Beowulf*. University of California Press, 1959. Copyright © 1959 by The Regents of the University of California. Reprinted by permission of the publisher.

Brooke, Stopford A. From *English Literature: From the Beginning to the Norman Conquest*. The Macmillan Company, 1898.

Bryant, William Cullen. From a preface to *The Iliad of Homer*. Translated by William Cullen Bryant. Fields, Osgood and Co., 1870.

Butler, Samuel. From *The Trapanese Origin of the Odyssey*. Metcalfe & Co., 1893.

Chambers, R. W. From a foreword to *Beowulf*. Translated by Archibald Strong. Constable & Co., 1925.

Chapman, George. From *Achilles Shield.* John Windet, 1598.

Chesterton, G. K. From an introduction to *The Song of Roland.* Translated by Charles Scott Moncrieff. Chapman & Hall, Ltd., 1919.

Čiževskij, Dmitrij. From *History of Russian Literature from the Eleventh Century to the End of the Baroque.* Mouton, 1960. © copyright Mouton & Co., Publishers. Reprinted by permission of Mouton de Gruyter, a Division of Walter de Gruyter & Co.

Conybeare, John Josias. From *Illustrations of Anglo-Saxon Poetry.* Edited by William Daniel Conybeare. Harding and Lepard, 1826.

Courthope, W. J. From *A History of English Poetry: The Middle Ages, Vol. I.* Macmillan and Co., 1895.

de Montaigne, Michel. From "Of the Most Outstanding Men," in *The Complete Works of Montaigne: Essays, Travel Journal, Letters.* Translated by Donald M. Frame. Stanford University Press, 1957. Copyright © 1943 by Donald M. Frame. © 1948, 1957 by the Board of Trustees of the Leland Stanford Junior University. Excerpted with the permission of the publishers, Stanford University Press.

Dinsmore, Charles Allen. From *The Great Poets and the Meaning of Life.* Houghton Mifflin, 1937. Copyright, 1937, by Charles Allen Dinsmore. All rights reserved. Reprinted by permission of Houghton Mifflin Company.

Disraeli, Isaac. From *Amenities of Literature, Consisting of Sketches and Characters of English Literature.* Edward Moxon, 1841.

Dryden, John. From "A Discourse Concerning the Original and Progress of Satire," in *The Satires of D. J. Juvenalis.* By Juvenal, translated by John Dryden and others, N.p., 1693.

Dryden, John. From a preface to *Fables Ancient and Modern.* Translated by John Dryden. Jacob Tonson, 1700.

Earle, John. From an introduction to *The Deeds of Beowulf: An English Epic of the Eighth Century Done into Modern Prose.* Translated by John Earle. Oxford at the Clarendon Press, Oxford, 1892.

Enright, D. J. From *A Mania for Sentences.* Chatto & Windus/The Hogarth Press, 1983. © D. J. Enright, 1983. All rights reserved. Reprinted by permission of the author and Chatto & Windus/The Hogarth Press.

Fedotov, George P. From *The Russian Religious Mind: Keivan Christianity, the Tenth to the Thirteenth Centuries.* Cambridge, Mass.: Harvard University Press, 1946. Copyright 1946 by the President and Fellows of Harvard College. Renewed 1973 by Nina Rojankovsky. All rights reserved. Excerpted by permission of the publishers.

Fennell, John. From "'The Tale of Igor's Campaign'," in *Early Russian Literature.* By John Fennell and Anthony Stokes. University of California Press, 1974. Copyright © 1974 by John Fennell and Anthony Stokes. All rights reserved. Reprinted by permission of the publisher.

Festugière, André-Jean. From *Personal Religion Among the Greeks.* University of California Press, 1954.

Gaselee, Stephen. From an introduction to *The Golden Ass: Being the Metamorphoses of Lucius Apuleius.* By Lucius Apuleius, translated by William Adlington, revised by S. Gaselee. The Macmillan Company, 1915.

Geddes, J., Jr. From *La chanson de Roland: A Modern French Translation of Theodor Müller's Text of the Oxford Manuscript.* Edited by J. Geddes, Jr. The Macmillan Company, 1906.

Gladstone, W. E. From *Studies on Homer and the Homeric Age.* Oxford at the University Press, 1858.

Goldin, Frederick. From an introduction to *The Song of Roland.* Translated by Frederick Goldin. Norton, 1978. Copyright © 1978 by W. W. Norton & Company, Inc. All rights reserved. Reprinted by permission of W. W. Norton & Company, Inc.

Goldsmith, Margaret E. From *The Mode and Meaning of 'Beowulf'.* The Athlone Press of the University of London, 1970. © Margaret E. Goldsmith 1970. Reprinted by permission of the publisher.

Gosse, Edmund. From *More Books on the Table.* Charles Scribner's Sons, 1923.

Gradon, Pamela. From *Form and Style in Early English Literature.* Methuen, 1971. © 1971 Pamela Gradon. All rights reserved. Reprinted by permission of Methuen & Co. Ltd.

Grant, Michael. From *Roman Literature.* Cambridge at the University Press, 1954.

Graves, Robert. From an introduction to *The Transformations of Lucius, Otherwise Known as The Golden Ass.* By Lucius Apuleius, translated by Robert Graves. Farrar, Straus & Young, 1951. Copyright © 1951 by International Authors N.V. All rights reserved. Reprinted by permission of Farrar, Straus and Giroux, Inc.

Graves, Robert. From an introduction to *The Anger of Achilles: Homer's Iliad.* Translated by Robert Graves. Cassell, 1960. © Robert Graves 1959. Reprinted by permission of A P Watt Ltd on behalf of the Executors of the Estate of Robert Graves.

Gray, Wallace. From *Homer to Joyce*. Macmillan Publishing Company, 1985. Copyright © 1985 by Wallace Gray. All rights reserved. Reprinted with permission of Macmillan Publishing Company.

Greenfield, Stanley B. From *A Critical History of Old English Literature*. New York University Press, 1965. Copyright © 1965 by New York University. Reprinted by permission of the publisher.

Grierson, Herbert J. C. and J. C. Smith. From *A Critical History of English Poetry*. Chatto & Windus, 1944.

Griffin, Jasper. From *Homer on Life and Death*. Clarendon Press, Oxford, 1980. © Jasper Griffin 1980. All rights reserved. Reprinted by permission of Oxford University Press.

Grunmann-Gaudet, Minnette. From "The Representation of Time in 'La chanson de Roland'," in *The Nature of Medieval Narrative*. Edited by Minnette Grunmann-Gaudet and Robin F. Jones. French Forum, 1980. Copyright © 1980 by French Forum, Publishers, Incorporated. All rights reserved. Reprinted by permission of the publisher.

Gudzy, N. K. From *History of Early Russian Literature*. Translated by Susan Wilbur Jones. Macmillan, 1949. Copyright 1949, renewed 1977, by American Council of Learned Societies. All rights reserved. Reprinted with permission of Macmillan Publishing Company.

Hadas, Moses. From *A History of Latin Literature*. Columbia University Press, 1952. Copyright 1952 Columbia University Press. Renewed 1980 by Elizabeth S. Hadas. Reprinted by permission of the publisher.

Haight, Elizabeth Hazelton. From *Essays on Ancient Fiction*. Longmans, Green and Co., 1936.

Harrison, Robert. From an introduction to *The Song of Roland.* Translated by Robert Harrison. New American Library, 1970. Copyright © 1970 by Robert Harrison. All rights reserved. Reprinted by arrangement with NAL Penguin Inc., New York, NY.

Havelock, Eric A. From "The Sophistication of Homer," in *I. A. Richards: Essays in His Honor*. Reuben Brower, Helen Vendler, John Hollander, eds. Oxford University Press, 1973. Copyright © 1973 by Oxford University Press. Reprinted by permission of the publisher.

Havelock, Eric A. From *The Greek Concept of Justice: From Its Shadow in Homer to Its Substance in Plato*. Cambridge, Mass.: Harvard University Press, 1978. Copyright © 1978 by Eric A. Havelock. All rights reserved. Excerpted by permission of the publishers.

Heiserman, Arthur. From *The Novel before the Novel: Essays and Discussions About the Beginnings of Prose Fiction in the West*. University of Chicago Press, 1977. © 1977 by The University of Chicago. All rights reserved. Reprinted by permission of The University of Chicago Press.

Highet, Gilbert. From *The Classical Tradition: Greek and Roman Influences on Western Literature*. Oxford University Press, 1949. Copyright 1949 by Oxford University Press, Inc. Renewed 1976 by Gilbert Highet. Reprinted by permission of the publisher.

Howes, Robert C. From an introduction to *The Tale of the Campaign of Igor: A Russian Epic Poem of the Twelfth Century*. Translated by Robert C. Howes. Norton, 1973. Copyright © 1973 by W. W. Norton & Company, Inc. All rights reserved. Reprinted by permission of W. W. Norton & Company, Inc.

Hull, Denison Bingham. From an introduction to *Homer's Iliad*. Translated by Denison Bingham Hull. N.p., 1982. Copyright © 1982 by Denison Bingham Hull. All rights reserved. Reprinted by permission of the author.

Irving, Edward B. Jr. From *A Reading of "Beowulf."* Yale University Press, 1968. Copyright © 1968 by Yale University. All rights reserved. Reprinted by permission of the publisher.

Jenkins, T. Atkinson. From an introduction to *La chanson de Roland*. Edited by T. Atkinson Jenkins. Revised edition. D. C. Heath, 1924. Copyright, 1924 by D. C. Heath and Company. Renewed 1951 by Marian Magill Jenkins.

Jones, George Fenwick. From *The Ethos of "The Song of Roland."* Johns Hopkins Press, 1963. © 1963 by the Johns Hopkins Press. Reprinted by permission of the publisher.

Jones, Gwyn. From *Kings Beasts and Heroes*. Oxford University Press, London, 1972. © Oxford University Press 1972. Reprinted by permission of Oxford University Press, London.

Kato, Shuichi. From *A History of Japanese Literature: The First Thousand Years*. Translated by David Chibbett. Macmillan Press Ltd., 1979. © Shuichi Kato, 1979. Translation © Paul Norbury Publications Limited, 1979. All rights reserved. Reprinted by permission of Macmillan, London and Basingstoke.

Keene, Donald. From *Approaches to the Oriental Classics: Asian Literature and Thought in General Education*. Edited by William Theodore de Bary. Columbia University Press, 1959. Copyright © 1959 Columbia University Press, New York. Reprinted by permission of the publisher.

Kennedy, Charles W. From *The Earliest English Poetry: A Critical Survey of the Poetry Written before the Norman Conquest with Illustrative Translations*. Oxford University Press, 1943. Copyright 1943 by Oxford University Press, Inc. Reprinted by permission of the publisher.

Ker, W. P. From *Epic and Romance: Essays on Medieval Literature*. Macmillan and Co., Limited, 1897.

Ker, W. P. From *The Dark Ages*. Charles Scribner's Sons, 1904.

Kirk, G. S. From *Homer and the Epic: A Shortened Version of The Songs of Homer*. Cambridge at the University Press, 1965. © Cambridge University Press, 1965. Reprinted by permission of the publisher.

Klaeber, Friederich. From *Beowulf and The Fight at Finnsburg*. Edited by Friederich Klaeber. D. C. Heath and Company, 1922. Copyright, 1922 by D. C. Heath & Company. Renewed 1950 by Friederich Klaeber. Reprinted by permission of the publisher.

Konishi, Jin'ichi. From *A History of Japanese Literature: The Early Middle Ages, Vol. II*. Edited by Earl Miner, translated by Aileen Gatten. Princeton University Press, 1986. Copyright © 1986 by Princeton University Press. All rights reserved. Reprinted with permission of the publisher.

Lattimore, Richmond. From an introduction to *The Iliad of Homer*. By Homer, translated by Richmond Lattimore. University of Chicago Press, 1951. Copyright 1951 by The University of Chicago. Renewed 1979 by Richmond Lattimore. All rights reserved. Reprinted by permission of The University of Chicago Press.

Lawrence, William Witherle. From *Beowulf and Epic Tradition*. Cambridge, Mass.: Harvard University Press, 1928. Copyright © 1928 by the President and Fellows of Harvard College. Renewed 1956 by William Witherle Lawrence. Excerpted by permission of the publishers.

Le Bossu, René. From *Treatise of the Epick Poem*. Thomas Bennet, 1695.

Le Gentil, Pierre. From *The Chanson de Roland*. Translated by Frances F. Beer. Cambridge, Mass.: Harvard University Press, 1969. Copyright © 1969 by the President and Fellows of Harvard College. All rights reserved. Excerpted by permission of the publishers.

Lee, Alvin A. From *The Guest-Hall of Eden: Four Essays on the Design of Old English Poetry*. Yale University Press, 1972. Copyright © 1972 by Yale University. All rights reserved. Reprinted by permission of the publisher.

Lewis, C. S. From *A Preface to Paradise Lost*. Oxford University Press, 1942. Reprinted by permission of Oxford University Press.

Lewis, C. S. From *The Discarded Image: An Introduction to Medieval and Renaissance Literature*. Cambridge at the University Press, 1964. © Cambridge University Press 1964. Reprinted by permission of the publisher.

Likhachov, Dmitry. From *The Great Heritage: The Classical Literature of Old Rus*. Translated by Doris Bradbury. Progress Publishers, 1981. English Translation © Progress Publishers 1981. Reprinted by permission of the publisher.

Longfellow, Henry Wadsworth. From *The Poets and Poetry of Europe with Introduction and Biographical Notices*. Revised edition. Carey & Hart, 1845.

Lord, Albert B. From *The Singer of Tales*. Cambridge, Mass.: Harvard University Press, 1960. Copyright © 1960 by the President and Fellows of Harvard College. All rights reserved. Excerpted by permission of the publishers.

Lowell, Amy. From an introduction to *Diaries of Court Ladies of Old Japan*. Translated by Annie Shepley Omori and Kochi Doi. Houghton Mifflin Company, 1920.

Mackail, J. W. From *Lectures on Greek Poetry*. Longmans, Green and Co., 1911.

Macrobius, Ambrosius Theodosius. From *Commentary on the Dream of Scipio*. Translated by William Harris Stahl. Columbia University Press, 1952. Copyright 1952 Columbia University Press. Renewed 1980 by Mattie L. Stahl. Reprinted by permission of the publisher.

Magnus, Leonard A. From *The Tale of the Armament of Igor: A Russian Historical Epic, A.D. 1185*. Oxford University Press, London, 1915.

McNamee, Maurice B., S. J. From *Honor and the Epic Hero: A Study of the Shifting Concept of Magnanimity in Philosophy and Epic Poetry*. Holt, Rinehart and Winston, Inc., 1960. Copyright © 1960 by Maurice B. McNamee, S. J. All rights reserved. Reprinted by permission of Henry Holt and Company, Inc.

Mirsky, Prince D. S. From *A History of Russian Literature: From the Earliest Times to the Death of Dostoyevsky (1881)*. Alfred A. Knopf, 1927.

Moorman, Charles. From *Kings & Captains: Variations on a Heroic Theme*. The University Press of Kentucky, 1971. Copyright © 1971 by The University Press of Kentucky. Reprinted by permission of the publisher.

Morris, Ivan. From *The World of the Shining Prince: Court Life in Ancient Japan*. Alfred A. Knopf, 1964. Oxford University Press, Oxford, 1964. Copyright © 1964 by Ivan Morris. All rights reserved. Reprinted by permission of Alfred A. Knopf, Inc. In Canada by Oxford University Press.

Murray, Gilbert. From *The Rise of the Greek Epic*. Oxford University Press, 1934.

Nabokov, Vladimir. From a foreword to *The Song of Igor's Campaign: An Epic Twelfth Century*. Translated by Vladimir Nabokov. Vintage Books, 1960. © Copyright, 1960, by Vladimir Nabokov. All rights reserved. Reprinted by permission of the Literary Estate of Vladimir Nabokov.

Nichols, Stephen G., Jr. From *Formulaic Diction and Thematic Composition in the "Chanson de Roland."* Studies in the Romance Languages and Literatures, No. 36. The University of North Carolina Press, 1961. Reprinted by permission of the publisher and the author.

Niles, John D. From *Beowulf: The Poem and Its Tradition*. Cambridge, Mass.: Harvard University Press, 1983. Copyright © 1983 by the President and Fellows of Harvard College. All rights reserved. Excerpted by permission of the publishers.

Norinaga, Motoori. From "Good and Evil in the 'Tale of Genji'," translated by Ryusaku Tsunoda, in *Sources of Japanese Tradition*. Ryusaku Tsunoda, William Theodore de Bary, Donald Keene, eds. Columbia University Press, 1958. Copyright © 1958, renewed 1986 Columbia University Press, New York. Reprinted by permission of the publisher.

Ogilvy, J. D. A. and Donald C. Baker. From *Reading Beowulf: An Introduction to the Poem, Its Background, and Its Style*. University of Oklahoma Press, 1983. Copyright © 1983 by the University of Oklahoma Press, Norman, Publishing Division of the University. Reprinted by permission of the publisher.

Owen, D. D. R. From an introduction to *The Song of Roland*. Translated by D. D. R. Owen. Allen & Unwin Ltd., 1972. © D. D. R. Owen. All rights reserved. Reprinted by permission of the author.

Pater, Walter. From *Marius the Epicurean: His Sensations and Ideas, Vol. I*. Macmillan and Co., Limited, 1885.

Pei, Mario A. From *French Precursors of the "Chanson de Roland."* Columbia University Press, 1948. Copyright 1948 Columbia University Press. Renewed 1976 by Mario A. Pei. Reprinted by permission of the publisher.

Pekarik, Andrew. From *Ukifune: Love in "The Tale of Genji."* Edited by Andrew Pekarik. Columbia University Press, 1982. Copyright © 1982 Columbia University Press. All rights reserved. Reprinted by permission of the publisher.

Perry, Ben Edwin. From *The Ancient Romances: A Literary-Historical Account of Their Origins*. University of California Press, 1967. Copyright © 1967 by The Regents of the University of California. Reprinted by permission of the publisher.

Plato. From *The Republic*. Translated by Desmond Lee. Revised edition. Penguin Books, 1974. Copyright © H. D. P. Lee, 1955, 1974. Reproduced by permission of Penguin Books Ltd.

Poggioli, Renato. From *The Spirit of the Letter: Essays in European Literature*. Cambridge, Mass.: Harvard University Press, 1965. Copyright © 1965 by the President and Fellows of Harvard College. All rights reserved. Excerpted by permission of the publishers.

Pope, Alexander. From the preface to *The Iliad of Homer*. Translated by Alexander Pope. Bernard Lintott, 1715.

Pound, Ezra. From *The Spirit of Romance: An Attempt to Define Somewhat the Charm of the Pre-Renaissance Literature of Latin Europe*. J. M. Dent & Sons, Ltd., 1910.

Powys, John Cowper. From *Homer and The Aether*. Macdonald, 1959. © John Cowper Powys, 1959. Reprinted by permission of the Literary Estate of John Cowper Powys.

Pritchett, V. S. From *The Tale Bearers: Literary Essays*. Random House, 1980. Published in England as *The Tale Bearers: Essays on English, American and Other Writers*. Chatto & Windus, 1980. Copyright © 1980 by V. S. Pritchett. Reprinted by permission of Random House, Inc. In Canada by Chatto & Windus/The Hogarth Press and the author.

Puette, William J. From *Guide to 'The Tale of Genji' by Murasaki Shikibu*. Charles E. Tuttle Company, 1983. Copyright in Japan, 1983 by Charles E. Tuttle Co., Inc. All rights reserved.

Quiller-Couch, Sir Arthur. From *On the Art of Writing*. G. P. Putnam's Sons, 1916. Copyright, 1916 by G. P. Putnam's Sons. Renewed 1943 by Arthur Quiller-Couch. Reprinted by permission of The Putnam Publishing Group.

Rapin, René. From *The Whole Critical Works of Monsieur Rapin, Vol. I*. Translated by Several Hands. H. Bonwicke, 1706.

Rascoe, Burton. From *Prometheans: Ancient and Modern*. G. P. Putnam's Sons, 1933.

Renoir, Alain. From "The Heroic Oath in 'Beowulf', the 'Chanson de Roland', and the 'Nibelungenlied'," in *Studies in Old English Literature in Honor of Arthur G. Brodeur*. Edited by Stanley B. Greenfield. University of Oregon Books, 1963.

Rexroth, Kenneth. From *Classics Revisited*. Quadrangle Books, 1968, New Directions, 1986. Copyright © 1968 by Kenneth Rexroth. All rights reserved. Reprinted by permission of New Directions Publishing Corporation.

Robinson, Fred C. From an introduction to *Beowulf: A Verse Translation with Treasures of the Ancient North*. Translated by Marijane Osborn. University of California Press, 1983. Copyright © 1983 Marijane Osborn. Reprinted by permission of the publisher.

Saint Augustine. From *The City of God*. Translated by Marcus Dods with Rev. J. J. Smith and Rev. George Wilson. The Modern Library, 1950.

Sayers, Dorothy L. From an introduction to *The Song of Roland*. Translated by Dorothy L. Sayers. Penguin Books Inc., 1957. Copyright © 1957, renewed 1985 by Executors of Dorothy L. Sayers. Reprinted by permission of David Higham Associates.

Schein, Seth L. From *The Mortal Hero: An Introduction to Homer's "Iliad."* University of California Press, 1984. © 1984 by Seth L. Schein. Reprinted by permission of the publisher.

Schücking, Levin L. From "The Ideal of Kingship in 'Beowulf'," in *An Anthology of Beowulf Criticism*. Edited by Lewis E. Nicholson. University of Notre Dame Press, 1963. Copyright © 1963 by University of Notre Dame Press; Notre Dame, IN 46556. Reprinted by permission of the publisher.

Shippey, T. A. From *Beowulf*. Edward Arnold, 1978. © T. A. Shippey 1978. All rights reserved. Reprinted by permission of the author.

Sisam, Kenneth. From *The Structure of Beowulf*. Oxford at the Clarendon Press, Oxford, 1965. © Oxford University Press 1965. Reprinted by permission of the publisher.

Steiner, George. From "Homer and the Scholars," in *Language and Silence: Essays on Language, Literature and the Inhuman*. Atheneum, 1967. Copyright © 1963, 1967 by George Steiner. All rights reserved. Reprinted with the permission of Atheneum Publishers, a division of Macmillan, Inc.

Taine, H. A. From *History of English Literature, Vol. I*. Translated by H. Van Laun. Holt & Williams, 1871.

Taylor, Thomas. From an introduction to *The Metamorphoses of Golden Ass, and Philosophical Works of Apuleius*. By Lucius Apuleius, translated by Thomas Taylor. Robert Triphook and Thomas Rodd, 1822.

Tillyard, E. M. W. From *The English Epic and Its Background*. Chatto & Windus, 1954. Copyright 1954 by E. M. W. Tillyard. Renewed 1982 by Stephen Tillyard. Reprinted by permission of the Literary Estate of E. M. W. Tillyard and Chatto & Windus.

Uitti, Karl D. From *Story, Myth, and Celebration in Old French Narrative Poetry, 1050-1200*. Princeton University Press, 1973. Copyright © 1973 by Princeton University Press. All rights reserved. Reprinted with permission of the publisher.

Vance, Eugene. From *Reading the Song of Roland*. Prentice-Hall, 1970. Copyright © 1970 by Prentice-Hall, Inc. All rights reserved. Excerpted by permission of Prentice-Hall, Inc., Englewood Cliffs, NJ 07632.

Van Doren, Mark. From *The Noble Voice: A Study of Ten Great Poems*. Henry Holt and Company, 1946. Copyright, 1946, by Henry Holt and Company, Inc. Renewed 1973 by Dorothy G. Van Doren. Reprinted by permission of the Literary Estate of Mark Van Doren.

Very, Jones. From *Poems and Essays*. Revised edition. Houghton, Mifflin and Company, 1886.

Vinaver, Eugène. From *The Rise of Romance*. Oxford at the Clarendon Press, Oxford, 1971. © Eugène Vinaver, 1971. Reprinted by permission of Oxford University Press.

Voltaire. From *An Essay upon the Civil Wars of France, Extracted from Curious Manuscripts, and Also upon the Epick Poetry of the European Nations from Homer Down to Milton*. Samuel Jallasson, 1727.

Waley, Arthur. From an introduction to *The Sacred Tree: Being the Second Part of "The Tale of Genji"*. Translated by Arthur Waley. George Allen & Unwin Ltd., 1926.

Waliszewski, K. From *A History of Russian Literature*. Heinemann, 1900.

Warburton, William. From his *The Divine Legation of Moses Demonstrated, Vol. I*. N.p., 1738.

Whibley, Charles. From an introduction to *The Golden Ass of Apuleius*. Translated by William Adlington. D. Nutt, 1893.

Whitelock, Dorothy. From *The Audience of Beowulf*. Oxford at the Clarendon Press, Oxford, 1951.

Whitman, Cedric H. From *Homer and the Heroic Tradition*. Cambridge, Mass.: Harvard University Press, 1958. Copyright © 1958 by the President and Fellows of Harvard College. Renewed 1986 by Leda Whitman-Raymond and Rachel C. Whitman. Excerpted by permission of the publishers.

Winkler, John J. From *Auctor & Actor: A Narratological Reading of Apuleius's "Golden Ass."* University of California Press, 1985. Copyright © 1985 by The Regents of the University of California. Reprinted by permission of the publisher.

Wrenn C. L. From *Beowulf, with the Finnesburg Fragment*. Edited by C. L. Wrenn. Third edition, fully revised by W. F. Bolton. St. Martin's Press, 1973, Harrap, 1973. Copyright © George C. Harrap & Co., Ltd., and the executors of C. L. Wrenn, 1973. All rights reserved. Used with permission of St. Martin's Press, Inc. In Canada by Thomas Nelson and Sons Limited, assignees of Harrap Ltd.

Yarmolinsky, Avrahm. From "The 'Slovo' in English," in *Russian Epic Studies*. Edited by Roman Jakobson and Ernest J. Simmons. American Folklore Society, 1949.

Yourcenar, Marguerite. From *With Open Eyes: Conversations with Matthieu Galey*. Translated by Arthur Goldhammer. Beacon Press, 1984. English translation copyright © 1984 by Beacon Press. All rights reserved. Reprinted by permission of Beacon Press.

Literary Criticism Series Cumulative Author Index

Author Index

This index lists all author entries in the Gale Literary Criticism Series and includes cross-references to other Gale sources. For the convenience of the reader, references to the *Yearbook* in the *Contemporary Literary Criticism* series include the page number (in parentheses) after the volume number. References in the index are identified as follows:

AITN: *Authors in the News,* Volumes 1-2
CAAS: *Contemporary Authors Autobiography Series,* Volumes 1-5
CA: *Contemporary Authors* (original series), Volumes 1-121
CABS: *Contemporary Authors Bibliographical Series,* Volumes 1-2
CANR: *Contemporary Authors New Revision Series,* Volumes 1-21
CAP: *Contemporary Authors Permanent Series,* Volumes 1-2
CA-R: *Contemporary Authors* (revised editions), Volumes 1-44
CDALB: *Concise Dictionary of American Literary Biography*
CLC: *Contemporary Literary Criticism,* Volumes 1-45
CLR: *Children's Literature Review,* Volumes 1-14
CMLC: *Classical and Medieval Literature Criticism,* Volume 1
DLB: *Dictionary of Literary Biography,* Volumes 1-59
DLB-DS: *Dictionary of Literary Biography Documentary Series,* Volumes 1-4
DLB-Y: *Dictionary of Literary Biography Yearbook,* Volumes 1980-1986
LC: *Literature Criticism from 1400 to 1800,* Volumes 1-6
NCLC: *Nineteenth-Century Literature Criticism,* Volumes 1-16
SAAS: *Something about the Author Autobiography Series,* Volumes 1-4
SATA: *Something about the Author,* Volumes 1-48
SSC: *Short Story Criticism,* Volume 1
TCLC: *Twentieth-Century Literary Criticism,* Volumes 1-26
YABC: *Yesterday's Authors of Books for Children,* Volumes 1-2

Author Index

Author Index

Author Index

Author Index

Author Index

Author Index

CMLC Title Index

CMLC Critic Index